Wells

Hand Bach en Dr Antonio
Foot

800-
733 1717

817-
792 3432 SPC
Bill Dahl

Tom Clinger

WHAT DO *YOU* WANT FROM TECHNOLOGY?

When HRW decided to develop technology products, we started by asking teachers what they needed in the classroom. We polled thousands of educators, and their ideas and advice became our starting point.

The first thing we learned is that most technology products available today share a common flaw — they aren't integrated with the curriculum. Most of them were created by people who know a great deal about technology, but not very much about education. The result for teachers: frustration and hours of planning time wasted trying to mix and match.

Because HRW has been creating educational curriculum since 1866, we know that the focus of the classroom is the student, not the technology. That's why we've organized our new technology materials around your curriculum, and that's why we want to show you the instructional content and value that characterize every product from HRW. At HRW, technology is not an extra; it's part of an integrated approach to classroom management and instruction.

Order the **Komm mit! Video Program** or **Expanded Video Program** today and see for yourself the difference it makes when a technology product is developed with the student and teacher in mind.

Like all HRW materials, the **Komm mit! Video Program** and **Expanded Video Program** —

- *Require less planning time because we've already matched its content to fit your curriculum goals and sequence*

- *Address the diversity of learning styles found in today's classroom*

- *Offer a Video Guide containing all the information you need to use the program — teaching strategies, ideas for customizing instruction, scripts and activity sheets — all correlated directly to Komm mit!*

That's our story. To motivate your students as they meet German-speaking people, experience the culture and learn German in context, please order the **Komm mit! Video Programs** or **Expanded Video Programs.** Just complete the attached order form and either fax or mail it to us today.

William A. Talkington
President
Holt, Rinehart and Winston

**HOLT
RINEHART
WINSTON**

122H94A10
9-99-707544-7

Komm mit!

HOLT GERMAN LEVELS 1, 2, and 3

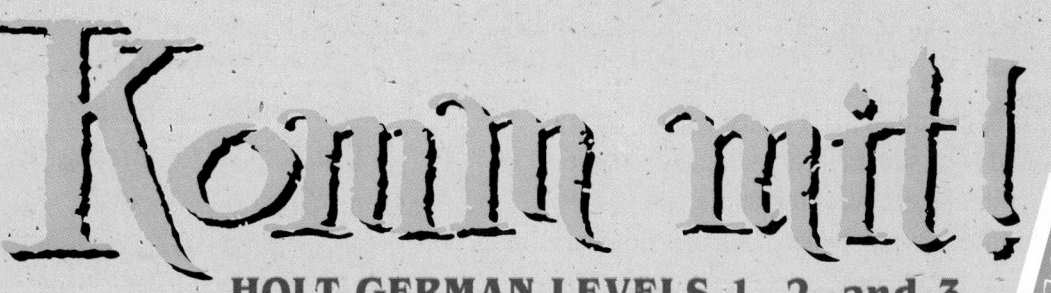

SO SAGT MAN DAS!

Making plans

You have been using the **möchte**-forms (*would like to*) to express y
Er möchte Musik hören. You can also use **wollen** (*to want to*).

Talking to someone:
Heiko, was willst du machen?

Talking about yourself:
Ich will in ein Caf

Talking about someone:

Wohin will Birte gehen?

Sie will ins Schw

A ROAD MAP TO PROFICIENCY

Komm mit!'s **functionally driven scope and sequence** gives students reasons to communicate. As a result, they develop proficiency in the four language **skills** (listening, speaking, reading, and writing) and build their critical-thinking skills.

Plus, Komm mit! presents **grammar** in context to support the functions, enhancing your students' ability to communicate with accuracy and confidence.

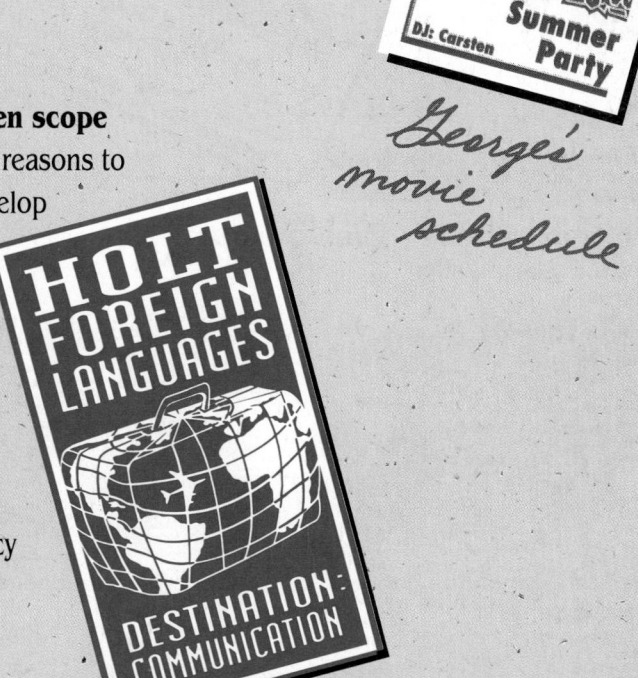

George's movie schedule

JOURNEY AT A REALISTIC PACE

Komm mit!'s **manageable chapters** set a realistic pace, so you and your students can complete each level of this three-level program in one year—without sacrificing language development.

Komm mit!'s **spiraling** of functions, vocabulary, and grammar increases your students' retention of newly acquired language and presents opportunities for using the language in various situations. And, with only 60 to 70 active **vocabulary** words per chapter, your students can use the core vocabulary with greater ease, yet still personalize their own communication.

Best of all, Komm mit!'s variety of activities, strategies, and supplementary materials **meets individual student needs**—ensuring the success of all students.

WORTSCHATZ

Wohin gehen? Was machen? Lies, was Katja und Julia planen! Julia sagt: „Katja und ich, wir wollen ..."

in ein Café gehen,
ein Eis essen

ins Schwimmbad gehen,
baden gehen

ins Kino gehen,
einen Film sehen

EXPLORE CULTURE

Develop your students' appreciation of the German-speaking world with **Komm mit!**'s **authentic** dialogues, interviews, realia, photos, and videos. **Komm mit!**'s strong cross-cultural perspective enriches students' understanding of the **multicultural** nature of the German-speaking world.

shown 75% of actual size

In der Freizeit

What do you think students in Germany like to do when they have time to spend with their friends? We have asked a number of students from different places this question, but before you read their responses, write down what you think they will say. Then read these interviews and compare your ideas with what they say.

LANDESKUNDE

EIN WENIG LANDESKUNDE

The prices on German menus include the tip. However, most people will round the check up to the next mark or to the next round sum, depending on the total of the bill.

Had a great time!

YOU'RE READY FOR ANYTHING!

Lesson plans, activities, strategies, scripts, and more highlight the Teacher's Edition, providing a **variety of instructional materials**.

Chapter Resource blackline masters—including realia, situation cards, and listening activities—are **organized by chapter** for ease of use. Students sharpen their language skills as they see and hear German in context via **integrated technology**: the high-interest audio program and on-location **videos** they'll have fun with while they learn.

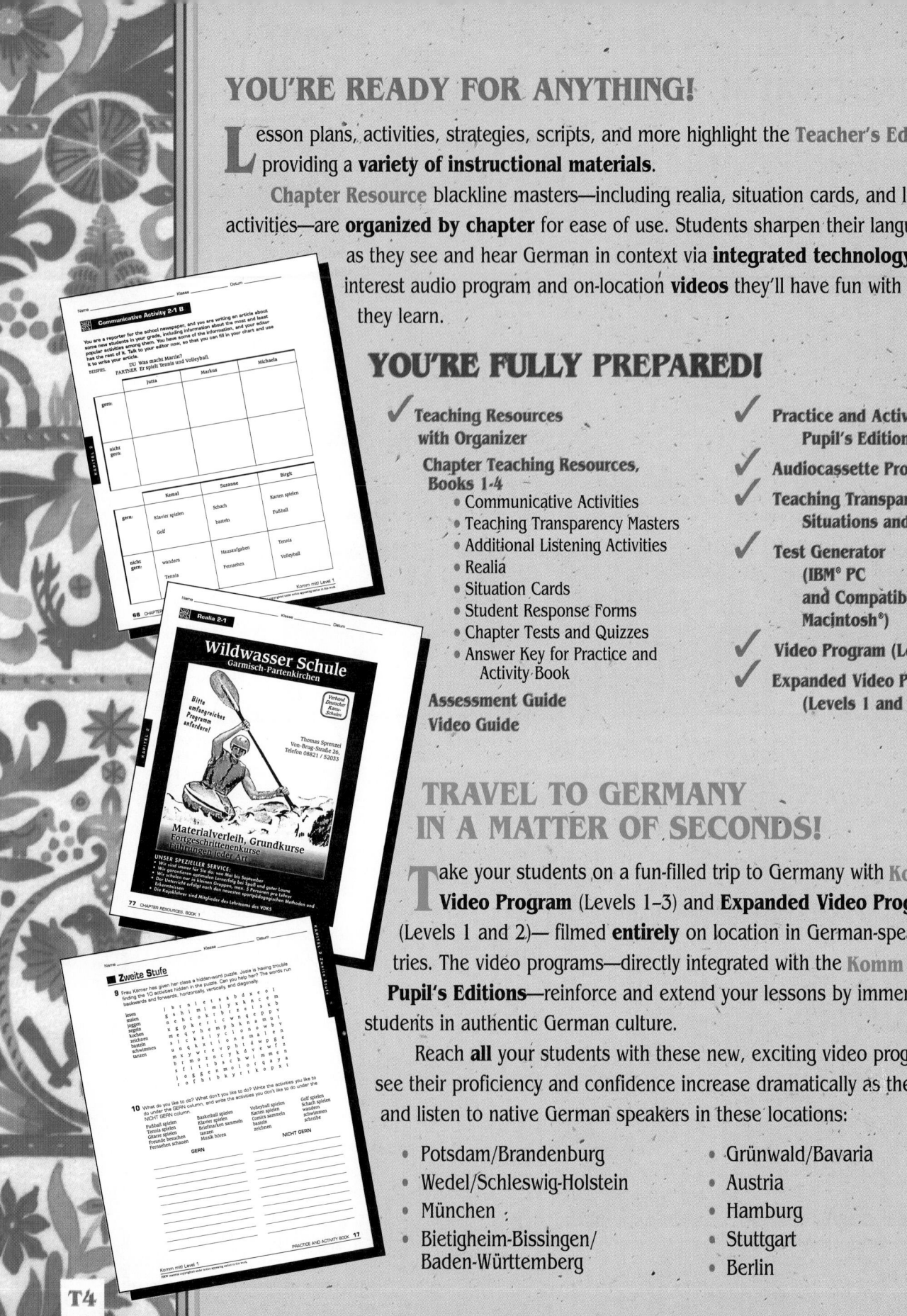

YOU'RE FULLY PREPARED!

✓ **Teaching Resources with Organizer**

Chapter Teaching Resources, Books 1-4
- Communicative Activities
- Teaching Transparency Masters
- Additional Listening Activities
- Realia
- Situation Cards
- Student Response Forms
- Chapter Tests and Quizzes
- Answer Key for Practice and Activity Book

Assessment Guide

Video Guide

✓ **Practice and Activity Book, Pupil's Edition**

✓ **Audiocassette Program**

✓ **Teaching Transparencies: Situations and Maps**

✓ **Test Generator (IBM® PC and Compatibles and Macintosh®)**

✓ **Video Program (Levels 1-3)**

✓ **Expanded Video Program (Levels 1 and 2)**

TRAVEL TO GERMANY IN A MATTER OF SECONDS!

Take your students on a fun-filled trip to Germany with Komm mit! **Video Program** (Levels 1–3) and **Expanded Video Program** (Levels 1 and 2)— filmed **entirely** on location in German-speaking countries. The video programs—directly integrated with the Komm mit! **Pupil's Editions**—reinforce and extend your lessons by immersing your students in authentic German culture.

Reach **all** your students with these new, exciting video programs. And see their proficiency and confidence increase dramatically as they watch and listen to native German speakers in these locations:

- Potsdam/Brandenburg
- Wedel/Schleswig-Holstein
- München
- Bietigheim-Bissingen/ Baden-Württemberg
- Grünwald/Bavaria
- Austria
- Hamburg
- Stuttgart
- Berlin

Komm mit!

Holt German
Level 2

HOLT, RINEHART AND WINSTON
Harcourt Brace & Company

Austin • New York • Orlando • Atlanta • San Francisco • Boston • Dallas • Toronto • London

Printed in the United States of America

ISBN 0-03-032553-6

2 3 4 5 6 7   041   99 98 97 96 95

For permission to reprint copyrighted material, grateful acknowledgment is made to the following sources:

ABDA: From "Wenn Kinder feiern ..." from *Neue Apotheken-Illustrierte,* 6/93, p. 28.

Berlin Programm Rimbach Verlag GmbH: "Oper & Theater" from *Berlin Programm,* September 1993. Reviews of "Blau-Rot," "Britzer Mühle," "Istanbul," "Restaurant El Pharaoh," "Restaurant Hardtke," "Restaurant Pferdestall," and "Restaurant Seaside" from *Berlin Programm,* September 1993.

Berliner Bären Stadtrundfahrt GmbH: Logo for Berliner Bären Stadtrundfahrt GmbH and "Tägliche Stadtrundfahrten Daily Sightseeingtours + Potsdam" advertisement from *Berlin Programm,* September 1993, p. 58.

Berliner Dom: From advertisement, "Berliner Dom" from *Berlin Programm,* September 1993, p. 41.

Berliner Symphoniker: Advertisement, "Berliner Symphoniker" from *Berlin Programm,* September 1993, p. 43.

Burda Publications: "Sechs Tips, die für Sie so wichtig sind wie für Boris" with photographs from "Warum ist Dr. Müller-Wohlfahrt nie krank?" from *BUNTE,* no. 22, May 27, 1993, p. 40. "Jetzt ein Eis!" from *BUNTE,* no. 33, August 12, 1993, p. 83.

Club La Santa: Photograph of "Club La Santa auf Lanzarote" from *Sport-Scheck Reisen,* Summer 1993, pp. 172–173.

Concert Concept GmbH: Advertisement, "Peter Hofmann, Anna Maria Kaufman singen Musical Classics" from *Berlin Programm,* September 1993, p. 39.

Globus-Kartendienst GmbH: Graphs, "Globus Graphik 9680—Was das Auto wirklich kostet," "Globus Graphik 9133— Beliebte Auto-Extras," and "Globus Graphik 9400—Europa auf Reisen."

Gruner + Jahr AG & Co.: "Das Pausenklingeln ist die schönste Musik!" from *Eltern,* October 1990, pp. 208–211. Copyright © 1990 by Gruner + Jahr AG & Co. From "Reich ist, wer nix mehr lernen muß!" from *Eltern,* July 1991, pp. 168, 169, 171. Copyright © 1991 by Gruner + Jahr AG & Co. "Gesucht: Bauernhof zum Ausschlafen!" from *Eltern,* August 1991, pp. 146–148. Copyright © 1991 by Gruner + Jahr AG & Co. From "Alles, Was Recht Ist" from *stern-tv magazin,* July 15, 1993, p. 19. Copyright © 1993 by Gruner + Jahr AG & Co.

Ho-Lin-Wah: Advertisement, "Ho-Lin-Wah" from *Berlin Programm,* September 1993.

International Press Syndicate: "Der neue Trend: 'Bleich ist beautiful'" from *Focus—Das moderne Nachrichtenmagazin,* no. 28, 1993, p. 81.

Kartographischer Verlag Busche GmbH: "Baden-Baden" from *Aral Auto-Reisebuch,* 1994/95.

Pop/Rocky: From "Ich bin kein Wunderkind!" and from "Nudeln mit Biss" from *Pop/Rocky,* no. 18, 1993, pp. 42, 49.

ACKNOWLEDGMENTS continued on page 396, which is an extension of the copyright page.

CONTRIBUTING WRITER

Ulrike Puryear
Austin, TX
Mrs. Puryear wrote background information, activities, and teacher suggestions for all chapters of the *Teacher's Edition*.

CONSULTANTS

The consultants conferred on a regular basis with the editorial staff and reviewed all the chapters of the Level 2 *Teacher's Edition*.

Dorothea Bruschke
Parkway School District
Chesterfield, MO

Diane E. Laumer
San Marcos High School
San Marcos, TX

REVIEWERS

The following educators reviewed one or more chapters of the *Teacher's Edition*.

Nancy Butt
Washington and Lee
High School
Arlington, VA

Frank Dietz
The University of Texas
at Austin
Austin, TX

Connie Frank
John F. Kennedy High School
Sacramento, CA

Patrick T. Raven
School District of Waukesha
Waukesha, WI

John Scanlan
Arlington High School
Arlington, OR

Rolf Schwägermann
Stuyvesant High School
New York, NY

Jim Witt
Grand Junction High School
Grand Junction, CO

FIELD TEST PARTICIPANTS

We express our appreciation to the teachers and students who participated in the field test. Their comments were instrumental in the development of the entire *Komm mit!* program.

Eva-Marie Adolphi
Indian Hills Middle School
Sandy, UT

Connie Allison
MacArthur High School
Lawton, OK

Dennis Bergren
West High School
Madison, WI

Linda Brummett
Redmond High School
Redmond, WA

M. Beatrice Brusstar
Lincoln Northeast High School
Lincoln, NE

Jane Bungartz
Southwest High School
Fort Worth, TX

Devora D. Diller
Lovejoy High School
Lovejoy, GA

Margaret Draheim
Wilson Junior High School
Appleton, WI

Kay DuBois
Kennewick High School
Kennewick, WA

Elfriede A. Gabbert
Capital High School
Boise, ID

Petra A. Hansen
Redmond High School
Redmond, WA

Christa Hary
Brien McMahon High School
Norwalk, CT

Ingrid S. Kinner
Weaver Education Center
Greensboro, NC

Diane E. Laumer
San Marcos High School
San Marcos, TX

J. Lewinsohn
Redmond High School
Redmond, WA

Linnea Maulding
Fife High School
Tacoma, WA

Judith A. Nimtz
Central High School
West Allis, WI

Jane Reinkordt
Lincoln Southeast High School
Lincoln, NE

Elizabeth A. Smith
Plano Senior High School
Plano, TX

Elizabeth L. Webb
Sandy Creek High School
Tyrone, GA

PROFESSIONAL ESSAYS

Using Portfolios in the Foreign Language Classroom
Jo Anne S. Wilson
Consultant
Glen Arbor, MI

Teaching Culture
Nancy A. Humbach
Miami University
Oxford, OH

Dorothea Bruschke
Parkway School District
Chesterfield, MO

The Student-Centered Classroom
Patrick T. Raven
School District of Waukesha
Waukesha, WI

Learning Styles and Multi-Modality Teaching
Mary B. McGehee
Louisiana State University,
Laboratory School
Baton Rouge, LA

Higher-Order Thinking Skills
Audrey L. Heining-Boynton
The University of North
Carolina at Chapel Hill, NC

Multi-Level Classrooms
Joan H. Manley
University of Texas at
El Paso, TX

AUTHOR

George Winkler
Austin, TX

Mr. Winkler developed the scope and sequence and framework for the chapters, created the basic material, selected realia, and wrote activities.

CONTRIBUTING WRITERS

Carolyn Roberts Thompson
Abilene Christian University
Abilene, TX

Mrs. Thompson was responsible for the selection of realia for readings and for developing reading activities.

CONSULTANTS

The consultants conferred on a regular basis with the editorial staff and reviewed all the chapters of the Level 2 textbook.

Dorothea Bruschke
Parkway School District
Chesterfield, MO

Margrit Meinel Diehl
Syracuse, NY

Diane E. Laumer
San Marcos High School
San Marcos, TX

Phyllis Manning
Vancouver, WA

Ingeborg R. McCoy
Southwest Texas State University
San Marcos, TX

REVIEWERS

The following educators reviewed one or more chapters of the *Pupil's Edition*.

Nancy Butt
Washington and Lee High School
Arlington, Va

Connie Frank
John F. Kennedy High School
Sacramento, CA

Patrick T. Raven
School District of Waukesha
Waukesha, WI

John Scanlan
Arlington High School
Arlington, OR

Rolf Schwägermann
Stuyvesant High School
New York, NY

Linda Wiencken
The Austin Waldorf School
Austin, TX

Scott Williams
The University of Texas at Austin
Austin, TX

Jim Witt
Grand Junction High School
Grand Junction, CO

FIELD TEST PARTICIPANTS

We express our appreciation to the teachers and students who participated in the field test. Their comments were instrumental in the development of the entire **Komm mit!** program.

Eva-Marie Adolphi
Indian Hills Middle School
Sandy, UT

Connie Allison
MacArthur High School
Lawton, OK

Dennis Bergren
West High School
Madison, WI

Linda Brummett
Redmond High School
Redmond, WA

M. Beatrice Brusstar
Lincoln Northeast High School
Lincoln, NE

Jane Bungartz
Southwest High School
Fort Worth, TX

Devora D. Diller
Lovejoy High School
Lovejoy, GA

Margaret Draheim
Wilson Junior High School
Appleton, WI

Kay DuBois
Kennewick High School
Kennewick, WA

Elfriede A. Gabbert
Capital High School
Boise, ID

Petra A. Hansen
Redmond High School
Redmond, WA

Christa Hary
Brien McMahon High School
Norwalk, CT

Ingrid S. Kinner
Weaver Education Center
Greensboro, NC

Diane E. Laumer
San Marcos High School
San Marcos, TX

J. Lewinsohn
Redmond High School
Redmond, WA

Linnea Maulding
Fife High School
Tacoma, WA

Judith A. Nimtz
Central High School
West Allis, WI

Jane Reinkordt
Lincoln Southeast High School
Lincoln, NE

Elizabeth A. Smith
Plano Senior High School
Plano, TX

Elizabeth L. Webb
Sandy Creek High School
Tyrone, GA

ACKNOWLEDGMENTS

We are very grateful to the German students who participated in our program and are pictured in this textbook. We wish to express our thanks also to the parents who allowed us to photograph these young people in their homes and in other places. There are many teachers, school administrators, and merchants whose cooperation and patience made an enormous difference in the quality of these pages; we are grateful to them as well.

MAIN CHARACTERS

Hamburg: David Ene, Saskia Geddat, Max Jentzen, Isolde Rüter, Renate Sprick, Horst Stahl, Finn Thor Stracen, Jutta Thassler, Cornelia Vogt, Julien Walter, Saskia Zimmermann

Stuttgart: Michael Beiser, Nina Buhre, Jochen Friedrick, Frieder Gauger, Sigrun Gauger, Ulrich Gauger, Adolf Gerst, Rosemarie Gerst, Katharine Kronberg, Anne Künzlen, Björn Künzlen, Christine Müller, Vanessa Philipps, Eric Schäfer, Nadine Schaefer, Dirk-Michael Schulz, Michael Tischer, Hussein Ulhu

München: Hadi Assassa, Thomas Austria, Sabine Brucker, Bärbel Doermer, Ralf Doermer, Lucretia Guggemos, Max Hüber, Florian Kraemer, Susi Krauth, Mathias Müller, Georg Portenlänger, Carol Seyboth

Berlin: Yvonne Barenz, Ismar Hadziefendic, Klaus-Jürgen Hintzler, Thieu-Binh Hoang, Nico Klemm, Barbara Manguoglu-Wittwer, Berta Nieszen, Katharine Proft, Nicole Sattler, Lars Ulrich

TEACHERS AND FAMILIES

Cordula and Eduard Böhm, Liv and Christoph Künzlen, Barbara and Harald Manguoglu-Wittwer, Janet and Peter Seyboth, Giesela and Karl-Heinz Simon, Renate and Karl-Heinz Sprick, Jutta and Jochen Thassler

SCHOOLS

Bismarck-Gymnasium, Hamburg; Ellenthal-Gymnasium, Bietigheim-Bissingen; Helene-Lange-Gymnasium, Hamburg; Max-Beckmann-Oberschule, Berlin; Rudolf-Diesel-Realschule, München

TEACHER'S EDITION

Contents

Komm mit!

Come along— to a world of new experiences!

Komm mit! offers you the opportunity to learn the language spoken by millions of people in several European countries and around the world. Let's find out about these people and their culture.

TEACHING SUGGESTIONS FOR THE BAYERN LOCATION OPENER ...T68–T69

Komm mit nach

Bayern!

LOCATION FOR KAPITEL 1, 2, 3 1

VISIT THE SOUTHERN STATE OF BAYERN AND —

Get to know a Bavarian family • KAPITEL 1

Find out how German teenagers help at home • KAPITEL 2

Travel to German and Austrian cities • KAPITEL 3

TEACHING SUGGESTIONS FOR KAPITEL 1 ....3A–3R

KAPITEL 1
WIEDERHOLUNGSKAPITEL

Bei den Baumanns 4

KAPITEL 2
WIEDERHOLUNGSKAPITEL

KAPITEL 3

Komm mit nach
Hamburg!

VISIT GERMANY'S LARGEST PORT CITY,
HAMBURG AND —

Get in shape "German style" • KAPITEL 4

Eat at school with
German students • KAPITEL 5

Visit a pharmacy • KAPITEL 6

KAPITEL 4

Gesund leben 82

Komm mit nach

§tuttgart!

VISIT STUTTGART, THE CAPITAL
OF BADEN-WÜRTTEMBERG AND —

Talk about life in the city and life in the country • KAPITEL 7

Express concerns about fashion and clothes • KAPITEL 8

Make alternate vacation plans • KAPITEL 9

KAPITEL 7

Stadt oder Land? 158

TEACHING SUGGESTIONS FOR THE BERLIN LOCATION OPENER.....229A–229

Komm mit nach

Berlin!

LOCATION FOR KAPITEL **10, 11, 12 . . . .230**

VISIT BERLIN, THE CAPITAL OF GERMANY, AND —

Discuss television programs and cars • KAPITEL **10**

Plan a birthday party • KAPITEL **11**

Invite friends for a casual get-together • KAPITEL **12**

TEACHING SUGGESTIONS FOR KAPITEL 10...............233A–233R

KAPITEL 10

Viele Interessen! 234

Cultural References

To The Teacher

*S*ince the early eighties, we have seen significant advances in modern foreign language curriculum practice: (1) a redefinition of the objectives of foreign language study involving a commitment to the development of proficiency in the four skills and in cultural awareness; (2) a recognition of the need for longer sequences of study; (3) a new student-centered approach that redefines the role of the teacher as facilitator and encourages students to take a more active role in their learning; (4) the inclusion of students of all learning abilities.

The new Holt, Rinehart and Winston foreign language programs take into account not only these advances in the field of foreign language education but also the input of teachers and students around the country.

PRINCIPLES AND PRACTICES

As nations become increasingly interdependent, the need for effective communication and sensitivity to other cultures becomes more important. Today's youth must be culturally and linguistically prepared to participate in a global society. At Holt, Rinehart and Winston, we believe that proficiency in a foreign language is essential to meeting this need.

The primary goal of the Holt, Rinehart and Winston foreign language programs is to help students develop linguistic proficiency and cultural sensitivity. By interweaving language and culture, our programs seek to broaden students' knowledge of other languages while at the same time deepening their appreciation of other cultures.

We believe that all students can benefit from foreign language instruction. We recognize that not everyone learns at the same rate or in the same way; nevertheless, we believe that all students should have the opportunity to acquire language proficiency to a degree commensurate with their individual abilities.

By appealing to a variety of learning styles, the Holt, Rinehart and Winston foreign language programs are designed to accommodate all students.

We believe that effective foreign language programs should motivate students. Students deserve an answer to the question they often ask, "Why are we doing this?" They need to have goals that are interesting, practical, clearly stated, and attainable.

The Holt, Rinehart and Winston foreign language programs promote success. They present relevant content in manageable increments that encourage students to attain achievable functional objectives.

We believe that proficiency in a foreign language is best nurtured by programs that encourage students to think critically and to take risks when expressing themselves in the language. We also recognize that students should strive for accuracy in communication. While it is important that students have a knowledge of the basic structures of the language, it is also important that they go beyond simple manipulation of forms.

Holt, Rinehart and Winston's foreign language program reflects a careful progression of activities that guides students from comprehensible input of authentic language through structured practice to creative, personalized expression. This progression, accompanied by consistent re-entry and spiraling of functions, vocabulary, and structures, provides students with the tools and the confidence to express themselves in their language.

Finally, we believe that a complete program of foreign language instruction should take into account the needs of teachers in today's increasingly demanding classrooms.

At Holt, Rinehart and Winston we have designed programs that offer practical teacher support and provide multiple resources to meet individual learning and teaching styles.

Using Portfolios in the Foreign Language Classroom

*T*he promise of portfolios is one of a more realistic and accurate way to assess the process of language teaching and learning.

A communicative, whole-language approach describes today's foreign language instruction. This approach requires methods of assessment that closely parallel the daily teaching and learning strategies in the proficiency-oriented classroom. We know that language acquisition is a process. Portfolios are process-oriented and provide for authentic assessment of both learning and instruction.

What Is a Portfolio?

A portfolio is a purposeful, systematic, and organized collection of a student's work. It shows the student's efforts, progress, and achievements for a given period of time, usually a semester or a school year. The portfolio is a tool to assist you in developing a student profile. It may be used as a basis for periodic evaluation, for final grades, for overall evaluation, even for placement. It may also be used to enhance or provide alternatives to traditional assessment measures, such as formal tests, quizzes, class participation, and homework.

Why Use Portfolios?

Portfolios are of great benefit to both students and teachers, because they

- **Are ongoing and systematic.** A language learner acquires skill in the language by trial and error. A portfolio reflects the real-world process of production, assessment, revision, and reassessment. It parallels the natural rhythm of learning.

- **Offer an incentive to learn.** Students have a vested interest in creating their portfolios because portfolios give them the opportunity to showcase their ongoing efforts and tangible achievements. Students select the work to be included and have a chance to revise, perfect, evaluate, and explain the contents.

- **Are sensitive to individual needs.** There is a wide diversity in the pace and manner of language development. Language learners bring varied abilities to the classroom and do not acquire skills in a uniformly neat and orderly fashion. Portfolios offer a way of personalizing and individualizing assessment that responds to this diversity.

- **Provide documentation of language development.** Language learning is a process. The material in a student portfolio is evidence of student progress in this process. The contents of the portfolio make it easier for you to discuss student progress with the students as well as with parents and others interested in the student's progress.

- **Offer multiple sources of information.** A portfolio presents a way to collect and analyze information from multiple sources that reflect a student's efforts, progress, and achievements in the language. This information gives valuable feedback to both teachers and students that allows them to assess and improve both the teaching and learning processes.

Portfolio Components

For the foreign language portfolio to be of value, it should include both oral and written work, student self-evaluation, and documentation of teacher observation. For example, a Level One portfolio might contain audio tapes of a student's description of family members or the acting out of an everyday situation, such as shopping for clothing. Writing samples could include a shopping list or labeling of items pictured on a poster or sketch of a classroom setting. Teacher observation should be included in the portfolio, too, perhaps in the form of brief, non-evaluative, anecdotal comments of student performance written on adhesive notes.

The Oral Component

The oral component of a portfolio might be an audio or video cassette. It may contain both rehearsed and extemporaneous dialogues and monologues. For a rehearsed speaking activity, give a specific communicative task that students can personalize according to their individual interests (for example, ordering a favorite meal in a restaurant).

Rehearsing with other members of the class gives students an opportunity for peer coaching and revision prior to the final recording. For an extemporaneous speaking activity, first acquaint students with some possible topics for discussion or the specific task they will be expected to perform. (For example, tell them they will be asked to discuss a picture showing a sports activity or a restaurant scene.)

The Written Component
Portfolios offer an excellent opportunity to incorporate process-writing strategies into the foreign language classroom. Evidence of the writing process—documentation of prewriting brainstorming, multiple drafts, and peer comments—should be included along with the finished product.

Involve students in the selection of a writing task. At the beginning levels of learning, the task might include some structured writing in the target language, such as labeling or listing. Evidence of cultural sensitivity can be included in pieces written by the student in English. Keeping a journal in the target language is also a valuable way for students to see progress in their ability to use the written language. Letter-writing is another appropriate way for students to become involved in the writing process. Final drafts of a specific writing assignment could even be displayed on bulletin boards or reproduced in a newsletter.

Student Self-Evaluation
Students are not only major contributors of material to their portfolios, but they should also be involved in critiquing and evaluating their portfolios as well. It is appropriate that students monitor their own progress; therefore, the process and procedure for student self-evaluation should be considered in planning the contents of the portfolio. Students should work with you and their peers to design the exact format. Self-evaluation encourages them to think about what they are learning (content), how they learn (process), why they are learning (purpose), and where they are going in their learning (goals).

Teacher Observation
A crucial component of a foreign language portfolio is documentation of teacher observations. Results of these systematic, regular, and ongoing observations are placed in the portfolio only after discussing them with the student. They are not intended to be evaluative, but rather to provide expert-witness feedback on the process of language learning.

With portfolios, you become a distanced observer of student behavior, recording observations with an established set of criteria that has been developed earlier with input from the student. Observation techniques may include the following:

- Jotting notes in a journal to be discussed with the student and then placed in the portfolio
- Using a checklist of observable behaviors such as the willingness to take risks when using the target language, demonstrations of strategic or linguistic competence, and an indication of the degree to which the learner is engaged in the linguistic task

- Making observations on adhesive notes that can be easily placed in folders
- Recording anecdotal comments, during or after class, using a small hand-held voice-activated cassette recorder.

What about subjectivity? The reality of subjectivity is present whenever the human element, however appropriate, is a part of evaluation. Nothing should be placed in a permanent portfolio that cannot be substantiated. Knowledge of the criteria you use in your observation gives students a framework for their performance. You are the expert in the classroom. Your expert observation, with appropriate documentation, utilizes your professional skills in a way that is missing from traditional testing methods.

How Are Portfolios Evaluated?
The portfolio should reflect the process of student learning over a specific period of time. At the beginning of that time period, determine the criteria by which you will assess the final product and convey them to the students. Make this evaluation a collaborative effort by seeking students' input as you formulate these criteria and your instructional goals.

Students need to understand that evaluation based on a predetermined standard is but one phase of the assessment process; demonstrated effort and growth are just as important. As you consider correctness and accuracy in both oral and written work, also consider the organization, creativity, and improvement revealed by the student's portfolio over the time period. The portfolio provides a way to monitor the growth of a student's knowledge, skills, and attitudes. The contents should show the student's efforts and progress, as well as achievements.

How to Implement Portfolios

Teacher/teacher collaboration is as important to the implementation of portfolios as teacher/student collaboration. Confer with your colleagues to determine the answers to questions such as the following: What kinds of information do you want to see in the student portfolio? How will the information be presented? What is the purpose of the portfolio? Will it be used for grading, placement, or a combination of both? What are the criteria for evaluating the portfolio? Answers to these and other questions can help create a strong foreign language department and foster a departmental cohesiveness and consistency that will ultimately benefit the students.

The Promise of Portfolios

As teachers and students work together to develop portfolios and to decide how they will be used, there is a high degree of student involvement. This involvement promises renewed student enthusiasm for learning and improved achievement. As students compare portfolio pieces done early in the year with work produced later, they can take pride in their progress as well as reassess their motivation and work habits.

Portfolios also provide a framework for periodic assessment of teaching strategies, programs, and instruction. They offer schools a tool to help solve the problem of vertical articulation and accurate student placement. The promise of portfolios is one of a more realistic and accurate way to assess the process of language teaching and learning that is congruent with the strategies that should be used in the proficiency-oriented classroom.

Komm mit! supports the *use of portfolios* in the following ways:

The Pupil's Edition
▶ Includes numerous oral and written activities that can be easily adapted for student portfolios.

The Teacher's Edition
▶ Identifies in the *Portfolio Assessment* feature activities that may serve as portfolio items.

The Ancillary Program
▶ Includes in the *Assessment Guide* criteria for evaluating portfolios.

Teaching Culture

*W*e must integrate culture and language in a way that encourages curiosity, stimulates analysis, and teaches students to hypothesize.

Ask students what they like best about studying a foreign language. Chances are that learning about culture, the way people live, is one of their favorite aspects. Years after language study has ended, adults remember with fondness the customs of the target culture, even pictures in their language textbooks. It is this interest in the people and their way of life that is the great motivator and helps us sustain students' interest in language study.

That interest in other people mandates an integration of culture and language. We must integrate culture and language in a way that encourages curiosity, stimulates analysis, and teaches students to hypothesize and seek answers to questions about the people whose language they are studying. Teaching isolated facts about how people in other cultures live is not enough. This information is soon dated and quickly forgotten. We must attempt to go a step beyond and teach students that all behavior, values, and traditions exist because of certain aspects of history, geography, and socio-economic conditions.

There are many ways to help students become culturally knowledgeable, and to assist them in developing an awareness of differences and similarities between the target culture and their own. Two of these approaches involve critical thinking, that is, trying to find reasons for a certain behavior through observation and analysis, and relating these observations to larger cultural patterns.

First Approach: Questioning

The first approach involves *questioning* as the key strategy. At the earliest stages of language learning, students learn ways to greet peers, elders, strangers, as well as the use of **du, ihr,** and **Sie.** Students need to consider questions such as: How do German-speaking people greet each other? Are there different levels of formality? Who initiates a handshake? What's considered a good handshake? Each of these questions leads students to think about the values that are expressed through words and gestures. They start to "feel" the other culture, and at the same time, understand how much of their own behavior is rooted in their cultural background.

Magazines, newspapers, advertisements, and television commercials are all excellent sources of cultural material. For example, browsing through a German magazine, one finds an extraordinary number of advertisements for health-related products. Could this indicate a great interest in staying healthy? To learn about customs involving health, reading advertisements can be followed up with viewing videos and films, or by interviewing native speakers or people who have lived in German-speaking countries. Students might want to find answers to questions such as: "How do Germans treat a cold? What is their attitude toward fresh air? Toward exercise?" This type of questioning might lead students to discover that some of the popular leisure-time activities, such as **einen Spaziergang machen** or **eine Wanderung machen,** are related to health consciousness.

An advertisement for a refrigerator or a picture of a German kitchen can provide an insight into practices of shopping for food. Students first need to think about the refrigerator at home, take an inventory of what is kept in it, and consider when and where their family shops. Next, students should look closely at a German refrigerator. What is its size? What could that mean? (Smaller refrigerators might mean that shopping takes place more often, stores are within walking distance, and people eat more fresh foods.)

Food wrappers and containers also provide cultural insight. For example, in German-speaking countries, bottled water is preferred to tap water even though tap water is safe to drink in most places. Why, then, is the rather expensive bottled water still preferred? Is it a tradition stemming from a time when tap water was not pure? Does it relate to the Germans' fondness of "taking the waters," i.e., drinking fresh spring water at a spa?

Second Approach: Associating Words with Images

The second approach for developing cultural understanding involves *forming associations of words with the cultural images they suggest.* Language and culture are so closely related that one might actually say that language *is* culture. Most words, especially nouns, carry a cultural connotation. Knowing the literal equivalent of a word in another language is of little use to students in understanding this connotation. For example, **Freund** cannot be translated simply as *friend,* **Brot** as *bread,* or **Straße** as *street.* The German word **Straße,** for instance, carries with it such images as people walking, sitting in a sidewalk café, riding bicycles, or shopping in specialty stores, and cars parked partly over the curb amid dense traffic. There is also the image of **Fußgängerzone,** a street for pedestrians only.

When students have acquired some sense of the cultural connotation of words—not only through explanations but, more

importantly, through observation of visual images—they start to discover the larger underlying cultural themes, or what is often called deep culture.

These larger cultural themes serve as organizing categories into which individual cultural phenomena fit to form a pattern. Students might discover, for example, that Germans, because they live in much more crowded conditions, have a great need for privacy (cultural theme), as reflected in such phenomena as closed doors, fences or walls around property, and shutters on windows. Students might also discover that love of nature and the outdoors is an important cultural theme as indicated by such phenomena as flower boxes and planters in public places, well-kept public parks in every town, and people going for a walk or hiking.

As we teach culture, students learn to recognize elements not only of the target culture but also of their American cultural heritage. They see how elements of culture reflect larger themes or patterns. Learning what makes us Americans and how that information relates to other people throughout the world can be an exciting discovery for a young person.

As language teachers, we are able to facilitate this discovery of our similarities with others as well as our differences. We do not encourage value judgments about others and their culture, nor do we recommend adopting other ways. We simply say to students, "Other ways exist. They exist, just as our ways exist, due to our history, geography, and what our ancestors have passed on to us through traditions and values."

Komm mit! develops *cultural understanding and cultural awareness* in the following ways:

The Pupil's Edition

▶ Informs students about daily life in German-speaking countries through culture notes.

▶ Provides deeper insight into cultural phenomena through personal interviews in the **Landeskunde** section.

▶ Helps students associate language and its cultural connotations through authentic art and photos.

The Teacher's Edition

▶ Provides additional cultural and language notes.

▶ Suggests critical thinking strategies that encourage students to hypothesize, analyze, and discover larger underlying cultural themes.

The Ancillary Program

▶ Includes realia that develops cultural insight by serving as catalyst for questioning and discovery.

▶ Offers activities that require students to compare and contrast cultures, as well as to find reasons for certain behavior.

Implementing Komm mit! in the Middle Grades

Remember that planning a variety of tactile, kinesthetic, and visual activities that invite participation will help students be successful.

Students in the middle grades are at different levels of cognitive development than are high school and elementary students. In addition, middle school students are at markedly different levels of development from one another and have many different learning styles. Many sixth and seventh graders, especially, are tactile and kinesthetic, with a particular need for opportunities for movement. Seventh and eighth graders are more capable of formal cognitive operations and are increasingly preoccupied with social issues. They need and demand to know that what they learn in school relates to their lives. For all middle school students, self-esteem can be particularly fragile because of the many developmental changes they are undergoing.

The wide variety of activities in the various components of *Komm mit!* Level 1 enables teachers to adapt the many materials to their students' needs.

Scheduling
Komm mit! Level 1 can best be taught as a two-year program in the middle grades. Covering six chapters and two Location Openers each year allows five to six weeks for each chapter. This scheduling affords ample time to include varied activities that the diversity of the students demands.

Instruction
A number of proposals for teaching **Kapitel 3** are presented below as examples of activities especially well suited to middle school students. Many of these suggestions are either directly excerpted or adapted from those in the *Teacher's Edition* and ancillary materials. As you plan your own lessons, remember that planning a variety of tactile, kinesthetic, and visual activities that invite participation will help students be successful. Remember, too, that varying the type of activity often within each class and offering students choices will augment enthusiasm and motivation.

Los geht's!
Visual and concrete learners enjoy and learn from the videos. Show them the video segment **Los geht's!** without sound and ask them to watch for things that seem to be different in Germany.
- After briefly discussing what they think happened in the segment, write the title **Nach der Schule** on the board, and then draw three sets of spokes branching from the themes **Was wir tun, Was wir essen,** and **Was wir trinken**. Ask the students in English about what they like to do after school, and put their answers into German in the word webs on the board. Creating the web personalizes the material, makes it visual, and also helps students anticipate what they are about to see and hear as the video is presented a second time.
- As suggested on p. 63H, the activities that follow **Los geht's!** on p. 68 can be completed in cooperative learning groups after viewing the video.
- Occasionally, have groups briefly speculate about what will happen in the **Fortsetzung** before showing it. This activity is fun and encourages the students to anticipate what they may see and hear.

Erste Stufe
Before beginning the **Erste Stufe**, offer students a concrete, hands-on project. For example, share with them a list of foods and beverages that you would like to have as props in the classroom for presentations and role-playing, and have them sign up to make the life-size prop of their choice, using chenille stems, construction paper, fabric, papier-maché, plastic cups, and more. Have them make more than one of whatever they choose so that you will have props for all of the cooperative learning groups.
- To introduce the **Wortschatz** on p. 71, give each group a basket full of props, and then use TPR as suggested on p. 63J. Call on one student from each group as you request each prop.
- The **möchte**-forms are introduced on p. 71; Activity 11 on p. 72 provides a brief opportunity to practice them. Another opportunity particularly suited to visual, kinesthetic, and social learners is a team game requiring dry erase boards, dry erase markers preferably of the low odor variety, and rags. Show a glass of mineral water and ask **Was möchtet ihr trinken?** The cooperative learning groups work silently as teams to write **Wir möchten ein Glas Mineralwasser, bitte,** or **Wir möchten ein Mine-**

ralwasser. The student in each group who has possession of the board when the question is given should write the first word of an appropriate response and then pass the materials to the next person. That person can choose either to correct the one word that has been written or to add the word that should follow. The third student, in turn, may choose either to correct a word or to add the word that should follow. Allow a designated amount of time to pass, and then award each group a point for each word correctly written.

- Have students use the props they made to do Activity 12 on p. 72.
- The students very much enjoy seeing and hearing kids close to their own ages in the **Landeskunde** segments, and the activities in the Activity Masters define clear tasks for them to accomplish as they listen.

Zweite Stufe

In the **Zweite Stufe**, students learn to describe bedrooms and the furniture in them; personalize the material by asking students how they would like to furnish their bedrooms if money were no object.

- Presenting the grammar introduced on p. 75 and elsewhere in the book in the way suggested on p. 63L encourages students to draw their own inferences, and this process promotes self-esteem as it encourages students to use higher-order thinking skills and empowers them to construct their own knowledge.
- Many learners in the middle grades especially enjoy games such as the opposites game suggested on p. 63M which involves movement.
- A number of activities present-

ed in the teacher's suggestions, such as Activitiy 15 on p. 63L, Activity 18 on p. 63M, and the Suggested Project on p. 63E, are suitable for middle school students.

Dritte Stufe

In the **Dritte Stufe**, students learn to describe people and talk about family members. To introduce the new vocabulary, talk about and show pictures of your own family as you put the words for relations onto the board in a family tree. Instead of simply using chalk, color code the new words according to whether they refer to male or female relations.

- Have students work in groups to ask one another about their families using possessives, pronouns, and the new vocabulary for describing people. To help students organize their notes on what they learn from one another, prepare a grid like the one proposed in Group Work suggestion for Activity 20 on p. 63O.

- The numbers 21-100 are introduced on p. 79, and p. 63O suggests playing Bingo. Model the game by playing as a class, then break into small groups to allow more students to be callers and thus practice pronouncing the new vocabulary.
- Seventh grade students especially enjoy playing Buzz when they can stand at their desks until they are eliminated, and addition games such as the one on p. 63O can also be good fun.
- A number of activities presented in the teacher's suggestions, such as **Anwendung 8c** on p. 85, Activity 20, *Chapter Resources Book 1*, p. 146, the TPR game and the game of *Twenty Questions* on p. 63P, are suitable for the middle school students.

Komm mit! addresses the *needs of learners in the middle grades* in the following ways:

The Pupil's Edition
▶ Offers a sequence of activities in each **Stufe** that guides students from structure practice to open-ended activities promoting personalized, meaningful expression.
▶ Provides tips in the **Lerntrick** and **Lesetrick** features that help students become autonomous learners.
▶ Includes a **Zum Lesen** section at the end of each chapter that offers prereading, reading, and postreading activities to help students develop reading strategies.
▶ Features many photos and drawings.

The Teacher's Edition
▶ Proposes a variety of activities that target auditory, kinesthetic, tactile, and visual learners; features many cooperative learning activities.
▶ Offers **Family Link** suggestions that younger students enjoy.
▶ Presents game ideas at the beginning of each chapter that can easily be made active and can often be used just as well with other chapters.

The Ancillary Program
▶ The extensive ancillary program provides both extensive auditory and visual exposure to the language and many activities that help learners simplify complex learning tasks.

Learning Styles and Multi-Modality Teaching

*I*ncorporating a greater variety of teaching and learning activities to accommodate the learning styles of all students can make the difference between struggle and pleasure in foreign language learning.

The larger and broader population of students who are enrolling in foreign language classes brings a new challenge to foreign language educators, calling forth an evolution in teaching methods to enhance learning for all our students. Educational experts now recognize that every student has a preferred sense for learning and retrieving information: visual, auditory, or kinesthetic. Incorporating a greater variety of teaching and learning activities to accommodate the learning styles of all students can make the difference between struggle and pleasure in foreign language learning.

Accommodating Different Learning Styles

A modified arrangement of the classroom is one way to provide more effective and more enjoyable learning for all students. Rows of chairs and desks must give way at times to circles, semicircles, or small clusters. Students may be grouped in fours or in pairs for small group work, cooperative work, or peer teaching. It is important to find a balance of arrangements, thereby providing the most comfort in varied situations.

Since auditory, kinesthetic, and visual learners will be present in the class, and also because every student's learning will be enhanced by a multi-sensory approach, lessons must be directed toward all three learning styles. Any language lesson content may be presented auditorially, visually, and kinesthetically.

Visual presentations and practice may include the chalkboard, charts, posters, television, overhead projectors, books, magazines, picture diagrams, flash cards, bulletin boards, films, slides, or videos. Visual learners need to see what they are to learn. Lest the teacher think he or she will never have the time to prepare all those visuals, Dickel and Slak (1983) found that visual aids generated by students are more effective than ready-made ones.

Auditory presentations and practice may include stating aloud the requirements of the lesson, oral questions and answers, paired or group work on a progression of oral exercises from repetition to communication, tapes, CDs, dialogues, and role-playing. Jingles, catchy stories, and memory devices using songs and rhymes are good learning aids. Having students record themselves and then listen as they play back the cassette allows them to practice in the auditory mode.

Kinesthetic presentations entail the students' use of manipulatives, chart materials, gestures, signals, typing, songs, games, and role-playing. These lead the students to associate sentence constructions with meaningful movements.

A Sample Lesson Using Multi-Modality Teaching

A multi-sensory presentation on greetings might proceed as follows. As the teacher begins oral presentation of greetings and introductions, he or she simultaneously shows the written forms on transparencies, with the formal expressions marked with an adult's hat, and the informal expressions marked with a baseball cap. The teacher then distributes cards with the hat and cap symbols representing the formal or informal expressions. As the students hear taped mini-dialogues, they hold up the appropriate card to indicate whether the dialogues are formal or informal. On the next listening, the students repeat the sentences they hear. A longer taped dialogue follows, allowing students to hear the new expressions a number of times. The students next write from dictation several sentences containing the new expressions. They may work in pairs, correcting each other's work as they "test" their own understanding of the lesson at hand. Finally, students respond to simple questions using the appropriate formal and informal responses cued by the cards they hold.

For additional kinesthetic input, members of the class come to the front of the room, each holding a hat or cap symbol. As the teacher calls out situations, the students play the roles, using gestures and props appropriate to the age group they are portraying. Non-cued, communicative role-playing

BY MARY B. McGEHEE

with props further enables the students to "feel" the differences between formal and informal expressions.

Helping Students Learn How to Use Their Preferred Mode

Since we require students to perform in all language skills, part of the assistance we must render is to help them develop strategies within their preferred learning modes to carry out an assignment in another mode. For example, visual students hear the teacher assign an oral exercise and visualize what they must do. They must see themselves carrying out the assignment, in effect watching themselves as if there were a movie going on in their heads. Only then can they also hear themselves saying the right things. Thus, this assignment will be much easier for the visual learners who have been taught this process, if they have not already figured it out for themselves. Likewise, true auditory students, confronted with a reading/writing assignment, must talk themselves through it, converting the entire process into sound as they plan and prepare their work. Kinesthetic students presented with a visual or auditory task must first break the assignment into tasks and then work their way through them.

Students who experience difficulty because of a strong preference for one mode of learning are often unaware of the degree of their preference. In working with these students, I prefer the simple and direct assessment of learning styles offered by Richard Bandler and John Grinder in their book *Frogs into Princes,* which allows the teacher and student to quickly determine how the student learns. In an interview with the

student, I follow the assessment with certain specific recommendations of techniques to make the student's study time more effective.

It is important to note here that teaching students to maximize their study does not require that the teacher give each student an individualized assignment. It does require that each student who needs it be taught how to prepare the assignment using his or her own talents and strengths. This communication between teacher and student, combined with teaching techniques that reinforce learning in all modes, can only maximize pleasure and success in learning a foreign language.

References

Dickel, M.J. and S. Sleek. "Imaging Vividness and Memory for Verbal Material." *Journal of Mental Imagery 7*, i(1983):121-6

Bandler, Richard, and John Grinder. *Frogs into Princes,* Real People Press, Moab, Utah. 1978

Komm mit! accommodates *different learning styles* in the following ways:

The Pupil's Edition
► Presents basic material in video, audio, and printed format.
► Includes role-playing activities and a variety of multi-modality activities.

The Teacher's Edition
► Provides suggested activities for auditory, visual, and kinesthetic learners.
► Offers Total Physical Response activities.

The Ancillary Program
► Meets individual needs of students with additional reinforcement activities in a variety of modes.

Higher-Order Thinking Skills

*I*ntroduce students to the life skills they need to become successful, productive citizens in our society.

Our profession loves acronyms! TPR, ALM, OBI, and now the HOTS! HOTS stands for **h**igher-**o**rder **t**hinking **s**kills. These thinking skills help our students listen, speak, read, write, and learn about culture in a creative, meaningful way, while providing them with necessary life skills.

What Are Higher-Order Thinking Skills?

Higher-order thinking skills are not a new phenomenon on the educational scene. In 1956, Benjamin Bloom published a book that listed a taxonomy of educational objectives in the form of a pyramid similar to the one in the following illustration:

Bloom's Taxonomy of Educational Objectives

Evaluation
Synthesis
Analysis
Application
Comprehension
Knowledge

Knowledge is the simplest level of educational objectives, and is not considered a higher-order thinking skill. It requires the learner to remember information without having to fully understand it. Tasks that students perform to demonstrate knowl-edge are recalling, identifying, recognizing, citing, labeling, listing, reciting, and stating.

Comprehension is not considered a higher-order thinking skill either. Learners demonstrate comprehension when they paraphrase, describe, summarize, illustrate, restate, or translate.

Foreign language teachers tend to focus the most on knowledge and comprehension. The tasks performed at these levels are important because they provide a solid foundation for the more complex tasks at the higher levels of Bloom's pyramid. However, offering our students the opportunity to perform at still higher cognitive levels provides them with more meaningful contexts in which to use the target language.

When teachers incorporate **application, analysis, synthesis,** and **evaluation** as objectives, they allow students to utilize **higher-order thinking skills.**

Application involves solving, transforming, determining, demonstrating, and preparing.

Analysis includes classifying, comparing, making associations, verifying, seeing cause and effect relationships, and determining sequences, patterns, and consequences.

Synthesis requires generalizing, predicting, imagining, creating, making inferences, hypothesizing, making decisions, and drawing conclusions.

Finally, **evaluation** involves assessing, persuading, determining value, judging, validating, and solving problems.

Most foreign language classes focus little on higher-order thinking skills. Some foreign language educators mistakenly think that all higher-order thinking skills require an advanced level of language ability. Not so! Students can demonstrate these skills by using very simple language available even to beginning students. Also, higher-order thinking tasks about the target culture or language can be conducted in English. The use of some English in the foreign language classroom to utilize higher cognitive skills does not jeopardize progress in the target language.

Higher-order thinking skills prepare our students for more than using a foreign language. They introduce students to the life skills they need to become successful, productive citizens in our society. When we think about it, that *is* the underlying purpose of education.

Why Teach Higher-Order Thinking Skills?

There is already so much to cover and so little time that some teachers may question the worth of adding this type of activities to an already full schedule. Yet we know from experience that simply "covering" the material does not help our students acquire another language. Incorporating higher-order thinking skills in the foreign language classroom can help guide students toward language acquisition by providing meaningful experiences in a setting that can often feel artificial.

Also, we now know that employing higher-order thinking skills assists all students, including those who are at risk of failing. In the past, we felt that at-risk students were incapable of higher-order thinking, but we have since discovered that we have been denying them the opportunity to experience what they are capable of doing and what they need to do in order to be successful adults.

Sample Activities Employing Higher-Order Thinking Skills

There are no limitations to incorporating higher-order thinking skills into the foreign language classroom. What follows are a few sample activities, some of which you may already be familiar with. Use *your* higher-order thinking skills to develop other possibilities!

Listening

HOTS: Analysis
Tasks: Patterning and sequencing
Vocabulary Needed: Three colors
Materials Required: Three colored-paper squares for each student

After reviewing the colors, call out a pattern of colors and have the students show their comprehension by arranging their colored pieces of paper from left to right in the order you give. Then have them finish the pattern for you. For example, you say: **rot, grün, blau, rot, grün, blau, rot, grün,**... now what color follows? And then what color?

This is not only a HOTS activity; it also crosses disciplines. It reviews the mathematical concept of patterning and sequencing. You can have the students form patterns and sequences using any type of vocabulary.

Reading

HOTS: Synthesis
Tasks: Hypothesizing and imagining
Vocabulary Needed: Determined by level of students
Materials Required: Legend or short story

After the students have read the first part of the story, have them imagine how the story would end based on the values of the target culture.

Speaking

HOTS: Evaluation
Tasks: Assessing and determining value
Vocabulary Needed: Numbers 0-25, five objects students would need for school
Materials Required: Visuals of five school-related objects with prices beneath them

Tell students that they each have twenty-five dollars to spend on back-to-school needs. They each need to tell you what they would buy with their money.

Writing

HOTS: Analysis
Tasks: Classifying
Vocabulary Needed: Leisure activities

Materials Required: Drawings of leisure activities on a handout

From the list of activities they have before them, students should write the ones that they like to do on the weekend. Then they should write those that a family member likes to do. Finally, students should write a comparison of the two lists.

Commitment to Higher-Order Thinking Skills

Teaching higher-order thinking skills takes no extra time from classroom instruction since language skills are reinforced during thinking skills activities. What teaching higher-order thinking skills does require of teachers is a commitment to classroom activities that go beyond the knowledge/comprehension level. Having students name objects and recite verb forms is not enough. Employing HOTS gives students the opportunity to experience a second language as a useful device for meaningful communication.

References

Bloom, Benjamin. *Taxonomy of Educational Objectives. Handbook 1: Cognitive Domain.* New York: David McKay Company, 1956.

Komm mit! encourages *higher-order thinking* in the following ways:

The Pupil's Edition
▶ Develops higher-order thinking skills through a variety of activities.

The Teacher's Edition
▶ Includes the feature *Thinking Critically* that requires students to draw inferences, compare and contrast, evaluate, and synthesize.

The Ancillary Program
▶ Incorporates higher-order thinking skills in activities that help students use the language in a creative, meaningful way.

Multi-Level Classrooms

There are positive ways, both psychological and pedagogical, to make this situation work for you and your students.

So you have just heard that your third-period class is going to include both Levels 2 and 3! While this is never the best news for a foreign language teacher, there are positive ways, both psychological and pedagogical, to make the multi-level classroom work for you and your students.

Relieving student anxieties
Initially, in a multi-level class environment, it is important to relieve students' anxiety by orienting them to their new situation. From the outset, let all students know that just because they "did" things the previous year, such as learn how to conjugate certain verbs, they may not yet be able to use them in a meaningful way. Students should not feel that it is demeaning or a waste of time to recycle activities or to share knowledge and skills with fellow students. Second-year students need to know they are

not second-class citizens and that they can benefit from their classmates' greater experience with the language. Third-year students may achieve a great deal of satisfaction and become more confident in their own language skills when they have opportunities to help or teach their second-year classmates. It is important to reassure third-year students that you will devote time to them and challenge them with different assignments.

Easing your own apprehension
When you are faced with both Levels 2 and 3 in your classroom, remind yourself that you teach students of different levels in the same classroom every year, although not officially. After one year of classroom instruction, your Level 2 class will never be a truly homogeneous group. Despite being made up of students with the

same amount of "seat time," the class comprises multiple layers of language skills, knowledge, motivation, and ability. Therefore, you are constantly called upon to make a positive experience out of a potentially negative one. Your apprehension will gradually diminish to the extent that you are able to...
- make students less dependent on you for the successful completion of their activities.
- place more responsibility for learning on the students.
- implement creative group, pair, and individual activities.

How can you do this? Good organization will help. Lessons will need to be especially well-planned for the multi-level class. The following lesson plan is an example of how to treat the same topic with students of two different levels.

Teaching a lesson in a multi-level classroom

Lesson objectives:

Relate an incident in the past that you regret.

- Level 2: Express surprise and sympathy.
- Level 3: Offer encouragement and make suggestions.

Lesson plan

1. **Review and/or teach the past tense.**
   Present the formation of the past tense. Model its use for the entire class or call upon Level 3 students to give examples.

2. **Practice the past tense.**
   Have Level 3 students who have mastered the past tense teach it to Level 2 students in pairs or small groups. Provide the Level 3 student instructors with several drill and practice activities they may use for this purpose.

3. **Relate your own regrettable past experience.**
   Recount a personal regrettable incident—real or imaginary—to the entire class as a model. For example, you may have left your automobile lights on, and when you came out of school, the battery was dead and you couldn't start your car. Or you may have scolded a student for not doing the homework and later discovered the student had a legitimate reason for not completing the assignment.

4. **Prepare and practice written and oral narratives.**
   Have Level 2 students pair off with Level 3 students. Each individual writes about his or her experience, the Level 3 partner serving as a resource for the Level 2 student. Partners then edit each other's work and listen to each other's oral delivery. You might choose to have students record their oral narratives.

5. **Present communicative functions.**
   A. Ask for a volunteer to recount his or her own regrettable incident for the entire class.
   B. Model reactions to the volunteer's narrative.
      (1) Express surprise and sympathy (for Level 2): "Really! That's too bad!"
      (2) Offer encouragement and make suggestions (for Level 3): "Don't worry!" "You can still...."

6. **Read narratives and practice communicative functions.**
   Have Level 2 students work together in one group or in small groups, listening to classmates' stories and reacting with the prescribed communicative function. Have Level 3 students do the same among themselves. Circulate among the groups, listening, helping, and assessing.

7. **Assess progress.**
   Repeat your personal account for the entire class and elicit reactions from students according to their level. Challenge students to respond with communicative functions expected of the other level if they can.

Every part of the above lesson plan is important. Both levels have been accommodated. The teacher has not dominated the lesson. Students have worked together in pairs and small groups, while Level 3 students have helped their Level 2 classmates. Individual groups still feel accountable, both within their level and across levels.

Any lesson can be adapted in this way. It takes time and effort, but the result is a student-centered classroom where students share and grow, and the teacher is the facilitator.

Komm mit! addresses the *multi-level classroom* in the following ways:

The Pupil's Edition
▶ Provides creative activities for pair and group work that allow students at different levels to work together and learn from one another.

The Teacher's Edition
▶ Offers practical suggestions for *Projects* and *Cooperative Learning* that engage students of different levels.
▶ Provides a clear, comprehensive outline of the functions, vocabulary, and grammar that are recycled in each chapter. The *Chapter Overview* of each chapter is especially helpful to the teacher who is planning integrated or varied lessons in the multi-level classroom.

The Ancillary Program
▶ Provides a variety of materials and activities to accommodate different levels in a multi-level classroom.

Professional References

The Professional References section provides you with information about many resources that can enrich your German class. Included are addresses of German government and tourist offices, pen pal organizations, subscription agencies, and many others. Since addresses change frequently, you may want to verify them before you send your requests.

PEN PAL ORGANIZATIONS

The Student Letter Exchange will arrange pen pals for your students. For the names of other pen pal groups, contact your local chapter of AATG. There are fees involved, so be sure to write for information.

Student Letter Exchange
630 Third Avenue
New York, NY 10017
(212) 557-3312

EMBASSIES AND CONSULATES

Embassy of the Federal Republic of Germany
4645 Reservoir Rd. N.W.
Washington, D.C. 20007-1998
(202) 298-4000

Consulate General of the Federal Republic of Germany
460 Park Avenue
New York, NY 10022
(212) 308-8700
(also in Atlanta, Boston, Chicago, Detroit, Houston, Los Angeles, San Francisco, Seattle)

Embassy of Austria
3524 International Court N.W.
Washington, D.C. 20008
(202) 895-6700

Austrian Consulate General
950 Third Avenue
New York, NY 10022
(212) 737-6400
(also in Los Angeles and Chicago)

CULTURAL AGENCIES

For historic and tourist information and audiovisual materials relating to Austria, contact:

Austrian Institute
11 East 52nd Street
New York, NY 10022
(212) 759-5165

Material on political matters is available from **Bundeszentrale für politische Bildung**, a German federal agency.

Bundeszentrale für politische Bildung
Berliner Freiheit 7
53111 Bonn, GERMANY
(0228) 5150

For free political, cultural, and statistical information, films, and videos, contact:

German Information Center
950 Third Avenue
New York, NY 10022
(212) 888-9840

For various materials and information about special events your classes might attend, contact the **Goethe Institut** nearest you. For regional locations, contact:

Goethe Haus, German Cultural Center
1014 Fifth Avenue
New York, NY 10028
(212) 439-8700

The **Institut für Auslandsbeziehungen** provides cultural information to foreigners. The institute offers books and periodicals on a limited basis as well as a variety of two- and three-week professional seminars which allow educators to learn about the people, education, history, and culture of German-speaking countries.

Institut für Auslandsbeziehungen
Charlottenplatz 17
70173 Stuttgart, GERMANY
(0711) 22250

Inter Nationes, a nonprofit German organization for promoting international relations, supplies material on all aspects of life in Germany (literature, posters, magazines, press releases, films, slides, audio and video tapes, records) to educational institutions and organizations abroad.

Inter Nationes
Kennedyallee 91-103
53175 Bonn, GERMANY
(0228) 8800

TOURIST BUREAUS

Write to the following tourist offices for travel information and brochures.

German National Tourist Office
122 East 42nd St., 52nd Floor
New York, NY 10168
(212) 661-7200
(also in Chicago and San Francisco)

Deutsche Zentrale für Tourismus e.V.
Beethovenstraße 69
60325 Frankfurt GERMANY
(0611) 75720

PROFESSIONAL ORGANIZATIONS

The two major organizations for German teachers at the secondary school level are

The American Council on the Teaching of Foreign Languages (ACTFL)
6 Executive Plaza
Yonkers, NY 10701
(914) 963-8830

The American Association of Teachers of German (AATG)
112 Haddontowne Court
Suite 104
Cherry Hill, NJ 08034
(609) 795-5553

PERIODICALS

Listed below are some periodicals published in German. For the names of other German magazines and periodicals contact a subscription agency.

Deutschland-Nachrichten, a weekly newsletter available in both German and English, is published by the German Information Center *(see address under Cultural Agencies).*

Goethe Haus *(see address under Cultural Agencies)* publishes **Treffpunkt Deutsch,** a magazine of information, bibliographies, and ideas for teachers.

Bundeszentrale für politische Bildung *(see address under Cultural Agencies)* publishes **Politische Zeitung (PZ),** a quarterly magazine covering issues of social interest.

The Austrian Press and Information Service publishes a monthly newsletter. Write to:
Austrian Information
3524 International Court N.W.
Washington, D.C. 20008

Juma classroom magazine is a free publication to which you can subscribe. You can order multiple copies. Write to:
Redaktion Juma
Frankfurter Straße 128
5000 Köln, GERMANY
(0221) 693061

SUBSCRIPTION SERVICES

German magazines can be obtained through subscription agencies in the United States. The following companies are among the many which can provide your school with subscriptions:

EBSCO Subscription Services
P.O. Box 1943
Birmingham, AL 35201-1943
(205) 991-6600

Continental Book Company
8000 Cooper Ave. Bldg. 29
Glendale, NY 11385
(718) 326-0572

MISCELLANEOUS

(ADAC) Allegemeiner Deutscher Automobil Club
Am Westpark 8
81373 München, GERMANY

For students who want to find a summer job in Germany, write to:

Zentralstelle für Arbeitsvermittlung
Dienststelle 2122
Postfach 70545
60079 Frankfurt, GERMANY
(069) 71110
(Applicants must have a good knowledge of German.)

For international student passes and other student services contact:

CIEE Student Travel Services
205 E. 42nd Street
New York, NY 10018
(212) 661-1414
(has branch offices in several other large cities)

A Bibliography for the German Teacher

This bibliography is a compilation of many resources available to enrich your German class.

SELECTED AND ANNOTATED LIST OF READINGS

I. Methods and Approaches

Cohen, Andrew, D. *Assessing Language Ability in the Classroom*, 2/e. Boston, MA: Heinle, 1994.

Presents various principles to guide teachers through assessment processes, such as oral interviews, role-playing situations, dictations, and portfolio assessment. The discussions are fully accessible to novice teachers, and touch upon some innovative means of assessing reading ability, evaluation of written and oral portfolios, and computer-based tests.

Hadley, Alice Omaggio. *Teaching Language in Context 2/e.* Boston, MA: Heinle, 1993.

An updated edition reviewing past and present language acquisition theories and models as they apply to successful teaching in the second language classroom. Discusses the nature of language proficiency, how adult learners develop second language proficiency, and how technology affects language learning. Generally used for teacher training at the university level.

Krashen, Stephen, and Tracy D. Terrell. *The Natural Approach: Language Acquisition in the Classroom.* New York: Pergamon, 1983.

Provides a brief overview of Krashen's Optimal Input Theory and its applications to teaching in the second language classroom. Suggestions and examples for curriculum, classroom activities, oral communication development, and testing are applicable to high school classes.

Oller, John W., Jr. *Methods That Work. Ideas for Language Teachers, 2/e.* Boston, MA: Heinle, 1993.

A revised collection of teaching methods including extensive selections of current methods. Shows how to keep pace with the current changes in language and culture instruction. Addresses topics such as literacy in multicultural settings, cooperative learning, peer teaching, and CAI (computer-assisted instruction).

Shrum, Judith L., and Eileen W. Glisan. *Teacher's Handbook: Contextualized Language Instruction.* Boston, MA: Heinle, 1993.

Focuses on practical application of the most recent language teaching theory at the high school level, including teaching grammar, testing, using video texts, and cooperative learning. Contains microteaching situations, case studies, and observational episodes. Samples of unit plans, daily lessons, different types of tests, and cooperative tasks are contained in a useful appendix. The book features extensive references and a resource list. Used in many teacher training programs at universities and in school districts.

II. Second Language Theory

Krashen, Stephen. *The Power of Reading.* New York: McGraw, 1994.

Updates Krashen's Optimal Input Hypothesis—which originally focused on listening—by applying it to reading in the second language classroom. This is an important book to read, because it emphasizes authentic reading texts for developing efficient use of oral language. Contains many suggestions and strategies for more effective reading comprehension.

Liskin-Gasparro, Judith. *A Guide to Testing and Teaching for Oral Proficiency.* Boston, MA: Heinle, 1990.

Provides important historical and other background information about the oral proficiency interview. An application section features sample oral activities based on each level of the ACTFL Proficiency Guidelines. Extensive commentaries on the taped interviews offer detailed analysis of the speech samples and the interviewer's techniques. An excellent book for understanding the foundations of the current proficiency model for second language acquisition.

Rubin, Joan, and Irene Thompson. *How To Be a More Successful Language Learner 2/e.* Boston, MA: Heinle, 1993.

Presents the latest research about learner strategies and language learning including psychological, linguistic, and practical matters surrounding the successful development of a second language. Also includes discussions and samples of cognitive and metacognitive learner strategies.

III. Video and CAI

Altmann, Rick. The Video Connection: Integrating Video into Language Teaching. Boston: Houghton, 1989.

Contains valuable discussions about using video texts to support second language learning. Author explains why authentic video texts are necessary and how to present them successfully to students. Diverse strategies for students before and after viewing are offered as practical suggestions.

Dunkel, Patricia A. Computer-Assisted Language Learning and Testing. Boston, MA: Heinle, 1992.

Examines the effectiveness of CAI and computer-assisted language learning (CALL) in the foreign language classroom. Has a very clear format and provides an insightful overview of the computer's effect on foreign language.

Kenning, M.J., and M.M. Kenning. Computers and Language Learning: Current Theory and Practice. New York: E. Horwood, 1990.

Offers an array of theoretical discussions as well as practical suggestions. Excellent overview of how CAI (computer-assisted instruction) can support successful second language development.

IV. Professional Journals

Calico (Published by Duke University, Charlotte, N.C.)

Dedicated to the intersection of modern language learning and high technology. Research articles on videodiscs, using computer-assisted language learning, how-to articles, and courseware reviews. Examples of articles:

Complain, Jean, Lise Duquette, and Michel Laurier. "Video and Software Self-Development Tools for the Language Teacher." Calico 10 (1992): 5-15.

Hendricks, Harold H. "Models of Interactive Videodisc Development." Calico 11 (1993): 53-67.

The Foreign Language Annals (Published by the American Council on the Teaching of Foreign Languages)

Consists of research and how-to-teach articles. Examples of articles:

VanPatten, Bill. "Grammar Teaching for the Acquisition-Rich Classroom." FLA 26 (1993): 435-50.

Young, Dolly Jesusita. "Processing Strategies of Foreign Language Readers: Authentic and Edited Input." FLA 26 (1993): 451-68.

German Quarterly (Published by the American Association of Teachers of German)

Articles on literary interpretations of German-language literature. An example of a published article:

Mehigan, Tim. "Eichendorff's Taugenichts; or, The Social Education of the Private Man." German Quarterly 66 (1993): 60-70.

The IALL Journal of Language Learning Technologies, (Published by the International Association for Learning Laboratories)

Research articles as well as practical discussions pertaining to technology and language instruction. Examples of articles:

Kuettner, D., J. Toth and K. Landahl, eds. "Report on IALL '93: Defining the Role for the Language Lab." IALL Journal 26 (1993): 9-17.

Salay, Susan. "Secondary School Update." IALL Journal 26 (1993): 141-44.

The Modern Language Journal

Primarily features research articles. Examples of articles:

DeKeyser, Robert M. "The Effect of Error Correction on L2 Grammar Knowledge and Oral Proficiency." MLJ 77 (1993): 501-14.

Glisan, Eileen W. and Victor Drescher. "Textbook Grammar: Does It Reflect Native Speaker Speech?" MLJ 77 (1993): 23-33.

Hulstijn, Jan H. "When do Foreign-Language Readers Look Up the Meaning of Unfamiliar Words? The Influence of Task and Learner Variable." MLJ 77 (1993): 139-51.

Riley, Gail L. "A Story Approach to Narrative Text Comprehension." MLJ 77 (1993): 417-32.

Die Unterrichtspraxis (published by the American Association of Teachers of German)

Articles about teaching German successfully. Examples of articles:

Fraser, Catherine C. "What is Technology Really Doing for Language Teaching and Learning?" Die Unterrichtspraxis 26 (1993): 127-31.

Myers, Michael. "Production and Use of Slides for Language and Culture Classes." Die Unterrichtspraxis 25 (1992): 75-79.

Pentecost, Gislind, E. "Deutschlandspiegelvideos." Die Unterrichtspraxis 26 (1993): 196-99.

Saur, Pamela S. "Teaching the Adjective Endings in 1992: A Survey." Die Unterrichtspraxis 26 (1993): 56-61.

Scope and Sequence: German Level 1

VORSCHAU
- Das Alphabet
- Wie heißt du?
- Im Klassenzimmer
- Die Zahlen von 0 bis 20

KAPITEL 1   WER BIST DU?
Functions:
- Saying hello and goodbye
- Asking someone's name and giving yours
- Asking who someone is
- Talking about places of origin
- Talking about how someone gets to school

Grammar:
- Forming questions
- Definite articles **der, die, das**
- Subject pronouns and **sein**

Culture:
- Greetings
- Using **der** and **die** in front of people's names
- Map of German states and capitals
- **Wie kommst du zur Schule?**

Re-entry:
- Asking someone's name
- Numbers 0-20
- Geography of German-speaking countries

KAPITEL 2   SPIEL UND SPASS
Functions:
- Talking about interests
- Expressing likes and dislikes
- Saying when you do various activities
- Asking for an opinion and expressing yours
- Agreeing and disagreeing

Grammar:
- The singular subject pronouns and present tense verb endings
- The plural subject pronouns and verb endings
- The present tense of verbs
- Word order: verb in second position
- Verbs with stems ending in **d, t, n,** or **-eln**

Culture:
- Formal and informal address
- **Was machst du in deiner Freizeit?**
- German weekly planner

Re-entry:
- Question formation
- Greetings
- Expressions **stimmt/stimmt nicht** used in a new context

KAPITEL 3   KOMM MIT NACH HAUSE!
Functions:
- Talking about where you and others live
- Offering something to eat and drink and responding to an offer
- Saying please, thank you, and you're welcome
- Describing a room
- Talking about and describing family members
- Describing people

Grammar:
- The **möchte**-forms
- Indefinite articles **ein, eine**
- The pronouns **er, sie, es,** and **sie**
- The possessive adjectives **mein, dein, sein,** and **ihr**

Culture:
- The German preference for **Mineralwasser**
- **Wo wohnst du?**

Re-entry:
- Definite articles **der, die, das**
- Asking someone's name and age
- Asking who someone is
- Talking about interests

KAPITEL 4   ALLES FÜR DIE SCHULE!
Functions:
- Talking about class schedules
- Using a schedule to talk about time
- Sequencing events
- Expressing likes, dislikes, and favorites
- Responding to good news and bad news
- Talking about prices
- Pointing things out

Grammar:
- The verb **haben**
- Using **Lieblings-**
- Noun plurals

Culture:
- The German school day
- 24-hour time system
- The German grading system
- **Was sind deine Lieblingsfächer?**
- German currency

Re-entry:
- Numbers
- Likes and dislikes: **gern**
- Degrees of enthusiasm
- The pronouns **er, sie, es,** and **sie**

KAPITEL 5   KLAMOTTEN KAUFEN
Functions:
- Expressing wishes when shopping
- Commenting on and describing clothes
- Giving compliments and responding to them
- Talking about trying on clothes

Grammar:
- Definite and indefinite articles in the accusative case
- The verb **gefallen**
- Direct object pronouns
- Separable prefix verbs
- Stem-changing verbs **nehmen** and **aussehen**

Culture:
- Exchange rates
- German store hours
- German clothing sizes
- **Welche Klamotten sind „in"?**

Re-entry:
- Numbers and prices
- Colors
- Pointing things out
- Expressing likes and dislikes
- Asking for and expressing opinions
- The verb **aussehen**

KAPITEL 6   PLÄNE MACHEN
Functions:
- Starting a conversation
- Telling time and talking about when you do things
- Making plans
- Ordering food and beverages
- Talking about how something tastes
- Paying the check

Grammar:
- The verb **wollen**
- The stem-changing verb **essen**

Culture:
- Clocks on public buildings
- **Was machst du in deiner Freizeit?**
- Tipping in Germany

Re-entry:
- Expressing time when referring to schedules
- Vocabulary: School and freetime activities
- Inversion of time elements
- Sequencing events
- Accusative case
- The verb nehmen
- Using **möchte** to order food

KAPITEL 7   ZU HAUSE HELFEN

Functions:
- Extending and responding to an invitation
- Talking about how often you do things
- Offering help and explaining what to do
- Talking about the weather

Grammar:
- The modals **müssen** and **können**
- The separable prefix verb **abräumen**
- The accusative pronouns
- Using present tense to refer to the future

Culture:
- **Was tust du für die Umwelt?**
- German weather map and weather report
- Weather in German-speaking countries

Re-entry:
- Separable prefix verbs
- Time clauses
- Vocabulary: Free-time activities
- Using numbers in a new context, temperature

KAPITEL 8   EINKAUFEN GEHEN

Functions:
- Asking what you should do
- Telling someone what to do
- Talking about quantities
- Saying you want something else
- Giving reasons
- Saying where you were and what you bought

Grammar:
- The modal **sollen**
- The **du**-commands
- The conjunctions **weil** and **denn**
- The past tense of **sein**

Culture:
- Specialty shops and markets
- **Was machst du für andere Leute?**
- Weights and measures
- German advertisements

Re-entry:
- The **möchte**-forms
- Numbers used in a new context, weights and measures
- Responding to invitations
- Vocabulary: Activities
- Vocabulary: Household chores

KAPITEL 9   AMERIKANER IN MÜNCHEN

Functions:
- Talking about where something is located
- Asking for and giving directions
- Talking about what there is to eat and drink
- Saying you do/don't want more
- Expressing opinions

Grammar:
- The verb **wissen**
- The verb **fahren**
- The formal commands with **Sie**
- The phrase **es gibt**
- Using **kein**
- The conjunction **daß**

Culture:
- The German **Innenstadt**
- **Was ißt du gern?**
- Map of a German neighborhood
- **Imbißstube** menu
- **Leberkäs**

Re-entry:
- Vocabulary: Types of stores
- **Du**-commands
- Vocabulary: Food items
- Indefinite articles: accusative case

KAPITEL 10   KINO UND KONZERTE

Functions:
- Expressing likes and dislikes
- Expressing familiarity
- Expressing preferences and favorites
- Talking about what you did in your free time

Grammar:
- The verb **mögen**
- The verb **kennen**
- **Lieber, am liebsten**
- The stem changing verb **sehen**
- The phrase **sprechen über**
- The stem-changing verbs **lesen** and **sprechen**

Culture:
- The German movie rating system
- A German pop chart
- German movie ads
- **Welche kulturellen Veranstaltungen besuchst du?**
- German upcoming events poster
- German best-seller lists
- German video-hits list
- Popular German novels

Re-entry:
- Expressing likes and dislikes
- The verb **wissen**
- The stem-changing verb **aussehen**
- Vocabulary: Activities
- The stem-changing verbs **nehmen** and **essen**
- Talking about when you do things

KAPITEL 11   DER GEBURTSTAG

Functions:
- Using the telephone in Germany
- Inviting someone to a party
- Talking about birthdays and expressing good wishes
- Discussing gift ideas

Grammar:
- Introduction to the dative case
- Word order in the dative case

Culture:
- Using the telephone
- Saints' days
- German good luck symbols
- **Was schenkst du zum Geburtstag?**
- German gift ideas

Re-entry:
- Numbers 0-20
- Time and days of the week
- Months
- Accusative case
- Vocabulary: Family members

KAPITEL 12   DIE FETE (Wiederholungskapitel)

Functions (Review):
- Offering help and explaining what to do
- Asking where something is located and giving directions
- Making plans and inviting someone to come along
- Talking about clothing
- Discussing gift ideas
- Describing people and places
- Saying what you would like and whether you do or don't want more
- Talking about what you did

Grammar (Review):
- The verb **können**; the preposition **für**; accusative pronouns; and **du**-commands
- The verb **wissen** and word order following **wissen**
- The verbs **wollen** and **müssen**; word order
- Nominative and accusative pronouns; definite and indefinite articles
- Dative endings
- The nominative pronouns **er, sie, es,** and **sie** (pl); possessive pronouns
- The **möchte**-forms; **noch ein** and **kein**

Culture:
- **Spätzle** and **Apfelküchle**
- **Mußt du zu Hause helfen?**
- German gift ideas
- Photos from furniture ads
- Menu from an **Imbißstube**

T45

Scope and Sequence: German Level 2

KAPITEL 1   BEI DEN BAUMANNS
(Wiederholungskapitel)

Functions (Review):
- Asking for and giving information about yourself and others; describing yourself and others; expressing likes and dislikes; identifying people and places
- Giving and responding to compliments; expressing wishes when buying things
- Making plans; ordering food; talking about how something tastes

Grammar (Review):
- Present tense forms of **haben** and **sein**
- The possessive adjectives **mein, dein, sein,** and **ihr** (nominative)
- The nominative and accusative forms of the definite and the indefinite articles
- The third person pronouns
- The verb **wollen**
- The **möchte**-forms

Culture:
- Questionnaire: **Was für eine Person bist du?**
- Article: **Sebastian über seine Familie**
- Article: **Popstars machen Mode**
- **Und was hast du am liebsten?**
- Advertisements

KAPITEL 2   BASTIS PLAN
(Wiederholungskapitel)

Functions (Review):
- Expressing obligations; extending and responding to an invitation; offering help and telling what to do
- Asking and telling what to do; telling that you need something else; telling where you were and what you bought
- Discussing gift ideas; expressing likes and dislikes; expressing likes, preferences, and favorites; saying you do or don't want more

Grammar (Review):
- The present tense forms of **müssen, können, sollen,** and **mögen**
- The interrogative **warum**
- Clauses introduced by **weil** and **denn**
- Personal pronouns: accusative case
- The possessives **mein, dein, sein,** and **ihr** (accusative)

- The **du**-commands
- The past tense forms of **sein**
- The dative case of **mein, dein, sein,** and **ihr**
- **Noch ein**, nominative and accusative
- **Kein**, nominative and accusative

Culture:
- **Was nimmst du mit, wenn du irgendwo eingeladen bist?**
- Grocery advertisements
- German gift ideas

KAPITEL 3   WO WARST DU IN DEN FERIEN?

Functions:
- Reporting past events, talking about activities
- Reporting past events, talking about places
- Asking how someone liked something; expressing enthusiasm or disappointment, responding enthusiastically or sympathetically

Grammar:
- The conversational past
- The past tense of **haben** and **sein**
- **An** and **in** with dative-case forms to express location
- The definite article, dative plural
- Personal pronouns, dative case
- The dative-case forms of **ein**

Culture:
- Information on Dresden
- Information on **Frankfurt am Main**
- **Was hast du in den letzten Ferien gemacht?**

Re-entry:
- Expressions of time/frequency
- **Weil**-clauses
- Expressing likes and dislikes

KAPITEL 4   GESUND LEBEN

Functions:
- Expressing approval and disapproval
- Asking for information and responding emphatically or agreeing with reservations
- Asking and telling what you may and may not do

Grammar:
- The verb **schlafen** (**schläft**)
- **Für** + accusative
- Reflexive verbs (accusative)
- **Jeder, jede, jedes** (nominative)
- The accusative forms of **kein**
- The verb **dürfen**

Culture:
- Interviews of German teenagers
- **Was tust du, um gesund zu leben?**
- Survey on health habits
- **Bioläden** and **Reformhäuser**

Re-entry:
- Modals: **sollen/müssen**
- **Daß**-clauses
- Conjunctions **weil** and **denn**
- Expressions of place, time, frequency, and quantity
- Giving reasons
- **Für** and **kein**
- Responding to an invitation
- The irregular verb **essen**

KAPITEL 5   GESUND ESSEN

Functions:
- Expressing regret and downplaying; expressing skepticism and making certain
- Calling someone's attention to something and responding
- Expressing preference and strong preference

Grammar:
- **Dieser, diese, dieses**
- The possessives (summary)
- Verbs used with dative case
- The interrogatives **welcher, welche, welches**
- The preposition **zu**

Culture:
- **Was ißt du, was nicht?**
- Nutritious snacks for **Gymnasiasten**
- German meals

Re-entry:
- Talking about quantities
- The possessives
- Talking about how food tastes
- Comparatives and superlatives
- Saying you want more
- The interrogative **was für**

KAPITEL 6   GUTE BESSERUNG!

Functions:
- Inquiring about someone's health and responding; making suggestions
- Asking about and expressing pain
- Asking for and giving advice; expressing hope

Grammar:
- Reflexive pronouns in dative
- The inclusive command
- Verbs used with dative case
- The verbs **brechen, waschen, messen, weh tun**

- The dative case to express the idea of something too expensive, too large, too small for you

Culture:
- **Was machst du, wenn dir nicht gut ist?**
- The difference between an **Apotheke** and a **Drogerie**
- Article about sun exposure

Re-entry:
- The verb **sich fühlen**
- The accusative reflexive pronouns
- Expressing obligations
- The conversational past
- **Daß**-clauses

KAPITEL 7   STADT ODER LAND?

Functions:
- Expressing preference and giving a reason
- Expressing wishes
- Agreeing with reservations; justifying your answers

Grammar:
- Comparative forms of adjectives
- The verb **sich wünschen**
- Adjective endings following **ein**-words
- Adjective endings of comparatives

Culture:
- **Wo wohnst du lieber? Auf dem Land? In der Stadt?**
- Letter from a German pen pal

Re-entry:
- Talking about where something is located
- Reflexive dative verbs
- Expressing opinions
- Dative verb **gefallen**

KAPITEL 8   MODE? JA ODER NEIN?

Functions:
- Describing clothes
- Expressing interest, disinterest, and indifference; making and accepting compliments
- Persuading and dissuading

Grammar:
- Adjective endings following **der** and **dieser**-words
- The verbs **tragen** and **interessieren**
- The conjunction **wenn**

Culture:
- **Was trägst du am liebsten?**
- Clothes typically worn by German-speaking youths
- Interviews about fashion

Re-entry:
- Talking about what you bought
- Accusative reflexive verbs
- **Für** + accusative
- Giving reasons
- Word order with subordinate conjunctions

KAPITEL 9   WOHIN IN DIE FERIEN?

Functions:
- Expressing indecision; asking for and making suggestions
- Expressing doubt, conviction, and resignation
- Asking for and giving directions

Grammar:
- **Nach, an, in**, and **auf**
- **Ob**-clauses
- Expressing direction and location (Summary)
- Prepositions followed by dative
- The prepositions **durch, um, vor**, and **neben**

Culture:
- **Wohin fährst du in den nächsten Ferien?**
- Statistics on transportation
- Students talk about vacations
- **Stadtrundgang durch Bietigheim**

Re-entry:
- Inclusive commands
- The modal **können**
- The stem-changing verb **fahren**
- The verb **wissen** with subordinate prepositions
- Giving directions
- Inviting someone and responding to an invitation

KAPITEL 10   VIELE INTERESSEN!

Functions:
- Asking about and expressing interest
- Asking for and giving permission; asking for information and expressing an assumption
- Expressing surprise, agreement, and disagreement; talking about plans

Grammar:
- Verbs with prepositions
- **Wo**-compounds and **da**-compounds
- The verbs **lassen** and **laufen**
- The use of **kein** to negate a noun
- The future tense with **werden**

Culture:
- Television companies
- **Was machst du, um zu relaxen?**
- Statistics on television programs
- Getting a driver's license in Germany

Re-entry:
- The conjunctions **weil** and **daß**
- Word order with modals
- Time expressions
- The interrogative **was für**
- Expressing future events with present tense
- Making plans

KAPITEL 11   MIT OMA INS RESTAURANT

Functions:
- Asking for, making, and responding to suggestions
- Expressing hearsay
- Ordering in a restaurant; expressing good wishes

Grammar:
- The **würde**-forms
- Unpreceded adjectives
- The **hätte**-forms

Culture:
- **Für welche kulturellen Veranstaltungen interessierst du dich?**
- State-supported art in Germany
- International cuisine
- Menu

Re-entry:
- Cultural activities and sights
- The impersonal pronoun **man**
- Talking about favorites
- The modal **sollen**
- Saying what's available
- Ordering and asking for the bill

KAPITEL 12   DIE REINICKENDORFER CLIQUE
(Wiederholungskapitel)

Functions (Review):
- Reporting past events; asking for, making, and responding to suggestions
- Ordering food, expressing hearsay and regret; persuading and dissuading
- Asking for and giving advice; expressing preference, interest, disinterest, and indifference

Grammar (Review):
- The past tense
- **Sollen** and the **würde**-forms
- Prepositions
- The command forms of strong verbs
- Adjective endings
- Comparative forms of adjectives

Culture:
- **Welche ausländische Küche hast du gern?**
- Etiquette in German restaurants
- Franziska van Almsick

Scope and Sequence: German Level 3

KAPITEL 1 DAS LAND AM MEER (Wiederholungskapitel)

Functions (Review):
- Reporting past events
- Asking how someone liked something; expressing enthusiasm or disappointment; responding enthusiastically or sympathetically
- Asking and telling what you may or may not do
- Asking for information
- Inquiring about someone's health and responding; asking about and expressing pain
- Expressing hope

Grammar (Review):
- Prepositions followed by dative-case forms
- Past tense
- Dative-case forms
- Forms of **dieser** and **welcher**
- Reflexive pronouns

Culture:
- **Insel Rügen**
- **Fit ohne Fleisch**
- **Währungen und Geld wechseln**

KAPITEL 2 AUF IN DIE JUGENDHERBERGE! (WIEDERHOLUNGSKAPITEL)

Functions (Review):
- Asking for and making suggestions
- Expressing preference and giving a reason
- Expressing wishes
- Expressing doubt, conviction, and resignation
- Asking for information and expressing an assumption
- Expressing hearsay
- Asking for, making, and responding to suggestions
- Expressing wishes when shopping

Grammar (Review):
- Two-way prepositions (**So sagt man das!**)
- Word order in **daß**- and **ob**-clauses (**So sagt man das!**)
- Adjective endings
- The verb **hätte** (**So sagt man das!**)

Culture:
- Explanation of **Jugendherbergen**
- **Einkaufsliste**
- **Programm für eine 6-Tage-Reise nach Weimar**
- **Weimar im Blickpunkt**

KAPITEL 3 AUSSEHEN: WICHTIG ODER NICHT?

Functions:
- Asking for and expressing opinions
- Expressing sympathy and resignation
- Giving advice
- Giving a reason
- Admitting something and expressing regret

Grammar:
- **Da**- and **wo**-compounds (Summary)
- Infinitive clauses

Culture:
- **Die deutsche Subkultur**
- Teenagers talking about what they do to feel better

Re-entry:
- Expressing interest
- Sequencing events
- Expressing opinions
- Verbs requiring prepositional phrases
- Hobby and clothing vocabulary
- **Wo**- and **da**-compounds
- Responding sympathetically
- Asking for and giving advice
- Making suggestions
- Giving reasons
- Infinitives
- **Weil**-clauses

KAPITEL 4 VERHÄLTNIS ZU ANDEREN

Functions:
- Agreeing
- Giving advice
- Introducing another point of view
- Hypothesizing

Grammar:
- Ordinal numbers
- Relative clauses
- **Hätte** and **wäre**
- The genitive case

Culture:
- Importance of **Cliquen** for young people
- **Die verschiedenen Bildungswege in Deutschland**

Re-entry:
- Agreeing
- **Wenn-**, **weil-**, and **daß**-clauses
- Cardinal numbers
- Pronouns (nom., acc., and dat. case)
- Giving advice
- **Wenn**-phrases
- Subjunctive (**würde-**, **hätte-**, **wäre**-forms)
- The preposition **von** + dative

KAPITEL 5 RECHTE UND PFLICHTEN

Functions:
- Talking about what is possible
- Saying what you would have liked to do
- Saying that something is going on right now
- Reporting past events
- Expressing surprise, relief, and resignation

Grammar:
- The **könnte**-forms
- Further uses of **wäre** and **hätte**
- Use of verbs as neuter nouns
- The past tense of modals (the imperfect)

Culture:
- **Artikel 38/2. Absatz des Grundgesetzes**
- Cartoon
- **Gleichberechtigung im deutschen Militär?**
- **Wehrpflicht**

Re-entry:
- **Hätte**-forms and **wäre**-forms
- **Weil**-clauses
- Giving reasons
- The modals **können, wollen,** and **müssen**
- Reporting past events
- Expressing surprise
- Expressing resignation
- Expressing hearsay

KAPITEL 6 MEDIEN: STETS GUT INFORMIERT?

Functions:
- Asking someone to take a position
- Asking for reasons
- Expressing opinions
- Reporting past events
- Agreeing or disagreeing
- Changing the subject
- Interrupting
- Expressing surprise or annoyance

Grammar:
- Narrative past (imperfect)
- Superlative forms of adjectives

Culture:
- **Die TV-Kids**
- **Die Schülerzeitung**
- **Leserbriefe an die Redaktion der Pepo**

Re-entry:
- Talking about favorites

- Leisure-time activities
- Expressing opinions
- The conversational past
- Agreeing and disagreeing
- Television vocabulary
- Expressing surprise
- The comparative forms of adjectives
- Time expressions
- Words of quantity

KAPITEL 7 OHNE REKLAME GEHT ES NICHT!

Functions:
- Expressing annoyance
- Comparing
- Eliciting agreement and agreeing
- Expressing conviction, uncertainty, and what seems to be true

Grammar:
- **Derselbe, der gleiche**
- Adjective endings following determiners of quantity
- Relative pronouns
- Introducing relative clauses with **was** and **wo**
- **Irgendein** and **irgendwelche**

Culture:
- **Werbung—pro und contra**
- **Warum so wenig Unterbrecherwerbung?**
- Excerpt from *Frankfurter Allgemeine*
- Cartoon

Re-entry:
- Expressing annoyance
- The conjunctions **wenn** and **daß**
- Comparative and superlative
- Adjective endings
- Agreeing
- Relative pronouns
- Word order in dependent clauses
- Expressing conviction
- Expressing uncertainty

KAPITEL 8 WEG MIT DEN VORURTEILEN!

Functions:
- Expressing surprise, disappointment, and annoyance
- Expressing an assumption
- Making suggestions and recommendations; giving advice

Grammar:
- The conjunction **als**
- Coordinating conjunctions
- Verbs with prefixes (Summary)

Culture:
- Cartoon
- **Verständnis für Aüslander?**
- **Der sympathische Deutsche**

Re-entry:
- Expressing surprise
- Expressing disappointment
- **Daß-clauses**

- Narrative past
- Conversational past
- Coordinating conjunctions
- Expressing an assumption
- Prepositions followed by dative
- Separable prefix verbs
- Making suggestions
- Giving advice

KAPITEL 9 AKTIV FÜR DIE UMWELT!

Functions:
- Expressing concern
- Making accusations
- Offering solutions
- Making polite requests
- Saying what is being done about a problem
- Hypothesizing

Grammar:
- Subjunctive forms of **müssen, dürfen, sollen,** and **sein**
- The passive voice, present tense
- Use of a conjugated modal verb in the passive
- Conditional sentences

Culture:
- Environmental concerns
- **Ein unweltfreundlicher Einkauf**

Re-entry:
- Adjective endings
- **Daß-, wenn-** and **weil-clauses**
- **Hätte-, würde-,** and **könnte-** forms
- **Werden** and **sollen**
- Environmental vocabulary
- Subjunctive forms

KAPITEL 10 DIE KUNST ZU LEBEN

Functions:
- Expressing preference, given certain possibilities
- Expressing envy and admiration
- Expressing happiness and sadness
- Saying that something is or was being done

Grammar:
- Prepositions with genitive
- **Da-** and **wo-**compounds
- The passive voice (Summary)

Culture:
- **Aphorismen**
- **Kultur findet man überall!**

Re-entry:
- Expressing preference
- **Würde-forms**
- Genitive-case forms
- Prepositions
- **Da-** and **wo-**compounds
- Past participles
- Subjunctive forms of modals
- **Von** + dative case

KAPITEL 11 DEINE WELT IS DEINE SACHE!

Functions:
- Expressing determination or indecision
- Talking about whether something is important or not important
- Expressing wishes
- Expressing certainty and refusing or accepting with certainty
- Talking about goals for the future
- Expressing relief

Grammar:
- The use of **wo-**compounds to ask questions
- Two ways of expressing the future tense
- The perfect infinitive with modals and **werden**

Culture:
- German universities
- **Wie findet man eine Arbeitsstelle in Deutschland?**
- **Umfragen und Tests**

Re-entry:
- Reflexive verbs
- Expressing indecision
- Conversational past and conditional
- **Ob-** and **daß-**clauses
- **Um … zu**
- **Wo-**compounds
- Expressing wishes
- **Wäre**
- Determiners of quantity
- Negation with **kein**
- Future tense formation

KAPITEL 12 DIE ZUKUNFT LIEGT IN DEINER HAND!
(Wiederholungskapitel)

Functions (Review):
- Reporting past events
- Expressing surprise and disappointment
- Agreeing; agreeing with reservations; giving advice
- Giving advice and giving reasons
- Expressing determination or indecision
- Talking about what is important or not important
- Hypothesizing

Grammar (Review):
- Narrative past
- The **würde-**forms
- Infinitive forms of verbs
- Direct and indirect object pronouns
- Subjunctive

Culture:
- **Kummerkasten**
- **Pauken allein reicht nicht**
- **Claudias Pläne für die Zukunft**
- **Textbilder**

The Pupil's Edition

Proficiency is the goal of language instruction in Komm mit! Every chapter begins with authentic situations that model communicative needs common among young people: ordering from a menu, asking someone for a date, shopping for clothes. In the ensuing situations, students learn the functions, vocabulary, and grammar that support natural expression. They also become interested, involved, and responsive—in short, they answer the invitation to Komm mit! and to communicate.

An Overview

Komm mit! Level 2, opens with a two-chapter review of the functions, vocabulary, and grammar learned in Level 1. Following this comprehensive review, Chapters 3-11 provide a carefully sequenced program of balanced skills instruction in the four areas of listening, speaking, reading, and writing. In addition, every chapter is rich in authentic language and culture. Most chapter photographs were taken on location and reflect the characters and settings featured in the videos that accompany *Komm mit!*

Chapter 12 is a review of the second year's study of German. It provides an opportunity to reinforce skills and remediate deficiencies before the end of the school year. This opportunity to pause and reflect on what has been learned provides closure and gives students a sense of accomplishment and renewed purpose.

At the end of the *Pupil's Edition*, a Reference Section summarizes functions and grammar rules for quick reference. It also provides a list of Additional Vocabulary as well as German>English and English>German glossaries. Throughout the year, students are encouraged to consult the Reference Section to review and expand their choices of functional expressions, vocabulary, and structures.

Activity-Based Instruction

In *Komm mit!*, language acquisition is an active process. From the first day, students are using German. Within each lesson, a progression of activities moves students from discrete point use of language to completely open-ended activities that promote personalized, meaningful expression. This sequence allows students to practice receptive skills before moving on to language production. It is this carefully articulated sequence that ensures success.

A Guided Tour

On the next several pages, you will find a guided tour of *Komm mit!* On these pages (the pages shown are from Level 1) we have identified for you the essential elements of the textbook and the various resources available. If, as you are using *Komm mit!*, you encounter any particular problems, please contact your regional office for information or assistance.

Location Openers

In *Komm mit!*, students visit four locations. Each locale is introduced with photographs, text, and authentic cultural video footage shot at the location site.

Inset maps show the location within Germany and its relationship to neighboring countries. *The Teacher's Edition* suggests activities that strengthen students' understanding of the geography of the region.

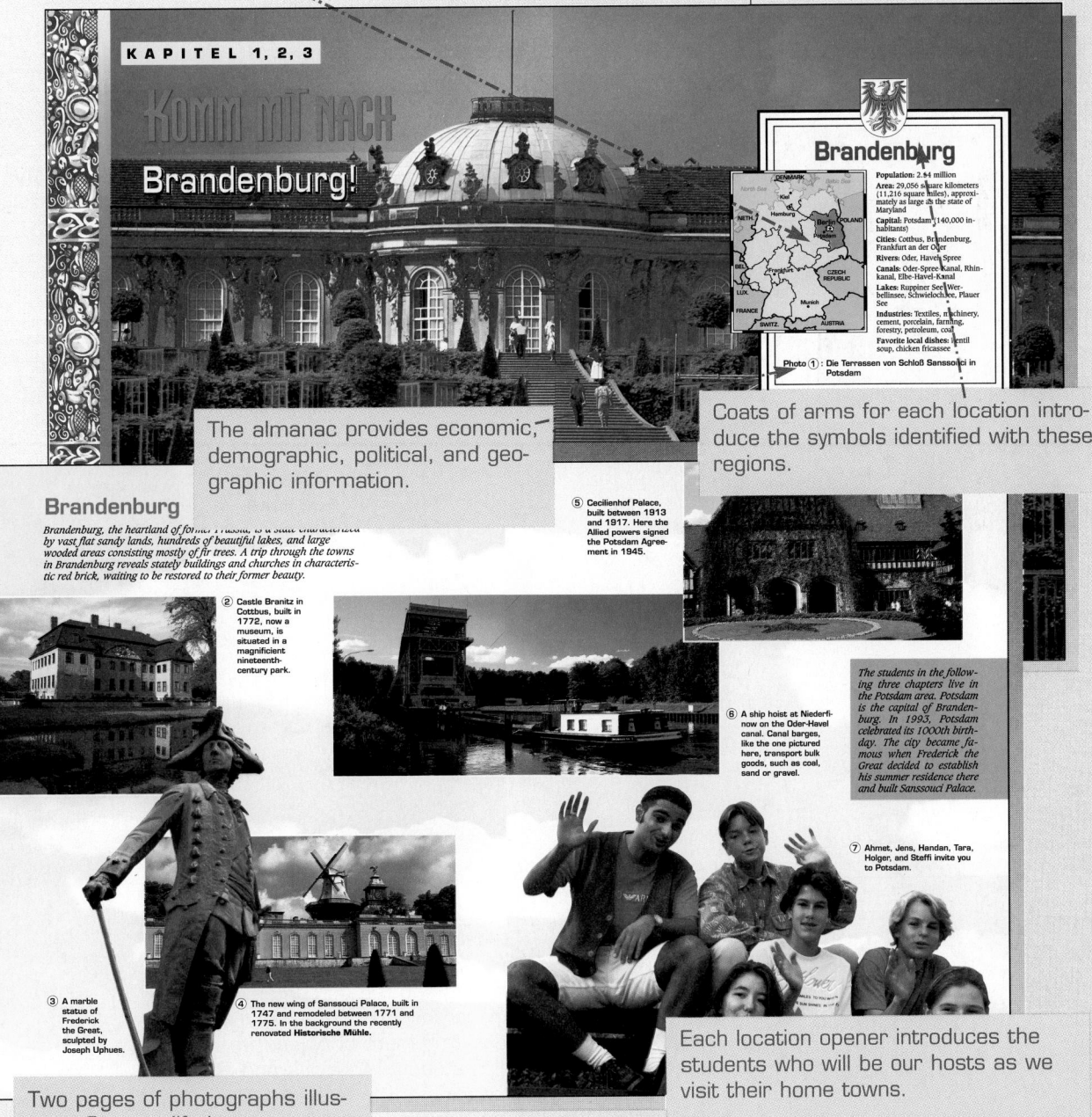

KAPITEL 1, 2, 3

Komm mit nach

Brandenburg!

Brandenburg

Population: 2.54 million
Area: 29,056 square kilometers (11,216 square miles), approximately as large as the state of Maryland
Capital: Potsdam (140,000 inhabitants)
Cities: Cottbus, Brandenburg, Frankfurt an der Oder
Rivers: Oder, Havel, Spree
Canals: Oder-Spree-Kanal, Rhinkanal, Elbe-Havel-Kanal
Lakes: Ruppiner See, Werbellinsee, Schwielochsee, Plauer See
Industries: Textiles, machinery, cement, porcelain, farming, forestry, petroleum, coal
Favorite local dishes: lentil soup, chicken fricassee

Photo ① : Die Terrassen von Schloß Sanssouci in Potsdam

The almanac provides economic, demographic, political, and geographic information.

Coats of arms for each location introduce the symbols identified with these regions.

Brandenburg

Brandenburg, the heartland of former Prussia, is a state characterized by vast flat sandy lands, hundreds of beautiful lakes, and large wooded areas consisting mostly of fir trees. A trip through the towns in Brandenburg reveals stately buildings and churches in characteristic red brick, waiting to be restored to their former beauty.

② Castle Branitz in Cottbus, built in 1772, now a museum, is situated in a magnificent nineteenth-century park.

⑤ Cecilienhof Palace, built between 1913 and 1917. Here the Allied powers signed the Potsdam Agreement in 1945.

⑥ A ship hoist at Niederfinow on the Oder-Havel canal. Canal barges, like the one pictured here, transport bulk goods, such as coal, sand or gravel.

The students in the following three chapters live in the Potsdam area. Potsdam is the capital of Brandenburg. In 1993, Potsdam celebrated its 1000th birthday. The city became famous when Frederick the Great decided to establish his summer residence there and built Sanssouci Palace.

⑦ Ahmet, Jens, Handan, Tara, Holger, and Steffi invite you to Potsdam.

③ A marble statue of Frederick the Great, sculpted by Joseph Uphues.

④ The new wing of Sanssouci Palace, built in 1747 and remodeled between 1771 and 1775. In the background the recently renovated Historische Mühle.

Two pages of photographs illustrate German life in towns, cities, and countryside.

Each location opener introduces the students who will be our hosts as we visit their home towns.

Chapter Opener

Each chapter is organized around a topic with intrinsic appeal for teenagers—school, sports, leisure activities. As the topic is developed through a variety of situations, students will learn and practice the functions necessary for real-life communication.

LIVELY PHOTOGRAPHS
Colorful pictures shot on location illustrate authentic scenes tied to the chapter theme.

REALISTIC SITUATIONS
Each chapter topic is immediately placed in a realistic context, a situation that encourages exploration and interest.

KAPITEL

4 Alles für die Schule!

When a new school year begins, students are often curious about their friends' classes: When do they meet? Which ones are their favorites? What school supplies do they need? There are some similarities and some differences in what students in German-speaking countries and in the U.S. experience in school. Let's find out what they are.

In this chapter you will learn
- to talk about class schedules; to use a schedule to talk about time; to sequence events
- to express likes, dislikes, and favorites; to respond to good news and bad news
- to talk about prices; to point things out

And you will
- listen to German-speaking students talk about their schedules
- read ads for school supplies and become familiar with German money
- write a report card for yourself in German
- find out what German students have to say about school

② Was kosten die Hefte?

① Wann habt ihr Sport?

92 zweiundneunzig

③ Am Freitag haben wir Mathe.

dreiundneunzig 93

APPROPRIATE FUNCTIONS
Students are immediately alerted to the functions they will be learning and the outcomes expected from their study. This clear statement of objectives helps students to focus and organize.

Los geht's!

The first step in every chapter is to provide authentic cultural and linguistic input. In each opening episode situations are developed that will require students to generate language as they discuss the characters' actions and motives.

RECEPTIVE SKILLS

Recognition activities following the opening story reinforce receptive skills. Students work with the episode—exploring the new language presented, relating it to their own experiences, and making new combinations based on their accumulated language base.

AUTHENTIC INPUT

The natural language and situations of the conversations build interest and provide language models. Auditory and visual learners also have access to both video and audio recordings of the dialogue.

---

1 Was passiert hier?

Do you understand what is happening in the **Foto-Roman**? Check your comprehension by answering these questions. Don't be afraid to guess.

1. What plans have Julia and Katja made for the afternoon?
2. What is Heiko going to do?
3. Where do the three friends meet Michael?
4. Why does Michael apologize to Katja? How does Katja react?

2 Genauer lesen

Reread the conversations. Which words or phrases do the characters use to

1. ask how someone is doing
2. talk about time
3. name food or drinks
4. tell a waiter they want to pay
5. apologize

3 Was paßt zusammen?

Match each statement or question on the left with an appropriate response on the right.

1. Wie geht's denn?   a. Er ist für mich.
2. Wohin gehst du?   b. So lala.
3. Wie spät ist es jetzt?   c. Das macht zusammen vierzehn Mark zehn.
4. Wer bekommt den Cappuccino?   d. Viertel nach drei.
5. Ich möchte zahlen.   e. Zu Katja.

4 Was fehlt hier?

Based on the **Foto-Roman** that you've just read, complete each of the sentences below with an appropriate item from the list.

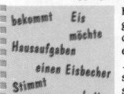

bekommt   Eis
möchte
Hausaufgaben
einen Eisbecher
Stimmt
zahlen   halb

Katja und Julia machen zuerst die __1__. Dann wollen sie in ein Café gehen, ein __2__ essen. Sie wollen so um __3__ fünf gehen. Im Café fragt der Kellner: „Was __4__ ihr?" Katja __5__ einen Cappuccino. Julia sagt: „Ich bekomme __6__, Fruchteis." Michael will gehen. Er sagt: „Ich möchte __7__, bitte." Der Kellner sagt: „Vierzehn Mark zehn." Und Michael antwortet, „Fünfzehn Mark. __8__ schon."

Café am Markt

Nudelsuppe	DM	4,50
Käsebrot		5,20
Wurstbrot		5,60
Wiener mit Senf		5,80
Pizza		8,00
Apfelkuchen		2,00
Eis		1,10
Mineralwasser		3,50
Kaffee		4,20
Cola		3,00

5 Und du?

Look at the menu from the **Café am Markt**. Which items are foods, and which are beverages? If you were with your friends at the **Café am Markt**, what would you order? Make a list, including the prices.

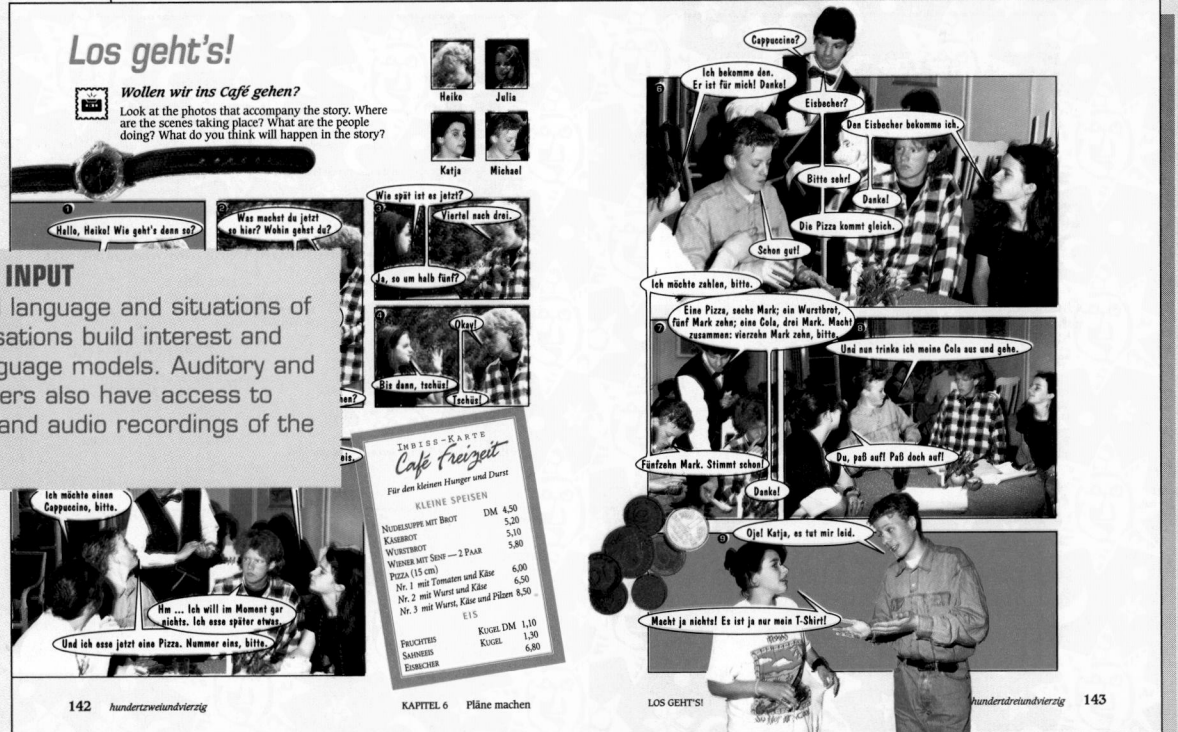

T53

Stufen

Each chapter is divided into three Stufen, short manageable lessons that provide a carefully planned progression of activities. Within each Stufe, activities are sequenced from structured practice to open-ended communication in individual, pair, and group activities that accommodate many different learning styles.

FORM FOLLOWS FUNCTION

Grammatical structures that support the communicative functions appear under the headings **Grammatik** and **Ein wenig Grammatik**. This carefully planned integration of grammar with a communicative purpose helps students communicate with increasing accuracy.

VOCABULARY IN CONTEXT

Theme-related, functional vocabulary is presented visually in the **Wortschatz** and then re-entered in the activities of the **Stufe**.

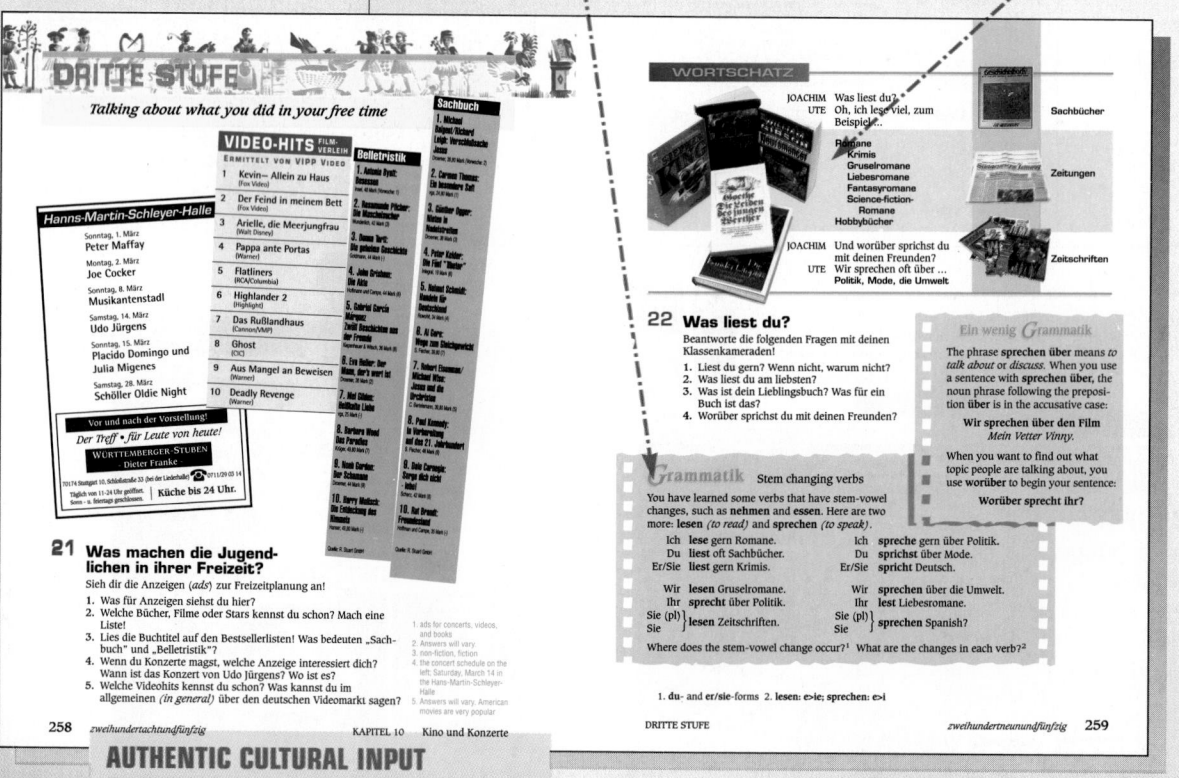

AUTHENTIC CULTURAL INPUT

Realia provide authentic linguistic and cultural input. Students gain cultural insight and increasing confidence in their ability to read and comprehend authentic material.

SPEAKING AND WRITING

A pronunciation activity, **Aussprache** (Level 1 only), appears in each chapter at the end of the third **Stufe**. After pronunciation and reading practice, students write sentences containing these sounds from dictation.

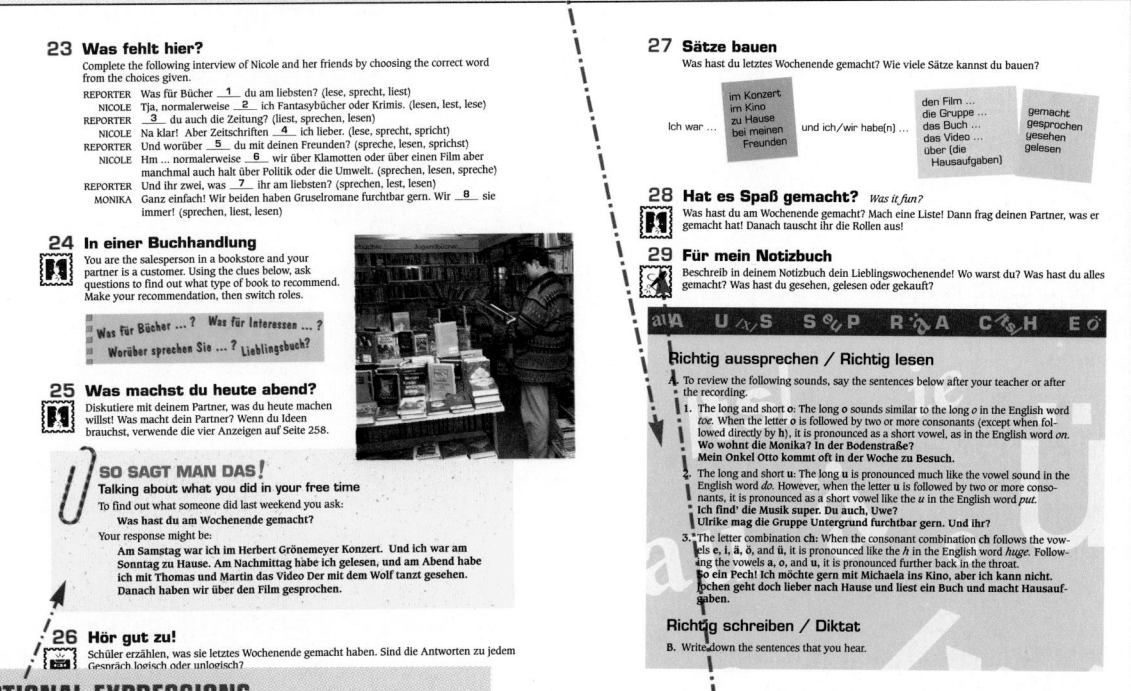

FUNCTIONAL EXPRESSIONS

In each **Stufe**, the expressions that students need in order to develop proficiency are summarized in **So sagt man das!** These functional expressions, supported by the necessary vocabulary and grammar, are the main focus of the lesson.

PERSONAL JOURNALS

Students practice new structures and vocabulary while reinforcing previously learned skills by keeping a **Notizbuch** or personal journal.

LERNTRICK

When you are learning a lot of new words, group them together in meaningful categories: group baked goods under **die Bäckerei**, meat items under **die Metzgerei**, etc. Putting the words in context will help you recall them more easily.

SPRACHTIP

Denn, mal, halt, and **doch** are words that you've seen a lot throughout this book. None of these words has a direct translation, but they are often used in everyday conversations to give emphasis to a question, command, or statement. For example, **Wie sieht er denn aus? Sag mal, wann gehst du? Das hat halt nicht jeder.** and **Wir gehen doch um vier.** Using these words in your conversations will help your German sound more natural.

QUICK TIPS

Two recurring features, **Sprachtip** and **Lerntrick**, encourage students to improve their study skills and their ability to speak more naturally.

Landeskunde

Landeskunde is an integrated approach to culture that enriches students' cultural awareness and language skills. These informal, spontaneous interviews with people of all ages illustrate aspects of daily life in German-speaking countries. The **Landeskunde** is also available in both audio and video formats, and this allows students to sharpen their listening and pronunciation skills by becoming familiar with a variety of regional dialects.

PREPARING TO LISTEN
A brief introduction presents the topic and explains the subject of the interview.

AUTHENTIC LANGUAGE
The names and photographs of each of the people interviewed remind students that the views expressed and the language used are real. As students listen to people from various regions and countries, they will heighten their awareness of differences in attitudes and interests, as well as speech.

REINFORCING COMPREHENSION
Questions following the interviews encourage students to compare and contrast the opinions of the people interviewed and to consider how their views match or differ from those of Americans. This cross-cultural analysis builds personal as well as global understandings.

EIN WENIG LANDESKUNDE

Although there are many large, modern supermarkets in Germany, many people still shop in small specialty stores or at the open-air markets in the center of town. Many Germans shop frequently, buying just what they need for one or two days. Refrigerators are generally much smaller than in the United States, and people prefer to buy things fresh.

CULTURAL AWARENESS
The **Ein wenig Landeskunde** are small cultural notes that appear wherever useful to explain some point of German culture that might be puzzling to an American teenager.

Zum Lesen

Even reluctant readers will be motivated by the eye-catching format and appealing realia of Zum Lesen. These intriguing lessons help students develop reading skills and simultaneously acquire more information about German life.

READING TIPS
The **Lesetrick** notes provide useful hints that ease reading anxieties and develop valuable reading strategies.

INNOVATIVE ACTIVITIES
Activities suggest the use of pertinent skills such as skimming or looking for visual clues. Questioning strategies become more complex as students master a variety of skills.

REALIA
Students build reading confidence by working with authentic materials such as German recipes, travel brochures, entertainment guides, or excerpts from newspapers and magazines.

A system of icons is used throughout the *Pupil's Edition* to identify activities that are specifically designed to promote certain skills or that might be particularly useful in pair or group work.

Anwendung

The end-of-chapter review, Anwendung, offers the same level of interest and challenge as the instructional pages. Students are engaged in a series of activities that measure their ability to comprehend and generate language.

COMPLETE SKILLS REVIEW
Each **Anwendung** covers all four skill areas: listening, speaking, reading, and writing. These activities require students to recombine language and are a true measure of their growth in proficiency.

Listening

This icon indicates the listening activities that range from global comprehension to discrete tasks. Teachers can use the audiocassette for authentic input or read from the scripts available in the *Teacher's Edition* interleaf before each chapter.

Writing

Komm mit! offers a variety of writing activities, many of which are intended to be placed in the student's ***Notizbuch*** Teachers may decide how formal they wish the ***Notizbuch*** or journal to be, but students who are able to look back at their own writing periodically are reassured and encouraged by seeing their own growth and improvement.

Pair Work

Activities with this icon are ideal for pair work. It may be helpful to assign pairs for a certain period of time, preferab a week or two. This also promotes students' social growth as they learn to interact with a variety of people.

Group Work

Group activities are particularly successful in alleviating students' stress and inhibitions. Students will benefit from bein assigned to groups at times and allowed to choose their ow groups at others. The choice of how these groups will repor is the teacher's, and direction lines may be varied so that groups report orally or in writing, or both.

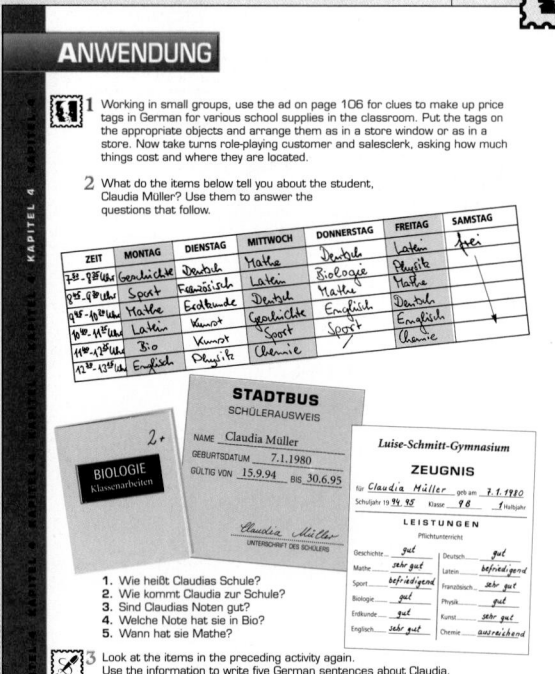

ROLE-PLAYING
Every chapter review culminates in a **Rollenspiel**. These dramatic activities encourage students to use language in imaginative and creative expression.

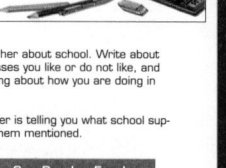

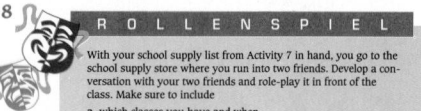

KANN ICH'S WIRKLICH?

Can you extend and respond to an invitation? (p. 174)

1 How would you invite a friend to go
   a. to a movie   b. to a Café   c. shopping   d. swimming

2 Accept or decline the following invitations. If you decline, give a reason why you can't go.
   a. Wir gehen jetzt in eine Disko. Komm doch mit!
   b. Ich muß in die Stadt gehen. Möchtest du mitkommen?
   c. Wir spielen jetzt Tennis. Kannst du mitkommen?

Can you express obligation using müssen? (p. 174)

3 Say that the people below have to do the things indicated.

Bernd   Leyla   Pedro und Felipe   Karin

Can you talk about how often you have to do things? (p. 178)

4 How would you ask a classmate how often he or she has to
   a. washes the windows   c. clears the table
   b. vacuums   d. does the dishes

5 How would you tell a classmate how often you have to do each of the things above?

Can you offer help and tell someone what to do using expressions with "für"? (p. 179)

6 How would you ask a classmate if you could help him or her? How would you ask two classmates?

7 Using können, explain to each of these people what they can do to help you:
   a. Sara: das Geschirr spülen
   b. Silke und Peter: das Zimmer aufräumen
   c. Markus: das Bett machen
   d. Claudia und Daniel: den Tisch decken

8 How might a friend respond if he or she agreed to do some chores for you?

Can you talk about the weather? (p. 183)

9 How would you tell a classmate what the weather is like today? How would you tell him or her the weather forecast for tomorrow?

10 How would you tell someone new to your area what the weather is like in
   a. January   c. June   e. December
   b. March   d. October

WORTSCHATZ

ERSTE STUFE

EXTENDING AND RESPONDING TO INVITATIONS
mitkommen (sep)   *to come along*
Komm doch mit!   *Why don't you come along!*
Ich kann leider nicht.   *Sorry, I can't.*
Das geht nicht.   *That won't work.*

EXPRESSING OBLIGATION
tun   *to do*
helfen   *to help*

zu Hause helfen   *to help at home*
müssen   *to have to*
ich muß ...   *I have to...*
mein Zimmer aufräumen (sep)   *clean up my room*
Staub saugen   *vacuum*
den Müll sortieren   *sort the trash*
den Rasen mähen   *mow the lawn*
die Katze füttern   *feed the cat*
den Tisch decken   *set the table*
den Tisch abräumen (sep)   *clear the table*

das Geschirr spülen   *wash the dishes*
die Blumen gießen   *water the flowers*
das Bett machen   *make the bed*
meine Klamotten aufräumen   *pick up my clothes*
die Fenster putzen   *clean the windows*
Ich habe keine Zeit.   *I don't have time.*

ZWEITE STUFE

SAYING HOW OFTEN YOU HAVE TO DO THINGS
Wie oft?   *How often?*
nie   *never*
manchmal   *sometimes*
oft   *often*
immer   *always*
einmal, zweimal, dreimal ...   *once, twice, three times...*
in der Woche   *a week*
im Monat   *a month*

jeden Tag   *every day*

ASKING FOR AND OFFERING HELP AND TELLING SOMEONE WHAT TO DO
können   *can, to be able to*
Was kann ich für dich tun?   *What can I do for you?*
Kann ich etwas für dich tun?   *Can I do something for you?*
Du kannst ...   *You can...*

Gut! Mach' ich!   *Okay! I'll do that!*
für   *for*
Für wen?   *For whom?*
mich   *me*
dich   *you*
uns   *us*
euch   *you (pl)*

OTHER USEFUL WORDS AND EXPRESSIONS
ungefähr   *about, approximately*

DRITTE STUFE

TALKING ABOUT THE WEATHER
Was sagt der Wetterbericht?   *What does the weather report say?*
Wie ist das Wetter?   *How's the weather?*
Es ist...   *It is...*
heiß   *hot*
warm   *warm*
kühl   *cool*
kalt   *cold*
trocken   *dry*
naß   *wet*
sonnig   *sunny*

wolkig   *cloudy*
der Schnee   *snow*
Es schneit.   *it's snowing*
der Regen   *rain*
Es regnet.   *it's raining*
das Eis   *ice*
das Gewitter   *thunder-storm*
Die Sonne scheint.   *The sun is shining.*
heute   *today*
morgen   *tomorrow*
heute abend   *this evening*
Wieviel Grad haben wir?   *What's the temperature?*
der Grad   *degree (s)*

zwei Grad   *two degrees*
der Monat, -e   *month*
der Januar   *January*
im Januar   *in January*
Februar   *February*
März   *March*
April   *April*
Mai   *May*
Juni   *June*
Juli   *July*
August   *August*
September   *September*
Oktober   *October*
November   *November*
Dezember   *December*

The Teacher's Edition

The **Komm mit!** *Teacher's Edition is designed to help you meet the increasingly varied needs of today's students by providing an abundance of suggestions and strategies. The Teacher's Edition includes the pages of the Pupil's Edition, with annotations, plus interleaf pages before each location and chapter opener.*

Using the Location Opener Interleaf

Preceding each location opener is a two-page interleaf section with specific background information on each photograph. In addition, teaching suggestions help you motivate students to learn more about the history, geography, and culture of German-speaking countries.

Using the Chapter Interleaf

The Chapter Interleaf includes background information, a list of resources, additional culture notes, and suggestions on how to motivate students, present material, and adapt activities to accommodate different learning styles.

Getting Started

At the beginning of each chapter you'll find a chapter overview chart, listening scripts, a suggested project, and several games.

Chapter Overview outlines the chapter in a concise chart that includes the functions, grammar, and culture presented in each **Stufe**, as well as a list of corresponding resource materials. The re-entry column lists previously presented material that is recycled in the chapter.

Textbook Listening Activities Scripts provide scripts of the recorded chapter listening activities for your reference or use in class.

Suggested Project proposes an extended four-skills activity based on the theme of the chapter or the location opener.

Games allow students to apply and reinforce the functions, structures, vocabulary, and culture in an informal, non-threatening atmosphere.

Teaching Cycle

For each **Stufe**, a logical instructional sequence enables you to:

motivate students by personalizing and contextualizing the topic;

teach the functions, vocabulary, structures, and culture with a variety of approaches;

close each **Stufe** with activities that combine the communicative goals;

assess students' progress with a quiz and/or performance assessment.

The teaching cycle contains the following sections:

Meeting Individual Needs

The following features suggest alternate approaches to help you address the diverse needs and abilities of students.

Visual, Auditory, Tactile, Kinesthetic Learners benefit from activities that accommodate their unique learning styles.

A Slower Pace provides ideas to break the presentation of information into smaller steps to facilitate comprehension.

Challenge includes creative, open-ended activities that encourage students to extend their reach.

Making Connections

To help students appreciate their membership in a global community, suggestions for linking German with other disciplines and cultures appear under the following categories:

Math (History, . . .) **Connections** relate the chapter topic to other subject areas, making German relevant to the students' experiences.

Multicultural Connection compares and contrasts the language and culture of German-speaking countries with those of other parts of the world.

Community/Family Link encourages students to seek opportunities for learning outside of the classroom by interacting with neighbors and family members.

Developing Thinking Skills

Thinking Critically helps students develop their higher-order thinking skills by drawing inferences, comparing and contrasting, analyzing, and synthesizing.

Establishing Collaborative Learning

Cooperative Learning allows students to work in small groups to attain common goals by sharing responsibilities.

Actively Involving Students

Total Physical Response techniques visually and kinesthetically reinforce structures and vocabulary.

Teaching *Zum Lesen*

Teacher's notes in **Zum Lesen** offer prereading, reading, and post-reading activities to help students develop reading strategies and improve comprehension.

Komm mit! Ancillaries

The Komm mit! *Holt German program offers a state of the art ancillary package that addresses the concerns of today's teachers. Because foreign language teachers are providing for all types of students, our ancillaries are designed to accommodate all learners. The* Komm mit! *ancillary materials are innovative, relevant to students' lives, and full of variety and fun.*

Teaching Resources with Professional Organizer

HRW has taken an innovative approach to organizing our **Teaching Resources**. The *Komm mit!* ancillaries are conveniently packaged in time-saving **Chapter Resources** books with a **Teaching Resource Organizer**. Each Chapter Resources book puts a wealth of resources at your fingertips!

Chapter Resources, Books 1-4

♦ Oral communication is the language skill that is most challenging to develop and test. The *Komm mit!* **Situation Cards** and **Communicative Activities** are designed to help students develop their speaking skills and give them opportunities to communicate in a variety of situations.

♦ **Additional Listening Activities**, in combination with the textbook audiocassette program, provide students with a unique opportunity to actively develop their listening comprehension skills in a variety of authentic contexts.

♦ The *Komm mit!* **Realia** reproduce real documents to provide your students with additional language practice in authentic cultural contexts. Included with the **Realia** are suggestions for their use.

♦ The **Student Response Forms** are provided for your convenience. These copying masters enable you to reproduce standard answer forms for the listening activities in the textbook.

♦ The *Komm mit!* **Assessment Program** responds to your requests for a method of evaluation that is fair to all students, and that encourages students to work toward realistic, attainable goals. The **Assessment Program** includes the following components:

♦ Three **Quizzes** per chapter (one per **Stufe**)
♦ One **Chapter Test** per chapter; each **Chapter Test** includes listening, speaking, reading, writing, and culture. Part of each test can be corrected on ScanTron®.

♦ Also included in the *Chapter Resources:*

♦ **Teaching Transparency Masters** for use in a variety of activities
♦ **Listening Scripts** for the Additional Listening Activities and the Assessment Program
♦ **Answer Key** for the *Practice and Activity Book*

Assessment Guide

The **Assessment Guide** describes various testing and scoring methods. This guide also includes:

♦ **Portfolio Assessment** suggestions and rubrics
♦ **Speaking Tests** to be used separately or as part of the Chapter Test
♦ A cumulative **Midterm Exam**
♦ A comprehensive **Final Exam**

Teaching Resource Organizer

A tri-fold binder helps you organize the ancillaries for each chapter.

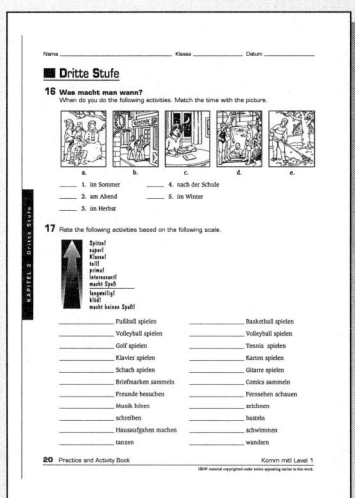

Teaching Transparencies

The **Teaching Transparencies** benefit the visual learner as well as all students. These colorful, situational transparencies add variety and focus to your classroom. The **Chapter Resources** books include suggestions to help you integrate the 24 transparencies and two full-color map transparencies into your lesson plans.

Audiocassette Program

The listening activities in the **Audiocassette Program** help students develop their listening and pronunciation skills by providing opportunities to hear native speakers of German in a variety of authentic situations and to practice the sounds of the language.

Practice and Activity Book

The **Practice and Activity Book** is filled with imaginative, challenging activities that will motivate students to learn German. In addition, there are exercises that reinforce the grammatical structures. Extension activities allow students to explore culture and language in a personally relevant context.

Test Generator

The **Test Generator** is a software program that enables you to create customized worksheets, quizzes, and tests for each chapter in *Komm mit!* The **Test Generator** is available for IBM© PC and Compatibles and Macintosh © computers.

Komm mit! Video

Komm mit! *Video Program* and *Komm mit!* *Expanded Video Program* bring the German-speaking world right into your classroom! Filmed entirely on location in Germany and Austria, these video programs feature native speakers of German in realistic, high-interest situations.

Video is the ideal medium for providing authentic input and increasing proficiency in German. With the **Video Program** and **Expanded Video Program,** students both see and hear speakers of German interacting with one another naturally in realistic settings. Students' comprehension of authentic speech is enhanced by the rich visual cues that the video provides. Moreover, the video is entertaining as well as educational.

Komm mit! Video Program

The **Video Program** correlates with the *Komm mit!* *Pupil's Edition:*

♦ Chapter Opener Filmed on location in the chapter setting, these images preview the chapter theme and reflect the functions and vocabulary of the chapter. This dynamic collage of people in real situations is a motivating introduction to the chapter.

♦ **Los geht's!** A contemporary, dramatic episode, thematically linked to the chapter, models the functional expressions, vocabulary, and grammar, and also spirals material from previous chapters in new contexts. This video episode can be used either as the primary or supplemental means of presenting the chapter.

♦ **Landeskunde** Authentic interviews with native speakers of German on a variety of cultural topics complement the information presented in the chapter. German culture comes to life as real people talk about themselves, their country, and their way of life.

Komm mit! Expanded Video Program

Komm mit! *Expanded Video Program offers the teacher an even wider variety of video materials, directly related to the textbook, which will enhance and expand students' proficiency in the German language and their knowledge of people, places, and culture.*

The **Expanded Video Program** includes all of the material provided in the **Video Program,** and more.

♦ **Location Opener** A narrated tour of the region presented in the Location Opener expands students' acquaintance with the geography and people of that area.

♦ **Fortsetzung** continues the dramatic episode begun in **Los geht's!** to further motivate and challenge students. The episodes of **Los geht's!** end in ways that suggest several possible sequels. In **Fortsetzung**, the dramatic episodes continue the story lines and resolve the situations. **Fortsetzung** not only provides additional high-interest input related to the functions and vocabulary of each chapter, but also offers opportunities for students to go a step beyond. Confidence and proficiency increase as **Fortsetzung** spirals functions, vocabulary, and structures from previous chapters, and previews content of upcoming chapters.

♦ **Landeskunde** interviews are presented in their entirety and additional people are interviewed in the **Expanded Video Program**. These interviews with a wide variety of native speakers of German give students exposure to regional variations in speech, the diversity of the German people, and varying points of view. This assortment of interviews from the German-speaking countries enriches students' appreciation of German culture.

♦ **Video realia** provide short segments of video that include authentic footage from German television, music videos, news broadcasts, commercials, and more. Students will gain confidence as they realize that they can understand and enjoy material not expressly designed for language learners, but produced for native speakers of German!

Komm mit! Video Guide

Komm mit! Video Guide provides background information and suggestions for pre- and post-viewing activities for all portions of the **Video Program** and the **Expanded Video Program**. In addition, the **Video Guide** contains a transcript and synopsis of each **Los geht's!** dramatic episode, a supplemental vocabulary list, and reproducible student activity sheets.

Chapter 3 Sample Lesson Plan

DAILY PLANS	RESOURCES

DAY 1   **OBJECTIVE:** To learn how German students tell about their vacations

Chapter Opener, pp. 52-53 Discussion (p. 51G)
Los geht's! pp. 54-55:
  Motivating Activity, p. 51H
  Basic Material: **Unser Film- und Fotoclub**
  Activities 1/2/4, p. 56
Closure: p. 51I
Assignment: Activity 3, p. 56
	Video Program OR *Expanded*
	  Video Program, Videocassette 1
	Video Guide, **Kapitel 3**
	Textbook Audiocassette 2A
	
	Practice and Activity Book

DAY 2   **OBJECTIVE:** To report on past events and talk about activities

Focus: Activity 3, p. 56
Erste Stufe, p. 57
  Motivating Activity, p. 51I,
  Activity 5, p. 57
  Presentation: **So sagt man das!** (p. 57), p. 51I
  Presentation: **Wortschatz!** (p. 57), p. 51I
  Activities 6/7, p. 58
Assignment: Activity 8, p. 58
	Chapter Resources, Book 1
	Textbook Audiocassette 2A
	Additional Listening Activities,
	  Audiocassette 9A
	
	Practice and Activity Book

DAY 3   **OBJECTIVE:** To report on past events and talk about places

Focus: Activity 8, p. 58 Presentation: **Grammatik** (pp. 58-59), p. 51J Activity 9, p. 59 Activity 10, p. 60 Text: **Dresden, Haupstadt von Sachsen,** p. 61 Activity 12, p. 61 Assessment: p. 51K Closure: p. 51K Assignment: Activity 11, p. 60	*Chapter Resources*, Book 1 *Practice and Activity Book*

DAY 4   **OBJECTIVE:** To report on past events and talk about places

Focus: Activity 11, p. 60
Quiz: 3-1
Zweite Stufe, p. 62
  Motivating Activity, p. 51L
  Text: **Frankfurt a.M.**, p. 62
  Activities 13/14, p. 62
  Activities 15/16, p. 63
  Presentation: **So sagt man das!** (p. 63), p. 51L
  Presentation: **Wortschatz** (p. 63), p. 51M
Assignment: Activity 17, p. 64
	Chapter Resources, Book 1
	Assessment Items,
	  Audiocassette 7A
	  Textbook Audiocassette 2A
	
	Practice and Activity Book

DAY 5   **OBJECTIVE:** To tell about where you were and to find out about students' vacations

Focus: Activity 17, p. 64 Presentation: **Grammatik** (p. 64), p. 51M Activities 18/19, p. 64 Presentation: **Grammatik** (p. 65), p. 51M Activities 20/21, p. 65 Activities 22/23, p. 66 **Landeskunde**, p. 67: Discussion Assessment: p. 51N Assignment: Activity 24, p. 66	*Chapter Resources*, Book 1 *Video Program* OR *Expanded* *Video Program,* Videocassette 1 *Video Guide,* **Kapitel 3** *Practice and Activity Book*

DAILY PLANS

RESOURCES

DAY 6   OBJECTIVE: **To report on places visited and to express enthusiasm or disappointment**

Daily Plans	Resources

Focus: Activity 24, p. 66
Quiz: 3-2
Dritte Stufe, p. 68
  Motivating Activity, p. 51O
  Activity 25, p. 68
  Presentation: **So sagt man das!** (p. 68), p. 51O
  Activity 26, p. 68
  Presentation: **Grammatik** (p. 69), p. 51O
  Activities 27/28, p. 69
Assignment: Activity 29, p. 70
	Chapter Resources, Book 1
	Assessment Items
	  Audiocassette 7A
	Textbook Audiocassette 2A
	
	Practice and Activity Book

DAY 7   OBJECTIVE: **To tell where one stays and where one eats on vacation**

Daily Plans	Resources
Focus: Activity 29, p. 70 Presentation: **Wortschatz** (p. 70), p. 51O Activities 30-32, p. 71 Assessment: p. 51P Closure: p. 51P Assignment: Activity 33, p. 71	*Chapter Resources*, Book 1 *Practice and Activity Book*

DAY 8   OBJECTIVE: **To express enthusiasm, talk about where you were; to read for main idea**

Daily Plans	Resources
Focus: Activity 33, p. 71 Quiz: 3-3 **Zum Lesen**, Activities 1-6, pp. 72-73; p. 51Q Closure: p. 51P Assignment: Activity 7, p. 73	*Chapter Resources*, Book 1 *Assessment Items* *Audiocassette* 7A *Practice and Activity Book*

DAY 9   OBJECTIVE: **To use what you have learned to prepare for Chapter Test**

Daily Plans	Resources
Focus: Activity 7, p. 73 **Anwendung**, pp. 74-75, p. 51R Activities 1-3: partner practice Activities 5-6: listening **Kann ich's wirklich?** p. 76 Assignment: **Wortschatz**, p. 77; p. 51R	*Chapter Resources*, Book 1 *Video Program* OR *Expanded* *Video Program*, Videocassette 1 *Video Guide*, **Kapitel 3** *Textbook Audiocassette* 2A *Practice and Activity Book*

DAY 10   OBJECTIVE: **To assess progress**

Daily Plans	Resources
Focus: Activity 7, p. 73 **Kapitel 3** Chapter Test Speaking Test	*Chapter Resources*, Book 1 *Assessment Items* *Audiocassette* 7A *Assessment Guide*, **Kapitel 3**

▣ Location Opener

Bayern, pages 1-3
Expanded Video Program, Videocassette 1

*U*sing the Photograph,
p. 1

Background Information

Schloß Kranzbach was built between 1913 and 1915 near the Kranz brook (hence the name **Schloß Kranzbach**) for Miss Portmann, an Englishwoman. A hall with an orchestra pit was specifically designed for performances by musicians from all over the world. Unfortunately, World War I kept Miss Portmann from ever visiting her castle, and it stayed empty for 18 years. Today the estate is used for church retreats and is also open year-round to the public as a resort.

Thinking Critically

Drawing Inferences Ask students why World War I kept Miss Portmann from living in her estate. (The conflict with Germany during World War I put England on the opposing side.)

Geography Connection

Ask students what visitors can expect to do during their stay at **Schloß Kranzbach.** (Examples: spring/summer/fall: hiking, mountain climbing, visits to nearby Mittenwald; winter: cross-country skiing, downhill skiing)

Teacher Notes

• You may want to point out to students that although Germany has many state-owned castles of historical and architectural significance, many more, such as **Schloß Kranzbach,** are privately owned. In order to maintain such enormous castles financially, many owners allow some or all of their estates to become museums or resorts.

• The Karwendel Mountains (9,040 ft/2,756 m) in the background of the photo are a national park. They are located between the Isar and Inn rivers and are part of a chain of mountains called the **Nordtiroler Kalkalpen.**

*U*sing the Almanac and Map,
p. 1

The Bavarian coat of arms was originally the crest of the powerful Duke of Bogen on the Danube. The diagonal rows of blue and white diamonds symbolize the unity of the Free State of Bavaria and the colors of the sky over Bavaria—blue and white.

Terms in the Almanac

• **Nürnberg** (482,000 inhabitants): the second largest city of Bavaria (after Munich), dating back to the Middle Ages. **Nürnberg** is known for being the originating point of the first German railroad in 1835. Between 1945 and 1949 the city was the site of the Nuremberg trials.

• **Rhein-Main-Donau-Kanal:** also called the **Europa-Kanal**. It runs through Bavaria, connecting the Danube with the Main. This extensive system of waterways is an inland route between the Black Sea and North Sea. It was completed in 1993.

• **Synthesizing** Ask students why this canal is important to other European countries as well as to Germany. (This waterway facilitates the increased transport of goods between western Europe and the countries of central and southeastern Europe.)

• **Zugspitze:** the highest mountain in the German Alps. It is 9,719 feet (2,962 meters) high. It is easily accessible by cable car.

• **Richard Strauss** (1864-1949): composer who wrote such famous operas as *Elektra* and *Der Rosenkavalier*. He was born in Munich and died in Garmisch.

- **Bertolt Brecht** (1898-1956): considered one of the most influential playwrights of the twentieth century. Brecht is known for his socially critical writings such as *Mutter Courage und ihre Kinder* and *Die Dreigroschenoper.*

- **Radi:** Bavarian term for **Rettich. Radi** is a white vegetable that resembles a long radish or a carrot and tastes like a radish. This vegetable was originally brought to central Europe by Roman soldiers.

- **Kalbshaxe:** veal shank which is cooked in water, browned, and often served with tomatoes and dumplings

- **Starnberger See:** Located south of Munich, this lake is a popular recreational destination for swimming, sailing, and windsurfing. A cross stands in the lake, marking the point where Ludwig II drowned mysteriously in 1886.

Teaching Suggestion

Ask students if they know the name of Ludwig II's most famous castle. (**Neuschwanstein**)

Using the Map

- Have students use the map on p. 394 to identify the German states that border Bavaria. (**Hessen, Thüringen**, and **Sachsen** to the north; **Baden-Württemberg** to the west) You may also want to use Map Transparency 1.
- Have students identify the countries that share a border with Bavaria. (**Österreich** to the south, the **Tschechische Republik** to the east)
- Have students locate and trace the new **Rhein-Main-Donau-Kanal.**
- Have students locate the Danube and the Main.

↗nterpreting the Photo Essay, pp. 2-3

- **Group Work** Have students work in small groups to study the pictures. They should come up with things that they think might be unique to this area.

② In 1330 Emperor **Ludwig der Bayer** founded this monastery. It was modeled after the Church of the Holy Sepulcher in Jerusalem. The dome was added between 1745 and 1752. The main entrance hall to the church is considered one of the masterpieces of the German rococo style.

③ The **Pfarrkirche St. Peter und Paul** in Mittenwald was built in the baroque style by Joseph Schmuzer between 1737 and 1740 and was dedicated in 1749. The ceiling painting as well as the painting at the high altar were done by Matthäus Günther (1705-1788), a well-known painter who decorated the interior of many churches in southern Germany. Günther was trained by the famous baroque artist Cosmas Damian Asam, and his work marks the transition from the baroque to the rococo style.

④ This memorial is located in front of the **Pfarrkirche St. Peter und Paul** and is a monument to the violin maker Matthias Klotz. After learning his trade under Stradivari in Italy, Klotz returned to his native Mittenwald to continue his work. To this day, this town is known for the outstanding craftsmanship of the violins produced there.

⑤ This castle was built for **König Ludwig II. von Bayern**, who chose the style of the French King Louis XIV's Versailles as a model. Behind the castle is a beautiful park with many monuments. In the front is the **Neptunbrunnen**, which has a fountain that is 105 feet (32 meters) high. The **Wasserspiele** in the park fountain can be seen every hour.

⑥ Robert, Christiane, and Sebastian were born in Bavaria; their Bavarian accents attest to it. Thomas is from Poland.

⑦ **Zwiebeltürme**, onion shaped towers, are also called **Zwiebelhauben** *(onion shaped caps).* **Lüftlmalerei** is common in the southern parts of Germany where the facades of houses and churches are often painted with brightly colored scenes. **Lüftlmalerei** is also known as **Freskomalerei**, a term coming from the Italian *al fresco*, which means *on fresh*, because paint is applied to fresh plaster on walls before the plaster hardens.

Komm mit nach

Bayern!

Bayern

Einwohner: 11,4 Millionen

Fläche: 70 500 Quadratkilometer (27 200 Quadratmeilen; etwa halb so groß wie Iowa)

Landeshauptstadt: München

Große Städte: Nürnberg, Regensburg, Augsburg, Erlangen, Würzburg, Fürth, Passau

Flüsse: Donau, Main, Iller, Lech, Isar, Inn

Seen: Bodensee, Ammersee, Starnberger See, Chiemsee, Tegernsee

Kanäle: Rhein-Main-Donau-Kanal

Berge: Zugspitze (2962 m), Watzmann (2713 m)

Bedeutende Bayern: Richard Strauss (1864-1949, Komponist), Ludwig Thoma (1867-1921, Schriftsteller), Bertolt Brecht (1898-1956, Schriftsteller), Carl Orff (1895-1982, Komponist), Luise Rinser (1910-, Schriftstellerin)

Industrie: Maschinenbau, Elektroindustrie, Automobilindustrie, Textilindustrie, Tourismus

Beliebte Gerichte: Schweinshaxe, Kalbshaxe, Knödel, Karpfen, Radi, Leberkäs, Zwetschgenkuchen

Foto ① Schloß Kranzbach bei Mittenwald. Im Hintergrund das Karwendelgebirge

Bayern

Bayern, das größte Land der Bundesrepublik Deutschland, ist das beliebteste Reiseziel Deutschlands. Jedes Jahr besuchen Millionen von Touristen die zahlreichen Attraktionen Bayerns, von den barocken Städten Frankens bis zu den malerischen Bergen Oberbayerns. Land- und Forstwirtschaft sind immer noch sehr wichtig in Bayern, doch spielen moderne Industrien eine zunehmend größere Rolle.

2 Das Benediktiner-
kloster Ettal
in Oberbayern

3 Die Pfarrkirche St. Peter und
Paul in Mittenwald

4 Ein Denkmal für
Mathias Klotz
(1653 - 1743),
den Begründer
des Mittenwalder
Geigenbaus

Die ersten zwei Kapitel spielen in Grünwald, einer Vorstadt von München, wo die Baumanns wohnen. Im dritten Kapitel erzählt Sebastian von seiner Reise nach Österreich, und zwei von seinen Freunden berichten über Frankfurt und Dresden. Die Schüler in diesen Kapiteln gehen aufs Gymnasium in Grünwald.

5 Schloß Linderhof, 1874 - 78 für König Ludwig II. von Bayern erbaut

6 Robert, Thomas, Christiane und Sebastian

7 Eine typisch bayrische Kirche mit Zwiebelturm und typisches Gasthaus mit Lüftlmalerei

Kapitel 1: Bei den Baumanns *Wiederholungskapitel*

Los geht's! pp. 6-8	Sebastian stellt seine Familie vor, *p. 6*		*Video Guide*
	REVIEW OF FUNCTIONS	**REVIEW OF GRAMMAR**	**CULTURE**
Erste Stufe pp. 9-15	• Asking for and giving information about yourself and others; describing yourself and others; expressing likes and dislikes, *p. 11* • Identifying people and places, *p. 13*	• The verbs **sein** and **haben**, *p. 11* • Regular and stem-changing verbs, *p. 12* • The singular possessive adjectives, *p. 13*	• Questionnaire: **Was für eine Person bist du?** *p. 9* • Article: **Sebastian über seine Familie**, *p. 14*
Zweite Stufe pp. 16-19	• Giving and responding to compliments, *p. 18* • Expressing wishes when buying things, *p. 18*	• The **möchte**-forms, *p. 19* • The nominative and accusative forms of the definite and the indefinite articles, *p. 19* • The third person pronouns, *p. 19*	• Article: **Popstars machen Mode**, *p. 16* • Department store ad, *p. 19*
Dritte Stufe pp. 23-25	• Making plans, *p. 23* • Ordering food and beverages, *p. 25* • Talking about how something tastes, *p. 25*	• The verb **wollen**, *p. 23* • The **möchte**-forms, *p. 23*	• **Landeskunde: Und was hast du am liebsten?** *p. 22* • Advertisements, *p. 24*

Zum Lesen pp. 20-21 — **Cousin und Kusine verständigen sich, oder?**
Reading Strategy: Using prereading strategies (looking at visual clues, reading the title and subtitles, looking for cognates and other familiar words while skimming)

Review pp. 26-27
• **Kann ich's wirklich?** *p. 26*
• **Wortschatz**, *p. 27*

Assessment Options

Stufe Quizzes
• *Chapter Resources*, Book 1
  Erste Stufe, Quiz 1-1
  Zweite Stufe, Quiz 1-2
  Dritte Stufe, Quiz 1-3
• *Assessment Items, Audiocassette* 7 A

Kapitel 1 Chapter Test
• *Chapter Resources*, Book 1
• *Assessment Guide*, Speaking Test
• *Assessment Items, Audiocassette* 7 A

Test Generator, Kapitel 1

Chapter Overview

Video Program **OR**
Expanded Video Program, Videocassette 1

Textbook Audiocassette 1 A

RESOURCES Print	**RESOURCES** Audiovisual

Textbook Audiocassette 1 A

Practice and Activity Book
Chapter Resources, Book 1
- Additional Listening Activities 1-1, 1-2 ....*Additional Listening Activities, Audiocassette* 9 A
- Student Response Forms
- Realia 1-1
- Situation Card 1-1
- Teaching Transparency Master 1-1 ....*Teaching Transparency* 1-1
- Quiz 1-1 ....*Assessment Items, Audiocassette* 7 A

Textbook Audiocassette 1 A

Practice and Activity Book
Chapter Resources, Book 1
- Communicative Activity 1-1
- Additional Listening Activities 1-3, 1-4 ....*Additional Listening Activities, Audiocassette* 9 A
- Student Response Forms
- Realia 1-2
- Situation Card 1-2
- Teaching Transparency Master 1-2 ....*Teaching Transparency* 1-2
- Quiz 1-2 ....*Assessment Items, Audiocassette* 7 A

Textbook Audiocassette 1 A

Practice and Activity Book
Chapter Resources, Book 1
- Communicative Activity 1-2
- Additional Listening Activities 1-5, 1-6 ....*Additional Listening Activities, Audiocassette* 9 A
- Student Response Forms
- Realia 1-3
- Situation Card 1-3
- Quiz 1-3 ....*Assessment Items, Audiocassette* 7 A
Video Guide ....*Video Program/Expanded Video Program,* Videocassette 1

Video Guide ....*Video Program/Expanded Video Program,* Videocassette 1

Alternative Assessment
- Performance Assessment
  Teacher's Edition
  Erste Stufe, p. 3L
  Zweite Stufe, p. 3M
  Dritte Stufe, p. 3R
- Portfolio Assessment
  Written: **Dritte Stufe,** Activity 37, *Pupil's Edition,* p. 23; *Assessment Guide* p. 14
  Oral: **Dritte Stufe,** Activity 44, *Pupil's Edition,* p. 25; *Assessment Guide* p. 14
- **Notizbuch,** *Pupil's Edition,* pp. 11, 14, 15, 23; *Practice and Activity Book,* p. 145

Kapitel 1: Bei den Baumanns
Textbook Listening Activities Scripts

Erste Stufe
Activity 6, p. 9

1. Immer freundlich, sehr sympathisch und vor allem immer gut gekleidet. Liebt vor allem bunte Sachen; geht sehr gern aus.
2. Nicht sehr groß, blond, sehr ruhig und vor allem sehr tierlieb. Reitet furchtbar gern und hat sogar ein eigenes Pferd.
3. Nett und freundlich. Steht auf Jeanskleidung. Alle lieben die blonden Locken. Hilft anderen Leuten furchtbar gern; repariert die Fahrräder von Familie und Freunden.
4. Schlank und sehr attraktiv, immer lächelnd, braune Haare, die gewöhnlich mit einem Stirnband zusammengehalten werden. Liebt schicke Sachen, vor allem Lederklamotten.
5. Superschlank und sportlich. Ein Stirnband hält beim Skilaufen die dunklen Haare zusammen — hier natürlich beim Grasskilaufen.

Answers to Activity 6
a. 4; b. 3; c. 5; d. 2; e. 1

Activity 10, p. 11

1. Also, ich heiße Johannes, bin 16 Jahre alt, 1,70 groß, schlank, und ich habe braune Haare. Ich spiele Squash … ja, was noch? Mein Hobby ist, ja, das hört sich vielleicht komisch an: ich sammle Ansichtskarten. Ich habe schon so viele Karten, Karten aus der ganzen Welt. Das Hobby ist toll: ich lerne sehr viel über Geographie und wie es in der Welt aussieht.

2. Mein Name ist Monika. Ich bin 15, werde aber im nächsten Monat 16. Ja, wie sehe ich aus? Blonde, lockige Haare hab' ich, ich trag' eine Brille. Meine Klassenkameraden sagen, ich bin furchtbar intelligent. Warum, das weiß ich auch nicht. Vielleicht, weil ich gut in Mathe bin und eigentlich immer eine Eins schreibe.

3. Heike ist mein Name, und ich bin 17 Jahre alt. Ich bin nicht sehr groß, nur 1,55, aber vielleicht wachse ich noch. Ich habe schwarze Haare, ja, was soll ich noch über mich sagen? Ach ja, ich sehe schlecht, sehr schlecht sogar, und ich muß Kontaktlinsen tragen. Mein Hobby ist Kochen — ich koche sogar sehr gern. Das hab' ich von meinem Vater; er ist Chefkoch in einem großen, noblen Restaurant. Ja, und wie sieht's mit Sport aus? Radfahren, und ab und zu spiele ich auch Tennis.

4. Ich heiße Dieter Maier — Maier mit *a i* — ich bin 16 Jahre alt. Wie ich aussehe? Meine Freunde sagen: blöd! Na ja, ich hab' lange, blonde Haare, die ich mir hinten zusammenbinde. Ich habe braune Augen, sehe sehr gut; dann bin ich ein guter Basketballspieler und spiele in unserer Schulmannschaft. Hobbys? Ich lese sehr gern, alles über Tiere. Tiergeschichten aus Afrika, Indien und so — ja, das ist es wohl. Tja!

Answers to Activity 10

1. **Johannes:** 16; 1,70 groß; braune Haare; schlank; spielt Squash; sammelt Ansichtskarten. 2. **Monika:** 15; blond; trägt eine Brille; furchtbar intelligent; gut in Mathe. 3. **Heike:** 17; nicht sehr groß, 1,55; schwarze Haare; trägt Kontaktlinsen; kocht sehr gerne; fährt sehr gerne Rad; spielt Tennis. 4. **Dieter:** 16; sieht blöd aus; lange, blonde Haare; braune Augen; guter Basketballspieler in Schulmannschaft; liest gern Tiergeschichten.

SCRIPTS

Activity 20, p. 15

1. Mein Name ist Erika. Ich bin 16 und gehe aufs Gymnasium. Meine Lieblingsfächer sind Deutsch und Englisch, ja auch Biologie. In Bio hab' ich sogar 'ne Eins. Physik hab' ich überhaupt nicht gern, das Fach interessiert mich nicht.

2. Ich heiße Walter Neumann und bin 17 Jahre alt. Was ich in der Schule gern hab'? Ja, das sind zuerst einmal die beiden Pausen, weil ich da … da kann ich mit meinen Klassenkameraden im Schulhof Tischtennis spielen. Na ja, Mathe hab' ich schon gern, auch Geschichte, aber Biologie ist absolut furchtbar.

3. Ich bin der Jörg, bin 16 Jahre alt und gehe hier auf die Realschule. Meine Lieblingsfächer sind Musik, weil ich später mal in einer Band spielen möchte. Andere Fächer? Deutsch ist so so, und Englisch geht gerade noch. Aber Mathe — furchtbar! Ich bekomme immer 'ne Fünf!

Answers to Activity 20

1. Erika: 16; Gymnasium; Lieblingsfächer Deutsch, Englisch und Biologie; hat eine Eins in Bio; interessiert sich nicht für Physik.
2. Walter: 17; hat die beiden Pausen gern; Tischtennis; mag Mathe und Geschichte, aber nicht Bio. 3. Jörg: 16; Realschule; Lieblingsfach Musik; will mal in einer Band spielen; mag Deutsch und Englisch ein bißchen; hat eine 5 in Mathe.

Activity 24, p. 15

JÖRG Mein Zimmer ist sehr nett. Es ist groß, hat zwei große Fenster. Ich hab' also viel Sonne im Zimmer. Meine Möbel sind okay, Bett, Schrank, der Sessel ist ganz neu, hab' ich zum Geburtstag bekommen. Jetzt kann ich also ganz bequem im Sessel sitzen und Video schauen, wenn ich nicht selbst Musik mache.

ERIKA Ja, ich habe ein schönes Zimmer, klein, aber sehr gemütlich. Ich habe einen super Schrank, ganz alt, den hab' ich von meiner Oma. Dann hab' ich noch einen kleinen Schreibtisch im Zimmer, zwei Stühle und eine Couch — das ist mein Bett. Muß ich jeden Abend aufmachen, damit ich schlafen gehen kann.

Answers to Activity 24

Jörg: Bett, Schrank, Sessel; Erika: Schrank, Schreibtisch, Stühle, Couch

Zweite Stufe
Activity 34, p. 19

Der Sommerschlußverkauf beginnt offiziell nächsten Montag, aber wir haben schon jetzt unsere Preise reduziert — für Sie, liebe Kunden — damit Sie jetzt schon in Ruhe bei uns einkaufen können. Unser Angebot ist groß: T-Shirts in allen Größen und Farben und schon ab 12 Mark. Die Sensation in unserer Jugendabteilung sind Polohemden aus reiner Baumwolle, mit halbem Ärmel, ideal für die heißen Sommertage. Und auch der Preis ist heiß: nur 18 Mark 50! In der Jeansabteilung finden Sie alle Marken und Größen — aber zu kleinen Preisen. Jeans schon ab 36 Mark! Eine Sensation im Junior-Shop: Pullover für die kühlen Herbsttage. Aus Polyacryl. Leider nur in drei Farben, Blau, Grün und Rot. Aber dafür zum einmaligen Preis von nur 20 Mark! Und noch ein ganz heißer Tip: Cowboystiefel — die Sensation — in Braun und in Schwarz. Viele Größen und schon ab 120 Mark! Sie fühlen sich wie im Westen Amerikas! Also, nichts wie zum Sport-Bauer, das moderne Sportgeschäft, das Ihre Wünsche erfüllt!

Dritte Stufe
Activity 36, *p. 23*

PETRA   Also, meistens gehe ich am Samstag nachmittag schwimmen. Wenn das Wetter schön ist, zum Beispiel im Sommer, dann gehen wir ins Freibad, sonst ins Hallenbad. Danach gehen wir meistens in die Stadt zum Bummeln oder Eis essen.

SVEN   Ich hab' jeden Samstag Fußballtraining von drei bis halb fünf. Entweder fahre ich mit dem Rad oder ich jogge dorthin, als Aufwärmtraining, bevor wir mit dem Spiel anfangen. Nach dem Training gehen wir meistens 'was trinken.

MARTINA   Also, ich geh' samstags immer mit meiner Freundin in die Nachmittagsvorstellung ins Kino. Vorher lese ich immer die Wochenendausgabe der Zeitung. Da sind auch alle Kinoprogramme drin.

Answers to Activity 36

Petra: schwimmen; bummeln; Eis essen. Sven: Fußballtraining; radfahren; joggen; etwas trinken gehen. Martina: Kino, Zeitung lesen.

Activity 42, *p. 24*

1. A: Worauf hast du denn Appetit?
   B: Du, ich weiß nicht! Ich hab' aber großen Hunger.
   A: Also, ich möchte heute mal etwas Italienisches, eine Pizza vielleicht. Ich glaube, ich nehme die zu acht fünfzig.
2. A: Wo kann ich nur einen Spitzer und einen Radiergummi kaufen?
   B: Komm mit! Da an der Ecke ist ein Schreibwarengeschäft. Da kriegst du alles, was du brauchst.
3. A: Ich brauch' unbedingt etwas, was zu meiner Jeans paßt, eine Bluse oder ein T-Shirt vielleicht.
   B: Geh doch zum Sport-Bauer! Der hat diese Woche tolle Sonderangebote. Die Ware ist echt gut, und die Preise sind stark reduziert.
4. A: Wie spät ist es denn?
   B: Du weißt doch, meine Uhr ist kaputt.
   A: Dann kauf dir halt eine neue! Ich weiß, wo du sogar eine Solaruhr für 12 Mark bekommst.
5. A: Ich sitz' gern in diesem Café. Der Kaffee riecht hier immer so gut.
   B: Stimmt! — Hm, ich glaube, daß ich heute einen Eiskaffee trinke. Es ist so heiß draußen, und ich möchte unbedingt etwas Kaltes.

Answers to Activity 42

a. 3; b. 4; c. 5; d. 1; e. 2

Answers to Activity 43

Ich möchte heute mal ... ; ich glaube, ich nehme ... ; wo kann ich ... kaufen?; ich brauch' unbedingt ... ; ich möchte unbedingt ...

Kapitel 1: Bei den Baumanns
Projects and Games

PROJECT

Students will write an autobiographical sketch called **Mein Lebenslauf.** *Begin this project after students have reviewed and practiced the vocabulary and functions in the* **Erste Stufe** *and have done Activity 19* (**Beatrices Steckbrief**) *on p. 15. This project is a great way for students to learn about one another at the beginning of the new school year.*

Materials Students may need poster board or a large sheet of paper, glue, and photographs of themselves.

Suggested Sequence

1. Begin by brainstorming with students as to what kind of information should be included in their **Lebenslauf.** (Examples: first, middle, and last name; date of birth; place of birth; names of parents; siblings; schools attended; address; hobbies) Remind students to use the vocabulary on pp. 9 and 10.
2. Ask students to make an outline of the facts to be included in their autobiographical sketch.
3. Have students write their **Lebenslauf** on poster board or on a sheet of paper and attach a photograph of themselves.
4. Students present their project and read their **Lebenslauf** to the classroom.
5. Display all **Lebensläufe** in your classroom.

Grading the Project

Suggested point distribution (total = 100 points)

Written work	60
Originality, Neatness, Appearance	40

Teacher Note

When giving assignments that entail the disclosure of personal information, keep in mind that some students and their families may consider family matters private. In some cases, you may want to give an alternate assignment in which students discuss a make-believe family.

 GAME

Bildkarten

In this game students practice the articles **der, die,** *and* **das** *as they apply to the nouns to be reviewed.*

Preparation Write nouns from a particular vocabulary group on small index cards. (Examples: foods, clothing) You could also glue or tape pictures of the objects on index cards instead of writing the words. You will need a set of at least twelve cards for each group.

Procedure Students play in groups of five; four students will play, while the fifth student is the leader. Each of the four players receives a blank sheet of paper on which he or she writes the three direct articles.

der	die	das

The leader receives a list with all the nouns, including the corresponding articles, as well as a set of index cards which show the picture or word. The leader places the deck of cards face down. Students take turns drawing a card from the top of the deck. Each student tries to name the correct definite article for the noun written on the card he or she has drawn. If he or she is correct, the card is placed on the sheet in front of him or her under the corresponding article. If the student names the wrong article, the leader receives the card. Once all cards in the deck have been used, the leader reshuffles the remaining cards and continues until all articles have been named correctly. The student with the most cards on his or her sheet (**der-die-das**) wins. To expand this activity, students could also be required to create a complete sentence using each of the nouns. Play the game several times to help students learn all the vocabulary with the correct articles.

Kapitel 1: Bei den Baumanns
Lesson Plans, pages 4-27

Teacher Notes

- Chapter 1 is a review chapter that reintroduces functions, grammar, and vocabulary from *Komm mit!* Level 1.

- Some activities suggested in the *Teacher's Edition* ask students to contact various people, businesses, and organizations in the community. Before assigning these activities, it is advisable to request parental permission. In some cases, you may also want to obtain permission from the parties the students will be asked to contact.

*U*sing the Chapter Opener, *pp. 4-5*

Motivating Activity

Divide the class into six groups and ask each group to sit together and choose one designated writer. On six index cards write the following categories: clothing, places in Germany, foods, adjectives (characteristics), family members, and sports and activities. Mix the six cards and have one member of each group take one card. Once each group has its card, members try to come up with as many German words as they can for the category listed on their card. The writer records the words. You may want to set a time limit for this activity. (Example: two minutes) Then ask the groups to read their category and the words they listed.

Teaching Suggestion

To reacquaint students with one another as well as to introduce new students, ask students to walk around the classroom asking the following five questions which you have written on the board:

Wie heißt du?
Wo wohnst du?
Was machst du gern in deiner Freizeit?
Was hast du diesen Sommer gemacht?
Was ißt du gern/nicht gern?

After students have returned to their seats, call on several students to share at least three items of information about a classmate.

Building on Previous Skills

Ask students to name and describe in German people, objects, or places that they see in the three pictures, using vocabulary they remember from their previous German class. (Examples: clothing, furniture, physical attributes, activities)

Thinking Critically

③ **Drawing Inferences** This photo looks like a snap shot from a summer vacation. Ask students to imagine why Basti had this photo taken. Have students talk about it in German.

③ **Comparing and Contrasting** Ask students what they typically wore during their summer vacation. For what types of occasions did they vary their outfits? How do they compare their typical summer clothing with what Basti is wearing? Ask students if they think there is appropriate dress for different occasions. Students should justify their answers.

Focusing on Outcomes

Have students preview the learning outcomes listed on p. 5. Ask them what the people in the photographs might say that would represent each function. (Example: Photo 2—giving compliments— **Ich finde dein Halstuch toll!**) NOTE: Each of these outcomes is modeled in the video and evaluated in **Kann ich's wirklich?** on p. 26.

Teaching Los geht's!
pp. 6-8

Resources for Los geht's!

- *Video Program* **OR**
  Expanded Video Program, Videocassette 1
- *Textbook Audiocassette* 1 A
- *Practice and Activity Book*

▶ **pages 6-7**

Video Synopsis

In this segment of the video, Sebastian gives a tour of his house and introduces his family. The student outcomes listed on p. 5 are modeled in the video: asking for and giving information about yourself and others, describing yourself and others, expressing likes and dislikes, identifying people and places, giving and responding to compliments, expressing wishes when buying things, making plans, ordering food and beverages, and talking about how something tastes.

Motivating Activity

Ask each student to introduce himself or herself to one other student in the class. They should each talk about themselves, their family, and where they live.

Teaching Suggestion

After students have watched this video segment ask them to recall
    a. three facts about Sebastian,
    b. two things about his home, and
    c. two things about his family.

Thinking Critically

Comparing and Contrasting Ask students how their living rooms (**Wohnzimmer**) are similar to or different from Sebastian's.

▶ **page 8**

Teaching Suggestion

1 Ask students to work with a partner as they go over the **Foto-Roman** on p. 6 again and answer Questions 1-8 in writing. Have students report their answers. Ask two or three students to give their responses to questions that can have more than one answer.

For Individual Needs

3 Auditory Learners Write the names of possible speakers in random order on the board (**Frau Baumann, Herr Baumann, Beatrice, Großvater, Robert, Basti, Artus**). Have students close their books as you read each statement. Ask students to identify the speaker of each statement from the choices on the board.

Teaching Suggestions

4 Have students work with a partner and come up with a different response to each of the stimuli. Then have students reverse roles and again respond differently.

5 You may want to assign this activity as homework.

Closure

Refer students back to the outcomes listed on p. 5 and ask them to name at least one German phrase or expression from the **Foto-Roman** that they believe corresponds to each of the functions.

LOS GEHT'S!

*T*eaching Erste Stufe, *pp. 9-15*

Resources for Erste Stufe

Practice and Activity Book
Chapter Resources, Book 1
- Additional Listening Activities 1-1, 1-2
- Student Response Forms
- Realia 1-1
- Situation Card 1-1
- Teaching Transparency Master 1-1
- Quiz 1-1

Audiocassette Program
- *Textbook Audiocassette* 1 A
- *Additional Listening Activities, Audiocassette* 9 A
- *Assessment Items, Audiocassette* 7 A

▶ **page 9**

MOTIVATE

Teaching Suggestion

Ask students to name several people from the sports and entertainment world. Write the names on the board and then ask students to describe these people.

TEACH

PRESENTATION: Wortschatz

To present the vocabulary in this box:
  A. Read vocabulary in each category.
    Have students repeat after you.
    Stress new words and cognates which are always hard to pronounce.
  B. Ask either/or and open-ended questions.

Examples:
Bist du sportlich oder unsportlich?
Wer in der Klasse hat kurzes Haar?
Wie sieht dein Freund/deine Freundin aus?
Was für Hobbys hast du?

▶ **page 10**

PRESENTATION: Wortschatz

Ask students to give one situation in which the adjectives (**neugierig, lustig, gut gelaunt,** and **schlecht gelaunt**) would apply to them. Example: **Ich bin gut gelaunt, wenn ich gute Noten in Mathe bekomme.**

Ask students:
  1. Which of the three hobbies shown is a hobby that someone they know would enjoy?
  2. Which of the eight featured track and field events are they good at, enjoy, or do not like?

 Culture Note

Leichtathletik, soccer, and tennis are the most popular sports in Germany.

Physical Education Connection

Do students know of any famous American track and field athletes? Can they name the events these athletes compete(d) in?
  1. Carl Lewis   (**100m-Lauf, Weitsprung**)
  2. Jackie Joyner-Kersee (**Weitsprung, Hürdenlauf**)
  3. Evelyn Ashford   (**100/200m-Lauf**)
  4. Florence Joyner   (**100m-Lauf**)
  5. Michael Stuice   (**Kugelstoßen**)
  6. Dick Fosbury   (**Hochsprung**)

▶ **page 11**

PRESENTATION: So sagt man das!

Ask students to work with a partner to review the questions presented in this function box. Allow students time to find out about each other and their siblings. Call on several students and ask them to recall what they found out about their partner.

For Individual needs

8 Tactile learners In addition to this activity or as an alternative activity, describe a well-known person to students in as much detail as possible. Have students try to draw this character as you describe him or her. Let students share and compare their pictures. (Examples: Garfield; the president)

Teacher Note

9 The **Notizbuch** is a personal diary in which students will be asked to write in German. There will be at least one **Notizbuch** activity per chapter.

PRESENTATION: Ein wenig Grammatik

Write the conjugated verb forms of **haben** and **sein** in random order on a transparency. Ask students to create sentences using the forms listed. Write several of the students' sentences on the transparency.

▶ *page 12*

 ## For Individual Needs

11 Challenge After students have completed their description of the student, ask them to add at least two additional questions they would like to ask that student to find out more about him or her.

PRESENTATION: Grammatik

Divide the class in two groups and ask the groups to take turns giving examples of regular and stem-changing verbs. Write the verbs on large sheets of newsprint as students call them out. Give a sheet to each group and have them write sentences with the verbs listed. Afterwards hang the papers up to display.

Teaching Suggestion

12 You may want to limit the questions (to 5 for example) or time (not to exceed 30 seconds). If the team cannot guess, it must give up, and the other team gets a turn.

 ## For Individual Needs

13 A Slower Pace Review the vocabulary on p.9 to help students with their questions and answers. Give them some examples as to how the vocabulary should be used.

▶ *page 13*

PRESENTATION: So sagt man das!

On a transparency, reintroduce family members by constructing a family tree for a fictitious family or for a popular TV family. Begin by explaining the relationship between the members, then ask several students how certain members of the family are related.

PRESENTATION: Ein wenig Grammatik

Help students to refamiliarize themselves with the possessive adjectives through question-answer practice using objects that students have or that are near them.
Examples:
—**Michael, ist das deine Sportuhr?**
—**Ja, das ist meine Uhr.** or **Nein, das ist nicht meine Uhr.**

—**Wem gehören die zwei Deutschbücher?**
—**Das sind unsere Bücher!**

—**Ist das sein Taschenrechner oder ihr Taschenrechner?**
—**Das ist sein Taschenrechner.**

ERSTE STUFE

♜ Game

Give students additional practice with possessive adjectives by playing *Pass the Buck*. The goal is to pass ownership to another person and to keep the exchange going for several turns.

Examples:

A	**Das ist dein Geld, nicht wahr?**
B	**Nein, das ist sein Geld.** (Pointing to a boy)
A	**Harold, ist das dein Geld?**
C	**Nein, das ist ihr Geld.** (Pointing to a girl)
A	**Tracy, ist das dein Geld?**
D	**Ja, das ist mein Geld. Danke!**

A	**Sind das eure Bücher, Alan und Michelle?**
B + C	**Nein, das sind ihre Bücher.** (Pointing to two other students)
A	**Susan und Barbara, sind das eure Bücher?**

▶ page 14

✦ For Individual Needs

Challenge After reading **Sebastian über seine Familie,** ask students to bring a family portrait which shows as many members of their family as possible. They could also make up a family portrait with cutouts from magazines. Students then introduce and explain the relationships among their family members to their group.

✦ For Individual Needs

• **A Slower Pace** Have students identify all the family members in the picture, giving their relationship to the other people pictured.

17 Auditory Learners As an additional activity, students could bring two pictures of the same person taken many years apart. They could then elaborate on the contrast, using the vocabulary from p. 9.

Example: **meine Mutter als Dreijährige**
meine Mutter heute

• **Challenge** After reading **Sebastian über seinen Bruder,** ask students to describe a sibling, a parent, or someone they admire in as much detail as possible, emphasizing physical appearance, attributes, and interests. This can be done orally or in writing.

▶ page 15

Teaching Suggestion

19 Ask students to write their own **Steckbrief.** If possible they can include a small school picture. After students have read their **Steckbrief** to the class, display them on the bulletin board under the title **SUCHE BRIEFFREUND/IN**

✦ For Individual Needs

22 A Slower Pace Before students proceed with this activity, you may want to (a) review time-telling, using a clock with movable hands and stressing especially the starting times of class periods in your school; and (b) ask students to brainstorm and name all the school subjects that are offered at their school. Write these on the board or on a transparency.

25 Tactile Learners Ask pairs of students to come up with a sketch which would resemble one of the rooms described in the listening activity. Students should also label all furniture and then compare their drawings with others in the class.

CLOSE

Teaching Suggestion

Put the following two incomplete statements on the board or on a transparency. Ask students to choose one statement and complete it.
Ein(e) beste(r) Freund(in) muß ... sein.
Ich mag Leute nicht, die ...

Focusing on Outcomes

Refer students back to the learning outcomes on p. 5. They should recognize that they now know how to ask for and give information about themselves and others, describe themselves and others, express likes and dislikes, and identify people and places.

ASSESS

- **Performance Assessment** Ask students to describe orally or in writing
  - a. their best friend
    - or
  - b. their favorite relative

Students should include physical attributes, interests, and at least one interesting or unusual fact about the person being described.

- Quiz 1-1, *Chapter Resources*, Book 1

Teaching Zweite Stufe,
pp. 16-19

Resources for Zweite Stufe

Practice and Activity Book
Chapter Resources, Book 1
- Communicative Activity 1-1
- Additional Listening Activities 1-3, 1-4
- Student Response Forms
- Realia 1-2
- Situation Card 1-2
- Teaching Transparency Master 1-2
- Quiz 1-2
Audiocassette Program
- *Textbook Audiocassette* 1 A
- *Additional Listening Activities, Audiocassette* 9 A
- *Assessment Items, Audiocassette* 7 A

▶ *page 16*

MOTIVATE

Teaching Suggestion

Ask students if they bought new clothes at the beginning of the school year. What did they buy? What would they still like to buy? What types of clothes are "in" at the moment?

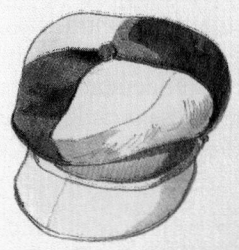

TEACH

Building on Previous Skills

Collect some cut-out pictures of stars, fashion models, and teenagers from teen magazines and show them to the class. Ask students to describe what the people in the pictures are wearing. At the end, have students vote on the best and worst dressed. Have students put them in order from *like* to *dislike*.

Teaching Suggestion

Ask students to recall at least one item of clothing for each of the five stars mentioned in the reading selection.

Group Work

29 Ask students to work with a partner or in groups of three and have them answer the questions in writing. Then ask all groups to share their answers and discuss them.

▶ *page 17*

PRESENTATION: Wortschatz

Bring a bag full of items of clothing and accessories including the ones featured in this vocabulary box. Begin by pulling out one item at a time and telling the class what it is. Once the bag has been emptied, continue with several other teacher-guided activities to help students practice the vocabulary. Ask yes/no, either/or, and open-ended questions. To encourage students to use all new items, ask them to tell you in which order to place the items back into the bag. Tell students to use sequencing words such as **zuerst, dann, nun, danach, jetzt,** and **zum Schluß.** You may want to have those words on the board or on a transparency.

 Total Physical Response

Use the bag of accessories you used to present the **Wortschatz.** Give commands to the class or to individual students. These commands should include the vocabulary students have just learned, words from previous chapters, and verbs such as **nehmen, geben, anprobieren, anziehen, aufsetzen** and **umbinden.**
Examples:
Carol, nimm einen Hut!
Ben, setz die Mütze auf!

ZWEITE STUFE

▶ *page 18*

 For Individual Needs

31 Challenge After students have read the conversation **Wer ist Christiane?** and completed Activity 31, ask them to work with a partner to come up with a dialogue that is based on the one given here but has a different twist. The new dialogue could, for example, be about Sebastian wearing a shirt he just bought and telling Christiane where he got it and how much he paid for it.

PRESENTATION: So sagt man das!

After reading this function box with the class, ask students to turn to their neighbors and comment on their clothing using the expressions in the box as models. Partners should respond accordingly. Students alternate giving compliments and responding to compliments.

For Additional Practice

32 Ask students to walk around and mingle with other students and try to compliment as many classmates as possible on something they are wearing. Students should always try to respond.

▶ *page 19*

Building on Previous Skills

33 Before students proceed with the role-play activity you may want to review fabrics. (Examples: **aus Wolle, Baumwolle, Seide, Polyester**)

 For Individual Needs

35 Challenge Ask students to create their own short **Radioreklame**, similar to the one in Activity 34. Ask several students to tape their radio commercials and then play them for the class.

Reteaching: Clothing

Ask students to name the types of clothing they would wear during different seasons for occasions such as a party, a dance, a family reunion, or the theater.

CLOSE

Game

Begin this game by making the following statement: **Ich packe meinen Koffer und nehme eine Sonnenbrille mit.** The student closest to you repeats your statement and must add his or her own item. That student then turns to the next student who must repeat all that was said previously and then add a new item — and so on. If a student makes a mistake, he or she is out of the game. The winner is the student who can remember all the items that were packed in the correct order.

Focusing on Outcomes

Refer students back to the learning outcomes listed on p. 5. Students should see that they now know how to give and respond to compliments and express wishes when buying clothes.

ASSESS

- **Performance Assessment** To prepare for this activity, have a bag of clothes on hand which includes all items of clothing and accessories reviewed or introduced in this **Stufe**. Give students commands using verbs such as **geben, anprobieren, nehmen, aufsetzen, anziehen, ausziehen**, and the clothing and accessories vocabulary.
  Example:
  Mark, nimm bitte den Hut aus dem Beutel und gib ihn Erica! Erica, setz bitte den Hut auf!

- Quiz 1-2, *Chapter Resources*, Book 1

Teaching Zum Lesen,
pp. 20-21
Reading Strategy

The targeted strategy in this reading is using pre-reading strategies (looking at visual clues, reading the title and subtitles, looking for cognates and other familiar words while skimming) to help readers understand a text. Students should learn about these strategies before beginning Questions 1, 2, and 3.

PREREADING

Motivating Activity

Ask students to name different ways to communicate and get in touch with friends. After you have made a list of these different means of communication, ask students which of these they like and why. (Examples: letters, phone calls, faxes)

Teacher Note

Activities 1 and 2 are prereading activities.

READING

Skimming and Scanning

After students have completed Activity 3, put the words they recognized on the board or on a transparency as a visual aid. Quickly go over the list to familiarize everybody with the meanings, using synonyms and paraphrasing rather than translations.

Teacher Note

Teaching compound nouns is a great way to help students apply reasoning skills and infer meaning. Compound nouns were introduced in the **Zum Lesen** section of Chapter 4, Level 1. Here, they are reintroduced and expanded upon.

Cooperative Learning

Divide students into groups of three. Each group should have a writer, a reporter, and a discussion leader. Set a time limit for this assignment of approximately 30 minutes. Ask each group to do Activities 5 and 6. Once students have completed the activities, ask two or three group reporters to share their groups' answers with the rest of the class.

Thinking Critically

5/6 Drawing Inferences Draw two columns on the board, one for each of the questions (5 and 6). Ask students to reread the letters and elicit specific words or phrases which would help answer each of the questions. What types of words helped them out with their answers?

POST-READING

Teacher Note

Activity 8 is a post-reading task that will show whether students can apply what they have learned.

Closure

Game

This game will help students practice the vocabulary in the reading section. On a transparency, write several nouns that could be part of a compound that you feel students could recognize. In addition, write the three definite articles on top of the transparency. (See layout as an example.)

	Rad	Garten
Fuß		
	Stadt	Turnier
	Tennis	Farbe
Hof		
	Haus	Zentrum
	Training	Ball
Fußball		
	Freizeit	
Fahrrad		
	Haar	Bummel
	Clique	
Tour		
		Aufgaben

Students work in teams of two or three with a sheet of paper and a pencil in front of them. Within a given amount of time (1-2 minutes), teams write down as many compounds as they can build, using the nouns on the transparency. When time is called, pencils must be put away, and teams read out the words they came up with. You are the final judge as to the authenticity of the word. The team that builds the most correct compound nouns wins. This game can also be played with the vocabulary on pp. 340-354 of Level 1 as a review.

Answers to Activity 1
letters

Answers to Activity 2
title indicates who is writing (two cousins)

Answers to Activity 3
b

Answers to Activity 4
Benjamin is writing because Andrea is coming to Munich. He informs her of his busy weekend schedule. Andrea responds by listing her plans for the weekend.

Answers to Activity 5
Their schedules do not match.

Answers to Activity 6
It does not seem that Benjamin is very excited to see his cousin. He does not try to change his plans for the weekend because of Andrea's visit. She should not count on seeing him.

Answers to Activity 7
Answers will vary.

▶ **page 22**

📼 PRESENTATION: Landeskunde

Teacher Notes

- The **Landeskunde** interviews are recorded on audiocassette and videocassette. Before doing the activities on this page, go over the prereading activity with your students. Then play the audiocassette or have students watch the interviews on the video.

- You may want to introduce the following vocabulary before students read the interviews:
  Schlaghosen *bell bottom pants*
  Frutti di Mare *Italian appetizer which includes an assortment of seafood*
  der Sakko (**das Sakko** in southern Germany and Austria) *sports coat*

Group Work
Have students work in groups of four. Students take turns reading the interviews and then answer Questions 1 through 3 of Activity A. Have two or three groups share their information with the rest of the class, using as much German as possible.

Thinking Critically
Drawing Inferences Do Activity B with the whole class. Ask students to go over the four interviews again scanning the interviews for connectors, sequencing words, and phrases that express reasoning. Make a list on the board or on a transparency as students call these words and phrases out.

Teacher Note
Mention to your students that the **Landeskunde** will also be included in Quiz 1-3 given at the end of the **Dritte Stufe**.

Teaching Dritte Stufe, pp. 23-25

▶ **page 23**

MOTIVATE

Teaching Suggestion

Ask students what their favorite weekend activities are. Remind them to use expressions such as **gern,** and **Lieblings-,** as well as sequencing words.

TEACH

Building on Previous Skills

37 Before students make their lists, review sequencing words and discuss their usefulness. You should emphasize to your class the importance of such words and how they enhance the quality of language.

📁 Portfolio Assessment

37 You may want to suggest this activity as a written portfolio item for your students. See *Assessment Guide,* p. 14.

Teaching Suggestion

38 Monitor pair work by asking pairs to model their conversations as you walk around the classroom.

PRESENTATION: So sagt man das!

After reading the function box, give students the opportunity to practice the expressions with a partner. Have some expressions on the board or on a transparency such as
wenn es regnet
am Donnerstag
samstagabend
am 4. Juli
zu deinem Geburtstag.
Students can use these phrases when asking each other about making plans.

PRESENTATION: Ein wenig Grammatik

To review the forms of **wollen** and **möchte,** prepare a *Tic-Tac-Toe* grid on a transparency, using conjugated forms of these two verbs. Divide the class into two groups and ask students to come up with correct sentences using the verb forms shown.

▶ **page 24**

Group Work

41 Ask students to work in groups of three to practice reading the two conversations above Activity 41. After several readings, have the groups answer the questions in Activity 41.

DRITTE STUFE

For Individual Needs

41 Challenge After students have worked through Activity 41 in groups, ask each group to create a new dialogue to accompany the two pictures. To complete the activity, each group has to come up with two questions about their new dialogue, which the rest of the class should be able to answer.

▶ *page 25*

PRESENTATION: So sagt man das!

To practice the expressions for ordering food, have students role-play the conversation with a partner. Ask students to read with expression and switch roles for additional practice.

 For Individual Needs

44 Challenge As students role-play this situation, have them add a variation in which the customer cannot make up his or her mind what to order and asks a lot of questions. The waiter is in a hurry and impatient. Monitor groups' activities as you walk around. If time permits, call on some of the pairs to recreate their conversation for the class.

 Portfolio Assessment

44 You might want to suggest this activity as an oral portfolio item for your students. See *Assessment Guide*, p. 14.

PRESENTATION: So sagt man das!

After reviewing the expressions which are used to talk about how something tastes, reinforce this vocabulary by asking students to share their likes and dislikes of certain foods. Most students should be familiar with the food groups pyramid. Ask the home economics teacher to lend you a large poster. Ask students about their likes and dislikes as you point to different foods.

Reteaching: Foods

Use visual aids and props to review the food vocabulary with your students. (Examples: transparencies, food magazines, cutouts, posters from the home economics department, advertisements from local grocery stores)

CLOSE
Teaching Suggestion

To prepare for this activity, make a number of flash cards on which you write types of foods from the four categories listed below. Write one food item on each card.
Examples:

Vorspeisen:	**Frutti di Mare, Käse, Tomatensalat, Gurkensalat, Suppe**
Getränke:	**Limo, Mineralwasser, Kaffee, Tee, Milch**
Hauptspeisen:	**Bratwurst, gegrilltes Hähnchen, Spaghetti, Pizza, Leberkäs**
Nachspeisen:	**Kuchen, Obst, Obstsalat, Eis, Pudding**

Distribute the cards among students (one per student). Students are then asked to walk around the class and find a student who has a food from the same category on his or her card.
Example:

—**Hast du auch eine Vorspeise?**
—**Nein, tut mir leid, ich habe eine Nachspeise.**

Have the four categories written on the board. Once all students have found the other students who belong into their food category, they share the names of those students with the rest of the class.

Focusing on Outcomes

Refer students back to the learning outcomes listed on p. 5. Students should recognize that they now know how to make plans, how to order food and beverages, and how to talk about how something tastes.

ASSESS

- **Performance Assessment** Provide students with a copy of the arts and entertainment section of a local newspaper including the names of shows, games, concerts and movies, and where and when they take place. Ask students to tell you what they plan for the upcoming weekend. Encourage students to use sequencing words.

- Quiz 1-3, *Chapter Resources*, Book 1

📼 Video Wrap-Up

At this time, you might want to use the *Video Program* or the *Expanded Video Program,* Videocassette 1 for additional review and enrichment. See *Video Guide* for suggestions regarding:
- **Sebastian stellt seine Familie vor** (Dramatic episode)
- **Landeskunde** Interviews
- **Videoclips** (Authentic footage—*Expanded Video Program* only)

*K*ann ich's wirklich?
p. 26

This page helps students prepare for the test. It is a brief checklist of the major points covered in the chapter. The students should be reminded that it is only a checklist and not necessarily everything that will appear on the test.

*U*sing Wortschatz,
p. 27

Teaching Suggestions

- At this level you should try to give definitions in German whenever possible to help build vocabulary through synonyms and definitions.

- To review family members, students could write the definition of each word in the form of a riddle. Have each student read his or her riddle to the rest of the class and have them guess who that person is.
Example: **Vater—Diese Person ist der Onkel von meinem Cousin.**

- Arrange all the adjectives of the **Erste Stufe** randomly on a transparency. Give students a predetermined amount of time to categorize the words under certain headings. (Examples: **Größe, Haarfarbe, Interessen**)

♖ Game
Play the game **Bildkarten** to review the vocabulary of the **Zweite Stufe**. See p. 3F for the procedure.

Teacher Note
Give the **Kapitel 1** Chapter Test, *Chapter Resources*, Book 1.

1
Bei den Baumanns

1 Die Fotos sind prima! Aber wer ist das, Basti?

German teenagers are often curious about life in the United States. They will ask you all sorts of questions, such as where you live, and what your friends and family members look like. They may also ask you about your school, your favorite hangouts, and the kind of clothes you like to wear.

In this chapter you will review and practice

- asking for and giving information about yourself and others; describing yourself and others; expressing likes and dislikes; identifying people and places
- giving and responding to compliments; expressing wishes when buying things
- making plans; ordering food and beverages; talking about how something tastes

In reviewing these functions, you will

- listen to German-speaking students talk about their interests
- read about clothing trends among rock stars
- write about your personality traits
- find out about some German students' favorite things in different categories

② Das Halstuch sieht lässig aus!

③ Willst du mit ins Café gehen?

IMBISS-KART

Café Fre

Für den kleinen Hunger und

KLEINE SPEISEN

	DM 4,50	1 TASSE
	5,20	1 KÄNN
	5,60	1 TASSE
...AR	5,80	1 GLAS
...d Käse	6,00	
...Käse	6,50	AL
...e und Pilzen	8,50	MINE
		LIMON
		APFEL
		COLA
...HEN		
...UCK	DM 2,80	
...UCK	3,00	

EIS

FRUCHTEIS   KUGEL
            KUGEL

Los geht's!

Sebastian

Robert

Sebastian stellt seine Familie vor.

You are about to meet Sebastian Baumann.
Where do you think he is? Judging from these
photos, what is he probably talking about?

Hallo!

Ich heiße Sebastian Baumann. Ich bin fünfzehn Jahre alt und wohne hier in
Grünwald; das ist ein Vorort von München.

In diesem Haus haben wir eine schöne Wohnung, hier oben im zweiten Stock.

Das ist unser Wohnzimmer. Wie ihr seht,
es ist ziemlich groß, aber es ist doch ganz
gemütlich. Schaut mal, die vielen Bücher!
Meine Eltern lesen gern. Sie lesen
eigentlich alles, von Grass bis Goethe.

Und sie hören gern Musik. Hier: die vielen
Platten und CDs. Hören wir mal, was
aufliegt! — Ich hab's gewußt: etwas
Klassisches!

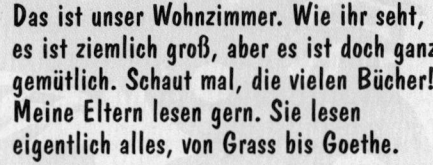

Hier sind unsere Familienfotos. Meine
Großeltern, meine Eltern, meine
Geschwister: mein Bruder Robert, das
hier bin ich, und meine Schwester,
Beatrice. Und Artus, unser ... nein,
Vatis Hund.

1 Was passiert hier?

Verstehst du alles, was Basti und Robert sagen? Beantworte die Fragen!

1. Wo wohnen die Baumanns? 1. In Grünwald, München
2. Haben sie ihr eigenes Haus oder eine Wohnung?
3. Wie groß ist die Familie? 3. Sieben Personen, ein Hund.
4. Was erzählt Basti von seinen Eltern? 4. Hören gern Musik und lesen
5. Sieht Robert seinen Bruder gern? Was meinst du? 5. Nein.
6. Was für ein Schüler ist Robert? 6. Fleißig.
7. Sebastian sagt: „Das ist mein Reich." Was meint er damit? 7. Er hat ein eigenes Zimmer.
8. Welche Hobbys und Interessen hat Basti? 8. Gitarre, Schach, Lesen, Tennis, Fußball

2 Genauer lesen

Lies den Text noch einmal und beantworte diese Fragen!

1. Mit welchen Wörtern beschreibt Basti das Wohnzimmer und sein Zimmer? 1. Groß, gemütlich; Nicht sehr groß, gemütlich.
2. Mit welchen Wörtern beschreibt er seine Familie?
3. Robert hat es nicht gern, daß Basti in sein Zimmer kommt. Was sagt er, damit *(so that)* Basti wieder geht? 3. „Dann kannst du wieder gehen."
4. Wie beschreibt Basti seinen Bruder? 4. Fleißig, gut in Schule, Sport besonders Tennis.
5. Was sagt Basti über sein Zimmer, seine Pokale und seine Hobbys? 5. Mein Reich; Pokale: Tennis, Fußball; Hobbys: Gitarre, Schach, lese gern Action.
2. Eltern: lesen, Musik; Robert: fleißig, gut in Schule u. Sport.

3 Wer ist das?

Lies die Personenbeschreibungen und rate, wer das ist!

1. Ich wohne in einer ziemlich großen Wohnung in Grünwald. Mein Mann und ich hören gern klassische Musik und lesen gern. Wir lesen alles — von Grass bis Goethe! Ich habe drei Kinder: zwei Söhne und eine Tochter. Wer bin ich? 1. Frau Baumann (Bastis Mutter).
2. Ich wohne mit meiner Familie in einem Vorort von München. Meine Eltern sind sehr nett, und ich habe auch zwei Brüder, Sebastian und Robert. Wer bin ich? 2. Beatrice (Bastis Schwester).
3. Mein Sohn und seine Familie wohnen in Grünwald, also nicht weit von hier. Ab und zu besuchen sie uns, und das macht viel Spaß. Meine Frau und ich haben die drei Kinder — Sebastian, Robert und Beatrice — sehr gern. Wer bin ich? 3. Bastis Großvater.
4. Ich wohne bei einer sehr netten Familie in Grünwald. Wir haben eine große Wohnung, und das gefällt mir. Die Kinder in der Familie sind sehr nett und spielen oft mit mir, aber eigentlich liebe ich den Vater der Familie! Wer bin ich? 4. Artus, der Hund.

4 Was paßt zusammen?

Welche Sätze passen zusammen?

1. Die vielen Bücher! c.
2. Hört mal, was aufliegt! e.
3. Was gibt's? d.
4. Der Robert ist ein super Tennisspieler. a.
5. Das ist mein Zimmer. b.

a. Super nicht, aber ganz gut.
b. Nicht groß, aber es gefällt mir.
c. Meine Eltern lesen gern.
d. Ich will nur „Grüß Gott" sagen.
e. Etwas Klassisches!

5 Und du?

Schreib folgendes auf eine Liste! Answers may vary.

1. wo du wohnst
2. wie groß deine Familie ist
3. welche Hobbys deine Familie hat
4. wie dein Zimmer aussieht

Asking for and giving information about yourself and others; describing yourself and others; expressing likes and dislikes; identifying people and places

Was für eine Person bist du?

Aussehen
- [ ] groß
- [ ] klein
- [ ] schlank
- [ ] vollschlank
- [ ] attraktiv
- [ ] nicht sehr attraktiv
- [ ] hübsch

Haarfarbe
- [ ] schwarz
- [ ] blond
- [ ] hellbraun
- [ ] dunkelbraun
- [ ] rötlich

Haarlänge
- [ ] kurz
- [ ] lang
- [ ] mittellang

Augenfarbe
- [ ] braun
- [ ] blau
- [ ] grün
- [ ] grau

Brille
- [ ] habe eine Brille
- [ ] trage Kontaktlinsen

Eigenschaften
- [ ] nett
- [ ] nicht nett
- [ ] freundlich
- [ ] unfreundlich
- [ ] intelligent
- [ ] sympathisch
- [ ] unsympathisch
- [ ] ruhig
- [ ] nervös

- [ ] kinderlieb
- [ ] tierlieb
- [ ] langweilig
- [ ] sportlich
- [ ] unsportlich
- [ ] faul
- [ ] fleißig

Sport
- [ ] Fußball
- [ ] Football
- [ ] Volleyball
- [ ] Basketball
- [ ] Tennis
- [ ] Skilaufen
- [ ] Schwimmen
- [ ] Golf
- [ ] Radfahren
- [ ] Schlittschuhlaufen
- [ ] Rollschuhlaufen

Interessen
- [ ] ausgehen
- [ ] tanzen
- [ ] lesen
- [ ] reisen
- [ ] Musik hören
- [ ] kochen
- [ ] fotografieren
- [ ] Musik machen
- [ ] basteln
- [ ] zeichnen
- [ ] malen
- [ ] (Briefmarken) sammeln

Lies den Text! Welche Wörter und Ausdrücke kennst du schon? Welche sind neu? Kannst du raten, was die neuen Wörter und Ausdrücke bedeuten? Wie beschreibst du dich?

6 Hör gut zu!
For answers, see listening script in TE Interleaf.

Welche Beschreibung *(description)* paßt zu welchem Foto? — Schreib die Zahlen 1-5 auf ein Blatt Papier und daneben den Buchstaben (a., b., c., d., e.) des Fotos, das zur Beschreibung paßt!

a.   b.   c.   d.   e.

Wie charakterisierst du diese Leute? Er/Sie ist ...

| neugierig | lustig | sympathisch | unsympathisch | gut gelaunt | schlecht gelaunt |

Welche Hobbys haben diese Leute? Was machen sie?

  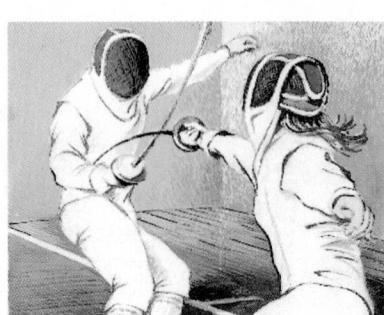

| Er rodelt. | Sie macht Bogenschießen. | Die beiden fechten. |

Diese Leute machen Leichtathletik. Was machen sie?

| Kugelstoßen | Speerwerfen | Diskuswerfen | Langstreckenlauf |

| 100-Meter-Lauf | Weitsprung | Hürdenlauf | Stabhochsprung |

7 Und du? Answers may vary. E.g.: Ich mache ... ; sie macht ...

Sag deiner Partnerin, welche Hobbys du hast und welchen Sport du machst! Was macht deine Partnerin?

SO SAGT MAN DAS!

Asking for and giving information about yourself and others; describing yourself and others; expressing likes and dislikes

When talking about yourself and others, you have used a number of words and expressions.

If someone asks:

Wer ist das?

Wie alt ist sie?

Du hast auch einen Bruder. Wie sieht er aus?

Macht er Sport?

Beschreibe deine Schwester!

Und du? Was machst du gern, was machst du nicht gern?

Your response might be:

Das ist meine Schwester.

Sie ist 19 Jahre alt.

Er ist groß und ziemlich schlank und hat braune Haare und dunkle Augen.

Nein, er ist faul.

Sie ist intelligent, freundlich und sehr fleißig.

Ich lese gern und höre gern Musik. Aber ich koche nicht gern.

Remember: you don't always have to answer with a complete sentence. How might you answer these questions more informally, using phrases?

8 Wer ist das? Rate mal!

Beschreibe einen Klassenkameraden oder eine Klassenkameradin! Erwähne Alter, Aussehen, Haarfarbe, Augenfarbe, Eigenschaften und Sport und Hobbys! Deine Mitschüler sollen dann erraten, wer das ist. Answers may vary.

9 Für mein Notizbuch

Beschreibe dich selbst! Erwähne alle Eigenschaften, die du hast, und erwähne alle Sportarten und Hobbys, die du hast! Answers may vary.

10 Hör gut zu!

For answers, see listening script in TE Interleaf.

Vier deutsche Schüler und Schülerinnen erzählen über sich selbst. Mach dir Notizen, damit du über einen Schüler berichten kannst! Verwende die folgenden Kategorien, um deine Notizen zu organisieren: Augen, Haare, Eigenschaften, Interessen, usw.!

Schon bekannt
Ein wenig Grammatik

When you describe yourself or someone else, you use the verb **sein**. To talk about what you have or someone else has, you need the present tense forms of **haben**. To review the forms of **sein** and **haben**, see the Grammar Summary.

11 Über einen Schüler berichten

Such dir einen von den vier Schülern aus und berichte über ihn oder sie! Deine Mitschüler erraten, wen du beschreibst.

Answers may vary.

12 Ratespiel

Bildet zwei Gruppen! Gruppe A sieht zur Tafel hin, Gruppe B sieht auf die Wand hinten in der Klasse. Gruppe A wählt eine Schülerin aus. Alle Schüler von Gruppe B stellen jetzt Fragen, um die Schülerin aus der Gruppe A zu identifizieren. Tauscht dann die Rollen aus!

Gruppe B		Gruppe A	
Schüler 1	Ist das ein Junge?	Schüler 1	Nein.
Schüler 2	Hat sie blonde Haare?	Schüler 2	Ja.
Schüler 3	Hat sie lange Haare?	Schüler 3	Ja.
Schüler 4	Hat sie graue Augen?	Schüler 4	Nein.
Schüler 5	Ist sie ...		...
Schüler 6	...		...
Schüler 7	...		...
Schüler 8	Ist das die (Jessica)?	Schüler 8	Ja!

Kennst du auch Zwillinge? Wie sehen sie aus?

Herbert und Günther sind Zwillinge. Sie sind gleich alt, und sie sehen sich sehr ähnlich. Zwillinge haben oft auch die gleichen Eigenschaften und die gleichen Interessen.

13 Was wollt ihr von den Zwillingen wissen?

Zwei Klassenkameraden übernehmen die Rollen von Herbert und Günther. Fragt die „Zwillinge", was ihr von ihnen wissen wollt! Einer antwortet für die beiden. Tauscht die Rollen aus!

Questions and answers may vary.

14 Jetzt spielt ihr Zwillinge

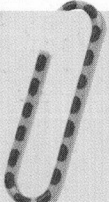

Bildet Gruppen zu dritt! Zwei von euch sind „Zwillinge", und der dritte fragt die beiden nach Aussehen, Haarfarbe, Augenfarbe, Eigenschaften und Interessen. Tauscht dann die Rollen aus! Questions and answers may vary.

SO SAGT MAN DAS!

Schon bekannt

Identifying people and places

When you want to know who someone is, you might ask:

Wer ist das, Sebastian?
Und wer ist das Mädchen?
Ist das dein Großvater?
Und das ist deine Mutter, ja?
Und wo ist dein Zimmer?

The response might be:

Das ist mein Bruder, der Robert.
Meine Schwester, die Beatrice.
Ja, das ist mein Großvater.
Stimmt!
Hier! Das ist mein Zimmer.

---

15 Die Familie Baumann

Schau dir die Fotos der Familie Baumann an! Dann beantworte die Fragen mit mehreren Sätzen!

──────── **die Kinder** ────────

Beatrice
Tochter
Schwester

Sebastian
Sohn
Bruder

Robert
Sohn
Bruder

──────── **die Eltern** ────────

Hans Baumann, Vater
Elfriede Baumann, Mutter

1. Die Eltern von Sebastian, Beatrice und Robert.
1. Wer sind Hans und Elfriede Baumann?
2. Wer ist Beatrice? 2. Die Tochter von ...;
die Schwester von ...
3. Wer ist Robert?
4. Beschreibe zwei Familienmitglieder!
3. Der Sohn von ...; der Bruder von ... 4. Answers may vary.

Schon bekannt
Ein wenig *G*rammatik

When you want to identify *whose* father, mother, etc. someone is, you use the possessive adjectives, **mein, dein, sein,** and **ihr.** Remember that the ending of the possessive adjectives is determined by the noun it refers to. You can review the singular possessive adjectives in the Grammar Summary.

16 Klamotten beschreiben

Sag deinem Partner, was die Baumanns in diesen Fotos anhaben! Tauscht die Rollen aus! E.g.: **Beatrice hat eine Jeansjacke an.**

Sebastian über seine Familie

Das hier ist meine Familie, meine Eltern, meine Geschwister und meine Großeltern. Die Oma und der Opa sitzen hier in der ersten Reihe. Neben dem Opa kniet mein Vater, und neben ihm liegt Artus, unser ... nein, Vatis Hund! Hinter meinem Vater steht meine Mutter und neben ihr der Robert und die Beatrice. Und der da ganz links in der zweiten Reihe, das bin ich!

Erzähle, was Sebastian über seine Familie sagt!

17 Meine Familie und Freunde

1. Bring Fotos von zwei Familienmitgliedern mit in die Klasse und beschreibe sie! Zeig deiner Partnerin ein Foto und sag ihr, wer diese Person ist, wie alt sie ist, wie sie aussieht und welche Interessen sie hat! 1. E.g.: **Das ist mein Bruder. Er ist 10 Jahre alt.**
2. Jetzt zeigst du deinem Partner das zweite Foto. Dein Partner stellt Fragen über diese Person, und du beantwortest sie. Tauscht dann die Rollen aus! 2. E.g.: **Wer ist das Mädchen?**
3. Erzähle jetzt einem Partner, was du über die Familie eines anderen Partners weißt!
  3. E.g.: **Er/sie hat zwei Brüder. Die Familie hat einen Hund.**

18 Für mein Notizbuch

Beschreibe einen Freund oder jemanden aus deiner Familie! Schreib, wer die Person ist und erwähne Alter, Aussehen, Eigenschaften, Sport und Hobbys!

Answers may vary.

Sebastian über seinen Bruder

Mein Bruder, der Robert, ist immer fleißig. Er ist gut in der Schule, bekommt immer gute Noten. Er ist auch gut in Sport. Ein super Tennisspieler!

Erzähle, was Sebastian über seinen Bruder sagt!

19 Beatrices Steckbrief

Lies zuerst diesen Steckbrief, und beantworte die folgenden Fragen auf deutsch.

1. Wo wohnt Beatrice? 1. Sie wohnt in Grünwald.
2. Was sind ihre Lieblingsfächer?
3. Welches Fach hat sie nicht gern? 3. Geschichte.

Dann erzähle einem Partner, was du über Beatrice gelesen hast! 2. Musik, Deutsch u. Physik.

20 Hör gut zu!

Hör zu, was diese Schüler über sich sagen! Mach dir Notizen! For answers, see listening script in TE Interleaf.

21 Über wen sprichst du?

Such dir einen Schüler aus, über den du dir Notizen gemacht hast, und erzähle deinem Partner über diesen Schüler! Dein Partner verbessert dich, wenn du etwas sagst, was nicht stimmt. Tauscht dann die Rollen aus! For answers, see listening script in TE Interleaf.

Name: Beatrice Baumann, 17
Wohnort: Grünwald
Schule: Gymnasium in Grünwald
Lieblingsfächer: Musik, Deutsch, Physik,
nicht gern: Geschichte
Sport: Tennis

22 Mein Stundenplan

Such dir einen anderen Partner! Jeder nimmt seinen Stundenplan in die Hand. Fragt euch jetzt gegenseitig (*in turns*), welche Fächer ihr in welcher Stunde habt! Fragt euch auch, welche Fächer ihr gern und welche ihr nicht gern habt!

BEISPIEL **Was hast du um (8 Uhr 10)?**

23 Für mein Notizbuch

Schreib in dein Notizbuch, auf welche Schule du gehst, welche Fächer du gern hast und welche nicht! Bist du gut in Sport? Bist du vielleicht ein(e) super Volleyballspieler(in)?

24 Hör gut zu!

Zwei Schüler beschreiben ihr Zimmer. Schreib auf, welche Möbel jeder in seinem Zimmer hat!
For answers, see listening script in TE Interleaf.

25 Wie sieht das Zimmer aus?

Such dir eine Partnerin! Nimm deine Notizen von Übung 24 in die Hand, und beschreibe eins von den beiden Zimmern! Deine Partnerin muß raten, welches Zimmer du beschrieben hast.

26 Für mein Notizbuch

Schreib, wie dein Zimmer aussieht! Welche Möbel hast du? Sind sie alt oder neu? Gefallen sie dir?

Giving and responding to compliments; expressing wishes when buying things

POPSTARS MACHEN MODE

Bei Popstars spielt der Look eine wichtige Rolle — und du kannst die Styling-Ideen deiner Idole leicht kopieren.

Pop-Superstar Madonna hat immer wieder einen neuen Look. Durch Styling und Klamotten macht sie ihr Image. Ihre Fans sind begeistert! Typisch: Hot Pants, geknotetes Hemd und ganz viele Metallketten.

Bist du ein Prinz-Fan? Na, dann sollst du unbedingt seine Lieblingsfarbe Lila tragen. Und sonst? Viel Glitter, hohe Stiefel, Satinmäntel und Rüschenhemden.

Die Beatles — eine Legende wird wieder modern! Mit dem Beatle-Revival sind die bunten Paradejacken von „Sergeant Pepper's Lonely Hearts Club Band" heute in.

Magst du das Outfit von Ex-Punker Billy Idol, oder findest du vielleicht das Minikleid der sensationellen Rock-Lady Tina Turner gut? Den Look kannst du haben — und oft viel billiger als bei den Stars! Mach mal einen Bummel durch den Flohmarkt oder schau mal in einen Secondhand-Laden rein!

27 Über Popstars

What is the main idea of this article? What words do you recognize?

1. Many popstars like to wear bizarre, flashy clothes.
2. If you dress like the popstars you admire, you will be more like them.
3. It is relatively easy to imitate the look of many popstars.

28 Wer ist das?

Scan the article again, then decide which description fits with which Popstar.

1. Madonna c.
2. Prinz d.
3. Beatles b.
4. Billy Idol e.
5. Tina Turner a.

a. sensationelle Rock-Lady
b. eine Legende, die wieder modern wird
c. trägt Hot Pants, geknotetes Hemd und ganz viele Metallketten.
d. viel Glitter, hohe Stiefel, Satinmäntel
e. Ex-Punker

29 Beantworte die Fragen!

Read the article again, then answer these questions.

1. How does Madonna create her image?
2. What would you need to wear in order to look like Prinz?
3. What is a good way to find what you need in order to look like your favorite popstar?

1. Sie hat immer wieder einen neuen Look.
2. Lila tragen; viel Glitter; hohe Stiefel; Satinmäntel u. Rüschenhemden.

3. Bummel durch den Flohmarkt oder in einen Secondhand-Laden reinschauen.

Was brauchst du? — Ich brauche ...

ein Stirnband

einen Schal

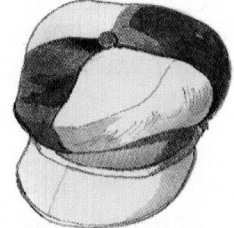

eine Mütze

einen Hut

eine Halskette

ein Paar Ohrringe

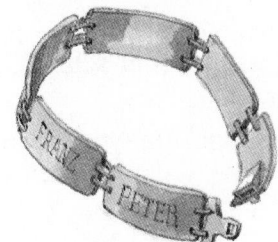

ein Armband

eine Handtasche

30 Was trägst du, wenn du ausgehst?

Frag einen Partner, was er trägt, wenn er ausgeht!
Du sagst ihm dann, was du trägst. Questions and answers may vary.

WER IST CHRISTIANE?

Sebastian weiß, wo er heute seine Schwester finden kann, denn die Beatrice sitzt an diesem Tag immer mit Freunden in einem Café.

CHRISTIANE	Basti, du siehst heute so fesch aus! Das Tuch da, das ist echt schick!
SEBASTIAN	Wirklich?
CHRISTIANE	Wirklich! Ist das neu?
SEBASTIAN	Das hab' ich schon lange.
CHRISTIANE	Wirklich?
SEBASTIAN	Ja, das ist schon alt.

31 Was ist passiert?

Beantworte diese Fragen auf englisch oder auf deutsch!

1. Wie begrüßt Christiane den Sebastian? Was bedeutet das?
2. Freut sich der Basti über das Kompliment? Was sagt er? 2. „Wirklich?"
3. Warum fragt Christiane, ob das Tuch neu ist? 3. Sie kennt es nicht. Sie sieht das Preisschild.
4. Was antwortet Sebastian? Warum sagt er wohl das?

1. „Basti, du siehst heute so …"
   Ein Kompliment.

4. „Ja, das ist schon alt."
   Er hat es gerade gekauft.

SO SAGT MAN DAS!

Schon bekannt

Giving and responding to compliments

When you want to compliment someone
you might say:

Du siehst heute so fesch aus!
Das Tuch da, das ist echt schick!
Es gefällt mir.

Your friend might respond:

Meinst du?
Wirklich?
Ehrlich?

How might you respond after your friend asks **Wirklich?** or **Meinst du?**

32 Komplimente machen   Answers may vary. E.g.: **Die Jeans gefällt mir. — Ehrlich?**

Such dir an deinem Partner etwas aus, was dir gefällt, und mach ihm oder ihr ein Kompliment! Dein Partner reagiert auf dein Kompliment und macht dir dann auch ein Kompliment. — Die Wörter im Kasten sind nur zur Anregung da.

die Jeans   das Kleid   das T-Shirt   die Weste
der Schal   der Hut   die Stiefel   das Stirnband
das Tuch   die Halskette   der Rock   die Mütze
die Jacke   die Handtasche   die Ohrringe   das Armband

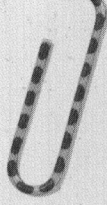

SO SAGT MAN DAS!

Schon bekannt

Expressing wishes when buying things

When you want to buy new clothes, there are a number of expressions you have already learned to use.

The salesclerk might ask you:

Was möchten Sie bitte?
Was bekommen Sie?
Haben Sie einen Wunsch?

Ja sicher. Welche Größe brauchen Sie?

Your response might be:

Ich brauche einen Schal.
Den Taschenrechner da.
Ja, ich suche eine Mütze. Haben Sie diese Mütze in Schwarz?

Größe L.

33 Im Warenhaus Möller

Lies zuerst die Reklame für das Warenhaus Möller! Welche Wörter kennst du? Welche sind dir neu? Dann such dir zwei Sachen aus, die du brauchst! Spielt mit einem Partner die Rollen von Verkäufer und Kunde! Führt ein Verkaufsgespräch! Dann tauscht die Rollen aus! Nicht vergessen: Fragt nach Farbe, Größe und Eigenschaft (z.B., aus Wolle), wenn ihr Kleidungsstücke kauft, und fragt immer nach dem Preis! Answers may vary.

IM ANGEBOT
In unserer Bekleidungsabteilung

Gürtel, echt Leder, circa 3 cm breit, in Braun und in Schwarz
DM 17,00

Polohemden, 6 aktuelle Farben, mit halbem Ärmel, alle Größen, 100% Baumwolle
DM 28,50

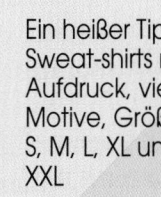

Ein heißer Tip: Sweat-shirts mit Aufdruck, viele Motive, Größen: S, M, L, XL und XXL
DM 19,95

Im Junior-Shop: Pullis für Jungen und Mädchen, 100% Polyacryl, Farben: blau, weiß, rot, pink
DM 24,95

IN UNSERER SCHULABTEILUNG

Taschenwörterbücher	DM 20,00
Taschenrechner	ab DM 24,95
Schultaschen	ab DM 13,50
Etuis	ab DM 6,80
Kugelschreiber	DM 1,50
Filzstifte	DM 1,20
Bleistifte, 6 Stück	DM 2,10

Nur diese Woche!
Warenhaus G. Möller

34 Hör gut zu!

Du brauchst ein paar Klamotten. Da hörst du zufällig eine Reklame im Radio für Sachen, die du gern haben möchtest. Schreib dir vier Dinge auf, die du dir gern kaufen möchtest! For answers, see listening script in TE Interleaf.

35 Was brauchst du? Answers may vary.

Such dir eine Partnerin! Beschreibe ihr zwei Sachen, die du in der Reklame gehört hast und die du gern kaufen möchtest! Sag ihr auch, warum du diese Sachen haben möchtest!

Schon bekannt
Ein wenig Grammatik

For the **möchte**-forms, for nominative and accusative forms of the definite and the indefinite articles, and for third person pronouns, see the Grammar Summary.

Cousin und Kusine verständigen sich, oder?

20, FEB. 94   12:15   5.002

LESETRICK

Using prereading strategies. There are several things you can do before you begin to read a new text in order to get an idea of what the reading is about. You do these things all the time when reading texts in English without even thinking about it. First, look for visual clues, such as format. Next, read the title and any subtitles. Then skim the text once, looking for cognates and other words you already know. These strategies should give you a good idea of what the reading is about and the kinds of information you can expect to find.

Liebe Andrea,

   Mutti sagt, Du kommst nach München. Prima! Ich möchte Dich gern sehen, nur habe ich dieses Wochenende so viel vor. Lies: Am Samstag von 10 bis 12 Fußballtraining. Von halb zwei bis 4 Uhr ist unser Fußballspiel. Danach fahren wir an den Starnberger See. Dort wollen wir segeln, denn das Wetter wird ideal sein! Dann komm' ich erst um 9 Uhr zurück.

   Am Sonntag vormittag, von 9 bis 12 Uhr, will ich mit meiner Fahrradclique eine kleine Radtour machen. Zu Mittag bin ich dann wieder zu Hause! So gegen 3 Uhr treff' ich mich aber mit meiner Schulclique im Café am Hofgarten. Dort bleib' ich bis halb 6. Dann muß ich nach Hause und Hausaufgaben machen.

   Ich hoffe, daß ich Dich doch irgendwie sehen kann. Ruf doch mal an, wenn Du in München bist!

Dein Benjamin

Getting Started

1. Based on the format of the readings, what kind of texts are these?
2. Now read the title. What two pieces of information does the title provide that will help you understand the content of the faxes?

Tip As in English, German uses many compound nouns. The difference is that in German these compound nouns are written as one word: **Tennisturnier**, *tennis tournament*; **Fußballspiel**, *soccer game*. Remember: the gender of the compound noun is that of the last noun in the compound: **das Spiel: das Fußballspiel.** If you understand one or more words within a compound noun, you can usually guess the meaning of the new word.

For answers, see TE Interleaf.

Fußball-

Tennis- **spiel** Karten-

Handball-

Tennis-

Schach- **turnier** Reit-

Tanz-

21. FEB. 94   10:45   5.002

Lieber Benjamin!

Danke für Dein Fax! Schade, daß Du dieses Wochenende so viel zu tun hast. Ist das immer so bei Dir?

Meine Freundin und ich, wir wollen auch viel unternehmen. Vielleicht willst Du irgendwohin mitgehen?

Hier sind unsere Pläne: Am Samstag komm' ich so gegen 10 Uhr 30 an. Dann geh' ich gleich mit Renate zum Tennisturnier, bis so um 2 Uhr. Um 3 Uhr wollen wir ins Kino gehen, und um 6 Uhr gehen wir ins Freizeitzentrum. Dort bleiben wir bis halb 10.

Am Sonntag, so zwischen 11 und 12 Uhr, wollen wir einen kleinen Stadtbummel machen. Dann gehen wir in ein Café, etwas essen. Von halb vier bis 5 Uhr sind wir dann zu Hause beim Kaffeetrinken. Um halb 7 Uhr geht mein Zug.

Also, was meinst Du, können wir uns sehen?

Deine Kusine Andrea

3. Skim both texts quickly using cognates or other words you already know to help you get the gist of each letter. Place a piece of paper over the readings and, with a partner, try to remember all the words you saw which meant something to you. Based on this information, the most likely topic of this fax exchange is
   a. **eine Einladung**
   b. **Pläne fürs Wochenende**
   c. **was man in den Ferien gemacht hat**
   d. **Schule und neue Freunde**

A Closer Look

4. Reread each letter.
   Together with your partner, try to answer the following questions. Why is Benjamin writing to Andrea? What kind of information is Benjamin giving to Andrea? With what kind of information does Andrea respond?

5. Make a weekend calendar page for Benjamin and another for Andrea. List the times mentioned and next to each, the activity planned. What is the problem?

6. Do you think that Benjamin is very excited about his cousin coming to visit? Why or why not? On what are you basing this inference? Should Andrea count on seeing him?

7. If you received this letter from your cousin, how would you interpret it?

8. Write a letter to a relative of yours who wants to visit you on a busy weekend. Detail all of your plans for him or her. In your letter, you must state explicitly (or outright), whether you plan to see your relative or not. Think of a way to express the following clearly, but politely: a) you do not want to see your relative, b) you do want to get together with him or her. Choose one of these options and write your letter.

Und was hast du am liebsten?

We asked several German-speaking students about some of their favorite things in a number of categories. First listen to their interviews, then read the texts.

Sandra, *Berlin*

„Volleyball ist mein Lieblingssport, und ich spiel's so gern, weil man da nicht mit dem Gegner zusammentrifft, und es deswegen auch keine Fouls und so gibt wie beim Fußball ... und ... ja deswegen find' ich's ganz gut. Ich ess' gern Spaghetti und Pizza, alles was so richtig schön viel Kalorien hat, Schokolade auch, und, ja, Kaugummi kau' ich auch ab und zu, nur so süßsaure chinesische Gerichte ess' ich nicht so gern."

Tim, *Berlin*

„Mein Lieblingssport ist Fitneß und Jiu-Jitsu, das ist eine Selbstverteidigung, Vollkontakt, macht mir sehr viel Spaß. Ich ... meine Lieblingsfächer sind Deutsch, Sport und Physik. Biologie mag ich nicht so. Ja, meine Lieblingsbücher stammen zum größten Teil von Stephen King. Die sind recht spannend und ... also, da hab' ich fast alle von. Ja, also meine Lieblingskleidung sind also T-Shirts, Jeans, Turnschuhe."

Eva, *Bietigheim*

„Also, ich reite, und ich spiel' Handball. Und Lieblingsessen, alles, was italienisch ist, so Nudeln, Spaghetti und so was. Und Lieblingskleidung ... es muß gemütlich sein und bequem."

1. **Sport; Essen; Kleidung; Schulfächer; Bücher.** Possible question: **Was ißt du gern?**

A. 1. Under which five categories do these students' favorites fall? What questions might the interviewer have asked each student to get these responses? Make a grid with the names of the students interviewed and the different categories. Fill in the grid for each student. Identify the phrases in each interview in which a reason is given and add these to your grid.

2. Interview your partner to find out what his or her favorites are in each category and why. Continue the chart. Then switch roles.

3. Are there any students who mentioned the same things as you or your partner? Are the things mentioned very similar to or different from things teenagers in the United States might say?

B. Choose one of the students above who is most like you (Sandra or Tim). Use this interview as a framework and rewrite it for yourself, changing the information to fit you. Use the words and phrases from the chart your partner made about you.

DRITTE STUFE

Making plans; ordering food and beverages; talking about how something tastes

36 Hör gut zu!

Drei Schüler erzählen, was sie alles am Samstag tun. Schreib auf, was jeder zwischen drei Uhr und fünf Uhr macht! For answers, see listening script in TE Interleaf.

37 Was willst du am Wochenende machen?

Mach eine Liste und schreib auf, was du am Wochenende machen willst! Schreib auf, wann du das alles machst!

38 Was machst du gewöhnlich am Samstag?

Such dir einen Partner und sag ihm, was du gewöhnlich am Samstag zwischen drei und sechs Uhr machst — oder am Sonntag, zwischen sechs Uhr und neun Uhr abends!

SO SAGT MAN DAS!

Schon bekannt

Making plans

When you make plans to do something with your friends, you might ask your friend:

Was möchtest du machen?
or **Und was willst du machen?**

What do you think **faulenzen** means?

Your friend might respond:

Ins Kino gehen.
Du, ich will mal echt faulenzen!

Ein wenig *G*rammatik

When you make plans, you need to know the forms of the verbs **wollen** and **möchte**. To review these forms, see the Grammar Summary.

39 Mein Wochenende

Such dir zwei Aktivitäten aus, die du gern am Wochenende machen willst. Frag deinen Partner, ob er mitmachen will! Er fragt dich wann. Tauscht dann die Rollen aus! Dann erzählt euern Mitschülern eure Pläne fürs Wochenende!

Wann?

am Nachmittag	am Abend
von 14 bis 16 Uhr	
am Sonntag	um 15 Uhr

Was?

joggen 100-Meter-Lauf Schach
Bogenschießen wandern
Leichtathletik Tennis Klavier

40 Für mein Notizbuch

Schick deinem Freund ein Fax! Berichte, was du am Wochenende alles machen willst! Du hast bestimmt so viele Pläne wie Benjamin und Andrea!

Bestell was, Basti!

Sebastian sitzt da und weiß nicht recht, was er tun soll. Lies den Text!

BEATRICE Bestell was zu trinken, Basti!
SEBASTIAN Hallo!
BEDIENUNG Ja, bitte?
SEBASTIAN Eine Limo, bitte!
BEDIENUNG Alles?
SEBASTIAN Ja.

BEATRICE Etwas zu essen, Basti?
SEBASTIAN N ... nein.

BEATRICE Komm, iß doch etwas! Ich zahl's dir. Ich lade dich ein.
SEBASTIAN Na gut! – Ein Stück Torte, Himbeertorte für mich.

41 Wer bezahlt?

Lies den Text und beantworte diese Fragen!

1. Was bestellt Basti zu trinken? Was sagt er? — Welche Ausdrücke könnte (*could*) er auch gebrauchen? **1. Eine Limo;** e.g.: **ich möchte ...**
2. Dann bestellt er etwas zu essen. Was sagt er? — Was könnte er auch sagen?
3. Warum, glaubst du, will Basti zuerst gar nichts essen?

2. **Ein Stück Torte;** e.g.: **ich nehme ...**

3. Possible answer: **Er hat nicht genug Geld mit.**

42 Hör gut zu!

Zwei Schüler sprechen über Dinge, die in den Fotos abgebildet sind. — Schreib die Zahlen 1- 5 auf ein Blatt Papier und daneben den Buchstaben (a. b. c. d. e.) des Fotos, das zu dem Gespräch paßt! For answers, see listening script in TE Interleaf.

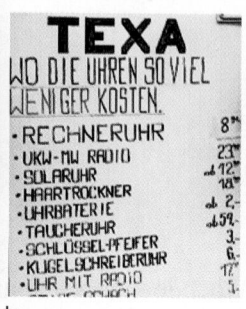

a.   b.   c.   d.   e.

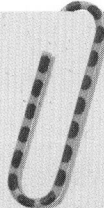

SO SAGT MAN DAS!

Ordering food and beverages

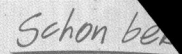

When ordering at a café or
restaurant, the waiter might ask:

> **Was bekommen Sie?**
> **Und Sie? Was essen Sie?**
> **Und was möchten Sie?**

You might ask a friend:

> **Was nimmst du?**
> **Und du?**

Your response might be:

> **Ich möchte eine Suppe, bitte!**
> **Für mich ein Wurstbrot, bitte!**
> **Ich esse ein Käsebrot.**

And the response might be:

> **Ja, ich nehme den Eisbecher.**
> **Ich will im Moment gar nichts.**

43 Hör gut zu!

Hör dir noch einmal die Schüler von Übung 42 an! Schreib jetzt auf, was jeder sagt, wenn
er etwas bestellt oder kauft! For answers, see listening script in TE Interleaf.

44 Was möchtest du essen und trinken?

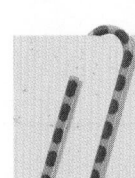

Such dir einen Partner! Einer von euch ist die Bedienung (*waiter* or *waitress*), der andere
bestellt etwas zu essen und zu trinken. Gebraucht bei euerm Gespräch die Reklame (*advertisements*) auf Seite 24! Die Bedienung macht dann die Rechnung fertig. Answers may vary.
E.g.: **Was bekommen Sie? — Ich möchte eine Pizza, bitte!**

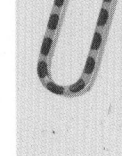

SO SAGT MAN DAS!

Talking about how something tastes

Wie schmeckt's?	**Lecker! Gut! Echt prima!** *oder*
	Es schmeckt nicht, weil es zu salzig ist.
	Der Kaffee schmeckt nicht, weil er zu bitter ist.
Schmeckt's?	**Ja, gut! Ausgezeichnet. Sagenhaft!** *oder*
	Nicht besonders.

45 Wie schmeckt's?

Such dir einen Partner! Seht euch die Reklame auf Seite 24 an! Dein Partner fragt dich, was
du da ißt. Du sagst es ihm. Dann fragt er dich, wie es schmeckt, und du sagst es ihm auch.
Tauscht dann die Rollen aus!

46 Es war echt super!

Such dir zwei Partner! Arbeitet zusammen an einem Gespräch in einem Café! Ihr seid zwei
Kunden und eine Bedienung. Denkt an folgendes:

a. Was wollt ihr essen und trinken?
b. Wie bestellt ihr alles bei der Bedienung?
c. Die Bedienung fragt, was jeder bestellt hat.

d. Ihr fragt, wie es schmeckt.
e. Ihr wollt zahlen, aber einer
hat kein Geld mit.

Das Gespräch soll echt lustig sein. Führt das beste Gespräch auf!

1 How would you say what your name is, how old you are, and where you live?   1. E.g.: **Ich heiße Tom. Ich bin sechzehn Jahre alt und wohne in Austin, Texas.**

2 How would you ask someone what his or her friend's name, age, and place of residence are?   2. E.g.: **Wie heißt deine Freundin? Wie alt ist sie? Wo wohnt sie?**

3 How would you ask a friend what a member of his or her family looks like? What would your friend answer if that person is tall and thin, has brown hair and dark eyes, and is very intelligent? 3. E.g.: **Wie sieht dein Bruder aus? - Er ist groß und schlank, hat braune Haare und dunkle Augen. Er ist sehr intelligent.**

4 How would you ask someone what he or she likes and doesn't like to do? What would you answer if someone asked you that question? 4. E.g.: **Was machst du gern, was machst du nicht gern? - Ich lese gern. Ich koche nicht gern.**

5 How would you ask a friend who someone is? Where his or her room is? What might your friend's answers be? 5. E.g.: **Wer ist das Mädchen? Wo ist dein Zimmer? - Das ist meine Schwester. Mein Zimmer ist neben dem Wohnzimmer.**

6 How would you say to someone that he or she looks elegant? How would you respond if someone gave you the same compliment? 6. E.g.: **Du siehst heute fesch aus. - Wirklich? Vielen Dank!**

7 How would you tell a salesclerk you would like to buy a hat and a scarf?   7. E.g.: **Ich möchte einen Hut und einen Schal kaufen.**

8 How would you ask a friend what his or her plans are? What might your friend answer?   8. E.g.: **Was möchtest du am Wochenende machen? - Ins Kino gehen.**

9 How would you order soup, a sandwich, ice-cream, and a lemon-flavored drink? What would you tell the waiter if you didn't want anything?   9. E.g.: **Ich möchte eine Suppe, ein Sandwich, Eis und eine Limo. Ich will im Moment gar nichts.**

10 How would you ask someone if his or her food tastes good? How would he or she respond if it did? If it didn't? What reasons might he or she give? 10. E.g.: **Schmeckt's? - Echt prima! / Es schmeckt nicht, weil es zu salzig ist.**

Can you describe yourself and others? (p. 11)

Can you express likes and dislikes? (p. 11)

Can you identify people and places? (p. 13)

Can you give and respond to compliments? (p. 18)

Can you express wishes when buying things? (p. 18)

Can you make plans? (p. 23)

Can you order food and beverages? (p. 25)

Can you talk about how something tastes? (p. 25)

ERSTE STUFE
ASKING FOR AND GIVING INFORMATION ABOUT YOURSELF AND OTHERS

faul *lazy*
fleißig *hard-working*
freundlich *friendly*
intelligent *intelligent*
neugierig *curious*
lustig *funny*
sympathisch *nice, pleasant*
unsympathisch *unfriendly, unpleasant*
gut gelaunt *in a good mood*
schlecht gelaunt *in a bad mood*
schlank *slender*
dunkel *dark*

FAMILY MEMBERS

beschreiben *to describe*
der Sohn, ¨e *son*
die Tochter, ¨ *daughter*
der Zwilling, -e *twin*
das Kind, -er *child*

EXPRESSING LIKES AND DISLIKES

Hobbys *hobbies*
  rodeln *sledding*
  fechten *fencing*
  kochen *cooking*
  Bogenschießen *archery*

die Leichtathletik *track and field*
der Sport *sports*
  Kugelstoßen *shot put*
  Speerwerfen *javelin throw*
  Diskuswerfen *discus throw*
  Langstreckenlauf *long-distance run*
  100-Meter-Lauf *100 yard dash*
  Weitsprung *long jump*
  Hürdenlauf *hurdling*
  Stabhochsprung *pole vault*
das Hobby, Hobbys *hobby*

ZWEITE STUFE
DESCRIBING AND COMMENTING ON CLOTHES

das Stirnband, ¨er *head band*
der Schal, -s *scarf*
die Mütze, -n *cap*

der Hut, ¨e *hat*
die Halskette, -n *necklace*
der Ohrring, -e *earring*
ein (das) Paar Ohrringe *pair of earrings*

das Armband, ¨er *bracelet*
die Handtasche, -n *handbag*

DRITTE STUFE
MAKING PLANS

Was willst du machen? *What do you want to do?*
Ich will faulenzen! *I want to be lazy!*

TALKING ABOUT HOW SOMETHING TASTES

Wie schmeckt's? *How does it taste?*
ausgezeichnet *excellent*
zu bitter *too bitter*
zu salzig *too salty*
die Suppe, -n *soup*

OTHER USEFUL WORDS AND EXPRESSIONS

echt *really*

Kapitel 2: Bastis Plan *Wiederholungskapitel*

CHAPTER OVERVIEW

Los geht's! pp. 30-32	Basti, das Schlitzohr! *p. 30*		*Video Guide*
	REVIEW OF FUNCTIONS	**REVIEW OF GRAMMAR**	**CULTURE**
Erste Stufe pp. 33-37	• Expressing obligations, *p. 33* • Extending and responding to an invitation, *p. 34* • Offering help and telling what to do, *p. 36*	• The forms of **müssen**, *p. 33* • The interrogative **warum** and the conjunctions **weil** and **denn**, *p. 35* • The forms of **können**, *p. 36* • The accusative forms of the personal pronouns and of the possessives, *p. 37*	Teenagers doing chores, *p. 37*
Zweite Stufe pp. 40-43	• Asking and telling what to do, *p. 41* • Telling that you need something else, *p. 42* • Telling where you were and what you bought, *p. 42*	• The forms of **sollen** and the **du**-commands, *p. 41* • The past tense forms of **sein**, the **war**-forms, *p. 43*	• Grocery advertisement, *p. 40* • **Landeskunde: Was nimmst du mit, wenn du irgendwo eingeladen bist?** *p. 44*
Dritte Stufe pp. 45-49	• Discussing gift ideas, *p. 46* • Expressing likes and dislikes, *p. 46* • Expressing likes, preferences, and favorites, *p. 47* • Saying you do or don't want more, *p. 48*	• The dative forms of **mein** and **dein** and dative personal pronouns, *p. 46* • The forms of **mögen**, *p. 47* • The phrase **noch ein**- and the forms of **ein** and **kein**, *p. 48*	German gift ideas, *p. 45*

Zum Lesen pp. 38-39	Macht Schule Spaß? Reading Strategy: Using context to derive the meaning of new words

Review pp. 50-51	• Kann ich's wirklich? *p. 50* • Wortschatz, *p. 51*

Assessment Options	**Stufe Quizzes**
	 • *Chapter Resources,* Book 1
	    Erste Stufe, Quiz 2-1
	    Zweite Stufe, Quiz 2-2
	    Dritte Stufe, Quiz 2-3
	 • *Assessment Items, Audiocassette* 7 A
		Kapitel 2 Chapter Test
		 • *Chapter Resources,* Book 1
		 • *Assessment Guide,* Speaking Test
		 • *Assessment Items, Audiocassette* 7 A
		
		 Test Generator, Kapitel 2

Chapter Overview

Video Program **OR**
Expanded Video Program, Videocassette 1

Textbook Audiocassette 1 B

RESOURCES Print	**RESOURCES** Audiovisual

Textbook Audiocassette 1 B

Practice and Activity Book
Chapter Resources, Book 1
- Additional Listening Activities 2-1, 2-2 ....*Additional Listening Activities, Audiocassette* 9 A
- Student Response Forms
- Realia 2-1
- Situation Card 2-1
- Teaching Transparency Master 2-1...............................*Teaching Transparency* 2-1
- Quiz 2-1 ....*Assessment Items, Audiocassette* 7 A

Textbook Audiocassette 1 B

Practice and Activity Book
Chapter Resources, Book 1
- Communicative Activity 2-1
- Additional Listening Activities 2-3, 2-4 ....*Additional Listening Activities, Audiocassette* 9 A
- Student Response Forms
- Realia 2-2
- Situation Card 2-2
- Quiz 2-2 ....*Assessment Items, Audiocassette* 7 A
Video Guide ....*Video Program/Expanded Video Program,* Videocassette 1

Textbook Audiocassette 1 B

Practice and Activity Book
Chapter Resources, Book 1
- Communicative Activity 2-2
- Additional Listening Activities 2-5, 2-6 ....*Additional Listening Activities, Audiocassette* 9 A
- Student Response Forms
- Realia 2-3
- Situation Card 2-3
- Teaching Transparency Master 2-2...............................*Teaching Transparency* 2-2
- Quiz 2-3 ....*Assessment Items, Audiocassette* 7 A

Video Guide ....*Video Program/Expanded Video Program,* Videocassette 1

Alternative Assessment
- Performance Assessment
Teacher's Edition
  Erste Stufe, p. 27K
  Zweite Stufe, p. 27P
  Dritte Stufe, p. 27R

- Portfolio Assessment
  Written: **Zweite Stufe,** Activity 29, *Pupil's Edition,* p. 42; *Assessment Guide,* p. 15
  Oral: **Zweite Stufe,** Activity 28, *Pupil's Edition,* p. 42; *Assessment Guide,* p. 15
- **Notizbuch,** *Pupil's Edition,* pp. 35, 37; *Practice and Activity Book,* p. 146

Kapitel 2: Bastis Plan
Textbook Listening Activities Scripts

Erste Stufe
Activity 5, p. 33

1. JUTTA   Ja, ich muß zu Hause schon was helfen. Also, ich putze das Badezimmer ein- oder zweimal in der Woche. Dann gehe ich nachmittags auch einkaufen oder zur Post, je nach dem was so anfällt. Außerdem sortiere ich den Müll und bringe die Glasflaschen zum Container. Das geht nur bis 18 Uhr, danach darf man's nicht mehr, wegen Lärmschutz!

2. ROLF   Ja, also ich hab' noch zwei Geschwister, und bei uns muß jeder was zu Hause machen. Diese Woche bin ich mit der Küche dran, das heißt Tisch decken, Geschirr spülen, abtrocknen und so. Besonders Spaß macht das nicht, aber ich find's okay, damit meine Eltern nach ihrem Job auch mal relaxen können und nicht direkt zu Hause weiterarbeiten müssen.

3. FRANZ   Helfen? Ja, direkt helfen muß ich eigentlich nicht so viel. Wir haben nämlich eine Putzfrau. Die kommt zweimal pro Woche und macht eigentlich alles sauber. Meine Eltern wollen lieber, daß ich für die Schule lerne. Aber ab und zu mache ich schon etwas zu Hause, zum Beispiel den Rasen mähen und die Garage aufräumen.

4. CHRISTIANE   Ja, ich muß 'ne ganze Menge zu Hause machen. Das find' ich echt nicht fair, denn von meinen Freundinnen muß niemand so viel zu Hause machen wie ich! Ich muß mein Zimmer aufräumen, das versteh' ich ja noch, aber dann muß ich auch Staub wischen, Staub saugen, den Geschirrspülautomaten leer machen, die Wäsche zusammenfalten und manchmal auch bügeln. Andauernd gibt es was zu tun. Das nervt mich ehrlich!

Answers to Activity 5

1. Badezimmer putzen; einkaufen; zur Post gehen; Müll sortieren; Glasflaschen zum Container bringen
2. Tisch decken, Geschirr spülen, abtrocknen.
3. Rasen mähen; Garage aufräumen
4. Zimmer aufräumen; Staub wischen; Staub saugen; Geschirrspülautomaten leermachen; Wäsche falten; bügeln

Activity 11, p. 34

1. DANIELA   Hast du Lust, am Samstag abend ins Kino zu gehen? Der neue Steven-Spielberg-Film läuft im Roxi.
   ILSE   Du, ich kann leider nicht, ich bin auf eine Fete eingeladen.
2. PETER   Hallo Martin! Am Sonntag fahr' ich nach Garmisch zum Skilaufen. Du kannst mitfahren, wenn du willst.
   MARTIN   Super! Danke für die Einladung!
3. KLAUS   He, wir wollen am Wochenende mit der Clique segeln gehen. Willst du mitkommen?
   MAX   Oh Mann, ich kann überhaupt nicht segeln! Aber ich komm' doch mit, okay?
4. CHRISTINE   Ich hab' gehört, daß *Guns 'n Roses* bald auf Konzerttour gehen. Die kommen auch nach München. Ich geh' auf jeden Fall hin. Kommst du mit?
   ANNETTE   Nein, ganz bestimmt nicht! Ich find' die Musik schrecklich!

Answers to Activity 11

1. declines; 2. accepts; 3. accepts; 4. declines

Activity 18, p. 36

-Sag mal, wie kann ich dir helfen? Was kann ich für dich tun?

1. CORDULA   Du kannst mir beim Einkaufen helfen. Meine Mutter hat hier eine Liste gemacht von allem, was sie braucht. Hol das Brot und den Kuchen beim Bäcker und geh auch zum Metzger, wenn du noch Zeit hast! Den Rest besorg' ich dann im Supermarkt.
2. ULRICH   Kannst du meinen kleinen Bruder für mich aus dem Kindergarten holen? Ich habe nämlich heute einen Termin beim Frisör und schaffe es einfach nicht rechtzeitig.

3. LUTZ Weißt du, was du tun kannst? Du kannst mir bei meinen Hausaufgaben helfen! Die Matheaufgaben sind mir viel zu kompliziert. Und wenn du damit fertig bist, kannst du mir helfen, meine Englischvokabeln zu lernen. Danach können wir dann zusammen den Tisch für das Abendessen decken.

Answers to Activity 18

1. Beim Bäcker und Metzger einkaufen
2. Bruder aus dem Kindergarten holen
3. bei Matheaufgaben helfen; bei Englischvokabeln helfen; Tisch decken

Zweite Stufe
Activity 24, p. 40

1. BRUNO Ja, also heute hab' ich Küchendienst und muß was zu essen kochen. Wir haben zu Hause nur noch zwei oder drei Kartoffeln. Das reicht nicht. Also muß ich einen 3-Kilo-Beutel Kartoffeln besorgen und noch etwas anderes Gemüse dazu, am liebsten mag ich grüne Bohnen. Und dann brauch' ich noch ein Hähnchen. Ich glaub', ich hole außerdem noch Tomaten und einen Bund Radieschen. Das Gemüse kaufe ich im Gemüseladen, und das Hähnchen hole ich vom Supermarkt um die Ecke.

2. HEIDI Also, ich kaufe heute nur das ein, was der Supermarkt Bausinger im Sonderangebot hat! Heute sind die Erdbeeren billig, die hol' ich ganz bestimmt. Außerdem gibt es dort den Kopfsalat für nur 99 Pfennig! Ja, und dann nehme ich noch das Hackfleisch und die Butter aus dem Angebot. Eigentlich brauch' ich auch noch ein Brot, aber das hol' ich lieber beim Bäcker!

Answers to Activity 24

1. Kartoffeln, grüne Bohnen, Tomaten, Radieschen: im Gemüseladen; Hähnchen: im Supermarkt
2. Erdbeeren, Kopfsalat, Hackfleisch, Butter: im Supermarkt Bausinger; Brot: beim Bäcker

Activity 27, p. 42

Frische Radieschen, ein Bund nur 79 Pfennig! Knackfrischer Kopfsalat! Garantiert ohne Pestizide! Zwei Köpfe für eine Mark! Neue Kartoffeln, frisch aus der Erde! Pro Beutel nur 2,99! Holländische Treibhaustomaten! Ein halbes Pfund für zwei Mark! Junge Zucchinis! Direkt vom Gemüsebauer! Vier Stück für nur drei Mark zwanzig! Zwiebeln und Karotten im 5-Kilo-Beutel für jeweils drei Mark!

Answers to Activity 27

Radieschen; Kopfsalat; Kartoffeln; Tomaten; Zucchinis; Zwiebeln; Karotten

Activity 29, p. 42

1. GABI Also, ich habe mir gerade ein halbes Pfund süße italienische Trauben auf dem Markt am Rathausplatz gekauft. Dort ist das Obst immer frisch, und man kann es vorher auch probieren!

2. WOLFGANG Die Kirschtorte hier ist von der Bäckerei am Stadttor. Die haben die leckersten Backwaren der ganzen Stadt! Jeder sagt, daß sie dort am besten schmecken.

3. UDO Ich war heute beim Metzger Gutmann und habe einen Haufen Aufschnitt gekauft, also Salami, Kalbsleberwurst, gekochten Schinken und Corned Beef. Ich kaufe Wurst lieber beim Metzger als im Supermarkt, weil der Metzger viele verschiedene Sachen hat.

4. URSULA Heute bin ich für meine Mutter einkaufen gegangen, lauter Konservendosen, als Vorrat für die Speisekammer! Also, Pilze, grüne Bohnen, Tomatenpüree, Mais, alles in Dosen. Ich hab' das ganze Zeug bei Aldo-Discount geholt. Dort ist es am billigsten!

Answers to Activity 29

a. 1: Markt am Rathausplatz; 2: Bäckerei am Stadttor; 3: Metzger Gutmann; 4: Supermarkt Aldo-Discount
b. 1: Obst frisch und man kann es probieren; 2: schmeckt lecker; 3: viele verschiedene Sachen; 4: billig

Dritte Stufe

Activity 31, p. 45

1. VOLKER   Meine Schwester hat nächste Woche Geburtstag. Ich hol' ihr einen Tennisschläger. Den wünscht sie sich schon lange, damit sie mit ihrer Freundin Tennis spielen kann.

2. RÜDIGER   Meine Oma und mein Opa feiern heute ihren 40-jährigen Hochzeitstag. Wir schenken ihnen ein Gemälde, das total gut in ihr Wohnzimmer paßt.

3. ANJA   Ich bin am Samstag auf 'ne Fete beim Jürgen, 'nem Schulkameraden, eingeladen, aber ich kenn' den Typ leider überhaupt nicht so gut. Ich glaub', ich schenke ihm nichts, ich bring' einfach nur Cola und Kartoffelchips oder Salzstangen mit!

4. CHRISTA   Zu Weihnachten schenken meine Geschwister und ich meinen Eltern einen neuen Radiowecker. Der alte funktioniert nämlich manchmal nicht mehr!

Answers to Activity 31

1. Tennisschläger für die Schwester; 2. Gemälde für Oma und Opa; 3. nichts; 4. Radiowecker für Eltern.

Activity 34, p. 46

1. RENATE   Also, zum Geburtstag mag ich als Geschenk zum Beispiel eine CD, oder ein Abonnement für 'ne Zeitschrift, die ich gut finde. Was ich überhaupt nicht mag, sind so traditionelle Sachen wie Blumen oder Pralinen.

2. TANJA   Ich mag Blumen unheimlich gern. Mein ganzes Zimmer ist voll von Pflanzen und Blumen, und ich freue mich immer, wenn ich welche zum Geburtstag kriege. Aber zum Beispiel neue Klamotten als Geschenk, mag ich überhaupt nicht. Mode ist mir nämlich total egal.

3. KONRAD   Ich mag es gern, wenn es zu meinem Geburtstag eine Torte gibt, eine Schwarzwälder Kirschtorte genauer gesagt. So einen normalen Kuchen, wie zum Beispiel Nußkuchen, mag ich nicht. Es muß schon eine richtige Torte sein!

Answers to Activity 34

1. mag: CD, Abonnement für Zeitschrift; mag nicht: Blumen und Pralinen
2. mag: Blumen und Pflanzen; mag nicht: Klamotten
3. mag: Torte; mag nicht: Nußkuchen

Activity 37, p. 47

1. OTTO   Also, ich hab' zum Geburtstag drei CDs geschenkt bekommen. Die mit der Country-Musik mag ich lieber als die von der Techno-Gruppe. Aber am liebsten hör' ich die Heavy Metal CD.

2. HANS   Wenn ich ins Kino gehe, seh' ich mir normalerweise nur Actionfilme an. Die mag ich am liebsten. Aber wenn gerade keiner läuft, guck' ich schon mal Slapstick-Komödien. Die mag ich auf jeden Fall lieber als so'n kitschiges romantisches Zeug wie *Bodyguard!*

3. INGE   Also, wenn mir jemand Bücher oder CDs zum Geburtstag schenken will, dann würde ich lieber Bücher haben. Mein Musikgeschmack ändert sich so schnell, aber wenn ich ein Buch gut finde, dann mag ich es eigentlich für längere Zeit. Am liebsten lese ich Science-fiction-Romane.

4. MONIKA   In der Pause hol' ich mir am liebsten 'ne Pizza vom Imbiß. Aber wenn ich mir was von zu Hause mitbringe, dann nehm' ich lieber Brezeln als ein langweiliges Butterbrot.

Answers to Activity 37

1. Country lieber als Techno; Heavy Metal am liebsten
2. Slapstick-Komödien lieber als Romanzen; Actionfilme am liebsten
3. Bücher lieber als CDs; Science-fiction-Romane am liebsten
4. Brezeln lieber als Butterbrot; Pizza am liebsten

Activity 40, p. 48

1. SABINE   Hm, die Schokoladentorte ist wahnsinig lecker! Ich glaub', ich nehme noch ein Stück!

2. THOMAS   Also, dieser Hamburger war echt gigantisch! Ich bin total satt und mag meinen Joghurt nicht mehr!

3. SILKE   Ich habe gerade fast eine ganze Flasche Mineralwasser ausgetrunken. Jetzt habe ich keinen Durst mehr!

4. MARKUS   Ich nehme noch ein Brötchen mit Ei. Heute bin ich tierisch hungrig!

Answers to Activity 40

1. mehr; 2. nichts mehr; 3. nichts mehr; 4. mehr

Kapitel 2: Bastis Plan
Projects and Games

PROJECT

Students will produce a magazine of a survey on topics of interest to teenagers. Start this project after the **Zum Lesen** *on pp. 38 and 39.*

Materials Students may need a small tape recorder, magazine pictures, poster board, glue, scissors, and markers.

Suggested Topics

Wie schmeckt das Essen in unserer Schule?
Soll unsere Schule Schuluniformen haben?
Wie verbringen Teenager ihre Freizeit?
Sollen Teenager Taschengeld bekommen?
Sollen Teenager für ihre Hilfe zu Hause bezahlt werden?

Suggested Sequence

1. Students choose a topic from the list of suggestions and make an outline of the questions they feel should be part of their survey.
2. Students interview other students throughout the school during lunch and before or after school.
3. Once students have sufficient data, they organize and evaluate the information.
4. Have students draft their surveys and turn them in for suggestions.
5. Students complete their surveys by writing or typing them and placing them onto the poster board. They should include visuals to resemble an authentic magazine layout.
6. Students present their projects to the class and explain the results of their surveys.

Grading the Project

Suggested point distribution (total = 100 points)
Originality and design   30
Written assignment   40
Oral presentation   30

 GAMES

Das tut mir leid

This game will help students review and practice nouns at the end of the **Dritte Stufe**.

Preparation Make a list of categories of all the nouns or expressions learned so far. (Examples: foods, gift ideas, chores, school subjects, family members, hobbies)

Procedure Have students form a line. Ask each of them to name a word that belongs in the category that you announce. Write the words on the board or on a transparency. Once a student has given a word from the category, he or she goes to the end of the line. If a student makes a mistake or waits more than five seconds to give an answer, he or she is dismissed, and you say **Das tut mir leid.** That student returns to his or her seat. Keep the game going depending on the number of categories and vocabulary you plan to practice. The three remaining students are the winners.

Fang den Ball!

This game will help students review the verbs that have been introduced so far.

Preparation Decide on the verbs you would like to review and write the infinitives on the board. (Examples: **sollen, können, mögen, müssen,** and the past tense of **sein**)

Procedure Ask students to stand up. Use a foam ball or any other soft ball and throw it to one of the students. Name the infinitive of one of the verbs listed and tell the student the conjugated form that you want him or her to say. (Example: **sollen—du**) The student says the verb in its correct form and then throws the ball to another student. This student must give the correct form of the verb called by the student who threw the ball. If a student says the incorrect verb form, he or she drops out of the game and sits down. The last student standing wins.

Kapitel 2: Bastis Plan
Lesson Plans, pages 28-51

Teacher Note

Chapter 2 is a review chapter that reintroduces functions, grammar, and vocabulary from *Komm mit!* Level 1.

Using the Chapter Opener, pp. 28-29

Motivating Activity

Ask students how they have to help around the house and how the work is divided up among family members. Which chores do they not mind and which ones do they dislike? Are there any they enjoy?

Building on Previous Skills

① Ask students to name some of the foods on the table.

Thinking Critically

Comparing and Contrasting Ask students about some of the things their families discuss during breakfast or dinner. (Examples: chores, events of the day, upcoming events)

 Culture Note

② In the German-speaking countries, it is very common to bring a small gift when visiting friends or relatives. This can be a bouquet of flowers (**ein Blumenstrauß**) for the hostess or a box of chocolates (**eine Schachtel Pralinen**). Ask students what they would take when visiting relatives or friends.

 For Individual Needs

③ **Challenge** Have students work with a partner and write a brief dialogue that could accompany this photo. Give a time limit of five minutes then call on several pairs to read their conversations.

Focusing on Outcomes

To help students focus on the learning outcomes listed on p. 29, ask students to name several gifts they bought recently and to tell why they chose each particular gift. **NOTE:** Each of these outcomes is modeled in the video and evaluated in **Kann ich's wirklich?** on p. 50.

Teaching Los geht's! pp. 30-32

Resources for Los geht's!

- *Video Program* **OR**
  Expanded Video Program, Videocassette 1
- *Textbook Audiocassette 1 B*
- *Practice and Activity Book*

▶ **page 30**

 Video Synopsis

In this segment of the video, the family discusses the children's chores for the day. Sebastian offers to switch chores with his brother Robert who was supposed to help his grandparents. Later, they discover that Sebastian's grandparents didn't need any help. The student outcomes listed on p. 29 are modeled in the video: expressing obligations, extending and responding to an invitation, offering help and telling what to do, asking and telling what to do, telling that you need something else, telling where you were and what you bought, discussing gift ideas, expressing likes and dislikes, expressing likes, preferences, and favorites, saying you do or don't want more.

Motivating Activity

Ask students if and how they have tried to get out of doing chores around the house. What excuses have worked for them? Which ones haven't?

Language Note

Schlitzohr means *rascal*. The word originated years ago when swindlers were punished by having their ears slit.

Building on Previous Skills

Ask students to briefly look at the **Wochenplan**. Whose chores would they prefer to do and why? (Encourage students to use **denn** or **weil** in their responses.)

Teaching Suggestion

To practice the reading, put students in groups of five and have them "role-play" the **Foto-Roman**. Have students change roles to give them additional practice. As a variation, you may want to ask students to pantomime the **Foto-Roman**.

▶ *page 32*

Teaching Suggestion

1 Ask students to work in pairs as they answer questions 1-8 in writing. Once students are finished, go over their responses.

✦ For Individual Needs

2 A Slower Pace Ask students to quietly read the **Foto-Roman** as they try to answer questions 1-7 orally.

3 Challenge After students have completed Activity 3, have them extend their answers for both the **Stimmt** and **Stimmt nicht** categories.
Examples:
Heute will Sebastian in der Küche helfen.
Stimmt nicht! Er will nicht helfen. Er will mit
  Robert tauschen und zum Opa gehen.

Heute nachmittag gibt es keinen Regen.
Stimmt! Das Wetter ist gut. Die Familie kann
  bei den Großeltern im Garten sitzen.

4 Auditory Learners Put the eight words in the box on a transparency or the board. Then ask students to close their books as you read each sentence to the class. After each sentence, students choose the word that best completes the statement. Repeat, but this time take groups of sentences and not necessarily in sequence.
Example: 6., 7., 8.; then 1., 2., 3.; then 4., 5.

Closure

Refer students back to the learning outcomes listed on p. 29, and ask students to list one German phrase from the **Foto-Roman** that corresponds to each function.

Teaching Erste Stufe,
pp. 33-37

Resources for Erste Stufe

Practice and Activity Book
Chapter Resources, Book 1
 • Additional Listening Activities 2-1, 2-2
 • Student Response Forms
 • Realia 2-1
 • Situation Card 2-1
 • Teaching Transparency Master 2-1
 • Quiz 2-1
Audiocassette Program
 • *Textbook Audiocassette* 1 B
 • *Additional Listening Activities,*
   Audiocassette 9 A
 • *Assessment Items, Audiocassette* 7 A

▶ *page 33*

MOTIVATE

Teaching Suggestion

Have students list in German at least three things that they have to do this week. (Examples: chores, activities, appointments)

TEACH

✦ For Individual Needs

5 Comparing and Contrasting After students have listened to the activity, ask them whose chores their own resemble the most. What are the things they also have to do?

ERSTE STUFE

PRESENTATION: Ein wenig Grammatik

Review the forms of **müssen** with a fast-paced question-answer practice that focuses on form but is still communicative. Using the same phrase through several exchanges, point to students to signal second or third person. Nod or shake your head to indicate a positive or a negative response.
Examples:

Ich muß jetzt gehen.

Mußt du auch gehen? **Ja, ich muß auch gehen.**

Und er, muß er gehen? **Nein, er muß nicht gehen.**

Ihr beide, müßt ihr jetzt gehen? **Ja, wir müssen jetzt gehen.**

Stella und Meredith müssen sicher gehen, ja? **Nein, sie müssen nicht gehen.**

PRESENTATION: So sagt man das!

After reading the **So sagt man das!** box with the class, ask students for information, using sentences that contain the verb **müssen**.
Examples:

Was mußt du nachmittags nach der Schule tun?

Was müßt ihr heute im Sportunterricht machen?

Was muß dein Bruder zu Hause alles tun?

▶ *page 34*

Building on Previous Skills

9 After students have answered the questions, ask students to describe the chores in the three photographs on p. 34.

Teaching Suggestion

10 Remind students to use sequencing words in their answers. (Examples: **zuerst, dann, danach**)

PRESENTATION: So sagt man das!

To practice the expressions, make many suggestions for which students may either choose an accepting or declining phrase from the function box.
Example:

Hannah, willst du heute mit deiner Schwester ins Einkaufszentrum gehen?

▶ *page 35*

For Additional Practice

12 After students have decided on the two places they would like to go, ask them to use **denn** or **weil** as they give reasons for deciding on the two places.

Teaching Suggestion

13 Monitor students' work and ask several pairs to give you an example of their conversations.

Reteaching: 24-Hour Time

14 Using a clock with moveable hands, review 24-hour time (Level 1, Chapter 4, p. 99). Show several different times and indicate whether it is **nachts, morgens, mittags, nachmittags,** or **abends.** Ask students to give the time accordingly.

Teaching Suggestion

15 On the left side of a transparency or work sheet, write several questions that begin with the interrogative **warum**. On the right side, write possible answers for each of the questions in random order. Ask students to combine the sentences first using **weil**, then using **denn**.
Examples:

Warum schenkst du Dieter einen Fußball zum Geburtstag? **Das ist sein Lieblingssport.**

Ich schenke Dieter einen Fußball, weil das sein Lieblingssport ist.

Warum lernst du Deutsch? **Wir reisen im Sommer nach Deutschland.**

Ich lerne Deutsch, denn wir reisen im Sommer nach Deutschland.

Thinking Critically

Analyzing Ask students to compare the word order before and after the changes they made. What can they conclude about the word order of dependent clauses?

▶ *page 36*

For Additional Practice

18 Continue with further question-answer practice. Ask students about their daily routine and have them include the words and phrases from the box in their responses.

PRESENTATION: So sagt man das!

After reading the expressions introduced in the function box, tell students to imagine that their best friend owes them a favor. What would the students like their friends to do for them? Go around the class and ask students what they might tell their friends.

PRESENTATION: Ein wenig Grammatik

Review the forms of **können** with fast-paced question-answer practice involving the whole class. Use the same phrase so that attention is on producing the right form. Point to students to signal second or third person. Nod or shake your head to signal positive or negative responses.
Examples:
Ich habe am Samstag eine Party.

Kannst du kommen?	**Ja, ich kann kommen.**
Könnt ihr kommen?	**Nein, wir können nicht kommen.**
Kann (Jill) kommen?	**Ja, sie kann kommen.**

After reviewing the forms of **können,** ask students to create complete sentences using the following clues. Prepare this activity ahead of time on a transparency or a handout.

Ich	conjugated forms	Auto fahren
Du	of **können**	die Küche schnell
Er	(in random order)	aufräumen
Sie		gut Deutsch sprechen
Wir		Schlittschuh laufen
Ihr		einkaufen gehen
Bernd und Dieter		besonders gut kochen

▶ *page 37*

For Individual Needs

20 A Slower Pace To practice the accusative forms, write your students' names on small raisin boxes or on any box the size of a small gift. Or you may want to ask students to each bring a small box to class with the name of a classmate written on it. Students could decorate their boxes to make them look like a real present. Then call students to the front and ask them to give the "present" to the student whose name appears on the box. The student presenting the item says **Das Geschenk ist für dich, Abdul!** Ask other students in the class to repeat the statement in the third person: **Das Geschenk ist für ihn!**

Reteaching: Accusative Pronouns

Review the accusative pronouns with fast-paced substitution practice. Use the same phrase for a number of substitutions so that attention is on form. Point to students to signal to which person(s) the statement is directed.
Examples:
Ich habe hier viele schöne Geschenke.

Das ist für Peter.	**Das ist für *ihn*.**
Das ist für Ann.	**Das ist für *sie*.**
Das ist für Mary und dich.	**Das ist für *euch*.**
Das ist für Gene und mich.	**Das ist für *uns*.**
Das ist für Patty und Jeff.	**Das ist für *sie*.**

Next, do a similar pronoun practice using questions. This forces students to respond rather than merely substitute. Use pictures of foods or actual foods as you offer them to students.
Examples:

Ist das für dich?	**Ja, das ist für *mich*.**
Ist das für euch?	**Ja, das ist für *uns*.**
Ist das für die Barbara?	**Ja, das ist für *sie*.**
Ist das für den George?	**Ja, das ist für *ihn*.**
Ist das für die beiden?	**Ja, das ist für *sie*.**

ERSTE STUFE

ZUM LESEN

Next, practice accusative pronouns by writing sentences on a transparency which include prepositional phrases with **für**. Students should restate the sentences using pronouns.

Personal			seine Mutter
Pronouns	chores	für	Andy und dich
or			Bea und Jean
Proper Names			Michael
			Erin und mich

Examples:
Er putzt die Fenster für Erin und mich.
Er putzt die Fenster für uns.

Wir mähen den Rasen für seine Mutter.
Wir mähen den Rasen für sie.

CLOSE

♜ Game
Divide the class into two teams. Team A sends a student to the front of the class to act out a vocabulary word that you show him or her on an index card (chores for this **Stufe**). A student from Team B tries to guess the word or expression correctly. Only German can be used. Teams receive one point for each correct guess.

Focusing on Outcomes
Refer students back to the learning outcomes listed on p. 29. They should recognize that they now know how to express obligations, extend and respond to an invitation, offer help and tell what to do.

ASSESS

• **Performance Assessment** On index cards or small pieces of paper write questions that represent the functions of this **Stufe**.

Examples:
Kannst du den Müll bitte sortieren?
Willst du zu Ming Chins Fete gehen?

Hand out these cards to half of your students. Students with cards should direct their questions to students without a card. That student responds to each question with an excuse using **denn** or **weil**.

• Quiz 2-1, *Chapter Resources*, Book 1

Teaching Zum Lesen, *pp. 38-39*

Reading Strategy
The targeted strategy in this reading is using context to derive the meaning of new words. Students should learn about this strategy before doing Activity 4.

PREREADING

Motivating Activity
Go around the classroom and ask several students to talk about what they really like about being at school.

Building on Previous Skills
In Chapter 5 of Level 1, on p. 125, students learned to use the word **gefallen** when describing clothing. Help students infer the meaning of **mißfallen** based on this knowledge.

Thinking Critically
Drawing Inferences Ask students where this type of text could be found. Can they determine the title of the magazine and who this text is intended for? (*Eltern;* intended for parents)

Teacher Note
Activities 1 and 2 are prereading activities.

READING

Teaching Suggestion
3 Before doing the reading activities, ask students what facts or information are given about the participants of the survey. (type of school and age) How many are boys and how many are girls? (7/5) How were students able to tell? (-**in** ending for female)

Teacher Note
In Chapter 4 of Level 1 students were introduced to the German school day and grading system. Many of the students featured in the videos and the book are students at local **Gymnasien**.

Thinking Critically

Comparing and Contrasting Ask students how most school systems in the United States are structured. Make a chart on the board or transparency. Have students tell the corresponding age for each school. (elementary, middle school or junior high, and senior high school) Then introduce the German school system. Use the following Culture Note as a transparency or make a handout for students. Explain to students that, in Germany, at the end of the 4th or 6th grade (depending on the **Bundesland** they live in), parents and teachers decide which of the three secondary schools a student should attend (based on academic performance). Discuss how these three schools differ.

Teacher Note

The following Culture Note gives a general description of the German school system.

Culture Note

The Grundschule is the first school that German students attend (after **Kindergarten**). After completing four or six years in the **Grundschule**, students (together with their teachers and parents) must decide which of several possible secondary schools they will attend:

1. the **Hauptschule,** which prepares students mainly for blue-collar jobs;
2. the **Realschule,** which concludes with the **Mittlere Reife** at the end of 10th grade and prepares students for work in clerical and administrative jobs; or
3. the **Gymnasium,** which is a nine-year program that ends with a rigorous exam called the **Abitur,** successful completion of which qualifies students to attend a **Universität.**

For those who choose the **Hauptschule,** the next step (at age 16) is the **Berufschule,** which is a state-sponsored vocational school. The **Berufschule** offers students training in their chosen craft or trade, as well as general clerical training. Graduates of the **Berufschule** may go on to attend a **Fachschule**; graduating from the **Fachschule** qualifies students to attend a **Fachhochschule** where they can obtain advanced degrees.

Successful completion of the **Realschule** program (ending with the acquisition of the **Mittlere Reife** diploma) qualifies students either to become employed in a clerical or administrative position, to begin an apprenticeship, or to attend a **Fachgymnasium** (called **Fachoberschule** in some areas). After graduating from a **Fachgymnasium,** students can choose to attend a **Universität** or a **Fachhochschule.**

The **Gymnasium** has the highest academic standards of the German secondary schools. Students attend the **Gymnasium** for nine years and receive a diploma called the **Abitur** ("Abi"), which entitles them to enter a **Universität** (though some subjects, such as medicine, only admit students with a very good **Abitur.**) At the **Universität,** German students do not take basic courses, but concentrate solely on their major.

In the 1980s, a new type of school was introduced in Germany: the **Gesamtschule.** The **Gesamtschule** has all the above mentioned types of schools in one complex, and students who attend these schools have a better chance of changing from one "track" to another. Students who start out in the **Hauptschule** program or track and do very well have the opportunity to switch either to a **Gymnasium** or to a **Realschule** track.

Teaching Suggestion

Since the reading selections have many words and constructions that students don't know, remind students to use the **Lesetrick,** the prereading activities, and the context to derive the meaning of the new words.

Cooperative Learning

Assign small groups of three students to do Activities 4-6 as a cooperative learning activity within a specific amount of time. Each group member has a task as part of this activity as leader/reader, recorder, and reporter. Upon completion of the assignment, call on the reporters of several groups to share their answers with the rest of the class.

POST-READING

Teacher Note

Activity 8 is a post-reading task that will show whether students can apply what they have learned.

Thinking Critically

Drawing Inferences Have students do Activity 7 in pairs. Then ask them to think of synonyms for the words **aufdrehen, ausquatschen,** and **Heimfahrt.** Students can also describe each word, by paraphrasing. (Example: **aufdrehen —> lauter machen**). Do students know what **db** stands for? (**Dezibel**)

Examples:
ausquatschen —> reden, sprechen
Heimfahrt —> nach Hause fahren

Give students other unknown words from the interviews that they should be able to infer from context. Have students work in pairs and try to find synonyms or other words and phrases to explain the new words.

Klaus: das Mieseste; Tim: das Schwitzen; Dieter: scharf denken, sich leicht vertun; Sara: Dreck abladen; Nicole: saumäßig; abgestandene (Buttermilch); (alte) Pantoffeln

For Individual Needs

Challenge Based on Christa's description of a teacher, ask students to describe a teacher they like.

Closure

Ask students about their overall impression of German students' attitudes toward school. Is it similar or different from the way American students feel about school?

Teaching Zweite Stufe,
pp. 40-43

Resources for Zweite Stufe

Practice and Activity Book
Chapter Resources, Book 1
- Communicative Activity 2-1
- Additional Listening Activities 2-3, 2-4
- Student Response Forms
- Realia 2-2
- Situation Card 2-2
- Quiz 2-2
Audiocassette Program
- *Textbook Audiocassette* 1 B
- *Additional Listening Activities, Audiocassette* 9 A
- *Assessment Items, Audiocassette* 7 A
Video Program or *Expanded Video Program*

▶ **page 40**

MOTIVATE

Teaching Suggestion

Ask students in German to recall what foods and beverages are in their refrigerator and pantry at home.

TEACH

Teaching Suggestions

These ads are a good source of cultural information. Here are several suggestions on how to present the ads.

1) Have students scan the ads for weights and liquid measurements. (**g = Gramm; kg = Kilogramm**)
2) Have students scan the ads for quality indicators or descriptors. (**Kl. I = Klasse I; Kl. II = Klasse II; Spitzenqualität; täglich frisch; ohne Knochen**)
3) Have students find references to the countries or regions of origin of certain products. What do these references imply? (**aus Italien; aus Holland; aus dem Allgäu; deutscher Schnittkäse;** references imply that the products are of good quality)
4) Have students find references to amounts other than weight and infer the meaning of these words. (**Stück, Bund, Schale, Becher, Beutel**)
5) Have students compare the store hours in German supermarkets to the hours in American stores. Have them look at opening and closing times, lunch time, and Saturday hours. Remind students that **langer Samstag** occurs only once a month.
6) Have students discuss how their families' shopping habits would have to be changed if they lived in Germany. What responsibilities would they as teenagers have?

✦ For Individual Needs

24 A Slower Pace Have students listen to the activity twice. The first time have them record where the two students plan to do their shopping. The second time, have students list the foods they need to buy underneath the names of the stores or places they plan to go to.

24 Challenge Ask students to mention at least two more items that could be purchased at each of those stores.

PRESENTATION: Wortschatz

Introduce the new fruits and vegetables by modeling them and having students repeat. Some are difficult to pronounce (**Pfirsiche, Zwetschgen, Erbsen, Spinat**). Next, ask questions about *likes* and *dislikes.*

Examples:
Welches Obst von den drei Obstarten ißt du gern?
Welches Gemüse von den drei Gemüsearten ißt du gern? nicht gern?

▶ *page 41*

Teaching Suggestion

26 Have two or three pairs perform their conversations for the class.

▶ *page 42*

PRESENTATION: So sagt man das!

Using the lists the students made in Activity 27, ask a student **Was bekommen Sie?**, then, **Was bekommen Sie noch? Haben Sie noch einen Wunsch?, Sonst noch etwas?**, working through students' lists. Ask these questions to one more student. Then have students ask each other similar questions, using the function box as a model.

Thinking Critically

27 Comparing and Contrasting In German rural areas, delivery trucks are still very common. Can students think of a similar service in their areas? What type of merchandise is delivered?

Language Note

A **Kombi** (**Kombiwagen**) is a station wagon or a delivery truck.

Teaching Suggestion

28 After students have completed their dialogues, ask for volunteer pairs to act out their skits in front of the class. As a follow-up activity, ask the audience one or two questions per skit to check for comprehension.
Example:
Wieviel Pfund Erdbeeren will Mark kaufen?

📁 Portfolio Assessment

28 You might want to use this activity as a written portfolio item for your students. See *Assessment Guide*, p. 15.

29 You might want to use this activity as an oral portfolio item for your students. See *Assessment Guide*, p. 15.

PRESENTATION: So sagt man das!

After reading the examples in the function box, ask students questions based on their skits from Activity 28. Students should respond using the past tense.
Examples:
Sag mal Robin, wo warst du?
Was hast du vom Christopher gekauft?

▶ *page 43*

Thinking Critically

30 Synthesizing Once students have completed the activity, ask them to name advantages and disadvantages of buying at specialty stores versus large supermarkets. Make a chart on the board or on a transparency. Expand the activity by asking students why it is more popular in Germany to patronize specialty stores than supermarkets.

Reteaching: Past Tense of *Sein*

Have the following sentences listed on a transparency. Ask students to restate the sentences in the past tense using the adverbial phrases in parentheses.
Examples:
Jetzt bist du 15 Jahre alt. (Letztes Jahr)
Michael ist durstig. (Nach dem Tennisspiel)
Ich bin so müde. (Vorgestern)
Angela und Rüdiger sind mit Freunden im Kino. (Gestern)
Diana und du, ihr seid oft im Schwimmbad. (Im Sommer)

▶ *page 44*

📼 PRESENTATION: Landeskunde

Teacher Note

The **Landeskunde** interviews are recorded on audiocassette and videocassette.

Teaching Suggestion

Begin the **Landeskunde** page by having students do the prereading activity. Then play the audiocassette or have students watch the video. Before putting students in groups of three and having them practice reading the interviews, practice some of the more difficult passages with the class.

Group Work

Divide students into groups of three or four and have each group work on Activities A1 and A2. Then have each group share the information with the rest of the class, using as much German as possible.

Teaching Suggestions

- Ask students to look at the interviews again. What word often appears following a **wenn**-clause? What do they notice about the word order in these sentences? Write the sentences on a transparency or on the board. Ask students to infer a rule about the word order of **wenn**-clauses.

- Ask students to think of three occasions, such as a birthday or an invitation to someone's house for dinner, and to list what they would bring (or not bring) if they were invited on each of these occasions. Ask students to use these elements to create their own sentences, joining them together with **wenn** and **dann** and giving their own answers to the interview question. Students should then switch papers with their partners and correct each other's answers. Ask students how similar their answers are to what the people interviewed said.

- Ask students how traditional they think society in the United States is. Are there any customs regarding social courtesies that are important today? Students should write a brief essay in English on this topic and include any observations about other countries or cultures with which they have come in contact. The essay could be assigned to students for extra credit.

Multicultural Connection

Ask students from other countries to share when and what they typically exchange or bring for gifts. Students in class could get information about other countries' customs from exchange students, other foreign language students, or other foreign language teachers.

Teacher Note

Mention to your students that the **Landeskunde** will also be included in Quiz 2-2 given at the end of the **Zweite Stufe.**

CLOSE

Teaching Suggestion

Present students with the following situation: Their doctor has informed them that they need to improve their diet. Based on the major food groups of a balanced diet ask students to imagine what else the doctor might suggest.
Example:
Du sollst täglich Obst essen!

Focusing on Outcomes

Refer students back to the learning outcomes listed on p. 29. They should recognize that they now know how to ask and tell what to do, tell that they need something else, and tell where they were and what they bought.

ASSESS

• **Performance Assessment** Ask students to tell you why they were at one of the following stores today. What purchases did they make and why?

beim Metzger
in der Bäckerei
im Reformhaus
im Obst- und Gemüseladen
im Kaufhaus
im Buchgeschäft
im Geschenkladen

• Quiz 2-2, *Chapter Resources*, Book 1

Teaching Dritte Stufe,
pp. 40-43

Resources for Dritte Stufe

Practice and Activity Book
Chapter Resources, Book 1
• Communicative Activity 2-2
• Additional Listening Activities 2-5, 2-6
• Student Response Forms
• Realia 2-3
• Situation Card 2-3
• Teaching Transparency Master 2-2
• Quiz 2-3
Audiocassette Program
• *Textbook Audiocassette* 1 B
• *Additional Listening Activities, Audiocassette* 9 A
• *Assessment Items, Audiocassette* 7 A

▶ *page 45*

MOTIVATE

Teaching Suggestion

Ask students to name some of the gifts they have received for their last birthday. Which ones did they like and what was it?

TEACH

Total Physical Response

To get students warmed up for this activity, give students the commands using verbs such as **geben, nehmen, reichen, einpacken, auspacken,** and **aufmachen.**
Examples:
Pam, reich Kimberly bitte die Bücher!
Dianne, pack die Bücher in Papier ein!
Mark, mach den Kalender auf Seite dreißig auf und schreib deinen Namen und deine Adresse rein!

For Additional Practice

31 In addition to this activity ask students for whom they would buy each of the pictured gifts and why.

▶ *page 46*

PRESENTATION: So sagt man das!

Ask students to read the questions and answers in class. Then help students identify the indirect object in the questions and answers and the changes that occur.

Group Work

32 Ask students to work in small groups and set a time limit of three minutes in which groups build as many sentences or questions as they can. One member in each group is the writer and lists all sentences. Ask students to read some of their sentences to the class.

Teaching Suggestion

33 Start by brainstorming the different types of occasions for which students might purchase gifts.
Examples: **zum** Muttertag, **zum** Vatertag, **zum** Geburtstag, **zu** Weihnachten, **zu einer** Hochzeit)

PRESENTATION: So sagt man das!

After reading the expressions in this function box, ask students to work with a partner, using the questions as listed but giving their own responses. Then call on several students to tell the class what their partner likes and dislikes.

▶ *page 47*

PRESENTATION: Ein wenig Grammatik

Practice the forms of **mögen** by providing students with patterned sentences.
Examples:

Zum Geburtstag	form of	du	nicht so gern
	mögen		Klamotten
Zum Muttertag		er	gern Bücher
Zum Vatertag		ich	lieber Rosen
			als Pralinen
		sie	

 For Individual Needs

36 A Slower Pace Before students work with their partners, work with students on a list of possible reasons they would use in this activity. Write these suggestions on a transparency to help students with the interview. Monitor students' work as you walk around the class.

PRESENTATION: So sagt man das!

Ask students to read the function box with a partner and then to further practice the expressions by talking about music, clothing, and sports.

 For Individual Needs

38 Challenge Once students have completed their lists, take a survey of the entire class and record the findings on the board or on a transparency. Help students elicit information from each other, using ordinal numbers. (Example: **Auf dem ersten Platz steht...**) Have students make a general conclusion based on the information. (Example: **Was haben viele Schüler am liebsten? nicht so gern?**)

▶ *page 48*

Teaching Suggestion

39 Call on several students and ask them to restate their partners' preferences about foods and beverages.

PRESENTATION: So sagt man das!/Ein wenig Grammatik

To review the functions and the grammar in these boxes, use props or show pictures of foods and ads from grocery stores. Then ask students if they would like more of the foods pictured.

Reteaching: *Mögen* and Gift Ideas

Prepare a chart on a transparency or on a handout. Give students a time limit to write as many sentences as possible.

Subject	Verb	Object	Dependent Clause
Er	form	**Semmeln** weil	**gut schmecken**
Sie	of	**Pralinen**	**Schokolade gern**
	mögen	**Turnschuhe**	**essen**
		CDs	**täglich joggen**
Wir		**Blumenstrauß**	**ein Musikfan sein**
Ich			**Blumen gern haben**
Ihr			
Dawn und Chris			

Example: **Sie mag Semmeln, weil sie gut schmecken.**

CLOSE

Teaching Suggestion

Make a class set of the weekly school cafeteria menu. Ask students to express their likes and dislikes for the foods offered using the scale at the top of p. 48.

Focusing on Outcomes

Refer students back to the learning outcomes listed on p. 29. Students should recognize that they now know how to discuss gift ideas, express likes and dislikes, express likes, preferences, and favorites, and say they do and don't want more.

ASSESS

- **Performance Assessment** Tell students to imagine they have received a $50.00 gift certificate for their favorite store. Ask students in German what they would buy and why.

- Quiz 2-3, *Chapter Resources*, Book 1

Video Wrap-Up

At this time, you might want to use the *Video Program* or the *Expanded Video Program*, Videocassette 1 for additional review and enrichment. See *Video Guide* for suggestions regarding:
- **Basti, das Schlitzohr!**
   (Dramatic episode)
- **Landeskunde**
   Interviews
- **Videoclips**
   (Authentic footage—*Expanded Video Program* only)

Kann ich's wirklich?
p. 50

This page helps students prepare for the test. It is a brief checklist of the major points covered in the chapter. The students should be reminded that it is only a checklist and not necessarily everything that will appear on the test.

Using Wortschatz,
p. 51

Teaching Suggestions

- Give vocabulary definitions in German and have students try to guess the word or expression.
- Ask students to group vegetables and fruits by degrees of likes and dislikes.
- Use pictures from food magazines to practice names of foods.

Game

Ask students to work in groups of four or five. Using the vocabulary of the **Dritte Stufe**, one student describes to the others in his or her group the item he or she has misplaced or lost. The others have to guess the name of the item. Students can also include gift items from the **Landeskunde.**

Teacher Note

Give the **Kapitel 2** Chapter Text, *Chapter Resources*, Book 1.

2
Bastis Plan

① Nein, danke! Sag mir lieber, was wir heute tun müssen!

In German families, chores are often shared among family members. Sometimes a plan is drawn up to remind everyone of his or her duties. What are some of the chores you perform at home? Do you sometimes swap chores with other members of the family?

In this chapter, you will review and practice

- expressing obligations; extending and responding to an invitation; offering help and telling what to do
- asking and telling what to do; telling that you need something else; telling where you were and what you bought
- discussing gift ideas; expressing likes and dislikes; expressing likes, preferences, and favorites; saying you do or don't want more

And you will

- listen to German-speaking students talk about helping others
- read about what students like and don't like about their school
- write your plans for the weekend
- find out what German students take when they are invited to someone's house

② Schenkst du dem Opa Pralinen?

③ Möchtest du noch ein Stück Kuchen?

Los geht's!

Beatrice

Robert

Sebastian

Vater

Mutter

Basti, das Schlitzohr!

The Baumanns are having their breakfast.
What are they talking about? What is Basti's plan?

VATER Iß, iß, mein Sohn! Du mußt heute noch viel arbeiten.

ROBERT Was muß ich denn heute machen?

BEATRICE Schau halt mal auf den Plan drauf!

SEBASTIAN Wenn du willst, können wir tauschen! Du kannst für mich in der Küche helfen, und ich gehe für dich zum Opa.

ROBERT He, prima! Danke dir.

Wochenplan	Robert	Beatrice	Basti
		Oma, Opa	Garage
Mo.			
Di.	einkaufen	einkaufen	einkaufen
Mi.	Küchendienst	Küchendienst	Küchendienst
Do.		Fenster!	Müll
Fr.	Oma/Opa		
Sa.	Rasen		
So.			

SEBASTIAN Wie soll das Wetter sein?

BEATRICE Schön. Das hab' ich schon gestern gehört.

MUTTER   Kein Regen! Das paßt prima. Da können wir uns bei den Großeltern in den Garten setzen.

ROBERT   Was? Wir gehen zur Oma?

MUTTER   Wir sind zum Kaffee eingeladen.

SEBASTIAN   Okay, wir sehen uns dann heute nachmittag bei Oma und Opa.

MUTTER   Ja, aber mach dich nicht schmutzig bei der Arbeit!

SEBASTIAN   Aber Mama, kein Problem! Tschau!

VATER   Ja, stimmt! Nein, nein. Ich weiß, um drei Uhr. Was sagst du? Das mußt du noch mal wiederholen! Der Basti? So ein Schlitzohr! Na, warte! Ja, bis später! Tschüs!

VATER   Der Basti! Man kann es nicht glauben, so ein Schlitzohr! Er ist gar nicht beim Opa. Der Opa kann ihn heute gar nicht brauchen, er hat gar nichts zu tun. Aber unser Sohn geht zu den Großeltern zum Mittagessen!

MUTTER   Jetzt weiß ich's! Deshalb hat er so schnell mit dem Robert getauscht.

1 Was passiert hier?

Verstehst du alles, was die Leute in der
Foto-Story sagen? Beantworte die Fragen!

1. Worüber sprechen die Baumanns?
2. Was muß Robert heute tun?
3. Was sagt Sebastian zu Robert?
4. Was sagt Beatrice über das Wetter?
5. Was meint die Mutter über das Wetter?
6. Wohin gehen die Baumanns am Nachmittag? Warum?
7. Warum ist Basti nicht beim Opa?
8. Welche Aufgaben haben Beatrice, Robert und Basti in
   dieser Woche?

1. Über das, was sie heute alles machen müssen.
2. Oma u. Opa helfen.
3. „Wenn du willst, können wir tauschen…"
4. Schön.
5. Paßt prima.
7. Opa braucht ihn nicht.
6. Großeltern; zum Kaffee eingeladen.
8. Bea.: Oma u. Opa helfen, einkaufen, Küchendienst, Fenster putzen.
Robert: einkaufen, Küchendienst, Oma u. Opa helfen, Rasen. Basti: Garage, einkaufen, Küchendienst, Müll.

2 Genauer lesen

Lies den Text noch einmal und beantworte die Fragen!

1. Warum soll Robert viel essen?
2. Welche Aufgaben haben die drei Geschwister heute?
3. Was möchte Basti heute lieber tun?
4. Warum gehen die Baumanns heute nachmittag zur Oma?
5. Wo können sie heute bei den Großeltern sitzen? Warum?
6. Warum nennt Herr Baumann seinen Sohn ein Schlitzohr?
7. Was bedeutet der Ausdruck „Schlitzohr"? Was meinst du?

1. Er muß noch viel arbeiten.
2. Oma u. Opa helfen; Fenster putzen; Küchendienst.
3. Oma u. Opa helfen.
4. Sie sind eingeladen.
5. Garten; Wetter ist schön.
6. Weil Basti gefaulenzt hat.
7. sly fox

3 Stimmt oder stimmt nicht?

Stimmen diese Sätze? Wenn nicht, mußt du die richtige Antwort geben.

1. Heute will Sebastian in der Küche helfen.
2. Heute nachmittag gibt es keinen Regen.
3. Die Baumanns haben die Großeltern zum Kaffee eingeladen.
4. Der Opa ruft Herrn Baumann an.
5. Der Sebastian ist beim Opa und hilft ihm.

1. Stimmt nicht; er will den Großeltern helfen.
2. Stimmt.
3. Stimmt nicht; (the other way around).
4. Stimmt.
5. Stimmt nicht; er faulenzt.

4 Welches Wort paßt?

Welche Wörter auf der rechten Seite passen in die Satzlücken?

1. Basti will mit Robert _____.
2. Er möchte für Robert zum Opa _____.
3. Robert muß jetzt in der Küche _____.
4. Die Baumanns sind zum Kaffee _____.
5. Alle können heute im Garten _____.
6. Aber Basti ist nicht beim Opa.
   Herr Baumann kann es nicht _____.
7. Der Opa hat für Basti nichts zu _____.
8. Deshalb hat Basti mit Robert _____.

1. tauschen
2. gehen
3. helfen
4. eingeladen
5. sitzen
6. glauben
7. tun
8. getauscht

eingeladen   gehen
tun   getauscht
glauben   helfen
sitzen   tauschen

Expressing obligations; extending and responding to an invitation; offering help and telling what to do

5 Hör gut zu!

Schüler erzählen, was sie so zu Hause alles machen müssen. Mach dir Notizen! (Schreib auf, wer was macht!) <small>For answers, see listening script on TE Interleaf.</small>

6 Was müssen die Schüler tun?

Ordne jetzt deine Notizen nach drei Gruppen von Arbeiten: Küchendienst, Gartenarbeiten und Persönliches! Dann vergleiche mit einem Partner, was ihr beide aufgeschrieben habt!

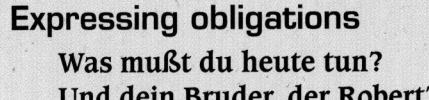

SO SAGT MAN DAS!

Schon bekannt

Expressing obligations

Was mußt du heute tun?	**Ich muß heute den Rasen mähen.**
Und dein Bruder, der Robert?	**Er muß in der Küche helfen.**

7

Nimm die Liste, die du für Übung 6 gemacht hast, in die Hand, und berichte vor der Klasse, welche Arbeiten die Schüler von Übung 5 machen müssen! Fang mit den Gartenarbeiten an!

> **Schon bekannt**
> **Ein wenig Grammatik**
> To review the forms of **müssen**,
> see the Grammar Summary.

8 Basti sagt, er hat so viel zu tun!

Christiane ruft Basti an. Sie möchte irgendwohin gehen, vielleicht ins Kino. Aber der Basti kann heute nicht mitgehen. Er sagt, er hat heute so viel zu tun. Was muß er alles machen? — Such dir einen Partner und spielt die Rollen von Christiane und Basti!

ins Kino	zu (Monika)
ins Café Fröhlich	
ins Kaufhaus	in die Stadt

WORTSCHATZ

Things to do around the house

putzen   *to clean*
in der Küche helfen   *to help in the kitchen*
die Garage aufräumen   *to clean the garage*
das Auto polieren   *to polish the car*
den Müll wegtragen   *to take out the garbage*
Staub wischen   *to dust*
die Wäsche waschen   *to wash clothes*
die Wäsche trocknen   *to dry clothes*
die Wäsche bügeln   *to iron clothes*

9 Was macht der Basti? Und die anderen?

Lies, was Sebastian sagt, und beantworte die Fragen!

> Ach, wie schön das Leben ist! Ich kann faulenzen, und die anderen müssen arbeiten!

1. Was macht Sebastian? Warum?
2. Warum kann der Basti faulenzen?
3. Was müssen seine Geschwister und sein Vater tun?

1. Faulenzen; Opa hat nichts für ihn zu tun.   2. Er hat mit Robert getauscht.   3. Fenster putzen, Tisch abräumen; Staub saugen.

10 Was mußt du zu Hause alles tun?

Mach eine Liste von Arbeiten, die du zu Hause machen mußt! Erzähle dann deiner Klasse, was du alles machen mußt!

11 Hör gut zu!

You will hear four brief conversations. In each one, someone is being invited somewhere. Determine who accepts and who declines the invitation.

For answers, see listening script on TE Interleaf.

SO SAGT MAN DAS!

Schon bekannt

Extending and responding to an invitation

When extending an invitation, you might say:

Ich gehe heute abend ins Kino. Kommst du mit?

When accepting you might say:

Ja, gern!
Ich gehe gern mit!

Na, klar!

When declining you might say:

Das geht nicht.
Das geht leider nicht, weil (ich so viele Hausaufgaben hab'.)
Ich kann leider nicht, denn (ich muß in die Stadt.)

12 Wohin gehst du?

Schreib zwei Orte auf, wo du heute hingehen möchtest! Rechts im Kasten stehen ein
paar Ideen.

Answers may vary. E. g.: **Ich möchte heute gern ins Kino gehen.**

ins Kino   zum Tennisplatz

in die Disko   in ein Café

in ein Konzert

ins Museum   ins
                    Einkaufszentrum

ins Schwimmbad

13 Kommst du mit?

Such dir einen Partner! Lade ihn ein! Dein
Partner geht mit oder nicht.

a. Wenn dein Partner mitgeht, muß er
   einen Grund angeben.
b. Wenn dein Partner nicht mitgeht, muß
   er drei Gründe angeben. Er muß sagen,
   was er zuerst tun muß, dann und danach!

14 Für mein Notizbuch

Mach einen Stundenplan für jeden Nachmittag in der Woche und für das ganze Wochenende! Trag ein, was du wirklich an jedem Tag und zu welcher Zeit tust!

	Montag	Dienstag	Mittwoch	Donnerstag
14–15	–	–		
15–16	Klavier			
16–17	–	Rasenmähen		
17–18	Tennis	Hausaufgaben		
18–19	Küchend.	Fußball		
19–20				

Wann geht's?

Geht's am Montag?

Geht's zwischen 17 und 18 Uhr?

Geht's am Montag?

15 Wann geht's?

Du möchtest nächste Woche an irgendeinem Tag etwas unternehmen, aber nicht allein. Du
möchtest, daß ein Klassenkamerad oder eine Klassenkameradin mitgeht. — Such dir also
einen Partner! Nimm dein Notizbuch zur
Hand und frag deinen Partner, wann er
mitkommen kann! Wenn es nicht geht, muß
dein Partner einen Grund angeben. Tauscht
dann die Rollen aus!

> **Schon bekannt**
> **Ein wenig _Grammatik_**
>
> The interrogative **warum?** asks for
> reasons. When giving reasons the
> conjunctions **weil** or **denn** can be
> used. For word order after **weil** and
> **denn**, see the Grammar Summary.

16 Wann geht's jetzt?

Wiederhol Übung 15 noch einmal! Jetzt
mußt du aber deine Ausreden mit einem
weil-Satz begründen.

E.g.: **..., weil ein neuer Film läuft.**

17 Wie oft mußt du helfen?

Such dir eine Partnerin! Frag sie, wie oft sie bestimmte Tätigkeiten machen muß! Sie sagt es dir. Tauscht dann die Rollen! — Im Kasten stehen einige „wie oft" Antworten.

> einmal
> zweimal
> in der Woche
> im Monat
> am Tag

> oft
> nie
> manchmal
> jeden Tag

> Staub saugen
>
> den Großeltern helfen
>
> den Tisch decken
>
> den Rasen mähen
>
> Staub wischen
>
> einkaufen gehen
>
> die Katze füttern
>
> das Geschirr spülen

18 Hör gut zu!

Drei Schüler beantworten die Frage: Sag mal, wie kann ich dir helfen, oder was kann ich für dich tun? — Schreib auf, was jeder Schüler tun kann und für wen!

For answers, see listening script on TE Interleaf.

SO SAGT MAN DAS !

Schon bekannt

Offering help and telling what to do

When someone wants to help you, he or she might ask:

Kann ich etwas für dich tun?
Was kann ich für dich tun?
Für wen kann ich etwas tun?

Your response might be:

Ja, du kannst in der Küche helfen.
Du kannst für mich Staub saugen.
Du kannst für die Oma einkaufen gehen.

---

19 Sätze bauen

Wie viele Sätze kannst du bauen? Für wen kannst du etwas tun?

> Schon bekannt
> ### Ein wenig *G*rammatik
> For the forms of **können**, see the Grammar Summary.

Wer?

> ihr
> du
> ich
> wir
> Basti

> können
> könnt
> kann
> kannst

Für wen?

> Opa
> Oma
> Eltern
> mich
> Christiane

Was?

> einkaufen gehen
> Staub wischen
> Müll wegtragen
> Tisch decken
> Geschirr spülen
> Fenster putzen
> Wäsche bügeln

Various possibilities.
E.g.: **Basti kann für den Opa Staub wischen.**

20 Alle möchten helfen.

Setzt euch in Gruppen von vier oder fünf Personen zusammen! Einer von euch hat sehr viel zu tun, und ihr anderen fragt, was ihr für diese Person tun könnt. Hier sind ein paar Ideen:

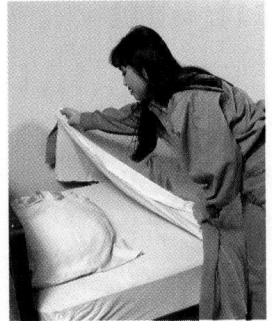   

a. Kann ich für dich das Bett machen? b. ... die Klamotten aufräumen? c. ... das Geschirr spülen? d. ... die Blumen gießen?

21 Was könnt ihr für andere tun?

Bildet eine neue Gruppe von vier oder fünf Personen! Jeder fragt einmal, einer antwortet! Die Frage ist: „Was tun wir für andere?" — Tauscht dann die Rollen aus!

Ich geh' für meine Mutter einkaufen.

Für wen?

für dich? für deine Kusine? für deine Oma? für euch? Opa?

Schon bekannt

Ein wenig *Grammatik*

For the accusative forms of the personal pronouns and of the possessives, see the Grammar Summary.

22 Viel zu tun!

Frag deine Partnerin, was sie für andere Leute tut! Sie muß dir drei Dinge nennen und sagen, wann sie etwas für andere tut und warum. — Tauscht dann die Rollen aus!

Wann?

einmal im Monat

einmal in der Woche

am Montag

am Dienstag

nach der Schule

nach den Hausaufgaben

Warum?

hat keine Zeit

arbeitet den ganzen Tag

kann das nicht mehr tun

ist schon sehr alt

23 Für mein Notizbuch

Schreib in dein Notizbuch, was du für andere Leute tust und warum!

Macht Schule Spaß?

LESETRICK

Using context to derive meaning. You can often make an intelligent guess about the meaning of new words by looking at the context (the surrounding words). Read the following sentence. **Im Restaurant schmeckt das Essen köstlich, nicht wie das Essen im Café, das schmeckt scheußlich. Köstlich** is probably a new word to you. Notice it is describing the food at a restaurant. Reading on, you find the speaker says it doesn't taste like the food at the café, which is described as **scheußlich.** Any adjective which means the opposite of **scheußlich** would be a good guess for the meaning of **köstlich,** which means *tasty.*

Getting Started

1. Use the prereading strategies you reviewed in Chapter 1 to find out what kind of text this is and what it is about. Try to state in your own words (in German) the two-part question that is the focus of the article.

2. Together with your classmates brainstorm for words and phrases that you know in German which you might expect to find in the student responses.

3. Now skim the interviews and note whether each student mentions what he or she likes, dislikes, or if he or she mentions both. Write each student's name under the correct heading: MENTIONS LIKES, MENTIONS DISLIKES, MENTIONS BOTH.

5. **Musikraum;** to turn up the volume
6. drive home

Eltern - UMFRAGE

Das Pausenklingeln ist die schönste Musik!

*Was Schülern an der Schule gefällt und mißfällt — das zeigt die neue **ELTERN**-Umfrage*

*P*rima ist der Musikraum unserer Schule, weil man dort die Stereo-Anlage auf 100 db aufdrehen kann.

Tanja, Gymnasiastin, 14 Jahre

*I*m Schulbus bekommen wir immer viel Spaß. Besonders die Heimfahrt ist gut. Da ist man froh, daß wieder so ein doofer Schultag vorüber ist und ein freier Nachmittag beginnt.

Rolf, Realschüler, 12 Jahre

*S*chön sind nur die Ferien. Morgens wacht man auf und denkt: Schule und Lehrer, gibt es die überhaupt noch?

Eva, Realschülerin, 14 Jahre

*D*as Schönste: daß man in der Pause so laut sein darf, wie man will, und sich mit seinen Freunden ausquatschen kann. Das Mieseste: im Unterricht stundenlang still sein müssen, nur antworten, aber sich nicht unterhalten dürfen.

Klaus, Realschüler, 13 Jahre

*E*s geht nichts über einen fröhlichen, lachenden Lehrer, der nur das Gute für seine Schüler will. Wir haben Herrn Jansen. Wenn er in die Klasse kommt, lacht er gleich. Er hat immer Verständnis, wenn einer einen Fehler macht. Strafe ist für ihn ein Fremdwort.

Christa, Realschülerin, 13 Jahre

M eine Mutter macht mir immer ein Super-Pausenbrot. Zum Beispiel ein Dreikörnerbrot mit Zungenwurst und ganz zarten Gurkenscheiben darunter. Das schmeckt so gut, daß ich den sonstigen Mist in der Schule vergesse.

Bernd, Grundschüler, 10 Jahre

D as Beste an der Schule ist, daß man morgens etwas zu tun hat. Sonst müßte man zu Hause bei der Hausarbeit helfen. Das wäre noch schlimmer.

Volker, Realschüler, 13 Jahre

A m besten: die Getränkeautomaten. Am schlechtesten: das Diktatschreiben.

Werner, Grundschüler, 9 Jahre

F ür mich könnte der ganze Lehrplan nur aus Sport bestehen: Badminton, Handball, Fußball, Schwimmen, Turnen, Leichtathletik. Beim Sport fühle ich mich gut. Das Schwitzen dabei ist sogar gesund. Das Schwitzen bei einer Klassenarbeit dagegen macht krank.

Tim, Gymnasiast, 14 Jahre

A m besten ist Biologie, weil man da so viel über Tiere und Pflanzen erfährt. Am schlechtesten ist Mathematik, weil man da so scharf denken muß, nichts versteht und sich so leicht vertut.

Dieter, Gymnasiast, 14 Jahre

D as Schlimmste ist für mich der Müllhaufen auf dem Schulhof, wenn viele Mitschüler ihren ganzen Dreck abladen: Dosen von Joghurt und Pudding, Papier von Schokolade und Tüteneis.

Sara, Realschülerin, 14 Jahre

S aumäßig ist die Luft in unserem Klassenzimmer. Es riecht immer nach faulen Eiern, nach abgestandener Buttermilch oder alten Pantoffeln. Schön ist, wenn unsere Deutschlehrerin reinkommt und einen herrlichen Duft verbreitet. Sie steht nämlich auf Chanel.™

Nicole, Realschülerin, 14 Jahre

4. For those who mention both likes and dislikes, find out which sentence(s) expresses the negative and which the positive aspects of school. Cognates and words you already know should give you enough information.

A Closer Look

5. What does Tanja like best at school? Notice she says one can do something with the stereo. What might **aufdrehen** mean?

6. Rolf mentions riding the schoolbus and says the **Heimfahrt** is especially good. He can either be referring to the ride to school or home again. Read the next sentence and try to determine the meaning of **Heimfahrt**.

7. Read the interviews more closely and use context and the chart you made to help you determine the meaning of the following words:

Klaus: **ausquatschen**   to talk one's heart out
Christa: **Verständnis**   understanding
Völker: **Hausarbeit**   housework
Tim: **Schwitzen**   sweating
Dieter: **Pflanzen**   plants

8. During **Austauschwoche** a group of Austrian students will be paired up with the students interviewed here. You've been given information about the Austrian students, and you must pair each person below with one of the students interviewed.

BEATE: very athletic   Tim
HANS: an understanding   Christa   teacher is the best thing
ULRIKE: dislikes doing housework   Volker
MARIO: interested in zoology,   Dieter   botany.
NORBERT: enjoys talking with   Klaus   friends
SONJA: likes to listen to loud   Tanja   music

ZWEITE STUFE

Asking and telling what to do; telling that you need something else; telling where you were and what you bought

24 Hör gut zu!

Zwei Schüler haben Küchendienst. Sie sagen, was sie heute einkaufen müssen und wo sie alles kaufen! For answers, see listening script on TE Interleaf.

Bausinger

SUPERANGEBOT:

Trauben blau, Kl.I, 1 kg	**1,90**
Erdbeeren aus Italien, 250g	**1,49**
Himbeeren 200g Schale	**2,99**
Äpfel Jonathan, 1kg	**2,98**
Bananen 1kg	**2,29**
Hackfleisch täglich frisch!, 100g	**1,99**
Aufschnitt Spitzenqualität!, 100g	**1,89**
Hähnchen 1kg	**7,99**
Schweinebraten ohne Knochen, 1 kg	**8,99**

STARK IM PREIS!

Kartoffeln 3 kg-Beutel	**2,39**
Tomaten aus Holland 500g	**1,99**
Kopfsalat Klasse I Stück	**-,99**
Radieschen Bund	**-,80**
Zwiebeln Klasse II 1kg	**-,79**

Tilsiter deutscher Schnittkäse 100g	**1,39**
Frische Milch 3,8% Fett 1 Liter	**1,49**
Markenbutter Kl. I, aus dem Allgäu 250g	**1,99**
Sahnejoghurt verschiedene Sorten 150 g-Becher	**-,69**
Diätmargarine 250 g-Becher	**-,99**

Unsere Öffnungszeiten:

Mo, Di, Mi, Fr	9.00—12.30 14.00—18.30	Samstag	8.30—13.00
Donnerstag	9.00—12.30 14.00—20.30	langer Samstag	8.30—16.00
		Für Druckfehler keine Haftung!	

WORTSCHATZ

Obst und Gemüse

    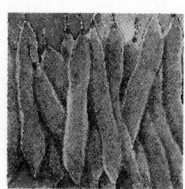 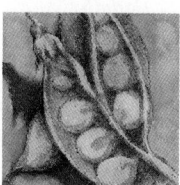

Bananen	Zwetschgen	Pfirsiche	Spinat	grüne Bohnen	Erbsen

40 *vierzig*   KAPITEL 2   Bastis Plan

25 Was gibt's im Angebot?

Such dir einen Partner! Du bewunderst verschiedene Angebote bei Bausinger. Dein Partner stimmt zu und sagt, daß die Ware auch gar nicht so teuer ist. Tauscht dann die Rollen aus!

BEISPIEL — **Die Pfirsiche sehen lecker aus!**
— **Stimmt! Und sie sind sehr preiswert. Nur zwei zwanzig das halbe Kilo!**

SO SAGT MAN DAS!

Schon bekannt

Asking and telling what to do

Someone who wants to help you might ask:

Was soll ich jetzt tun?
Wo soll ich das Brot kaufen?

Your response might be:

Geh bitte für mich einkaufen!
Kauf es doch beim Bäcker!

---

26 Was soll ich kaufen?

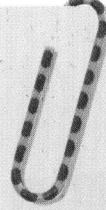

Du mußt einkaufen gehen. Deine Mutter gibt dir einen Einkaufszettel. Du liest, was du alles kaufen sollst, und du willst wissen, wo du alles kaufen sollst. — Such dir einen Partner und spielt diese Rollen! Tauscht dann die Rollen aus!

> 1/2 Pfd. Butter
> 1 kg Trauben
> 250 g Erdbeeren
> 100 g Aufschnitt
> 1 kg Zwiebeln
> 1 Liter Milch

> Sag mal, wo soll ich die Trauben kaufen? Im Supermarkt?

> Nein, kauf sie lieber im Obstladen!

Schon bekannt
Ein wenig Grammatik

For the forms of **sollen** and the **du**-commands, see the Grammar Summary.

Wo?

beim Bäcker?
im Supermarkt?
im Obst- und Gemüseladen?
beim Metzger?

27 Hör gut zu!

Der Gemüsemann kommt auch heute noch mit seinem Kombi in viele Wohngegenden und ruft mit lauter Stimme seine Ware und die Preise aus. — Schreib fünf Artikel auf, die du kaufen willst! For answers, see listening script on TE Interleaf.

SO SAGT MAN DAS!

Schon bekannt

Telling that you need something else

To ask if someone needs something else, you might ask:

Was bekommen Sie noch?

Haben Sie noch einen Wunsch?
Sonst noch etwas?

Your response might be:

Ein Kilo Tomaten, und dann bekomme ich noch eine Gurke.
Nein, danke!
Danke, das ist alles.

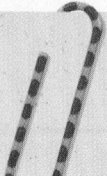

28 Sonst noch etwas?

Such dir einen Partner! Dein Partner spielt den Gemüsemann oder die Gemüsefrau, und du kaufst die Artikel, die du auf den Zettel geschrieben hast. Tauscht dann die Rollen aus!

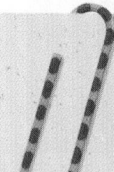

29 Hör gut zu!

Vier Schüler sagen, was sie gekauft haben, in welchen Geschäften sie waren und warum sie dort eingekauft haben. Mach dir Notizen!

a. Schreib auf, in welchen Geschäften jeder war!
b. Schreib auf, warum sie dort eingekauft haben!
For answers, see listening script on TE Interleaf.

SO SAGT MAN DAS!

Schon bekannt

Telling where you were and what you bought

To ask a friend where he was and what he did, you might ask:

Wo warst du?
Was hast du im Supermarkt gekauft?
Warst du auch beim Metzger?

His response might be:

Beim Bäcker und im Supermarkt.

Die Milch und die Eier.
Ja, dort hab' ich das Fleisch gekauft.

---

30 Das Angebot ist groß!

Du kommst vom Einkaufen zurück und hast die Lebensmittel, die unten abgebildet sind, gekauft. Wo warst du? Warst du im Supermarkt? Im Obst- und Gemüseladen? Beim Metzger? Deine Mutter will es wissen. Wenn du die Artikel woanders gekauft hast, dann sag warum! — Such dir einen Partner und spielt diese Rollen!

MUTTER **Wo hast du das Brot gekauft? Im Supermarkt?**

DU **Nein, ich war beim Bäcker.**

MUTTER **Du warst beim Bäcker?**

DU **Dort ist das Brot immer frisch!**

> ### Schon bekannt
> ### Ein wenig *G*rammatik
>
> For the past tense forms of **sein,** the **war**-forms, see the Grammar Summary.

Warum?

Dort ist alles nicht so teuer!

Dort ist (das Brot) immer frisch!

Dort muß ich nicht lange warten.

Die Verkäufer sind so nett.

Der (Bäcker) ist nicht so weit.

Was nimmst du mit, wenn du irgendwo eingeladen bist?

We asked people from around Germany what they bring with them when they are invited somewhere. First listen to the interviews, then read the texts.

Sandra, *Stuttgart*

„Also, wenn ich zu 'ner Geburtstagsfete eingeladen bin, dann nehm' ich meistens ein Geschenk mit, zum Beispiel 'ne CD, also gerade von der Lieblingsgruppe, oder 'ne Single einfach, oder wenn die Person halt gerne was liest, dann ein Buch. Wenn's 'ne ganz normale Party ist, dann nehmen wir irgendwas zum Knabbern, oder 'nen Salat, oder irgendwelche Snacks halt mit."

Martina, *München*

„Also, wenn ich zu 'ner Fete eingeladen bin und ein Geschenk mitbringe, dann richte ich mich eigentlich immer nach dem Gastgeber und versuche dann, also eigentlich schon so seinem ... Dings ... zu entsprechen, daß das für ihn was Schönes ist. Also nicht nur 'nen Blumenstrauß oder 'ne Flasche Wein, das sollte dann schon irgendwie passen."

Julia, *Hamburg*

„Also, wenn es ein Geburtstag ist, dann überlege ich mir ein Geschenk, was zu der Person paßt. Und wenn es einfach so 'ne Einladung ist zu 'ner Feier, dann nehm' ich eigentlich gar nichts mit, also nur für mich, wenn ich etwas zum Mitnehmen brauche, oder so. Also, sonst eigentlich nur zum Geburtstag oder zu irgendeinem Anlaß."

A. 1. Skim over the interviews again and find as many words as you can that are mentioned as possible gifts. Julia and Sandra mention two different types of occasions that would influence what they would bring. What are the two kinds of occasions? (*Hint:* they state under what conditions they would bring certain gifts. Do you remember the conjunction that signals a condition?) What gifts would they bring for each kind of occasion?

2. Although social customs are always changing, many long-held traditions are still important in German-speaking countries today, especially those concerning social courtesies. In general, when one is invited to someone's home, it is customary to bring flowers for the host or hostess. Read Martina's interview again. What does she say she would not give as a present? Why does she say this? How well do you think she knows the people she has in mind? 1. Gifts are underlined in interviews. Occasions: **Geburtstag u. normale Party/Fete/Feier** 2. **Blumenstrauß oder Flasche Wein.** She knows people well enough to bring a personalized gift.

B. Think about how you would answer the interview question. Are there any particular customs where you live or where your family is from? How do these customs compare to German customs?

DRITTE STUFE

Discussing gift ideas; expressing likes and dislikes; expressing likes, preferences, and favorites; saying you do or don't want more

31 Hör gut zu!

Vier Schüler brauchen Geschenke. Sie sagen, was sie schenken möchten und wem. Mach dir Notizen! Schreib auf, was für ein Geschenk jeder Schüler kauft und wem er es schenkt!

For answers, see listening script on TE Interleaf.

WORTSCHATZ

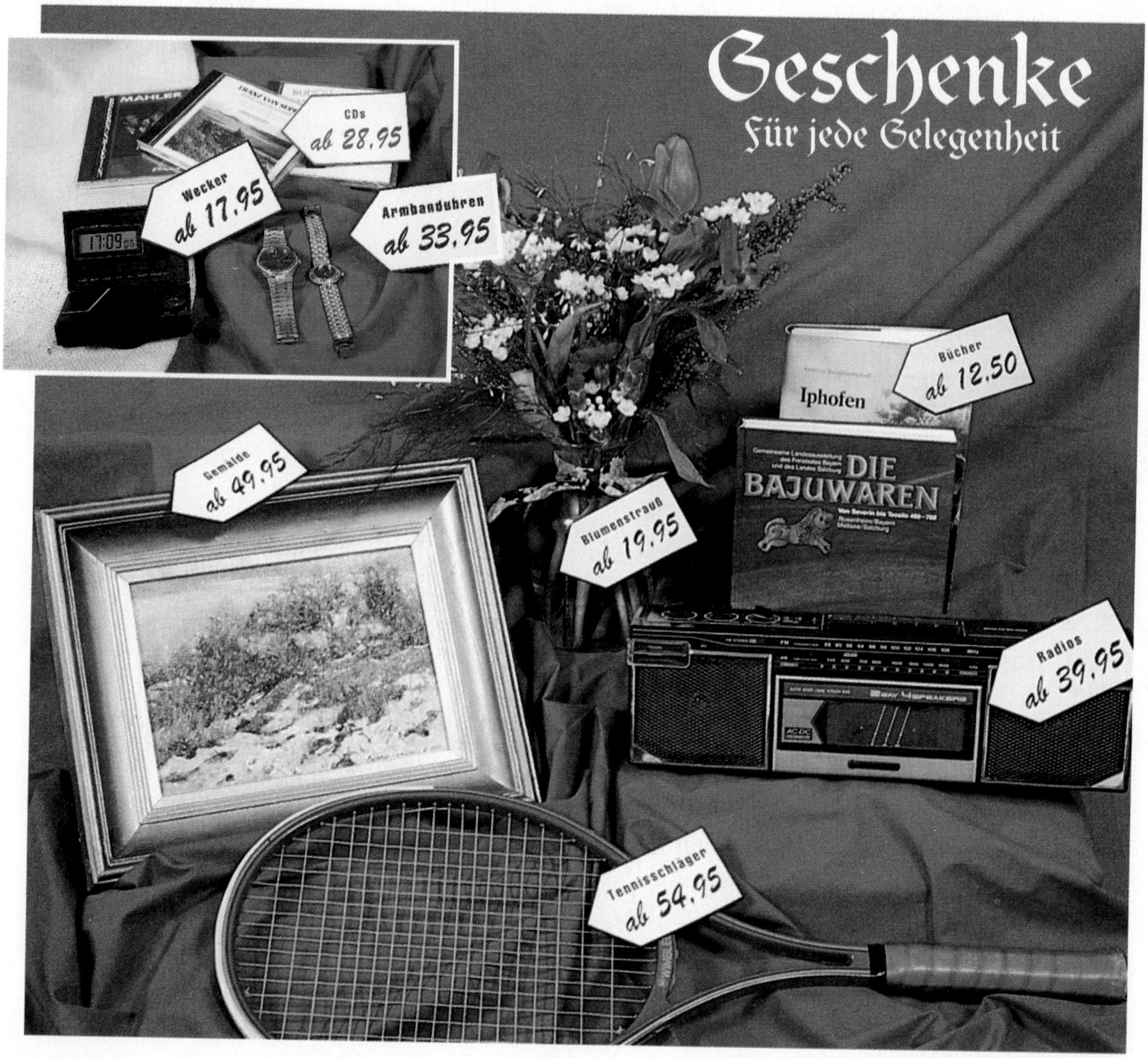
Geschenke
Für jede Gelegenheit
MAHLER
CDs
ab 28.95
Wecker
ab 17.95
Armbanduhren
ab 33.95
Bücher
ab 12.50
Iphofen
DIE BAJUWAREN
Gemälde
ab 49.95
Blumenstrauß
ab 19.95
Radios
ab 39.95
Tennisschläger
ab 54.95

...IAN DAS!

...ideas

...meone is giving
...t ask:

...du deiner Mutter
...stag?

...deinem Vater?
...den Blumenstrauß?
...u deinem Opa?

Your response might be:
Ich schenke **ihr** Schokolade.

Ich kauf' **ihm** ein Gemälde.
Meiner Oma.
Ich weiß noch nicht. Hast du eine
Idee?

32 Wer? Wem? Was?

Wie viele Sätze kannst du bauen?

wer?

meine Schwester
ich
mein Bruder
wir

schenken
kaufen
geben

wem?

meine Mutter
mein Freund
meine Oma
meine Freundin
mein Vater
meine Kusine
mein Opa

was?

Buch
Tennisschläger
Wecker
Klamotten
Ring aus Silber
Blumenstrauß
Armbanduhr
Gemälde

Various possibilities.
E.g.: **Ich gebe meinem Opa ein Buch.**

33 Was schenkst du?

Schreibe deine eigene Geschenkliste! Wem
schenkst du was? — Dann such dir einen
Partner! Frag ihn, was er schenkt und
wem! Tauscht dann die Rollen aus!

Schon bekannt
Ein wenig *G*rammatik
For the dative forms of **mein** and
dein, and the dative personal pronouns, see the Grammar Sum-
mary.

34 Hör gut zu!

Drei Schüler sagen, was sie mögen und
was sie nicht mögen. Mach dir Notizen!
For answers, see listening script on TE Interleaf.

SO SAGT MAN DAS!

Expressing likes and dislikes

You might ask someone what he or she
likes or does not like by saying:
Was für Geschenke **magst du?**

Was **magst du nicht?**
Magst du Horrorfilme?

His or her response might be:
Ich **mag** alles: Bücher, CDs,
Klamotten und so.
Pralinen **mag** ich **nicht.**
Und wie!

35 Eine Umfrage in der Klasse

Setzt euch in einer großen Gruppe zusammen! Das Thema lautet: „Wer mag was für Geschenke?"

a. Einer von euch fragt alle anderen Mitschüler, und ein anderer schreibt das Ergebnis auf.

b. Ein dritter liest dann das Ergebnis der Klasse vor. Zum Beispiel: Drei mögen ...

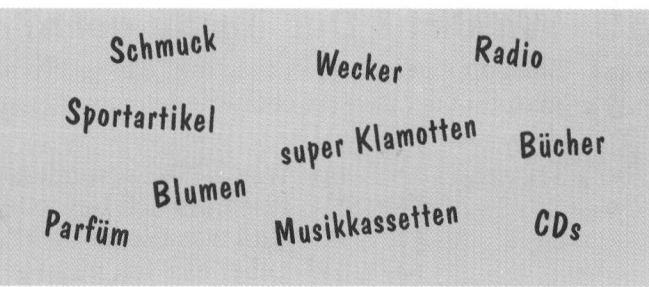

Schmuck Wecker Radio
Sportartikel super Klamotten Bücher
Blumen
Parfüm Musikkassetten CDs

Schon bekannt
Ein wenig *G*rammatik
For the forms of **mögen**, see the Grammar Summary.

36 Was magst du?

Such dir einen Partner! Frag ihn, was er alles mag und warum! Er muß einen Grund angeben.

BEISPIEL

DU **Was magst du zum Geburtstag?**

PARTNER **Eine CD mit Country, denn das hör' ich gern. Oder ja, ein Buch, weil ich gern lese und Bücher sammle.**

37 Hör gut zu!

Vier Schüler sagen, was sie lieber mögen und was sie am liebsten mögen. Mach dir Notizen! Vergleiche dann deine Notizen mit den Notizen von deinem Partner!

For answers, see listening script on TE Interleaf.

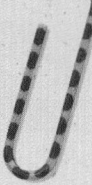

SO SAGT MAN DAS!

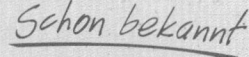
Schon bekannt

Expressing likes, preferences, and favorites

To find out what someone likes or prefers, you might ask:

Was für Filme **siehst** du **gern?**

Magst du zum Geburtstag **lieber** eine CD oder ein Buch?

Welche CDs **magst** du **am liebsten?**

The response might be:

Ich **sehe gern** Actionfilme.

Lieber ein Buch.

Am liebsten mag ich die CDs von Matthias Reim.

38 Was magst du gern? Nicht gern?

Schreib auf eine Liste die Dinge, die du gern und nicht gern ißt oder trinkst! Dann ordne die einzelnen Posten (items) auf deiner Liste! Was steht ganz oben? Was steht ganz unten?

Cola Kaffee Kuchen
Pizza Fleisch Pralinen
Fisch Milch Äpfel
Leber Spinat Brokkoli

39 Wirklich? Das ißt du gern?

Such dir einen Partner! Frag ihn, was er besonders gern ißt oder trinkt und was er nicht gern ißt oder trinkt! Gebrauche in deinen Fragen die Wörter im Kasten rechts! — Tauscht dann die Rollen aus!

BEISPIEL	DU	**Was ißt du besonders gern?**
	PARTNER	**Fisch ess' ich besonders gern.**
	DU	**Und was ißt du nicht gern?**
	PARTNER	**Leber ess' ich nicht gern.**

furchtbar gern
besonders gern
sehr gern
—— gern ——
nicht gern
gar nicht gern
überhaupt nicht gern

40 Hör gut zu!

Vier Schüler sind beim Essen. Wer mag mehr? Wer mag nichts mehr? Welche Gründe geben sie an? Mach dir Notizen!

For answers, see listening script on TE Interleaf.

Schon bekannt

SO SAGT MAN DAS!

Saying you do or don't want more

Here's how someone might ask you if you want more of something:

Möchtest du **noch etwas?**

Und du? Auch **noch eine Semmel?**
Magst du **noch einen Saft?**

Your response might be:

Ja, bitte! Ich nehme **noch eine Semmel!**
Nein, danke! **Keine Semmel mehr.**
Nein, **keinen Saft mehr.** Ich habe **keinen Durst mehr.**

Schon bekannt
Ein wenig *G*rammatik

The phrase **noch ein** means *another.* For the forms of **ein** and **kein,** used to "negate" nouns, see the Grammar Summary.

Semmeln

Eis

Cappuccino

Bratwurst

Saft

Leberkäs

Brezel

Kartoffelsalat

Answers may vary. E.g.: **Magst du noch eine Limo? - Ja, ich nehme noch eine Limo!**

41 Noch etwas?

Du sitzt mit deinem Freund oder mit deiner Freundin in einem Café. Mag er oder mag sie noch etwas zu essen oder zu trinken? Frag mal! — Tauscht dann die Rollen aus!

42 Ein kurzer Besuch in München

Nach einer Fahrt mit dem Nachtzug bist du mit deiner Deutschklasse eben in München angekommen. Ihr habt ein großes Programm vor! Ihr wollt euch die Innenstadt ansehen und vielleicht auch ein Museum besuchen. Aber alle haben erst mal großen Hunger, und ihr wollt zuerst etwas essen. Ihr geht an einen Imbißstand und lest die Anschlagtafeln. Such dir einen Partner, und schreib mit ihm ein Gespräch auf, das folgendes enthalten muß!

1. was es zu essen und zu trinken gibt
2. was ihr mögt und was ihr nicht mögt
3. was euch zu teuer ist
4. was ihr bestellt
5. wie alles schmeckt
6. wer noch etwas bestellen will

43

ROLLENSPIEL

Such dir zwei Partner und spielt die folgende Szene! Entwerft zuerst einen Speisezettel für eine Imbißstube! Benützt dazu ein großes Stück festes Papier! Danach übernimmt einer die Rolle vom Verkäufer, die beiden anderen die Rollen von zwei Kunden.

a. Die Kunden lesen den Speisezettel und unterhalten sich darüber. Dann bestellt jeder etwas. Frag, was jedes Gericht kostet, und ob du von einem noch etwas haben kannst.

b. Beim Essen unterhaltet ihr euch darüber, wie alles schmeckt, ob ihr mehr von einem Gericht haben oder lieber noch etwas anderes essen wollt.

c. Danach sprecht ihr über euere Pläne, denn ihr wollt ja noch viel sehen. Was müßt ihr noch alles tun, bevor ihr München wieder verlassen müßt?

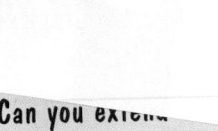

1 How would you ask a friend what he or she has to do at home? How would your friend say he or she has to help in the kitchen, wash clothes, and take out the garbage? 1. E.g.: **Was mußt du heute zu Hause tun? - Ich muß in der Küche helfen, die Wäsche waschen und den Müll wegtragen.**

2 How would you tell someone you are going to the movies, and ask that person if he or she is coming along? How would that person

    a. accept your invitation?

    b. decline your invitation and give a reason? 2. E.g.: **Ich gehe heute ins Kino. Kommst du mit? - a. Ja, gern.; b. Das geht leider nicht, weil ich zu Hause helfen muß.**

3 How would you ask your mother what you can do for her? How would she say you can polish her car and go grocery shopping? 3. E.g.: **Was kann ich für dich tun? - Du kannst für mich das Auto polieren und einkaufen gehen.**

4 How would you ask your grandmother where you are supposed to buy the bread? How would she tell you to buy it at the baker's? 4. E.g.: **Wo soll ich das Brot kaufen? - Kauf es doch beim Bäcker!**

5 How would a salesperson ask you if you want something else? How would you say

    a. that you need one kilo of plums? **b.** that "that will be it"? 5. E.g.: **Sonst noch was? - a. Ja, ich bekomme noch ein Kilo Pflaumen.; b. Danke, das ist alles.**

6 How would your grandmother ask you where you were and what you bought there? How would you answer that you bought meat at the butcher's and beans and peaches at the supermarket? 6. E.g.: **Wo warst du? - Ich habe das Fleisch beim Metzger gekauft und die Bohnen und Pfirsiche im Supermarkt.**

7 How would you ask a friend what he or she is giving

    a. his father? **b.** her mother? **c.** his grandparents? 7. E.g.: **a. Was schenkst du deinem Vater?; b. Was kaufst du deiner Mutter?; c. Was gibst du deinen Großeltern?**

8 How would your friend answer that she is giving

    a. a radio to her father? 8. E.g.: **a. Ich schenke meinem Vater ein Radio.; b. Ich kaufe meiner Mutter einen Ring aus Silber.; c. Ich schenke meinen Großeltern Tennisschläger.**

    b. a silver ring to her mother?

    c. tennis rackets to her grandparents?

9 How would you ask someone what kind of movies he or she likes? How would that person say he or she likes action movies but doesn't like horror movies? 9. E.g.: **Was für Filme siehst du gern? - Ich sehe gern Actionfilme, aber Horrorfilme mag ich nicht.**

10 How would you say you like reading books but you like listening to CDs the best? 10. E.g.: **Ich lese gerne Bücher, aber am liebsten höre ich CDs.**

11. E.g.: **Möchtest du noch eine Banane? - a. Ja, ich möchte noch eine Banane!; b. Nein danke! Keine Banane mehr.**

11 How would you ask a friend if he or she wants another banana? How would your friend answer that he or she

    a. wants another one? **b.** doesn't want another one?

Can you extend and respond to an invitation? (p. 34)

Can you offer help and tell what to do? (p. 36)
Can you ask and tell what to do? (p. 41)

Can you tell that you need something else? (p. 42)

Can you tell where you were and what you bought? (p. 42)

Can you discuss gift ideas? (p. 46)

Can you express likes and dislikes? (p. 46)

Can you express likes, preferences, and favorites? (p. 47)
Can you say you do or don't want more? (p. 48)

ERSTE STUFE
THINGS TO DO AROUND THE HOUSE

putzen   *to clean*
in der Küche helfen   *to help in the kitchen*
die Garage aufräumen   *to clean the garage*

das Auto polieren   *to polish the car*
den Müll wegtragen   *to take out the garbage*
Staub wischen   *to dust*
die Wäsche waschen   *to wash clothes*

die Wäsche trocknen   *to dry clothes*
die Wäsche bügeln   *to iron clothes*

ZWEITE STUFE
FOOD ITEMS

die Zwetschge, -n   *plum*
die Banane, -n   *banana*
der Pfirsich, -e   *peach*
die (grüne) Bohne, -n   *(green) bean*

die Erbse, -n   *pea*
der Spinat   *spinach*
die Gurke, -n   *cucumber*

TELLING YOU NEED SOMETHING ELSE

Sonst noch etwas?   *Anything else?*

DRITTE STUFE
GIFT IDEAS

das Gemälde, -   *painting*
der Ring, -e   *ring*
  aus Silber   *made of silver*
  aus Gold   *made of gold*

die Schokolade   *chocolate*
das Radio, -s   *radio*

der Tennisschläger, -   *tennis racket*
der Wecker, -   *alarm clock*

Kapitel 3: Wo warst du in den Ferien?

Los geht's! pp. 54-56	Unser Film- und Fotoclub, *p. 54*			*Video Guide*
	FUNCTIONS	**GRAMMAR**	**CULTURE**	**RE-ENTRY**
Erste Stufe pp. 57-61	Reporting past events, talking about activities, *p. 57*	The conversational past, *p. 58*	Information on Dresden, *p. 61*	• Past participles, *pp. 57, 58* (from **Kap. 10,** I) • Activity vocabulary, *p. 58* (from **Kap. 2/6,** I) • Talking about when you do things, *p. 60* (from **Kap. 4,** I) • Using a schedule to talk about time, *p. 60* (from **Kap. 4,** I) • Sequencing events, *p. 60* (from **Kap. 4,** I)
Zweite Stufe pp. 62-66	Reporting past events, talking about places, *p. 63*	• The past tense of **haben** and **sein**, *p. 64* • The dative case with the prepositions **in** and **an**, *p. 65*	• Information on **Frankfurt am Main,** *p. 62* • Landeskunde: **Was hast du in den letzten Ferien gemacht?** *p. 67*	• Accusative case, *p. 62* (from **Kap. 5,** I) • Past tense of **sein**, *pp. 63, 64* (from **Kap. 8,** I) • The **möchte**-forms, *p. 64* (from **Kap. 3,** I) • **Weil**-clauses, *p. 64* (from **Kap. 8,** I) • City vocabulary, *pp. 65, 66* (from **Kap. 6/9,** I)
Dritte Stufe pp. 68-71	Asking how someone liked something, expressing enthusiasm or disappointment, responding enthusiastically or sympathetically, *p. 68*	• The personal pronouns, dative case, *p. 69* • The definite article, dative plural, *p. 69* • The dative case forms of **ein**, *p. 71*		• Talking about likes and dislikes, *p. 68* (from **Kap. 2/10,** I) • Dative pronouns, *p. 69* (from **Kap. 5/11,** I) • The verb **gefallen**, *p. 69* (from **Kap. 5,** I) • Time expressions, *p. 71* (from **Kap. 7,** I)

Zum Lesen pp. 72-73	In Tirol Reading Strategy: Identifying the main idea and supporting details

Review pp. 74-77	• **Anwendung,** *p. 74* • **Kann ich's wirklich?** *p. 76* • **Wortschatz,** *p. 77*

Assessment Options	**Stufe Quizzes**
	 • *Chapter Resources,* Book 1
	    Erste Stufe, Quiz 3-1
	    Zweite Stufe, Quiz 3-2
	    Dritte Stufe, Quiz 3-3
	 • *Assessment Items, Audiocassette* 7 A
		Kapitel 3 Chapter Test
		 • *Chapter Resources,* Book 1
		 • *Assessment Guide,* Speaking Test
		 • *Assessment Items, Audiocassette* 7 A
		
		 Test Generator, Kapitel 3

Chapter Overview

Video Program **OR**
Expanded Video Program, Videocassette 1

Textbook Audiocassette 2 A

RESOURCES **Print**	RESOURCES **Audiovisual**

Textbook Audiocassette 2 A

Practice and Activity Book
Chapter Resources, Book 1
- Additional Listening Activities 3-1, 3-2................................Additional Listening Activities, Audiocassette 9 A
- Student Response Forms
- Realia 3-1
- Situation Card 3-1
- Teaching Transparency Master 3-1....................................Teaching Transparency 3-1
- Quiz 3-1 ....Assessment Items, Audiocassette 7 A

Textbook Audiocassette 2 A

Practice and Activity Book
Chapter Resources, Book 1
- Communicative Activity 3-1
- Additional Listening Activities 3-3, 3-4................................Additional Listening Activities, Audiocassette 9 A
- Student Response Forms
- Realia 3-2
- Situation Card 3-2
- Quiz 3-2 ....Assessment Items, Audiocassette 7 A

Video Guide..Video Program/Expanded Video Program, Videocassette 1

Textbook Audiocassette 2 A

Practice and Activity Book
Chapter Resources, Book 1
- Communicative Activity 3-2
- Additional Listening Activities 3-5, 3-6................................Additional Listening Activities, Audiocassette 9 A
- Student Response Forms
- Realia 3-3
- Situation Card 3-3
- Teaching Transparency Master 3-2....................................Teaching Transparency 3-2
- Quiz 3-3..Assessment Items, Audiocassette 7 A

Video Guide..Video Program/Expanded Video Program, Videocassette 1

Alternative Assessment
- Performance Assessment
Teacher's Edition
  Erste Stufe, p. 51K
  Zweite Stufe, p. 51N
  Dritte Stufe, p. 51P

- Portfolio Assessment
  Written: **Anwendung**, Activity 3, *Pupil's Edition*, p. 75;
  Assessment Guide, p. 16
  Oral: **Anwendung**, Activity 3, *Pupil's Edition*, p. 75;
  Assessment Guide, p. 16
- **Notizbuch**, *Pupil's Edition*, pp. 60, 65, 71; *Practice and Activity Book*, p. 147

Kapitel 3: Wo warst du in den Ferien?
Textbook Listening Activities Scripts

Erste Stufe
Activity 5, p. 57

JAN Was ich in den Ferien so gemacht habe? Also ich bin mit zwei Freunden nach Südtirol gefahren, mit dem Zug natürlich. Wir haben bei Verwandten von uns auf 'nem Bauernhof gewohnt, mitten in den Bergen. Tagsüber sind wir meistens gewandert und abends dann runter ins Dorf. Da gab es 'ne Disco, da sind wir dann immer zum Tanzen hingegangen. Wir waren die Hälfte der Sommerferien dort, also drei Wochen lang. Die anderen drei Wochen war ich zu Hause und hab' meistens im Jugendzentrum rumgehangen.

ANJA Ja, also ich war mit meiner Volleyballmannschaft im Schwarzwald. Da waren auch andere Mannschaften aus Bayern, und wir haben ein paar Wettbewerbsspiele gemacht, aber nur so zum Spaß. Zweimal sind wir auch nach Freiburg gefahren, alle zusammen mit dem Reisebus. Dort haben wir uns die Stadt angesehen und den Dom, also ich meine das Freiburger Münster. Und dann sind wir fast jeden Tag schwimmen gegangen. In der Nähe von der Jugendherberge gab es nämlich ein riesiges Freibad.

UDO Ich war in den Ferien das erste Mal in Amerika, mit meinen Eltern. Wir sind nach Washington geflogen und haben uns da 'ne ganze Menge angeschaut. Ich war sogar im Weißen Haus und auch im Pentagon! Dann sind wir weiter nach Virginia gefahren mit einem Mietwagen. Wir waren da in einem Hotel am Strand, um ein paar Tage zu relaxen, weil wir den totalen Jet-lag hatten! Ja, und als ich dann wieder zu Hause war, habe ich noch 'ne kurze Radtour mit meiner Freundin gemacht am letzten Wochenende in den Ferien.

JÖRG Wir waren diesmal nicht weg, weil mein Vater zur Zeit arbeitslos ist. Also war ich die ganzen Ferien lang zu Hause. Das war aber nicht schlecht, denn wir haben ziemlich viel im Garten gemacht und einen Fischteich angelegt. Aber nicht nur einfach ein normales Plastikbecken, sondern einen Teich mit Ökosystem, also mit Wasserpflanzen, Insekten, Fröschen und so. Das hat echt Spaß gemacht. Ja, und sonst war ich mit 'nem Klassenkameraden, der auch zu Hause geblieben ist, ab und zu im Kino, oder wir haben uns ein Video ausgeliehen.

Answers to Activity 5
JAN: gewandert; in die Disco gegangen; im Jugendzentrum rumgehangen
ANJA: Volleyball gespielt; die Stadt Freiburg u. den Dom angesehen; schwimmen gegangen
UDO: das Weiße Haus u. Pentagon besichtigt; am Strand relaxt; eine Radtour gemacht
JÖRG: einen Fischteich im Garten angelegt; ins Kino gegangen; ein Video ausgeliehen

Zweite Stufe
Activity 15, p. 63

LISA Ja, also ich war mit meinen Eltern in Lindau am Bodensee. Wir haben den ganzen Tag Wassersport gemacht, also schwimmen, segeln, tauchen und so. War echt super!

EVA Ich bin in Paris gewesen, und hab' so einen Französischkurs mitgemacht. Ich glaub' ich hab' eine ganze Menge neue Vokabeln gelernt, aber eigentlich war ich immer froh, wenn der Unterricht zuende war und wir uns die Stadt ansehen konnten.

KURT Ich bin mit einer Jugendgruppe in Holland gewesen, in so einem kleinen Nest in der Nähe von Rotterdam, direkt am Meer. Wir haben alle auf dem Campingplatz gezeltet. Am letzten Abend haben wir ein riesiges Lagerfeuer gemacht, Lieder gesungen, und ein paar Leute haben Gitarre gespielt. Das hat mir echt gut gefallen.

INGE Ich war in den Ferien zu Hause. Ich bin aus Trier, das liegt an der Mosel. Die Landschaft ist echt toll hier. Jedes Jahr kommen Tausende von Touristen an die Mosel, um hier ihren Urlaub oder die Ferien zu verbringen. Also, warum soll ich irgendwo anders hinfahren?

Answers to Activity 15
LISA: Lindau am Bodensee; EVA: Paris;
KURT: in der Nähe von Rotterdam, in Holland;
INGE: zu Hause in Trier an der Mosel

Dritte Stufe
Activity 25, p. 68

GRETE Mir hat es wahnsinnig gut in den Ferien gefallen. Ich habe so viele neue Leute kennengelernt. Es war echt super!

LUTZ Also, mir hat's leider überhaupt nicht gefallen. Wir hatten die meiste Zeit nur Regen und konnten gar nichts unternehmen. Das war furchtbar!

ELKE Ach, das tut mir leid. Aber bei mir war es fast genauso. Wir haben in den Ferien nur so ein langweiliges Zeug gemacht. Es hat mir nicht besonders gefallen.

UTE Meine Ferien waren phantastisch! Ich war mit einer ganz tollen Jugendgruppe im Schwarzwald. Nächstes Jahr möchte ich auch wieder mit denen zusammen in die Ferien fahren.

ERIK Mir hat es auch ziemlich gut in den Ferien gefallen! Ich habe zwar nichts Besonderes gemacht, nur gefaulenzt, aber das war ja gerade das Gute daran!

Answers to Activity 25
GRETE: gefallen; LUTZ: nicht gefallen; ELKE: nicht gefallen; UTE: gefallen; ERIK: gefallen

Awendung
Activity 5, p. 75

1. In der Nähe gibt es einen großen, modernen Freizeitpark mit einem Schwimmbad, Tennisplätzen und einer Minigolf-Anlage. In der Stadt gibt es mehrere Kinos, ein Schauspielhaus und die Oper. Wer gern wandert, kann raus aufs Land fahren. Dort gibt es mehrere Wanderwege, oder man kann eine Bootstour auf dem See machen.

2. Die Stadt ist ziemlich klein, so ungefähr 50 000 Einwohner. Aber nur etwa 3 Kilometer von hier gibt es ein riesiges Waldgebiet. Und etwas außerhalb liegt der Kaarster See. Ganz in der Nähe von der Stadt sind ein paar Bauernhöfe. Die Felder reichen bis zum Stadtrand.

3. Das größte Hotel der Stadt ist das Seehotel. Es gibt dort über 200 Zimmer, mehrere Konferenzräume, einen großen Speisesaal, ein Schwimmbad und vieles mehr. Es ist fast immer ausgebucht, besonders im Sommer, wenn alle Touristen kommen, um Ferien zu machen.

SCRIPTS

4. Hier in der Stadt gibt es viele Sehenswürdigkeiten. Man kann sich zum Beispiel die
sogenannte Altstadt ansehen. Sie fängt am
Marktplatz an und geht weiter durch die
kleinen Gassen bis hin zur Dominikanerkirche.
Direkt hinter der Kirche ist das Archäologische
Museum, mit Funden, die hier aus der Gegend
stammen. Und wenn man sich für Kunst interessiert, dann muß man sich unbedingt die
Engelskulptur im Rokokostil auf dem
Stadtbrunnen ansehen!

Answers to Activity 5

1. c
2. a
3. d
4. b

Activity 6, p. 75

1. Wir waren zum Camping am Burger See. Das
Wetter war echt toll, und wir haben ein Boot
gemietet. Dann sind wir angeln gewesen. Am
Abend haben wir dann die Fische gegrillt. Es
hat uns wirklich gut gefallen.

2. Wir sind nach Paris geflogen. Es hat das ganze
Wochenende geregnet, und wir haben uns ein
Museum nach dem anderen angesehen. Echt
langweilig. Vom Eiffelturm aus konnte man gar
nichts sehen, es war total nebelig und verreg-
net. Es hat mir überhaupt nicht gefallen.

3. Ich bin zu meiner Tante nach Hamburg gefahren. Schon im Zug habe ich echt nette Leute
kennengelernt. Und wir haben uns dann verab-
redet, zusammen ins Kino zu gehen, uns die
Stadt anzusehen und so. Ich war fast kaum zu
Hause. Meine Tante fand es nicht so gut, aber
mir hat es gefallen.

4. Ich war zum Skilaufen in der Schweiz. Es gab
kaum Schnee, viel zu viel Sonne und steigende
Temperaturen. Ich habe kein einziges Mal
Skilaufen können. Ich war echt sauer. Es hat
mir gar nicht gefallen.

Answers to Activity 6

1. Burger See; gefallen
2. Paris; nicht gefallen
3. Hamburg; gefallen
4. Schweiz; nicht gefallen

Kapitel 3: Wo warst du in den Ferien?
Projects and Games

PROJECT

*In this activity students will describe their dream vacation (**Meine Traumreise**). It should be started after completion of the **Zum Lesen** section of this chapter. Students will create a poster which includes visual and written information. They will also give a brief oral presentation.*

Materials Students may need brochures from travel agencies, maps, magazine ads, scissors, poster board, paper, and glue or tape.

Suggested Sequence

1. Students choose the destination of their dream vacation.
2. Students look for sources and materials. (Examples: library books, old magazines, travel agency brochures)
3. Once all materials have been gathered, each student should make an outline of the information and realia he or she wants to include in the report.
4. Students begin the layout of their poster, leaving space for the paper they write about their **Traumreise**. The realia and other visuals should support and illustrate the written part of the assignment.
5. Students present their **Traumreise** to the class.
6. Optional: At the end of all presentations the class votes via secret ballot for the best **Traumreise**, the place they have been convinced would be the best place to visit.

Grading the Project

Suggested point distribution (total = 100 points)

Oral presentation	30
Appearance of project/Originality	40
Accuracy of language	30

♜ GAMES

Mal doch schnell!

This game will help tactile learners review the vocabulary learned in the chapter.

Procedure Make a list of the words from the **Wortschatz** of this Chapter that are suitable for illustrating. Write the words on small pieces of paper and put them all in a hat. Have students take turns coming to the board or to the overhead projector. Ask students to take a piece of paper from the hat. Give them a few seconds to think about how to draw the word. Then give the signal for the student to begin drawing. The rest of the class tries to guess what is being drawn using German only. The student who first says the word or phrase correctly wins a point.

Stadt, Land, Fluß

This game is a popular game among German teenagers and can be adapted to a variety of teaching needs.

Materials Students will need a ruler, some paper, and a pen.

Procedure Ask each student to make a chart like the one below.

Stadt	Land	Fluß	Substantiv	Verb	Adjektiv	Punkte

Go through the alphabet, beginning by saying "A" aloud and then continuing silently. A designated student says "**Halt!**", and the letter that you are thinking of becomes the beginning letter for the words. If, for example, the letter is **F**, students must write a word that begins with the letter **F** in each category. The student who completes his or her chart first says "**Fertig!**" and all students stop writing and mark their empty spaces with a zero. Then students share their words and get one point per correct entry. The total points per game are added to the far right. Continue the game as time permits. At the end, students total their points under the heading "**Punkte**", and the student with the highest score wins.

Kapitel 3: Wo warst du in den Ferien?
Lesson Plans, pages 52-77

$\mathcal{U}$sing the Chapter Opener, *pp. 52-53*

Motivating Activity
Ask students where they would like to go on vacation if they had unlimited time and the money to do so.

Culture Note
German students get a similar amount of vacation time as students in the United States, but the time is distributed differently. German students generally get six weeks off in the summer (**Sommerferien**), two weeks in the fall (**Herbstferien**), two weeks at Christmas (**Weihnachtsferien**), and two weeks around Easter time (**Osterferien**). Holidays vary slightly throughout the **Bundesländer**.

Thinking Critically
① **Drawing Inferences** German students can participate in many after-school activities as can students in the United States. Can students tell from the photograph what club or organization these German teenagers belong to? When does the club meet? (Film and Photo Club/Tuesdays in 7th and 8th periods) You might want to look at Frame 1 of the **Foto-Roman** on p. 54 for a clearer picture.

Geography Connection
② Ask students to look at a map of Europe and have them locate **Tirol**. Based on what they see in the photograph, where should students look? (mountains such the Alps) What types of activities could they expect to be offered in that area? (Examples: skiing, hiking)

Background Information
② **Tirol** is one of Austria's **Bundesländer** (4,882 square miles or 12,648 square kilometers, comparable in size to the state of Connecticut). Its state capital is Innsbruck. It is a mountainous area and is known as a great winter sport region. Many resorts are located in this alpine state. The mountains in the background are called the Tyrolean Alps.

Thinking Critically
② **Drawing Inferences** Ask students to read the caption of the photo and ask them if they can deduce the meaning of the word **Bergen** from the picture.

Geography Connection
Ask students to scan the maps of Germany, Austria, and Switzerland for towns with the suffix -**berg**. Students should notice that these towns and cities are often located in mountainous areas.

Language Note
The suffix -**berg** should not be confused with -**burg**, which means *castle*. (Examples: Würzburg, Hamburg vs. Heidelberg, Nürnberg)

Thinking Critically
Drawing Inferences Ask students to look at the postcard next to Picture 3. Can students tell by looking at the stamp where the card originated and how much it cost to mail it? (**Österreich; 7 Schilling**) Have students check exchange rates for the equivalent of seven schillings in U.S. dollars.

Focusing on Outcomes
Ask students about their most memorable vacation. What was so memorable about it? Then have students preview the learning outcomes listed on p. 53. **NOTE:** Each of these outcomes is modeled in the video and evaluated in **Kann ich's wirklich?** on p. 76.

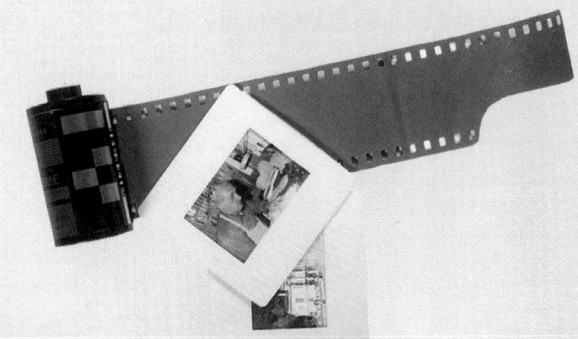

Teaching Los geht's!
pp. 54-56

Resources for Los geht's!

- *Video Program* OR
  Expanded Video Program, Videocassette 1
- *Textbook Audiocassette* 2 A
- *Practice and Activity Book*

▶ **pages 54-55**

Video Synopsis

In this segment of the video, members of the **Film- und Fotoclub** are meeting for the first time after the summer break. The club members talk about the places they visited during their vacation. The student outcomes listed on p. 53 are modeled in the video: reporting past events, talking about activities and places, asking how someone liked something, expressing enthusiasm or disappointment, and responding enthusiastically or sympathetically.

Motivating Activity

Ask students about their extra-curricular activities. Do they belong to any clubs or organizations? If so, what do they do?

Teaching Suggestion

As an advance organizer to the **Foto-Roman**, do the prereading activity at the top of p. 54 with the class. Then have students scan the text and the pictures, looking for visual clues and cognates to help them anticipate what they are going to hear and see.

Art and Media Connection

If your school has a photography club, ask a member of the club to tell the class what the club does, where and when members meet. The speaker could also bring some of the equipment and samples of the club's work to show students.

Geography Connection

Ask students to look in an atlas and locate Dresden, Frankfurt, and St. Ulrich.

▶ **page 56**

✦ For Individual Needs

1 Auditory Learners Have students read Questions 1 through 6. Replay the video or the audiocassette of **"Unser Film- und Fotoclub"** and have students answer the questions while they listen to the story. Suggest that students take notes. You might want to tell them that their answers do not have to be in complete sentences.

1 A Slower Pace Have students answer the questions in one or two complete English sentences.

Teaching Suggestion

2 Ask students to work with a partner. Students go over the text and answer the questions in German in writing. Remind students to use the reading strategies they have learned so far to help them complete the assignment.

✦ For Individual Needs

3 Challenge Ask students to rewrite the paragraphs as if Sebastian and Christiane were planning trips to Tyrol and Frankfurt and are telling someone what they are going to do.

Building on Previous Skills

4 You may want to continue Activity 4, using locations students learned about in Level 1. Prepare a handout or transparency with information from the Location Openers in Level 1. Use the box below as a suggestion for the cities Munich, Potsdam, and Lübeck.

die Frauenkirche	der Olympiapark
Thomas Mann	das Holstentor
Schloß Sanssouci	
	Friedrich der Große
der Cecilienhof	
der Viktualienmarkt	das Oktoberfest

LOS GEHT'S!

Thinking Critically

4 Comparing and Contrasting Ask students to recreate this activity for German students who are learning about the United States. Which three cities would they choose and what information would they associate with each city? Encourage students to use as much German as possible and if necessary describe a place rather than give the English equivalent. (Example: **das Weiße Haus —> wo der Präsident wohnt**)

Closure

Ask students to list the new facts or phrases they have learned in **Los geht's!**

Teaching Erste Stufe
pp. 57-61

Resources for Erste Stufe
Practice and Activity Book
Chapter Resources, Book 1
• Additional Listening Activities 3-1, 3-2
• Student Response Forms
• Realia 3-1
• Situation Card 3-1
• Teaching Transparency Master 3-1
• Quiz 3-1
Audiocassette Program
• *Textbook Audiocassette* 2 A
• *Additional Listening Activities, Audiocassette* 9 A
• *Assessment Items, Audiocassette* 7 A

▶ page 57

MOTIVATE
Teaching Suggestion

Make a chart on a transparency on which you write names of vacation places on one side and a typical gift idea from each place in random order on the other side.
Examples:

Schwarzwald	Lebkuchen
Lübeck	eine Freiheitsstatue aus Plastik
New York	Marzipan
Nürnberg	eine Kuckucksuhr

Have students make up as many sentences as they can.
Example:
In den Ferien war ich in ... und habe ... gekauft.

Encourage students to make up other places and gift ideas as long as they continue in German.

TEACH
Building on Previous Skills

Ask students which words or phrases they used in the motivating activity to express past events. (**war** and **habe gekauft**)

PRESENTATION: So sagt man das!

After reading the questions and phrases in the function box, ask students what they notice about the verbs. How many parts do they have? Which part changes to agree with the subject? Can students point out where the second part of the verb is located in the sentences?

PRESENTATION: Wortschatz

Introduce the new vocabulary by acting out the phrases. Use props if available. Then give commands to the class or individual students.
Examples:
Helen, leg das Video bitte ein!
Travis, nimm das Video heraus!
Hier Patty, nimm die Kamera und fotografiere unsere Klasse!
Gib Gary bitte diesen Film!

Total Physical Response

Bring several props to class. Give students commands based on the vocabulary in the **Wortschatz** box.
Examples:
Catherine, leg ein Video ein!
Russ, nimm das Video heraus und gib es Amy!
Gregg, nimm diese Kamera und fotografiere die zwei Schüler da drüben!

▶ *pages 58-59*

Teaching Suggestion

6 Ask students to take the key ideas from their answers to the six questions and write a brief report about

- the kind of camera they have,
- the kind of pictures they usually take,
- their favorite photo subjects, and
- the last photos they took.

✤ For Individual Needs

7 Challenge Ask a student what he or she did during summer vacation. Then call on another student to restate what that student did using the third person.

Teaching Suggestion

8 After students have found all the sentences, ask them to group the sentences, naming all the phrases that use **sein** and the ones that use **haben**.

PRESENTATION: Grammatik

Before introducing this grammar box, ask students how they express past events in English. Write students' responses on the board. Since they will probably come up with several different ways, ask them to point out the one that most resembles the German conversational past.

Ask students to explain the function of a past participle (expressing a completed action) then underline the past participle in the sample phrases. Ask students to name several regular and several irregular past participles used in English.

After going over the conversational past with students, take time to practice saying the verb phrases in Activity 9.

- Go from present to past, using different pronouns. Focus especially on the irregular or strong verbs.
- Have students find the common denominator in most of the verbs in the box that take **sein** as an auxiliary in the conversational past. (All but **sein** and **bleiben** are verbs of motion, showing motion towards a place.)
- Go from past to present. Say a complete sentence in the past (Example: **Er ist nach Hause gegangen.**) and ask students to give the same sentence in the present.
- Ask students to identify all the strong verbs in the box that do <u>not</u> have a vowel change in the past participle (Example: **geben** - **gegeben**). Then have them identify the strong verbs that <u>do</u> have a vowel change (Example: **bleiben** - **geblieben**).

▶ *page 60*

Teaching Suggestion

10 Monitor student activities as you move around the room.

For Individual Needs

10 Challenge Once students have completed Activities a through c, ask them to add one additional activity to Sebastian's daily calendar.
Example:
Was hat der Sebastian noch am Montag gemacht?

ZWEITE STUFE

▶ *page 61*

Teaching Suggestion

12 Have students preview Questions 1-5 before they read about Dresden. If you find the text too challenging for your students, you may want to read each paragraph aloud, using various strategies to establish meaning when necessary, for example, giving definitions and examples, stressing key concepts, paraphrasing, and simplifying sentence structures.

Reteaching: Conversational Past

On a transparency, prepare a chart like the example below. Give students a set amount of time to come up with as many sentences as they can using the conversational past. Have students read their sentences aloud and ask the rest of the class to listen for correct usage.

Subject	Aux. Verb	Object	Infinitive
Ihr	haben	meine Mutter	sehen
Frieda	sein	ein Auto	kaufen
Helmut		ein Buch	arbeiten
Wir		in Dresden	essen
Ich		ins Museum	lesen
Du		ein Wurstbrot	gehen
Ernst und Eva			sein

CLOSE

Teaching Suggestion

Ask students to share with the class in German how they or their family documented their last trip and vacation. Did they take photographs, buy postcards, or make movies with video cameras? What were some of the souvenirs they brought back from their trip?

Focusing on Outcomes

Refer students back to the learning outcomes listed on p. 53. They should recognize that they now know how to report past events when talking about activities.

ASSESS

• **Performance Assessment** As students walk into the classroom, hand each of them a blank page of a weekly **Taschenkalender**. Ask students to fill in at least two activities per day that they did during the past week. Ask three to four students what they did on certain days.

• Quiz 3-1, *Chapter Resources,* Book 1

Teaching Zweite Stufe,
pp. 62-66

Resources for Zweite Stufe

Practice and Activity Book
Chapter Resources, Book 1
  • Communicative Activity 3-1
  • Additional Listening Activities 3-3, 3-4
  • Student Response Forms
  • Realia 3-2
  • Situation Card 3-2
  • Quiz 3-2
Audiocassette Program
  • *Textbook Audiocassette* 2 A
  • *Additional Listening Activities, Audiocassette* 9 A
  • *Assessment Items, Audiocassette* 7 A
Video Program or Expanded Video Program

▶ *page 62*

MOTIVATE

Teaching Suggestion

Ask students to recall as many German cities as they can, including those introduced in Level 1. If they had to pick one, which would they choose to visit and what would they like to do and see there?

TEACH

Geography Connection

Ask students to look in an atlas for towns named Frankfurt in the United States. (Examples: Frankfurt, Michigan and Frankfort, Kentucky)

Teaching Suggestion

Ask students to research the heritage and the background of one of those American cities. This could be done as a brief written assignment or for extra credit.

Thinking Critically

Drawing Inferences Ask students why **a.M.** (**am Main**) follows the name **Frankfurt.** Remind students that there is another city named Frankfurt in Germany (**Frankfurt an der Oder**). Have students look up these two cities on a map.

Background Information

• **Frankfurt am Main** dates back to 794, which makes it over 1200 years old. Its original name was **Francono Furd.** The city is located in **Hessen,** and its population currently is around 635,000. **Frankfurt an der Oder** was founded in 1226 and has a current population of 87,500 people. It is located in Brandenburg.

• Students might be interested in the two specialties mentioned in the reading. **Zwiebelkuchen** resembles quiche. It is made of puff pastry, browned onions, bacon, eggs, sour cream, salt, and cumin. It is baked and traditionally served with wine and beer. **Äbbewoi** is the name in the Hessian dialect for **Apfelwein,** a hard cider. (**der Äbbewoi**)

▶ *page 63*

PRESENTATION: So sagt man das!

Ask students in English how they would ask a person where he or she was last weekend. Since students might give two versions (Where were you? and Where have you been?), mention to students that those two ways of expressing this question are also used in the German language. Then read the expressions in the function box with the students.

ZWEITE STUFE

PRESENTATION: Wortschatz

As you go over the photos, give simple and brief facts about each one in German (see Background Information below). Then practice the words.

Background Information

Der Dom Dating back to 1356, this is where the coronation of German kings took place.

Der Römer (das Rathaus) It got its name for being the oldest in the set of 11 **Giebelhäuser** on the **Römerberg**. It is actually a group of three buildings whose steep step gables are a symbol of Frankfurt. The upper floor of the **Römer** was used for banquets following the coronation of kings. Today the **Römer** is Frankfurt's city hall.

Das Goethehaus is the famous writer's birthplace and childhood home. It was destroyed in World War II and rebuilt between 1946 and 1951. It features the workroom where Goethe wrote *Werther, Götz von Berlichingen,* and parts of *Faust.* The house is connected to the **Goethe-Museum**.

Der Main This river should be familiar to students from the Almanac of Chapter 1. It is part of the **Rhein-Main-Donau-Kanal**. The **Main** is 524 kilometers (325.4 miles) long.

Fachwerk is a building style consisting of a framework of straight and crosstimbered beams in which the area between the beams is filled in with clay or bricks. This style of architecture reached its high point in the 16th and 17th centuries.

Die Zeil is a modern pedestrian zone that houses many large department stores and smaller shops. This is Germany's busiest shopping area.

▶ *page 64*

Teaching Suggestion

17 Ask students to imagine that they have one day to spend in Frankfurt. What three things would they want to see and why?

PRESENTATION: Grammatik

Read the explanations and go over the verb forms with students. Prepare a transparency with many possible ways to create meaningful sentences. Have students practice the forms.

Ich	haben	in Frankfurt
Wir	sein	nur zwei Tage Zeit
Der Dom		interessant
Die Fachwerkhäuser		sehr schön
die Zeil		nicht viel Geld mit
		auch im Goethe-haus
		keine Karten für die Oper
		toll zum Ein-kaufen

Example: **Die Zeil war toll zum Einkaufen.**

 For Individual Needs

18 Challenge Ask students to react to what their partner says, using the phrases **noch nie, schon oft,** and **auch schon** presented in the Wortschatz.

Example: — **Wo warst du in den Ferien?**
— **Ich war in Kalifornien.**
— **Ja? Ich war noch nie da! Wie war es?**

Teaching Suggestion

19 Suggest that students take notes while they work with their partner. After students finish the activity, call on several students to tell the reasons their partners gave for not being at certain places.

▶ *page 65*

PRESENTATION: Grammatik

It will take much practice before students can easily respond to questions involving prepositions of place. To practice the four different uses featured, use visual aids such as posters, photographs, large wall maps, and postcards. This is also a good way to review names of **Bundesländer**, rivers, cities, and other points of interest from Level 1.

▶ *page 66*

For Individual Needs

22 Visual Learners If possible, use photographs and realia representing places and points of interest in each of the listed cities. Talk about the pictures with students. Then hang them up so students can see them as they work on the activity.

Reteaching: Dative Case with *in* and *an*

Have students look at the maps of Germany, Liechtenstein, Switzerland, and Austria on pp. 394 and 395 or use Map Transparencies 1 and 2. Prepare a list of questions which students can answer using the maps.
Examples:
In welchem Bundesland liegt München? (in Bayern)
Wo liegt die Stadt Bern? (in der Schweiz)
An welchem Fluß liegt Hamburg? (an der Elbe)

You can later ask questions such as **Wo ißt du meistens Frühstück?** (in der Küche) or **Wo schaust du meistens Fernsehen?** (im Wohnzimmer).

▶ *page 67*

PRESENTATION: Landeskunde
Teacher Note
The **Landeskunde** interviews are recorded on audiocassette and videocassette

Teaching Suggestion
Begin the presentation of **Landeskunde** by doing the prereading activity with your class. Then have students listen to the audiocassette or watch the video segment of the interviews.

For Individual Needs

A Slower Pace Make a chart on the board with the following heads:

Wer? **Woher?** **Wohin?** **Was?**

Then ask students to scan each interview and note the names of the persons interviewed, where he or she is from, where that person spent his or her vacation, and the activities that person took part in.

Language Note
The word **Ferien** is used when talking about vacations for **Schüler** and **Studenten**. The word **Urlaub** applies when talking about vacations for people in the working world (**arbeitstätige oder berufstätige Leute**). You may want to explain these terms in German.

Teaching Suggestion
Ask students if they can recall any mishaps they had (**Pech haben**) while they were on a trip. Where were they and what happened? Have them try to tell the story in German.

Teacher Note
Mention to your students that the **Landeskunde** will also be included in Quiz 3-2 given at the end of the **Zweite Stufe**.

CLOSE

Game
Play the game **Stadt, Land, Fluß**. See p. 51F for the procedure.

Focusing on Outcomes
Refer students back to the learning outcomes listed on p. 53. They should recognize that they now know how to report past events when talking about places.

ASSESS

• **Performance Assessment** Draw a calendar page for a three-day weekend on a transparency or on the board, including three consecutive dates of the past month. Ask students to imagine where they went and what they did. They should list a minimum of three activities per day.

• Quiz 3-2, *Chapter Resources*, Book 1

*T*eaching Dritte Stufe, *pp. 68-71*

Resources for Dritte Stufe

Practice and Activity Book
Chapter Resources, Book 1
- Communicative Activity 3-2
- Additional Listening Activities 3-5, 3-6
- Student Response Forms
- Situation Card 3-3
- Teaching Transparency Master 3-2
- Quiz 3-3

Audiocassette Program
- *Textbook Audiocassette* 2 A
- *Additional Listening Activities, Audiocassette* 9 A
- *Assessment Items, Audiocassette* 7 A

▶ *page 68*

MOTIVATE

Teaching Suggestion

Ask students to list as many expressions in English as they can to describe their last summer break (last birthday, last concert they attended).

TEACH

Building on Previous Skills

25 In the **Zum Lesen** section of Chapter 2, students were introduced to the verbs **gefallen** and **mißfallen**. To help students prepare for the listening activity, ask them for synonyms of **gefallen** and make a list of the words and phrases that students suggest. (Examples: **mögen, gern haben**)

PRESENTATION: So sagt man das!

After you have read the expressions, give the students several situations to practice these new functions. Ask them to respond to questions about:
- a movie they saw
- a book they read
- a sports event they attended
- a party they attended.

Language Note

You might want to give students the literal meaning of **Es hat mir gefallen**. *(It was pleasing to me.)* You may also want to mention that **gefallen** is one of the many verbs that require an object in the dative case.

▶ *page 69*

PRESENTATION: Grammatik

After introducing the first and second person dative pronouns, have students practice these pronouns as well as the third person pronouns. Ask students, for example, how they liked books they have read, movies or concerts they have attended, or a party they went to.

For Additional Practice

28 After students have completed the activity, have them ask an additional question. (Example: **Und was habt ihr da gemacht?**)

PRESENTATION: Grammatik

Read the explanations with students. Give additional examples of nominative plurals ending in -**n** such as **Studenten, Jungen,** and **Mädchen**. Ask students to use these nouns to create sentences.

▶ *page 70*

◆ For Individual Needs

29 Challenge Give students three to four minutes to do this activity. Encourage them to add any words or phrases they feel would make their sentences sound as natural as possible. Ask four or five students to read their sentences in class.

PRESENTATION: Wortschatz

Present the new vocabulary, then write open-ended phrases on a transparency. Ask students to complete the sentences using the new vocabulary. Examples:
Wenn wir nach Frankfurt reisen, schlafen wir gern …
Wenn ihr in Dresden esst, esst ihr oft …
Wenn ich in London bin, wohne ich immer …

Culture Note

Jugendherbergen originated in Germany, the first being the youth hostel in Altena, founded in 1909 by Richard Schirrmann and Wilhelm Münker. In 1910, the German youth Hostel Association came into being. Since 1925, youth hostels also have been established in other countries, and in 1932 the International Youth Hostel Federation was founded. Today there are over 5,000 youth hostels worlwide.

▶ *page 71*

For Individual Needs

30 Challenge Have students imagine that they are taking a survey for a travel magazine to find out people's lodging preferences. Students should take notes and then report their findings to the class.

Teaching Suggestion

31 Ask students to use several adverbial expressions from the box beside the activity in their **Notizbuch** entry.

For Individual Needs

32 Auditory Learners To involve the listening student actively in this activity, ask him or her to put the pictures in the order they are described by the partner. At the end, the listening student verifies the sequence with his or her partner. You may also want to call on several students to repeat their reports and have the rest of the class listen to see if the order of the pictures matches the description that students gave.

Community Link

33 Suggest that students videotape or interview local celebrities or feature local merchants or organizations in their reports. Tell students that they can get information from the Chamber of Commerce to help them with their projects.

Reteaching: Past Tense of *Sein*

Use the pictures of places from this chapter and places from Level 1. (Examples: **der Cecilienhof, das Schloß Neuschwanstein, Kiel, Potsdam**) Give students a picture or an index card with the name of a location. One of the students then says **Ich bin (in Kiel) gewesen.** The next student asks: **Wie war's denn?** The first student replies, using the functions from the **So sagt man das!** box on p. 68.

CLOSE

Game

In this activity students review and practice in German the places and points of interest that they have learned up to this point. Begin the game by making the following statement:

Im Sommer reisen wir nach Frankfurt, denn wir wollen den Dom besichtigen.

The first student repeats your sentence and reason for visiting and adds another location. The next student must remember both places with the reasons given and then add his or her own, and so on. If students make a mistake or forget a place, they drop out of the game. The student who can repeat the most places wins.

Focusing on Outcomes

Refer students back to the learning outcomes listed on p. 53. Students should recognize that they now know how to ask how someone liked something, to express enthusiasm or disappointment, and to respond enthusiastically or sympathetically.

ASSESS

- **Performance Assessment** On a map, have students point out three to five locations they have visited. Then ask them what they did there and how they liked the location.
  Wo warst du/wart ihr?
  Wie hat es dir/euch dort gefallen?
  Was hast du/habt ihr da gemacht?

- Quiz 3-3, *Chapter Resources*, Book 1

DRITTE STUFE

ZUM LESEN

*T*eaching Zum Lesen,
pp. 72-73

Reading Strategy

The targeted strategy in this reading is identifying the main idea and supporting details of a text. Students should learn about this strategy before doing Question 2.

PREREADING

Motivating Activity

Get several brochures from a travel agency. Ask students to work in pairs or in small groups. Each group receives one brochure. Give groups about two minutes to skim their brochures, then call on two or three groups to tell the class in German why they think their vacation destinations would appeal to travelers. Allow students to keep the brochures until they have done the additional activities suggested for Activity 1.

Teacher Note

Activities 1-3 are prereading activities.

Teaching Suggestions

1 Before starting the activity, ask students about postcards and announcements. What types of information do the writers of postcards usually give? What information is usually contained in a public announcement?

1 After doing Activity 1, ask students to look again at the travel brochure they used for the motivating activity. Ask them to compare the format of the brochure with the format of the brochure for the **Pillersee.**

READING

Skimming and Scanning

Give students three minutes to skim over each text. Then give them three more minutes to scan for words or phrases they think are some of the main points of the readings. Write students' ideas on the board or on a transparency.

Geography Connection

Earlier in this chapter, students were asked to locate **Tirol** and St. Ulrich. Now, have them locate the **Pillersee.**

Thinking Critically

Drawing Inferences What type of activities might students expect to find in the **Pillersee** area? Compile a list of students' suggestions. Remind students that if they don't know the name of an activity in German, they should try to describe it rather than give the English word.

Cooperative Learning

5/6 Divide students into groups of three. Each group should have a reader, a writer, and a reporter. The reader reads Questions 5 and 6 aloud, then all group members answer the questions together while the writer takes notes. Give groups ten minutes to finish their assignments. Encourage students to discuss their findings in German. Once groups have completed their assignments, call on two or three reporters to present their answers to the class.

POST-READING

For Individual Needs

Challenge Tell students that they have been invited to St. Ulrich. Based on what students have learned about this town and its surrounding area, what would they like to do there and why?

Teacher Note

Activity 7 is a post-reading task that will show whether students can apply what they have learned.

Closure

Based on the different texts, students should list at least five things the town of St. Ulrich has to offer visitors.

Answers to Activity 5

They have seen a lot in three days; Yesterday they were being lazy; They walked around the **Pillersee**; They swam in the lake; Tomorrow there is a town festival.

Answers to Activity 6

The event took place in St. Ulrich; It is a small town (village); located at the **Pillersee** in **Tirol**, Austria; supporting details for main event: e.g. day, time, people attending, food, music

*U*sing Anwendung,
pp. 74-75

🎞 Video Wrap-Up

At this time, you might want to use the *Video Program* or the *Expanded Video Program*, Videocassette 1 for additional review and enrichment. See *Video Guide* for suggestions regarding:
- **Unser Film- und Fotoclub**
  (Dramatic episode)
- **Landeskunde**
  Interviews
- **Videoclips**
  (Authentic footage—*Expanded Video Program* only)

Thinking Critically

1 **Drawing Inferences** Based on what the Stegmüllers have checked off, can students describe the family's interests?

📁 Portfolio Assessment

3 You might want to suggest this activity as a written and oral portfolio item for your students. See *Assessment Guide*, p. 16.

✣ For Individual Needs

5 **Visual Learners** Before students listen to the script ask them what words or phrases they would expect to hear in each one of the summaries. Then make a list and leave it on the transparency or board for students to see as they listen to the activity.

After students have listened to the summaries ask them which of the listed phrases they actually heard.

*K*ann ich's wirklich?
p. 76

This page helps students prepare for the test. It is a brief checklist of the major points covered in the chapter. The students should be reminded that it is only a checklist and not necessarily everything that will appear on the test.

*U*sing Wortschatz,
p. 77

♜ Game

Play the game **Mal doch schnell!** See p. 51F for the procedure.

Group Work

Divide students into groups of three or four. Give students a list of interesting headlines from newspapers from German-speaking countries. (Examples: *Frankfurter Allgemeine, Dresdener Rundschau, Süddeutsche Zeitung*) Students should use the vocabulary of the **Zweite Stufe** to write brief, humorous stories to fit the headlines.

✣ For Individual Needs

Tactile Learners Use sentence strips to practice the sentences and expressions from the **Dritte Stufe**. Put the sentence strips into numbered envelopes. Give one envelope to each student or pair of students. Students then put the sentence strips in the correct order, write the sentence, and pass their envelope to the next student or pair of students until all envelopes have been to each person. Then students self-check their sentences.

Teacher Note

Give the **Kapitel 3** Chapter Test, *Chapter Resources*, Book 1.

KAPITEL 3

Wo warst du in den Ferien?

① Was hast du fotografiert?

German students have many opportunities to travel, sometimes with their families, sometimes with friends. They like to take photos or make films of the exciting new places they visit. Do you like to travel? What kinds of places do you like to visit? To talk about places you have seen and how much you liked them, you need to learn several new expressions.

In this chapter you will learn

- to report past events, talking about activities
- to report past events, talking about places
- to ask how someone liked something, to express enthusiasm or disappointment, to respond enthusiastically or sympathetically

And you will

- listen to students talk about their vacations
- read reports about such places as Frankfurt, Dresden, and St. Ulrich, Austria
- write about your own weekend and vacation activities
- find out how Germans spend their vacation time

② Ich war in den Bergen, in Tirol.

③ Was habt ihr in den Ferien gemacht?

Los geht's!

Unser Film- und Fotoclub

You are going to meet some members
of the Film and Photo Club at Basti's school.
What do you think these young people
are talking about?

 Lehrerin  Frank  Sebastian  Christiane

> Nun, wie waren eure Ferien? Habt ihr viel gesehen?
> Habt ihr auch viel gefilmt und fotografiert?

An Sebastians Gymnasium gibt es einen Film-
und Fotoclub. Frau Sabine Brucker, die Biologie-
und Sportlehrerin, leitet den Klub. Die langen
Sommerferien sind vorüber, und heute sind die
Klubmitglieder zum ersten Mal im neuen Schuljahr
zusammengekommen. Die Schüler unterhalten sich
angeregt: heute können sie nämlich zeigen, was sie
in den Ferien gefilmt oder fotografiert haben. Drei
Leute haben sogar ein Video mitgebracht.

> Mein Vater hatte in Dresden zu
> tun, und ich bin mitgefahren.

> Wie hat dir Dresden gefallen?

> Phantastisch!

> Das freut mich! Dann erzähl
> uns mal etwas über Dresden!

FRANK August der Starke hat Dresden im 18. Jahrhundert zu
einer der schönsten deutschen Barockstädte gemacht. Ich hab'
das Schloß gesehen, den Zwinger — das ist ein phantastisches
Kunstmuseum, weltbekannt! Ich bin in Dresden mit meinem Vater
in die Oper gegangen, in die berühmte Semperoper. Wir haben
Beethovens „Fidelio" gehört. Überall baut man in Dresden, denn
die Stadt wurde 1945 fast total zerstört. Über 35 000 Menschen
verloren in einer Nacht das Leben.

④ *Dresden*

> Nun, Christiane, was hast du in den Ferien gemacht?

Christiane erzählt, wo sie war.

CHRISTIANE Ich habe meine Tante in Frankfurt besucht. Ich bin oft im Römer gewesen; meine Tante arbeitet dort. Ich hab' natürlich den Dom besichtigt, und ich bin oft durch die Zeil spaziert. In der Oper war ich auch einmal. Ach ja, ich bin natürlich auch im Goethehaus und im Goethemuseum gewesen. Was mir am besten gefallen hat, das sind die Fachwerkhäuser auf dem Römerberg.

⑥

⑤ *Frankfurt*

Jetzt ist Sebastian dran. Er legt seine Kassette ein.

SEBASTIAN Ich war mit meinem Freund Thomas in Tirol. Wir haben in St. Ulrich gewohnt, in einer netten Pension für junge Leute. Jeden Tag sind wir gewandert, durch die Wälder, durch die Wiesen. Wir sind auch oft um den See gegangen oder sind auf einen Berg gestiegen. Zu Mittag haben wir gewöhnlich in einem Gasthof gegessen, irgendeine Tiroler Spezialität, wie zum Beispiel einen „Strammen Max", das ist Schinken mit Spiegelei.

⑧

⑦ *St. Ulrich*

⑨

1 Was passiert hier?

Hast du „Unser Film- und Fotoclub" verstanden? Versuch es, die folgenden Fragen (auf deutsch oder englisch) zu beantworten!

1. Warum kommen heute die Schüler zusammen? 1. Zeigen, was sie in den Ferien gefilmt/fotografiert haben.
2. Wer ist Frau Brucker? 2. Biologie- und Sportlehrerin; leitet den Klub.
3. Was erzählen die drei Schüler? 3. Was sie in den Ferien gemacht haben.
4. Wo war Frank und warum? 4. Dresden; sein Vater hatte dort zu tun.
5. Was hat Christiane während der Ferien gemacht? 5. Tante in Frankfurt besucht.
6. Wo war Sebastian und mit wem? 6. Tirol; mit seinem Freund.

2 Genauer lesen

1. Was hat Frank in Dresden gesehen und gemacht? 1. Schloß u. Zwinger gesehen; in die Oper gegangen.
2. Warum erwähnt Frank das Jahr 1945? 2. Zerstörung der Stadt im Zweiten Weltkrieg.
3. Was hat Christiane besichtigt? Was hat ihr am besten gefallen? 3. Dom; Fachwerkhäuser auf dem Römerberg.
4. Wo hat Basti in Tirol gewohnt? 4. Pension für junge Leute in St. Ulrich.
5. Was haben er und sein Freund gemacht? 5. Gewandert, um den See gegangen, auf Berg gestiegen.
6. Warum erwähnt er den „Strammen Max"? 6. Tiroler Spezialität.

3 Was paßt?

Welche Wörter auf der rechten Seite passen in die Satzlücken?

SEBASTIAN Mein Freund Thomas und ich, wir haben in St. Ulrich __1__. Jeden Tag sind wir __2__. Wir sind um den See __3__ oder auf einen Berg __4__. Zu Mittag haben wir gewöhnlich in einem Gasthaus __5__.

CHRISTIANE Ich habe meine Tante in Frankfurt __6__. Ich bin im Römer __7__, ich hab' den Dom __8__ und bin durch die Zeil __9__. Die Fachwerkhäuser am Römerberg haben mir am besten __10__.

besichtigt	gestiegen
besucht	
	gewandert
gefallen	
	gewesen
gegangen	gewohnt
	gegessen
gelaufen	spaziert

1. gewohnt; 2. gewandert;
3. gegangen/gelaufen/spaziert;
4. gestiegen; 5. gegessen;
6. besucht; 7. gewesen; 8. besichtigt; 9. spaziert/gelaufen/gegangen; 10. gefallen.

4 Wo ist das?

Such dir einen Partner! Nenne ihm ein Wort aus dem Kasten, und er muß dir sagen, mit welcher Stadt oder mit welchem Ort dieses Wort assoziiert ist. Die drei Orte sind: Dresden, Frankfurt und St. Ulrich. — Tauscht dann die Rollen aus!

BEISPIEL   DU eine Barockstadt
PARTNER **Das ist Dresden.**

August der Starke   Gasthof   kleine Pension   Wiesen
Goethe   Fachwerkhäuser   Römer   Zwinger   Zeil
Barockstadt   Oper   See   Schloß   Elbe
Dom   Berge   Main   Goethehaus   Semperoper

Reporting past events, talking about activities

5 Hör gut zu!

Vier Schüler haben sehr aktive Ferien gehabt und berichten darüber. Schreib von jedem Schüler drei Dinge auf, die er gemacht hat!

For answers, see listening script on TE Interleaf.

SO SAGT MAN DAS!

Reporting past events, talking about activities

When asking someone about
something in the past, you ask:

**Was hast du in den
Ferien gemacht?**

**Was hat Sebastian in
Tirol gemacht?**

And the response might be:

**Ich habe meine Tante in Frankfurt besucht.
Ich habe den Dom besichtigt und bin oft
durch die Stadt spaziert.**

**Er hat in St. Ulrich gewohnt. Er ist dort
viel gewandert, und er hat gefilmt und
fotografiert.**

WORTSCHATZ

Was macht ihr im Filmclub?

Wir sprechen über:

Wir fotografieren mit einer Kamera.

Ich filme mit einer Videokamera.

Ich bediene den Videorecorder/die Kamera.

Ich lege ein Video ein.

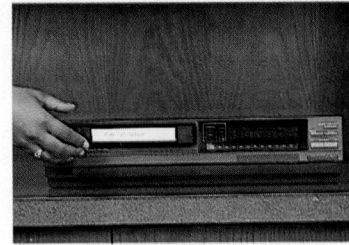

Ich nehme das Video heraus.

Videos

Filme

Dias

Farbbilder

6 Und du?

Such dir einen Partner! Stellt euch diese Fragen und beantwortet sie!

1. Was filmst du oder fotografierst du gewöhnlich?
2. Was für eine Kamera hast du? War das ein Geschenk, oder hast du die Kamera selbst gekauft?
3. Kaufst du einen Film für Dias oder für Farbbilder?
4. Hast du einen Videorecorder? Was für einen?
5. Was sind deine Lieblingsmotive, wenn du fotografierst?
6. Wann hast du die letzten Fotos gemacht? Was hast du fotografiert?

7 Was hast du in den Ferien gemacht?

Sag vier Dinge, die du in den Ferien gemacht hast! Im Kasten sind ein paar Ideen.

ICH HABE ...	ICH BIN ...
☐ Freunde besucht	☐ viel geschwommen
☐ viel gearbeitet	☐ zu Hause geblieben
☐ eine große Fete gemacht	☐ viel gewandert
☐ viel Tennis gespielt	☐ oft ins Kino gegangen
☐ viel gelesen	☐ nach (Denver) gefahren
☐ viele Videos geschaut	☐ Wasserski gelaufen
☐ sehr oft gefaulenzt	☐ in (Kalifornien) gewesen
☐ eine Reise gemacht	☐ viel schwimmen gegangen
☐ (Orlando) besichtigt	
☐ einen Sommerkurs besucht	

8 Was war los?

Lies den Text **Los geht's!** noch einmal! Welche Sätze erkennst du, die die Vergangenheit (*past*) ausdrücken? Schreib die Sätze in gekürzter Form auf einen Zettel!

BEISPIEL　　**Die Klubmitglieder sind zusammengekommen.**
Sie haben in den Ferien gefilmt.
Ich bin in die Oper gegangen.

Grammatik　The conversational past

1. When talking about past events, the conversational past tense is used. It consists of the present tense forms of **haben** or **sein** and a form of the verb, called the *past participle*.

> Ich **habe** meine Tante **besucht.**
> Ich **bin** um den See **gegangen.**

2. Most past participles have the prefix **ge-**: **gemacht, gelesen.**
3. The past participles of so-called regular or weak verbs end in **-t**: **machen, er macht, er hat (Ferien) gemacht.**
4. The past participles of so-called irregular or strong verbs end in **-en**, like the infinitive: **lesen, liest, er hat (Zeitung) gelesen.** Some have other changes: **gehen, geht, er ist gegangen; bleiben, bleibt, sie ist geblieben.**

5. The past participles of verbs ending in **-ieren** do not have the prefix **ge-**: fotografieren, er fotografiert, er hat (viel) fotografiert.

6. The past participles of verbs that already have an inseparable prefix do not add the prefix **ge-**: besuchen, er besucht, er hat besucht; gefallen, es gefällt mir, es hat mir gefallen.

7. The past participle of verbs that have a separable prefix keep the **ge-**: mitkommen, er kommt mit, er ist mitgekommen; aussehen, sie sieht (nett) aus, sie hat (nett) ausgesehen.

8. Most verbs in German are regular or weak. Therefore, unless you have learned otherwise, form the past participle with **-t**, the prefix **ge-**, and the auxiliary **haben**.

9. Here are some past participles of verbs that you should know.

WEAK VERBS	STRONG VERBS	VERBS WITH **sein**
hat gearbeitet	hat gegeben	ist gekommen
hat gefaulenzt	hat gegessen	ist gefahren
hat gefilmt	hat gelesen	ist gelaufen
hat gehabt	hat gesehen	
hat gehört	hat geholfen	ist geblieben
hat gekauft	hat getrunken	ist geschwommen
hat gemacht		ist gewesen
hat gemäht		ist gegangen
hat geschenkt		
hat gespielt		ist gewandert
hat gewohnt		ist spaziert
hat fotografiert		
hat besucht		
hat besichtigt		

9 Was hast du in den Ferien gemacht?

Such dir einen Partner! Frag ihn, was er in den Ferien gemacht hat! Er sagt es dir. Dann fragt er dich. Benutzt die Ausdrücke im Kasten als Anregung *(as suggestions)*!

viel schwimmen gehen   viel wandern

meine Oma besuchen   viel Musik hören

nach (Kanada) fahren   in Mexiko sein

die Natur fotografieren   gar nicht arbeiten

Klamotten kaufen   Volleyball spielen

viel lesen

viel essen und trinken   ziemlich viel faulenzen

Answers may vary. E.g.: **Was hast du … ? — Ich habe meine Oma besucht.**

10 Was hat Sebastian letzte Woche gemacht?

Hier ist ein Blatt aus Sebastians Tischkalender vom Juli.

a. Lies, was er alles gemacht hat!

b. Such dir dann einen Partner! Sag ihm, was Sebastian am Montag gemacht hat! Dein Partner sagt dir dann, was Sebastian am Dienstag gemacht hat und so weiter.

c. Zur Abwechslung (*for variety*) nennt jetzt mal nicht die Uhrzeit, sondern gebraucht die Reihenwörter wie: zuerst, dann, danach und zuletzt!

JULI		30. Woche
23 MONTAG	10.00–12.00 13.30–16.00 17.00	mit Robert schwimmen gehen Volleyball Rasen mähen
24 DIENSTAG	9.00–11.00	einen Stadtbummel machen Neue Jeans!
25 MITTWOCH	9.00 10.00–12.00 14.00–15.30	zum Frisör! Thomas besuchen Fußball
26 DONNERSTAG	8.00 20.30	mit Vati nach Tirol, wandern, schwimmen, gut essen nach Hause fahren
27 FREITAG	10.00–12.00 14.30–15.30 16.00	dem Opa im Garten helfen dort zu Mittag essen Flöte spielen Freunde besuchen
28 SAMSTAG	9.00–12.00 14.00–16.30 ab 19.00	Stadtbummel mit Christiane zu Mittag essen lesen, Musik hören, faulenzen Rockkonzert besuchen
29 SONNTAG	7.00–8.00 10.00–11.00 14.00–16.00 ab 19.00	Tennis mit Rad zum See Großeltern besuchen fernsehen (Krimi)

11 Für mein Notizbuch

Schreib in dein Notizbuch, was du letztes Wochenende (am Samstag und am Sonntag) gemacht hast! Schreib mindestens fünf Sätze. Verwende dabei auch Zeitausdrücke wie: am Nachmittag, am Abend, zuerst, zuletzt, und so weiter.

KAPITEL 3   Wo warst du in den Ferien?

Marienkirche

Zwinger

August I.

Dresden, Hauptstadt von Sachsen

Dresden, Kunst- und Kulturstadt an der oberen Elbe, war bis zur Zerstörung im Jahre 1945 eine der schönsten Städte Europas. Dresden war — und ist — weithin als „Elbflorenz" bekannt, weil die Stadt mit ihrer wundervollen Architektur an Florenz erinnert.

Kurfürst Friedrich August I. (August der Starke) war Landesfürst von Sachsen. Als konvertierter Katholik war er auch König von Polen. Unter seiner Herrschaft wurde Dresden in die schönste Barockstadt seiner Epoche verwandelt.

Der Zwinger, ein Meisterstück des Barocks, beherbergt die berühmte Gemäldegalerie „Alte Meister" (Raffael, Giorgione, Tizian, Tintoretto, u.a.). Die „Neuen Meister" hängen in einem anderen Museum, im Albertinum. Dort, im sogenannten Grünen Gewölbe, ist auch die königliche Sammlung ausgestellt: Gefäße, Schmuck und Waffen.

Zur Zeit wird Dresden renoviert. Die total zerstörte Marienkirche wird wieder aufgebaut. Bis zur 1000-Jahr-Feier im Jahre 2008 soll Dresden völlig renoviert sein und wieder in alter Pracht glänzen.

Blick auf die Elbe

12 Und du? Was weißt du über Dresden?

Lies den Bericht über Dresden! Dann such dir einen Partner, stellt euch abwechselnd diese Fragen und beantwortet sie!

1. Was für eine Stadt ist Dresden, und wo liegt sie?
2. Warum wird Dresden auch „Elbflorenz" genannt?
3. Wer war August der Starke? Was hat er gemacht?
4. Wo hängen die „Alten Meister"? Und die „Neuen Meister"?
5. Wie sieht Dresdens Zukunft *(future)* aus?

1. Kunst- und Kulturstadt; an der oberen Elbe.
2. Wundervolle Architektur erinnert an Florenz.
3. Landesfürst von Sachsen und König von Polen; machte aus Dresden die schönste Barockstadt seiner Epoche.
4. Im Zwinger; im Albertinum.
5. Dresden wird renoviert.

Reporting past events, talking about places

Frankfurts Skyline

Frankfurt a. M.

Frankfurt am Main ist Deutschlands Finanzmetropole und seit 1993 auch Sitz der Zentralbank der Europäischen Gemeinschaft. In Frankfurts Skyline sitzen nicht nur deutsche Banken, sondern viele ausländische Firmen, die in Deutschlands fünftgrößter Stadt ihre Büros haben. Der Rhein-Main-Flughafen außerhalb Frankfurts ist einer der größten Europas.

Frankfurt ist eine alte Stadt und wird 794 zum ersten Mal als einer der Sitze Karls des Großen erwähnt. Seit 1356 wurden hier im Dom der deutsche Kaiser und die deutschen Könige gewählt und zwischen 1562 und 1792 auch hier gekrönt.

In den Jahren 1848/49 war die Paulskirche in Frankfurt auch der Tagungsort der ersten deutschen Nationalversammlung.

In Frankfurt wurde am 28. August 1749 Johann Wolfgang von Goethe geboren. Der große Dichter, auf den die Frankfurter besonders stolz sind, hat hier seine Kindheit und Jugend verbracht.

Frankfurt hat auch eine sehr freundliche Seite: hier gibt es viele gemütliche Lokale, wo man sich nach einem vollen Arbeitstag mit Freunden treffen kann, bei leckerem Zwiebelkuchen und Äbbewoi, zwei Frankfurter Spezialitäten.

Der Dom

1. Sitz der Zentralbank der EG; viele ausländische Firmen; internationaler Flughafen.

13 Und du? — Was weißt du über Frankfurt?

Lies den Bericht über Frankfurt! Dann such dir eine Partnerin! Stellt euch abwechselnd diese Fragen und beantwortet sie!

1. Warum nennt man die Stadt Frankfurt „Deutschlands Finanzmetropole"? Was gibt es dort?
2. Was sind die Hauptpunkte in der langen Geschichte Frankfurts? Gib die Antwort in Stichwörtern *(by mentioning keywords)*!
3. Was interessiert dich am meisten an Frankfurt?

Goethe (1749–1832)

2. Sitz Karls des Großen; im Dom Wahl und Krönung deutscher Kaiser und Könige; in der Paulskirche Tagung der 1. deutschen Nationalversammlung.

14 Ich war in Frankfurt

Du warst in Frankfurt! Schreib auf eine Liste, was du gesehen hast, welche Gebäude du besichtigt hast, wo und was du gegessen hast und was du gefilmt oder fotografiert hast! Erzähl einem Partner über deinen Besuch in Frankfurt! Tauscht dann die Rollen aus!

Auf dem Römerberg

15 Hör gut zu!

Schüler erzählen, wo sie in den Ferien waren. Schreib dir auf, wo sie waren! Wer ist am meisten gereist? Hör dann noch einmal zu und schreib auf, was du hörst!

For answers, see listening script on TE Interleaf.

16 Wo waren die Schüler?

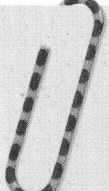

Such dir einen Partner! Vergleicht *(compare)* eure Notizen! Du fragst: „Wo war . . .?" Dein Partner antwortet dir. Dann fragt er dich, und du antwortest ihm.

SO SAGT MAN DAS!

Reporting past events, talking about places

When asking someone where he or she was, you ask:

Wo bist du gewesen?

Und wo warst du?

And the answer may be:

**Ich bin in Frankfurt gewesen.
Ich war dort im Römer — das ist das Rathaus.**

Ja, zuerst war ich in der Stadt. Ich war mit Robert im Kino. Danach waren wir im Café Mozart und haben dort Eis gegessen.

WORTSCHATZ

LEHRERIN **Sag mir mal, was du alles in Frankfurt gesehen hast!**
CHRISTIANE **Ich hab'... gesehen.**

die Fachwerkhäuser
(am Römerberg)

die Oper

das Rathaus
(den Römer)

den Dom

die Zeil

den Main

das Goethehaus

den Zoo

---

17 Und du?

Was möchtest du sehen, wenn *du* nach Frankfurt kommst?

> ### Grammatik — The past tense of haben and sein
>
> For the conversational past tense of **haben** or **sein**, the forms of the **Imperfekt** or simple past tense are often preferred, especially in northern Germany. These forms are shorter.
>
> | | | | | | | | |
> |---|---|---|---|---|---|---|---|
> | ich | **hatte** | wir | **hatten** | ich | **war** | wir | **waren** |
> | du | **hattest** | ihr | **hattet** | du | **warst** | ihr | **wart** |
> | er/sie/es | **hatte** | sie (*pl*) } Sie | **hatten** | er/sie, es | **war** | sie (*pl*) } Sie | **waren** |
>
> you may say: Ich **habe** keine Zeit **gehabt.**
> *or* Ich **hatte** keine Zeit.
>
> Ich **bin** in der Stadt **gewesen.**
> *or* Ich **war** in der Stadt.

18 Wo warst du?

Such dir eine Partnerin und frag sie, wo sie in den Ferien war! Dann fragt sie dich. Ihr könnt die Ausdrücke im Kasten gebrauchen, wenn ihr wollt.

Answers may vary. E.g.: **Wo warst du in den Ferien? — Ich war in Kalifornien. Dort war ich schon oft.**

> im Gebirge   am Michigansee
> in den Rockies   an der (Ost)küste
> in Kalifornien
> am Meer   in (Virginia) bei (meiner Tante)

WORTSCHATZ

noch nie	*never*
schon oft	*often*
auch schon	*already*

19 Warum warst du nicht dort?

Dein Partner war nicht dort und sagt dir warum.

DU **Du warst nicht (im Kino). Warum nicht?**
PARTNER **Ich war nicht im Kino, weil ich (zu viel zu tun hatte).**

Wo?

> im Schülercafé
> im Einkaufszentrum
> im Kino
> im Klub   in der Schule

Warum nicht?

> Karten fürs Fußballspiel haben   keinen Hunger haben
> das Wetter schlecht sein   kein Geld haben
> keine Zeit haben
> zu viel zu tun haben

*G*rammatik — The dative case with the prepositions **in** and **an**

In answer to a question beginning with **wo**, the prepositions **in** and **an** (and some others) indicate location and are followed by dative case forms.

1. The preposition **in** can be followed by the name of a city or town, state or country.

Wo warst du? ⎰ Ich war in Dresden. (city)
⎱ Ich war in Sachsen. (state)
⎱ Ich war in Deutschland. (country)

2. When the name of the country is feminine or used in the plural, the noun phrase is in the dative case.

Wo warst du? ⎰ Ich war in der Schweiz.
⎱ Ich war in der Türkei.
⎱ Ich war in den Vereinigten Staaten.

3. The preposition **in** is followed by dative case forms with all specific locations, such as areas, buildings, rooms. Note that **im** is a contraction of **in + dem**.

Wo warst du? ⎰ Ich war im Gebirge, in den Bergen …
⎱ Ich war im Museum, im Rathaus, in der Oper …
⎱ Ich war im Garten, in der Küche …

4. The preposition **an**, *at,* is followed by dative case forms when indicating location. Note that **am** is a contraction of **an + dem**.

Wo liegt das? ⎰ Am See, am Meer, an der Nordsee
⎱ Am Main, an der Elbe

20 Sag mal, wo warst du denn?

Ihr hattet ein besonders langes Wochenende, vier Tage!
— Such dir einen Partner! Frag ihn, wo er am letzten Wochenende war und was er dort alles gemacht hat! Danach fragt er dich, und du sagst es ihm. Ihr könnt die Wörter im Kasten in euren Antworten gebrauchen.
Answers may vary. E.g.: Sag mal, wo …? — Ich bin in New York gewesen.
— Was hast du dort alles gemacht? — Ich war in der Oper.

New York   Schweiz
Stadt   Museum
Café (Mozart)   Oper
Eriesee   Gebirge
Restaurant (Koch)   Kino

21 Für mein Notizbuch

Schreib in dein Notizbuch, wo du letzte Woche warst und was du dort alles gemacht hast!

22 Eine Stadtbesichtigung

Stell dir vor, du warst für zwei Tage zu Besuch in einer deutschen Stadt, in Berlin, Dresden, Frankfurt, Hamburg oder München!

a. Schreib auf, was du alles gesehen oder besichtigt hast! Minimum: 5 Dinge!

b. Such dir einen Partner und frag ihn, wo er war und was er da alles gesehen hat! Dein Partner fragt dich, wo du warst.

c. Such dir einen anderen Partner! Diesmal wart ihr beiden in derselben Stadt, aber ihr habt nicht dasselbe gesehen oder gemacht. Einer von euch ist sehr kulturell interessiert, der andere geht lieber einkaufen, liebt die Natur und Tiere.

Was sehen wir uns gewöhnlich in einer Stadt an?

das Rathaus • die Universität • den Zoo
den Dom • den Marktplatz • den ... Park
das ... Stadion • die Innenstadt
die Einkaufsstraße
die ...kirche • das Einkaufszentrum • den Botanischen Garten
das ...Museum • die Oper

SPRACHTIP

When talking about sightseeing, one can use the verbs **besichtigen, besuchen,** and **sehen.**

Besichtigen is used for sight-seeing of buildings, where one takes a close view of the inside (churches, museums).
Besuchen is used for performances that one attends (opera, theater, concert).
Sehen is used in general with everything, but implies that one sees it without close inspection.

23 Ich war so beschäftigt!

Deine Eltern sind ärgerlich, daß du am Wochenende nur selten zu Hause warst. Aber du hattest so viel zu tun, für die Schule, für deinen Job und mit deinen Freunden.

a. Schreib auf eine Liste, was du alles am Wochenende gemacht hast!

b. Spiel mit einem Partner die Rollen von Vater/Mutter und Sohn/Tochter! Zeig deinem Vater/deiner Mutter die Liste und erzähle, was du alles gemacht hast! Es gibt viele Fragen, die du beantworten mußt, aber am Ende sind deine Eltern stolz auf dich.

c. Vergleiche deine Liste mit der Liste deines Partners! Was habt ihr beide gemacht? Was hat nur einer von euch gemacht?

24 Meine Ferien

Schreib, wo du in den letzten Ferien warst und was du alles gesehen und gemacht hast!

Was hast du in den letzten Ferien gemacht?

We asked several German-speaking people where they spent their last vacation and what they did. Listen. Before you read the interviews, write down your last vacation spot and the activities in which you participated during your vacation.

Hans, *Hamburg*

„Ich hab' gearbeitet, ich hab' ja … trainiert auch, Volleyball trainiert, und ja … mehr eigentlich nicht."

Monika, *Hamburg*

„Ich war in den Ferien in Kanada, und … hab' einen Sprachkurs gemacht, in Englisch. Ich bin nach Montreal gefahren und hab' Toronto und die Niagara Fälle auch gesehen. Hm, ja, was war noch? Ja, ich wollte nach New York, weil … es ist nur sechs Stunden von Montreal entfernt, wo ich gewohnt habe, und das ging dann leider nicht."

Sandra, *Berlin*

„Also, ich war in Spanien, und ich hab' da auch Granada besucht, und ansonsten lag ich eigentlich meistens am Strand, und hab' die Sonne genossen, aber ich hatte da dummerweise eine Sonnenallergie: da ging es dann auch nicht mehr so gut; na ja, also, ich hab' viel Spaß mit meiner Freundin gehabt, und dann waren die Ferien auch schon vorbei."

Brigitte, *Berlin*

„Wir waren, wann war das? … im März … drei Wochen in Midwest City, das ist ein Stadtteil von Oklahoma City, weil wir von unserer Schule aus, von unserem Gymnasium, alle zwei Jahre einen Schüleraustausch machen."

Herr Troger, *St. Ulrich, Österreich*

„Der letzte Urlaub war in Mallorca; da haben wir uns bei einer Radfahrgruppe angeschlossen und sind da eine Woche Rad gefahren. Es war aber eigentlich ein schlechtes Wetter, und trotzdem war das Wetter für uns nicht so schlecht, weil wir mit den Rädern ziemlich nach oben gefahren sind, und wieder runter, und wir waren dann eher froh, wenn es nicht zu heiß war, nicht wahr …"

A1. Monika: Montreal, Kanada - Sprachkurs. Sandra: Granada, Spanien - Strand und Sonne. Brigitte: Midwest City, USA - Schüleraustausch. Herr Troger: Mallorca, Spanien - Radfahren.

A. 1. On a map, locate the places where these people went on vacation. Jot these places down on a list along with the reason each gives for his or her trip.
2. Which two different words do Monika and Herr Troger use for "vacation"? Can you figure out the difference between these two words based on who uses them? A2. Ferien - Schule; Urlaub - Arbeit.
3. Three interviewees had some bad luck on their vacation. What happened to each?

A3. Monika: wollte nach N.Y. - es ging nicht. Sandra: hatte Sonnenallergie. Herr Troger: es war schlechtes Wetter.

B. What do all these vacations have in common? Sandra's and Herr Troger's trips are typical vacation goals for Germans. Why do you think that is?

B. Urlaub/Ferien im Ausland; schlechtes Wetter in Deutschland.

Asking how someone liked something, expressing enthusiasm or disappointment, responding enthusiastically or sympathetically

25 Hör gut zu!

Vier Schüler sprechen über ihre Ferien. Wo waren sie? Wem hat es gefallen? Wem hat es nicht gefallen? Warum wohl? Mach dir Notizen! Vergleiche dann deine Notizen mit den Notizen eines Partners! For answers, see listening script on TE Interleaf.

SO SAGT MAN DAS!

Asking how someone liked something, expressing enthusiasm or disappointment, responding enthusiastically or sympathetically

Here are some ways to ask how someone liked something or some place:

> **Wie war's?**
> **Wie hat dir Dresden gefallen?**
> **Wie hat es dir gefallen?**
> **Hat es dir gefallen?**

If you liked it, you may say:

> **Phantastisch!**
> **Es war echt super!**
> **Es hat mir gut gefallen.**
> **Wahnsinnig gut!**

If you didn't like it, you may say:

> **Na ja, soso!**
> **Nicht besonders.**
> **Es hat mir nicht gefallen.**
> **Es war furchtbar!**

The other person asking may respond enthusiastically:

> **Na, prima!**
> **Ja, Spitze!**
> **Das freut mich!**

Or sympathetically:

> **Schade!**
> **Tut mir leid!**
> **Das tut mir aber leid!**

26 Na, wie war's?

Such dir einen Partner! Stell dir vor, du warst an den Orten, die hier rechts im Kasten stehen! Dein Partner fragt dich, wie es war. Du antwortest, und dein Partner reagiert darauf. — Tauscht dann die Rollen aus!

PARTNER **Wo warst du in den Ferien?**
    DU **Ich war in/an . . .**
PARTNER **Wie war's?**
    DU **. . .**
PARTNER **. . .**

> San Francisco   in den Alleghenies
>   Meer   Ostküste
>   Minnesota   Michigansee
>   Disneyland   Swamps von Florida
>   Key West   Mojave Wüste

*G*rammatik Personal Pronouns, Dative Case (Summary)

You already know the third person dative pronouns **ihm** and **ihr**. Here are the others. With the verb **gefallen,** you always use dative case forms for the person.

second person		*first person*	
Wie hat es **dir**	gefallen?	Es hat **mir**	gut gefallen.
Wie hat es **euch**	gefallen?	Es hat **uns**	echt prima gefallen.
Wie hat es **Ihnen**	gefallen?	Es hat **mir**	nicht gefallen.
third person			
Wie hat es **dem Sebastian**	gefallen?	Es hat **ihm**	gut gefallen.
Wie hat es **der Beatrice**	gefallen?	Es hat **ihr**	echt prima gefallen.
Wie hat es **den Baumanns**	gefallen?	Es hat **ihnen**	nicht gefallen.

27 Wie hat es ihnen gefallen?

Such dir einen Partner! Du weißt, wo die Baumanns in den Ferien waren. (Das steht hier rechts!) Dein Partner fragt dich, wo sie waren. Du antwortest und sagst ihm, wie es ihnen gefallen hat. — Tauscht dann die Rollen aus!

Sebastian war mit einem Freund in Österreich.

Beatrice war in den Bergen, in den Alpen.

Die Großeltern waren am Rhein und an der Mosel.

Robert war an der Ostsee, auf der Insel Rügen.

Bastis Eltern waren in den USA, in Minnesota.

28 Wie hat es euch gefallen?

Such dir jetzt zwei Partner! Frag sie, wo sie in den Ferien waren! (Sie waren zusammen weg.) Einer antwortet für beide. Dann frag sie, wie es ihnen gefallen hat, und der andere antwortet für beide. Tauscht dann die Rollen aus!

DU	**Wo wart ihr denn in den Ferien?**
EIN PARTNER	**Wir waren . . .**
DU	**Wie hat es . . .**

*G*rammatik Definite Article, dative plural

1. The dative plural form of the definite article is **den.**

> Es hat **den** Eltern in Amerika echt gut gefallen.

2. The dative plural of almost all nouns end in -**n.** If the nominative plural form already ends in -**n,** the dative plural form is the same.

nominative plural	dative plural
die Eltern	Es hat **den** Eltern gut gefallen.
die Schüler	Es hat **den** Schülern gut gefallen.
die Kinder	Es hat **den** Kindern gut gefallen.

29 Wem hat es gefallen und wem nicht?

Bau Sätze mit den Wörtern im Kasten!

Various answers possible. E.g.: **Amerika hat den Baumanns sehr gut gefallen.**

der Stadtbummel die Berge Amerika Dresden Tirol das Meer der Film	hat haben	Baumanns Beatrice Opa Sebastian Kinder Geschwister Großmutter Schüler ich	besonders gut sehr gut ganz gut nicht besonders nicht so gut überhaupt nicht	gefallen

WORTSCHATZ

Basti war mit einem Freund, dem Thomas, in Tirol. Die beiden haben in einer Pension gewohnt und haben oft in einem Café gegessen, im Café Troger.

Wo übernachtet man gewöhnlich?

in einem Privathaus   in einer Pension   in einer Jugendherberge   in einem Hotel

Wo ißt man gewöhnlich?

in einer Imbißstube   in einem Lokal   in einem Gasthof   in einem Restaurant

30 Und du?

Such dir einen Partner! Frag ihn, wo er gewöhnlich übernachtet und wo er gewöhnlich ißt, wenn er mit (seinen Eltern) unterwegs ist!

31 Für mein Notizbuch

Schreib in dein Notizbuch etwas über deine Ferien! Wo bist du gewesen? Was hast du alles gemacht? Wie hat es dir gefallen und warum? Wo hast du übernachtet? Wo hast du gegessen?

32 Bastis Ferien

Sebastian hat einige Fotos von seinen Ferien ausgesucht, die er seinen Klassenkameraden im Film- und Fotoclub zeigen möchte. Spiel die Rolle von Basti und erzähle, wo du warst, was du gemacht hast und wie es dir gefallen hat! Dein Bericht muß zu den Fotos passen. Gebrauche auch die Wörter im Kasten oben rechts.

WORTSCHATZ

Schon bekannt
- jeden Tag
- oft
- einmal
- dreimal
- am Wochenende

Neu
- am letzten Tag
- jeden Abend
- nach dem Mittagessen
- jeden Morgen

1.

2.

3.

4.

5.

33 Klassenprojekt

Teilt eure Deutschklasse in Gruppen von vier oder fünf Leuten! Jede Gruppe hat die Aufgabe, etwas über eure Stadt zu berichten. Nehmt eine Kamera oder eine Videokamera mit! Jede Gruppe muß dann den anderen Gruppen erzählen und zeigen, was sie alles gemacht und gesehen hat.

Loferer Steinberge
St. Ulrich a.P.

Liebe Eltern!
Grüße aus St. Ulrich! Wir
sind erst 3 Tage da und
haben schon viel gesehen.
Nur gestern haben wir ge-
faulenzt, sind nur um den
Pillersee spaziert und haben
im See gebadet. Der ist
aber noch zu kalt!
Alles Gute Euer Basti
P.S. Morgen ist ein Dorffest

Fam.
Hans Baumann
Wolfratshausenerstr. 17
82031 Grünwald

Deutsch!

St. Ulrich/Tirol Der Dorfplatz in St. Ulrich am Pillersee hat jetzt einen Brunnen. Am Sonntag, den 4. Juli, um 9 Uhr 45, hat die Dorfplatzeinweihung stattgefunden. Nach einer Messe in der Dorfkirche mit Bischof Eder ist die Dorfgemeinde auf den Dorfplatz marschiert. Nach einer Ansprache von Bürgermeister Schlechter wurde der Dorfplatz von Bischof Eder offiziell eingeweiht.

Die Gastronomie St. Ulrich hatte für eine gute Jause gesorgt, und die Musikkapelle St. Ulrich, unter Leitung von Musikkapellmeister Alois Brüggel, für gute Stimmung und Unterhaltung. (Österreichische Landeszeitung)

SONNTAG, 4. JULI
ca. 9.45 Uhr
DORFPLATZEINWEIHUN
mit anschl.
Schmanggerlfest
der Gastronomi
Frühschoppenkonzert
Musikkapelle ca. 11.00 Uhr
und musikalischer
Unterhaltung
mit dem TIROL DUO

LESETRICK
Identifying the main idea and supporting details. When you read a text, it is important to be able to identify the main idea (or ideas). This will enable you to determine the global meaning of the text (the "big picture"), and then to find the details that support the global idea.

Getting Started
1. Look at the pictures, then look at the different formats of the texts and match each text with one of the formats below.
   1. excerpt from a brochure/advertisement
   2. announcement
   3. newspaper article
   4. postcard

   Based on the formats, what kind of information would you expect to find in each text?

   a. report of an event   3.
   b. news about someone's vacation   4.

Bischof Eder aus Salzburg

Im Pillerseetal
ist immer was los!

- Pillersee mit Badestrand
- Angeln im fischreichen See
- Tretboote, Ruderboote
- 60 km Wanderwege
- Tennis und Kegelbahnen
- Minigolf und Hallenbad
- Reithalle (Islandpferde)
- 7 Golfplätze in der Nähe

Die Musikkapelle St. Ulrich

Besonders für Kinder!

- Besuch auf einem Bauernhof
- Kindergrillparty
- Kinderdisco
- Ponyreiten mit unseren Ponies Amigo, Bibi und Sarah
- Kinder-Pizzaessen
- Basteln, Malen, Zeichnen, Singen und vieles mehr

Familien- und Sporthotel
Pillerseehof

Thomas u. ich am Pillersee

c. factual information, e.g. time, date 2.
d. promotion of something 1.

2. Does anything in the brochures above help you distinguish immediately between the main idea and the supporting details?

3. Where do you usually find the main idea of a newspaper article? 3. headline

> **Tip:** Sometimes the main idea is not stated directly, but only implied. You have to make an inference by looking at the supporting details.

4. Skim the postcard. What is the main idea?

A Closer Look For answers, see TE Interleaf.

5. What are some of the details Basti writes about in his postcard?

6. Look at the newspaper article more closely. Where did the event that is being reported take place? Is that a large city or a small town? Where is it? If the main idea is the dedication of the fountain, can you find four or five supporting details in the article?

7. Jetzt erzähle von deinen letzten Ferien! Bring entweder Dias, Fotos oder ein Video mit und zeig deinen Mitschülern, wo du warst und was du da alles gemacht hast!

1 Die Stegmüllers aus Düsseldorf haben mit ihren Kindern Melissa (7) und Jochen (9) den Sommerurlaub in St. Ulrich am Pillersee verbracht. Am Ende ihres Urlaubs haben sie den Fragebogen des Fremdenverkehrsvereins ausgefüllt. Lies diesen Fragebogen! Was haben die Stegmüllers abgehakt?

FRAGEBOGEN
Fremdenverkehrsverein St. Ulrich
Liebe Gäste!
Im Interesse aller Gäste bei uns möchten wir von Ihnen erfahren, welche Quartiere und Unterhaltungsmöglichkeiten Sie am meisten benutzt haben und was Ihnen bei uns am besten gefallen hat.

1. Wo haben Sie gewohnt?
   ☐ Hotel   ☐ Gasthof   ☑ Pension   ☐ Privatquartier

2. Wie hat Ihnen die Unterkunft gefallen?
   ☐ ausgezeichnet   ☑ sehr gut   ☐ gut
   ☐ nicht besonders   ☐ nicht gut

3. Wo haben Sie gewöhnlich gegessen?
   ☐ Hotel   ☑ Gasthaus   ☐ Café   ☐ Restaurant   ☐ selbst gekocht

4. Wie war die Qualität des Essens in unseren Lokalen?
   ☐ ausgezeichnet   ☑ sehr gut   ☐ gut   ☐ nicht gut

5. Wie haben Sie Ihren Urlaub verbracht? Kreuzen Sie bitte die Dinge an, die Sie am meisten gemacht haben!
   ☑ wandern   ☐ angeln   ☑ Minigolf
   ☐ bergsteigen   ☑ Boot fahren   ☐ Tennis
   ☐ spazierengehen   ☐ radfahren   ☑ Tischtennis
   ☑ baden gehen   ☐ reiten   ☐ kegeln

6. Was hat den Kindern am meisten Spaß gemacht?
   a. _Ponyreiten_
   b. _Grillparty_
   c. _____

7. Welche Unterhaltungsprogramme haben Ihnen am besten gefallen? Kreuzen Sie bitte nur drei Programme an!
   ☑ Musikabende   ☐ Tanzveranstaltungen   ☐ Vorträge
   ☑ Theateraufführungen   ☐ Dia-Vorführungen

8. Wie lange waren Sie bei uns?
   ☐ eine Woche   ☑ zwei Wochen   _____

Vielen Dank! Ihr Fremdenverkehrsverein A-6393 St. Ulrich am Pillersee in Tirol Telefon 05354-88176

2 Such dir einen Partner! Diskutiert gemeinsam die folgenden Fragen!

  1. Hat es den Stegmüllers in St. Ulrich gefallen? Wenn ja, warum? Wenn nein, warum nicht?

  2. Warum, glaubt ihr, hat die Familie in einer Pension gewohnt? In einem Gasthaus gegessen?

  3. Warum, glaubt ihr, sind die Stegmüllers nicht bergsteigen gegangen?

  4. Was meint ihr: Welche Freizeitbeschäftigungen kosten Geld? Welche nicht?

 3 **a.** Setzt euch in kleinen Gruppen zusammen und entwerft einen Fragebogen, der für einen Ferienort in den Vereinigten Staaten (Florida, Kalifornien) bestimmt ist! Gebraucht den Fragebogen von St. Ulrich als Muster! Euer Fragebogen muß auch Auskunft erfragen über: Wohnen, Essen, Freizeit, usw.

  b. Stellt euch vor, daß alle in eurer Gruppe die letzten Ferien zusammen verbracht haben! (Die Eltern von einem von euch haben die anderen mitgenommen.) Füllt gemeinsam euern Fragebogen aus!

  c. Teilt jetzt leere Fragebögen an die Mitglieder einer anderen Gruppe aus! Die Mitglieder dieser Gruppe fragen euch jetzt über eure Ferien, und ihr antwortet. — Tauscht dann die Rollen aus!

 4 Schreib einen Bericht über deine letzten Ferien mit deinen Eltern oder Freunden oder Verwandten, oder du erfindest einen Ferienort! In deinem Bericht mußt du erwähnen, wo du gewohnt hast, wo du gewöhnlich gegessen hast, was für Freizeitbeschäftigungen du gehabt hast und wie dir alles gefallen hat.
For answers, see listening script on TE Interleaf.

 5 Listen to the reports and decide what they are all about. Match each report to one of these summaries:

  a. description of a town or area

  b. description of sightseeing in a town

  c. description of activities one can undertake

  d. description of a hotel
For answers, see listening script on TE Interleaf.

 6 Listen to these people talking about a trip they recently took. Find out where they were and how they liked it.

7

R O L L E N S P I E L

Together with two other classmates, role-play the following scene.

You are a travel agent working in a travel agency. You have a customer who wants suggestions from you about where he could spend his vacation and information about what various vacation spots offer. As you make your suggestions, another customer joins in and tells of his experiences at a particular vacation spot. Have some brochures at your disposal, either from German vacation spots or vacation spots in the United States.

Can you report
past events, talk-
ing about activi-
ties? (p. 57)

1 How would you ask a classmate what he or she did during his or her vacation?   1. E.g.: **Was hast du in den Ferien gemacht?**

2 How would you tell someone about the things you did, using the verbs **spielen, lesen, wandern, besuchen, besichtigen, sein, gehen, laufen, fahren,** and **schwimmen?**
2. E.g.: **Ich habe meine Tante in Tirol besucht und bin dort viel gewandert.**

3 How would you report what someone else did, using the same verbs?
3. E.g.: **Er/sie hat den Dom in Frankfurt besichtigt.**

4 How would you ask someone where he or she was, using two differ-ent past tense forms? How would that person answer?
4. a. **Wo bist du gewesen? — Ich bin ... gewesen.** b. **Wo warst du? — Ich war ... .**

5 How would you say that you didn't have any time, using two different past tense forms? 5. a. **Ich habe keine Zeit gehabt.** b. **Ich hatte keine Zeit.**

6. a. E.g.: **Wo bist du gewesen?**   b. E.g.: **Was hast du alles gemacht?**   c. E.g.: **Was hast du dort alles gesehen?**

6 How would you invite someone to tell you
d. E.g.: **Wie hat es dir gefallen?**

   a. where he or she was?   **c.** what he or she saw?

   b. what he or she did?   **d.** how he or she liked it?

Can you report
past events, talk-
ing about places?
(p. 63)

7 How would you say that you were at each of these places? Use com-plete sentences.   7. **Ich war ... ; Ich bin ... gewesen.**
in   in   in   in der   in den
Dresden, Sachsen, Deutschland, Schweiz, Vereinigte Staaten, Schule, Kirche, Stadt, Museum, Park, Gebirge, Ostsee, Meer, Main
in der   in der   in der   im   im   im   an der   am   am

Can you ask some-
one how he or she
liked something
and respond enthu-
siastically or sym-
pathetically?
(p. 68)

8 How would you ask someone how they liked the city of Frankfurt? How they liked it in Tirol? How would you say that you liked it? That you didn't like it?   8. E.g.: **Wie hat dir Frankfurt gefallen? Wie hat es dir in Tirol gefallen? Es war echt super! Es hat mir nicht gefallen.**

9 How would you respond to someone who
— tells you that he or she liked his or her vacation?
— tells you that he or she did not like it?   9. E.g.: **Das freut mich!**
E.g.: **Tut mir leid!**

10 How would you tell someone that your parents liked Dresden but that they didn't like Leipzig?

10. E.g.: **Meinen Eltern hat Dresden gut gefallen, aber Leipzig hat ihnen überhaupt nicht gefallen.**

ERSTE STUFE
REPORTING PAST EVENTS, TALKING ABOUT ACTIVITIES

Was hast du in den Ferien gemacht?   *What did you do on your vacation?*
die Ferien (pl)   *vacation*
besichtigen   *to sightsee, visit a place*
Ich habe (den Dom) besichtigt.   *I visited (the cathedral).*
fotografieren   *to photograph*
Ich habe ... fotografiert.   *I photographed ...*

spazieren   *to walk, stroll*
filmen   *to film, videotape*
die Videokamera/die Kamera bedienen   *to use a video camera/a camera*
ein Video einlegen   *to insert a video cassette*
das Video herausnehmen   *to take out the video cassette*
die Kamera, -s   *camera*
der Film, -e   *roll of film*
das Dia, -s   *slide*
das Farbbild, -er   *color photograph*

der Videorecorder, -   *video cassette recorder*

VERBS AND PAST PARTICIPLES

arbeiten, gearbeitet   *to work*
faulenzen, gefaulenzt   *to be lazy*
laufen, (ist) gelaufen   *to run*
er/sie läuft   *he/she runs*
bleiben, (ist) geblieben   *to stay, remain*
(See p. 59 for a more complete list of past participles.)

ZWEITE STUFE
REPORTING PAST EVENTS, TALKING ABOUT PLACES

Wo bist du gewesen?   *Where were you?*
  Am (Main).   *On (the Main River).*
  In (London).   *In (London).*
  Im (Zoo).   *At (the zoo).*
besuchen   *to visit (a place)*

der Dom, -e   *cathedral*
die Oper, -n   *opera house*
das Museum, Museen   *museum*
der Römer   *name of city hall in Frankfurt*
die Fachwerkhäuser   *cross-timbered houses*
die Zeil   *name of main shopping street in Frankfurt*
der Main   *Main River*

das Goethehaus   *Goethe's birthplace*
der See, -n   *lake*
  um den See   *around the lake*

OTHER USEFUL WORDS AND EXPRESSIONS

noch nie   *not yet, never*
schon oft   *a lot, often*
auch schon   *also*

DRITTE STUFE
ASKING HOW SOMEONE LIKED SOMETHING

Wie war's?   *How was it?*
Wie hat dir Dresden gefallen?   *How did you like Dresden?*
Es hat mir gut gefallen!   *I liked it a lot!*
Wie hat es dir gefallen?   *How did you like it?*
Hat es dir gefallen?   *Did you like it?*
Es hat mir nicht gefallen.   *I didn't like it.*
Phantastisch!   *Fantastic!*
Echt super!   *Really great!*
Wahnsinnig gut!   *Extremely well!*
Na ja, soso!   *Oh, all right.*
Nicht besonders.   *Not especially.*

RESPONDING ENTHUSIASTICALLY OR SYMPATHETICALLY

Das freut mich!   *I'm really glad!*
Tut mir leid!   *I'm sorry.*
Das tut mir aber leid!   *I'm so sorry.*

PERSONAL PRONOUNS, DATIVE CASE

dir   *to/for you*
euch   *to/for you (plural)*
Ihnen   *to/for you (formal)*
mir   *to/for me*
uns   *to/for us*
ihnen   *to/for them*

PLACES TO STAY

übernachten   *to spend the night*
in einem/in einer ...   *in/at a ...*

das Privathaus, ̈-er   *private home*
die Pension, -en   *inn, bed and breakfast*
die Jugendherberge, -n   *youth hostel*
das Hotel, -s   *hotel*

PLACES TO EAT

die Imbißstube, -n   *snack stand*
das Lokal, -e   *small restaurant*
der Gasthof, ̈-e   *restaurant, inn*
das Restaurant, -s   *restaurant*

TIME EXPRESSIONS

am letzten Tag   *on the last day*
jeden Abend   *every evening*
jeden Morgen   *every morning*
nach dem Mittagessen   *after lunch*

🎬 Location Opener
Hamburg, pages 78-81
Expanded Video Program, Videocassette 2

𝒰sing the Photograph,
pp. 78-79

Background Information
The **Binnenalster** is an artificial lake in the shape of a trapezoid. It is located in the heart of Hamburg and encompasses an area of **18 Hektar** (44 acres). Its four banks make it unique. The **Jungfernstieg** on one side is the main boulevard of the city and houses many famous stores and hotels. The picture was taken from the bridge that was once known as the **Lombardsbrücke.** Parallel to this bridge runs the **Kennedy-Brücke** named in memory of the late U.S. president.

Thinking Critically
Comparing and Contrasting Ask students to compare the architecture of the buildings alongside the **Binnenalster.** (They are very similar in style and size.) Tell students that the uniform look is no accident. Street building codes required architects and builders to aim for a very connected and unified appearance.

𝒰sing the Almanac and Map,
p. 79

Hamburg's coat of arms dates back to the 12th and 13th centuries and depicts a silver gate tower with two silver stars above the outer towers, all on a red background. The crest represents the port of Hamburg's historical role as gateway to the world.

Terms in the Almanac
• **St. Michaelis-Kirche:** Better known as **der Michel,** the church is one of the symbols of Hamburg. It was built between 1751 and 1762 and stands 132 meters (433 feet) tall. It burned down in 1906, was rebuilt, then was destroyed during World War II. It was rebuilt the second time using the original plans of architects J.L. Prey and E.G. Sonnin.

• **Felix Mendelssohn-Bartholdy:** famous German pianist and composer who founded the Leipzig conservatory. He was the grandson of Moses Mendelssohn, a well-known German philosopher.

• **Carl von Ossietzky:** German writer who was imprisoned by the Nazis in 1933 and then received the Nobel Peace Prize in 1935. He published the **Weltbühne,** a famous cultural and political newspaper. Since 1962, **Carl-von-Ossietzky-Medaillen** have been given annually to outstanding artists and writers who contribute to human rights awareness.

• **Verlage:** The city is home to many publishers and printing businesses. Many of the country's magazines and newspapers, such as *Bild, Die Zeit, Deutsches Allgemeines Sonntagsblatt,* and *Der Spiegel* are published in Hamburg.

• **Hamburger Aalsuppe:** soup made of fresh eel, potatoes, soup greens, onions, lemon juice, and various herbs and spices

• **Matjeshering:** salted filet of young herring that is considered a great delicacy in northern Germany. It is often eaten on pumpernickel bread.

Using the Map
• Have students use the map on p. 394 to identify the German states that border on the Free Hanseatic City of Hamburg. (**Schleswig-Holstein** and **Niedersachsen**) You may also want to use Map Transparency 1.

• Have students locate and trace the Elbe and Alster rivers in an atlas.

Background Information
Originally named **Hammaburg,** the city was founded in the 9th century by the son of **Karl der Große,** Emperor **Ludwig der Fromme.** Hamburg is called the *Free Hanseatic City.* It received this status in the 13th century when Hamburg, together with Lübeck, founded the Hanseatic League. Bremen later joined the League in 1358.

The Hanseatic League was a collective union of merchants from dozens of cities from Norway to Russia. The merchants formed the League to strengthen their economic position. Hamburg was almost completely destroyed during World War II and rebuilt in the postwar years. Today the city is still called **Hansestadt Hamburg** and is a state in its own right. It is Germany's second largest city after Berlin.

Thinking Critically

Drawing Inferences Ask students to locate Hamburg, Lübeck, and Bremen on a map and ask them why they think these cities joined the **Hanse.** (Example: Each of these cities is located on a major body of water—**Elbe, Ostsee, Weser**— which facilitated trade.)

*I*nterpreting the Photo Essay,
pp. 80-81

② Hamburg is Germany's largest seaport. The port is one of the city's main attractions. Tourists as well as locals enjoy informative trips on tour boats as they cruise around small and large ships. Since harsh winters can freeze the port, ice-breakers must be used during part of the year to keep the port and its shipping channels open.

③ This spectacular city hall is located in the center of the city and is the seat of the state government as well as the senate of the city. The senate occupies the right side of the building, and the state parliament has its chamber and workrooms on the other side. A group of nine architects under the direction of **Baumeister Haller** built the **Rathaus** between 1886 and 1897 in the German Renaissance style. The front facade features 18 statues of German emperors.

• **Community Link** Ask students about the city hall in their community. Have them find out when it was built and by whom.

④ The community of Övelgönne attracts many visitors interested in seeing its many small houses with small windows and large wooden shutters. Most of the homes are those of retired river pilots, sea captains, and sailors. They are located along the banks of the Elbe river, and it is said that these retirees spend most of their time behind large telescopes viewing passing ships.

⑤ Blankenese is an exclusive residential area that is considered by many the most beautiful neighborhood in Hamburg. Homes are built on slopes and are surrounded and concealed by trees. Sea captains, ship owners, and heads of trading firms make up a good part of the residents of the area.

⑥ The SS Rickmer Rickmers is a sailing ship that was built in Bremerhaven in 1896. It was named after the grandchild of the shipyard's founder. It is 97 meters (318 feet) long and 12.20 meters (40 feet) wide. On its maiden voyage, it sailed to Hong Kong and returned loaded with rice and bamboo. During its history, it has relied on three major sources of power: it began with wind power, then added steam engines, and was finally converted to diesel engines. The SS Rickmer Rickmers was retired in 1987. It is now docked in Hamburg and open to the public for tours.

⑦ The **Speicherstadt** was designed and built at the end of the 19th century by 42 architects and 15 engineers. It is architecturally unique in that it is a city within a city. It is a 10 km^2 (3.86 square miles) large free port and storage facility in which goods are stored without customs clearance. Goods such as coffee, tea, tobacco, or spices are kept in huge, gothic-style brick buildings that form one big warehouse facility, the largest of its kind in the world. Today the **Speicherstadt** is also a historical landmark.

⑧ Maike, Thorsten, Wiebke, and David were born in Hamburg. Nicolas' parents are French. They both work for French companies in Hamburg. David's father is a Nigerian official who works in Hamburg. David went to school in Nigeria for five years, but he has been back in Hamburg for several years.

• **Drawing Inferences** The students in Photo 8 go to a bilingual school. Ask students why it might be helpful to be fluent in English or another foreign language in a city such as Hamburg. (Example: As a large seaport that also attracts many tourists, Hamburg hosts thousands of visitors from foreign countries each year.)

Komm mit nach

Hamburg!

Hamburg

Einwohner: 1,6 Millionen

Fläche: 755 Quadratkilometer (292 Quadratmeilen; etwa viermal so groß wie der District of Columbia)

Flüsse: Alster, Elbe

Berühmte Gebäude: Rathaus, St. Michaelis-Kirche, Chilehaus

Bedeutende Hamburger: Johannes Brahms (1833-1897, Komponist), Felix Mendelssohn-Bartholdy (1809-1847, Komponist), Carl von Ossietzky (1888-1938, Schriftsteller), Wolfgang Borchert (1921-1947, Schriftsteller), Helene Lange (1848-1930, Frauenrechtlerin)

Industrie: Handel, Verlage, Nahrungsmittel, Chemie

Beliebte Gerichte: Hamburger Aalsuppe, Matjeshering, Scholle

Foto ① Blick auf Hamburg, von der Lombards-brücke aus gesehen

DÄNEMARK
Nordsee
Ostsee
Hamburg
NIEDER-LANDE
POLEN
Berlin
BEL.
TSCHECH. REPUBLIK
LUX.
FRANK-REICH
SCHWEIZ
ÖSTERREICH

Hamburg

Die Freie und Hansestadt Hamburg, nach Berlin die größte Stadt Deutschlands, ist auch ein Bundesland. Schon im Mittelalter war die Stadt an der Elbe ein wichtiger Handelsplatz. Heute ist Hamburg, das „Tor zur Welt", Deutschlands bedeutendster Hafen. Die Konzentration von Zeitungen, Verlagen, Rundfunk- und Fernsehanstalten macht Hamburg zum kulturellen Zentrum Norddeutschlands.

2 Touristen machen eine Hafenrundfahrt.

3 Das Hamburger Rathaus, 1886-1897 im Renaissancestil erbaut

4 In Övelgönne an der Elbe wohnen pensionierte Schiffskapitäne. Typische Haustür

Die folgenden drei Kapitel führen uns nach Hamburg, in die Wirtschafts- und Kulturmetropole an der Elbe. Die Schüler in diesen Kapiteln gehen auf eine zweisprachige Schule, das Helene-Lange-Gymnasium.

(5) Villen in Blankenese

(6) Die „Rickmer Rickmers", ein stolzes Segelschiff

(7) Die Speicherstadt, heute eine Freie Handelszone

(8) Maike, Nicolas, Thorsten, Wiebke und David

Kapitel 4: Gesund leben

CHAPTER OVERVIEW

Los geht's! pp. 84-86	Wie fühlst du dich? *p. 84*			*Video Guide*
	FUNCTIONS	**GRAMMAR**	**CULTURE**	**RE-ENTRY**
Erste Stufe pp. 87-91	Expressing approval and dis-approval, *p. 88*	• The verb **schlafen**, *p. 88* • The accusative-case forms after the preposition **für**, *p. 89* • The reflexive verbs, *p. 90*	• Interviews of German teen-agers, *p. 87* • **Landeskunde: Was tust du, um gesund zu leben?** *p. 92*	• The modals **sollen/müssen**, *p. 87* (from **Kap. 7/8**, I) • Saying how often you do things, *p. 88* (from **Kap. 7**, I) • **Daß**-clauses, *pp. 88, 89* (from **Kap. 9**, I) • Expressing opinions, *p. 89* (from **Kap. 9**, I) • Responding to good and bad news, *p. 89* (from **Kap. 4**, I) • Greeting someone, *p. 91* (from **Kap. 1**, I) • The conjunctions **weil** and **denn**, *p. 91* (from **Kap. 8**, I) • Giving reasons, *p. 91* (from **Kap. 8**, I)
Zweite Stufe pp. 93-96	Asking for infor-mation and re-sponding emphat-ically or agreeing with reservations, *p. 95*	The determiner **jeder**, *p. 94*	• Survey on health habits *p. 93* • **Ein wenig Landeskunde: Bioläden** and **Reformhäuser**, *p. 96*	• Saying how often you do things, *p. 93* (from **Kap. 7**, I) • Telling someone what to do, *p. 94* (from **Kap. 8**, I) • The conjunction **aber**, *p. 95* (from **Kap. 1**, I) • The **Sie**-form of address, *p. 95* (from **Kap. 2**, I) • Agreeing, *p. 95* (from **Kap. 2**, I)
Dritte Stufe pp. 97-99	Asking and telling what you may or may not do, *p. 98*	• The accusative forms of **kein**, *p. 98* • The verb **dür-fen**, *p. 99*		• Expressing likes and dislikes, *p. 97* (from **Kap. 2**, I) • The irregular verb **essen**, *p. 97* (from **Kap. 6**, I) • Saying how often you do things, *p. 97* (from **Kap. 7**, I) • The conjunctions **weil** and **denn**, *p. 98* (from **Kap. 8**, I) • Talking about how things taste, *p. 98* (from **Kap. 6**, I) • Giving reasons, *p. 98* (from **Kap. 8**, I) • **Kein**, *p. 98* (from **Kap. 9**, I) • The impersonal pronoun **man**, *p. 99* (from **Kap. 3**, I)

Zum Lesen pp. 100-101	Bleibt fit und gesund! Reading Strategy: Activating your background knowledge

Review pp. 102-105	• **Anwendung**, *p. 102* • **Kann ich's wirklich?** *p. 104* • **Wortschatz**, *p. 105*

Assessment Options	**Stufe Quizzes**
	 • *Chapter Resources*, Book 2
	    Erste Stufe, Quiz 4-1
	    Zweite Stufe, Quiz 4-2
	    Dritte Stufe, Quiz 4-3
	 • *Assessment Items, Audiocassette* 7 B
		Kapitel 4 Chapter Test
		 • *Chapter Resources*, Book 2
		 • *Assessment Guide*, Speaking Test
		 • *Assessment Items, Audiocassette* 7 B
		
		 Test Generator, Kapitel 4

Chapter Overview

Video Program **OR**
Expanded Video Program, Videocassette 2

Textbook Audiocassette 2 B

RESOURCES Print	RESOURCES Audiovisual

Textbook Audiocassette 2 B

Practice and Activity Book
Chapter Resources, Book 2
- Additional Listening Activities 4-1, 4-2 ....*Additional Listening Activities, Audiocassette* 9 B
- Student Response Forms
- Realia 4-1
- Situation Card 4-1
- Teaching Transparency Master 4-1 ....*Teaching Transparency* 4-1
- Quiz 4-1...*Assessment Items, Audiocassette* 7 B

Video Guide ....*Video Program/Expanded Video Program,* Videocassette 2

Textbook Audiocassette 2 B

Practice and Activity Book
Chapter Resources, Book 2
- Communicative Activity 4-1
- Additional Listening Activities 4-3, 4-4 ....*Additional Listening Activities, Audiocassette* 9 B
- Student Response Forms
- Realia 4-2
- Situation Card 4-2
- Quiz 4-2...*Assessment Items, Audiocassette* 7 B

Textbook Audiocassette 2 B

Practice and Activity Book
Chapter Resources, Book 2
- Communicative Activity 4-2
- Additional Listening Activities 4-5, 4-6 ....*Additional Listening Activities, Audiocassette* 9 B
- Student Response Forms
- Realia 4-3
- Situation Card 4-3
- Teaching Transparency Master 4-2 ....*Teaching Transparency* 4-2
- Quiz 4-3...*Assessment Items, Audiocassette* 7 B

Video Guide ....*Video Program/Expanded Video Program,* Videocassette 2

Alternative Assessment

- Performance Assessment, *Teacher's Edition*
  Erste Stufe, p. 81M
  Zweite Stufe, p. 81N
  Dritte Stufe, p. 81P

- Portfolio Assessment
  Written: **Anwendung,** Activity 3, *Pupil's Edition,* p. 102; *Assessment Guide,* p. 17
  Oral: **Anwendung,** Activity 6, *Pupil's Edition,* p. 103; *Assessment Guide,* p. 17
- **Notizbuch,** *Pupil's Edition,* pp. 88, 89, 95; *Practice and Activity Book,* p. 148

Kapitel 4: Gesund leben
Textbook Listening Activities Scripts

Erste Stufe

Activity 8, p. 88

Der Gesundheitsmuffel! Ja, ich kenne einen. Er treibt selbst überhaupt keinen Sport. Na ja, Fußball liebt er heiß und innig, aber nur als Zuschauer. Er schaut den ganzen Tag Fernsehen. Dabei raucht er eine Zigarette nach der anderen. Wenn er müde wird, trinkt er literweise Kaffee. Er mag am liebsten Schweinefleisch. Außer Kartoffeln ißt er kein Gemüse, und Obst schmeckt ihm nur mit viel Zucker und Schlagsahne oben drauf. Kennst du auch so einen Gesundheitsmuffel?

Answers to Activity 8

Treibt keinen Sport; schaut den ganzen Tag Fernsehen; raucht; trinkt Kaffee; mag Schweinefleisch am liebsten; ißt kein Gemüse außer Kartoffeln; ißt viel Zucker und Schlagsahne.

Activity 12, p. 89

1. JASMIN Ich bin sehr sportlich! Dreimal pro Woche geh' ich direkt nach der Schule schwimmen. Und wenn das Wetter schön ist, mache ich oft am Wochenende eine Fahrradtour mit Freunden.

   KLAUS Spitze! Darf ich nächstes Wochenende mitfahren?

2. ELKE Ich esse fast kein Fleisch, eigentlich nur Gemüse, Obst, Käse, Brot, und so weiter. Alkohol trinke ich nicht gern, schmeckt mir normalerweise nicht. Ich tanze sehr gern und mache zweimal die Woche Gymnastik.

   KLAUS Das finde ich toll, Elke! Du siehst auch ziemlich fit aus.

3. PETER Eigentlich brauche ich jeden Tag meine acht Stunden Schlaf, sonst fühle ich mich nicht wohl. Meistens aber schlafe ich nur sechs Stunden oder so. Normalerweise trainiere ich zweimal pro Woche morgens in einer Fußballmannschaft, aber ich bin oft zu müde dazu.

KLAUS Das ist schade! Mensch, geh' doch früher ins Bett!

Answers to Activity 12

1. positiv 2. positiv 3. negativ

Activity 16, p. 90

Ich schlafe immer genügend und halte mich sehr fit. Jeden Morgen laufe ich zwei Kilometer. Dann esse ich frisches Obst und Müsli zum Frühstück. Man soll sich schließlich richtig ernähren. Bei der Arbeit trinke ich keinen Kaffee mehr, nur Saft und Wasser. Ich esse sehr viel Gemüse und Fisch, und selten auch mal Rindfleisch. Ich bin zwar gern draußen, aber ich vermeide die Sonne.

Answers to Activity 16

schläft genügend; läuft jeden Morgen; ißt Obst und Müsli; trinkt nur Saft und Wasser; ißt viel Gemüse und Fisch; selten Rindfleisch; vermeidet die Sonne

Zweite Stufe

Activity 23, p. 93

Guten Abend, meine Damen und Herren! Unsere heutige Sendung informiert Sie über die Sportgewohnheiten der deutschen Bevölkerung. Bei den Männern steht dabei Fußball an erster Stelle. 43% aller sporttreibenden deutschen Männer spielen mindestens einmal pro Woche Fußball, aber nur 4% aller sporttreibenden Frauen! Aber 50% der Frauen machen wöchentlich Aerobik und Jazztanz; die Männer sind hier nur mit 2% repräsentiert. Dafür liegt die Zahl der Teilnehmer am Bodybuilding am höchsten! 80% der gesamten sporttreibenden deutschen Bevölkerung sind Mitglied in einem Klub; Männer und Frauen sind mit jeweils 40% dabei. Sie trainieren im Durchschnitt zweimal die Woche.

Answers to Activity 23

Fußball: 43% Männer; 4% Frauen
Aerobik/Jazztanz: 50% Frauen; 2% Männer
Bodybuilding: 40% Männer; 40% Frauen

Activity 27, p. 95

Im Vergleich zu den Amerikanern gehen die meisten Deutschen ziemlich oft zu Fuß, weil sie es gesund finden, viel an der frischen Luft zu sein. Der Sonntagsspaziergang nach dem Mittagessen ist nach wie vor sehr beliebt. Außerdem spielen die Deutschen auch gern Squash und Tennis, weil es einen fit hält. An den Schulen gibt es normalerweise keine Mannschaften. Deshalb sind viele Deutsche Mitglieder in einem Fitneßklub oder Sportverein. Heutzutage vermeiden die Deutschen es auch, so viel zu rauchen, denn es ist total ungesund!

Answers to Activity 27

1. walk
2. squash; tennis; it keeps you fit
3. have school teams; members in a sport club
4. smoking; it is unhealthy

Dritte Stufe

Activity 31, p. 97

BETTINA Mein Lieblingsessen ist Fisch. Fisch schmeckt toll, und hier in Hamburg kriegt man die Salzwasserfische ganz frisch. Am liebsten mag ich Krabben!

ROLAND Ich mag keine Grapefruit! Die sind meistens viel zu sauer. Aber dafür esse ich Kirschen unheimlich gern! Die sind viel süßer.

RICHARD Blumenkohl finde ich gar nicht lecker. Er schmeckt mir nicht, aber sonst esse ich alle Gemüsesorten gern. Ja, und dann Fleisch, besonders Rind- und Schweinefleisch mag ich überhaupt nicht. Ich will Kühe und Schweine nicht essen, weil sie nette Tiere sind!

Answers to Activity 31

Bettina: mag Fisch und Krabben, weil sie frisch sind.
Roland: mag Grapefruit nicht, weil sie sauer sind; mag Kirschen, weil sie süß sind.
Richard: mag Blumenkohl nicht, weil er nicht schmeckt; mag Fleisch nicht, weil Tiere nett sind und er sie nicht essen will.

Activity 34, p. 98

ANNELIESE Ich darf noch gar nicht mit dem Auto fahren, weil ich noch nicht 18 bin!

ULRIKE Ich darf nicht so spät abends ausgehen und soll schon um 10 Uhr wieder zu Hause sein!

NORBERT Ich darf kein Fleisch essen.

JÖRG In der Klasse darf ich meine Lieblingszeitschrift nicht lesen.

SCRIPTS

SCRIPTS

*A*nwendung
Activity 1, *p. 102*

1. Der Gesundheitsminister appelliert an die Raucher: Aus gesundheitlichen Gründen vermeiden Sie es bitte, in Zimmern zu rauchen, in denen sich auch Nichtraucher aufhalten!
2. Tanzen Sie sich fit! Das City-Sportstudio lädt zu einer kostenlosen Stunde im Jazztanz oder Jitterbug ein! Machen Sie mit! Unsere Kurse laufen täglich! Schauen Sie noch heute bei uns herein!
3. Guten Abend, liebe Zuhörer! Hier ist Ihr Sender WDR-Y mit dem 9-Uhr-Abendprogramm. Relaxen Sie heute eine Stunde lang bei Mozarts *Kleiner Nachtmusik* bevor Sie ins Bett gehen, damit Sie morgen früh um sechs frisch und ausgeschlafen den Tag beginnen können!
4. Haben Sie heute schon Ihre Vitamine bekommen? Wenn nicht, dann auf zum Aldo-Markt! Wir haben für Sie eine große Auswahl von gartenfrischem Obst und Gemüse. Täglich neue Sonderangebote!

Answers to Activity 1
1. d; 2. a; 3. c; 4. b

Activity 5, *p. 103*

Hallo! Hier ist Peter Buschmann. Ich rufe an, weil ich ein Problem habe. Es geht mir nämlich gar nicht gut. Mir ist total schlecht geworden, nachdem ich eine große Tüte Kartoffelchips gegessen habe. Vorher habe ich mir, wie auch sonst jeden Tag, eine Portion Pommes frites mit Mayonnaise vom Imbiß geholt. Ich weiß echt nicht, warum mir schlecht ist, denn ich habe sonst nichts gegessen. Ich war den ganzen Tag in der Wohnung und habe nur Fernsehen geschaut! Wir haben nämlich Schulferien. Also, hoffentlich habe ich nichts Schlimmes! Ich bin doch erst 14 Jahre alt!

Answers to Activity 5
Peter Buschmann; 14 Jahre alt; Schüler; ihm ist schlecht; hat sich ungesund ernährt; soll Sport machen und frisches Obst und Gemüse essen

Kapitel 4: Gesund leben
Projects and Games

PROJECT

In this project students will create a fitness program advertised by a fictional health center.

Materials Students may need a large piece of construction paper, ads from fitness magazines and health food stores, scissors, markers, and some glue or tape.

Outline

Students' programs should include the following information
- Introduction to new members
- Outline for an exercise program
- Nutritional information and program
- At least 2 seminars which are offered. They should include a topic and a brief (2-3 sentences) summary of the lecture.

Suggested Sequence

1. Students decide to work individually or with a partner.
2. Students begin by making an outline of what they plan to include in the various parts of their programs. They should look at several magazines and ads for ideas.
3. Students then gather all information to make their program appealing to potential members. Encourage students to use some realia in each part of their program.
4. Students do the actual layout and write-up of their program and glue or tape it on the construction paper.
5. Students present their final project to the class in a short oral presentation.
6. Optional: Ask students to vote on whose program provided the best overall choices for improving their physical fitness.

Grading the Project

Suggested point distribution (total = 100 points)

Originality and design	30
Written assignment	40
Oral presentation	30

 GAME

Ratet mal, was ich bin!

This game will help students review the food and health vocabulary presented in this chapter.

Preparation Write the names of food items from this chapter and previous chapters on index cards.

Procedure Ask one of the students to come to the front of the class and pick a card. He or she "becomes" the food item on that card and tells the class **Ratet mal, was ich bin!** The other students then ask **ja/nein** questions in order to determine what food item he or she is.
Examples:
Hast du viele Kalorien?
Bist du gesund?
Ißt man dich zum Mittagessen?
Kann man dich beim Bäcker kaufen?
Bist du eine Obstsorte?
Bist du eine Gemüsesorte?
The student who guesses the correct food item comes to the front of the class, and the game begins again.

PROJECTS AND GAMES

Kapitel 4: Gesund leben
Lesson Plans, pages 82-105

Using the Chapter Opener, pp. 82-83

Motivating Activity

Go around the classroom and ask students what they do to stay fit outside of school. What types of activities do they enjoy the most? Are the other members of their family also involved in these activities? What are their reasons for staying fit?

Building on Previous Skills

① Ask students to describe in German what these two girls are doing and what they are wearing. Continue by asking your students what they usually wear when they jog or exercise and where they do this.

 Culture Note

Trimmdichpfade *(trails with suggested fitness activities marked along the path)* are very popular and can be found all over Germany.

Thinking Critically

Comparing and Contrasting Make a transparency of one of the **Stundenpläne** in the Level I *Pupil's Edition* on p. 97 or 112. Ask students to look for the physical education classes the German students have each week. How does the number of hours per week compare with their own schedules?

Group Work

Ask students to work in groups of three or four. Have each group make a list of as many team sports (**Mannschaftsport**) and individual sports (**Einzelsport**) they can think of. Set a time limit for this activity. Call on groups to share their sports with the class.

Building on Previous Skills

② In German, ask students to describe the foods featured in the photograph and have them tell you which ones they like or dislike. You may also want to ask students to recall the last time they ate the pictured foods.
Wann hast du das letzte Mal … gegessen?

Teaching Suggestions

② Read the caption of Photo 2 with students. Then ask them to answer the following question.
- **Daniel, wovon ißt du viel?**
- **Ich esse viel …**

③ On one side of the board or a transparency, write the word **OBST**. On the other side, write the word **GEMÜSE**. Ask students to come up with as many items for each group as they can.

Home Economics Connection

Have students consult the home economics teacher to find out the daily recommended servings for fruits and vegetables. (Four to five servings) Then ask students which of the pictured items they typically eat and how many servings of fruits and vegetables they eat each day.

Focusing on Outcomes

To get students to focus on the chapter objectives, ask them what kind of suggestions they would make to somebody who is trying to get into shape and improve his or her eating habits. Then preview the learning outcomes listed on p. 83.
NOTE: Each of these outcomes is modeled in the video and evaluated in **Kann ich's wirklich?** on p. 104.

Teaching Los geht's!
pp. 84-86

Resources for Los geht's!

- *Video Program* OR
  Expanded Video Program, Videocassette 2
- *Textbook Audiocassette* 2 B
- *Practice and Activity Book*

▶ **pages 84-85**

📼 Video Synopsis

In this segment of the video, four friends are asked what they do to stay healthy. The student outcomes listed on p. 83 are modeled in the video: expressing approval and disapproval, asking for information and responding emphatically or with reservations, asking and telling what you may or may not do.

Motivating Activity

Ask students what kinds of things they do to stay healthy. Do any of them exercise, eat special foods, or avoid certain foods? Try to discuss as much as possible in German. Encourage students to paraphrase or describe things for which they don't know the appropriate vocabulary.

Teaching Suggestions

- To introduce students to the **Foto-Roman,** do the prereading activity at the top of p. 84 with the class. You may also want to have students scan the text for cognates or previously learned phrases and expressions. Then show the video to students or have them listen to the audiocassette.

- After watching **Wie fühlst du dich?** once or twice, play each segment again and have students follow along in the book. Then go through the following steps.
a) Read the **Foto-Roman** with the class, alternating roles.
b) In German, explain or demonstrate any new words or phrases.
c) Have pairs of students read the interviews.
d) Ask simple open-ended questions.

▶ **page 86**

Teaching Suggestions

1 After students have seen the video, use these five questions to check for comprehension. This can be done orally. If some students are insecure about answering the questions, have them look back at the **Foto-Roman.**

2 Ask students to read the **Foto-Roman** with a partner. Monitor students' pronunciation and intonation and make suggestions when needed. Students then answer the six questions in writing. When students are finished call on several to read their answers.

✦ For Individual Needs

3 Auditory Learners Ask students to close their books. Write the names of the German students on the board. Read the six statements in Activity 3 to the class in German. After each statement, ask students who this statement best fits. Students choose one of the names on the board. (**geht zu Bett gewöhnlich um zehn Uhr; ißt keine Schokolade; wohnt gern in Hamburg; ißt Obst und Gemüse; spielt in der Basketballmannschaft; ißt nur mageres Fleisch**)

For Additional Practice

5 Once students have completed the seven sentences, have them write down which of the German students each statement refers to. Students should look at the text to verify their answers. Then have students write in narrative form what happens in the **Foto-Roman.**

Closure

Refer students back to the learning outcomes listed on p. 83 and ask students to list one German phrase or word from the **Foto-Roman** that corresponds to each function.

ERSTE STUFE

Teaching Erste Stufe,
pp. 87-91

Resources for Erste Stufe

Practice and Activity Book
Chapter Resources, Book 2
- Additional Listening Activities 4-1, 4-2
- Student Response Forms
- Realia 4-1
- Situation Card 4-1
- Teaching Transparency Master 4-1
- Quiz 4-1

Audiocassette Program
- *Textbook Audiocassette* 2 B
- *Additional Listening Activities, Audiocassette* 9 B
- *Assessment Items, Audiocassette* 7 B

Video Program or *Expanded Video Program*

▶ **page 87**

MOTIVATE

Teaching Suggestion

Ask students what one piece of advice they would give somebody to keep healthy and stay fit.

TEACH

Teaching Suggestion

Ask four volunteers to read the four interviews. Then ask your class which statement they can most identify with. Ask them to read that statement to their partner, making minor changes or deletions as necessary to fit their own situation. Call on several students to read their own report.

PRESENTATION: Wortschatz

To introduce the new expressions, use visual aids such as the symbols on p. 87, flash cards, magazine cutouts, or other pictures. Hold up each visual and give the corresponding expression from the **Wortschatz** box. Repeat the expressions several times. Then ask yes/no and either/or questions to help students practice the new vocabulary.

Building on Previous Skills

7 Before students write the 7 **Gebote**, mention that they can also use modal verbs such as **sollen, dürfen,** and **müssen.**
Examples:
Man soll vernünftig essen!
Man muß viel Obst essen!
Man darf nicht rauchen!

 For Individual Needs

7 **Visual Learners** Ask students to match each of the sentences they have written to accompany the symbols to one of the four interviews, according to how well each sentence fits that German student's tips.

▶ *page 88*

 For Individual Needs

8 **Challenge** To expand this activity, ask students what they would suggest to the **Gesundheitsmuffel** to help him overcome his vices. Students should use the new **Wortschatz** expressions.

PRESENTATION: Ein wenig Grammatik

In Level 1 students learned the words **fahren** and **einladen,** two verbs that have stem-vowel changes: **a** changes to **ä** in the **du-** and **er/sie-** forms. Review those two verbs before introducing **schlafen.**

For Additional Practice

9 Give a blank page from a weekly **Taschenkalender** to each student and ask students to fill in the fitness activities they plan for the upcoming week. Then ask students to share their fitness plans with the class.

PRESENTATION: So sagt man das!

Ask students about expressions of approval and disapproval they commonly use in English and then write some on the board or on a transparency. Have students look at the examples in the **So sagt man das!** box and ask them what the expressions mean. Use the familiar phrase **Ich glaube, daß ...** to review the verb position in dependent clauses. Can students recall another conjunction that requires the verb to be in final position? (**weil**)

For Individual Needs

11 Challenge After students have chosen the correct replies to Markus' statements, ask them to restate his statements using the conjunction **daß.** This can be done orally or in writing.
Examples:
Das ist prima, daß du regelmäßig Sport machst!
Das finde ich nicht gut, daß du nicht richtig ißt!

11 Challenge On a transparency, list additional statements that refer to healthy or unhealthy habits. Uncover one statement at a time and have students react to each of them using **daß**-clauses.
Examples:
Ich liege oft in der Sonne, denn ich will braun werden.
Mein Bruder raucht zwanzig Zigaretten am Tag.
In meiner Familie essen wir viel Obst, Gemüse und Salat.
Meine Eltern trinken gar keinen Alkohol.
Meine Mutter trinkt sehr viel Kaffee.

 **► page 89**

Teaching Suggestion

12 Have students listen to the recording twice before they write down which remarks are positive and which are negative. Then play each of the monologues again, one at a time. Ask students to summarize what Jasmin said. Do the same for Elke's and Peter's reports.

Group Work

13 Students work in groups of three. Ask each group to write down as many logical sentences as they can within a set time limit. Call on two or three groups to read some of their sentences to the class.

Teaching Suggestion

14 After students have finished Activity 14, ask them to form groups according to the **Laster** they share. Then ask students in each group to design a plan to improve their health. They should make fitness as well as dietary changes.

PRESENTATION: Wortschatz

Give several examples to complete the phrases.
Ich fühle mich wohl, wenn ich richtig esse.
Ich ernähre mich richtig, wenn ich viel Obst und Gemüse esse.
Ich halte mich fit, indem ich dreimal in der Woche jogge.
Then ask students to practice these new expressions by completing the phrases themselves.

Teaching Suggestion

16 Have students number lines from 1 to 7 in their notebooks. Then ask them to listen to Mr. Dingsda's report and jot down any information they can understand. Play the tape at least twice. Then play it again, stopping repeatedly so students can fill in the information they have missed. Next, ask students to write the report in short sentences. Have students compare their versions with their partners' versions and make up a composite report. Select several pairs to read their reports to the class.

ERSTE STUFE

▶ *page 90*

PRESENTATION: Grammatik

To present the reflexive verb structures, bring several hand-held mirrors to class. Also prepare flash cards with adhesive tape on the back. Make one flashcard using the same color for each subject pronoun in the nominative and another card for each corresponding reflexive pronoun.

ich   ——> **mich** (in red)
du   ——> **dich** (in blue)
er/sie ——> **sich** (in green)
wir   ——> **uns** (in orange)
ihr   ——> **euch** (in purple)
sie *(pl)* ——> **sich** (in brown)

Then write the different verb conjugations for the verb **sehen** on six different cards, all in black. Look in the mirror and say **Ich sehe mich.** Then hand the mirror to a student and ask him or her to look into it. Tell the student **Du siehst dich** (**im Spiegel**). Turn to the class and, pointing to the student, say **Er/sie sieht sich** (**im Spiegel**). Hand the mirror to two students, have them look at themselves in the mirror, and tell them **Ihr seht euch** (**im Spiegel**). Turn to the class and, pointing at the two students, say **Sie sehen sich** (**im Spiegel**). Finally, look into the mirror with students and say **Wir sehen uns** (**im Spiegel**). Repeat all the sentences you just introduced, and as you do so, tape the corresponding flash cards onto the board. Have different students come to the board and circle each subject pronoun and draw a line to the corresponding reflexive pronoun. Tell students that **ich** and **mich**, **du** and **dich**, **er** and **sich**, and so on, refer to the same person. Explain that a reflexive verb is a verb whose action is turned back (reflected like in the mirror activity) to the subject of the verb.

 For Individual Needs

17 A Slower Pace Have students do Activity 17 with a partner. They should read the dialogue and use the **Grammatik** box to complete the sentences. You may also want to keep the flashcards taped to the board so students can refer to them as needed. Partners should then switch roles and go over the conversations again.

Teaching Suggestions

18 Have partners make a list of all the things they think a health conscious person would do and not do. Then as each pair reports, keep track of their ideas on a transparency or on the board. Each idea mentioned by other groups gets five points, each idea mentioned only once gets ten points. The pair with the most points wins.

19 After students have completed the basic task, ask them to do it again expanding on their answers and telling why they feel good or bad. Examples:
— **Wie fühlst du dich in dieser Schule?**
— **Ich fühle mich sehr wohl. Ich habe viele Freunde und die Lehrer sind nett.**
or
— **Ich fühle mich sehr wohl, weil ich viele Freunde habe und die Lehrer nett sind.**

▶ *page 91*

PRESENTATION: Wortschatz

When people are asked in English how they feel about something, their answers usually vary greatly; they use different expressions to express their feelings. Go over the expressions under the heading **wie?** and give their meanings through synonyms, if possible. Then ask students:
Wie fühlst du dich in dieser Klasse?
Wie fühlst du dich an dieser Schule?
Wie fühlst du dich in dieser Stadt?
Students should use one of the expressions under the heading **wie?** to answer the questions.

Teaching Suggestions

21 After students have completed the written part of this activity, have them get together with another student to exchange what they have written down. Then call on several students to share with the class what their partners wrote about themselves and where they feel most comfortable.

22 Ask students to conduct this conversation as though one of them is being interviewed for an article on teen fitness. Both students should write down the questions and answers from their interview. For additional practice, students could ask two or three more questions than the activity calls for. Since this is a lengthy assignment, you may want to have students work on it during two class periods. Then call on three or four pairs to read their interviews to the rest of the class. To ensure that all students are listening, each pair should ask the class two questions related to the interview to check comprehension.

▶ *page 92*

 PRESENTATION: Landeskunde

Teacher Note

The **Landeskunde** interviews are recorded on audiocassette and videocassette.

Teaching Suggestion

Do the prereading activity at the top of p. 92. Then make a chart on the board or on a transparency and write on one side **Fitneß in den U.S.A.** and on the other side **Fitneß in Deutschland.** Have students brainstorm what they think might be popular fitness activities in both countries. This will help students build expectancies for the **Landeskunde** interviews.

🌐 Culture Notes

- Physical fitness is made important to Germans early in life. The German Sports Federation (**DSB = Deutscher Sportbund**), for example, challenges people of all ages to try for the gold, silver, and bronze **Sportabzeichen,** sports medals for which participants test and challenge their own level of fitness in a number of disciplines.
- **Volksmarsch,** also called **Volkswanderung,** is also a very popular way for Germans to stay fit, enjoy nature, and meet other people. It is an organized hike that varies in length and time (5, 10, or 20 km) for which participants sign up and receive awards for attending.

Language Note

Herr Troger is from St. Ulrich, in **Tirol.** Ask students if they can guess what the word **bissel** means. Do they see or hear a resemblance to the word **bißchen?** Regina uses the word **arg** at the end of her interview. It is a synonym for **sehr.**

Teaching Suggestion

Ask students how they can combine staying fit with doing something for the environment. Can students list some of the things they do regularly to help in this matter? (Example: riding bikes) Encourage students to use as much German as possible in their discussion. Many of the phrases and expressions they will need to answer this question were taught in Chapter 7 of Level 1. (Examples: **radfahren = keine Abgase in der Luft; Biokost essen = keine Pestizide in der Erde; mindestens acht Stunden am Tag schlafen = Licht aus: weniger Energie verbrauchen)**

Teacher Note

Mention to your students that the **Landeskunde** will also be included in Quiz 4-1 given at the end of the **Erste Stufe.**

CLOSE

Teaching Suggestion

To prepare for this activity, cut out several pictures from magazines that show people involved in physical fitness activities or ads for local health food stores. You may want to paste these on construction paper for future activities. Hold up one picture at a time and ask students in what way these people are staying fit or are taking care of themselves. Encourage students to use expressions of approval or disapproval about the featured activities or ads.

Focusing on Outcomes

Refer students back to the learning outcomes listed on p. 83. They should recognize that they now know how to express approval and disapproval.

ASSESS

- **Performance Assessment** Ask students to state three activities they need to do or changes they should make to feel better and live a healthier lifestyle.

- Quiz 4-1, *Chapter Resources,* Book 2

Teaching Zweite Stufe, pp. 93-96

Resources for Zweite Stufe

Practice and Activity Book
Chapter Resources, Book 2
- Communicative Activity 4-1
- Additional Listening Activities 4-3, 4-4
- Student Response Forms
- Realia 4-2
- Situation Card 4-2
- Quiz 4-2
Audiocassette Program
- *Textbook Audiocassette* 2 B
- *Additional Listening Activities, Audiocassette* 9 B
- *Assessment Items, Audiocassette* 7 B

▶ *page 93*

MOTIVATE

TPR Total Physical Response

To get students' attention and increase their awareness of physical fitness, introduce them to the **Fünf-Minuten Herzclub!** Give commands, using reflexive verbs such as **sich setzen, sich drehen, sich stellen, sich kämmen,** and other verbs such as **gehen, laufen, bringen, springen, stampfen, klatschen,** and **aufstehen.** Model each of the commands. Give commands to the class as a whole and to individual students.
Examples:
Stellt euch an die Wand!
Dreht euch um!
Klatscht in die Hände!
Kämm dich!
Springt vorwärts!
At the end you may want to ask a few students:
Und wie fühlst du dich jetzt?

TEACH

For Additional Practice

24 Ask students to use their answers to the questionnaire to write a short, coherent paragraph. Encourage students to use connectors. This could be assigned for homework. You might want to ask two or three students to read their paragraphs in class the following day.

▶ *page 94*

PRESENTATION: Grammatik

Write the sentence **Jeden Tag esse ich um 12 Uhr.** Underline the ending **-en.** Ask students
a) the gender of the word **Tag,** (masculine) and
b) in what case **jeden** is used. (accusative) Tell students that **jeder** has ending changes just like definite articles. Give other common examples of expressions with **jeder.**
Examples:

Welche Musik hörst du gern?	**Ich höre jede Musik gern.**

For Individual Needs

25 Challenge After students have done the five sentences, ask them to add similar phrases their parents use. Make a list of several phrases and then ask students to rephrase them as they did the five previous sentences, beginning each response with **doch.**

▶ *page 95*

PRESENTATION: So sagt man das!

Ask students to look back at the **Foto-Roman** on p. 84 and to list the various ways the interviewer initiates the interviews with Nicolas, Maike, David, and Thorsten. After they have made a list of the different ways she asked questions, ask students to provide English equivalents.

▶ *page 96*

 For Individual Needs

30 Challenge As an alternative, you may want to collect all the index cards after students have written down their three health related vices and their names. Read several cards to the class. Elicit student reactions as you read the vices and ask them for advice to help student X overcome his or her health-related vice.

PRESENTATION: Wortschatz

Go over the new words and phrases and help students practice them by asking them how often they do certain activities.
Examples:
Wie oft liest du Bücher?
Wie oft gehst du schwimmen?

PRESENTATION: Ein wenig Landeskunde

Students have learned reading strategies to help them determine the meaning of compound words. Put the following words on the board and help students infer the meaning of the words before they read the interviews (**Bioläden, Vollwertkost, Reformhäuser, Umweltbewußtsein**).

Reteaching: Asking for information and responding

On index cards, write questions similar to those in the **So sagt man das!** function box on p. 95 and those in the **Foto-Roman** on p. 84. Hand out the cards to students. Have each student read the question on his or her card aloud and ask another student in class to answer the question.

CLOSE

 Game

Play the game **Ratet mal, was ich bin!** See p. 81 F for the procedure.

Focusing on Outcomes

Refer students back to the learning outcomes listed on p. 83. They should recognize that they now know how to ask for information and respond emphatically or agree with reservations.

ASSESS

• **Performance Assessment** Prepare a list of questions similar to the questions in the **Fragebogen** on p. 93 and in the **So sagt man das!** box on p. 95. Include vocabulary from the **Zweite Stufe.** Call on individual students. They should answer your questions, using the expressions they have learned in the **Zweite Stufe.**
Examples:
Sag mal, machst du viel Sport? Wie oft denn?
Darf ich mal fragen? Ernährst du dich richtig?
Ich habe eine Frage! Wie oft treibst du Sport?
Wie steht's mit Tennis? Spielst du es gern?

• Quiz 4-2, *Chapter Resources,* Book 2

ZWEITE STUFE

*T*eaching Dritte Stufe
pp. 97-99

Resources for Dritte Stufe

Practice and Activity Book
Chapter Resources, Book 2
- Communicative Activity 4-2
- Additional Listening Activities 4-5, 4-6
- Student Response Forms
- Realia 4-3
- Situation Card 4-3
- Teaching Transparency Master 4-2
- Quiz 4-3

Audiocassette Program
- *Textbook Audiocassette* 2 B
- *Additional Listening Activities, Audiocassette* 9 B
- *Assessment Items, Audiocassette* 7 B

▶ *page 97*

MOTIVATE

Teaching Suggestion

As a warm-up for the upcoming activities, put the following incomplete statement on the board and ask students to think about how they would complete it.
Meine Mutter sagt, daß ich kein ... essen soll, weil ...

TEACH

PRESENTATION: Wortschatz

Introduce the new vocabulary using visual aids or a transparency of the items. Point to the foods and tell students what they are. Then ask yes/no questions and either/or questions. Once you think students feel comfortable with the words, ask open-ended questions such as the following.

Wie ißt du die Möhren? Roh oder gekocht?
Wie oft ißt du Rindfleisch?
Wie schmeckt dir Forelle?
Trinkst du Magermilch? Warum? or Warum nicht?
Wie viele Eier ißt du pro Woche?
Was kommt denn so alles in eine gute Hühnersuppe?

▶ *page 98*

PRESENTATION: Wortschatz

Use props or other visual aids to teach the new phrases. For example, hold up a candy bar and tell students: **Die Schokolade will ich nicht essen, denn sie hat zu viel Fett, zu viel Zucker, zu viele Kalorien.** Checking the information on the wrapper, say: **Laß mal sehen,... 500 Kalorien! Das ist zu viel!** Then hold up a carrot and ask students: **Was hat weniger Kalorien die Möhre oder die Schokolade?** For each of the new expressions, try to use visual aids and make comparisons with previously learned food items to give students plenty of practice.

PRESENTATION: So sagt man das!

As you introduce the verb **dürfen,** you may want to explain the difference between **dürfen** and **können.** Usually **dürfen** implies permission and **können** implies ability. Read through the examples in the function box, then provide practice for students by asking questions such as the following.

Was darf ein Diabetiker essen/nicht essen?
Was darf ein Vegetarier essen/nicht essen?
Jim ist allergisch gegen Orangen. Was darf er nicht essen?

For Additional Practice

34 To expand this listening activity, ask students to react to the comments made by the German students. Students should tell which of the mentioned activities they are or are not allowed to do either.

▶ *page 99*

PRESENTATION: Grammatik

To practice the forms of **dürfen,** make index cards with pronouns and nouns and combine them with pictures of foods and beverages or activities to prompt students to produce sentences.

Multicultural Connection

Ask students to find out from exchange students what types of rules they have in their schools and with individual teachers. Ask a few students to report their findings in German to the class.

Family Link

37 After completing this activity, have students interview their family members or friends about allergies. Or you may choose to have a few students interview the school nurse to find out about common allergies among the students at school. Have the students report back to the class and add their findings to the allergies listed on p. 99.

Thinking Critically

37 **Drawing Inferences** Discuss allergies your students or members of their families might have. Write the following words on the board or on a transparency and see if students can guess their meaning:

> Blütenstaub, Katzenhaare, Wolle, Medikamente, synthetische Stoffe

CLOSE

Teaching Suggestion

Divide the class into two groups to play *Tic-Tac-Toe.* Fill the nine squares of the grid with nine infinitive verbs such as **dürfen, können, sollen, müssen, wollen, sich fühlen, sich fit halten, schlafen,** and **sich freuen.** Teams must form sentences in the present tense, using the verb indicated in the square, in order to get an X or an O in a square. The first team to get three in a row wins.

X: **Ich darf Erdbeeren nicht essen, denn ich bin allergisch gegen Erdbeeren.**

O: **Wir halten uns fit: Wir joggen und wir essen auch vernünftig.**

Reteaching: *Dürfen* and dependent-clause-word order

Ask certain students to perform chores around the room, then ask a few other students to help a classmate with a chore, and finally ask some students if they would like to eat some of the foods you have brought to class. Students should answer, using an excuse why they cannot do the chore or eat the food.

Examples:

- **Pat, kannst du nach der Schule die Fenster zumachen?**
- **Ich darf leider nicht nach der Schule bleiben, weil ich zum Zahnarzt muß.**

ASSESS

- **Performance Assessment** Write the following incomplete sentence on the board or on a transparency.

> _____ darf kein _____ essen, weil ...

Ask students to complete the sentence, using vocabulary and expressions they learned in the **Dritte Stufe.**

- Quiz 4-3, *Chapter Resources,* Book 2

*T*eaching Zum Lesen, *pp. 100-101*

Reading Strategy

The targeted strategy in this reading is activating your background knowledge. Students should learn about this strategy before beginning Question 1.

PREREADING

Motivating Activity

Ask students to jot down four things they consider important to staying healthy.

Teacher Note

Activity 1 is a prereading activity.

Building on Previous Skills

Ask students to scan the pictures and have them give each a title. Call on several students to share their work with the class.

READING

Teaching Suggestions

- Ask students to scan the pictures and titles. Which article would they read first? Ask them to list the words that caught their eye. What type of words are they?

- As an advance organizer to the article on **Nichtraucher,** read Activities 2 and 3 with students. Then ask students to reread the article and to identify the main idea or the topic sentence.

ZUM LESEN

Thinking Critically

- **Comparing and Contrasting** Ask students if they know of any companies in the United States that provide incentives for their employees to improve their health or encourage physical activity. Students could call companies in their area and make inquiries about such incentives. (Example: Large companies often help pay for membership dues to health clubs.)

- **Drawing Inferences** Ask students to think of some reasons that might have made the German company owner promise money to his non-smoking employees. (Example: some employees might have complained about second-hand smoke.)

Thinking Critically

Drawing Inferences After students read the article about **Salat,** ask them to look for specific words that indicate **Salat** isn't necessarily a choice for Germans.

Cooperative Learning

Divide the class into groups of three. Group members choose a reader, a recorder, and a reporter. Students then work through Questions 4-7 within a set amount of time. Once the groups have completed their assignments, call on the reporters of several groups to present their answers. You may want to collect the papers at the end to verify that the task has been completed by all groups.

POST-READING

Teacher Note

Activity 8 is a post-reading task that will show whether students can apply what they have learned.

Closure

In preparation for this game, make a list of words from the **Zum Lesen** section. (Examples: **Nichtraucher, Reue, Aufwärmen**) Scramble the letters of the words and write them on a transparency. The student who guesses the word correctly first, wins a point.
Example: AUCHTHRNERIC = **Nichtraucher**

Answers to Activity 1
Examples: eating healthy, no smoking, exercising

Answers to Activity 2
An employer rewards his employees who quit smoking by giving them DM 100.

Answers to Activity 3
a. The offer has been very successful, all but one smoker gave up smoking.
b. One employee uses the extra money to pay for his vacation every year.

Answers to Activity 4
a. no reason given
b. no reason implied or hinted at
c. Examples: Non-smokers are healthier and will, therefore, miss fewer days at work.

Answers to Activity 5
A meal without a salad; it's not important whether we like it or not; eating a healthy salad makes up for guilty feelings after eating a hearty pork roast; in general, it is implied that Germans probably prefer the main course to a salad, but a lot of people tend to choose eating healthy foods such as salads these days.

Answers to Activity 6
1. **richtig aufwärmen;** 2. **richtiges Schuhwerk;** 3. **richtig essen;** 4. **richtig laufen;** 5. **richtig kühlen;** 6. **richtig sitzen**

Answers to Activity 7
gymnastics and stretching (**Gymnastik und Stretching**); Italian soccer players (**italienische Fußballstars**); out: ice cubes to cool injuries; in: "hot ice"; water near the freezing point

Using Anwendung,
pp. 102-103

Video Wrap-Up

At this time, you might want to use the *Video Program* or the *Expanded Video Program*, Videocassette 2 for additional review and enrichment. See *Video Guide* for suggestions regarding:
- **Wie fühlst du dich?**
  (Dramatic episode)
- **Landeskunde**
  Interviews
- **Videoclips**
  (Authentic footage—*Expanded Video Program* only)

◆ For Individual Needs

1 A Slower Pace Ask students to read the four summary statements before listening to the audiocassette. Have students come up with words and phrases they expect to hear.

Building on Previous Skills

2 Ask students to use the reading skills they have learned to find key phrases in the letter. This will help them answer Questions 1-3. Put students in pairs and give each pair a copy of the letter. Have them decide together on the key phrases and highlight them.

Teaching Suggestion

3 To help students prepare for this assignment, brainstorm with them a brief outline of what the response letter should entail. Remind them to use words and expressions from the **Gesundheitstips** on p. 87, from the **Wortschatz** on pp. 97 and 98, and expressions of approval and disapproval on p. 88 to help them write their response letter.

Portfolio Assessment

3 You may want to suggest this activity as a written portfolio item for your students. See *Assessment Guide*, p. 17.

Portfolio Assessment

6 You may want to suggest this activity as an oral portfolio item for your students. See *Assessment Guide*, p. 17.

Health Connection

7 You might want to suggest that students use their health textbooks to look up information on nutrition. They should follow guidelines to ensure that their menus include all major food groups.

Kann ich's wirklich?
p. 104

This page helps students prepare for the test. It is a brief checklist of the major points covered in the chapter. The students should be reminded that it is only a checklist and not necessarily everything that will appear on the test.

Using Wortschatz,
p. 105

Teaching Suggestion

Since many of the new vocabulary items are expressions and phrases, suggest that students write the new phrases on index cards. They should give a context to each phrase by including it in a sentence.

For Individual Needs

Tactile Learners Ask students to bring a healthy dish to class. You may want to suggest simple dishes such as appetizers or desserts. Tell students that some of the ingredients have to be foods that were introduced in this chapter. Students must also tell the class in German why this food is healthy, using the expressions they learned in the **Dritte Stufe**.

Teacher Note

Give the **Kapitel 4** Chapter Test, *Chapter Resources, Book 2*.

KAPITEL 4

Gesund leben

1 Wie haltet ihr euch fit?

Most German students exercise regularly, pay attention to what they eat and drink, and try to get enough sleep. Do you and your friends try to keep fit? When you talk about fitness, you might praise your friends for what they do well — or express disappointment about what they don't do. There are also other things you need to learn in order to talk with your friends about staying healthy.

In this chapter you will learn

- to express approval and disapproval
- to ask for information and respond emphatically or agree with reservations
- to ask and tell what you may or may not do

And you will

- listen to German students talk about their health and about what they do and don't eat
- read "health tips" offered by German teenagers
- write about what you do to stay healthy
- find out what students do to keep fit

② Es freut mich, daß es dir schmeckt.

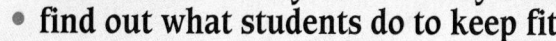

③ Ich esse viel Obst und Gemüse.

Los geht's!

Wie fühlst du dich?

Look at the photos that accompany the story.
Who are the students pictured?
What do you think they are talking about?

Nicolas   Maike   David   Thorsten

Wir haben junge Hamburger Gymnasiasten interviewt. Nicolas stellt uns seine Freunde vor.

> Das ist unsere Clique, Thorsten, ich, Wiebke, David und Maike. Wir gehen aufs Helene-Lange-Gymnasium. Das ist ein zweisprachiges Gymnasium.

①

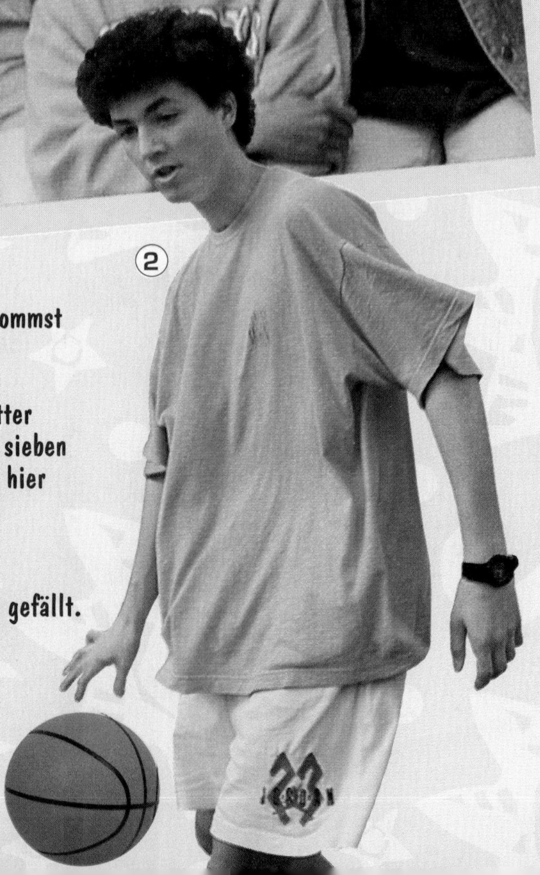

②

INTERVIEWERIN	Kann ich dich mal etwas fragen? Wo kommst du her, und wie fühlst du dich hier in Hamburg?
NICOLAS	Ich komme aus Frankreich. Meine Mutter arbeitet für Air France. Ich bin schon sieben Jahre in Hamburg, und ich fühle mich hier sehr wohl.
INTERVIEWERIN	Hast du kein Heimweh?
NICOLAS	Nein, überhaupt nicht!
INTERVIEWERIN	Das freut mich, daß es dir hier so gut gefällt.

③

INTERVIEWERIN Ihr seht alle so gesund aus! Könnt ihr mir mal sagen, was ihr für eure Gesundheit tut?

MAIKE Ja, also, ich lebe eigentlich sehr gesund. Ich mache jeden Morgen Gymnastik, und ich jogge, wenn ich Zeit habe. Und ich schlafe auch genug. Jeden Tag gehe ich gewöhnlich um zehn Uhr zu Bett.

INTERVIEWERIN Ich finde es prima, Maike, daß du so gesund lebst.

④

INTERVIEWERIN Na, David, dann sag uns mal, wie du dich fit hältst!

DAVID Tja, auch Sport, gesund essen, genügend schlafen. Ich spiele Basketball. Ich freue mich, daß ich auch in der Mannschaft bin. Ich fühle mich sehr wohl in der Mannschaft. Aber leider sind wir dieses Jahr nicht so gut.

INTERVIEWERIN Ach, das wird schon wieder!

⑤

INTERVIEWERIN Und Thorsten, wie ist es mit dir? Wie lebst du? Wie hältst du dich fit?

THORSTEN Nachmittags, zum Beispiel, spiele ich Basketball. Ich spiele in unserer Mannschaft. Wir trainieren zweimal die Woche, immer montags und donnerstags. Ja, und dann esse ich vernünftig.

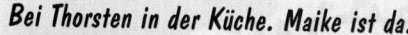

Bei Thorsten in der Küche. Maike ist da.

⑥

Und was ißt du so?

Ach, alles, was gesund ist: Obst und Gemüse ... und Fisch.

Und Fleisch? Wie steht's mit Fleisch?

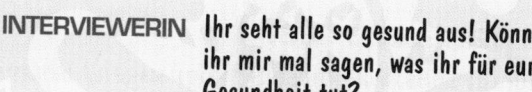

⑦

Gibt es etwas, was du nicht essen darfst?

Ja, Schokolade.

Warum nicht?

Ich bin allergisch gegen Schokolade.

Schade! Ich esse Schokolade gern.

Hier! Kannst du haben!

Danke schön!

Natürlich esse ich Fleisch! Warum nicht? Aber es muß mager sein!

1 Was passiert hier?

Verstehst du alles, was diese Schüler sagen? Beantworte die Fragen!

1. Where is Nicolas from? Why is he living in Hamburg?
2. What do Maike, David, and Thorsten do to keep fit?
3. What kinds of food does Thorsten eat?
4. What doesn't he eat? Why not?
5. Judging by her comments, what do you think the interviewer's attitude towards staying healthy is?

1. France. His mother works for Air France in Hamburg. 2. Exercise, eat healthy food, and get plenty of sleep.

3. Fruit, vegetables, fish, and lean meat.

4. Chocolate. He is allergic to it.

5. Positive.

2 Genauer lesen

Lies den Text noch einmal und beantworte diese Fragen!

1. Wie heißt die Schule? In welcher Stadt ist sie? 1. Helene-Lange-Gymnasium; in Hamburg.
2. Wie lange wohnt Nicolas schon in Hamburg? 2. Sieben Jahre.
3. Was für einen Sport macht Maike? 3. Gymnastik, joggen.
4. Wann geht sie gewöhnlich zu Bett? 4. Um zehn Uhr.
5. David nennt drei Sachen, die wichtig sind zum Fithalten. Was sind sie? 5. Sport, gesund essen, genügend schlafen.
6. Was spielt Thorsten? Wie oft? 6. Basketball; zweimal die Woche.

3 Wer macht was?

On a piece of paper, mark the statements with the initial of the person to whom they most logically apply: N=Nicolas; M=Maike; D=David; T=Thorsten. (Each statement might apply to more than one person.)

1. M usually goes to bed at 10:00 pm.
2. T doesn't eat chocolate.
3. N likes living in Hamburg.
4. T eats fruit and vegetables.
5. D&T plays on a basketball team.
6. T eats only lean meat.

4 Stimmt oder stimmt nicht?

Wenn der Satz nicht stimmt, schreib die richtige Antwort!

1. Stimmt nicht. Es ist ein zweisprachiges Gymnasium.

1. Auf dem Helene-Lange-Gymnasium lernen die Schüler keine Sprachen.
2. Nicolas' Mutter arbeitet in Hamburg. 2. Stimmt.
3. Maike geht immer sehr spät zu Bett, um 12 Uhr oder so. 3. Stimmt nicht. Um 10 Uhr.
4. David spielt Basketball und ist in der Mannschaft. 4. Stimmt.
5. Thorsten ißt kein Fleisch. 5. Stimmt nicht. Er ißt mageres Fleisch.
6. Er darf auch keine Schokolade essen. 6. Stimmt.

5 Wie geht der Satz zu Ende?

1. Ich halte mich 1. b
2. Ich schlafe 2. d
3. Ich gehe um zehn 3. g
4. Ich esse 4. e
5. Ich mache viel 5. f
6. Ich esse auch Fleisch, aber 6. a
7. Ich bin allergisch 7. c

a. es muß mager sein.
b. fit.
c. gegen Schokolade.
d. genug.
e. vernünftig.
f. Sport.
g. zu Bett.

6 Und du?

Welche Sätze passen auch für dich? Answers will vary.

Expressing approval and disapproval

Gesundheitstips

6 Dez 98

Ich tu' eigentlich recht viel für meine Gesundheit. Jeden Morgen mache ich Gymnastik, ich trinke keinen Alkohol, und ich rauche auch nicht."

Ganz oben steht bei mir: richtige Ernährung, viel Obst, Gemüse und Salat, wenig Fett. Ich schlafe wenigstens acht Stunden, und ich vermeide die Sonne. Die ist schlecht für meine Haut."

Ich halte mich fit durch Fitneßtraining. Ich trinke keinen Alkohol, ich trinke auch wenig Kaffee. Ich ernähre mich richtig, ja ich esse auch langsam und kaue richtig."

Nach der Schule relaxe ich erst einmal, ich lese etwas, oder ich fahre Rad. Ich kleide mich auch richtig, nicht zu warm und nicht zu kalt!"

WORTSCHATZ

sehr gesund leben	Gymnastik machen	viel Obst essen
viel für die Gesundheit tun	keinen Alkohol trinken	jeden Morgen joggen
vernünftig essen	die Sonne vermeiden	radfahren
genügend schlafen	nicht rauchen	

7 Lebst du gesund?

Lies, was diese Schüler zum Thema Gesundheit sagen! Dann beantworte die Fragen!

1. Welche Gesundheitstips sind dir neu? Schreib die Verben auf, die diese Schüler verwenden, wenn sie über ihre Gesundheit reden! Was bedeuten sie?

2. Schau die Logos oben an! Was bedeuten sie? Schreib einen Satz für jedes Logo — „Die 7 Gebote (*commands*) der Gesundheit!" Paß auf! Wie drückt man im Deutschen die Idee *one, people in general* aus? Welche zwei Modalverben kannst du hier gebrauchen?

2. E.g.: **Man soll nicht rauchen. Man muß vernünftig essen.**

8 Hör gut zu!

Der Gesundheitsmuffel: ein Muffel ist ein Mensch, der sich für nichts interessiert. Ein Gesundheitsmuffel ist also jemand, der sich wenig für seine Gesundheit interessiert. Hör mal zu, wie ein Muffel beschreibt, was er alles gegen seine Gesundheit macht! Schreib eine Liste von seinen Lastern (*vices*)!

For answers, see listening script on TE Interleaf.

> ### Ein wenig *Grammatik*
>
> The verb **schlafen** has a stem vowel change in the **du-** and **er/sie**-forms.
>
> Wie lange **schläfst** du?
> Er **schläft** acht Stunden.

9 Was tust du für die Gesundheit?

Frag deine Partnerin, was sie für ihre Gesundheit tut! Sie erzählt dir mindestens drei Sachen. Dann tauscht die Rollen aus! E.g.: Ich rauche nicht. Ich schlafe genug. Ich esse viel Obst und Gemüse.

10 Für mein Notizbuch

Schreib in dein Notizbuch, was du für deine Gesundheit tust! Schreib auch, wie oft du verschiedene Sportarten machst, und verwende dabei Wörter wie „ansonsten" (*otherwise*) und „auch", um deinen Text interessanter zu machen!

SO SAGT MAN DAS !

Expressing approval and disapproval

When expressing approval of what a friend or family member does, you might say:

Es ist prima, daß du nicht rauchst.
Ich finde es toll, daß du regelmäßig Sport machst.
Ich freue mich, daß du in der Mannschaft bist.
Ich bin froh, daß es dir hier gefällt.

When expressing disapproval, you might say:

Es ist schade, daß du nicht viel Rad fährst.
Ich finde es nicht gut, daß du so wenig schläfst.

Which of these expressions are new to you? What do you notice about the verbs in the **daß**- clauses?

---

11 Ich bin froh, daß ...

Markus spricht mit Freunden über seine Gewohnheiten, was er für seine Gesundheit macht und was er nicht macht. Seine Freunde reagieren darauf. Welche Bemerkungen sind logisch?

1. **Markus:** Ich mache regelmäßig Sport!
   a. Ich finde das nicht gut.
   b. Das ist aber schade!
   c. Das ist prima!

2. **Markus:** Ich esse aber nicht richtig.
   a. Ich bin froh, daß du richtig ißt!
   b. Das finde ich nicht gut!
   c. Das freut mich!

3. **Markus:** Ich rauche aber nicht!
   a. Du, das ist aber prima!
   b. Das finde ich nicht gut!
   c. Das ist aber wirklich schade!

4. **Markus:** Und ich spiele in einer Mannschaft.
   a. Das finde ich nicht gut.
   b. Das ist toll!
   c. Das ist aber wirklich schade!

12 Hör gut zu!

Hör zu, wie verschiedene Schüler einem Freund erzählen, was sie machen oder nicht machen, um gesund zu bleiben! Schreib für jedes Gespräch auf, ob der Freund positiv oder negativ darauf reagiert!

For answers, see listening script on TE Interleaf.

13 Sätze bauen

Denk an einen Freund in der Klasse und sag ihm, was du über seine Gewohnheiten denkst!

nicht gut
prima
toll
schade
wirklich gut
wirklich schade
froh

Es ist
Ich bin
Ich finde es

daß du ...

rauchen
nicht rauchen
gesund sein
regelmäßig Sport machen
richtig essen
wenig schlafen
genug schlafen
in einer Mannschaft sein

Schon bekannt
Ein wenig Grammatik

Remember that after the preposition **für,** accusative case forms are used:
Einen Cappuccino für **mich!**
Was machst du für **deine Gesundheit?**
And remember that in **daß**-clauses the conjugated verb is in the last position:

Es freut mich, daß du vernünftig lebst.
Es ist schade, daß du dich nicht fit hältst!

WORTSCHATZ

—Wie geht's Ihnen, Herr Dingsda?
—Danke, ich . . .

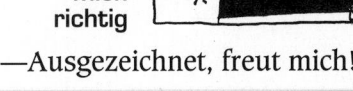

ernähre mich richtig

fühle mich wohl

halte mich fit

—Ausgezeichnet, freut mich!

---

14 Das finde ich ...

Deine Partnerin erzählt dir, was sie für ihre Gesundheit tut und auch welche Laster sie hat. Reagier darauf entweder positiv oder negativ! Schau auf den **So sagt man das!** Kasten und such dir die richtigen Ausdrücke aus! Tauscht dann die Rollen aus! Berichte danach, was deine Klassenkameradin gesagt hat! Alle Mitschüler dürfen darauf reagieren.

Grammatik   Reflexive verbs

1. Reflexive verbs are verbs that require a reflexive pronoun, such as in the sentence *I cut myself.* or *He enjoys himself.* The reflexive verbs used in this section, **sich fühlen, sich freuen, sich ernähren,** and **sich fit halten,** require a reflexive pronoun in the accusative case.

Ich	fühle	**mich**	hier sehr wohl.
Du	fühlst	**dich**	hier nicht wohl.
Er,(sie, man)	fühlt	**sich**	großartig.
Wir	fühlen	**uns**	hier wohl.
Ihr	fühlt	**euch**	hier wohl, ja?
Sie, sie	fühlen	**sich**	hier wohl.

2. In questions, the reflexive pronoun follows the subject pronoun.

> Wie hältst **du dich** fit?
> Wie fühlt **ihr euch** hier in Hamburg?

3. When a reflexive verb is used in a **daß**-clause, the reflexive pronoun also follows the personal pronoun.

> Ich freue mich, daß **du dich** hier wohl fühlst.
> Meine Mutter freut sich, daß **sie sich** fit hält.

Look at the sentences with the verb **sich fit halten.** What do you notice about the **du** and **er/sie**-forms?

15 Für mein Notizbuch

Schreib alles in dein Notizbuch, was du machst, was für dich ungesund ist! Reagiere entweder positiv oder negativ auf deine eigenen Laster! Findest du sie okay, oder möchtest du anders leben?

16 Hör gut zu!   For answers, see listening script on TE Interleaf.

Herr Dingsda erzählt seinen Freunden ganz stolz, was er für seine Gesundheit tut. Hör gut zu und schreib auf, was er macht, daß er sich so wohl fühlt!

17 Wie fühlst du dich?

As a waiter in the restaurant „Zum Hirschen" you overhear many conversations, but not everything that's said. Complete these conversations by filling in the correct reflexive pronoun.

1. — Fühlt ihr ===== hier wohl?
   — Ich, ja. Aber mein Bruder freut ===== nicht, hier in München zu sein. Und seine Frau fühlt ===== auch nicht wohl.   1. euch / sich / sich
2. — Mensch, wie siehst du aus! Du hältst ===== aber fit!   2. dich / uns / mich
   — Ja. Mein Mann und ich, wir halten ===== fit, und ich fühle ===== dabei sehr wohl!
3. — Fühlen Sie ===== hier in Bayern wohl, Herr Krause?
   — Sehr wohl, danke! Ich freue ===== sehr, hier zu sein.   3. sich / mich

wo?	wie?
an der Schule	ganz wohl
in der Klasse	nicht wohl
in der Clique	sehr wohl
in dieser Stadt	nicht sehr wohl
in der (Basketball-) mannschaft	großartig
in ...	überhaupt nicht wohl
	super-toll

18 Der Gesundheitsfanatiker

Sag deiner Partnerin, was Herr Dingsda wahrscheinlich alles macht, um gesund zu bleiben, zum Beispiel, was er ißt, um sich richtig zu ernähren!

19 Wie fühlt ihr euch?

Such dir einen Klassenkameraden und fragt euch gegenseitig, wie ihr euch fühlt! Verwendet dabei die Wörter im Wortschatzkasten oben, die beschreiben, wie gut oder schlecht man sich fühlen kann!

20 Was erzählen die Schüler?

Lies noch einmal, was die Schüler Maike, Thorsten, David und Nicolas über sich sagen! Wählt mit zwei anderen Mitschülern einen von den vier aus und schreibt eine Zusammenfassung von seinen Aussagen! Einer von euch liest dann allen Mitschülern diese Zusammenfassung vor, ohne den Namen des Schülers zu sagen. Die anderen Mitschüler müssen raten, wen ihr beschreibt.

21 Wo fühlst du dich am wohlsten?

a. Es gibt verschiedene Plätze, wo man sich am wohlsten fühlt. Füll die Tabelle rechts aus! Wie fühlst du dich an den Orten, die oben im Wortschatzkasten aufgelistet sind? Schreib auch warum!

b. Schreib jetzt zwei Sätze in dein Notizbuch und verwende dabei die Information aus deiner Tabelle! Schreib einen Satz darüber, wo du dich am wohlsten fühlst, und einen darüber, wo du dich am unwohlsten fühlst (verwende dabei entweder „weil" oder „denn")!

Wo?	Wie?	Warum?
Schule		
Klasse		
Mannschaft		
Clique		

22 Grüß dich!

Grüß deinen Partner und frag ihn, wie er sich fühlt oder fit hält! Er erzählt dir drei Dinge über sich. Reagier auf seine Aussagen! Tauscht dann die Rollen aus!

Was tust du, um gesund zu leben?

Health habits play an important role in German-speaking cultures. However, the focus and the trends have changed from one generation to the next. Let's find out what these people do for their health.

Herr Troger, *St. Ulrich*

„Ja, wenn Sie mich fragen, ob ich gesund lebe, muß ich sagen eigentlich schon. Einmal zuallererst darf ich vielleicht sagen, ich rauche nicht, wobei ich aber nicht unbedingt ein Raucherfeind bin. Ich rauche nicht, und ich trinke auch wenig und mache gerne Sport, ich fahre also sehr gern Rad. Im Winter gehen wir zum Langlauf, oder ein bissel Ski-fahren. Also, ich muß sagen, ich lebe gesund.

Regina, *Bietigheim*

„Ich esse am lieb-sten sehr viel Obst und Gemüse, weil ich glaub', daß das sehr gesund ist. Ich esse es am liebsten aus dem eigenen Garten, weil ich da weiß, daß es nicht ir-gendwie gespritzt ist oder mit chemischen Düngemitteln be-handelt ist. Fleisch esse ich nicht so gerne, weil ich ... erstens mal, weil ich mir denk' ... ich habe oft Filme im Fernsehen gesehen, wie die Tiere behandelt werden und so weiter, und ich kann ehrlich gesagt auch darauf verzichten, es muß echt nicht sein. Ja, so Schnellimbiß und so was mag ich auch nicht so arg."

Gerd, *Bietigheim*

„Oh, um gesund zu leben ... das ist schwer. Also, ich esse einfach das, was mir Spaß macht. Ich esse halt gerne Obst, und ansons-ten viel zum Gesundleben fällt mir eigentlich nicht ein. Also ich fahr' halt Skate-board. Also das bringt auch teilweise Kondi-tion, aber mehr fällt mir halt nicht ein."

A.
1. Which two types of things do these people do to stay healthy? Under each category, list what each person mentions.
2. From where does Regina like to get her food? What does she not like to eat? What reason does she give for this?
3. Does it sound like staying healthy is very important to Gerd? Why or why not?
4. Does Herr Troger do anything different from what the younger interviewees do for their health?

B. A number of America's favorite health pastimes, such as jogging or in-line skating, are becoming increasingly popular among the younger generation in Germany. Eating or-ganic foods is also quite popular. How prevalent are these trends, and the things the in-terviewees mentioned, among your friends? Do your parents do different kinds of things for their health than you do?

Asking for information and responding emphatically or agreeing with reservations

23 Hör gut zu!

Du hörst gerade im Radio eine Sendung über Sport, und es kommen Statistiken darüber, wie oft Deutsche verschiedene Sportarten treiben und wieviel Prozent der Bevölkerung an diesen Sportarten teilnimmt. Mach dir Notizen! Schreib dann mit einer Partnerin die Informationen in eine Tabelle um! Glaubst du, daß diese Tabelle auch für Amerikaner stimmt? Warum? Warum nicht? For answers, see listening script on TE Interleaf.

	Fußball	Aerobic	Jazztanz	Bodybuilding
Wie oft?				
Wieviel Prozent?				

24 Gesünder leben

a. Der folgende Ausschnitt stammt aus einer Umfrage mit dem Titel „Gesünder leben", die in einem Gesundheitsmagazin erschienen ist. Lies den Fragebogen und, auf einem Stück Papier, fülle den Fragebogen für dich selbst aus!

FRAGEBOGEN

Machen Sie wirklich genug Sport?

1. Wie oft machen Sie Sport?
❑ nie   ❑ oft
❑ fast nie   ❑ sehr oft
❑ selten   ❑ fast immer
❑ manchmal   ❑ immer

2. Wie oft?
❑ jeden Tag
❑ jeden zweiten Tag
❑ einmal am Tag
❑ zweimal am Tag
❑ einmal in der Woche
❑ zweimal in der Woche

Ernähren Sie sich richtig?

3. Ich esse ... Fleisch und Wurst.
❑ zu viel   ❑ wenig
❑ viel   ❑ ganz wenig
❑ ziemlich viel ❑ kein

4. Ich esse ... Obst und Gemüse.
❑ kein   ❑ viel
❑ wenig   ❑ sehr viel
❑ genug   ❑ nur

b. Such dir einen Partner! Fragt euch gegenseitig über eure Antworten in dem Fragebogen! Oder: Einer fragt über Sport, der andere über Ernährung.

Grammatik The determiner **jeder**

1. You have seen different forms of the word **jeder** throughout this chapter. What does it mean? What endings does it take? What other words or groups of words have you learned that have the same endings?[1]

	masculine	feminine	neuter	plural
Nominative	**jeder**	**jede**	**jedes**	**alle**
Accusative	**jeden**			
Dative	**jedem**	**jeder**	**jedem**	**allen**

Ich mache **jeden** Sport.
Ich mag **jedes** Gemüse.
Wir fragen **alle** Klassenkameraden.

2. Look at the two sentences below. Which *case* is used when **jeder** is in a time expression, expressing definite time?[2]

Wir schwimmen **jeden** Montag.
Wir wandern **jedes** Wochenende.

S P R A C H T I P

25 Das mache ich jeden Tag!

Deine Mutter glaubt nicht, daß du alles tust, was du tun sollst. Sag ihr, daß du das doch tust! Verwende die Zeitausdrücke, die mit jedem Satz gegeben sind! (Begin your sentences with **doch**! where appropriate.)

BEISPIEL **Du ißt kein Obst. (Tag)**
Doch! Ich esse jeden Tag Obst!

1. Du machst keinen Sport! (Woche)
2. Du ißt selten Obst und Gemüse! (Tag)
3. Du gehst nie schwimmen! (Wochenende)
4. Du sollst deine Großmutter besuchen! (Sonntag)
5. Du gehst selten ins Konzert! (Monat)

26 Beschreibungen

Such dir aus Zeitschriften bunte Fotos von Leuten aus, die Sport machen oder etwas Gesundes essen! Beschreib mit ein paar Sätzen, was jede Person macht, und stell dir vor, wie oft die Person die Aktivität macht! Dann reagiere entweder positiv oder negativ darauf! Danach mach folgendes:

a. Zeig deinen Mitschülern dein Foto und beschreibe es ihnen! *oder*
b. Du und deine Mitschüler hängen eure Fotos auf. Dann liest einer von euch eine Beschreibung vor, und die andern versuchen, das Foto zu erraten.

You have heard and seen the word **doch** used a lot by Germans in everyday conversations. One purpose **doch** serves is to soften the impact of a command: **Geh doch für mich einkaufen! Doch** has other meanings as well. If someone erroneously tells you that you don't do something, you can respond positively using **doch**.

Read the following sentences and determine what **doch** means in this context:

Du räumst nie auf!
Doch! Ich räume fast jede Woche auf.

How would you respond if someone said to you **Du ißt überhaupt kein Obst!** or **Du machst nie Sport!**

1. the definite articles; You may also remember seeing **dieser**- words with the same endings.
2. accusative case

SO SAGT MAN DAS!

Asking for information and responding emphatically or agreeing with reservations

You want to find out something specific about some of your friends. There are several ways to initiate your questions. You can say:

Ich habe eine Frage: Ißt du Obst und Gemüse?
Sag mal, trinkst du jeden Tag Milch?
Wie steht's mit Fleisch? **Ißt du eigentlich** viel Fleisch?
Darf ich dich etwas fragen? Wie hältst du dich fit?

To respond emphatically, your friend might say:

Ja, natürlich! or **Na klar!** or **Aber sicher!**

To agree with your statements, but with reservations, your friend might say:

(Du ißt viel Kuchen!)	**Ja, das kann sein, aber** ich esse auch viel Obst!
(Du schaust oft Fernsehen!)	**Das stimmt, aber** ich mache auch Sport!
(Du ißt gern Fleisch?)	**Eigentlich schon, aber** ich esse wenig Fleisch.

How would you begin your questions if you were speaking to two friends? Look at the last three responses. How do we express these same ideas in English?

27 Hör gut zu!

Hör gut zu, wenn Simone, eine Studentin in Krefeld, über die Fitneßgewohnheiten der Deutschen redet. Lies zuerst die englische Zusammenfassung unten, dann hör zu und versuche, die Zusammenfassung zu ergänzen!

1. According to Simone, most Germans ===== in order to stay healthy.
2. Simone says that Germans also enjoy playing ===== and =====, because =====.
3. Although Germans don't =====, they are often =====.
4. Today, Germans avoid ===== more and more, because =====.

For answers, see listening script on TE Interleaf.

28 Was tun die Amerikaner für ihre Gesundheit?

Your school newspaper has asked you to interview your peers regarding their health habits. Think of at least six questions in German that you could ask on this topic. Three should be addressed to the group and three to individuals. Get together in groups of four, use your questions to interview your partners, but initiate your questions appropriately (refer to the **So sagt man das!** box). Then prepare similar questions in order to interview your teacher. Take turns with your classmates finding out his or her health habits.

29 Für mein Notizbuch

Using the information from Activity 28, summarize your findings, in German, in a paragraph which describes what your friends and teacher do to stay healthy.

EIN WENIG LANDESKUNDE

Among the younger generation there are several new trends. For instance, teenagers, far more than their parents, shop and consume foods from **Bioläden,** where they can get everything for **Vollwertkost. Bioläden** specialize in organically grown products, whole-grain foods, and the like. These shops are different from those called **Reformhäuser**, which have been around a lot longer. Usually frequented by older consumers, **Reformhäuser** specialize in products for people with special diets or medical needs. For many people in Germany, healthy eating goes hand in hand with **Umweltbewußtsein.** And don't bother coming to a **Bioladen** without your own bag! Students favor carrying groceries in burlap bags or wicker baskets on the back of their bicycles. They also have to bring their own containers to fill up on bulk products. And you might see a strange sight when shopping at any regular store in Germany: people removing the excess packaging from products they buy and leaving it in a pile at the front of the store. What do you think is going on here?

30 Eigentlich schon, aber ...

You and your partner each write down three of your health-related vices on index cards and then trade cards. Your partner should fuss at you about your bad habits, stating what you do or don't do for your health. You have to agree, but with reservation, using statements from the **So sagt man das!** box.

Asking and telling what you may or may not do

WORTSCHATZ

Für jeden etwas! Oder?

Gemüse

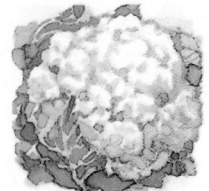

Blumenkohl · Brokkoli · Möhren · Pilze

Obst

Kirschen · Aprikosen

Beeren

Erdbeeren · Blaubeeren

Fisch

Forelle

Fleisch

Rindfleisch · Huhn/Hähnchen

Fisch- Hühner- Gemüse- *Nudel- Kartoffel- Reis-*

SUPPE

Suppe

Welche von diesen Speisen essen Amerikaner oft?
Selten? Gar nicht? Wie steht's mit Hühnersuppe?

Und dann noch . . .

Pudding   Magermilch
Vollmilch Sahne
Joghurt   Eier
Milch   Butter

31 Hör gut zu!

Schüler erzählen, was sie gern und was sie nicht gern
essen und warum. Mach dir Notizen! Vergleiche deine
Notizen mit den Notizen eines Partners!

For answers, see listening script on TE Interleaf.

32 Was ißt du?

Mach eine Liste von deinen Eßgewohnheiten! Ordne deine Liste in drei Gruppen: **1.** Was
ißt du (sehr) oft? **2.** Was ißt du manchmal? **3.** Was ißt du nie? — Teil diese Information
deinen Klassenkameraden mit!

Warum nicht?

hat zu viele Kalorien
hat zu viel Zucker
hat zu viel Fett
macht dick
nicht gut für die Gesundheit
schmeckt mir nicht
ungesund

Welche Speisen von Seite 97 passen zu diesen Gründen?

BEISPIEL   **Ich esse keinen Blumenkohl, weil er mir nicht schmeckt.**

Schon bekannt
Ein wenig *G*rammatik

Do you remember which case forms go with **kein** when it is a direct object?

Ich esse **keinen** Fisch. (der Fisch)
Ich mag **keine** Suppe. (die Suppe)
Ich esse **kein** Gemüse. (das Gemüse)
Ich mag **keine** Möhren. (plural)

33 Was ißt du nicht?

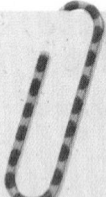

Gibt es etwas, was du nicht gern ißt? Such dir einen Partner! Er fragt dich, was du nicht ißt und warum. Du sagst es ihm.
— Tauscht dann die Rollen aus!

SO SAGT MAN DAS!

Asking and telling what you may or may not do

If you want to know what a friend is allowed to eat or to do, you could ask:

Was darfst du essen?
Darfst du alles essen?
Was darfst du tun?

The answer might be:

Fleisch, Gemüse, ...
Klar! Ich darf alles essen.
Ich darf Auto fahren.

To find out what your friend is not allowed to eat or to do, you could ask:

Was darfst du nicht tun?
Was darfst du nicht essen?

Ich darf nicht joggen.
Ich darf keine Schokolade essen.

What do you think the words **darf** and **darfst** mean? What other verbs do they remind you of?

34 Hör gut zu!

Schüler in Deutschland erzählen, was sie nicht machen dürfen. Hör gut zu! Welche Aussage paßt zu welchem Bild?   For answers, see listening script on TE Interleaf.

a.

b.

c.

d.

35 Klar darf ich das!

Sag deinem Partner, ob du auch die Dinge (von Übung 34) machen darfst oder nicht! Er sagt es dir.

Grammatik The verb **dürfen**, present tense

The verb **dürfen**, *to be allowed* or *permitted to,* has these forms in the present tense:

Ich	**darf** alles essen!	Wir	**dürfen** gehen!
Du	**darfst** nicht rauchen!	Ihr	**dürft** alles essen!
Er/Sie/Es/Man	**darf** nicht joggen!	Sie (pl), Sie	**dürfen** keine Schokolade essen!

---

36 Das darf man nicht machen!

Welche Regeln gibt es in eurem Klassenzimmer? Was darf man nicht machen? Schreib eure Klassenregeln auf deutsch, damit auch die Austauschschüler sie verstehen können und nicht in Schwierigkeiten geraten (*get into trouble*)!

37 Blöde Allergien!

Setz dich mit drei Klassenkameraden zusammen! Unterhaltet euch über Allergien! Wer darf gewisse Lebensmittel nicht essen oder trinken und warum? Wer hat Allergien gegen andere Speisen? —Unten stehen ein paar Dinge, gegen die manche Menschen allergisch sind. Sagt den anderen Gruppen, welche Allergien in eurer Gruppe am meisten vorkommen!

allergisch gegen:

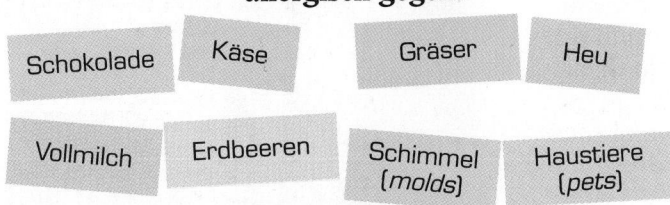

Schokolade   Käse   Gräser   Heu

Vollmilch   Erdbeeren   Schimmel (*molds*)   Haustiere (*pets*)

auch gegen die Sonne!

38 Was darfst du zu Hause machen?

a. Schreib drei Sachen auf, die du zu Hause nicht machen darfst! Frag danach deine Partnerin darüber, und sie fragt dann auch dich.

b. Macht jetzt eine Umfrage! Einer geht an die Tafel und fragt ein paar Schüler, was ihre Partner gesagt haben und schreibt dann die Ergebnisse auf. Welches Verbot kommt am häufigsten (*the most*) vor?

ZUM LESEN

Bleibt fit und gesund!

Getting Started

For answers, see TE Interleaf.

1. Judging by the pictures and titles of the readings, what do these authors consider important for staying healthy? Which of these concerns were also addressed by the people who were interviewed for this chapter (see p. 92)? With your classmates, brainstorm for German vocabulary or phrases that you would expect to find in texts on these health topics.

Tip: Some German prefixes carry their own meaning. Whether at the beginning of a noun or verb, they will change the meaning of the word in a certain way. For example, the prefix **auf** at the beginning of a verb often means *up*. You already know the phrases **das Zimmer aufräumen** and **den Hörer auflegen**; if you know the verb **geben,** what do you think the verb **aufgeben** might mean?

Warum ist Dr. Müller-Wohlfahrt nie krank?

Sechs Tips, die für Sie so wichtig sind wie für Boris

1 Richtig aufwärmen. „Nicht gleich loslegen, sondern in jeder Sportart sich vorher gezielt auf Touren bringen" — das rät der „Doc" dringend. Gymnastik und Stretching verhindern Verletzungen. „Am besten einen Sportarzt fragen, was individuell richtig ist."

2 Richtiges Schuhwerk. „Die meisten Sportler brauchen Einlegesohlen nach Maß. Solche Gehhilfen vom orthopädischen Schuhmacher verhindern Zerrungen, Muskelrisse, Ermüdungsbrüche. Eigentlich sollte jeder mit »seiner« Sohle Sport treiben."

3 Richtig essen. „Die italienischen Fußballstars haben die besten Werte, was Spurenelemente, Mineralien, Enzyme betrifft. Die mediterrane Küche ist die ideale Ernährung", schwört der „Doc". „Sie sollten Wert auf ausgewogene und leichte Kost legen".

4 Richtig laufen. „Es kommt auf den Stil an: Mit dem vorderen Mittelfuß aufsetzen, leicht abfedern, den Schritt leicht überlang machen, sich harmonisch nach vorne entwickeln, abrollen. Sie müssen das Gefühl haben, daß Sie vollkommen »rund« und mühelos laufen".

5 Richtig kühlen. Eiswürfel sind out — ideal zum Kühlen von Verletzungen ist „hot ice": Wasser in Gefrierpunktnähe. Verhindert spätere Überwärmung. Besonders effektiv: auf das „hot ice" ein paar Stöße Eisspray. Das garantiert dann dauerhafte Kühlung.

6 Richtig sitzen. Der „Doc" verpaßt seinen Patienten, die viel im Büro sitzen müssen, einen Sitzkeil aus hartem Schaumstoff. „Dadurch ergibt sich von vornherein die richtige Stellung der Wirbelsäule".

100 MARK FÜR NICHTRAUCHER

Foto: Exclusiv

„100 Mark für jeden, der das Rauchen aufgibt", sagte der Bielefelder Fahrradfabrikant Hans-Werner Schreiber zu seinen Angestellten. Gesagt, getan. Jeden Monat zahlt der Fabrikant 100 Mark an seine Nichtraucher. Das verlockende Angebot wirkte: Zwei Männer und drei Frauen hörten sofort mit dem Rauchen auf. Nach und nach folgten alle anderen Mitarbeiter - bis auf einen. Die Nichtraucher freuen sich natürlich über das zusätzliche Geld. Sven Harter (22 Jahre): „Ich bezahle damit jedes Jahr meinen Urlaub."

HER MIT DEM SALAT!

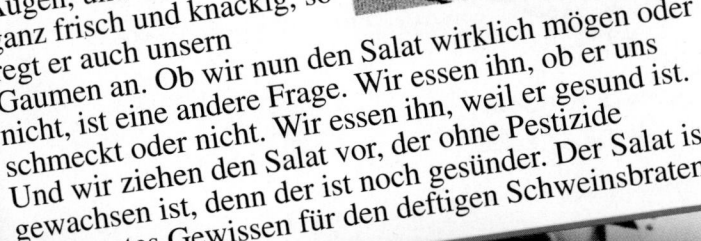

Eine Mahlzeit ohne Salat, das ist wie Brot ohne Butter oder Tee ohne Zucker, eins gehört zum andern. Das Grün eines Salats erfreut unsere Augen, und ist er noch ganz frisch und knackig, so regt er auch unsern Gaumen an. Ob wir nun den Salat wirklich mögen oder nicht, ist eine andere Frage. Wir essen ihn, ob er uns schmeckt oder nicht. Wir essen ihn, weil er gesund ist. Und wir ziehen den Salat vor, der ohne Pestizide gewachsen ist, denn der ist noch gesünder. Der Salat ist unser gutes Gewissen für den deftigen Schweinsbraten.

2. Read the first sentence of the article about **Nichtraucher.** What is the topic? (*Hint:* What did Hans-Werner promise his employees?)

A Closer Look

3. Before you read the rest of the article on **Nichtraucher,** try to predict: a) how successful the manufacturer's offer has been, and b) what the employees might do with their 100 DM. Then read the article to confirm or correct your predictions.

4. Now think about the following questions: a) Was any reason given explicitly for the manufacturer's offer? b) Was a reason implied or hinted at? c) If not, could you assume, using your background knowledge, what the reason(s) might be?

5. Read the article about **Salat.** What does the author compare to bread without butter and tea without sugar? According to the author, what is not important when eating salad? If you know that **Gewissen** means *conscience,* what might the last sentence mean? How serious do you think the author is about how Germans view salad?

6. What are the six **Tips** that Dr. Müller-Wohlfahrt offers? Read the boldface print after each number.

7. Read the first tip from Dr. Müller-Wohlfahrt. What two things help prevent injuries? Now skim over the third tip. According to the doctor, which athletes have the best diet? Look at the fifth tip. What is "out"? What is "in"? If you know that **Gefrier-** is freezing, what is "hot ice"?

8. Such dir einen Partner. Fragt die Schüler und Lehrer an eurer Schule, wie sie sich fithalten! Schreibt die Resultate auf deutsch um! Schreibt danach einen Bericht über die Ergebnisse! Entwerft ein Poster mit Tips dazu.

Friday

ANWENDUNG

1 You will hear four radio ads trying to persuade you to do different things for your health and fitness. Match each of the summary statements below with one of the ads that you hear. For answers, see listening script on TE Interleaf.

a. Du sollst so oft wie möglich Sport machen!

b. Man soll jeden Tag Obst und Gemüse essen!

c. Du sollst jeden Tag mindestens sieben Stunden schlafen!

d. Rauchen ist nicht gesund!

2 Read this letter to Dr. Müller-Meier, health columnist for the Dietzburger Zeitung. Then answer the questions below.

1. Warum schreibt Hans Giecht?   1. Er weiß nicht, was mit ihm los ist.

2. Was ist sein Problem?   2. Kopfschmerzen; Magenschmerzen; keine Energie.

3. Beschreib sein tägliches Leben!   3. Sitzt am Schreibtisch; liest und lernt.

3 As Dr. Müller-Meier's assistant, you often respond to the letters from his readers. Write a response to Hans Giecht, telling him what to do — or what not to do — in order to improve his health and regain his energy. Your response will appear in next Sunday's "Dietzburger Zeitung."

4 Your younger siblings look to you for advice. How often would you tell them to do or not to do the following?

Sport machen
Kuchen essen
Obst und Gemüse essen
Milch trinken
rauchen
Alkohol trinken
schwimmen

Lieber Dr. Müller-Meier!
Ich weiß nicht, was mit mir los ist! Vielleicht können Sie mir helfen. Ich fühle mich nie so richtig wohl — ich habe immer Kopfschmerzen, oder Magenschmerzen oder irgend etwas! Und das Schlimmste ist — ich habe überhaupt keine Energie! Ich bin Student an der Uni (ich studiere Germanistik), und ich muß jeden Tag lange am Schreibtisch sitzen und lesen und lernen. Ich brauche dafür viel Energie! Was soll ich tun? Ich esse genug, glaube ich — ich esse jeden Tag Brot, Nudeln, Fleisch — was es so eben in der Mensa gibt. Und ich rauche und trinke nicht viel. Ich rauche etwa fünf Zigaretten am Tag, und ich trinke ab und zu abends mit Freunden. Was soll ich tun, um meine Energie zurückzubekommen? Hilfe!!!

Mit bestem Dank
Hans Giecht

5 You work as an assistant in a clinic. A student who hasn't been feeling well calls you to seek your advice. As he describes his symptoms, you fill out the following form for your records. For answers, see listening script on TE Interleaf.

Name: _____

Alter: _____

Beruf: _____

Beschwerden: _____

_____

Diagnose: _____

_____

Empfehlung: _____

_____

Unterschrift _____

6 This couch potato obviously needs help. First describe what he is doing wrong, then describe what he should do in order to become fit again.

7 You have the job of planning the weekly menu at your high school cafeteria. You want to make it as healthful as possible, yet also interesting and tasty. Write in German what you think should be included in the lunch menu for one week.

8

R O L L E N S P I E L

Do the following activity with a partner or small group.

You work for a German marketing firm and need some good ideas for health-related advertisements to send to your firm back in Germany. Make a list of commercials you see on American television or hear on American radio that reflect health and fitness consciousness. Write down the ad (or the product being advertised) and, in German, tell what the health problem is and the basic message related to its cure. With your partner or group, select the commercial that you think is most effective, write it in German, and present it to the class. Use props and sound effects to make your commercial more interesting and fun. The rest of the class can serve as the "advisory board" in your German firm and select the commercial that they would most like to show on German television.

KANN ICH'S WIRKLICH?

Can you express approval? (p. 88)

1 How would you react if your friend told you that he or she

   a. lives in a healthy way?   a. E.g.: **Es ist prima, daß du gesund lebst.**
   b. eats properly?   b. E.g.: **Ich bin froh, daß du richtig ißt.**
   c. exercises regularly?   c. E.g.: **Ich finde es toll, daß du regelmäßig Sport machst.**

Can you express disapproval? (p. 88)

2 How would you react if your friend told you that he or she

   a. does not live in a healthy manner?   a. E.g.: **Es ist schade, daß du nicht gesund lebst.**
   b. does not get enough exercise?   b. E.g.: **Ich finde es nicht gut, daß du nicht genug Sport machst.**
   c. doesn't eat right?   c. E.g.: **Es ist schade, daß du nicht richtig ißt.**
   d. gets too little sleep?   d. E.g.: **Es ist nicht gut, daß du so wenig schläfst.**

Can you ask for information and respond to a question emphatically? (p. 95)

3 How would someone ask you if you

   a. play sports?   a. E.g.: **Machst du Sport?**
   b. eat correctly?   b. E.g.: **Ernährst du dich richtig?**
   c. exercise?   c. E.g.: **Machst du Gymnastik?**

4 How would you respond emphatically to the questions in Activity 3 by saying that you

    a. E.g.: **Ja, natürlich! Ich mache jede Woche Sport.**
   a. play sports every week?   b. E.g.: **Na klar! Ich esse jeden Tag Obst und Gemüse.**
   b. eat fruit and vegetables every day?
   c. exercise every morning?   c. E.g.: **Aber sicher! Ich mache jeden Morgen Gymnastik.**

Can you agree with reservation? (p. 95)

5 How would you respond in the following situations?   a. E.g.: **Ja, das kann sein, aber ich esse auch viel Obst!**

   a. Your mom accuses you of eating too much chocolate, but you know that you also eat a lot of fruit.
    b. E.g.: **Das stimmt, aber ich mache auch dreimal die Woche Gymnastik!**
   b. Your friend tells you that you watch too much television, but you also exercise three times a week.
   c. Your doctor says that you eat too much meat, but you tell him that you eat only lean meat.   c. E.g.: **Ja, das stimmt, aber ich esse nur mageres Fleisch!**

Can you ask and tell what you may and may not do, using dürfen? (p. 98)

6 How would you tell someone that you

   a. may not eat meat?   a. **Ich darf kein Fleisch essen.**
   b. may not drink alcohol?   b. **Ich darf keinen Alkohol trinken.**
   c. may eat cheese?   c. **Ich darf Käse essen.**
   d. may not eat chocolate because you are allergic to it?   d. **Ich darf keine Schokolade essen, weil ich allergisch dagegen bin.**

ERSTE STUFE
EXPRESSING APPROVAL

Es ist prima, daß ... *It's great that...*
Ich finde es toll, daß ... *I think it's great that...*
Ich bin froh, daß ... *I'm happy that...*
Ich freue mich, daß ... *I'm happy that...*

EXPRESSING DISAPPROVAL

Es ist schade, daß ... *It's too bad that...*
Ich finde es nicht gut, daß ... *I think it's bad that...*

FOR YOUR HEALTH

sich fit halten *to keep fit*
sehr gesund leben *to live in a very healthy way*
sich ernähren *to eat and drink*

viel für die Gesundheit tun *to do a lot for your health*
vernünftig essen *to eat healthy foods*
genügend schlafen *to get enough sleep*
er/sie schläft *he/she sleeps*
Gymnastik machen *to exercise*
keinen Alkohol trinken *not to drink alcohol*
die Sonne vermeiden *to avoid the sun*
nicht rauchen *not to smoke*
viel Obst essen *to eat lots of fruit*
jeden Morgen joggen *to jog every morning*
radfahren (sep) *to bicycle*

WHERE?

an der Schule *at school*
in der Klasse *in class*
in der Clique *in the clique*
in dieser Stadt *in this city*

in der (Basketball-) mannschaft *on the (basketball) team*

TALKING ABOUT HOW YOU FEEL

sich fühlen *to feel*
ganz wohl *extremely well*
sehr, nicht, nicht sehr wohl *very, not, not very well*
überhaupt nicht wohl *not well at all*
großartig *wonderful*
super-toll *really great*

REFLEXIVE PRONOUNS, ACCUSATIVE CASE

mich *myself*
dich *yourself*
sich *herself, himself*
uns *ourselves*
euch *yourselves*
sich *themselves, yourself, yourselves*

ZWEITE STUFE
ASKING FOR INFORMATION

Ich habe eine Frage: ... *I have a question:...*
Sag mal, ... *Tell me,...*
(Essen Sie) eigentlich ...? *Do you really (eat)...?*
Wie steht's mit ...? *So what about...?*
Darf ich euch etwas fragen? *May I ask you something?*

RESPONDING EMPHATICALLY

Ja, natürlich! *Certainly!*
Na klar! *Of course!*
Doch! *Yes, I do!*

AGREEING WITH RESERVATIONS

Ja, das kann sein, aber ... *Yes, maybe, but...*

Das stimmt, aber ... *That's true, but...*
Eigentlich schon, aber ... *Well yes, but...*

WHEN?

selten *seldom*
meistens *most of the time*
gewöhnlich *usually*
normalerweise *normally*

DRITTE STUFE
FOOD ITEMS

die Speise, -n *food*
der Blumenkohl *cauliflower*
der Brokkoli *broccoli*
die Möhre, -n *carrot*
der Pilz, -e *mushroom*
die Kirsche, -n *cherry*
die Aprikose, -n *apricot*
die Erdbeere, -n *strawberry*
die Blaubeere, -n *blueberry*

die Forelle, -n *trout*
das Rindfleisch *beef*
das Huhn, ¨er *chicken*
der Reis *rice*

SAYING WHY YOU DON'T EAT SOMETHING

hat zu viel Fett *has too much fat*
hat zu viele Kalorien *has too many calories*
macht dick *is fattening*

nicht gut für die Gesundheit *not good for your health*
ungesund *unhealthy*

ASKING OR TELLING WHAT YOU MAY OR MAY NOT DO

dürfen *to be allowed to, may* (for the forms of **dürfen**, see page 99.)

Kapitel 5: Gesund essen

CHAPTER OVERVIEW

Los geht's! pp. 108-110	Wiebkes Pausenbrot, *p. 108*			*Video Guide*
	FUNCTIONS	**GRAMMAR**	**CULTURE**	**RE-ENTRY**
Erste Stufe pp. 112-115	• Expressing regret and downplaying, *p.113* • Expressing skepticism and making certain, *p. 114*	The demonstrative **dieser**, *p. 114*	• **Landeskunde: Was ißt du, was nicht?** *p. 111* • **Ein wenig Landeskunde:** Students' mothers sell nutritious snacks to **Gymnasiasten,** *p. 112*	• Talking about prices, *p. 112* (from **Kap 4**, I) • Saying what you would like to eat or drink, *p. 112* (from **Kap 3**, I) • Expressing regret, *p. 113* (from **Kap 9**, • Talking about quantities, *p. 113* (from **Kap 8**, I) • Giving reasons, *p. 113* (from **Kap 8**, I) • The modal **sollen**, *p. 114* (from **Kap 8**, • The verb **essen**, *p. 114* (from **Kap 6**, I)
Zweite Stufe pp. 118-121	Calling someone's attention to something and responding, *p. 118*	• The preposition **auf**, *p. 119* • The possessives (Summary), *p. 120*	German meals, *p. 119*	• The possessives **mein, dein sein,** and **ihr,** *p. 119* (from **Kap 3/11**, I) • Ordering food, *p. 121* (from **Kap 6**, I) • The **möchte**-forms, *p. 121* (from **Kap 3**, I) • The verb **essen**, *p. 121* (from **Kap 6**,
Dritte Stufe pp. 122-125	Expressing preference and strong preference, *p. 123*	• Verbs used with dative-case forms, *p. 123* • The interrogative **welcher,** *p. 124* • The preposition **zu,** *p. 125*	German mealtimes, *p. 124*	• Talking about how food tastes, *p. 122* (from **Kap 6**, I) • Expressing preferences and favorites, *p. 122* (from **Kap 10**, I) • The comparative and superlative **lieber** and **am liebsten,** *p. 122* (from **Kap 10**, • Saying you want more of something, *p. 122* (from **Kap 8**, I) • The modal **mögen,** *p. 123* (from **Kap 10**, I) • Food vocabulary, *pp. 122, 124* (from **Kap 8**, I) • The interrogative **was für,** *p. 125* (from **Kap 10**, I)
Zum Lesen pp. 116-117	**Wo ruht ihr euch aus?** Reading Strategy: Understanding the tone of a text			
Review pp. 126-129	• **Anwendung,** *p. 126* • **Kann ich's wirklich?** *p. 128* • **Wortschatz,** *p. 129*			

Assessment Options	**Stufe Quizzes**
	 • *Chapter Resources*, Book 2
	   Erste Stufe, Quiz 5-1
	   Zweite Stufe, Quiz 5-2
	   Dritte Stufe, Quiz 5-3
	 • *Assessment Items, Audiocassette* 7 B
				Kapitel 5 Chapter Test
				 • *Chapter Resources*, Book 2
				 • *Assessment Guide*, Speaking Test
				 • *Assessment Items, Audiocassette* 7 B
				
				 Test Generator, Kapitel 5

Chapter Overview

Video Program **OR**
Expanded Video Program, Videocassette 2

Textbook Audiocassette 3 A

RESOURCES Print	RESOURCES Audiovisual

Textbook Audiocassette 3 A

Practice and Activity Book
Chapter Resources, Book 2
- Additional Listening Activities 5-1, 5-2 .... *Additional Listening Activities, Audiocassette* 9 B
- Student Response Forms
- Realia 5-1
- Situation Card 5-1
- Teaching Transparency Master 5-1 .... *Teaching Transparency* 5-1
- Quiz 5-1 .... *Assessment Items, Audiocassette* 7 B
Video Guide .... *Video Program/Expanded Video Program,* Videocassette 2

Textbook Audiocassette 3 A

Practice and Activity Book
Chapter Resources, Book 2
- Communicative Activity 5-1
- Additional Listening Activities 5-3, 5-4 .... *Additional Listening Activities, Audiocassette* 9 B
- Student Response Forms
- Realia 5-2
- Situation Card 5-2
- Quiz 5-2 .... *Assessment Items, Audiocassette* 7 B

Textbook Audiocassette 3 A

Practice and Activity Book
Chapter Resources, Book 2
- Communicative Activity 5-2
- Additional Listening Activities 5-5, 5-6 .... *Additional Listening Activities, Audiocassette* 9 B
- Student Response Forms
- Realia 5-3
- Situation Card 5-3
- Teaching Transparency Master 5-2 .... *Teaching Transparency* 5-2
- Quiz 5-3 .... *Assessment Items, Audiocassette* 7 B

Video Guide .... *Video Program/Expanded Video Program,* Videocassette 2

Alternative Assessment
- Performance Assessment,
Teacher's Edition
  Erste Stufe, p. 105K
  Zweite Stufe, p. 105N
  Dritte Stufe, p. 105Q
- Portfolio Assessment
  Written: **Anwendung,** Activity 5, *Pupil's Edition,* p. 127;
  Assessment Guide, p. 18
  Oral: **Anwendung,** Activity 4, *Pupil's Edition,* p. 127;
  Assessment Guide, p. 18
- **Notizbuch,** *Pupil's Edition,* pp. 115, 125; *Practice and Activity Book,* p. 149

CHAPTER OVERVIEW

Kapitel 5: Gesund essen
Textbook Listening Activities Scripts

Erste Stufe
Activity 6, *p. 112*

REGINA Ich nehme einen kleinen Orangensaft, ein Schinkencroissant und einen Vanillejoghurt.

VERKÄUFER Alles klar. Das macht dann zusammen zwei Mark fünfzig.

MAX Ich hätte gern einen Kakao und zwei Eibrötchen. Das ist alles.

VERKÄUFER Gut, also einmal Kakao und zweimal Eibrötchen. Zwei Mark achtzig, bitte!

KATJA Für mich bitte eine Banane, einen Müslijoghurt und eine kleine Flasche Milch. Mmmh, die Quarkbrötchen sehen lecker aus. Ich nehme auch noch ein Quarkbrötchen dazu!

VERKÄUFER Also, Banane, Joghurt, Milch und Quarkbrötchen. Da bekomme ich dann genau drei Mark.

FELIX Ich nehme zwei Äpfel und ein Salamibrötchen. Ist noch ein Bananenjoghurt da?

VERKÄUFER Ja, hier ist noch einer. Der letzte übrigens! Da hast du Glück gehabt. Also, alles zusammen kostet zwei Mark vierzig.

Answers to Activity 6

Regina: Orangensaft, Schinkencroissant, Vanillejoghurt; DM 2,50
Max: Kakao, zwei Eibrötchen; DM 2,80
Katja: Banane, Müslijoghurt, Milch, Quarkbrötchen; DM 3,00
Felix: zwei Äpfel, Salamibrötchen, Bananenjoghurt; DM 2,40

Activity 9, *p. 113*

1. MICHI Du, Mutti, haben wir etwas Leckeres im Kühlschrank? Ich möchte so gern etwas Süßes essen, ein Eis zum Beispiel!

MUTTER Schauen wir doch mal nach! Ja, also Eis haben wir nicht, aber hier ist ein Joghurt. Den kannst du haben, wenn du willst. Der ist bestimmt genauso lecker wie ein Eis.

MICHI Ach nein, einen Joghurt mag ich nicht. Der schmeckt doch ganz anders als Eis!

2. EVI Vati, haben wir noch Cola im Kühlschrank?

VATER Nein, ich glaube, du hast gestern die letzte Dose ausgetrunken, und der Apfelsaft ist leider auch schon alle. Aber, wie wäre es mit einem Glas Milch?

EVI Milch? Ach Papa, ich bin doch kein Baby mehr. Nein, also Milch mag ich nicht!

3. GRETCHEN Papa, ist noch etwas von der Schokoladentorte übrig? Deine Geburtstagstorte war so lecker!

VATER Nein, ich glaube, von der Torte ist nichts mehr übrig. Wir haben gestern alle Stücke aufgegessen. Aber hier sind noch ein paar Schokoladenplätzchen. Willst du die?

GRETCHEN Ja, danke. Die schmecken zwar nicht genauso gut wie deine Torte, aber ich mag sie trotzdem!

4. ULLI Mama, ich möchte so gern eine Portion Erdbeeren mit Schlagsahne essen. Haben wir welche im Kühlschrank?

MUTTER Mal sehen! Ja, also Schlagsahne haben wir, aber leider keine Erdbeeren mehr. Tut mir leid. Aber schau mal, wir haben Milch und wir haben auch Bananen. Du kannst dir einen Bananenmilchshake machen mit Schlagsahne oben drauf! Also, was hältst du davon?

ULLI Au ja, super! Möchtest du auch einen? Dann mach' ich gleich zwei!

MUTTER Ja, gern!

Answers to Activity 9

Michi: will Eis; mag keinen Joghurt
Evi: will Cola; mag keine Milch
Gretchen: will Schokoladentorte; mag auch Schokoladenplätzchen
Ulli: will Erdbeeren mit Schlagsahne; mag auch Bananenmilchshake

Activity 12, *p. 115*

1. **HEINZ** Sag mal, Richard, was hast du denn heute auf deinem Pausenbrot?

RICHARD Ich habe heute Salami drauf!

HEINZ Du hast immer nur Wurst auf deinem Pausenbrot! Ißt du nie was anderes? Käse, zum Beispiel! Oder mal was Süßes wie Marmelade oder so!

RICHARD Nein, Käse ist nicht mein Fall. Auf meinem Pausenbrot mag ich nun mal gerne Wurst. Salami, Schinken und Leberwurst mag ich am liebsten. Und wenn ich mal was Süßes will, dann nur Eis!

2. **ULRIKE** Hallo, Claudia! Kommst du in der Pause mit in den Supermarkt? Oder hast du dir was von zu Hause mitgebracht?

CLAUDIA Nein, du weißt doch, ich bringe mir selten was von zu Hause mit. Aber ich komme trotzdem nicht mit in den Supermarkt. Ich hole mir heute ein Fischbrötchen vom Fischstand. Freitags esse ich nämlich immer Fisch!

3. **HEIKE** He, Gerhard! Was hast du denn da in der Tragetasche?

GERHARD Da ist mein Pausensnack drin!

HEIKE Zeig doch mal, was hast du denn alles mitgebracht?

GERHARD Ja, also heute habe ich meinen Obsttag. Zwei Bananen, einen Apfel und ein Pfund blaue Trauben. Die sind echt lecker.

HEIKE Ißt du denn heute sonst nichts, nur Obst?

GERHARD Doch! Ich gehe gleich noch zum Bäcker und hole mir ein Stück Strudel. Aber Obst esse ich jeden Tag, der Vitamine wegen!

Answers to Activity 12

Richard: b, c
Claudia: e
Gerhard: a, d

Zweite Stufe

Activity 16, *p. 118*

UWE Martina, was hast du denn immer so auf deinem Pausenbrot?

MARTINA Also, meistens habe ich irgendeine Wurst drauf, zum Beispiel Salami, oder ich mag auch gern Corned Beef. Manchmal streiche ich auch Senf oder Mayonnaise auf die Wurst, das schmeckt mir auch gut. Ich hab' selten auch mal Marmelade drauf, aber normalerweise nicht auf einer Scheibe Brot, sondern nur wenn's ein Brötchen ist.

UWE Angelika, erzähl du uns doch mal, was du so gewöhnlich auf deinem Pausenbrot hast!

ANGELIKA Ja, also ich mag wahnsinnig gern Tofu mit Sojasprossen. Am liebsten auf einem Stück Knäckebrot. Und meistens habe ich auch noch ein paar Radieschen- oder Gurkenscheiben drauf auf dem Tofu. Das ist echt lecker.

UWE Und Klaus, wie sieht denn dein Pausenbrot so aus?

KLAUS Ja, also ich bin der totale Käsefreak! Ich hab, jeden Tag eine andere Sorte Käse drauf. Was das Brot anbetrifft, ist es mir eigentlich egal, welche Sorte es ist, also Vollkorn, Weiß- oder Schwarzbrot … esse ich alles gern. Aber auf den Käse kommt es an! Holländischen Edamer mag ich total gern und auch französischen Camembert. Ach ja, Margarine mag ich auf meinem Brot nicht. Butter schmeckt viel besser!

Answers to Activity 16

Martina: Salami und Corned Beef mit Senf und Mayonnaise; Marmelade
Angelika: Tofu mit Sojasprossen, Radieschen- und Gurkenscheiben
Klaus: holländischen Edamer, französischen Camembert, Butter

Activity 20, *p. 121*

1. - Hallo, Frau Becker! Dieser Kugelschreiber hier ist Ihnen gerade aus der Tasche gefallen.
   - Danke, Horst. Das war sehr aufmerksam von dir.
2. - Habt ihr Lust, heute abend zu mir zu kommen? Wir können uns die neuen CDs anhören, die ich von euch zum Geburtstag bekommen habe!
   - Au ja, Klasse! Wir kommen gern, oder was meinst du, Martin?

SCRIPTS

3. - Du, Britta, schau mal! Da hinten kommt die neue Biologielehrerin. Sie soll ganz nett sein, hab' ich gehört.
   - Ja, das hab' ich auch gehört.
4. - Entschuldigung, können Sie mir sagen, wo der Hausmeister ist? In unserer Klasse ist die Tafel kaputtgegangen.
   - Ja, natürlich. Er hat sein Büro gleich hinter dem Lehrerzimmer.
5. - He Frank, ich glaube, daß ich aus Versehen dein Mathebuch eingesteckt habe. Ich habe nämlich zwei in meiner Schultasche. Guck doch mal nach, ob dir deins fehlt!
   - Ja, du hast recht. Es gehört tatsächlich mir. Danke!

Answers to Activity 20

1. einer älteren Person; 2. zwei Freunden;
3. einem Freund; 4. einer älteren Person;
5. einem Freund

Dritte Stufe
Activity 26, p. 123

ILSE   Also, wenn ich Obst esse, dann mag ich Bananen lieber als Äpfel. Aber im Sommer mag ich Melonen am liebsten. Am besten schmeckt mir eisgekühlte Wassermelone mit Parmaschinken! Das haben wir zum erstenmal in Italien gegessen, als wir dort in den Ferien waren. Und jetzt machen wir es auch oft zu Hause, weil es uns so gut geschmeckt hat.

ULF   Wir essen sehr viel Gemüse zu Hause. Mein Vater macht eine ganz tolle Gemüsesuppe, mit frischen Kräutern und saurer Sahne und so. Da sind ganz viele verschiedene Gemüsesorten drin, eigentlich alles, was ich gerne mag. Also, Zucchini, Karotten und grüne Bohnen. Die mag ich lieber als zum Beispiel Paprika. Am liebsten mag ich es, wenn auch Tomaten drin sind.

UWE   An meinem Geburtstag darf ich mir aussuchen, was es zu essen gibt. Ich weiß noch nicht, ob ich mir lieber ein chinesisches Reisgericht oder italienische Pasta wünschen soll. Ja, eigentlich mag ich die chinesische Küche lieber. Aber, ehrlich gesagt, schmecken mir die deutschen Gerichte am besten, besonders wenn meine Oma kocht.

ANJA   Ich esse Obst nicht so gern, aber dafür trinke ich alle Fruchtsäfte, die es so gibt. Also, zum Beispiel, Orangensaft, Apfelsaft und Grapefruitsaft. Am liebsten mag ich Traubensaft. Der schmeckt immer richtig süß und fruchtig. Ja, und sonst, wenn ich total durstig bin oder viel Sport gemacht habe, dann trinke ich am liebsten literweise Wasser, Mineralwasser natürlich! Das löscht den Durst am besten.

Answers to Activity 26

Ilse: mag Bananen lieber als Äpfel; mag Melone am liebsten
Ulf: mag Zucchini, Karotten und grüne Bohnen lieber als Paprika; mag Tomaten am liebsten
Uwe: mag chinesische Küche lieber als italienische; mag deutsche Gerichte am liebsten
Anja: mag Traubensaft lieber als Orangen-, Apfel- und Grapefruitsaft; mag am liebsten Mineralwasser

Anwendung
Activity 1, p. 126

MUTTER   Also, Bernd, was möchtest du trinken?

BERND   Ah, ich freue mich schon auf den leckeren Orangensaft hier. Der schmeckt so gut, weil er immer aus frisch gepreßten Apfelsinen ist. Eigentlich mag ich den Apfelsaft ja auch gern, aber der Orangensaft schmeckt mir doch viel besser. Und du, Annette, was trinkst du?

ANNETTE   Ach, Bernd! Saft! Saft! Immer trinkst du nur Saft! Nimm doch mal was anderes, eine Cola zum Beispiel, so wie ich! Und dann bestelle ich mir jetzt die Gemüseplatte. Die haben ja sonst hier nicht so viel ohne Fleisch. Entweder Salatbuffet oder Gemüseplatte. Na ja, hoffentlich sind auch meine Lieblingspilze mit dabei. Mutti, nimmst du wieder die Krabben wie letztes Mal?

MUTTER   Ja, also, ich nehme wieder die frischen Krabben mit Kräuterbutter und Petersilienkartoffeln. Und dazu noch ein paar Scheiben Baguette. Das habe ich schon lange nicht mehr gehabt. Oder nein, ich glaube, ich lasse mal das Brot weg und nehme lieber nachher noch ein Dessert. Und was nimmst du, Hans-Peter?

VATER   Ja also, der Kuchen soll hier ausgezeichnet sein. Schau mal auf die Karte, was die alles haben: Apfeltorte, Kirschstreusel, Rosinennapfkuchen. Mmmh, und alles hausgemacht, ach, und auch noch Zitronencremeschnitten. Schokoladentorte mit Sahne hört sich nun auch gut an! Na ja, aber zuerst nehme ich mal die Aalsuppe, und dann sehen wir weiter!

Answers to Activity 1

1. Annette; 2. Bernd; 3. Nein, sie ißt vegetarisch; 4. Ja, denn er liest zuerst, welche Kuchen/Torten es auf der Speisekarte gibt.

Kapitel 5: Gesund essen
Projects and Games

PROJECT

In this activity students write a composition in which they describe the place where they feel safest and most comfortable. This assignment should be started after students have completed the **Zum Lesen** *section. Students work individually on the project. They may include pictures or drawings to support and illustrate the content of their writing.*

Materials Students may need paper, a pen or pencil, some photos or pictures, and a ruler.

Suggested Sequence

1. During the prewriting stage, help students focus on their writing skills. Have them brainstorm, make lists of words and phrases, and come up with drawings as they plan a rough draft. Students may want to reread some of the articles of the **Zum Lesen** section to help them get started.
2. Students begin to focus on specific ideas and come up with a main idea for their compositions.
3. Students study their notes again to ensure that their ideas are all relevant to the main idea of their composition.
4. Students use their outline to write their compositions in the present tense. They should use connectors and intensifiers such as the ones introduced in the **Zum Lesen** section.
5. Students edit their compositions (encourage peer editing) to identify and correct grammatical or mechanical errors.
6. Students write the final copy of their compositions and add visual aids to accompany their projects.
7. Students turn in the projects for a grade.

Grading the Project

Suggested point distribution (total = 100 points)

Content	25
Correct usage (grammar, vocabulary)	50
Originality	25

GAMES

Wörter kreuz und quer

This game will help students review the vocabulary they have learned thus far.

Procedure Divide the class into three or four teams and draw a large grid on the board. Write a word in the grid. The first team sends one member to the board and writes a word in the grid which intersects with the first word. Then the next team adds a word which again has to intersect with an existing word. Give one point per vowel, two points for most consonants, three points for umlauts, and four points for any consonants you consider more difficult. Points are added after each team's turn and are totalled at the end of the game or after a set amount of time has elapsed.

Entschuldigung, eine Frage bitte ...!

This game will help students review and practice vocabulary and verb tenses.

Provide each student in your class with a list of 20 items based on the vocabulary or expressions they have previously studied.
Example:
Finde jemanden, der ...
  Eier zum Frühstück gegessen hat.
  keinen Joghurt mag.
With the list and a pen or pencil, all students walk around the classroom and try to find someone who can affirmatively answer each of the questions. If a student answers with **ja**, the student who asked the question writes that student's name next to the item. Students may not use their own names for any of the items. The student who first completes his or her list is the winner.

Kapitel 5: Gesund essen
Lesson Plans, pages 106-129

Using the Chapter Opener,
pp. 106-107

Motivating Activity
Ask students what healthy snack foods and beverages are for sale and those they would like to see for sale at their school.

Building on Previous Skills
Make a transparency or a handout of the **Stundenplan** from p. 97 of Chapter 4, Level 1. Ask students what the word **Pause** means and how often it appears on the schedule. What might this time be allotted for, and can students guess what German students do during this time? (two 15-minute breaks in which students have time to eat snacks, socialize with friends, or do school work)

Thinking Critically
Comparing and Contrasting Ask students in German how often they have breaks and how long their breaks are. What do they typically do during their breaks?

Culture Note
① During breaks, German students are encouraged to leave the school building but remain on school grounds. Several teachers are assigned to monitor (**Schulhofaufsicht**) students outside, and, depending on the school size, some teachers have **Aufsicht** *(hall monitor duty)* inside the school.

Teaching Suggestion
② Ask students to look at the **Brötchenpreise** list. Using German, can they describe the different types of **Brötchen** offered and comment on the suggested prices? (Example: **Das ist billig/teuer.**) Then have students tell you what they would choose from the **Brötchenliste** and **Obstliste**.

Culture Note
② Many schools (elementary and secondary schools alike) offer a service in which students can put in a weekly drink order. Usually the **Hausmeister** *(head custodian)* takes the orders. Students make their selections (Examples: juices, milk, chocolate milk) and pay for the week. They get a card indicating what item they paid for, and they present this card daily to pick up their drink.

Background Information
③ Generally, Germans do not eat waffles, pancakes with syrup, or eggs and bacon for breakfast. They may eat **weichgekochte Eier** *(soft-boiled eggs)* or **hartgekochte Eier** *(hard-boiled eggs)*, especially on Sunday. **Frische Brötchen** are often part of the breakfast meal, and they are served along with butter or margarine, cold cuts, cheese, jam, honey, or **Nutella**® (a chocolate and hazelnut spread which is a favorite among younger children).

For Individual Needs
③ **Tactile Learners** Bring the items featured in this photograph to class. You may want to ask students to bring some of the foods. Have students set the table as in the picture and hold a typical German breakfast with your class.

Thinking Critically
③ **Comparing and Contrasting** Discuss with your students the differences between a typical German and a typical American breakfast.

Language Note
Students have seen the diminutive form -**chen** in words such as **Mädchen** or **Päckchen.** You might want to remind them that this ending denotes something small or young. Can students infer the meaning of **Brötchen?** (literally: *small bread*)

Multicultural Connection

Have students find out from exchange students, students from other countries, and foreign language teachers what a typical breakfast in each of those countries consists of. Have students report the information to the class.

Focusing on Outcomes

Ask students what they typically like to snack on and how important they think it is to have a snack. Then have students preview the learning outcomes on p. 107. **NOTE:** Each of these outcomes is modeled in the video and evaluated in **Kann ich's wirklich?** on p. 128.

Teaching Los geht's!
pp. 108-110

> ### Resources for Los geht's!
>
> - *Video Program* **OR**
>   *Expanded Video Program*, Videocassette 2
> - *Textbook Audiocassette* 3 A
> - *Practice and Activity Book*

▶ **pages 108-109**

 ## Video Synopsis

In this segment of the video, students buy healthy snacks at school. Wiebke has packed her own snack: a **Brötchen** with Tofu and bean sprouts. She tells her friends about the foods she ate for breakfast that morning and about a nutritious meal she once cooked. The student outcomes listed on p. 107 are modeled in the video: expressing regret and downplaying, expressing skepticism and making certain, calling someone's attention to something and responding, expressing preference and strong preference.

Motivating Activity

As an advance organizer to the **Foto-Roman**, ask students to describe a healthy
a) breakfast
b) lunch they would pack for school
c) lunch they would prepare for friends.

 ## For Individual Needs

Challenge Have students watch the video again and/or have them read along in their books. When finished, ask students in which of the scenes the foods you just listed are mentioned. Note beside each food whether it is for **Pausenbrot, Frühstück,** or **Mittagessen.** Then ask students to compare this list to the foods they listed in the motivating activity.

 ## Culture Notes

- When Germans have dessert after lunch, it usually is a fruit dish—fresh fruit—or steamed fruit in syrup. They usually do not eat pastries or cake right after lunch. They prefer to wait until around four o'clock to have cake or pastries, which they usually have with coffee. They call this time **die Kaffeezeit.**

- In the **Foto-Roman,** David requests a **Quarkbrötchen. Quark** is a soft, fresh cheese that looks much like yogurt. It is used in the preparation of **Käsekuchen,** dips, or eaten as a spread on bread. It comes in many flavors. **Quark** is hard to find in American stores, but delicatessen or specialty health food stores occasionally carry it.

▶ **page 110**

For Individual Needs

1 A Slower Pace To ensure comprehension of the text, go through each individual frame of the **Foto-Roman,** eliciting responses to the five questions from students.

2 Auditory Learners Ask students to look at the **Foto-Roman** as you read Questions 1-7 to the class. Students then look for the answers in the **Foto-Roman.** Add other questions to check comprehension.

LOS GEHT'S!

 For Individual Needs

3 Challenge Put students in pairs or small groups and have them make up a similar list of statements, some of which are factually correct and some which are not. Have each group put its list on an overhead transparency and present it to the class. The class has to decide whether each of the statements is true. If a statement is not true, students should restate it with correct information.

4 Challenge After students have successfully matched the sentences, have them think of a different response to each of the sentences or questions on the left.

Example:

- Hier sind zehn Mark.   - Es tut mir leid. Ich habe nicht genug Wechselgeld.

      or

      - Haben Sie es kleiner?

Closure

Ask students to describe a typical German snack, lunch, and breakfast.

▶ *page 111*

PRESENTATION: Landeskunde

Teacher Note

The **Landeskunde** interviews are recorded on audiocassette and videocassette.

Teaching Suggestions

• Ask students to help you make a list of foods that are representative of particular areas or regions in the United States. Then ask students if they would eat the foods that were just mentioned by the class, if not why?

• You may want to introduce the following vocabulary to help students better understand the interviews.
 der Auflauf *casserole*
 das Gericht *dish*
 die Hausmannskost *simple, but tasty meal*
 die Küche *cuisine*

Building on Previous Skills

In the Location Openers of Level I, students were introduced to some favorite local dishes. Ask students if they can name and describe some of the dishes from Brandenburg (lentil soup, chicken fricassee), Schleswig-Holstein (**Matjes, Krabben, Aale, Räucherspeck, Buttermilchsuppe, rote Grütze**), Munich (**Schweinshaxe, Leberkäs, Weißwürste**), and Baden-Württemberg (**Spätzle, Schwarzwälder Kirschtorte, Maultaschen, Schinken**).

Thinking Critically

Comparing and Contrasting In Activity B, students are introduced to German and Austrian table manners (**Tischmanieren**). Ask students what is considered appropriate in the United States for the hand that is not being used. (Americans generally keep that hand in their laps.)

Teaching Suggestion

Ask students to share in German some of the table manners or rules in their families. (Examples: Do not lick your knife; do not slurp; ask to be excused before leaving)

TPR Total Physical Response

After having discussed some of the rules of table manners, use several of those commands with your students. Here are some examples:
Ruth, nimm, den Ellbogen vom Tisch!
Linda, gerade sitzen, bitte!
George, halt bitte die Hände auf dem Tisch!
Scott, wasch deine Hände! (student pretends)
Susi, nimm die Gabel in die linke Hand, das Messer in die rechte!

Teacher Note

Mention to your students that the **Landeskunde** will also be included in Quiz 5-1 given at the end of the **Erste Stufe**.

*T*eaching Erste Stufe,
pp. 112-115

ERSTE STUFE

Resources for Erste Stufe

Practice and Activity Book
Chapter Resources, Book 2
  • Additional Listening Activities 5-1, 5-2
  • Student Response Forms
  • Realia 5-1
  • Situation Card 5-1
  • Teaching Transparency Master 5-1
  • Quiz 5-1
Audiocassette Program
  • *Textbook Audiocassette* 3 A
  • *Additional Listening Activities, Audiocassette* 9 B
  • *Assessment Items, Audiocassette* 7 B
Video Program or *Expanded Video Program*

▶ *page 112*

MOTIVATE

Teaching Suggestion

Have students imagine they need to raise money for a club by selling fresh fruit. Which fruits would sell well? Which would keep well and not require refrigeration? How much would they have to pay for the fruit? What would they charge per piece?

TEACH

PRESENTATION: Wortschatz

• Ask students to look back at Photo 2 of the Chapter Opener on p. 107. Go over the list of foods German students can choose from. Then ask questions such as **Was können die deutschen Schüler in der Pause kaufen?** Then ask students to read the items listed in the **Wortschatz** box and tell you how much each item costs.
• Ask students to choose a snack from the menu in Photo 2. The snack should consist of at least two items.

Building on Previous Skills

6 After students have completed their charts, ask them which of the German students' choices they like and why. Remind students to use **denn** or **weil** and the phrases expressing how something tastes. (Chapter 6 of Level I)

Group Work

7 Students work in groups of three: one student is the **Verkäufer(in)** and the other two are students going through the line at the snack counter. Ask students to make up a conversation using the **Wortschatz** on p. 112 and the vocabulary from Photo 2 on p. 107. They may want to ask how much things cost. They could even ask a friend for extra money and explain that an item might be sold out (**alle; ausverkauft**). Ask two or three groups to read or perform their conversations for the class.

▶ *page 113*

PRESENTATION: So sagt man das!

• Go over the new expressions with your students. Then ask them to look at the three captions of the Chapter Opener and at the frames of the **Foto-Roman** and find examples of the expressions they just learned.
• To provide students with practice using the new expressions, ask students questions to make them use an appropriate phrase from the **So sagt man das!** box.
  Examples:
  Margaret, wir haben leider keine Milch mehr!
  Carl, ich dachte, der Apfel kostet nur 50 Pfennig!

Teaching Suggestion

9 After completing the listening task as suggested in the activity, do a follow-up activity. This time ask students to write down what each of the four children wants and what each is being offered instead. On a transparency, make a simple chart with the names of the four children down the left side and two columns labeled **Was das Kind möchte** and **Was die Eltern anbieten**. After listening to the conversations twice, call on students to help fill in the chart.

Teaching Suggestion

10 Have students help you make a list of things that can be found at these markets. Students should use this list as they work on Activity 10.

▶ *page 114*

PRESENTATION: So sagt man das!

- Before introducing the new phrases, ask students how they express skepticism in English about something they see or hear. Ask students how intonation affects these types of remarks.

- Next, ask students how they make certain in English. What expressions do they use? Does intonation play a role? Now practice the expressions in the function box using the given examples and adding more. Reinforce especially the new vocabulary from **Los geht's!** and the **Erste Stufe.** Have students respond affirmatively or negatively using the expressions from the right side of the function box and any others they have learned. (**Natürlich! Ja, sehr gern! Nein, absolut nicht! Nein, überhaupt nicht!**)

PRESENTATION: Grammatik

On a table, place several familiar items such as foods, classroom objects, and accessories. Tell students that you are a customer in a store. Point to each item and use the phrase **Ich möchte dies(en/e/es) ... gern kaufen/haben.** Ask students to listen carefully and repeat what you just said. Have students point out the various endings and compare them to the endings of the definite articles in the accusative. Do a similiar demonstration with the nominative: **Dieser ... schmeckt gut (ist teuer, kommt aus ...).** Then demonstrate the dative with the location. **Was ist alles in diesem Salat? In dieser Suppe? In diesem Fertiggericht?** Finally, go over the grammar box with the class.

▶ *page 115*

CLOSE

♟ Game
Play the game **Wörter kreuz und quer**. See page 105F for the procedure.

Focusing on Outcomes

Refer students back to the learning outcomes listed on p. 107. They should recognize that they now know how to express regret, to downplay, to express skepticism, and make certain.

ASSESS

- **Performance Assessment** Using the new food vocabulary of the **Erste Stufe,** prepare a list of questions such as
  Du ißt wohl gern vegetarisch, oder?
  Du magst Blaubeeren, nicht?
  Address the questions to individual students. They should use responses such as **Ja!** or **Nein!, Nicht unbedingt!, Na klar!,** and **Sicher!** to reply to your questions.

- Quiz 5-1, *Chapter Resources,* Book 2

*T*eaching Zum Lesen,
pp. 116-117

Reading Strategy
The targeted strategy in this reading is understanding the tone of a text. Students should learn about this strategy before beginning Question 6.

PREREADING

Motivating Activity
Ask students why people sometimes prefer to be alone, without friends or other family members around them. When or how often does this happen to them?

Thinking Critically
Comparing and Contrasting After reading the Lesetrick, ask students for examples of intensifiers in English. Can students think of intensifiers their parents or other relatives use and how these vary from generation to generation?

Teacher Note
Activity 2 is a prereading activity.

READING

Thinking Critically

3 Drawing Inferences Before students scan the texts to find the German students' favorite places, remind them of the reading strategy in the reading section of Chapter 4. There they learned to activate their background knowledge. To help students build expectations for the text, brainstorm with them on places where students would typically like to go to be by themselves. Then do Activity 3.

Cooperative Learning

Divide students into groups of three. Each group should have a writer, a discussion leader, and a reporter. Set a time limit of approximately 20 minutes to complete Activities 5-8. When students are finished, ask each group reporter to share his or her group's discussion outcomes with the class.

For Individual Needs

6 Challenge Ask students to substitute synonyms for the words in bold in the three sentences. You may help students by providing them with a list of phrases which students should be able to recognize. (Examples: **wirklich, sicher, zwei Stunden oder mehr/länger, bestimmt, ziemlich**)

Thinking Critically

Drawing Inferences Ask students to skim the four interviews again and then make up an appropriate title for each of them. Titles should reflect the students' choices for a quiet place.

POST-READING

Teacher Note

Activity 9 is a post-reading task that will show whether students can apply what they have learned.

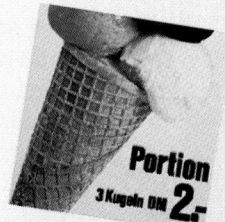

Closure

Divide the class into groups of three students. Each group should have a recorder and a reporter. Draw a flower like the one below on a transparency or the board and fill in each of the petals with a word from the reading selection. Each group creates a description using the words in the petals. Set a time limit for this activity. Then call on two or three groups and have the reporter read his or her group's story to the class.

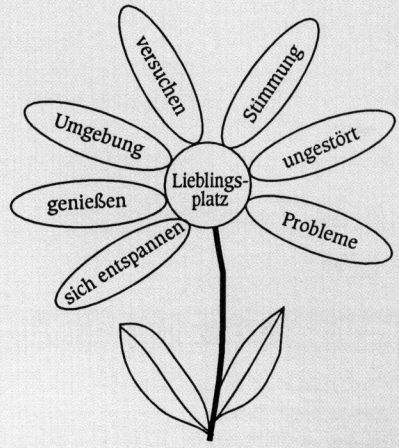

Answers to Activity 1
Favorite "get-away-spots" of young people

Answers to Activity 2
Answers will vary.

Answers to Activity 3
Markus: Café; Tanja: eigenes Zimmer; Nicole: Turm; Christian: Schülervertretungsbüro
Answers will vary.

Answers to Activity 4
Markus: abgelegen, nicht viele Leute / trinkt etwas, liest, schreibt Gedichte; Tanja: klein, unterm Dach / liegt im Bett, hört Musik, liest, bummelt herum, schläft lange, sortiert Flaschensammlung, blättert Zeitschriften durch; Nicole: im Stadtwald, es ist ruhig um den Turm, wenige Leute / denkt nach, unterhält sich mit Hund, genießt die Sonne; Christian: in der Schule, ruhig in den Pausen / denkt nach, entspannt sich, liest Briefe, verschönert den Raum

Answers to Activity 5
Answers will vary.

ZWEITE STUFE

Answers to Activity 6

a. The word **eigentlich** is a filler with various meanings. In this case it conveys the notion of "basically", "actually", or "really", and allows the speaker more time to think.
b. Using **mindestens** *(at least)* in this case, indicates an extension of the time period stated.
c. **Ganz schön** intensifies the adjective **eng**.

Answers to Activity 7

now and then; from time to time

Answers to Activity 8

Crazy as it may sound - sometimes I talk with him then.

*T*eaching Zweite Stufe, *pp. 118-121*

Resources for Zweite Stufe

Practice and Activity Book
Chapter Resources, Book 2
- Communicative Activity 5-1
- Additional Listening Activities 5-3, 5-4
- Student Response Forms
- Realia 5-2
- Situation Card 5-2
- Quiz 5-2

Audiocassette Program
- *Textbook Audiocassette* 3 A
- *Additional Listening Activities, Audiocassette* 9 B
- *Assessment Items, Audiocassette* 7 B

▶ page 118

MOTIVATE

Group work

In groups of three, have students brainstorm all the sandwiches they could make using the many foods they already know. Have them think of meat, cheese, eggs, vegetables, and jams, or honey. How many can they think of?
Examples: **Wurstbrötchen, Tomatenbrot, Quarkbrötchen**

TEACH

PRESENTATION: Wortschatz

Ask students to bring the foods from the vocabulary box to class. You may also want to bring a small selection of different types of German breads. (Examples: **Schwarzbrot, Mischbrot, Roggenbrot, Bauernbrot**) Label each food with the appropriate German word and display them on a table in front of the class. Introduce the items to the class. Repeat each word several times to ensure comprehension.

 For Individual Needs

Kinesthetic Learners Once you feel that students are familiar with the new words, ask students to make their own sample **Pausenbrot,** using the ingredients available. Students can form a line, preparing their **Pausenbrote.** Once all students are finished, ask several students **Was hast du denn auf dem Brot?**

 Culture Note

You might want to remind students that Germans usually eat open-faced sandwiches (except when prepared ahead of time for school or work). They often spread unsalted butter on the bread and then cover it with cold cuts, cheese, or jam. There are many varieties of breads available such as **Mischbrot,** which is made from wheat and rye flour, **Weißbrot,** which Germans generally use to make toast, and **Vollkornbrot** which is made from coarsely ground rye and wheat grains.

Thinking Critically

17 Comparing and Contrasting After students have talked to their partners, ask the class to make a list of the typical ingredients used for a **Pausenbrot** in the United States and in Germany. Have students compare the two.

PRESENTATION: So sagt man das!

Ask students to look back at the **Foto-Roman** on p. 108. Have them reread Frames 3 and 7 where the phrases **guck mal!** and **schau mal da!** are first introduced. Can students infer from the context the meaning of those two expressions? Then go over the expressions in the function box with students.

► *page 119*

For Individual Needs

18 A Slower Pace Write the sentences on the board. To help students see the relationship between the possessive pronoun and the subject, ask several students to come to the board and underline or connect the two elements.
Example:

Was haben sie denn auf ihrem Pausenbrot?

► *page 120*

PRESENTATION: Grammatik

After reviewing the possessive adjectives and their endings, ask individual students questions like those examples below. Students have to answer, using possessive pronouns with their correct endings.

James, wem gehört denn dieses Buch?
Mario, was ist denn in deiner Tasche?
John, wie heißen eure Nachbarn?

For Individual Needs

19 Challenge As an additional activity, you may want to ask students to rewrite the eight sentences from direct into indirect speech, changing the possessives accordingly.

► *page 121*

Total Physical Response

23 Once students have correctly identified the owner of the belongings, give commands to individual students, using such verbs as **nehmen, geben, hinlegen, bringen, weitergeben, aufheben, zeigen, reichen, suchen,** or **finden** as well as possessive adjectives.
Examples:

Marie, gib Andrew bitte deinen Kuli!
Hier ist Morgans Buch. Reich ihm bitte sein Buch!

Reteaching: Possessives

Make a chart of sentence fragments as in the following example. Have students create as many sentences as possible.

Ich	kaufen	mein	Freund	meistens	Blumen
Wir	geben	dein	Freundin	wirklich	Konzertkarten
Ihr	finden	sein	Geschwistern	gewöhnlich	Ratschläge
Sie	schenken	ihr	Zimmer	manchmal	CD-Sammlung
Er	leihen	euer	Mutter		
Bob		ihr	Eltern		
Jill		unser			

CLOSE

For Individual Needs

Visual Learners The day you plan to do this activity, ask students to leave one item belonging to them on your desk on their way to their seat. (Examples: comb, watch, pen, book, photo, snack) Hold up one item at a time, and ask students whose item it is.
Examples:

Grace, gehört dir dieser Kamm?
Diego, ist dies deine Uhr?

If the item doesn't belong to the student you just asked, that student may know who the owner is and should answer with **Nein, das ist nicht meine Uhr, das ist ihre Uhr.** (pointing to another student).
Continue until all items have been returned to their owners.

Focusing on Outcomes

Refer students back to the learning outcomes listed on p. 107. They should recognize that they now know how to call someone's attention to something and respond.

ASSESS

• **Performance Assessment** Ask students to prepare a short oral description of how they make their favorite sandwich. Students should use sequencing words as well as the vocabulary items learned in the **Zweite Stufe**.

• Quiz 5-2, *Chapter Resources,* Book 2

ZWEITE STUFE

DRITTE STUFE

*T*eaching Dritte Stufe, *pp. 122-125*

Resources for Dritte Stufe

Practice and Activity Book
Chapter Resources, Book 2
- Communicative Activity 5-2
- Additional Listening Activities 5-5, 5-6
- Student Response Forms
- Realia 5-3
- Situation Card 5-3
- Teaching Transparency Master 5-2
- Quiz 5-3

Audiocassette Program
- *Textbook Audiocassette 3 A*
- *Additional Listening Activities, Audiocassette 9 B*
- *Assessment Items, Audiocassette 7 B*

▶ *page 122*

MOTIVATE

Teaching Suggestion

Tell students that they are going to shop for a family dinner at the local supermarket. They will go to both the meat department and the fish department. What foods can they recall in German that can be found in these two places? Write the two heads **Fleischabteilung** and **Fischabteilung** on a transparency and have small groups of students brainstorm all the items that would fit under either one of the two heads.

TEACH

Thinking Critically

Drawing Inferences Ask students to look at the **KAUFMANNS** advertisement and have them find the five imported food items. Can students tell from the abbreviations where the items are from? (grapes/France, bananas/Guatemala, chicken and carrots/Holland, lamb/Australia)

Math Connection

Ask students to calculate all the prices given per **Pfund**. Do prices seem higher than, lower than, or similar to prices in U.S. supermarkets?

 For Individual Needs

Challenge In addition to the notations for imports, have students find all the words and phrases in small print that are used as qualifiers for various items. Some of these words should already be familiar to students. Have students first guess at the others and then verify their meaning. (Examples: **aus dem Faß, vom Schwein, Kl. A, gefroren, zart, mager, abgehangen, 1000 g Beutel, 500 g Packung**) Have students work in pairs and present their findings to the class.

▶ *page 123*

PRESENTATION: So sagt man das!

Using visual aids such as realia, transparencies, or photos, introduce the new functions by holding up the visual aid and asking directed questions that incorporate the new expressions. Elicit responses from individual students. This is also a great way to recycle vocabulary from different content areas you feel students need to review.

 For Individual Needs

26 A Slower Pace Inform students that they will hear the recording twice. The first time, students should try to take notes of the food and drink items mentioned. When students listen the second time, they should make notes on the preferences mentioned by the different students.

For Additional Practice

27 For extra practice, have students interview each other about the foods they prefer for different occasions. (Examples: **Fete, Grillparty, Picknick**)

 For Individual Needs

27 Challenge Have students make up pairs of beverages that could logically be compared. (Examples: **Kaffee/Tee, Milch/Saft, Leitungswasser/Mineralwasser, Cola/Eistee**) Then have students use these choices in practice with their partner.

▶ *page 124*

PRESENTATION: Grammatik

To introduce the interrogative **welcher**, recycle such phrases as **gern haben, gut finden, lieber machen, gern sehen,** and **gern hören.** Question students about their interests, tastes, likes, dislikes, and preferences. As you ask some of the questions, write them on a transparency as well. Then ask students to examine the new question word and determine why they think **welch-** has different endings.

Building on Previous Skills

29 Before students begin with the activity, write the six food categories on the board and have students brainstorm as many items for each of the listed categories as they can remember. Students can later refer to this list as they work with their partners.

Teaching Suggestion

30 Students should use the list you prepared for Activity 29 as they work on Activity 30. Point out to students that they can use the phrases underneath the word **Warum?** to give a reason for selecting a food as their favorite.

▶ *page 125*

PRESENTATION: Grammatik

On a transparency, make a list of phrases that students know. First ask them to shorten each phrase using a contraction.

> **zu der Schule —> zur Schule**
> **zu dem Supermarkt —> zum Supermarkt**
> **zu dem Mittagessen —> zum Mittagessen**

Then ask students to tell you what **zu der** (**zur**) and **zu dem** (**zum**) mean. (*to:* to school, to the supermarket, etc; *for:* (with meals) for lunch)

Teaching Suggestion

Tell students that they are all going to visit relatives this weekend. They need to tell you whom they are going to see. Make a list of all suggestions on a transparency. Try to elicit some plurals, too. Examples:
Ich gehe zu meinem Onkel.
Ich gehe zu meiner Kusine.
Ich gehe zu meinen Großeltern.

For Additional Practice

32 Ask students to come up with other possible answers beyond those offered in the word boxes. (Examples: **Schokoladeneis, Scholle, Mohnbrötchen, Brokkoli, Erdbeerjoghurt, Gurkensalat**)

Reteaching: Using the interrogative *welcher*

Ask students to look back at the **KAUFMANNS** advertisement on p. 122. Then ask students to imagine that they are the salesclerk at that supermarket. They didn't quite understand what a customer ordered and ask him or her about the order. Examples:
Welchen Fisch möchten Sie, bitte?
Welches Fleisch wünschen Sie?
Welche Äpfel dürfen es sein?

CLOSE

Teaching Suggestion

Play the following skit with students. In German, ask students to join you for an after-school study lesson. Students then try to get out of staying after school by telling you that they already have to go somewhere else. Here are some possible responses students might give you.
Das tut mir leid, aber ich muß zum Zahnarzt.
Ich bedauere, aber ich muß zum Kaufmann.
Es ist schade, aber ich muß zu meiner Oma.
Have each student try to talk himself or herself out of joining in on the study session. If possible, you might want to display a variety of pictures depicting reasons for excuses which students can refer to for this activity.

Focusing on Outcomes

Refer students back to the learning outcomes listed on p. 107. They should recognize that they now know how to express preference and strong preference.

ASSESS

- **Performance Assessment** Prepare a class set of index cards. Each card has a question on it reflecting the functions and phrases introduced in this **Stufe**. Hand a card to each student. Student A then begins to call on another student (B) and reads the question to him or her. Student B answers the questions and goes on by reading his or her question to a student who hasn't been asked yet. All students should get a turn.

- Quiz 5-3, *Chapter Resources*, Book 2

Using Anwendung,
p. 126-127

Video Wrap-Up

At this time, you might want to use the *Video Program* or the *Expanded Video Program*, Videocassette 2 for additional review and enrichment. See *Video Guide* for suggestions regarding:
- **Wiebkes Pausenbrot**
  (Dramatic episode)
- **Landeskunde**
  Interviews
- **Videoclips**
  (Authentic footage—*Expanded Video Program* only)

For Individual Needs

1 **A Slower Pace** On a transparency or the board, write in random order all the foods that are mentioned in the listening activity. As students listen to the activity, they can refer to the list to help them complete the chart.

Group Work

2 Read the text with students and go over unfamiliar words or phrases. Then divide the class into groups of three to four students. Ask each group to answer Questions 1-4 within a set amount of time. One student should write down the answers. When students are finished, call on several groups to share their answers with the class.

Teaching Suggestion

4 As a variation to this activity, you could have each student write one question on a piece of paper. Collect all papers and put them into a hat. Then have one student come to the front, pull a paper and direct the question to another student. The same student calls on different students to answer the questions until all questions have been read.

Portfolio Assessment

4 You might want to suggest this activity as an oral portfolio item for your students. See *Assessment Guide*, p. 18.

5 You might want to suggest this activity as a written portfolio item for your students. See *Assessment Guide*, p. 18.

𝒦ann ich's wirklich?

p. 128

This page helps students prepare for the test. It is a brief checklist of the major points covered in the chapter. The students should be reminded that it is only a checklist and not necessarily everything that will appear on the test.

𝒰sing Wortschatz,

p. 129

◈ For Individual Needs

26 Tactile Learners Use sentence strips to practice sentences that include the expressions or phrases from each **Stufe.** Write each sentence on a piece of paper, cutting each sentence into its word components. Put the fragments of each sentence into a numbered envelope. Write the corresponding sentence on a separate sheet of paper beside the number. Give one envelope to each pair of students who will try to put the sentences back together.

♜ Game

Play the game **Zeichenspiel,** using the food vocabulary from this chapter. See p. 167F in the Level 1 *Teacher's Edition* for the procedure.

Teaching Suggestion

To practice the names of foods, ask students to name foods that can be found in certain sections of a grocery store.
Examples:
Was kann man in der Fischabteilung kaufen?
Welche Sorte Fleisch gibt es in der Fleischabteilung?
Was für Obst findet man gewöhnlich bei dem Obsthändler?
Nenne einige Produkte in der Tiefkühlkostabteilung.

Teacher Note

Give the **Kapitel 5** Chapter Test, *Chapter Resources,* Book 2.

REVIEW

① Ich mag Tofu mit Sojasprossen am liebsten.

Since most German students have a late lunch, their two morning snacks — a sandwich, yogurt, or some fruit, and perhaps something to drink, such as milk or juice — are important to them. Do you and your schoolmates have a break during the morning when you can buy something to eat? When you talk about what snacks there are and what you want or prefer to eat or drink, you will need a number of expressions.

In this chapter you will learn

- to express regret and downplay; to express skepticism and make certain
- to call someone's attention to something and respond
- to express preference and strong preference

And you will

- listen to German students talk about their mid-morning snacks
- read about the importance given in Germany to the mid-morning snack
- write about your own choice of snacks
- find out what some German students like to eat

② **Macht nichts! Dann nehm' ich eben ein Quarkbrötchen.**

③ **Zum Frühstück ess' ich Brot mit Honig oder Wurst und Käse, manchmal auch ein Ei.**

Los geht's!

Wiebkes Pausenbrot

Look at the photos that accompany the story.
In how many different places does this story take place?
Can you name these places by looking at the photos?

Am Helene-Lange-Gymnasium in Hamburg können sich die Schüler in der Pause etwas zu essen und zu trinken kaufen. Alles ist gut, gesund und billig. Die „Verkäuferinnen" sind nämlich die Mütter der Schüler. Sie kaufen alles billig ein, sie bereiten die belegten Brötchen vor und stehen dann auch hinter der Theke.

Ein Eibrötchen!

Ich bedaure, die Eibrötchen sind alle.

Macht nichts! Dann nehm' ich eben eine Banane.

20 Pfennig!

Ich hab' leider nur einen Zehnmarkschein.

Das ist in Ordnung! Ich hab' genug Wechselgeld.

Ich möchte ... eine Milch ... und ein Quarkbrötchen, bitte!

Was ißt du denn da, Wiebke?

Das ist mein Pausenbrot. Das hab' ich mir mitgebracht.

Und, was hast du denn auf dem Brot?

Guck mal! Lecker, nicht?

Und was soll denn das sein, dieses Gemüse?

Tofu mit Sojasprossen!

Igitt! Du ißt wohl vegetarisch, was?

Nö, nicht unbedingt. Manchmal ess' ich auch Fleisch.

Heute morgen beim Frühstück.

5

Ich hab' hier noch ein Ei, Wiebke. Willst du es?

Nein, danke! Gib es doch dem Bernie! Aber ich nehme jetzt noch ein Stück Brot mit ... hm ...

Hier ist Honig, Marmelade, Wurst ...

Ich nehme mir eine Scheibe Wurst. Der Aufschnitt sieht echt prima aus.

Tofu ist gesund, Thorsten! Willst du mal probieren?

6

Hm, wirklich prima! Fast wie Quark.

Schaut mal da, der David! Du, David, wie willst du denn das alles essen? Da brauchst du ja drei Hände!

Einfach: Die Flasche in die Tasche; die Schokolade in die andere Tasche, und jetzt hab' ich meine Hände frei für mein Quarkbrötchen.

Einmal hat Wiebke für ihre Freunde ein prima Mittagessen gemacht.

8

Was ist das für eine Suppe?

Eine Gemüsesuppe. Kommt aus dem Kühlschrank! Es ist ein Fertiggericht, man braucht sie nur noch aufwärmen.

Hm, gut! Ich mag Gemüse.

Welches Gemüse magst du am liebsten?

Eigentlich alles. Nur Spinat mag ich nicht.

9

Und dann gibt es Huhn, mit Nudeln oder Reis. Hier ist die Soße. Ach ja, und dann gibt es noch Salat, Kopfsalat mit Tomaten.

Und zum Nachtisch gibt es Obst. Und nun wünsch' ich euch einen guten Appetit!

Mensch, da bin ich aber froh, daß ich keinen Spinat gemacht habe.

LOS GEHT'S!

1 Was passiert hier?

1. during the break; students' mothers

Verstehst du alles, was diese Leute sagen? Beantworte die Fragen!

1. When do the students buy something to eat and drink? Who sells it to them?
2. What does Thorsten ask for? What does he buy? Why? 2. egg sandwich; a banana; egg sandwiches are sold out
3. What does Wiebke have on her sandwich? 3. Tofu
4. What did Wiebke have for breakfast? 4. bread and sausage
5. What did Wiebke serve her friends the day she made lunch for them?

5. vegetable soup, chicken with noodles or rice, salad and fruit

2 Genauer lesen

Lies den Text noch einmal, und beantworte diese Fragen!

1. Was kostet die Banane? 1. 20 Pfennig
2. Was hat Wiebke von zu Hause mitgebracht? 2. Pausenbrot
3. Was ißt Wiebke zum Frühstück? 3. Stück Brot, Scheibe Wurst
4. Wie findet Thorsten den Tofu? 4. prima, fast wie Quark
5. Was ißt David alles? 5. Schokolade, Quarkbrötchen
6. Was hat Wiebke für ihre Freunde nicht gemacht?
7. Welches Gemüse mag David nicht? 6. Spinat
   7. Spinat

3 Stimmt oder stimmt nicht?

Wenn der Satz nicht stimmt, schreib die richtige Antwort!
1. stimmt nicht; eine Banane
1. Thorsten kauft ein Eibrötchen. 2. stimmt nicht; Eibrötchen sind
2. Das Eibrötchen kostet zehn Mark. 3. stimmt   alle
3. Wiebke hat Tofu mit Sojasprossen auf ihrem Pausenbrot.
4. Wiebke ißt immer vegetarisch. 4. stimmt nicht; sie ißt auch Fleisch
5. Auf ihrem Frühstücksbrot hat sie immer Honig. 5. stimmt nicht;
6. Thorsten probiert den Tofu. 6. stimmt   sie ißt auch Wurst
7. Wiebke braucht die Gemüsesuppe nur aufwärmen. 7. stimmt
8. David mag jedes Gemüse.
   8. stimmt nicht; Spinat mag er nicht

4 Was paßt zusammen?

Welche Sätze auf der rechten Seite passen zu den Sätzen auf der linken Seite?

1. Die Eibrötchen sind leider alle. a
2. Hier sind zehn Mark. c
3. Du ißt wohl nur vegetarisch? f
4. Willst du mal den Tofu probieren? e
5. Die Suppe schmeckt gut! b
6. Was gibt's heute zum Mittagessen? d

a. Dann nehme ich eben eine Banane.
b. Das ist ein Fertiggericht, kommt aus dem Kühlschrank.
c. Und du bekommst neun achtzig zurück.
d. Huhn mit Nudeln und Reis.
e. Hm, lecker! Fast wie Quark.
f. Nein, manchmal esse ich auch Fleisch und Wurst.

5 Und du?

Beantworte die Fragen! Answers will vary.

1. Kaufst du dein Essen in der Schule, oder bringst du etwas von zu Hause mit?
2. Ißt du nur vegetarisch?
3. Hast du schon mal Tofu mit Sojasprossen gegessen? Wie hat er dir geschmeckt?
4. Magst du Spinat?
5. Was kostet die Milch in deiner Schule?

Was ißt du, was nicht?

We have asked people from around Germany and Austria what kinds of food they usually eat and why. Before you read the responses, think about the most popular and unpopular foods in the United States. What do most teenagers like? Listen to the interviews, then read the texts.

LANDESKUNDE

Jens und Sabine, *Berlin*

Sabine: „Ich esse gerne Nudeln, Gemüse, Obst, besonders in Aufläufen, sehr gern auch Reisgerichte, Risotto, schmeckt sehr gut."
Jens: „Ja, und wir haben uns gerade ein Buch gekauft über italienische Nudelgerichte, weil wir sehr gerne kochen, vor allem italienisch, wollen wir das einmal ausprobieren."

Heidemarie, *München*

„Also, ich mag die italienische Küche und die chinesische Küche, und, also, chinesisch ist auch manchmal sehr interessant, hat 'nen interessanten Geschmack. Und nicht so gern esse ich Meeresfrüchte und so was mit Meeres ... Fisch und so was zu tun hat."

Gerhard, *St. Ulrich*

„Essen tu' ich alles sehr gern, bis auf Innereien, Fisch weniger. Mehlspeisen essen wir überhaupt sehr gern. Alles, was so Hausmannskost ist, das ist alles gefragt."

A. 1. Gerhard; predominantly meat and starches with sides of traditional vegetables (e.g. peas, carrots); innards; sea food

A. **1.** Which person mentions "home cooking" as his or her favorite? What might a typical home cooked meal in Germany look like? What do you think **Innereien** are, judging by the sound of it? If **Meer** means *sea* or *ocean,* what do you think **Meeresfrüchte** means? Read the interviews again and make a list of the different kinds of foods mentioned. Which foods do people say they like? Which don't they like?

2. Make a list of popular and unpopular foods in the United States. Are there any similarities between the two cultures with respect to food?

B. Both in Germany and Austria it is considered good manners to leave your lower arm (the one you're not eating with) on the edge of the table. It is also polite to eat with your fork in your left hand while holding your knife in your right hand. When your host is serving you food or a drink, you should let him or her know when to stop by saying **Danke!** Otherwise your host will keep on pouring!

Expressing regret and downplaying; expressing skepticism and making certain

Was gibt es heute in der Pause? Und wie teuer ist es?

Milch

Kakao

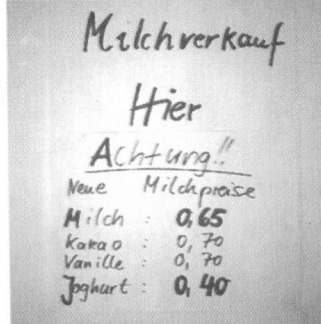

Vanillemilch

Joghurt

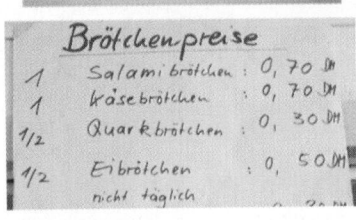

Welche von diesen Speisen und Getränken kannst du an deiner Schule kaufen? Was kosten sie?

6 Hör gut zu! For answers, see listening script on TE Interleaf.

Vier Schüler kaufen sich in der Pause etwas zu essen und zu trinken. Schreib auf, was jeder kauft und was das kostet! Wieviel hat jeder Schüler ausgegeben?

	Was?	Wieviel?	insgesamt
1			
2			

7 Und du? Was möchtest du?

Was möchtest du in der Pause essen und trinken? Wähl einige Sachen aus! Du hast nur drei Mark dabei. Sag deinen Mitschülern, was du möchtest! Wieviel Geld bekommst du zurück?

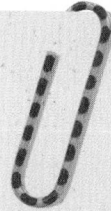

SO SAGT MAN DAS!

Expressing regret and downplaying

When you need to express regret, you could say:

Ich bedaure, die Eibrötchen sind alle.
Es tut mir leid, die Milch kostet jetzt 70 Pfennig.
Was für ein Pech! Kein Joghurt mehr.
Ich hab' **leider** nur Quarkbrötchen.

To respond to an expression of regret and to downplay your response, you could say:

Das macht nichts! *or* **Schon gut!** *or* **Nicht so schlimm!**

To indicate you'll do something else instead, use **eben** or **halt.**

Dann nehm' ich **eben** ein Salamibrötchen.
Dann trink' ich **halt** ein Mineralwasser.

Which of the expressions of regret sounds the most formal? The least formal?
How would you express the last two statements in English?

---

8 Es tut mir leid!

Together with a partner, choose a store that specializes in something, for example food, clothing, instruments, furniture, pets, or gifts. See page 319 for additional vocabulary. Bring in photos or props of things that your shop sells. Your partner will make a shopping list of things she would like to buy at your store. Your partner asks if you have the things on her list. If you happen to be out of stock, express your regret and give a reason why. Your partner then responds, downplaying her response. Role-play your conversation in front of the class.

9 Hör gut zu!

For answers, see listening script on TE Interleaf.

Listen as four children ask their parents about what there is in the refrigerator to eat. Write down which children are satisfied with the parent's answer (and decide to have something else), and which are not.

10 Was für ein Pech!

Such dir einen Partner! Stell dir vor, du bist auf einem Marktplatz, wo es gewöhnlich alles zu kaufen gibt! Aber jetzt ist es Samstag nachmittag, so um halb zwei. Vieles ist schon alle, denn die Stände machen um zwei Uhr zu. — Du bist jetzt der Verkäufer, dein Partner kauft bei dir ein. Tauscht dann die Rollen aus! Gebraucht die Wörter im Kasten, wenn ihr wollt!

Answers will vary. E.g.: Ich möchte 200 g Erdbeeren, bitte. —
Ich bedaure, die Erdbeeren sind alle.

1. **Ich möchte bitte zwei Pfund Pflaumen. Ein Kilo Kartoffeln, bitte!**

SPRACHTIP

Remember that when you ask for certain quantities, you do so by weight: **200 Gramm Wurst, bitte!** How would you ask for two pounds of plums? One kilogram of potatoes?[1]

Brokkoli	Aprikosen
Pflaumen	Möhren
Erdbeeren	Blaubeeren
Wurst Käse	Birnen
Äpfel	Kartoffeln

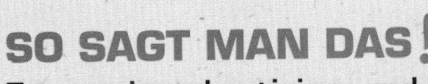

SO SAGT MAN DAS!

Expressing skepticism and making certain

You may be skeptical about something you see or hear. You could say:

> **Was soll denn das sein, dieser Quark und dieses Gemüse?**

You want to make certain and ask:

> Du ißt wohl vegetarisch, **was?**
> Du ißt wohl viel Fleisch, **ja?**
> Du magst Joghurt, **oder?**
> Du magst doch Quark, **nicht wahr?**

An answer may be:

> **Das ist Tofu, und das sind Sojasprossen.**

And the response might be:

> **Ja!** *or* **Nein!**
> **Nicht unbedingt!**
> **Na klar!**
> **Sicher!**

What do you think the first question means? How would you express this idea in English? What could **dieser** and **dieses** mean? How does adding a question (such as **was?**) at the end of the four statements change their meaning? How is **nicht unbedingt** different from the other responses?[1]

Was soll denn das sein, dieses Gemüse?

Grammatik The demonstrative **dieser**

1. Dieser, diese, dieses (*this*), and **diese** (*pl*) (*these*), are called demonstratives. They are used to indicate specific items.

> Was soll denn das sein, **dieses Gemüse?**
> Kann ich bitte **diesen Apfel** haben?

2. Dieser has the following forms:

	Masculine	Feminine	Neuter	Plural
Nominative	dieser	diese	dieses	diese
Accusative	diesen	diese	dieses	diese
Dative	diesem	dieser	diesem	diesen

What other group of words that you have learned has similar endings?[2]

---

1. **Nicht unbedingt** means *not necessarily* and leaves open the possibility the statement could be true.
2. The definite articles **der, die, das** have the same endings, as well as **jeder**.

11 Im Schulhof gehört

Schreib diese Sätze ab, und setz dabei die richtigen Endungen ein! Vergleiche dann deine Sätze mit den Sätzen eines Partners!

A: Dies ══1══ Eibrötchen sehen lecker aus! Schau!   1. diese   2. dieses   3. diesem

B: Stimmt! Ich nehme dies ══2══ Brötchen, denn auf dies ══3══ Brötchen liegt mehr Ei drauf!

A: Hm, dies ══4══ Pausenbrot sieht gut aus! Dies ══5══ Sojasprossen, prima! Aber was ist denn dies ══6══ Pudding da drunter?   4. dieses   5. diese   6. dieser

B: Dies ══7══ Pudding ist Tofu!   7. dieser

A: Willst du mal probieren? Dies ══8══ Schokolade schmeckt echt prima.   8. diese

B: Nein, danke! Dies ══9══ Apfel schmeckt auch sehr gut.   9. dieser

A: Was ist in dies ══10══ Flasche, David? Orangensaft? Darf ich mal probieren?   10. dieser

B: Hm, dies ══11══ Saft schmeckt lecker. Dies ══12══ Orangensaft kauf' ich mir auch!

      11. dieser   12. diesen

12 Hör gut zu!   For answers, see listening script on TE Interleaf.

Three students are asking their friends about the snacks they brought to school. Each also asks his or her friends about their eating habits. Match each of the friend's eating habits with the most appropriate photo below.

a.   b.   c.   d.   e.

13 Schreib mal eine Geschichte!

Was sagt Calvin zu seinem Vater? Calvin betrachtet skeptisch, was auf seinem Teller ist. Schreib Sätze, die in die Sprechblasen passen!

Answers may vary. E.g.: **Was soll denn das grüne Ding da sein? — Ach, Calvin, das ist doch dein Rindersteak.**

14

Take a minute and draw on a piece of paper an item of food that you especially like to eat. Your partner, quite skeptical in nature, asks what it could be. After you tell what it is, she can make a general assumption about your eating habits, giving the statement one of the question tags from the **So sagt man das!** box. Switch roles.

Answers may vary. E.g. **Was soll denn das sein? — Das ist Schinken. — Ach, du ißt nicht vegetarisch, was?**

15 Für mein Notizbuch

Was gibt es in deiner Schule zu essen und zu trinken? Was kaufst du, und was kostet das? Was bringst du von zu Hause mit? Oder ißt du nur in der Schulcafeteria?

Wo ruht ihr euch aus?

LESETRICK

Understanding the tone of a text. When looking at a German text, you can spot the nouns quickly because they are capitalized, and you can locate the verbs in the second and/or last position of a sentence. If you recognize the nouns and verbs (or at least some of them), you've probably got the gist of the text. But sometimes you will also want to look at adjectives, conjunctions, and adverbs in order to understand the "tone", that is, how the author feels about the subject. What is the difference between the following pairs of sentences?

Wie alt ist er?   Das weiß ich nicht.

Wie alt ist er **denn?**   Das weiß ich **gar** nicht.

The words **denn** and **gar** act as intensifiers. **Denn** indicates interest on the part of the speaker, and **gar** shows totality. Look for this type of word in the readings which follow to help you understand more fully the feelings of the writers.

Getting Started   For answers, see TE Interleaf.

1. Read the introduction to this article from JUMA. What and who is the focus of the article?

2. Where do you go when you want to get away? What do you like to do there to relax? Do **Ruhe** and **ungestört sein** play a role in your choice?

3. Scan the articles on these pages to find the favorite place for each student. Which place do you think was the most pre-

Hier hab ich meine Ruhe

Mal ganz für sich alleine sein, in Ruhe nachdenken oder lesen. Nicht gestört werden und machen können, was man will. Oder ganz einfach überhaupt nichts tun müssen, herumsitzen und an gar nichts denken. Das alles sind Dinge, die Jugendliche von ihrem Lieblingsplatz erwarten. Sehr viele verschiedene Aspekte sind ihnen wichtig. Genauso wie jeder von ihnen einen ganz bestimmten Platz hat, wohin er sich am liebsten zurückzieht. Dabei ist erstaunlich, wie unterschiedlich diese sein können: Billardsalon oder Café, ein Baum im Wald, ein Strand am Meer, das eigene Zimmer, der Keller im Elternhaus, der Trainingsraum im Fitneß-Studio, eine Bibliothek, die Garage, das Büro, die Schulaula . . . JUMA stellt Euch vier Jugendliche und ihre Lieblingsplätze vor.

Markus (18), Student: „Ich mag dieses Café. Es ist etwas abgelegen, und darum kommen nicht so viele Leute hierher. Das ist genau das Richtige für mich – man ist relativ ungestört. Ich komme zwei bis dreimal pro Woche ins Café. Was ich hier liebe, ist die Atmosphäre: Gedämpftes Licht, schöne alte Möbel, ruhige Leute, das Rascheln von Zeitungen.

Ich trinke Tee oder Kaffee, denke nach, lese Zeitungen oder ein Buch. Ich habe hier auch schon mal versucht, Gedichte zu schreiben. Vielleicht probiere ich es noch einmal. Ob ich gut bin, weiß ich nicht, aber es macht Spaß und lenkt ab. Die Umgebung inspiriert mich jedenfalls. Wie lange ich hier durchschnittlich sitze, kann ich eigentlich nicht so genau sagen. Mindestens eine Stunde, manchmal auch zwei Stunden. Am schönsten ist es, wenn ich genau weiß, daß ich am Nachmittag nichts mehr machen muß. Dann genieße ich meine Zeit so richtig."

6 JUMA 3/93

Nicole (19), Handelsschülerin: „Mein Lieblingsplatz ist ein alter Turm im Stadtwald. Meistens gehe ich nach der Berufsschule dorthin. Am meisten genieße ich die Ruhe rund um den Turm. Nur wenige Leute kommen wochentags hierher.

Ich kann dort ungestört über alles mögliche nachdenken – über mich selbst, meine Freunde oder über Streß in der Schule. Ab und zu nehme ich auch unseren Hund mit. Auch wenn es verrückt klingt – manchmal unterhalte ich mich dann mit ihm. Ich stelle mir halt vor, daß er mir zuhört.

Dann gibt es Tage, da sitze ich hier und denke über gar nichts nach. Ich genieße einfach die Sonne und freue mich, daß es hier im Wald so schön ist.

Am meisten liebe ich den Platz im Frühling, wenn es grün wird und sich der Wald jede Woche verändert."

Christian (16), Schüler: „Mein Lieblingsplatz ist vielleicht ein bißchen ungewöhnlich. Ich sitze gerne im Schülervertretungs-Büro unserer Schule. Man denkt vielleicht, daß hier viel los ist — ein ständiges Kommen und Gehen von Schülern, deren Interessen wir vertreten sollen — aber das ist gar nicht so. Am liebsten bin ich in den Pausen hier. Draußen toben die Schüler, hier im Büro ist es ruhig. Ich kann nachdenken, mich zwischen den Stunden ein bißchen entspannen. Wenn wir Post von Schülern haben, lese ich deren Briefe. Das lenkt auch von eigenen Problemen ab — man denkt über die Lage seiner Mitschüler nach.

Manchmal verschönere ich auch den Raum ein bißchen, hänge Plakate, Poster und Fotos auf. Auch dabei entspannt man sich, finde ich. Wenn ich hier aus dem Büro komme, habe ich eigentlich immer gute Laune. Und das ist der Zweck eines Lieblingsplatzes, denke ich."

Tanja (19), Auszubildende: „Mein Lieblingsplatz? Ganz einfach: Das ist mein eigenes kleines Zimmer unter dem Dach. Den Raum habe ich seit rund vier Jahren. Davor hatte ich zusammen mit meinen Schwestern ein Zimmer. Das war manchmal ganz schön eng.

In meinem Zimmer bin ich sehr gerne. Besonders dann, wenn ich Ärger an meiner Arbeitsstelle hatte. Ich will dann meine Ruhe haben. Je nach Stimmung liege ich auf meinem Bett, tue gar nichts oder höre Musik per Kopfhörer. Ab und zu lese ich auch, um auf andere Gedanken zu kommen — meistens nichts „Hochgeistiges". Am liebsten so ein paar richtig schöne Liebesromane mit Happy-End.

In den Ferien bummele (herumbummeln: umgangssprachlich für „etwas langsam machen") ich hier oben herum. Lange ausschlafen, meine Flaschensammlung sortieren, alte Zeitschriften durchblättern — das ist richtig schön."

Die interessantesten Lieblingsplätze stellen wir im JUMA vor. Die Gewinner erhalten wertvolle Bücher. Schreibt an:

> Redaktion JUMA
> Stichwort: Lieblingsplatz
> Frankfurter Straße 128
> 51065 Köln

---

dictable? And the most unusual?

A Closer Look

4. Read the articles more carefully. For each student jot down key words and phrases which describe the place and his or her favorite activities.

5. Search each article for occurrences of **Ruhe, ruhig,** and **ungestört.** Carefully read the contexts in which these words occur. What, if anything, is the writer seeking peace from? Specific people? Specific situations?

6. Notice the words which express tone in the sentences. Look at the following pairs of sentences and determine how the words in bold print give the second sentence of each pair a slightly different tone.
   a. Das weiß ich nicht.
      Das weiß ich **eigentlich** nicht.
   b. Da sitze ich zwei Stunden.
      Da sitze ich **mindestens** zwei Stunden.
   c. Mein Zimmer war eng.
      Mein Zimmer war **ganz schön** eng.

7. Locate the phrase **ab und zu** in Tanja's statement. What do you think **ab und zu** means?

8. What do you think Nicole means when she says: **Auch wenn es verrückt klingt — manchmal unterhalte ich mich dann mit ihm.**

9. Jeder in der Klasse schreibt an JUMA, unterläßt aber seinen Namen. Beschreib deinen Lieblingsplatz, und was du da gern tust! Zeichne ein Bild dazu, oder mach ein Foto! Häng die Beschreibung und Zeichnung an die Wand. Die Klasse übernimmt die Rolle von der JUMA Redaktion. Wählt die interessantesten Lieblingsplätze aus!

Calling someone's attention to something and responding

WORTSCHATZ

Was hast du denn auf dem Brot?

Margarine und
Wurst, Aufschnitt

Quark mit
Schnittlauch

Tofu mit
Sojasprossen

Was für Marmelade?

Was für Käse?

Erdbeermarmelade
Himbeermarmelade

Schweizer   Tilsiter
Camembert

Und dann noch . . .

Erdnußbutter
saure Gurken
Thunfischsalat
Schinkensalat
Eiersalat
Mayonnaise

Was hast du gewöhnlich auf deinem Brot?

---

16   Hör gut zu!   For answers, see listening script on TE Interleaf.

Was haben die Schüler gewöhnlich auf ihrem Pausenbrot? — Schreib die Namen von den Schülern auf, und schreib neben den Namen, was jeder Schüler auf seinem Pausenbrot hat!

17   Also, das schmeckt mir!

Was hast du gewöhnlich auf deinem Brot oder Sandwich? Sag es einem Mitschüler! Dann frag einen Mitschüler, was er gewöhnlich ißt, und so weiter!

SO SAGT MAN DAS!

Calling someone's attention to something and responding

If you want to call someone's attention to
something, you may say: And the response may be:

Schau mal!	**Ja? Was denn?**
Guck mal!	**Ja, was bitte?**
Sieh mal!	**Was ist denn los?**
Hör mal!	**Was ist?**
Hör mal zu!	**Was gibt's?**

How would you say these expressions in English? Are there other similar expressions
in English? How would you call two friends' attention to something? An adult's?

EIN WENIG LANDESKUNDE

What Germans eat for a particular meal probably differs somewhat from your own habits. For breakfast, **das Frühstück,** they might eat a grain cereal, **das Müsli,** but you will generally find fresh rolls, **Brötchen,** on every table. Germans like to spread butter on them, adding honey, cheese, or even slices of meat or sausage. A boiled egg is also common. Lunch, **das Mittagessen,** is typically the only warm meal of the day, and usually includes meat or fish, potatoes, and a salad. Closing out the day is **das Abendbrot (das Abendessen),** usually a cold, less heavy meal consisting of bread, cold cuts, cheese, salad, and maybe soup, or even some heated-up leftovers from lunch.

18 Was haben alle auf ihrem Pausenbrot?

Die Schüler freuen sich auf die Pause. Sie können miteinander sprechen und auch etwas essen. Lies, was diese Schüler fragen! Achte dabei genau auf die Wörter, die vor dem Wort „Pausenbrot" stehen! Was bedeuten diese Wörter?

euer = your (pl.); **unser** = our; **sein** = his; **ihr** = her; **ihr** = their

Ein wenig Grammatik

You learned in **Kapitel 4** that the prepositions **an** and **in** are followed by the dative case when the phrase indicates location. The same is true for the preposition **auf** (*on, on top of*). To express where something is, you can say:

Wo ist der Käse? Er ist schon auf meinem Brot.

Germans also use **auf** when referring to what is *in* their sandwiches:

Und was willst du auf deinem Sandwich?

— Ist das euer Pausenbrot? Was habt ihr denn auf euerem Pausenbrot?
— Auf unserem Pausenbrot haben wir Käse, Schweizer Käse.

David ißt jetzt sein Pausenbrot. Ich weiß, was er auf seinem Brot hat.

Wiebke ißt ihr Pausenbrot. Weißt du, was sie auf ihrem Pausenbrot hat?

Die Schüler essen ihr Pausenbrot. Was haben sie denn auf ihrem Pausenbrot?

Grammatik The possessives (Summary)

1. You have been using some possessives, such as **mein, dein, sein,** and **ihr.**
   Here is a summary and the meaning of all of them.

	Singular			Plural	
my	**mein**		*our*	**unser**	
your	**dein**		*your*	**euer**	
his, its	**sein**				
her, its	**ihr**		*their*	**ihr**	
your, formal	**Ihr**		*your, formal*	**Ihr**	

2. These are the endings you need when you use the possessives, using **mein** as
   a model. What other group of words has the same endings?[1]

	NOMINATIVE	ACCUSATIVE	DATIVE
masculine	Das ist **mein Kakao.**	Ich mag **meinen Kakao.**	Was ist in **meinem Kakao?**
feminine	Das ist **meine Milch.**	Ich mag **meine Milch.**	in **meiner Milch?**
neuter	Das ist **mein Brötchen.**	Ich mag **mein Brötchen.**	auf **meinem Brötchen?**
plural	Das sind **meine Brötchen.**	Ich mag **meine Brötchen.**	auf **meinen Brötchen?**

3. The dative plural of almost all nouns ends in **-n.**

   Was kaufst du deinen Freunde**n**?

   If the plural form of the noun already ends in **-n,** no further **-n** is added.

   Was ist auf deinen Brötchen? (das Brötchen, die Brötchen)

19 Wer ißt was?

Schreib, was alle auf ihren Brötchen haben! Gebrauche dabei die
richtige Form des Possessivpronomens!

    1. deinem

A: David fragt Wiebke: „Was hast du auf ══1══ Brot?"

B: Wiebke antwortet: „Auf ══2══ Brot? Da hab' ich Tofu drauf!"
    2. meinem

A: David fragt die Lehrerin: „Was haben Sie auf ══3══ Brötchen,
Frau Weber?"
    3. Ihrem

B: „Auf ══4══ Brötchen? Nur Käse."   4. meinem

A: Wiebke fragt David: „Was hat Frau Weber auf ══5══ Brot?"

B: „Auf ══6══ Brot hat sie nur Käse."   5. ihrem 6. ihrem
    7. euren

A: David fragt Nicolas und Thorsten: „Was habt ihr auf ══7══ Brötchen?"

B: Thorsten antwortet: „Auf ══8══ Brötchen haben wir Quark mit Schnittlauch."
    8. unseren

1. the indefinite articles **ein, eine, ein**

20 Hör gut zu!

Hör die folgenden Gespräche während der Pause im Schulhof an! Entscheide für jedes Gespräch, ob der Schüler mit einem Freund, zwei Freunden oder einer älteren Person spricht!

For answers, see listening script on TE Interleaf.

	mit: einem Freund	zwei Freunden	einer älteren Person
1			
2			
3			

21 Ist das dein ...?

Setzt euch in Gruppen von vier oder fünf Personen zusammen! Jeder muß einen oder mehrere Artikel von sich und von anderen Schülern in der Hand haben. Jetzt fragt ihr abwechselnd (*in turns*), wem das gehört.

 Ist das dein ...?

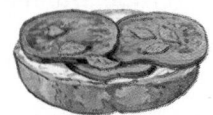 Nein, das ist ihr ...

Ist das euer ...? Das ist nicht mein ...

Heft Radiergummi Taschenrechner Deutschbuch Spitzer Schultasche Brille Volleyball Pausenbrot

Answers may vary. E.g.: **Ist das deine Brille? — Nein, das ist ihre Brille.**

22 Und auf eurem Sandwich?

You and two friends are at an **Imbißstube** and want to order from the vendor. Unfortunately, it's very crowded and you have to order for your friends. Follow these guidelines:

a. the vendor asks for your order
b. you ask your friends for their wishes
c. they decide and one answers for both
d. the other friend asks you what you want
e. you tell the vendor all of your orders
f. the vendor repeats them

Was möchtest du auf deinem Sandwich?

Schinken Käse Quark mit Tomaten Aufschnitt Erdnußbutter Mayonnaise Marmelade Butter Senf Schnittlauch Sojasprossen

23 Klar! Das ist mein ...

Identify and make a list of several objects you see around you, marking down to whom each belongs. Then describe each item, saying "his/her/their/our... is..." Now go to various students and see if you were right about the ownership: „Das ist doch dein ...?"

Answers may vary. E.g.: **Das ist doch dein Heft, oder? — Klar, das ist mein Heft.**

24 Was planst du heute fürs Mittagessen?

Fragt euch gegenseitig, ob ihr etwas zum Mittagessen mitgebracht habt oder ob ihr heute in der Cafeteria eßt! Wenn du etwas mitgebracht hast, kannst du allen erklären „Schaut mal!" und zeigen, was du hast. Oder wenn du heute in der Cafeteria ißt, dann sag ihnen „Hört mal zu!" und erkläre ihnen, was du dort essen willst!   Answers may vary. E.g.: **Hast du etwas von zu Hause mitgebracht? - Ja, schau mal! Ich habe Joghurt und ein Brot mitgebracht. Und du? — Hör mal zu! Ich esse in der Cafeteria. Heute gibt es Fischstäbchen.**

WORTSCHATZ

KAUFMANNS

Wir garantieren Qualität
Alle Angebote sind gültig ab Montag, den 3. September

TÄGLICH FRISCH		
Trauben aus Frankr.	kg **4.60**	
frische Bohnen	kg **2.90**	
Bananen aus Guatem.	kg **3.80**	
holländ. Möhren	kg **1.85**	
Sauerkraut aus dem Faß	kg **2.10**	
Äpfel Schwarzwald	kg **4.10**	

TIEFKÜHLKOST
AUS UNSERER FLEISCHABTEILUNG

Fischstäbchen gefroren 300 g Packung **1.99**	**Rindersteak** zart, abgehangen 100 g **1.49**	
Rindfleisch mager kg **9.99**	**Holl. Hühner** Kl. A per kg **2.22**	
Pommes frites 1000 g Beutel **0.88**	**Schnitzel** vom Schwein 100 g **1.12**	
Lamm aus Austral. kg **8.40**	**Spinat** gefroren 500 g Packung **1.78**	
Schweinefleisch kg **7.60**	**Schweinekoteletts** 100 g **0.98**	
Gemüsesuppe 500 g Packung **2.16**		

IN UNSERER
FISCHABTEILUNG

Heilbutt	100 g **1.40**
Forellen	100 g **1.25**
Karpfen	100 g **0.85**

Für Druckfehler
keine Haftung!

Auf zu Kaufmanns!

Which of these foods do you recognize? Can you guess the meaning of words you don't know? What does **Tiefkühlkost** mean? Which food items confirm that? Which different places have shipped food to Kaufmanns? Which specialty stores would you go to if you didn't want to go to the **Supermarkt?**

25 Abendessen zu viert

Answers will vary. E.g.: **Ich möchte bitte 200 Gramm Schnitzel. — Tut mir leid, aber die Schnitzel sind schon alle! — Macht nichts. Dann geben Sie mir ...**

a. You and your partner are planning to invite two other friends to dinner and want to serve the following: a fish entrée, two vegetables, potatoes or noodles, and a fruit salad for dessert. Have a look at Kaufmanns' specials. With only twenty marks, decide what and how much to buy of each thing (enough to feed four people). Make a shopping list.

b. Go to Kaufmanns' with your list. Your partner is the vendor. Order everything over the counter. Unfortunately, Kaufmanns' is out of some things on your list. Downplay your disappointment and ask for a different item. Be polite!

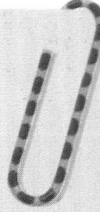

SO SAGT MAN DAS!

Expressing preference and strong preference

When asking about someone's preference, you could ask:

> Welche Suppe magst du **lieber**?
> Nudelsuppe oder Gemüsesuppe?
> Welches Fleisch schmeckt dir **besser**? Schwein oder Rind?

Asking for strong preference:

> Welches Gemüse magst du **am liebsten**?
> Welche Suppe schmeckt dir **am besten**?

And the answer may be:

> Nudelsuppe mag ich **lieber**.
>
> Rind schmeckt mir **besser**.
>
> **Am liebsten** mag ich Spinat.
> Nudelsuppe schmeckt mir **am besten**.

---

26 Hör gut zu!

Im Schulhof sprechen einige Schüler über Essen und Trinken. Schreib auf, wer was lieber oder am liebsten ißt, wem was besser oder am besten schmeckt!

For answers, see listening script on TE Interleaf.

27 Was schmeckt dir am besten?

Such dir eine Partnerin! Frag sie, was ihr besser schmeckt! Du mußt zwei Dinge nennen, und sie muß auswählen. Frag sie dann, was ihr am besten schmeckt! — Tauscht dann die Rollen aus!

Answers will vary. E.g.: **Was schmeckt dir besser: Pudding oder Joghurt? - Mir schmeckt Pudding besser.**

Reis
Äpfel
Fisch
Pudding
Tomaten
Kuchen
Schnitzel
Forelle

oder

Nudeln
Birnen
Fleisch
Joghurt
Möhren
Eis
Steak
Karpfen

28 Eine Umfrage: Was schmeckt euch?

Stellt euch vor, ihr müßt einen Brunch für alle Deutschschüler an der Schule organisieren! Was gibt es alles zu essen? Schreibt eure Gerichte auf ein Poster! — Vergleicht eure Posters und sagt, was euch besser und am besten schmeckt! Fragt auch euern Lehrer, was ihm besser schmeckt. Am Ende wählt ihr das schönste Poster aus.

Was schmeckt Ihnen besser, die Bohnen oder das Kraut?

Wem schmeckt das Rindfleisch?

Was schmeckt dir am besten?

Was schmeckt euch nicht?

Ein wenig *Grammatik*

There are some verbs that are always used with dative case forms, such as **gefallen.**

> Dresden hat **mir** gut gefallen.

The verb **schmecken** can be used with or without a dative object.

> Die Nudeln schmecken gut.
> Die Suppe schmeckt **dem David.**
> Die Soße hat **mir** nicht geschmeckt.

Grammatik The interrogative **welcher**

1. The question word **welcher (welche, welches)**, *which,* asks for specific information concerning two or more choices.

   Welche Suppe möchtest du? Die Nudelsuppe oder die Gemüsesuppe?

2. The interrogative **welcher** is used in front of nouns and has these forms:

	Masculine	*Feminine*	*Neuter*	*Plural*
Nominative	**welcher**	**welche**	**welches**	**welche**
Accusative	**welchen**	**welche**	**welches**	**welche**
Dative	**welchem**	**welcher**	**welchem**	**welchen**

Welcher Joghurt schmeckt gut? **Welches Obst** magst du?
Welchen Salat magst du am liebsten? Auf **welche Schule** gehen diese Schüler?
How would you express the last sentence in English? Of which word and forms does **welcher** remind you?[1]

29 Welches Obst magst du?

Ask your partner which of these general categories of food he likes: **Fleisch, Salat, Fisch, Gemüse, Obst,** or **Wurst.** When your partner says he likes a certain category of food, find out which foods in that category he likes.

Answers will vary. E.g.: **Magst du Gemüse? Welches Gemüse magst du?**

30 Welches magst du lieber?

Behalte (*keep*) den gleichen Partner von Übung 29 und frag ihn, welche von zwei Speisen er lieber mag oder welche von zwei Speisen ihm besser schmeckt und warum!

BEISPIEL   DU   **Was magst du lieber, ══ oder ══?**
      PARTNER   ══
            DU   **Und welch-══ magst du am liebsten?**
      PARTNER   ══
            DU   **Und warum?**

Warum?

schmeckt mir am besten

ist nicht so teuer

ist gesund für mich

hat nicht so viele Kalorien

ist besser für mich

geht schnell zu kochen

EIN WENIG LANDESKUNDE

Für viele Deutsche besteht die Hauptmahlzeit noch immer aus einem warmen Mittagessen, das gewöhnlich zwischen 12 und 13 Uhr serviert wird. In kleineren Orten schließen die meisten Geschäfte zur Mittagszeit, und die Schulkinder kommen zu dieser Zeit von der Schule nach Hause. In größeren Betrieben gibt es Betriebskantinen, die ihren Angestellten eine kleine Auswahl an warmen Gerichten anbieten. Wer zu Mittag kalt essen möchte, der muß lange suchen, denn in Restaurants gibt es zur Mittagszeit keine kalte Küche.

1. **dieser, jeder**

Grammatik The preposition zu

The preposition **zu** (*to*) is always followed by dative case forms. **Zu** and the definite articles **der** and **dem** contract to **zur** and **zum**.

> Ich gehe jetzt **zum Großvater.** (zu + dem = zum)
> Jetzt fahr' ich immer mit dem Moped **zur Schule.** (zu + der = zur)
> **Zum Nachtisch** ess' ich gewöhnlich Obst.
> Was gibt's heute **zum Mittagessen**?

Zu has other meanings as well. Look at the last two sentences. Can you guess the meaning of **zu** in these sentences? Which other prepositions are always followed by the dative case?[1]

31 Und du?

Such dir eine Partnerin! Stell ihr diese Fragen! Dann fragt sie dich.

1. Was ißt du gewöhnlich zum Frühstück?
2. Und was trinkst du zum Frühstück?
3. Was ißt du meistens zum Mittagessen?
4. Was eßt ihr gewöhnlich zum Abendessen?
5. Was eßt ihr zu Hause zum Nachtisch?
6. Wenn es bei euch Fleisch gibt, was gibt es dazu?

ein Stück Käse
ein Glas Milch
eine Scheibe Wurst
ein Stück Brot

Antworten

Vanilleeis
Karpfen
Vollkornbrötchen
Salami
Schweinefleisch
Spinat
Vanillejoghurt

Käsekuchen
Erdbeermarmelade
Gemüsesuppe
Tomatensalat

32 Was ist das für ein ...?

Du gehst mit einem deutschen Schüler durch einen Supermarkt in deiner Stadt. Er sieht sich alles an, weiß aber oft nicht, was das ist, und er hat viele Fragen. Du beantwortest sie. Gebrauch dabei die Wörter in den Kästen!
— Tauscht dann die Rollen aus!

PARTNER **Was ist das für (ein ...) ... ?**
DU **Das ist ...**

Fragen

Suppe
Kuchen
Salat
Marmelade

Fleisch
Eis
Brötchen
Fisch

Gemüse
Joghurt
Wurst

SPRACHTIP

When asking for a certain kind of information, you have been using the interrogative **was für ein**, as in:
Was für ein Film ist das?
In colloquial German, the interrogative is often split:
Was ist das **für ein** Film?
Was ist das **für eine** Suppe?

33 Für mein Notizbuch

Schreib deinem deutschen Briefpartner, was du gewöhnlich zum Frühstück, Mittagessen und Abendessen ißt! Ist das typisch für die meisten Amerikaner?

1. **bei, mit, nach, von**

ANWENDUNG

1 Bernd und seine Familie sind heute abend im **Café an der Elbe** zum Abendessen. Sie haben die Speisekarte gelesen und wollen bestellen. Hör ihrem Gespräch gut zu und schreib auf, was jedes Familienmitglied (Bernd, Vater, Mutter, Bernds Schwester Annette) mag, nicht mag, lieber mag und am liebsten mag! Stell deine eigene Tabelle her, und füll sie dann aus! Dann beantworte die Fragen!

	mag	mag nicht	mag lieber	mag am liebsten
Bernd				

1. Wer mag nur vegetarische Gerichte?
2. Wer trinkt wohl zu Hause am liebsten Saft? Was meinst du?
3. Glaubst du, daß die Annette auch Krabben mag? Warum oder warum nicht?
4. Glaubst du, daß Bernds Vater ein Stück Kuchen mit Sahne zum Nachtisch möchte? Warum oder warum nicht?   For answers, see listening script on TE Interleaf.

2 Lies diesen Text und beantworte die Fragen!

1. Hier sind einige Tips für eine Party. Was für eine Party soll das sein? Woher weißt du das?   1. eine Geburtstagsparty; „ … wenn sie Geburtstag haben … "
2. Was soll man nach der Kuchenschlacht (*run for the cake*) tun?   2. essen
3. Was ist „Fleischsalat"? Was soll man mit dem Fleischsalat tun?
4. Was empfiehlt man hier zum Trinken? In welcher Jahreszeit soll man das servieren?   3. Salat aus Wurst oder Aufschnitt; Tomaten füllen
   4. Eistee; im Sommer

Wenn Kinder feiern...

hat was los zu sein! Von klein auf wünschen sich Kinder Gäste, wenn sie Geburtstag haben: die Spielfreunde, die Kinder aus der Schule. Da sind Eltern gefordert, zu planen, zu organisieren, sich Spiele auszudenken und für Überraschungen zu sorgen, die eine Kinderparty zu einem richtigen Erlebnis machen.

Nach der Kuchenschlacht und dem Spielprogramm kommt Hunger auf — wetten daß? Gegen den gibt es:

Gefüllte Tomaten
Zutaten: 4 feste, mittelgroße Tomaten, wenig Salz, etwas Pfeffer, 200g Fleischsalat, 4 Scheiben Salatgurken, 4 Scheiben hartgekochte Eier, etwas leichte Mayonnaise, einige Salatblätter.

Zubereitung: Tomaten waschen, abtrocknen, einen Deckel abschneiden und vorsichtig mit einem Teelöffel aushöhlen. Die Innenräume mild würzen und gleichmäßig den Fleischsalat einfüllen. Jede Tomate mit einer Gurken- und Eischeibe belegen, den Tomatendeckel aufsetzen und mit einigen Tupfern

Mayonnaise versehen. Eine Platte mit gewaschenen Salatblättern auslegen, und die Tomaten daraufsetzen. Dazu steht aufgeschnittenes Stangenbrot bereit.

Was gibt es hier zu trinken? Kinder haben immer Durst, weil ihr Wasserhaushalt einen viel höheren Pegel hat als der von Erwachsenen. Im Sommer, wenn draußen gefeiert wird, gibt es leicht gekühlten Eistee, der mit Orangen- und Zitronensaft angereichert und mit Süßstoff oder wenig Zucker gesüßt wird. Außerdem empfiehlt sich — weil es irgendwie „erwachsen" wirkt — eine Früchte-Bowle.

Früchte-Bowle
Zutaten und Zubereitung: 200g Erdbeeren (auch aufgetaute Tiefkühlerdbeeren), 4 Kiwis, 1 kleine Melone, 4 Orangen, 4 EL Traubenzucker, 2 Päckchen Vanillezucker, Saft von 4 Zitronen, 1 Orangensaft, 2 Flaschen Mineralwasser.

Erdbeeren putzen und in Stückchen schneiden, das Fruchtfleisch der Melone herauslösen und ebenfalls stückeln, Orangen schälen, die Filets zwischen den Häuten herausschneiden. Alle Früchte in ein Bowle-Gefäß geben, mit den Zuckersorten bestreuen und etwa eine Stunde ziehen lassen. Dann mit Orangensaft und Mineralwasser aufgießen, noch einmal gut verrühren — und „Zum Wohl"!

3 a. Zwei Klassenkameraden und du, ihr plant eine Geburtstagsparty für kleine Kinder. Ihr macht die gefüllten Tomaten und die Früchte-Bowle. Zuerst müßt ihr einkaufen gehen. Schreibt zuerst eine Einkaufsliste! Dann geht ihr zu verschiedenen Geschäften. In jedem Geschäft spielt einer von euch die Rolle vom Verkäufer. Als Kunden seid ihr ab und zu nicht sicher, was verschiedene Sachen sind. Ihr müßt den Verkäufer danach fragen.　　a. **Was soll das sein, dieses Gemüse? — Das sind Tomaten!**

b. Dann willst du noch eine Speise für die Party machen. Erzähl deinem Partner, was du machst und was alles drin ist. Dein Partner stellt dir dann Fragen über das Gericht: **Das ist wohl vegetarisch, was?** Dann tauscht ihr die Rollen aus!

　　b. **Ich mache Kartoffelsalat. — Das ist wohl vegetarisch, oder? — Nein, es ist auch Wurst in dem Salat.**

4 Du und dein Partner, ihr spielt jetzt ein Spiel, das „Zwanzig Fragen" heißt. Du willst wissen, was für ein Mensch dein Partner ist: Lebt er gesund oder ungesund? Kocht er normalerweise zu Hause? Was kocht er? Zuerst mußt du 20 Fragen auf ein Stück Papier schreiben. Die Fragen müssen nur Ja/Nein - Fragen sein, z.B. **Ißt du gewöhnlich Obst?** Dann stell deinem Partner die Fragen! Du kannst dabei die Fotos verwenden, wenn du willst.

5 Verwende die Information von Übung 4, und schreib einen Bericht über deinen Partner! Was kann er kochen? Ist er Vegetarier, oder ißt er auch Fleisch? Schreib alles über ihn, was du weißt!

6

R O L L E N S P I E L

Spiel mit drei Klassenkameraden die folgende Szene der Klasse vor!

Du und ein Freund, ihr habt eine kleine Imbißstube. Entwerft eine Speisekarte für alle Speisen, die ihr verkauft! Illustriert die Speisekarte! Die anderen zwei Schüler sind die Kunden bei euch. Sie müssen sich entscheiden (*to decide*), was sie essen und trinken möchten. Dein Partner oder du, ihr sagt, ob ihr diese Speise noch habt oder nicht. Die zwei Kunden sprechen darüber, was sie wollen und was für Speisen sie normalerweise essen.

Can you express regret and downplay something? (p. 113)

1 How would you tell someone that

a. Es tut mir leid, die Milch ist alle.

a. you're sorry that there isn't any more milk?

b. Ich bedaure, die Salamibrötchen kosten jetzt DM 1, 50.

b. you're sorry that **Salamibrötchen** now cost 1,50 DM?

c. he or she is out of luck — there isn't any more pudding?

c. Was für ein Pech! Der Pudding ist alle.

d. you unfortunately only have trout?

d. Ich habe leider nur Forelle.

2 How would you respond to the above by saying that it doesn't matter or that it is all right?   Das macht nichts!; Schon gut!; Nicht so schlimm!

3 How would you say that you'll just take a **Käsebrot** instead?

3. Dann nehme ich eben nur ein Käsebrot.

4 How would you ask a friend what in the world he has on his sandwich?   Was hast du auf deinem Brot? Was soll denn das sein auf deinem Brot?

Can you express skepticism and make certain? (p. 114)

5 How would you make certain that

a. your friend is a vegetarian?   a. Du ißt vegetarisch, nicht wahr?

b. someone you know likes apples?   b. Du magst Äpfel, ja?

c. someone you know likes chocolate milk?   c. Du magst Kakao, was?

6 How might the persons in 5a., 5b., and 5c. above respond to your questions?   E.g.: a. Ja, das stimmt. b. Nein, Äpfel schmecken mir nicht. c. Ja, Kakao mag ich.

Can you call someone's attention to something and respond? (p. 118)

7 How would you point something out to a friend? How would you tell him or her to listen?   Schau mal!; Guck mal!; Hör mal zu!

8 How would you respond to the above and ask what is going on?   Ja? Was denn? Was ist?

9 How would you ask someone

a. what fish he or she eats often?   a. Welchen Fisch ißt du oft?

b. what fruit there is?   b. Welches Obst gibt es?

c. what soup costs 3.75 DM?   c. Welche Suppe kostet DM 3,75?

Can you express preference and strong preference? (p. 123)

10 How would you say that

a. you like grapes?   a. Ich mag Trauben.

b. you prefer apples?   b. Ich mag Äpfel lieber.

c. you like bananas the best?   c. Ich mag Bananen am liebsten.

ERSTE STUFE

EXPRESSING REGRET

Ich bedaure, ...   *I'm sorry,...*
bedauern   *to be sorry about*
Was für ein Pech!   *That's too bad!*
Ich hab' leider nur ...   *I only have...*

DOWNPLAYING

(Das) macht nichts!   *That's all right!*
Schon gut!   *It's okay.*
Nicht so schlimm!   *That's not so bad.*

ADJUSTING

Dann nehm' ich eben ...   *In that case I'll take...*
Dann trink' ich halt ...   *I'll drink ... instead.*

EXPRESSING SKEPTICISM AND MAKING CERTAIN

Was soll denn das sein?   *What's that supposed to be?*
Du ißt wohl vegetarisch, was?   *You eat vegetarian, right?*
Du ißt wohl viel Fleisch, ja?   *You eat a lot of meat, right?*
Du magst Joghurt, oder?   *You like yogurt, don't you?*
Du magst doch Quark, nicht wahr?   *You like quark, don't you?*
Nicht unbedingt!   *Not entirely!/Not necessarily!*

FOOD ITEMS

die Milch   *milk*
der Kakao   *chocolate milk*
die Vanillemilch   *vanilla flavored milk*
der Joghurt   *yogurt*

OTHER USEFUL WORDS AND EXPRESSIONS

dies-   *this*

ZWEITE STUFE

CALLING SOMEONE'S ATTENTION TO SOMETHING AND RESPONDING

Schau mal!   *Look!*
Guck mal!   *Look!*
Sieh mal!   *Look!*
Hör mal!   *Listen!*
Hör mal zu!   *Listen to this!*
Ja? Was denn?   *Okay, what is it?*
Ja, was bitte?   *Yes, what?*
Was ist?   *What is it?*
Was gibt's?   *What is it?*
Was ist denn los?   *What's going on?*

FOOD ITEMS

Was hast du denn auf dem Brot?   *What do you have in your sandwich?*
das Sandwich, -es   *sandwich*
die Margarine   *margarine*
der Quark   *a soft cheese similar to ricotta or cream cheese*
der Schnittlauch   *chives*
der Tofu   *tofu*
die Sojasprossen (pl)   *bean sprouts*
die Marmelade   *marmalade*
die Erdbeermarmelade   *strawberry marmalade*
die Himbeermarmelade   *raspberry marmalade*
der Schweizer Käse   *Swiss cheese*
der Tilsiter Käse   *Tilsiter cheese*
der Camembert Käse   *Camembert cheese*

POSSESSIVE PRONOUNS

Ihr   *your (formal, singular)*
Ihr   *your (formal, plural)*
ihr   *their*
unser   *our*
euer   *your (informal, plural)*

DRITTE STUFE

EXPRESSING PREFERENCES AND STRONG PREFERENCES

Welche Suppe magst du lieber?   *Which soup do you prefer?*
Rind schmeckt mir besser.   *Beef tastes better to me.*
Welches Gemüse magst du am liebsten?   *Which vegetable is your favorite?*
Welche Suppe schmeckt dir am besten?   *Which soup tastes the best to you?*

TALKING ABOUT WHAT YOU EAT AT MEALS

Zum Nachtisch ess' ich ...   *For dessert I eat...*
Zum Mittagessen gibt es ...   *For lunch there is...*

FOOD ITEMS

das Sauerkraut   *sauerkraut*
die Pommes frites (pl)   *French fries*
das Fischstäbchen, -   *fish stick*
der Heilbutt   *halibut*
das Rindersteak, -s   *steak (beef)*
das Schnitzel, -   *cutlet (pork or veal)*
das Schweinekotelett, -s   *pork chop*
das Schweinefleisch   *pork*
das Lammfleisch   *lamb*
die Traube, -n   *grape*
der Karpfen, -   *carp*

Kapitel 6: Gute Besserung!

CHAPTER OVERVIEW

Los geht's! pp. 132-134	Was fehlt dir? *p. 132*			*Video Guide*
	FUNCTIONS	**GRAMMAR**	**CULTURE**	**RE-ENTRY**
Erste Stufe pp. 136-139	• Inquiring about someone's health and responding *p. 137* • Making suggestions *p. 138*	• Reflexive pronouns in dative, *p. 137* • **Sollen** used to make suggestions, *p. 139* • The inclusive command, *p. 139*	• **Landeskunde: Was machst du, wenn dir nicht gut ist?** *p. 135* • **Ein wenig Landeskunde:** The difference between an **Apotheke** and a **Drogerie**, *p.139*	• The verb **sich fühlen**, *p. 136* (from **Kap. 4**, II) • Talking about how often you do something, *p. 136* (from **Kap. 7**, I) • Giving reasons, *p. 137* (from **Kap. 8**, I) • The accusative reflexive pronouns, *p. 138* (from **Kap. 4**, II) • The particle **mal**, *p. 138* (from **Kap. 6**) • The modal **sollen** *p. 139* (from **Kap. 8**) • Responding to an invitation, *p. 139* (from **Kap. 7**, I) • Expressing obligations, *p. 139* (from **Kap. 7**, I) • The conversational past, *p. 139* (from **Kap. 3**, II) • The dative pronouns, *p. 136* (from **Kap. 3**, II)
Zweite Stufe pp. 142-145	Asking about and expressing pain, *p. 143*	• Verbs used with dative-case forms, *p. 143* • The verb **weh tun**, *p. 143* • Reflexive verbs used with dative-case forms, *p. 144* • The verb **brechen**, *p. 145* • The verb **waschen**, *p. 145*		• The dative pronouns, *p. 143* (from **Kap. 3**, II) • Time expressions, *pp. 143, 145* (from **Kap. 7**, I) • Family members, *p. 143* (from **Kap. 3**, I) • The conversational past, *p. 144* (from **Kap. 3**, II) • Accusative reflexive verbs, *p. 145* (from **Kap. 4**, II) • Asking what you should do, *p. 145* (from **Kap. 8**, I)
Dritte Stufe pp. 146-149	• Asking for and giving advice, *p. 147* • Expressing hope, *p. 148*	• The verb **messen**, *p. 148* • The dative case to express the idea of something too expensive, too large, too small for you, *p. 149*	Article about sun exposure, *p. 146*	• Asking what you should do, *p. 147* (from **Kap. 8**, I) • **Du**-commands, *p. 148* (from **Kap. 8**, I) • **Daß**-clauses, *p. 148* (from **Kap. 9**, I) • Using the telephone, *p. 148* (from **Kap. 11**, I) • Talking about likes and dislikes, *p. 149* (from **Kap. 5**, I)
Zum Lesen pp. 140-141	**Viel los unter der Sonne!** Reading Strategy: Deciphering charts and graphs			
Review pp. 150-153	•**Anwendung**, *p. 150* •**Kann ich's wirklich?** *p. 152* •**Wortschatz**, *p. 153*			

Assessment Options
 ___
 Mid-term Exam, *Assessment Guide* Audiocassette 7 B
	Stufe Quizzes
	 •*Chapter Resources*, Book 2
	  Erste Stufe, Quiz 6-1
	  Zweite Stufe, Quiz 6-2
	  Dritte Stufe, Quiz 6-3
	 •*Assessment Items, Audiocassette* 7 B
			Kapitel 6 Chapter Test
			 • *Chapter Resources*, Book 2
			 • *Assessment Guide*, Speaking Test
			 • *Assessment Items, Audiocassette* 7 B
			
			 Test Generator, Kapitel 6	

Chapter Overview

Video Program **OR** *Expanded Video Program*, Videocassette 2	*Textbook Audiocassette* 3 B

RESOURCES Print	**RESOURCES** Audiovisual

Textbook Audiocassette 3 B

Practice and Activity Book
Chapter Resources, Book 2
- Additional Listening Activities 6-1, 6-2 ....*Additional Listening Activities, Audiocassette* 9 B
- Student Response Forms
- Realia 6-1
- Situation Card 6-1
- Teaching Transparency Master 6-1......................................*Teaching Transparency* 6-1
- Quiz 6-1 ....*Assessment Items, Audiocassette* 7 B
Video Guide ....*Video Program/Expanded Video Program*, Videocassette 2

Textbook Audiocassette 3 B

Practice and Activity Book
Chapter Resources, Book 2
- Communicative Activity 6-1
- Additional Listening Activities 6-3, 6-4 ....*Additional Listening Activities, Audiocassette* 9 B
- Student Response Forms
- Realia 6-2
- Situation Card 6-2
- Teaching Transparency Master 6-2......................................*Teaching Transparency* 6-2
- Quiz 6-2 ....*Assessment Items, Audiocassette* 7 B

Textbook Audiocassette 3 B

Practice and Activity Book
Chapter Resources, Book 2
- Communicative Activity 6-2
- Additional Listening Activities 6-5, 6-6 ....*Additional Listening Activities, Audiocassette* 9 B
- Student Response Forms
- Realia 6-3
- Situation Card 6-3
- Quiz 6-3 ....*Assessment Items, Audiocassette* 7 B

Video Guide..*Video Program/Expanded Video Program*, Videocassette 2

Alternative Assessment
- Performance Assessment, *Teacher's Edition*
  Erste Stufe, p. 129K
  Zweite Stufe, p. 129O
  Dritte Stufe, p. 129Q
- Portfolio Assessment
  Written: **Anwendung**, Activity 5, *Pupil's Edition*, p. 151; *Assessment Guide*, p. 19
  Oral: **Anwendung**, Activity 8, *Pupil's Edition*, p. 151; *Assessment Guide*, p. 19
- **Notizbuch**, *Pupil's Edition*, p. 139; *Practice and Activity Book*, p. 150

Kapitel 6: Gute Besserung!
Textbook Listening Activities Scripts

*E*rste Stufe
Activity 6, *p. 136*

1. JÜRGEN Meine Stirn ist so furchtbar heiß! Mir ist schlecht. Ich habe bestimmt Fieber.

2. KARIN Mir geht es überhaupt nicht gut! Ich habe Bauchschmerzen und gar keinen Appetit! Der Arzt war gerade da und hat mir ein Rezept geschrieben.

3. STEFAN Ich treffe mich gleich mit ein paar Freunden. Wir gehen zum Fußballtraining. Ich bin heute gut in Form!

4. ULRIKE Ich fühl' mich heute nicht wohl! Ich habe Halsschmerzen und kann kaum schlucken.

Answers to Activity 6
a. 4; b. 1; c. 2; d. 3

*Z*weite Stufe
Activity 15, *p. 142*

ROSI Zuerst habe ich in der Nacht angefangen zu husten, weil mein Hals gekratzt hat. Und heute morgen, als ich aufgewacht bin, konnte ich vor lauter Halsschmerzen gar nicht schlucken.

JAN Schon seit Tagen tun mir die Zähne weh, wenn ich Schokolade oder Eis esse. Heute ist es besonders schlimm. Ich glaube, ich muß wohl endlich mal zum Zahnarzt gehen. Ich kann die Schmerzen kaum noch aushalten!

SANDRA Gestern abend habe ich Fisch gegessen, und heute habe ich starke Bauchschmerzen. Mir ist so übel. Hoffentlich muß ich mich nicht übergeben!

TOBIAS Ahh, ich habe tierische Kopfschmerzen. Und ausgerechnet heute, wo ich einen Mathetest in der Schule habe. Ich kann mich gar nicht konzentrieren.

Answers to Activity 15
a. **Tobias**; b. **Rosi**; c. **Sandra**; d. **Jan**

Dritte Stufe

Activity 23, p. 147

MARKUS Markus Weber hier. Hallo?

UWE Guten Morgen, Markus! Ich bin's, Uwe. Du, ich wollte dich fragen, ob es dir etwas besser geht. Kommst du heute zur Schule? Soll ich dich abholen?

MARKUS Ach Uwe, nee, ich kann heute nicht zur Schule kommen. Ich hab' wirklich schlimme Zahnschmerzen. Meine Wange ist sogar ein bißchen geschwollen. Es hat gestern nachmittag angefangen.

UWE Ja, also, das tut mir echt leid. Ich hab' gestern in der Schule schon gemerkt, daß du nicht so gut drauf warst! Gehst du heute denn zum Zahnarzt?

MARKUS Nein, ich bleibe lieber im Bett. Meine Eltern kommen morgen aus dem Urlaub zurück, bis dahin warte ich noch! Dann kann mich meine Mutter zum Arzt hinfahren.

UWE Das finde ich aber nicht so gut! Du solltest sofort zum Zahnarzt gehen. Ich hol' dich nach der Schule mit meinem Moped ab und fahr' dich zu Doktor Dressler, okay?

MARKUS Also gut, wenn du meinst. Und vielen Dank für deinen Anruf!

UWE Nichts zu danken. Tschüs dann, bis nachher!

Answers to Activity 23

Markus hat Zahnschmerzen; er soll zum Zahnarzt gehen; Uwe holt ihn ab und bringt ihn hin.

Activity 27, p. 148

KLAUS Ja also, das Spiel war echt sensationell! Beide Mannschaften waren ziemlich gut in Form! Ich glaube aber, daß es bei uns mehr Verletzungen gegeben hat. Der Lothar zum Beispiel hat sich ganz schön den Knöchel verstaucht, gleich nach den ersten zehn Spielminuten!

THOMAS Ja stimmt! Ich glaube aber, daß es bei ihm nicht so schlimm ist, wie beim Rudi. Der hat sich nämlich in der zweiten Halbzeit das Knie verletzt. Es hat sogar geblutet. Das war ein ziemlich blödes Foul von der anderen Mannschaft! Hoffentlich kann er nächste Woche wieder beim Training mitmachen.

ANDREAS Ach ja, das kann er bestimmt. Der Rudi ist ganz schön „tough"! Mir tut der Marco echt leid. Ausgerechnet unser bester Spieler muß sich den Fuß brechen! Ich hoffe, daß er in dieser Saison überhaupt wieder spielen kann. Es sieht ziemlich schlecht für ihn aus. Das dauert bestimmt lange, bis der Fuß wieder in Ordnung ist!

Answers to Activity 27

Lothar: Knöchel verstaucht; Rudi: Knie verletzt; Marco: Fuß gebrochen

*A*wendung
Activity 1, *p. 150*

SONJA   Ich fahre in den Ferien ans Meer und brauche unbedingt eine gute Sonnencreme. Am besten mit einem hohen Lichtschutzfaktor, denn ich will auf keinen Fall einen Sonnenbrand bekommen!

MELANIE   Ich habe schon seit ein paar Tagen Kopfschmerzen. Mein Arzt hat mir ein Rezept für Tabletten gegeben, aber ich hatte noch keine Zeit, sie abzuholen.

UTE   Meine Hustenmedizin ist alle. Ich muß mir neue kaufen.

JÖRG   Ich brauche unbedingt eine neue Zahnpasta. Heute morgen habe ich den letzten Rest verbraucht.

Answers to Activity 1
1: Wenn man Sonnencreme braucht, muß man zur Drogerie.
2: Wenn man Tabletten braucht, muß man zur Apotheke.
3: Wenn man Medizin braucht, muß man zur Apotheke.
4: Wenn man Zahnpasta braucht, muß man zur Drogerie.

Kapitel 6: Gute Besserung!
Projects and Games

PROJECT

In this activity, students will prepare and write an advice column for a health magazine. After completing the **Zum Lesen** *section of this chapter students should begin the projects in pairs.*

Materials Students may need paper, writing utensils, and advice columns from health magazines to familiarize themselves with the format.

Outline

The project should include at least two letters in the physician's advice column (**Ratgeberspalte des Doktor Tutgut**): a request for advice and a response.

- The first letter should include complaints about a physical problem, a description of symptoms, and a request for **Doktor Tutgut's** help and advice.
- The second letter should be a response to the first letter. It should offer advice and solutions for the writer's problems and might include a suggestion for visiting a certain **Kurort**.
- Students should include as much of the vocabulary from Chapter 6 as possible.

Suggested Sequence

1. Pair students up and give them the guidelines explained in the outline above.
2. Have pairs write their letters.
3. Have three or four pairs read their letters to the rest of the class.
4. Prepare a simple handout with one heading on each half of the paper: **Probleme/Lösungen.** As students listen to the presentations, have them jot down key information contained in the letter.

Grading the Project

Suggested point distribution (total = 100 points)
Completion of assignment requirements   40
Correct language usage   40
Oral presentation   20

 **GAME**

Wörter bilden

Students will enjoy reviewing vocabulary with the following game.

Procedure Choose several words from the **Wortschatz** section. (Example: **Fieber**) Then ask students to think of one new word that begins with each letter of that word. (Example: **Fieber— Fuß, ich, Ellbogen, Bauch, Eltern, Rücken**) The student who finishes first shouts **Halt!**, and all students must put their pens down. The student who called **Halt!** reads out his or her words. If the words are all correct, this round of the game is over. If the student has an incorrect word (or words), the game continues until another student finishes and calls **Halt!** The caller now reads his or her words, one at a time. The rest of the students also give their words for each letter. If a word has been thought of by only one person, it receives ten points. If more than one person thought of the word, it reveives five points. The person with the most points wins.

Kapitel 6: Gute Besserung!
Lesson Plans, pages 130-153

Using the Chapter Opener, pp. 130-131

Motivating Activity

Ask the students if they have ever had a serious illness or an accident or know someone who has. Ask if any of them are familiar with first aid procedures and what should be done in case of an emergency.

Background Information

In Germany, there are numbers to call in case of emergency that are similar to the 911 number in the United States. Germans can dial 110 to reach the police and 112 to call the local fire department.

Thinking Critically

① **Analyzing** Ask students to look at the photo and determine where these students might be. Can students guess what might have happened in the photo? (in a park; one of the students fell and hurt himself)

① **Drawing Inferences** Ask students to imagine they are one of the three students surrounding the injured student. What are some of the questions they could ask him in order to find out what happened or how they might be able to help?

② **Drawing Inferences** Can students infer the meaning of the compound noun **Sonnenmilch** in the caption of the photograph? Ask students to look at what the girl is holding in her hand to help them guess the meaning of this word.

Teaching Suggestion

③ Ask students to scan the photo for visual clues and cognates to help them figure out what type of store this is. (pharmacy)

Language Note

Some students may be familiar with the noun *apothecary* (from the Greek *apotheke*) meaning *pharmacist*. Ask students if they can infer the meaning of the sign **MANSTEIN APOTHEKE** at the top of the photograph. Teach students the terms **der Apotheker** and **die Apothekerin.** Ask: **Wer sind die Personen im Foto?**

Focusing on Outcomes

To get students to focus on the chapter objectives listed on p. 131, ask them if they have ever had to go to the school nurse. If so, what kind of questions does he or she typically ask? Then have students preview the learning outcomes. **NOTE:** Each of these outcomes is modeled in the video and evaluated in **Kann ich's wirklich?** on p. 152.

Teaching Los geht's! pp. 132-134

> ### Resources for Los geht's!
> - *Video Program* **OR** *Expanded Video Program*, Videocassette 2
> - *Textbook Audiocassette* 3 B
> - *Practice and Activity Book*

▶ *pages 132-133*

🔲 Video Synopsis

In this segment of the video, Thorsten and David call Maike to hear why she was not at school. Maike tells them about her ailments and asks them to get her some medicine at the pharmacy. Meanwhile, Wiebke and Nicolas are at a **Drogerie** buying toiletries for Wiebke. The student outcomes listed on p. 131 are modeled in the video: inquiring about someone's health and responding, making suggestions, asking about and expressing pain, asking for and giving advice, and expressing hope.

Motivating Activity

Ask students about the last time they had to stay home from school because they were sick. What was wrong and what did they do to get better? Did friends do something to help?

Teaching Suggestion

Ask students to scan each frame for cognates or previously learned phrases. Have them list two or three per frame. Then have students watch the video segment or listen to the recording of the **Foto-Roman.**

Math Connection

The standard German fever thermometer measures degrees in Celsius. Have students determine how high Maike's fever is. To convert Celsius to Fahrenheit, multiply by 9, divide by 5, and add 32. (Maike has a fever of 102° F.)

▶ *page 134*

 For Individual Needs

1 Auditory Learners Ask students to look again at the eight frames of the **Foto-Roman.** Read Questions 1-5 to students while they scan the text for the answers. Repeat the questions if necessary.

2 A Slower Pace Ask students to do this activity in writing as they refer to the **Foto-Roman** for the answers. When finished, call on several students to read their sentences.

3 Challenge After students have completed this activity, have them use the sentences on the left side to come up with a different completion or follow-up sentence for each one.

 Culture Note

Explain to students the difference between **Apotheke** and **Drogerie** or have students read the **Ein wenig Landeskunde** box on p. 139.

Thinking Critically

4 Analyzing To expand this activity, ask students to think of another way to describe each of the six people. Their descriptions should not be based on something that is stated explicitly, but rather should reflect an impression they got about that person after having watched the video segment and read the **Foto-Roman.**

Teaching Suggestion

5 This activity could also be done as a written assignment in pairs. Students will need to change the text from direct discourse to a narrative. This will require students to concentrate on the main ideas of the text. Students will have to use connectors, change word order, and replace nouns with pronouns. Completing this task will assure that students have a good understanding of the content of the **Foto-Roman.**

Closure

Remind students of the functions targeted in this chapter. Have them look again at each outcome and try to find expressions in the **Foto-Roman** that carry out that function.

▶ *page 135*

PRESENTATION: Landeskunde

Teacher Note

The **Landeskunde** interviews are recorded on audiocassette and videocassette.

Thinking Critically

Comparing and Contrasting In German, ask students to look at the symbol used to represent pharmacies in Germany. Do students notice a difference between the symbol used in Germany and the one used in the United States? (symbol in the United States: Rx, mortar and pestle)

ERSTE STUFE

Teaching Suggestion

In German, ask students what the procedure is at their school when they need to go home early due to illness. Encourage students to give a description using the impersonal pronoun **man.** You might want to introduce the following additional vocabulary to help students understand the interviews:

etwas dabei haben *to have something along or nearby*
der Magen *stomach*
die Tablette *pill*
Tabletten einnehmen *to take pills*

Background Information

German students who have to go home from school because of illness must inform the teacher of the class they are leaving. That teacher notes the absence in the **Klassenbuch.** The day the student returns to school, he or she must bring a note from home (**eine Entschuldigung**).

Teaching Suggestion

C You may want to assign Activity C for extra credit and let students present a report to the class.

Teacher Note

Mention to your students that the **Landeskunde** will also be included in Quiz 6-1 given at the end of the **Erste Stufe.**

*T*eaching Erste Stufe
pp. 136-139

Resources for Erste Stufe

Practice and Activity Book
Chapter Resources, Book 2
- Additional Listening Activities 6-1, 6-2
- Student Response Forms
- Realia 6-1
- Situation Card 6-1
- Teaching Transparency Master 6-1
- Quiz 6-1
Audiocassette Program
- *Textbook Audiocassette* 3 B
- *Additional Listening Activities, Audiocassette* 9 B
- *Assessment Items, Audiocassette* 7 B
Video Program or *Expanded Video Program*

▶ *page 136*

MOTIVATE
Teaching Suggestion

Ask students to tell you how their voice sounds when they tell someone that they are not feeling well. Let them give you several examples in English.

TEACH
PRESENTATION: Wortschatz

- Teach the new expressions by acting them out. For example, you could cup your hand over your ear, indicate that you have pain, and say **Ich habe Ohrenschmerzen!** Have students repeat after you, also acting out the new phrases and putting much expression into their voices.

- To further practice the new expressions, use pantomime. Act out some kind of pain and have students tell you or ask you what your ailment is. Examples:
Sie haben Zahnschmerzen.
Haben Sie eine Erkältung?

▶ *page 137*

PRESENTATION: So sagt man das!

Ask students what expressions they use in English to inquire about someone's health. Then go over the expressions in the function box, emphasizing the intonation of each question and response. Have students repeat. Explain that the tone communicates how concerned the speaker is. Ask students to practice these new phrases with a partner, taking turns asking and responding. After students feel comfortable with the new material, the person answering should expand the response by adding what is wrong with him or her in particular, using phrases just learned in the **Wortschatz**. The person who initiated the exchange should respond to what is being said.

Teaching Suggestion

9 Before starting this activity, review the reflexive pronouns and dative pronouns for persons other then **du** and **ich**. Use the photos and captions in the **Wortschatz** box on p. 136 for the review. Have students respond accordingly.

Examples:
— **Wie geht es dem Jungen im Foto 1?**
— **Ihm ist nicht gut. Er ist krank.**

— **Was hat das Mädchen im Foto 2?**
— **Sie hat Halsschmerzen. Sie kann kaum schlucken.**

Continue with the rest of the pictures. Then ask about the whole group so that students get practice with the third person plural.
Example:
Wie geht es den Jungen und Mädchen in diesen Fotos? Wie fühlen sie sich?

Teaching Suggestion

9 Gather photographs from magazines featuring teenage idols or other famous people who look unwell in that particular shot (you may want to glue the photo on construction paper for later use). Give each pair of students a picture. Looking at one of the pictures, student A asks questions modeled after those in the **So sagt man das!** box but changed to third person. Student B answers accordingly. When a pair finishes with a picture, it should pass it to the next pair. Monitor students' work as you move around the classroom.

▶ *page 138*

Teaching Suggestion

11 Have students play this situation as a telephone conversation with person A expressing real concern about person B's health, asking several questions, and at the end wishing him or her well. After students have exchanged roles and practiced both conversations, have them record their "telephone conversations." Play some of the conversations in class and use them for third person questions and responses.

✦ For Individual Needs

11 Challenge Have students play out a similar situation but after the classmate's illness is over, and he or she has returned to school. Person A does not know why person B was absent. This situation will require both partners to use the past tense for at least part of the exchange. Again, an audio or video recording of the exchanges could be made and used for teaching purposes and then become part of the students' portfolios.

11 Challenge Once students have completed their dialogues, ask several students to tell in German what their partner said. Example: **Michael hat gesagt, daß er nicht in der Schule war, weil er Zahnschmerzen hatte.** Since this may be a difficult construction for some students, you may give an example first or put an example on the board.

ERSTE STUFE

ERSTE STUFE

PRESENTATION: So sagt man das!

Before students look at this function box, ask them to look back at the first photo of the **Foto-Roman** in which Thorsten and David each make a suggestion. Ask students to point out and compare the two ways suggestions are made. Then go over the expressions in the **So sagt man das!** box.

▶ *page 139*

For Additional Practice

12 After students have had ample practice with making suggestions and responding, have them extend their dialogues by at least one more exchange beyond the reply.

Examples:
— Sollen wir mal den Thorsten besuchen?
— Warum nicht?
— Gut, wann gehen wir?
— Heute nach der Schule.
or
— Sollen wir mal den Thorsten besuchen?
— Tut mir leid. Ich hab' keine Zeit.
— Kannst du vielleicht morgen?
— Ja, wie wär's um vier?
— Prima!

Multicultural Connection

Have students find out whether the distinction between **Apotheke** and **Drogerie** exists in other countries.

PRESENTATION: Grammatik

Before introducing the inclusive command, review the **du-** and **Sie-** command forms. You can review these commands using TPR. (Examples: **Steve, geh bitte zur Tafel!** or **Fräulein Norwood, gehen Sie bitte zur Tür!**) Ask students how those commands are formed. Then introduce the new forms, giving additional examples using "chore" verbs, such as **das Zimmer aufräumen, den Tisch decken, abwaschen, abtrocknen,** and **Fenster putzen.**

Reteaching: The Inclusive Command

Prepare a chart similar to the one below. Ask students to choose activities from the list to make suggestions about things their partners could do in the Hamburg area.

besuchen	mal	zuerst	eine Hafenrundfahrt
besichtigen	wir doch	später	den Michel
machen		danach	Matjeshering
essen		zum Schluß	in der Övelgönne
spazieren			das Rathaus
fahren			durch Blankenese
bummeln			an der Binnenalster entlang

CLOSE

♜ Game

Play the game **Kettenspiel** to review vocabulary for types of stores and items found in stores. Begin by saying: **Ich gehe heute in die Drogerie und kaufe Parfüm.** The first student repeats your sentence and adds another store and one item he or she will buy there, and so on.

Focusing on Outcomes

Refer students back to the learning outcomes listed on p. 131. They should recognize that they now know how to inquire about someone's health and respond, and how to make suggestions.

ASSESS

- **Performance Assessment** Ask students to think of a way to decline an invitation to an event they'd rather not attend, using an ailment or illness as an excuse.
  Example:
  Das tut mir sehr leid, aber ich habe Kopfschmerzen.

- Quiz 6-1, *Chapter Resources,* Book 2

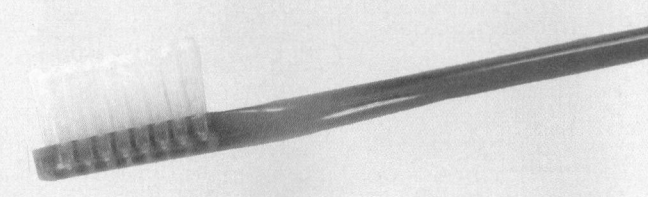

Teaching Zum Lesen, pp. 140-141

Reading Strategy

The targeted strategy in this reading is deciphering charts and graphs. Students should learn about this strategy before beginning Question 2.

PREREADING

Motivating Activity

Ask students what Americans do to take care of their health. Then ask them what role concerns for health play when they and their families are planning a vacation. What criteria are taken into consideration as they choose where to go?

Teacher Note

Activity 1 is a prereading activity.

Geography Connection

After doing Activity 1, have students look up Baden-Baden, Gaggenau-Bad Rotenfels, Schwangau, Todtmoos, and Bad Wurzach in an atlas. Ask students to give the general location of these towns. (southern Germany)

Background Information

- Located in Baden-Württemberg, Baden-Baden is one of the best known spa towns possessing saltwater springs. The Romans, over 2,000 years ago, already knew of Baden-Baden's mild climate and valued the soothing effects of its hot springs.
- Bad Wurzach is known as the oldest mud-bath resort in Baden-Württemberg and also possesses the largest continuous bog in Central Europe. The bog encompasses an area of 16 km^2 (6.2 square miles).
- Located in the **Voralpen** of Bavaria, Schwangau is a popular climatic health resort as well as ski resort. Schwangau has a population of 3,300. The area surrounding Schwangau is a **Naturschutzgebiet** *(national preserve)*.

Thinking Critically

- **Drawing Inferences** Ask students in what ways a health spa such as Schwangau might be beneficial to people.
- **Analyzing** Ask students where they might find the kind of articles and survey found in this **Zum Lesen** section. (Examples: health magazine, health section of a newspaper)

READING

 For Individual Needs

3 A Slower Pace After students have read the two survey questions, have them brainstorm for the kind of responses they might find. Make a list of students' ideas on butcher paper taped to the board. Use this paper to gather students input for the other **Zum Lesen** activities.

Teaching Suggestion

3 The task of summarizing the data could be done orally or in writing. Either way, it requires students to draw from previously learned language elements. (Examples: connectors, dependent clauses, paraphrasing) To simplify the activity, you could provide students with a completion paragraph or cloze passage. (See the following Teacher Note.)

Teacher Note

In a cloze passage, you would provide a partial summary and a set of words (in a list below the text) from which students could choose in order to correctly summarize the data. This format would enable you to check students' reading comprehension, as well as any grammatical structures you wish to review.

Teaching Suggestion

5 Treat this as a scanning activity where students look for the information needed under the five headings suggested. You may have to help students find the necessary information in one or two of the articles and see to it that they do not get bogged down in all the detail the articles provide.

Teaching Suggestion

5 After students have completed this activity with their partners, use the butcher paper from Activity 3 or a transparency and make an outline of the chart. Have individual students come up to the board and fill in the chart using the information they compiled with their partners. The rest of the class can make suggestions to delete or add information.

Background Information

6 The costs of **Kuren** are paid (in part or full) through the health care system if prescribed by a physician. **Kuren** are considered to be therapeutic and part of health maintenance. They help patients protect their health as they cope with the stresses of daily life or recurring illnesses. **Kuren** are not only for wealthy people; most people whose physicians have recommended this type of treatment have part or all of their expenses paid by their **Krankenkasse.**

POST-READING

Teacher Note

Activity 6 is a post-reading task that will show whether students can apply what they have learned.

Closure

Ask students which of the featured health spas they would choose to visit, and why. (Example: **Wenn du einen Badekurort besuchen könntest, welchen von diesen hier würdest du wählen und warum?**)

Answers to Activity 1

chart: combination of health and fashion; articles: combination of health and leisure

Answers to Activity 2

One will look beautiful when following the new trend; people questioned (male and female, male, female); percentage scale; percentages

Answers to Activity 3

For results, see colored bars in chart.

Answers to Activity 4

Kurstadt; Kochsalzquellen

Answers to Activity 6

Health treatment using natural resources such as saltwater spas, mineral springs, and mud baths under supervision of a physician; healthy diet; exercise; costs of **Kur** paid in part or full by health insurance. Health spas in the United States are generally much more expensive and are not covered by health insurance.

*T*eaching Zweite Stufe,
pp. 142-145

▶ *page 142*

MOTIVATE

Building on Previous Skills

Have students prepare for this section by thinking of common pains and injuries (a) they have (b) athletes have (c) older people have. List students' suggestions in German on a tranparency. Examples:

Schmerzen haben/weh tun: der Rücken, die Hüfte, der Kopf

sich etwas brechen: den Fuß, die Hüfte, den Arm

sich etwas verstauchen: den Knöchel, den Finger

sich etwas verletzen: das Knie, die Schulter

TEACH

PRESENTATION: Wortschatz

- To teach the new body parts, introduce them by pointing to them on yourself or on a drawing. Name the body parts as you point to them.
- Teach the new expressions using cause and effect situations as examples.

Example:

Ich habe gestern zu viel Chili con carne gegessen, und heute tut mir der Bauch weh.

- Use a doll for practicing the phrases and communicative functions. Act as if the doll were speaking. For example, make her fall and break her leg and say: **Ich habe mir das Bein gebrochen!**
- If students know of athletes who are injured, use their names and the expressions that fit their injury.

Language Note

In German, people often wish others good luck by saying: **Hals- und Beinbruch!** *(Break a leg!)* Another expression using a body part is **Lügen haben kurze Beine!** *(Lies won't get you anywhere.)*

For Additional Practice

16 To provide students with further practice, write the following question on the board or on a transparency. **Hast du dich schon mal verletzt?** Have students ask their partners this question and then switch roles.

▶ *page 143*

PRESENTATION: So sagt man das!

Introduce the new expressions to the class, then ask students to think of other ways to answer each of the questions posed in the **So sagt man das!** box.
Examples:

Tut's weh?	Ja, sehr.
	Ja, aber nur ein bißchen.
	Nein, nicht sehr.
Tut dir der Kopf weh?	Nein, aber der Hals.
	Ja, er tut sehr weh.

 Multicultural Connection

If possible, have students find out about other languages and the expressions people use to communicate pain. Example: When they hurt themselves, French speakers often yell out *aïe!* (pronounced like the English word *eye*).

 For Individual Needs

17 Challenge For each of the sentences students come up with, ask them to add a reason or the cause of the pain. (Example: **Meiner Mutter tun oft die Knie weh, denn sie arbeitet viel im Garten.**) This activity can be done orally or in writing.

PRESENTATION: Grammatik

Before presenting the verbs that require a direct object in the dative, review verbs from Level 1 which have indirect objects in the dative case. (Examples: **schenken, geben, kaufen, glauben, sagen**) To review the dative case personal pronouns, refer students to p. 334 in the Grammar Summary.
Practice each of the verbs from the **Grammatik** box in brief activities. Set up "situations" and ask questions to which students can respond on their own.
Examples:

Ich habe gehört, daß deine Mutter krank war. Wie geht es ihr jetzt?

Du bist immer so nett und hilfst allen Leuten. Wem hast du am letzten Wochenende geholfen?

PRESENTATION: Grammatik

Simplify the idea of the dative reflexive pronoun by telling students that the verb's action is turned back on the subject of the verb. Then give examples of previously introduced verbs used reflexively and non-reflexively. Examples:

Er hat seinen Bleistift kaputt gebrochen.

Er hat sich das Bein beim Fußballspiel gebrochen.

DRITTE STUFE

Group Work

18 Divide students in groups of three and ask them to imagine that they just returned from their **Klassenfahrt in den Alpen** where they went skiing. Ask them to come up with a creative narrative, using the sentence fragments to tell what happened to students and teachers on that trip. Students can replace the pronouns with proper names for this activity.

Teaching Suggestion

19 Ask students to answer the questions in the form of a narrative in which they describe in chronological order what happened. Call on several students to read their narrative to the class.

▶ page 145

PRESENTATION: Wortschatz

Waschen, kämmen, and **putzen** are three common verbs that can be used reflexively or non-reflexively. Model them by demonstrating the actions depicted in the pictures and several others, each time contrasting action directed toward another person or thing with action directed toward oneself. Then ask questions about the pictures.
Examples:
Was macht das Mädchen im Rollstuhl?
Was machen die beiden Jungen im Badezimmer?
Wie hilft der Junge seiner Mutter in Bild 5?

For Individual Needs

21 Tactile Learners Write the six sentences on the board and ask students to draw lines from the reflexive pronouns to the subject pronouns to emphasize that these people are doing something for themselves.

PRESENTATION: Ein wenig Grammatik

Write the verbs **geben, sehen, lesen, essen,** and **nehmen** on the board and remind students that these are stem-vowel changing verbs. Introduce **brechen** and ask students to infer what the stem-vowel change should be. Do the same for **waschen** by reintroducing verbs such as **fahren** and **einladen.**

Reteaching: Reflexive and Non-Reflexive Verbs

Prepare a transparency or handout with columns listing the following expressions from the **Zweite Stufe.** Then ask students to create as many sentences as possible using appropriate expressions from the various columns. This activity can be done orally or in writing.

Am Wochenende	waschen	ich	mir	die Haare
Wenn (ich)	putzen	wir	uns	die Hände
Zeit habe	kämmen	ihr	euch	das Auto
Nach jeder Mahlzeit	bürsten	er	sich	den Hund
Einmal pro Woche		sie		die Zähne
Abends				die Katze
				die Fenster
				die Wäsche

CLOSE

ⓉⓅⓇ Total Physical Response

Give commands to the class or to individual students using vocabulary that focuses on body parts.
Examples:
Heb den linken Arm!
Zeig auf das rechte Knie!
Stampf mit beiden Beinen!
Leg die Hände auf die Schultern!

Focusing on Outcomes

Refer students back to the learning outcomes listed on p. 131. They should recognize that they now know how to ask about and express pain.

ASSESS

• **Performance Assessment** Have students form groups of three to role-play a scene in an emergency room. One of the students plays the nurse, another one the doctor, and the third one the patient. The patient answers the nurse's questions and then the doctor's questions. The questions should relate to what brought the patient to the emergency room.

• Quiz 6-2, *Chapter Resources,* Book 2

*T*eaching Dritte Stufe,
pp. 146-149

Resources for Dritte Stufe

Practice and Activity Book
Chapter Resources, Book 2
- Communicative Activity 6-2
- Additional Listening Activities 6-5, 6-6
- Student Response Forms
- Realia 6-3
- Situation Card 6-3
- Quiz 6-3

Audiocassette Program
- *Textbook Audiocassette* 3 B
- *Additional Listening Activities, Audiocassette* 9 B
- *Assessment Items, Audiocassette* 7 B

▶ **page 146**

MOTIVATE

Group Work

Divide the class into three to four large groups. Each of the groups should choose a writer who will have to go to the board once the game is underway. Groups are given one to two minutes to tell their writers the phrases or ideas they come up with for the topic at hand. The group with the most suggestions or ideas wins. Here are some sample topics you may want to use.

Gründe, warum man zum Doktor gehen soll
Gründe, warum man nicht mit zum Rockkonzert gehen soll
Was einem alles wehtun kann

TEACH

Cooperative Learning

22 Divide students into groups of three. Each group should have a writer, a group leader, and a reporter. Set a time limit of approximately 10-15 minutes for this activity. Ask each group to use the questions and answers from this activity to create a public service announcement warning people about the dangers of frequent exposure to the sun. Groups should brainstorm, outline, and then write their announcements. When groups are finished, ask each group reporter to read his or her announcement to the rest of the class as if he or she were reading a public radio announcement.

▶ **page 147**

PRESENTATION: Wortschatz

Introduce the new expressions by making a transparency of the **Wortschatz** box and leaving out the captions. Then ask students what captions they would use if asked **Was soll ich tun?** Based on the pictures, have students complete the phrase **Du mußt unbedingt ... !** Then show the class a transparency containing the captions from the book. Have students compare the expressions they came up with with the expressions in the **Wortschatz** box.

For Individual Needs

24 Tactile Learners Ask students to work with a partner to create an advice pamphlet or a handout for concert goers, focusing on what one should and should not do while attending outdoor concerts in the summer heat. Students can use pictures from magazines, photos, or they can draw their own pictures. When finished, students can display their pamphlets on the bulletin board in the class.

DRITTE STUFE

▶ *page 148*

PRESENTATION: So sagt man das!

Point out to students that there are several ways to express hope. Lead the students to discover how the following sentences differ in structure but not in meaning.

Ich hoffe, du hast kein Fieber.
Ich hoffe, daß du kein Fieber hast.
Hoffentlich hast du kein Fieber.

▶ *page 149*

Teaching Suggestion

28 As students prepare the dialogue, ask them to add words that don't change the meaning drastically but add emphasis to the statement. (Examples: **unbedingt, bloß, denn, wohl, mal, doch**).

PRESENTATION: Wortschatz

To teach the new vocabulary, you may want to bring the actual items to class with price stickers still attached if possible.

Math Connection

Provide students with an approximate current exchange rate and ask them to convert and then compare the German product prices to American prices.

Teaching Suggestion

31 You could also add alternatives such as **das Reformhaus** and **die Apotheke** and let students choose among the three options. When students act out their conversation, stress that they should not read the script and that they can improvise new lines if they can't remember the text they have prepared.

CLOSE

♖ Game

Each student needs a pen and paper for this game. Give students several minutes to look through the **Dritte Stufe** and pick out a new word or phrase. Tell students to make up a sentence in which that new word is omitted intentionally. The blank space is called **Dingsda**. For example, a student may choose the word **Sonnenschutzmittel** and use it as follows:

Im Sommer benutze ich immer (Sonnenschutzmittel), denn ich habe empfindliche Haut.

Each student gets a turn to call on another classmate to whom he or she reads the sentence, substituting the word **Dingsda** for the new word. The challenged student tries to complete the sentence by identifying the missing word. If that student guesses correctly, he or she challenges another student.

Focusing on Outcomes

Refer students back to the learning oucomes listed on p. 131. They should recognize that they now know how to ask for and give advice and express hope.

ASSESS

- **Performance Assessment** Compile a list of ailments and complaints on index cards, the chalkboard, or a transparency. Ask students to play the role of a physician who gives advice to a patient. You can point to a particular ailment (Example: **einen Sonnenstich haben**) and ask individual students what they would recommend a patient do, using the expressions learned in the **Dritte Stufe**.

- Quiz 6-3, *Chapter Resources,* Book 2

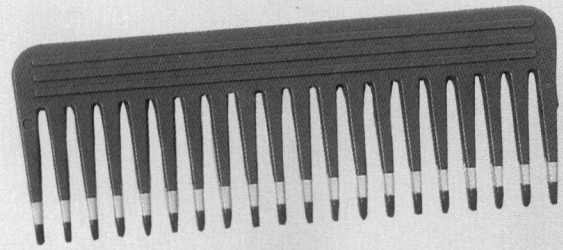

Using Anwendung,
pp. 150-151

▣ Video Wrap-up

At this time, you might want to use the *Video Program* or the *Expanded Video Program*, Videocassette 2 for additional review and enrichment. See *Video Guide* for suggestions regarding:
- **Was fehlt dir?**
  (Dramatic episode)
- **Landeskunde**
  Interviews
- **Videoclips**
  (Authentic footage—*Expanded Video Program* only)

Language Note

2 Point out to students how the impersonal pronoun **man** (*one*) is used in the instructions for this activity. Remind students that **man** is often used in German when describing a process or how something should be done.

Group Work

3 Divide the class into groups of three or four students. One of the students should play the part of the doctor; the others are the patients. Monitor students' conversations. You may want to call on several groups to act out their conversations for the rest of the class.

Teaching Suggestion

5 You may want to brainstorm with students for expressions and phrases appropriate for an official pamphlet. Examples:
Wir raten Ihnen ...
Am besten gehen/machen Sie ...
Sie müssen unbedingt ...
Man soll dafür ...

▣ Portfolio Assessment

5 You may want to suggest this activity as a written portfolio item for your students. See *Assessment Guide*, p. 19.

▣ Portfolio Assessment

8 You may want to suggest this activity as an oral portfolio item for your students. See *Assessment Guide*, p. 19.

Kann ich's wirklich?
p. 152

This page helps students prepare for the test. It is a brief checklist of the major points covered in the chapter. The students should be reminded that it is only a checklist and not necessarily everything that will appear on the test.

Using Wortschatz,
p. 153

Teaching Suggestion

Ask students to work with a partner and come up with as many words, phrases, or expressions as possible associated with the following topics.
- Advice a doctor might give
- Complaints by a patient
- Body parts

Each pair of students will write down as many words as they can think of within a specific amount of time. When time is up students can check their words and phrases against the vocabulary on p. 153, or you may want to call on several pairs to read their vocabulary words to the class.

◆ For Individual Needs

Kinesthetic Learners Ask students to take turns acting out or pantomiming an expression from the **Wortschatz** page (especially the section marked "talking about health" and the reflexive verbs). The rest of the class tries to guess the word or expression.

Teacher Note

Give the **Kapitel 6** Chapter Test, *Chapter Resources*, Book 2.

6
Gute Besserung!

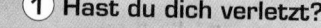
1 Hast du dich verletzt?

Everyone gets sick or injured occasionally. When that happens, you need to be able to tell someone what is wrong, and you need to know what to do to remedy the situation. You might have to talk to your doctor or pick up a prescription from the pharmacy. In order to communicate what is wrong — or what you or someone else needs — there are several things you should know how to say.

In this chapter you will learn

- to inquire about someone's health and respond; to make suggestions
- to ask about and express pain
- to ask for and give advice; to express hope

And you will

- listen to German students talk about what is wrong with them and how they feel
- read some tips for taking care of yourself in the sun
- write about the last time you were sick and what you did to get better
- find out the difference between an *Apotheke* and a *Drogerie*

② Ich muß unbedingt eine Sonnen-milch benutzen.

③ Ich hoffe, daß sich Maike bald wieder wohl fühlt.

Los geht's!

Was fehlt dir?

Look at the photos that accompany the story.
What do you think is happening?
Why was Maike not at school on this day?
What do the boys do to help her?

Maike

David   Thorsten

Nicolas

Wiebke

David und Thorsten sitzen im Alsterpark. Sie lernen zusammen ihre Englischvokabeln für den Englischtest.

①
THORSTEN	Wollen wir aufhören?
DAVID	Nie! Aber machen wir mal eine Pause!
THORSTEN	Okay! Übrigens, wollen wir mal die Maike anrufen? Was meinst du?
DAVID	Klar! Die Maike, die war heute nicht in der Schule. Hoffentlich ist sie nicht krank.

②

MAIKE	Tag, Thorsten! Was gibt's?
THORSTEN	Du warst heute nicht in der Schule. Ist was mit dir?
MAIKE	Mir ist nicht gut. Mir tut der Hals weh, und ich kann kaum schlucken.

Maike mit ihrer Mutter früh am Morgen

Mir ist so heiß!

Mit Fieber kannst du nicht in die Schule gehen. Deine Stirn ist auch ganz schön heiß. Willst du dich wieder in dein Bett legen? 38,9°! Das ist ganz schön hoch!

Ich glaub', du hast Fieber. Du mußt heute unbedingt zu Hause bleiben!

③ ④

Aber ich hab' heute eine Klassenarbeit!

Ich mess' mal, wie hoch deine Temperatur ist ...

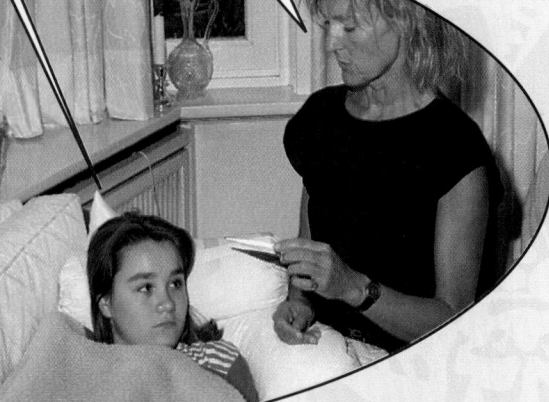

Maike weiter am Telefon

MAIKE Der Hals tut noch weh, aber es geht mir schon besser. Ich glaube, ich habe kein Fieber mehr.

THORSTEN Können wir etwas für dich tun?

MAIKE Ihr könnt mir die Medizin aus der Apotheke holen, aus der Manstein Apotheke. Aber kommt erst vorher hier vorbei! Ihr müßt den Abholschein noch mitnehmen.

In der Apotheke

APOTHEKERIN Guten Tag! Ja bitte?

THORSTEN Einmal die Medizin für Johannsen, bitte! Hier ist der Abholschein.

APOTHEKERIN Einen Moment mal!

THORSTEN Danke! Bin ich Ihnen etwas schuldig?

APOTHEKERIN Nein, es war schon bezahlt. Wiedersehen!

Zu dieser Zeit sind Wiebke und Nicolas in einer Drogerie. Die beiden wollen sich später mit Maike, David und Thorsten treffen und Ball spielen.

WIEBKE Das ist meine Marke. Die nehme ich.

NICOLAS So eine große Tube?

WIEBKE Ja, nach jeder Mahlzeit putze ich mir die Zähne. Schau! Und da geht so eine Tube schnell weg.

NICOLAS Da, Sonnencreme, Schutzfaktor acht!

WIEBKE Das ist nicht hoch genug für mich. Meine Haut ist sehr empfindlich. Ich nehme gewöhnlich Schutzfaktor zwanzig.

NICOLAS Da, sogar fünfundzwanzig! Für dreiundzwanzig Mark neunundneunzig.

WIEBKE Das ist mir zu teuer. Hier ist eine Sonnencreme für zwölf Mark vierzig. Die nehme ich.

1 Was passiert hier?

Verstehst du alles, was diese Schüler sagen? Beantworte die Fragen!

1. Warum rufen Thorsten und David die Maike an?   1. Sie war heute nicht in der Schule.
2. Warum will Maike heute in die Schule gehen? Warum kann sie nicht gehen?   2. Hat heute eine Klassenarbeit; hat Fieber.
3. Was machen Thorsten und David für Maike? Was müssen sie zuerst tun?   3. Medizin aus der Apotheke holen; Abholschein von Maike holen.
4. Was braucht Wiebke in der Drogerie? Warum braucht sie jeden Artikel?   4. Zahnpasta, weil sie sich nach jeder Mahlzeit die Zähne putzt;
5. Warum kauft Wiebke die Sonnenmilch nicht?   Sonnencreme, weil
   5. zu teuer   sie eine sehr empfindliche Haut hat.

2 Genauer lesen

Lies den Text noch einmal und beantworte diese Fragen!

1. Was tut Maike weh?   der Hals
2. Was kann sie kaum tun?   schlucken
3. Was meint Maikes Mutter, was Maike hat?   Fieber
4. Wo holen Thorsten und David die Medizin?   Apotheke
5. Was macht die Wiebke nach jeder Mahlzeit?   Zähne putzen
6. Welchen Schutzfaktor braucht Wiebke gewöhnlich?
   zwanzig

3 Was paßt zusammen?

Welche Ausdrücke auf der rechten Seite passen zu den Ausdrücken auf der linken Seite?

1. Maikes Hals tut ihr noch weh, aber   c
2. Du hast Fieber.   d
3. Maike war heute nicht in der Schule.   a
4. Die kostet 23,99 DM.   f
5. Schutzfaktor acht!   g
6. Du kannst mir die Medizin aus der Apotheke holen.   e
7. Machen wir mal eine Pause!   b

a. Hoffentlich ist sie nicht krank.
b. Okay!
c. es geht ihr schon besser.
d. Du mußt unbedingt zu Hause bleiben.
e. Aber du brauchst erst den Abholschein.
f. Das ist mir zu teuer.
g. Nicht hoch genug für mich.

4 Beschreibungen

Welche Beschreibung paßt zu welcher Person?

1. Maike   d
2. Thorsten   f
3. David   b
4. Nicolas   e
5. Wiebke   a
6. Maikes Mutter   c

a. braucht eine große Tube Zahnpasta, weil sie sich nach jeder Mahlzeit die Zähne putzt.
b. will nicht mit dem Englischlernen aufhören, sondern will nur eine Pause machen.
c. mißt Maikes Temperatur und sagt ihr, daß sie zu Hause bleiben muß.
d. hat heute Halsweh und geht nicht in die Schule.
e. will wissen, warum Wiebke soviel Zahnpasta braucht.
f. spricht mit Maike am Telefon und holt dann für sie die Medizin in der Apotheke.

5 Nacherzählen

Erzähle einem Partner, was in dieser Fotogeschichte passiert!

Was machst du, wenn dir nicht gut ist?

What do German students do when they don't feel well? Is it that different from what we do in the United States? Let's find out.

Trudi, *Bietigheim*

„Also, wenn's mir in der Schule halt schlecht wird, dann geh' ich nach Hause, und wenn ich halt stark krank bin, dann geh' ich zum Arzt."

Tim, *Berlin*

„Es kommt öfters vor, daß ich Magenprobleme habe, daß ich Magen-krämpfe habe. Und dage-gen hab' ich von meinem Arzt ein paar Tabletten bekommen, die ich dann also auch meistens nicht dabei habe, also so schnell wie möglich nach Hause fahre und die Tabletten einnehme."

A. 1. home, doctor; **wenn mir schlecht wird … / wenn ich krank bin …**

A. 1. Where does Trudi go when she is sick? What phrases does she use to describe how she feels?
2. What kind of problems does Tim describe? What does he do when he has this problem? A. 2. stomach-ache, stomach cramps; goes home and takes pills

B. You may have heard that Germany has a national health care system. Did you know that the first health care system was introduced in Germany in 1883? Because of this long history, Germans have come to expect that every person has some kind of insurance. If you're an exchange student or visit Germany for any length of time, you are required to have insur-ance in order to stay in the country. For the average German, the amount paid for health insurance is relatively small. The government and employers carry much of the cost in this system.

C. What is the status of health care reform in the United States? Do you think everyone should be insured? Who should pay for it? The individual, the government, or employers? Do you think America's tradition of individualism has influ-enced our views on this issue?

Inquiring about someone's health and responding; making suggestions

WORTSCHATZ

Wie geht's dir denn? Was ist los mit dir?

Mir ist überhaupt nicht gut. Ich glaube, ich bin krank.

Ich habe Halsschmerzen. Ich kann kaum schlucken.

Ich fühl' mich nicht wohl. Mir ist nicht gut.

Kopfschmerzen

Zahnschmerzen

Mir ist so schlecht. Ich habe Fieber.

Mir ist gar nicht gut. Ich hab' eine Erkältung.

Ich hab' Husten und Schnupfen.

Ohrenschmerzen

Bauchschmerzen

6 Hör gut zu!

Vier Schüler erzählen, wie sie sich fühlen. Mach dir Notizen, dann beantworte die folgenden Fragen!

a. Wer hat Halsschmerzen? **c.** Wer muß in die Apotheke gehen?
b. Wer hat hohes Fieber? **d.** Wer fühlt sich heute wohl?

For answers, see listening script on TE Interleaf.

7 Was ist los mit dir?

Was hast du, wenn du krank bist? Schreib auf, was du gewöhnlich hast und wie oft! Such dir dann einen Partner und fragt euch gegenseitig, was ihr manchmal habt!

oft   manchmal
gewöhnlich
                nie
ab und zu

SO SAGT MAN DAS!

Inquiring about someone's health and responding

You have used the expression **Wie geht's?** to ask about general well-being. As a response to this question, you used such expressions as **Danke, gut! Danke, es geht! Nicht gut!** and **Miserabel!**

Here are some specific ways to inquire about someone's health.

You may ask:

Wie fühlst du dich?
Wie geht es dir?
Ist dir nicht gut?
Ist was mit dir?
Was fehlt dir?

And the response may be:

Ich fühl' mich wohl!
Es geht mir nicht gut!
Mir ist schlecht.
Mir ist nicht gut.
Nichts!

If someone tells you that he or she is not doing well, you might say:

Ach schade!
Gute Besserung!
Hoffentlich geht es dir bald besser!

How many dative pronouns do you recognize?

8 Wie fühlst du dich?

Such dir einen Partner! Frag ihn, wie er sich fühlt! Er sagt es dir. — Tauscht dann die Rollen aus! Dann beschreibt die beiden hier unten!

9 Was ist mit ...?

Such dir einen Partner! Dein Partner möchte wissen, was mit jemandem (*someone*) in der Klasse los ist, warum er so schlecht aussieht. Du sagst es ihm. — Tauscht dann die Rollen aus!

1. **mich, dich, sich, uns, euch**
2. **Fühlen Sie sich wohl? Fühlt ihr euch wohl?**

Ich fühl' ▬▬ nicht wohl. Es geht ▬▬ nicht gut. ▬▬ ist schlecht, ich fühl' ▬▬ miserabel!

Maike

Gestern hab' ich ▬▬ nicht wohl gefühlt. ▬▬ war furchtbar schlecht, aber heute geht es ▬▬ viel besser!

David

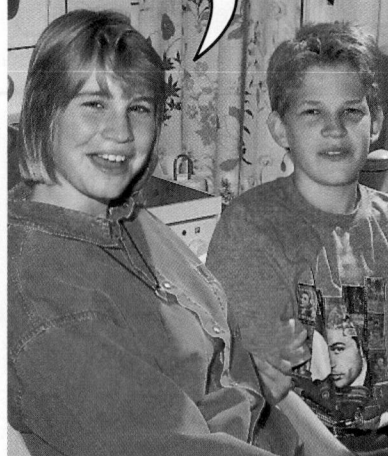

Wir fühlen ▬▬ absolut prima. Es geht ▬▬ echt gut! ▬▬ fehlt nichts!

Saskia und Finn

10 Was ist los?

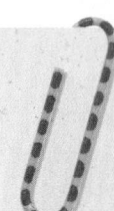

Was sagen diese Schüler?

a. Maike: mich/mir/Mir/mich; David: mich/Mir/mir; Saskia und Finn: uns/uns/Uns
b. Maike: sich/ihr/Ihr/sich; David: sich/Ihm/ihm; Saskia und Finn: sich/ihnen/Ihnen

a. Schreib, was diese Schüler sagen! Welche Pronomen kommen in die Lücken?

b. Jetzt schreib, was diese Schüler gesagt haben! Fang so an: Maike hat gesagt, sie fühlt ...

11 Was hast du?

Deine Partnerin war heute nicht in der Schule! Frag sie, warum sie nicht in der Schule war, was sie hat und wie sie sich jetzt fühlt! — Tauscht dann die Rollen aus!

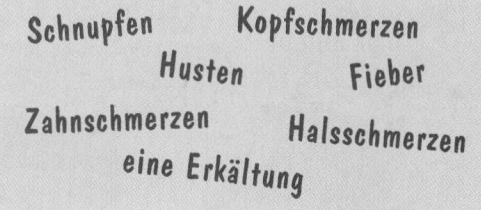

Schnupfen   Kopfschmerzen
        Husten   Fieber
Zahnschmerzen   Halsschmerzen
        eine Erkältung

SO SAGT MAN DAS!

Making suggestions

Here are some ways you have learned to make suggestions so far:

Möchtest du ins Kino gehen?   *or*   **Willst du** ins Café Freizeit gehen?

Du kannst für mich Brot **holen.**   *or*   **Kauf** es doch beim Bäcker!

Here are two other ways to make suggestions:

Rufen wir mal die Maike an!

Sollen wir mal die Maike anrufen?

What are the English equivalents of the last two sentences? What purpose does the word **mal** serve in these suggestions?

12 Sollen wir mal ...?

Such dir einen Partner! — Du weißt nicht so recht, was du tun sollst, und du fragst deshalb deinen Partner. Gebraucht die Ausdrücke im Kasten! — Tauscht dann die Rollen aus!

DU	**Sollen wir mal ...?**
PARTNER	**Prima Idee!**

Was tun?

in den Alsterpark gehen
die Englischvokabeln lernen
die ... anrufen
den ... besuchen
zu Hause bleiben
in die Drogerie gehen
in die Apotheke gehen
einkaufen gehen
nach ... fahren

Ja?

Prima Idee!
Na klar!
Ja, gern!
Warum nicht?
Machen wir!

Nein?

Es geht nicht.
Ich hab' keine Zeit.
Ich muß zu Hause bleiben.
Ich hab' zu viel zu tun.
Ich ...

Schon bekannt
Ein wenig *Grammatik*

Read the following sentence.

Ich soll einkaufen gehen.

What does the modal verb **sollen** mean here? **Sollen** is often used to express obligation, but it has other meanings as well.

Sollen wir ein Eis essen?

In what way is **sollen** being used in the sentence above?[1]

Grammatik The inclusive command

1. When making suggestions, the inclusive command can be used. It consists of the **wir**-form of the verb with the verb itself in first position followed by **wir**.

gehen: wir gehen   **Gehen wir** mal ins Kino!
Let's go to the movies!

2. If a verb has a separable prefix, the prefix is at the end of the command.

anrufen: wir rufen an   **Rufen wir** mal Maike **an**!
Let's call Maike!

EIN WENIG LANDESKUNDE

Traditionally, the **Apotheke** and the **Drogerie** in German towns and cities serve two different purposes. If you need medicine, whether prescription or over-the-counter, you go to the **Apotheke.** You can also get vitamins, herbal teas, and other health-related items at the **Apotheke.** If you need shampoo, toothpaste, or other such items, you would go to the **Drogerie.** In many larger cities, the **Drogerie** is being replaced by larger stores that sell everything from toiletries to books.

13 Schade, es geht leider nicht!

Such dir eine Partnerin! Ruf sie an und lade sie ins Kino oder ins Konzert ein! Sie kann aber leider nicht mitgehen. Sie fühlt sich nicht wohl, ihr ist nicht gut. Du fragst sie, was sie hat, und sie sagt es dir. — Tauscht dann die Rollen aus!

14 Für dein Notizbuch

a. Schreib in dein Notizbuch, wann du das letzte Mal krank warst, was du gehabt hast, wie du dich gefühlt hast und wie lange du nicht in der Schule warst!

b. Sag es dann auch einer Partnerin!

1. To make a suggestion.

Kuren und Bäder

Baden-Baden

Bundesland:
Baden-Württemberg
Kfz-Kennzeichen: BAD
Höhe: 183 m ü.d.M. - Einwohnerzahl:
50 000
Postleitzahl: #76530
Telefonvorwahl: 07221

ⓘ Kurdirektion
(Gäste-Information),
Augustaplatz 1;
Tel.: 27 52 00

⓮ **Baden-Baden**

Baden-Baden besitzt als Kurstadt Weltruf.
Seit zweitausend Jahren werden die heißen
Kochsalzquellen genutzt.
Friedrichsbad (→ Marktplatz): Der
Renaissancebau ist eines der prächtigsten
und traditionsreichsten Badehäuser der Welt.
Das „Römisch-Irische Bad" bietet u. a.
Heißluft-Dampfbad, Thermal-Vollbad,
Sprudelbad und Tauchbad.
Römische Badruinen (unter dem →
Römerplatz): Etwa 2000 Jahre alt sind die
Reste einer römischen Badeanlage für die
Legionäre, ein anschauliches Bild antiker
Thermen.

Schwangau

Gesundzeit mit Heubad

Unter dem Motto „Gesundzeit in
Bayern" bietet der heilklimatische

Kurort Schwangau 1994 Gesund-
heitsurlaube von einwöchiger Dauer an.
Darin enthalten sind: ärztliche
Untersuchung mit Gesundzeitplan, drei
medizinische Anwendungen (davon ein
Heubad aus ungedüngtem Bergwiesen-
heu, eine Kneippsche Anwendung, eine
Massage), zweimal Gymnastik, je eine
geführte Wanderung zu den beiden
Königsschlössern Hohenschwangau und
Neuschwanstein. Außerdem gibt es Tips
und Anleitungen vom Gesundheitsbe-
rater. Preis pro Person ab 385 Mark.
Gültig ist die „Gesundzeit" ganzjährig.
Infos: Kurverwaltung Schwangau,
Münchener Str. 2,
87645 Schwangau,
Tel. 08362/8198-0

Bad Rotenfels

Neuer Saunapark lädt ein

Der Thermal-Mineral-Badeort
Gaggenau-Bad Rotenfels im romanti-
schen Murgtal präsentiert bis zum 30.
April 1994 ein Bade- und
Saunavergnügen zum Supersparpreis.
Im Mittelpunkt stehen dabei das
Thermal-Mineral-Badezentrum
Rotherma mit über 600 qm
Wasserfläche und der neue Saunapark
mit einer Größe von über 3000 qm. Das
Sparangebot ab 189 Mark beinhaltet
fünf Übernachtungen mit Frühstück in
Privat- oder Gästehäusern. Weiter sind
vier Thermalbäder und ein
Saunabesuch sowie Kurtaxe enthalten.
Infos: Gaggenau-Tourist-Info,
Rathausstr. 11, 76571
Gaggenau-Bad Rotenfels,
Tel. 07225/62301

Todtmoos

Schlittenhunde unterwegs

Am Wochenende vom 28. bis 30.
Januar 1994 sind in Todtmoos im
Südschwarzwald wieder die Hunde los!
Bei den schon traditionellen
Schlittenhunderennen, die bereits zum
19. Mai in Todtmoos ausgetragen wer-
den, laufen die schnellsten Hunde
Europas. Zu diesem Hundespektakel
hat die Kurverwaltung Todtmoos ein
interessantes Pauschalangebot zusam-
mengestellt: Gültig vom 28. bis 30.
Januar ab 96 Mark für Übernachtung
mit Frühstück in Privatzimmern mit
Dusche und WC. Die Kurtaxe ist im
Preis inbegriffen. Das Pauschalpaket
enthält außerdem die Eintritte für die
Rennen, den großen Countryabend am
29. Januar und den Bustransfer zur
Rennstrecke.
Infos: Kurverwaltung, 79682
Todtmoos, Tel. 07674/534

Bad Wurzach

Moor und vieles mehr

Zur Bad Wurzacher Gesundheitswoche
lädt das älteste Moorheilbad Baden-
Württembergs in der Zeit vom 9. Januar
bis 30. April 1994 ein. Dabei werden
nicht nur Mooranwendungen, sondern
auch Wassergymnastik, Massagen und
Gesundheitsvorträge angeboten. Zur
Behandlung von rheumatischen
Erkrankungen, Bandscheiben- und
Wirbelsäulenschäden,
Gelenkerkrankungen.
Infos: Städtische Kurverwaltung,
Mühltorstr. 1, 88410 Bad Wurzach,
Tel. 07564/302150

LESETRICK

Deciphering charts and graphs.
Charts and graphs can be confus-
ing, even in your native language,
but if you follow a few important steps before
answering any questions, you can master the
information: 1) read titles and subtitles;
2) check for a legend and become familiar with
it; 3) understand what the numbers represent
(percents, parts per thousand, etc.); and 4)
check the source and the way survey questions
are worded. Remember, charts and graphs require careful reading—short cuts won't work.

Getting Started

1. Skim over the headline areas of the chart and
the articles. What general concern do these
texts all have in common? Is this information
about work? fashion? health? leisure? Or
some combination of topics?

2. Look at the title area of the chart. Notice that
the chart depicts the results of an **Umfrage**.
What does the slogan „Bleich ist beautiful"
tell you to expect of the new trend? Locate
the legend. What do the colored bars indicate? And the vertical lines? What do the
numbers represent? Make sure you feel comfortable with the organization of information.

For answers, see TE Interleaf.

Der neue Trend:

„Bleich ist beautiful"

Wenn Sie in der Sonne baden und ein Sonnenschutzmittel benutzt haben: Glauben Sie, daß das Sonnenbaden...

... für Ihre Gesundheit auf jeden Fall schädlich ist?
- 17 %
- 20 %
- 14 %

Gesamt
Frauen
Männer

... nur schädlich ist, wenn Sie zu lange in der Sonne bleiben?
- 60 %
- 65 %
- 57 %

... nicht schädlich ist?
- 11 %
- 7 %
- 14 %

Oder sind Sie sich nicht ganz sicher, ob es für Ihre Gesundheit schädlich ist?

weiß nicht/keine Angabe
- 11 % — 0 %
- 8 % — 0 %
- 14 % — 1 %

Wenn Sie einmal an die Zeit vor 10 Jahren denken: Würden Sie sagen, daß Sie heute häufiger, gleich oft oder seltener als vor 10 Jahren sonnenbaden?

häufiger

weiß nicht/keine Angabe
- 16 % — 1 %
- 16 % — 1 %
- 16 % — 1 %

gleich oft
- 30 %
- 25 %
- 35 %

seltener
- 52 %
- 57 %
- 47 %

FOCUS-Magazin

A Closer Look

> **Tip:** If you know how to divide long compound words, you can usually guess their meaning. An **-s** following a masculine or neuter noun belongs with that word. The same is often true of **-n** following feminine nouns, as in **Sonnenbaden**. Also be aware of common prefixes, such as **er-** or **be-**. How would you divide **Alterserscheinungen?**

3. Read the two survey questions. What were the results? Try to summarize the data in two sentences.

4. Read the description of Baden-Baden. Give two reasons why it is world famous.
5. Read the articles from **Kuren und Bäder** and, together with a partner, fill out a chart with the following headings as you read: Place, Main Feature of **Kur,** Other Attractions, Cost, and Number of Days.
6. **Kuren** have long been a part of Germany's health traditions. How would you describe a typical **Kur** based on the information from the four descriptions you read? What are the general characteristics of a **Kur?** Is there anything comparable in the United States?

ZWEITE STUFE

Asking about and expressing pain

WORTSCHATZ

Was tut dir weh? — Mir tut / tun ... weh!

Mir tut der
Hals weh.

Der Kopf tut
mir weh.

Der Bauch tut
mir weh.

die Schulter

der Rücken

die Hüfte

die Beine

der Arm

Hast du dich verletzt? Hast du dir etwas gebrochen?

Ich hab' mir den
Fuß gebrochen.

Ich hab' mir den
Knöchel verstaucht.

Ich hab' mir das
Knie verletzt.

---

15 Hör gut zu! For answers, see listening script on TE Interleaf.

Was ist mit diesen Leuten los? Schau diese Bilder an und hör gleichzeitig die Kassette an!
Welches Bild paßt zu welcher Beschreibung?

a.

b.

c.

d.

16 Tut dir was weh?

Such dir einen Partner! Frag ihn, was ihm manchmal weh tut! Er muß dir zwei Dinge
sagen, die ihm weh tun. — Tauscht dann die Rollen aus!

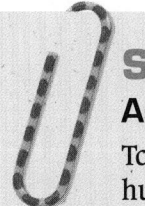

Asking about and expressing pain

To ask a friend if he or she is hurting, you say:

Tut's weh?
Tut es noch weh?

To inquire what hurts, you ask:

Was tut dir weh?
Tut dir der Kopf weh?

Why do you think the verb form **tut** is used sometimes, and sometimes the form **tun**?[1] What other verb does **weh tun** remind you of?

The response might be:

Au! *or* **Aua! Es tut weh!**
Nein, es geht!

And the response might be:

Die Ohren tun mir weh.
Ja, ich hab' Kopfschmerzen.

Ein wenig *Grammatik*

The verb **weh tun** acts like a separable prefix verb, with the adverb **weh** in last position in a simple statement. **Tun** is an irregular verb, but you need only two forms in this phrase:

Der Hals **tut** mir weh.
Die Augen **tun** ihm weh.

17 Was tut ihnen weh?

Wie viele Sätze kannst du machen?

BEISPIEL **Meinem Opa tun oft die ... weh.**

Wem?

(mein) Opa
Oma
Mutter
Vater
Bruder
Schwester
Eltern
ich

weh tun

Wie oft?

ab und zu
oft
sehr oft
häufig
manchmal
nie

Was?

Arm   Beine
Schulter   Hals
Ellbogen   Hüfte
Kopf   Hand
Knöchel   Füße
Bauch   Rücken
        Knie

Grammatik Verbs used with dative case forms

There are verbs that require the direct object to be in the dative case.

weh tun	Was tut **dir** weh? — Der Hals tut **mir** weh.
(gut) gehen	Wie geht es **dir**? — Danke, es geht **mir** gut.
gefallen	Dresden hat **dem Frank** gut gefallen.
helfen	Der Robert hilft **seiner Oma** gern.
schmecken	Die Quarkbrötchen schmecken **den Schülern** gut.
fehlen	Was fehlt **dir**? — **Mir** fehlt nichts.

Name all the direct objects in these questions and statements. Can you express these sentences in English?

---

1. **Tut** is used with a singular subject, **tun** if the subject is in the plural.

Grammatik Reflexive verbs used with dative case forms

1. You already know some reflexive verbs that require a reflexive pronoun in the accusative case, such as **sich freuen** and **sich fühlen.**

Ich freue **mich,** daß du **dich** wohl fühlst.

2. When there is another object, a direct object, in the accusative case, the reflexive pronoun must be in the dative case.

Ich habe **mir** *das Knie* verletzt.

3. Look at the chart. Are the dative reflexive pronouns the same as the personal pronouns? What difference do you observe?

Ich habe	**mir**	
Du hast	**dir**	
Er/ Sie/Es hat	**sich**	das Bein gebrochen.
Wir haben	**uns**	
Ihr habt	**euch**	
Sie (pl)/Sie haben	**sich**	

4. Also note the use of the definite article with the direct object:

Ich habe mir **das** Bein gebrochen. *I broke* my *leg.*
Er hat sich **den** Fuß verstaucht. *He sprained* his *ankle.*

What do you notice about the positions of the pronoun and the direct object?[1]

18 Sätze bauen

Wie viele Sätze kannst du bauen?

ich	haben	uns	Ellbogen		verletzt
wir	habt	euch	Arm		gebrochen
unser Lehrer	habe	sich	Knöchel		verstaucht
du	hast	mir	Hand	Bein	
meine Oma	hat	dir	Knie	Finger	
ihr			Fuß	Auge	
			Daumen	Hüfte	
			Nase		

19 Und du?

Lies die folgenden Fragen! Schreib, was für dich zutrifft (*what pertains to you*)!

1. Wie oft verletzt du dich?
2. Was hast du dir schon öfter verletzt?
3. Hast du dir schon einmal etwas verstaucht? Was? Wievielmal?
4. Was hast du dir schon einmal gebrochen?

---

1. The reflexive pronoun precedes the direct object.

20 Hast du dir etwas gebrochen?

Frag jetzt einen Partner, ob er sich schon einmal etwas gebrochen, verstaucht oder verletzt hat! — Tauscht dann die Rollen aus! Erzähl danach deinen Mitschülern, was dein Partner gesagt hat!

WORTSCHATZ

Er wäscht das T-Shirt.

Er wäscht sich die Hände.

Sie kämmt den Hund.

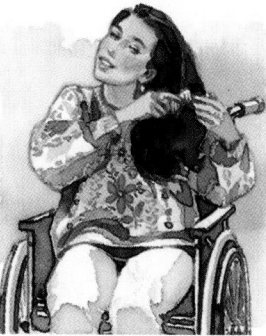

Sie kämmt sich.

21 Wie oft machst du das?

Such dir einen Partner! Frag ihn:

a. wie oft er sich die Hände wäscht
b. wie oft er sein Auto wäscht
c. wie oft er sich die Haare kämmt
d. wie oft er (seine Katze) kämmt
e. wie oft er sich die Zähne putzt
f. wie oft er sein Fahrrad putzt
Danach fragt er dich.

Er putzt die Fenster.

Er putzt sich die Zähne.

wann? und wie oft?

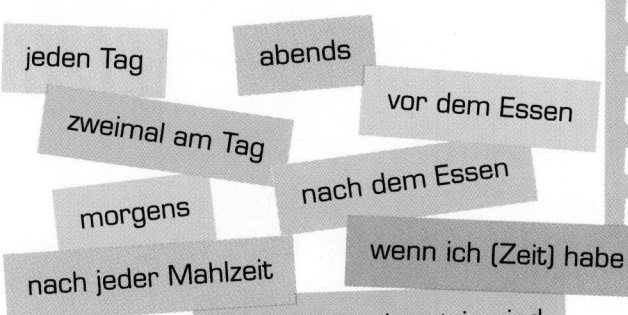

jeden Tag
abends
vor dem Essen
zweimal am Tag
nach dem Essen
morgens
nach jeder Mahlzeit
wenn ich (Zeit) habe
wenn (sie) schmutzig sind

Vorsicht vor Sonnenstrahlen!

Ein Sonnenbad kann ein Genuß sein. Aber zu intensive Sonneneinstrahlung schadet nicht nur der Haut, sondern kann einen Sonnenstich oder sogar Hitzschlag verursachen.

Zu viel Sonne! Was passiert?

Die Symptome eines Sonnenstichs treten schon beim Sonnenbaden oder manchmal kurz danach auf. Die Haut ist heiß und trocken, der Kopf hochrot, der Puls läuft schnell. Die Körpertemperatur ist hoch. Es kommt zu Kopfschmerzen, Ohrensausen — der Patient fühlt sich unwohl.

Wann müssen Sie zum Arzt?

Bei erhöhter Temperatur nach einem Sonnenbad und bei eintretenden Kopfschmerzen unbedingt den Arzt anrufen. Nur er kann die Tätigkeit von Herz und Kreislauf stabilisieren.

Wie kann man sich schützen?

* Setzen Sie sich nie zu lange intensiver Sonneneinstrahlung aus!
* Trinken Sie viel Wasser, bis zu vier Liter am Tag, damit Sie genug schwitzen können!
* Vermeiden Sie körperliche Anstrengung in der Hitze!
* Vermeiden Sie Alkohol und essen Sie nur leichte Speisen!

Helfen Sonnenschutzmittel?

Einen absolut sicheren Sonnenschutz gibt es nicht. Wenn Sie unbedingt in der Sonne sein müssen, so schützen Sie Ihre Haut mit einer guten Sonnencreme! Eine Creme mit einem hohen Lichtschutzfaktor schützt die Haut vor schädlichen UV-Strahlen!

22 Was hast du verstanden?

Lies den Bericht! Dann diskutier die Antworten zu den folgenden Fragen mit deinen Mitschülern!

1. Was kann zu intensive Sonneneinstrahlung verursachen?
2. Was sind die Symptome eines Sonnenstichs?
3. Wann soll man sofort den Arzt anrufen?
4. Wie kann man sich vor einem Sonnenstich schützen?
5. Wie helfen Sonnenschutzmittel?

23 Hör gut zu! For answers, see listening script on TE Interleaf.

Ein Schüler kann heute nicht zur Schule kommen, weil er krank ist. Hör zu, als ein Freund ihn anruft und fragt, wie es ihm geht! Schreib dann auf, was dem Schüler fehlt, was er machen soll und wie sein Freund ihm helfen will!

Was soll ich tun? — Du mußt unbedingt …!

die Sonne vermeiden

Alkohol vermeiden

viel Wasser trinken

nur Sonnencreme mit hohem Lichtschutzfaktor benutzen

nur leichte Speisen essen

den Arzt anrufen

24 Bist du vorsichtig?

Frag deine Partnerin, was sie macht, wenn sie im Sommer in der großen Hitze zu einem Konzert unter freiem Himmel (*open-air concert*) geht! Und was machst du? Wie schützt du dich?

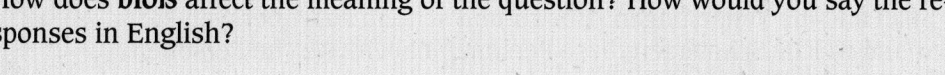

SO SAGT MAN DAS!

Asking for and giving advice

When asking for advice, you say:

Was soll ich machen?
Was soll ich bloß tun?

When giving advice, you say:

Du gehst am besten zum Arzt.
Geh doch mal zum Arzt!
Du mußt unbedingt zum Arzt gehen!

How does **bloß** affect the meaning of the question? How would you say the responses in English?

25 Du mußt unbedingt ...!

Such dir eine Partnerin! — Deine Partnerin hat viele Beschwerden (*complaints*). Du sagst ihr, was sie tun muß. Gebraucht die Ideen in beiden Kästen! Eure Antworten müssen aber stimmen! — Tauscht dann die Rollen aus!

Beschwerden
Was soll ich bloß machen?

Ich bin krank.
Ich brauche Medizin.
Ich glaub', ich hab' einen Sonnenstich.
Meine Haut ist ja ganz rot.
Ich fühl' mich nicht wohl.
Ich bin so müde.
Ich habe Hunger.
Meine Stirn ist so heiß.

WORTSCHATZ

das Fieber messen *to measure one's temperature*
müde *tired*
der Sonnenstich *sun stroke*
die Haut *skin*
die Temperatur *temperature*

Was tun?
Du mußt unbedingt . . .

die Sonne vermeiden
den Arzt anrufen
eine gute Sonnencreme benutzen
etwas essen
eine Pause machen
in die Apotheke gehen
(dein) Fieber messen
zu Hause bleiben
zum Arzt gehen

26 Geh doch mal zum Arzt!

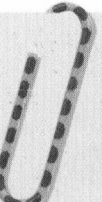

Such dir einen neuen Partner! — Macht jetzt die gleiche Übung noch einmal, aber diesmal mit der **du**-Form des Imperatives!

BEISPIEL   PARTNER   **Ich bin so müde.**
            DU   **Mach doch mal eine Pause!**
      PARTNER   **Gute Idee!**

Ein wenig *Grammatik*

The verb **messen**, as in **Fieber messen**, has a stem vowel change in the **du**- and **er/sie**-forms.

   Mißt du mal mein Fieber?
   Er **mißt** jetzt sein Fieber.
The **du**-command is **miß**!
   Miß doch mal deine Temperatur!

SO SAGT MAN DAS!

Expressing hope
To express hope, you may say:

   Ich hoffe, du hast kein Fieber.
   Wir hoffen, daß du dir nichts gebrochen hast.
   Hoffentlich hast du dir nur den Fuß verstaucht.

What do you notice about the word order in the **daß**-clause? What do you think **hoffentlich** means?

27 Hör gut zu!   For answers, see listening script on TE Interleaf.

Nach dem großen Fußballspiel am Samstag sprechen drei Schüler über das Spiel und die Verletzungen. Hör zu und schreib auf, über wen sie reden und welche Schmerzen diese Personen haben! Welche Personen drücken auch Hoffnungen aus?

28 Was hoffst du?

Sprich mit einem Partner am Telefon darüber, wie er sich fühlt und was ihm fehlt! Drück Hoffnungen aus und sage ihm, wie du ihm helfen kannst! Wenn ihr wollt, könnt ihr die Wörter rechts als Hilfe benutzen.

kein Fieber mehr haben

morgen wieder in die Schule gehen können

wieder besser gehen

die Medizin nehmen

der Hals nicht mehr weh tun

nichts gebrochen haben

WORTSCHATZ

Warum kaufst du dir nicht ...?

Sonnencreme

Die Sonnencreme ist mir zu teuer.

Sonnenmilch

Schutzfaktor 8 ist mir nicht hoch genug.

Haarshampoo

Das Shampoo ist mir nicht gut genug.

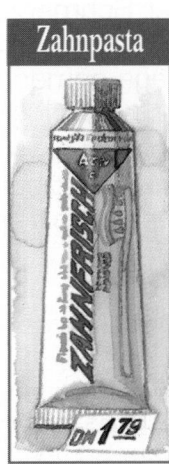

Zahnpasta

Die Zahnpasta ist mir zu süß.

Seife

DM 2.50

Die Seife ist mir zu parfümiert.

Handcreme

DM 3.90

Die Handcreme ist mir zu fett.

29 Warum kaufst du das nicht?

Such dir eine Partnerin! — Ihr seid in einer Drogerie! Sag ihr, daß du hoffst, daß sie sich etwas kauft, was dir gefällt, aber sie hat für alles eine Ausrede (*an excuse*).

30 In der Drogerie

Du bist in einer Drogerie. Dein Partner ist der Drogist. Du brauchst drei ganz bestimmte Artikel. Du fragst, ob er diese Artikel hat und was sie kosten. Wenn es einen Artikel nicht gibt, sag, daß du etwas anderes nimmst!

31 Sie wünschen, bitte?

Schreib jetzt mit deinem Partner ein Gespräch, das du mit ihm in der Drogerie gehabt hast! Führt dann dieses Gespräch in der Klasse vor!

Das ist mir zu teuer!

Ein wenig *G*rammatik

You also use the dative case forms to express the idea of something being "too expensive, too large, too small for you."

Die Creme ist **mir** zu teuer.
Die Seife ist **ihr** zu parfümiert.

ANWENDUNG

For answers, see listening script on TE Interleaf.

1 Einige Leute erzählen, was sie haben, was ihnen fehlt und was sie brauchen. Wo muß jeder hingehen, um das zu bekommen, was er braucht? (Zum Beispiel: Wenn man Brot braucht, muß man zur Bäckerei.) Schreib auf, wo jeder hingehen muß!

2 Ab und zu mal hat jeder Schmerzen und muß etwas dagegen tun. In diesem Artikel von *Bunte* werden Vorschläge gemacht, wie man mit Schmerzen zurechtkommt.
What is this article about? 2. c
  a. If you have pain, think about something like ice cream and the pain won't seem so severe.
  b. If you force yourself to think about something else, your body will forget about the pain and it will go away.
  c. If you concentrate on whatever is causing you pain, it will make it easier for the pain to go away.

Jetzt ein Eis!

Sie lesen diese Überschrift – und plötzlich können Sie gar nicht anders: Immer wieder denken Sie an ein Eis. Und je mehr Sie versuchen, nicht daran zu denken, desto stärker wird der Gedanke. Forscher der Uni Houston haben dieses Phänomen untersucht und festgestellt: Machen Sie es genau andersrum – denken Sie bewußt an etwas, das Sie verdrängen wollen, und Sie werden es bald vergessen. So lassen sich auch Schmerzen „wegdenken". Je mehr Sie sich auf den Schmerz konzentrieren, desto leichter vergeht er.

3 Viele Schüler sind heute krank oder haben sich verletzt.
  a. Wie würden (*would*) diese Schüler die Fragen **Wie geht es dir denn?** oder **Was ist los mit dir?** beantworten? a. E.g.: **Mir ist nicht gut. Ich habe Husten.**
  b. Was sagt der Arzt wahrscheinlich zu diesen Schülern? Gib jedem Schüler einen Ratschlag! b. E.g.: **Nimm dieses Rezept, und hol dir Hustensaft aus der Apotheke.**

4 Was für Schmerzen hast du gehabt? Was machst du, wenn du Schmerzen hast? Schreib mindestens vier Sätze darüber in dein Notizbuch!

 5 You are the health official in a new resort opening up soon. It is your responsibility to prepare a pamphlet informing tourists what they should and should not do in order to stay healthy and safe while they are at the resort, and what they should do in case of sickness or an accident. Work with two other students, your team of health workers, to prepare this document. Use drawings or photos from magazines to illustrate your ideas.

 6 Dein Brieffreund in Dresden will wissen, wie dein tägliches (*daily*) Leben in den U.S.A. aussieht. Schreib ihm einen Brief und erzähl ihm alles, was du an einem Tag machst — von früh morgens bis abends!

BEISPIEL   **Ich stehe um 7 Uhr auf (*get up*). Dann wasche ich mich, putze mir die Zähne, . . .**

 7 Tell a friend about several things you are planning to do. Your friend expresses hope that you will take care of yourself so that nothing bad happens.

Du willst:

a. acht Stunden in Kalifornien am Strand liegen
b. ein hartes Fußballspiel gegen eine College-Mannschaft spielen
c. eine tolle Party in einer anderen Stadt besuchen
d. heute abend gar nicht für den großen Test lernen

8

ROLLENSPIEL

Work with several students to act out the following situation. You are an **Apotheker** in a German city. Several people come to you during the day and explain their injuries, aches or pains. You listen to their explanations, ask questions to get more specific information, then make recommendations about what they can do to remedy the situation. Take turns playing the **Apotheker**. Bring props to make the situation livelier.

7. a. — Ich will acht Stunden in Kalifornien am Strand liegen.
　　— Hoffentlich bekommst du keinen Sonnenstich.
　b. — Ich werde ein hartes Fußballspiel gegen eine College-Mannschaft spielen.
　　— Ich hoffe, du verletzt dich nicht.
　c. — Ich werde eine tolle Party in einer anderen Stadt besuchen.
　　— Hoffentlich kommst du nicht so spät nach Hause.
　d. — Ich werde heute abend gar nicht für den großen Test lernen.
　　— Ich hoffe, daß du keine schlechte Note bekommst.

Can you inquire about someone's health and respond? (p. 137)

1 How would you ask someone how he or she is doing? How would you ask if something is wrong?   E.g.: **Wie fühlst du dich? Fehlt dir etwas?**

2 How would you respond to the question above in the following situations?

a. **Ich habe Halsschmerzen und kann kaum schlucken.**

a. You have a sore throat and can hardly swallow.

b. You have an earache.   b. **Ich habe Ohrenschmerzen.**

c. You have a toothache.   c. **Ich habe Zahnschmerzen.**

d. You have a cold, with coughing and a stuffy nose.   d. **Ich habe eine Erkältung mit Husten und Schnupfen.**

Can you make suggestions? (p. 138)

3 How would you tell the following people what they should do?

a. Hanna / go to the pharmacy   a. **Geh mal zur Apotheke!**

b. your little brother / not to go to school   b. **Geh mal nicht zur Schule!**

c. your good friend / stay at home   c. **Bleib mal zu Hause!**

d. Thorsten and Wiebke / go to the **Drogerie**   d. **Geht mal in die Drogerie!**

e. you and your friends / go to the movies   e. **Gehen wir mal ins Kino!**

Can you ask about and express pain? (p. 143)

4 How would you ask someone what is hurting him or her? How would you say that these people have the following problems?   4. **Was tut dir/Ihnen weh?**

a. your mother's arm hurts often   a. **Meiner Mutter tut oft der Arm weh.**

b. your throat hurts   b. **Mein Hals tut mir weh.**

c. your sister's head hurts sometimes   c. **Meiner Schwester tut manchmal der Kopf weh.**

d. your dad's tooth hurts   d. **Meinem Vater tut ein Zahn weh.**

5 How would you say that you are doing great — that nothing hurts?
E.g.: **Ich fühle mich wohl. Mir tut nichts weh.**

Can you ask for and give advice? (p. 147)

6 What advice would you give to these people?
Du mußt unbedingt ... (Answers will vary).

Can you express hope? (p. 148)

7 How would you express hope that

a. **Ich hoffe, Birgits Hals tut nicht mehr weh.**
b. **Hoffentlich hat sich meine Schwester nicht das Bein gebrochen.**
c. **Ich hoffe, daß ich kein Fieber mehr habe.**
d. **Hoffentlich kann Wiebke morgen zur Schule gehen.**

a. Birgit's throat doesn't hurt anymore

b. your sister hasn't broken her leg

c. you don't have a fever anymore

d. Wiebke can go to school tomorrow

ERSTE STUFE

INQUIRING ABOUT SOME-ONE'S HEALTH AND RESPONDING

Wie fühlst du dich? *How do you feel?*
Wie geht es dir? *How are you?*
Ist dir nicht gut? *Are you not feeling well?*
Ist was mit dir? *Is something wrong?*
Was fehlt dir? *What's wrong with you?*
Ich fühle mich wohl! *I feel great!*
Es geht mir (nicht) gut! *I'm (not) doing well.*
Mir ist schlecht. *I'm feeling sick.*

Mir ist nicht gut. *I'm not doing well.*
Ach schade! *That's too bad.*
Gute Besserung! *Get well soon!*
Hoffentlich geht es dir bald besser! *I hope you'll get better soon.*

TALKING ABOUT HEALTH

Ich kann kaum schlucken. *I can hardly swallow.*
Ich habe Husten und Schnupfen. *I have a cough and stuffy nose.*
das Fieber *fever*
die Erkältung *cold*
die Halsschmerzen, (pl) *sore throat*

die Kopfschmerzen, (pl) *headache*
die Zahnschmerzen, (pl) *toothache*
die Ohrenschmerzen, (pl) *earache*
die Bauchschmerzen, (pl) *stomachache*
krank *sick*

WHAT TO DO WHEN YOU ARE SICK

zu Hause bleiben *to stay at home*
in die Drogerie gehen *to go to the drugstore*
in die Apotheke gehen *to go to the pharmacy*

ZWEITE STUFE

ASKING ABOUT AND EXPRESSING PAIN

Tut's weh? *Does it hurt?*
Au!, Aua! *Ouch!*
Es tut weh! *It hurts!*
Was tut dir weh? *What hurts?*
Tut dir ... weh? *Does your...hurt?*
... tut mir weh. *My...hurts.*
der Hals, ⸚e *throat*
der Kopf, ⸚e *head*
der Bauch, ⸚e *stomach*
die Schulter, -n *shoulder*
der Rücken, - *back*

die Hüfte, -n *hip*
das Bein, -e *leg*
der Arm, -e *arm*
der Fuß, ⸚e *foot*
der Knöchel, - *ankle*
das Knie, - *knee*
sich etwas brechen *to break something*
er/sie/es bricht sich *he/she/it breaks*
sich verstauchen *to sprain (something)*
sich verletzen *to injure (oneself)*

REFLEXIVE PRONOUNS, DATIVE CASE

See p. 144

VERBS THAT CAN BE BOTH REFLEXIVE AND NON-REFLEXIVE

(sich) waschen *to wash*
er/sie/es wäscht *he/she/it washes*
(sich) kämmen *to comb*
(sich) putzen *to clean*
sich die Zähne putzen *to brush one's teeth*

DRITTE STUFE

TALKING ABOUT HEALTH

nur leichte Speisen essen *to only eat light foods*
Ich bin so müde. *I am so tired.*
Ich habe Hunger. *I am hungry.*
der Arzt, ⸚e *doctor*
der Lichtschutzfaktor, -en *sun protection factor*
der Sonnenstich, -e *sunstroke*
die Haut *skin*

die Temperatur *temperature*
Fieber messen *to take one's temperature*
er/sie/es mißt *he/she measures*

EXPRESSING HOPE

Ich hoffe, (daß) ... *I hope that...*
hoffentlich ... *hopefully...*

OTHER USEFUL WORDS

die Sonnenmilch *sun tan oil*
die Sonnencreme *sun tan oil*
das Shampoo, -s *shampoo*
die Zahnpasta *toothpaste*
die Seife, -n *soap*
die Handcreme *hand cream*
süß *sweet*
fett *greasy*
parfümiert *perfumed*

[📼] **Location Opener**

Stuttgart, pages 154-157
Expanded Video Program, Videocassette 3

Using the Photograph,
pp. 154-155

Background Information

Stuttgart, the largest city in southwestern Germany, is also the capital of Baden-Württemberg (see Location Opener, Level 1, pp. 240-243). This panoramic view of the city shows modern buildings juxtaposed to wooded hills and vineyards. Economically and culturally, it is the focal point of southwestern Germany because it is home to more than 500 businesses. Numerous technical institutes, agricultural schools, and the Institute of Music and Art indicate the educational and cultural importance of the city as well.

Thinking Critically

Drawing Inferences Point out the tower at the top center of the photograph and ask students what it might be used for. (It is the **Fernsehturm,** *TV tower,* which was built in 1956 on the side of the mountain called **der Bopser.** It measures 217 meters (711 feet), including the antenna, and sends out TV signals for the **Süddeutscher Rundfunk.**)

Geography Connection

To get an idea of the size of the population of Stuttgart, ask students to compare it to a U.S. city of equal or similar size. (Examples: Cleveland, Ohio—573,000; Jacksonville, Florida—541,000)

Using the Almanac and Map,
p. 155

It is said that the depiction of the horse on the Stuttgart coat of arms emerged around the year 950 when Duke Ludolf of Swabia founded a studfarm in the area that is now Stuttgart. It was then referred to as **stuotgarte,** (could be translated as **Stuten-Garten** in modern German), and later became known as Stuttgart around 1250. Today, the emblem of Stuttgart is commonly referred to as **Stuttgarter Rößle.**

Terms in the Almanac

- **Neckar:** A tributary river of the **Rhein.** It originates in the Black Forest and ends at the city of Mannheim. It is 367 kilometers (223.5 miles) long.
- **Schloß Solitude:** This castle was built for Duke Carl Eugen by the French architect La Guépière as a place for reflection and solitude. It is built in the rococo style and is situated on the edge of a plateau west of the city.
- **Stiftskirche:** The **Evangelische Stiftskirche Heiliges Kreuz** was built between 1433 and 1460 following plans of the builder Aberlin Jörg. The structure emerged from the expansion of a pre-existing tower and basilica which dates back to 1230. Inside the church are the tombs of the counts of Württemberg. The tombs were sculpted by S. Schlör during the 17th century and are some of the most famous sculptures of that time.
- **Weißenhofsiedlung:** This group of housing complexes was built in 1927 by a group of 16 architects from five European countries under the direction of Mies van der Rohe. Each of the houses showcased new ideas and styles for the home. Ten of these homes were destroyed during World War II.
- **Staatsgalerie:** The **Staatsgalerie** was originally opened in 1843. It contains a large collection of European art from periods ranging from the Middle Ages to the present. They are works of old German masters as well as French, Dutch, Spanish, and Italian artists, including Hals, Rembrandt, Rubens, and Picasso.
- **Georg Wilhelm Friedrich Hegel:** He was one of the major figures in nineteenth-century philosophy, and his dialectical method influenced Marx and Engels. He taught in Heidelberg and Berlin.
- **Wilhelm Hauff:** Hauff, who was born and also died in Stuttgart, was a well-known writer and novelist who created an extensive collection of writing in his short life. He was well known for his fairy tales *Kalif Storch, Zwerg Nase, Der kleine Muck,* and *Das kalte Herz.* He also wrote a historical novel, *Lichtenstein.*

- **Robert Bosch:** Bosch was an electrical engineer who invented the high-tension electric ignition for the **Ottomotor** in 1902. He was the first to design and invent electrical equipment for automobiles.
- **Automobilindustrie:** Stuttgart is especially well known for its high-quality automobile production. It is often referred to as **die Stadt des guten Sterns,** not only because it has the highest per capita income of all German cities, but also because of the silver Mercedes star attached to the hood of every Mercedes manufactured. Daimler-Benz and Porsche produce their cars here, and both companies have museums where visitors can follow the history of early automobile engineering and see various original models of the cars manufactured by the respective companies.
- **Elektrotechnik:** IBM Germany in Stuttgart manufactures integrated circuits such as DRAM chips (dynamic random access memory) and logic chips for computers.
- **Verlage:** Publishing companies also make up a large percentage of Stuttgart's industry, with Klett being one of the best known.
- **Flädlesuppe:** Flädle is a sweet egg dough that is rolled out and cut into thin strips. The dough strips are then added to a pot of soup stock or bouillon.

Using the Map

- Have students locate and trace the path of the Neckar river on the map on p. 394. You may also want to use Map Transparency 1.
- Have students compare the location and industry of Stuttgart with that of Hamburg (see p. 79 of the *Pupil's Edition*). What are the differences? (Examples: different geographic location; Hamburg depends on its seaport for its industry; Stuttgart's geographic location makes it one of Germany's largest wine growing regions.)

Industrial Arts Connection

Find out from your industrial arts teacher what type of electrical components were used in Bosch's invention and how Bosch's invention improved the automobile. Try to get a diagram or illustration to share with students if possible.

Interpreting the Photo Essay, pp. 156-157

② In 1984 the **Staatsgalerie** was expanded, moved into a new building behind the **Staatstheater,** and became known also as the **Neue Staatsgalerie.**

③ This memorial to Friedrich von Schiller, the famous German writer and poet, was erected in 1839. The square is surrounded by significant buildings such as the **Stiftskirche** and the **Alte Kanzlei,** which dates back to the 16th century. Schiller wrote such plays as *Die Räuber* and *Don Carlos.*

④ The **Königstraße** is a pedestrian zone similar to the one in Munich that students saw in Level 1, p. 167 (Photo 5).

⑤ In 1746 Duke Carl Alexander and his son Carl Eugen commissioned the building of the **Neues Schloß** based on the plans of the Palace of Versailles. After a fire in 1944, the interior was completely remodeled and refurbished in a more contemporary style between 1958 and 1963.

⑥ Boris, Katrin, Roland, and Judith attend the same school and are good friends. All of them are interested in foreign languages, and — when we were filming — they were just about to go on vacations with their parents. Boris was on his way to see parts of the United States, and Katrin was going to Sweden, where her mother is from.

⑦ The concert hall houses three music halls; the **Beethovensaal** which seats 2,000 people, the **Mozartsaal** with a seating capacity of 750, and the **Silchersaal** with 350 seats. The **Konzerthaus** was built in 1955/56.

⑧ The city of Stuttgart is also often referred to as **Die Großstadt zwischen Wald und Reben.** Long before the city achieved a leading position in manufacturing goods, its economic foundation was based on wine-making.

KAPITEL 7, 8, 9

Komm mit nach

Stuttgart!

Stuttgart

Einwohner: 550 000

Flüsse: Neckar

Berühmte Gebäude: Schloß Solitude, Stiftskirche, Weißenhofsiedlung, Staatsgalerie

Bedeutende Stuttgarter: Georg Wilhelm Friedrich Hegel (1770-1831, Philosoph), Wilhelm Hauff (1802-27, Schriftsteller), Robert Bosch (1861-1942, Erfinder), Marcia Haydée (1937-, Choreographin)

Industrie: Automobilindustrie, Elektrotechnik, Maschinenbau, Textilindustrie, Verlage

Beliebte Gerichte: Spätzle, Maultaschen, Flädlesuppe

Foto ① Stuttgart, in einem Talkessel gelegen, ist von Obstgärten und Weinbergen umrahmt

Stuttgart

Stuttgart, die Hauptstadt des südwestdeutschen Bundeslandes Baden-Württemberg, hat viele Attraktionen. Institutionen wie die Staatsgalerie, die Württembergische Landesbibliothek, das Stuttgarter Ballett, sowie der Süddeutsche Rundfunk bezeugen die kulturelle Bedeutung dieser Stadt. Der Großraum Stuttgart ist außerdem ein Industriestandort ersten Ranges. Neben Weltfirmen in der Automobilbranche gibt es hier auch hunderte von hochspezialisierten kleinen Betrieben in den Bereichen Feinmechanik und Maschinenbau.

(2) **Vor der Staatsgalerie eine Bronzefigur von Henry Moore**

(4) **Die Königstraße, eine populäre Einkaufsstraße in der Stuttgarter Innenstadt**

(3) **Der Blumenmarkt auf dem Schillerplatz**

In den Kapiteln 7, 8, und 9 besuchen wir Stuttgart, die Großstadt zwischen „Wald und Reben". Dort treffen wir Boris, Katrin, Roland und Judith, die auf das Dillmann-Gymnasium gehen.

5 Schloßplatz mit dem Neuen Schloß

6 Boris, Katrin, Roland und Judith

7 Konzerthaus Stuttgarter Liederhalle

8 Weinberge am Neckar

Kapitel 7: Stadt oder Land?

Los geht's! pp. 160-162	Das Interview, *p. 160*			*Video Guide*
	FUNCTIONS	**GRAMMAR**	**CULTURE**	**RE-ENTRY**
Erste Stufe pp. 163-166	Expressing preference and giving a reason, *p. 165*	Comparative forms of adjectives, *p. 166*	**Landeskunde: Wo wohnst du lieber? Auf dem Land? In der Stadt?** *p. 167*	• Talking about where you live, *p. 164* (from **Kap. 3**, I) • Places to live, *p. 164* (from **Kap. 3**, I) • Talking about where something is located, *p. 164* (from **Kap. 9**, I) • Expressing preferences and favorites, *p. 165* (from **Kap. 10**, I) • **Weil**-clauses, *p. 165* (from **Kap. 8**, I) • Giving reasons, *p. 165* (from **Kap. 8**, I) • The verb **gefallen**, p. 166 (from **Kap. 3**, II)
Zweite Stufe pp. 168-171	Expressing wishes, *p. 168*	• Adjective endings following **ein**-words, *p. 170* • The verb **sich wünschen**, *p. 168*	Letter from a German pen pal, *p. 171*	• The **möchte**-forms, *p. 168* (from **Kap. 3**, I) • Reflexive dative verbs, *p. 168* (from **Kap. 6**, II) • Parts of a house, *p. 169* (from **Kap. 3**, I) • Talking about where you live, *p. 171* (from **Kap. 3**, I)
Dritte Stufe pp. 174-177	• Agreeing with reservations, *p. 175* • Justifying your answers, *p. 177*	Adjective endings of comparatives, *p. 176*		• Transportation vocabulary, *p. 174* (from **Kap. 1**, I) • Agreeing, *p. 175* (from **Kap. 2**, I) • Expressing opinions, *p. 175* (from **Kap. 2/9**, I) • Giving reasons, *p. 177* (from **Kap. 8**, I) • The verb **gefallen**, *p. 177* (from **Kap. 3**, II)
Zum Lesen pp. 172-173	**Und dein Traumhaus?** Reading Strategy: Using grammatical and lexical clues to derive meaning			
Review pp. 178-181	• **Anwendung,** *p. 178* • **Kann ich's wirklich?** *p. 180* • **Wortschatz,** *p. 181*			
Assessment Options	**Stufe Quizzes** • *Chapter Resources*, Book 3 **Erste Stufe**, Quiz 7-1 **Zweite Stufe**, Quiz 7-2 **Dritte Stufe**, Quiz 7-3 • *Assessment Items, Audiocassette* 8 A		**Kapitel 7 Chapter Test** • *Chapter Resources*, Book 3 • *Assessment Guide*, Speaking Test • *Assessment Items, Audiocassette* 8 A **Test Generator, Kapitel 7**	

Chapter Overview

Video Program **OR**
Expanded Video Program, Videocassette 3

Textbook Audiocassette 4 A

RESOURCES Print	**RESOURCES** Audiovisual

Textbook Audiocassette 4 A

Practice and Activity Book
Chapter Resources, Book 3
- Additional Listening Activities 7-1, 7-2 ....*Additional Listening Activities, Audiocassette* 10 A
- Student Response Forms
- Realia 7-1
- Situation Card 7-1
- Teaching Transparency Master 7-1 ....*Teaching Transparency* 7-1
- Quiz 7-1 ....*Assessment Items, Audiocassette* 8 A
Video Guide ....*Video Program/Expanded Video Program*, Videocassette 3

Textbook Audiocassette 4 A

Practice and Activity Book
Chapter Resources, Book 3
- Communicative Activity 7-1
- Additional Listening Activities 7-3, 7-4 ....*Additional Listening Activities, Audiocassette* 10 A
- Student Response Forms
- Realia 7-2
- Situation Card 7-2
- Quiz 7-2 ....*Assessment Items, Audiocassette* 8 A

Textbook Audiocassette 4 A

Practice and Activity Book
Chapter Resources, Book 3
- Communicative Activity 7-2
- Additional Listening Activities 7-5, 7-6 ....*Additional Listening Activities, Audiocassette* 10 A
- Student Response Forms
- Realia 7-3
- Situation Card 7-3
- Teaching Transparency Master 7-2 ....*Teaching Transparency* 7-2
- Quiz 7-3 ....*Assessment Items, Audiocassette* 8 A

Video Guide..*Video Program/Expanded Video Program*, Videocassette 3

Alternative Assessment
- Performance Assessment, *Teacher's Edition*
  - **Erste Stufe**, p. 157K
  - **Zweite Stufe**, p. 157M
  - **Dritte Stufe**, p. 157Q
- Portfolio Assessment
  - Written: **Anwendung**, Activity 6, *Pupil's Edition*, p. 179; *Assessment Guide*, p. 20
  - Oral: **Anwendung**, Activity 3, *Pupil's Edition*, p. 178; *Assessment Guide*, p. 20
- **Notizbuch**, *Pupil's Edition*, pp. 165, 171, 177; *Practice and Activity Book*, p. 151

Kapitel 7: Stadt oder Land?
Textbook Listening Activities Scripts

Erste Stufe
Activity 9, p. 165

SABINE Ich wohne seit zwei Jahren in Stuttgart, und es gefällt mir sehr gut hier. In Stuttgart ist immer was los! Konzerte, Theater, viele Discos! Man kann jeden Abend woanders hingehen. Vorher habe ich in Bietigheim gewohnt, 'ne typische Kleinstadt, viel zu ruhig, nicht viel los. Ich würde sogar sagen, es ist ziemlich langweilig dort ...

BORIS Also, ich seh' das nicht so. Im Gegenteil! Kleinstädte sind viel gemütlicher, nicht so hektisch wie die Großstadt. Je weiter weg von der Großstadt, desto besser! Wir wohnen schon seit ein paar Jahren in Schönaich, einem kleinen Dorf mitten auf dem Lande! Die Luft ist total frisch hier, es gibt eine tolle Landschaft, viele Wiesen und Wälder. Man kann eine Menge draußen unternehmen, wandern, Fahrrad fahren und so ...

SABINE Ja, aber was ist, wenn man mal dringend in die Stadt muß, ins Krankenhaus zum Beispiel? Das dauert ja ewig, bis man dort ist! Nein, also da wohne ich doch lieber direkt in der Großstadt. In Stuttgart gibt es einen schönen Stadtpark, viele Cafés und Restaurants. Und außerdem gibt es noch ein ganz großes Einkaufszentrum mit tollen Boutiquen, die immer supermodische Klamotten haben. Und nicht zu vergessen: Stuttgart hat ziemlich gute Verkehrsverbindungen in alle Richtungen mit Bussen, Straßenbahnen und der U-Bahn.

BORIS Das ist genau der Punkt, der mich an einer Großstadt so stört: zu viel Verkehr! Überall verstopfte Straßen und dreckige Luft! Deshalb sind wir auch von Esslingen weggezogen. Das ist zwar nicht direkt in der Stadt, aber die Vororte wachsen so schnell mit der Großstadt zusammen, da gibt es kaum einen Unterschied.

SABINE Also, ich würde lieber in einem Vorort wie Esslingen wohnen, als auf einem Dorf. In einem Vorort gibt es zwar kein großes Kulturangebot, aber man kann schnell in die Stadt rein. Andererseits hat man den Vorteil, in einer etwas ruhigeren Umgebung zu wohnen, wenn man nach einem langen Tag gestreßt nach Hause kommt.

BORIS Also, am liebsten mag ich Schönaich. Auf dem Land in der Natur zu leben, ist mir tausendmal wichtiger, als alles, was die Großstadt jemals zu bieten hat!

Answers to Activity 9

1. **Stuttgart (Großstadt):** immer was los, Konzerte, Theater, Discos, Stadtpark, Cafés, Restaurants, großes Einkaufszentrum, gute Verkehrsverbindungen; zu viel Verkehr, verstopfte Straßen, dreckige Luft
2. **Bietigheim (Kleinstadt):** gemütlich, nicht so hektisch; zu ruhig, nicht viel los, langweilig
3. **Esslingen (Vorort):** schnelle Verbindung in die Stadt, ruhige Wohngegend; wächst mit der Großstadt zusammen, kein großes Kulturangebot
4. **Schönaich (Dorf):** frische Luft, tolle Landschaft, wandern, Fahrrad fahren; Fahrt in die Stadt dauert zu lange in dringenden Fällen

Zweite Stufe
Activity 14, p. 169

RALF Ich bin der Ralf und wünsche mir, daß es keinen Krieg mehr auf der Welt gibt, keinen Hunger und keine Armut. Aber zuerst wünsche ich mir einen guten Schulabschluß, damit ich auf die Uni gehen kann, um Politik zu studieren.

CLAUDIA Ich heiße Claudia. Mein größter Wunsch ist ein eigenes Zimmer. Ich muß ein Zimmer mit meiner Schwester teilen, und das ist katastrophal! Überall läßt sie ihre Klamotten rumliegen, macht nie ihr Bett und benutzt andauernd meine Sachen. Ein eigenes Zimmer ganz für mich alleine, das ist mein Traum!

MATTHIAS Ja, also ich heiße Matthias. Ich wünsche mir mal einen ganz tollen Job, der mir in erster Linie Spaß macht und auch viel Geld einbringt. Am liebsten wär' ich Manager in einer Computer- oder Hightechfirma oder so. Auf jeden Fall was mit Zukunft!

ANNE Ich bin die Anne und wünsch' mir, daß wir in einer sauberen und natürlichen Umwelt leben könnten, wo die Luft nicht dreckig ist, das Wasser nicht verseucht ist und keine Chemikalien in den Nahrungsmitteln sind.

Answers to Activity 14
Ralf: keinen Krieg, keinen Hunger, keine Armut, einen guten Schulabschluß
Claudia: ein eigenes Zimmer
Matthias: einen tollen Job
Anne: eine saubere und natürliche Umwelt

Dritte Stufe
Activity 20, p. 174

MARKUS Also, wenn mein Bruder abends immer mit dem Motorrad nach Hause kommt, dann kann man ihn schon von weitem hören! Am lautesten ist es, wenn er direkt bis vor die Haustür fährt!

UTE Sag ihm doch, er soll das Motorrad schon ein paar Meter vor dem Haus ausmachen und es den Rest des Weges einfach nur rollen lassen. Dann würde man ihn gar nicht hören, wenn er kommt.

MARKUS Super! Ich schlage es ihm gleich heute abend vor! Aber noch schlimmer als laute Motorräder, finde ich eigentlich den Lärm von den Flugzeugen hier. Der Flughafen ist fast mitten in der Stadt! Dort, wo wir wohnen, fliegen die Flugzeuge schon ziemlich tief herunter, bevor sie landen. Und wenn ich nachmittags meine Hausaufgaben mache, stört mich der Lärm ganz besonders.

UTE Ja, das kann ich verstehen. Das würde mich auch nerven. Setz dir doch einen Kopfhörer auf mit deiner Lieblingsmusik. Dann hörst du den Flugzeuglärm bestimmt nicht mehr.

MARKUS Also, ich glaub', das ist keine gute Idee. Ich hör' am liebsten Heavy Metal. Aber dabei kann ich mich echt nicht auf meine Hausaufgaben konzentrieren.

UTE Na ja, das ist schade. Versuch's doch mal mit Mozart oder Bach!

MARKUS Niemals! So was Langweiliges! Lieber ertrage ich den Flugzeuglärm!

Answers to Activity 20
Motorradlärm; Flugzeuglärm
Motorrad abstellen und rollen lassen; Kopfhörer aufsetzen
Vorschlag ist super; Vorschlag ist keine gute Idee

SCRIPTS

*A*nwendung,
Activity 1, p. 178

OLAF Ich wohne lieber mitten in der Großstadt als auf dem Land. Ich gehe nämlich gern abends aus, zum Beispiel in ein Restaurant, ins Theater oder ins Kino. In einer Stadt ist garantiert immer was los.

SIGRID Also, ich wohne ganz gern hier in Unterlingen. Das ist ein kleines Nest, wo jeder jeden kennt. Es gibt ein paar Bauernhöfe hier, viele Tiere, eine schöne Landschaft, also viel Natur. Das gefällt mir.

HEIDI Also, ich brauch' beides: viel Action einerseits und meine Ruhe andererseits. Deswegen wohne ich am liebsten hier in Oberkassel, das ist ein Vorort von Düsseldorf. Wenn ich ausgehen will, dann bin ich schnell im Stadtzentrum. Und wenn ich mal ein gemütliches Wochenende zu Hause verbringen möchte, dann sitze ich auf meinem Balkon und höre nichts von dem Lärm in der Stadt.

FRED Also ich wohne in Bad Homburg, das ist eine nette Kleinstadt nicht weit von Frankfurt. Es gibt hier ein ziemlich gutes Kulturangebot und viele Restaurants, fast wie in einer Großstadt. Nur viel Verkehr haben wir nicht, und die Luft ist besser. Deswegen wohne ich lieber in Bad Homburg als in Frankfurt.

Answers to Activity 1

1. Olaf: Großstadt; geht gern abends aus
2. Sigrid: Dorf; ihr gefällt die Natur
3. Heidi: Vorort; braucht die Nähe zur Stadt, aber auch eine ruhige Umgebung
4. Fred: Kleinstadt; hat gutes Kulturangebot, wenig Verkehr, bessere Luft

Kapitel 7: Stadt oder Land?
Projects and Games

PROJECT

In this activity students will design, label, and describe an ideal place to live. This project could be called **Hier läßt es sich leben!** *You should begin this project after students have covered the vocabulary and functions introduced in the* **Dritte Stufe.** *This project can be done individually or in pairs.*

Materials Students may need travel magazines, tour brochures, city maps, real estate magazines, poster board, scissors, glue, markers, paper, and pens.

Suggested Sequence

1. Ask students to write down their initial ideas of what this dream area might look like, including where it is located (examples: city, village, mountain, island), what type of facilities are nearby or available (examples: stores, services), and what type of transportation people can use to get around.
2. Once students have finished this task, they should gather pictures, ads, photos from magazines, guides, maps, etc. to illustrate their place.
3. Students should design the area (example: **Kleinstadt**) and label each place once it has been pasted on the poster board. (Provide students with additional vocabulary or make dictionaries available.)
4. After students have completed the artistic part of the project (designing and labeling), they must write an essay describing their place and give it its own unique name. The essay should describe the area and point out its advantages, as well as specific reasons why it is so appealing to the student.
5. Students should present their project to the class upon completion.
6. Display the projects in the classroom.

Grading the Project

Suggested point distribution (total = 100 points)

Poster content and originality	30
Oral presentation	30
Written information (labels and essay)	40

 ## GAME

Gegenteile nennen

Playing this game will help your students review the vocabulary of **Vor- und Nachteile,** *as well as previously learned expressions.*

Procedure Divide your class into two groups, Team A and Team B. Give each student an index card on which you have written an adjective with its opposite in parentheses. The first student on Team A uses the adjective on his or her card in a sentence. Example: **schnell: Meine Eltern fahren einen schnellen Wagen.**
A player from Team B responds with the same sentence except that he or she must replace the adjective with its opposite. Example: **Meine Eltern fahren einen langsamen Wagen.**
If the student gives the correct opposite, his or her team receives a point; if he or she also uses the correct adjective ending, the team receives an additional point. Then Team B has its turn. If the opposing team does not provide the correct opposite, a member of the reader's team may restate the sentence. The game may end in one of two ways. Either you call time and each team tallies up its points to determine the winner, or you can wait until all the cards have been used.

Kapitel 7: Stadt oder Land?
Lesson Plans, pages 158-181

*U*sing the Chapter Opener, *pp. 158-159*

Motivating Activity

Ask students to describe where they live, including their city or town, their neighborhood, and their home.

Background Information

① **Das Neue Schloß** was built as a residence for **Herzog Carl Alexander** in the 18th century. The **Jubiläumsäule,** which stands in the middle of the **Schloßplatz,** was added in 1841. The palace was almost completely destroyed during World War II and rebuilt afterward. Today the palace houses two government offices and is used by the **Landesregierung** for official and social purposes.

Building on Previous Skills

Make an enlarged transparency or a class set of the city map of Stuttgart from p. 313 of Level 1. Ask students to imagine they are students at the university on **Keplerstraße.** Where would they like to have an apartment and why? (You may want to keep the maps for other activities in this chapter.)

Culture Note

② Since the cost of housing is extremely high in Germany, owning or living in a house such as the one pictured is a source of great pride to those living there. Germans often keep flowers and potted plants on window sills and balconies. For those who would like a garden but live in an apartment, **Schrebergärten** are a good alternative. People can lease a small plot of land, usually located at the edge of town, and use it for gardening purposes.

Thinking Critically

Comparing and Contrasting Ask students if their parents enjoy yard work, have many plants in their home, or if they know of anybody who does. Have students ask these people why they enjoy working with plants or in their yards.

Teaching Suggestion

③ Ask students to focus on the caption of this photo. Then ask them to work with a partner and make a list of three reasons for living in the city and three reasons for living in the country. Call on students to read what they came up with.

Thinking Critically

Drawing Inferences Based on what students learned about Stuttgart in the Location Opener, ask students to think of three reasons why somebody would like to live there.

Focusing on Outcomes

To get students to focus on the chapter objectives, ask them where they would like to live if they could choose any place in the United States and why. Then have students preview the learning outcomes listed on p. 159. **NOTE:** Each of these outcomes is modeled in the video and evaluated in **Kann ich's wirklich?** on p. 180.

*T*eaching Los geht's!

pp. 160-162

Resources for Los geht's!

- *Video Program* **OR**
  Expanded Video Program, Videocassette 3
- *Textbook Audiocassette* 4 A
- *Practice and Activity Book*

▶ **pages 160-161**

📼 Video Synopsis

In this segment of the video, Katrin stops two passers-by to interview them for her German class. She asks them if they enjoy living where they are. Later, Katrin meets her friend Judith at her house and talks about her own home. The student outcomes listed on p. 159 are modeled in the video: expressing preference and giving a reason, expressing wishes, agreeing with reservations, and justifying your answers.

Motivating Activity

Ask students what type of questions they would ask somebody to find out more about a) the area they live in, b) their home, and c) how they feel about living there. Have students compile a list of possible questions and write them on the board or on a transparency.

Thinking Critically

Analyzing After students have watched the video, ask them to look at the first frame of the **Foto-Roman**. What can students say about interview etiquette? How do Germans make polite inquiries?

Group Work

After students have watched the video segment a second time, divide students into groups of four. Ask each group member to assume the role of one of the characters and role-play the **Foto-Roman**.

▶ **page 162**

✥ For Individual Needs

1 Challenge After students have watched the video or listened to the audiocassette, use these eight questions to check for comprehension. Do this orally. If you feel some students are insecure about answering the questions, let them look at the text.

2 Visual Learners Make a chart on the board with two columns for the **Vorteile** and **Nachteile** of living in a **Großstadt** and two columns for the **Vorteile** and **Nachteile** of a **Kleinstadt**. Ask students to look for relevant phrases in the text and record them on the chart on the board. Review all expressions with the class.

Teaching Suggestions

4 Have students work in pairs to answer the questions. Upon completion, call on students to share their answers with the class.

4 This activity could be assigned for homework. Students could begin an outline in class and then complete the final draft at home.

Closure

Ask students to go back to the Stuttgart Location Opener on pp. 154-157. Have them list three advantages and three disadvantages of living in this city.

ERSTE STUFE

*T*eaching Erste Stufe,
pp. 163-166

Resources for Erste Stufe

Practice and Activity Book
Chapter Resources, Book 3
- Additional Listening Activities 7-1, 7-2
- Student Response Forms
- Realia 7-1
- Situation Card 7-1
- Teaching Transparency Master 7-1
- Quiz 7-1

Audiocassette Program
- *Textbook Audiocassette* 4 A
- *Additional Listening Activities, Audiocassette* 10 A
- *Assessment Items, Audiocassette* 8 A

Video Program or *Expanded Video Program*

▶ *page 163*

MOTIVATE

Teaching Suggestion

Ask students in German how long they have lived in their present home and ask them to tell one thing they like and one thing they dislike about their home. Survey students as to how often they have moved from one home to another.

TEACH

Teaching Suggestion

Ask several students to take turns reading the interview with Britta and Norbert aloud in class. Other students should jot down any words or expressions they do not recognize. Explain new vocabulary, giving German definitions or synonyms when possible.

Thinking Critically

Drawing Inferences Ask students to use the reading strategy of understanding the tone of a text that they learned in Chapter 5. Britta compares the homes in the former East to those in the West. Can students tell how she feels by looking at the adverbs and adjectives she uses?

Language Note

The adjective **piekfein** is a colloquial expression used to describe immaculate conditions. Britta's tone is somewhat defensive, but she also expresses hope for change by using the adverb **noch**.

Background Information

A **Gesellenprüfung**, which Norbert plans to take in another year, is an examination that follows two to three years of apprenticeship in a professional trade under the guidance of a **Meister**. The apprentice system requires all apprentices to undergo several years of practical on-the-job training, with additional vocational theory classes. Apprentices receive **Ausbildungsgeld,** a minimal salary, while undergoing their training.

Thinking Critically

Drawing Inferences After students have read the two interviews, ask them with which of the two German students they can best identify.

▶ *page 164*

❖ For Individual Needs

6 Visual Learners Outline the **Fragebogen** for this activity on a transparency or a large piece of construction paper and tape it on the wall or board. After students have completed the information on their own paper, ask several volunteers to complete the chart. Go over the **Fragebogen** with the class.

PRESENTATION: Wortschatz

To introduce the new vocabulary, use names of cities, towns, suburbs, and villages you think students will be familiar with. Once you feel students are comfortable with the new expressions, ask them to give you an example of **ein Dorf, eine Großstadt, eine Kleinstadt,** etc.

▶ *page 165*

PRESENTATION: So sagt man das!

To practice previously learned material as well as new expressions, ask students to express preferences in a different context, for example, **essen, trinken, spielen, lesen,** or **hören.** Have them use the expressions from the function box in short sentences.

Examples:

Ich finde die Musik von U2 besser als die Musik von den Beatles.

Mir gefallen Abenteuerromane besser als Liebesromane.

Geography Connection

9 Before students begin the listening activity, ask them to locate the four places on a map or in an atlas. (All four places are located in the state of Baden-Württemberg, ranging in size as follows: **Stuttgart, Esslingen, Bietigheim, Schönaich.**)

▶ *page 166*

PRESENTATION: Grammatik

A simple way to teach comparisons is by using concrete examples. Be prepared to bring several items of equal and unequal size and teach the comparatives by contrasting the items.

Example:

Schuhe: **kleiner als**
             länger als
             größer als
             so groß wie

To provide further practice, ask students to make comparisons using the same items. Encourage them to make comparisons using other objects in the classroom.

ⓉⓅⓇ Total Physical Response

To further practice the comparative forms of adjectives, give students commands such as

Kim, zeig auf Schuhe in der Klasse, die größer als deine sind!

Richard, finde einen Schüler, der Schuhe trägt, die kleiner als deine sind!

Kelli, gib Wendy eine Schultasche, die so groß wie deine ist!

Teaching Suggestions

11 After groups have completed the activity, call on each group to share with the rest of the class an advantage and a disadvantage. Write these down as students call them out. Continue discussing and contrasting the points listed on the board with the entire class.

12 To make this activity more realistic, ask students to review the interview in the **Foto-Roman** on pp. 160-161. Then have students do this activity in a similar way. Students may want to record their interviews on audio or videocassette.

Reteaching: Making comparisons

Tell students to imagine that their parents are planning a trip to Europe and want to visit either Hamburg or Stuttgart. Since they only have time to visit one of these cities, students must compare the two cities to help their parents decide which one they should visit.

▶ *page 167*

🔊 PRESENTATION: Landeskunde

Teacher Note

The **Landeskunde** interviews are recorded on audiocassette and videocassette.

Teaching Suggestion

Begin the **Landeskunde** page by having students do the prereading activity. Then have students listen to the audiocassette or watch the interviews on the video.

Building on Previous Skills

Ask students to look at the name of the place where each of the students is from. Can students recall in what general part of Germany each place is located and in what **Bundesland?**

ERSTE STUFE

Group Work

Divide the class into groups of three or four students. Have each group member read one of the interviews, then ask the group to work through Activities A1-A2. Have each group share its answers with the rest of the class.

Teaching Suggestion

A3 Do this activity together in class, using as much German as possible.

Thinking Critically

Drawing Inferences Based on what students know of these four locations, have them place each in a category (**Großstadt, Kleinstadt, Dorf**) assuming that a **Großstadt** has a population of at least 100,000, a **Kleinstadt** between 5,000 and 20,000 inhabitants, and a **Dorf** under 5,000. (Berlin: **Großstadt**, Hamburg: **Großstadt**, Wedel: **Kleinstadt**, Bietigheim: **Kleinstadt**)

Background Information

When visitors travel around Germany for the first time, they might be struck by the sight of a typical German city. Visitors will notice that only the very large cities have skyscrapers. Even in cities considered **Großstädte**, the tallest buildings are generally no more than about ten stories high.

Geography Connection

Have students use an atlas, almanac, or encyclopedia to find out the populations of the six largest cities in Germany. Then have students compare the list to cities of similar size in the United States. (1. Berlin: 3,400,000, 2. Hamburg: 1,600,000, 3. Munich: 1,200,000, 4. Cologne: 1,000,000, 5. Frankfurt a. M: 635,000, 6. Essen: 624,000)

Teacher Note

Mention to your students that the **Landeskunde** will also be included in Quiz 7-1 given at the end of the **Erste Stufe.**

CLOSE

♜ Game

Play the game **Gegenteile nennen.** See p. 157F for the procedure.

Focusing on Outcomes

Refer students back to the learning outcomes listed on p. 159. Students should recognize that they now know how to express preferences and give reasons.

ASSESS

• **Performance Assessment** Reuse the class set of the city map of Stuttgart from pp. 313 of Level 1. Ask students to look at the map again and choose one or two sites they would like to visit if they were in Stuttgart. They should also give a reason for their choices.

• Quiz 7-1, *Chapter Resources,* Book 3

Teaching Zweite Stufe, pp. 168-171

Resources for Zweite Stufe

Practice and Activity Book
Chapter Resources, Book 3
  • Communicative Activity 7-1
  • Additional Listening Activities 7-3, 7-4
  • Student Response Forms
  • Realia 7-2
  • Situation Card 7-2
  • Quiz 7-2
Audiocassette Program
  • *Textbook Audiocassette* 4 A
  • *Additional Listening Activities, Audiocassette* 10 A
  • *Assessment Items, Audiocassette* 8 A

▶ page 168

MOTIVATE

Teaching Suggestion

Ask students to think about their room at home. Is there anything they wish they could change to improve the room? Is there anything they would like to get for their room to make it perfect?

TEACH

Teaching Suggestion

13 Ask six students to read the six bubbles on this page. Then ask students to work with a partner to answer Questions 1 and 2. Students should then take turns telling a partner which students they can identify with and why.

PRESENTATION: So sagt man das!

Students should already be familiar with the **möchte**-forms in the context of saying what they would like to eat (see Chapter 9, Level 1). Ask students to practice the new expressions by telling the class what they would like for their next birthday. Ask students to look back at the **Foto-Roman** and find what Katrin wished for to improve her room. How were the expressions used in the context of the **Foto-Roman**?

Teaching Suggestion

Have students look back at the six speech bubbles at the beginning of this section and tell what each of the students wishes for.
Examples:
Sven wünscht sich einen guten Wagen, einen tollen Job ...
Britta wünscht sich und ihren Mitmenschen eine saubere Umwelt, ...

▶ page 169

PRESENTATION: Wortschatz

The items in this vocabulary box provide students with the vocabulary to discuss abstract concepts and ideas. After introducing the vocabulary, have students choose at least two or three non-material things they wish for most.

Teaching Suggestion

You may also introduce the following additional vocabulary for further practice:
ein Leben
  ohne Krankheit
  ohne Familienkonflikte
  ohne (finanzielle) Probleme.

For Individual Needs

15 A Slower Pace You may want to offer some specific suggestions to make this activity more concrete for students. (Examples: this school year, your family, the year you graduate, your first job)

▶ page 170

PRESENTATION: Grammatik

The students will better understand the reason for the different adjective endings if you first show them the change from definite article to indefinite article and adjective:
der Garten —> ein großer Garten
die Wohnung —> eine nette Wohnung
das Zimmer —> ein schönes Zimmer
For practice, ask students to repeat Activity 16, this time adding a second adjective to their wish.

▶ page 171

For Individual Needs

18 Tactile Learners Along with the letter students write describing where they live, ask them to draw a map of their neighborhood or area which indicates such places as parks, schools, stores, churches. In addition, students should draw the floor plan of their house or apartment, labeling each room.

Reteaching: Adjective endings following *ein*-words

Prepare a class set of pictures and ads from catalogs for this activity. (Examples: colorful clothes, stereo equipment, sports cars, jewelry) Give one photo or ad to each student and ask each **Was wünschst du dir zum Geburtstag?** In response, the student describes the picture or ad in as much detail as possible, using at least one adjective.
Example: **Ich wünsche mir ein fesches T-shirt.**
Occasionally you may repeat a statement by asking **Was hat sich Anne zum Geburtstag gewünscht?** and having other students report what was said.

ZWEITE STUFE

ZUM LESEN

 For Individual Needs

Challenge Ask all students to give a detailed response to the question: **Sag mal, wo wohnst du denn?** Students should write the longest descriptive sentence they can think of, such as the one below:

Ich wohne in einem netten Haus mit einem schönen Garten in einer ruhigen Straße in einem kleinen Dorf an einem schönen See, nicht weit von einer kleinen Kirche.

Call on a few individual students to read their sentences aloud.

Focusing on Outcomes

Refer students back to the learning outcomes listed on p. 159. Students should recognize that they now know how to express wishes.

ASSESS

- **Performance Assessment** Tell students to imagine that they will be granted three wishes. Ask them to tell you what their three wishes are.

- Quiz 7-2, *Chapter Resources,* Book 3

Teaching Zum Lesen,
pp. 172-173

Reading Strategy

The targeted strategy in this reading is using grammatical and lexical clues to derive meaning. Students should learn about this strategy before beginning Question 2.

PREREADING

Motivating Activity

Ask several students to tell the class where they would build their dream house if they were a millionaire and why.

Teacher Note

Activity 1 is a prereading activity.

READING
Teacher Notes

1 Students who answered Question B in the **Landeskunde** will have done some thinking about overcrowding in Germany and how it might affect personal living space; because of the scarcity of space in some areas, there is no room for many teenagers to have their own room.

1 While students may be able to generalize about a typical German teen's **Traumzimmer,** much of the material in this chapter indicates that it would certainly depend on the individual. Some students prize peace and quiet while others like the fast pace of city life. You might point particularly to the variety shown in **Wunschträume** in Activity 13 on p. 168 (**Wer wünscht sich was?**).

Teaching Suggestions

- Tell students that the format of a text clues the reader in on the intent of the writer and should influence how the reader approaches it. When you read a poem, for example, you need to be sensitive to the emotions the images evoke. But when taking a test, you need to read every sentence carefully for comprehension.
- Letting one or more volunteers read the poem aloud to the class while the others just listen may help bring out the quality of a child's song (regular rhyme and almost sing-song rhythm).
- Give students the following guidelines to help them read the poem:
Read the poem slowly two or three times. If possible, just listen while someone else reads it aloud. What visual impression does the pattern **X aus Y** *(something made of something)* invoke? Could you sketch the **Traumhaus?** How do the **zwei Türme** *(towers)* fit into your picture? Are they an expected element or do they shift the picture into a slightly different focus?

Thinking Critically

4 **Drawing Inferences** After students have read the poem, ask them who the author of this poem might be and how old he or she might be. Then ask students on what evidence they based their guesses.

For Individual Needs

4 Tactile Learners Ask students to use the images created by the author to draw a picture of this **Traumhaus.**

Cooperative Learning

Divide students into groups of three. Each student has a specific role: writer, discussion leader, or reporter. Set a time limit of at least 30 minutes for students to complete Activities 5-7. Ask each group to read the test and then answer each question to find out what **Wohntyp** they are. Encourage students to keep their discussion in the target language. Once students have added up their score and interpreted it using the **Lösung,** the reporter uses the information the writer recorded to share his or her group's test outcomes with the rest of the class.

Thinking Critically

Analyzing Ask students where they might find this type of a quiz.

Teaching Suggestion

Pair students up and ask them to write one new multiple-choice question that could be added to the quiz. Then have pairs share their questions with the class. Write all of the new questions on a transparency and have the class "take the test" by responding to each question orally.

POST-READING

Teacher Note

Activity 8 is a post-reading task that will show whether students can apply what they have learned.

Closure

Based on what students have learned in previous chapters and this reading selection, ask students to compare a typical American student's room to that of a German student. Make a list of comparisons on the board or butcher paper. Then discuss advantages and disadvantages of both rooms.

Answers to Activity 1
Answers will vary.

Answers to Activity 2
furniture; article, poem, self-test

Answers to Activity 3
approx. 88-132 square feet; answers will vary

Answers to Activity 4
furnishing a dream house; sweets

Answers to Activity 5
teenagers from Munich; what kind of person you are in regard to living conditions

Answers to Activity 6
sich vorstellen (reflexive verb) - *to imagine*
Himmelbett (noun) - *canopy bed*
Umzug (noun) - *move*
sich verhalten (reflexive verb) - *to behave*
verkaufen (verb) - *to sell*
wählen (verb) - *to choose*
schädlich (adverb) - *harmful*

Answers to Activity 7
Kuschelecke (noun) - *quiet corner*
giftfrei (adjective) - *non-toxic*
anbieten (verb) - *to offer*
vertreiben (verb) - *to drive away*
einschüchtern (verb) - *to intimidate*
Schmuse Typ (noun) - *cuddly type*
einrichten (verb) - *to furnish*

Teaching Dritte Stufe,
pp. 174-177

Resources for Dritte Stufe

Practice and Activity Book
Chapter Resources, Book 3
- Communicative Activity 7-2
- Additional Listening Activities 7-5, 7-6
- Student Response Forms
- Realia 7-3
- Situation Card 7-3
- Teaching Transparency Master 7-2
- Quiz 7-3

Audiocassette Program
- *Textbook Audiocassette* 4 A
- *Additional Listening Activities, Audiocassette* 10 A
- *Assessment Items, Audiocassette* 8 A

▶ **page 174**

MOTIVATE

Building on Previous Skills

In Chapter 7, Level 1, students were introduced to expressions concerning the environment. Ask students what they do to help protect the environment. (Examples: **Müll sortieren, radfahren anstatt Auto fahren**) Go around the classroom to hear each student's response.

TEACH

PRESENTATION: Wortschatz

Use realia such as pictures from magazines or newspapers to teach various modes of transportation, including new as well as previously learned vocabulary. Ask students if they can think of other sources of undesirable noise. (Examples: **Straßenbau, Heavy-Metal-Musik, Sirenen, Feuerwerk**) If students can't think of a particular word, encourage them to describe it in German.

For Individual Needs

Challenge After students are familiar with the three sentences in the **Wortschatz** box, including the **man**-construction and **wenn**-clauses, have them manipulate the vocabulary in the following ways:
- Change the last three picture captions into the same pattern.
  Example: **Man vermeidet Lärm, wenn man langsam fährt.**
- Make up other sentences using **man** and **wenn**-clauses.
  Example: **Man produziert Lärm, wenn man den Rasen mäht.**

Thinking Critically

20 Drawing Inferences As an advance organizer to the activity, write the opposites **laut** and **leise** on the board. Ask students to think of words and phrases that they associate with each of these adjectives.

▶ **page 175**

Teaching Suggestion

21 After students have read the selection **Der Lärm wird größer!**, ask them to find the various modes of transportation that were mentioned. Make a list. Ask students if they can think of synonyms for the following words from the reading: **Bevölkerung, Personenkraftwagen, Kraftfahrer, zuschlagen,** and **Lärm machen**. Ask students to work with a partner to answer Questions 1-3.

For Individual Needs

21 A Slower Pace Help students understand the reading selection by giving them German synonyms and definitions for difficult or unknown words and phrases.
Examples:
Der Lärm nimmt zu. —> Der Lärm wird immer größer.
Lärmminderung —> Lärmreduzierung

Thinking Critically

Drawing Inferences Ask students if they can think of places where road signs encourage noise reduction. (Examples: hospitals or senior citizen homes)

Community Link

Ask students to contact the local government to ask if the area has a problem with noise pollution and, if so, what measures have been taken so far to decrease or reduce the noise. Have students report to the class what they have learned.

PRESENTATION: So sagt man das!

To help students become familiar with the new ways to express reservation, ask them to react to what you say. Repeat the same statement several times in order to get several different responses.

Examples:

Es ist ideal, in einem Vorort zu wohnen.

• **Ja schon, aber der Verkehr ist furchtbar.**
• **Ja, aber es ist so weit in die Stadt.**
• **Da stimme ich dir zu, aber es ist auch sehr teuer.**

Remind students of other phrases they have learned that could be used to agree with reservations.

Examples:

Das finde ich auch, aber...
Ja, ich glaube aber, daß...

To allow students to practice the expressions, ask them to work with a partner discussing such topics as the latest trends in music, clothing, movies, books, and cars.

Examples:

— **Findest du Rock nicht besser als Country-musik?**
— **Ja schon, aber Rock geht mir manchmal auf die Nerven!**

▶ *page 176*

PRESENTATION: Grammatik

Review the adjective endings of all genders and cases the students have learned. Then have them list all the adjectives they know that could be applied to cars.

Examples: | sportlich | schön | ruhig |
| teuer | neu | bequem |
| sicher | schnell | flott |

Students then go through the list, using the adjectives in the comparative form (where appropriate) to talk about the topic **Auto.**

For Additional Practice

23 Ask students to express other advantages of living in a city, using comparative forms. This activity will help students recycle previously learned vocabulary such as places around town and other adjectives.

▶ *page 177*

PRESENTATION: So sagt man das!

After presenting the questions and responses in this function box, have students refer to the Stuttgart Location Opener on pp. 154-157 to find some other reasons why people might like to live in Stuttgart. Students should express these reasons with a statement containing **halt** or **eben.**

Family Link

Have students interview members of their family about all the places they have lived. Students should ask the relative being interviewed to give a detailed description of the different places he or she has lived, as well as the advantages and disadvantages of each location.

DRITTE STUFE

REVIEW

Reteaching: Adjective Endings of Comparatives

Ask students to imagine that they had a terrible experience on their last vacation. Prepare a chart like the one below and have students say how their next vacation is going to be better than the last one, using the suggested phrases.

In	unseren	nächsten Ferien	werden wir	gutes Wetter haben
	meinen	nächsten Urlaub	werde ich	bequeme Betten haben
	unserem			Museen besuchen
	meinem			viel Geld ausgeben
				kleine Pensionen besuchen
				ein schnelles Auto mieten

Ask students to use the fragments to create as many sentences as possible.

CLOSE

Focusing on Outcomes

Refer students back to the learning outcomes listed on p. 159. Students should recognize that they now know how to agree with reservations and justify their answers.

ASSESS

• **Performance Assessment** On the day you plan to do this activity, hand each student a blank family tree and give students a few minutes to fill it out. Then have students describe their family in terms of who is older and younger.
Example:
Meine Mutter hat eine jüngere Schwester, die Tante Barbara.

• Quiz 7-3, *Chapter Resources,* Book 3

*U*sing Anwendung, *pp. 178-179*

Video Wrap-up

At this time, you might want to use the *Video Program* or the *Expanded Video Program,* Videocassette 3 for additional review and enrichment. See *Video Guide* for suggestions regarding:
• **Das Interview**
(Dramatic episode)
• **Landeskunde**
Interviews
• **Videoclips**
(Authentic footage—*Expanded Video Program* only)

For Individual Needs

1 A Slower Pace Tell students that they will hear the tape twice. As they listen the first time, they should listen only for the information answering the question **wo.** As they listen the second time, students should listen for information answering the question **warum.**

For Additional Practice

2 If you feel that students need more practice using these functions, give each pair of students photos from home furnishing magazines or catalogs and let them contrast the pictures. (Examples: one teen bedroom vs. another; a typical German teen room vs. an American teen bedroom)

Portfolio Assessment

3 You might want to suggest this activity as an oral portfolio item for your students. See *Assessment Guide,* p. 20.

History Connection

4 Have students assume the persona of a well-known figure from the past. Ask students to imagine how that person would answer the same questions. You may have to replace the word **Auto** with **Fortbewegungsmittel** to fit the time period.

📁 Portfolio Assessment

6 You might want to suggest this activity as a written portfolio item for your students. See *Assessment Guide*, p. 20.

𝒦ann ich's wirklich?
p. 180

This page helps students prepare for the test. It is a brief checklist of the major points covered in the chapter. The students should be reminded that it is only a checklist and not necessarily everything that will appear on the test.

𝒰sing Wortschatz,
p. 181

Teaching Suggestion

To practice talking about where you live, give students an example, such as New York, and ask them: **Was für eine Stadt ist New York?** They should respond with: **New York ist eine Großstadt.** Use locations in Germany, Austria, Switzerland, and Liechtenstein for this activity to increase geography skills.

◈ For Individual Needs

• **Tactile Learners** Provide students with a blank copy of a floor plan of a house including front and back yard and ask them to label all rooms and places you have numbered. Time this activity.

• **Visual Learners** Show pictures of all the modes of transportation students have studied so far. Ask students to name each, including the articles that accompany the nouns. Write each noun on the board or on a transparency. In addition, you may ask students to describe the vehicles in more detail in order to recycle descriptive adjectives and the use of adjectives following **ein**-words.

♜ Game

Play the game **Scavenger-Jagd** to review the places, phrases, and expressions in this chapter. The game, in which students test their knowledge of facts, vocabulary, and expressions learned in this chapter can be played individually or in pairs. You can adapt this game to any chapter or **Stufe** you plan to review.

Preparation Prepare a list of questions, incomplete statements, or words and phrases from the materials you plan to review. Make copies of this list for each student or pair of students.
Here are some suggestions for this chapter.
Welcher Fluß fließt durch Stuttgart?
Nenne einen berühmten deutschen Erfinder aus Stuttgart!
Welche zwei Autohersteller gibt es in Stuttgart?
Wie heißt die populäre Einkaufstraße in Stuttgart?
Was ist das Gegenteil von Kleinstadt?
Was ist das Gegenteil von Vorteil?
Was ist das Gegenteil von sauber?
Nenne drei Fortbewegungsmittel!
Give the signal to begin the **Scavenger-Jagd.** The first student or pair to complete the list correctly is the winner.

Teacher Note

Give the **Kapitel 7** Chapter Test, *Chapter Resources*, Book 3.

7
Stadt oder Land?

1 Eine Großstadt hat viele Vorteile. Da ist immer viel los.

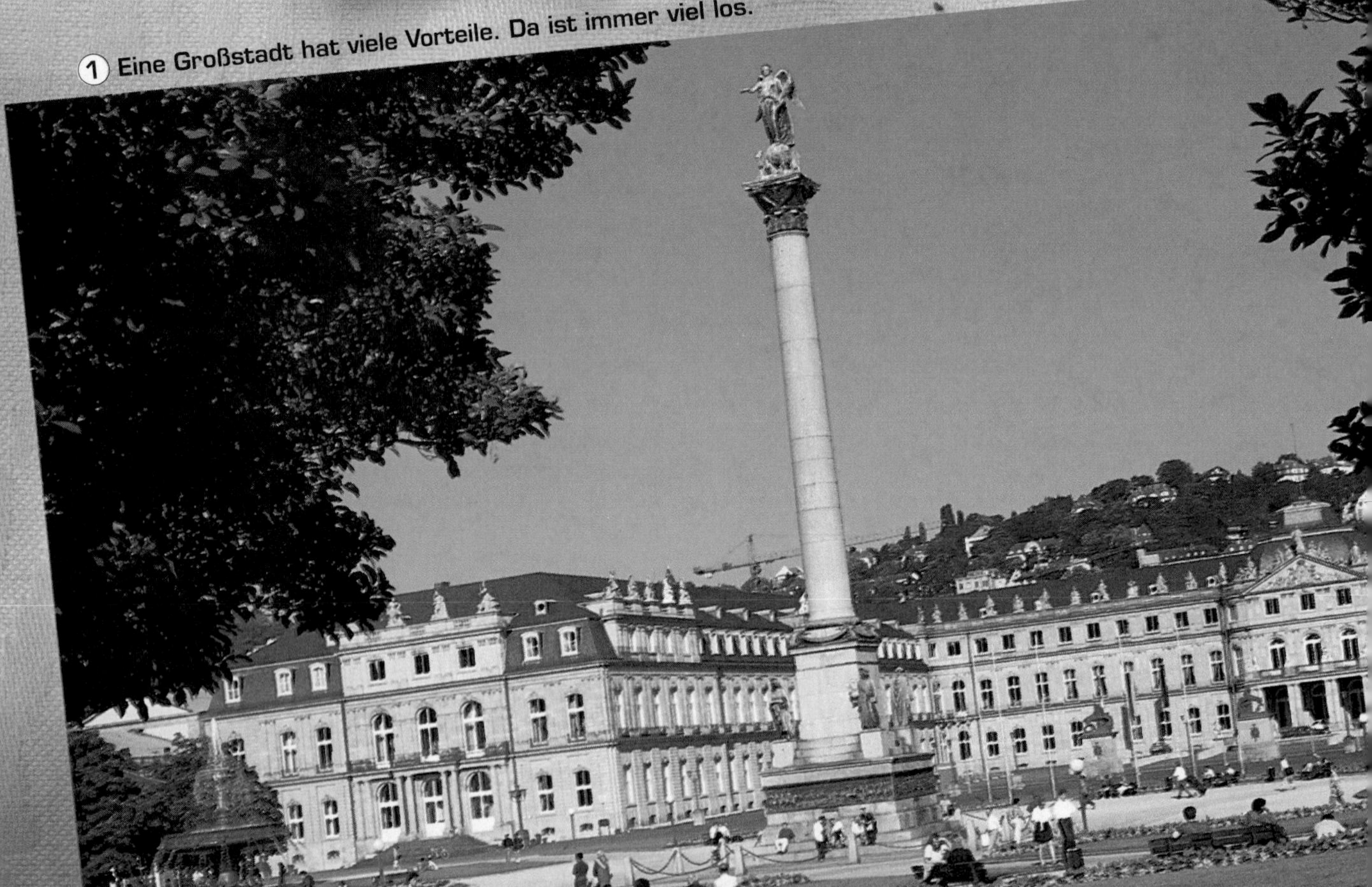

Students usually like the places where they have lived and grown up. However, each place may offer advantages as well as disadvantages. Students also have very specific dreams about their future. — In order to talk about that, there are several things that you should know how to say.

In this chapter you will learn

- to express preference and give a reason
- to express wishes
- to agree with reservations; to justify your answers

And you will

- listen to German students talk about where they live and what they like or dislike about it
- read about where students live and about their wishes and dreams for the future
- write about the advantages and disadvantages of living in your community
- find out what German students wish for the future

② Wir haben ein schönes Haus mit einem großen Garten.

③ Wohnst du lieber in der Stadt oder auf dem Land?

Los geht's!

Katrin   Frank   Bettina   Judith

Das Interview

Look at the photos that accompany the story.
What do you think is happening?

KATRIN Hallo! — Hallo, darf ich dich mal etwas fragen? Und dürfen wir dich filmen?

FRANK Ja, schon. Aber erst mal, worum geht's?

② Wir machen eine Umfrage für unsern Deutschunterricht. Ich möchte dich fragen, wo du wohnst, wohnst du gern dort und warum oder warum nicht?

KATRIN Aber erst mal, wie heißt du?

FRANK Ja, ich heiße Frank Härtle, und ich wohne hier in Stuttgart — wir, das ist meine Mutter und ich, meine Mutter ist geschieden. Wir haben eine nette Wohnung in der Innenstadt.

KATRIN Und du wohnst gern in der Stadt?

FRANK Ja, eigentlich schon. Alles ist eben in der Nähe, die Geschäfte und so ...

④ Ja, das sind schon Vorteile, wenn man in der Stadt wohnt. Aber leider gibt es auch Nachteile. Es sind oft zu viele Leute in der Stadt. Und der Verkehr ist größer, und damit ist die Luft auch schmutziger als in der Umgebung. Aber, ehrlich gesagt, ich möchte nicht fort von hier, nicht fort von Stuttgart!

KATRIN Wo wohnst du, und wie gefällt dir dein Wohnort?

BETTINA Ich heiße Bettina, und ich wohne in der Umgebung von Stuttgart, in Bietigheim. Also, ich möchte nicht in einer großen Stadt wie Stuttgart wohnen. Ich ziehe eine kleine Stadt wie Bietigheim vor. Das Leben ist hier ruhiger, wir haben weniger Verkehr, und die Luft ist hier besser als in einer großen Stadt.

BETTINA Tja, was wünsche ich mir noch? Was es hier in Bietigheim nicht gibt, gibt es in Stuttgart. Und Stuttgart ist mit der Bahn nur fünfundzwanzig Minuten entfernt.

KATRIN Vielen Dank, Bettina! Das war ein toller Bericht!

BETTINA Das freut mich. Viel Glück! Tschüs!

Bei Katrin zu Hause

Hallo! Übrigens, ich bin die Katrin. Und das ist die Judith, eine Klassenkameradin von mir.

Hallo, Oma, Opa! Meine Großeltern wohnen auch bei uns. Sie sind gern im Garten, immer aktiv! Ja, hier bin ich zu Hause. Ein schönes Haus, nicht? — Komm! Meine Eltern sind nicht da. Sie arbeiten.

Wie viele Zimmer habt ihr denn?

Ach ja, was haben wir? Eine Küche, ein großes Wohnzimmer, vier Schlafzimmer, ja ... ein Badezimmer und zwei Toiletten. — Aber komm! Ich zeig' dir mein Zimmer.

Toll! Ein eigenes Zimmer!

Ja, das ist schon prima! Aber ich wünsch' mir noch so viele Dinge: einen größeren Schreibtisch, einen bequemeren Sessel und einen größeren Schrank für meine vielen Klamotten.

Wirklich? Der ist doch groß genug!

1 Was passiert hier?

Verstehst du alles, was diese Leute sagen? Beantworte die Fragen!

1. Wer macht eine Umfrage?   1. Katrin
2. Wofür ist diese Umfrage?   2. für den Deutschunterricht
3. Wen hat Katrin interviewt?   3. Frank und Bettina
4. Woher ist Frank?   4. aus Stuttgart
5. Wo wohnt Bettina?   5. in Bietigheim
6. Was hast du über Katrins Familie gehört?   6. Großeltern wohnen im gleichen Haus; Eltern arbeiten
7. Und über Katrins Haus?
8. Was wünscht sich Katrin?   8. größeren Schreibtisch, bequemeren Sessel, größeren Schrank

7. großes Haus mit einer Küche, einem Wohnzimmer, vier Schlafzimmern, einem Badezimmer und zwei Toiletten

2 Genauer lesen

Lies den Text noch einmal und beantworte diese Fragen!

1. Frank wohnt gern in Stuttgart. — Welche Vorteile hat Stuttgart?   1. Alles ist in der Nähe, z.B. Geschäfte.
2. Er nennt auch drei Nachteile. Was sind diese?   2. zu viele Leute in der Stadt; viel Verkehr; schmutzigere Luft
3. Bettina zieht das Leben in einer Kleinstadt vor. Welche Vorteile nennt sie?   3. ruhigeres Leben; weniger Verkehr; bessere Luft
4. Was tut Bettina, wenn sie etwas braucht, was es in ihrer Stadt nicht gibt?   4. Sie fährt mit der Bahn nach Stuttgart.

3 Was ist richtig?

Ergänze die folgenden Aussagen mit der besten Antwort!

1. Frank wohnt __b__ .
   a. in Bietigheim   **b.** bei seiner Mutter   **c.** gern in einer Kleinstadt.
2. Es gibt in Stuttgart Nachteile wie __a__ .
   a. viel Verkehr   **b.** nicht genug Geschäfte   **c.** bessere Luft
3. Bettina fährt nach Stuttgart __b__ .
   a. ..., wenn es viel Lärm in Bietigheim gibt   **b.** mit der Bahn   **c.** ..., weil es ruhiger ist
4. Katrin wünscht sich __a__ .
   a. einen größeren Schrank   **b.** immer mehr Klamotten   **c.** ihr eigenes Zimmer

4 Ein Interview

Beantworte die folgenden Fragen auf deutsch, bitte!

1. How does Katrin initiate her interview with Frank? What does she say? How does he respond?   1. Hallo! Darf ich dich mal etwas fragen? Und dürfen wir dich filmen? — Ja, schon.
2. What does Frank want to know first? What does he ask her?   2. Aber erst mal, worum geht's?
3. What does Katrin give as a reason for the interview?   3. Umfrage für den Deutschunterricht
4. What does Katrin say to Bettina at the close of the interview?   4. Vielen Dank! Das war ein toller Bericht!
5. Using your answers to these questions as a guide, write a "framework" for an interview that you will do later in this chapter.

5 Und du?

Das Leben in einer Großstadt hat Vorteile (*advantages*) und Nachteile (*disadvantages*), auch das Leben auf dem Land. Wohnst du in der Stadt oder auf dem Land? In einer Großstadt oder in einer Kleinstadt? Welche Vorteile und Nachteile hat dein Wohnort? Schreib sie auf!

Expressing preference and giving a reason

Wo wohnst du lieber?
In der Stadt oder auf dem Land?

Diese Frage haben wir zwei jungen **L**euten gestellt.
Lies, was sie gesagt haben!

Britta
17 Jahre

„Ich heiße Britta Wegener, bin 17 Jahre alt und gehe hier auf die Oberschule in Weißensee. Weißensee ist ein Stadtteil hier im Osten Berlins, also — ich meine auch im früheren Osten."

Wohnst du gern hier in Weißensee?

„Eigentlich schon, aber ... na ja, die Gegend sieht im Moment noch nicht sehr schön aus. Unsere Häuser sind alt, alles sieht halt noch ziemlich grau aus und ist nicht so piekfein wie im Westen."

Möchtest du lieber woanders wohnen?

„Nö. Berlin gefällt mir. Berlin ist eine internationale Stadt; hier ist eben immer was los! Mir gefällt zum Beispiel Berlin besser als Hamburg oder sogar München. Berlin hat so viele Seen und Kanäle. Wir können segeln und Kajak fahren, im Winter können wir sogar Ski laufen auf unserm Teufelsberg.[1] Und es gibt billige öffentliche Verkehrsmittel: U-Bahn, S-Bahn, Busse."

Norbert
17 Jahre

„Ich bin Norbert Seemüller, bin 17 Jahre und lerne Schreiner. Ich bin im zweiten Lehrjahr. Ich wohne auf dem Land außerhalb von Besigheim."

Wo wohnst du? Und bist du dort zufrieden?

„Ja, klar! Ich wohne bei meinen Eltern, und wir haben ein schönes Haus mit einem großen Garten. Ja, und ich habe meine Lehrstelle hier — ich muß noch ein Jahr lernen, bis ich meine Gesellenprüfung machen kann."

Du möchtest also nicht woanders wohnen, zum Beispiel in Stuttgart?

„Nein. Und warum denn? Ich hab' hier halt alles, was ich brauche: eine schöne Umgebung, viel mehr Platz als in der Stadt. Ja, was noch? Die Luft ist eben hier viel sauberer als in einer großen Stadt und der Verkehr geringer. Ja, ich bin hier schon sehr zufrieden."

---

1. The **Teufelsberg,** an artificial mountain in the Grunewald section of Berlin, was built after World War II from the rubble of the destroyed city. Now beautifully landscaped, it is the sight of many sports events, grass-skiing in the summer, and skiing and sledding in the winter.

6 Ein Fragebogen: Britta und Norbert

Nimm ein Blatt Papier zur Hand und mach deinen eigenen Fragebogen! Schreib auf, was du über Britta und Norbert gelesen hast!

1. **Nachname**   1. Wegener; Seemüller
2. **Alter**   2. 17; 17
3. **Wohnort**   3. Weißensee; außerhalb von Besigheim
4. **Beschreibung des Wohnorts**
5. **Vorteile des Wohnorts**
6. **Nachteile des Wohnorts**
   6. Die Gegend sieht nicht sehr schön aus.

	Britta	Norbert
Nachname		
Alter		

4. alte Häuser, alles sieht grau aus, nicht so piekfein; auf dem Land   5. international, immer was los, Seen u. Kanäle, billige Verkehrsmittel; schöne Umgebung, mehr Platz, sauberere Luft, geringerer Verkehr

7 Britta oder Norbert?

Such dir einen Partner! — Nimm deinen ausgefüllten Fragebogen zur Hand und sag deinem Partner, was du alles über Britta weißt! — Dann sagt dir dein Partner, was er über Norbert weiß. Stimmt das, was dein Partner sagt?

WORTSCHATZ

Wo wohnst du? Ich wohne ...

in einer Großstadt

in einem Dorf

in einer Kleinstadt

Und dann noch . . .

am Stadtrand
mitten in der Stadt
im Stadtzentrum
im Stadtteil (Degerloch)
im Kreis (Ludwigsburg)
in Ludwigsburg County

in einem Vorort
in den Bergen
an einem See
an einem Fluß

8 Wo wohnst du?

Erzähl deinen Mitschülern möglichst genau (*in as much detail as possible*), wo du wohnst! Gebrauche auch die Wörter rechts, die dir schon bekannt sind!

auf dem Land

in der Innenstadt

in der ...straße

in der Stadt

in (Chicago)

(nicht) weit von hier

am ...platz

in der Nähe von ...

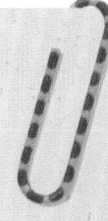

SO SAGT MAN DAS!

Expressing preference and giving a reason

You already know some ways to express preference and favorites:

> **Ich sehe lieber einen Actionfilm.**
> **Am liebsten lese ich Science-fiction.**
> **Mein Lieblingsstar ist Tom Cruise.**

Here are some other ways to express preference:

> **Mir gefällt Berlin besser als Hamburg.**
> **Ich finde die Innenstadt von Hamburg schöner.**
> **Ich ziehe eine kleine Stadt wie Bietigheim vor.**

You may also want to give a reason for your preference:

> **Ich wohne lieber in einem Dorf. Da ist die Luft besser.**
> **Wir ziehen die Stadt vor, weil da einfach mehr los ist.**

Which words or phrases help to make a comparison and show preference? What might the verb **vorziehen** mean? Where is the conjugated verb in a **weil**-clause?

WORTSCHATZ

————— Vorteile —————		————— Nachteile —————	
Land:	**Stadt:**	**Stadt:**	**Land:**
Wohnungen billiger	mehr los	mehr Menschen	weniger Geschäfte
Umgebung schöner	mehr zu tun	Wohnungen teurer	weniger los
weniger Verkehr	Geschäfte in der Nähe	mehr Verkehr	keine Theater, Museen
weniger Lärm	Theater, Museen,	Lärm größer	keine Oper, kein Ballett
Luft sauberer	Oper, Ballett	Luft schmutziger	keine U-Bahn oder
Leben ruhiger	öffentliche Verkehrsmittel		S-Bahn
	(Bus, U-Bahn)		

9 Hör gut zu! For answers, see listening script on TE Interleaf.

In der Radiosendung „Guten Morgen!" diskutieren zwei Zuhörer über das Thema: Stadt oder Land? Vorteile oder Nachteile. Schreib die Vorteile und Nachteile auf, die diese Leute für jeden dieser Orte erwähnen!

1. Stuttgart
2. Bietigheim
3. Eßlingen
4. Schönaich

10 Für mein Notizbuch

Schreib in dein Notizbuch

a. warum dir dein Wohnort gefällt!
b. warum dir dein Wohnort besser gefällt als dein Nachbarort!

1. Words such as *larger, cleaner,* and *more beautiful* are called comparatives. In English, most comparatives have the ending *-er.* In German, all comparatives end in **-er.**

Positive	Comparative
Die Umgebung ist schön.	**Die Umgebung hier ist aber schöner.**
Die Wohnungen sind billig.	**Die Wohnungen hier sind billiger.**

2. Most one-syllable adjectives with stem-vowels **a, o, u,** add an umlaut in the comparative:

alt **älter**   groß **größer**   jung **jünger**

3. As in English, some comparative forms are completely different from the positive forms.

gern **lieber**   gut **besser** · viel **mehr**

4. To compare two things that are equal, the words **so ... wie** are used:

Die Luft ist hier **so** schlecht **wie** in der Großstadt.

5. To compare two things that are not equal, the comparative form and the word **als** are used.

Die Luft ist hier **schlechter als** in der Großstadt.

11 Wo ist es schöner?

Setzt euch in Gruppen von vier oder fünf Personen zusammen! Ihr vergleicht euren Heimatort mit einem Nachbarort.

a. Macht zuerst zusammen eine Liste mit Vor- und Nachteilen von euerm Heimatort! Dann macht eine Liste mit Vor- und Nachteilen von dem Nachbarort! Schreibt dann alle Vor- und Nachteile auf kleine Karteikarten. Legt die Karten in vier Stapel (*piles*)!
b. Ein Partner in der Gruppe fragt dann einen anderen Schüler, welchen Ort er schöner findet. Dieser Schüler gibt eine Antwort und zieht (*draws*) eine Karte von einem der vier Stapel. Er sagt dann seinen Grund dafür.
c. Macht weiter, bis alle ihre Meinungen gesagt haben!

BEISPIEL   DU **Welche Stadt gefällt dir besser, Denver oder Colorado Springs?**
       PARTNER **Colorado Springs** (Zieh eine Karte!)
                   ... , weil es dort weniger Verkehr gibt.

12 Und du? Wo wohnst du lieber?

Am Anfang des Kapitels hast du einen Grundriß (*framework*) für ein Interview gemacht. Verwende ihn jetzt, um deine Partnerin zu interviewen. Frag sie, wo sie wohnt, wie es ihr dort gefällt und welche Vor- und Nachteile ihr Wohnort hat! Möchte sie lieber woanders wohnen? Wo und warum?

Wo wohnst du lieber? Auf dem Land? In der Stadt?

Where do teenagers in Germany like to live? In the big cities, in the country, or somewhere in between? We asked many students about their preferences and this is what some of them said.

Ilse, *Wedel*

„Ja, also, ich wohne gerne in Wedel, weil Wedel also 'ne nette Kleinstadt ist, es ist nicht allzu dreckig, es ist nicht dieser Streß mit dem vielen Verkehr, und … es ist einfach lustig. Man kann viel unternehmen, dafür, daß es so 'ne Kleinstadt ist, und … na ja, es ist einfach nett hier."

Hans, *Hamburg*

„Ja, Hamburg ist schön, hat viele grüne Flächen, aber ich würde eigentlich auch mal gerne auf dem Lande leben, für 'ne Weile auf jeden Fall, weil hier eben viel Verkehr ist, stickige Luft auch, eben typische Großstadt."

Iwan, *Bietigheim*

„Also, ich würde lieber in 'ner Kleinstadt wohnen, so wie hier in Bietigheim, weil hier es doch ruhiger ist, und es ist besser … ich meine besser für kleine Kinder, weil die besser hier aufwachsen können als in der Großstadt. In 'ner großen Stadt ist auch schlecht, daß die Luftverschmutzung dort groß ist. Aber andererseits, in der großen Stadt kann man natürlich alles bekommen, was in der kleinen Stadt nicht zu haben ist."

Heide, *Berlin*

„Ich leb' eigentlich gerne in Berlin, obwohl Berlin sowohl Nachteile als auch Vorteile hat. Die Nachteile sind halt, daß immer relativ schlechtes Wetter ist, und dann die Luft stickig ist und man Kopfschmerzen hat. Aber dann der Vorteil ist auch, daß in Berlin immer relativ viel los ist, so konzertmäßig und partymäßig, und von daher ganz schön ist, hier zu leben."

A. 1. small town; big city; Ilse and Iwan: **Kleinstadt**; Heide and Hans: **Großstadt**

A. 1. What do you think a **Kleinstadt** is? And a **Großstadt**? In which categories do the places where these students live belong?

2. Which advantages and disadvantages does each student mention? What seems to be the big disadvantage to living in a large city, according to most of these students? Did that surprise you? A. 2. various; air pollution caused by too much traffic; answers will vary

3. Think about where you live and places you've visited in the United States. What would you say are the advantages and disadvantages of living in a) cities, b) small towns, and c) the country? Are they similar to what these students said?

B. Germany's population density is 583 people per square mile compared to sixty-nine per square mile in the United States. How do you think Germany's population density might affect Germans' daily lives, their habits and their concerns? Write a short essay on this question. Be sure to include any facts or first-hand information from Germans which help to illustrate the effects of Germany's dense population.

Expressing wishes

Nicco, 15

„Ich wünsch' mir erst mal ein eigenes Zimmer mit neuen Möbeln, eine größere Stereoanlage und vor allem meinen eigenen Fernseher mit einem Video-Recorder."

Nadine, 16

„Ich möchte gern mal ein großes aber gemütliches Haus haben mit bequemen Möbeln. Dann wünsch' ich mir einen großen Garten mit vielen Blumen und Sträuchern und vielen Bäumen, und ein kleiner Pool wäre auch nicht schlecht."

Sven, 17

„Meine Wünsche? Ja, einen guten Wagen, einen tollen Job, später einmal eine nette Frau, gute Freunde, ja, ich wünsch' mir mal ein schönes Leben. Warum nicht?"

André, 16

„Was ich mir wünsche und was ich dringend brauche sind gute Noten in der Schule, damit ich später eine gute Ausbildung bekomme und einmal einen guten Job."

Jeanine, 16

„Mein großer Wunsch ist ein guter Schulabschluß, das heißt bei mir ein gutes Abitur, damit ich einen Platz an der Uni bekomme und studieren kann. Dann wünsch' ich mir einen netten Freundeskreis, ein schönes Familienleben und vor allem ein gutes und sicheres Einkommen."

Britta, 16

„Ich wünsche mir und meinen Mitmenschen vor allem eine saubere Umwelt und ein friedliches Leben, ohne Armut, ohne Hunger und ohne Krieg."

13 Wer wünscht sich was?

Lies, was sich diese Schüler wünschen und beantworte die Fragen!
1. Welche Schüler wünschen sich mehr materielle Dinge? Welche nicht?
2. Mit welchen Schülern kannst du dich identifizieren? Warum?
   1. Nicco, Nadine / Sven, André, Jeanine, Britta

Ein wenig *Grammatik*

Look again at the first interview above. What do you notice about the pronoun that follows the verb **wünschen**? Here, **wünschen** is used reflexively (**sich wünschen**), and the reflexive pronoun is always in the dative case.

Was wünschst du **dir**?
Ich wünsche **mir** einen großen Garten.

SO SAGT MAN DAS!

Expressing wishes

When asking someone about his or her wishes, you may ask:

> **Was möchtest du gern mal haben?**
> *or* **Was wünschst du dir mal?**

> **Und was wünscht ihr euch?**

And the answer may be:

> Ich möchte gern mal einen tollen Wagen!
> Ich wünsche mir mal eine schöne Wohnung!

> Wir wünschen uns ein eigenes Zimmer.

Name the noun phrases in the right-hand column. What are the genders of the three nouns? How do you know? To how many people is the third question addressed?

Für mein Traumhaus wünsch' ich mir

einen kleinen Pool

einen Garten mit Blumen,
Sträuchern und Bäumen

auch:

eine moderne Küche
ein nettes Wohnzimmer
ein gemütliches Eßzimmer
ein hübsches Schlafzimmer
ein eigenes Badezimmer
einen hellen Flur
zwei Toiletten
einen kühlen Keller
eine ruhige Terrasse

Ich wünsch' mir auch:

eine gute Ausbildung *a
good education*
einen tollen Job
a great job
ein friedliches Leben
a peaceful life
eine saubere Umwelt
a clean environment
ein sicheres Einkommen
a secure income
keine Armut
no poverty
keinen Hunger
no hunger
keinen Krieg
no war

Sag deinen Klassenkameraden, was du dir wünschst!

---

14 Hör gut zu! For answers, see listening script on TE Interleaf.

Hör zu, was sich diese Schüler wünschen! Wer wünscht sich was? Schreib zuerst die Namen auf, die du hörst! Dann schreib neben jeden Namen, was sich diese Person wünscht!

15 Was sind deine Wunschträume?

Such dir einen Partner! Er fragt dich nach deinen Wunschträumen, und du sagst ihm, was du dir wünschst. Tauscht dann die Rollen aus!

Was du dir wünschst:

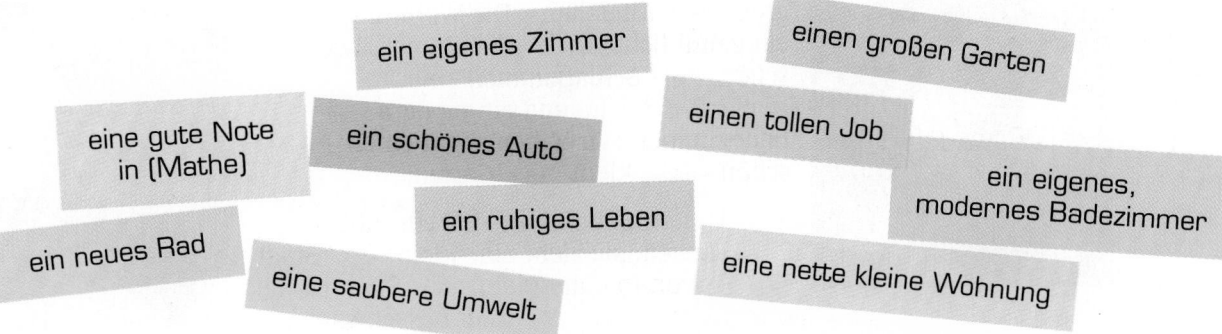

ein eigenes Zimmer

einen großen Garten

eine gute Note in (Mathe)

ein schönes Auto

einen tollen Job

ein eigenes, modernes Badezimmer

ein ruhiges Leben

ein neues Rad

eine saubere Umwelt

eine nette kleine Wohnung

Grammatik Adjective endings following **ein**-words

1. Adjectives following **ein**-words (**ein, kein,** and the possessives **mein, dein, sein, ihr,** etc.) have these endings:

Nominative	Das ist ein	groß**er**	Garten.	*masculine nouns*
Accusative	Ich wünsche mir einen	groß**en**	Garten.	
Nominative	Das ist eine	nett**e**	Wohnung.	*feminine nouns*
Accusative	Ich wünsche mir eine	nett**e**	Wohnung.	
Nominative	Das ist ein	schön**es**	Zimmer.	*neuter nouns*
Accusative	Ich wünsche mir ein	schön**es**	Zimmer.	
Nominative	Das sind keine	modern**en**	Möbel.	*plural nouns*
Accusative	Ich möchte keine	modern**en**	Möbel.	

2. Since **ein** has no plural form itself, the plural adjective ending is **e** in both the nominative and the accusative.

	Singular	Plural
Nominative	Das ist ein toll**er** Garten!	Das sind toll**e** Gärten!
Accusative	Ich habe eine neu**e** Lampe.	Ich habe zwei neu**e** Lampen.

3. In the dative case, the adjective endings are **-en** for nouns of all gender and for plural nouns.

	einem klein**en** Vorort	
Ich möchte mal in	einer groß**en** Stadt	wohnen.
	einem schön**en** Haus	
	groß**en** Städten	

4. When more than one adjective is used, both have the same ending.

Das ist aber ein schön**es**, klein**es** Haus, nicht?

16 Was wünschen sich diese Schüler?

Schreib, was sich diese Schüler wünschen und setz dabei die richtigen Endungen ein!

Ich habe alles, was ich brauche. Wir haben eine nett___e___ Wohnung in einem groß___en___ Mietshaus. Die Wohnung hat ein gemütlich___es___ Wohnzimmer, zwei schön___e___ Schlafzimmer, eine groß___e___ Küche und ein modern___es___ Badezimmer. Wir haben sogar einen schön___en___, klein___en___ Garten.

Bettina wünscht sich ein ruhig___es___ Leben; sie zieht eine klein___e___ Stadt vor. In einer klein___en___ Stadt ist die Luft besser, sagt sie.

17 Ein Briefpartner schreibt

Stell dir vor, dein Briefpartner aus Deutschland hat dir geschrieben! Lies das Ende seines Briefes! Dann beantworte die Fragen!

1. What is Jochen talking about in the first part of the letter?   1. sports
2. How does Jochen describe where he lives?   2. small suburb, nice house, big garden, modern kitchen, sunny living room, 3 big bedrooms
3. Does he have his own room?   3. yes
4. What is special about the cellar?   4. hobby-room

> immer Tennis spielen.
>   Nun, genug über Sport. Jetzt möchte ich deine Fragen beantworten. Also, wir wohnen in einem kleinen Vorort von Stuttgart, in Eßlingen. Dort haben wir ein schönes Haus mit einem großen Garten. Wir haben eine moderne Küche, ein sonniges Wohnzimmer und drei große Schlafzimmer. Mein Bruder und ich, wir haben jeder unser eigenes Schlafzimmer.
>   Ach ja, im Keller haben wir einen schönen Hobbyraum.
>   Schreib mal, wie Du wohnst!
>   Viele Grüße
>   Dein Jochen

18 Lieber Jochen!

Schreib deinem Briefpartner Jochen, wie du wohnst! Lies danach deinem Partner deinen Brief vor, und er tut das gleiche (*the same*)!

19 Für mein Notizbuch

Überleg dir (*think about*), was du dir wirklich einmal wünschst, und schreib deine Wünsche in dein Notizbuch!

Wo wohnst du?

Stadtrand
Kleinstadt
Vorort
Dorf
Großstadt

Was habt ihr?

Haus
Wohnung
Garten
Schlafzimmer
Wohnzimmer
Küche
Toilette
Bad
Terrasse
Garage

Und dein Traumhaus?

LESETRICK

Using grammatical and lexical clues to derive meaning. You can guess the meaning of many words and phrases by looking at cognates, the context, and words you know within compounds. You can also look for variations of root words, for example, the addition of prefixes (**bieten, verbieten**) or suffixes (**Person, persönlich**). And you can look at the part of speech (noun, verb, etc.) to help you guess the meaning.

For answers, see TE Interleaf.

Getting Started

1. Do you think having one's own room might be something German teenagers dream about? Considering what you have learned about the kinds of clothes German teens wear and their lifestyles in general, could you make any predictions about what a **Traumzimmer** would look like? Or would it depend on the individual?

2. Skim quickly over the readings. What theme do they all have in common? What are the different formats? How will you adjust your reading strategy to get the most out of each text?

A Closer Look

3. Read the paragraph about **Kinderzimmer.** Convert the size of the average child's room in Germany from square meters to square feet (1 square meter equals approximately 11 square feet). Do you think the average child's room in the United States

MEIN TRAUMHAUS IST AUS SCHOKOLADE

Kinderzimmer in deutschen Mietwohnungen sind zwischen 8 und 12 Quadratmeter groß. Zieht man die notwendigen Flächen für Bett, Schrank und Tisch ab, bleiben 1,20m x 1,80m für Spiel und Bewegung übrig. In Wohn- und Schlafzimmern, tagsüber meistens leer, dürfen nur wenige Kinder spielen.

Keine Grenzen für die Fantasie: Mit viel Eifer und Energie entstanden die Objekte der Kinder

Traumhaus

Mein Traumhaus ist aus Schokolade,
und im Schwimmbecken fließt Limonade.
Aus Marzipan sind die Gardinen,
und das Bett ist aus Rosinen.
Mein Sofa ist aus Kaubonbons,
und daran hängen Luftballons.
Die Treppe ist aus Joghurteis,
da lauf' ich rauf mit sehr viel Fleiß.
Zwei Türme, die sind auch noch dran,
worin man sehr gut zeichnen kann.

16 JUMA 1/92

TEST

(von Susi, Anette, Dani und Julie aus München. Alle Vier sind 14 Jahre alt.)

Was bist Du für ein Wohntyp?

1. Stell Dir vor, Du kannst Dein neues Bett selber aussuchen. Was wählst Du?
- a) Ein rosarotes Himmelbett in Herzform.
- b) Eine neonfarbene Couch.
- c) Du würdest am liebsten auf dem Fußboden schlafen, weil das alle tun.
- d) Dir ist das Design egal — Hauptsache bequem.

2. Wie würdest Du Dich bei einem Umzug verhalten?
- a) Der Umzug ist Dir egal. Hauptsache, Dein Teddybär kommt mit.
- b) Du würdest Deinen Hamster mit Punkfrisur mitnehmen. Was sonst!
- c) Du nimmst keine Möbel mit. Du kaufst neue, die gerade „in" sind.
- d) Du nimmst alles Brauchbare mit, was Dir zur Verfügung steht.

3. Du brauchst Geld und mußt etwas verkaufen.
Wovon trennst Du Dich als erstes?
- a) Von dem Drahtbett, das Dir ein Freund geschenkt hat.
- b) Von dem braunen Kleiderschrank, den Deine Eltern gekauft haben.
- c) Von Deiner Zahnbürste, weil Zähneputzen „uncool" ist.
- d) Von Deinem Computer, weil er schädlich für Dich ist.

4. Du bist umgezogen. Mit wem freundest Du Dich zuerst an?
- a) Mit Lisa, weil sie eine schöne Kuschelecke hat.
- b) Mit dem Punker von nebenan, weil Du seine Klamotten „cool" findest.
- c) Mit dem Typen, der den Schaukelstuhl (siehe Bild) entworfen hat, weil Du solche Sachen gut findest.
- d) Mit Hannelore, weil sie Dir giftfreie Farbe für Deine Wände geschenkt hat.

5. Du hast nach Deiner dritten Mahnung die Miete noch nicht gezahlt.
Nun klingelt der Vermieter. Wie verhältst Du Dich?
- a) Du versuchst, ihn mit echten Tränen einzuschüchtern.
- b) Du vertreibst ihn mit einem Heavy-Metal-Song.
- c) Du sagst: „Mann, ich bin Kick-Boxer. Das schwöre ich Dir!"
- d) Du bietest ihm Deinen selbstgebackenen Bio-Kuchen an.

Lösung

Du hast **a)** am meisten angekreuzt. Du bist ein verspielter Schmuse-Typ. Dein Zimmer würdest Du am liebsten nur mit Stofftieren einrichten. *Du träumst davon, in einem großen Stofftier zu leben.*

Du hast **b)** am meisten angekreuzt. Du liebst grelle Farben und Verrücktes. Sanfte Farben findest Du langweilig. *Bist Du vielleicht ein Punker?*

Du hast **c)** am meisten angekreuzt. Du magst moderne Möbel, die nicht unbedingt bequem sein müssen. *Man findet bei Dir das Nagelbett eines Fakirs — wenn es gerade modern ist.*

Du hast **d)** am meisten angekreuzt. Du bist der praktische Öko-Typ. Du faßt nichts an, was Du nicht vorher desinfiziert hast. Wer mit Dir reden will, muß sich mindestens fünfmal täglich waschen. *Frage: Übertreibst Du da nicht ein bißchen?*

is bigger or smaller? What about your own room?

4. Now read the poem slowly two times. Then listen as a classmate reads it aloud. What is it about? What terms does the writer use in his or her description? Could you sketch the **Traumhaus**?

5. Look at the self-test. Who wrote it, and what is it designed to reveal?

6. Read the first three questions of the test once. Then look back at the individual sentences and try to guess the meanings of the following words from the words on the right. First determine the part of speech, then look for clues to its meaning.

sich vorstellen	*to sell*
Himmelbett	*to choose*
Umzug	*to imagine*
sich verhalten	*harmful*
verkaufen	*move*
wählen	*to behave*
schädlich	*canopy bed*

7. Reread the questions and answer them for yourself. Follow the same procedure with questions four and five and the solutions. What type are you?

Kuschelecke	*non-toxic*
giftfrei	*to intimidate*
anbieten	*to offer*
vertreiben	*to drive away*
einschüchtern	*quiet corner*
Schmuse-Typ	*to furnish*
einrichten	*cuddly type*

8. Schreib jetzt nach dem Muster unten dein eigenes, fünfzeiliges Gedicht über dein Traumhaus!

a noun	*Apfel*
two adjectives	*rot, vergiftet*
three verbs	*essen, schmecken, geben*
an idea	*Ein schöner Apfel ist nicht immer gut.*
a noun	*Schein*

WORTSCHATZ

Was produziert Lärm?

LKWs (Lastkraftwagen)

Flugzeuge

Motorräder

Und dann noch . . .

PKWs (Personenkraft-
wagen)
Mofas und Mopeds
Busse
zuviel Verkehr
Motorboote

Man produziert auch Lärm, wenn man ...

zu schnell in die Kurven fährt

die Autotür oder den Kofferraumdeckel zuschlägt

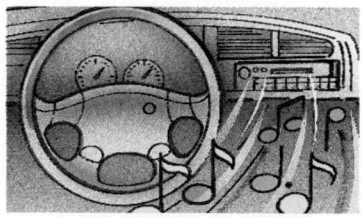

das Autoradio zu laut spielt

Sieh dir die Illustrationen an! Was kann man tun, um
Lärm zu vermeiden?

langsam fahren

den Motor abstellen

nicht hupen

20 Hör gut zu! For answers, see listening script on TE Interleaf.

Zwei Schüler, Markus und Ute, sprechen über den Lärm in ihrer Stadt. Markus nennt einige
Probleme, und Ute macht Vorschläge (*suggestions*), wie man das Problem lösen (*solve*)
kann. Wie reagiert Markus auf Utes Vorschläge? Hör dem Gespräch zweimal zu! Schreib
zuerst die Probleme auf, die Markus erwähnt! Dann schreib Utes Vorschläge auf und wie
Markus darauf reagiert!

Der Lärm wird größer!

Der Lärm in unseren größeren Städten nimmt zu.

Mehr als 50 Prozent der Bevölkerung fühlt sich durch Lärm belästigt. Verkehrslärm steht mit 70% an erster Stelle. Lastkraftwagen und Busse verursachen einen größeren Lärm als Personenkraftwagen. Unsere motorisierten Zweiräder, besonders die Leichtkrafträder und Motorräder, machen einen größeren Lärm als zum Beispiel Mofas und Mopeds. Als Kraftfahrer können Sie aber durch ein lärmbewußtes Verhalten zur Lärmminderung beitragen.

Hier sind einige Tips:

- Vermeiden Sie Kavalierstarts!
- Fahren Sie nicht zu schnell in Kurven!
- Schlagen Sie Ihre offene Autotür und den Kofferraumdeckel nicht zu!
- Drehen Sie Ihr Autoradio auf Normalstärke!
- Machen Sie keine unnötigen Fahrten, vor allem in Wohngebieten!
- Stellen Sie den Motor an Bahnübergängen ab!
- Beachten Sie strikt die Geschwindigkeitsbeschränkungen aus Lärmschutzgründen!

21 Was tun, um Lärm zu beseitigen?

Beantworte die folgenden Fragen!   Answers will vary.

1. Welcher Lärm belästigt die Bevölkerung am meisten?
2. Welche Fahrzeuge machen den größten Lärm? Welche machen weniger Lärm?
3. Bist du ein Lärmmuffel? — Was tust du selbst, um Verkehrslärm zu mindern? Schau dir die Tips an und nenne zwei Dinge, die du selbst tust!

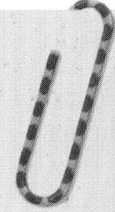

SO SAGT MAN DAS!

Agreeing with reservations

If someone wants to know about your preference, he or she might ask:

> **Findest du Boston schöner als New York?**
> **Ich finde die Innenstadt von Baltimore schöner. Du auch?**
> **Wohnst du auch lieber in der Stadt als auf dem Land?**
> **Das Leben auf dem Land ist todlangweilig, nicht wahr?**

In your answer, you may want to express reservations by saying:

> **Ja schon, aber ... (Boston hat im Winter mehr Schnee).**
> **Ja, aber ... (New York hat bessere Theater).**
> **Eigentlich schon, aber ... (in einer Großstadt gibt es schönere Museen).**
> **Ja, ich stimme dir zwar zu, aber ... (es ist viel gesünder).**

Which words or phrases show that the speaker has reservations?

22 Eigentlich schon, aber ...

Schreib drei Dinge auf einen Zettel, die du in deiner Heimatstadt schön findest. Deine Partnerin schreibt drei Nachteile auf. Sag ihr jetzt, was du über deine Heimatstadt denkst! Sie stimmt dir zwar zu, aber sie hat dazu auch etwas anderes zu sagen. — Tauscht dann die Rollen aus!

Grammatik Adjective endings of comparatives

Read the following pairs of sentences.

Adjectives before nouns	Comparatives before nouns
Das ist ein **groß** er Garten.	Aber dort ist ein viel **größer** er Garten!
Wir haben einen **groß** en Garten.	Schmitts haben einen **größer** en Garten.
Frank hat ein **klein** es Zimmer.	Sein Bruder hat ein **kleiner** es Zimmer.
Wir wohnen in einer **klein** en Stadt.	Webers wohnen in einer **kleiner** en Stadt!
Meiers haben keine **modern** en Möbel.	Sie wollen keine **moderner** en Möbel.

What do you notice about the endings of the comparative forms of adjectives?[1]

23 Was glaubt Peter?

Peter glaubt, in der Stadt ist alles besser. Schreib auf, was er sagt!

1. In der Stadt gibt es modern═ere═ Häuser!
2. Ihr wohnt bestimmt in einer bess═eren═ Gegend.
3. In der Stadt gibt es immer größ═ere═ Wohnungen.
4. Hier gibt es auch ein bess═eres═ Theater.
5. Es gibt auch einen schön═eren═ Tennisplatz als bei uns.

24 Ich stimme dir zwar zu, aber ... !

Such dir eine Partnerin! — Du sagst deiner Partnerin etwas über deine Wohnung. Deine Partnerin stimmt dir zuerst zu, aber dann sagt sie, daß bei ihr doch alles besser, schöner oder größer ist! Tauscht dann die Rollen aus!

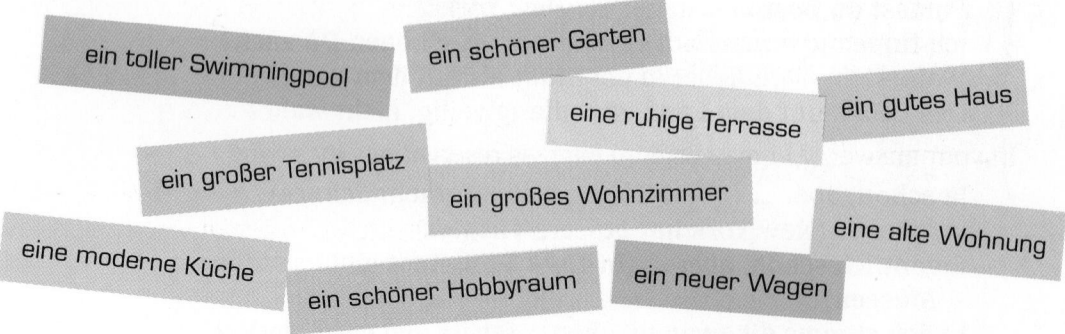

ein toller Swimmingpool
ein schöner Garten
eine ruhige Terrasse
ein gutes Haus
ein großer Tennisplatz
ein großes Wohnzimmer
eine alte Wohnung
eine moderne Küche
ein schöner Hobbyraum
ein neuer Wagen

1. The endings are the same for both comparative and positive adjectives.

25 Nach Gründen suchen

Lies noch einmal, was Britta und Norbert auf Seite 163 gesagt haben! Such beim Lesen die Gründe heraus, die die Wörter „eben" und „halt" enthalten! Welche Aufgabe, glaubst du, erfüllen diese beiden Wörter? emphatic confirmation of justification or explanation

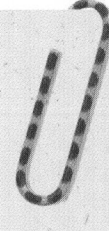

SO SAGT MAN DAS!
Justifying your answers

If someone asked you about your preferences, for example:
> **Warum gefällt es dir in Stuttgart besser als in Bietigheim?**

You might answer:
> Mir gefällt es in Stuttgart besser, weil da **halt** alles in der Nähe ist. Hier kann man **eben** schnell einmal ins Theater gehen.

Eben and **halt** are often used when giving a reason, justifying something, or giving an explanation.

26 Ein guter Grund?

Für jede Aussage auf der linken Seite gibt es einen guten Grund auf der rechten Seite. Für jeden Grund gebrauche entweder „eben" oder „halt".

1. Wir wohnen jetzt in einer kleinen Stadt in der Nähe von Stuttgart.   1. e
2. Wir wohnen jetzt in einer wirklich schönen Gegend.   2. d
3. Wir haben jetzt viel mehr Platz, und einen Garten. Die Großeltern können jetzt auch bei uns wohnen.   3. c
4. Ich hab' jetzt mein eigenes Zimmer.   4. a
5. Und einen kleinen Swimmingpool haben wir auch!   5. b

a. Da hab' ich alles, was ich brauche.
b. Da kann ich schnell mal schwimmen gehen.
c. Da können wir alle zusammen sein.
d. Aber da sind die Häuser und die Wohnungen teurer.
e. Die Luft ist da viel besser als in Stuttgart.

27 Bei uns ist alles besser, oder?

a. Bildet zuerst zwei Gruppen! Eure Aufgabe ist, etwas über eure Gegend zu berichten oder über eine Gegend, in der ihr gern wohnen möchtet. Welche Vor- und Nachteile bietet diese Gegend?
b. Dann trägt jemand aus der Gruppe den Bericht vor, den ihr gemeinsam erarbeitet habt. Die Mitglieder der anderen Gruppe dürfen sich dabei Notizen machen.
c. Sprecht eure Vorbehalte (*reservations*) aus!

28 Für mein Notizbuch

Frag zuerst deine Eltern (oder andere Verwandte oder Bekannte), ob sie gern oder nicht gern in deiner Gegend wohnen! Welche Vor- und Nachteile erwähnen sie? Schreib danach in dein Notizbuch, was sie gesagt haben!

ANWENDUNG

1 Ein paar Leute sagen, wo sie lieber wohnen und warum. Mach eine Tabelle wie diese und füll sie dann aus! For answers, see listening script on TE Interleaf.

Person	wo?	warum?
1		
2		

2 Vergleiche (*compare*) mit deinem Partner diese zwei Illustrationen. Erzählt einander alles, was ihr bemerkt!

BEISPIEL **Die Küche im Haus in der Stadt ist kleiner als die Küche im Haus auf dem Land.**

3 Zeichne dein Traumhaus! Zeichne zuerst das Haus auf ein großes Blatt Papier! Danach beschreibe deinem Partner das Haus! Dein Partner hört dir zu und zeichnet dein Traumhaus. Vergleicht dann die beiden Zeichnungen! Hat dein Partner alles richtig gehört? Dann erzählt dir dein Partner, wie sein Traumhaus aussieht, und du zeichnest sein Traumhaus auf ein Blatt Papier.

4 Was machst du in zehn Jahren? Was für eine Welt soll das sein? Du schreibst jetzt einen Bericht für dein Schuljahrbuch über dich selbst und die Welt in zehn Jahren. Auf was für einen Job hoffst du? Wo willst du wohnen? In was für einem Haus willst du wohnen? Was für ein Auto möchtest du haben? Was für eine Welt wünschst du dir? Schreib mindestens zehn Sätze!

5 Lies den Text unten und beantworte die folgenden Fragen!

1. Worüber berichtet der Text?   1. Schüler arbeiten in ihrem eigenen Garten.
2. Wo ist der Garten?   2. in der Schule
3. Was wächst im Garten?   3. Gemüse, Blumen, Kräuter, Obst
4. Wie finden die Schüler den Garten? Warum? Was sagen sie?
5. Was, meinst du, lernen die Schüler von der „Schule im Garten"?

4. Es macht ihnen Spaß, weil etwas Eigenes entsteht.
5. Sie lernen etwas Praktisches.

Schüler ziehen mit Spaten, Hacken, Heckenscheren und Schubkarren hinaus ins Freie, um an „ihrer" Oase zu arbeiten. Und wie die blüht und wächst! Es gibt Gemüse- und Blumenbeete sowie einen Kräutergarten. Die Schüler beliefern die Schulküche mit Zwiebeln, Karotten, Tomaten, Kartoffeln und Erdbeeren. Nicht nur der Garten, auch die Klassenzimmer werden immer grüner: Im Sommer gibt es dort jetzt frische Blumensträuße. Die jungen Hobbygärtner sind ganz begeistert. „Die Penne (Schule) macht viel mehr Spaß, weil etwas ganz Eigenes entsteht", meint Lizzy. „Klar kostet das Arbeit, aber dann siehst du etwas wachsen, kannst riechen, es anschauen." Am Ende kann man einiges sogar schmecken, essen und davon satt werden.

6 Die Schüler im Bericht haben einen Garten gepflanzt, um ihr Schulerlebnis zu verbessern (*improve*). Was kannst du tun, um deine Schule oder dein Schuler-lebnis zu verbessern? Such dir zwei Klassenkameraden! Ihr macht ein Poster von allem, was ihr wünscht, um die Schule zu verbessern. Auf der linken Seite schreibt die Verbesserungsvorschläge auf, und auf der rechten Seite schreibt Ideen, wie ihr diese Wünsche erfüllen könnt! Dann erzählt euren Klassenkame-raden etwas über eure Ideen!

7

Using props, role-play the following scene in front of the class.

You and three of your classmates are participants in a television talk-show. The topic of the day is "The best place in the world to live." One of you will play the role of the host and ask questions of the others, who will play the guests. Everyone in the class writes the name of a large city anywhere in the world on a slip of paper and puts it in a box. Each guest draws a city from the box. He or she must think of some reasons and justifications for why he or she thinks this city is the best place in the world to live. The host will ask specific questions about the guest's interests to try to find out more information about why each person thinks he or she lives in the best place in the world.

KANN ICH'S WIRKLICH?

Can you express preference and give a reason? (p. 165)

1 How would you say you prefer to live in the following places and give a reason for it?   Ich wohne lieber …

  a. in a small town   a. in einer Kleinstadt, weil …
  b. in a big city   b. in einer Großstadt, weil …
  c. in the country   c. auf dem Land, weil …
  d. in the mountains   d. in den Bergen, weil …
  e. by a river   e. an einem Fluß, weil …
  f. by a lake   f. an einem See, weil …

2 How would you ask a friend's opinion about different locations, using the following expressions?

  a. **lieber**   a. E.g.: Wo wohnst du lieber? In der Stadt oder auf dem Land?
  b. **gefallen**   b. E.g.: Wo gefällt es dir besser? In Bonn oder in Berlin?

Can you express your wishes, and ask others about their own? (p. 168)

3 How would you say you wish for the following things?   Ich wünsche mir, …

  a. a television and a VCR   a. einen Fernseher und einen Video-Recorder.
  b. a great job   b. einen guten Job.
  c. a secure income   c. ein sicheres Einkommen.
  d. a peaceful life   d. ein friedliches Leben.
  e. a clean environment   e. eine saubere Umwelt.
  f. no war   f. keinen Krieg.

4 How would you ask someone what he or she wishes for?
E.g.: Was wünschst du dir?

Can you agree with reservations? (p. 175)

5 How would you say to your friend that you agree that he or she does everything possible to avoid making excessive noise, but that you have the following reservations? He or she…

  a. drives too fast around curves   a. E.g.: Ja schon, aber du fährst zu schnell in die Kurven.
  b. slams the car door   b. E.g.: Ja, aber du schlägst deine Autotür zu.
  c. plays the car radio too loud   c. E.g.: Eigentlich schon, aber du spielst dein Autoradio zu laut.

Can you justify your answers, using halt and eben? (p. 177)

6 How would you now tell your friend he or she actually does make too much noise, and use the same arguments to justify your opinion?
Du machst zu viel Lärm, weil du halt/eben …
… zu schnell in die Kurven fährst.
… deine Autotür zuschlägst.
… dein Autoradio zu laut spielst.

ERSTE STUFE
EXPRESSING PREFERENCE

Mir gefällt ... besser als ...
  I like... better than...
vorziehen *(sep)* *to prefer*
Ich ziehe ... vor *I prefer...*
so ... wie *as... as*
(schlechter) als *(worse) than*
älter *older*
größer *bigger*
jünger *younger*

TALKING ABOUT WHERE YOU LIVE

in einer Großstadt *in a big city*

in einem Vorort *in a suburb*
der Vorort, -e *suburb*
in einer Kleinstadt *in a town*
in einem Dorf *in a village*
das Dorf, ̈er *village*
in den Bergen *in the mountains*
der Berg, -e *mountain*
an einem See *on a lake*
der See, -n *lake*
an einem Fluß *on a river*
der Fluß, Flüsse *river*

LIVING IN YOUR COMMUNITY

der Vorteil, -e *advantage*

der Nachteil, -e *disadvantage*
öffentliche Verkehrsmittel (pl)
  public transportation
die Wohnung, -en *apartment*
die Umgebung, -en *surrounding
  area*
der Verkehr *traffic*
der Lärm *noise*
die Luft *air*
das Leben *life*
sauber *clean*
schmutzig *dirty*
ruhig *calm*

ZWEITE STUFE
AROUND THE HOUSE

das Haus, ̈er *house*
der Flur, -e *hallway*
das Wohnzimmer, - *living room*
das Eßzimmer, - *dining room*
die Küche, -n *kitchen*
das Schlafzimmer, - *bedroom*
das Badezimmer, - *bathroom*
die Toilette, -n *bathroom, toilet*
der Keller, - *cellar*
die Terrasse, -n *terrace, porch*
der Garten, ̈ *garden, yard*

der Pool, -s *pool*
der Strauch, ̈er *bush*
der Baum, ̈e *tree*

EXPRESSING WISHES

sich wünschen *to wish*
Was wünschst du dir (mal)?
  What would you wish for?
Ich wünsche mir ... *I wish
  for...*
die Ausbildung, -en *education*
der Job, -s *job*

das Einkommen *income*
die Umwelt *environment*
die Armut *poverty*
der Krieg, -e *war*

USEFUL WORDS FOR DESCRIBING THINGS

friedlich *peaceful*
gemütlich *comfortable, cozy*
hell *bright*
sicher *secure*
eigen *(one's) own*

DRITTE STUFE
TALKING ABOUT NOISE POLLUTION

der Lärm *noise*
Was produziert Lärm? *What
  produces noise?*
der Lastkraftwagen (LKW), -
  truck
das Flugzeug, -e *airplane*
das Motorrad, ̈er *motorcycle*
langsam *slow, slowly*
abstellen *(sep)* *to switch off*
der Motor, -en *motor*
Stellen Sie den Motor ab! *Turn
  your engine off!*
hupen *to honk the horn*

Du fährst zu schnell in die
  Kurve! *You're taking the
  curve too fast!*
Er schlägt die Autotür (den Kofferraumdeckel) zu! *He's
  slamming the car door (the
  trunk)!*
He, Sie da! Sie spielen das Autoradio zu laut! *Hey you
  there! You're playing your radio
  too loud!*

AGREEING, BUT WITH RESERVATIONS

Ja schon, aber ... *Well yes,
  but...*

Eigentlich schon, aber ...
  I suppose so, but...
Ja, ich stimme dir zwar zu,
  aber ... *Yes, I do agree with
  you, but...*

GIVING REASONS OR JUSTIFICATIONS

halt: Die Kleinstadt gefällt mir
  gut, weil es da halt ruhiger
  ist. *I like a small town because it's just quieter there.*
eben: Man kann eben den Groß-
  stadtlärm vermeiden. *You
  can really avoid big city noise.*

Kapitel 8: Mode? Ja oder nein?

CHAPTER OVERVIEW

Los geht's! pp. 184-186	Ein starkes Outfit, *p. 184*			*Video Guide*
	FUNCTIONS	**GRAMMAR**	**CULTURE**	**RE-ENTRY**
Erste Stufe pp. 188-191	Describing clothes, *p. 189*	Adjectives following **der** and **dieser**-words, *p. 189*	• **Landeskunde: Was trägst du am liebsten?** *p. 187* • **Ein wenig Landeskunde:** Clothes typically worn by German-speaking youths, *p.191*	• Clothing vocabulary, *pp. 188-189* (from **Kap. 5,** I) • Expressing wishes when buying thing *p. 189* (from **Kap. 5,** I) • Commenting on clothes, *p. 190* (from **Kap. 5,** I) • Talking about what you bought, *p. 19* (from **Kap. 8,** I) • Talking about prices, *p. 191* (from **Kap. 4,** I)
Zweite Stufe pp. 192-195	• Expressing interest, disinterest, and indifference, *p. 193* • Making and accepting compliments, *p. 194*	• The verb **sich interessieren,** *p. 194* • The verb **tragen,** *p. 194* • Further uses of the dative case, *p. 195*	Interviews with German students about fashion, *p. 192*	• Accusative reflexive verbs, *p. 194* (from **Kap. 4,** I) • The preposition **für** + accusative, *p. 194* (from **Kap. 7,** I) • Giving reasons, *p. 194* (from **Kap. 8,** I) • Complimenting someone, *p. 194* (from **Kap. 5,** I) • Dative pronouns, *p. 195* (from **Kap. 3,** II) • Commenting on clothing, *p. 195* (from **Kap. 5,** I)
Dritte Stufe pp. 196-199	Persuading and dissuading, *p. 198*	• The verb **kaufen** with dative reflexive pronouns, *p. 198* • The conjunction **wenn,** *p. 199*	Excerpt from a clothing catalog, *p. 196*	• Vocabulary: clothing items and fabrics *pp. 196, 197* (from **Kap. 5,** I) • The **möchte**-forms, *pp. 197, 198* (from **Kap. 3,** I) • Giving reasons, *p. 197* (from **Kap. 8,** I) • Expressing likes with **gefallen,** *p. 19* (from **Kap. 3,** II) • Expressing opinions, *p. 198* (from **Kap. 2,** I) • Dative reflexive verbs, *p. 198* (from **Kap. 6,** II) • The **du**-commands, *p. 198* (from **Kap. 8,** I) • Word order with subordinate conjunctions, *p. 199* (from **Kap. 8/9,** I)

Zum Lesen pp. 200-201	Was bedeutet „reich und schön sein"? Reading Strategy: Understanding relationships between and within sentences

Review pp. 202-205	• **Anwendung,** *p. 202* • **Kann ich's wirklich?** *p. 204* • **Wortschatz,** *p. 205*

Assessment Options	**Stufe Quizzes**
	• *Chapter Resources,* Book 3
	  Erste Stufe, Quiz 8-1
	  Zweite Stufe, Quiz 8-2
	  Dritte Stufe, Quiz 8-3
	• *Assessment Items, Audiocassette* 8 A
		Kapitel 8 Chapter Test
		• *Chapter Resources,* Book 3
		• *Assessment Guide,* Speaking Test
		• *Assessment Items, Audiocassette* 8 *F*
		
		Test Generator, Kapitel 8

Chapter Overview

Video Program **OR**
Expanded Video Program, Videocassette 3

Textbook Audiocassette 4 B

RESOURCES	RESOURCES
Print	Audiovisual

Textbook Audiocassette 4 B

Practice and Activity Book
Chapter Resources, Book 3
●Additional Listening Activities 8-1, 8-2 ....*Additional Listening Activities, Audiocassette* 10 A
●Student Response Forms
●Realia 8-1
●Situation Card 8-1
●Teaching Transparency Master 8-1 ....*Teaching Transparency* 8-1
●Quiz 8-1 ....*Assessment Items, Audiocassette* 8 A
Video Guide..*Video Program/Expanded Video Program,* Videocassette 3

Textbook Audiocassette 4 B

Practice and Activity Book
Chapter Resources, Book 3
●Communicative Activity 8-1
●Additional Listening Activities 8-3, 8-4 ....*Additional Listening Activities, Audiocassette* 10 A
●Student Response Forms
●Realia 8-2
●Situation Card 8-2
●Quiz 8-2 ....*Assessment Items, Audiocassette* 8 A

Textbook Audiocassette 4 B

Practice and Activity Book
Chapter Resources, Book 3
●Communicative Activity 8-2
●Additional Listening Activities 8-5, 8-6 ....*Additional Listening Activities, Audiocassette* 10 A
●Student Response Forms
●Realia 8-3
●Situation Card 8-3
●Teaching Transparency Master 8-2 ....*Teaching Transparency* 8-2
●Quiz 8-3 ....*Assessment Items, Audiocassette* 8 A

Video Guide..*Video Program/Expanded Video Program,* Videocassette 3

Alternative Assessment

● Performance Assessment,
Teacher's Edition
  Erste Stufe, p. 181L
  Zweite Stufe, p. 181M
  Dritte Stufe, p. 181O

● Portfolio Assessment
  Written: **Anwendung,** Activity 6, *Pupil's Edition,* p. 203;
  Assessment Guide, p. 21
  Oral: **Anwendung,** Activity 4, *Pupil's Edition,* p. 203;
  Assessment Guide, p. 21
● **Notizbuch,** *Pupil's Edition,* pp. 195, 199; *Practice and Activity Book,* p. 152

CHAPTER OVERVIEW

Kapitel 8: Mode? Ja oder nein?
Textbook Listening Activities Scripts

Erste Stufe
Activity 7, p. 189

KLAUS Also, der Lutz sieht immer total ordentlich aus: weißes Hemd, schicke Hose, glänzende Lederschuhe. Und wenn er mal 'ne Jeans trägt, dann hat die garantiert 'ne Bügelfalte! Die Katrin hat immer tolle Klamotten an, je nach dem, was gerade so „in" ist. Enger Minirock, „cooles" Lederoutfit und hohe Stöckelschuhe. Sie sieht fast aus wie Claudia Schiffer! Die Silke sieht auch ganz klasse aus. Sie hat zwar nicht immer den neuesten Look, aber dafür zieht sie sich echt originell an! Große, silberne Ohrringe, ein buntes Stirnband, 'ne fetzige Jeans und das geknotete Männerhemd, … eigentlich viel zu weit, steht ihr aber toll! So wie der Udo, lauf' ich gerne selber 'rum. Er trägt die bequemsten Klamotten: ausgewaschene Jeans und alte Turnschuhe. Heute sieht er echt lässig aus in dem T-Shirt von seiner Lieblingsfußballmannschaft!

Answers to Activity 7

a. Katrin: toll, eng, „cool", hoch
b. Udo: bequem, verwaschen, alt
c. Silke: groß, silbern, bunt, fetzig, geknotet, weit
d. Lutz: weiß, schick, glänzend
Answers will vary.

Activity 11, p. 190

ERIK Also, mein Freund, der Otto, hat immer wahnsinnig witzige Klamotten an. Er kombiniert die unmöglichsten Farben miteinander. Heute hat er zum Beispiel ein oranges Hemd an, drei Nummern zu groß natürlich! Das trägt er ganz lässig über der Hose. Am Kragen steht es offen, und um den Hals hat er locker eine alte Seidenkrawatte von seinem Opa geschlungen, weiß mit großen roten Punkten. Seine fetzigen Jeans sind an den Knien zerrissen und ganz hellblau verwaschen. Dazu trägt er knallgrüne Socken und, typisch Otto, die feinsten Schuhe aus schwarzem Leder! Tja, alle finden Otto supercool!

Zweite Stufe
Activity 17, p. 194

MIRIAM Ich interessiere mich für Sprachen. Französisch ist mein Lieblingsfach, und in den Sommerferien fahre ich nach Paris. Es macht mir Spaß, die Sprache eines anderen Landes zu lernen, um die Mentalität und Kultur dieser Menschen besser zu verstehen.

AXEL Mich interessiert klassische Musik. Ich höre Schumann, Bach und Tschaikowsky sehr gern, besonders wenn ich Hausaufgaben mache. Am meisten interessiere ich mich für die Klavierstücke von Chopin. Ich mag klassische Musik, weil ich selber ein klassisches Instrument spiele.

TINA Es gefällt mir, wenn ich Komplimente für mein Aussehen bekomme. Deswegen interessiere ich mich für Mode und Kosmetik. Es macht mir Spaß, mich zu stylen und immer die neuesten Klamotten zu haben. Am liebsten probiere ich verschiedene Frisuren aus. Wenn ich mit der Schule fertig bin, möchte ich irgendwas mit Mode und Design machen.

BEATE Ich interessiere mich für Politik. Ich finde es sehr wichtig, darüber informiert zu sein, was so alles in der Welt los ist. Ich sehe gern die Nachrichten im Fernsehen und lese jeden Morgen die Zeitung.

Answers to Activity 17

a. 1. Miriam: Sprachen, Französisch; 2. Axel: klassische Musik; 3. Tina: Mode und Kosmetik; 4. Beate: Politik

b. 1. Miriam: um Mentalität und Kultur zu verstehen; 2. Axel: weil er selbst ein klassisches Instrument spielt; 3. Tina: weil sie gern Komplimente für ihr Aussehen bekommt; 4. Beate: weil sie es wichtig findet, informiert zu sein

Dritte Stufe
Activity 26, p. 197

SYLVIA Hallo, Elke! Du hast es aber eilig. Wo willst du denn hin?

ELKE Ach, hallo, Sylvia! Hallo, Tina! Ich will den Bus um drei Uhr noch bekommen, um in die Stadt zu fahren. Heute kaufe ich mir endlich die schwarze Lederjacke aus der kleinen Boutique neben dem Kaufhaus. Morgen abend ziehe ich sie an, wenn wir zum Pop-Festival am Brandenburger Tor gehen. Hast du dir schon die fransige Jeansweste geholt, die du so gern haben wolltest, Sylvia?

SYLVIA Nein, und ich werde sie mir auch nicht kaufen. Ich hab' sie vor ein paar Tagen mal anprobiert. Die Tina und ich, wir waren letzten Donnerstag zusammen in der Stadt. Die Weste sah schrecklich an mir aus, stimmt's Tina? Viel zu weit und zu lang. Ich war echt enttäuscht.

TINA Ja, das stimmt, leider! Aber ich hatte auch ein ziemliches Pech an diesem Tag. Ich wollte mir so gern dieses gepunktete Outfit aus Seide kaufen, weißt du, so eins, wie die Julia Roberts in *Pretty Woman* anhatte. Im „Mode-Schlößchen" gab es nur noch eins in meiner Größe. Die Sylvia hat gesagt, daß es mir super steht. Aber dann, an der Kasse, haben wir bemerkt, daß es einen großen Fleck auf dem Ärmel hatte. Ich hab' mich vielleicht geärgert und war den ganzen Donnerstag lang schlecht gelaunt deswegen!

ELKE Du, Tina, ich hab' das gleiche Outfit im Heinemann-Katalog gesehen. Bestell es dir doch einfach dort!

TINA Echt? Das mach' ich bestimmt! Ich komm' heute abend mal bei dir vorbei und schau' mir den Katalog an, okay?

ELKE Ja, klar. Gern! Aber jetzt muß ich schnell zur Bushaltestelle laufen. Also tschüs dann, bis heute abend!

TINA Tschüs!

SYLVIA Tschüs, Elke!

Answers to Activity 26

Elke: will Lederjacke kaufen, fürs Pop-Festival
Sylvia: will Jeansweste nicht kaufen, weil sie
ihr nicht paßt
Tina: will gepunktetes Outfit kaufen, aber es
hat einen Fleck; will es dann aus dem Katalog
bestellen

Activity 32, p. 199

DORO Ich fahr' eigentlich nur mit dem Auto
zur Schule, wenn mein Fahrrad mal
kaputt ist. Das heißt, ich fahr' nicht
selber, sondern meine Mutter fährt
mich natürlich, weil ich noch keinen
Führerschein habe.

ROLAND Am Wochenende oder in den Ferien
gehe ich gern segeln, aber nur wenn
es sonnig und warm ist. Bei schlechtem
Wetter und stürmischer See segeln zu
gehen, ist viel zu gefährlich.

ANITA Wenn es draußen regnet, gehe ich
meistens ins Jugendzentrum, um
Schach zu spielen. Dort sind immer
zwei, drei Leute, die auch gern Schach
spielen. Ich finde es ziemlich langweilig, an einem regnerischen Tag zu
Hause herumzusitzen.

HOLGER Normalerweise muß ich mich bei uns
zu Hause nicht um den Einkauf küm-
mern, das besorgt alles meine Mutter.
Ich gehe eigentlich nur Lebensmittel
einkaufen, wenn ich meine Oma
besuche. Aber das mache ich gern, weil
sie nicht so schwere Sachen schleppen
kann.

Answers to Activity 32

1. b; 2. d; 3. c; 4. a

Anwendung,
Activity 1, p. 202

KATRIN Boris, kauf dir doch diese Jacke aus
Baumwolle hier! Die ist nicht so teuer
wie die Wildlederjacke dort, und außerdem sieht sie echt sportlich aus. Probier
sie doch mal an! Also, ich finde, du solltest sie unbedingt nehmen!

BORIS Wirklich? Ja, wenn du meinst, sie steht
mir, dann kauf' ich sie doch glatt!

KATRIN Du, Judith, gestern wollte ich mir Schuhe
in dem neuen Schuhgeschäft am
Bahnhof kaufen. Als ich ein Paar Stiefel
anprobiert habe, ist ein Absatz
kaputtgegangen und die Sohle war auch
schon lose. Kauf dir ja keine Schuhe
dort! Die haben eine ganz schlechte
Qualität.

JUDITH Ja, das habe ich auch schon gehört. Da
geh' ich bestimmt nichts kaufen.

Answers to Activity 1

Baumwolljacke kaufen; sieht sportlich aus
Keine Schuhe in dem neuen Schuhgeschäft
kaufen; schlechte Qualität

Kapitel 8: Mode? Ja oder nein?
Projects and Games

PROJECT

In this activity each student will design his or her ideal wardrobe by cutting out photos and ads from favorite clothing catalogs or advertisements. Each item or outfit will include a detailed description. Students should begin this project after they are familiar with the new phrases and expressions of all three **Stufen.**

Materials Students may need poster board, scissors, glue, old catalogs or advertisements, paper, and pens.

Suggested Sequence

1. After you have discussed the project with students, they should make an outline of what they would like to include in their ideal wardrobe.
2. With their wardrobes in mind, students should search through catalogs and ads to find pictures for their poster project.
3. Once students have collected their materials, they should design the layout and arrange the various outfits on the poster board.
4. For the writing component of this project, students should incorporate the new phrases and expressions they have learned in this chapter in written descriptions of each of the outfits.
5. Before students write a final description, they should ask a classmate to proofread what they have written.
6. The final descriptions should be placed underneath each outfit.
7. Finally, students present their ideal wardrobe to the rest of the class.

Grading the Project

Suggested point distribution (total = 100 points)

Appearance	25
Accurate descriptions and correct language usage	50
Presentation	25

 GAMES

Auf dem Kostümball

This game gives students an opportunity to use the vocabulary from Chapter 8 in a fun way and to review expressions from previous chapters.

Preparation Prepare a list of possible costumes one might see at a costume ball, including some that are currently popular.

Procedure Divide students into two teams. Have a member of team A come to the front of the class and show him or her the name of a costume. (Example: **ein Clown**) The student then describes the costume to the class in German within a set amount of time. The first team to guess the correct costume wins a point. After the student from team A is finished, a member of team B comes to the front to describe the next costume. The team with the highest score at the end of the game wins. Here are other suggestions for costumes: **Ärztin, Dracula, Cowboy, Hexe.**

Kleidungswettbewerb

This game is a fun and different way for students to review clothing vocabulary and adjectives.

Procedure The day you plan to play this game bring two bags filled with various items of clothing that students are familiar with. Place the two bags at the front of the class. Divide the class into two teams. Each team appoints one member to be the model. When you give the signal, one model from each group comes to the front of the room, takes out all the clothing in his or her bag and puts it on. His or her group makes a list of all the items in the order their model puts them on. The team to finish its list first wins. For extra points, have students choose an appropriate adjective to describe each item.

Kapitel 8: Mode? Ja oder nein?
Lesson Plans, pages 182-205

Using the Chapter Opener, pp. 182-183

Motivating Activity

Ask students about the latest fashions. What types of clothing are currently fashionable and trendy? How do their parents feel about the clothes students wear?

Teaching Suggestion

Ask students to look at the three photos and describe the clothing being worn in each.

Teacher Note

You may want to introduce the vocabulary for the items scattered on these two pages.
der Knopf *button*
der Reißverschluß *zipper*

Thinking Critically

① **Drawing Inferences** After students read the caption, ask them to look again at the clothes the two girls are wearing and make a guess as to what fabrics their clothes could be made of. Students may be able to recall some of the following vocabulary from Level 1: **Baumwolle, Leder, Seide, Leinen.**

Building on Previous Skills

Recycle some of the expressions for commenting on clothes that students learned in Chapter 5 of Level 1. Put these words in two columns on the board and ask students, after having read the caption, to use some of the words on the board in reaction to the clothes they see:

fesch	scheußlich
stark	blöd
schick	furchtbar
lässig	doof
prima	schlecht
toll	häßlich

Thinking Critically

③ **Drawing Inferences** Ask students to look at this **Schaufenster**, its display, and its logo. What is the name of the establishment and what type of clothing does it carry? (**Ponater Mode;** haute couture)

③ **Analyzing** Ask students if they can think of a reason why French is used as part of the store's name. (The French are known for their fashion houses.)

Focusing on Outcomes

To get students to focus on the chapter objectives, have them tell you how they usually decide what clothes to buy. What is involved in their decision to purchase a particular item of clothing? Then have students preview the learning outcomes listed on p. 183. **NOTE:** Each of these outcomes is modeled in the video and evaluated in **Kann ich's wirklich?** on p. 204.

*T*eaching Los geht's!
pp. 184-186

Resources for Los geht's!

- *Video Program* **OR**
  Expanded Video Program, Videocassette 3
- *Textbook Audiocassette* 4 B
- *Practice and Activity Book*

▶ **pages 184-185**

Video Synopsis

In this segment of the video, Katrin and Judith are talking about clothes and fashion. The student outcomes listed on p. 183 are modeled in the video: describing clothes, expressing interest, dis-interest, and indifference, making and accepting compliments, and persuading and dissuading.

Motivating Activity

Ask students to estimate how much of the cloth-ing in their closet they actually wear. Then ask them to give a reason why they do not wear some of their clothes.

For Individual Needs

Auditory Learners Have students watch the video segment of the **Foto-Roman.** Pause the tape after each frame and give students time to write down in English the gist of each conversation. After the last frame, ask students to share their findings. Based on these, have students try to summarize what is going on in the **Foto-Roman.** Then let students watch the **Foto-Roman** again.

▶ **page 186**

For Individual Needs

1 A Slower Pace Ask students to work with a partner to write down the answers to each of the eight questions. Beside each answer students must indicate specifically what led them to that answer. (Example: For Question 4 - **Ich kaufe mir jetzt nur noch Sachen aus Baumwolle oder Wolle.**)

3 Challenge After students have successfully matched the four pairs of sentences, ask them to rephrase each pair of statements by combining them into one. Students should use connectors such as **denn, und, deshalb,** or **weil.**

Teaching Suggestion

5 This activity can be assigned as homework. Students should write at least three sentences and give each sentence a different sentence structure.

LOS GEHT'S!

Closure

Replay the video segment of the **Foto-Roman**, this time without sound. Put students into groups of four and have them assume the roles of Katrin, Judith, Roland, and Boris. As you play the video, have them take turns filling in the dialogue. After each frame, call on one group to perform.

▶ **page 187**

[▣] PRESENTATION: Landeskunde

Teacher Note

The **Landeskunde** interviews are recorded on audiocassette and videocassette.

Teaching Suggestions

• Before students watch the video segment or listen to the tape, ask them to do the prereading activity. Ask students the question that was posed in the interview "**Was trägst du am liebsten?**" Ask students if they think the answers of the four German students will be similar to theirs.

• Help students with words and phrases they may not be able to guess from the context of the interviews.
gruftimäßig *dark; alternative*
zeckig; richtig links *slang terms to describe an alternative or punk style*

Thinking Critically

Comparing and Contrasting Monika talks about her interest in clothes from the seventies. You may want to try to get several yearbooks from the seventies from your school library and let students browse through the photo section. Then ask them to describe the clothes and compare them to what students typically wear at school today.

Multicultural Connection

Have students interview foreign exchange students or people they know from other countries. They should try and find out what teenagers in other countries like to wear. What is "in" and what is "out" in different countries?

Thinking Critically

B Drawing Inferences After discussing the questions, ask students how their own parents are involved in their clothes purchases and how their parents feel about the way they dress.

Teacher Note

Mention to your students that the **Landeskunde** will also be included in Quiz 8-1 given at the end of the **Erste Stufe**.

Teaching Erste Stufe, pp. 188-191

Resources for Erste Stufe

Practice and Activity Book
Chapter Resources, Book 3
 • Additional Listening Activities 8-1, 8-2
 • Student Response Forms
 • Realia 8-1
 • Situation Card 8-1
 • Teaching Transparency Master 8-1
 • Quiz 8-1
Audiocassette Program
 • *Textbook Audiocassette* 4 B
 • *Additional Listening Activities, Audiocassette* 10 A
 • *Assessment Items, Audiocassette* 8 A
Video Program or *Expanded Video Program*

▶ **page 188**

MOTIVATE

For Individual Needs

Visual Learners Bring a collection of mail-order catalogs, department store advertisements, or fashion magazines and let each student look for an outfit that he or she really likes. Ask students to describe the outfit to a partner, telling him or her in German why they like it.

TEACH

Cooperative Learning

6 Divide students in groups of four. Instruct each group to choose a discussion leader, a recorder, a proofreader, and a reporter. Give students a specific amount of time in which to complete Activity 6 (20-30 minutes). Each group should begin by reading the questions out loud. Monitor group work as you walk around, helping students with unfamiliar words or phrases. The recorder of each group can use a transparency to write his or her group's answers. Tape the paper on the wall or the blackboard with masking tape. Then call on a few group reporters to read what their groups wrote. You can decide whether or not to collect students' work for a grade at the end of the activity.

▶ *page 189*

For Individual Needs

7 A Slower Pace As an advance organizer to this activity, write the adjectives **modisch, sportlich, witzig**, and **konservativ** on the blackboard or on a transparency. Ask students what type of clothes or outfits they would label with each of the adjectives. Make a list of students' ideas underneath each adjective.

8 Challenge To expand this activity, you could tell students to imagine that they have a **DM 600** clothing allowance. How would they spend this money on clothes? Ask students to make a shopping list. When they complete the activity, call on several students to describe their planned purchases.

PRESENTATION: So sagt man das!

Go over the functions in the **So sagt man das!** box. Then remind students of the motivating activity they did at the beginning of this **Stufe**. See if any of their descriptions are similar to the German expressions introduced in this function box.

PRESENTATION: Grammatik

In the previous chapter, students learned the adjective endings following **ein**-words (see p. 170). Make transparencies of the two grammar boxes on pp. 170 and 189. Ask students to compare adjective endings and point out the differences in endings after **der**- and **ein**-words. Remind students that the -**er** and -**es** adjective endings are necessary where the **ein**-word gives no indication of gender.

▶ *page 190*

Building on Previous Skills

Recycle some of the colors by pointing and asking students to describe classroom objects, students' clothing, and photos if necessary. Then introduce the new colors in a similar manner. Reinforce the new colors by asking students to think of other objects which have these colors.

Thinking Critically

10 Drawing Inferences Take a survey asking students if their family takes any clothes or laundry items to the cleaner's. Have them name the items and give reasons why people take certain clothing items to the cleaner's.

Teaching Suggestion

11 Have students work in pairs to create Otto. One student is the note taker and the other is the artist. Play the tape several times. During the first and second listenings, stop the tape after each description so that one student can take notes and the other can draw the item. During the third listening, have students listen for colors. After pairs have finished their drawings, let them listen to the complete description one more time, making sure they included all details.

ERSTE STUFE

Background Information

Most German households have washing machines. Advertisements for washing machines and similar large appliances indicate that consumers are concerned about several things: water usage, electrical usage, and size. Before purchasing a washing machine, many Germans consult the German equivalent of *Consumer Reports* which is called *Test* and is published by **Stiftung Warentest.** Most German washing machines are smaller than those in the United States.

Thinking Critically

Analyzing Ask students to think of some reasons why Germans are so concerned about the size and performance of such an appliance. (Water and electricity are considerably more expensive in Germany than in the United States. Since homes, especially apartments, tend to be smaller in Germany, washing machines are often kept in the bathroom or kitchen.)

▶ *page 191*

Teaching Suggestion

12 If you are not sure that all students have access to or can bring pages from fashion catalogs, obtain the advertisement inserts from the Sunday edition of a large newspaper. Let students look through the advertisements for an outfit they would like to use for this activity.

For Individual Needs

13 Tactile Learners In preparation for this activity, place a suitcase of unusual clothing (you may want to ask the drama teacher if you could borrow some costumes) in front of the class. Encourage each group to take items of clothing for a **verrücktes Outfit** from the suitcase. One of the group members puts on the clothes the other members have picked out for him or her and becomes the **Mode-Freak.**

PRESENTATION: Ein wenig Landeskunde

Explain that with the recent introduction of **Kabelfernsehen** in Germany, German teens have a much higher exposure to current American fashion trends and thus are much faster to copy them.

Thinking Critically

Comparing and Contrasting Ask students how they would go about finding out about fashion trends among teenagers in other countries.

Background Information

In Germany, there aren't many public tennis courts, golf courses, or riding stables that are open to the general public.

Thinking Critically

Synthesizing Can students think of reasons why Germans are more aware of proper attire when they participate in a sport? (If Germans plan to participate in one of the above activities, they must often join a tennis or golf club, for example, and abide by a dress code.)

Teacher Note

15 After all teams have created their **Reklameseite**, you may want to collect their creations and make a catalog similar to those mailed out by department stores. Display it in your classroom or in the foreign language area.

Reteaching: Adjective Endings after *der/dieser*-words and Colors

Scatter the items of clothing from your suitcase (see Activity 13) on the floor. Students should request a particular piece of clothing from you. Examples:
Könnte ich bitte diesen gelben Anorak haben?
or
Bitte geben Sie mir den feuerroten Pulli da!

CLOSE

♜ Game

Play the game **Auf dem Kostümball.** See p. 181F for the procedure.

Focusing on Outcomes

Refer students back to the learning outcomes listed on p. 183. They should recognize that they now know how to describe different types of clothes.

ASSESS

- **Performance Assessment** Have students imagine that they have to report a lost suitcase to an airline's lost and found agent. They should give the agent a detailed written or oral description of the contents of the suitcase.

- Quiz 8-1, *Chapter Resources*, Book 3

*T*eaching Zweite Stufe, *pp. 192-195*

Resources for Zweite Stufe

Practice and Activity Book
Chapter Resources, Book 3
- Communicative Activity 8-1
- Additional Listening Activities 8-3, 8-4
- Student Response Forms
- Realia 8-2
- Situation Card 8-2
- Quiz 8-2
Audiocassette Program
- *Textbook Audiocassette* 4 B
- *Additional Listening Activities, Audiocassette* 10 A
- *Assessment Items, Audiocassette* 8 A

▶ **page 192**

MOTIVATE

Total Physical Response

To recycle clothing vocabulary, descriptive adjectives, and colors, give commands with the following phrases.

Steht bitte auf, wenn ihr ... anhabt!
Komm nach vorne, wenn du ... trägst!
Heb die Hand, wenn du ... heute anhast!
Zeigt auf einen Schüler in der Klasse, der ... anhat!

TEACH

◈ For Individual Needs

16 Auditory Learners Have students keep their books closed while you read all five interviews. Have the three questions and the names of the interviewees written on the board. Read each interview twice as students take notes to answer questions 1-3. Call on students to check for comprehension. Then ask students to answer the third question.

▶ **page 193**

PRESENTATION: Wortschatz

To teach this new vocabulary you may want to use realia, such as actual clothing, pictures from catalogs, or ads. Include the adjectives in the **Und dann noch ...** box in your presentation.

Teacher Note

To expand this vocabulary list you could also introduce:
kurzärmelig *short-sleeved*
langärmelig *long-sleeved*
die Garderobe *wardrobe*
kurze and **wadenlange Socken** *short and calf-length socks*
Marken-Jeans *designer jeans*

PRESENTATION: So sagt man das!

Ask students to look back at the five interviews in Activity 16 and identify as many expressions as they can find that indicate interest, disinterest, or indifference. To practice the new expressions, ask students to tell you their level of interest in:
a) **klassische Musik**
b) **Country-Western Musik**
c) **Sport**
d) **Autos**
e) **Kochen.**

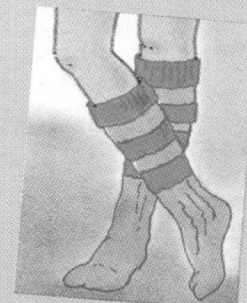

ZWEITE STUFE

▶ *page 194*

For Individual Needs

17 **A Slower Pace** On a transparency or on the board, list the interests mentioned in random order down one side and the reasons down the other side. As students listen to the reports, they should use the clues on the board to help them complete Activities 1a and 1b.

For Additional Practice

18 If you feel students need further practice, you can brainstorm with them to come up with further topics. Make a list on the board and then conduct a class survey to find out which topics students are interested or not interested in and reasons for their opinions.

PRESENTATION: So sagt man das!

Have students practice these expressions with a partner. One student should read the compliment and the other student the response. Ask students if they can think of other similar expressions which they learned in previous chapters. There are some other expressions students should be familiar with:

Die Jacke sieht lässig aus!   **Findest du?**
Die Jeans gefällt mir!   **Wirklich?**

▶ *page 195*

PRESENTATION: Grammatik

To reintroduce previously learned verbs that take the dative case, ask students to respond to questions such as:

Was schenkst du deiner Freundin zum Geburtstag?
Welche Musik gefällt dir am besten?
Was gibst du deinen Eltern gewöhnlich zum Geburtstag?
Wie geht es dir heute?
Use verbs such as
schenken, geben, helfen, gefallen, schmecken, and **gehen.**

For Individual Needs

22 **Challenge** To expand this activity, hang up large pictures from magazines. Ask students to address compliments to the people in the pictures, observing formal or familiar address forms of address. Other students should give appropriate responses.

Reteaching: Adjectives after *der/dieser*-words

In preparation for this activity, use old catalogs. Cut out a class set of pictures of colorful outfits and glue or tape these on construction paper (students can help you with this). Then give each student one picture. They should describe the outfit in detail using phrases such as:
Ich möchte gern ...
Ich finde ...
Ich kaufe ... für ...

CLOSE

For Individual Needs

Kinesthetic Learners Bring to class unusual outfits or costumes which you have borrowed from the drama department. Give students certain items of clothing to try on. Then ask other students to comment on them. (Examples: **zu eng, zu klein, zu lang, zu weit, zu groß, zu unpraktisch**)

Focusing on Outcomes

Refer students back to the learning outcomes listed on p. 183. Students should recognize that they now know how to express interest, disinterest, and indifference, and to make and accept compliments.

ASSESS

• **Performance Assessment** Use photographs of famous people or current stars. Show students one photo at a time and ask them to describe what that person is wearing, and how the clothes fit. In addition, they should make a comment about the outfit in general.

• Quiz 8-2, *Chapter Resources,* Book 3

Teaching Dritte Stufe, pp. 196-199

▶ page 196

Resources for Dritte Stufe

Practice and Activity Book
Chapter Resources, Book 3
- Communicative Activity 8-2
- Additional Listening Activities 8-5, 8-6
- Student Response Forms
- Realia 8-3
- Situation Card 8-3
- Teaching Transparency Master 8-2
- Quiz 8-3

Audiocassette Program
- *Textbook Audiocassette* 4 B
- *Additional Listening Activities, Audiocassette* 10 A
- *Assessment Items, Audiocassette* 8 A

▶ page 196

MOTIVATE

Teaching Suggestion

Take a class survey. Ask students where they and their family members purchase their clothes. Write a list of choices on the board. (Examples: **in Einkaufszentren, in Spezialgeschäften, in Boutiquen, aus Katalogen.**) Students should also give an explanation or reason for their preference.

TEACH

Group Work

25 Divide the class into groups of three. Assign one student in each group to be the writer. The group begins by reading the advertisements from the **Berger-Katalog.** Then the group answers Questions 1 through 3, and the writer records all answers. Set a time limit to complete this activity, then call on groups to share their findings with the rest of the class.

▶ page 197

PRESENTATION: Wortschatz

Use real pieces of clothing or pictures from magazines to introduce the new items of clothing pictured. For the details in the bottom row, show a pair of jeans and a jacket. In all cases, model the new word or phrase and have students repeat. Follow up with either/or and open-ended questions. Examples:

Wie macht man diese Jacke zu, mit einem Reißverschluß oder mit Knöpfen?
Wie wissen wir, daß man einen Gürtel zu dieser Hose braucht?

◆ For Individual Needs

27 Challenge To expand this activity, you can provide each pair of students with pages from a mail-order clothing catalog. Students tell each other what they would purchase with a $1000 shopping allowance. Monitor students' work as you walk from pair to pair. Occasionally ask one partner what the other one has chosen to buy and why.

Teacher Note

28 As an alternative, have students bring a magazine picture of a celebrity. (Examples: Princess Di, Steve Urkel, Bart Simpson) One of the partners plays the role of the famous person, while the other partner comments on, compliments, or criticizes his or her style. Though similar in task, this variation avoids students directly criticizing each other's clothing.

▶ page 198

PRESENTATION: So sagt man das!

Model the expressions of this function box by addressing individual students, using the phrases on the left side. Have students respond with the corresponding responses on the right side.

For Individual Needs

30 Tactile Learners Before beginning this activity, let students look at and feel several different swatches of material. (Examples: **Baumwolle, Seide, Wolle, Kunstfasern**) Have students try to guess what each material is.

▶ *page 199*

Family Link

34 Students can also interview different family members to find out about their clothing preferences. Students can point out and name the clothing that the family member is wearing to teach him or her some German words and phrases.

For Individual Needs

35 Visual Learners To expand this activity, let students take a look at the outfits they are wearing that day. Give students a minute to discuss their style, making use of any of the suggested words. Then have students volunteer to come to the front to model their outfits and give an ad-lib description of their style.

Reteaching: Persuading and Dissuading

Make a set of cards for half the students in your class. On each card write expressions and phrases like the ones in the **So sagt man das!** function box on p. 198.
Examples:
Warum kaufst du dir keine roten Shorts?
Kauf dir doch die Beatles Kassette!

Have students work with a partner. One person in each pair gets a card and reads the statement or question to his or her partner who then responds accordingly.
Examples:
Rote Shorts finde ich total scheußlich!
Du hast recht! Die Beatles sind echt super!

Then the card gets passed to the next pair of students. Pairs take turns reading the card they get and responding until all pairs have seen all the cards.

CLOSE

Teaching Suggestion

Provide students with the following **Lückensatz** which each one of them should try to complete in an interesting way.
Meine drei Lieblingskleidungsstücke bei mir im Schrank sind ..., weil ...
Students should take a few minutes to write out their sentence. Have several students read their sentence to the class.

Focusing on Outcomes

Refer students back to the learning outcomes listed on p. 183. They should recognize that they now know how to persuade and dissuade someone else.

ASSESS

- **Performance Assessment** Bring two large photos or ads from a clothing catalog, one of a female model and one of a male model. Ask students how they would try to persuade their best friend to buy the various pieces of one of the models' outfits.

- Quiz 8-3, *Chapter Resources,* Book 3

Teaching Zum Lesen,
pp. 200-201

Reading Strategy

The targeted strategy in this reading is understanding relationships between and within sentences. Students should learn about this strategy before beginning Question 4.

PREREADING

Motivating Activity

Take a survey asking students how important money is to them now and also for their future.

Language Note

The word **nix** in the title of the first text is colloquial for the pronoun **nichts**.

Thinking Critically

Drawing Inferences Ask students to think about the title **Reich ist, wer nix mehr lernen muß!** Do they agree or disagree with that statement? Have students give at least one reason for their opinion.

Teacher Note

Activity 1 is a prereading activity.

READING

 ## For Individual Needs

3 A Slower Pace On the board or a transparency, write the numbers 1 through 7 for each of the survey responses. Then elicit words or phrases from students which sum up each of the responses. Sometimes more than one word or phrase may be suggested. Have students come to a consensus as to which noun or phrase best summarizes the interviewee's opinion.

Teaching Suggestion

After students have determined how **sonst, damit,** and **besonders** affect the meanings of the responses referred to in Activities 4, 5, and 6, have them identify other transitional words that link thoughts together and indicate relationships within sentences. (Examples: **aber, leider, wenn**)

Thinking Critically

Comparing and Contrasting Ask students to take a closer look at the expression the thirteen-year-old **Hauptschüler** used when talking about money. **Mäuse in der Tasche haben.** Can students think of similar colloquial phrases used in English? (Examples: *to have lots of dough; to be loaded*)

 ## For Individual Needs

Challenge Ask students to reread the students' answers and decide under which category of the survey summary each answer would best fit.

Cooperative Learning

Do Activity 7 together with the class, then divide the class into cooperative groups of three to work on Activities 8 and 9. Assign students the roles of reader, recorder, and reporter. While students work on their assignments, put the five questions from Activities 8 and 9 on the board. When students are finished, ask the reporters to write the responses of their groups underneath each question.

Language Note

The German language has several proverbs that are related to money. Here are some examples you can share with your class:
Geld verdirbt den Charakter. *Money spoils character.*
Die Glücklichen sind reich, die Reichen nicht immer glücklich. *Money can't buy you happiness.*
Geld regiert die Welt. *Money rules the world.*

Thinking Critically

- **Comparing and Contrasting** Ask students if they know of any English proverbs, sayings, or expressions about money. (Examples: *A fortune is as fragile as glass. Money doesn't grow on trees.*)
- **Drawing Inferences** Tina considers her work as a model a **Nebenjob.** What do students think **Nebenjob** refers to? Survey your students as to what they consider to be **Nebenjobs.** Do any of them work part-time in addition to going to school? Tina works because she enjoys it. Do the students that do have jobs feel the same?

POST-READING

Teacher Note

Activity 10 is a post-reading task that will show whether students can apply what they have learned.

Teaching Suggestion

10 Since this is a comprehensive task and requires some time, you may consider the completed assignment an alternative to the suggested project for this chapter.

Closure

Ask students to look at the survey summary again and rank the items according to the student's personal preference from most important (1) to least important (12).

Answers to Activity 1

a survey; what must one have to be rich?; answers will vary; answers will vary

Answers to Activity 2

Minister, Fabrik, Personal

Answers to Activity 3

Zufriedenheit, Klamotten/Auto, nichts, Bungalow/Kunst, saubere Umwelt, Computer, Gesundheit

Answers to Activity 4

One must have good health, otherwise money and luxuries are worthless; **sonst** provides the contrast between good health and money and luxuries.

Answers to Activity 5

Damit expresses *for what purpose* the students want to have something.

Answers to Activity 6

He says he doesn't need anything; **besonders** *(especially)* emphasizes *when/on what occasions* he feels really good.

Answers to Activity 7

about 18-year-old student Tina who works as a model; on her beauty

Answers to Activity 8

modeling; yes; parents are happy to see her in pictures, but say that school is more important than looks

Answers to Activity 9

It's probably not so easy; e.g.: **Wenn man gut aussieht, hat man vielleicht nicht so viele Freunde, wie man glaubt.**

*U*sing Anwendung, pp. 202-203

▣ Video Wrap-up

At this time, you might want to use the *Video Program* or the *Expanded Video Program*, Videocassette 3 for additional review and enrichment. See *Video Guide* for suggestions regarding:
- **Ein starkes Outfit**
  (Dramatic episode)
- **Landeskunde**
  Interviews
- **Videoclips**
  (Authentic footage—*Expanded Video Program* only)

For Individual Needs

1 Challenge After students have completed the activity, ask them to think of another reason why Judith and Boris should or should not buy these same items.

Teaching Suggestion

2 Make a copy of the **Bestellkarte** for each student and have them answer Questions 1-5 on a separate piece of paper. Have students compare answers with a parner.

 For Individual Needs

3 Auditory learners After students have chosen three items and determined the rest of the information they need, ask students to continue working in pairs. Students take turns reading the information to each other. The student who is listening could pretend to be the catalog operator taking the order over the phone.

Teaching Suggestion

4 This activity could be added to the previous suggestion. Encourage students to act out the phone conversation, using props such as plastic phones and order forms.

 Portfolio Assessment

4 You may want to suggest this activity as an oral portfolio item for your students. See *Assessment Guide,* p. 21.

6 You may want to suggest this activity as a written portfolio item for your students. See *Assessment Guide,* p. 21.

Kann ich's wirklich?
p. 204

This page helps students prepare for the test. It is a brief checklist of the major points covered in the chapter. The students should be reminded that it is only a checklist and not necessarily everything that will appear on the test.

Using Wortschatz,
p. 205

Game
Play the game **Wer ist das?** to review the clothing vocabulary as well as the descriptive adjectives from this chapter. Students look around the classroom and secretly choose someone whose outfit they want to describe. They write that student's name on a small piece of paper and turn it face down. As each student names the items a classmate is wearing, the rest of the class tries to guess who it is. The first student to guess correctly wins a point. To verify the answer you can check the name on the paper. The student who guessed correctly then begins the next round.

Teaching Suggestions
- Ask students to pick at least 10 words or phrases from the **Wortschatz** to use at a fashion show to describe an outfit being modeled.
- Bring in photos or ads of the vocabulary items and ask students to give the word in German.

 For Individual Needs

Tactile Learners Each student should have a blank piece of paper and a pen or pencil. Use the vocabulary from the **Wortschatz** to describe an outfit. Students try to draw the outfit as you describe it. When students are finished, have them compare drawings.

Game
Play the game **Kleidungswettbewerb.** See p. 181F for the procedure.

Teacher Note
Give the **Kapitel 8** Chapter Test, *Chapter Resources, Book 3.*

REVIEW

KAPITEL

8

Mode? Ja oder nein?

(1) Kauf dir ja nichts aus Acryl!

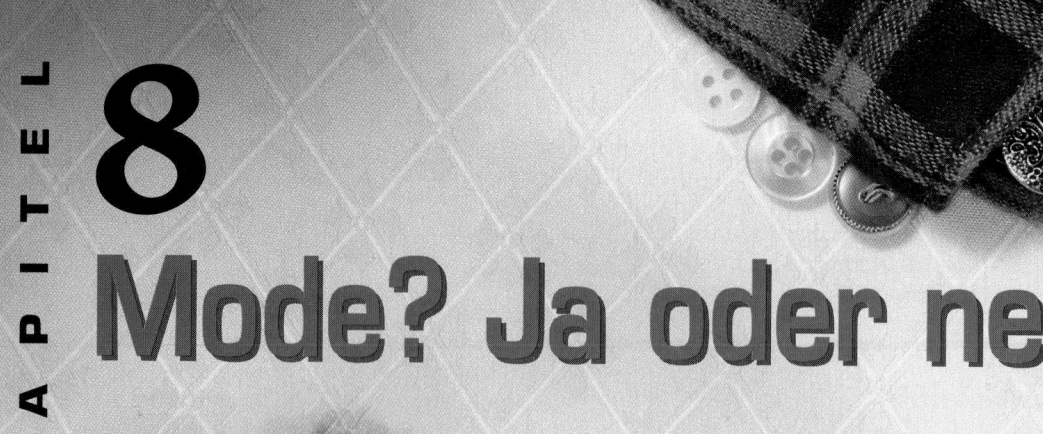

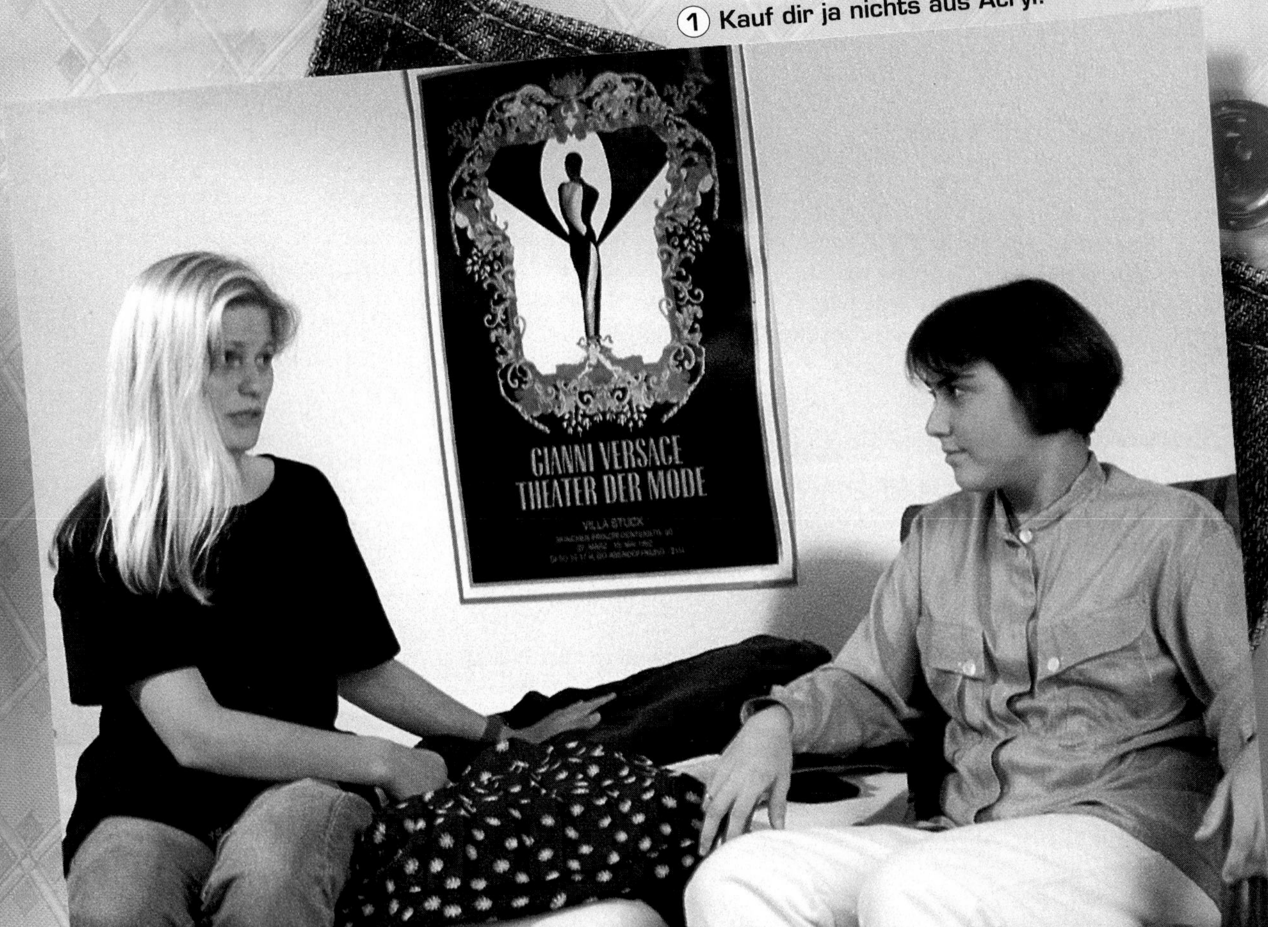

German students, like you and other American students, dress for the occasion; the outfit for school is likely to be different from the outfit for a bike ride or a picnic. The look and the style of the clothes they wear is heavily influenced by American styles. In order to talk about clothes and express specific interest in clothes, you need to know several new expressions as well as specific vocabulary.

In this chapter you will learn

- to describe clothes
- to express interest, disinterest, and indifference; to make and accept compliments
- to persuade and dissuade

And you will

- listen to students talk about clothes
- read about the kinds of clothes German students like to wear
- write your own clothing ads
- find out what German students think about fashion and clothes

② Dieser fesche Rollkragen-pulli steht dir gut!

③ Für Mode interessier' ich mich besonders.

Los geht's!

Ein starkes Outfit

Katrin   Judith   Roland   Boris

Look at the photos on the left. What might the topic of the conversation be? Now look at the photos on the right. What is the topic there? What roles do the two boys play?

1 Was passiert hier?

Verstehst du alles, was diese Leute sagen? Beantworte die Fragen!

1. What is this text about? *1. clothes and fashion* *2. because she is sorting through her clothes* *3. wash some,*
2. Why does Judith think that Katrin is going on a trip? *take some to the cleaners, throw some away*
3. What does Katrin intend to do with her clothes? *4. cotton and wool; acrylic*
4. What are her favorite materials? What clothes will she never buy again?
5. Which one of the two girls is interested in fashion? How does that show?
6. What does Judith's brother like to wear? *5. Judith; she dresses stylishly* *6. the color black*
7. Whom do the girls seem to like and why? *7. Boris; because he is so stylish*
8. What does this person like about Katrin? *8. she is natural, does*

not care about fashion, has sense of humor

2 Stimmt oder stimmt nicht?

Wenn der Satz nicht stimmt, schreib die richtige Antwort!

1. stimmt nicht; sie muß Ordnung

1. Katrin möchte verreisen. *in ihre Sachen bringen* *2. stimmt nicht; sie*
2. Sie möchte den Pulli in die Reinigung geben. *will ihn wegwerfen*
3. Sie kauft sich jetzt nur noch Klamotten aus Acryl. *3. stimmt nicht;*
4. Katrin interessiert sich sehr für Mode. *aus Baumwolle und Wolle*
5. Der Roland trägt am liebsten Schwarz. *4. stimmt nicht; sie interessiert sich*
6. Die Katrin mag den Boris nicht. *nicht dafür* *5. stimmt* *6. stimmt nicht; er*
7. Der Boris ist ein lässiger Typ. *gefällt ihr* *7. stimmt*

3 Welche Sätze passen zusammen?

Welche Sätze auf der rechten Seite passen zu den Sätzen auf der linken Seite?

1. Katrin bringt Ordnung in ihre Klamotten. c
2. Der grüne Pullover paßt ihr nicht. d
3. Judiths grüne Bluse paßt gut zu der
   weißen Jeans. a
4. Der Roland ist ein richtiger Mode-Freak. b

a. Das ist ein heißes Outfit.
b. Er ist stolz auf seine Klamotten.
c. Sie möchte sehen, was sie hat.
d. Er ist ihr viel zu weit, und er ist aus Acryl.

4 Welche Wörter passen in die Lücken?

1. Ich muß mal __1__ in meine Klamotten bringen.
2. Das muß ich waschen, und das muß in die __2__.
3. Diesen Pullover willst du __3__?
4. Der Roland ist ein __4__ Mode-Freak.
5. Er ist __5__ auf seine Klamotten.
6. Mode ist für ihn ziemlich __6__.
7. Der Boris ist ein wirklich lässiger __7__.

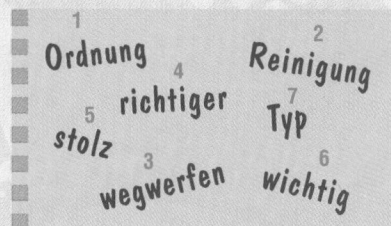

1 Ordnung 4 richtiger 2 Reinigung 5 stolz 7 Typ 3 wegwerfen 6 wichtig

5 Und du?

Wie beschreibst du dich selbst? Was ist dein Stil? Gebrauche drei Adjektive aus dem Kasten, um dich zu beschreiben.

modisch einfach sportlich schick lässig elegant verrückt natürlich fesch cool fetzig

Was trägst du am liebsten?

We asked several teenagers the question **Was trägst du am liebsten und warum?** Based on what you already know about what German students like to wear, think about the kinds of clothing these teenagers might mention. What reasons might they give for wearing certain kinds of clothing? Listen to and then read the interviews.

Monika, *Hamburg*

„Also ich wechsle mein Outfit auch je nach Gelegenheit. Entweder zieh' ich mich total gruftimäßig an oder siebziger Jahrestil, wie man es jetzt so sieht. Oder, na ja, ich geh' halt ganz normal zeckig, ganz normal richtig links."

Rosi, *Berlin*

„Ich trage am liebsten 'ne Jeans und T-Shirt, also, weil es ist in der Schule so, da zieht keiner schicke Sachen an, also mit Kleidern nur wenige Ausnahmen, ich fühl' mich dann am wohlsten."

Jens, *Berlin*

„Also, was ich gerne anziehe, kann ich nicht sagen. Ich ... kleide mich gerne sportlich, weil ich fein nicht so mag, weil es was Besonderes ist. Meine Lieblingsfarbe ist Dunkelblau."

Uli, *München*

„Also Kleidung muß natürlich bequem sein, in erster Linie, und es unterscheidet sich natürlich, ob ich abends weggehe mit Freunden oder ob ich arbeite. Also wenn man mich jetzt sieht, das ist eine typisch bequeme Arbeitsklamotte, sag' ich mal, die ich anhab', also mit Turnschuhen, in denen ich bequem laufen kann, weil ich doch viel unterwegs bin. Wenn ich abends weggehe, zieh' ich mich gerne etwas feiner an, also sprich weg, so daß ich meine, ich sehe besser aus, in dann engen Hosen oder mal ein ausgeschnittenes T-Shirt."

A. 1. Monika: changing; Jens: sporty; Rosi: Jeans and T-shirt; Uli: comfortable clothes. Uli: She wears comfortable clothes during the day and finer clothes in the evening. When going out she thinks she looks better in finer clothes. Comfortable clothes and tennis shoes for work; tight pants and low-cut T-shirt for the evening.

A. 1. What kind of clothing do each of these people say they like to wear the best? What kind of reasons do they give for their choices? Which person says he or she likes to dress up? Who mentions comfort? The athletic look? Does Uli make a distinction between clothes she wears every day and clothes she wears when she goes out in the evening? What does she say? Describe the two outfits she wears.

2. With a partner choose one of the interviews above and jot down a few notes about what that person said. Then summarize in German (in your own words) the interview. Describe that person to your classmates using the phrase **Diese Person ...** to identify him or her. Let your classmates guess which person you are describing.

B. What do these people's statements and their choice of clothes tell you about them? Do you think their parents would make the same choices? How does their taste in clothes compare to yours and your friends'?

Describing clothes

6 Hast du alles verstanden?

Lies zuerst den Text unten, und dann beantworte die Fragen!

1. Was ist heute in der jungen Mode anders als früher?
2. Die Jugend experimentiert. Wie zeigt sich das?
3. Nenne die Adjektive, die diese Modeartikel beschreiben!

1. Heute geht alles. Früher hat es nur zwei Stile gegeben. 2. Sie kombinieren verschiedene Stile und Farben. 3. cool, schwarz, bunt, lässig, gefüttert, kariert, „in", klassisch, toll, blau, weit, scharf, witzig

WORTSCHATZ

Was ist heute „in"?

Früher hat es in der jungen Mode gewöhnlich nur zwei Stile gegeben: konservativ und modisch. Und heute? — Heute geht alles. Die Jugend von heute experimentiert und kombiniert: Hosen aus den 60er Jahren mit geblümten Hemden aus den 70er Jahren. Und farblich? Alles geht! Aber Schwarz ist zur Zeit „in".

Richtig cool ist die schwarze Jeans und das bunte Shirt darüber, das am besten offen bleibt.

Jeans 129,40
Shirt 80,90

Für jeden sportlichen Typ: Käppis! Am liebsten natürlich von US-Baseball-Mannschaften.

Käppis ab 28,00

Immer noch „in": Die schon klassischen Turnschuhe gibt's jetzt in tollen Farben.

Turnschuhe 79,60

Echt toll ist dieser blaue Blazer und das lässige, weite Hemd darunter.

Blazer 189,00
Hemd 69,80

Lässig für den kalten Winter: diese gefütterte Wind- und Wetterjacke über der Jeansweste und dem karierten Wollhemd.

Windjacke 186,00
Jeansweste 96,00
Wollhemd

Diese bunten Krawatten passen besonders gut zu dem blauen Jeansshirt.

Krawatten ab 27,00

Dieser bunte Anorak sieht auch von hinten scharf aus – ein Anorak mit Patches! Darunter trägt man, was man will. Dieses witzige T-Shirt vielleicht?

Anorak 109,00
T-Shirt 39,90

Welche Adjektive beschreiben die Kleidungsstücke von deinen Klassenkameraden?

7 Hör gut zu! For answers, see listening script on TE Interleaf.

Ein Schüler beschreibt die Kleidung von vier neuen Klassenkameraden. Mach dir Notizen (zum Beispiel Adjektive) über die verschiedenen Kleidungsstile! Wer von den Klassenkameraden kleidet sich a. modisch? b. sportlich? c. witzig? d. konservativ?

8 Du und dein Partner

Du und dein Partner, ihr müßt euch jeder einen Artikel aus der Reklameseite (Seite 188) heraussuchen. Was gefällt euch? Was nicht? Was kauft sich dann jeder von euch?

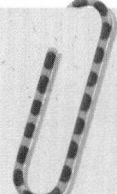

SO SAGT MAN DAS!

Describing clothes

When describing clothes, as well as other things, you want to use adjectives in your description.

Diese schwarze Jeans und das bunte Shirt sind echt cool.
Für den kalten Winter bei uns brauch' ich diese gefütterte Windjacke.
Dieser bunte Anorak sieht sehr gut aus.

Identify the adjectives in the noun phrases above. Why do you think **schwarze**, **bunte**, and **gefütterte** have an -e ending, but **kalten** an -en ending?

Grammatik Adjectives following der and dieser-words

1. Adjectives following **der** and **dieser**-words (**dieser, jeder, welcher**) have these endings.

Nominative: Dieser bunt e Anorak sieht toll aus. *Accusative:* Diesen bunt en Anorak kauf' ich mir.	*Masculine*
Nominative: Die schwarz e Jacke ist echt cool. *Accusative:* Die schwarz e Jacke kauf' ich mir auch.	*Feminine*
Nominative: Das weit e Hemd ist lässig. *Accusative:* Das weit e Hemd trag' ich gern.	*Neuter*
Nominative: Diese bunt en Krawatten sehen gut aus. *Accusative:* Diese bunt en Krawatten mag ich nicht.	*Plural*

2. In the dative case, the adjective endings are **-en** for all nouns of all genders, and for the plural.

Dative: Das paßt echt gut zu
- diesem grün en Anorak.
- dieser weiß en Jacke.
- diesem bunt en Hemd.
- diesen bunt en Turnschuhen.

3. When more than one adjective is used to describe a noun, all adjectives have the same ending: Du willst diese schöne, grüne Bluse wegwerfen?

---

9 Leute beschreiben

Setz dich mit einer Partnerin zusammen, und sprecht über die Leute in den Fotos! Welche Kleidungsstücke gefallen euch? Welche nicht? Sagt auch, welche Farben diese Kleidungsstücke haben!

Farben

Schon bekannt

rot blau
weiß
grün gelb
schwarz
grau braun

Und dann noch . . .

feuerrot
wollweiß
türkisblau
olivgrün
knallgelb
hellbraun
dunkelgrau
tiefschwarz

10 Waschen? In die Reinigung? Oder wegwerfen?

Katrin bringt Ordnung in ihre Klamotten. Aber was soll sie nur mit den vielen Klamotten tun? Welche Stücke soll sie waschen? Welche soll sie in die Reinigung bringen? Welche soll sie wegwerfen? Sag deinen Mitschülern, was Katrin machen soll!

waschen?

wegwerfen?

in die Reinigung bringen?

11 Hör gut zu! For answers, see listening script on TE Interleaf.

Hör zu, wie Erik ein Outfit von seinem Freund Otto beschreibt! Otto trägt nämlich gern ganz verrückte Klamotten. Mach eine Skizze von Ottos Outfit, in Farbe natürlich! Vergleiche dann deine Skizze mit denen deiner Mitschüler! Wer hat den schönsten Otto gezeichnet?

12 Reklame für Klamotten

Jeder in der Klasse muß eine Reklameseite aus einem Katalog mit in die Klasse bringen. Sprecht über die einzelnen Artikel! Was gefällt euch? Was gefällt euch nicht? Wo gibt es diese Sachen? Wie teuer sind sie?

13 Typen wie der Boris?

Bildet Gruppen von drei Personen! Jede Gruppe muß einen Mode-Freak haben, der gern „verrückte" Kleidung trägt. Wenn keiner ein Mode-Freak sein will, verwendet die beste Otto-Zeichnung! Sprecht jetzt über euren Mode-Freak oder Otto!

a. Beschreibt das Outfit!
b. Sagt, was euch besonders gefällt oder überhaupt nicht gefällt!
c. Wie passen die Klamotten?

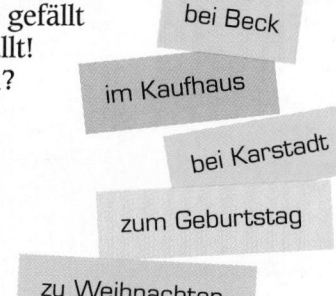

bei Beck

im Kaufhaus

bei Karstadt

zum Geburtstag

zu Weihnachten

EIN WENIG LANDESKUNDE

Heutzutage ist es fast unmöglich, junge Deutsche der Kleidung nach von jungen Amerikanern zu unterscheiden: die Jugend ist in ihrer Freizeit locker und lässig gekleidet.

Beim Sport legen die jungen Deutschen vielleicht ein bißchen mehr Wert auf richtige Kleidung. Man wandert in bequemen Wanderhosen mit den richtigen Schuhen dazu, man reitet in Reithosen und Stiefeln und man spielt Tennis in Weiß — vielleicht auch deshalb, weil man viele Tennisplätze nur im weißen Outfit betreten darf.

In manchen Gegenden, besonders in Bayern und in Österreich, trägt die Jugend auch Tracht, besonders an Sonntagen oder zu Festtagen, wie zum Beispiel beim Besuch von Volksfesten.

14 Dieses Hemd gefällt mir!

Get together with three other classmates. Find something about each person's outfit that you really like and tell him or her how much you like it. Then find out where each person bought that clothing article. Your classmate will tell you where he or she bought it or if he or she received it as a present. Try to find out how much it costs. The phrases above can help.

BEISPIEL   DU   **Das Kleid gefällt mir sehr. Wo hast du es gekauft?**

PARTNER   **Ich hab' das nicht gekauft, ich hab' es zum Geburtstag bekommen.**

15 Der tolle Sommerjob

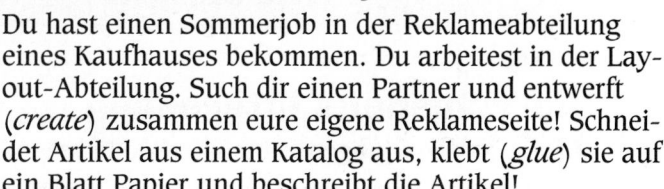

Du hast einen Sommerjob in der Reklameabteilung eines Kaufhauses bekommen. Du arbeitest in der Layout-Abteilung. Such dir einen Partner und entwerft (*create*) zusammen eure eigene Reklameseite! Schneidet Artikel aus einem Katalog aus, klebt (*glue*) sie auf ein Blatt Papier und beschreibt die Artikel!

Expressing interest, disinterest, and indifference; making and accepting compliments

HAST DU INTERESSE AN MODE?

Roland
„Mode ist für mich ziemlich wichtig. Ich trag' eigentlich schon, was ‚in' ist. Im Moment trage ich Schwarz."

Lin
„Es ist mir ziemlich egal, was ich anhab'. Es muß nur sauber sein. Ich lieb' aber fetzige Klamotten, bedruckte T-Shirts und Jacken mit bunten Prints."

Stefan
„Mode? — Nein. Ich zieh' mir auch Klamotten an, die nicht in Mode sind. Ich kauf' mir zum Beispiel viele Klamotten auf dem Trödelmarkt, weil sie dort billiger sind."

Johanna
„Ja, für Mode interessiere ich mich schon ein bißchen. Die Kleidung muß mir auch gut passen und gut stehen. Ich trag' furchtbar gern Kleider. Und zu diesem braunen Kleid trag' ich schwarze Strümpfe und schwarze Schuhe mit hohen Hacken."

Sandra
„Ich interessier' mich schon für Mode. Vor allem müssen die Farben passen. Zum blauen Hemd zum Beispiel passen die grüne Jacke und diese weiße Jeans. Toll! Was?"

16 Verschiedene Interessen

2. Mode ist wichtig, sie interessieren sich für
Mode; Mode — Nein, ist ihnen egal

Lies, was diese jungen Leute über Mode sagen! Beantworte die folgenden Fragen!

1. Wer interessiert sich für Mode? Wer nicht?   1. Roland, Sandra, Johanna; Stefan, Lin
2. Wie drücken die Schüler ihr Interesse oder Desinteresse aus? Was sagen sie?
3. Wer ist dir sympathisch? Warum?   3. Answers will vary.

Was trägst du zu deinen Klamotten? Ich trage ...

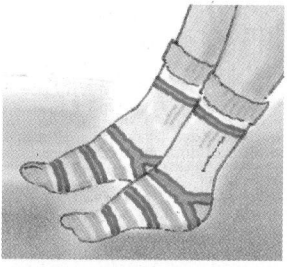

Socken

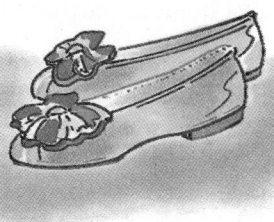

Schuhe mit flachen Absätzen

Schuhe mit hohen Absätzen

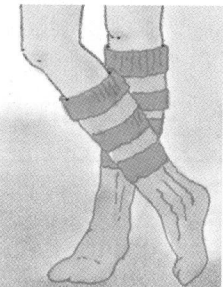

Strümpfe

Was gefällt dir ...

diese gepunktete Jeans? oder gestreifte, abgeschnittene Jeans?

die ärmellose Bluse?

diese weiche Lederjacke?

Und dann noch . . .

bedruckt	monoton
einfarbig	mehrfarbig
gemustert	locker

SO SAGT MAN DAS!

Expressing interest, disinterest, and indifference

When asking about someone's interests, you ask:

Interessierst du dich für Mode?
Wofür interessierst du dich?

When expressing disinterest, you may answer:

Mode interessiert mich nicht.
Ich hab' kein Interesse an Mode.

When expressing interest, you say:

Mode interessiert mich sehr.
Ich interessiere mich für Mode.

When expressing indifference, you may say:

Mode ist mir egal.

Which of the two questions is more general? What do you notice about the verb **interessieren**? What case follows the preposition **für**?[1]

1. **Für** is always followed by accusative case forms.

17 Hör gut zu! For answers, see listening script on TE Interleaf.

1. Schüler berichten über ihre Interessen. Hör dir die Berichte zweimal an!
   a. Schreib zuerst auf, welche Interessen jeder Schüler hat!
   b. Dann schreib die Gründe neben die Interessen der einzelnen Schüler!
2. Such dir dann einen Schüler aus und erzähl deinem Partner von ihm!

18 Man kann sich für vieles interessieren

Mach eine Liste mit mindestens drei Dingen, für die du dich interessierst und für die du dich nicht interessierst! Schreib auch Gründe dafür auf! Hier sind einige Ideen:

Umwelt —
die Natur lieben

Geografie —
gern reisen

Kameras —
gern fotografieren

Bücher —
gern lesen

Sport —
gern aktiv sein

Ein wenig Grammatik

Sich interessieren (*to be interested*) requires a reflexive pronoun in the accusative case. To talk about your or someone else's interest *in* something, the preposition **für** is used:

Ich interessiere mich für alte Autos.

How would you ask two classmates what they are interested in? How might they respond?[1]

19 Wofür interessierst du dich?

Such dir eine Partnerin! Frag sie nach ihren Interessen und Desinteressen! In ihrer Antwort muß sie dir auch einen Grund nennen. Verwende dabei die Information von Übung 18! — Tauscht dann die Rollen aus!

20 Was trägst du gern?

Frag einen Mitschüler, was er gern im Sommer trägt! Er sagt es dir. Dann darf er auch einen Mitschüler fragen, was dieser gern im Sommer, im Winter, usw. trägt. Frag auch, was deine Lehrerin gerne trägt!

Ein wenig Grammatik

The verb **tragen,** *to wear,* has a stem vowel change in the **du-** and **er/sie/es**-forms:

Was **trägst** du gern?
Und was **trägt** Roland?

There is no umlaut in the **du**-command.

Trag dieses Kleid nicht!

SO SAGT MAN DAS!

Making and accepting compliments

When making a compliment, you could say:

Deine Jeans steht dir gut.
Sie paßt dir auch echt gut.
Und diese Jacke paßt dir prima!
Sie paßt gut zu deiner blauen Bluse.

And the responses might be:

Meinst du wirklich?
Ist sie mir nicht zu eng?
Ehrlich?
Echt?

How would you reassure your friend that you really meant it?

---

1. **Wofür interessiert ihr euch? Wir interessieren uns für Politik.**

Grammatik Further uses of the dative case

1. In **Kapitel 6** you learned that there are certain verbs that are usually used with dative case forms, such as **passen,** *to fit,* and **(gut) stehen,** *to look (good).*

> Diese Jeans paßt **dir** sehr gut.
> Dieses fetzige Outfit steht **deinem Bruder** gut.

2. Dative case forms are always used after the preposition **zu.**

> Das grüne Hemd paßt gut **zu dieser blauen Jacke.**

3. When expressing personal comfort, dative case forms are also usually used.

> Diese Jacke ist **mir** viel zu eng.
> Sind **dir** diese Schuhe nicht zu groß?

21 Tolle Outfits, nicht wahr?

Du bist mit deiner Partnerin in der Stadt, und ihr seht diese Leute auf dem Marktplatz. Erzählt euch gegenseitig, was diese Leute tragen und wie ihnen die Kleidung paßt! Gefällt euch ihre Kleidung? Ist sie zu konservativ oder zu fetzig?

zu kurz
zu eng
zu klein
zu monoton

zu lang
zu weit
zu groß
zu bunt

zu fetzig
zu teuer
zu konservativ
zu unpraktisch

22 Komplimente machen

Such dir einen Partner und bewundere, was er anhat! Mach ihm Komplimente! — Tauscht dann die Rollen aus!

23 Für mein Notizbuch

Schreib in dein Notizbuch, ob du dich für Mode interessierst! Schreib, was du gern trägst und warum, und welche von deinen Klamotten besonders gut zusammenpassen oder dir gut stehen!

24 Dein Job: Modefachmann oder Modefachfrau

Du arbeitest in einem Modegeschäft. Ein Kunde hat keine Ahnung, was er sich kaufen soll. Er weiß nicht, was ihm gut steht und was nicht, was ihm gut paßt und was nicht, und welche Farben er tragen soll. Du berätst (*advise*) ihn. Entwickelt ein Rollenspiel und spielt es der Klasse vor!

1. 7, 13, 19, 21, 31, 41, 43, 47; 112, 126, 134; 116, 23, 37, 101, 103, 108
2. Naturfasern: 7, 13, 19, 23, 31, 47, 103, 112, 116, 126; Kunstfasern: 108, 134; Beides: 21, 37, 41, 43, 101, 127

25 Aus dem Modekatalog

Lies die folgende Werbung aus dem Katalog der Firma Berger! Dann beantworte die Fragen!

1. Welche Kleidungsstücke sind für Frauen? Für Männer? Für beide?
2. Welche Kleidungsstücke sind aus Naturfasern? Aus Kunstfasern?
3. Such dir zwei Angebote aus, und sag einem Partner, warum du diese Sachen haben möchtest!

7 Fischerhose. Mit Gummibund. Reine Baumwolle. **74.-**

13 Shorts. Gestreift. Mit Reißverschluß. 100% Baumwolle. **22.50**

19 Minirock. Reine Baumwolle. Mit Gürtelschlaufen. Ohne Gürtel. **25.-**

21 Jeans-Röhre. 5 Taschen. 98% Baumwolle, 2% Elasthan. Ohne Gürtel. **39.50**

23 Jeans-Jacke. Bund verstellbar. Denim. Stonewashed. **67.-**

31 Hemdbluse. Mit 2 Brusttaschen. 100% Viskose. **35.-**

37 Rollkragen-Pullover. Lang. 80% Polyacryl, 20% Wolle. **35.95**

41 Rock. 67% Polyester, 33% Viskose. Ohne Gürtel. **69.95**

43 Steghose. Mit Gürtelschlaufen. 63% Polyester, 30% Wolle, 7% sonstige Fasern. **79.95**

47 Träger-Top. Einfarbig. Mit Knöpfen. Hinten elastisch. 100% Viskose. **15.-**

101 Parka. Mit Brusttaschen. Ärmel mit Gummibund. 65% Polyester, 35% Baumwolle. **15.-**

103 Jeans. Fetzig u. fransig, wie's junge Leute mögen. Denim. Reine Baumwolle, stone-washed. **39.95**

108 Jacke. Mit vielen Taschen. Vorn mit Reißverschluß und Druckknöpfen. 100% Nylon. **49.95**

112 Sakko. Leichte Qualität. 55% Leinen, 45% Baumwolle. **89.-**

116 Shorts. Mit Bundfalten, Gürtelschlaufen, Taschen und Gesäßtasche. Ohne Gürtel. 100% Baumwolle. **35.-**

126 Anzug. Zweireiher. 2 Innentaschen, 1 Gesäßtasche. 55% Leinen, 45% Baumwolle. Ohne Gürtel. **129.-**

127 Anzug. Einreiher. 4 Innentaschen. 67% Polyester, 33% Viskose. Ohne Gürtel. **209.-**

134 Bundfaltenhose. Vollwaschbar, mit Reißverschluß. 100% Polyester. **59.-**

der Faltenrock

das Trägerhemd

die Steghose

der Sakko

der Anzug

der Blouson

Aus welchem Material?

Aus Naturfasern:

Wolle *wool*

Baumwolle *cotton*

Leinen *linen*

Seide *silk*

Viskose

Und dann noch . . .
Aus Kunstfasern: Polyester, Acryl, Polyacryl, Nylon, Kunstseide

mit kurzen Ärmeln

mit Kapuze

mit Gesäßtasche

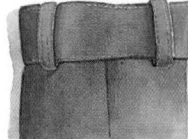

mit Schlaufen

mit Reißverschluß

mit Knöpfen

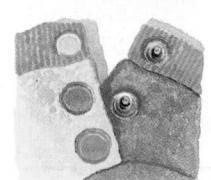

mit Druckknöpfen

Welches von diesen Kleidungsstücken hast du auch? Aus welchem Material ist es? Schau dir die Werbung auf Seite 196 an! Welche Kleidungsstücke haben Reißverschlüsse, Knöpfe oder Taschen?

---

26 Hör gut zu! For answers, see listening script on TE Interleaf.

Schüler sprechen über ihre Einkäufe. Wer von diesen Schülern will sich etwas kaufen und wer nicht? Warum? Warum nicht? Mach dir Notizen!

27 Was möchtest du dir kaufen?

Such dir eine Partnerin! Nenne ihr zwei Angebote aus dem Berger-Katalog und sag ihr, warum du dir diese Sachen kaufen möchtest!

BEISPIEL   **Ich möchte mir die Jacke kaufen, die Nummer hundertacht, weil sie viele Taschen hat und auch einen Reißverschluß und Druckknöpfe.**

28 Was trägt dein Klassenkamerad?

Such dir einen Partner und beschreibe seine Kleidung! Sag ihm, was dir gefällt und warum, und sag ihm, was dir nicht gefällt und warum nicht! — Tauscht dann die Rollen aus!

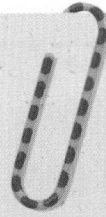

SO SAGT MAN DAS!

Persuading and dissuading

When trying to persuade someone, you may want to say:

> Warum kaufst du dir kein Woll-
> hemd?
> Kauf dir doch dieses karierte Hemd!
> Trag doch mal etwas Lustiges!

The response may be:

> Ich mag keine Wollhemden!
> Das ist mir zu teuer.
> Meinst du?

When trying to dissuade someone, you may want to say:

> Kauf dir ja kein Seidenhemd!
> Trag ja nichts aus Polyester!

The response may be:

> Ich finde Seide aber toll!
> Warum nicht?

Which words or phrases are used to persuade someone? And dissuade?

29 Soll ich das kaufen?

Such dir einen Kleidungsartikel aus dem Katalog oder aus dem Wortschatz aus, und sag deiner Partnerin, daß du dir diesen Artikel kaufen möchtest! Sie hat ihre eigene Meinung über diesen Artikel. Sie stimmt dir zu oder auch nicht und sagt dir, warum. Versuch es, sie zu überzeugen (*convince*)!

30 Aus welchem Material ist eure Kleidung?

Bildet kleine Gruppen und fragt euch gegenseitig, aus welchem Material eure Kleidungsstücke sind! Sind sie aus Naturfasern? Aus Kunst- oder Mischfasern?

Ein wenig Grammatik

The verb **kaufen** is often used with a reflexive pronoun in the dative case.

> Kauf **dir** doch ein Wollhemd!

Do you remember the reflexive pronouns?[1] How would you tell two friends to buy themselves jackets? How would you say you want to buy yourself shoes?[2]

aus Polyester
aus Kunstseide

aus Wolle:
Wollhemden, Wolljacken

aus Leinen:
Leinensakko, Leinenhosen

aus Seide:
Seidenhemden, Seidenschals

aus Baumwolle:
Baumwollsocken, Baumwollhosen

31 Eine Auswahl aus deinem Katalog

Such dir zu Hause einen Katalog mit Kleidungsreklame heraus! Dann such dir zwei Kleidungsstücke aus, für die du dich interessierst und zwei, für die du dich nicht interessierst! Bring die Reklame mit in den Deutschunterricht! Sag deiner Gruppe, für welche Klamotten du dich interessierst und warum, und für welche du dich nicht interessierst und warum! Erwähne Farbe, Material und Preis!

1. **mir, dir, sich, uns, euch, sich.** 2. **Kauft euch Jacken! Ich kaufe mir Schuhe.**

32 Hör gut zu!

For answers, see listening script on TE Interleaf.

Listen as four different students talk about what they like to do and under what conditions they usually do this. For each description you hear, match the activity with the condition the student mentions. Then listen again and write what you hear.

1. Mit dem Auto fahren
2. segeln
3. Schach spielen
4. Lebensmittel einkaufen

a. I visit Grandma
b. my bicycle is broken
c. it rains
d. it's warm and sunny

33 Das mache ich, wenn ...

Finde heraus, welche Satzteile logisch zusammenpassen, und verbinde sie dann mit einem wenn-Satz! E.g.: **Ich gehe ins Kino, wenn ich genug Geld habe.**

Ich gehe ins Kino.
Wir spielen alle Volleyball.
Ich muß mein Zimmer aufräumen.
Wir gehen ins Restaurant.
Ich fahre nach Deutschland.
Ich gehe nicht in die Schule.

Wir haben großen Hunger.
Das Wetter ist wunderbar.
Es ist Weihnachten.
Ich habe genug Geld.
Dort ist Chaos.
Das Wetter ist schlecht.

Ein wenig *Grammatik*

Read the following sentences:

**Ich spiele gern Fußball, wenn das Wetter schön ist.
Aber ich bastle zu Hause, wenn es regnet.**

What do you think the conjunction **wenn** means? How would you say these two sentences in English? Here, the conjunction **wenn** has the meaning of *whenever*. Don't confuse this word with the question-word **wann,** which asks about specific time. What do you notice about the word order in clauses beginning with **wenn?**[1] What other conjunctions have you seen which have the same word-order rule?[2]

34 Was trägst du, wenn ...?

Sag deiner Partnerin, welche Klamotten du gern trägst, wenn du ...

BEISPIEL   **Ich trage ... , wenn ich Sport mache.**

a. Sport machst
b. zur Schule gehst
c. arbeitest
d. zu Hause bist
e. in ein Konzert gehst
f. auf eine Fete gehst

35 Wie trägst du deine Sachen gern?

Sag deinem Partner, wie du deine Sachen gern trägst!

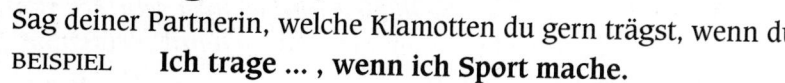

einfarbig *oder* mehrfarbig

weiter *oder* enger

länger *oder* kürzer

einfach *oder* gemustert

36 Für mein Notizbuch

Schreib in dein Notizbuch etwas über deine Kleidung! Deine Beschreibung muß folgende Fragen beantworten:

a. Wofür interessierst du dich und warum?
b. Was für Sachen kaufst du dir gewöhnlich und warum?
c. Wie gut müssen die Sachen passen, und welche Farben magst du gern?
d. Aus welchem Material sind deine Sachen und warum?

1. The conjugated verb is in last position. 2. **weil, daß,** and **ob.**

ZUM LESEN

Was bedeutet „reich und schön sein"?

LESETRICK

Understanding relationships between and within sentences.

Cohesive devices are words or phrases that help "glue" a text together and show relationships between ideas, such as time sequence or cause and effect. Cohesive devices can be pronouns, conjunctions (**aber, wenn**), or adverbs (**leider, danach**). Read the following sentences: *My mother is a banker. My mother does volunteer work. My mother is a banker, but she also does volunteer work.* Several words in the last sentence help tie the two ideas together. *But* is a conjunction that joins the two sentences, and *she* is a pronoun that refers back to (and thus forms a connection to) the subject of the first sentence.

Getting Started   For answers, see TE Interleaf.

1. Read the title, subtitle, and introduction to the list of results from the text on the left. What kind of article is this? What question is the focus of the article? Choose a German noun that would sum up your answer to this question. Now answer the question by completing this statement: **Um reich zu sein, muß man ...**

2. Look at the survey summary list. With a partner, see how many words you can understand. Can you identify the three false cognates?

Eltern-UMFRAGE

Reich ist, wer nix mehr lernen muß!

Realschüler, 12 Jahre

Neben Geld gibt es ganz andere Güter, die den Menschen reich machen – das finden unsere Kinder. Nachdenkenswertes Ergebnis der neuesten ELTERN-Umfrage

Das Wichtigste, was man braucht, um sich reich zu fühlen, ist die Zufriedenheit. Aber leider hat man immer neue Wünsche, die nicht erfüllt werden.
Orientierungsstufenschülerin, 12 Jahre

Tolle Klamotten und ein schnelles Auto, damit jeder sieht, daß da einer kommt, der Mäuse in der Tasche hat.
Hauptschüler, 13 Jahre

Ich brauche nichts, um reich zu sein. Ich fühl' mich sauwohl, besonders wenn ich mit meinen Eltern in Urlaub fahre.
Gesamtschüler, 11 Jahre

Einen tollen Bungalow mit viel Kunst an den Wänden. Möglichst ein Bild von Chagall und eines von Hundertwasser.
Gymnasiast, 15 Jahre

Eine saubere Umwelt. Was hab' ich vom Geld, wenn ich in Dreck ersticke?
Gymnasiastin, 14 Jahre

Einen Computer, damit ich immer genau ausrechnen kann, wieviel ich noch habe und wieviel ich ausgeben darf.
Gesamtschüler, 13 Jahre

Eine gute Gesundheit, sonst hat man nichts von all dem Geld und Luxus.
Hauptschülerin, 13 Jahre

Großes Herz und volle Kasse

ELTERN fragte 1880 Schülerinnen und Schüler, zehn bis 16 Jahre alt: Was muß man haben, um reich zu sein? Am häufigsten genannt:

1. soziale Einstellung (Hilfsbereitschaft, Großzügigkeit);
2. materieller Besitz (Geld, Aktien, Häuser, Fabriken);
3. Luxusgüter (teuerste Autos, Yachten, Schmuck, Kunstsammlungen);
4. gesunde Umwelt;
5. kluger Steuerberater;
6. Personal (Diener, Köchin, Chauffeur);
7. liebevoller Lebenspartner;
8. gute Freunde;
9. Bescheidenheit und Zufriedenheit;
10. Kinder;
11. Titel (Professor, Doktor, Minister);
12. Gesundheit

Tina

Das Mädchen aus dem Katalog

Zur Zeit arbeitet Tina (18) als Modell für eine Agentur. Was sagen sie, ihre Eltern, und ihre Freunde dazu? Tina meint: „Es macht mir Spaß. Ich mag meinen Nebenjob, denn man kann reisen und lernt viele interessante Leute kennen." Ihre Eltern freuen sich, Tina auf Fotos für Werbung oder Modenschauen zu sehen. Andererseits sagen sie: „Vergiß die Schule nicht. Sie ist wichtiger als gutes Aussehen." Und die Freunde? „Die finden mich ganz normal, auch wenn ich Modell bin. Am Anfang, als ich einen Schönheitswettbewerb gewonnen hatte, gab es sehr viele häßliche Bemerkungen. Viele Mädchen waren neidisch. Ich war darüber sehr geschockt. Denn ich habe doch meine Persönlichkeit nicht verändert. Und ein guter Charakter ist für mich bei Freunden viel wichtiger als Schönheit. Wenn man gut aussieht, hat man vielleicht nicht so viele Freunde, wie man glaubt." Simona (16), Tinas Freundin, sagt: „Ich finde wichtig, daß Tina trotz ihres Erfolgs als Modell genauso nett wie früher ist. Natürlich, sie ist wirklich sehr hübsch, und manche unserer Mitschüler denken: ‚Sie ist bestimmt eingebildet und arrogant.' Aber ich glaube, sehr viele Jugendliche sind neidisch oder haben Vorurteile. Wenn wir zusammen einkaufen gehen, wird Tina von vielen Jungen bewundert. Manchmal ist Schönheit auch lästig. Man fällt überall auf. Vielleicht möchten schöne Menschen viel lieber ganz normal aussehen und in ein Café gehen, ohne angestarrt zu werden."

3. Skim the survey responses to get the gist of each student's answer. Most answers contain one noun which sums up the person's opinion. Can you identify these words?

A Closer Look

4. What does the thirteen-year-old girl say about health? How does the word **sonst** affect the meaning of the sentence?

> **Tip:** If you see a word that looks like a form for *the* (**der, die, das,** etc.), but it is not followed by a noun, it is usually a pronoun. Try translating it as either *who* or *that*.

5. Look at the two 13-year-old boys' responses. What function does **damit** (*so that*) serve in their answers?

6. What does the eleven-year-old boy say about being rich? How does **besonders** affect the meaning of his sentence?

7. Now skim the article *Tina*. Who is the article about? On which characteristic of this person does the article focus?

8. Reread the article. What is Tina's job? Does she like it? What do her parents think about her job?

9. Do you think that Tina has an easy life because she is pretty? Which sentence(s) from the article can support your answer?

10. Together with your classmates, think of ten answers to the *Eltern* survey question. Form groups of four and, using these choices, design your own questionnaire. Be sure to include instructions on how people should fill out your form. Each person will survey four people (including oneself). With your group, tally the results, then do the same with your class as a whole. With the final results each group will design a summary chart like the one from the *Eltern* survey.

1 Katrin sagt ihren Freunden Judith und Boris, was sie kaufen und nicht kaufen sollen. Sie gibt auch Gründe dafür. Hör gut zu und schreib auf, was Judith und Boris kaufen und nicht kaufen sollen, und aus welchen Gründen!
For answers, see listening script on TE Interleaf.

2 Auf Seite 196 sind einige Sachen aus einem Modekatalog abgebildet. Schau dir mit einer Freundin diese Sachen an! Jeder von euch möchte zwei Sachen bestellen (*order*). Schau dir jetzt die Bestellkarte an und beantworte die folgenden Fragen zusammen mit einem Partner! 1. order number/size/quantity/total amount/page number
2. check the upper right box 3. 6 installments in 6 months; 3 installments in 3 months; total sum within 14 days; collect on delivery
4. date of birth and telephone number
5. telephone number printed crossways over the order form

1. What would you write in the columns with these labels: Bestellnummer? Größe? Anzahl/Menge? Gesamtpreis? Abb. Seite?
2. What should you do if you want to receive your order within three weeks?
3. What are the different possibilities for paying for your merchandise?
4. What information should you not forget (**Bitte nicht vergessen!**) to include?
5. What on the form tells you that you may order the merchandise more quickly?

 3 Such dir drei Sachen aus dem Katalog, Seite 196, aus! Schreib die Information auf, die du brauchst, um diese Sachen zu bestellen!

 4 Du möchtest die drei Sachen schneller bekommen. Ruf die Nummer an, die auf der Bestellkarte steht, und sag der Verkäuferin (deiner Partnerin), was du bestellen möchtest! Die Verkäuferin stellt Fragen, und du beantwortest sie, um die Bestellkarte auszufüllen.

 5 Deine Oma möchte dir etwas kaufen, aber sie weiß nicht genau, was dir gefällt. Schreib ihr einen Brief, und beschreib darin das neue „Outfit", das du gestern im Kaufhaus gesehen hast!

 6 Such dir einen Partner für dieses kleine Projekt! Entwerft zusammen eine Reklameseite, auf der ihr eure Lieblingskleidungsstücke zeichnet und genau beschreibt! Gebraucht dabei so viele Details wie nur möglich! — Zeigt eure Reklame den anderen Mitschülern! Wer hat die beste Reklameseite?

7  R O L L E N S P I E L

Get together with a classmate and role-play the following scene.

You are a salesperson in the clothing department of a large department store. A customer with really bizarre taste wants to buy certain items of clothing that either do not fit, do not match, or are simply not the right style for this person. Your job is to convince the customer to buy the right clothes, without being offensive.

KANN ICH'S WIRKLICH?

Can you describe clothes, using adjectives? (p. 189)

1 How would you ask a friend what he or she likes to wear?
1. Was trägst du gern?

2 How might your friend respond if he or she likes to wear the following clothes? 2. Ich trage gerne …

a. black jeans and a colorful shirt/blouse — a. eine schwarze Jeans und ein buntes Hemd/eine bunte Bluse.
b. a red skirt with white stockings and brown shoes — b. einen roten Rock mit weißen Strümpfen und braunen Schuhen.
c. a striped shirt and a leather bomber jacket — c. ein gestreiftes Hemd und einen Lederblouson.
d. a blue wool blazer and grey pants — d. einen blauen Blazer aus Wolle und eine graue Hose.

Can you ask someone about his or her interests and disinterests? Can you express indifference? (p. 193)

3 How would you ask a friend what he or she is interested in?
3. Wofür interessierst du dich?

4 How might your friend respond

a. that he or she is interested in soccer? — a. Ich interessiere mich für Fußball.
b. that he or she has no interest in fashion? — b. Ich interessiere mich nicht für Mode.
c. that he or she is indifferent to sports? — c. Sport ist mir egal.

Can you make and accept compliments? (p. 194)

5 How would you make the following compliments to someone?

a. this jacket looks great on you — a. Diese Jacke steht dir gut.
b. these socks go very well with your grey pants — b. Diese Socken passen sehr gut zu deiner grauen Hose.

6 How would that person respond?
6. E.g.: Meinst du wirklich? Echt?

Can you persuade and dissuade? (p. 198)

7 How would you try to persuade someone to buy a silk shirt or blouse?
7. Kauf dir doch ein Seidenhemd oder eine Seidenbluse.

8 How might that person respond

a. that silk shirts/blouses are too expensive for him or her? — a. Seidenhemden/Seidenblusen sind mir zu teuer.
b. that he or she doesn't like silk shirts/blouses? — b. Ich mag keine Seidenhemden/Seidenblusen.
c. that he or she is not sure? — c. Meinst du?

ERSTE STUFE
DESCRIBING CLOTHING

Wo hast du die neuen Stiefel gekauft? *Where did you buy the new boots?*
das Käppi, -s *(baseball) cap*
die Krawatte, -n *tie*
die Wind-, Wetterjacke, -n *windbreaker*
der Blazer, - *blazer*
das Wollhemd, -en *wool shirt*

der Anorak, -s *parka*
die Jeansweste, -n *jeans vest*

der Typ, -en *guy, type*
der Stil, -e *style*

USEFUL ADJECTIVES FOR DESCRIBING CLOTHING

konservativ *conservative*
modisch *fashionable*

cool *cool*
geblümt *flowery*
kariert *checked*
scharf *sharp*
gefüttert *padded*
sportlich *sporty*
bunt *colorful*
witzig *fun*
darunter *under it, underneath*
darüber *over it*
von hinten *from behind*

ZWEITE STUFE
EXPRESSING INTEREST

Die schöne Bluse paßt (toll) zu dem blauen Rock. *The nice blouse goes (really) well with the blue skirt.*
Interessierst du dich für Mode? *Are you interested in fashion?*
Wofür interessierst du dich? *What are you interested in?*

MORE CLOTHING AND DESCRIPTIONS

die Lederjacke, -n *leather jacket*
die Socke, -n *sock*

der Strumpf, ⸚e *stocking*
Schuhe mit flachen und hohen Absätzen *flats, high heels*
ärmellos *sleeveless*
abgeschnitten *cut-off*
weich *soft*
fetzig *really sharp*
tragen *to wear, carry*
   du trägst
   er/sie/es trägt

EXPRESSING DISINTEREST

Mode interessiert mich nicht. *Fashion doesn't interest me.*

Ich hab' kein Interesse an Mode. *I'm not interested in fashion.*

EXPRESSING INDIFFERENCE

Mode ist mir egal. *I don't care about fashion.*

MAKING AND ACCEPTING COMPLIMENTS

Das steht dir prima! *That looks great on you!*
Das ist dir zu eng. *It's too tight on you.*
Echt? *Really?*

DRITTE STUFE
PERSUADING AND DISSUADING

Kauf dir doch ...! *Why don't you just buy...*
Trag doch mal ...! *Go ahead and wear...*
Kauf dir ja kein ...! *Just don't buy...*
Trag ja nichts aus ...! *Just don't wear anything made of...*

MORE CLOTHING

der Faltenrock, ⸚e *pleated skirt*

die Steghose, -n *stirrup pants*
das Trägerhemd, -en *camisole*
der Sakko, -s *business jacket*
der Blouson, -s *bomber jacket*
der Anzug, ⸚e *suit*
die Kapuze, -n *hood*
das Seidenhemd, -en *silk shirt*
die Gesäßtasche, -n *back pocket*
die Tasche, -n *pocket*
die Schlaufe, -n *belt loop*
der Reißverschluß, -verschlüsse *zipper*
der Knopf, ⸚e *button*
der Druckknopf, ⸚e *snap*

mit langen, kurzen Ärmeln *with long, short sleeves*

TALKING ABOUT THE MATERIAL

aus Naturfasern *made from natural fibers*
die Wolle *wool*
die echte Seide *real silk*
das Leinen *linen*

OTHER USEFUL WORDS

wenn (conj.) *whenever*

Kapitel 9: Wohin in die Ferien?

Los geht's! pp. 208-210	Verpatzte Ferien, *p. 208*			*Video Guide*
	FUNCTIONS	**GRAMMAR**	**CULTURE**	**RE-ENTRY**
Erste Stufe *pp. 212-215*	Expressing indecision, asking for and making suggestions, *p. 213*	• -er endings with place names, *p. 213* • The prepositions **nach, an, in,** and **auf,** *p. 214*	• **Landeskunde: Wohin fährst du in den nächsten Ferien?** *p. 211* • **Reisetips,** *p. 212* • **Ein wenig Landeskunde:** Statistics on the means of transportation Germans use to go on vacation, *p. 215*	• Prepositions with location vs. direction, *p. 212* (from **Kap. 3,** II) • Talking about interests, *p. 212* (from **Kap. 8,** II) • Asking someone what to do, *p. 213* (from **Kap. 8,** I) • Inclusive commands, *p. 213* (from **Kap. 6,** II) • The modal **können,** *p. 213* (from **Kap. 7,** I) • The **möchte**-forms, *p. 214* (from **Kap. 3,** I) • The stem-changing verb **fahren,** *p. 214* (from **Kap. 9,** I) • Talking about free-time activities, *p. 215* (from **Kap. 2/6,** I)
Zweite Stufe *pp. 216-219*	Expressing doubt, conviction, and resignation, *p. 217*	• The conjunction **ob,** *p. 218* • Expressing direction and location (summary), *p. 218*	Students talk about vacations, *p. 216*	• **Daß**-clauses, *p. 217* (from **Kap. 9,** I) • Word order with subordinate clauses, *pp. 217-218* (from **Kap. 8/9,** I) • The verb **wissen** with subordinate prepositions, *p. 217* (from **Kap. 9,** I) • Accusative vs. dative case, *p. 218* (from **Kap. 3,** II) • Using the telephone, *p. 219* (from **Kap. 11,** I) • Saying where you were on vacation, *p. 219* (from **Kap. 3,** II) • Talking about free-time activities, *p. 219* (from **Kap. 2/6,** I)
Dritte Stufe *pp. 220-223*	Asking for and giving directions, *p. 222*	• Prepositions followed by dative-case forms, *p. 222* • The prepositions **durch** and **um,** *p. 222* • The prepositions **vor, neben,** and **zwischen,** *p.223*	**Stadtrundgang durch Bietigheim,** *p. 220*	• Giving directions, *pp. 221, 222* (from **Kap. 9,** I) • Asking where something is located, *pp. 222* (from **Kap. 9,** I) • Two-way prepositions, *p. 222* (from **Kap. 3,** II) • Preposition followed by the accusative case, *p. 222* (from **Kap. 7,** I) • Inviting someone and responding to an invitation, *p. 223* (from **Kap. 11,** I)

Zum Lesen *pp. 224-225*	**Was ist dein Lieblingsreiseziel?** Reading Strategy: Distinguishing between fact and opinion
Review *pp. 226-229*	•*Anwendung, p. 226* •*Kann ich's wirklich? p. 228* •*Wortschatz, p. 229*

Assessment Options	**Stufe Quizzes** •*Chapter Resources,* Book 3 Erste Stufe, Quiz 9-1 Zweite Stufe, Quiz 9-2 Dritte Stufe, Quiz 9-3 •*Assessment Items, Audiocassette* 8 A	**Kapitel 9 Chapter Test** •*Chapter Resources,* Book 3 •*Assessment Guide,* Speaking Test •*Assessment Items, Audiocassette* 8 A **Test Generator, Kapitel 9**

Chapter Overview

Video Program **OR**
Expanded Video Program, Videocassette 3

Textbook Audiocassette 5 A

RESOURCES Print	**RESOURCES** Audiovisual

Textbook Audiocassette 5 A

Practice and Activity Book
Chapter Resources, Book 3
- Additional Listening Activities 9-1, 9-2 ....*Additional Listening Activities, Audiocassette* 10 A
- Student Response Forms
- Realia 9-1
- Situation Card 9-1
- Teaching Transparency Master 9-1 ....*Teaching Transparency* 9-1
- Quiz 9-1 ....*Assessment Items, Audiocassette* 8 A
Video Guide ....*Video Program/Expanded Video Program,* Videocassette 3

Textbook Audiocassette 5 A

Practice and Activity Book
Chapter Resources, Book 3
- Communicative Activity 9-1
- Additional Listening Activities 9-3, 9-4 ....*Additional Listening Activities, Audiocassette* 10 A
- Student Response Forms
- Realia 9-2
- Situation Card 9-2
- Quiz 9-2 ....*Assessment Items, Audiocassette* 8 A

Textbook Audiocassette 5 A

Practice and Activity Book
Chapter Resources, Book 3
- Communicative Activity 9-2
- Additional Listening Activities 9-5, 9-6 ....*Additional Listening Activities, Audiocassette* 10 A
- Student Response Forms
- Realia 9-3
- Situation Card 9-3
- Teaching Transparency Master 9-2 ....*Teaching Transparency* 9-2
- Quiz 9-3 ....*Assessment Items, Audiocassette* 8 A

Video Guide ....*Video Program/Expanded Video Program,* Videocassette 3

Alternative Assessment
- Performance Assessment, *Teacher's Edition*
  Erste Stufe, p. 205K
  Zweite Stufe, p. 205M
  Dritte Stufe, p. 205P
- Portfolio Assessment
  Written: **Anwendung,** Activity 6, *Pupil's Edition,* p. 227; *Assessment Guide,* p. 22
  Oral: **Anwendung,** Activity 7, *Pupil's Edition,* p. 227; *Assessment Guide,* p. 22
- **Notizbuch,** *Pupil's Edition,* pp. 219, 223; *Practice and Activity Book,* p. 153

CHAPTER OVERVIEW

Kapitel 9: Wohin in die Ferien?
Textbook Listening Activities Scripts

Erste Stufe
Activity 6, p. 212

1. HORST Mit der Bahn drei Tage an die Nordsee in das kleine Fischerdorf Bensersiel. In diesem Dorf direkt an der Küste sind noch Zimmer frei. Entspannen Sie im Hallenbad, beim Reiten und Stadtwandern. Ein Besuch im Buddelschiffmuseum lohnt sich!

2. HANNI Einmalig preiswert! Eine Drei-Tage-Busfahrt nach Dresden und in die Sächsische Schweiz. In Dresden besuchen Sie den berühmten Zwinger, und Sie erleben die einmalig schönen Sandsteinfelsen der Bastei.

3. HORST Eine Tagesfahrt an den Bodensee nach Unteruhldingen und weiter mit dem Schiff auf die Insel Mainau, wo Sie unter Palmen spazieren und die Blumenwelt bewundern können. Abfahrt sechs Uhr.

4. HANNI Eine Wochenendfahrt (Samstag/Sonntag) in die Schweiz. Übernachtung in Brienz. Am nächsten Vormittag mit der Bergbahn aufs Brienzer Rothorn, die Schweizer Bergwelt genießen. Ein Superangebot!

5. HORST Sonderfahrt mit dem Bus nach Ulm zum bekannten Fischerstechen auf der Donau. Am Vormittag Gelegenheit zum Messebesuch im Dom. Mittagessen in einem soliden Gasthaus. Das Fischerstechen beginnt um 14 Uhr. Rückkehr gegen 19 Uhr 30.

6. HANNI Drei Tage mit dem Bus durch die schönsten Täler in der Schweiz. Im Emmental Besichtigung eines typischen Bauernhauses und Besuch einer Käserei.

7. HORST Drei Tage (von Dienstag bis Donnerstag) mit dem Bus nach Österreich, nach Alpbach in Tirol. Sehr preisgünstig. Ideal für Bergwanderer und solche, die's noch werden wollen!

Answers to Activity 6
1. f; 2. b; 3. d; 4. e; 5. g; 6. c; 7. a

Zweite Stufe
Activity 14, p. 217

1. TANJA Ich möchte so gern im Sommer nach Südfrankreich, an die Atlantikküste zum Zelten. Es gibt dort ganz tolle Campingplätze, hab' ich gehört! Aber in den Sommerferien ist da natürlich Hochsaison. Ich bezweifle, daß es dort noch einen freien Platz für ein 4-Personen-Zelt gibt.

   RUTH Ja also, wir waren letztes Jahr an der französischen Atlantikküste, auch mitten in den großen Ferien. Wir hatten überhaupt nicht im voraus gebucht und haben trotzdem einen Platz auf einem schönen großen Campingplatz direkt am Meer bekommen. Ich bin sicher, daß du auch etwas findest.

2. DIRK Ich habe zum Geburtstag eine neue Taucherausrüstung bekommen. Martin, hast du vielleicht Lust, am Wochenende mit mir an den Strümper See zu fahren? Ich weiß nur nicht genau, ob man dort auch tauchen darf.

   MARTIN Mein Bruder hat mir gesagt, dort gibt es Schilder, auf denen steht, daß man dort weder schwimmen noch angeln darf. Also, das mit dem Tauchen, das kannst du vergessen. Da kann man nichts machen.

3. **MARITA** Wir haben ein Zimmer in einem ganz modernen Sporthotel im Schwarzwald gebucht. Dort gibt es ein Schwimmbad, 'ne Sauna, ein Fitneßstudio und einen Golfplatz nebenan. Ich bin nur nicht sicher, ob es dort auch Tennisplätze gibt.

OLIVER Also, wenn es ein ganz modernes Sporthotel ist, dann gibt es dort bestimmt auch einen Tennisplatz. Das kannst du mir glauben!

4. **NINA** Ich freu' mich schon wahnsinnig auf unseren Urlaub. Wir fahren an die Nordsee, in ein kleines Fischerdorf am Meer. Ich werde jeden Tag an den Strand gehen, um zu schwimmen und ein Sonnenbad zu nehmen. Ich möchte auch gern unseren Hund, den Waldi, mitnehmen. Aber ich weiß nicht, ob er auch mit an den Strand darf.

BERT Also, ich bin ziemlich sicher, daß man Hunde nicht mit an den Strand nehmen darf. Besonders dann nicht, wenn es ein Badestrand ist und viele Touristen dort sind. Tja, das ist leider so.

Answers to Activity 14

1. ob sie noch einen Zeltplatz bekommen; hat andere Meinung
2. ob man im See tauchen darf; stimmt zu
3. ob es einen Tennisplatz gibt; hat andere Meinung
4. ob der Hund mit an den Strand darf; stimmt zu

Activity 16, p. 219

KATJA Ja, hallo Sandra! Katja hier. Du, die Fahrt nach Zürich ist endlos! Wir sind heute morgen ganz früh von Berlin losgefahren, so um vier Uhr! Jetzt sind wir gerade in Nürnberg und machen eine kleine Pause. Wir haben ungefähr noch fünf Stunden vor uns. Puh! Du kannst dir gar nicht vorstellen, wie froh ich bin, wenn wir endlich ankommen! Also, ich meld' mich wieder, wenn wir in Zürich sind. Tschüs!

BERND Hallo Sandra! Hier ist Bernd. Ja, also ich wollte eigentlich nur mal sehen, wie es dir so geht in Berlin. Echt schade, daß du die ganzen Ferien zu Hause bleiben mußt. Aber wir können ja was zusammen unternehmen, wenn der Patrick und ich wieder zurückkommen. Also, unser Zug ist gerade erst in Lindau angekommen, so ungefähr vor einer Minute! Wir sind noch auf dem Bahnhof und müssen jetzt erstmal herausfinden, wie wir zum Campingplatz kommen. Also, wir sehen uns dann in zwei Wochen! Tschüs!

PINAR Sandra! Hier ist die Pinar! Du, endlich sind wir in Antalya angekommen! Es ist einfach herrlich hier! Die Sonne, der Strand, traumhaft, sag' ich dir! Und ich hab' dir ja schon erzählt, daß meine Großeltern ein kleines Häuschen direkt am Meer haben! Einfach sagenhaft! Meine Eltern sind natürlich auch total happy, wieder hier zu sein. Das nächste Mal mußt du unbedingt mit in die Türkei kommen! Also, viel Spaß noch in Berlin. Bis nach den Ferien!

BORIS He Sandra! Hier ist Boris. Schade, daß du nicht zu Hause bist. Ich wollte dir halt nur schnell schöne Ferien wünschen. Wir haben uns ja gar nicht mehr gesehen, bevor ich losgefahren bin. Ach übrigens, der Enrico und ich, wir sind gerade unterwegs nach Thüringen. Wir wollen uns Weimar, Jena und Eisenach anschauen. Die Hälfte der Strecke haben wir schon hinter uns. Also, na ja, wie gesagt, schöne Ferien dann noch, und bis bald! Ach ja, und viele Grüße auch vom Enrico!

Answers to Activity 16
Katja: auf dem Weg dorthin
Bernd: aus dem Ferienort
Pinar: aus dem Ferienort
Boris: auf dem Weg dorthin

*D*ritte Stufe
Activity 22, p. 221

1. Beginnen Sie Ihren Rundgang durch das schöne Städtchen Bietigheim am großen Parkplatz an der Holzgartenstraße. Überqueren Sie die Metter und gehen Sie geradeaus, bis Sie auf der linken Seite das Stadttor sehen, ein imposantes Mauerwerk aus dem 14. Jahrhundert. Spazieren Sie durch das Stadttor und biegen Sie dann gleich nach rechts in die Fräuleinstraße ein. Gehen Sie in die zweite Straße links, dann die erste Straße rechts. Dort sehen Sie direkt an der Ecke das Kachelsche Haus aus dem 16. Jahrhundert. Direkt neben dem Kachelschen Haus auf der rechten Seite endet der Rundgang vor einem prächtigen Fachwerkhaus.

2. Treffpunkt für diesen Rundgang ist der Ulrichsbrunnen am Marktplatz. Gehen Sie von dort aus in die Farbstraße hinein, um auch die schönen Seitenfassaden des Bietigheimer Rathauses aus dem 16. Jahrhundert zu besichtigen. Hinter dem Rathaus biegen Sie in die nächste Straße rechts ein, und Sie werden auf der linken Seite eines der ältesten Wohnhäuser Bietigheims sehen, das Hormoldhaus. Gehen Sie nun wieder rechts und dann nach links. Halten Sie sich geradeaus, bis Sie auf der linken Seite ein imposantes Gebäude erblicken. Der Stadtrundgang endet mit einer Innenbesichtigung dieses Gebäudes.

3. Dieser Rundgang beginnt am alten Stadttor auf der Hauptstraße, die in die Innenstadt hineinführt. Gehen Sie hinter dem Stadttor nach rechts in die Fräuleinstraße. Biegen Sie dann in die vierte Straße links. Auf der rechten Seite befindet sich das alte, sehenswürdige Backhaus. Wenn Sie an dem Backhaus vorbei weiter geradeaus gehen, sehen Sie auf der linken Seite das stattliche Bürgerhaus, ein Fachwerkgebäude aus dem 17. Jahrhundert. Gehen Sie weiter die Schieringbrunnerstraße entlang, bis Sie zum Marktplatz kommen. Dort biegen Sie nach rechts in die Hauptstraße. Biegen Sie die erste Straße rechts ein, gehen Sie am Dom vorbei und überqueren Sie das Schwätzgäßle. Vor dem Fachwerkgebäude auf der rechten Seite endet der Rundgang.

Answers to Activity 22
1. Schieringerstraße, Bürgerhaus
2. Schieringsbrunnerstraße, Evangelische Kirche
3. Pfarrstraße, Kleines Bürgerhaus

*A*wendung
Activity 1, p. 226

Hi, ich bin's, die Gabi! Stell dir vor, ich war in den Sommerferien drei Wochen lang in Österreich. Es war ganz toll, ich bin gerade vor ein paar Tagen wieder zurückgekommen. Die Moni, das ist meine Freundin, und ich, wir sind zuerst mit dem Zug von München nach Salzburg gefahren. Dort haben wir uns erstmal die Innenstadt angeschaut und, ach ja, auch das Schloß Mirabell haben wir besichtigt! Wunderschön, sag' ich dir! Dann sind wir von Salzburg aus mit dem Reisebus nach Tirol gefahren. Auf dem Wolfgangsee haben wir eine super Bootsfahrt gemacht. Ach ja, und hab' ich dir schon von den wunderschönen Bergen in Österreich erzählt? Wir wollten so gern eine Bergtour in den Alpen machen, aber stell' dir mal vor, Moni und ich hatten leider keine richtigen Wanderschuhe mit, nur unsere Turnschuhe. So was Blödes! Damit kann man natürlich nicht wandern gehen! Na ja, aber dafür haben wir jeden Morgen Tennis gespielt. Wir haben übrigens in einer kleinen Pension gewohnt, die gleich in der Nähe von einer supermodernen Sportanlage war, sogar mit Schwimmbad. Aber Moni und ich sind lieber im See schwimmen gegangen. Das hat viel mehr Spaß gemacht. Und du, erzähl doch mal, was hast du denn alles in den Ferien gemacht?

Answers to Activity 1
Ist mit dem Zug nach Salzburg gefahren; hat die Innenstadt von Salzburg angeschaut; hat Schloß Mirabell besichtigt; ist mit dem Reisebus nach Tirol gefahren; hat eine Bootsfahrt auf dem Wolfgangsee gemacht; hat Tennis gespielt; ist im See schwimmen gegangen

Kapitel 9: Wohin in die Ferien?
Projects and Games

PROJECT

In this project each student will create an illustrated advertisement with the title ... **muß man gesehen und erlebt haben!** *Students will choose a city for which they will create a convincing advertisement.*

Materials Students may need poster board, paper, pens, travel magazines or travel sections from newspapers, and an encyclopedia for reference.

Suggested Cities

Hamburg, Bietigheim, München, Stuttgart, Leipzig, Vienna, Zurich, or any other city that you find appropriate for this project.

Suggested Sequence

1. Each student decides on a city for his or her advertisement and makes an outline showing how he or she plans to organize the project.
2. Students use resources such as travel brochures, reference materials, and travel ads to prepare a convincing visual and written report about their city.
3. The written part of the project should include facts and data. Realia, such as photos or graphs, should be incorporated into a convincing article that would invite people to visit that particular location.
4. As part of the oral component, students should be prepared to give a brief (1 minute) statement to the rest of the class to convince them to visit the city. This oral report should not be read directly from the written advertisement, but instead should be delivered as a sales pitch.

Grading the Project

Suggested point distribution (total = 100 points)
Originality and design   30
Written assignment (language
usage and accuracy)   40
Oral presentation   30

 GAME

Warum denn dahin?

This game tests students' knowledge of German cities and also the grammar structures introduced in this chapter.

Procedure Divide the class into two teams. Each team makes a list of ten to fifteen German cities, mountains, lakes, etc. that they have learned about. Students may use the book to look for names of cities, mountains, and lakes. The first player on team A chooses the first city on his or her group's list and asks a student on team B: **Warum fährst du denn nach** (**München**)? The student who was asked then replies by restating the question and also adding an interesting fact or point of interest that made him or her decide to visit the city.
Example: **Ich fahre nach München, weil ich zum Oktoberfest will.**
If the student answers with a correct point of interest or idea, he or she wins a point for the team. Then team B gets to ask the next question. The team with the most points at the end of the game wins.

Kapitel 9: Wohin in die Ferien?
Lesson Plans, pages 206-229

*U*sing the Chapter Opener, pp. 206-207

Motivating Activity

Ask students about their family vacations. How do they generally decide on a vacation destination? What are some of their most memorable vacations? Have there been any that did not turn out as planned?

Teaching Suggestions

- Much planning goes into organizing a vacation. Ask students to brainstorm how to best plan a vacation. What is involved in making plans and what resources could be used? Make a list.
- Ask students to look at the various objects that are pictured on the two pages: **Flugzeug, Tennisschläger, Angel, Golfschläger, Golfball, Bus,** and **Straßenkarte.** Have students make suggestions about how these objects relate to vacations.

Thinking Critically

① **Drawing Inferences** Have students focus on the picture of the Bavarian village. Can students guess why people might want to go there on their vacation? What are some of the recreational activities a visitor might find there? (Examples: **wandern, skilaufen**)

Background Information

① Many Germans prefer to vacation in small villages and towns such as the one pictured. Since large resorts or hotels cannot be found there, lodging is typically provided by bed and breakfast establishments (**Pension**). At a reasonable price visitors stay in a home, often share bathrooms with other guests, and receive a full breakfast included in the price.

Thinking Critically

① **Comparing and Contrasting** Ask students if they know of any bed and breakfasts in their area. You could bring a guidebook to class to have students find out about lodgings in their state.

③ **Drawing Inferences** Have students imagine that the family pictured is calling the proprietors of the **Pension** where they will be staying. They are not familiar with the area and need help planning some day trips. Have students come up with a list of questions these people might be asking.

Building on Previous Skills

② Throughout the chapters of Levels 1 and 2, students have been introduced to several historical downtown areas, referred to as **Altstädte.** (Examples: Stuttgart and Hamburg) Can students name some of the interesting places and sights in an **Altstadt?** (Examples: **altes Rathaus, Kirche, Schloß, Theater**)

Thinking Critically

Drawing Inferences Give students a synonym for the word **Bürger.** (Examples: **Einwohner; Leute, die in einem Ort wohnen.**) Can students then guess what the word **Bürgerhaus** refers to? See the following Teacher Note.

Teacher Note

A **Bürgerhaus** is an old apartment building in the historical part of a town which dates back to the 15th-17th centuries.

Focusing on Outcomes

To get students to focus on the chapter objectives, ask them to think of ways they would make suggestions for planning a vacation. How would they express their doubt, in English, about travel plans they are not too sure about? Then have students preview the learning outcomes listed on p. 207. **NOTE:** Each of these outcomes is modeled in the video and evaluated in **Kann ich's wirklich?** on p. 228.

Teaching Los geht's!
pp. 208-210

Resources for Los geht's!

- *Video Program* **OR**
  Expanded Video Program, Videocassette 3
- *Textbook Audiocassette* 5 A
- *Practice and Activity Book*

▶ **pages 208-209**

Video Synopsis

In this segment of the video, Katrin and her family are disappointed when their vacation plans fall through. Katrin and her friends come up with a plan to spend the holidays at home. The student outcomes listed on p. 207 are modeled in the video: expressing indecision, asking for and making suggestions, expressing doubt, conviction, and resignation, and asking for and giving directions.

Motivating Activity

Ask students if they ever had a trip or vacation cancelled or changed due to unforeseen problems. If so, can they tell the class what happened?

For Individual Needs

A Slower Pace Have students watch the video segment of this **Foto-Roman**, pausing the tape after each of the eight frames depicted in the book. Give students a moment to summarize in writing what happens in each frame, then continue with the next one. After all eight frames have been viewed, ask students to read what they have written down. Replay the entire **Foto-Roman** and ask students to make any final changes to their individual summaries.

Culture Note

Pfingstferien (*Whitsuntide* or *Pentecost vacation*) usually falls at the end of May and varies in length from **Bundesland** to **Bundesland** from four to seven days. **Pfingsten** is a Christian holiday.

▶ **page 210**

Thinking Critically

Drawing Inferences Ask students to explain what **Frau Simon** means when she says "**Unsere Reise ist wahrscheinlich ins Wasser gefallen.**" Can students think of a way to express the idea of **ins Wasser fallen** in English? (*to fall through, not to work out*)

For Individual Needs

1 Auditory Learners After students have watched the video segment of the **Foto-Roman**, ask the questions in Activity 1. Depending on students' comprehension you may or may not want to let them keep their books open.

1 Challenge Ask the questions in German immediately after students have watched the video segment without having them look at the script.

4 A Slower Pace Before students scan the story for this activity ask them to think of phrases they use in English to express each of the ideas listed. Make a list and have students compare it with the German expressions they found in the **Foto-Roman**.

Closure

Have students choose roles and act out the **Foto-Roman**. Students should choose to play a member of the Simon family (in groups of three) or a member of Katrin's circle of friends (in groups of five). Ask students to dramatize their roles using a lot of expression. Encourage students not to simply read the lines from the book, but to add their own lines to the conversation.

▶ **page 211**

PRESENTATION: Landeskunde

Teacher Note

The **Landeskunde** interviews are recorded on audiocassette and videocassette.

Teaching Suggestions

- After students have done the prereading activity, ask them to close their books. While students watch the video segment or listen to the audio-cassette, ask them to take notes about the vacation plans the four German teenagers talk about. If necessary, play the interviews two or three times. Then divide the board into four sections and write the name of each teenager at the top of each section. Ask students to tell you how the German teenagers spend their vacation. Then read the four interviews in the book and have students compare the information on the board with the actual readings.

- You might want to introduce the following definitions to help students better understand the video segment or listening script.

  aufgrund dessen - weil

  bissel (southern dialect) **- ein bißchen; ein wenig**

  der Verstärker - Teil einer Stereoanlage

 ## Culture Note

In Germany, every employee is entitled by law to a minimum of three weeks paid vacation each year. However, collective agreements with most employers give many employees six weeks or more of paid vacation (**bezahlter Urlaub**).

Thinking Critically

Synthesizing Ask students to describe the benefits of a six-week paid vacation for a German employer as well as for an employee. (Examples: promotes job stability, helps lower unemployment rate, increases employee morale, allows parents to spend time with kids) Then ask students to identify the downside of such a vacation policy for the employer and the employee. (Example: increases cost of doing business by forcing employer to compensate for loss of productivity of a vacationing work force)

 ## Multicultural Connection

Ask students to find information about the length of school vacations in foreign countries. If possible, have students interview foreign exchange students about their favorite vacation spots and the usual length of their stay.

Teacher Note

Mention to your students that the **Landeskunde** will also be included in Quiz 9-1 given at the end of the **Erste Stufe**.

Teaching Erste Stufe,
pp. 212-215

▶ *page 212*

MOTIVATE
Teaching Suggestion

Ask students where they would go if they were offered a round trip ticket to anywhere in the United States for the upcoming weekend. What would they do there?

TEACH

 ## For Individual Needs

6 Auditory Learners After students have listened to the descriptions and matched them with the corresponding photos, play the descriptions a second time. This time ask students to listen for the particular phrase or word that helped them match the description and photo. Students should write that phrase or word next to the number and its letter. (Example: 3. **Insel Palmen**)

▶ *page 213*

PRESENTATION: Wortschatz

Review previously learned means of transportation such as **Auto, Fahrrad, Mofa, Moped, S-Bahn, U-Bahn,** and **Bus** by asking questions such as: **Wie kommst du gewöhnlich zur Schule? Wie fährt dein Vater/deine Mutter zur Arbeit?**

Using a world map, introduce the new vocabulary through meaningful context. Example: **Von New York nach Frankfurt geht es am schnellsten mit dem Flugzeug.**

Practice using the vocabulary by asking students what type of transportation they use
a) to go on vacation,
b) to visit family,
c) to go into town.

Teaching Suggestion

You may want to introduce some vacation places students have not yet learned.
ins Ferienlager
aufs Land
ins Freibad
ins Wellenbad
auf einen Bauernhof
in den Vergnügungspark

PRESENTATION: Ein wenig Grammatik

Have students use an atlas or a map of Europe to find other examples of such mountain names.
Examples:
Wildspitze - Österreich
Rheinwaldhorn - Schweiz
Hochalmspitze - Österreich
Stanserhorn - Schweiz
Sustenhorn - Schweiz

PRESENTATION: So sagt man das!

Ask your students what other ways of making suggestions they remember. (In Chapter 6 students used modals as well as the inclusive command to make suggestions.) Students can practice the expressions in the function box with a partner as they discuss plans for the afternoon or the weekend.
Examples:
Was machen wir heute nachmittag?
Ich bin dafür, daß wir mal ins Kino gehen.

▶ *page 214*

PRESENTATION: Grammatik

To demonstrate the use of prepositions to express direction, use pictures of geographic features like the ones used in this grammar box. Then elicit answers to the question "**Wohin fährst du diesen Sommer?**" To emphasize the concept of direction, demonstrate the difference between **in** as a response to **wohin?** and **in** as a response to **wo?** Have one student leave the classroom and then walk back in. Ask the other students: **Wohin geht Thomas?** answer: **In die Klasse.** Then ask: **Und wo ist Thomas?** stressing **ist.** Elicit the answer or answer yourself: **In der Klasse.**

✦ For Individual Needs

9 Challenge To expand this activity, ask students to reuse their notes to compose a series of travel journal entries for an imaginary trip. Students should give an account of their daily activities for a minimum of three days.

▶ *page 215*

Building on Previous Skills

10 Before students begin this activity, write the twelve destinations on the board or a transparency. For each location, ask students to brainstorm what sights or activities might be of interest based on what they have learned in previous chapters, including Location Openers. Write students' suggestions next to each destination. Students then use the list they compiled to work on the activity.

ERSTE STUFE

Teacher Note

12 You may want to have a selection of travel brochures available for students to choose from. You can obtain these materials from local travel agencies or order materials from the **Deutsche Zentrale für Tourismus e. V.** or the German National Tourist Office. For addresses, see p. T41 of the *Teacher's Edition*.

Geography Connection

12 As an alternative to having students work on destinations in German-speaking countries, ask students to refer to foreign countries they have studied in Social Studies or Geography and have them incorporate that information into the **Reisebüro** conversation.

Background Information

Travel has become by far the most popular pastime for many Germans. Travel is viewed as a necessity to balance out busy work schedules and the stresses of everyday life. The most popular destinations for German tourists are Italy, Spain, Austria, France, Switzerland, and the United States.

Thinking Critically

Drawing Inferences Among the German population today, the highest percentage of travel occurs among former East Germans. Can students think of reasons for this? (Before unification, East Germans were not allowed to travel to the west and could only vacation in other Eastern block countries.)

Reteaching: Expressing direction

The day before you plan to do this activity, ask students to bring red, blue, green, and brown colored pens or pencils to class. To review the uses of **an, auf, in,** and **nach,** prepare a list of sentences like the following examples. Students receive a handout and are asked to underline all bodies of water in blue, all countries or geographic areas that require an article in green, all countries or geographic areas that do not require an article in red, and all areas referring to height or flat surfaces in brown. Then, based on what students learned on p. 214, have them decide which preposition to use to fill in the blanks. Examples:

Wir fahren im Sommer_____(die Ostsee).
Ihre Familie steigt jedes Jahr____(die Zugspitze).
Ich fliege nächste Woche_____(die Türkei).
Am Wochenende fährt er immer___(Hamburg).

CLOSE

♖ Game
Play the game **Warum denn dahin?** See p. 205F for the procedure.

Focusing on Outcomes

Refer students back to the learning outcomes listed on p. 207. Students should recognize that they now know how to express indecision and ask for and make suggestions.

ASSESS

- **Performance Assessment** Ask individual students to give an account of an excursion or trip that did not turn out as planned. Where did they plan to go and what happened?

- Quiz 9-1, *Chapter Resources*, Book 3

Teaching Zweite Stufe, pp. 216-219

▶ *page 216*

MOTIVATE

Teaching Suggestion

Ask students to describe the type of activities they like to do on vacation. Do they prefer quiet activities, such as reading, sunbathing, and fishing or more active things, such as playing tennis, running, and hiking?

TEACH

Group work

Divide the class into groups of three and assign each group one of the interviews on this page. After groups have read their paragraph, they should study the text to find out
a) what the original travel plans were,
b) why the person(s) cannot go,
c) what alternate plans are being considered.
Each group should make a list of words or phrases that support each of the three answers. Call on each group and ask them to share their ideas with the class. You may want to write the words and phrases from each interview on the board and have students compare them.

▶ *page 217*

PRESENTATION: Wortschatz

- Have students think of all the water sports they can do at the following locations.
  am/im Meer
  am/im See
  am/auf dem Fluß
  Have students write the names of the activities from the **Wortschatz** box under the appropriate headings. They should also include other vocabulary they have already learned. (Examples: **baden, schwimmen**)
- After introducing the hotel vocabulary, ask individual students to describe an ideal hotel, one they would like to stay in for a week-long vacation.

PRESENTATION: So sagt man das!

Before introducing the new expressions, ask students what they would say in English to convey doubt, conviction, and resignation. Then go over the German expressions in the function box. Demonstrate to students that intonation plays a big role in the perception of what is being said. Ask students to look back at the **Foto-Roman** on pp. 208-209 and determine where and how these functions are modeled. Have students make a list of the statements they find.

For Additional Practice

Give students several different statements to which they have to react, expressing either doubt, conviction, or resignation. Use situations from this chapter or previous chapters.
Examples:
In Tirol hat es Hochwasser gegeben.
Drei Tage mit dem Bus fahren? Das ist sehr lange!

✦ For Individual Needs

14 A Slower Pace In order for students to follow the conversations, play each conversation several times. Have students listen for the main idea expressed by each speaker. To check students' comprehension, make a chart on the board and elicit students' responses to complete it.

ZWEITE STUFE

ZWEITE STUFE

▶ *page 218*

Teaching Suggestion

15 Ask students to incorporate in their conversation as many of the new vocabulary items from the **Wortschatz** on p. 217 as possible. To make the role-playing situation more authentic, students can use a map to choose an interesting **Reiseziel**.

PRESENTATION: Grammatik

To teach the difference between expressing direction and location, ask students if they can think of other verbs to replace the ones in the grammar box. Here are some examples:

gehen	leben
reisen	wohnen
ziehen	sitzen
besuchen	zelten
sich befinden	

Ask students to rephrase the sentences in the box, replacing each verb with one of their own.

▶ *page 219*

Teaching Suggestion

17 With students, prepare a list of words that will help them improve their use of connected discourse.
Examples: **denn, dann, danach, zuerst, weil**

✦ For Individual Needs

18 Auditory Learners As an alternative, students could use a tape recorder and record their description on audiocassette, rather than writing in their **Notizbuch**.

Teaching Suggestion

20 You may want to provide students with some additional vocabulary to help them role-play this situation.

vorschlagen *to suggest*
übernachten *to spend the night*
reservieren *to reserve*
abfahren *to depart*
ankommen *to arrive*
erste und zweite Klasse *1st and 2nd class*

Reteaching: Vacation Vocabulary

To review the various water activities, ask students what type of activities one can do in and around the water, which of these activities they would like to try, and why.

CLOSE

♜ Game
The game **Kofferpacken** will help auditory learners review the vocabulary they have learned so far. Begin the game with the phrase: **Wenn ich diesen Sommer nach ... reise, nehme ich ... mit.** The first student repeats your sentence and adds another item he or she will take along. If a student misses a previously mentioned word, he or she drops out of the game. The game continues until only one student is left or time is called.

Focusing on Outcomes

Refer students back to the learning outcomes listed on p. 207. They should recognize that they now know how to express doubt, conviction, and resignation.

ASSESS

• **Performance Assessment** Prepare a class set of index cards or small pieces of paper. On each card write the name of a travel destination, preferably one by a lake or ocean so that students can use a lot of vocabulary from this **Stufe**. Give each student one of the cards. Then tell students to take 5-10 minutes to prepare a convincing argument (using expressions of conviction as well as vocabulary from the **Wortschatz** box) why this particular location is worth a visit.
Example:
Ocean City: **Es lohnt sich, Ocean City zu besuchen, weil ...**
Additional locations might include **Cancun, Acapulco, Ibiza, die italienische Riviera, die Côte d'Azur, Santa Barbara,** or **Miami.**

• Quiz 9-2, *Chapter Resources*, Book 3

*T*eaching Dritte Stufe,
pp. 220-223

Resources for Dritte Stufe

Practice and Activity Book
Chapter Resources, Book 3
- Communicative Activity 9-2
- Additional Listening Activities 9-5, 9-6
- Student Response Forms
- Realia 9-3
- Situation Card 9-3
- Teaching Transparency Master 9-2
- Quiz 9-3

Audiocassette Program
- *Textbook Audiocassette* 5 A
- *Additional Listening Activities, Audiocassette* 10 A
- *Assessment Items, Audiocassette* 8 A

▶ *page 220*

MOTIVATE

For Individual Needs

Tactile Learners On the day you plan to do this activity, bring a large piece of construction paper, rulers, and markers to class. Ask students to work together to create a map of a fictitious city, including at least ten different stores, sights, parks, street names, and street signs. Once the city plan (**Stadtplan**) has been designed, students should come up with a name for their city. You will be able to use this map as you teach the objectives of this **Stufe.**

TEACH

Teaching Suggestion

Before students read about the **Stadtrundgang durch Bietigheim,** have them familiarize themselves with the map by locating all the numbered items.

Teacher Note

Posthalterei is a word that dates back to the 18th century. It referred to the building where mail horses were changed and packages were loaded and unloaded.

Building on Previous Skills

Check to see if students can recall any information about Bietigheim and its location from previous lessons. (In the Location Opener of Chapter 10 in Level 1, students learned that Bietigheim is located in the **Bundesland** of Baden-Württemberg near the city of Stuttgart and the river Enz.)

Background Information

Suffixes of German town names often tell a great deal about a town's origin. Bietigheim, for example, is said to have been founded by Frankish settlers, as have other towns with the -**heim** suffix.

Teaching Suggestion

Ask students to look on a map for other German towns with names ending in -**heim.** (Examples: Mannheim, Heppenheim, Bad Mergentheim, Tauberbischofsheim, Rüsselsheim)

Thinking Critically

Drawing Inferences There is almost always a **Tor** *(gate)* and a **Brunnen** *(well)* in the old parts of German towns. Can students think of the significance of these two landmarks? (A **Tor** and a surrounding wall were usually built to protect a town from invaders. The **Brunnen** supplied water to the population.)

▶ *page 221*

PRESENTATION: Wortschatz

To teach the new expressions, use the fictitious map students designed in the Motivating Activity at the beginning of this **Stufe.** Use the new words and prepositional phrases along with words that students are already familiar with. Example: **Die Schule befindet sich in der Hauptstraße.** Repeat the new phrases several times, giving directions to different places.

DRITTE STUFE

For Additional Practice

22 After students have completed the activity, ask one student to choose another place on the map of Bietigheim on p. 220 as a starting point for a **Rundgang**. That student then gives directions to the rest of the class as he or she leads them on a city tour of the town. See if all students end up at the same place at the end of the activity.

▶ *page 222*

PRESENTATION: So sagt man das!

Introduce the expressions to the class. Then have students role-play them with a partner. To provide further practice, ask students to use the map of Bietigheim on p. 220 to review the new functions.

PRESENTATION: Grammatik

Write the dative prepositions **mit, zu, aus, bei, nach, von,** and **gegenüber** on the board or a transparency. Then ask students to turn to the description of Bietigheim on p. 220. Have students scan the text and make a list of all phrases that include these prepositions. Students can come up to the board and write each phrase next to the appropriate preposition. Discuss contractions and lead students to discover what each contraction is composed of.

▶ *page 223*

 ## For Individual Needs

24 **Challenge** After the "tourists" have received directions, the "local" should ask them what they plan to do or see at each place. Example: **Was möchten sie denn dort sehen?**

For Individual Needs

25 **Challenge** As an additional or alternate activity, have students think of as many ways as they can to turn down the requests for directions. These may include the following:

Das tut mir leid, ich bin nicht von hier. Ich weiß leider nicht!
Das müssen sie jemand anders fragen. Ich hab' leider keine Ahnung!

28 **Tactile Learners** In lieu of written directions, ask students to draw a map for the two classmates. The map should be as detailed as possible, including landmarks such as stores, parks, and street names. When students have completed their maps, they exchange them with their partners and give verbal instructions on how to get to their home. Students then switch roles.

Thinking Critically

29 **Comparing and Contrasting** After students have completed the project, ask them to compare the layout of their town to that of Bietigheim on p. 220. Perhaps students can even take a walking tour of their town and compare the list of characteristics.

Background Information

Finding your way around a German town or city is a challenge. The American checkerboard city would be hard to find in Germany. German cities grew and expanded in an irregular pattern over the centuries. Any **Altstadt** in a German town or city is a great model. Typically, the demands of the different historical periods shaped towns into patterns of interlaced streets, alleys, lanes, and squares. The **Tor(e), Brunnen, Marktplatz, Rathaus,** and **Kirche** can usually be found in a central location.

Reteaching: Dative Prepositions

In preparation for this activity, take out the map that the students designed for the Motivating Activity at the beginning of this **Stufe**. Then make a list of all the stores, places, or parks that students included on the map. Call on individual students and ask them how to get to various places from a specific location.

CLOSE

Total Physical Response

Practice the expressions in the **Wortschatz** box on p. 221 and the prepositions by asking individual students to follow your directions around the classroom.
Examples:
Michael, geh bitte am Tisch von der Karen vorbei, und stell dich gegenüber von Thomas hin!
Maria, geh bitte zwischen den Stühlen von Robert und Susan durch, dann geh an der Tafel entlang!

Focusing on Outcomes

Refer students back to the learning outcomes listed on p. 207. Students should recognize that they now know how to ask for and give directions.

ASSESS

- **Performance Assessment** Before beginning this activity, write the names of places and businesses in your area on slips of paper. Students should be familiar with the location of all the places. Place the slips of paper in a hat and have each student draw a slip. The first student calls on another student, reads the place written on his or her piece of paper (example: **die Post**), and asks that student to give directions from the school to that place. Some other places you could use are the nearest drugstore, grocery store, city hall, car wash, or hospital.

- Quiz 9-3, *Chapter Resources*, Book 3

Teaching Zum Lesen,
pp. 224–225

Reading Strategy

The targeted strategy in this reading is distinguishing between fact and opinion. Students should learn about this strategy before beginning Question 1.

PREREADING

Motivating Activity

Take a survey in class asking students to talk about the best vacation they have had. Where was it? What did they do there? Compile a list of students' responses on a transparency and keep it for a later activity.

Thinking Critically

Drawing Inferences After doing Activity 1, ask students what the source for each of the four sentences might be. (Examples: guidebook, advertisement, journal entry, excerpt from a conversation)

Teacher Note

Activity 1 is a prereading activity.

READING

Cooperative Learning

5 Assign small groups of students to do Activity 5 as a cooperative learning activity within a set amount of time. Each group member should have a specific task as part of this activity. (Examples: reader, recorder, reporter) Call on the reporters of several groups to share their findings with the class.

For Individual Needs

6 **A Slower Pace** Ask students to read the girl's interview again to find three facts that she gives to support her vacation paradise.

Geography Connection

Ask students to read the description made by the fifteen-year-old **Realschüler**. Have students look on a map to find out where he wants to take a bicycle trip. Using the scale on the map, can students tell approximately how far apart Passau and Vienna are? (476 km/295 miles) This student would be riding his bicycle along what river if he went from Passau to Vienna? (Danube)

Background Information

The fourteen-year-old **Gymnasiastin** talks about her family's **Ferienhaus** in the **Lüneburger Heide.** The **Lüneburger Heide** is a large national park located between the rivers Elbe and Aller and the towns of Lüneburg and Celle. It encompasses an area of 720 square kilometers (278 square miles) and consists mainly of fertile ground. To control the growth of heather, heath-sheep continually graze the area. The **Heide** is considered to be one of the most popular and tranquil areas in northern Germany.

POST-READING

Teacher Note

Activity 10 is a post-reading task that will show whether students can apply what they have learned.

Closure

Put up the transparency of the survey results from the Motivating Activity for students to review. Ask students to compare it to the top ten **Ferienparadiese** in the **Eltern-Umfrage.** How do the two surveys differ? Can students think of reasons why they are different?

Answers to Activity 1

a. opinion; b. fact; c. fact; d. opinion

Answers to Activity 2

Students are being interviewed about where they like to spend their vacation best; the results of a survey.

Answers to Activity 3

See "**Tiere sind Trumpf**" box on p. 224.

Answers to Activity 4

opinions; facts

Answers to Activity 6

Hawaii; She likes the village where her grandmother lives.

Answers to Activity 7

cycling along a river and on forest paths; Both the first and the last sentences are opinions; the second sentence is a fact.

Answers to Activity 8

Her parents like to go to tourist spots (Mallorca, Gran Canaria, etc.); She would like to spend her vacation at a small lake, camping in a tent and having a paddle boat; She has neither a boat nor a tent; fact.

Answers to Activity 9

in the Lüneburg Heath; Sometimes it is a little boring.

Answers to Activity 10

Answers will vary; 5/5, may be subject to discussion; Answers will vary.

*U*sing Anwendung, *pp. 226-227*

🎬 Video Wrap-up

At this time, you might want to use the *Video Program* or the *Expanded Video Program*, Videocassette 3 for additional review and enrichment. See *Video Guide* for suggestions regarding:
- **Verpatzte Ferien**
  (Dramatic episode)
- **Landeskunde**
  Interviews
- **Videoclips**
  (Authentic footage—*Expanded Video Program* only)

✦ For Individual Needs

1 Challenge After students have completed the listening activity and taken notes, ask them to restate the exchange student's report, using third person conjugations. This can be done orally or in writing. Remind students to use phrases that state facts and opinions in their reports whenever possible.

Teaching Suggestion

2/3 Make a mini-lesson out of these two activities. Remind students of the **Lesetrick** in Chapter 6 to help them decipher charts and graphs. This will help them especially with Activity 2. As an advance organizer to Activity 3, brainstorm with students about what they expect to find out in the article. Take down a few of their suggestions. Have students take turns reading the article aloud in class and remind them not to get distracted by words they don't understand. Rather, they should concentrate on what they can understand. If you need to give students additional vocabulary for clarification, try to give German definitions whenever possible. You may want to divide the questions among several groups. Give each group a few minutes to complete the assignment, then call groups to share their responses with the rest of the class.

Family Link

4 Ask students to extend the question of this activity to as many family members as they can. Students then summarize their results in a concise written statement which they later share with the class.

Teaching Suggestion

6 Remind students to use as many of the expressions from the function box on p. 217 as possible in their postcards.

📁 Portfolio Assessment

6 You might want to suggest this activity as a written portfolio item for your students. See *Assessment Guide*, p. 22.

7 You might want to suggest this activity as an oral portfolio item for your students. See *Assessment Guide*, p. 22.

*K*ann ich's wirklich?
p. 228

This page helps students prepare for the test. It is a brief checklist of the major points covered in the chapter. The students should be reminded that it is only a checklist and not necessarily everything that will appear on the test.

*U*sing Wortschatz,
p. 229

Teaching Suggestion

Ask students to work with a partner. Each partner picks five to ten vocabulary items from this page and writes them down. Students then take turns asking each other questions using the words from their list. Only one word can be used per question.

✦ For Individual Needs

• **Visual Learners** Provide each pair of students with a copy of the **Foto-Roman** with the dialogue whited out. Ask students to come up with an original script for this **Foto-Roman,** using as many words from the **Wortschatz** as possible. Students are not allowed to turn to the pages where the actual **Foto-Roman** is printed.

• **Challenge** Ask students to complete all open-ended phrases that are on this page in an original way. (Examples: expressing doubt, conviction, and asking for and making suggestions)

Teaching Suggestion

Students should have their books closed for this activity. Ask individual students to give you a definition of words you call out. (Examples: **Hallenbad, Verkehrsmittel**)

Teacher Note

Give the **Kapitel 9** Chapter Test, *Chapter Resources*, Book 3.

Wohin in die Ferien?

ICE SPARPREIS

① **Ich schlage vor, wir fahren nach Bayern.**

Germans enjoy their vacations, whether they spend them at home or traveling abroad. But sometimes vacation plans fall through for one reason or another and have to be improvised, as with the teenagers in this chapter. When you talk about vacations and vacation plans, there are words and expressions that you need to know.

In this chapter you will learn

- to express indecision; to ask for and make suggestions
- to express doubt, conviction, and resignation
- to ask for and give directions

And you will

- listen to students talk about places to go on their vacation and how to get around
- read about various vacation spots
- write about your own vacation plans and ways to get around in your community
- discover why Germans consider vacations a necessity and not a luxury

② Das Bürgerhaus? Das ist gleich hier rechts um die Ecke.

③ Die Brücke ist kaputt?! Da kann man wohl nichts machen.

Los geht's!

Verpatzte Ferien

 Boris    Katrin    Judith   Roland

 Mutter    Vater

Look at the photos on the left. Judging by Katrin's expressions, what might be happening in the story? Who is she speaking with? Now look at the photos on the right. What are the characters doing in each picture?

KATRIN   Ja, was macht ihr denn? Ihr seht fern so früh am Nachmittag!

MUTTER   Wir haben eben den österreichischen Wetterbericht gesehen. Unsere Reise nach Tirol ist wahrscheinlich ins Wasser gefallen.

KATRIN   Bist du sicher? Warum? Was ist passiert?

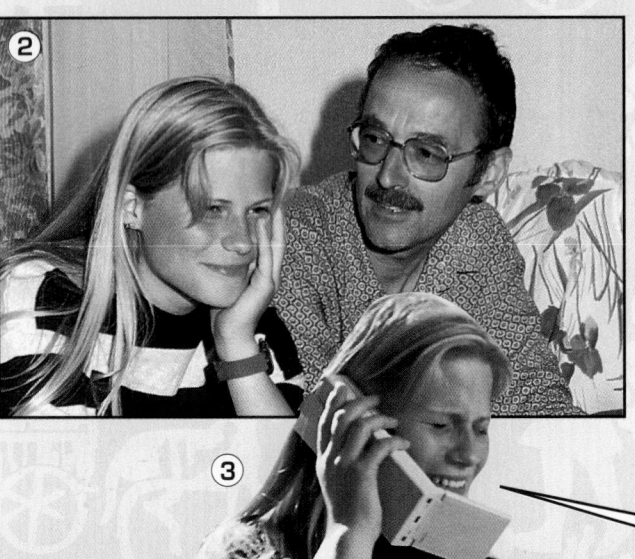

VATER   Die hatten ein Hochwasser, und die Brücke auf der Straße nach Mittersill ist kaputt.

KATRIN   Da gibt's doch bestimmt eine andere Straße.

VATER   Eben nicht.

KATRIN   Ruf doch mal an!

VATER   Das hab' ich schon zweimal probiert. Ich bezweifle, daß ich jetzt durchkomme.

> Katrin Simon. Ja, der ist da. Einen Moment!

VATER   Simon. Ja. Ja. Ja, das haben wir eben zufällig im Fernsehen gesehen. Glauben Sie, daß bis Freitag ... Ja, das ist sehr schade. Wir sind alle sehr enttäuscht. Aber da kann man nichts machen ... Gut! Vielleicht klappt's im nächsten Jahr ... Gut, Herr Mooslechner. Ade!

Katrin mit ihren Freunden

⑤ Ja, was machen wir jetzt? Jetzt mußt auch du die Pfingstferien zu Hause verbringen.

Ich bin dafür, daß wir einmal zusammen nach Ulm fahren.

Blödsinn! Das kennen wir doch schon alle.

⑥ Dann schlage ich vor, wir fahren nach Würzburg. Wir können uns dort die Stadt anschauen.

Das kostet zu viel Geld mit der Bahn.

Ich hab' eine bessere Idee! Wir spielen Touristen in einer Stadt. Ich weiß: in Bietigheim!

Spitze! Aber wie?

„Touristen" in Bietigheim

⑦ Entschuldigung! Wo ist bitte das Rathaus?

Da geht ihr diese Straße entlang bis zur nächsten Ecke nach rechts in die Hauptstraße, und dann seht ihr es schon.

⑧ Verzeihung! Wissen Sie vielleicht, wo das Kronenzentrum ist?

Ja, da geht ihr gleich links um die Ecke und dann die erste Straße rechts, und da steht ihr direkt vor dem Kronenzentrum.

1 Was passiert hier?

Verstehst du alles in der Fotostory? Beantworte die Fragen!

1. Why is Katrin surprised when she comes home?
2. Why do her parents feel disappointed?
3. Why can't the family go where it wanted to go?
4. Why doesn't Katrin's father call Austria again?
5. Who is calling and why?
6. What are Katrin and her three friends talking about?
7. What idea does one of her friends come up with?

1. Because her parents are watching TV in the early afternoon.
2. Because their vacation "fell through".
3. There is a flood in Tirol and a bridge collapsed.
4. He already tried twice and did not get through.
5. the landlord; to cancel their booking
6. about their vacation plans   7. to play tourists in Bietigheim

2 Stimmt oder stimmt nicht?

Wenn der Satz nicht stimmt, schreib die richtige Antwort!

1. Katrin wollte mit ihrer Familie nach Österreich fahren.   1. Stimmt.
2. Aber Österreich hatte furchtbar viel Regen.   2. Stimmt.
3. Es gibt viele Straßen nach Mittersill.   3. Stimmt nicht. Es gibt nur eine.
4. Katrins Vater hat Herrn Mooslechner angerufen.   4. Stimmt nicht. The other way around.
5. Die vier Freunde fahren jetzt nach Würzburg.
6. Am Ende spielen sie Touristen in einer kleinen Stadt in der Nähe von Stuttgart.

5. Stimmt nicht. Es kostet zu viel Geld mit der Bahn.   6. Stimmt.

3 Was paßt zusammen?

Welche Ausdrücke auf der rechten Seite passen zu den Satzanfängen auf der linken Seite?

1. Die Reise nach Tirol   1. b   a. Hochwasser.
2. Die Brücke nach Mittersill   2. c   b. kann nicht stattfinden.
3. Österreich hatte   3. a   c. ist kaputt.
4. Katrin und ihre Eltern   4. g   d. kostet zu viel Geld.
5. Aber da kann man nichts   5. e   e. machen.
6. Katrin will die Pfingstferien   6. f f. nicht zu Hause verbringen.
7. Nach Würzburg fahren   7. d   g. sind enttäuscht.
8. Jetzt spielen die Freunde   8. h   h. Touristen in Bietigheim.

4 Genauer lesen

Lies den Text noch einmal und beantworte diese Fragen!

1. Which word in the text expresses "probability"?   1. wahrscheinlich
2. Which word expresses "doubt"?   2. bezweifle
3. Which words and phrase express "disappointment"?   3. Das ist schade; ... enttäuscht
4. Which phrase expresses "resignation"?   4. ... da kann man nichts machen.
5. Which phrases are used to "make a proposal"?

5. Ich bin dafür, daß ... ; Ich schlage vor, daß ... ; Ich hab' eine bessere Idee.

5 Welche Wörter passen in die Lücken?

Welches Wort aus dem Kasten paßt in welche Lücke?

1. Katrins Eltern haben früh am Nachmittag __1__.
2. Im Wetterbericht haben sie __2__, daß Österreich Hochwasser __3__.
3. Katrin fragt, was __4__ ist.
4. Ihr Vater sagt, die Reise ist ins Wasser __5__.
5. Die Familie ist __6__, aber vielleicht __7__ die Reise im nächsten Jahr.

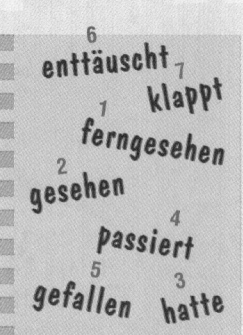

enttäuscht 7
klappt 1
ferngesehen 6
gesehen 2
passiert 4
gefallen 5
hatte 3

Wohin fährst du in den nächsten Ferien?

We asked students from around Germany where they were planning to go during their next school holidays. Before you read their answers, think about where students in the United States usually go or what they like to do during summer vacation. Come up with a list of the top ten most popular vacation spots for U.S. teenagers. Then listen to the interviews and read the texts.

Paolo, *Stuttgart*

„Also meistens verbring' ich meine Ferien in Italien aufgrund dessen, daß ich selber Italiener bin, aus Salerno komm', die Amalfi Küste gerne besuch', zum Beispiel Capri oder Pompeji, Paestum, das gehört ja alles dazu, das ist ['ne] sehr schöne Gegend."

Gerd, *Bietigheim*

„Also meistens fahr' ich in den Ferien überhaupt nicht in den Urlaub. Ich mach' halt dann 'nen Ferienjob und verdien' mir 'n bißchen Geld dazu. Da kann ich mir halt dann 'ne neue Gitarre oder 'nen neuen Verstärker, oder halt irgendwas kaufen, was ich halt haben möchte."

Gabi und Anja, *München*

Gabi: „Also ich, wir fahren in den Ferien zusammen eine Woche zum Reiten auf einen Bauernhof, in Niederbayern, ja, in den Urlaub."
Anja: „Ja, weil wir sehr gern reiten. Jetzt fahren wir zusammen weg." *Gabi:* „Genau. Und ich fahr' dann noch zwei Wochen nach Bad Gastein, in Österreich, auf Wandern und Schwimmen."
Anja: „Und ich fahr' a bissel vielleicht auch noch mit 'ner anderen Freundin auch noch nach Österreich, auch auf 'n Dorf, auch zum Wandern, Schwimmen."
Gabi: „Und nach den Ferien fahr' ich acht Wochen nach Washington D.C. — einen Schüleraustausch, Englisch lernen."

A. 1. Italy, Niederbayern, Bad Gastein, Austria, Washington; Gabi; two of them are vacation, one is a student exchange program; does not go anywhere for vacation, but works.

A.
1. Three of these students mention specific places where they are going. What are they? Which of these students mentions three different trips? Are all three trips vacations? What does the fourth student say he or she is going to do during vacation?
2. What do each of these students plan to do in each of the places they talked about?
3. How do their plans compare to what you thought most teenagers in the United States would do for summer vacation? Did any German teenagers mention something that was on your list of most popular vacation spots?

A. 2. enjoy the landscape; work; ride horses, hike, swim, study English

B. High school students in Germany attend school year round. Although each **Bundesland** has its own schedule, students typically have one or two weeks off for fall holidays, two weeks for Christmas, two weeks in the spring, and six weeks off during the summer. The summer vacation dates for **Bundesländer** are staggered, with the beginning dates about one week apart. Knowing that Germany is very densely populated, can you guess why this is done? How does this vacation schedule compare with your schedule? Who has more vacation time? What do you think the advantages and disadvantages of year-round school might be?

ERSTE STUFE

Expressing indecision, asking for and making suggestions

6 Hör gut zu! For answers, see listening script on TE Interleaf or box below right.

Hör dir die Beschreibung von jedem der sieben Ferienangebote an! Welches Angebot paßt zu welchem Foto? Trag die Lösung in den Rabattcoupon rechts unten ein!

URLAUB IN LETZTER MINUTE
Unsere heißen Reisetips

Für diese Kurzreisen sind noch Plätze erhältlich. Rufen Sie an und kommen Sie dann persönlich vorbei, um sich Ihren Platz zu sichern! Mit einem richtig ausgefüllten Coupon erhalten Sie 10% Rabatt:

1. Mit der Bahn drei Tage an die Nordsee in das kleine Fischerdorf Bensersiel. In diesem Dorf direkt an der Küste sind noch Zimmer frei. Entspannen Sie im Hallenbad, beim Reiten und Strandwandern. Ein Besuch im Buddelschiffmuseum lohnt sich!

2. Einmalig preiswert! Eine Drei-Tage-Busfahrt nach Dresden und in die Sächsische Schweiz. In Dresden besuchen Sie den berühmten Zwinger, und Sie erleben die einmalig schönen Sandsteinfelsen der Bastei.

3. Eine Tagesfahrt an den Bodensee nach Unteruhldingen und weiter mit dem Schiff auf die Insel Mainau, wo Sie unter Palmen spazieren und die Blumenwelt bewundern können. Abfahrt: 6.00.

4. Eine Wochenendfahrt (Sa/So) in die Schweiz. Übernachtung in Brienz. Am nächsten Vormittag mit der Bergbahn aufs Brienzer Rothorn, die Schweizer Bergwelt

genießen. Ein Superangebot!

5. Sonderfahrt mit dem Bus nach Ulm zum bekannten Fischerstechen auf der Donau. Am Vormittag Gelegenheit zum Messebesuch im Dom. Mittagessen in einem soliden Gasthaus. Das Fischerstechen beginnt um 14 h. Rückkehr gegen 19.30 h.

6. Drei Tage mit dem Bus durch die schönsten Täler in der Schweiz. Im Emmental Besichtigung eines typischen Bauernhauses und Besuch einer Käserei.

7. Drei Tage (Di. - Do.) mit dem Bus nach Österreich, nach Alpbach in Tirol. Sehr preisgünstig. Ideal für Bergwanderer und solche, die's noch werden wollen!

7 Wohin geht's? For answers, see TE Interleaf.

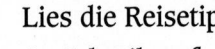

Lies die Reisetips und beantworte die Fragen!

1. Schreib auf, wohin diese sieben Reisen gehen!
2. Für wie viele Tage ist jede Reise?
3. Welche Reisen führen ans Meer oder an einen See? Welche in die Berge? Welche sind Stadtbesichtigungen?
4. Für welche Reise interessierst du dich? Warum?

10% RABATT!

1. f _____
2. b _____
3. d _____
4. e _____
5. g _____
6. c _____
7. a _____

Beliebte Verkehrsmittel:

die Bahn

das Flugzeug

das Schiff

Wohin gehst du in den Ferien?

auf den Tennisplatz

ins Hallenbad

Wer steigt auf einen Berg? Aufs Brienzer Rothorn? Auf die Zugspitze?

Mit welchem Verkehrsmittel fährst du gewöhnlich in die Ferien? Und was machst du in den Ferien? Wohin gehst du?

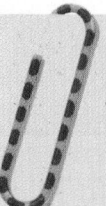

SO SAGT MAN DAS!

Expressing indecision, asking for and making suggestions

When expressing indecision about your plans, you could say:

>   **Was machen wir jetzt?**
>   **Was sollen wir bloß machen?**

If you need specific suggestions, you might ask:

>   **Wohin fahren wir? Hast du eine Idee?** *or* **Was schlägst du vor?**

When making suggestions, you might say:

>   **Wir können mal an die Nordsee fahren.**
> *or* **Fahren wir mal in die Schweiz!**
> *or* **Ich schlage vor, daß wir mal in die Schweiz fahren.**
> *or* **Ich bin dafür, daß wir an den Rhein fahren.**

Which of these expressions are new to you?

Ein wenig Grammatik

Many mountains in the German-speaking countries are named **(das) Horn** or **(die) Spitze**, as in **Matterhorn** and **Zugspitze**. Sometimes mountains are also named for near-by towns. In this case, the ending **-er** is added to the name of the town. For example, near the town of **Brienz** is the **Brienzer Rothorn**.

8 Wohin jetzt?

Katrins Familie kann nicht nach Mittersill fahren. Katrin hat die Reisetips gelesen und schlägt den Eltern ein paar Kurzreisen vor. Die Eltern haben keine große Lust dazu. Spiel die Rolle von Katrin, und such dir einen Partner für die Rolle von Katrins Vater oder Mutter!

Grammatik Expressing direction: The prepositions **nach, an, in,** and **auf**

To express directions toward a place, German uses different prepositions depending on the nature of the place. The prepositions **nach, an, in,** and **auf** all convey here the meaning of "to a place."

1. The preposition **nach** is used with names of cities, states, countries, and islands that are not preceded by an article (such as **die Schweiz**).

Wohin fahren wir?
- **Nach Ulm.** *(city)*
- Fahren wir mal **nach Bayern!** *(state)*
- Ich fahre **nach Österreich.** *(country)*
- Fahren wir heute **nach Mainau!** *(island)*

2. The preposition **in** is used with the names of countries and geographic areas that require the use of the definite article.

Wohin fahrt ihr?
- Ich fahre mal **in die Schweiz.**
- Wir fliegen **in die Vereinigten Staaten.** *(countries)*
- Wir fahren **in die Berge, in die Alpen.** *(areas)*
- Ihr fahrt **in den Schwarzwald?**

3. The preposition **an** is used when referring to bodies of water.

Wohin fahrt ihr?
- Ich fahre **an die Nordsee.**
- Wir fahren **an den Rhein.** *(bodies of water)*
- Wir fahren **an den Bodensee.**

4. The preposition **auf** is used when referring to heights or flat surfaces.

Was macht ihr? Wir steigen **auf einen Berg, aufs Brienzer Rothorn.**
Wohin geht ihr jetzt? **Auf den Tennisplatz.**

5. The prepositions **an, auf,** and **in** form contractions with the definite article **das.**

an + das = **ans**   auf + das = **aufs**   in + das = **ins**

Which case is used with noun phrases following **in, an,** and **auf** to express going somewhere?[1]

nach (Kalifornien)

an den (Michigansee)

9 Deine Reiseziele?

in die (Blue Ridge) Mountains

a. Schreib fünf Reiseziele auf einen Zettel! Diese Ziele können in Deutschland, in den Vereinigten Staaten oder irgendwo anders sein! Schreib auch auf, was du an jedem Ziel machen möchtest! Danach ordne deine Reiseziele! Wohin fährst du zuerst? Danach? Zuletzt? Mit wem fährst du? Im Kasten stehen ein paar Reiseziele in den Vereinigten Staaten.

an den Strand in (Mississippi)

auf den (Pikes) Peak

b. Such dir eine Partnerin! Frag sie über ihre Reisepläne für den nächsten Sommer! Frag sie, wohin sie fährt und mit wem, und ob sie mit dem Auto fährt oder fliegt! Frag sie auch, was sie überall macht!

1. the accusative case

10 Franks Reisepläne

Frank und seine Familie (sie wohnen in Stuttgart) haben für die großen Ferien eine lange Reise geplant. Schau auf diese Karte, auf die Frank die Reiseziele eingetragen hat! Sag, wohin er fährt, und was er an jedem Ort bestimmt macht! E.g.: **Frank fährt zuerst nach München und schaut sich dort bestimmt die Stadt an. Dann fährt er an den Starnberger See und geht bestimmt schwimmen.** Etc.

Die Reiseroute

1. München
2. Starnberger See
3. Garmisch
4. Tirol/Innsbruck
5. Zürich/Zürichsee
6. Bodensee
7. Schwarzwald
8. Frankfurt/Main
9. Hamburg
10. Lübeck/Ostsee
11. Insel Rügen
12. Potsdam
13. nach Hause

(Karte von Deutschland, Österreich, der Schweiz und Nachbarländern mit eingetragenen Orten: DÄNEMARK, Nordsee, Ostsee, Insel Rügen, Lübeck, Hamburg, Bremen, NIEDERLANDE, Düsseldorf, Bonn, BELGIEN, LUXEMBURG, FRANKREICH, Berlin, Potsdam, DEUTSCHLAND, POLEN, Leipzig, Dresden, TSCHECHISCHE REPUBLIK, SLOWAKISCHE REPUBLIK, Frankfurt, Stuttgart, Schwarzwald, München, Starnberger See, Garmisch, Zugspitze, Bodensee, Basel, Zürich, Zürichsee, St. Gallen, Bregenz, Vaduz, Innsbruck, Bern, Luzern, Chur, Davos, St. Moritz, Interlaken, Eiger, Zermatt, SCHWEIZ, ITALIEN, ÖSTERREICH, Salzburg, Linz, Großglockner, Großvenediger, Klagenfurt, ALPEN, Flüsse: Rhein, Mosel, Ems, Weser, Elbe, Havel, Oder, Spree, Neiße, Saale, Main, Neckar, Donau, Isar, Inn, Rhône, Salzach, Traun, Enns)

EIN WENIG LANDESKUNDE

Die Deutschen machen gerne Urlaub. Sie sind viel und gewöhnlich sehr lange unterwegs. Wie fahren die Deutschen in den Urlaub? Hier ist eine kleine Statistik darüber.

mit dem Auto	62,6%
mit dem Flugzeug	17,6%
mit der Bahn	8,6%
mit dem Bus	11,2%

11 Meine Sommerreise

a. Plane deine Sommerreise! Schreib auf, wohin du fahren und was du dort machen möchtest!
b. Dann erzähle deinen Klassenkameraden von deiner geplanten Reise! Zeig ihnen deine Reiseroute auf einer Landkarte!

12 Im Reisebüro

Du arbeitest in einem Reisebüro. Dein Partner ist ein Kunde. Er ist sehr enttäuscht, denn er kann nicht dorthin fahren, wohin er fahren wollte. Du schlägst ihm ein anderes Reiseziel vor und erzählst ihm, was er dort alles machen kann! Gefällt ihm dein Vorschlag? Wenn nicht, schlag etwas anderes vor! Bring Reisebroschüren mit in die Klasse, die du den Kunden zeigen kannst! — Tauscht dann die Rollen aus!

Expressing doubt, conviction, and resignation

13 Warum so unsicher?

1. Er und seine Eltern haben noch keine preiswerte Unterkunft gefunden.
2. Sie kann einen Segelkurs am Gardasee machen oder mit ihren Eltern nach Südfrankreich fahren.

Lies den Text und beantworte die folgenden Fragen!

1. Warum kann Boris vielleicht nicht nach Italien fahren?
2. Warum hat es Nadine dieses Jahr schwer, sich für einen Ferienort zu entscheiden?
3. Warum fliegt Katrins Familie gern nach Spanien?   3. Dort gibt es viel Sonne.

WEISST DU SCHON,

BORIS

„Ja, das ist so 'ne Sache. Wir wollen nach Italien, an die Adria. Aber meine Eltern haben zu spät gebucht, und wir glauben nicht, daß wir noch eine Unterkunft bekommen, also etwas, was einigermaßen preiswert ist. In teuren Hotels, da bin ich sicher, gibt's bestimmt noch Zimmer. Aber so viel Geld wollen wir auch wieder nicht ausgeben."

WO DU DIE FERIEN

NADINE

„Also ich hab's dieses Jahr sehr schwer. Ich kann von der Schule aus einen Segelkurs am Gardasee, also in Italien, mitmachen. Aber ich weiß nicht, ob das so eine gute Idee ist. Im Kurs sprechen alle Deutsch, und ich bezweifle, daß ich dort mein Italienisch verbessern kann. Also, ich fahr' wohl lieber mit meinen Eltern nach Südfrankreich. Dort kann ich auch segeln, und ich kann ganz bestimmt mein Französisch verbessern. Ich hab' in Französisch bloß 'ne Vier. Schlecht, was?"

VERBRINGST?

KATRIN

„Ja, wie ihr wißt, ist unsere Reise ins Wasser gefallen. Ins Hochwasser! Ich bezweifle, daß meine Eltern in den Bergen Urlaub machen wollen. Das Wetter ist eben zu unsicher. Ich bin nicht sicher, ob wir wieder in die Staaten fliegen, wie letztes Jahr. Das war eine sehr teure Reise. Aber vielleicht geht's nach Spanien. Dort gibt's viel Sonne, das könnt ihr mir glauben! Wir waren schon zweimal dort. Wir fahren immer ans Meer, an die Costa Brava und so. Echt super-toll!"

Ich fahr' ans Meer, denn dort kann ich ...

| segeln | windsurfen | tauchen | angeln | Boot fahren |

In unserm Hotel gibt es ...

| einen Pool | einen Golfplatz | einen Sandstrand | einen Fitneßraum | eine Diskothek |

| einen Tennisplatz | eine Liegewiese | eine Sauna | einen Whirlpool | einen Fernsehraum |

1. Wo übernachtest du gewöhnlich, wenn du mit deinen Eltern in die Ferien fährst?
2. Was gibt es gewöhnlich in dem Hotel oder Motel, wo ihr übernachtet?
3. Was machst du, wenn du an einem See oder am Meer Ferien machst?

Und dann noch . . .

rudern
schnorcheln
Kajak fahren
Tretboot fahren
River Rafting
   machen
Motorboot fahren

SO SAGT MAN DAS!

Expressing doubt, conviction, and resignation

When expressing doubt, you might say:

Ich weiß nicht, ob (wir die Reise schon gebucht haben).
Ich bezweifle, daß (es dort einen Golfplatz gibt).
Ich bin nicht sicher, daß (wir dort surfen können).

When expressing resignation, you might say:

Da kann man nichts machen.
or **Das ist leider so.**

When expressing conviction, you might say:

Du kannst mir glauben, daß (es dort einen Golfplatz gibt).
Ich bin sicher, daß (wir dort surfen können).

What do you think the conjunction **ob** means in the first sentence?

14 Hör gut zu! For answers, see listening script on TE Interleaf.

Einige Leute unterhalten sich über ihre Pläne für die Ferien und drücken dabei Zweifel (*doubts*) aus. Schreib zuerst auf, woran sie zweifeln und danach, ob ihre Gesprächspartner zustimmen oder eine andere Meinung haben!

15 Optimist? Pessimist?

Du und deine Partnerin, ihr streitet euch (*argue*) über eure Reiseziele. Sie bezweifelt, was du ihr sagst, aber du bist sicher, daß es an dem Ferienort alles gibt, was sie gern möchte. — Tauscht dann die Rollen aus!

DU   **Wohin fährst du denn?**
PARTNERIN   **Wir ...**
DU   **Dort kannst du/gibt es bestimmt ...**
PARTNERIN   **Ich weiß nicht, ob ...**
DU   **Aber ich bin sicher, daß ...**
PARTNERIN   **...**

Ein wenig Grammatik

The conjunction **ob** means *if* or *whether.* Look at the **So sagt man das!** box. What do you notice about the position of the verb in **ob**-clauses? What other conjunctions require verb-last position?[1]

Was?

teure Hotels   eine Unterkunft bekommen

eine Diskothek

viel Geld ausgeben   segeln/tauchen

einen Pool   Deutsch sprechen

Grammatik   Expressing Direction and Location (Summary)

Read these two blocks of sentences carefully. Which group refers to location? Which to direction? Which question word is used to elicit responses like the ones on the left? And on the right?

Wir fahren nach Frankfurt.	**Ich war auch schon mal in Frankfurt.**
Roland fährt in die Schweiz.	**Ich war auch schon in der Schweiz.**
Boris fliegt in die Vereinigten Staaten.	**Ich war letztes Jahr in den Vereinigten Staaten.**
Katrin fährt an die Nordsee.*	**Ich war auch schon an der Nordsee.**
Wir fahren morgen an den Bodensee.*	**Ich bin auch schon am Bodensee gewesen.**
Roland fährt aufs Brienzer Rothorn.	**Ich war auch schon mal auf dem Brienzer Rothorn.**

*Note the two meanings of the word **See: die See** means *sea,* **der See** means *lake.*

1. To answer a **wo**-question (a question that asks about location), dative case forms are used after the prepositions **an, in, auf,** and some others.

         Wo warst du in den Ferien? Ich war **an der Nordsee.**

2. To answer a **wohin**-question (a question that asks about direction), accusative case forms are used after these prepositions.

         Wohin fährst du? Ich fahre an **die Nordsee.**

1. **weil** and **daß**

16 Hör gut zu!

For answers, see listening script on TE Interleaf.

Einige Freunde haben angerufen und eine Nachricht auf dem Anrufbeantworter hinterlassen. Rufen sie aus dem Ferienort an oder auf dem Weg dahin? Mach dir Notizen!

	aus dem Ferienort	auf dem Weg dorthin
Katja		
Bernd		

17 Franks Reise

E.g.: **Frank war in München und hat sich dort wahrscheinlich die Stadt angeschaut. Etc.**

Frank ist von seiner Reise zurück. Er war mit seinen Eltern an allen Orten, die er auf der Landkarte eingetragen hat. — Schau auf die Karte auf Seite 215 und erzähle, wo Frank überall gewesen ist und was er wahrscheinlich dort gemacht hat!

18 Für mein Notizbuch

Wohin fährst du mit deinen Eltern oder Verwandten in die nächsten Ferien, oder wohin möchtest du mal fahren? — Beschreibe eine kurze Reise, die drei verschiedene Reiseziele hat! Erwähne:

a. mit wem du fährst
b. wohin ihr fahrt
c. wie ihr dorthin kommt
d. wo ihr übernachtet
e. was ihr dort alles tun könnt

19 Deine Pläne diskutieren

Such dir einen Partner! Erzähle ihm von deiner Reise!

20 Du arbeitest als Reiseberater

Du arbeitest in einem Reisebüro. Deine Partnerin, eine Kundin, möchte mit dir ihre Ferienpläne besprechen, eine Reise planen und bei dir buchen. Sie hat Fragen über verschiedene Reiseziele. Sie möchte zum Beispiel wissen, was sie an jedem Reiseort unternehmen kann. Als Reiseberater bist du bestens informiert, denn du bist schon überall gewesen und kannst deshalb ihre Fragen beantworten. Schreibt ein Rollenspiel und führt es der Klasse vor!

Asking for and giving directions

Stadtrundgang durch Bietigheim

Parken Sie Ihren Wagen auf dem Parkplatz am Japangarten. Von hier aus sind es nur zwei Gehminuten in die Stadt.

Vom Parkplatz gehen Sie auf der Holzgartenstraße über unser kleines Flüßchen, die Metter, und Sie kommen direkt in die Hauptstraße und damit in die Fußgängerzone in der Innenstadt.

An der Hauptstraße gehen Sie nach links. Vor Ihnen sehen Sie jetzt das

1. **Parkplatz**
2. **Stadttor**
3. **Backhaus**
4. **Bürgerhaus**
5. **Kachelsches Haus**
6. **Posthalterei**
7. **Marktbrunnen**
8. **Rathaus**
9. **Hormoldhaus**
10. **Evangelische Stadtkirche**
11. **Kleines Bürgerhaus**
12. **Bietigheimer Schloß**

einzige noch guterhaltene Stadttor. (Es hat einmal vier davon gegeben.) Das imposante Mauerwerk stammt aus dem Ende des 14. Jahrhunderts.

Sie gehen jetzt weiter durch dieses Tor, immer die Hauptstraße entlang bis zur Fräuleinstraße, wo Sie rechts in die Fräuleinstraße einbiegen. An der Ecke Schieringsbrunnerstraße sehen Sie das alte Backhaus auf der rechten Seite. Früher war dieses Haus außerhalb der Stadt.

Nach etwa 60 Metern kommen Sie zur Schieringerstraße. Hier biegen Sie links ein. Auf der linken Seite, Nr. 20, ist das stattliche Bürgerhaus, ein Fachwerkhaus aus dem 17. Jahrhundert.

Neben dem Bürgerhaus befindet sich das Kachelsche Haus, ein repräsentatives Wohnhaus aus dem 16. Jahrhundert.

Schräg gegenüber vom Kachelschen Haus ist die alte Posthalterei, ein schönes Fachwerkhaus aus dem 18. Jahrhundert.

Jetzt kommen Sie bald wieder auf die Hauptstraße. Sie gehen nach rechts, und gleich ein paar Schritte weiter kommen Sie zum Bietigheimer Rathaus mit dem schönen Marktbrunnen davor.

21 In Bietigheim

Lies zuerst den Text auf Seite 220! Dann such dir einen Partner, und beantwortet zusammen diese Fragen! Seht euch dabei den Stadtplan von Bietigheim an!

1. Wo kann man den Wagen parken, wenn man die Innenstadt von Bietigheim besuchen will?
2. Wie kommt man vom Parkplatz in die Hauptstraße?
3. Wie kommt man jetzt zum Stadttor?
4. Wie kommt man vom Stadttor in die Fräuleinstraße?
5. Wo steht das Alte Backhaus?
6. Wo ist das Bürgerhaus?
7. Wo befindet sich das Kachelsche Haus?
8. Wo ist die Posthalterei?
9. Wohin kommt man, wenn man wieder rechts in die Hauptstraße einbiegt?

> in der ... straße
>
> bis zum ... platz
>
> am ... platz
>
> bis zur ... straße
>
> nach rechts
>
> nach links
>
> dann geradeaus
>
> die erste (zweite) Straße nach rechts
>
> und dann wieder nach links

1. auf dem Parkplatz am Japangarten; 2. auf Holzgartenstraße über die Metter gehen; 3. an der Hauptstraße nach links gehen; 4. durch das Stadttor, die Hauptstraße entlang, dann rechts einbiegen; 5. an der Ecke Schieringsbrunnerstraße auf der rechten Seite; 6. Schieringer-straße Nr. 20; 7. neben dem Bürgerhaus auf der Schieringerstraße; 8. schräg gegenüber vom Kachelschen Haus auf der Schieringerstraße; 9. zum Bietigheimer Rathaus

WORTSCHATZ

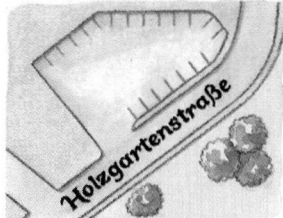

Der Parkplatz befindet sich an der Holzgarten-straße.

Die Metter läuft zwischen der Innenstadt und dem Palmengarten entlang.

Gehen Sie links um die Ecke; dann kommen Sie zum Stadttor!

Die Hauptstraße führt durch das Stadttor.

Das Rathaus ist aus dem 16. Jahrhundert.

Vor dem Rathaus steht der Ulrichsbrunnen.

Dieses Fachwerkhaus stammt aus dem 17. Jahrhundert.

Dieses Wohnhaus ist beim Rathaus.

Can you identify the prepositions above? What do you think they mean and how would you express them in English? What case follows each of these prepositions?

---

22 Hör gut zu! For answers, see listening script on TE Interleaf.

Du hörst drei Kurzbeschreibungen von einem Rundgang durch Bietigheim. Schau auf die Stadtkarte und schreib auf, wo sich der Tourist am Ende der Beschreibung befindet!

Grammatik   Prepositions followed by dative case forms

1. The prepositions **mit** and **zu** are always followed by dative case forms:
   Jens kommt **mit dem Moped zur Schule.** Ich muß jetzt **zum Bäcker** gehen.

2. There are other prepositions that must be used with dative case forms.

aus	*from*	Das Tor ist **aus dem 14. Jahrhundert.**
bei	*by, near*	Das Hormoldhaus ist **beim Rathaus.**
nach	*after*	**Nach 60 Metern** ist der Brunnen.
von	*from*	**Vom Parkplatz** sind es nur zwei Gehminuten.
gegenüber	*across from*	**Gegenüber dem Kachelschen Haus** ist die Posthalterei.

3. Like **zu**, the prepositions **bei** and **von** also form contractions.

   bei + dem = **beim**   von + dem = **vom**

23 Eine kurze Beschreibung

Your German pen pal is coming to visit. Send him a short description of your town. Rewrite your note with dative prepositions and the correct articles.

... Also, die Amtrakstation ist gar nicht weit vom Stadtzentrum. ~~Von~~ d ~~er~~ Station bis zur Innenstadt sind es nur zehn Minuten zu Fuß. Da ist das alte Rathaus. Es stammt ~~aus~~ d ~~em~~ neunzehnten Jahrhundert. Das ist schon alt in den Vereinigten Staaten! ~~Bei~~ d ~~em~~ Rathaus, direkt daneben, siehst du das alte Postgebäude. Auf der anderen Straßenseite, ~~gegenüber~~ d ~~em~~ Rathaus, ist ein schöner Park. Dort spiele ich Baseball ~~nach~~ d ~~er~~ Schule.

Ein wenig *Grammatik*

The prepositions **durch**, *through*, and **um**, *around*, are always followed by accusative case forms.

   Wir gehen **durch das Stadttor.**
   Das Rathaus ist **um die Ecke.**

Which other two prepositions do you know that are always followed by the accusative case?[1]

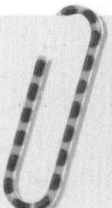

SO SAGT MAN DAS!
Asking for and giving directions

When asking for directions, you might ask:

   Entschuldigung! Wo ist bitte das Rathaus?

or   **Wie komme ich bitte zum Stadttor?**

or   **Verzeihung! Wissen Sie vielleicht, wie ich zur Post komme?**

When giving directions, you might say:

   Sie biegen hier rechts ein. Dann kommen Sie zum Rathaus.
   Das ist hier rechts um die Ecke.

   Tut mir leid. Ich weiß es leider nicht. Ich bin nicht von hier.

What do the prepositions **zum** and **zur** indicate? Look at the responses on the right. How would you say them in English?

1. **für** and **gegen**

24 Verzeihung! Wissen Sie, wo …?

Zwei Partner sind Touristen. Du kennst dich in Bietigheim aus, und gibst ihnen Auskunft.

Hier sind die Partner:	Sie wollen dorthin:
1. am Rathaus	Evangelische Stadtkirche
2. auf dem Parkplatz	Fußgängerzone
3. in der Fräuleinstraße	Marktbrunnen
4. bei der Stadtkirche	Hormoldhaus

25 Touristen in der Stadt

Zwei verschiedene Gruppen von Touristen sprechen dich auf dem Parkplatz in Bietigheim an. Eine Gruppe möchte zur Evangelischen Stadtkirche, die andere zum Bietigheimer Schloß. Sag ihnen, wie man dahin kommt!

26 Für mein Notizbuch

Schreib in dein Notizbuch

a. wie du mit dem Rad von zu Hause zur Schule kommst!

b. wie du von zu Hause zu einem Freund kommst!

Ein wenig *G*rammatik

In this chapter you learned that the prepositions **in, an** and **auf** can be followed by either accusative or dative noun phrases. Do you remember in which instances the accusative forms are used? And the dative forms? Here are three other prepositions that also follow this rule:

vor *in front of*
neben *next to*
zwischen *between*

Like **in, an,** and **auf**, these prepositions must be used with the accusative case when indicating direction and with the dative case when indicating location.

27 Geh vor den Schreibtisch!

Take turns with your classmates giving different students commands to move around your classroom. Use the prepositions **an, vor, zwischen,** and **neben.** Each student will do what you tell him or her. When he or she is in the proper place, that student will tell the class where he or she is now located using these same prepositions.

BEISPIEL   DU   **Geh an die Tafel!** *(classmate walks to the chalkboard)*
       MITSCHÜLER   **Ich stehe an der Tafel.**

28 So kommst du zu mir!

Du hast eine Party und lädst ein paar Klassenkameraden ein. Zwei Klassenkameraden wissen gar nicht, wo du wohnst. Du hast für sie auf einem Zettel eine Route vorbereitet, wie sie am besten zu dir kommen. Gib ihnen den Zettel und erklär es ihnen persönlich!

29 Ein Klassenprojekt: Unser Ort

An diesem Projekt können zwei oder drei Gruppen arbeiten, je nach Größe eurer Stadt. Jede Gruppe hat die Aufgabe, ein Layout zu erstellen, das eure Stadt zeigt.

a. Bereitet das Layout vor, zeichnet die wichtigsten Straßen und Gebäude ein und beschriftet diese!

b. Die fertigen Layouts dienen dann als offizielle Stadtkarte in euerm Informationszentrum. Ein Mitglied eurer Gruppe arbeitet im Infocenter und die andern in der Gruppe sind Touristen, die Auskunft nach verschiedenen Zielen in euerm Ort erfragen. Die Touristen wollen auch wissen, wie alt einige Gebäude sind.

ZUM LESEN

Was ist dein Lieblingsreiseziel?

LESETRICK

Distinguishing between fact and opinion. It is important to notice when an author is expressing a personal opinion or value as opposed to conveying facts. Understanding the values held by a group of people is a key to getting along in that culture. Here are some expressions that indicate when an author is giving a personal opinion:

Ich finde ...

Ich glaube ...

Für mich ...

Es soll ... sein.

Ich meine ...

Getting Started For answers, see TE Interleaf.

1. Read the following sentences and determine which ones are fact and which are opinion.
   a. Solche Ferien sind besser als nach Mallorca zu fahren.
   b. Nachts machen wir Waldspiele.
   c. Keine Autos fahren vorbei.
   d. Ein Ferienparadies soll ein Urlaub mit Freunden sein.
2. Look at the title, subtitle, and drawings on these two pages. What is the article about? Scan the article. What kind of information is summarized here?
3. Now read the summary of results **Tiere sind Trumpf**. What are the ten most popular vacations for German teenagers?
4. Does this survey focus on facts or opinions? If the question were

Eltern—UMFRAGE

Gesucht: Bauernhof zum Ausschlafen
Realschüler, 14 Jahre

Wo Mädchen und Jungen am liebsten Ferien machen

„Für die meisten Menschen ist wohl Hawaii der Urlaubstraum. Für mich ist es das Dorf, wo meine Großmutter wohnt. Da ist ein See mit dem Paddelboot von meinem Opa. Ich habe dort mehrere Freunde. Und Großmutter kocht nur, was mir wirklich schmeckt."
Realschülerin, 13 Jahre

„Es ist und bleibt ein Bauernhof. Es soll ein Urlaub mit Freunden, ohne Eltern sein. Man kann bei der Arbeit freiwillig helfen. Alles, was ich nicht muß wie in der Schule, macht mir Freude. Nachts darf ich mit Freunden schon mal auf dem Heuboden schlafen. Dann hört man plötzlich was. Ist es eine Maus oder ein Siebenschläfer oder ein Marder oder eine der vielen Katzen vom Hof? Dann wird's einem ganz gruselig. Solche Ferien sind besser als nach Mallorca zu müssen in den Ölsardinensitzen."
Realschüler, 13 Jahre

„Mein Ideal ist ein Pfadfinderlager. Nachts machen wir Waldspiele

Tiere sind Trumpf

Eltern fragte 2220 Schülerinnen und Schüler acht bis 16 Jahre alt. Was ist für dich ein Ferienparadies? Am häufigsten genannt wurden:
1. Bauernhof, Reiterhof
2. bei Großeltern oder anderen Verwandten
3. Zelten, Jugendlager, Wohnmobil
4. Trampen
5. Strand an südlichen Meeren
6. zu Hause (Ausschlafen)
7. Bergtour
8. Aktivferien (Surfen, Klettern, Angeln)
9. USA/Kanada (Nationalparks, Disney World)
10. Abenteuerreise (Dschungel, Wüste, Vulkane)

Rund zehn Prozent der Befragten bringen zum Ausdruck, daß für sie der Ferienort eigentlich Nebensache ist—sie empfinden es als viel wichtiger, daß die Eltern Zeit haben, entspannt und gutgelaunt sind.

mit Taschenlampen. Wir haben ein Lagerfeuer. Wenn der Wind ums Zelt heult, kuschelt man sich in seinen Schlafsack."
Realschüler, 14 Jahre

„Für mich muß es ganz, ganz weit weg sein. Wenn ich wieder zu Hause bin, kann ich allen meinen Freunden erzählen, wie weit weg ich war."
Hauptschüler, 14 Jahre

„Meine Eltern gehen immer ins Reisebüro und suchen sich was

Tolles aus. Meistens Urlaubsziele, wo sich Menschenmassen zusammenballen: Mallorca, Gran Canaria, Italien, Kreta, Meran usw. Mein Urlaubstraum aber ist ein kleiner See mit nettem Strand und dahinter etwas weg ein Dorf. Auf dem Strand steht mein Zelt, und daneben liegt mein Paddelboot. Leider habe ich weder ein Boot noch ein Zelt. Nur Träume."

Gymnasiastin, 15 Jahre

„*Für mich sind die schönsten Ferien, wenn wir eine Fahrradtour machen. An einem Fluß vorbei und über Waldwege. Daran sieht man, daß es im Urlaub nicht die Super-Luxus-Hotels machen, um echte Freude zu kriegen.*"

Gymnasiast, 13 Jahre

„*Wo keine Abgase sind. Wo man nachts schlafen kann, weil keine Autos und Lastwagen vorbeidonnern.*"

Realschüler, 13 Jahre

„*Viele Urlaubsparadiese kann man erleben, wenn man eine Radtour macht. Am schönsten war für mich der Weg von Passau nach Wien. Im Flugzeug, im Auto, im Bus sieht man doch alles nur hinter Glasscheiben. Aber auf dem Fahrrad ist alles ganz nahe. Die wunderbarsten Waldwege kann man fahren, und an Flüssen und Bächen vorbei.*"

Realschüler, 15 Jahre

„*Wir haben in der Lüneburger Heide ein kleines Ferienhaus. Das ist unser Urlaubsparadies. Wir wandern oder fahren mit einem Pferdewagen durch die Heide. Meine Eltern, meine Schwester und ich, wir fühlen uns dort sehr wohl. Nur manchmal ist es ein bißchen langweilig. Aber diese Stille ist am besten für die Erholung, für mich vom Schulstreß, für meine Eltern von der Firma.*"

Gymnasiastin, 14 Jahre

„*Ein Bauernhof wie in dem Roman ,Herbstmilch!' So ganz urgemütlich. Betten mit karierten hohen Plümos in einem ganz kleinen Zimmer mit zwei ganz kleinen Fenstern. Aus den Ställen hört man das Vieh brüllen. Pferde sind da und Schafe. Es ist einfach wunderbar, mitten in der Landwirtschaft zu leben. Abends sitzen alle an einem langen Holztisch und essen aus einem Topf und aus einer Pfanne. Es gibt herrliche Suppe, leckere Braten, feine Nachtische und viel Obst. Alles ist deftig gekocht. Und abends sitzen wir an einem alten Kamin. Ja, so erträume ich mir das.*"

Gymnasiastin, 15 Jahre

Wo warst du in den letzten Ferien? would the answers be facts or opinions?

5. Skim the interviews. For each interview, jot down the student's age, the main idea (in this case, usually the vacation place or the people with whom the vacation is spent), and one specific fact supporting that person's opinion.

A Closer Look

6. What does the thirteen-year-old **Realschülerin** think most people would describe as a vacation paradise? How does her own opinion differ?

7. What does the thirteen-year-old **Gymnasiast** like about bicycle tours? Which parts of his response are opinion and which are fact?

> **Tip:** You may not know the expression **weder ... noch,** but you can guess its meaning from context because you know the word **leider.**

8. How does the fifteen-year-old **Gymnasiastin**'s idea differ from her parents' idea about a vacation paradise? What does she say about a boat and tent? Is this a fact or opinion?

9. Where does the fourteen-year-old **Gymnasiastin**'s family have a vacation house? What is the only drawback, in her opinion?

10. You have probably formed some impressions and opinions of your own about the readings on these pages. How many of these students do you think are city-dwellers? (Why do you think so?) How many of them are describing vacations they have actually taken, and how many are describing a "daydream?" Which tells you more about a person: his or her real life or his or her hopes and dreams?

ANWENDUNG

For answers, see listening script on TE Interleaf.

1 The German exchange student who lived with your family last summer calls you early one morning and tells you about her trip to Austria. Take notes so that you can tell the rest of your family about her vacation.

1. ... Spanien 2. Die 17-19jährigen fahren nach Portugal; die 14-16jährigen nicht.

2 Schau die Tabelle unten an und dann diese Aussagen! Wenn eine Aussage nicht stimmt, ändere sie so, damit sie stimmt!

1. Die deutschen Jugendlichen fahren am liebsten nach Frankreich.
2. Die 17-19jährigen fahren nicht so oft nach Portugal wie die 14-16jährigen.
3. Die Niederlande sind ein sehr beliebtes Reiseziel.
3. Die Niederlande sind ein nicht sehr beliebtes Reiseziel.
4. Deutsche Jugendliche fahren lieber nach Jugoslawien als nach Spanien.
5. Nicht sehr viele Jugendliche fahren nach London.
4. Deutsche Jugendliche fahren lieber nach Spanien als nach Jugoslawien.
6. Die 14-28jährigen fahren genauso oft nach Dänemark wie nach Griechenland.
5. Stimmt. 6. Die 14-28jährigen fahren genauso oft nach Dänemark wie nach Portugal.

Das Ausland steht an erster Stelle

Wohin geht die Haupturlaubsreise der Jugendlichen? Im Inland bleibt nur jeder fünfte. Hier sind vor allem die Küsten von Schleswig-Holstein attraktiv.

Renner sind die Auslandsreisen. Spanien, Frankreich und Italien stehen an den ersten Stellen (siehe Tabelle).

In Spanien ist „schwer was los"

Die Niederlande, Italien, Jugoslawien und die Türkei sind für Deutsche preisgünstig. Großbritannien, Österreich, Italien, Griechenland und die USA bieten nach Ansicht von deutschen Jugendlichen gute Möglichkeiten, neue Leute kennenzulernen. Die Inseln Spaniens, Italien, Jugoslawien, Griechenland und die Türkei bieten eine prima Urlaubsatmosphäre. In Großbritannien, Spanien und Italien ist „schwer was los".

In die Sonne, ans Meer

Was ist entscheidend bei der Wahl des Urlaubsortes? Die deutschen Jugendlichen zögern nicht lange: Meer und schöne Strände zum Baden, viel Sonne und günstige Preise nennen sie zuerst. Freundliche Einheimische und viel Abwechslung vom Alltag sowie eine schöne Landschaft und interessante Kultur im Gastland sind ebenfalls wichtig.

Die Eltern entscheiden

Bei den 14- bis 19jährigen entscheiden oft die Eltern das Urlaubsziel, die auch meist die Organisation der Reise in die Hand nehmen und für die Kosten aufkommen. Allein reisen nur 15 Prozent der 14- bis

Die wichtigsten Reiseziele der deutschen Jugendlichen im Ausland (1993)			
	14-28 Jahre	14-16 Jahre	17-19 Jahre
Spanien (Inseln und Festland):	17,9	12	20
Frankreich:	11,4	7	12
Italien (mit Inseln):	10,8	7	13
Jugoslawien:	5,9	5	6
Griechenland:	5,4	3	3
Österreich:	5,4	7	6
Dänemark:	4,0	6	5
Portugal:	4,0	-	2
Niederlande:	3,7	2	6
Großbritannien:	3,5	7	6

(alle Angaben in Prozent; durch andere Reiseziele und Mehrfachnennungen ergeben sich keine 100 Prozent)

16jährigen und acht Prozent der 17- bis 19jährigen. Die anderen reisen mit Eltern, Gleichaltrigen, einer Jugendgruppe oder einem Verein. Mit der Freundin oder dem Freund verreisen 9 Prozent der 14- bis 16jährigen und 17 Prozent der 17- bis 19jährigen.

Welche Aktivitäten am Urlaubsort?

Auf der Hitliste der Urlaubsaktivitäten steht Schwimmen ganz oben. Beliebt sind auch Ausflüge in die Umgebung, Einkaufsbummel und Gespräche mit anderen Menschen. Einfach faulenzen, sich sonnen oder ausruhen sind weit weniger wichtig als bei Erwachsenen.

---

3 Lies den Artikel auf Seite 226 und beantworte die Fragen auf Englisch!

1. What is the topic of the article? 1. where young people from Germany spend their vacation 2. The Netherlands, Italy, Yugoslavia,

2. According to the report, what are the different advantages each country has to offer as a vacation spot? Turkey: inexpensive; Great Britain, Austria, Italy, Greece, USA: best to get to know new people; Islands of Spain, Italy, Yugoslavia, Greece, Turkey: great vacation at-

3. Do more Germans choose to travel to another country or to stay within Germany for their vacations? What statistics support your answer? mosphere; Great Britain, Spain, Italy: a lot going on

4. According to the article, do most teenagers travel alone or with friends and family? How does the article support its conclusion to this question?

5. Which activity is the most popular among teenage vacationers?

6. Look back at the table on page 224 that summarizes students' dream vacations. Read the table and compare it with the table on page 226. How could you explain the different results? 3. they travel to other countries; only every 5th stays in Germany 4. they travel with family and friends; for the most part parents choose, organize and bear the costs of the travel 5. swimming 6. Various answers possible.

4 **a.** Drei Schüler nehmen Stift und Notizblock in die Hand und befragen alle Schüler in der Klasse, was jeder für die zwei „heißesten" Ferienstaaten in den USA hält. Die drei Schüler schreiben die Resultate an die Tafel und nennen dann die drei Lieblingsreisestaaten der ganzen Klasse. Dann fragt euch gegenseitig, warum ihr diese Staaten wohl gewählt habt! E.g.: different age group; questions are different

b. Jeder schreibt jetzt einen kurzen Bericht, der die Information aus der Umfrage wiedergibt.

5 Get together with three other classmates. Each of you chooses (without telling others) one place to go or thing to do in your home town. Each begins by suggesting to the others his or her desire and tries to persuade them to come along. The other two should try to express some reservation about the idea. Everyone gets a turn to suggest and persuade. In the end, all of you must agree on one thing to do together.

6 Each student writes on a card one place where he or she would never want to be stuck on vacation (it must be a general place that everyone will recognize). All cards go into a hat and are then redistributed. The place you pick is where you actually have to go for one whole week of your precious vacation! Now write a postcard in German filled with doubt, displeasure and resignation to your best friend who is back home leading the grand life.

7 R O L L E N S P I E L

With two partners, pick a vacation spot in the United States which you will have to present to a group of German students who are prospective travelers to the United States. Market and "sell" the spot, making it as attractive as possible. Get photos of the area, find out the main attractions and conveniences. Orient your presentation to the interests of German students. Then make your presentation to the class.

KANN ICH'S WIRKLICH?

Can you express in-decision? (p. 213)

Can you ask for and make suggestions? (p. 213)

1 How would you ask someone what you should do?

E.g.: **Was soll ich bloß machen?**

2 How would you ask your friends for specific suggestions on what you all could do this evening? E.g.: **Was machen wir? Hast du eine Idee? Was schlägst du vor?**

3 How would your friend suggest that you go to these places?

a. to Switzerland   a. E.g.: **Ich schlage vor, daß wir mal in die Schweiz fahren.**

b. to New York   b. E.g.: **Fahren wir mal nach New York!**

c. to Lake Constance **(der Bodensee)**   c. E.g.: **Wir können mal an den Bodensee fahren.**

4 How might your friends respond if

a. they like the idea   a. E.g.: **Ja, Spitze! Das ist eine gute Idee.**

b. they do not like the idea   b. E.g.: **Ich bin nicht dafür.**

Can you express doubt, conviction, and resignation? (p. 217)

5 How would you convey to a friend

a. that you doubt you will be able to go on vacation?   a. E.g. **Ich bezweifle, daß ich in die Ferien fahre.**

b. that you are sure you will go to Florida?   b. E.g.: **Ich bin sicher, daß ich nach Florida fahre.**

6 How would you say to someone that it will rain all summer and that unfortunately nothing can be done about it?

E.g.: **Ich bin sicher, daß es den ganzen Sommer regnet. Da kann man nichts machen. Das ist leider so.**

Can you ask for and give directions? (p. 222)

7 How would you ask your teacher how to get to the post office?

E.g.: **Entschuldigung! Wie komme ich bitte zur Post?**

8 How would you give directions to someone   a. E.g.: **Gehen Sie von der Schule geradeaus und dann rechts um die Ecke. Dort ist die Post.**

a. who needs to go to the post office from your school?

b. who is looking for the shopping center?

b. Various possibilities. E.g.: **Biegen Sie hier rechts in die Hauptstraße ein. Auf der linken Seite ist das Einkaufszentrum.**

9 How would you answer if someone asked you for directions, but you were new in town?

E.g.: **Tut mir leid. Ich weiß es leider nicht. Ich bin neu in der Stadt.**

ERSTE STUFE
EXPRESSING INDECISION

Was machen wir jetzt? *What are we going to do now?*
Was soll ich bloß machen? *Well, what am I supposed to do?*

TALKING ABOUT GOING ON VACATION

das Verkehrsmittel, - *transportation*
die Bahn, -en *train*
das Flugzeug, -e *airplane*
das Schiff, -e *ship*
der Urlaub, -e *vacation (time off from work)*
die See, -n *ocean, sea*
  die Nordsee *the North Sea*
das Hallenbad, ̈er *indoor pool*
der Tennisplatz, ̈e *tennis court*
steigen *to climb*

ASKING FOR AND MAKING SUGGESTIONS

Wohin fahren wir? *Where are we going?*
Hast du eine Idee? *Do you have an idea?*
Was schlägst du vor? *What do you suggest?*
Ich schlage vor, daß ... *I suggest that...*
Ich bin dafür, daß ... *I am for doing...*
Fahren wir nach ... ! *Let's go to... !*

USEFUL PREPOSITIONS FOR EXPRESSING DIRECTION

nach *to, toward*
an *to, at*
in *in, into*
auf *to, onto*

ZWEITE STUFE
WORDS FOR DESCRIBING A VACATION BY THE WATER

das Meer, -e *ocean*
segeln *to sail*
windsurfen *to wind surf*
tauchen *to dive*
angeln *to fish*
Boot fahren *to go for a boat ride*
das Boot, -e *boat*

HOTEL ACTIVITIES

die Liegewiese, -n *lawn for relaxing and sunning*
der Golfplatz, ̈e *golf course*
der Strand, ̈e *beach*
der Sandstrand, ̈e *sand beach*
die Sauna, -s *sauna*
der Fitneßraum, ̈e *training and weight room*
der Whirlpool, -s *whirlpool*
die Diskothek, -en *discothek*
der Fernsehraum, ̈e *TV room*

EXPRESSING DOUBT

Ich weiß nicht, ob ... *I don't know whether...*
Ich bezweifle, daß ... *I doubt that...*
Ich bin nicht sicher, daß/ob ... *I'm not sure that/whether...*

EXPRESSING CONVICTION

Ich bin sicher, daß ... *I am certain that...*
Das kannst du mir glauben! *You can believe me on that!*

EXPRESSING RESIGNATION

Da kann man nichts machen. *There's nothing you can do.*
Das ist leider so. *That's the way it is unfortunately.*

DRITTE STUFE
ASKING FOR AND GIVING DIRECTIONS

Entschuldigung! *Excuse me!*
Verzeihung! *Pardon me!*
Das ist hier um die Ecke. *That's right around the corner.*
die Ecke, -n *corner*
Biegen Sie hier ein! *Turn in here!*
Tut mir leid. Ich bin nicht von hier. *I'm sorry. I'm not from here.*

DESCRIBING A CITY

der Parkplatz, ̈e *parking lot*
das Stadttor, -e *city gate*
die Hauptstraße, -n *main street*
aus dem (16.) Jahrhundert *from the (16th) century*
der Brunnen, - *fountain*
das Wohnhaus, ̈er *residence*
Das Fachwerkhaus ist aus dem fünfzehnten Jahrhundert. *The half-timbered house is from the fifteenth century.*
aus *from, out of*
bei *by, near*
nach *after*
von *from, of*
gegenüber *across from*
durch *through*
um *around*
neben *next to*
vor *in front of*
zwischen *between*

OTHER USEFUL WORDS AND EXPRESSIONS

Das ist gerade passiert. *That just happened.*
kaputt *ruined, broken*
eine andere, ein anderer, ein anderes *another (a different) one*
eben nicht *actually not*
das Jahrhundert, -e *century*

▣ Location Opener
Berlin, pages 230-233
Expanded Video Program, Videocassette 4

Using the Photograph,
p. 230-231

Background Information

The **Reichstagsgebäude,** located on the **Platz der Republik,** was built between 1884 and 1894 following the plans of the architect Paul Wallot. The building was severely damaged by a mysterious fire in 1933 and then by heavy bombing at the end of World War II. It was slowly rebuilt between 1957 and 1970 without its original glass dome. For the 20 years following its restoration, it contained exhibits depicting the history of Germany. Since the unification of Germany on October 3, 1990, it has been decided that the Parliament will return to its former home, the **Reichstag**, in Berlin.

Thinking Critically

Analyzing The return of the Parliament from Bonn to its original seat in Berlin has been much debated by the German public and politicians. Can students determine why the move was suggested in the first place and why it is controversial? (Berlin was the historic seat of German government. The move is controversial because of the extremely high cost of relocating the government.)

Using the Almanac and Map,
p. 231

The coat of arms of Berlin depicts a black bear on a white background. **Der Berliner Bär** originally symbolized the struggle for freedom by the people of Berlin from the rulers of Brandenburg. During the post-war era, both East Berlin and West Berlin kept the same flag, with one difference—a slight variation in the crown above the bear. Since the unification, the crest of West Berlin has become the coat of arms for the united city of Berlin.

Terms in the Almanac

- **Spree:** The Spree river is a tributary of the Havel river. It is 403 kilometers (250 miles) long, and 180 kilometers (112 miles) of the river can be navigated by ships. In the city of Berlin, where the river runs through various lakes, the river is a popular site for boat rides and water-sports.

- **Schloß Charlottenburg:** The original castle was commissioned by King Friedrich I in 1695 for his wife Sophie Charlotte. Between 1701 and 1707 the two wings and the tower with its crown-like roof were added. The castle burned almost completely in 1943, but most of the furnishings and art were saved. When the castle was rebuilt, most of the original structure was reconstructed and its contents returned.

- **Pergamon Museum:** This museum is considered one of the finest museums of ancient art in the world. Its treasures include the Market Gate of Miletus and the celebrated Altar of Athena (180-160 B.C.) from the ancient city of Pergamon (an ancient city founded by Greek colonists on the Aegean coast of Anatolia, modern Turkey). The altar's elaborate carvings represent a high point in hellenic sculpture.

- **Wilhelm von Humboldt:** He was a close friend of Schiller and Goethe. He founded the University of Berlin when he was the director of the education department.

- **Alexander von Humboldt:** He was one of the foremost scientists in Germany and the brother of Wilhelm von Humboldt. He traveled extensively in South America and Asia for his scientific studies.

- **Marlene Dietrich:** She was an actress who became famous for her dramatic films in the 1930s. In 1939 she became a U.S. citizen and used her influence to work against Nazi Germany during World War II. She is buried in Berlin.

- **Werner von Siemens:** He was an engineer, inventor, and industrialist who founded one of the major electrical manufacturing companies in Europe.

- **Berliner Pfannkuchen:** The famous **Pfannkuchen** are not pancakes as the name might suggest, rather, they are made from yeast dough, deep-fried, and filled with jam. They are similar to jelly doughnuts, but are heavier.

- **Eisbein:** pig's shanks cooked in boiling water with a variety of spices and served on sauerkraut

- **Buletten:** breaded meat patties served as a main dish or as a cold appetizer

Using the Map

- Have students locate and trace the path of the Havel and Spree rivers on the map on p. 394. You may also want to use Map Transparency 1.

- Ask students to compare the population of unified Berlin to a U.S. city or to any other city in the world of similar or equal size. (Examples: Washington D.C.: 3.2 million; Montreal: 2.9 million)

*I*nterpreting the Photo Essay,
pp. 232-233

② The **Brandenburger Tor,** the only remaining gate in Berlin, was designed by the German architect Carl Gotthard Langhans and built between 1788 and 1791. It was modeled after the Propylaea of the Acropolis in Athens, Greece. The gate was built as an imperial entrance to Berlin and was originally called the **Friedenstor.** It is crowned by Gottfried von Schadow's bronze Quadriga, showing the goddess of victory, **Viktoria,** in a chariot drawn by four horses. In 1807, Napoleon captured and moved the Quadriga to Paris. It was triumphantly returned to Berlin eight years later by Marshall Blücher. In November of 1989 the gate became the new symbol of freedom when Berliners began tearing down the Wall at the Brandenburg Gate.

③ **Das Mahnmal für die Opfer der Berliner Mauer** is one of the many memorials commemorating those who tried unsuccessfully to flee from the East across the wall to the West. The Wall was first erected on the night of August 12-13, 1961 by the communist government of East Germany, ostensibly to protect East Berliners from the influence of the West. The Wall, which divided the city for 28 years, was 45 kilometers (28 miles) long and stood 3 meters high (10 feet). It was dismantled in 1989; only a few sections remain standing today.

④ **Die Kaiser-Wilhelm-Gedächtniskirche** was built between 1891 and 1895. It stands in ruins as a reminder of the destruction caused during World War II. The ruins of the 68-meter high West Tower are all that remain of the original church. Between 1959 and 1961 a new flat-roofed, octagon-shaped church was built adjacent to the ruins by Egon Eiermann. The church is located on the **Kurfürstendamm,** or **Ku'damm,** a boulevard that dates back to the 16th century when it was referred to as the **Knüppeldamm.** It was then used as a hunting trail. In 1871, Chancellor Bismarck was inspired by the Champs-Elysées in Paris and decided to have the boulevard expanded.

⑤ The **Leierkastenmann,** here **Orgel-Hermi,** typically strolls along busy pedestrian zones, playing popular tunes on his mechanical organ. The organ-grinder accepts gratuities for the entertainment.

⑥ **Das Café Kranzler am Ku'damm** is a famous café dating back to the pre-war era. It is located in the center of the city and has historically been frequented by artists and writers.

⑦ These six students all belong to a theater group at the Max-Beckmann-Gymnasium, through which they have become close friends. Thieu-Binh Hoang's parents are from Vietnam, but she was born in Berlin. Ismar Hadziefendic was born in Bosnia, but has lived in Berlin most of his life.

- **Thinking Critically** Ask the class why the students in Photo 7 and their families may have come to Berlin to live.

Komm mit nach

Berlin!

Berlin

Einwohner: 3,4 Millionen

Flüsse: Spree, Havel

Berühmte Gebäude: Kaiser-Wilhelm-Gedächtniskirche, Schloß Charlottenburg, Pergamon-Museum, Brandenburger Tor, Reichstag, Kongreßhalle, Nationalgalerie

Bedeutende Berliner: Wilhelm von Humboldt (1767-1835, Diplomat und Linguist), Alexander von Humboldt (1769-1859, Naturforscher), Rahel Varnhagen (1771-1833, Schriftstellerin), Karl Friedrich Schinkel (1781-1841, Architekt), Werner von Siemens (1816-1892, Erfinder), Kurt Tucholsky (1890-1935, Schriftsteller), George Grosz (1893-1959, Maler), Marlene Dietrich (1901-1992, Schauspielerin)

Industrie: Elektrotechnik, Textilindustrie, Metallindustrie, Verlage, Pharmazeutische Industrie

Beliebte Gerichte: Berliner Pfannkuchen, Eisbein, Buletten, Grüner Aal

Foto ① Das nach der Kriegszerstörung wieder aufgebaute Reichstagsgebäude

Berlin

Berlin, das jahrzehntelang geteilt und dessen westlicher Teil von der kommunistischen DDR umgeben war, ist seit 1990 Hauptstadt des vereinten Deutschlands. Die größte deutsche Stadt ist zugleich eine Kulturmetropole von Weltruf. Die Vitalität dieser Stadt, die die Zerstörungen im Zweiten Weltkrieg ebenso überstand wie den Bau der Berliner Mauer, macht Berlin so faszinierend.

4 Die Kaiser-Wilhelm-Gedächtniskirche am Kurfürstendamm

2 Das Brandenburger Tor ist das Wahrzeichen Berlins.

3 Mahnmal für die Opfer der Berliner Mauer

6 Das berühmte Café Kranzler am „Ku'damm"

5 „Orgel-Hermi", ein typischer Berliner Leierkasten-mann

Die letzten Kapitel in unserem Buch zeigen uns Berlin, die alte und neue deutsche Hauptstadt. Die sechs Schüler in diesen Kapiteln gehen aufs Max-Beckmann-Gymnasium in Reinickendorf.

7 Sandra, Astrid, Andreas, Binh, Ismar und Lars

Kapitel 10 : Viele Interessen!

Los geht's! pp. 236-238	Mensch, zieh die Handbremse an! *p. 236*		*Video Guide*	
	FUNCTIONS	**GRAMMAR**	**CULTURE**	**RE-ENTRY**
Erste Stufe pp. 239-242	Asking about and expressing interest, *p. 240*	Verbs with prepositions; **wo-** and **da-**compounds, *p. 241*	• **Ein wenig Landeskunde:** Television companies in Germany, *p. 242* • **Landeskunde: Was machst du, um zu relaxen?** *p. 243*	• Expressing interest, *p. 239* (from **Kap. 8**, II) • Reflexive verbs, *p. 239* (from **Kap. 4**, II) • Types of movies, *p. 240* (from **Kap. 10**, I) • Giving reasons, *p. 240* (from **Kap. 8**, I) • The conjunction **weil**, *p. 240* (from **Kap. 8**, I) • Saying how often you do things, *p. 241* (from **Kap. 7**, I) • The prepositions **auf** and **für**, *p. 241* (from **Kap. 7**, I) • The reflexive verb **sich freuen**, *p. 241* (from **Kap. 4**, II) • Free-time interests, *p. 243* (from **Kap. 2**, I)
Zweite Stufe pp. 246-249	• Asking for and giving permission, *p. 247* • Asking for information and expressing an assumption, *p. 248*	• The verb **lassen**, *p. 247* • The verb **laufen**, *p. 249*	Statistics on television programs and viewing habits, *p. 246*	• The modal **dürfen**, *p. 247* (from **Kap. 4**, II) • The modal **können**, *p. 247* (from **Kap. 7**, I) • Word order with modals, *p. 247* (from **Kap. 3**, I) • Clauses following **wissen**, *p. 248* (from **Kap. 9**, I) • Yes/no question, *p. 248* (from **Kap. 1**, I) • The conjunction **daß**, *p. 248* (from **Kap. 8**, I) • Expressing wishes when buying, *p. 248* (from **Kap. 5**, I) • Time expressions, *p. 248* (from **Kap. 2**, I) • Saying how often you do things, *p. 249* (from **Kap. 7**, I)
Dritte Stufe pp. 250-253	• Expressing surprise, agreement, and disagreement, *p. 251* • Talking about plans, *p. 252*	• **Kein** used to negate a noun, *p. 251* • The future tense with **werden**, *p. 253*	**Ein wenig Landeskunde:** Getting a driver's license in Germany, *p. 252*	• The interrogative **was für**, *p. 251* (from **Kap. 10**, I) • Agreeing and disagreeing, *p. 251* (from **Kap. 2**, I) • **Kein**, *p. 251* (from **Kap. 9**, I) • The **möchte**-forms, *p. 251* (from **Kap. 3**, I) • Giving reasons, *p. 251* (from **Kap. 8**, I) • Expressing future events with present tense, *p. 252* (from **Kap. 7**, I) • Making plans, *p. 252* (from **Kap. 6**, I) • Word order with auxiliaries, *p. 252* (from **Kap. 3**, II)

Zum Lesen pp. 244-245	Was läuft im Fernsehen? Reading Strategy: Predicting the content of a text
Review pp. 254-257	• **Anwendung,** *p. 254* • **Kann ich's wirklich?** *p. 256* • **Wortschatz,** *p. 257*

Assessment Options	**Stufe Quizzes**
	• *Chapter Resources,* Book 4
	  Erste Stufe, Quiz 10-1
	  Zweite Stufe, Quiz 10-2
	  Dritte Stufe, Quiz 10-3
	• *Assessment Items, Audiocassette* 8 B
	
	Kapitel 10 Chapter Test
	• *Chapter Resources,* Book 4
	• *Assessment Guide,* Speaking Test
	• *Assessment Items, Audiocassette* 8 B
	
	Test Generator, Kapitel 10

CHAPTER OVERVIEW

Chapter Overview

RESOURCES Print	RESOURCES Audiovisual

Textbook Audiocassette 5 B

Practice and Activity Book
Chapter Resources, Book 4
- Additional Listening Activities 10-1, 10-2 ....*Additional Listening Activities, Audiocassette* 10 B
- Student Response Forms
- Realia 10-1
- Situation Card 10-1
- Teaching Transparency Master 10-1 ....*Teaching Transparency* 10-1
- Quiz 10-1 ....*Assessment Items, Audiocassette* 8 B
Video Guide..*Video Program/Expanded Video Program*, Videocassette 4

Textbook Audiocassette 5 B

Practice and Activity Book
Chapter Resources, Book 4
- Communicative Activity 10-1
- Additional Listening Activities 10-3, 10-4 ....*Additional Listening Activities, Audiocassette* 10 B
- Student Response Forms
- Realia 10-2
- Situation Card 10-2
- Quiz 10-2 ....*Assessment Items, Audiocassette* 8 B

Textbook Audiocassette 5 B

Practice and Activity Book
Chapter Resources, Book 4
- Communicative Activity 10-2
- Additional Listening Activities 10-5, 10-6 ....*Additional Listening Activities, Audiocassette* 10 B
- Student Response Forms
- Realia 10-3
- Situation Card 10-3
- Teaching Transparency Master 10-2 ....*Teaching Transparency* 10-2
- Quiz 10-3 ....*Assessment Items, Audiocassette* 8 B

Video Guide..*Video Program/Expanded Video Program*, Videocassette 4

Alternative Assessment
- Performance Assessment,
Teacher's Edition
  Erste Stufe, p. 233K
  Zweite Stufe, p. 233O
  Dritte Stufe, p. 233R
- Portfolio Assessment
  Written: **Anwendung**, Activity 1, *Pupil's Edition*, p. 254;
  Assessment Guide, p. 23
  Oral: **Anwendung**, Activity 1, *Pupil's Edition*, p. 254;
  Assessment Guide, p. 23
- **Notizbuch**, *Pupil's Edition*, p. 242; *Practice and Activity Book*, p. 154

Kapitel 10: Viele Interessen!
Textbook Listening Activities Scripts

Erste Stufe
Activity 6, p. 239

VERONIKA Welche Sendungen ich sehe? Tja, eigentlich gucke ich außer Sportsendungen fast gar nichts. Für Tennis interessiere ich mich am meisten. Bei den Australian Open habe ich sogar ganz früh morgens vor dem Fernseher gesessen, um ja nichts zu verpassen. Ich spiel' selber Tennis im Verein, hier bei uns in Leimen. Das ist übrigens der gleiche Club, in dem auch Boris Becker angefangen hat.

AXEL Ich guck' mir zwar auch mal ab und zu Sportsendungen an, weil ich mich für Fußball interessiere, aber eigentlich sehe ich am liebsten spannende Krimis. Am besten gefallen mir die alten Filme mit Sherlock Holmes. Es macht mir total Spaß, selbst Detektiv zu spielen und die Fälle vor dem Fernseher zu lösen.

PATRICK Also, wenn ich Fernsehen gucke, dann will ich mich in erster Linie informieren. Deswegen gucke ich am liebsten die Nachrichten und das Auslandsmagazin. Ich seh' auch gern mal eine Talkshow, in der Politiker über verschiedene aktuelle Themen diskutieren. Besonders vor den Bundestagswahlen! Der Meinungsaustausch ist dann fast so spannend wie ein Krimi!

TINA Ja, also die Nachrichten schau' ich mir natürlich auch fast jeden Tag an, aber eigentlich nur wegen dem Wetterbericht. Ich fahr' nämlich jeden Tag mit dem Rad zur Schule, und deswegen interessiert es mich, wie das Wetter jeden Tag wird. Na ja, und außer dem Wetterbericht schaue ich auch unheimlich gern Tier- und Natursendungen an. Wir wohnen ja hier mitten im Industriegebiet, da ist nicht viel los mit Natur und so. Deswegen gefallen mir alle Sendungen, die mit der Natur oder mit Tieren zu tun haben.

Answers to Activity 6

1. Veronika: Sportsendungen/Tennis, weil sie selber Tennis spielt
2. Axel: Sportsendungen, weil er sich für Fußball interessiert; Kriminalfilme, weil er selber gern Detektiv spielt
3. Patrick: Nachrichten/Auslandsmagazin, weil er sich informieren will; Talkshow/Politikerdiskussionen, weil er sie spannend findet
4. Tina: Nachrichten, weil sie den Wetterbericht sehen will; Tier- und Natursendungen, weil es nicht viel Natur in ihrer Umgebung gibt

Zweite Stufe
Activity 15, p. 247

ROLF Also, ich bin total begeistert von meiner neuen Anlage. Du mußt sie dir so vorstellen: die komplette Anlage ist in einem ganz tollen Fernseh- und Videowagen im Wohnzimmer untergebracht. Der Fernseh- und Videowagen hat vier Ablagefächer. Also, auf dem Regalfach ganz unten ist das Videogerät. Direkt darüber, also im zweiten Regalfach von unten, da stehen links alle meine Videokassetten und auf der rechten Seite die CDs. Auf dem zweiten Ablagefach von oben stehen der CD-Spieler und über dem CD-Spieler das Radio mit doppeltem Kassettendeck, alles Stereo natürlich! Ja, und ganz oben auf dem Wagen, da habe ich das Farbfernsehgerät hingestellt. Es hat achtundvierzig Programme und eine super Bildqualität! Auf dem Fernseher steht natürlich die Zimmerantenne. Ach ja, und links außen am Fernseh- und Videowagen, da ist ein Haken für den Kopfhörer. Also, meine neue Anlage sieht einfach fantastisch aus!

Answers to Activity 15

bottom shelf: video
second shelf from bottom: video cassettes on left
side; CDs on right side
second shelf from top: CD player and radio/cas-
sette deck
top shelf: TV
on top of TV: antenna

Dritte Stufe

Activity 24, p. 251

TILL   Hallo Silke! Komm steig ein!

SILKE   Ach, hallo Till! Das ist ja nett von dir, daß
du angehalten hast. Kannst du mich ein
Stück mitnehmen?

TILL   Ja klar! Wo mußt du denn hin?

SILKE   Ich muß in die Werkstatt, mein Auto
abholen. Es war kaputt. Hoffentlich läuft
es jetzt wieder!

TILL   Was war denn kaputt?

SILKE   Ach, irgendwas am Motor! Und die
Scheibenwischer haben auch nicht mehr
funktioniert. Na ja. — Aber sag mal, das
ist ja ein toller Wagen, den du hier fährst.
Ist der neu?

TILL   Ja, ich hab' ihn erst letzte Woche bekommen. Schau mal, er hat ganz tolle Extras:
Automatik und Klimaanlage ...

SILKE   Eine Klimaanlage hätte ich auch gern!
Aber dafür hat mein Auto wenigstens ein
Schiebedach.

TILL   Hier, Silke, hör dir mal den Sound von
meinem Stereo-Radio an! Toll, was?

SILKE   Spitze! Der Sound ist viel besser als bei
meinem Stereo. Du, Till, die Sitzschoner
sehen ja toll aus! Gehören die zur
Grundausstattung?

TILL   Nee! Die hab' ich extra dazubestellt,
genauso wie die Rallyestreifen außen.
Hast du nicht auch Rallyestreifen an
deinem Auto?

SILKE   Nee! Nur so'n paar blöde Aufkleber hinten. Aber mein Bruder hat mir vor ein paar
Tagen ganz tolle Breitreifen ans Auto
gemacht. Sieht echt super aus!

TILL   Ja, Breitreifen find' ich auch toll! Aber die
waren so teuer. Da hab' ich lieber die
Servolenkung als Extra genommen.

SILKE   Was? Auch noch Servolenkung? Du, läßt
du mich mal mit deinem Auto fahren?

TILL   Ja, gern! Ich halte gleich da drüben an der
Ecke an!

Answers to Activity 24

Stereo-Radio; Tills Auto: Automatik,
Klimaanlage, Sitzschoner, Rallyestreifen,
Servolenkung; Silkes Auto: Schiebedach,
Aufkleber, Breitreifen

Activity 27, p. 252

SVEN   Du, Jürgen, gestern habe ich einen tollen
Abenteuerfilm im Fernsehen gesehen!
Der Film hat von einem Rennfahrer
gehandelt, der sich auf den Grand Prix
in Monte Carlo vorbereitet hat. Der Film
war echt super! Nächste Woche kommt
der zweite Teil. Den werde ich mir bestimmt ansehen.

JÜRGEN   Ja, genau! Den Film hab' ich gestern
auch gesehen. Der war echt Klasse! Hast
du die tollen Autos im Film gesehen?
Super Sportflitzer mit 5-Gang-Getriebe,
Breitreifen und Rallyestreifen! Einfach
sagenhaft! So ein Auto zu haben,
Mensch, Sven, das wäre mein Traum!

SVEN   Hm, nicht schlecht. Aber damit kann
man ja nicht im normalen Straßen-
verkehr rumfahren!

JÜRGEN   Da hast du recht! Aber ich werde mir
trotzdem einen ganz tollen Sportwagen
mit Schiebedach kaufen, wenn ich 'nen
Job habe und Geld verdiene.

SVEN   Hast du gestern in den Nachrichten
dieses neue Solarmobil gesehen? Find'
ich echt stark, so ein Auto, das nur mit
Sonnenenergie betrieben wird!

JÜRGEN   Ja, Autos mit Sonnenenergie — das ist
ein tolles Konzept, was?

SVEN   Also, ich find' das echt super! Nur leider
gibt es noch nicht so viele Autos damit!
Aber in ein paar Jahren ist die Techno-
logie bestimmt so weit. Dann werde ich
mir ein Solarmobil kaufen.

Answers to Activity 27

Sven: nächste Woche den zweiten Teil des
Films gucken; ein Solarmobil kaufen
Jürgen: einen Sportwagen kaufen

SCRIPTS

Anwendung
Activity 3, p. 254

PETER Klasse! Heute kann sich jeder Krimi-Fan freuen! Es kommen gleich zwei Krimis heute abend!

FRAU BAUER So? Was kommt denn?

PETER Also, wir können erstmal um sechs Uhr *Mord ist ihr Hobby* mit Angela Lansbury sehen und später dann um acht Uhr den Agatha Christie-Film. Heute soll er besonders spannend sein!

HERR BAUER Ja, will denn keiner heute die Nachrichten sehen?

ANKE Doch, na klar, Vati! Aber die kommen doch genau dazwischen, um sieben Uhr! Das paßt doch prima!

FRAU BAUER Ja, heißt das etwa, daß wir heute den ganzen Abend vor dem Fernseher verbringen? Das kann doch nicht euer Ernst sein! Laßt uns lieber mal was anderes zusammen unternehmen!

ANKE Was schlägst du denn vor, Mutti?

FRAU BAUER Laßt uns doch mal wieder einen Spaziergang machen und zum See runter gehen.

HERR BAUER Ja, das ist eine gute Idee! Gleich nach dem Agatha-Christie-Krimi um neun können wir doch einen schönen Abendspaziergang machen!

PETER Ja, aber spätestens um halb elf müssen wir wieder zu Hause sein!

ANKE Wieso das denn?

PETER Weil ich dann unbedingt die Fußballberichte aus der ersten Liga sehen will!

Answers to Activity 3

18 Uhr: RTL; 19 Uhr: 3SAT; 20 Uhr: SW3; 22.30 Uhr: SAT1

Der Prinz von Bel-Air

13.²⁰ RTL Serie

Ist die Katze unterwegs, tanzten die Mäuse auf den Tischen – da macht Bel-Air keine Ausnahme

Will (M. hinten) sitzt ganz schön in der Klemme: Phil muß helfen

Vivian und Phil sind für zwei Tage unterwegs. Hilary übernimmt in ihrer Abwesenheit die Aufsicht über die Kinder. Will nutzt die Gelegenheit für einen Abstecher in die Stadt, läßt sich zu einem Billardspiel mit Einsatz überreden – und verliert prompt 500 Dollar. **25 Min.**

Praxis Bülowbogen

17.²⁵ ARD Serie

„Schuldgefühle" plagen Thomas: Nach dem Autounfall bleibt Freundin Susanne gelähmt

Behandeln Thomas: Dr. Katrin (l.) und Peter Brockmann (M.)

Seit Susanne durch seine Schuld im Rollstuhl sitzen muß, hat sich Thomas' ganzes Leben verändert. Er kümmert sich rührend um seine Freundin. Doch sie ist überzeugt, daß sie eines Tags verlassen wird. **65 Min.**

FILMB

70 TV GUIDE

Im Reich der wilden Tiere

13.¹⁵ PRO 7 Doku

Auf Flußpferdfang in Afrika und Karibus in Kanada

Flußpferden sieht man nicht an, wie gefährlich sie werden können. Die Wildhüter des Krüger-Nationalparks haben eine spezielle Fangmethode entwickelt: Eine schwere Straßenbauma- schine schützt die Männ bei ihrem gefährlichen J Bei den kanadischen Karib versuchen die Wissenscha ler, der hohen Sterblichk unter den Jungtieren auf d Spur zu kommen. **55 M**

Hippopotamus amphibius – das Flußpferd und seine Drohgebär

Kapitel 10: Viele Interessen!
Projects and Games

PROJECT

Students will create a "wall of information" about the city of Berlin. The project should be done in English. Begin this project soon after you have started Chapter 10 to allow the students time for research and revision. This project can be done individually or in pairs, depending on the number of topics and the size of your class. Final projects should be presented, collected, and attached to the "wall."

Materials Students may need poster board, paper, dictionaries, pencils, travel books, and an encyclopedia.

Suggested Topics

Brandenburg Gate	Berlin Wall
Pergamon Museum	**Schloß Charlottenburg**
Reichstag	Berlin Airlift
Kurfürstendamm	History of Berlin

Suggested Sequence

1. Students research the history of the topic of their choice using resources such as world reference books, guidebooks, periodicals, and almanacs.
2. Students give their project a title and begin compiling their materials.
4. Students organize their notes, materials, and any illustrations they want to use.
5. Students turn in their final project.
6. All projects become part of the "wall," a piece of butcher paper long enough to display all projects.

Grading the Project

Suggested point distribution (total = 100 points)
Content (accuracy of information)	40
Appearance (neatness and design)	30
Correct language usage	30

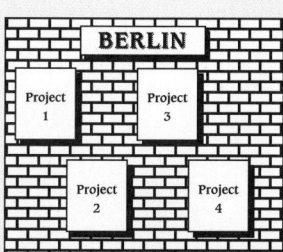

♜ GAMES

Beschriftungen

This game will help students review automobile vocabulary.

Preparation Prepare a handout of a car with all the parts visible but without labels.

Procedure Students may not use their books for this game but may work with a partner. Give each pair a handout. When you give the signal, students begin to identify and label as many parts as they can. The team that first labels all the parts correctly wins.

Heiße Kartoffel

This game is a good vocabulary review for auditory learners.

Procedure Divide the class into small groups of three to five students. Have each group form a circle with their chairs. Provide each group with a potato or a small ball: **die heiße Kartoffel.** Start the game by calling out a word or expression from the **Wortschatz** page. The student in each group with the **Kartoffel** in his or her hand calls out a word that is associated with the one you just called out. For example, you call out "**Fernsehen,**" and the student answers "**die Sendung**" or "**das Programm.**" He or she then throws the **Kartoffel** to another member of his or her group. The person who catches the potato also has to think of a related word, and so on. If a student cannot think of another word or uses one inappropriately, he or she drops out of the game. The last person remaining in each group wins.

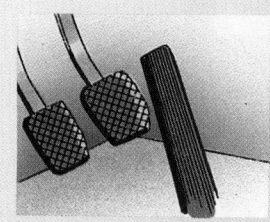
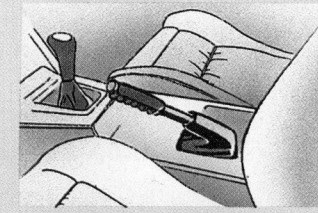

Kapitel 10: Viele Interessen!
Lesson Plans, pages 234-257

*U*sing the Chapter Opener,
pp. 234-235

Motivating Activity

Conduct a survey in German on your students' television viewing habits. Find out how many television sets they have in their homes and approximately how many hours per day or per week they watch TV. Write the information on the board and discuss it with students.

Building on Previous Skills

Ask students to name the last movie they watched on television and to say what type of film it was. (Examples: **Western, Krimi, Actionfilm, Abenteuerfilm**) How did they like the film? Did they watch it alone or with someone else?

Background Information

Students already know from Level 1 that the German school day is shorter than the American school day. Most German students are home by 12:30 or 1:00. Since after-school activities are not part of the school curriculum in Germany, students participate in a variety of other leisure time activities and often join clubs or organizations.

Teaching Suggestion

With your students, brainstorm the different extracurricular activities that they can participate in after school. Make a list on the board and ask students in which of these activities they actually participate.

✧ For Individual Needs

① **Visual Learners** Ask students to take a moment to look at the picture and write down all the things they recognize. Then ask students to create a mini-story surrounding the photo. Have one student begin with what he or she thinks preceded this scene. Let other students build on what the previous student said. Students should not repeat any information, but rather try to add to the story in a creative way. Encourage them to include the realia featured in this photo.

Thinking Critically

② **Drawing Inferences** Have students read the caption. You might have to explain the word **Ratesendungen** by giving examples of such programs on American television. (Examples: *Jeopardy*®, *Wheel of Fortune*®) Then ask students if they watch these types of programs. What makes these shows so popular? This discussion can take place in small groups or pairs.

③ **Drawing Inferences** Ask students to study the inscriptions on the vehicle. Can students tell which city the car is from and who sponsored it? (Karlsruhe; **S = Sparkasse,** a nationwide network of savings institutions; **Hotel Kübler,** a local hotel)

Focusing on Outcomes

To get students to focus on the chapter objectives, have them describe one extracurricular activity they participate in regularly. Then have students preview the learning outcomes listed on p. 235. **NOTE:** Each of these outcomes is modeled in the video and evaluated in **Kann ich's wirklich?** on p. 256.

Teaching Los geht's!
pp. 236-238

Resources for Los geht's!

- *Video Program* **OR**
  Expanded Video Program, Videocassette 4
- *Textbook Audiocassette* 5 B
- *Practice and Activity Book*

▶ **pages 236-237**

Video Synopsis

In this segment of the video, Ismar and Andreas decide to take a break from their studies to see what's on television. Later, while Ismar is helping Andreas wash his mother's car, a small accident occurs. The student outcomes listed on p. 235 are modeled in the video: asking about and expressing interest, asking for and giving permission, asking for information and expressing an assumption, expressing surprise, agreement, and disagreement, and talking about plans.

Motivating Activity

Ask students to name their favorite television program and say why they enjoy watching it. In addition, you might ask which type of program they like least and have them explain their answers.

Teaching Suggestion

Play the video segment of the **Foto-Roman** with the sound turned off. Pause the tape occasionally and have students comment on what might be happening in the story. Write down students' ideas. Then replay the video segment with sound. Have students compare their ideas with what actually happened in the segment.

Language Note

The verb **dahinflitzen** is a colloquial expression that means **schnell fahren**.

▶ **page 238**

For Individual Needs

1 Challenge Ask students to answer the questions. in German and summarize the **Foto-Roman**. The summary could be done orally or in writing.

Building on Previous Skills

2 Before students scan the text for phrases, have them think of constructions from previous chapters that could be used to express the six functions. Put the responses on a transparency. After students have read the **Foto-Roman** again, ask them to point out which expressions were familiar to them and which were new.

For Individual Needs

3 Challenge Have students replace the conjunction **denn** with **weil** and change the word order accordingly.

Closure

Ask students to write a brief report about what they think happens next in the **Foto-Roman**. This could be assigned as homework.

ERSTE STUFE

*T*eaching Erste Stufe,
pp. 239-242

Resources for Erste Stufe

Practice and Activity Book
Chapter Resources, Book 4
- Additional Listening Activities 10-1, 10-2
- Student Response Forms
- Realia 10-1
- Situation Card 10-1
- Teaching Transparency Master 10-1
- Quiz 10-1
Audiocassette Program
- *Textbook Audiocassette* 5 B
- *Additional Listening Activities, Audiocassette* 10 B
- *Assessment Items, Audiocassette* 8 B
Video Program or *Expanded Video Program*

▶ **page 239**

MOTIVATE

Teaching Suggestion

Have students make a list in English of the types of programs that are on American TV. Then, give students a list of program types in German. Ask them to try to match the German with the English.

TEACH

Teaching Suggestions

- The conversation on p. 239 contains several new vocabulary items. You might want to introduce some of the vocabulary before students read the text or after they have read it once. Give examples and use synonyms or descriptions.
- Have students role-play the conversation with a partner, then elicit responses from several students to the questions that follow.

Language Note

The German language has several words or phrases meaning *to watch television*. **Gucken** is a colloquial expression which could be replaced with verbs such as **sehen, ansehen,** and **anschauen**. **Glotzen** is a slang word meaning *to stare*. **Die Glotzkiste** or **die Glotze** is a humorous slang word for *television set*.

For Individual Needs

6 Auditory Learners After students have taken notes, play the audiocassette again and ask students to listen specifically for words that the speakers use to preface a clause giving reasons. (Examples: **weil, deswegen**)

▶ **page 240**

PRESENTATION: Wortschatz

To give students an opportunity to practice the names of different types of TV programs, prepare a list of popular shows on a transparency. You might want to translate some of the names into German. Ask students to classify the programs according to the categories in the **Wortschatz** box. Then ask students to give additional examples of shows in each category.

For Individual Needs

7 Challenge Ask students to give at least one additional reason why Ismar might be interested in each type of program.

PRESENTATION: So sagt man das!

To review and practice these expressions, ask students about the interests of various family members. Examples:
Wofür interessiert sich deine Mutter?
Was für Interessen hat dein Vater?

Building on Previous Skills

8 Ask students to incorporate previously learned functions to elaborate on their reasons for being interested in certain programs. Example: **Ich interessiere mich für Kriminalfilme, weil sie so spannend sind.**

▶ *page 241*

PRESENTATION: Grammatik

- Have students scan the **Foto-Roman** on pp. 236-237 and make a list of all the verbs that are followed by a preposition. Then ask students for the meaning of each verb with and without the preposition.
- To teach the usage of **wo-** and **da**-compounds, show students several examples, such as the ones listed below, and have them try to infer the rules of how and when they are used before you go over the explanation in the function box. Examples:

  Peter und ich sprechen über Mark.
  Peter und ich sprechen über ihn.

  Peter und ich sprechen oft über Sport.
  Peter und ich sprechen oft darüber.

- After students have learned about the **r** inserted in **darüber**, ask them if they can think of other such compounds that require that insertion. (Examples: **daraus, woraus, darum, worum**)

For Additional Practice

9 To provide students with additional practice of **da-** and **wo-** compounds, ask them to rephrase their sentences by replacing the object with the appropriate compound.

▶ *page 242*

Reteaching: The 24-hour clock

Before doing Activity 11, you may want to review the 24-hour clock with students. You could do this by asking them when their favorite programs are shown.

Teacher Note

The letters **SO** in the program overview stand for **Sonntag**.

Thinking Critically

11 Drawing Inferences After students have completed the partner activity, ask them to scan the listing again. Based on the title, can students tell what type of program each one is? Example: **Das Programm um 20 Uhr im BR3 ist eine Natursendung.**

For Individual Needs

11 Challenge To expand the activity, have partners exchange specific information about the programs they like to watch. On which day does the show air? At what time? What is the name of the program? What is it about?

Thinking Critically

13 Analyzing Since most students are familiar with television commercials, ask them to come up with some reasons why the type of products being advertised varies according to the time of day. (Advertisers target different viewing audiences depending on the product they are selling.)

PRESENTATION: Ein wenig Landeskunde

Based on what students have read, ask them to compare the television systems in Germany and in the United States. What are the main networks on American television and what are their logos? (NBC: peacock; CBS: eye; ABC: letters a, b, and c in a circle)

Reteaching: *Wo-* and *Da-* Compounds

Ask students to create at least three sentences from the sentence fragments in the following chart. Then have students rephrase their sentences using appropriate compounds.

Er	sich interessieren	über	Politik
Wir	sprechen	für	Mode
Ich	sich unterhalten	auf	die neue
Sie	sich freuen		Fernsehsendung
Die Mädchen	diskutieren		seinen Besuch
			die Sommerferien
			Sport

▶ *page 243*

PRESENTATION: Landeskunde

Teacher Note

The **Landeskunde** interviews are recorded on audiocassette and videocassette.

ERSTE STUFE

ERSTE STUFE

Teaching Suggestion

Based on students' knowledge of Berlin, Hamburg, and Stuttgart, ask students what types of outdoor activities people might enjoy in those three cities. You might want to introduce the following vocabulary to help students understand the interviews.

Fallschirmspringen	*parachuting*
Tandemsprung	*paired parachute jump*
vor allen Dingen	*above all*
dazwischen	*in between*
mitkriegen	*to learn, to find out*
beruflich einsteigen	*to get into a line of work*

Multicultural Connection

Ask students to interview foreign exchange students, other foreign language teachers, or anyone else they know from a different country about what teenagers in that country typically enjoy doing to relax in their free time.

Group Work

Ask students to work in groups of three. Have each group do Activities A1 through A4 in writing. When students are finished, ask the spokesperson from each group to share his or her answers with the rest of the class.

Teaching Activity

As a final activity, have students scan the three interviews for all the activities mentioned and list them with their infinitive form.

Thinking Critically

A5 Synthesizing To expand further on this question, have students come up with reasons why so many of these trends are similar. (Examples: exposure to American films; television and music give German teenagers insights into American culture and trends among young people.)

Family Link

Have students interview their family members about their free time interests and what they do to relax after work or school.

Teaching Suggestion

B2 Help students prepare for this writing assignment by reviewing phrases from previous chapters that they can use to state their opinion.

Examples:
Ich finde, daß ...
Ich glaube, daß ...
Ich meine, daß ...

Teacher Note

The Culture portion of Quiz 10-1 is based on **Ein wenig Landeskunde** on p. 242.

CLOSE

Teaching Suggestion

Ask students on which current television show they would like to guest star and why.
In welcher Fernsehsendung würdest du gerne mitspielen? Und warum?

Focusing on Outcomes

Refer students back to the learning outcomes listed on p. 235. They should recognize that they now know how to ask about and express interest.

ASSESS

- **Performance Assessment** On a transparency, prepare an evening lineup of television programs on two different channels. Ask students to choose the program that they would most like to watch at a certain time. Students must be able to explain why they chose that program over the other one airing at the same time on the other channel.

- Quiz 10-1, *Chapter Resources*, Book 4

*T*eaching Zum Lesen,
pp. 244-245

Reading Strategy

The targeted strategy in this reading is predicting the content of a text. Students should learn about this strategy before beginning Question 1.

PREREADING

Motivating Activity

Go around the classroom and ask several students how they find out what is on TV. How do they decide whether or not to watch a particular program?

Teaching Suggestion

Ask students where one would find program announcements such as the ones in this reading selection. (Examples: newspaper entertainment section, TV program guides)

Language Note

ARD is the acronym for **Arbeitsgemeinschaft der öffentlich-rechtlichen Rundfunkanstalten der Bundesrepublik Deutschland. RTL** stands for **Radio-Télévision Luxembourg.**

Teacher Note

Activities 1 and 2 are prereading activities.

READING

Building on Previous Skills

Based on the vocabulary students learned in the **Wortschatz** box on p. 240, have them classify the six programs described in the reading. (Example: **Die Eishockey WM ist eine Sportsendung.**)

Language Note

WM stands for **Weltmeisterschaft.** This acronym is used with other sports, as well, for example **Leichtathletik WM, Fußball WM,** and **Gymnastik WM.**

Thinking Critically

Synthesizing Students can see from these pages that Germans can see many American shows on television. Can students think of reasons to explain the fact that American shows are available on German TV, but German shows are rarely shown on American TV? (The German broadcasting industry is smaller than its American counterpart and often imports foreign programs to fill program demands. The American broadcasting industry is large enough to fill program demands without having to import much foreign programming.)

Have students do Activities 4-6 in pairs or small groups. Call on several groups to report back to the class.

POST-READING

Teacher Note

Activities 7 and 8 are post-reading tasks that will show whether students can apply what they have learned.

Teaching Suggestion

7 After students have written their preview, have them read it to the rest of the class. The reader should not mention the name of the program so that the class can try to guess what it is.

Multicultural Connection

Have students ask an exchange student, another foreign language teacher, or anybody else they know from another country about television programming in their country. Then have students report their findings to the rest of the class.

Closure

Ask students to give a reason why someone might enjoy watching each of the six programs described in the readings.

Answers to Activity 1
TV previews

Answers to Activity 2
Answers will vary.

ZWEITE STUFE

Answers to Activity 3

a. upper left hand corner of each review, first line of little box
b. upper left hand corner of each review, second line of little box
c. upper left hand corner of each review, third line of little box
d. at the end of each review text
e. at the very top
The initials refer to the stations/channels; Praxis Bülowbogen, Eishockey WM, Raumschiff Enterprise

Answers to Activity 4

Raumschiff Enterprise, Der Prinz von Bel-Air, Im Reich der wilden Tiere, Der Junge mit dem großen schwarzen Hund; predictions will vary.

Teaching Zweite Stufe, pp. 246-249

Resources for Zweite Stufe

Practice and Activity Book
Chapter Resources, Book 4
- Communicative Activity 10-1
- Additional Listening Activities 10-3, 10-4
- Student Response Forms
- Realia 10-2
- Situation Card 10-2
- Quiz 10-2

Audiocassette Program
- *Textbook Audiocassette* 5 B
- *Additional Listening Activities, Audiocassette* 10 B
- *Assessment Items, Audiocassette* 8 B

► page 246

MOTIVATE

Teaching Suggestion

Ask students which television program(s) they would recommend to an exchange student who is new to American television.

TEACH

 **Cooperative Learning**

14 Divide the class into groups of three students. Each group should have a writer, a discussion leader, and a reporter. Set a time limit of approximately 30 minutes for this activity. Before groups begin to read the two articles and the chart, you might want to introduce the vocabulary and give the information from the following Teacher Notes. Then ask each group to read the articles, examine the chart, and answer the questions. When students are finished, ask each group reporter to share the group's responses to Questions 1-4 with the rest of the class.

Teacher Notes

• Here are synonyms and explanations you might want to use to introduce some of the unfamiliar terms in the reading.

die Fernsehanstalt: ARD, ZDF, RTL sind Fernsehanstalten.

die Einschaltquote: Statistiken darüber, wieviele Leute den Fernseher anmachen

unentbehrlich: Für viele Leute ist der Fernseher unentbehrlich geworden. Sie *müssen* unbedingt Fernsehen schauen.

Vorsicht!: Achtung! Aufpassen!

• Help students interpret the chart "**Hitparade der Jüngsten**". Tell students that the percentages indicate the two age groups of viewers who watch a particular channel, those under fifty and those over fifty.

Thinking Critically

Comparing and Contrasting Ask students what the American equivalent to the German **GfK** in **Nürnberg** is. (A.C. Nielsen Company)

PRESENTATION: Wortschatz

Use a TV or VCR cart and equipment from your school's media department or library to introduce the **Wortschatz**. Have students gather around the equipment while you present the various items to them.

▶ *page 247*

 For Individual Needs

16 Challenge Encourage students to elaborate on each question. You might have them work with a partner. Use the first question as a model and direct it to a student. Ask additional questions based on the student's response.

For Additional Practice

16 Have students summarize their answers into one report, entitled: **Unser(e) Fernsehgerät(e).** Have them begin with the following phrase: **Bei uns zu Hause haben wir ...** Students should tell about the features of their TV(s). Remind them to use connecting words and phrases such as **und, auch, außerdem,** and **und dann noch.**

PRESENTATION: So sagt man das!

Have students give examples of how they ask their parents for permission to have or do something. What do they say? Write down the different ways students ask for permission and underline the verbs in these questions. Then go over the expressions in the function box with students.

For Additional Practice

17 To have students continue practicing the new expressions, ask them to role-play the following situations with their partners.

a. asking for an increase in their allowance (**Taschengeld**)
b. asking for permission to use the car for a date
c. asking for permission to attend a party at a friend's house on a weeknight

▶ *page 248*

PRESENTATION: So sagt man das!

Ask several yes/no questions with **ob**-clauses about school matters to which students can easily respond.
Examples:
Weißt du, ob Herr (Smith) heute in der Schule ist?
Wißt ihr, ob (John) noch krank ist?
Könnt ihr mir sagen, ob unsere (Fußball)mannschaft am Samstag spielt?
Next, ask students if they noticed how you formulated your questions. You might have to repeat some of the questions for students to really notice the **ob**-clauses. In order to make the word order more obvious, ask a few questions in two different ways.
Examples:
Braucht das Gerät eine Zimmerantenne?
Kannst du mir sagen, ob das Gerät eine Zimmerantenne braucht?
Finally, introduce the function box by going over all the phrases.

 For Individual Needs

18 Visual Learners Bring a TV or VCR cart to your classroom. Call on pairs to role-play this situation in front of the class, using the television set or the videorecorder (**Videogerät**) as the item to be purchased.

▶ *page 249*

PRESENTATION: Wortschatz

To practice the vocabulary, provide students with a copy of a television schedule for one week. Students should work in pairs and ask each other what programs are shown and at what times. Example: **Was gibt's im ZDF** (or ABC if you give them an American schedule) **montags um 15 Uhr?**

Teaching Suggestion

22 Encourage students to go beyond the A/B dialogue pattern and continue their conversation for at least one more exchange. They can ask for more information or comment on what their partner says.

Reteaching: Vocabulary

Ask students to describe the television sets in their homes. Have them describe some of the features (size, capabilities), using the vocabulary from p. 246 and other expressions from this **Stufe.**

CLOSE

🔵 Total Physical Response

Plan to have a TV/VCR cart in your classroom on the day you plan to do this activity. Ask individual students to follow your directions.
Examples:
Nimm die Fernbedienung und schalte den Fernseher ein!
Setz dir bitte diesen Kopfhörer auf!
Könntest du bitte messen, wie breit dieser Fernseher ist? Schreib' die Größe an die Tafel!
Leg bitte diese Kassetten auf das untere Ablagefach des Videowagens!

Focusing on Outcomes

Refer students back to the learning outcomes listed on p. 235. They should recognize that they now know how to ask for and give permission, ask for information, and express an assumption.

ASSESS

• **Performance Assessment** Ask students to prepare a brief statement about their viewing habits. They should describe which programs they watch regularly. What programs do they watch and when do they watch them? In addition, they could also tell with whom they watch certain programs and why they enjoy these programs.

• Quiz 10-2, *Chapter Resources*, Book 4

Teaching Dritte Stufe, pp. 250-253

Resources for Dritte Stufe

Practice and Activity Book
Chapter Resources, Book 4
• Communicative Activity 10-2
• Additional Listening Activities 10-5, 10-6
• Student Response Forms
• Realia 10-3
• Situation Card 10-3
• Teaching Transparency Master 10-2
• Quiz 10-3
Audiocassette Program
• *Textbook Audiocassette* 5 B
• *Additional Listening Activities, Audiocassette* 10 B
• *Assessment Items, Audiocassette* 8 B

▶ *page 250*

MOTIVATE

Teaching Suggestion

Ask students if they can recall makes of cars that are manufactured in Germany. Examples: Mercedes (built by Daimler-Benz), Porsche, Audi, VW (Volkswagen), BMW (**Bayerische Motorenwerke**), and Opel.

DRITTE STUFE

TEACH

Language Notes

- PKW is the common acronym for **Personenkraftwagen. LKW** stands for **Lastkraftwagen.**
- **Geld auf den Tisch legen** is a colloquial expression. Here, it could be translated as *to come up with the money.*

Thinking Critically

Analyzing Based on the information in the reading, ask students if they can think of reasons why people in German-speaking countries tend to drive smaller cars than people in the United States. (Fuel in Europe is very expensive; people in the German-speaking countries tend to be concerned about the environment.)

PRESENTATION: Wortschatz

To present the new vocabulary you may want to obtain a car brochure from an auto dealer that has close-up shots of auto parts, such as lights and windshield wipers. After you have gone over the new vocabulary, ask students to list the features of their own car, their parent's car, or a car they would like to have.

▶ *page 251*

For Individual Needs

24 Tactile Learners While students listen to the two descriptions, have them draw a sketch of the options (**Extras**) that the car owners mention. Then have students go back to the **Wortschatz** and write the corresponding word beside each sketch.

25 Visual Learners Ask students to bring a picture of their dream car that they have cut out of a magazine. Students can use these pictures as they exchange information with their partners. Students should take turns labeling the features.

PRESENTATION: So sagt man das!

- Ask students to work with a partner and have them write a statement to precede each functional expression. Call on several pairs to role-play what they came up with, using the expressions in the function box as responses.

- Prepare a list of additional statements for students to react to by showing surprise, agreement, or disagreement, depending on the situation. Examples:
  Autofahren ist sehr teuer!
  Ich finde, man braucht keine Klimaanlage. Das ist Luxus.

Teaching Suggestion

26 As an alternative activity, bring pictures of classic cars and older models to class on the day you plan to do this activity. Each pair of students should choose one picture as the basis for their dialogue.

▶ *page 252*

PRESENTATION: Ein wenig Landeskunde

- Ask students if they can recall the required driving age in Germany for a **Moped.** (16)
- Ask students to compare the age requirements for mopeds and cars in their own state with the requirements in Germany.
- If any of your students are or were enrolled in a driving school, ask them what they learn there.
- After students read the text, ask them questions to assure full understanding. Next, have students list all the requirements that trainees must fulfill to get a driver's license in Germany. Remind them to include costs and hours behind the wheel.

Background Information

In contrast to state procedures in the United States, once a driver's license is issued in Germany, it is valid in all areas of Germany. If a person relocates to another **Bundesland,** for example, he or she does not have to obtain another driver's license.

DRITTE STUFE

PRESENTATION: So sagt man das!

Ask students to list all the time expressions they have learned so far that can be used to refer to the future. (Examples: **morgen; am 3. Juli; nächsten Sommer; im April; in zwei Wochen; später; morgen abend**) Ask students to study the examples in the function box, and lead them to discover the similarities between the use of **werden** and the modal verbs. Finally, give students several pairs of sentences that use both **wollen** and **werden**, two verbs that are frequently mixed up. Ask students to explain the difference in meanings of the sentences.
Example:
Ich *will* das machen.
Ich *werde* das machen.

 ## For Individual Needs

27 A Slower Pace Have students listen to the conversation several times, paying special attention to specific time expressions that indicate the future. Students should make note of these expressions. Elicit phrases from students and write them on the board or a transparency.

▶ *page 253*

PRESENTATION: Grammatik

• Ask students to look at the forms of **werden** and examine how **werden** can be used as an auxiliary verb with another verb in the infinitive.
• Have students compare the two ways future can be expressed in German with the way future is expressed in English.

 ## For Individual Needs

A Slower Pace Prepare a list of conversation starters and have them ready as students start this activity. Put them on a transparency and uncover them one at a time. The students' task is to think of ways to improve or change the situation.
Examples:
Euer Wagen ist wirklich sehr alt.
O, du hast schon wieder eine Vier in Mathe!
Ich kann die Fernbedienung nicht finden!

Teaching Suggestion

30 Make sure students take notes on the information their partners share with them. Students should be prepared to share their partners' information with the rest of the class.

Reteaching: The Future Tense with *werden*

Prepare a list of statements using the present tense and ask students to restate them in the future tense using the correct form of **werden**.
Examples:
Morgen kommt er bestimmt nach Hause.
Morgen wird er bestimmt nach Hause kommen.

Ich komme heute später, weil ich noch einkaufe.
Ich werde heute später kommen, weil ich noch einkaufen werde.

CLOSE

Thinking Critically

Comparing and Contrasting The German language has proverbs related to the future: **Morgen, morgen, nur nicht heute, sagen alle faulen Leute. Was du heute kannst besorgen, das verschiebe nicht auf morgen.** Ask students if they know similar proverbs in English. (Example: *Don't put off until tomorrow what can be done today.*)

Game

Play the game **Beschriftungen** to review the vocabulary of auto parts. See p. 233F for the procedure.

Focusing on Outcomes

Refer students back to the learning outcomes listed on p. 235. They should recognize that they now know how to express surprise, agreement, and disagreement, and talk about plans.

ASSESS

• **Performance Assessment** Ask students to describe their ideal car. What type would it be and what are some of the options they would want their car to have?

• Quiz 10-3, *Chapter Resources*, Book 4

Using Anwendung,
pp. 254-255

Video Wrap-up

At this time, you might want to use the *Video Program* or the *Expanded Video Program*, Videocassette 4 for additional review and enrichment. See *Video Guide* for suggestions regarding:
• **Mensch, zieh die Handbremse an!**
  (Dramatic episode)
• **Landeskunde**
  Interviews
• **Videoclips**
  (Authentic footage—*Expanded Video Program* only)

Family Link

1 Ask students to expand their polling market by asking members of their family some of the same questions. Remind them that the larger the number of people being surveyed the more accurate the results will be.

Portfolio Assessment

1 You might want to suggest this activity as a written and oral portfolio item for your students. See *Assessment Guide*, p. 23.

For Individual Needs

3 **A Slower Pace** Make the listening script available to students as they listen to the activity a second time. Have them identify the name and type of each program the Bauer family plans to watch.

Thinking Critically

4 **Drawing Inferences** Ask students to think of one additional remark each of the characters could have made. This will ensure that students have a true understanding of each person's point of view. This activity could also lead to a lively discussion.

Kann ich's wirklich?
p. 256

This page helps students prepare for the test. It is a brief checklist of the major points covered in the chapter. The students should be reminded that it is only a checklist and not necessarily everything that will appear on the test.

Using Wortschatz,
p. 257

For Individual Needs

Visual Learners Number each program on an overview page from a TV program guide. To review the vocabulary of the **Erste Stufe**, ask students to identify the type of program of the number you call out.

Game

Play the game **Heiße Kartoffel** to review the vocabulary of this chapter. See p. 233F for the procedure.

Teacher Note

Give the **Kapitel 10** Chapter Test, *Chapter Resources*, Book 4.

10

Viele Interessen!

1 Das gibt's doch nicht!

What do German-speaking teenagers do when they need a break from homework? Though television in the German-speaking countries is different from American television, it is a source of information and entertainment for those teenagers who are tired of hitting the books. Cars are another area of interest to many teenagers. Most of them look forward to getting a driver's license and with it a certain amount of independence. To talk about these interests, you need to know a number of words and expressions.

In this chapter you will learn

- to ask about and express interest
- to ask for and give permission; to ask for information and express an assumption
- to express surprise, agreement, and disagreement; to talk about plans

And you will

- listen to students talk about television and cars
- read excerpts from a German television guide
- write about your interests in television and cars
- find out how the German television companies operate, and what is required to obtain a German driver's license

② Ich interessier' mich für Ratesendungen.

② Ich werde mir mal so einen tollen Wagen kaufen — ein Solarmobil!

Solarmobil Karlsruhe e.V.

HOTEL KÜBLER
Karlsruhe

Los geht's!

Mensch, zieh die Handbremse an!

Look at the photos on these two pages. What are the boys doing at first? What topics do you think they are discussing?

Ismar Andreas

Du, Ismar, laß mal sehen! Das kann doch nicht stimmen. Du hast dich ganz bestimmt verrechnet. Ich meine ...

Hier, du darfst nachrechnen.

①

Du, ich hab' ein ganz anderes Ergebnis. Das gibt's doch nicht! Was machen wir jetzt?

Ich meine, wir sind müde. Machen wir mal eine kleine Pause!

②

Einverstanden! — Schauen wir mal, was es jetzt im Fernsehen gibt! Um diese Zeit kommt gewöhnlich nichts Besonderes.

Du hast bestimmt recht, aber schauen wir mal! — Habt ihr ein Fernsehmagazin?

Ja schon. Aber ich weiß nicht, wo es liegt. Gib mir lieber mal die Fernbedienung rüber!

③

Hier!

Danke! Schauen wir mal, was es im Ersten Programm gibt!

Ach, etwas über die Umwelt. Normalerweise interessiert mich so was, aber nicht jetzt. Mach weiter!

Etwas über Politik! Das interessiert mich wenig.

④

Da stimm' ich dir zu.

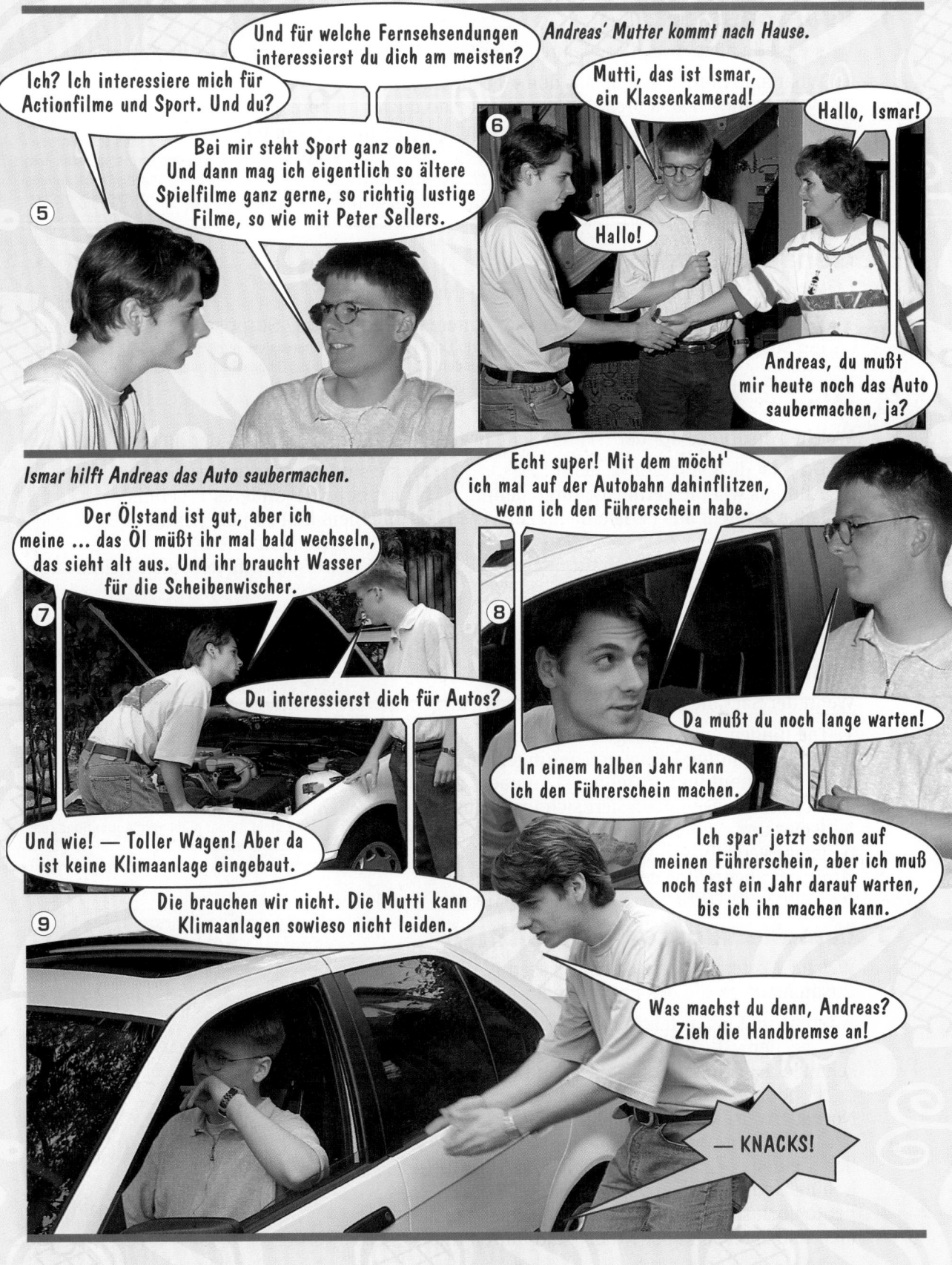

1 Was passiert hier?

Verstehst du alles, was diese Leute in der Foto-Story sagen? Beantworte die Fragen!

1. What are Andreas and Ismar doing at the beginning? *1. They are doing their math homework.*
2. Why do they take a break? What do they do during the break? *2. because they are tired; they watch TV*
3. What do you find out about Andreas and Ismar's interests in television? *3. Ismar likes action movies and sports shows; Andreas likes sports shows and old movies*
4. Who interrupts them? What does Andreas get reminded of? *4. Andreas' mother; to clean her car*
5. Does Ismar know a lot about cars? How do you know? *5. yes; he checks Andreas' mother's car*
6. What happens at the end? What do you think is going to happen next? *6. the car starts moving; it is going to roll over the nozzle of the vacuum cleaner*

2 Genauer lesen

Lies den Text noch einmal und beantworte diese Fragen!

1. Which phrases express compliments? Interest? Permission? Surprise? Agreement? Making suggestions? *1. Toller Wagen!; Echt super! / Laß mal sehen!; Ich interessiere mich ... / Du darfst ... / Das gibt's doch nicht! / Einverstanden!; Da stimm' ich dir zu; Du hast bestimmt recht; Ja schon / Machen wir mal ... ; Schauen wir mal ...*

3 Was paßt zusammen?

Welche Ausdrücke auf der rechten Seite beenden die Satzanfänge auf der linken Seite?

1. Du hast dich verrechnet, denn ... *1. b*
2. Andreas will die Fernbedienung, denn ... *2. e*
3. Ismar braucht das Fernsehmagazin, denn ... *3. d*
4. Andreas interessiert sich für ältere Spielfilme, denn ... *4. a*
5. Ismar darf bald Auto fahren, denn ... *5. c*

a. sie sind oft sehr lustig.
b. ich habe ein anderes Ergebnis.
c. in einem halben Jahr kann er den Führerschein machen.
d. er will wissen, was jetzt am Nachmittag kommt.
e. er will das Fernsehgerät einschalten.

4 Stimmt oder stimmt nicht?

Wenn der Satz nicht stimmt, schreib die richtige Antwort!

1. Die Jungen haben das gleiche Ergebnis in den Matheaufgaben. *1. Stimmt nicht. Sie haben beide ein anderes Ergebnis.*
2. Am Nachmittag kommen Sendungen im Fernsehen, für die sie sich interessieren. *2. Stimmt nicht. Sie interessieren sich nicht für die Sendungen am Nachmittag.*
3. Ismar schaut im Fernsehmagazin nach, um zu sehen, was am Nachmittag läuft. *3. Stimmt nicht. Andreas nimmt die Fernbedienung.*
4. Normalerweise interessiert sich Ismar für Umweltprobleme. *4. Stimmt.*
5. Ismar und Andreas sehen die gleichen Filme gern. *5. Stimmt nicht. Ismar sieht gern Actionfilme, und Andreas mag ältere Spielfilme.*
6. Ismar versteht viel von Autos. *6. Stimmt.*
7. Er hat auch schon seinen Führerschein. *7. Stimmt nicht. Er kann ihn in einem halben Jahr machen.*

5 Welche Wörter passen?

Welche Wörter aus dem Kasten passen in die Zusammenfassung des Foto-Romans?

Andreas und Ismar machen __1__ in Mathe zusammen. Sie machen __2__, weil sie müde sind. Sie wollen __3__ schauen aber finden __4__ nicht und versuchen mit der __5__ herauszufinden, was es im Ersten Programm gibt. Normalerweise interessieren sie sich für __6__, die mit der Umwelt zu tun haben, aber heute nicht. Sie wollen lieber einen __7__ oder Sport schauen. Die Mutter kommt und erinnert (*reminds*) Andreas daran, __8__ heute noch sauberzumachen. Sie machen das zusammen und sprechen über Autos, Autofahren und __9__.

8 das Auto   7 Actionfilm
4 das Fernsehmagazin
9 den Führerschein
3 Fernsehen   2 eine Pause
5 Fernbedienung
6 Sendungen   1 Hausaufgaben

Asking about and expressing interest

Wer guckt was?

Lies, worüber sich Ismar und Andreas unterhalten und beantworte die Fragen!

ISMAR Für welche Sendungen interessierst du dich am meisten?

ANDREAS Das ist leicht zu sagen, wofür ich mich interessiere: für Nachrichtensendungen und ab und zu vielleicht mal für einen tollen Krimi.

ISMAR Dann bist du ein wirklich typischer Fernsehgucker. — Schau, hier ist eine Statistik über die beliebtesten Fernsehsendungen der Deutschen.

ANDREAS Das gibt's doch nicht! — Interessant! Und wofür interessierst du dich?

ISMAR Wir sehen uns zu Hause Nachrichten, Sport und Politik an. Und danach diskutieren wir immer heftig über alles …

ANDREAS Das find' ich toll! — Aber jetzt checken wir schnell mal das Nachmittagsprogramm durch!

„Ich freu' mich schon immer auf ‚Tatort'. Das läuft sonntags um 20 Uhr 15 im Ersten Programm."

1. Wofür interessiert sich Andreas? Worauf freut sich Ismar?
2. Warum ist Andreas ein typischer Fernsehzuschauer?
3. Für welche Sendungen interessiert sich Ismars Familie?
4. Was passiert gewöhnlich nach einer Sendung bei ihm zu Hause?
5. Für welche Sendungen interessieren sich die Deutschen am meisten? Am wenigsten?
6. Welche amerikanischen Sendungen passen in diese Kategorien?

Die TV-Hits der Deutschen	
Nachrichtensendungen	74%
Kriminalfilme	57%
Wetterbericht	50%
Ratesendungen/Spielshows	43%
Sportübertragungen	43%
Tier-/Natursendungen	42%
Familiensendungen	42%
Lustspiele/Komödien	39%
Wildwest-/Abenteuerfilme	37%
Gesundheits-/Medizinthemen	37%
Talkshows	36%
Politikerdiskussionen	36%

6 Hör gut zu! For answers, see listening script on TE Interleaf.

Für welche Fernsehsendungen interessieren sich diese Leute und warum? Mach dir Notizen! Vergleiche dann deine Notizen mit den Notizen deiner Mitschüler!

die Nachrichten, Nachrichtensendungen

der Wetterbericht

Sportsendungen, Sportübertragungen

Natursendungen

Ratesendungen

Diskussionen über Politik

Und dann noch . . .

Familiensendungen	Tiersendungen
Kriminalfilme	Lustspiele
Wildwestfilme	Komödien
Abenteuerfilme	Sendungen über
Spielshows	Gesundheit
Talkshows	Werbesendungen

Für welche Sendungen interessierst du dich? Sag es deinen Klassenkameraden!

E.g.: Ismar interessiert sich für Kriminalfilme, weil er sie sehr spannend findet.

7 Wofür interessiert sich Ismar und warum?

Was paßt zusammen?

Ismar interessiert sich für ...

den Wetterbericht die Nachrichten

Sportsendungen Kriminalfilme

Natursendungen Komödien

weil er ...

gern lustige Sachen sieht

Tiere furchtbar gern hat

sie sehr spannend findet

wissen möchte, was in der Welt passiert

nur bei gutem Wetter im Gebirge wandert

selbst gern Sport macht

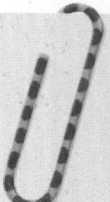

SO SAGT MAN DAS!

Schon bekannt

Asking about and expressing interest

You already know several ways of asking someone about his or her interests:

Was für Interessen hast du?
Wofür interessierst du dich?

and of expressing your interests:

Ich interessiere mich für Sport.

8 Wofür interessierst du dich und warum?

Bevor du mit deinem Partner die vielen Sendungen durchcheckst, frag ihn, wofür er sich besonders interessiert und warum! Danach sag ihm, wofür du dich interessierst und warum!

Grammatik Verbs with prepositions; wo- and da-compounds

1. As in English, German verbs are often followed by prepositions which convey specific meanings. Think of some examples in English. In German, you have to pay attention to the case (accusative or dative) that follows a preposition. Look at the sentences below. Which case follows each preposition?

> **sprechen über: Die Jungen sprechen über das Ergebnis.**
> **sich freuen auf: Andreas freut sich auf den Krimi.**
> **sich interessieren für: Er interessiert sich für lustige Filme.**

2. When using verbs with prepositions in a question or response, you must do the following:

   a. When referring to people, use the preposition plus the question word **wen** in your questions: **Für wen interessierst du dich?**

   > **Ich interessiere mich für ihn, den Ralph.**

   b. When referring to things or ideas, you use a **wo**-compound (**wo** + preposition) in your question:

   > **Wofür interessierst du dich?**   **Ich interessiere mich für Politik.**

   If you want to refer to the thing or idea in a statement using a pronoun (*it*), you have to use a **da**-compound (**da** + preposition):

   > **Ich interessiere mich für Politik. — Ja? Ich interessiere mich auch dafür.**
   > **Er freut sich auf den Krimi. — Ich freue mich auch darauf.**

3. If a preposition begins with a vowel, an **r** is inserted between **wo** and **da** and the preposition to facilitate pronunciation:

   > **auf: worauf, darauf**   **über: worüber, darüber**

9 Wie viele Sätze kannst du bauen?

Various possibilities. E.g.: **Ich diskutiere immer über Problemfilme.**

ich meine Freunde und ich, wir meine Eltern mein Freund	sprechen diskutieren s. freuen s. interessieren	gewöhnlich immer ab und zu ganz selten	auf für über	die Nachrichten Sportsendungen Natursendungen Ratesendungen Krimis Kultursendungen Problemfilme Kindersendungen Werbung

10 Wofür interessierst du dich?

Frag deine Partnerin, wofür sie sich interessiert! Sag ihr, ob du dich auch dafür interessierst oder nicht!

11 Was gucken wir?

Du möchtest mit deiner Partnerin heute abend Fernsehen gucken. Du weißt aber nicht genau, wofür sie sich interessiert. Habt ihr die gleichen Interessen? Auf welches Programm freust du dich? Und sie?

12 Für mein Notizbuch

Schreib in dein Notizbuch, für welche Sendungen du dich interessierst und was du gewöhnlich guckst! Wann kommen deine Lieblingssendungen? Auf welchem Fernsehsender (*channel*)? Gibt es eine Sendung, auf die du dich besonders freust?

13 Werbung im Fernsehen

Rang	Werbeartikel
1	Fast-foods
2	Geschirrspülmittel
3	Waschpulver
4	Kaffee
5	Video-Spiele
6	Textilien
7	Rasierklingen

Guck dir mal die Werbesendungen im Fernsehen an! Für welche Artikel werben die Sender am meisten? — Mach eine Rangliste mit Werbeartikeln, wie im Beispiel links! Erwähne auch deine Lieblingswerbung und beschreibe sie! Berichte deiner Klasse über dein Ergebnis!

SO ÜBERSICHT		
18.00 ZDF	Ein Heim für Tiere Bobby hat zwei Zuhause.	60 Min.
18.00 RTL	Mord ist ihr Hobby mit Angela Lansbury	45 Min.
19.00 3SAT	heute	30 Min.
19.00 RTL	Hans Meiser Audience Participation Show	70 Min.
20.00 BR3	Die Sterngucker Sind wir allein im Universum?	45 Min.
20.00 N3	Der amerikan. Bürgerkrieg Letzter Teil: Robert E. Lee	60 Min.
20.00 SW3	Agatha Christie Krimiserie: Hercule Poirot	60 Min.
20.00 PRO 7	Matlock Krimiserie	45 Min.
22.15 ZDF	Die Sport-Reportage	30 Min.
22.30 SAT1	Fußball Berichte der 1. Liga	30 Min.

EIN WENIG LANDESKUNDE

ARD

ZDF

RTL

SAT.1

In Germany there are public and private television companies. The public companies are financed by a monthly viewing fee based upon the number of TV sets in use in each household. The fee amounts to DM 23,80 a month. The programming of the public companies is scrutinized by a quasi-governmental agency, the **Rundfunk- und Fernsehrat**, that is composed of various interest groups. The two public television companies are **ARD**, producing the **Erstes Programm**, and the **ZDF**, producing the **Zweites Programm**. The **ARD** also produces regional programming, the **Regionalprogramm**, or the **Drittes Programm**. Advertising on these stations is restricted to two 15-minute periods a day.

A number of private TV companies that emerged in the eighties are financed by commercials. The most prominent companies are **RTL** and **SAT 1**. These private stations transmit, above all, sports, entertainment programs, and often controversial series. Other popular private companies are **PRO 7**, **n-tv**, **MTV**, and **Eurosport**.

PRO 7

3 SAT

RTL 2

VOX

Was machst du, um zu relaxen?

You've learned a lot already about the way German-speaking students like to spend their free time. Now we've asked people from around Germany what they do after school or work in order to relax and unwind. Think about what you've learned so far about Germans' free time interests. Then think about what you and your friends do after school or after work to relax. Afterwards, listen to the interviews, then read the text.

Sabine, *Berlin*

„In der Freizeit viel lesen, schwimmen gehen, Sport, und ich würde gern mal Fallschirmspringen, diese Tandemsprünge würde ich gerne mal machen. Und was ich vor allen Dingen in der Freizeit mache, ist Schlafen, das finde ich ganz besonders schön."

Uwe, *Hamburg*

„So, ich mach' Hausaufgaben, mit sehr viel Musik dazwischen, und, ja dann entweder treff' ich mich mit meinen Freunden, spiel' Basketball oder Fußball, oder etliches, ja, oder ich faulenze einfach, leg' mich aufs Bett und schlafe."

Philipp, *Stuttgart*

„In der Freizeit, also da fahr' ich speziell Rollerblade und fahr' Mountainbike, und das hab' ich mitgekriegt, weil mal welche aus Amerika da waren — von dem Film ‚Rollerboys', und dann hab' ich das angefangen. Rollerblade zu fahren macht mir ziemlich Spaß, ich finde das irgendwie ... andere Welten für mich, und das macht mir sehr viel Spaß. Mit [meinem Freund] speziell mach' ich hobbymäßig Computer, und da möchten wir später mal auch beruflich einsteigen."

A. 1. Write the names of the people interviewed on a piece of paper and next to each the activities or hobbies that he or she talks about.
2. What does Sabine like to do best? What phrase does she use to describe that? Name one thing Sabine would like to do, but has not yet done.
3. What else does Uwe like to do when he's doing homework?
4. When did Philipp first become interested in in-line skating?
5. Scan through the activities again. Which other activities are mentioned which are also popular in the United States? Based on what you already knew about German culture, were you surprised that so many trends popular in the United States are also popular in Germany?

B. 1. People often think the habits of other cultures are somewhat "strange" and difficult to understand. At some time in your life, you may have heard this about German culture. However, once people get to know the other culture (as you've gotten to know German culture) they find it's not so very different from their own. What's your impression? Think about everything you've learned about Germany so far. Are there more similarities between our two cultures or are there more differences?
2. Write an essay in German stating your own opinion. Be sure to support your opinion with several examples based on what you've learned in the **Landeskunde** sections.

ZUM LESEN

Was läuft im Fernsehen?

LESETRICK

Predicting the content of a text. You're likely to read more quickly and more easily if you are able to make some predictions ahead of time about the content of a text. You have already learned how to predict using pictures, format, titles, and subtitles as clues. In this lesson you will continue to practice predicting using pictures and titles, but you will also develop your ability to predict *while* reading a text.

For answers, see TE Interleaf.

Getting Started

1. Judging by their format, what kind of texts are these?
2. With your classmates, think of five different kinds of information that you would usually find in a TV schedule at home and list these on the board.

Tip: When reading a schedule you are usually looking for specific information, for instance, dates or times. To orient yourself, you need to scan the schedule to find out what kind of information is given and where it is located.

3. Locate the following kinds of information in the **Fernsehprogramm** excerpts:
   a. times
   b. channels
   c. types of shows
   d. length of shows
   e. day/date
   To what do the initials **ARD**, **ZDF**, etc. refer? If you had time

---

13.20 RTL Serie — Der Prinz von Bel-Air

Ist die Katze unterwegs, tanzen die Mäuse auf den Tischen – da macht Bel-Air keine Ausnahme

Will (M. hinten) sitzt ganz schön in der Klemme: Phil muß helfen

Vivian und Phil sind für zwei Tage unterwegs. Hilary übernimmt in ihrer Abwesenheit die Aufsicht über die Kinder. Will nutzt die Gelegenheit für einen Abstecher in die Stadt, läßt sich zu einem Billardspiel mit Einsatz überreden – und verliert prompt 500 Dollar. **25 Min.**

17.25 ARD Serie — Praxis Bülowbogen

„Schuldgefühle" plagen Thomas: Nach dem Autounfall bleibt Freundin Susanne gelähmt

Behandeln Thomas: Dr. Katrin (l.) und Peter Brockmann (M.)

Seit Susanne durch seine Schuld im Rollstuhl sitzen muß, hat sich Thomas' ganzes Leben verändert. Er kümmert sich rührend um seine Freundin. Doch sie ist überzeugt, daß er sie eines Tags verlassen wird. **65 Min.**

70   TV GUIDE   FILMR

13.15 PRO 7 Doku — Im Reich der wilden Tiere

Auf Flußpferdfang in Afrika und Karibus in Kanada

Flußpferden sieht man nicht an, wie gefährlich sie werden können. Die Wildhüter des Krüger-Nationalparks haben eine spezielle Fangmethode entwickelt: Eine schwere Straßenbaumaschine schützt die Männer bei ihrem gefährlichen Job. Bei den kanadischen Karibus versuchen die Wissenschaftler, der hohen Sterblichkeit unter den Jungtieren auf die Spur zu kommen. **55 Min.**

Hippopotamus amphibius – das Flußpferd und seine Drohgebärde

15.00 EURO. Sport

Eishockey WM

live!

Aus der Olympiahalle, München: Zweiter der Gruppe B gegen den Dritten der Gruppe A

Die Vorrunde ist ausgespielt. Nun werden im K.O.-System die Endspielgegner ermittelt: Die ersten vier Teams der beiden Vorrundengruppen kommen weiter. Die Deutschen haben bei dieser WM mit Heimvorteil gute Chancen. **180 Min.**

Eine Spielszene der Begegnung BRD – Kanada

16.09 ZDF Serie

Raumschiff Enterprise

„Illusion oder Wirklichkeit": Ein schwarzes Loch im Universum zieht die Enterprise magisch an

Opfer einer fremden Geisteskraft: Picard, Haskell, Data (o.)

Bei dem Versuch, ein Schwarzes Loch im All näher zu untersuchen, wird die Enterprise verschlungen. Gleich darauf kommt es zu seltsamen Sinnestäuschungen: Die Mannschaft kämpft gegen ein romulanisches Kriegsschiff, das gar nicht existiert! **51 Min.**

11.30 ZDF Kinder

Der Junge mit dem gro-ßen schwarzen Hund

Ulf und der Neufundländer – eine schwierige Freundschaft

Im Schrebergarten von Oskar hat Nepomuk genug Auslauf

Ulf ist zehn und will schon lange einen eigenen Hund. Eines Tages läuft ihm ein schwarzer Neufundländer hinterher. Ulf gibt ihm den Namen Nepomuk und nimmt ihn mit nach Hause. Seine Eltern sind nicht gerade begeistert, aber für eine Nacht darf er bleiben. **75 Min.**

---

between 3:00pm and 5:30pm on Saturday, what could you watch on German TV?

A Closer Look

4. If you're reading this section of the TV guide you probably want to figure out what these shows are about or if you've already seen them. For the following shows, look at the photos and read the captions, titles and subtitles: a science fiction series, an American sit-com, a documentary, and a children's TV show. Then, based on this information alone, predict what each show or episode is about.

5. Read the previews of these shows to confirm or adapt your original prediction. How close were you in predicting the content of the show?

6. Previews of TV shows never give the ending away. However, based on everything you know about the shows so far and on your own knowledge of different kinds of shows, predict the endings for the following shows. Then write, in German, one or two concluding sentences for each summary.
   a. *Raumschiff Enterprise*
   b. *Der Junge mit ...*
   c. *Praxis Bülowbogen*
   d. *Der Prinz von Bel-Air*

7. Write a preview for one episode of your favorite show. Write one sentence about the main idea of the episode and four sentences which develop the main idea. Use connecting words such as those in the texts on these pages. Be sure not to give away the ending!

8. Write a movie and TV trivia quiz. Everyone will write three trivia questions in German on three separate cards and then put all the cards in a container. Divide up into two teams and play trivia.

Asking for and giving permission; asking for information and expressing an assumption

Fernseh-Hits in Deutschland 1991

Rang	Sendung	Datum	Anstalt	Zuschauer (Mio)
1	Wetten daß .. ?	13. 4.	ZDF	17,56
2	Wetten daß .. ?	2. 3.	ZDF	17,50
3	Die Rudi Carrell Show	26. 1.	ARD	16,60
4	ARD-Sport Extra: EM-Qualifikation Deutschland–Wales	16. 10.	ARD	16,43
5	Die Rudi Carrell Show	26. 10.	ARD	16,12
6	Die Rudi Carrell Show	20. 4.	ARD	15,90
7	Wetten daß .. ?	14. 12.	ZDF	15,89
8	Wetten daß .. ?	2. 11.	ZDF	15,72
9	Das Traumschiff	1. 1.	ZDF	15,57
10	Die Rudi Carrell Show	7. 12.	ARD	15,51
11	ZDF-Sport Extra: Fußball Belgien – BRD	20. 11.	ZDF	15,38
12	Tagesschau	3. 2.	ARD	15,35
13	Tagesschau	20. 1.	ARD	15,25
14	Derrick	15. 3.	ZDF	15,09
15	Ein Fall für zwei	25. 1.	ZDF	14,76

Quelle: Media Control GmbH

PRO 7 und RTL haben das jüngste Publikum

Wenn im Vorabendprogramm die „Real Ghostbusters" oder „Lassie", die „Little Wizards" oder „Doogie Howser" auftauchen, dann ist entweder PRO 7, RTL 2 oder der Kabelkanal eingeschaltet, die Sender mit dem „jüngsten" Publikum (siehe Tabelle rechts). Vor allem Kinder

Die erfolgreichsten Sendungen

In den Fernsehanstalten weiß man morgens ganz genau, für welche Fernsehprogramme sich die meisten Haushalte am Abend zuvor interessiert haben, denn für alle Sendungen werden die Einschaltquoten gemessen.

Solche Statistiken sind heutzutage für alle Fernsehanstalten für die Planung von neuen Programmen unentbehrlich. Auch wollen die Werbesponsoren diese Einschaltquoten wissen.

Die Gesellschaft für Konsum-, Markt- und Absatzforschung (GfK) in Nürnberg ermittelt diese Einschaltquoten. Fernsehgeräte von ausgewählten Haushalten werden mit kleinen Computern versehen, die der Zentrale sekundengenau anzeigen, wann und wie viele Haushalte die verschiedenen Fernsehprogramme eingeschaltet haben.

und Jugendliche sehen sich die US-Produktionen an — und die Werbespots für „McDonald's", „Murmel-Mikado" und das Elektronikspiel „Super Nintendo".

Aber Vorsicht mit diesen Zahlen! Die „jüngsten" TV-Sender haben zwar die meisten Zuschauer unter 50 Jahren, doch ist ihr Marktanteil wesentlich geringer als der von ARD und ZDF.

HITPARADE der „jüngsten" TV-Sender im Juni 1993

RANG	SENDER	ZUSCHAUER unter 50 Jahre	über 50 Jahre
1	PRO 7	76,6%	23,3%
2	RTL 2	74,4%	25,6%
3	KABK	65,1%	34,9%
4	VOX	56,1%	43,9%
5	RTL	56,1%	44,0%
6	DSF	54,5%	45,5%
7	SAT.1	51,2%	48,8%
8	NTV	45,8%	58,3%
9	ARD	43,7%	56,3%
10	ZDF	35,4%	64,6%

1. sie sprechen über Einschaltquoten 2. für die Fernsehanstalten; zur Planung von neuen Programmen

14   Beliebte Sendungen

Lies die beiden Artikel und beantworte die Fragen!

1. Was haben beide Artikel gemeinsam (*in common*)?
2. Für wen sind die Einschaltquoten von Interesse und warum?
3. Welche Sendungen sehen sich die jüngeren Zuschauer an? Auf welchen TV-Sendern kommen diese Sendungen?   3. US-Produktionen; PRO7, RTL2, Kabelkanal
4. Welche sind die beiden größten deutschen Fernsehanstalten?   4. ARD und ZDF

WORTSCHATZ

Stereo-Farbfernsehgerät

- 68 cm, 2×30 Watt
- Kabeltuner für 39 Programme
- LED-Programmanzeige
- Kopfhöreranschluß
- Fernbedienung
- mit Videotext

Dieser **Fernseh- und Video- wagen** kommt mit zwei **Ablagefächern** für Ihre **Videocassetten**

Diese **Fernbedienung** steuert bequem Ihr Gerät.

Dieser **Stereo-Kopfhörer** kommt mit einem Lautstärkeregler

Eine **Zimmerantenne** für UHF und VHF

15 Hör gut zu! For answers, see listening script on TE Interleaf.

Rolf has just bought himself a new entertainment system with all the latest features. On a separate piece of paper, draw the outlines of a **Fernseh- und Videowagen**. Then listen to Rolf's description and sketch what you hear. Draw in all the equipment and features he mentions and pay attention to where the features are located.

16 Und du?

Beantworte die Fragen!

1. Was für ein Fernsehgerät habt ihr? Wie groß ist es?
2. Wie viele Programme könnt ihr empfangen (*receive*)?
3. Welche Ausstattung (*features*) hat euer Fernsehgerät?
4. Habt ihr Kabelfernsehen oder eine Zimmerantenne?
5. Wie steuert ihr euer Fernsehgerät?
6. Wie viele Fernsehgeräte habt ihr? Wo stehen sie?
7. Wann gebrauchst du einen Kopfhörer?
8. Hast du einen eigenen Fernseher? Wenn ja, was für einen?

SO SAGT MAN DAS!

Asking for and giving permission

You have been using the helping verbs **dürfen** and **können** in questions such as:

> **Warum darfst du keine Bananen essen?**
> **Kann ich bitte Andrea sprechen?**

When asking for permission, you could say:

> **Darf ich (bitte) das Fernsehgerät einschalten?**
>
> **Kann ich bitte mal die Fernbedienung haben?**
>
> **He, du! Laß mich mal das Fernsehmagazin sehen!**

When giving permission, you may say:

> **Ja, natürlich! Bitte schön!**
>
> **Bitte! Hier!**
>
> **Gern! Hier ist es!**

Which one of these questions seems to be the most formal or polite?

---

17 Laß mal ...!

Frag deinen Partner, ob du die folgenden Sachen sehen oder haben darfst! Er erlaubt es dir.

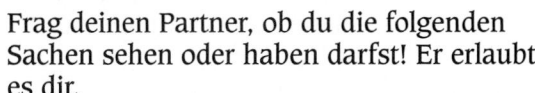

Fernbedienung   Zimmerantenne
Kopfhörer   Wetterbericht
Fernsehgerät   Fernsehmagazin
Sportsendung   Programmanzeige

Ein wenig Grammatik

One of the many meanings of the verb **lassen** is *to let,* in questions and statements asking for permission.

> **Laß mich bitte mal sehen!**
> **Läßt du mich bitte fernsehen?**

The verb **lassen** has a stem vowel change in the **du**- and **er/sie**-forms.

SO SAGT MAN DAS!

Asking for information and expressing an assumption

You already know one way of asking for information using *yes/no* questions:

Hat das Gerät eine Fernbedienung?

Here is another way of asking a *yes/no* question, using an **ob**-clause:

Wissen Sie, ob das Gerät eine LED-Programmanzeige hat?
Können Sie mir sagen, ob das Gerät einen Kopfhöreranschluß hat?

As a response, you may express an assumption by saying:

Ich glaube schon, daß (er eine LED-Programmanzeige hat).
Ich meine doch, daß (das Gerät einen Kopfhöreranschluß hat).

What position does the conjugated verb occupy in the **daß**-clause? And in the **ob**-clause? How would you ask a friend the above questions, using **ob**-clauses? What about two friends?

18 Du brauchst Information

Du brauchst einen neuen Fernseher*, aber bevor du ihn kaufst, hast du viele Fragen. Spielt die Rollen von Kunde und Verkäufer mit einem Klassenkameraden und frag, welche Ausstattung der Fernseher hat!

BEISPIEL   KUNDE   **Können Sie mir sagen, ob ...**

19 Weißt du, ob ...?

Die neue Fernsehsaison beginnt bald. Du möchtest etwas über deine Lieblingssendung wissen. Dein Partner hat ein Fernsehprogramm von zu Hause mitgebracht. Du möchtest folgendes wissen (verwende dabei ob-*clauses*):

a. wann die Sendung kommt
b. um welche Zeit sie kommt
c. wer wieder mitspielt

BEISPIEL   DU   **Weißt du, ob . . . noch am Samstag kommt?**

> **Ausstattung**
> **Farbfernsehgerät**
> **Stereogerät**
> **Kabeltuner**
> **LED-Programmanzeige**
> **Fernbedienung**
> **Kopfhöreranschluß**

20 Und du?

Eure Schule macht eine Umfrage über die Fernsehgewohnheiten (*viewing habits*) von Schülern! Beantworte die Fragen des Reporters der Schülerzeitung! Such dir einen Partner und spielt die Rollen von Reporter und Schüler! Mach dir Notizen!

1. Wieviel Zeit verbringst du vor dem Fernsehgerät?
2. Welches Programm siehst du am meisten?
3. Zu welcher Zeit siehst du fern?
4. Welches sind deine Lieblingssendungen? Warum?
5. Welche Sendungen siehst du dir nur ab und zu an? Warum?
6. Wofür interessierst du dich überhaupt nicht?
7. Schaust du dir die Werbespots an? Warum? Warum nicht?

*Fernseher is a popular way of referring to a **Fernsehgerät.**

21 Was steht im Fernsehprogramm?

Lies, was Andreas über das Fernsehprogramm sagt! Was bedeuten die Wörter **montags**, **dienstags**, usw.?

> Montags läuft immer eine Krimiserie. Die kommt abends im ARD. Dienstags kommt auf SAT 1 das „Glücksrad" ... und samstags kommt im ZDF immer „Das aktuelle Sport-Studio."

WORTSCHATZ

montags	freitags
dienstags	samstags
mittwochs	sonntags
donnerstags	

22 Was läuft so im Fernsehen?

Dein Partner, ein deutscher Austauschschüler, möchte wissen, wann in der Woche im Fernsehen etwas läuft, wofür er sich vielleicht interessiert. Sieh in deinem Fernsehmagazin nach und sag es ihm! Tauscht dann die Rollen aus!

BEISPIEL   PARTNER   **Was läuft denn samstags so im Fernsehen?**

DU   **Samstags läuft fast nie etwas Besonderes. Aber sonntags läuft immer ...**

Ein wenig *Grammatik*

The verb **laufen,** *to walk* or *run,* is also used to talk about what *is on* TV. How would you say the following sentence in English?

Läuft *60 Minutes* **noch am Sonntag?**

Laufen has a stem-vowel change in the **du** and **er/sie**-forms:

Läufst du schnell zum Zeitungsstand? Ich will sehen, was im Fernsehen läuft.

Wann?

montags
dienstags
mittwochs
donnerstags
freitags
samstags
sonntags

Wie oft?

immer   regelmäßig
fast immer   manchmal
meistens   kaum
häufig   fast nie
sehr oft   selten
oft   nie

Was?

etwas/nichts Besonderes
etwas ganz Tolles: ...
eine super Sendung: ...
ein ganz gutes Programm: ...
ein toller Film

23 Eine Reportage

Du mußt jetzt einen kurzen Bericht über die Fernsehgewohnheiten von deinem Partner, einem typischen Schüler, für deine Schülerzeitung schreiben. Schau auf deine Notizen von Übung 20, und schreib einen kurzen Bericht über ihn!

Expressing surprise, agreement, and disagreement; talking about plans

Autofahren kostet viel Geld!

Für einen neuen Wagen muß man heute so um die 20 000 Mark auf den Tisch legen, und der Preis kann noch höher sein, wenn man sich eine Menge Auto-Extras dazu kauft, wie zum Beispiel eine Servolenkung oder Breitreifen. Auch sind die monatlichen Unterhaltungskosten ziemlich hoch, was die Statistik nebenan beweist.

1. Wie viele Extras haben deutsche PKWs?
2. Wieviel muß der Autofahrer monatlich für sein Auto zahlen?

Beliebte Auto-Extras

Von je 100 Pkw haben als Sonderausstattung:

Radio 94

44	Metallic-Lack
35	Schiebedach
28	Servolenkung
26	Zentralverriegelung
26	Wärmedämmendes Glas
22	Breitreifen
21	Leichtmetallräder
12	Automatik
12	Anhängerkupplung
10	Elektrische Fensterheber
8	ABS

Quelle: DAT
© Globus 9133

Was Autofahren wirklich kostet

Monatsausgaben 1992 für einen VW Golf CL 1,8

Beispielrechnung für einen Neuwagen, der 20 000 km pro Jahr zurücklegt und 5 Jahre behalten wird

Kfz-Steuer 20
Nebenausgaben 25
Waschen, Pflege 33
Versicherung 50
Garage 70
Wartung, Reparaturen, Reifen 139
Öl, Benzin 191
Wertverlust 229 DM

insgesamt 757 DM

Quelle: ADAC
© Globus 9680

WORTSCHATZ

Jedes Auto hat ...

Scheinwerfer

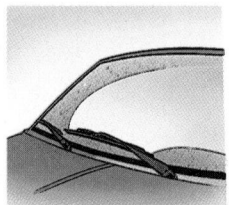

Scheibenwischer

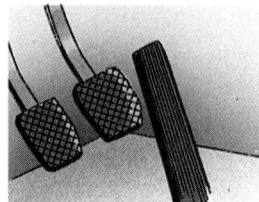

eine Fußbremse

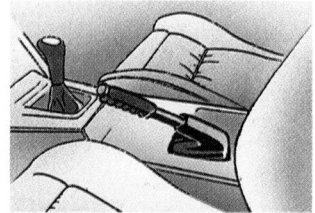

eine Handbremse

Es gibt auch Extras, zum Beispiel . . .

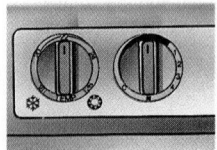

eine Klimaanlage

ein Schiebedach

Breitreifen

Und dann noch . . .

ein Stereo-Radio, einen Kassettenspieler
eine Automatik *automatic transmission*
eine Servolenkung *power steering*
Servobremsen *power brakes*
ein 5-Gang Getriebe *five-speed transmission*
eine Zentralverriegelung *automatic locks*
eine Alarmanlage *an alarm system*
Sitzschoner *seat covers*
Alufelgen *aluminum rims*
Rallyestreifen *rally stripes*
Aufkleber *(bumper) stickers*

24 Hör gut zu!

For answers, see listening script on TE Interleaf.

Zwei Leute beschreiben ihre Autos. Mach dir Notizen! Welche Extras haben beide Autos? Welche Extras hat ein Auto, die das andere nicht hat?

25 Und du?

Such dir eine Partnerin und tauscht Informationen zu den folgenden zwei Fragen aus!

1. Welche Ausstattung hat euer Auto zu Hause?
2. Was für ein Auto wünschst du dir einmal? Was für ein Auto muß es sein? Welche Extras muß es haben? Welche Extras brauchst du nicht?

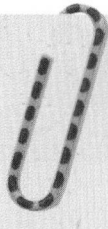

SO SAGT MAN DAS!

Expressing surprise, agreement, and disagreement

You already know many expressions to express surprise, such as:

Was? Wirklich?

Here are some others:

Das ist ja unglaublich!
Das ist nicht möglich!
Das gibt's doch nicht!

You also know many expressions for expressing agreement, such as:

Gut! Na klar! Gern! Ja, das stimmt!

Here are some others:

Da stimm' ich dir zu!
Da hast du (bestimmt) recht!
Einverstanden!

When expressing disagreement, you may say:

Das finde ich nicht.
Das stimmt (überhaupt) nicht!

26 Ja, das gibt's doch nicht!

Bring Werbung für Autos mit in die Klasse! Zeig deinem Partner, welches Auto du dir gern kaufen möchtest und warum! Dein Partner ist überrascht, daß dieses Auto nicht viele Extras hat. Du sagst ihm, daß du das nicht brauchst und nennst einen Grund dafür. Dein Partner stimmt dir zu oder auch nicht.

> Schon bekannt
> ### Ein wenig Grammatik
> Remember to use **kein**, *not, not any, no,* to negate a noun rather than an entire sentence.
>
> Es hat **keine** Klimaanlage.
> Ich brauche **kein** Schiebedach.

BEISPIEL   DU   **Ich möchte mir gern dieses Auto kaufen; es sieht toll aus und ist nicht so teuer.**

PARTNER   **Aber schau! Es hat keine (Klimaanlage). Das gibt's doch nicht!**

DU   **Ich brauch' keine. Es ist nicht so heiß bei uns.**

PARTNER   **Da hast du recht.** *oder* **Das finde ich nicht. Ich ...**

In Deutschland muß man 18 Jahre alt sein, um den Führerschein für einen PKW machen zu können. Jeder Bewerber muß erst einmal eine Fahrschule besuchen. Der theoretische Unterricht besteht aus mindestens zehn Doppelstunden zu je 90 Minuten. Für die Fahrpraxis sind heute 20 normale Fahrstunden vorgeschrieben und zehn Sonderfahrten — auf Landstraßen, auf der Autobahn, auch Fahrten bei Regen und in der Nacht. Um den Führerschein zu bekommen, braucht man also ziemlich viel Zeit — und auch viel Geld. Die Durchschnittskosten für einen PKW-Führerschein liegen heute bei DM 3 000,00. — Wie bekommt man einen Führerschein in den Vereinigten Staaten?

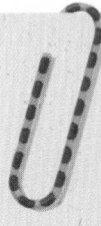

SO SAGT MAN DAS!

Talking about plans

You have been talking about plans in sentences that contain a word referring to future time, such as:

Morgen gehe ich schwimmen. or **Wir gehen am Samstag ins Kino.**

If you want to express your future plans in a very definite manner, you can say:

Ich werde mir einmal einen tollen Wagen kaufen.
In einem halben Jahr werde ich den Führerschein machen.

Name the verbs used in each of these two sentences. Which one is the conjugated verb? The infinitive? How would you say these sentences in English?

---

27 Hör gut zu! For answers, see listening script on TE Interleaf.

Zwei Schüler unterhalten sich übers Fernsehen und über Autos. Hör ihrem Gespräch gut zu, und schreib nur die Dinge auf, die jeder ganz bestimmt machen wird!

28 Was wirst du dir kaufen?

Du sagst einem Partner, was du dir ganz bestimmt kaufen wirst. Er ist überrascht, aber du gibst ihm einen guten Grund.

BEISPIEL

DU **Ich werde mir mal ein Auto mit einem Schiebedach kaufen.**

PARTNER **Wirklich? Was willst du denn mit einem Schiebedach?**

DU **Ein Schiebedach ist sehr praktisch — Luft und Sonne können ins Auto!**

PARTNER **Das finde ich nicht. Ich meine, daß ...**

Was?

ein Auto

mit einem Schiebedach
mit einer Klimaanlage
mit Zentralverriegelung
mit einer Alarmanlage
mit ...

einen Fernseher

mit einer Fernbedienung
mit einem Kabeltuner
mit einer LED-Anzeige
mit ...

Grammatik   The future tense with **werden**

1. Future time can be expressed by using the present tense with a word indicating future time, such as **morgen, nächste Woche**, etc.

   Morgen gehen wir schwimmen.

2. Another way to express future events is to use the verb **werden** as an auxiliary verb together with another verb in the infinitive.

   In einem halben Jahr **werde** ich den Führerschein **machen.**

3. The present tense forms of **werden** are:

ich	werde	wir	werden
du	wirst	ihr	werdet
er, sie, es, man	wird	sie, Sie	werden

4. In clauses beginning with **daß, ob, wenn, weil,** the conjugated form of **werden** is in last position, preceded by the infinitive.

   Ich weiß nicht, ob ich mir diesen Wagen kaufen **werde.**

29   Was wirst du tun?

Dein Partner macht eine Bemerkung, oder er fragt dich etwas. Du sagst ihm, was du tun wirst. Denk an so viele Antworten wie möglich!

PARTNER   **Du bist wirklich sehr müde.**

DU   **Das stimmt! Und ich werde gleich mal eine kleine Pause machen.**

30   Du und dein Partner

1. Frag deinen Partner, was er sich dieses Wochenende im Fernsehen ganz bestimmt ansehen wird! Er nennt dir mindestens drei Sendungen, und er sagt dir auch, warum er sich diese Programme ansehen wird.

2. Dein Partner fragt dich, was für ein Auto du dir einmal kaufen wirst. Du sagst es ihm, und du sagst ihm auch, was für eine Ausstattung und welche Extras es haben wird und warum.

3. Frag deine Partnerin, ob sie schon ihren Führerschein hat oder wann sie ihn machen wird! Frag sie auch, wie man sich auf den amerikanischen Führerschein vorbereiten muß! Würdest du lieber den deutschen Führerschein machen? Warum oder warum nicht?

31   Wie geht's meinem Brieffreund?

Schreib deinem Brieffreund über deine Freizeitinteressen, besonders übers Fernsehen! Schreib ihm etwas über deine Fernsehgewohnheiten und über deine Lieblingssendungen! Und wenn du dich für Autos interessierst, schreib ihm, was für ein Auto du dir einmal kaufen wirst!

ANWENDUNG

1 Umfrage halten! The German channel ZDF is planning a satellite feed into German classes across the United States, and they have hired you to do market research of TV viewing habits. In groups of three, choose one of the categories below and design a questionnaire with at least three questions relating to your topic. Poll the class, tally your results in the group and present them (in German) to the class.

- Fernsehkonsum (wie viele Stunden? an welchen Tagen? usw.)
- beliebte und unbeliebte Programme
- beliebte Werbesendungen
- Sportsendungen
- Musiksendungen
- Spielfilme
- Serien (*Sit-coms*)
- Spielshows

E.g.: **Welche Serien schaust du gerne?; Wie oft schaust du amerikanische Sit-coms?; Wann kommt deine Lieblingsserie? etc.**

2 Your partner will describe to you the dream car he or she will one day buy (using **werden**). As your partner describes it, draw a picture according to his or her description. When you're finished, find out if you understood everything by describing the drawing in front of you back to your partner. Then switch roles. Below are types of cars and features your dream car might have.

Aufkleber (bumper stickers) Schiebedach Rallyestreifen Kombiwagen (station wagon)

große Boxen (big loudspeakers) Sportwagen Truck

Breitreifen Kabriolett (convertible) Alufelgen (mag wheels)

3 Listen to the Bauer family discuss the evening lineup on TV. As you listen, look at the schedule on page 242 and fill in a grid like the one on the right. For each time slot write in the channel the family decides to watch.

For answers, see listening script on TE Interleaf.

18.00	
19.00	
20.00	
22.30	

4 Lies, was die Leute auf Seite 255 über die Vorteile und Nachteile vom Kabelfernsehen sagen! Danach beantworte die folgenden Fragen!

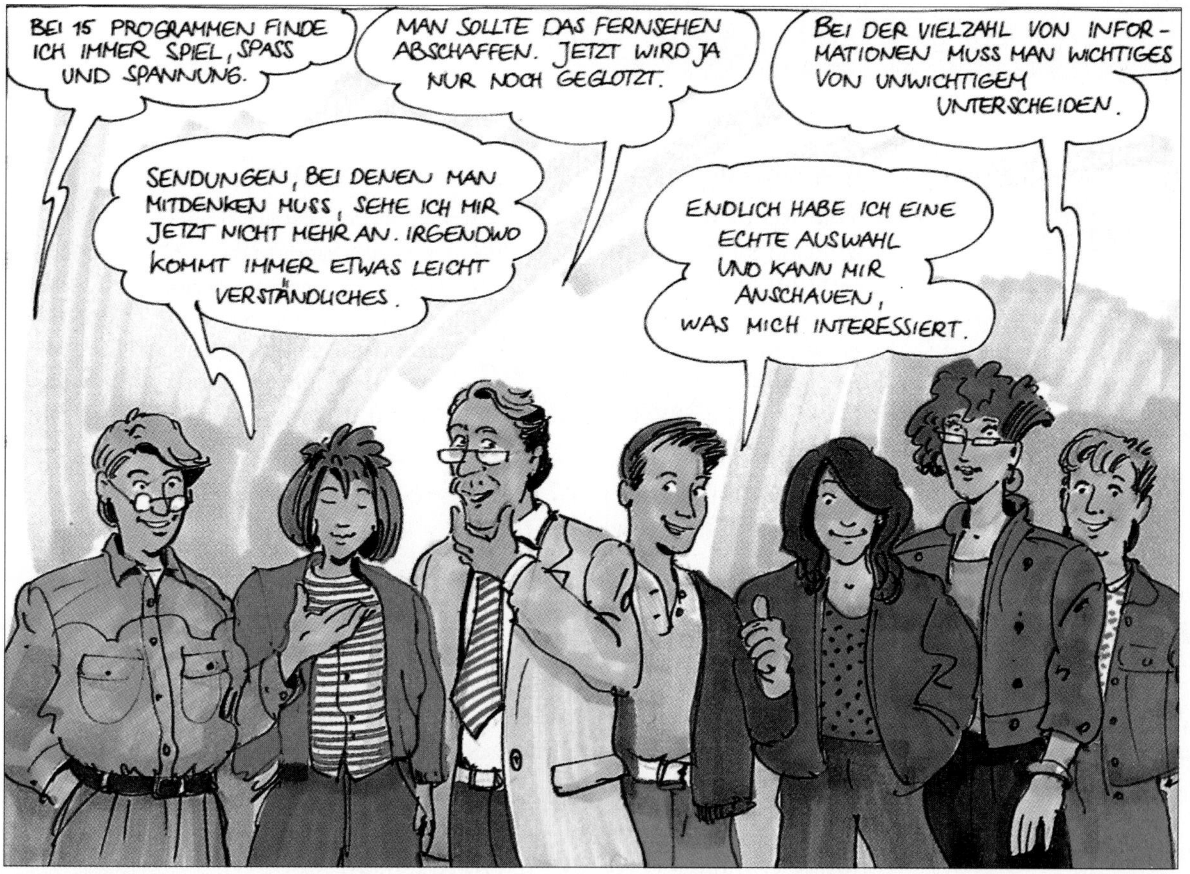

1. Lothar, Traude, Sepp; Rudolf, Udo; advantages: large selection (15 channels), variety of shows (difficult, easy, important, unimportant etc.), lots of information 2. Udo's statement 3. people just watch/stare without thinking

1. Which people mention an advantage of cable TV? Which mention a disadvantage? What are the specific advantages and disadvantages?

2. Which of the five statements can be interpreted either way?

3. If **glotzen** means *to stare blankly,* what is Rudolf trying to say?

4. Which two people express a generalization? *(Hint:* which German pronoun expresses the idea of *people in general?)* Which verbs are used in these generalizations? 4. Rudolf and Udo; **man; sollen, müssen**

5 Schreib in dein Notizbuch deine eigene Meinung zum Thema: Was sind die Vorteile und Nachteile vom Kabelfernsehen?

6 ROLLENSPIEL

In groups of three, pick any product and produce your own commercial for German TV. Try to sell your product to your German audience using the phrases you've learned in this chapter. Be sure to use props or glossy photos!

Can you ask about and express interests? (p. 240)

1 How would you ask a friend, using a **wo**-expression,

a. what his or her interests are?   a. Wofür interessierst du dich?
b. what he or she is talking about?   b. Worüber sprichst du?
c. what he or she is looking forward to?   c. Worauf freust du dich?

2 How would you ask your friend who he or she is interested in?
Für wen interessierst du dich?

3 How would you say, using a **da**-expression, that

a. that interests you?   a. Ich interessiere mich dafür.
b. you don't talk about that?   b. Ich spreche nicht darüber.
c. you are looking forward to that?   c. Ich freue mich darauf.

Can you ask for and give permission? (p. 247)

4 How would you politely ask someone if you may turn on the TV?
How might that person respond?   Darf (Kann) ich bitte das Fernsehgerät einschalten? — Ja natürlich! Bitte schön!

5 How might you be less polite when asking to have the headphones?
5. He, du! Laß mich mal den Kopfhörer haben!

Can you ask for information and express an assumption? (p. 248)

6 How would you ask   a. Weißt du, ob wir heute Deutsch haben? — Ich glaube schon, daß wir heute Deutsch haben.

a. a classmate if he or she knows whether you have German today, using an **ob**-clause? How would that person answer that he or she thinks you have class, using a **daß**-clause?

b. a salesman if a particular car has a lot of extras? How would he respond?   b. Wissen Sie, ob dieses Auto (dieser Wagen) viele Extras hat? — Ich meine doch, daß das Auto viele Extras hat.

Can you express surprise, agreement, and disagreement? (p. 251)

7 How would you respond if someone told you that

a. E.g.: Was? Wirklich! Das ist ja unglaublich!
a. he or she won $10,000,000 in a sweepstakes?
b. winning $10,000,000 is difficult?   b. E.g.: Da stimm' ich dir zu! Da hast du recht!
c. winning $10,000,000 is very easy?   c. E.g.: Das finde ich nicht. Das stimmt (überhaupt) nicht!

Can you talk about plans? (p. 252)

8 How would you say that

a. In einem Jahr werde ich den Führerschein machen.
a. you will get your driver's license in a year?
b. your sister will travel to Berlin soon?   b. Meine Schwester wird bald nach Berlin fahren.

9 How would you ask a friend if he will buy himself a color TV-set?
Wirst du dir mal ein Farbfernsehgerät kaufen?

ERSTE STUFE
TALKING ABOUT TELEVISION PROGRAMS

Sehen wir nachher fern? *Are we going to watch TV afterwards?*
fernsehen (sep) *to watch TV*
Fernseh gucken *to watch TV (colloquial)*
die Sendung, -en *show, program*

das Programm, -e *schedule of shows*
der Sender, - *station, transmitter, channel*
die Nachrichten (pl) *the news*
der Wetterbericht, -e *weather report*
die Sportübertragung, -en *sport telecast*

die Übertragung, -en *telecast, transmission*
die Natursendung, -en *nature program*
die Ratesendung, -en *quiz show*
eine Diskussion über Politik *political discussion*
die Diskussion, -en *discussion*
wo- and **da-**compounds *(see page 241)*

ZWEITE STUFE
TALKING ABOUT A TV SET

Habt ihr ein Farbfernsehgerät zu Hause? *Do you have a color television set at home?*
das Stereo-Farbfernsehgerät, -e *color stereo television set*
der Fernseher, - *television*
die Fernbedienung, -en *remote control*
der (Stereo-)Kopfhörer, - *(stereo) headphones*
die Zimmerantenne, -n *indoor antenna*
der Lautstärkeregler, - *volume control*
der Fernseh- und Videowagen, - *TV and video cart*
das Ablagefach, ¨er *storage shelf*

die Videocassette, -n *video cassette*

ASKING FOR AND GIVING PERMISSION

Darf ich (bitte) ...? *May I (please)...?*
Kann ich bitte ...? *Can I (please)...?*
Laß mich mal ... *Let me...*
Ja, natürlich! *Yes, of course!*
Bitte! Hier! *Here you go!*
Gern! Hier ist es! *Here! I insist!*
lassen *to let, allow*
  er/sie läßt *he/she lets, allows*

ASKING FOR INFORMATION

Weißt du, ob ...? *Do you know whether...?*

Können Sie mir sagen, ob ...? *Can you tell me whether...?*
Was läuft im Fernsehen? *What's on TV?*

EXPRESSING AN ASSUMPTION

Ich glaube schon, daß ... *I do believe that...*
Ich meine doch, daß ... *I really think that...*

EXPRESSING RECURRING TIME: DAYS OF THE WEEK

montags *Mondays*
dienstags *Tuesdays*
mittwochs *Wednesdays*
donnerstags *Thursdays*
freitags *Fridays*
samstags *Saturdays*
sonntags *Sundays*

DRITTE STUFE
TALKING ABOUT CARS

der Scheinwerfer, - *headlight*
der Scheibenwischer, - *windshield wiper*
die (Fuß-, Hand-)Bremse, -n *(foot, hand) brake*
die Klimaanlage, -n *air conditioning*
das Schiebedach, ¨er *sunroof*
der Breitreifen, - *wide tire*
der Führerschein, -e *driver's license*

EXPRESSING SURPRISE

Das ist ja unglaublich! *That's really unbelievable!*
(Das ist) nicht möglich! *(That's) impossible!*
Das gibt's doch nicht! *There's just no way!*

EXPRESSING AGREEMENT AND DISAGREEMENT

Da stimm' ich dir zu! *I agree with you on that!*
Da hast du (bestimmt) recht! *You're right about that!*

Einverstanden! *Agreed!*
Das finde ich nicht. *I don't think so.*
Das stimmt (überhaupt) nicht! *That's not right (at all)!*

TALKING ABOUT PLANS

Ich werde mir einen tollen Wagen kaufen. *I'm going to buy myself a great car.*
werden *will*
  du wirst *you will*
  er/sie/es wird *he/she will*

Kapitel 11: Mit Oma ins Restaurant

CHAPTER OVERVIEW

Los geht's! pp. 260-262	Pläne für Omas Geburstag, *p. 260*		*Video Guide*	
	FUNCTIONS	**GRAMMAR**	**CULTURE**	**RE-ENTRY**
Erste Stufe pp. 264-267	Asking for, making, and responding to suggestions, *p. 266*	The **würde**-forms, *p. 267*	• **Landeskunde: Für welche kulturellen Veranstaltungen interessierst du dich?** *p. 263* • **Ein wenig Landeskunde:** State-supported arts in Germany, *p. 267*	• Cultural activities and sights in a large city, *p. 265* (from **Kap. 9,** I) • The modal **können**, *p. 265* (from **Kap. 7,** I) • The impersonal pronoun **man**, *p. 265* (from **Kap. 7,** I) • Talking about interests, *p. 265* (from **Kap. 8/9,** II) • Making suggestions, *p. 266* (from **Kap. 7,** I)
Zweite Stufe pp. 268-271	Expressing hearsay, *p. 270*	Unpreceded adjectives, *p. 271*	**Ein wenig Landeskunde:** International cuisine, *p. 270*	• Restaurants and other eating opportunities, *pp. 268* and *270* (from **Kap. 6,** I) • Talking about favorites, *p. 270* (from **Kap. 10,** I) • The conjunction **daß**, *p. 270* (from **Kap. 9,** I) • The modal **sollen**, *p. 270* (from **Kap. 8,** I) • Giving reasons, *p. 270* (from **Kap. 8,** I) • The conjunctions, **weil** and **denn**, *p. 270* (from **Kap. 8,** I)
Dritte Stufe pp. 272-275	• Ordering in a restaurant, *p. 274* • Expressing good wishes, *p. 275*	The **hätte**-forms, *p. 274*	Menu from **Haus Dannenberg am See**, *p. 272*	• The interrogative **was für**, *p. 273* (from **Kap. 10,** I) • Saying what's available, *p. 273* (from **Kap. 9,** I) • Talking about favorites, *p. 273* (from **Kap. 4,** I) • Giving reasons, *p. 273* (from **Kap. 8,** I) • Ordering in a restaurant, *p. 274* (from **Kap. 6,** I) • Ways of addressing people, *p. 275* (from **Kap. 2,** I) • Asking for the bill, *p. 275* (from **Kap. 6,** I)

Zum Lesen pp. 276-277	Das Leben im fremden Land Reading Strategy: Reading for comprehension

Review pp. 278-281	•Anwendung, *p. 278* •Kann ich's wirklich? *p. 280* •Wortschatz, *p. 281*

Assessment Options	**Stufe Quizzes**
	 •*Chapter Resources*, Book 4
	   Erste Stufe, Quiz 11-1
	   Zweite Stufe, Quiz 11-2
	   Dritte Stufe, Quiz 11-3
	 •*Assessment Items, Audiocassette* 8 B
		Kapitel 11 Chapter Test
		 •*Chapter Resources*, Book 4
		 •*Assessment Guide*, Speaking Test
		 •*Assessment Items, Audiocassette* 8 B
		
		 Test Generator, Kapitel 11

Chapter Overview

Video Program **OR** *Expanded Video Program*, Videocassette 4	*Textbook Audiocassette* 6 A

RESOURCES Print	**RESOURCES** Audiovisual

Textbook Audiocassette 6 A

Practice and Activity Book
Chapter Resources, Book 4
- Additional Listening Activities 11-1, 11-2 ....*Additional Listening Activities, Audiocassette* 10 B
- Student Response Forms
- Realia 11-1
- Situation Card 11-1
- Teaching Transparency Master 11-1 ....*Teaching Transparency* 11-1
- Quiz 11-1 ....*Assessment Items, Audiocassette* 8 B

Video Guide ....*Video Program/Expanded Video Program*, Videocassette 4

Textbook Audiocassette 6 A

Practice and Activity Book
Chapter Resources, Book 4
- Communicative Activity 11-1
- Additional Listening Activities 11-3, 11-4 ....*Additional Listening Activities, Audiocassette* 10 B
- Student Response Forms
- Realia 11-2
- Situation Card 11-2
- Quiz 11-2 ....*Assessment Items, Audiocassette* 8 B

Textbook Audiocassette 6 A

Practice and Activity Book
Chapter Resources, Book 4
- Communicative Activity 11-2
- Additional Listening Activities 11-5, 11-6 ....*Additional Listening Activities, Audiocassette* 10 B
- Student Response Forms
- Realia 11-3
- Situation Card 11-3
- Teaching Transparency Master 11-2 ....*Teaching Transparency* 11-2
- Quiz 11-3 ....*Assessment Items, Audiocassette* 8 B

Video Guide..*Video Program/Expanded Video Program*, Videocassette 4

Alternative Assessment
- Performance Assessment, *Teacher's Edition*
  Erste Stufe, p. 257K
  Zweite Stufe, p. 257N
  Dritte Stufe, p. 257P
- Portfolio Assessment
  Written: **Anwendung**, Activity 2, *Pupil's Edition*, p. 278; *Assessment Guide*, p. 24
  Oral: **Anwendung**, Activity 4, *Pupil's Edition*, p. 279; *Assessment Guide*, p. 24
- **Notizbuch**, *Pupil's Edition*, p. 271; *Practice and Activity Book*, p. 155

Kapitel 11: Mit Oma ins Restaurant
Textbook Listening Activities Scripts

Erste Stufe
Activity 7, p. 266

SIMONE Ich gehe sehr gerne ins Theater. Zum Geburtstag habe ich von meinen Großeltern ein Abonnement für das Landestheater in unserer Stadt bekommen. Es gefällt mir sehr, ganz vorne in einer der ersten Reihen im Theater zu sitzen und die Schauspieler aus der Nähe zu sehen. Letzte Woche habe ich eine bayerische Bauernkomödie gesehen. Das Publikum hat Tränen gelacht. Also, ich finde die Atmosphäre in einem Theater tausendmal besser als zu Hause vor dem Fernseher zu sitzen.

ARNO Also, wenn ich mal am Wochenende was ganz Besonderes machen will, dann geh' ich in ein Musical. Vor ein paar Monaten habe ich „Das Phantom der Oper" gesehen. Einfach sagenhaft! Ich hab' mir sofort danach die CD gekauft! Leider werden bei uns in der Stadt keine Musicals aufgeführt. Da muß man schon bis nach Hamburg reinfahren. Das dauert so ungefähr zwei Stunden, bis man dort ist. Aber der weite Weg lohnt sich auf jeden Fall! Ich finde Musicals einfach toll!

JUTTA Ich liebe Opern! Wagner, Mozart, Verdi ... ich höre alles gern. Am liebsten mag ich es, wenn die Oper in italienisch gesungen wird. Die italienische Sprache ist so temperamentvoll und dramatisch! Aber an einer Oper gefällt mir nicht nur der Gesang, mich faszinieren auch die schönen Kostüme der Sänger. Leider sind Opernkarten so teuer, und deswegen gehe ich nur selten ins Opernhaus. Die meisten Opern hab' ich im Fernsehen gesehen.

Answers to Activity 7

Simone: Theaterstück „Andorra" von Max Frisch

Arno: Musical „Oklahoma" von Hammerstein

Jutta: Oper „Die Zauberflöte" von Mozart

Activity 10, p. 267

1. PAUL Was sollen wir denn heute unternehmen, Thomas? Hast du Lust, in den Stadtpark zu gehen und Frisbee zu spielen? Oder wir können auch einfach nur so in den Park gehen, uns auf die Wiese legen und faulenzen.

THOMAS Nee, das ist mir zu langweilig! Hast du keine andere Idee?

PAUL Ja, also gehen wir doch wieder zum Hafen runter und gucken, welche Schiffe dort liegen.

THOMAS Mensch, Paul! Das haben wir doch erst letzte Woche gemacht. Ich bin nicht dafür, daß wir schon wieder dorthin gehen.

2. KARSTEN He, Dominik! Sollen wir mal das neue argentinische Steakhaus an der Ecke ausprobieren? Hast du am Samstag Zeit? Danach können wir uns den neuen Action Thriller mit Mel Gibson im Cinemax ansehen. Also, was meinst du?

DOMINIK Ja, das wär' nicht schlecht!

3. ULRIKE Hi, Moni! Du, mein Opa hat mir zwei Karten für „Cats" geschenkt. Wie wär's? Willst du mitkommen?

MONI Ach, ich weiß nicht. Ich interessiere mich nicht so sehr für Musicals. Frag doch mal die Alexandra! Ich glaube, die mag so was. Ich bin dafür, daß wir lieber mal zusammen ins Theater gehen.

Answers to Activity 10

1. nicht einverstanden; 2. einverstanden;
3. nicht einverstanden

Zweite Stufe
Activity 16, p. 270

MARITA Du, Beate, wo wollen wir denn heute abend hin? Ich hätte Lust, essen zu gehen.

BEATE Ja, laß uns doch mal wieder zu dem Türken an der Kreuzberger Straße gehen. Weißt du noch, der hat diese tolle Joghurtsoße zu dem gebratenen Lammfleisch!

MARITA Ja, stimmt! Dort ist das Essen wirklich schön würzig, und viel Knoblauch ist überall drin! Aber könnten wir nicht mal was Neues ausprobieren? Wie wäre es zum Beispiel mit dem mexikanischen Restaurant, das vor kurzem auf der Bismarckstraße aufgemacht hat? Acapulco heißt das oder so!

BEATE Ach, Marita, ich weiß nicht. Mexikanisch hab' ich noch nie probiert. Das soll doch ziemlich scharf sein, oder?

MARITA Ja, ich glaub' schon. Aber vielleicht gibt es dort auch milde Gerichte. Was meinst du?

BEATE Ja, bestimmt. Aber heute möchte ich eigentlich lieber zum Türken. Ich habe dort noch nie den gegrillten Fisch gegessen.

MARITA Also gut, gehen wir halt dorthin. Bis jetzt hat es mir dort immer gut geschmeckt. Ich glaub', ich weiß auch schon, was ich nehme.

BEATE Was denn?

MARITA Ich probiere mal den gebratenen Reis mit den kleinen deftigen Fleischbällchen, die der Johannes hatte, als wir das letzte Mal dort waren.

BEATE Ja, prima! Komm, wir gehen los!

Answers to Activity 16

türkisch und mexikanisch;
Sie gehen türkisch essen, weil ...
   ... das Essen dort würzig ist.
   ... Beate noch nie den gegrillten Fisch
gegessen hat.
   ... es Marita bis jetzt immer gut dort
geschmeckt hat.

Activity 18, p. 271

OLIVER Na endlich sind wir in Berlin! Du, ich freue mich schon auf die Stadtrundfahrt. Oder sag mal, Kati, sollen wir zuerst etwas essen gehen?

KATI Also, weißt du, Oliver, eigentlich würde ich lieber zuerst die Stadtrundfahrt machen, um halt soviel wie möglich von Berlin zu sehen. Hunger hab' ich noch keinen.

OLIVER Also gut! Dann gehen wir erst heute abend essen. Die Manuela hat mir zwei Restaurants empfohlen, die sie ziemlich gut fand, als sie hier in Berlin war. Das eine heißt „Zum Anker". Dort gibt es hauptsächlich Fischgerichte. Es soll ganz toll eingerichtet sein. Sie hat gesagt, daß an der Eingangstür ein richtig schwerer Anker befestigt ist, und an der Decke sollen Fischernetze hängen. Also, eine richtige Seemannsatmosphäre.

KATI Hat Manuela auch etwas über die Preise und die Bedienung gesagt?

OLIVER Ja, also über die Preise weiß ich nichts. Ach ja, über die Bedienung hat sie auch etwas gesagt. Und zwar kommt der Chef persönlich an den Tisch, um das Tagesgericht zu empfehlen.

KATI Und welches Restaurant hat Manuela dir noch empfohlen?

OLIVER Ja, warte mal, das heißt „Schanghai", ein Chinese natürlich. Dort soll es die beste Pekingente geben, die Manuela jemals gegessen hat. Und die Preise sollen völlig okay sein.

KATI Und was ist mit der Bedienung?

OLIVER Ja, also die Bedienung soll nicht so gut sein. Manuela hat erzählt, daß alle Kellner unfreundlich sind.

KATI Ach, du meine Güte!—Du, der Tobias hat mir hier ein Restaurant empfohlen, das ausschließlich hausgemachte, ostdeutsche Spezialitäten serviert. Also zum Beispiel Thüringer Rostbratwurst oder Leipziger Allerlei. Ist übrigens mein Lieblingsgericht! Tobias hat gesagt, daß man dort ziemlich große Portionen für wenig Geld bekommt!

OLIVER Mhm. Nicht schlecht! Richtig gute Hausmannskost! Wie ist es mit der Atmosphäre? Hat Tobias auch etwas über die Einrichtung gesagt? Wie heißt das Restaurant überhaupt?

KATI Ja, also das Restaurant heißt „Ossi", ist rustikal eingerichtet mit alten Holztischen und Bänken. Ziemlich einfach, aber dafür urgemütlich!

OLIVER Du, Kati, ich glaub', da würd' ich gern mal hingehen. Das scheint genau das richtige für heute abend zu sein, wenn wir von der Besichtigungstour zurückkommen.

KATI Ja, das find' ich auch. Aber nun mal los, auf in die Stadt!

Answers to Activity 18

Zum Anker — Essen: Fischgerichte; Bedienung: Chef; Atmosphäre: Seemannsatmosphäre; Preise: (Oliver doesn't know anything about the prices.)
Schanghai — Essen: beste Pekingente; Bedienung: unfreundlich; Atmosphäre: (not mentioned); Preise: okay
Ossi — Essen: hausgemachte, ostdeutsche Spezialitäten, große Portionen; Bedienung: (not mentioned); Atmosphäre: rustikal, einfach, urgemütlich; Preise: nicht teuer

Dritte Stufe
Activity 24, p. 274

DAGMAR Mhm! Seebarschfilet! Hast du das hier schon mal gegessen, Lutz?

LUTZ Nein, ich bin kein Fischfan! Ich esse lieber Fleisch! Aber Manuela, du magst doch gerne Fisch, oder?

MANUELA Ja schon, aber ich war vorher noch nie im Haus Dannenberg. Also, ich weiß nicht, wie es hier schmeckt.

KELLNER Guten Tag! Haben Sie schon gewählt?

DAGMAR Ja, ich hätte gerne das gegrillte Seebarschfilet mit Salzkartoffeln und gemischtem Gemüse. Und bringen Sie mir bitte auch einen Salatteller dazu!

KELLNER Gern! Was möchten Sie trinken?

DAGMAR Ein Mineralwasser, bitte!

KELLNER Möchten Sie auch einen Nachtisch bestellen?

DAGMAR Ach ja, ich nehme zum Nachtisch die frischen Erdbeeren mit Sahne. Und du Lutz, nimmst du auch die Erdbeeren zum Nachtisch?

LUTZ Nein, ich nehme nur das Wiener Schnitzel, ohne Beilage bitte, und einen Apfelsaft dazu!

KELLNER Apfelsaft und Wiener Schnitzel ohne Beilage.—Und was darf ich Ihnen bringen?

MANUELA Ich bekomme die Seezunge nach Art des Hauses. Und bringen Sie mir doch bitte eine Scheibe Brot dazu!

KELLNER Ja, unsere Seezunge ist ausgezeichnet. Was hätten Sie gern zu trinken?

MANUELA Also, ich nehme eine Fruchtlimo, bitte!

KELLNER Zum Nachtisch kann ich Ihnen die Rote Grütze sehr empfehlen. Sie ist hausgemacht und wird mit feiner Vanillesoße serviert.

MANUELA Für mich keinen Nachtisch, bitte!

KELLNER Sehr wohl!—Die Getränke kommen sofort.

Answers to Activity 24

1. Lutz: Wiener Schnitzel
2. Dagmar: Seebarschfilet mit Salatteller; Manuela: Seezunge mit einer Scheibe Brot
3. Lutz und Manuela

Activity 27, p. 275

Gruppe 1

HERR GÖTZ Na, wo bleibt denn der Herr Neumann? Wissen Sie, ob er noch kommt, Frau Jäger? Schließlich haben wir ja vor allem ihm zu verdanken, daß wir heute den Abschluß unseres Projektes hier feiern! Da sollte er doch auf keinen Fall fehlen, finden Sie nicht?

FRAU JÄGER Ach, der Herr Neumann wird bestimmt in einer halben Stunde hier sein. Er kommt doch direkt vom Flughafen hierher.

HERR GÖTZ Wieso Flughafen? War er denn heute noch auf einer Geschäftsreise?

FRAU JÄGER Ja, natürlich! Heute morgen ist er doch nach Hamburg geflogen, um den neuen Vertrag zu unterschreiben. Wir können gleich am Montag mit der Planung anfangen!

HERR GÖTZ Ja, dann können wir ja schon mal auf das nächste Projekt anstoßen. Zum Wohl, Frau Jäger!

FRAU JÄGER Prost, Herr Götz!

Gruppe 2

ARNO Achtung! Alle mal aufpassen! Hier kommt die Torte mit den Kerzen drauf! Susi, zähl mal, ob es auch wirklich sechzehn sind!

SUSI Zwei, vier, sechs ... vierzehn, fünfzehn, sechzehn! Stimmt genau! Find' ich ja super von euch, daß ihr mir eine Torte bestellt habt. Also, wer will das erste Stück?

ANITA Mensch, Susi, das erste Stück ist doch für dich! Komm, gib mal das Messer her! Ich schneide die Stücke für die anderen ab.—Hier, Arno, probier mal! Volker und Andrea, gebt mir mal eure Teller rüber!

ARNO Mhm, echt lecker! Schokolade mit Erdbeeren und Vanillecreme!—Also, herzlichen Glückwunsch, Susi! Ach, da kommen ja auch schon die Getränke!

ANITA Ja, also dann ... auf dein Wohl, Susi!

ARNO Prost, Susi!

SUSI Danke! Prost alle zusammen!

Gruppe 3

ONKEL NORBERT Also, weil's so schön ist, wollen wir doch noch einmal einen Toast auf das neue Ehepaar aussprechen! Auf eine glückliche Zukunft, Kinder! Prost!

CLAUDIA Ach, Onkel Norbert. Nun hast du uns schon zum dritten Mal gratuliert! Komm, Stefan, sprich du doch mal einen Toast auf unsere Gäste aus! Vati hat doch auch schon seine Rede gehalten. Jetzt bist du dran!

STEFAN Äh, also, vielen Dank, daß Ihr heute alle ins Haus Dannenberg gekommen seid. Claudia und ich, äh, wir freuen uns, daß alle die Einladung zu unserer Hochzeitsfeier angenommen haben. Äh, und ganz besonders möchten wir uns bei Onkel Norbert und Tante Hiltrud bedanken, die die weite Reise aus Österreich gemacht haben, nur um heute mit uns zu feiern. Also, äh, auf das Wohl unserer Gäste!

ONKEL NORBERT Prost!

TANTE HILTRUD Danke! Zum Wohl!—Claudia und Stefan, ihr müßt uns recht bald in Salzburg besuchen kommen!

CLAUDIA Versprochen, Tante Hiltrud!

Answers to Activity 27

Gruppe 1: Abschluß eines Projektes; Geschäftsleute

Gruppe 2: Geburtstag; Freunde

Gruppe 3: Hochzeit; Familienmitglieder

*A*wendung
Activity 1, p. 278

OLIVER Also, ich bin dafür, daß wir zuerst einmal eine Stadtrundfahrt durch Berlin machen. Ich finde, daß man so die Stadt ziemlich gut kennenlernen kann. Und man sieht eine ganze Menge.

LARS Ja, da hast du recht. Nur leider hält so ein Bus nicht überall an. Ich möchte zum Beispiel unheimlich gerne die Nationalgalerie sehen — aber nicht nur von außen! Ich glaube, daß der Bus bei einer Stadtrundfahrt einfach nur an dem Gebäude vorbeifährt. Also, ich fahr' dann schon lieber selbst mit der U-Bahn zur Museumsinsel, wo die Nationalgalerie ist.

JUTTA Ich will unbedingt zum Ku'damm! Dort gibt es tolle Geschäfte, und ich möchte ein paar Souvenirs einkaufen.

SILKE Zum Ku'damm? Nee, da ist es mir zu voll! Hat denn keiner von euch Lust, Schloß Charlottenburg zu besichtigen? Ich möchte da auf jeden Fall hingehen!

OLIVER Also, es scheint, als ob jeder etwas anderes machen will. Ich habe einen Vorschlag. Jeder sieht sich das an, wofür er sich interessiert, und am Abend, wenn wir alle wieder zurück sind, gehen wir zusammen essen. Einverstanden?

LARS Ja! Das ist eine prima Idee! Also, treffen wir uns dann um halb sieben in dem kleinen Café neben dem Hotel!

JUTTA Gut! Ich bin auch dafür! Also, dann, bis um halb sieben!

SILKE Tschüs, und viel Spaß!

Answers for Activity 1

Oliver: Stadtrundfahrt; Lars: Nationalgalerie; Jutta: Ku'damm; Silke: Schloß Charlottenburg / Jeder macht, was er will. Am Abend gehen sie dann zusammen essen.

Kapitel 11: Mit Oma ins Restaurant
Projects and Games

PROJECT

In this activity students will do a report about a famous German-speaking person. Begin this project before you start Chapter 11, allowing students time for research and revision of their projects. This project is designed for students to do individually. The final project should consist of a written report and a brief oral presentation.

Materials Students may need encyclopedias and other reference materials.

Suggested Sequence

1. Students do research at a library on the person they choose.
2. Students compile and organize their notes and materials.
3. Students find one piece of realia to support their reports. For example, if the subject of the report is an author, the student might want to bring in a book that the author wrote. For a report on a composer, the student might bring a recording of one of the composer's works, or even try to play part of a piece.
4. Students prepare their written reports and oral presentations.
5. After the oral presentation, students turn in their final projects which can then be displayed in class or in the foreign language area.

Grading the Project

Suggested point distribution (total = 100 points)
Written report (content, correct
usage, appearance)　　　　60
Oral presentation (including realia) 40

GAME

Was wird beschrieben?

This game is a good way to review the vocabulary for cultural events.

Preparation Write the names of famous pieces of music, operas, and plays on index cards.

Procedure Have one student at a time come to the front of the room to draw from the stack of index cards. The student looks at the card and then describes the piece without giving away the title. The rest of the class may then ask yes/no questions to which the student responds with **ja** or **nein**. The student who guesses the name of the piece correctly wins a point. This game can also be played in teams, in which case the person who guesses correctly scores a point for his or her team.

PROJECTS AND GAMES

Kapitel 11: Mit Oma ins Restaurant
Lesson Plans, pages 258-281

*U*sing the Chapter Opener, *pp. 258-259*

Motivating Activity

In German, ask students if their family has a favorite restaurant that they like to go to when they eat out. How often do they eat there and what type of food is the restaurant known for?

Background Information

Although German cooking is often thought of as bland and heavy, contemporary German cuisine has a variety of tastes. Culinary diversity began to develop in the 1970s when Germany's standard of living improved enough to create a demand for more exotic foods and greater variety.

Thinking Critically

Analyzing What type of ethnic cooking would students expect to be popular in Germany today based on what they have learned about the German population? (Examples: Italian, Turkish, Greek, Asian)

① **Drawing Inferences** Ask students to describe the type of information they think would be contained in a magazine such as the *Berlin Programm* which the girl is reading. Who would be especially interested in this kind of magazine? Have students list the types of activities and events that might be listed in the *Berlin Programm.*

Building on Previous Skills

② Ask students what dishes the grandmother (**Oma**) could order in a typical **Berliner Lokal** based on what they learned about specialties of Berlin in the Location Opener on p. 231. (**Berliner Pfannkuchen, Eisbein, Buletten, Grüner Aal**)

Teaching Suggestion

② Ask students how their family typically celebrates a grandparent's or other older person's birthday.

✦ For Individual Needs

③ **Visual Learners** Ask students to take a closer look at the photograph and describe what the people are eating. Have them make a list of the foods they see.

Teaching Suggestions

③ Have students recall the most memorable dishes that they have ordered at a restaurant.

• For each picture, have students think of a question or statement that could have triggered the caption.
Example:
Foto 3 (Der Fisch soll hier ausgezeichnet sein.)
Warum gehen wir in dieses Lokal?

Focusing on Outcomes

To get students to focus on the chapter objectives, ask them what they would do in Berlin if they had the opportunity to visit the city. Then have students preview the learning outcomes listed on p. 259. **NOTE:** Each of these outcomes is modeled in the video and evaluated in **Kann ich's wirklich?** on p. 280.

Teaching Los geht's!
pp. 260-262

Resources for Los geht's!

- *Video Program* **OR**
  Expanded Video Program, Videocassette 4
- *Textbook Audiocassette* 6 A
- *Practice and Activity Book*

▶ **pages 260-261**

Video Synopsis

In this segment of the video, Astrid and Andreas are having trouble making plans for their grandmother's birthday. Andreas decides to ask **Oma** what she wants to do. The whole family ends up celebrating in a restaurant. The student outcomes listed on p. 259 are modeled in the video: asking for, making, and responding to suggestions, expressing hearsay, ordering in a restaurant, and expressing good wishes.

Motivating Activity

Ask students about the last birthday celebration they planned or helped to plan for a family member. Whose birthday was it, and what did they do to celebrate?

Teaching Suggestion

After students have read, watched, or listened to the **Foto-Roman**, ask them where the Schmidt family took **Oma** on her birthday. Where is the restaurant located? (on a lake) What is the name of the restaurant? (**Haus Dannenberg am See**) How can someone who does not have a car get to the restaurant? (busses number 13 and 14) Why did they choose that restaurant? (**Oma** wanted to sit on an outside terrace.)

Thinking Critically

Analyzing After students have watched the video, ask them to look at the fifth and seventh frames of the **Foto-Roman**. What can students say about the etiquette of ordering in a restaurant? How do Germans order in a restaurant?

Thinking Critically

Drawing Inferences Have students look at the eighth frame and ask them how Germans make a toast. What expression does this family use? (**Zum Wohl!**)

For Individual Needs

A Slower Pace Have students write down what each of the five people ordered, including the beverage and the main dish.

▶ **page 262**

For Individual Needs

1 Challenge Ask students to work in pairs and take notes as they answer the questions. Based on the notes and the storyline in the video, students should summarize the events in German. This can be done orally or in writing.

2 A Slower Pace For each of the eight statements, ask students to look back at the **Foto-Roman** on pp. 260-261 and point out the specific frame that each statement refers to.

4 Challenge After students have matched the phrases correctly, ask them to use these expressions in a story entitled **Die Überraschung**. Students can work on an outline in class and then complete the final draft as written homework.

Closure

Refer students back to the outcomes listed on p. 259. Ask them to write down German phrases or words from the **Foto-Roman** they think correspond to each of the functions.

▶ **page 263**

PRESENTATION: Landeskunde
Teacher Note

The **Landeskunde** interviews are recorded on audiocassette and videocassette.

Teaching Suggestion

Ask each student to name the last cultural event he or she attended. What was it? When and where did it take place?

 For Individual Needs

A1 Auditory Learners Before students look at the text on p. 263, play the audiocassette or have them watch the interviews on video. Ask students to make a list of all the cultural events that were mentioned. As students tell you the cultural events they identified, make a list on the board or on a transparency. After students have read the interviews, have them check to see how many of the cultural activities they were able to understand.

Music Connection

Herr and **Frau Heine** referred to the **Philharmonie** in their interview. Have students do some research to find out more about the famous Berlin Philharmonic Orchestra.

Background Information

Berlin has more than 50 museums and almost 100 public and private galleries. Several of these museums and galleries are located on the **Museumsinsel** in the center of Berlin. The **Pergamon Museum** is one of the most famous museums.

Thinking Critically

Comparing and Contrasting Ask students to identify a city in the United States which offers a similar concentration of major museums and galleries in a central area. (Example: The Mall in downtown Washington, D.C. has an impressive variety of museums, such as the Smithsonian Institution, the National Gallery of Art, the National Air and Space Museum, and the National Museum of American History.)

Teacher Note

Mention to your students that the **Landeskunde** will also be included in Quiz 11-1 given at the end of the **Erste Stufe**.

Teaching Erste Stufe,
pp. 264-267

▶ **page 264**

MOTIVATE

Teaching Suggestions

- Ask students to list the different cultural activities that are available in their area. Have them bring in concert or theater programs they might have kept after attending a cultural event.
- Ask students to recall the last play their school put on. What was the name of it, who wrote it, and which students played the leading roles?

TEACH

Background Information

Berlin offers a rich variety of entertainment, including theater, opera, operetta, orchestra, chamber music, jazz, and film. The city's architecture further enhances the elegant atmosphere in the staging of these performances. Orchestral and chamber music concerts, including performances of the world-renowned Berlin Philharmonic Orchestra, take place in Philharmonic Hall (**Die Philharmonie**) and at **Schloß Charlottenburg.** Operas and operettas are performed in three opera houses (**Deutsche Oper, Staatsoper, Komische Oper**) and theatrical productions are staged at theaters such as the **Renaissance-Theater, Volksbühne, Schiller Theater, Hansa Theater,** and the **Deutsches Theater,** to name a few.

Group Work

5 Ask students to work on this activity in groups of three. They should first look over the opera and theater program listings and then read the concert excerpt, **Berlin ist eine Reise wert.** Remind students that they are not expected to know every word but should make use of previously learned reading strategies such as scanning for information. One of the group members should record the responses to the questions. If you feel some vocabulary explanations are necessary, clarify them with synonyms and paraphrasing whenever possible. When groups have completed the activity, call on individual students to share their groups' answers with the class.

Thinking Critically

5 Drawing Inferences Can students identify the two operas that will be performed in Italian? (*Aida; Romeo und Julia*)

▶ *page 265*

PRESENTATION: Wortschatz

- To introduce the different types of musical and theatrical productions, play excerpts from these musical scores and have a copy of Max Frisch's play on hand.
- To explore the **Und dann noch ...** expressions, ask students about the last time they visited one of the events listed.

Building on Previous Skills

Ask students if they can recall another German city where sightseeing by boat is very popular among tourists. (Hamburg)

Geography Connection

Ask students to look at a map of Germany to find other cities in which boat tours are likely to be of interest to visitors. (Examples: Kiel, Lübeck, Bremerhaven, Wilhelmshaven)

Teacher Note

Restoration of the **Berliner Synagoge** pictured in the **Wortschatz** box began in the summer of 1991. It was first built in the 1860s, and then set on fire during **Kristallnacht** in November 1938.

◆ For Individual Needs

6 Challenge To expand the activity, ask students to choose four activities from the list that they would like to do while visiting Berlin. Have students also explain why they are interested in each sight or activity.

▶ *page 266*

For Additional Practice

8 Have students work with a partner to choose a few completed conversations to read aloud in class.

◆ For Individual Needs

A Slower Pace Play the role of Ulf and give students a chance to respond. Repeat several times, each time changing your questions in order to show students a range of possible stimuli. This will prepare students to develop the dialogue on their own.

9 Tell students that their itinerary also takes them to the cities of Hamburg and Stuttgart. Have them look over the Location Openers on pp. 78-81 for Hamburg and 154-157 for Stuttgart and continue making suggestions to the tour guide.

PRESENTATION: So sagt man das!

Use the three different ways of making suggestions with the **Wortschatz** on p. 265. Have students respond in any way they wish but using one of the functional expressions.

 ## Total Physical Response

Review the functions with this TPR activity. Have all students stand, then give commands using the functions from the **So sagt man das!** box. At the end of the activity, all students should be seated. Examples:

Setz dich, wenn du gern in einem italienischen Restaurant essen würdest!

Setz dich, wenn du dafür bist, daß wir alle nach Berlin fliegen!

▶ *page 267*

 ## For Individual Needs

10 **A Slower Pace** Inform students that they will hear the conversation twice. During the first listening, ask them to listen for the suggestions that students make and only take notes on that information. When the conversation is played a second time, students should listen for the friend's responses. Finally, ask students to identify the phrase or expression that showed whether or not the friend liked the suggestion.

PRESENTATION: Grammatik

• **Würde**, like **möchte**, is a subjunctive verb form. Using **würde**-forms is the most polite way to express what you would like to do. Show students the following sentences for contrast:
  Ich würde gern mal das Pergamon Museum besuchen.
  Ich möchte das Pergamon Museum besuchen.
  Ich will das Pergamon Museum besuchen.
• Ask third person questions to give students practice using **würde**.
  Example:
  Wohin würde deine Familie gern mal reisen?

 ## For Individual Needs

11 **Challenge** Ask students to combine their sentences into a cohesive paragraph in which they describe their friend's interests in Berlin. This can be done orally or in writing.

PRESENTATION: Ein wenig Landeskunde

Students may be interested to know that German classes often attend a performance of a literary or musical piece after having studied it in school. **Schülerkarten** are at greatly reduced prices.

Reteaching: Vocabulary

Ask students to look back at the opera and theater programs at the top of p. 264. Tell students that they will be in charge of evening entertainment for their family on a visit to Berlin. For each of the four nights, they should choose a program. Students should then share the suggestions with the rest of the class.

CLOSE

 ### Game

Play the game **Was wird beschrieben?** See p. 257F for the procedure.

Focusing on Outcomes

Refer students back to the learning outcomes listed on p. 259. They should recognize that they now know how to ask for, make, and respond to suggestions.

ASSESS

• **Performance Assessment** Ask students to complete the following statement: **Am Wochenende würde ich gern ... , denn ...** The day before you plan to do this activity, ask students to bring the entertainment page from the weekend newspaper. Then ask students to tell the rest of the class what they would like to do, based on what is being offered for that weekend.

• Quiz 11-1, *Chapter Resources,* Book 4

*T*eaching Zweite Stufe,
pp. 268-271

▶ *page 268*

MOTIVATE

Teaching Suggestion

Ask students about their interest in ethnic foods. What type of foods do they like to eat? Where do they go to eat ethnic foods?

Thinking Critically

Drawing Inferences Ask students how they would find out about the different ethnic restaurants located in their area.

TEACH

Background Information

Berlin has more than 7,000 cafés, restaurants, and bars, thus offering the greatest variety in culinary tastes of all the German cities.

Teaching Suggestion

13 Since the advertisements include many unfamiliar words and abbreviations, you may want to have students use the questions as an advance organizer to help them focus only on the information in each restaurant description.

▶ *page 269*

PRESENTATION: Wortschatz

- As you introduce and practice the new vocabulary, have students concentrate on correct pronunciation of the names of various dishes.
- Ask students to recall from previous chapters one additional dish for each category (**chinesisch, ägyptisch, mediterran, gutbürgerlich**).

Teaching Suggestion

14 On the day you plan to do this activity, you could bring to class several cookbooks on ethnic cooking from your school or local library. This will help students explore the foods of the various countries listed.

▶ *page 270*

◆ For Individual Needs

16 Visual Learners For this activity, you could provide students with a copy of restaurant listings featuring ethnic cooking from your local newspaper. Students can use the listings to describe their culinary tastes and reasons for them. Take a survey of the most popular of the listed restaurants at the conclusion of the activity.

PRESENTATION: Wortschatz

To introduce these descriptive adjectives you could have a sample tasting of different foods with the characteristics described. Write each adjective on an index card and label each food with the appropriate adjective. You could also review and add other adjectives such as **süß, sauer, salzig, bitter**, and **saftig**.

Friedrich
Altberliner Restaurant
Neue deutsche & vegetarische Küche
Büffet & Veranstaltungsservice
auch außer Haus
Täglich 16-1 Uhr·Küche 16-24 Uhr
Tel.: 421 65 27
Sophie-Charlotten-Str. 80
1000 Berlin 19

ZWEITE STUFE

PRESENTATION: So sagt man das!

- Ask students to look back at the the sixth frame of the **Foto-Roman** on p. 261. Have them scan the dialogue to find the statement that is used to express hearsay.
- To practice the new expressions, ask students to tell what they have heard about a movie that just came out or the latest CD from a popular singer or group.
- Make up some rumors or hearsay about people and events in your school and present it to the class. Have students react to what you tell them and either agree that they too heard it or disagree, telling you what they know.

Thinking Critically

Analyzing Ask students to account for the high number of Italian, Greek, and Turkish restaurants that can be found in Berlin and all across Germany. (When **Gastarbeiter** arrived in Germany in the 1960s, they brought with them their own national dishes. Gradually, these ethnic restaurants became popular with the Germans as well.)

▶ *page 271*

For Additional Practice

19 To provide students with further practice with the new functions and vocabulary, students could also make suggestions as to what cultural events a German visitor might enjoy attending in their area.

PRESENTATION: Grammatik

The students have already learned to use adjectives following **der-** and **ein**-words. Tell them that unpreceded adjectives have to assume the role of an article: their endings must signal the gender, number, and case of the noun that follows.

Thinking Critically

Analyzing Have students deduce the gender of each of the nouns in the grammar box from the descriptive adjective.

Background Information

20 German-American Day, usually celebrated on October 6, was first officially proclaimed and signed into law on October 2, 1987 by President Ronald Reagan. The day honors all Americans of German descent and their contributions to life and culture in the United States.

Social Studies Connection

Ask students to identify cities, streets, schools, and public institutions named after German Americans.

History Connection

Ask students to research the history of German immigrants to their state.

Building on Previous Skills

Ask students when the first German immigrants came to the United States and where they settled. (See *Komm mit!* Level 1, **Vorschau**, p. 10 and the following Culture Note.)

Culture Note

The first German immigrants arrived at Penn's Landing in Philadelphia in 1683. They had been invited to the New World by the Quaker William Penn. Their first settlement was Germantown, Pennsylvania, northwest of Philadelphia.

好年華酒樓

CHINA RESTAURANT

»HO LIN WAH«

Chinesische Spezialitäten und
»DIM SAM«-Köstlichkeiten.
Auch außer Haus Verkauf.
Täglich von 12 bis . . . Uhr geöffnet.

Kurfürstendamm . . .
(in der Passage)

SURYA

INDISCHES RESTAURANT

Genießen Sie in indischer
Atmosphäre unsere Spezialitäten,
Huhn, Lamm, vegetarische
Speisen zu kleinen Preisen.

Grolmanstr. 22 · 10623 Berlin-Charlottenbg.
(am Savignyplatz) ☎ 312 91 23
täglich geöffnet 12.00 - 1.00 Uhr

Reteaching: Vocabulary and Unpreceded Adjectives

Provide students with a selection of pictures cut out of magazines or drawings of food items. Ask them to each choose one picture and then come up with a phrase that could be used to advertise the characteristics of the food item they have chosen.

CLOSE

For Individual Needs

Kinesthetic Learners To review the adjectives from p. 270 (**scharf, würzig,** etc.), prepare the following activity. Bring sample foods that have the characteristics of each of the adjectives. Ask a volunteer to come up to the board, blindfold the volunteer, then ask him or her to sample various foods and comment on how they taste, using the new adjectives.

Focusing on Outcomes

Refer students back to the learning outcomes listed on p. 259. They should recognize that they now know how to express hearsay.

ASSESS

- **Performance Assessment** Have the following incomplete statement written on the board or on a transparency when students come into class. **Ich habe neulich gehört, daß ... und deshalb will ich mal ...**
  After students have had a few minutes to look at the statement, call on individual students to find out how they completed it.

- Quiz 11-2, *Chapter Resources*, Book 4

Teaching Dritte Stufe, *pp. 272-275*

Resources for Dritte Stufe

Practice and Activity Book
Chapter Resources, Book 4
- Communicative Activity 11-2
- Additional Listening Activities 11-5, 11-6
- Student Response Forms
- Realia 11-3
- Situation Card 11-3
- Teaching Transparency Master 11-2
- Quiz 11-3
Audiocassette Program
- *Textbook Audiocassette* 6 A
- *Additional Listening Activities, Audiocassette* 10 B
- *Assessment Items, Audiocassette* 8 B

▶ **page 272**

MOTIVATE

For Individual Needs

Visual Learners To prepare for this activity, gather photos of various food items (appetizers, main dishes, side dishes, and desserts) from magazines. Select dishes that students will be able to talk about in German. Stack the pictures in categories on a table in the front of the class. Ask students to work in pairs or groups of three. Let each group come up to the front and choose a picture from each stack. They should take these back to their desks and use them to organize an original menu. When groups are finished ask them what they will be serving, using the following vocabulary: **Vorspeise, Hauptgericht, Beilage, Nachtisch, Getränke.**

 DRITTE STUFE

TEACH

Teaching Suggestions

- Have students look at the **Speisekarte** from **Haus Dannenberg am See** while you replay the video segment of the **Foto-Roman**. Have students listen for and identify the dishes the family ordered. Then have students make out the bill (**die Rechnung**), listing all the items and prices based on what the family ordered.
- Help students with the pronunciation of the various dishes, especially the names of the main dishes.

▶ *page 273*

 For Individual Needs

22 Challenge After students have completed this activity, ask them to look at the **Speisekarte** again, this time choosing what they would like to eat. Students should be prepared to share their choices with the rest of the class. Remind students to use sequencing words as they describe their elaborate meal.

PRESENTATION: Wortschatz

To practice the vocabulary, ask students to name their favorite item for each of the categories listed. Which ones are their least favorite?

Teaching Suggestion

You might want to refer students back to the recipe for **gefüllte Eier** on p. 311 of *Komm mit!* Level 1.

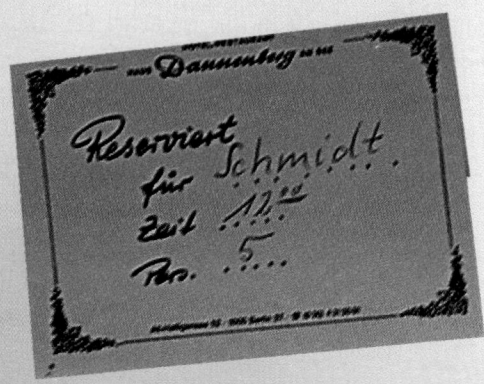

 Culture Note

Bratkartoffeln are similar to hash browns, except that they are sliced instead of grated. They are usually served at lunchtime or in the evening.

▶ *page 274*

PRESENTATION: So sagt man das!

After you have introduced the new expressions, replay frames five through seven of the **Foto-Roman** with the sound turned off. Ask several students to take on the roles of the people in the story and to ad-lib the conversation, incorporating the new functions. Students should not try to remember what each person actually ordered; they should make up the storyline as they go along.

Teaching Suggestion

Have students think of all the things a waiter or waitress might say in the following situations. Get several expressions for each function.
- to greet people
- to offer the menu
- to ask for the drink order
- to ask for the main order
- to make suggestions
- to serve the food
- to ask if people want dessert
- to bring the bill
- to end the service

Teaching Suggestion

25 Have each group prepare a skit based on the situation. Encourage students to use realia and props as much as possible.

PRESENTATION: Grammatik

Explain to students that the addition of an **Umlaut** to the vowel of a past-tense verb signals the subjunctive. Remind them also of the forms of **würde** presented in the **Erste Stufe**. The students should recall that **würde** was used to express what one would like to do.

▶ *page 275*

❖ For Individual Needs

26 Visual Learners Ask each group to design a **Speisekarte** for the restaurant, including a name for the establishment and prices for each item. Students should use the **Speisekarte** in their skits.

PRESENTATION: So sagt man das!

Have students practice toasting each other. Have plastic cups available and juice or water. Students walk around the classroom with their cup in hand, toasting the health of another student.

Thinking Critically

Comparing and Contrasting Ask students how Americans express good wishes at the table. How is the ritual of toasting used? Do Americans wish **Guten Appetit!** before a meal? Ask students about their customs at home.

Teaching Suggestion

29 You might want to pick up a menu from a favorite German restaurant in your area. Copy it for students and have them use it to practice the functions in this activity or use the menu students made for Activity 26.

Reteaching: The *hätte*-forms

Ask students to tell you one thing that they, their best friend, a parent, and a sibling would like to have for their next birthday.

CLOSE

Teaching Suggestion

To review the vocabulary and expressions presented in the **Dritte Stufe**, design a crossword puzzle that contains enough spaces for the words needed to complete the expressions listed below.
Rote Grütze ist ein ... (Nachtisch)
Nenne ein warmes Getränk. (Tee)
Seezunge ist ein ... (Fischgericht)
Antwort auf: Guten Appetit! (Danke!)
Nenne eine typische deutsche Beilage. (Kloß)

Focusing on Outcomes

Refer students back to the outcomes listed on p. 259. They should recognize that they now know how to order in a restaurant and to express good wishes.

ASSESS

- **Performance Assessment** Ask students to imagine calling the hotel restaurant for room service late at night. How and what would they order?

- Quiz 11-3, *Chapter Resources*, Book 4

𝒯eaching Zum Lesen, *pp. 276-277*

Reading Strategy

The targeted strategy in this reading is reading for comprehension. Students should learn about this strategy before beginning Question 3.

PREREADING

Motivating Activity

Ask students if they know of any people from other countries—in their school, in their neighborhood, and maybe even in their family. Where are these people from and what languages do they speak? How do others react to their accents? How are they treated in general?

Building on Previous Skills

Ask students to recall the word **Gastarbeiter** from Level 1. Ask someone to explain what it means.

ZUM LESEN

Teacher Note

Activities 1 and 2 are prereading activities.

READING

Thinking Critically

3 Drawing Inferences After completing this activity, ask students to name the role of each person in the conversation. (taxi driver; passenger)

Teaching Suggestion

You might want to go over the following vocabulary to help students understand the story.

der Kollege *co-worker*
der Kanacke *derogatory slang word referring to a Turkish person*
etwas gestehen *to admit something*
ausprobieren *to try out*
danebengehen *to go amiss*

 Cooperative Learning

Once students feel comfortable with the text, assign small groups of students to complete Activities 5 through 7 within a set amount of time. Each group member should have a specific task (reader, recorder, or reporter). Call on two or three groups to share their answers and ideas with the class.

Thinking Critically

Comparing and Contrasting Emigration occurs for various reasons. In the case of the **Gastarbeiter** in Germany, the ethnic groups left their homes to fill a labor shortage in postwar Germany. Today many people go to Germany to escape persecution or economic hardship in their home countries. Based on what students learn through the news media, what are some of the reasons people want to immigrate to the United States?

POST-READING

Teacher Note

Activity 8 is a post-reading task that will show whether students can apply what they have learned.

 For Individual Needs

8 Auditory Learners You might ask students to record their summary on a tape recorder. Remind students to use connecting words as appropriate.

Closure

Ask students to share their impressions about some of the misconceptions Turkish and German people seem to have about each other.

Answers to Activity 1

a German and a Turk; **Seltsam** and **komisch** both mean *strange, odd, peculiar,* or *weird;* Dashes indicate a change of speaker.

Answers to Activity 2

Answers will vary.

Answers to Activity 3

It is a conversation between a German and a Turk; in a taxi; most likely assumption: Turk—passenger, German—taxi driver

Answers to Activity 4

e.g.: car, work, colleagues at work, weather, relationship between Germans and Turks in Germany

Answers to Activity 5

The taxi driver answers the passenger in Turkish; The passenger is a German pretending to be a Turk so that he can find out how a German taxi driver would treat a Turkish passenger.

Answers to Activity 6

It fails because the taxi driver is not a German but a Turk; The passenger is confused and embarrassed; He is surprised that the Turkish taxi driver speaks excellent German.

Answers to Activity 7

One should not be too quick to judge people by their appearances, for appearances are often deceiving; After the German passenger gets out of the taxi, another German gets in. When the Turkish driver makes a comment about the "strange Turk" he has just had as a passenger, the German (not realizing the driver is a Turk) uses the derogatory term **Kanacken** to refer to the Turks. The author does not need to state explicitly that prejudice is bad.

*U*sing Anwendung,
pp. 278-279

▶ Video Wrap-up

At this time, you might want to use the *Video Program* or the *Expanded Video Program*, Videocassette 4 for additional review and enrichment. See *Video Guide* for suggestions regarding:
• **Pläne für Omas Geburtstag**
   (Dramatic episode)
• **Landeskunde**
   Interviews
• **Videoclips**
   (Authentic footage—*Expanded Video Program* only)

Teaching Suggestion

1 As an advance organizer for the listening activity, ask students to list at least eight points of interest in Berlin.

Math Connection

2 After students have decided on the sights they plan to see in Berlin, ask them to figure out how much it would cost to do everything they have planned. Once students have come up with a figure, have them give an approximate equivalent in U.S. dollars based on the latest available exchange rate.

▶ Portfolio Assessment

2 You might want to suggest this activity as a written portfolio item for your students. See *Assessment Guide,* p. 24.

4 You might want to suggest this activity as an oral portfolio item for your students. See *Assessment Guide,* p. 24.

Teaching Suggestion

5 Before starting this activity, review the expressions for reporting hearsay.

*K*ann ich's wirklich?
p. 280

This page helps students prepare for the test. It is a brief checklist of the major points covered in the chapter. The students should be reminded that it is only a checklist and not necessarily everything that will appear on the test.

*U*sing Wortschatz,
p. 281

Teaching Suggestion

To practice the vocabulary of cultural events, ask students to categorize the titles of plays or music scores that you call out. Example:
— **Was ist** *Carmen?*
— *Carmen* **ist eine Oper.**

◆ For Individual Needs

• **Visual Learners** To practice the international adjectives (**chinesisch, französisch, russisch,** etc.), bring several flags or a large poster featuring the flags of the world to class (ask a teacher in the Social Studies or Geography department for such realia). Point to or hold up a flag and ask students: **Welche Flagge ist diese hier?** and students respond with: **Das ist die russische Flagge.**

• **Challenge** To practice the food vocabulary, ask students to write riddles for one or two of the vocabulary words related to food. Each student reads his or her riddle, and the rest of the class tries to guess the word.

Teacher Note

Give the **Kapitel 11** Chapter Test, *Chapter Resources,* Book 4.

KAPITEL 11

Mit Oma ins Restaurant

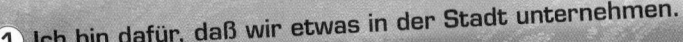

1 Ich bin dafür, daß wir etwas in der Stadt unternehmen.

Going to a play, a concert, or an opera, or even going to a nice restaurant is something special. That is especially true if it marks an occasion to celebrate — an anniversary, a birthday, or another family event. If you had to make plans in Germany for a special occasion, you would need to know several new expressions in German.

In this chapter you will learn

- to ask for, make, and respond to suggestions
- to express hearsay
- to order in a restaurant; to express good wishes

And you will

- listen to students talk about their plans to attend cultural events and to go out for dinner
- read excerpts from city guides and restaurant menus
- write about your cultural and culinary tastes
- find out what cultural events are offered in cities and what kinds of specialties Germans like to eat

② Ich würde gern mal in ein typisches Berliner Lokal gehen.

③ Der Fisch soll hier ausgezeichnet sein.

Los geht's!

Pläne für Omas Geburtstag

Andreas

Astrid

Oma

Bedienung

Vater

Mutter

Look at the photos on these two pages. Who do you think these people are and what do you think they are doing?

ASTRID Hier ist etwas, was Oma vielleicht gefallen würde, ein Sommerkonzert in der Philharmonie.

ANDREAS Ja, Musik mag sie gerne. Vati möchte ja am liebsten nach Schwerin fahren, um dort essen zu gehen.

ASTRID Wirklich? Bei diesem Verkehr? Ich bin dafür, daß wir hier etwas unternehmen.

ANDREAS Ich schlage vor, daß ich die Oma mal fragen werde, was sie am liebsten machen möchte.

ASTRID Das ist doch keine Überraschung mehr!

ANDREAS Das weiß ich.

ASTRID Na gut! Wie du meinst.

ANDREAS Hallo, Omi! Ich hab' dir ein paar Blumen mitgebracht, aus unserm Garten.

OMA Hallo, Andreas! Schön, daß du mich besuchst.

ANDREAS Du hast doch Geburtstag, Omi. Astrid und ich, wir möchten wissen, was du am liebsten machen möchtest. Da läuft so viel.

OMA Ach, ich liebe so viele Dinge.

ANDREAS Eben! Nun, Omi, sag schon! Möchtest du vielleicht ein Konzert besuchen, oder möchtest du in eine Oper oder Operette gehen?

OMA Ich möchte gern ins Theater gehen, aber nicht im Sommer, sondern später, wenn es kühler ist.

ANDREAS Möchtest du vielleicht in ein griechisches oder italienisches Restaurant? Oder wie wär's mit einem typischen Berliner Lokal?

OMA Ich würde am liebsten in ein Lokal gehen, wo wir draußen sitzen können.

ANDREAS Prima, Oma! Aber, sag nichts dem Vati, daß ich dich gefragt habe! Tschüs!

OMA Auf Wiedersehen, Andreas! Und noch mal vielen Dank für die Blumen!

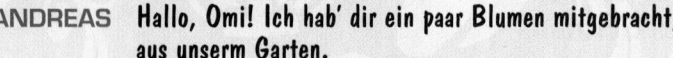

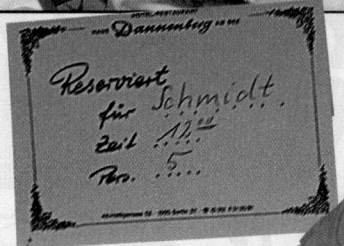

Ja, hier ist Schmidt. Ich möchte einen Tisch bestellen, beziehungsweise reservieren, für Samstag, für 12 Uhr 30, und wir sind fünf Personen ... Ja, der Name ist Schmidt, mit d-t. Danke! Tschüs!

BEDIENUNG	So, bitte schön, die Karte! Möchten Sie zuerst etwas trinken?
MUTTER	Ich hätte gern einen Weißwein, aber trocken.
OMA	Ich auch.
ASTRID	Ein Mineralwasser, bitte!
ANDREAS	Und ich hätte gern einen Apfelsaft.
VATER	Für mich ein Bier, ein alkoholfreies, bitte!

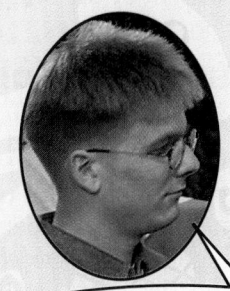

Der Fisch hier soll sehr gut sein, hab' ich gehört. Worauf hättest du denn Appetit, Mutter?

Ich nehme mal die Seezunge.

Ich würde gern das Wiener Schnitzel essen, aber ich weiß nicht, ob ich Salzkartoffeln oder Pommes frites dazu bestellen soll.

Ich würde die Salzkartoffeln nehmen.

Ja, du!

BEDIENUNG	Haben Sie schon gewählt?
VATER	Ja, ich denke, wir sind so weit.
MUTTER	Ja, ich hätte gern ein Schweinerückensteak, mit Käse überbacken.
OMA	Ich nehme die Seezunge mit Salzkartoffeln und Salat.
VATER	Bringen Sie mir bitte das Seebarschfilet mit Salzkartoffeln und einem kleinen Salat!
ASTRID	Ich hätte gerne … Königsberger Klopse und einen kleinen gemischten Salat.
ANDREAS	Und ich hätte gern das Wiener Schnitzel, aber mit Pommes, bitte!

VATER	Also, jetzt trinken wir erst einmal auf dein Wohl, Mutter. Alles Gute!
MUTTER	Zum Wohl! Und bleib uns recht lange gesund!
OMA	Zum Wohle, meine Lieben!
ASTRID	Prost, Oma! Alles Gute!
ANDREAS	Alles Gute, Oma! Prost!

1 Was passiert hier?

1. grandmother 2. go to a restaurant in Schwerin; concert 3. to find out what she wants to do for her birthday 4. go to a restaurant where one can sit outside

Verstehst du alles, was diese Leute sagen? Beantworte die Fragen!

1. For whom are Astrid and Andreas making plans?
2. What does their father want to do? What does Astrid suggest?
3. Why does Andreas go to Oma's?
4. What does Oma like to do on her birthday?
5. Why is Oma not to say anything about Andreas' visit?
6. What does Andreas do after he gets home from Oma's?
7. What does the family order first in the restaurant?
8. What has the father heard about this place?
9. What does Andreas have trouble deciding about?
10. What kinds of side dishes do they order?
11. What happens at the end of the story?

5. it is supposed to be a surprise for her
6. reserve a table in a restaurant
7. beverages
8. fish is supposed to be good
9. whether to order potatoes or French fries 10. potatoes, salad, French fries 11. they drink to grandmother's health

2 Stimmt oder stimmt nicht?

Wenn der Satz nicht stimmt, schreib die richtige Antwort!

1. Der Vater würde am liebsten zu Omas Geburtstag nach Schwerin fahren. 1. Stimmt.
2. Astrid möchte lieber etwas in Berlin unternehmen. 2. Stimmt.
3. Die Oma würde gern mal in eine Oper gehen. 3. Stimmt nicht. Sie würde gern mal ins Theater gehen.
4. Sie würde aber auch gern in ein griechisches Lokal gehen. 4. Stimmt nicht. Sie möchte in ein typisches Berliner Lokal.
5. Andreas bestellt einen Tisch für vier Personen.
6. Andreas' Vater trinkt im Restaurant ein alkoholfreies Bier.
7. Als Hauptgericht bestellt sich die Oma Königsberger Klopse.
8. Alle trinken auf Vaters Wohl.

5. Stimmt nicht. Er bestellt ihn für fünf Personen. 6. Stimmt. 7. Stimmt nicht. Sie bestellt Seezunge.
8.. Stimmt nicht. Alle trinken auf Omas Wohl.

3 Welche Sätze passen zusammen?

Welche Satzteile auf der rechten Seite passen zu den Satzteilen auf der linken Seite?

1. Die beiden Geschwister planen etwas Besonderes, 1. f
2. Ihr Vater möchte nach Schwerin fahren 2. e
3. Andreas schlägt vor, 3. b
4. Die Oma freut sich sehr, 4. a
5. Andreas möchte die Omi fragen, was sie zum Geburtstag tun will, 5. d
6. Am liebsten möchte die Oma in ein Lokal gehen, 6. g
7. Die Oma soll dem Vater nichts von Andreas' Besuch bei ihr sagen, 7. c

a. daß Andreas sie besucht und ihr Blumen mitbringt.
b. daß er die Oma besucht und sie fragt, was sie tun will.
c. denn die Geburtstagsfeier soll eine Überraschung sein.
d. denn in Berlin läuft so viel.
e. und dort ins Restaurant gehen.
f. weil ihre Oma bald Geburtstag hat.
g. wo sie alle draußen sitzen können.

4 Was paßt?

Welches Wort im Kasten paßt zu welchem Ausdruck unten?

1. Musik ═══
2. eine Operette ═══
3. den Geburtstag ═══
4. mit dem Auto ═══
5. in ein Konzert ═══
6. einen Tisch ═══
7. Appetit ═══
8. auf das Wohl ═══
9. Blumen ═══

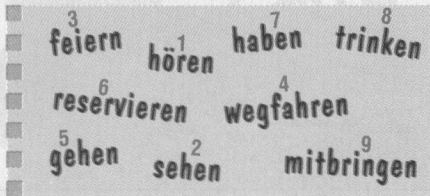

feiern ³ hören ¹ haben ⁷ trinken ⁸
reservieren ⁶ wegfahren ⁴
gehen ⁵ sehen ² mitbringen ⁹

Für welche kulturellen Veranstaltungen interessierst du dich?

We asked people from around Germany what kinds of cultural interests they have. Listen to the interviews, then read the texts.

Herr und Frau Heine, *Goslar*

„Ja, also Kultur ... wir gehen ganz gerne mal in ein Konzert, ins Theater ... und das ist natürlich etwas, was man in der Kleinstadt nicht so hat, das ist ganz klar. In der Kleinstadt müssen wir eine Fahrzeit von ein bis eineinhalb Stunden rechnen, um in die nächstgrößere Stadt zu kommen, die dann etwa so 250 bis 500 000 Einwohner hat. In der Großstadt Berlin, oder in 'ner anderen Stadt der Größe oder ähnlicher Größe, wär' das eben so, daß man ein viel höheres Angebot in der Stadt an Kulturangeboten bekommt — da sind Museen, Theater, Schauspielhäuser, Konzerte. Die Philharmonie hier hab' ich vor einigen Monaten das erste Mal besuchen können, das ist schon sehr beeindruckend, überwältigend, auch vom Klang her."

Günther, *Berlin*

„Zu Konzerten und Ausstellungseröffnungen, und zwar Martin Gropius Bau ‚Amerikanische Kunst im zwanzigsten Jahrhundert'. Zu sowas. Ab und zu ein Musical, aber eher selten, eigentlich Konzerte mehr."

Claudia und Ursel, *Düsseldorf*

Claudia: „Also, wir zeigen eigentlich sehr vielseitige Interessen, zum Beispiel auch Kino oder Theater, und ..."
Ursel: „Dann abends gehen wir auch ganz gerne in 'ne Disko zum Beispiel."
Claudia: „Oder wir sind hier nach Hamburg gekommen, um uns das *Phantom der Oper* anzuschauen, also Musicals auch, also das ist eigentlich sehr breit gefächert."

A. 1. Kino, Theater, Disko, Musicals, Konzerte, Ausstellungen
A. 2. Konzert, Theater; Museen, Theater, Schauspielhäuser, Konzerte; höheres Angebot an Kultur in Großstadt.

A. 1. What different kinds of cultural events do these people mention?
2. Reread Mr. Heine's interview. To what is he referring when he says **Das ist etwas, was man in einer Kleinstadt nicht hat?** What does a city like Berlin have to offer? What phrase does he use to sum this up and make a comparison?

B. Berlin has always been a diverse city with something exciting for everyone. Since unification there is more to see in Berlin than ever. How many of the places below do you recognize? Test your cultural and geographic savvy by matching each name with one of the photos below.

Das Pergamon Museum

Schloß Charlottenburg

Die Weltzeituhr am Alexanderplatz

Mahnmal (Opfer der Mauer)

Asking for, making, and responding to suggestions

Berlin ist eine Reise wert. Ein deutsches Sprichwort heißt: „Wer die Wahl hat, hat die Qual." Das trifft besonders auf Berlin zu, denn die neue Metropole Deutschlands macht es den Berlinern selbst und den vielen Besuchern nicht leicht, sich für einige von den vielen kulturellen Möglichkeiten zu entscheiden, die diese Stadt bietet. Sie wollen Berlin ja nicht nur sehen, sondern es auch wirklich erleben.

Ein kleiner Auszug aus dem kulturellen Programm:

BERLINER SYMPHONIKER

Sonntag, 5.9., 16 Uhr
SFB, Großer Sendesaal

1. Konzert für die ganze Familie. In Zusammenarbeit mit dem JugendKulturService.

„Geschichten von Trollen, Abenteuern und Lügen"

Dirigentin: **Konstantia Gourzi** – Moderatorinnen: **Imke Fischbeck-Griese: Ulrike Föster-Greig:** Peer-Gynt-Suite Nr. 1 op. 46, Peer-Gynt-Suite Nr. 2 op. 55.

Karten zum Preise von DM 7,- erhältlich bei den Bezirksämtern, Abteilung Jugendpflege, über das „Theater der Schulen", den JugendKulturService - Telefon 242 44 65, bei den bekannten Vorverkaufskassen und im Kartenbüro der Berliner Symphoniker. Telefon: 8 82 52, 87, Mo.-Fr.10-14 Uhr.

Sa, 4.9., Deutschlandhalle, 20 Uhr Berlin 88,8 präsentiert

«Das Phantom Traumpaar ist zurück»

Peter Hofmann
Anna Maria **Kaufmann**

singen

Musical Classics

mit Mitgliedern des

NDR-Sinfonieorchesters
Leitung:
Carl Robert Helg

BERLINER DOM

Sonnabend, 4. August, 19.30 Uhr
Streichkonzert
Israel Camerata
Women's String Orchestra
Werke von Bach u.a.

Sonntag, 5. August, 17 Uhr
Orgelkonzert
Dr. Dieter Hiller (Berlin)
Werke von Schumann, Liszt, Guilmant u.a.

		Deutsche Oper Berlin	Staatsoper Unter den Linden	Theater am Kurfürstendamm	Komödie	Hansa Theater	Berliner Kammerspiele
		Charlottenburg, Bismarck-str. 35, ☎ 3 41 02 49; ☎ 34 38-1 (Zentrale); Ⓤ Dt. Oper; Bus: 101	Mitte, Unter den Linden 7, ☎ 2 00 47 62; Ⓤ Friedrichstraße; Bus: 100, 157	Charlottenburg, Kurfürstendamm 206, ☎ 8 82 78 93; Ⓤ Uhland-straße; Bus: 119, 129	Charlottenburg, Kurfürstendamm 206, ☎ 8 82 78 93; Ⓤ Uhland-straße; Bus: 119, 129	Tiergarten, Alt-Moabit 48, ☎ 3 91 44 60; Ⓤ Turmstraße; Bus: 101, 123, 245	Tiergarten, Alt-Moabit 99, ☎ 3 91 55 43; Ⓤ Turm-straße; Bus: 123, 245
2.	Do	19.30 Aida (in ital. Sprache)	20.00 Romeo und Julia (in ital. Sprache)	Keine Vorstellung	20.00 Ausreißer	20.00 Don Camillo und Peppone	19.00 Andorra
3.	Fr	19.30 Ballett: Dornröschen	19.30 Hoffmanns Erzählungen	20.00 Herr im Haus bin ich (Premiere)	20.00 Ausreißer	20.00 Don Camillo und Peppone	19.00 Andorra
4.	Sa	18.30 Liederabend (siehe 'Konzerte')	19.30 Ballett: Nacht/ Verklärte Nacht/Der wunderbare Mandarin	20.00 Herr im Haus bin ich	20.00 Ausreißer	19.00 Don Camillo und Peppone	19.00 Andorra
5.	So	17.00: Der Ring des Nibelungen: Götterdämmerung	19.00: Ballett: Nacht/ Verklärte Nacht/Der wunderbare Mandarin	20.00 Herr im Haus bin ich	18.00 Ausreißer	15.30 Don Camillo und Peppone	Keine Vorstellung

5 Viel zu tun in Berlin!

Lies den Text „Berlin ist eine Reise wert", und beantworte die folgenden Fragen!

1. Was bedeutet das Sprichwort „Wer die Wahl hat, hat die Qual"? *1. It's difficult to choose when the options are equally good.*
2. In welcher Weise paßt das Sprichwort zu Berlin? *2. In Berlin gibt es ein großes kulturelles Angebot.*
3. Für welche kulturellen Veranstaltungen ist dieser Auszug aus dem Berlin Programm?
4. Wohin mußt du gehen, wenn du folgendes sehen oder hören willst? *3. Konzerte, Oper & Theater*
   a. am Sonnabend „Herr im Haus bin ich" *a. Theater am Kurfürstendamm*
   b. am Donnerstag „Romeo und Julia" *b. Staatsoper*
   c. am Sonntag das Orgelkonzert *c. Berliner Dom*

Was kann man in Berlin alles sehen?

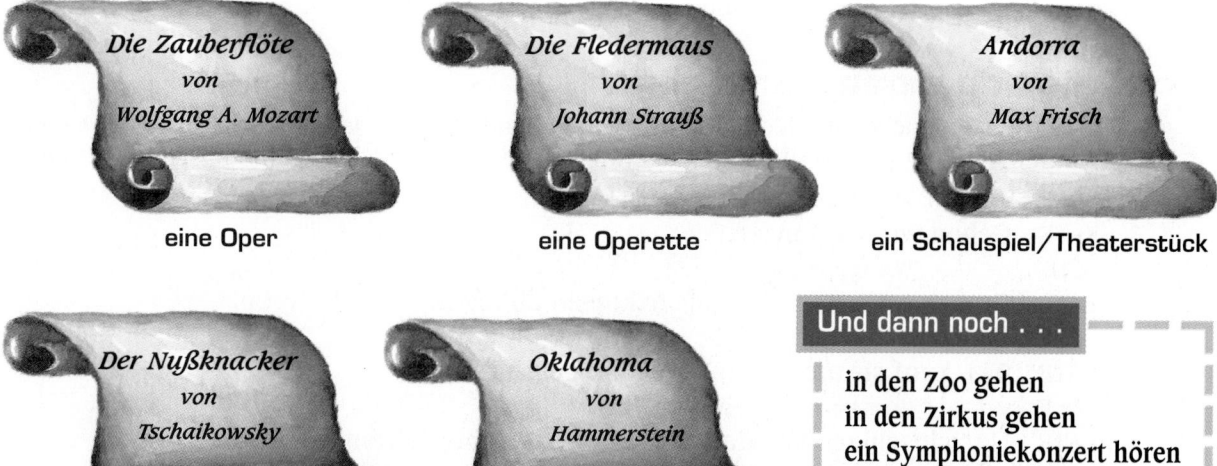

Die Zauberflöte
von
Wolfgang A. Mozart

eine Oper

Die Fledermaus
von
Johann Strauß

eine Operette

Andorra
von
Max Frisch

ein Schauspiel/Theaterstück

Der Nußknacker
von
Tschaikowsky

ein Ballett

Oklahoma
von
Hammerstein

ein Musical

Und dann noch . . .
in den Zoo gehen
in den Zirkus gehen
ein Symphoniekonzert hören
ein Chorkonzert hören
ins Kabarett gehen

Und man kann Stadtrundfahrten machen — mit dem Bus oder mit dem Schiff — und sich die vielen kulturellen Baudenkmäler Berlins ansehen.

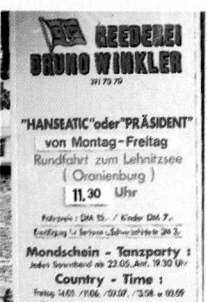

Busausflug   Ausflugsschiff   Anschlag für Ausflüge   Berliner Synagoge

6 Was kann man alles machen?

Erzähl deinen Freunden alles, was man in Berlin machen kann, indem (*by connecting*) du die Verben mit den richtigen Hauptwörtern verbindest.

Man kann ...

in den Zoo	gehen
den Dom	machen
eine Stadtrundfahrt	besichtigen
ein Symphoniekonzert	besuchen
ein Schauspiel	sehen
ins Kabarett	hören
Baudenkmäler	
eine Kunstausstellung	
ein Schloß	

7 Hör gut zu! For answers, see listening script on TE Interleaf.

Einige Schüler erzählen, für welche kulturellen Veranstaltungen sie sich interessieren und warum. Wähle für jede Beschreibung eine Aktivität aus dem Wortschatzkasten auf Seite 265 aus, die dieser Person besonders gefallen würde!

8 Hast du einen Vorschlag?

Ulf und Beate machen gerade Pläne für heute abend, aber Ulf ist gar nicht sicher, wie das ablaufen soll und fragt nach Vorschlägen. Für jede Antwort schreib eine passende Frage!

ULF	Was sollen wir heute abend machen?
BEATE	**Gehen wir ins Konzert!**
ULF	Was kann ich tun?
BEATE	**Du kannst schon die Konzertkarten abholen.**
ULF	Wo soll ich sie kaufen?
BEATE	**Tja, kauf sie am besten im Musikgeschäft!**
ULF	Wann fahren wir? Was schlägst du vor?
BEATE	**Na, ich schlage vor, daß wir um sechs dahin fahren.**
ULF	Und was möchtest du jetzt machen?
BEATE	**Ich? Ich möchte mal einfach nach Hause fahren. Also, bis dann!**

9 Ich schlage vor, …

Du bist mit deiner Familie und einigen Freunden in Berlin, und alle wollen etwas Tolles unternehmen. Als einziger, der Deutsch spricht, mußt du eurem Reiseleiter Vorschläge machen. Schau den Wortschatzkasten auf Seite 265 an, und sage, für welche Veranstaltungen sich deine Eltern interessieren und für welche sich deine Freunde interessieren! Teile deine Ideen deinen Mitschülern mit! Danach mach dem Reiseleiter vier Vorschläge, und schreib sie auf ein Blatt Papier!

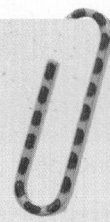

SO SAGT MAN DAS!

Asking for, making, and responding to suggestions

Here are some new ways of asking for, making, and responding to suggestions:

You could ask for a suggestion by saying:

> **Was sollen wir mit der Oma machen? Wofür bist du?**

When making suggestions, you might say:

> **Würdest du gern mal in ein italienisches Restaurant gehen?**
> **Wie wär's mit einem typischen Berliner Lokal?**

And you could make a suggestion by saying:

> **Ich bin dafür, daß wir in Berlin etwas unternehmen.**

When responding to suggestions, you might say:

> **Nein, ich würde am liebsten in ein deutsches Lokal gehen.**
> **Das wär' nicht schlecht.**

Identify the verb forms in the second and third questions and answers. Of what do these constructions remind you? How would you express these in English? Which case always follows the preposition **mit**?[1]

1. **Mit** is always followed by the dative case.

10 Hör gut zu!  For answers, see listening script on TE Interleaf.

Verschiedene Schüler versuchen, mit Freunden Pläne zu machen. Die Schüler machen einige Vorschläge. Für jedes Gespräch, das du hörst, entscheide dich, ob der Freund mit dem Vorschlag einverstanden ist oder nicht.

---

*G*rammatik   The **würde**-forms

1. Using a form of **würde** followed by **gern, lieber,** or **am liebsten** and an infinitive lets you make suggestions and express wishes in a new way.

   Würdest du gern mal in ein italienisches Restaurant **gehen?**
   Ich würde gern mal wieder eine Scholle **essen.**

2. Here are the **würde**-forms:

ich	**würde**	wir	**würden**
du	**würdest**	ihr	**würdet**
er, sie, es	**würde**	sie, Sie	**würden**

---

11 Wer möchte was?   E.g.: **Ich würde gern mal die Mauerreste sehen.**

Wofür würdet ihr euch (du, deine Familie und Freunde) in Berlin interessieren?

Meine Eltern Mein Bruder Meine Schwester Ich Meine Freunde und ich, wir	bin dafür ist dafür sind dafür würde würden	daß wir gern mal am liebsten	eine Stadtrundfahrt machen ein Konzert im Berliner Dom hören eine Ausstellung besuchen die Mauerreste sehen einen Ausflug nach Potsdam machen Schloß Sanssouci besichtigen in den Zirkus gehen in ein typisches Berliner Restaurant gehen

---

EIN WENIG LANDESKUNDE

In Germany the arts are state supported. This enables most cities and even smaller towns to offer most cultural events at reasonable prices. The arts receive such generous support due to a long tradition of art patronage in German-speaking countries.

High school students can also take advantage of inexpensive tickets that schools acquire to performances that are not sold out, and university students can make use of sharply reduced tickets at the box office just prior to performances.

---

12 Was würdest du gern mal tun?

 Frag deinen Partner, was er mal gern in Berlin tun würde und warum! Er muß dir drei verschiedene Dinge aufzählen! — Danach fragt er dich.

Berliner und ausländische Küche

... von 11-24 (außer montags; Küche bis 23 Uhr): Folgen Sie einer Empfehlung: Schisch-Kebab - Lammlachs, 24 Stunden in einer Spezialmarinade eingelegt, die einen besonderen Geschmack verspricht. Er wird auf Lavastein gegrillt und mit gebratenen Kartoffeln oder Reis, dazu Sesamsauce und gemischter frischer Salat auf ägyptische Art, serviert für DM 25,-. Restaurant El Pharao-Wiesenbaude, Steglitz, Goerzallee 1 ☎ 8 33 78 74.

... von 11-24 Uhr: Ausgewählte Köstlichkeiten, mediterrane Delikatessen, Vollwertkost und vegetarische Speisen erwarten Sie im Restaurant Seaside, Reinickendorf, An der Mühle 5-9, Reservierung ☎ 3 61 90 27.

... von 12-24 Uhr: (Küche bis 22 Uhr): deutsche und internationale Spezialitäten sowie zahlreiche Fischgerichte im gepflegten Restaurant mit maritimer Einrichtung. Yachthafen-Restaurant Blau-Rot, das Restaurant mit Terrasse direkt an der Havel. Spandau, Scharfe Lanke 103-107, Reservierung: ☎ 3 61 90 21.

... von 12-24 Uhr: türkische Köstlichkeiten in Berlins erstem türkischen Speiserestaurant Istanbul. Charlottenburg, Knesebeckstr. 77 ☎ 8 83 27 77.

... von 12-1 Uhr: gutbürgerliche Küche und vorzügliche Pfannengerichte, z.B.: 1/2 Bauernente mit Rotkohl und Kartoffelkloß für DM 25,60. Restaurant Hardtke, Wilmersdorf, Hubertusallee 48 ☎ 8 92 58 48.

... ab 18 Uhr: herzhafte Spezialitäten im rustikalen Pferdestall im Haus Dannenberg am See. Reinickendorf, Alt-Heiligensee 52-54 ☎ 4 31 30 91.

... von 9-14 Uhr: Brunch im Sommergarten (nur bei schönem Wetter) - warme Braten, deftige Wurst- und Käsespezialitäten, Schinken, Lachs, Eier, Rollmops, Salate, dazu süßer Aufstrich und Obst, außerdem Cornflakes oder Müsli und Rote Grütze, Kaffee, Tee oder Fruchtsaft für DM 16,90, 1/2 Portion DM 9,90. Britzer Mühle, Neukölln, Buckower Damm 130, neben der restaurierten Mühle am Britzer Garten ☎ 6 04 10 05.

RESTAURANTS

13 Lies diese Anzeigen und beantworte die Fragen!

1. Wohin kann man gehen, wenn man chinesisch essen will?   1. Ho Lin Wah
2. Wo bekommt man neue deutsche und vegetarische Küche?   2. Friedrich
3. Was bekommt man alles im Restaurant „Blau-Rot"?   3. deutsche und internationale Spezialitäten, Fischgerichte
4. Was bekommt man zum Brunch im Sommergarten? Nenne fünf Gerichte!
5. Was für ein Restaurant ist „Istanbul"? Was gibt es dort?   5. türkisches Restaurant; türkische Köstlichkeiten
6. Wo kann man indische Atmosphäre genießen und indisch essen?   6. Surya

4. E.g.: Braten, Schinken, Lachs, Eier, Rollmops

Ausländische und deutsche Spezialitäten:

eine chinesische Spezialität ist Peking Ente

Was gibt's zum Brunch?

deftige Wurst- und Käsespezialitäten

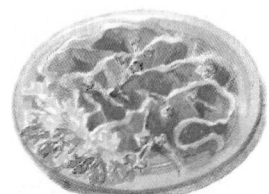

rohen Schinken

eine ägyptische Köstlichkeit ist Schisch-Kebab

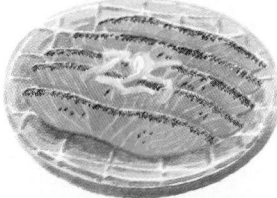

marinierten Lachs

Rote Grütze

mediterrane Delikatessen sind Hummer, Austern, Krabben

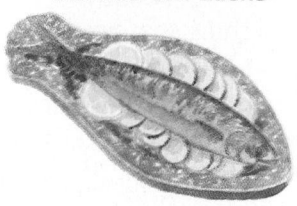

geräucherten Fisch

kalten Braten

eine gutbürgerliche Küche: Pfannengerichte, z.B. Mastente mit Rotkohl und Kartoffelkloß

ägyptisch	italienisch
chinesisch	mexikanisch
deutsch	russisch
französisch	spanisch
griechisch	türkisch
indisch	typisch Berlin

14 Typische Gerichte

Nenne drei typische Gerichte der Länder, für die im Kasten ein Adjektiv steht!

BEISPIEL **Ein typisches französisches Gericht ist ...**

15 Worauf hast du Appetit?

Ihr seid den ganzen Tag in Berlin herumgelaufen und habt viel gesehen. Ihr habt großen Hunger und wollt essen gehen. Aber wohin? Die Auswahl ist so furchtbar groß! Mach deinem Partner einen Vorschlag von den Restaurants auf Seite 268! Akzeptiert er ihn? Oder würde er lieber woanders essen? Warum oder warum nicht? Frag ihn mal!

16 Hör gut zu!

For answers, see listening script on TE Interleaf.

Zwei Berliner Schüler unterhalten sich darüber, in welches Lokal sie zum Essen gehen wollen. Schreib die verschiedenen Möglichkeiten auf, über die sie sprechen! Wohin gehen sie schließlich und warum?

17 Ißt du mal gern ein ausländisches Gericht?
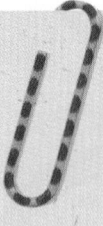

Frag deinen Partner, welche ausländische Küche er am liebsten mag und warum! Schau in den Kasten rechts als Hilfe! Dann soll er dich fragen!

SO SAGT MAN DAS!

Expressing hearsay

To pass on something that you have heard, you may say in informal conversation:

Ich habe gehört, daß das Essen dort sehr gut ist.
Man hat mir gesagt, daß die Musik dort toll sein soll.
Der Fisch **soll** dort ausgezeichnet **sein.**

How would you express these ideas in English?

EIN WENIG LANDESKUNDE

In den deutschen Großstädten hat es schon immer eine große Anzahl von ausländischen Restaurants gegeben. Ausländische Besucher sollen sich wie zu Hause fühlen, und die Deutschen wollen die internationale Küche genießen.

Heute kann man auch sehr viele ausländische Restaurants und Lokale in kleinen Städten und Dörfern finden, besonders italienische, griechische und türkische Lokale. Und diese findet man sogar in Häusern, die typisch deutsch aussehen, und wo früher mal ein deutsches Lokal war.

18 Hör gut zu!

For answers, see listening script on TE Interleaf.

Two students from Potsdam are visiting Berlin. Listen as they discuss a restaurant where they might go for dinner and what they have heard about it from their friends. For each category, write what they heard from their friends.

Essen	Bedienung	Atmosphäre	Preise

19 Wo sollen wir heute abend hingehen?

Together with your partner, decide where you might take a German visitor out for dinner in your town or a large city nearby. Make a suggestion and tell him or her the things you have heard about the restaurant. Your partner will also make a suggestion and say what he or she has heard. Come to a consensus and share your results with your classmates. Ask them if they have heard anything about the restaurant you decided on.

---

*G*rammatik   Unpreceded adjectives

1. When an adjective is not preceded by an article (**ein, der, dieser,** etc.), the adjective must show gender and case. Such adjectives get the same endings as the **der** and **dieser**-words would in their place.

Der Salat schmeckt prima.	Griechisch**er** Salat schmeckt prima.
Ich mag **den** Käse nicht.	Ich mag französisch**en** Käse nicht.
Dies**e** Milch schmeckt gut.	Kalt**e** Milch schmeckt gut.
Dies**es** Obst ist gesund.	Frisch**es** Obst ist gesund.
Wir empfehlen dies**e** Wurst-spezialitäten.	Wir empfehlen deftig**e** Wurst-spezialitäten.

2. When there are two or more adjectives in a series, they both share the same ending.

Ich esse gern gemischt**en** grün**en** Salat.

---

20 Internationales Essen!

It's German-American Day and the German chancellor's personal chef is coming to your class to cook an international meal. Tell him one thing you like and one thing you don't like from the list of possibilities. (Be sure to use the correct adjective endings!)

E.g.: Ich mag italienisches Eis gerne. Norwegischer Lachs schmeckt mir nicht.

bulgarisch	Schisch-Kebab	
kalifornisch	Salat	
italienisch	Eis	
hausgemacht	Wurst	
polnisch	Lachs	schmeckt mir (nicht).
griechisch	Brot	
norwegisch	Käse	
französisch	Spezialitäten	
deutsch	Gulasch	
türkisch	Trauben	
ungarisch	Kuchen	

21 Für mein Notizbuch

Schreib auf, was für Spezialitäten du am liebsten ißt, was du gewöhnlich zum Brunch ißt und welche Spezialitäten du nicht gern ißt!

HOTEL-RESTAURANT
HAUS *Dannenberg* AM SEE
Speisenkarte

VORSPEISEN
Gefülltes Ei auf Gemüsesalat	5,40
Geräuchertes Forellenfilet	6,50

SUPPEN
Nudelsuppe mit Huhn	4,20
Frische Gemüsesuppe	4,00

BEILAGEN
Portion Sauerkraut	3,80
Portion Pommes frites	3,50
Portion Gemüse	4,20
Salatteller	4,50
Kloß	3,00
Scheibe Brot	0,70

HAUPTGERICHTE

FISCHGERICHTE
Mit Lachs gefüllte Seezungenröllchen mit Brokkoli-Rahmsauce	25,00
Filets vom Babysteinbutt mit Walnußsauce auf einem Gemüsebett serviert	22,50
Gegrilltes Seebarschfilet m. Salzkartoffeln und gemischtem Gemüse	24,60
Frische Seezunge nach Art des Hauses m. Salzkartoffeln u. gem. Salat	26,50

FLEISCHGERICHTE
Wiener Schnitzel m. Salzkartoffeln oder Pommes frites	22,50
Königsberger Klopse m. Nudeln und gemischtem Salat	16,80
Ungarisches Gulasch mit Kloß	11,90
Frische mecklenburgische Mastente mit Kartoffelkloß	18,50
Schweinerückensteak mit Kräuterbutter u. Pommes frites	21,30

NACHSPEISEN
Rote Grütze mit Vanillesauce	4,60
Apfelstrudel	3,80
Frische Erdbeeren mit Sahne	6,90

GETRÄNKE

WARME GETRÄNKE
1 Tasse Kaffee	3,80
1 Kännchen Kaffee	6,00
1 Tasse Tee	3,80
1 Tasse Kaffee Hag	4,30

ALKOHOLFREIE GETRÄNKE
Mineralwasser	0,3l	3,80
Apfelsaft	0,4l	3,60
Orangensaft	0,3l	3,00
Fruchtlimo	0,3l	3,00

ALKOHOLISCHE GETRÄNKE
Verlangen Sie bitte unsere Getränkekarte

22 Was steht auf der Speisekarte?

Such dir einen Partner! Stellt euch gegenseitig Fragen über die Speisekarte* von „Haus Dannenberg am See"!

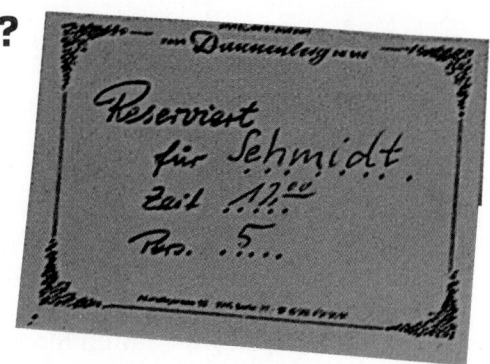

1. Was für ein Gericht ist (Seezunge)?
2. Was für Suppen gibt es?
3. Was für Hauptgerichte gibt es?
4. Welche Fischgerichte gibt es? Welche Fleischgerichte?
5. Welche Beilagen gibt es? Und was für Getränke? Nenne drei!
6. Welche Vor- und Nachspeisen gibt es? Nenne eine Vorspeise und eine Nachspeise!

WORTSCHATZ

Was bestellt man gewöhnlich in einem Restaurant?

eine Vorspeise

gefülltes Ei

ein Hauptgericht

Schweinerückensteak mit Kartoffelkroketten

eine Beilage

Klöße

eine Nachspeise

Rote Grütze

ein Getränk

Spezi

Und dann noch ...

Bratkartoffeln
gemischter Salat
eine Scheibe Brot
Erdbeeren mit Sahne

Was bestellst du gewöhnlich?

23 Beantworte die Fragen!

Such dir einen anderen Partner und beantwortet abwechselnd diese Fragen!

1. Was möchtest du dir bestellen? Welche Vorspeise? Eine Suppe? Welches Gericht? Eine Beilage dazu? Welche Nachspeise? Welches Getränk?
2. Welches von diesen Gerichten möchtest du am liebsten essen? Warum? Welches möchtest du nicht essen? Warum nicht?

*Both words **Speisenkarte** (usually printed on a German menu) and **Speisekarte** are acceptable, the latter being used in everyday speech.

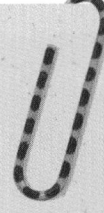

SO SAGT MAN DAS!

Ordering in a restaurant

You have been using various expressions to order food in a restaurant.
Here are some other ways to order:

The waitperson may ask:

Haben Sie schon gewählt?

Und was hätten Sie gern?

You could order by saying:

Ja, bringen Sie mir bitte das Seebarschfilet!

Ich hätte gern das Wiener Schnitzel.

Identify the verb forms in the last question and response. What do these verb forms remind you of? Do these statements refer to the past? What do you think these forms express? How would the waitperson ask several customers at the same time for their order?

24 Hör gut zu!

For answers, see listening script on TE Interleaf.

Die Schüler aus der Beckmann Oberschule machen heute ihre Schulfeier und fahren zum Haus Dannenberg am See. Hör zu, wie sie ihr Essen und ihre Getränke bestellen! Schreib auf, was drei Schüler bestellen, und dann beantworte diese Fragen!

1. Wer bestellt nur ein Hauptgericht?
2. Wer möchte auch eine Beilage zum Hauptgericht?
3. Wer bestellt keinen Nachtisch?

25 Was hättet ihr gern?

Such dir vier Partner! Frag drei von ihnen, was jeder gern zu essen oder zu trinken hätte! Jeder Partner wählt etwas auf der Speisekarte aus. Du gibst die Bestellung weiter an den vierten Partner. — Tauscht dann die Rollen aus!

SPRACHTIP

When ordering from a menu, Germans normally use the definite article before the name of the dish, even though the item may not be listed with an article.

Here is how the dish may be listed on the menu:

Geräuchertes Forellenfilet

Gegrilltes Seebarschfilet

Frische Erdbeeren

Here is how you would order that dish:

Ich hätte gern das geräucherte Filet.

Das gegrillte Seebarschfilet, bitte!

Ich nehme die frischen Erdbeeren.

Grammatik The hätte-forms

When ordering a meal you can use the **hätte**-forms together with **gern** or **lieber**.

Ich **hätte gern** eine Suppe.
Was **hättest** du denn **gern**?
Andreas **hätte gern** Rote Grütze.

Wir **hätten gern** Bratkartoffeln.
Und was **hättet** ihr **gern** dazu?
Die Kinder **hätten lieber** einen Salat.

From what verb are the **hätte** forms derived? How are they like the imperfect form of this verb? What is different? How would you express **hätte gern** in English?

26 Und was hätten Sie gern?

Du bist mit deinem Partner in einem guten Restaurant in Berlin. Du feierst deinen Geburtstag und bestellst dir deshalb ein großes Essen, mit Vorspeise, Hauptgericht, Beilage, Nachspeise und Getränk. Ein dritter Schüler übernimmt die Rolle der Bedienung. Was bestellst du alles? Was bestellt dein Partner? Entwickelt ein Rollenspiel und spielt die Szene der Klasse vor!

27 Hör gut zu! For answers, see listening script on TE Interleaf.

Einige Gruppen feiern heute im Haus Dannenberg am See. Als Kellner hörst du verschiedene Gespräche. Was feiert jede Gruppe, und was ist das Verhältnis (*relationship*) der Leute in jeder Gruppe zueinander? Sind es Familienmitglieder, Freunde oder Geschäftsleute (*business people*)?

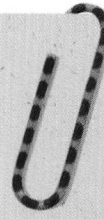

SO SAGT MAN DAS!

Expressing good wishes

When toasting someone, you say:

Zum Wohl!
Auf dein Wohl!
Prost!
Auf euer Wohl!

Before beginning your meal, you say:

Guten Appetit!
Mahlzeit!

In response to a toast you say:

Prost!
Zum Wohl!
Auf Ihr Wohl!
Danke! Zum Wohl!

In response you can say:

Danke! Dir auch!
oder **Danke, gleichfalls!**
oder **Mahlzeit! Guten Appetit!**

Which of these expressions would you use with an older person whom you do not know well? Which ones would you use with friends and family?

28 Zum Wohl!

Du bist mit verschiedenen Leuten in einem Restaurant. Du trinkst auf ihr Wohl. Was sagst du zu ihnen? Was sagst du …

a. zu einem Freund?
b. zu deinen Eltern?
c. zu zwei Klassenkameraden?
d. zu deiner Deutschlehrerin?

a. Auf dein Wohl!
b. Auf euer Wohl!
c. Auf euer Wohl!
d. Auf Ihr Wohl!

29 Wir gehen zusammen aus

At the end of the school year you and your classmates and German teacher go out to a German restaurant where the waitstaff speaks German. With the people at your table and/or the waiter

— discuss what you will order and why
— suggest to your friends what they should order
— order your food and drink
— toast each other
— begin the meal with good wishes
— talk about how the food tastes
— order dessert and more drinks
— ask for and pay the bill
— arrange for a decent tip!

Das Leben im fremden Land

LESETRICK

Reading for comprehension. When reading a short story in German, you need to focus on understanding ideas rather than isolated words. You'll be surprised to find out how much you can understand if you use the following strategy: 1) read at least one-third of the text without looking up any words; 2) reread the same passage and ask yourself what you *do* understand; 3) if you have a general idea of what is happening, read to the end without stopping; and 4) read the story a third time, pausing at intervals to see if you can summarize what you have read.

Getting Started For answers, see TE Interleaf.

> **Weißt du noch?** Always look at the title before you begin to read a story or poem.

1. Who are the two people in the title of this story? What does **seltsam** mean? And **komisch**? Knowing that there are two people in the story, can you guess the purpose of the dashes?

2. Use your background knowledge about ethnic groups in Germany and the United States to come up with three possible characteristics of life for Turks in Germany. How do you think they fit into society?

Seltsamer Deutscher, komischer Türke

- Grüßgott! Du fahren mich das Adresse?
- Ja mei, wozu sind wir denn da, geben's mir mal den Zettel her . . . (halblaut) Mehmet Öztürk. Klugstr. 19. (laut) Aha, die Klugstraße, in Neuhausen ist die. Steigen S' ein, ich bring Sie hin! (abgewendet) Also, Sepp, Servus. Ich fahr' grad mal nach Neuhausen rüber, vielleicht sehn wir uns noch, die Nacht . . .
- (Sepp: Wenn nicht, funk mich halt an!)

- Dein Auto gutes Auto. Ich arbeite auch in der BMW. Schichtarbeit. Nach der Arbeit mit Kollegen Bier trinken gehen. Jetzt Alkohol trinken, nix Auto fahren.
- Mit wem sind Sie denn zum Biertrinken gegangen — mit deutschen oder türkischen Kollegen?
- Türkische Kollegen. Deutsche Kollegen sagen immer: Keine Zeit, keine Zeit! Meine alte Freunde erzählen, 1960, 1965, 1968 Deutsche immer freundlich; aber jetzt nix freundlich, immer schimpfen, immer sagen „Kanacke" . . .
- Tja, schön ist das nicht, wie sich manche Deutsche im Alltag gegenüber Türken benehmen . . .
  (Pause)
- Scheißwetter! Die ganze Nacht regnet's schon! Würden Sie mal bitte mit dem Tuch hier das Fenster abwischen. Damit ich an der Kreuzung die rechte Seite sehen kann. So, es reicht schon, danke schön.
- In Türkei jetzt sehr heiß, sehr schön, immer Sonne.
- Jaja, das glaube ich Ihnen schon, daß in der Türkei sehr schönes Wetter ist . . .
- Deutschland immer Regen, kalt. Die Deutsche sagen immer „Türken raus!" — warum? Wir keine schlechte Menschen. Wir immer arbeiten.
- Tja, wissen Sie, die Frage kann ich auch nicht so recht beantworten. Wir sind alle Menschen, da mach' ich überhaupt keinen Unterschied, ob einer Türke ist, Grieche oder Deutscher . . .
- Sie sind aber ein guter deutsche Mensch. Du sagen nicht, Ausländer nehmen mir Arbeit weg.

- Ja mei, es gibt halt solche und solche . . . Wir alle versuchen eben, irgendwie über die Runden zu kommen. So, jetzt sind wir gleich da!
- Du sehr gut fahren Auto!
- Danke für das Kompliment!
- Was muß ich bezahlen?
- Yediseksen ediyor arkadasim?
- Was bitte?
- Dedim ya yediseksen ediyor.
- Hier nehmen Sie, 10 Mark, reicht es?
- Moment mal, ich hab's Ihnen doch schon auf türkisch gesagt. Sagen Sie, sind Sie jetzt eigentlich Türke, oder was!
- Hm, um ehrlich zu sein . . . Ich muß Ihnen gestehen, ich bin gar kein Türke, äh, ich bin Deutscher, also ich meine . . .
- Ja um Gottes willen, wieso haben Sie dann die ganze Zeit dieses Theater gespielt?
- Tja, ich wollt' eben mal ausprobieren, wie ein deutscher Taxifahrer einen türkischen Fahrgast behandelt und wollt' mal wissen, wie Sie auf mein Verhalten reagieren würden. Aber sagen Sie mal, was haben Sie da gerade zu mir gesagt? War das tatsächlich Türkisch? Jetzt sagen Sie bloß, Sie sind wirklich Türke!
- Ja, ja, ich bin ein Türke.
- Aber warum sprechen Sie denn so ausgezeichnet Deutsch?
- Tja, ganz einfach. Ich lebe seit 23 Jahren hier in Deutschland, beziehungsweise, ich bin hier geboren.
- Ja! Da mußte mein Versuch ja danebengehen! Es war trotzdem eine lustige Fahrt, oder?
- Jaja, kann man wohl sagen.
- Hier, das Geld. Stimmt schon so! Also dann — Viel Glück noch heut nacht! Wiedersehen!
- Ja, danke, danke! Wiederschaun!

- (aus dem Hintergrund) Hallo, sind Sie frei?
- Ja freilich. Steigen Sie ein!
  Hab gerade so einen „komischen Türken" gefahren . . .
- Jaja. Unsere Kanacken sind halt so komisch!

Cengiz Kip

3. Complete steps 1 and 2 of the strategy outlined in the **Lese-trick** box. In one sentence, summarize what the story is about thus far. Where is it taking place? Which character do you think is the Turk? Which is the German?

A Closer Look

> **Tip:** Summarizing the action of a story every paragraph or so will help you determine how much you understand and what you might need to read again.

4. Complete steps 3 and 4 of the reading strategy. As you read through the third time, try to summarize the action or topics of the dialogue at regular intervals. What are some of the topics of conversation between the German and the Turk?

5. What is the sudden twist in the dialogue? Who is the passenger really and why is he riding in a taxi?

6. Why does the passenger's experiment fail? How does the passenger react when he finds out who the driver really is? What is he so surprised about?

7. What do you think the point of this story is? That is, what message is the author trying to get across? What happens in the final scene to illustrate the author's point?

8. Schreib eine Zusammenfassung (*summary*) von der Geschichte, die du gerade gelesen hast, mit sieben bis acht Sätzen! Verwende dabei so viele *connecting words* wie möglich, zum Beispiel Pronomen (er, sie, es usw.) und Zeitausdrücke (zuerst, dann, zuletzt usw.)!

ANWENDUNG

1 Einige Touristen sprechen über ihre Pläne für Berlin. Hör gut zu! Was wollen sie sich ansehen? Was schlagen sie vor? — Schreib auf, wo jeder gern mal hingehen würde! Aber was tun sie wirklich?   *For answers, see listening script on TE Interleaf.*

2 Ein Slogan heißt: Berlin ist eine Reise wert! Sieh dir diesen Auszug für Stadtrundfahrten aus dem Berlin Programm an! Welche Sehenswürdigkeiten kennst du schon?
Schlag deinem Partner vor, was du dir gern mit ihm ansehen würdest! Was meint er dazu? Hat er bessere Vorschläge?

3 Schreib drei Sehenswürdigkeiten auf, die du dir gern einmal ansehen würdest! Schreib auch auf, warum du daran interessiert bist!

Tägliche Stadtrundfahrten
Daily Sightseeingtours
+ Potsdam

Tickets in Ihrem Hotel und am Bus/ in your hotel and at the bus

In unserer **BBS City Tour** zeigen und erklären wir unter anderem:
In our **BBS City Tour** you will see and have explained among others:

- Gedächtniskirche
- Europa Center
- KaDeWe
- Urania
- Checkpoint Charlie
- Gendarmenmarkt
- Schauspielhaus
- Deutscher Dom
- Französischer Dom
- Friedrichsw. Kirche
- Nicolaiviertel
- Rotes Rathaus
- Alexanderplatz
- T.V.Tower
- Museumsinsel

- Siegessäule
- Schloß Bellevue
- Berliner Dom
- Staatsbibliothek
- Humboldt Universität
- Unter den Linden
- Staatsoper
- Kronprinzenpalais
- Prinzessinnenpalais
- St. Hedwigs Kathedrale
- Forum Fredericianum
- Brandenburger Tor
- Reichstag
- Haus der Kulturen
- Tiergarten

- Charlottenburger Tor
- Technische Universität
- Ernst-Reuter-Platz
- Deutsche Oper
- Rathaus Charlottenburg
- Schloß Charlottenburg
- Ägyptisches Museum
- Funkturm
- ICC
- Messegelände
- Ku'damm Carée
- Kempinski
- Ku'damm Eck
- Kurfürstendamm
- Café Kranzler

Kinderermäßigung / child reduction: Außer/except Kombi-Ticket
0-6 Jahre/years: frei/free
7-13 Jahre/years: Ermäßigung/reduction 50%
Ausflüge/excursions: Ermäßigung/reduction DM 10,-

Zeit	Tour		Dauer	Preis
10.00	Gr. / Big Berlin-Tour	täglich / daily	3	38,-
11.00	Berlin City-Tour	täglich / daily	2	30,-
11.30	Berlin in Kürze/in brief	täglich / daily	1,5	25,-
13.30	Berlin City-Tour	täglich / daily	2	30,-
14.00	* Potsdam / Sanssouci¹⁾	täglich / daily	ca. 4	49,-
14.00	Super Berlin-Tour incl. Pergamon-Museum	täglich / daily	4	45,-
14.30	Berlin in Kürze/in brief	täglich / daily	1,5	25,-
16.00	Berlin City-Tour	täglich / daily	2	30,-
21.00	Nightclub-Tour	Sa / Sat	ca. 5	99,-
	Superspar/Discount Ticket 10.00 Gr./ Big Berlin Tour + 14.00 Potsdam / Sanssouci			79,-
	Kinder / children			69,-

Berlin - Touren: Kinderermäßigung / Reduction for children
0 bis 6 Jahre / Years gratis / free of charge, 7–13 Jahre / Years 50%.
Ausflüge / Excursions: Kinderermäßigung / Reduction for children DM 10,-
* **Platzreservierung erforderlich / Advance booking required.**
¹⁾ Siehe Tourbeschreibung / see description.

Abfahrt aller Rundfahrten/ Departure of all tours:
Kurfürstendamm 216 / Fasanenstr.,
Nähe / near U-Bhf. Uhlandstr.
Tel. (030) 883 10 15 · Fax (030) 882 56 18 · Telex 184 642

BBS   Berliner Bären Stadtrundfahrt GmbH
Rankestraße 35 · D-10789 Berlin · Tel. 213 40 77 · Fax 213 73 54 · Telex 183 794 bbs · Alexanderplatz · D-10178 Berlin · Tel. 242 43 62

 **4** Such dir eine Partnerin! Schlag ihr vor, daß sie sich mit dir die Sehenswürdigkeiten ansieht, die du dir ausgesucht hast! Sag ihr auch, was du darüber schon gehört hast! Geht sie mit dir mit? Sie muß ihre Antwort begründen.

 **5** Schau mit drei Partnern die Speisekarte hier rechts an! Sprecht darüber, was ihr über die Gerichte gehört habt und was ihr bestellen wollt! Vergeßt auch die Getränke nicht! Dann beginnt das Essen mit den passenden Wünschen.

6 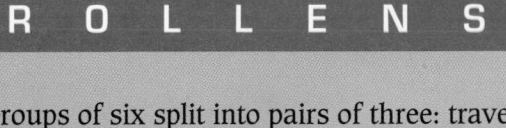 **ROLLENSPIEL**

Groups of six split into pairs of three: travelers and travel agents. Both groups should review by themselves what they know about famous Berlin places and reasons they have heard for going there. Set up rows of desks to simulate a travel agency. The travelers then have to go to the agents and ask about some sights they have heard of. The agents should corroborate that information, urging the travelers to go there (or not) and make suggestions of their own. The travel agents tell the travelers which of the city tours listed on page 278 they should take in order to see those sights, what time the tours are and how much they cost.

KANN ICH'S WIRKLICH?

Can you ask for, make, and respond to suggestions? (p. 266)

1 How would you ask a friend what he or she would like to do? Think of three different ways! 1. Was möchtest du machen? Was würdest du gerne machen? Was möchtest du tun?

2 How would you tell a friend you are in favor of eating at a Chinese restaurant? How would you ask your friend if he or she would like that, using **würde**? 2. Ich bin dafür, daß wir chinesisch essen gehen. Würdest du gern mal chinesisch essen gehen?

3 How would your friend respond that it wouldn't be bad, but that he or she would rather eat at a Mexican restaurant? How would you then say: "What about 'Los Compadres'?" 3. Das wär' nicht schlecht. Aber ich würde lieber in einem mexikanischen Restaurant essen gehen. — Wie wär's mit „Los Compadres"?

Can you express hearsay? (p. 270)

4 How would you say 4. a. Ich habe gehört, daß das Essen bei Hardtke sehr gut sein soll. b. Klaus hat mir gesagt, daß die Pizza im „La Bussola"

a. that you heard the food is very good at Hardtke's? ausgezeichnet sein soll.

b. that Klaus told you the pizza was excellent at "La Bussola"?

c. that the service is supposed to be very bad at "Jean-Marc's"?

c. Der Service bei „Jean Marc" soll sehr schlecht sein.

Can you order in a restaurant? (p. 274)

5 How would a waiter ask you

a. if you have made your choice? a. Haben Sie schon gewählt?

b. what you would like? b. Was hätten Sie gern?

6 How would you say a. Ich hätte gern eine Flasche Mineralwasser.

a. that you would like a bottle of mineral water?

b. "Please bring me the goulash!"? b. Bringen Sie mir bitte das Gulasch!

7 How would you ask your sister if she would prefer French fries?
7. Möchtest du lieber Pommes frites?

Can you express good wishes? (p. 275)

8 How would you say "Enjoy your meal!" to someone? How would that person respond? 8. Guten Appetit! Mahlzeit! — Danke gleichfalls!

9 How would you toast

a. a friend? a. Prost! Auf dein Wohl!

b. a group of friends? b. Auf euer Wohl!

c. a teacher? c. Auf Ihr Wohl!

How would those persons respond?
Prost!; Danke, gleichfalls!; Zum Wohl!

ERSTE STUFE
ASKING FOR, MAKING, AND RESPONDING TO SUGGESTIONS

Würdest du gern mal ...?
  Wouldn't you like to...?
Wie wär's mit ...?   *How about...?*
Ich bin dafür, daß ...   *I prefer that ...*

Nein, ich würde am liebsten ...
  No, I would rather...
Das wär' nicht schlecht.   *That wouldn't be bad.*

TALKING ABOUT CULTURAL EVENTS

die Operette, -n   *operetta*
das Schauspiel, -e   *play*
das Theaterstück, -e   *play*

das Ballett, -e   *ballet*
das Musical, -s   *musical*
die Stadtrundfahrt, -en   *city tour*
das Baudenkmal, ¨er   *monument*
die Synagoge, -n   *synagogue*
der Ausflug, ¨e   *excursion*
der Anschlag, ¨e   *announcement*
würde   *would*
  du würdest
  er/sie/es würde

ZWEITE STUFE
EXPRESSING HEARSAY

Ich habe gehört, daß ...   *I heard that...*
Man hat mir gesagt, daß ...   *Someone told me that...*
Der Fisch soll prima sein.   *The fish is supposed to be great.*

DESCRIBING INTERNATIONAL FOODS

chinesisch   *Chinese*
mediterran   *Mediterranean*
ägyptisch   *Egyptian*
italienisch   *Italian*
französisch   *French*
griechisch   *Greek*
indisch   *(Asian) Indian*
mexikanisch   *Mexican*

russisch   *Russian*
spanisch   *Spanish*
türkisch   *Turkish*
ausländisch   *foreign*

TALKING ABOUT GERMAN AND INTERNATIONAL FOODS

die Köstlichkeit, -en   *delicacy*
die Delikatesse, -n   *delicacy*
die Peking Ente, -n   *Peking duck*
die Mastente, -n   *fattened duck*
das Schisch-Kebab   *shish kebab*
der Hummer, -   *lobster*
die Auster, -n   *oyster*
die Krabbe, -n   *crab*
der Lachs, -e   *salmon*
gut bürgerliche Küche   *good home-cooked cuisine*
die Küche   *cuisine*

der Schinken   *ham*
das Pfannengericht, -e   *pan-cooked entrée*
der Braten, -   *roast*
der Rotkohl   *red cabbage*
der Kloß, ¨e   *dumpling*
der Knoblauch   *garlic*
Rote Grütze   *red berry dessert*

WAYS TO DESCRIBE FOOD

deftig   *robust*
herzhaft   *hearty*
roh   *raw*
mariniert   *marinated*
würzig   *spicy*
scharf   *spicy, hot*
mild   *mild*
gebraten   *fried*
gegrillt   *grilled*
geräuchert   *smoked*

DRITTE STUFE
ORDERING IN A RESTAURANT

Bringen Sie mir bitte ...   *Please bring me...*
Ich hätte gern ...   *I would like...*

ORDERING FROM FOOD CATEGORIES

die Vorspeise, -n   *appetizer*
die Beilage, -n   *side dish*
das Hauptgericht, -e   *main dish*
die Nachspeise, -n   *dessert*
das Getränk, -e   *drink*

MORE GERMAN SPECIALTIES

das Schweinerückensteak, -s   *pork loin steak*
das Wiener Schnitzel, -   *veal cutlet*
das Seebarschfilet, -s   *filet of perch*
die Kroketten (pl)   *potato croquettes*
die Bratkartoffeln (pl)   *fried potatoes*
das gefüllte Ei, -er   *deviled egg*
das Spezi, -s   *mix of cola and lime soda*

EXPRESSING GOOD WISHES

Zum Wohl!   *To your health!*
Auf dein/Ihr/euer Wohl!   *To your health!*
Prost!   *Cheers!*
Guten Appetit!   *Bon appétit!*
Mahlzeit!   *Bon appétit!*
Danke! Dir/Ihnen auch!   *Thank you! The same to you!*
Danke, gleichfalls!   *Thank you and the same to you!*

Kapitel 12: Die Reinickendorfer Clique *Wiederholungskapitel*

CHAPTER OVERVIEW

Los geht's! *pp. 284-286*	Echt toll, Ismar! *p. 284*		*Video Guide*

	REVIEW OF FUNCTIONS	**REVIEW OF GRAMMAR**	**CULTURE**
Erste Stufe *pp. 288-292*	• Reporting past events, *p. 290* • Asking for, making, and responding to suggestions, *p. 291*	• The past tense, *p. 289* • Two-way prepositions, *pp. 291, 292* • The verb **sollen**, *p. 291* • The **würde**-forms, *p. 291*	• **Landeskunde: Welche aus- ländische Küche hast du gern?** *p. 287* • German vacation habits, *p. 288* • Report on a popular vacation resort, *p. 288*
Zweite Stufe *pp. 293-296*	• Ordering food, expressing hearsay and regret, *p. 295* • Persuading and dissuad- ing, *p. 296*	The command forms of strong verbs, *p. 296*	**Ein wenig Landeskunde:** Etiquette in German restaurants, *p. 295*
Dritte Stufe *pp. 297-301*	• Asking for and giving advice, *p. 299* • Expressing preference, *p. 299* • Expressing interest, disin- terest, and indifference, *p. 300*	• Adjective endings, *p. 297* • More adjective endings, *p. 299* • Comparative adjectives, *p. 300*	Franziska van Almsick, *p. 297*

Zum Lesen *pp. 302-303*	Nach dem Krieg Reading Strategy: Note-taking		

Review *pp. 304-305*	• **Kann ich's wirklich?** *p. 304* • **Wortschatz,** *p. 305*		

Assessment Options Final Exam, *Assessment Guide* *Audiocassette* 8 B	**Stufe Quizzes** • *Chapter Resources,* Book 4 **Erste Stufe,** Quiz 12-1 **Zweite Stufe,** Quiz 12-2 **Dritte Stufe,** Quiz 12-3 • *Assessment Items, Audiocassette* 8 B		**Kapitel 12 Chapter Test** • *Chapter Resources,* Book 4 • *Assessment Guide,* Speaking Test • *Assessment Items, Audiocassette* 8 B **Test Generator, Kapitel 12**

Chapter Overview

Video Program **OR**
Expanded Video Program, Videocassette 4

Textbook Audiocassette 6 B

RESOURCES Print	RESOURCES Audiovisual

Textbook Audiocassette 6 B

Practice and Activity Book
Chapter Resources, Book 4
- Additional Listening Activities 12-1, 12-2.........................*Additional Listening Activities, Audiocassette* 10 B
- Student Response Forms
- Realia 12-1
- Situation Card 12-1
- Teaching Transparency Master 12-1.........................*Teaching Transparency* 12-1
- Quiz 12-1 ....*Assessment Items, Audiocassette* 8 B

Video Guide ....*Video Program/Expanded Video Program,* Videocassette 4

Textbook Audiocassette 6 B

Practice and Activity Book
Chapter Resources, Book 4
- Communicative Activity 12-1
- Additional Listening Activities 12-3, 12-4.........................*Additional Listening Activities, Audiocassette* 10 B
- Student Response Forms
- Realia 12-2
- Situation Card 12-2
- Quiz 12-2 ....*Assessment Items, Audiocassette* 8 B

Textbook Audiocassette 6 B

Practice and Activity Book
Chapter Resources, Book 4
- Communicative Activity 12-2
- Additional Listening Activities 12-5, 12-6.........................*Additional Listening Activities, Audiocassette* 10 B
- Student Response Forms
- Realia 12-3
- Situation Card 12-3
- Teaching Transparency Master 12-2.........................*Teaching Transparency* 12-2
- Quiz 12-3 ....*Assessment Items, Audiocassette* 8 B

Video Guide...*Video Program/Expanded Video Program,* Videocassette 4

Alternative Assessment
- Performance Assessment
Teacher's Edition
  Erste Stufe, p. 281K
  Zweite Stufe, p. 281M
  Dritte Stufe, p. 281P
- Portfolio Assessment
  Written: **Zweite Stufe,** Activity 18, *Pupil's Edition,* p. 294; *Assessment Guide* p. 25
  Oral: **Zweite Stufe,** Activity 18, *Pupil's Edition,* p. 294; *Assessment Guide* p. 25
- **Notizbuch,** *Pupil's Edition,* p. 292; *Practice and Activity Book,* p. 156

Kapitel 12: Die Reinickendorfer Clique
Textbook Listening Activities Scripts

Erste Stufe

Activity 6, *p. 289*

MIRIAM Ach, war die Reise fantastisch! Die fünf Tage sind so schnell vergangen. Das war wirklich ein toller Geheimtip von meiner Tante. Das nächste Mal müssen wir unbedingt länger dort bleiben. Ich hab' echt nicht gewußt, daß Schweden so ein tolles Land ist. Das Meer, der Strand, ach ja, und die steilen Klippen direkt am Wasser …

GABI Ja, stimmt! Schweden hat mir auch wahnsinnig gut gefallen. Die Ostsee ist viel sauberer an den skandinavischen Küsten als hier bei uns. Ich wäre so gern dort segeln gegangen. Aber, naja, das Segelboot, das wir gemietet hatten, war halt zu klein für uns alle.

MIRIAM Ach, Gabi, es war doch nicht so schlimm. Der Lars und du, ihr seid dann doch zu der kleinen Insel hingeschwommen. Das war doch gar nicht so weit. Dafür brauchte man nun wirklich extra kein Boot mieten, um dahin zu kommen.

GABI Ja, es war zwar nicht weit, aber das Wasser war doch ziemlich kalt! Und außerdem gehe ich nun mal gern segeln. Du hast echt Glück gehabt, daß du noch einen Platz im Boot bekommen hast! Aber, naja, ist ja jetzt auch egal. Warum bist du eigentlich keinmal mit uns schwimmen gegangen?

MIRIAM Tja, ich war halt lieber auf dem Tennisplatz. Das macht mir mehr Spaß als schwimmen zu gehen. Und gewandert bin ich auch einmal, weißt du, zusammen mit den Engländern, die auch in unserer Pension waren.

GABI Ach, das wußte ich gar nicht. Da wär' ich aber auch gern mitgekommen. Warum hast du denn nichts gesagt?

MIRIAM Ganz einfach! Du warst ja nie da, sondern hast nur den ganzen Tag am Strand gelegen. Ach, schau mal! Jetzt sind wir an der Reihe! Komm, gib mir auch dein schwedisches Geld, damit wir gleich alles zusammen umtauschen können.

Answers to Activity 6

Sie haben eine Reise nach Schweden unternommen; Miriam hat am meisten Spaß gehabt; Sie tauschen ihr schwedisches Geld um.

Activity 10, *p. 291*

MUTTER Also, Markus und Annette, Vati und ich haben uns gestern abend mal die Urlaubsbilder vom letzten Jahr angesehen. Vati meint, daß es schön wäre, wieder in die Schweiz zu fahren …

MARKUS Oh nein, nicht schon wieder!

ANNETTE Ja, ich finde, der Markus hat recht. Nur weil ihr gern in den Bergen wandern geht, heißt das noch lange nicht, daß wir das auch gern machen! Können wir nicht mal was anderes machen?

VATER Also, dann sagt doch mal, wohin ihr gern fahren möchtet!

ANNETTE Nach Griechenland!

VATER Also, ich weiß nicht. Wir fahren doch jedes Jahr nach Interlaken in die Schweiz, und jedes Mal verbringen wir eine herrliche Zeit in den Bergen und am See. Dieses Jahr wird es auch nicht anders sein.

MARKUS Ja eben! Jedes Jahr das gleiche! Ich bin echt dafür, daß wir mal woanders hinfahren. In Griechenland gibt es tolle Strände, klares blaues Wasser … ideal zum Surfen. Das würd' ich gern mal machen! Wir könnten doch auf einer Insel Urlaub machen, auf Kreta zum Beispiel!

ANNETTE   Ja, oder auf Rhodos! Eine Insel mit wahnsinnig viel Kultur und wunderschönen alten Tempelruinen. Ach, das wäre schön, wenn ich die mal besichtigen könnte. In unserem Geschichtsbuch sind sie alle abgebildet! Und Vati, außerdem gibt es in Griechenland auch Berge, wenn du unbedingt wandern willst!

VATER   Hmm! Also, ich befürchte, daß mir in Griechenland das Essen bestimmt nicht schmecken wird. Außerdem spricht keiner von uns Griechisch! Was meinst du denn dazu, Helga?

MUTTER   Ja also, Günther, ich finde, die Kinder haben recht! Wir fahren immer nur in die Schweiz! Es wird langsam mal Zeit, daß wir uns was anderes anschauen!

VATER   Und was schlägst du vor?

MUTTER   Wie wäre es mit ... Afrika? Eine richtig abenteuerliche Safari in Kenia, das ist mein Traum!

ANNETTE   Ui, Mutti, was für eine super Idee!

VATER   Ja, wenn das so ist, dann gehe ich morgen mal ins Reisebüro und hole uns die neuesten Sommerkataloge für Kenia und Griechenland.

MARKUS   Prima, Vati! Ich komm' mit!

Answers to Activity 10

Vater: Interlaken, Schweiz; wandert gern in den Bergen und am See
Markus: Kreta, Griechenland; will an den Strand und im Meer surfen
Annette: Rhodos, Griechenland; interessiert sich für Kultur und die Tempelruinen
Mutter: Kenia, Afrika; möchte auf eine abenteuerliche Safari

Zweite Stufe
Activity 19, *p. 295*

KARSTEN   Find' ich echt super von dir, Jutta, daß du mich heute abend einlädst! Guck dir nur mal diese Speisekarte an! Die haben hier echt alles Mögliche! Du, das meiste kenn' ich überhaupt nicht.

JUTTA   Ja, genau deswegen hab' ich dieses Restaurant ja ausgesucht. Ich möchte gern mal was völlig Neues ausprobieren. Schau mal, Karsten, die Gerichte auf der Karte sind alle aus Ländern am Mittelmeer. Griechenland, Türkei, Italien, Spanien und sogar Portugal!

KARSTEN   Aha! Jetzt weiß ich auch, warum das Restaurant „Mediterraneo" heißt!

KELLNER   Guten Abend! Haben Sie schon etwas ausgewählt?

KARSTEN   Wir sind gerade dabei! Ich möchte gerne wissen, was Mousaka ist.

KELLNER   Mousaka ist unser beliebtestes griechisches Gericht. Es besteht aus Kartoffeln und Auberginen und wird im Ofen mit Käse überbacken. Sehr zu empfehlen!

JUTTA   Und was ist Calzone?

KELLNER   Calzone ist eine zusammengeklappte Pizza mit verschiedenen Füllungen, ganz nach Ihrem Geschmack!

JUTTA   Ach so! So ähnlich wie 'ne Pizza ... also, nee, was Italienisches esse ich eigentlich öfters, also Pizza und Spaghetti und so ... Heute möchte ich lieber etwas anderes ausprobieren. Was ist denn alles in der Paella drin?

KELLNER   Paella ist ein köstliches spanisches Reisgericht aus der Pfanne. Es wird mit Hähnchen, Krabben, Muscheln und Gemüse zubereitet.

JUTTA   Mhm! Das hört sich lecker an. Ich mag Reis sehr gern. Also, ich nehme dann die Paella. Und du, Karsten, was nimmst du?

KARSTEN   Ich probiere lieber mal die Mousaka. Was Griechisches hab' ich noch nie gegessen!

KELLNER   Und was hätten Sie gern zu trinken?

JUTTA   Ein Mineralwasser für mich, bitte.

KARSTEN   Und ich nehme eine Limo.

KELLNER   Kommt sofort!

SCRIPTS

SCRIPTS

Answers to Activity 19

Jutta: Paella, spanisches Gericht; Sie mag Reis.
Karsten: Mousaka, griechisches Gericht; Er hat
noch nie was Griechisches gegessen.

Dritte Stufe
Activity 24, p. 298

ROLAND Also, heut' abend ziehe ich ein echt
klassisches Outfit an, das heißt: weiße
Shorts, weißes T-Shirt, weiße Socken
und ... ach so, meine Schuhe, die sind
natürlich auch weiß. Halt! Ich zieh'
auch noch ein neues Stirnband an. Es
ist total bunt und sieht völlig flippig
aus! Das gibt einen tollen Kontrast zum
traditionellen Weiß! Das Stirnband hat
mir die Silke geschenkt, um mir Glück
zu wünschen für das Doppel heute
abend mit Klaus, Andreas und Ralf.

KATJA Ich ziehe eine saloppe Hose, bequeme
Schuhe und eine kurzärmelige
Baumwollbluse an. Ja, ach so, einen
Pulli nehm' ich halt auch noch mit,
denn es wird manchmal ganz schön
kalt im Flugzeug. Den Rest meiner
Klamotten hab' ich schon in den Koffer
gepackt. Alles nur leichte Sommer-
sachen, genau richtig für den Strand.

AXEL Meine Schwester will, daß ich einen
schwarzen Smoking anziehe, mit
weißem Hemd und auch noch 'ne
passende Weste dazu! Also, echt schick
und elegant. Ist eigentlich überhaupt
nicht mein Stil, aber es ist nun mal
ein ganz besonderer Tag für meine
Schwester und ihren zukünftigen Mann!
Da trag' ich dann halt ausnahmsweise
mal diese edlen Klamotten!

BÄRBEL Zuerst wollte ich ja mein neues gepunktetes Kleid anziehen, aber dann hat mir
der Martin erzählt, daß die ganze Sache
draußen im Garten stattfindet! Also, das
Barbecue und das Buffet, alles draußen
auf der Terrasse! Ja, da ziehe ich lieber
meine Jeans an und meine gestreifte
Bluse, die mit den kurzen Ärmeln. Ach
so, meine Wildlederjacke nehm' ich
auch noch mit, falls es dann später kalt
wird, wenn der Martin dann um Mitter-
nacht seine Geschenke aufmacht.

Answers to Activity 24

Roland: zum Tennis; Katja: in die Ferien;
Axel: zur Hochzeit seiner Schwester; Bärbel:
zur Geburtstagsfete von Martin

Kapitel 12: Die Reinickendorfer Clique
Projects and Games

PROJECT

Students will compile and design a **Reiseführer** *for a city which has not been previously studied in Levels 1 or 2. Students may choose a city in Germany, Austria, Switzerland, or Liechtenstein.*

Outline

This project should be started as soon as you begin Chapter 12. Students can work in pairs or individually. The project should be written completely in German and should include the following:
- a brief history of the city;
- an overview of interesting and noteworthy landmarks, including background information;
- typical food and drinks served in this city, including some popular restaurants;
- other significant information that would be of interest to the class.

Materials Students may need poster board, glue or masking tape, scissors, markers, and travel brochures.

Suggested Sequence

1. Before students begin working on their project, have them look at the Chapter Opener on p. 282. Point out the two guidebooks. Discuss the title *Erlebnis Berlin.*
2. Once students have decided on a city they would like to research, they should begin to gather materials for their **Reiseführer** in the library.
3. Students prepare an outline of their report to show you for suggestions and approval.
4. Students begin their final draft using all gathered information, including visuals.
5. Students give a short presentation on the city they chose for their **Reiseführer.**

Grading the Project

Suggested point distribution (total = 100 points)
Appearance/originality	25
Completion of assignment requirements	25
Correct language usage	25
Oral presentation	25

♜ GAMES

Anziehwettbewerb

Play this game to review the clothing vocabulary from this and previous chapters.

Preparation Prepare for this game by filling two bags with clothing articles you would like to review. Each bag should have the same number of clothing items, but the items need not be identical.

Procedure Divide the class into two teams and place the two bags at the front of the classroom. A member of each team comes to the front of the class. When you give the signal, each of the two students should put on all of the clothing in his or her bag while the rest of the team writes down the clothing items in the order he or she puts them on. The first team that writes down all clothing items correctly wins.

Globus

This game will help students review names of countries, nationalities, adjective endings, and international dishes.

Preparation Bring a revolving globe to class on the day you plan to play this game.

Procedure Divide the class into two teams and ask one member of each team to come up to the front. Gently spin the globe. Stop the globe with your finger and immediately call out the country that your finger has landed on. (Example: **Italien**) The two students try to come up with a traditional dish from that country. (Example: **Ein italienisches Gericht ist Fettucine.**) The first student to correctly name an ethnic dish wins a point for his or her team.

Kapitel 12: Die Reinickendorfer Clique
Lesson Plans, pages 282-305

Using the Chapter Opener, pp. 282-283

Motivating Activity

Prior to the activity, set up your classroom to look like a travel agency. Write **REISEBÜRO WALTER** (or use your own last name) on the board, along with instructions such as **Nehmen Sie sich bitte eine Nummer! Man wird Ihnen schnellstens behilflich sein.** Set up the chairs along the walls. As students enter the classroom, point to the board to suggest that they are not sitting in a classroom but are waiting to speak to a travel agent. You play the role of the travel agent. Call on the students by number and ask each a few questions to help them plan their upcoming summer vacation.

Geography Connection

① Ask students to look at a map of Germany and have them think of several seaside resorts where this photo could have been taken. (Examples: Kiel, Travemünde, Sylt)

Building on Previous Skills

① Ask students for suggestions about activities that they associate with this picture. (Examples: **schwimmen, baden, sich sonnen, Ball spielen**)

Thinking Critically

Drawing Inferences Have students talk about what they would like to do for their summer vacation. Give students a few minutes to jot down some notes, then call on individual students and have them tell about their plans.

 ### For Individual Needs

Challenge After students have shared their plans for summer vacation with the class, have them get into pairs. Using their notes from the previous activity, students should try to persuade their partners to join them on their trips.

Teaching Suggestions

③ Have students report on what they typically eat and drink when they go to a friend's house for a party. Does everybody bring something to help out the host or hostess?

③ If you plan to have an end-of-year party with your German class or the German club, have students make suggestions about what they would like to do and what everybody should bring to eat and drink.

③ Have students imagine that they are planning an end-of-year get-together with their friends. They have decided to go out to eat, but would like to try a new place. Have students make suggestions about local restaurants based on what they have heard about them from other people.

Focusing on Outcomes

To get students to focus on the chapter objectives, ask them why they are looking forward to their summer vacation and how they plan to spend their time off. Then have students preview the learning outcomes listed on p. 283. **NOTE:** Each of these outcomes is modeled and evaluated in **Kann ich's wirklich?** on p. 304.

Teaching Los geht's!
pp. 284-286

Resources for Los geht's!

- *Video Program* **OR**
  Expanded Video Program, Videocassette 4
- *Textbook Audiocassette* 6 B
- *Practice and Activity Book*

▶ *pages 284-285*

Video Synopsis

In this segment of the video, Andreas and Astrid have invited some friends over for a party at their house. The student outcomes listed on p. 283 are modeled in the video: reporting past events, asking for, making, and responding to suggestions, ordering food, expressing hearsay and regret, persuading and dissuading, asking for and giving advice, expressing preference, and expressing interest, disinterest and indifference.

Motivating Activity

As an advance organizer for the storyline of the **Foto-Roman,** ask students what they usually talk about when they get together with their friends for a party.

Teaching Suggestion

After students have read and watched or listened to the **Foto-Roman,** ask them if they can determine from the context what the expression **Schwirr ab!** in Frame 3 could mean. *(Get lost, take a hike!)*

For Individual Needs

Visual Learners After watching the video and looking at the frames in the book, ask students to list the types of foods that the friends are going to have at their party.

Background Information

In Frame 5 Andreas is telling his friends that he will **den Vierer machen.** Tell students that he is referring to the moped license he is planning to get.

Thinking Critically

Comparing and Contrasting Ask students about the different classes of licenses that are required in the United States to operate various modes of transportation.

▶ *page 286*

Group Work

1 Ask students to work in groups of three as they answer Questions 1-10. Call on several groups to have them read their answers to the rest of the class.

For Individual Needs

2 Auditory Learners Instead of rereading the **Foto-Roman,** you might want to replay the video segment and have students listen for the four expressions. Students can call out the number (1-4) when they hear the corresponding expression.

3 Challenge Have students come up with an alternative coordinating or subordinating clause to complete each sentence.

Closure

Play the video of the **Foto-Roman** without sound. Have students take turns playing the roles of the five German teenagers ad-libbing the storyline as best they can.

▶ *page 287*

PRESENTATION: Landeskunde

Teacher Note

The **Landeskunde** interviews are recorded on audiocassette and videocassette.

Thinking Critically

Drawing Inferences Ask students to name some of their favorite and least favorite ethnic foods. Which of those would they most likely recommend to the rest of the class to try?

Teaching Suggestion

You might want to introduce this additional vocabulary to help students with the four interviews.

dazugehören *to belong to*
schmackhaft *tasty*
variationsreich *diverse*
drin=darin *in it*
ab und zu *now and then*

Building on Previous Skills

Ask students if they can recall some of the **beliebte Gerichte** from the Location Openers in this book from Stuttgart, Hamburg, and Berlin.

Teaching Suggestion

Take a survey in your class to find out the most popular ethnic food among your students. Ask students what ethnic foods they like and why they like them. Is their taste similar to that of the German teenagers?

 For Individual Needs

Challenge Ask students to explain the difference between the following groups of words:
die Gaststätte/die Imbißstube/das Restaurant/ der Biergarten/das Café

Teacher Note

Mention to your students that the **Landeskunde** will also be included in Quiz 12-1 given at the end of the **Erste Stufe.**

Teaching Erste Stufe, pp. 288-292

Resources for Erste Stufe

Practice and Activity Book
Chapter Resources, Book 4
• Additional Listening Activities 12-1, 12-2
• Student Response Forms
• Realia 12-1
• Situation Card 12-1
• Teaching Transparency Master 12-1
• Quiz 12-1
Audiocassette Program
• *Textbook Audiocassette* 6 B
• *Additional Listening Activities, Audiocassette* 10 B
• *Assessment Items, Audiocassette* 10 B
Video Program or *Expanded Video Program*

▶ **page 288**

MOTIVATE
Teaching Suggestion

As a warm-up activity, give a slip of paper to each student as he or she enters the classroom. Each slip of paper should have the name of a domestic or foreign travel destination on it. Students should use the destination on their paper to suggest to their neighbor where he or she should go for his or her next vacation.

TEACH
Teaching Suggestion

Remind students to use the various reading skills they have been taught throughout the school year as they work through this reading selection.

Europa auf Reisen
Ausgaben bei Auslandsreisen 1990 in Milliarden Dollar

► *page 289*

Group Work

5 Divide your class into five groups and assign each group two questions. Group members should share the responsibility of reading the text and helping each other as needed. One member of each group assumes the responsibility for writing down the responses to the questions the group has been assigned. When students are finished, call on groups to share their responses with the rest of the class.

Background Information

Ulrike Meifarth was one of Germany's best high-jumpers. She won the gold medal at the age of 16 in the 1972 Olympic Games in Munich. Guido Kratschmer and Jürgen Hingsen were world-class decathlon athletes in the 1980s.

Physical Education Connection

Ask students to name the ten events that make up a decathlon. (100-meter run, 400-meter run, 1500-meter run, 110-meter high hurdles, javelin throw, discus throw, shot put, pole vault, high jump, long jump)

PRESENTATION: Wortschatz

If possible, bring pictures that show the expressions featured in this vocabulary box. Introduce the vocabulary by holding up the pictures as you pronounce the words.

Geography Connection

Ask students to give an example of a geographic location for each of the five pictures.

 For Individual Needs

6 A Slower Pace After students have listened to the activity once, provide them with a copy of the listening script. Have them underline all verb forms and expressions that indicate the past tense.

► *page 290*

PRESENTATION: So sagt man das!

Ask students to read this excerpt and then make a list of all the verb phrases. There is one verb that uses **sein** as an auxiliary. Did students find it? (**sind gewandert**)

Geography Connection

7 Before students begin with the activity, have them locate the Canary Islands on a map.

For Additional Practice

7 Once students have compiled responses to Questions a-h, ask each group to compose a cohesive written summary of Astrid's and Andreas' vacation using the past tense.

For Individual Needs

8 Challenge Ask students to assume the role of a reporter for travel brochures and magazines. How would a favorable review of *La Santa* sound? Have students write a review from a travel agent's point of view.

► *page 291*

Teaching Suggestion

9 Ask students to retell the events in a postcard to their best friend back home. They should emphasize all the wonderful things they did in *La Santa*.

PRESENTATION: So sagt man das!

Review these expressions with students. Then have students look back at the plans of *La Santa* on p. 290. Pairs of students should take turns making and responding to a least five suggestions based on the activities and facilities that are available there.

ERSTE STUFE

For Individual Needs

11 Visual Learners Before students begin working with their partners, you may want to review the sports that are featured in this activity. Enlarge each symbol to a size that can be seen by each student. Show each symbol to the class and ask for the name of the sport it represents.

Teacher Note

11 The sports and activities represented by the symbols are as follows:

1. Reiten	7. Basketball	13. Fechten
2. Volleyball	8. Skilaufen	14. Tennis
3. Handball	9. Langlauf	15. Golf
4. Fußball	10. Diskuswerfen	16. Wasserski
5. Eishockey	11. Speerwerfen	17. Segeln
6. Hockey	12. Kugelstoßen	18. Schach

▶ *page 292*

Building on Previous Skills

12 To have students review what they have learned about various German cities and sights, have them work from a list of travel destinations that you have compiled. Use the Location Openers on pp. 1, 78, 154, and 230 for suggestions.

Teaching Suggestion

14 To review adverbial expressions, ask students to use some of the following time adverbs in their reports.

Examples:

regelmäßig	fast nie
häufig	manchmal
sehr oft	meistens

For Additional Practice

15 To provide students with additional practice in narrating past events, call on several students and ask them to tell the rest of the class what their partner did on his or her last vacation. Remind students to use third person pronoun forms.

Example:

Michael hat gesagt, daß er und seine Familie letztes Jahr ...

CLOSE
Teaching Suggestion

Ask students to complete the following statement. **Wenn ihr im kommenden Sommer nach La Santa (Berlin, Stuttgart, Hamburg) fahrt, vergeßt nicht, ...**

Focusing on Outcomes

Refer students back to the learning outcomes listed on p. 283. They should recognize that they now know how to report past events, and ask for, make, and respond to suggestions.

ASSESS

- **Performance Assessment** Advise students that they have been asked to take three to five photos in *La Santa* for a brochure advertising the resort. What three subjects would students suggest taking photos of and why?

- Quiz 12-1, *Chapter Resources*, Book 4

*T*eaching Zweite Stufe, *pp. 293–296*

Resources for Zweite Stufe

Practice and Activity Book
Chapter Resources, Book 4
- Communicative Activity 12-1
- Additional Listening Activities 12-3, 12-4
- Student Response Forms
- Realia 12-2
- Situation Card 12-2
- Quiz 12-2

Audiocassette Program
- *Textbook Audiocassette* 6 B
- *Additional Listening Activities, Audiocassette* 10 B
- *Assessment Items, Audiocassette* 8 B

▶ **page 293**

MOTIVATE

Teaching Suggestion

Ask students what foods come to mind that start with the following letters: **F, M, K, S, E.** You can use different letters as needed.

TEACH

 ### For Individual Needs

Tactile Learners Some students might want to prepare Andreas' spaghetti recipe at home. Have them follow up by writing a brief review of his recipe using the vocabulary on p. 270 (Chapter 11) to describe how the dish tasted.

Teaching Suggestion

Once students have read the article on p. 293, help them discover that the text is written in the narrative past. Next, have students identify at least five verbs in the narrative past and ask them to give the corresponding present tense forms for each.

▶ **page 294**

PRESENTATION: Wortschatz

Teach the vocabulary of **internationale Gerichte** by asking students questions such as **Was für ein Gericht ist denn Fettucine?** Students should respond with the appropriate category: **Fettucine ist ein italienisches Gericht.**

Teacher Note

These are active vocabulary words which do not appear in the vocabulary list at the end of the chapter because their English names are the same as their German names. However, you might want to give students their genders.
die Mousaka
die Ćevapčići *(pl)*
die Paella
das/der Couscous (also **Kuskus**)
die Fettucine *(pl)*
die Crêpes Suzette *(pl)*
der Taco
das Steak
das Wiener Schnitzel

For Additional Practice

17 To review the dative preposition in adjective endings and the impersonal pronoun **man,** have students ask each other where one could find the ethnic dishes listed. Students should answer with statements such as **Man kann Tacos in ein*em* mexikanisch*en* Restaurant essen.**

Portfolio Assessment

18 You might want to suggest this activity as a written and oral portfolio item for your students. See *Assessment Guide,* p. 25.

▶ **page 295**

PRESENTATION: So sagt man das!

To practice the expressions in this function box, ask pairs of students to role-play a restaurant scene using the vocabulary from the **Wortschatz** box on p. 294. One partner should play the role of the waiter while the other partner plays the customer.

ZWEITE STUFE

 For Individual Needs

19 Visual Learners Try to find pictures in food magazines to represent each of the dishes mentioned. Display the pictures in random order at the front of the class. Allow students to look at the pictures as they listen to the audiocassette.

Thinking Critically

Drawing Inferences After students have read the **Ein wenig Landeskunde** box, ask them in what type of restaurant one would typically find a **Stammtisch**. (**Gaststätte, Lokal**) Once students understand the meaning of **Stammtisch**, ask them to infer the meaning of other related nouns such as **Stammkunde** and **Stammlokal**. Encourage students to give a definition or description in German.

▶ *page 296*

PRESENTATION: So sagt man das!

To practice the functions in this box, give each student a slip of paper and have them write the name of a local restaurant, diner, cafeteria, or fast food chain on it. Put all the slips in a hat and have each student take one. Call on students to persuade someone else in the class to eat at the place written on their slip of paper. The other students should respond favorably or unfavorably depending on their own opinions of the food offered at that particular establishment. Use the same slips of paper to have students dissuade each other to go there or to eat a certain type of food there.

Teaching Suggestion

21 If you feel students also need writing practice, you could have them convey their suggestions in the form of a letter to the cousin. This could be assigned as written homework.

Language Note

22 The German language has a saying related to hunger: **Ich habe einen Bärenhunger.** *(I'm as hungry as a bear.)*

Thinking Critically

22 Comparing and Contrasting Ask students if they know any English sayings related to being hungry.

Example: *I am so hungry I could eat a horse.*

Reteaching: Command Forms

To reteach various command forms, ask students to look back at the plan of *La Santa* (or the Location Opener for Berlin) and come up with suggestions of what to do there, following the example below. **Wenn du Berlin besuchst, iß im Café Kranzler am Kurfürstendamm!**

CLOSE

Game

Play the game *Tic-Tac-Toe*. In each of the nine squares of the *Tic-Tac-Toe* grid, write an adjective that refers to a nationality. Divide the class into teams. In order to get an X or O in a square, team members must come up with a sentence using the adjective in that square. The first team to get three in a row wins.

französisch	italienisch	mexikanisch
spanisch	chinesisch	deutsch
~~griechisch~~	(bosnisch)	russisch

X: Mousaka ist ein griechisches Gericht.
O: Cevapcici ist ein bosnisches Gericht.

Focusing on Outcomes

Refer students back to the learning outcomes listed on p. 283. They should recognize that they now know how to order food, express hearsay and regret, and to persuade and dissuade.

ASSESS

• **Performance Assessment** Conduct a survey addressing the functions introduced in this **Stufe**. Ask individual students how they would persuade somebody to eat at their favorite restaurant despite that person's dislike for the food.

• Quiz 12-2, *Chapter Resources*, Book 4

Teaching Dritte Stufe,
pp. 297-301

Resources for Dritte Stufe

▶ **page 297**

MOTIVATE
Teaching Suggestion
Ask students to list as many German-speaking athletes (or athletes from other countries) as they can think of. Also have them say which sport the athlete participates in. (Examples: Katharina Witt—**Eiskunstlauf**, Ulrike Meifarth—**Hochsprung**, Boris Becker—**Tennis**, Steffi Graf—**Tennis**, Guido Kratschmer— **Zehnkampf**, Franz Beckenbauer—**Fußball**)

TEACH
Teaching Suggestion
Instead of having students use their books to work on the reading selection „**Ich bin kein Wunderkind!**" photocopy the text and white out a number of words to create a **Lückentext.** Distribute copies of the skeletal text to students, then write the missing words in random order on a transparency or on the board. Give students three to five minutes to read through the **Lückentext** and complete it by filling in the corresponding words from the transparency. Have students check their text against the article on p. 297.

Teacher Note
Swimmer Franziska van Almsick is from Berlin. She is the European Champion and holds the world record in short distance swimming. In 1993, she was voted "Athlete of the Year" by the world association of sports journalists. They chose her over track and field World Champion Wang Junxia and tennis player Steffi Graf.

❖ For Individual Needs
23 Challenge Ask students to use their answers to the four questions as the basis for a summary of this article. The summary can be done orally or in writing.

Language Note
The German language has a colloquial expression referring to having fun which is used in this article. The expression is **Jux machen** or **herumjuxen.**

▶ **page 298**

PRESENTATION: Wortschatz
After introducing the new expressions, provide each student or pair with a picture of a person cut out of a magazine or catalog. Ask each student to study the outfit the person is wearing and then describe it to the rest of the class. In addition, each student should come up with one piece of advice for the person pictured on how the outfit or his or her appearance could be improved.

❖ For Individual Needs
24 A Slower Pace As an advance organizer for the listening activity, ask students to go over the list of occasions and suggest one outfit for each.

DRITTE STUFE

For Additional Practice

25 To provide students with further practice, ask them to describe an outfit a parent would probably wear for a specific occasion.

▶ *page 299*

For Individual Needs

26 **Tactile Learners** Once students are seated with a partner, provide each pair with several colored markers, crayons, or pencils and two blank pieces of paper. As one student describes the clothing he or she likes to wear around the house, the other student should sketch it on the paper. After the student is done with the drawing, he or she should show it to his or her partner to see if it resembles the outfit described. Then students switch roles.

PRESENTATION: So sagt man das!

To review the expressions in the function box, bring several pieces of clothing to class (sweaters, shirts, slacks, jackets, scarves, hats, etc.). Ask students to give you advice on what to wear.

For Additional Practice

27 Have students continue practicing the functions of asking and giving advice by changing the occasion. Suggest occasions such as **Strandfete,** **Maskenball,** or **das Hochzeitsjubiläum der Eltern.** Students should give additional suggestions for appropriate outfits.

PRESENTATION: So sagt man das!

Prior to reviewing these functions, compile a list of contrasting topics. Review the expressions in the function box before students start working in pairs. They should use the examples from a list which you have prepared on a transparency or a handout. Examples are ethnic foods (**chinesisch** vs. **mexikanisch**), art (**moderne** vs. **traditionelle Kunst**), and music (**Rock** vs. **klassische Musik**).

▶ *page 300*

For Individual Needs

28 **A Slower Pace** Before students begin with the activity, brainstorm with them all the different types of fabrics they have learned. Make a list of the fabrics on the board or on a transparency for students to use when describing their outfits. It might also help students to review colors and patterns before starting the activity.

PRESENTATION: So sagt man das!

Ask students to think of some typical questions a salesperson in the following stores might ask a customer to find out what he or she is looking for: **Buchhandlung, Schuhgeschäft, Geschenkwarenladen, Schreibwarenladen,** and **Musikgeschäft.** Once students have compiled a list of questions, have them come up with possible responses using expressions of interest, disinterest, and indifference when possible.

Teaching Suggestion

30 To expand this activity, students could prepare a skit using props such as clothing, accessories, and shoes. Encourage students to make an outline with their partner but to perform their skit without any notes.

▶ *page 301*

Cooperative Learning

31 Divide students into groups as suggested and have each group member take the role of a reader, writer, proofreader, discussion leader, or reporter. Since this is an extensive activity, you might want to break it into a two or three day assignment using some class time each day. Each day, groups work together to answer the questions, and the writer takes notes for the group. On the last day of the activity, the proofreader checks the assignment for accuracy. Once all groups have completed Questions a-j, they should continue with Activity 32 in which the reporter tells about his or her group's plans.

DRITTE STUFE

Reteaching: Vocabulary for Occasions and Clothing

Have a collection of magazine pictures on hand that show people dressed for different occasions. Hold up each picture and ask students to describe the outfit and determine for what occasion the outfit might be worn. Finally, have students express their preference for the outfit using one of the functions reviewed in the function box on p. 299.

CLOSE

 ### Total Physical Response

Prior to this activity you may want to ask the home economics teacher if you could use the mannequin that is often used in sewing classes to fit clothing. Also bring a bag of clothing and some accessories that represent all the clothing vocabulary students have learned so far. Call on students to come to the front of the class. Give them specific instructions on what to pick from the bag of clothing to dress the mannequin. Once the mannequin is completely dressed, ask students to give each other specific directions to undress the mannequin again.

Focusing on Outcomes

Refer students back to the learning outcomes listed on p. 283. They should recognize that they now know how to ask for and give advice, express preference, and express interest, disinterest, and indifference.

ASSESS

• **Performance Assessment** Ask students what kind of advice they would have for an exchange student who is unfamiliar with the clothing styles and customs of American teenagers. How would students advise this student to dress for the following occasions?
- dinner at the host family's home
- a field trip to the coast
- a hiking trip
- watching a football game

• Quiz 12-3, *Chapter Resources*, Book 4

Teaching Zum Lesen,
pp. 302-303

Reading Strategy

The targeted strategy in this reading is note-taking. Students should learn about this strategy before beginning Question 2.

PREREADING

Motivating Activity

Ask students the following questions. What kinds of sounds wake you up at night? How do you react when you are awakened? Have you ever gotten out of bed to go to the kitchen in the middle of the night? Were you hungry or just restless? Did you try to hide what you were doing? Why do you think someone might try to hide doing this?

Teaching Suggestion

Ask students to think about the words they would need to know in order to read a story involving the scenario you discussed in the Motivating Activity. Have them work in pairs to make a list of words they already know in German and a list in English of words they might need to know but don't already.

Thinking Critically

Drawing Inferences Tell students that the author of this story does not state the main point directly. Ask them what they need to do or look at to infer what the author is implying. (word choice and arrangement of ideas)

Literature Connection

Ask students to name the literary era that occurred during the lifetime of Wolfgang Borchert (1921-1947). (Expressionism)

Background Information

Wolfgang Borchert was a German poet and short-story writer. He was born on May 20, 1921 in Hamburg. He published newspaper articles while still in high school, then worked in a book store to support himself while studying drama. At age twenty he was drafted and sent to the eastern front, where he was twice arrested and imprisoned on suspicion of "malingering," and for making fun of the Nazis. He is known for portraying the devastation and absurdity of war. He died shortly after World War II of wounds he suffered during the war. Today he remains one of the most read and celebrated writers in German literature.

Teacher Note

Activity 1 is a prereading activity.

READING

History Connection

To help students gain a better understanding of the story, you may want to have them do some research about the time during which Borchert lived. Have students check their history books for relevant dates, political figures, and events that occurred during that time period.

 ## For Individual Needs

4 A Slower Pace To help students better understand the text, break it into sections and have them try to briefly summarize each section.

Teaching Suggestion

While students read the story, ask them to make notes of words or phrases they might want to know. If available, provide students with a German dictionary to look up the definitions of unknown words and phrases.

 ## For Individual Needs

Kinesthetic Learners After students have completed Activity 8, ask them to work with a partner to reenact this story based on what they have read. One student assumes the role of the husband, the other of the wife. Allow students time to review the sequence of events and plan for props. The following day, ask several pairs to role-play *Das Brot* in class. Encourage students to ad-lib their lines as best they can to allow for more spontaneity.

POST-READING

Teacher Note

Activity 9 is a post-reading task that will show whether students can apply what they have learned.

Closure

Ask students to come up with one question they would like to ask the male character and one question they would like to ask the female character in this story. Ask students to take a few moments to write down their questions, then read them aloud in class. Encourage others to come up with possible answers from both the man's and the woman's perspective.

Answers to Activity 1

The traditional German dinner, **das Abendbrot**, consists of bread and cold cuts. The title suggests simplicity, sparseness.

Answers to Activity 2

Summaries will vary; The story takes place in the kitchen (of a flat) at 2:30 A.M.; There are two characters: **sie** and **er** (no names are given).

Answers to Activity 3

1. g; 2. b; 3. f; 4. h; 5. a; 6. e; 7. c; 8. d

Answers to Activity 6

The noise must have come from outside; it must have been the wind against the gutter; He was lying to her.

Answers to Activity 7

She heard his chewing; She realized he was hungry, so the next night she gave him part of her portion of the bread.

Answers to Activity 8

The woman's (third person partially omniscient); The bread (or lack of it) was the source of the conflict, and it was also the resolution; He was hungry; They may have been poor for a long time, but more likely the story reflects the immediate post-war era when food was scarce.

Video Wrap-up

At this time, you might want to use the *Video Program* or the *Expanded Video Program*, Videocassette 4 for additional review and enrichment. See *Video Guide* for suggestions regarding:
- **Echt toll, Ismar!**
  (Dramatic episode)
- **Landeskunde**
  Interviews
- **Videoclips**
  (Authentic footage—*Expanded Video Program* only)

*K*ann ich's wirklich?
p. 304

This page helps students prepare for the test. It is a brief checklist of the major points covered in the chapter. The students should be reminded that it is only a checklist and not necessarily everything that will appear on the test.

*U*sing Wortschatz,
p. 305

Teaching Suggestions
- Ask students to make a list of five facilities that their ideal ocean resort would have.
- Show students some photos or ads from clothing catalogs or fashion magazines featuring the vocabulary of the **Dritte Stufe**. Ask students to work with a partner to write down as many of the items in the pictures as they can recall. Have students read their lists aloud in class.

Games
- Play the games **Anziehwettbewerb** and **Globus**. See p. 281F for the procedure.
- Play the game **Wörter kreuz und quer**. See p. 105F for the procedure.

Teacher Note
Give the **Kapitel 12** Chapter Test, *Chapter Resources*, Book 4.

12
Die Reinickendorfer Clique

① Wir haben die meiste Zeit am Strand verbracht. Es war toll!

German teenagers often get together at someone's home to talk, to listen to music, and to just have fun. This is especially true after a long summer vacation when everyone wants to see each other again and talk about the events of the past six weeks. If you were to get together with some German friends, there are many things you would want to talk about.

In this chapter you will learn

- to report past events; to ask for, make, and respond to suggestions
- to order food, to express hearsay and regret; to persuade and dissuade
- to ask for and give advice; to express preference; to express interest, disinterest and indifference

And you will

- listen to reports about vacations, favorite foods, and clothes
- read about vacation resorts, international cuisine, and clothes
- write about vacation plans and interesting vacation experiences
- find out where Germans like to spend their vacations, what clothes they take, and what kinds of cuisine they enjoy

② Wohin gehen wir? Was schlägst du vor?

③ Ich hab' gehört, der Ismar hat die belegten Brote gemacht. Stimmt's?

Los geht's!

Echt toll, Ismar!

Look at the photos on these two pages.
What are these students doing? What do you
think they are talking about?

 Andreas  Astrid  Ismar

 Lars  Binh

ASTRID	Das machst du echt toll, Ismar! Du wirst bestimmt mal ein bekannter Chefkoch werden!
ISMAR	Du wirst es mir nicht glauben, aber Kochen macht mir großen Spaß. Du mußt mal zu uns kommen, dann mach' ich für dich ein bosnisches Gericht, Ćevapčići. Echt super!
ASTRID	Du mußt mich eben mal einladen.
ISMAR	Mach' ich!

ANDREAS	Hm, prima! Das sieht echt lecker aus.
ASTRID	Hat Ismar gemacht. — He, Finger weg! Du darfst dir nichts vom Teller nehmen.
ANDREAS	Ich hab' aber Hunger.
ASTRID	Pech gehabt!

ASTRID	Na gut! Ich mach' dir ein belegtes Brot. Was willst du denn drauf haben?
ANDREAS	Käse und Schinken! Doppelt gemoppelt hält besser.
ASTRID	So, hier! Schwirr ab!

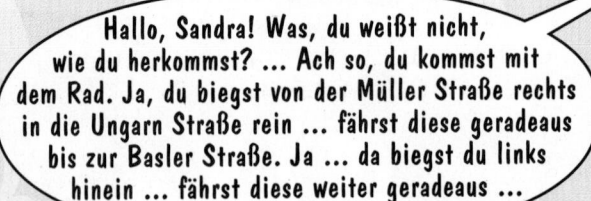

> Hallo, Sandra! Was, du weißt nicht, wie du herkommst? ... Ach so, du kommst mit dem Rad. Ja, du biegst von der Müller Straße rechts in die Ungarn Straße rein ... fährst diese geradeaus bis zur Basler Straße. Ja ... da biegst du links hinein ... fährst diese weiter geradeaus ...

ANDREAS	Hallo! — Das ist also dein neues Moped. Echt super! Wie lange hast du es jetzt schon?
LARS	Seit ich den Führerschein hab', also seit Anfang der Ferien. Gefällt dir, was?
ANDREAS	Ich mach' den Vierer in sechs Monaten. Du läßt mich doch dann mal fahren, oder?
LARS	Na klar!
ANDREAS	So, kommt rein! Ismar ist schon da, schwer am Arbeiten, und Sandra wird auch gleich da sein.

⑥ Rohes Gemüse, hm! Wohl für mich?

Warum? Bist du jetzt eine Vegetarierin? Das ist mir neu.

Nein, so schlimm ist das nicht. Ich ess' eben gern Obst und Gemüse. Nur Bananen kann ich nicht essen.

Warum nicht?

Ich bin allergisch gegen Bananen.

Echt? Das hab' ich nicht gewußt.

Macht nichts!

⑦ Mensch, Lars, du siehst heute so anders aus. Ich erkenn' dich kaum wieder: weißes Hemd, schwarze Hosen ...

Tja, ich hatte es einfach satt, in Jeans und T-Shirt rumzurennen.

Wirklich? Das soll ich dir glauben?

⑧ Mensch, Binh, deine Jacke gefällt mir. Die sieht echt toll aus. Und die steht dir auch. Ist sie neu?

Die hab' ich mir vor den Ferien gekauft.

Super, echt super! So eine würde ich auch gern mal haben. Darf ich sie mal anprobieren?

Natürlich! Hier, probier sie an!

⑨ Was hast du denn mit deinem Arm? Hast du dich verletzt?

Ich bin vom Fahrrad gefallen.

Das hat wohl weh getan.

Am Anfang schon. Aber jetzt geht's.

⑩ So, greift zu!

Hm, super! Die hast du aber mit viel Liebe vorbereitet.

Ehrlich gesagt hab' ich gar nichts gemacht. Das hat alles Ismar gemacht — und so schön dekoriert!

1 Was passiert hier?

3. because he can't have the food they prepared; prepare a sandwich

Verstehst du alles, was diese Schüler sagen? Beantworte die folgenden Fragen!

1. Why are these students getting together? Where is the story taking place? **1. They will eat at Astrid's.**
2. What are Astrid and Ismar discussing in the opening scene? **2. Ismar's cooking talents.**
3. Why does Astrid say **Pech gehabt** to Andreas? What does Astrid do for him instead?
4. Why is Sandra calling? What kind of information does Andreas give her?
5. What do Andreas and Lars discuss when Lars and Binh arrive? What kind of deal does Andreas make with Lars? **4. she doesn't know how to get there; directions 5. They talk about the moped. When Andreas gets his license, Lars will let him ride his moped. 6. She is allergic to them.**
6. Why does Binh mention bananas?
7. In what way does Lars look different today? Does Ismar believe the reason Lars gives for the change? **7. He is dressed up.; He does not really believe it.**
8. What does Astrid say to Binh about her jacket? **8. Astrid says that she likes the jacket.**
9. Why does Andreas ask Binh about her arm? What happened to her? **9. Binh has a bandage on her arm; She fell off her bike.**
10. In what way does Astrid compliment Ismar at the end of the story?
10. She says that Ismar has prepared all the food.

2 Genauer Lesen

a. Lies den Text noch einmal! Such die Wörter oder Ausdrücke aus, die das Folgende ausdrücken! **1. E.g.: Echt toll! 2. E.g.: Finger weg! 3. E.g.: Echt? 4. E.g.: Das hat wohl weh getan.**
   1. compliments or praise
   2. a warning or reprimand
   3. surprise
   4. concern for someone else

b. Beantworte die folgenden Fragen! **1. Ismar will become a famous chef.**
   1. Astrid makes a prediction. What is it? **3. E.g.: Kommt rein!; Probier sie an!; Schwirr ab!**
   2. What wish does Astrid express? What words does she use to say this?
   3. Several people instruct others to do something. Find at least three examples.
   4. Find three instances in which people ask for specific information. Which phrases do they use to do this? **4. E.g.: Ist sie (die Jacke) neu?; Was willst du drauf?; Wie lange hast du es schon?**
   2. She would like to be invited by Ismar; Du mußt mich eben mal einladen.

3 Welche Sätze passen zusammen?

Welche Nebensätze auf der rechten Seite passen zu den Satzanfängen auf der linken Seite?

1. Du darfst dir nichts vom Teller nehmen,   a. denn ich bin vom Rad gefallen. **1. d**
2. Du darfst noch nicht Moped fahren, **2. e**   b. weil du alles mit viel Liebe vorbereitet hast.
3. Ich darf das nicht essen, **3. c**   c. denn ich bin dagegen allergisch.
4. Ich trage heute mal etwas anderes, **4. f**   d. denn das ist für unsere Gäste.
5. Der Arm tut mir weh, **5. a**   e. weil du noch keinen Führerschein hast.
6. Das schmeckt echt gut, **6. b**   f. weil ich es satt habe, immer in denselben Klamotten herumzulaufen.

4 Nacherzählung

Erzähl die Geschichte nach, indem du die folgenden Sätze in die richtige Reihenfolge bringst! Zuerst hilft Ismar der Astrid in der Küche.

8 Am Ende sitzen alle am Tisch und essen.
3 Danach ruft die Sandra an.
6 Andreas findet es toll und möchte bald damit fahren.
4 Andreas sagt Sandra, wie man zu ihm kommt.
7 Später sprechen die Schüler über das Essen, Klamotten, und wie Binh sich verletzt hat.
1 Dann kommt der Andreas und will schon ein Sandwich probieren.
5 Kurz danach kommen Lars und Binh mit dem Moped an.
2 Das geht aber nicht. Astrid macht ihm aber schnell ein belegtes Brot.

Welche ausländische Küche hast du gern?

What kinds of ethnic cuisine do Germans enjoy? Before you read the responses below, think about what you know about popular foods in Germany. Which foreign cuisine do you think is the most popular among German teenagers?

Werner, *Berlin*

„Ja, ausländische Küche ... würde ich sagen mit Vorliebe italienisch, Spaghetti in jeder Variante, mit Tomatensoßen, mit Cremesoßen, mit Joghurtsoßen, und alles, was zur italienischen Küche dazugehört."

Monika, *Hamburg*

„Ich esse gerne chinesisch, griechisch, ja auch italienisch, weil es ist ... schmeckt halt gut. Und Fast food esse ich auch gerne, weil so schön viele Kalorien drin sind. Wenn du richtig gut Fast food essen willst, mußt du nach Berlin, und dann gehst du ins Hard Rock Café, und dann bestellst du dir 'nen Hamburger."

Margit, *Stuttgart*

„Ich interessier' mich am meisten für die italienische Küche, koch' das auch sehr gern, les' gerne viel darüber. Am meisten viel Nudelgerichte oder auch spezielle Nachspeisen von dort, weil die sehr schmackhaft sind, und sehr variationsreich auch."

Hans, *Hamburg*

„Amerikanische Küche mag ich eigentlich nicht, kein Fast food, kein Big Mac, mal ab und zu, aber eben so typisch deutsche Gerichte mag ich auch eigentlich gerne, Kartoffeln mit 'nem Steak und Bohnen ... und, ja, eigentlich alles."

A.
1. Which ethnic cuisines do these people say they like? Which is the most popular cuisine? Is this what you guessed beforehand? A. 1. Italian, Chinese, Greek, American; most popular: Italian
2. What does Hans think of as American food? Why might he think this? How do you feel about this stereotype? A. 2. Fast food
3. What other foreign cuisines are popular in Germany which were not mentioned by these particular people? A. 3. E.g.: Spanish, Yugoslav, Japanese, Turkish

B.
1. There are many different kinds of eateries in Germany, and you are already familiar with some of them. Which ones can you recall and what are their characteristics? You already know about **Fast food Restaurants** from your own experience, and there are many American franchises now in Germany. Germany also has some of its own chains, for example, **Nordsee.** Can you guess what kind of food they serve?
2. In addition to fast food, you'll find in every village and town at least one **Gaststätte. Gaststätten** reflect the local color and traditions of the region they are in, both in terms of decor and the type of food served. When the weather is good, Germans flock to the outdoors and often congregate in **Biergärten.** These have a definite family atmosphere, much like the English pub. By custom, patrons can buy food there or bring their own, but must purchase beverages from the establishment.

Reporting past events; asking for, making, and responding to suggestions

---

Die Deutschen – die Weltmeister im Reisen

DIE DEUTSCHEN SIND ein reiselustiges Volk. Allein im Jahr 1990 gaben sie bei Auslandsreisen fast 49 Milliarden DM aus. Damit stehen sie mit weitem Abstand an der Spitze der Europäer. Das liegt wohl zum einen daran, daß die Deutschen ein wohlhabendes Volk sind und über viel Freizeit verfügen. Zum andern suchen sie ihr Urlaubsglück häufiger jenseits der Grenzen als daheim. Andere Europäer verbringen ihre Ferien bevorzugt im eigenen Land.

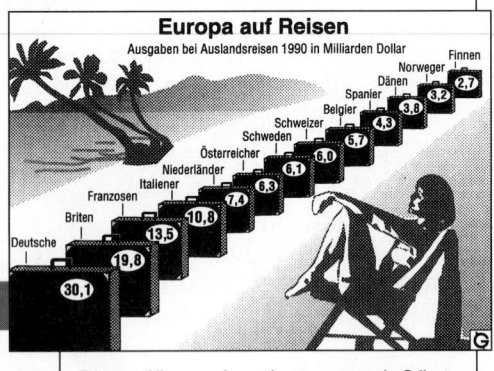

Europa auf Reisen
Ausgaben bei Auslandsreisen 1990 in Milliarden Dollar

Finnen 2,7 · Norweger · Dänen 3,2 · Spanier 3,8 · Belgier · Schweizer · Schweden 5,7 · Österreicher 6,0 · Niederländer 6,1 · Italiener 6,3 · Franzosen 7,4 · Briten 10,8 · 13,5 · 19,8 · Deutsche 30,1

| Spanien | Kanarische Inseln | Lanzarote |

Sport, Spaß und Erholung

Eine Entdeckungsreise auf der ca. 795 Quadratkilometer großen Insel führt Sie vorbei an kleinen, sauberen Dörfern mit weißen Häusern, abwechslungsreichen Stränden mit hellem oder dunklem Sand, Klippen und einsamen Buchten.

Club „La Santa"

Unter Insidern und Top-Athleten gilt er längst als Geheimtip. Jetzt steht der exklusive Club „La Santa", auf der schwarzen Insel Lanzarote, nur etwa 4 Flugstunden von Deutschland entfernt und ca. 150 km vor der afrikanischen Küste, auch den Gästen von Sport-Scheck Reisen offen. Werfen Sie einen Blick hinein in die Traumanlage der fast unbegrenzten Sportmöglichkeiten, wo sich Olympiasieger wie Claudia Losch, Ulrike Meifarth, die Zehnkämpfer Guido Kratschmer, Jürgen Hingsen und ganze Bundesligateams erholen und auf neue Erfolge vorbereiten — Sie werden begeistert sein.

Um den Club „La Santa" zu besuchen, müssen Sie aber kein Spitzensportler sein — Kinder, Erholungssuchende, Aktive, Familien, Gruppen … im „Club La Santa" ist jeder herzlich willkommen.

Das „Grüne Team"

Junge, profitrainierte Sportleute (vorwiegend englischsprechend) stehen im „Club La Santa" den Gästen mit Rat und Tat zur Seite. Angeboten wird Unterricht im Squash, Badminton, Tennis, Schwimmen, Schnorcheln, Windsurfen, sowie Fitneß-Test und Gewichttraining — je nach Programm unterteilt in Gruppen für Anfänger, Fortgeschrittene, Erfahrene und Kinder.

Weltklasse Einrichtungen für mehr als 20 Sportarten

„La Santa" ist ausgerüstet wie eine kleine Olympiastadt: Mit Fußball- und Leichtathletikstadion, 50-Meter-Swimmingpool, Badminton- und Handballhalle, Squashcourts, Tauchschule, Surfstation, Tennisplätzen, Fitneß-Studio, Tischtennisräumen, Basketballplatz, großes Fahrrad-Depot. Oft beginnen Fitneß und Entspannung auf Lanzarote mit Entdeckungstouren auf Rennrad oder Mountainbike.

Wohnen im Club „La Santa"

Sämtliche Sportanlagen und Einrichtungen sind um das gepflegte Appartement-Dorf, etwa 250 Meter vom offenen Meer entfernt, gruppiert. Obwohl die 400 Wohnungen Platz für mehr als tausend Gäste bieten, entsteht nie der Eindruck von Enge. Restaurants, Bars, Disco, Shops, Video-Kino, Friseur … sorgen für eine dörfliche Atmosphäre. Der Supermarkt in der Anlage ist sehr gut sortiert — auch die verwöhnten Genießer und ernährungsbewußten Sportler können dort gut einkaufen.

Die Appartements (Varianten von 1 bis 3 Personen) sind einfach und zweckmäßig eingerichtet. Sie verfügen über Bad/WC, Kitchenette mit Kühlschrank, Schlafraum und Wohnraum sowie Patio (keine Aussicht). Ganz nach Lust und Laune wird selbst gekocht oder in einem der zahlreichen Restaurants innerhalb oder außerhalb des Clubs gespeist. Oder aber Sie nehmen die Halb- bzw. Vollpension, die aus europäischem Frühstücksbuffet und wahlweise Mittag- oder Abendbuffet besteht, in Anspruch. Auch am Abend braucht „Jung und Alt" sich nicht zu langweilen. Grill- und Strandfeste, Kinoabende und Kinder-Bühnen-Show, Ausflüge und Turniere verschiedenster Art erwarten Sie. Das „Grüne Team" stellt sich zweimal wöchentlich einmal ganz anders vor — lassen Sie sich überraschen. Selbstverständlich ist auch in den Bars und in der Club-Disco immer was los.

| das Meer und der Strand | die Küste und die Klippen | eine Insel | eine Bucht | eine Oase |

auf deutsch erklärt:

der Anfänger = Schüler, Greenhorn

der Fortgeschrittene = weiß mehr als ein Anfänger

der Erfahrene = Experte

der Olympiasieger = hat in der Olympiade gewonnen

der Zehnkämpfer = kämpft in zehn verschiedenen Sportarten

der Geheimtip = nicht alle sollen das wissen

abwechslungsreich = nicht langweilig

s. langweilen = nichts zu tun haben

zahlreiche = viele

Sportanlagen
der Court
der Platz
der Pool
die Anlage
die Halle
das Fahrrad-Depot

Was würdest du auf dieser Insel tun? Welche Sportanlagen würdest du benutzen und warum?

5 Der Ferien Club

Lies den Artikel auf Seite 288! Schreib die Antworten zu den folgenden Fragen auf ein Blatt Papier! Such dir dann einen Partner! Stellt euch abwechselnd diese Fragen und beantwortet sie!

1. Wer gibt am meisten für Auslandsreisen aus?
2. Wo verbringen die meisten Deutschen ihren Urlaub?
3. Warum können die Deutschen so viel Geld für ihren Urlaub ausgeben?
4. Warum besuchen die Urlauber gern den Club „La Santa"?
5. Was kann man alles beim „grünen Team" lernen?
6. Welche Einrichtungen gibt es im Club „La Santa"?
7. Was gibt es alles im Appartement-Dorf?
8. Wie sind die Appartements eingerichtet?
9. Warum braucht sich niemand im Club zu langweilen?

6 Hör gut zu!

For answers, see listening script on TE Interleaf.

Du stehst in der Schlange vor dem Bankschalter und hörst, wie sich zwei junge Leute über ihr letztes Wochenende unterhalten. Sind sie in der Stadt geblieben, oder haben sie eine längere Reise unternommen? Wer hat am meisten Spaß gehabt? Warum müssen sie jetzt auf die Bank?

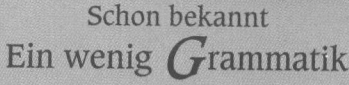

Schon bekannt
Ein wenig *Grammatik*

When talking about the past, you generally use two verb forms, a helping verb and a past participle.

Wo **bist** du **gewesen**?
Wir **haben** Tennis **gespielt**.

For past participles of verbs that you should know, see the Grammar Summary. You know two verbs that also have a single verb form to refer to the past. What are these verbs? And their forms?

SO SAGT MAN DAS!

Reporting past events

When reporting past events, you use special verb forms. Pay special attention to the verbs here:

> Die Osterferien habe ich mit meinen Eltern in der Schweiz verbracht. Wir waren in Brienz, in den Bergen. Wir hatten wunderschönes Wetter und haben viel unternommen. Nach dem Frühstück sind wir gewöhnlich ein paar Stunden gewandert und haben irgendwo zu Mittag gegessen. Nach dem Essen haben wir ein bißchen gefaulenzt, und dann ...

When would you use **haben** with the past tense? And **sein**?

7 Andreas' und Astrids Ferien

Die letzten Weihnachtsferien haben Astrid und Andreas mit ihren Eltern auf den Kanarischen Inseln verbracht. Du willst von ihnen wissen, wie es war und was sie dort alles gemacht haben. — Such dir zwei Partner, die die Rollen von Astrid und Andreas spielen!

Du willst folgendes wissen:

a. wo sie waren
b. wo das liegt
c. wo sie gewohnt haben
d. wie das Appartement eingerichtet war
e. welche Sporteinrichtungen es gibt

f. was sie neu gelernt haben
g. welche Spitzensportler sie kennengelernt haben
h. wie sie ihre Abende verbracht haben

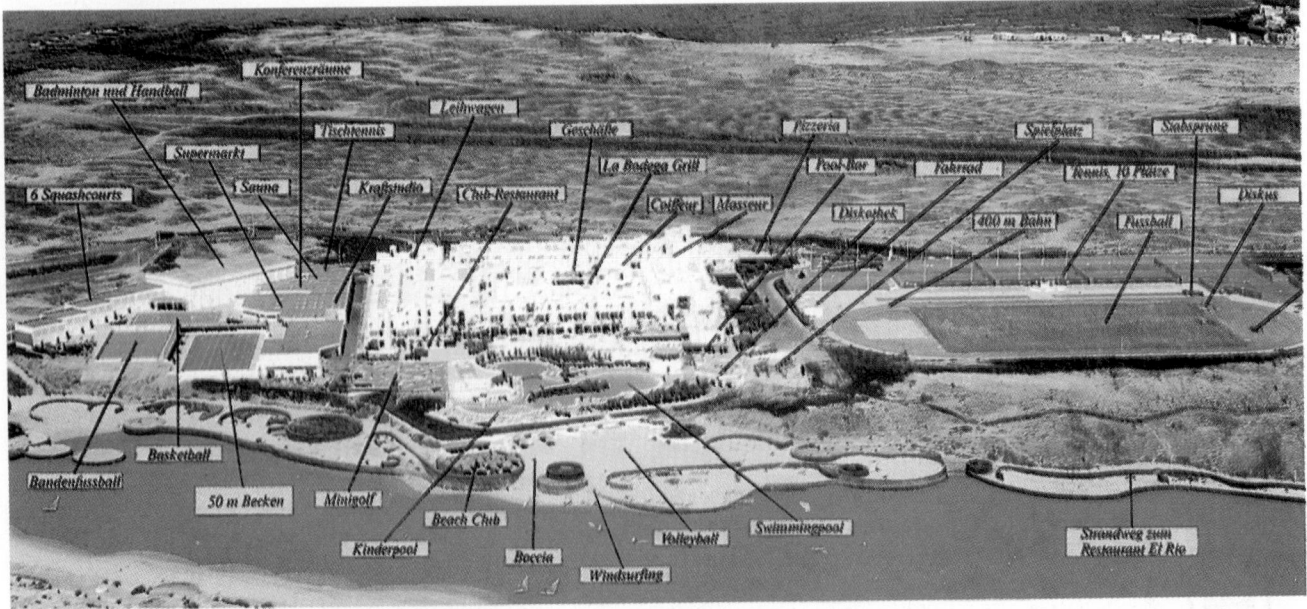

8 Ein großes Angebot

„La Santa" ist ausgerüstet wie eine kleine Olympiastadt, und für mehr als 20 Sportarten gibt es Weltklasse Einrichtungen. Sieh dir diesen Plan von „La Santa" an, und schreib sechs Sportarten auf, die du dort gern machen würdest!

9 Was hast du dort gemacht?

Erzähl deinem Partner, wo du überall im Club gewesen bist und was du dort alles gemacht hast und wie oft!

Wo?

in der Minigolfanlage

in der Pizzeria

im Kraftstudio

am Strand

am Meer

am Pool

im Stadion

in der Diskothek

im Beach Club

in der Sauna

im Squashcourt

in der Basketballhalle

in der Bucht

im Supermarkt

auf dem Tennisplatz

Schon bekannt
Ein wenig *G*rammatik

You have used questions and statements such as:

Wart ihr am Pool?
Nein, in der Minigolfanlage.

What case follows these two prepositions? Why? For more on two-way prepositions, see the Grammar Summary.

10 Hör gut zu! For answers, see listening script on TE Interleaf.

Die Familie Kohl bespricht ihren kommenden Urlaub. Leider würden die Kinder, Markus und Annette, lieber ganz andere Dinge machen als ihre Eltern. Schreib auf, welche Vorschläge die Eltern und die Kinder machen. Welche Gründe geben sie an?

SO SAGT MAN DAS!

Schon bekannt

Asking for, making, and responding to suggestions

When asking for suggestions, you could say:

Wohin sollen wir fahren? Was schlägst du vor?

When making suggestions, you could say:

Würdest du gern mal an die Küste fahren?
Wie wär's denn mit einem Flug nach Spanien?

And you could respond by saying:

Eine gute Idee!
Das wäre toll! Super!

Schon bekannt
Ein wenig *G*rammatik

For the forms of **sollen** and the **würde**-forms, see the Grammar Summary.

11 Was würdest du gern mal tun?

Sag deinem Partner, was du gern mal in den kommenden Ferien tun würdest und warum! Er sagt dir dann, was er gern tun würde.

12 Auf in die Ferien!

Deine Eltern haben dich und deine Schwester gebeten, zahlreiche Reiseprospekte zu besorgen, damit ihr zusammen am Wochenende eure Pläne für die kommenden Ferien machen könnt.

a. Schreib drei Ferienziele auf ein Blatt Papier!

b. Schreib daneben ein oder zwei Gründe, warum du gern dorthin fahren würdest!

c. Such dir jetzt drei Partner für die Rollen von deinen Eltern und deiner Schwester! Schlag den Eltern einen Ferienort vor und begründe deinen Vorschlag! Was meinen die Eltern dazu?

> Schon bekannt
> ## Ein wenig *G*rammatik
>
> Read these questions and statements:
>
> **Fahrt ihr wieder ans Meer?**
> **Wir waren im Juli am Meer.**
> **Fahren wir heute in die Berge?**
> **In den Bergen regnet es.**
> **Fliegst du nach Österreich?**
> **Ich war schon in Österreich.**
>
> What case follows these prepositions and why? What kind of preposition is **nach**? For more on prepositions, see the Grammar Summary.

13 Im Reisebüro

Ihr habt euch in der Familie auf drei Reiseziele geeinigt, aber bevor ihr euch endgültig für einen Ferienort entscheidet, braucht ihr noch mehr Information. Du sollst diese Information besorgen.

a. Schreib die drei Reiseziele auf eine Liste und trag die Sehenswürdigkeiten (*sights*) ein, die ihr an jedem Ziel besuchen wollt!

b. Schreib mindestens acht Dinge auf, über die du Auskunft möchtest, zum Beispiel, ob der Ferienort einen großen Swimmingpool hat oder ob die Pension einen schönen Tennisplatz hat!

c. Such dir jetzt einen Partner! Er übernimmt die Rolle von einem Angestellten im Reisebüro. Er fragt dich, wofür du dich interessierst, und du sagst es ihm. Leider muß der Angestellte dir sagen, daß es nicht alles gibt, was du willst.

BEISPIEL   ANGESTELLTER **Ja, wofür interessieren Sie sich denn?**
                  DU **Ich interessiere mich für eine Reise nach ... und ich möchte wissen, ob ...**

14 Für mein Notizbuch

Du warst mit deiner Familie in einem schönen Ferienort. Schreib einen Bericht über deine Ferien in dein Notizbuch! Er muß Antworten zu folgenden Fragen enthalten (*include*):

1. Wo wart ihr und wie lange?
2. Wo habt ihr gewohnt, und wie waren die Zimmer?
3. Was für Sportarten habt ihr dort ausgeübt?
4. Wo habt ihr gegessen, und wie hat es euch geschmeckt?
5. Wie habt ihr die Abende verbracht?
6. Was hat euch gefallen und was nicht?
7. Würdet ihr gern noch einmal dorthin fahren oder fliegen? Warum? Warum nicht?

15 Und wo bist du gewesen?

Frag deine Partnerin über ihre letzten Ferien! Wo ist sie gewesen, und was hat sie alles gemacht? Danach erzählst du ihr von deinen Ferien.

Ordering food, expressing hearsay and regret; persuading and dissuading

Andreas Elsholz präsentiert sein bestes Spaghettirezept!

Man nehme 300 Gramm italienische Nudeln, ein halbes Pfund Hackfleisch, einen großen Topf und — natürlich einen begabten Koch . . .

„Seit ich in meiner eigenen Bude in Berlin-Köpenick wohne, bin ich der perfekte Koch geworden", erzählt Andreas Elsholz (21) stolz beim POP/Rocky-Interview. „Spaghetti sind meine besondere Stärke." Das wollten wir genauer wissen — und stellten Andreas mit einem Kochtest auf die Probe. Null problemo für Andi, der sich beim Nobel-Italiener „La Locanda" in München-Giesing sofort begeistert in die Küche verdrückte. Chefkoch Nicola staunte nicht schlecht, als Andreas ganz fachmännisch zunächst einige Spritzer Olivenöl in das Spaghettiwasser tat. „Nudeln dürfen nicht zu lange kochen, müssen „al dente" sein, das heißt, sie müssen noch Biß haben", erklärt Andreas seine Nudelphilosophie. Und dann legte er wie ein Wirbelwind los: Er hackte die Zwiebeln und den Paprika für die Sauce, rührte zwischendrin die Nudeln um, würzte den Tomatenfond — so, als wäre er in einer Restaurantküche großgeworden. Nach zwanzig Minuten stand das Gourmetgericht dampfend auf dem Tisch. Koch Nicola durfte als erster kosten. Sein Urteil: „Molto bene, grandioso!" Doch das Jobangebot als Koch mußte der „Heiko" aus „Gute Zeiten — schlechte Zeiten" leider ablehnen. „Ich präsentiere meinen Fans dafür einen Ohrenschmaus mit meinem ersten Hit, „Immer noch verrückt nach dir ..."

SPAGHETTI
MIT PAPRIKA UND PILZEN
❀ ✳ ❀

225 g Pilze,
in Scheiben geschnitten
115 g kleingeschnittene
Paprika
60 g Butter oder Margarine
300 g Spaghetti
Salz und Pfeffer
1 EL gehackte Petersilie
60 g geriebener Parmesan

Die Pilze und die Paprika in der Hälfte der Butter anbraten. Inzwischen die Spaghetti in reichlich Salzwasser zehn Minuten kochen. Dann ablaufen lassen und zurück in den Topf geben. Den Rest der Butter, Salz, reichlich frisch gemahlenen schwarzen Pfeffer, die Pilze und den Paprika zugeben. Alles gut vermengen. Anschließend die gehackte Petersilie darüberstreuen und geriebenen Parmesan dazu servieren. **Die Rezeptmenge reicht für vier Personen.**

16 Beantwortet diese Fragen!

2. im „La Locanda"
3. Nudeln müssen „al dente" sein.

Lies den Artikel auf Seite 293! Dann such dir einen Partner! Stellt euch abwechselnd diese Fragen und beantwortet sie!

1. Wo wohnt Andreas, und was tut er besonders gern?   1. in Berlin; kochen
2. Wo hat Andis Kochtest stattgefunden?
3. Was ist Andis „Nudelphilosophie"?
4. Woraus besteht sein Gourmetgericht?
5. Wie beurteilt Chefkoch Nicola das Gericht?   5. ausgezeichnet
6. Warum hat Andi das Jobangebot als Koch nicht angenommen?   6. er singt lieber

4. Paprika, Pilze, usw.

17 Ausländische Gerichte

Such dir eine Partnerin und stell ihr folgende Fragen!

1. Was für ein Gericht ist (Paella)?
2. Welches ist ein (russisches) Gericht?
3. Welche von diesen Gerichten hast du schon gegessen?
4. Welches Gericht würdest du gern einmal probieren? Warum?
5. Welches Gericht wirst du dir bestimmt bestellen, wenn du einmal nach (Griechenland) kommst?

18 Gerichte beschreiben

Alle sollen ein internationales Kochbuch zur Schule bringen. Jeder von euch sucht sich ein Gericht aus, das er den Mitschülern genauer beschreiben soll. Die drei Mitschüler müssen an Fragen denken, um herauszufinden, was das ist.

BEISPIEL	FRAGE	**Was ist Paella?**
	ANTWORT	**Paella ist ein spanisches Reisgericht.**
	FRAGE	**Woraus besteht dieses Gericht?**
	ANTWORT	**Aus Huhn, Wurst, Krabben, Muscheln ...**
	FRAGE	**Wie macht (kocht) man das?**
	ANTWORT	**Man ...**

Internationale Gerichte

Mousaka

Ćevapčići

Paella

Fettucine

Crêpes Suzette

Tacos

Wiener Schnitzel

Steak

Couscous

In was für ein Lokal würdest du gern einmal gehen? Was würdest du dir dort bestellen? Welche Gerichte kennst du? Welche hast du schon gegessen?

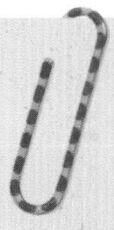

SO SAGT MAN DAS!

Schon bekannt

Ordering food, expressing hearsay and regret

When you order food, you may say:

Ich hätte gern die Paella.

You might tell your friend what you heard about it:

Ich habe gehört, die Paella soll hier ausgezeichnet sein.

But the waiter may have bad news:

Tut mir leid. Die Paella ist heute schon alle.

19 Hör gut zu!   For answers, see listening script on TE Interleaf.

Zwei Leute sind in einem Restaurant, wo es viele internationale Gerichte gibt. Sie kennen einige Gerichte überhaupt nicht und unterhalten sich mit der Bedienung darüber. Schreib auf, welches Gericht sich jeder am Ende bestellt, was für ein Gericht das ist und warum sich jeder dieses Gericht bestellt hat!

20 Macht nichts! Dann nehme ich eben …

Zu deinem Geburtstag gehen deine Eltern mit dir in ein nettes Restaurant, wo du schon ab und zu warst. Du erinnerst dich (*recall*) an ein Gericht, das dir besonders gut geschmeckt hat, und du möchtest es wieder bestellen.

a. Schreib auf einen Zettel, was du damals gegessen und getrunken hast! Vorspeise, Hauptgericht, Beilage, Nachspeise, Getränk.

b. Such dir einen Partner, der die Rolle der Bedienung übernimmt! Du bestellst das Gericht, das dir so gut geschmeckt hat, aber leider ist es schon alle. Deshalb bestellst du dir eben ein anderes Gericht, das auch sehr gut sein soll.

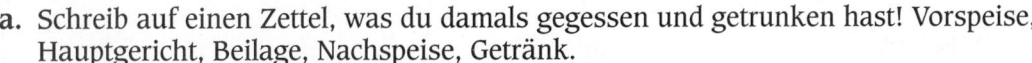
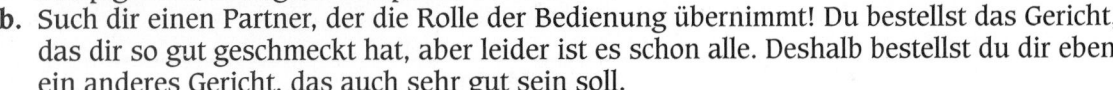

EIN WENIG LANDESKUNDE

In den meisten deutschen Lokalen sucht man sich selbst den Tisch aus. Man muß nur darauf achten, daß man sich nicht an einen reservierten Tisch setzt oder an einen „Stammtisch", der immer für eine bestimmte Gruppe reserviert ist. Wenn man keinen leeren Tisch findet, dann setzt man sich eben zu anderen Leuten, nachdem man vorher höflich gefragt hat: „Ist hier noch frei?" Es ist daher nicht ungewöhnlich, daß drei oder vier verschiedene Gruppen am gleichen Tisch essen und sich miteinander unterhalten. Und unter dem Tisch liegt oft ganz friedlich des Menschen „bester Freund", der Hund, denn in den meisten Lokalen ist es gestattet, seinen Vierbeiner mitzubringen. Gastwirte sind hundelieb. Im Sommer, wenn es sehr heiß ist, stellen viele Wirte einen Wassernapf neben die Eingangstür, damit sich vorbeigeführte Hunde erfrischen können.

SO SAGT MAN DAS!

Schon bekannt

Persuading and dissuading

When trying to persuade someone, you might say:

> **Geh doch einmal griechisch essen!**
>
> **Iß doch mal etwas, was du noch nie gegessen hast!**

The response might be:

> **Du, die griechische Küche ist mir zu scharf.**
>
> **Das ist ein guter Vorschlag.**

When trying to dissuade someone, you might say:

> **Iß dort ja keinen Fisch!**
>
> **Trink dort ja kein ungekochtes Wasser!**

The response might be:

> **Warum nicht?**
>
> **Gut! Mach' ich nicht!**

21 Iß ja kein ...!

Deine Verwandten fahren in Urlaub. Sie fahren dorthin, wo du mit deinen Eltern letztes Jahr warst. Such dir eine Partnerin, die die Rolle von deiner Kusine übernimmt! — Sag ihr zwei Dinge, die sie am Ferienort unbedingt tun soll und zwei, die sie nicht tun soll! Begründe deine Aussagen! Einige Ideen stehen im Kasten unten. — Tauscht dann die Rollen aus!

> *Schon bekannt*
> ## Ein wenig *Grammatik*
>
> Do you remember the command forms of various strong verbs? Here are some you should recognize: **Iß! Lies! Nimm! Vergiß!** For command forms, see the Grammar Summary.

Einige Ideen

ja:

> sich richtig ausruhen
> etwas Sport machen
> in die Disko gehen
> Sonnenschutz nicht vergessen
> die tollen Fischgerichte essen

nein:

> nicht zu viele Klamotten mitnehmen
> nicht zu lange in der Sonne liegen
> kein ungekochtes Wasser trinken

22 Mensch, hab' ich einen Bärenhunger!

Deine Eltern haben am Ferienort ein Appartement gemietet, und ihr bereitet euer eigenes Frühstück und Abendessen vor.

a. Schreib mindestens zehn Speisen auf, die deine Familie im Kühlschrank haben würde! Zum Beispiel: frisches Obst, geräucherten Fisch, usw.

b. Du bringst einen Freund mit nach Hause ins Appartement. Ihr habt Basketball gespielt, und ihr seid jetzt hungrig und durstig. Du schlägst vor, ein paar belegte Brote zu machen, und du fragst deinen Freund, was er gern drauf hätte. Er sagt dir, was er gern mag und was nicht. Frag ihn, ob es etwas gibt, was er nicht essen darf! Er sagt es dir. — Tauscht dann die Rollen aus!

Asking for and giving advice; expressing preference; expressing interest, disinterest, and indifference

ICH BIN KEIN WUNDERKIND!

Ihr Hippie-Outfit soll beweisen, daß sie auch als Schwimmstar auf dem Boden bleibt . . .

In Action: Franzi ist im Wasser nicht zu bremsen

Supercool: Franziska van Almsick beim Jux mit Bruder Sebastian

„Peace"— nein, mit dem Hippie-Gruß aus den sechziger Jahren, der prima zu ihrem Outfit passen würde, empfängt Franzi unseren Fotografen nicht. Die vierfache Medaillengewinnerin der Olympischen Spiele von Barcelona 1992 fährt neuerdings völlig auf Kluft à la Woodstock ab. Strickstirnband, Schlabberpulli im Ringelmuster, John-Lennon-Sonnenbrille, Schlaghosen-Jeans mit zerissenem Saum, die eher einer Patchworkdecke gleichen: der Jungstar des deutschen Schwimmsports (geboren am 5. April 1978), der bereits im zarten Alter von fünf Jahren mit dem Hochgeschwindigkeitsbaden begann, zeigt allen Beobachtern sein wahres Ich. Viele haben versucht, ihr das Image eines Nesthäkchens und Wunderkindes anzuhängen. „Alles Quatsch", meint Franzi ganz cool dazu. Und unsere Bilder beweisen es. Franziska ist ein ganz normales Mädchen — und dazu noch total süß und natürlich. Sie kann halt nur ein bißchen schneller schwimmen als die meisten anderen . . .

23 Habt ihr alles verstanden?

1. von Franziska
3. Hippie-Klamotten
4. „Alles Quatsch."

Lies den obigen Artikel und beantworte die Fragen!

1. Wovon handelt dieser Artikel?
2. Wer ist die Franziska, auch Franzi genannt? 2. Schwimmerin u. Medaillengewinnerin bei der Olympiade '92
3. Was für Klamotten trägt Franzi zur Zeit?
4. Manche Leute nennen sie ein Wunderkind. Was meint sie dazu?

Schon bekannt
Ein wenig *G*rammatik

Be careful to watch the adjective endings! Can you explain why these endings are correct?

Kalt**er** Kaffee schmeckt mir nicht! Ich mag dies**es** frisch**e** Brot.

For adjective endings, see the Grammar Summary.

Wie bist du gekleidet? Bist du ...

salopp angezogen, mit Pulli und Jeans, die Löcher haben?

gut angezogen, mit weißem Hemd, schwarzer Hose?

elegant angezogen, mit weißem Hemd und Fliege?

Was ziehst du gern an? Vielleicht ...

einen Pulli mit Ringelmuster?

ein Hemd mit großen Karos?

eine braune Wildlederjacke?

eine Bluse mit Streifen?

Was ziehst du zu Festlichkeiten an?

schwarze Lackschuhe?

ein modisches Abendkleid mit weitem Rock und Schleife?

einen dunkelblauen Smoking, mit weißem Hemd, Fliege und Kummerbund?

Wie kleidest du dich gewöhnlich? Was ziehst du zu Festlichkeiten an?

---

24 Hör gut zu! For answers, see listening script on TE Interleaf.

Schüler erzählen, was sie sich heute abend anziehen. Rate, für welchen Anlaß sich jeder anzieht! Anlässe stehen in den beiden Kästen unten.

25 Was trägst du gern?

Mach eine Liste mit den Kleidungsstücken, die du gern zu drei verschiedenen Anlässen anziehst! Schreib daneben, warum du dir diese Sachen anziehst!

Anlässe

zu Hause
in der Schule
zum Sport
in den Ferien
zum Einkaufen
zu einer Geburtstagsfete

zu Festlichkeiten, wie:
zu einer Hochzeit
zu einem Ball
zu einer Schulfeier

26 Was ziehst du dir gern an?

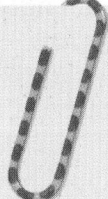

Frag deine Partnerin, was sie gern anzieht, wenn sie zu Hause ist und wenn sie zu einer Geburtstagsfete geht! Was zieht sie an und warum? Danach fragt sie dich.

SO SAGT MAN DAS!

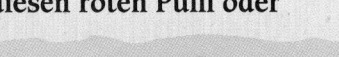
Schon bekannt

Asking for and giving advice

When asking for advice, you might say:

> **Welchen Pulli soll ich mir zur Fete anziehen, diesen roten Pulli oder den blauen?**

When giving advice, you may say:

> **Zieh doch deinen blauen Pulli an!**
> *or* **Ich würde mir diesen blauen Pulli anziehen. Der paßt besser zu deiner weißen Jeans.**

Ein wenig *Grammatik*

Look at the adjectives in these sentences. What are their endings? What do these endings indicate?

> **Zieh doch den blauen Pulli an!**
> **Der blaue Pulli ist schöner.**
> **Ich zieh' das grüne Hemd an.**
> **Ein grünes Hemd paßt gut zu dieser bunten Hose.**

For adjective endings, see the Grammar Summary.

27 Was soll ich mir anziehen?

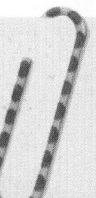

A classmate has invited you to his birthday. Ask your partner which of the different clothing items or styles you should wear to the party. He or she will advise you and say why you should choose one or the other. To get an idea of how the whole outfit will look, sketch a picture as your partner advises you. Then switch roles. Afterwards, share your pictures with the class. Who has given the best advice, judging by the pictures?

— saloppe Kleidung oder gut angezogen?
— Hemd: einfarbig, gestreift oder kariert?
— T-Shirt: einfach oder modisch?
— Bluse: lange oder kurze Ärmel?

— Jeans oder dunkle Hose?
— bunte Krawatte oder (rote) Fliege?
— hübsches Kleid oder Rock und Bluse?
— Lackschuhe oder einfache Sneakers?

SO SAGT MAN DAS!

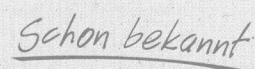
Schon bekannt

Expressing preference

When asking what someone prefers, you might say:

> **Welches Hemd findest du schöner, dieses weiße Hemd oder das gestreifte?**
> **Welche Schuhe gefallen dir besser?**
>
> **Welches Muster ziehst du vor?**
>
> **Was soll ich anziehen? Jeans oder ein Kleid? Was meinst du?**

When expressing preference, you might say:

> **Ich finde das gestreifte Hemd schöner.**
> **Also, mir gefallen eigentlich diese schwarzen Schuhe besser.**
> **Du, ich ziehe den Pulli mit dem Karomuster vor.**
> **Also, ich würde mir ein Kleid anziehen.**

28 Wer die Wahl hat ...

Du hast einfach zu viele Klamotten und weißt nicht, welches Outfit du zum Sting-Konzert anziehen sollst. — Zeichne drei Outfits auf ein Blatt Papier, die du dir gern anziehen würdest! Beschreibe jedes Outfit und notiere den Namen, Farbe und Stoff von jedem Kleidungsstück! Zeig deinen Mitschülern die Zeichnungen!

Schon bekannt
Ein wenig *Grammatik*

How would you compare two things in German? Is it the same as in English? Some adjectives are irregular. Can you name some? For comparative adjectives, see the Grammar Summary.

29 Was findest du schöner?

Du hast dich noch nicht entschieden, was du zur Fete anziehst. Du beschreibst deinem Partner die drei Outfits, die du dir in Übung 28 ausgesucht hast und fragst ihn, welches Outfit er schöner findet. Dein Partner vergleicht die Outfits. Stimmst du ihm zu? Warum? Warum nicht? — Tauscht dann die Rollen aus!

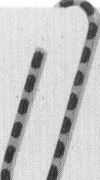

SO SAGT MAN DAS!

Schon bekannt

Expressing interest, disinterest, and indifference

When asking about someone's interests, you might say:

Wofür interessieren Sie sich?

When expressing interest, you might say:

Ich interessiere mich für nette Klamotten, nicht zu salopp, nicht zu fein.

When expressing disinterest, you might say:

Soll die Bluse aus Acryl sein?

Nein, ich interessier' mich nicht für Acryl.

When expressing indifference, you might say:

Welche Farbe soll es sein?

Ach, das ist mir eigentlich egal.

30 Also doch etwas Neues kaufen!

Du hast beschlossen, daß du wirklich kein flottes Outfit für die Fete hast und daß du dir lieber ein neues Kleidungsstück kaufen möchtest.

a. Schreib dir zwei Kleidungsstücke auf, die du dir kaufen möchtest! Welche Farbe? Welches Material? Welche Accessoires?

b. Deine Partnerin ist Verkäuferin in einem Bekleidungsgeschäft. Sie fragt dich, wofür du dich interessierst. Sag es ihr! Sag ihr auch, wofür du dich nicht interessierst!

31 Für eine lange Reise planen

Nächsten Sommer darfst du mit deiner Klasse und deiner Deutschlehrerin vier Wochen lang die deutschsprachigen Länder besuchen. Aber bevor ihr fliegt, müßt ihr gemeinsam die Reise planen, und jeder von euch muß sich individuell auf diese Reise vorbereiten. Setzt euch in Gruppen von vier oder fünf Personen zusammen, und arbeitet gemeinsam einen detaillierten Reiseplan aus, den ihr aufschreibt und später der ganzen Klasse vortragt! Euer Plan muß folgendes enthalten:

a. Wie sieht eure Reiseroute aus? Welche Orte wollt ihr besuchen, und was würdet ihr dort machen?
b. Würdet ihr nur Städte besuchen, oder möchtet ihr auch viel von der schönen deutschen Landschaft sehen? Was interessiert euch am meisten und warum?
c. Was für Kleidung müßt ihr mitnehmen, denn es kann ziemlich kühl oder auch sehr warm sein?
d. Wo würdet ihr wohnen? Bei deutschen Familien? In Jugendherbergen oder Pensionen?
e. Wie würdet ihr euch ernähren? Möchtet ihr immer nur in Gasthäusern essen, oder würdet ihr euch auch oft Lebensmittel in Läden und Supermärkten kaufen? Warum?
f. Welche einheimischen Gerichte möchtet ihr unbedingt einmal probieren? Habt ihr von diesen Gerichten gehört oder gelesen?
g. Wie würdet ihr euch auf der Reise fit halten?
h. Was würdet ihr tun, wenn ihr euch in Deutschland plötzlich nicht wohl fühlt?
i. Welche Fernsehsendungen würdet ihr euch in Deutschland ansehen?
j. Welche sportlichen oder kulturellen Veranstaltungen würdet ihr gern besuchen? In welchen Städten? Welche Gründe habt ihr für den Besuch von solchen Veranstaltungen?

32 Reisebericht an die Klasse

Nun tragen abwechselnd die einzelnen Mitglieder jeder Gruppe ihren detaillierten Reiseplan der ganzen Klasse vor. Ist der Rest der Klasse mit dem Plan einverstanden? Welche Teile des Plans gefallen oder mißfallen den andern in der Klasse? Diskutiert dann über die einzelnen Teile des Plans! — Nachdem jede Gruppe ihren Plan vorgetragen hat, muß ein gemeinsamer Plan von allen Schülern ausgearbeitet werden!

Nach dem Krieg

LESETRICK

Note-taking. In this chapter you will practice taking notes that summarize a short story. Note-taking is a strategy that you can use in all of your classes. When you take summarizing notes as you read, you can gauge whether or not you understand what is going on, and you'll remember the content better and longer. You can also use those same notes to save time when studying for a test.

Getting Started   For answers, see TE Interleaf.

1. Another word for **Abend-**

> **Tip:** The title of a short story often holds the key to what the story is about. If the title refers to an object, the key is usually the relationship of the object to the main character(s).

essen is **Abendbrot.** Does this tell you anything about the role of **das tägliche Brot** in German life? If the title were *Der Apfelkuchen* or *Die Pommes frites,* you might expect certain kinds of characters or a certain atmosphere. What kind of atmosphere does *Das Brot* suggest?

2. Use the reading strategy you learned in **Kapitel 11** (p. 276) to get a general idea of what the story is about. On your third reading, try to summarize the story in three or four sentences. Where and when is the action taking place? How many characters are there?

Das Brot
VON
Wolfgang Borchert

Plötzlich wachte sie auf. Es war halb drei. Sie überlegte, warum sie aufgewacht war. Ach so! In der Küche hatte jemand gegen einen Stuhl gestoßen. Sie horchte nach der Küche. Es war still. Es war zu still und als sie mit der Hand über das Bett neben sich fuhr, fand sie es leer. Das war es, was es so besonders still gemacht hatte: sein Atem fehlte. Sie stand auf und tappte durch die dunkle Wohnung zur Küche. In der Küche trafen sie sich. Die Uhr war halb drei. Sie sah etwas Weißes am Küchenschrank stehen. Sie machte Licht. Sie standen sich im Hemd gegenüber. Nachts. Um halb drei. In der Küche.

Auf dem Küchentisch stand der Brotteller. Sie sah, daß er sich Brot abgeschnitten hatte. Das Messer lag noch neben dem Teller. Und auf der Decke lagen Brotkrümel. Wenn sie abends zu Bett gingen, machte sie immer das Tischtuch sauber. Jeden Abend. Aber nun lagen Krümel auf dem Tuch. Und das Messer lag da. Sie fühlte, wie die Kälte der Fliesen langsam an ihr hochkroch. Und sie sah von dem Teller weg.

„Ich dachte, hier wär was", sagte er und sah in der Küche umher.

„Ich habe auch was gehört", antwortete sie und dabei fand sie, daß er nachts im Hemd doch schon recht alt aussah. So alt wie er war. Dreiundsechzig. Tagsüber sah er manchmal jünger aus. Sie sieht doch schon alt aus, dachte er, im Hemd sieht sie doch ziemlich alt aus. Aber das liegt vielleicht an den Haaren. Bei den Frauen liegt das nachts immer an den Haaren. Die machen dann auf einmal so alt.

„Du hättest Schuhe anziehen sollen. So barfuß auf den kalten Fliesen. Du erkältest dich noch."

Sie sah ihn nicht an, weil sie nicht ertragen konnte, daß er log. Daß er log, nachdem sie neununddreißig Jahre verheiratet waren.

„Ich dachte, hier wäre was", sagte er noch einmal und sah wieder so sinnlos von einer Ecke in die andere, „ich hörte hier was. Da dachte ich, hier wäre was."

„Ich hab auch was gehört. Aber es war wohl nichts." Sie stellte den Teller vom Tisch und schnippte die Krümel von der Decke.

„Nein, es war wohl nichts", echote er unsicher.

Sie kam ihm zu Hilfe. „Komm man. Das war wohl draußen. Komm man zu Bett. Du erkältest dich noch. Auf den kalten Fliesen."

Er sah zum Fenster hin. „Ja, das muß wohl draußen gewesen sein. Ich dachte, es wäre hier."

Sie hob die Hand zum Lichtschalter. Ich muß das Licht jetzt ausmachen, sonst muß ich nach dem Teller sehen, dachte sie. Ich darf doch nicht nach dem Teller sehen. „Komm man", sagte sie und machte das Licht aus, „das war wohl draußen. Die Dachrinne schlägt immer bei Wind gegen die Wand. Es war sicher die Dachrinne. Bei Wind klappert sie immer."

Sie tappten sich beide über den dunklen Korridor zum Schlafzimmer. Ihre nackten Füße platschten auf den Fußboden.

„Wind ist ja", meinte er. „Wind war schon die ganze Nacht."

Als sie im Bett lagen, sagte sie: „Ja, Wind war schon die ganze Nacht. Es war wohl die Dachrinne."

„Ja, ich dachte, es wäre in der Küche. Es war wohl die Dachrinne." Er sagte das, als ob er schon halb im Schlaf wäre.

Aber sie merkte, wie unecht seine Stimme klang, wenn er log.

„Es ist kalt", sagte sie und gähnte leise, „ich krieche unter die Decke. Gute Nacht."

„Nacht", antwortete er und noch: „Ja, kalt ist es schon ganz schön."

Dann war es still. Nach vielen Minuten hörte sie, daß er leise und vorsichtig kaute. Sie atmete absichtlich tief und gleichmäßig, damit er nicht merken sollte, daß sie noch wach war. Aber sein Kauen war so regelmäßig, daß sie davon langsam einschlief.

Als er am nächsten Abend nach Hause kam, schob sie ihm vier Scheiben Brot hin. Sonst hatte er immer nur drei essen können.

„Du kannst ruhig vier essen", sagte sie und ging von der Lampe weg. „Ich kann dieses Brot nicht so recht vertragen. Iß du man eine mehr. Ich vertrag es nicht so gut."

Sie sah, wie er sich über den Teller beugte. Er sah nicht auf. In diesem Augenblick tat er ihr leid.

„Du kannst doch nicht nur zwei Scheiben essen", sagte er auf seinen Teller.

„Doch. Abends vertrag ich das Brot nicht gut. Iß man. Iß man."

Erst nach einer Weile setzte sie sich unter die Lampe an den Tisch.

3. Using context as a clue, determine the meaning of the words below.
   1. überlegen   a. *to lie*
   2. Atem   b. *breath*
   3. verheiratet   c. *gutter*
   4. ertragen   d. *to chew*
   5. lügen   e. *to listen to*
   6. horchen nach   f. *married*
   7. Dachrinne   g. *to think about*
   8. kauen   h. *to endure*

A Closer Look

4. Read the story again. As you read, you and your partner will take summarizing notes in English, jotting down the main points under these categories: Actions/Dialogues and Thoughts.

5. Compare your summary chart (**Zusammenstellung**) with those of your classmates. Did you understand, in general, the sequence of events and the thoughts of the woman?

6. What excuse did the woman make up for coming down to the kitchen? Why was she upset with her husband?

7. After they went back to bed, what did she hear? What did she seem to have realized by the next day?

8. From whose perspective is the story told? What is the significance of the title? What is implied about the man's motives, but never stated? What kind of social conditions might give rise to the kind of conflict portrayed in this story?

9. Schau noch einmal auf deine Zusammenstellung und stell fest, was durch die Gedanken der Frau erzählt wurde! Rekonstruiere jetzt die Erzählung aus der Perspektive des Mannes! (Vergiß nicht, Zeitausdrücke, wo nötig, zu verwenden!)

KANN ICH'S WIRKLICH?

1 How would you tell a friend what you did yesterday after school? How would you tell someone about the last vacation you enjoyed?
1. E.g.: Gestern nach der Schule habe ich … ; In den letzten Ferien war ich …

2 How would you ask your father to suggest a place to go on vacation? How would you suggest that you would like to fly to Austria? How could your father respond positively? 2. E.g.: Wo sollen wir in den Ferien hinfahren? Was schlägst du vor?; Ich würde gern mal nach Österreich fliegen.; Eine gute Idee!

3 How would you say that you would like to order a veal cutlet and a glass of mineral water?
3. Ich würde gern ein Wiener Schnitzel und ein Glas Mineralwasser bestellen.

4 How would you say that you heard   a. Ich habe gehört, die Pommes frites sollen sehr scharf sein.

a. that the French fries are very spicy?

b. that the shish-kebab at "The Slovenia" is excellent?
b. Ich habe gehört, das Schisch-Kebab im „Slovenia" soll ausgezeichnet sein.

5 How would a waiter say that there are no more meatballs?
5. Tut mir leid. Die Fleischklöße sind schon alle.

6 How would you persuade someone to go eat Mexican food? How would a friend dissuade you from eating a salad?
6. Geh doch einmal mexikanisch essen!; Iß ja keinen Salat!

7 How would you ask a friend's advice on what to wear

a. to a birthday party?   a. E.g.: Welche Bluse soll ich mir zur Geburtstagsparty anziehen, die rote oder die blaue?

b. for a day at the beach?   b. E.g.: Welches T-Shirt soll ich für einen Tag am Strand anziehen, das kurze oder das lange?

8 How would you suggest the same things to your friend?
8. Zieh doch die rote Bluse an!; Ich würde das kurze T-Shirt anziehen.

9 How would you ask a friend if she prefers

a. the blue blouse or the green one?   a. Welche Bluse findest du schöner, die blaue oder die grüne?

b. the striped pants or the checkered ones?   b. Welche Hose ziehst du vor, die gestreifte oder die karierte?

10 How would you say that

a. you really prefer the brown leather shoes?   a. Mir gefallen eigentlich die braunen Lederschuhe besser.

b. you prefer the T-shirt with the Germany motif?   b. Ich ziehe das T-Shirt mit dem Deutschland-Motiv vor.

11 How would you ask someone what he or she is interested in? How would you say you're interested in colorful ties, but don't care for sweaters made of wool?   11. Wofür interessierst du dich?; Ich interessiere mich für bunte Klamotten, aber ich interessiere mich nicht für Pullover aus Wolle.

12 How would you say to your friend that it doesn't really matter to you which shoes he or she wears?   12. Es ist mir eigentlich egal, was für Schuhe du trägst.

ERSTE STUFE

REPORTING PAST EVENTS

Ich bin gern im Mittelmeer geschwommen. *I enjoyed swimming in the Mediterranean Sea.*
Ich habe auch viel gesehen. *I saw a lot, too.*

TALKING ABOUT TRAVEL

Ich war (in, an, auf) ... *I was (in, at, on)...*
die Küste, -n   *coast*
die Klippe, -n   *cliff*
die Insel, -n   *island*
die Bucht, -en   *bay*
die Oase, -n   *oasis*

die Sportanlage, -n   *sport facility*
die Anlage, -n   *grounds, site*
der Court, -s   *court*
der Platz, ⸚e   *place*
der Pool, -s   *swimming pool*
die Halle, -n   *hall*
das Fahrrad-Depot, -s   *bicycle racks*

OTHER USEFUL WORDS

der Anfänger, -   *beginner*
der Fortgeschrittene, -n   *advanced (person)*
der Erfahrene, -n   *experienced (person)*

der Olympiasieger, -   *olympic champion*
der Zehnkämpfer, -   *decathlete*
der Geheimtip, -s   *secret tip*
abwechslungsreich   *varied, diversified*
sich langweilen   *to be bored*
zahlreich   *numerous*

RESPONDING TO SUGGESTIONS

Gute Idee! *Good idea!*
Das wäre toll! *That would be great!*

- - -

ZWEITE STUFE

TALKING ABOUT INTERNATIONAL FOODS
see page 294

EXPRESSING REGRET

Tut mir leid, aber der Couscous ist leider schon alle. *Sorry, but unfortunately we're all out of couscous.*

RESPONDING TO PERSUASION

Das ist ein guter Vorschlag. *That's a good suggestion.*
der Vorschlag, ⸚e   *suggestion*

- - -

DRITTE STUFE

TALKING ABOUT CLOTHING

salopp   *casual*
elegant   *elegant*
weit   *big, broad*
fein   *fine, exquisite*
der Ringel, -   *ringlet*

das Muster, -   *pattern*
das Karo, -s   *check, diamonds*
der Streifen, -   *stripe*
das Loch, ⸚er   *hole*
die Schleife, -n   *loop, bow*
die Fliege, -n   *bow tie*
die Wildlederjacke, -n   *suede jacket*

das Abendkleid, -er   *evening gown*
der Smoking, -s   *tuxedo*
der Kummerbund, -e   *cummerbund*
der Lackschuh, -e   *patent-leather shoe*

REFERENCE SECTION

SUMMARY OF FUNCTIONS

ADDITIONAL VOCABULARY

GRAMMAR SUMMARY

GERMAN-ENGLISH VOCABULARY

ENGLISH-GERMAN VOCABULARY

GRAMMAR INDEX

SUMMARY OF FUNCTIONS

Functions are probably best defined as the ways in which you use a language for specific purposes. When you find yourself in specific situations, such as in a restaurant, in a grocery store, or at school, you will want to communicate with those around you. In order to do that, you have to "function" in the language so that you can be understood: you place an order, make a purchase, or talk about your class schedule.

Such functions form the core of this book. They are easily identified by the boxes in each chapter that are labeled SO SAGT MAN DAS! These functions are the building blocks you need to become a speaker of German. All the other features in the chapter—the grammar, the vocabulary, even the culture notes—are there to support the functions you are learning.

Here is a list of the functions from both Levels 1 and 2, accompanied by the German expressions you will need in order to communicate in a wide range of situations. The level of the book is indicated by a Roman numeral I or II. The chapter and page on which the expressions were introduced is also indicated.

You have learned to communicate in a variety of situations. Using these expressions, you will be able to communicate in many other situations as well.

SOCIALIZING

Saying hello
I, Ch. 1, p. 21

Guten Morgen!
Guten Tag!
Morgen! ⎤
Tag! ⎦ *shortened forms*
Hallo! ⎤
Grüß dich! ⎦ *informal*

Saying goodbye
I, Ch. 1, p. 21

Auf Wiedersehen!
Wiedersehen! *shortened form*
Tschüs!
Tschau! ⎤ *informal*
Bis dann! ⎦

Offering something to eat and drink
I, Ch. 3, p. 70

Was möchtest du trinken?
Was möchte *(name)* trinken?
Was möchtet ihr essen?

Responding to an offer
I, Ch. 3, p. 70

Ich möchte *(beverage)* trinken.
Er/Sie möchte im Moment gar nichts.
Wir möchten *(food/beverage)*, bitte.

Saying please
I, Ch. 3, p. 72

Bitte!

Saying thank you
I, Ch. 3, p. 72

Danke!
Danke schön!
Danke sehr!

Saying you're welcome
I, Ch. 3, p. 72

Bitte!
Bitte schön!
Bitte sehr!

Giving compliments
I, Ch. 5, p. 127

Der/Die/Das *(thing)* sieht *(adjective)* aus!
Der/Die/Das *(thing)* gefällt mir.

II, Ch. 8, p. 194

Dein/Deine *(clothing item)* sieht echt fetzig aus.
Sie/Er/Es paßt dir auch echt gut.
Und dieser/diese/dieses *(clothing item)* paßt dir prima!
Sie/Er/Es paßt gut zu deiner/deinem *(clothing item)*.

Responding to compliments
I, Ch. 5, p. 127

Ehrlich?
Wirklich?
Nicht zu *(adjective)*?
Meinst du?

II, Ch. 8, p. 194

Meinst du wirklich?
Ist er/sie/es mir nicht zu *(adjective)*?
Das ist auch mein/meine Lieblings*(clothing item)*.
Echt?

Starting a conversation
I, Ch. 6, p. 145

Wie geht's?
Wie geht's denn? ⎤ *Asking how someone is doing*

Sehr gut!
Prima!
Danke, gut!
Gut!
Danke, es geht.
So lala. *Responding to* **Wie geht's?**
Nicht schlecht.
Nicht so gut.
Schlecht.
Sehr schlecht.
Miserabel. ⎦

Making plans
I, Ch. 6, p. 150

Was willst du machen?   Ich will *(activity)*.
Wohin will *(person)* gehen?   Er/Sie will in/ins *(place)* gehen.

Ordering food and beverages
I, Ch. 6, p. 154

Was bekommen Sie?   Ich bekomme *(food/beverage)*.
Ja, bitte?
Was essen Sie?   Einen/Eine/Ein *(food)*, bitte.
Was möchten Sie?   Ich möchte *(food/beverage)*, bitte.
Was trinken Sie?   Ich trinke *(beverage)*.
Was nimmst du?   Ich nehme *(food/beverage)*.
Was ißt du?   Ich esse *(food)*.

II, Ch. 11, p. 274

Haben Sie schon gewählt?   Ja, bringen Sie mir bitte den/die/das *(menu item)*.
Und was hätten Sie gern?   Ich hätte gern den/die/das *(menu item)*.

Talking about how something tastes
I, Ch. 6, p. 156

Wie schmeckt's?   Gut!
    Prima!
    Sagenhaft!
    Der/Die/Das *(food/beverage)* schmeckt lecker!
    Der/Die/Das *(food/beverage)* schmeckt nicht.
Schmeckt's?   Ja, gut!
    Nein, nicht so gut.
    Nicht besonders.

Paying the check
I, Ch. 6, p. 156

Hallo! Ich will/ möchte zahlen.   Das macht (zusammen) *(total)*.
Stimmt schon!

Extending an invitation
I, Ch. 7, p. 174; Ch. 11, p. 277

Willst du *(activity)*?
Wir wollen *(activity)*. Komm doch mit!
Möchtest du mitkommen?
Ich habe am *(day/date)* eine Party. Ich lade dich ein. Kannst du kommen?

Responding to an invitation
I, Ch. 7, p. 174; Ch. 11, p. 277

Ja, gern!
Toll!
Ich komme gern mit. ⎤ *accepting*
Aber sicher!
Natürlich! ⎦
Das geht nicht. ⎤ *declining*
Ich kann leider nicht. ⎦

Expressing obligations
I, Ch. 7, p. 175

Ich habe keine Zeit. Ich muß *(activity)*.

Offering help
I, Ch. 7, p. 179

Was kann ich für dich tun? ⎤
Kann ich etwas für dich tun? ⎟ *asking*
Brauchst du Hilfe? ⎦
Gut! Mach' ich!   *agreeing*

Asking what you should do
I, Ch. 8, p. 198

Was soll ich für dich tun?   Du kannst für mich *(chore)*.
Wo soll ich *(thing/things)* kaufen?   Beim (Metzger/Bäcker). In der/Im *(store)*.
Soll ich *(thing/things)* in der/im *(store)* kaufen?   Nein, das kannst du besser in der/im *(store)* kaufen.

Getting someone's attention
I, Ch. 9, p. 222

Verzeihung!
Entschuldigung!

Offering more
I, Ch. 9, p. 230

Möchtest du noch etwas?
Möchtest du noch einen/eine/ein *(food/beverage)*?
Noch einen/eine/ein *(food/beverage)*?

Saying you want more
I, Ch. 9, p. 230

Ja, bitte. Ich nehme noch einen/eine/ein *(food/beverage)*.
Ja, bitte. Noch einen/eine/ein *(food/beverage)*.
Ja, gern.

Saying you don't want more
I, Ch. 9, p. 230

Nein, danke! Ich habe keinen Hunger mehr.
Nein, danke! Ich habe genug.
Danke, nichts mehr für mich.
Nein, danke, keinen/keine/kein *(food/beverage)* mehr.

Using the telephone
I, Ch. 11, p. 274

Hier *(name)*.
Hier ist *(name)*.
Ich möchte bitte *(name)*
  sprechen.   *starting a conversation*
Kann ich bitte *(name)*
  sprechen?
Tag! Hier ist *(name)*.

Wiederhören!
Auf Wiederhören!   *ending a conversation*
Tschüs!

Talking about birthdays
I, Ch. 11, p. 278

Wann hast du Geburtstag? Ich habe am *(date)*
                               Geburtstag.
                               Am *(date)*.

Expressing good wishes
I, Ch. 11, p. 278

Alles Gute zum/zur *(occasion)*!
Herzlichen Glückwunsch zum/zur *(occasion)*!

II, Ch. 11, p. 275

Zum Wohl!
Prost!
Auf dein/euer/Ihr Wohl!
Guten Appetit!
Mahlzeit!

EXCHANGING INFORMATION

Asking someone his or her name and giving yours
I, Ch. 1, p. 22

Wie heißt du?   Ich heiße *(name)*.
Heißt du *(name)*?   Ja, ich heiße *(name)*.

Asking and giving someone else's name
I, Ch. 1, p. 22

Wie heißt der Junge?   Der Junge heißt *(name)*.
Heißt der Junge *(name)*?   Ja, er heißt *(name)*.
Wie heißt das Mädchen?   Das Mädchen heißt
                           (name).
Heißt das Mädchen *(name)*?   Nein, sie heißt *(name)*.

Asking and telling who someone is
I, Ch. 1, p. 23

Wer ist das?   Das ist der/die *(name)*.

Asking someone his or her age and giving yours
I, Ch. 1, p. 25

Wie alt bist du?   Ich bin *(number)* Jahre alt.
                   Ich bin *(number)*.
                    (Number).
Bist du schon *(number)*?   Nein, ich bin *(number)*.

Asking and giving someone else's age
I, Ch. 1, p. 25

Wie alt ist der Peter?   Er ist *(number)*.
Und die Monika? Ist
  sie auch *(number)*?   Ja, sie ist auch *(number)*.

Asking someone where he or she is from and telling where you are from
I, Ch. 1, p. 28

Woher kommst du?   Ich komme aus *(place)*.
Woher bist du?   Ich bin aus *(place)*.
Bist du aus *(place)*?   Nein, ich bin aus *(place)*.

Asking and telling where someone else is from
I, Ch. 1, p. 28

Woher ist *(person)*?   Er/Sie ist aus *(place)*.
Kommt *(person)* aus *(place)*?   Nein, sie kommt aus
                            (place).

Talking about how someone gets to school
I, Ch. 1, p. 31

Wie kommst du
  zur Schule?   Ich komme mit der/dem
                    (mode of transportation).

Kommt Ahmet zu Fuß
  zur Schule?   Nein, er kommt auch mit
                   der/dem *(mode of
                   transportation)*.

Wie kommt Ayla
  zur Schule?   Sie kommt mit der/dem
                    (mode of transportation).

Talking about interests
I, Ch. 2, p. 46

Was machst du in
  deiner Freizeit?   Ich *(activity)*.
Spielst du *(sport/
  instrument/game)*?   Ja, ich spiele *(sport/
                   instrument/game)*.
                   Nein, *(sport/instrument/
                   game)* spiele ich nicht.
Was macht *(name)*?   Er/Sie spielt *(sport/
                   instrument/game)*.

Asking about interests
II, Ch. 8, p. 193; Ch. 10, p. 240

Interessierst du dich für *(thing)*?
Wofür interessierst du dich?
Was für Interessen hast du?

Expressing interest
II, Ch. 8, p. 193; Ch. 10, p. 240

Ja, *(thing)* interessiert mich.
Ich interessiere mich für *(thing)*.

Expressing disinterest
II, Ch. 8, p. 193

(Thing) interessiert mich nicht.
Ich hab' kein Interesse an *(thing)*.

Expressing indifference
II, Ch. 8, p. 193

(Thing) ist mir egal.

Saying when you do various activities
I, Ch. 2, p. 53

Was machst du nach der Schule?	Am Nachmittag *(activity)*.
	Am Abend *(activity)*.
Und am Wochenende?	Am Wochenende *(activity)*.
Was machst du im Sommer?	Im Sommer *(activity)*.

Talking about where you and others live
I, Ch. 3, p. 69

Wo wohnst du?	Ich wohne in *(place)*.
	In *(place)*.
Wo wohnt der/die *(name)*?	Er/Sie wohnt in *(place)*.
	In *(place)*.

Describing a room
I, Ch. 3, p. 75

Der/Die/Das *(thing)* ist alt.	
Der/Die/Das *(thing)* ist kaputt.	
Der/Die/Das *(thing)* ist klein, aber ganz bequem.	
Ist *(thing)* neu?	Ja, er/sie/es ist neu.

Talking about family members
I, Ch. 3, p. 78

Ist das dein/deine *(family member)*?	Ja, das ist mein/ meine *(family member)*.
Und dein/deine *(family member)*? Wie heißt er/sie?	Er/Sie heißt *(name)*.
Wo wohnen deine *(family members)*?	In *(place)*.

Describing people
I, Ch. 3, p. 80

Wie sieht *(person)* aus?	Er/Sie hat *(color)* Haare und *(color)* Augen.

Talking about class schedules
I, Ch. 4, p. 98

Welche Fächer hast du?	Ich habe *(classes)*.
Was hast du am *(day)*?	*(Classes)*.
Was hat die Katja am *(day)*?	Sie hat *(classes)*.
Welche Fächer habt ihr?	Wir haben *(classes)*.
Was habt ihr nach der Pause?	Wir haben *(classes)*.
Und was habt ihr am Samstag?	Wir haben frei!

Using a schedule to talk about time
I, Ch. 4, p. 99

Wann hast du *(class)*?	Um *(hour)* Uhr *(minutes)*.
Was hast du um *(hour)* Uhr?	*(Class)*.
Was hast du von *(time)* bis *(time)*?	Ich habe *(class)*.

Sequencing events
I, Ch. 4, p. 101

Welche Fächer hast du am *(day)*?	Zuerst hab' ich *(class)*, dann *(class)*, danach *(class)*, und zuletzt *(class)*.

Talking about prices
I, Ch. 4, p. 107

Was kostet *(thing)*?	Er/Sie kostet nur *(price)*.
Was kosten *(things)*?	Sie kosten *(price)*.
Das ist (ziemlich) teuer!	
Das ist (sehr) billig!	
Das ist (sehr) preiswert!	

Pointing things out
I, Ch. 4, p. 108

Wo sind die *(things)*?	Schauen Sie!
	Dort!
	Sie sind dort drüben!
	Sie sind da hinten.
	Sie sind da vorn.

Expressing wishes when shopping
I, Ch. 5, p. 122

Was möchten Sie?	Ich möchte einen/eine/ein *(thing)* sehen, bitte.
	Ich brauche einen/eine/ein *(thing)*.
Was bekommen Sie?	Einen/Eine/Ein *(thing)*, bitte.
Haben Sie einen Wunsch?	Ich suche einen/eine/ein *(thing)*.

Describing how clothes fit
I, Ch. 5, p. 125

Es paßt prima.
Es paßt nicht.

Talking about trying on clothes
I, Ch. 5, p. 131

Ich probiere den/die/das *(item of clothing)* an.
Ich ziehe den/die/das *(item of clothing)* an.

If you buy it:	*If you don't:*
Ich nehme es.	Ich nehme es nicht.
Ich kaufe es.	Ich kaufe es nicht.

Telling time
I, Ch. 6, p. 146

Wie spät ist es jetzt? Es ist *(time)*.
Wieviel Uhr ist es? Es ist *(time)*.

Talking about when you do things
I, Ch. 6, p. 146

Wann gehst du *(activity)*? Um *(time)*.
Um wieviel Uhr *(action)* du? Um *(time)*.
Und du? Wann *(action)* du? Um *(time)*.

Talking about how often you do things
I, Ch. 7, p. 178

Wie oft *(action)* du? (Einmal) in der Woche.
Und wie oft mußt
du *(action)*? Jeden Tag.
  Ungefähr (zweimal) im Monat.

Explaining what to do
I, Ch. 7, p. 179

Du kannst für mich *(action)*.

Talking about the weather
I, Ch. 7, p. 183

Wie ist das Wetter heute? Heute regnet es.
  Wolkig und kühl.
Wie ist das Wetter morgen? Sonnig, aber kalt.
Regnet es heute? Ich glaube schon.
Schneit es am Abend? Nein, es schneit nicht.
Wieviel Grad haben wir heute? Ungefähr 10 Grad.

Talking about quantities
I, Ch. 8, p. 202

Wieviel *(food item)*
bekommen Sie? 500 Gramm *(food item)*.
  100 Gramm, bitte.

Asking if someone wants anything else
I, Ch. 8, p. 203

Sonst noch etwas?
Was bekommen Sie noch?
Haben Sie noch einen Wunsch?

Saying you want something else
I, Ch. 8, p. 203

Ich brauche noch einen/eine/ein
  (food/beverage/thing).
Ich bekomme noch einen/eine/ein
  (food/beverage/thing).

Telling someone you don't need anything else
I, Ch. 8, p. 203

Nein, danke.
Danke, das ist alles.

Giving a reason
I, Ch. 8, p. 206

Jetzt kann ich nicht, weil ...
Es geht nicht, denn ...

Saying where you were
I, Ch. 8, p. 207

Wo warst du heute morgen? Ich war in/im/an/am
  (place).

Wo warst du gestern? Ich war in/im/an/am
  (place).

Saying what you bought
I, Ch. 8, p. 207

Was hast du gekauft? Ich habe *(thing)* gekauft.

Talking about where something is located
I, Ch. 9, p. 222

Verzeihung, wissen Sie,
  wo der/die/das *(place)* ist? In der Innenstadt.
  Am *(place name)*.
  In der *(street name)*.
Wo ist der/die/das *(place)*? Es tut mir leid. Das
  weiß ich nicht.
Entschuldigung! Weißt du,
  wo der/die/das *(place)* ist? Keine Ahnung! Ich bin
  nicht von hier.

Asking for directions
I, Ch. 9, p. 226

Wie komme ich zum/zur *(place)*?
Wie kommt man zum/zur *(place)*?

II, Ch. 9, p. 222
Entschuldigung! Wo ist bitte *(place)*.
Verzeihung! Wissen Sie vielleicht, wie ich zum/zur
  (place) komme?

Giving directions
I, Ch. 9, p. 226

Gehen Sie geradeaus bis zum/zur *(place)*.
Nach rechts/links.
Hier rechts/links.

II, Ch. 9, p. 222
Sie biegen hier *(direction)* in die *(streetname)* ein.
Dann kommen Sie zum/zur *(place)*.
Das ist hier *(direction)* um die Ecke.
Ich weiß es leider nicht. Ich bin nicht von hier.

Talking about what there is to eat and drink
I, Ch. 9, p. 229

Was gibt es hier zu essen? Es gibt *(foods)*.
Und zu trinken? Es gibt *(beverage)* und
  auch *(beverage)*.

Talking about what you did in your free time
I, Ch. 10, p. 260

Was hast du *(time phrase)* gemacht?   Ich habe ...
(person/thing) gesehen.
(book, magazine, etc.)
gelesen.
mit *(person)* über *(subject)*
gesprochen.

Discussing gift ideas
I, Ch. 11, p. 282

Schenkst du *(person)*
einen/eine/ein *(thing)*
zum/zur *(occasion)*?   Nein, ich schenke ihm/ihr
einen/eine/ein *(thing)*.

Was schenkst du *(person)*
zum/zur *(occasion)*?   Ich weiß noch nicht. Hast
du eine Idee?

Wem schenkst du
den/die/das *(thing)*?   Ich schenke *(person)*
den/die/das *(thing)*.

Asking about past events
II, Ch. 3, p. 57; Ch. 3, p. 63

Was hast du *(time phrase)* gemacht?
Was hat *(person)* *(time phrase)* gemacht?

Asking what someone did
II, Ch. 3, p. 57

Was hast du *(time phrase)* gemacht?
Was hat *(person)* *(time phrase)* gemacht?

Telling what someone did
II, Ch. 3, p. 57

Ich habe *(activity + past participle)*.
Er/Sie hat *(activity + past participle)*.

Asking where someone was
II, Ch. 3, p. 63

Wo bist du gewesen?
Und wo warst du?

Telling where you were
II, Ch. 3, p. 63

Ich bin in/im/an/am *(place)* gewesen.
Ich war in/im/an/am *(place)*.
Ich war mit *(person)* in/im/an/am *(place)*.

Asking for information
II, Ch. 4, p. 95; Ch. 10, p. 248

Ich habe eine Frage: ...?
Sag mal, ...?
Wie steht's mit *(thing)*?
Darf ich dich etwas fragen? ...?
Wissen Sie, ob ...?
Können Sie mir sagen, ob ...?

Stating information
II, Ch. 10, p. 248

Ich glaube schon, daß ...
Ich meine doch, daß ...

Responding emphatically
II, Ch. 4, p. 95

Ja, natürlich!
Na klar!
Aber sicher!

Agreeing with reservations
II. Ch. 4, p. 95

Ja, das kann sein, aber ...
Das stimmt, aber ...
Eigentlich schon, aber ...

Asking what someone may or may not do
II, Ch. 4, p. 98

Was darfst du (nicht) tun?
Was darfst du (nicht) essen/trinken?
Darfst du *(activity)*?

Telling what you may or may not do
II, Ch. 4, p. 98

Ich darf (nicht) *(activity)*.
Ich darf *(food/drink)* (nicht) essen/trinken.

Expressing skepticism
II, Ch. 5, p. 114

Was soll denn das sein, dieser/diese/dieses *(thing)*?

Making certain
II, Ch. 5, p. 114

Du ißt nur vegetarisch, was?   Ja/Nein.
Du ißt wohl viel Fleisch, ja?   Nicht unbedingt!
Du magst Joghurt, oder?   Na klar!
Du magst doch Quark, nicht wahr?   Sicher!

Calling someone's attention to something and responding
II, Ch. 5, p. 118

Schau mal!   Ja, was denn?
Guck mal!   Ja, was bitte?
Sieh mal!   Was ist denn los?
Hör mal!   Was ist?
Hör mal zu!   Was gibt's?

Inquiring about someone's health
II, Ch. 6, p. 137

Wie fühlst du dich?
Wie geht es dir?
Ist dir nicht gut?
Ist was mit dir?
Was fehlt dir?

Responding to questions about your health
II, Ch. 6, p. 137

Ich fühl' mich wohl!
Es geht mir (nicht) gut!
Mir ist schlecht
Mir ist nicht gut.

Responding to statements about someone's health
II, Ch. 6, p. 137

Ach schade!
Gute Besserung!
Hoffentlich geht es dir bald besser!

Asking about pain
II, Ch. 6, p. 143

Tut's weh?
Was tut dir weh?
Tut dir was weh?
Tut dir *(body part)* weh?

Expressing pain
II, Ch. 6, p. 143

Au!
Aua!
Es tut weh!
Der/Die/Das *(body part)* tut mir weh.
Ja, ich hab' *(body part)* schmerzen.

Expressing wishes
II, Ch. 7, p. 168

Was möchtest du gern
mal haben?   Ich möchte gern mal
                        einen/eine/ein *(thing)*!
Was wünschst du dir mal?   Ich wünsche mir mal ...
Und was wünscht ihr euch?   Wir wünschen uns ...

Talking about plans
II, Ch. 10, p. 252

Ich werde *(activity)*.
(Time phrase) werde ich *(activity)*.

Expressing hearsay
II, Ch. 11, p. 270

Ich habe gehört, daß ...
Man hat mir gesagt, daß ...
(Thing) soll *(adjective)* sein.

EXPRESSING ATTITUDES AND OPINIONS

Asking for an opinion
I, Ch. 2, p. 55; Ch. 9, p. 232

Wie findest du *(thing/activity/place)*?

Expressing your opinion
I, Ch. 2, p. 55; Ch. 9, p. 232

Ich finde *(thing/activity/place)* langweilig.
(Thing/Activity/Place) ist Spitze!
(Activity) macht Spaß!
Ich finde es toll, daß ...
Ich glaube, daß ...

Agreeing
I, Ch. 2, p. 56

Ich auch!
Das finde ich auch!
Stimmt!
II, Ch. 10, p. 251
Da stimm' ich dir zu!
Da hast du (bestimmt) recht!
Einverstanden!

Disagreeing
I, Ch. 2, p. 56

Ich nicht!
Das finde ich nicht!
Stimmt nicht!
II, Ch. 10, p. 251
Das stimmt (überhaupt) nicht!

Agreeing with reservations
II, Ch. 7, p. 175

Ja, schon, aber ...
Ja, aber ...
Eigentlich schon, aber ...
Ja, ich stimme dir zwar zu, aber ...

Commenting on clothes
I, Ch. 5, p. 125

Wie findest du
den/die/das
(clothing item)?   Ich finde ihn/sie/es *(adjective)*.
                      Er/Sie/Es gefällt mir (nicht).

Expressing uncertainty, not knowing
I, Ch. 5, p. 125; Ch. 9, p. 222

Ich bin nicht sicher.
Ich weiß nicht.
Keine Ahnung!

Expressing regret
I, Ch. 9, p. 222

Es tut mir leid.

II, Ch. 5, p. 113

Ich bedaure, ...
Was für ein Pech, ...
Leider, ...

Downplaying
II, Ch. 5, p. 113

Das macht nichts!
Schon gut!
Nicht so schlimm!
Dann *(action)* ich eben *(alternative)*.
Dann *(action)* ich halt *(alternative)*.

Asking how someone liked something
II, Ch. 3, p. 68

Wie war's?
Wie hat dir Dresden gefallen?
Wie hat es dir gefallen?
Hat es dir gefallen?

Responding enthusiastically
II, Ch. 3, p. 68

Na, prima!
Ja, Spitze!
Das freut mich!

Responding sympathetically
II, Ch. 3, p. 68

Schade!
Tut mir leid!
Das tut mir aber leid!

Expressing enthusiasm
II, Ch. 3, p. 68

Phantastisch!
Es war echt super!
Es hat mir gut gefallen.
Wahnsinnig gut!

Expressing disappointment
II, Ch. 3, p. 68

Na ja, soso!
Nicht besonders.
Es hat mir nicht gefallen.
Es war furchtbar!

Expressing approval
II, Ch. 4, p. 88

Es ist prima, daß ...
Ich finde es toll, daß ...
Ich freue mich, daß ...
Ich bin froh, daß ...

Expressing disapproval
II, Ch. 4, p. 88

Es ist schade, daß ...
Ich finde es nicht gut, daß ...

Expressing indecision
II, Ch. 9, p. 213

Was machen wir jetzt?
Was sollen wir bloß machen?

Asking for suggestions
II, Ch. 9, p. 213; Ch. 11, p. 266

Hast du eine Idee?
Was schlägst du vor?
Was sollen wir machen?
Wofür bist du?

Making suggestions
II, Ch. 9, p. 213; Ch. 11, p. 266

Wir können mal *(activity)*.
Ich schlage vor, ...
Ich schlage vor, daß ...
Ich bin dafür, daß ...
Wie wär's mit *(activity/place)*?

Responding to suggestions
II, Ch. 11, p. 266

Das wäre nicht schlecht.

EXPRESSING FEELINGS AND EMOTIONS

Asking about likes and dislikes
I, Ch. 2, p. 48; Ch. 4, p. 102; Ch. 10, p. 250

Was *(action)* du gern?
(Action) du gern?
Magst du *(things/activities)*?
Was für *(things/activities)* magst du?

Expressing likes
I, Ch. 2, p. 48; Ch. 4, p. 102; Ch. 10, p. 250

Ich *(action)* gern.
Ich mag *(things/activities)*.
(Thing/Activities) mag ich (sehr/furchtbar) gern.

Expressing dislikes
I, Ch. 2, p. 48; I, Ch. 10, p. 250

Ich *(action)* nicht so gern.
Ich mag *(things/action)* (überhaupt) nicht.

Talking about favorites
I, Ch. 4, p. 102

Was ist dein
Lieblings *(category)*?   Mein Lieblings *(category)*
ist *(thing)*.

Responding to good news
I, Ch. 4, p. 104

Toll!
Das ist prima!
Nicht schlecht.

Responding to bad news
I, Ch. 4, p. 104

Schade!
So ein Pech!
So ein Mist!
Das ist sehr schlecht!

Expressing familiarity
I, Ch. 10, p. 252

Kennst du *(person/ place/thing)*?

Ja, sicher!
Ja, klar! *or*
Nein, den/die/das kenne ich nicht.
Nein, überhaupt nicht.

Expressing preferences
I, Ch. 10, p. 253

(Siehst) du gern ...?   Ja, aber ... (sehe) ich lieber.
Und am liebsten (sehe) ich ...

(Siehst) du lieber ...
oder ...?   Lieber ...

II, Ch. 5, p. 123; Ch. 7, p. 165

Welche *(thing)* magst du lieber?
(Thing) oder *(thing)*?   *(Thing)* mag ich lieber.
Welchen/Welche/Welches
(food item) schmeckt dir
besser? *(Food item)* oder
(food item)?   *(Food item)* schmeckt
mir besser.

Mir gefällt *(person/place/ thing)* besser als *(person/place/thing)*.
Ich finde die *(person/place/ thing)* schöner.
Ich ziehe *(person/place/ thing)* vor.

Expressing strong preference and favorites
I, Ch. 10, p, 253

Was (siehst) du am liebsten?   Am liebsten (sehe) ich ...
II, Ch, 5, p. 123
Welches *(thing)* magst
du am liebsten?   Am liebsten mag ich
(thing).

Welche *(food item)* schmeckt
dir am besten?   *(Food item)* schmeckt
mir am besten.

Expressing hope
II, Ch. 6, p. 148

Ich hoffe, ...
Wir hoffen, ...
Hoffentlich ...

Expressing doubt
II, Ch. 9, p. 217

Ich weiß nicht ob ...
Ich bezweifle, daß ...
Ich bin nicht sicher, ob ...

Expressing resignation
II, Ch. 9, p. 217

Da kann man nichts machen.
Das ist leider so.

Expressing conviction
II, Ch. 9, p. 217

Du kannst mir glauben: ...
Ich bin sicher, daß ...

Expressing surprise
II, Ch. 10, p. 251

Das ist ja unglaublich!
(Das ist) nicht möglich!
Das gibt's doch nicht!

PERSUADING

Telling someone what to do
I, Ch. 8, p. 199

Geh bitte *(action)*!
(Thing/Things) holen, bitte!

Making suggestions
II, Ch. 6, p. 138

Möchtest du *(activity)*?
Willst du *(activity)*?
Du kannst für mich *(activity)*.
(Activity) wir mal!
Sollen wir mal *(activity)*?

Asking for advice
II, Ch. 6, p. 147

Was soll ich machen?
Was soll ich bloß tun?

Giving advice
II, Ch. 6, p. 147

Am besten ...
Du mußt unbedingt ...

Persuading
II, Ch. 8, p. 198

Warum kaufst du dir keinen/keine/kein *(thing)*?
Kauf dir doch diesen/diese/diese *(thing)*!
Trag doch mal etwas *(adjective)*!

Persuading someone not to buy something
II, Ch. 8, p. 189

Kauf dir ja keinen/keine/kein *(thing)*!
Trag ja nichts aus *(material)*!

Asking for permission
II, Ch. 10, p. 247

Darf ich (bitte) *(activity)*?
Kann ich bitte mal *(activity)*?
He, du! Laß mich mal *(activity)*!

Giving permission
II, Ch. 10, p. 247

Ja, natürlich!
Bitte schön!
Bitte!
Gern!

ADDITIONAL VOCABULARY

ADDITIONAL VOCABULARY

This list includes additional vocabulary that you may want to use to personalize activities. If you can't find the words you need here, try the German–English and English–German vocabulary sections beginning on page 347.

SPORT UND INTERESSEN
(SPORTS AND INTERESTS)

angeln *to fish*
Baseball spielen *to play baseball*
Bodybuilding machen *to lift weights*
Brettspiele spielen *to play board games*
fotografieren *to take photographs*
Gewichtheben *lift weights*
Handball spielen *to play handball*
joggen *to jog*
Kajak fahren *to kayak*
kochen *to cook*
malen *to paint*
Münzen sammeln *to collect coins*
nähen *to sew*
radfahren *to ride a bike*
reiten *to ride (a horse)*
Rollschuh laufen *to roller skate*
rudern *to row*
schnorcheln *to snorkle*
segeln *to sail*
Skateboard laufen *to ride a skateboard*
Ski laufen *to (snow) ski*
stricken *to knit*
Tischtennis spielen *to play table tennis*
Videospiele spielen *to play video games*

ZUM DISKUTIEREN
(TOPICS TO DISCUSS)

die Armut *poverty*
die Gesundheit *health*
der Präsident *the president*
die Politik *politics*
die Reklame *advertising*
die Umwelt *the environment*
das Verbrechen *crime*
der Wehrdienst *military service*
der Zivildienst *alternate service*

HAUSTIERE
(PETS)

die Eidechse, -n *lizard*
der Fisch, -e *fish*
der Frosch, ⸚e *frog*
der Hamster, - *hamster*
der Hase, -n *hare*
der Kanarienvogel, ⸚ *canary*
das Kaninchen, - *rabbit*
die Maus, ⸚e *mouse*
das Meerschweinchen, - *guinea pig*
der Papagei, -en *parrot*
das Pferd, -e *horse*
die Schildkröte, -n *turtle*
die Schlange, -n *snake*
das Schwein, -e *pig*
der Vogel, ⸚ *bird*

FAMILIE (FAMILY)

der Halbbruder, ⸚ *half brother*
die Halbschwester, -n *half sister*
der Stiefbruder, ⸚ *stepbrother*
die Stiefmutter, ⸚ *stepmother*
die Stiefschwester, -n *stepsister*
der Stiefvater, ⸚ *stepfather*

GETRÄNKE (BEVERAGES)

die Limo, -s *lemon-flavored drink*
ein Glas Milch *a glass of milk*
ein Glas Tee *a glass of tea*
eine Tasse Kaffee *a cup of coffee*

SPEISEN (FOODS)

die Ananas, - *pineapple*
der Apfelstrudel, - *apple strudel*
die Banane, -n *banana*
die Birne, -n *pear*
die Bratkartoffeln (pl) *pan-fried potatoes*
der Chip, -s *potato chip*
das Ei, -er *egg*
der Eintopf *stew*
die Erdbeere, -n *strawberry*
die Erdnußbutter *peanut butter*
das Gebäck *baked goods*
der gemischte Salat, -e *tossed salad*
das Gulasch, -e *gulash*
die Gurke, -n *cucumber*
die Himbeere, -n *raspberry*
der Joghurt, - *yogurt*
die Karotte, -n *carrot*
die Magermilch *low-fat milk*
die Marmelade, -n *jam, jelly*
die Mayonnaise *mayonnaise*
die Melone, -n *melon*
die Möhre, -n *carrot*
das Müsli *muesli (cereal)*
die Nuß, (pl) Nüsse *nut*
die Orange, -n *orange*
das Plätzchen, - *cookie*
die Pommes frites (pl) *french fries*
der Pudding, -s *pudding*
die Sahne *cream*
der Spinat *spinach*
die Vollmilch *whole milk*
die Zwiebel, -n *onion*

FARBEN (COLORS)

beige *beige*
bunt *colorful*
gepunktet *polka-dotted*
gestreift *striped*
golden *gold*
lila *purple*
orange *orange*
rosa *pink*
silbern *silver*
türkis *turquoise*

KLEIDUNGSSTÜCKE (CLOTHING)

der Anzug, ̈e *suit*
der Badeanzug, ̈e *swimsuit*
der Blazer, - *blazer*
das Halstuch, ̈er *scarf*
der Handschuh, -e *glove*
der Hut, ̈e *hat*
die Krawatte, -n *tie*
der Mantel, ̈ *coat*
der Minirock, ̈e *miniskirt*
die Mütze, -n *cap*
der Parka, -s *parka*
der Rollkragenpullover, - *turtleneck sweater*
die Sandalen (pl) *sandals*
der Schal, -s *shawl*
die Steghose, -n *stirrup pants*
die Strumpfhose, -n *panty hose*
die Weste, -n *vest*

STOFFE (MATERIALS)

Acryl, *acrylic*
Kunstfasern, *synthetic fibers*
Kunstseide, *rayon*
Nylon, *nylon*
Polyacryl, *acrylic*
Polyester, *polyester*
Viskose, *viscose*

FÄCHER (SCHOOL SUBJECTS)

Algebra *algebra*
Band *band*
Chemie *chemistry*
Chor *chorus*
Französisch *French*
Hauswirtschaft *home economics*
Informatik *computer science*
Italienisch *Italian*
Japanisch *Japanese*
Latein *Latin*
Orchester *orchestra*
Physik *physics*
Russisch *Russian*
Spanisch *Spanish*
Sozialkunde *social studies*
Werken *shop*
Wirtschaftskunde *economics*

KÖRPERTEILE (PARTS OF THE BODY)

das Auge, -n *eye*
die Augenbraue, -n *eyebrow*
das Augenlid, -er *eyelid*
die Faust, ̈e *fist*
die Ferse, -n *heel*
das Gesicht, -er *face*
der Kiefer, - *jaw*
das Kinn, -e *chin*
der Nacken, - *neck*
der Oberschenkel, - *thigh*
die Stirn, -en *forehead*
der Unterschenkel, - *shin*
die Wade, -n *calf*
die Wange, -n *cheek*
die Wimper, -n *eyelash*

INSTRUMENTE (INSTRUMENTS)

die Blockflöte, -n *recorder*
die Bratsche, -n *viola*
das Cello (Violoncello), -s *cello*
die Flöte, -n *flute*
die Geige, -n *violin*
die Harfe, -n *harp*
die Klarinette, -n *clarinet*
der Kontrabaß, (pl) Kontrabässe *double bass*
die Mandoline, -n *mandolin*
die Mundharmonika, -s *harmonica*
die Oboe, -n *oboe*
die Posaune, -n *trombone*
das Saxophon, -e *saxophone*
das Schlagzeug, -e *drums*
die Trompete, -n *trumpet*
die Tuba, (pl) Tuben *tuba*

WETTER (WEATHER)

feucht *damp*
gewittrig *stormy*
halbbedeckt *partly cloudy*
heiter *bright*
kühl *cool*
neblig *foggy*
nieslig *drizzly*
trüb *murky*
windig *windy*

HAUSARBEIT *(HOUSEWORK)*

das Auto polieren *to polish the car*
das Auto waschen *to wash the car*
den Fußboden kehren *to sweep the floor*
den Müll wegtragen *to take out the trash*
putzen *to clean*
Staub wischen *to dust*
saubermachen *to clean*
die Wäsche waschen *to do the laundry*
       trocknen *to dry*
       aufhängen *to hang*
       zusammenlegen *to fold*
       bügeln *to iron*
       einräumen *to put away*

FERNSEHEN *(TELEVISION)*

der Abenteuerfilm, -e *adventure film*
die Familiensendung, -en *family program*
die Komödie, -n *comedy*
der Kriminalfilm, -e *detective film*
das Lustspiel, -e *comedy*
die Sendung, -en (über Gesundheit) *program (about health)*
die Spielshow, -s *game show*
die Talkshow, -s *talk show*
die Tiersendung, -en *animal program*
der Wildwestfilm, -e *western*
die Werbesendung, -en *commercial, advertisement*

MÖBEL *(FURNITURE)*

das Bett, -en *bed*
das Bild, -er *picture*
der Computer, - *computer*
die Couch, -es *or* -en *couch*
der Kleiderschrank, ˝e *wardrobe*
die Kommode, -n *chest of drawers*
die Lampe, -n *lamp*
der Nachttisch, -e *night stand*
das Regal, -e *bookshelf*
der Sessel, - *armchair*
der Schreibtisch, -e *desk*
das Sofa, -s *sofa*
der Stuhl, ˝e *chair*
der Teppich, -e *carpet, rug*
der Tisch, -e *table*
der Vorhang, ˝e *curtain*

IN DER STADT
(PLACES AROUND TOWN)

die Brücke, -n *bridge*
die Bücherei, -en *library*
die Diskothek, -en *dance club*
der Flughafen, (pl) Flughäfen *airport*
das Fremdenverkehrsamt,
   (pl) Fremdenverkehrsämter *tourist office*
der Frisiersalon, -s *beauty shop*
das Krankenhaus, (pl) Krankenhäuser *hospital*
der Kreis, -e *district; county*
die Minigolfanlage, -n *mini-golf course*
der Park, -s *park*
die Polizei *police station*
das Stadion, (pl) Stadien *stadium*
der Stadtrand, -̈er *outskirts*
der Stadtteil, -e *urban district*
das Stadtzentrum, (pl) Stadtzentren *downtown*
der Tennisplatz, -̈e *tennis court*
der Zoo, -s *zoo*

KULTURELLE VERANSTALTUNGEN
(CULTURAL EVENTS)

die Ausstellung, -en *exhibit*
das Chorkonzert, -e *choir concert*
das Kabarett, -e *cabaret*
das Symphoniekonzert, -e *symphony*
der Zirkus, (pl) Zirkusse *circus*

GEOGRAPHISCHE ADJEKTIVE
(GEOGRAPHIC ADJECTIVES)

amerikanisch *American*
ägyptisch *Egyptian*
chinesisch *Chinese*
deutsch *German*
englisch *English*
französisch *French*
griechisch *Greek*
indisch *Indian*
italienisch *Italian*
japanisch *Japanese*
mexikanisch *Mexican*
österreichisch *Austrian*
polnisch *Polish*
russisch *Russian*
Schweizer *Swiss*
spanisch *Spanisch*
türkisch *Turkish*

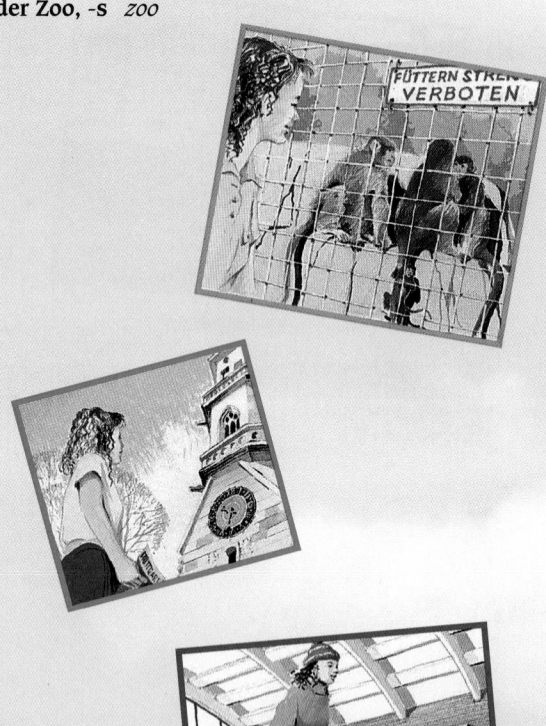

GESCHENKIDEEN
(GIFT IDEAS)

das Bild, -er *picture*
die Kette, -n *chain, necklace*
der Ohrring, -e *earring*
die Puppe, -n *doll*
das Puppenhaus, ¨-er *dollhouse*
der Ring, -e *ring*
... aus Silber *made of silver*
... aus Gold *made of gold*
die Schokolade, -n *chocolate*
das Spielzeug, -e *toy*

AUTO *(AUTOMOBILES)*

die Alarmanlage, -n *alarm system*
die Alufelge, -n *aluminum rims, mag wheels*
der Aufkleber, - *(bumper) sticker*
die Automatik, -en *automatic transmission*
die Lautsprecherbox, -en *speaker*
das 5-Gang Getriebe *five-speed (standard) transmission*
das Kabriolett, -s *convertible*
der Kassettenspieler *cassette player*
der Kombiwagen, - *station wagon*
der Rallyestreifen, - *racing stripes*
die Servolenkung, -en *automatic steering*
die Servobremsen (pl) *automatic brakes*
der Sitzschoner, - *seat cover*
das Stereo-Radio, -s *stereo*
die Zentralverriegelung, -en *automatic locks*

ERDKUNDE (GEOGRAPHY)

Here are some terms you will find on German-language maps:

LÄNDER (STATES)

Most of the states in the United States (**die Vereinigten Staaten**) have the same spelling in German that they have in English. Listed below are those states that have a different spelling.

Kalifornien	*California*
Neumexiko	*New Mexico*
Nordkarolina	*North Carolina*
Norddakota	*North Dakota*
Südkarolina	*South Carolina*
Süddakota	*South Dakota*

STAATEN (COUNTRIES)

Ägypten	*Egypt*
Argentinien	*Argentina*
Brasilien	*Brazil*
China	*China*
England	*England*
Frankreich	*France*
Griechenland	*Greece*
Indien	*India*
Indonesien	*Indonesia*
Italien	*Italy*
Japan	*Japan*
Kanada	*Canada*
Mexiko	*Mexico*
Polen	*Poland*
Rußland	*Russia*
Spanien	*Spain*
Türkei	*Turkey*
die Vereinigten Staaten	*The United States*

KONTINENTE (CONTINENTS)

Afrika	*Africa*
die Antarktik	*Antarctica*
Asien	*Asia*
Australien	*Australia*
Europa	*Europe*
Nordamerika	*North America*
Südamerika	*South America*

MEERE (BODIES OF WATER)

der Atlantik	*the Atlantic*
der Golf von Mexiko	*the Gulf of Mexico*
der Indische Ozean	*the Indian Ocean*
das Mittelmeer	*the Mediterranean*
der Pazifik	*the Pacific*
das Rote Meer	*the Red Sea*
das Schwarze Meer	*the Black Sea*

GEOGRAPHICAL TERMS

der Breitengrad	*latitude*
die Ebene, -n	*plain*
der Fluß, (pl) Flüsse	*river*
das ... Gebirge	*the ... mountains*
die Grenze, -n	*border*
die Hauptstadt, ⁻e	*capital*
der Kontinent, -e	*continent*
das Land, ⁻er	*state*
der Längengrad	*longitude*
das Meer, -e	*ocean, sea*
der Nordpol	*the North Pole*
der See, -n	*lake*
der Staat, -en	*country*
der Südpol	*the South Pole*
das Tal, ⁻er	*valley*

DEUTSCHE NAMEN *(GERMAN NAMES)*

Here are names that you will hear when you visit a German-speaking country.

MÄDCHEN *(GIRLS)*

Andrea	Gabriele (Gabi)	Marta
Angela, Angelika	Gertrud (Trudi(e))	Martina
Anja	Gisela	Meike
Anna	Grete	Michaela
Anneliese	Gudrun	Monika
Annette	Hannelore	Nicole
Antje	Heidi/Heidemarie	Petra
Barbara	Heike	Regina
Bärbel	Helga	Renate
Beate	Hilde	Roswitha
Birgit	Hildegard	Rotraud
Brigitte	Ilse	Sabine
Britta	Ina	Sara
Christa	Inge	Silke
Christiane	Ingrid	Simone
Christine	Irmgard	Stephanie
Claudia	Jennifer	Susanne
Connie	Julie	Silvia
Cordula	Jutta	Tanja
Dorothea	Karin	Ulrike (Uli)
Dorothee	Katharina	Ursel
Elfriede	Katja	Ursula (Uschi)
Elisabeth (Lisa)	Katrin	Ute
Elke	Kirstin	Veronika
Erika	Liselotte (Lotte)	Waltraud
Eva	Marie	

JUNGEN *(BOYS)*

Alexander	Hans-Georg	Martin
Andreas	Hans-Jürgen	Mathias
Axel	Hartmut	Max
Bernd(t)	Hauke	Michael
Bernhard	Heinrich	Norbert
Bruno	Heinz	Otto
Christian	Heinz-Dieter	Patrick
Christoph	Helmar	Paul
Daniel	Helmut	Peter
Detlev(f)	Ingo	Philipp
Dieter	Jan	Rainer (Reiner)
Dietmar	Jens	Ralf
Dirk	Joachim	Reinhard
Eberhard	Jochen	Reinhold
Erik	Johann	Rolf
Felix	Johannes	Rudi
Frank	Jörg	Rüdiger
Franz	Josef	Rudolf
Friedrich	Jürgen	Sebastian
Fritz	Karl	Stefan (Stephan)
Georg	Karl-Heinz	Thomas
Gerd	Klaus	Udo
Gerhard	Konrad	Ulf
Gottfried	Kurt	Ulrich (Uli)
Gregor	Lars	Uwe
Günter	Lothar	Volker
Gustav(f)	Lutz	Werner
Hannes	Manfred	Wilhelm (Willi)
Hans	Markus	Wolfgang

GRAMMAR SUMMARY

GRAMMAR SUMMARY
NOUNS AND THEIR MODIFIERS

In German, nouns (words that name a person, place, or thing) are grouped into three classes or genders: masculine, feminine, and neuter. All nouns, both persons and objects, fall into one of these groups. There are words used with nouns that signal the class of the noun. One of these is the definite article. In English there is one definite article: *the*. In German, there are three, one for each class: **der**, **die**, and **das**.

THE DEFINITE ARTICLE

SUMMARY OF DEFINITE ARTICLES

	NOMINATIVE	ACCUSATIVE	DATIVE
Masculine	der	den	dem
Feminine	die	die	der
Neuter	das	das	dem
Plural	die	die	den

When the definite article is used with a noun, a noun phrase is formed. Noun phrases that are used as subjects are in the nominative case. Nouns that are used as direct objects or the objects of certain prepositions (such as **für**) are in the accusative case. Nouns that are indirect objects, the objects of certain prepositions (such as **mit, bei**), or the objects of special verbs (see page 340) are in the dative case. Below is a summary of the definite articles combined with nouns to form noun phrases.

SUMMARY OF NOUN PHRASES

	NOMINATIVE	ACCUSATIVE	DATIVE
Masculine	der Vater der Ball	den Vater den Ball	dem Vater dem Ball
Feminine	die Mutter die Kassette	die Mutter die Kassette	der Mutter der Kassette
Neuter	das Mädchen das Haus	das Mädchen das Haus	dem Mädchen dem Haus
Plural	die Kassetten die Häuser	die Kassetten die Häuser	den Kassetten den Häusern

DIESER-WORDS

The determiners **dieser, jeder, welcher,** and **alle** are called **dieser**-words. Their endings are similar to those of the definite articles. Note that the endings of the **dieser**-words are very similar to the definite articles.

SUMMARY OF DIESER-WORDS

dieser	*this, that, these*
jeder	*each, every*
alle	*all*
welcher	*which, what*

	NOMINATIVE			ACCUSATIVE			DATIVE		
Masculine	dieser	jeder	welcher	diesen	jeden	welchen	diesem	jedem	welchem
Feminine	diese	jede	welche	diese	jede	welche	dieser	jeder	welcher
Neuter	dieses	jedes	welches	dieses	jedes	welches	diesem	jedem	welchem
Plural	diese	alle	welche	diese	alle	welche	diesen	allen	welchen

THE INDEFINITE ARTICLE

Another type of word that is used with nouns is the *indefinite article:* **ein, eine, ein** in German, *a, an* in English. There is no plural form of **ein**.

SUMMARY OF INDEFINITE ARTICLES

	NOMINATIVE	ACCUSATIVE	DATIVE
Masculine	ein	einen	einem
Feminine	eine	eine	einer
Neuter	ein	ein	einem
Plural	—	—	—

THE NEGATING WORD KEIN

The word **kein** is also used with nouns and means *no, not,* or *not any*. Unlike **ein**, **kein** has a plural form.

	NOMINATIVE	ACCUSATIVE	DATIVE
Masculine	kein	keinen	keinem
Feminine	keine	keine	keiner
Neuter	kein	kein	keinem
Plural	keine	keine	keinen

THE POSSESSIVES

These words also modify nouns and tell you *whose* object or person is being referred to (*my* car, *his* book, *her* mother). These words have the same endings as **kein**.

SUMMARY OF POSSESSIVES

	BEFORE MASCULINE NOUNS			BEFORE FEMININE NOUNS		BEFORE NEUTER NOUNS		BEFORE PLURAL NOUNS	
	Nom	Acc	Dat	Nom & Acc	Dat	Nom & Acc	Dat	Nom & Acc	Dat
my	mein	meinen	meinem	meine	meiner	mein	meinem	meine	meinen
your	dein	deinen	deinem	deine	deiner	dein	deinem	deine	deinen
his	sein	seinen	seinem	seine	seiner	sein	seinem	seine	seinen
her	ihr	ihren	ihrem	ihre	ihrer	ihr	ihrem	ihre	ihren
our	unser	unseren	unserem	usere	unserer	unser	unserem	unsere	unseren
your	euer	eueren	euerem	euere	euerer	euer	euerem	euere	eueren
their	ihr	ihren	ihrem	ihre	ihrer	ihr	ihrem	ihre	ihren
your	Ihr	Ihren	Ihrem	Ihre	Ihrer	Ihr	Ihrem	Ihre	Ihren

Commonly used short forms for unseren: unsren *or* unsern   *for* unsere: unsre
                                    eueren: euren *or* euern   euere: eure
                          for unserem: unsrem *or* unserm   *for* unserer: unsrer
                                    euerem: eurem *or* euerm   euerer: eurer

NOUN PLURALS

Noun class and plural forms are not always predictable. Therefore, you must learn each noun together with its article (**der, die, das**) and with its plural form. As you learn more nouns, however, you will discover certain patterns. Although there are always exceptions to these patterns, you may find them helpful in remembering the plural forms of many nouns.

Most German nouns form their plurals in one of two ways: some nouns add endings in the plural; some add endings and/or change the sound of the stem vowel in the plural, indicating the sound change with the umlaut ("). Only the vowels **a, o, u,** and the diphthong **au** can take the umlaut. If a noun has an umlaut in the singular, it keeps the umlaut in the plural. Most German nouns fit into one of the following five plural groups.

1. Nouns that do not have any ending in the plural. Sometimes they take an umlaut.
   NOTE: There are only two feminine nouns in this group: **die Mutter** and **die Tochter.**

der Bruder, die Brüder	der Schüler, die Schüler	das Fräulein, die Fräulein
der Lehrer, die Lehrer	der Vater, die Väter	das Mädchen, die Mädchen
der Onkel, die Onkel	die Mutter, die Mütter	das Poster, die Poster
der Mantel, die Mäntel	die Tochter, die Töchter	das Zimmer, die Zimmer

2. Nouns that add the ending -**e** in the plural. Sometimes they also take an umlaut.
   NOTE: There are many one-syllable words in this group.

der Bleistift, die Bleistifte	der Sohn, die Söhne	das Jahr, die Jahre
der Freund, die Freunde	die Stadt, die Städte	das Spiel, die Spiele
der Paß, die Pässe		

3. Nouns that add the ending -**er** in the plural. Whenever possible, they take an umlaut, i.e., when the noun contains the vowels **a, o,** or **u,** or the diphthong **au. NOTE:** There are no feminine nouns in this group. There are many one-syllable words in this group.

das Buch, die Bücher	das Haus, die Häuser
das Fach, die Fächer	das Land, die Länder

4. Nouns that add the ending -**en** or -**n** in the plural. These nouns never add an umlaut.
   NOTE: There are many feminine nouns in this group.

der Herr, die Herren	die Klasse, die Klassen	die Tante, die Tanten
der Junge, die Jungen	die Karte, die Karten	die Wohnung, die Wohnungen
die Briefmarke, die Briefmarken	der Name, die Namen	die Zahl, die Zahlen
die Familie, die Familien	der Vetter, die Vettern	die Zeitung, die Zeitungen
die Farbe, die Farben	die Küche, die Küchen	
die Frau, die Frauen	die Schwester, die Schwestern	

   Feminine nouns ending in -**in** add the ending -**nen** in the plural.

die Freundin, die Freundinnen	die Verkäuferin, die Verkäuferinnen
die Lehrerin, die Lehrerinnen	

5. Nouns that add the ending -**s** in the plural. These nouns never add an umlaut.
   NOTE: There are many words of foreign origin in this group.

der Kuli, die Kulis	das Auto, die Autos
die Kamera, die Kameras	das Hobby, die Hobbys

SUMMARY OF PLURAL ENDINGS

Group	1	2	3	4	5
Ending:	-	-e	-er	-(e)n	-s
Umlaut:	sometimes	sometimes	always	never	never

PRONOUNS

	NOMINATIVE	ACCUSATIVE	DATIVE	ACCUSATIVE	DATIVE
Singular					
1st person	ich	mich	mir	mich	mir
2nd person	du	dich	dir	dich	dir
3rd person *m.*	er	ihn	ihm		
f.	sie	sie	ihr	sich	sich
n.	es	es	ihm		
Plural					
1st person	wir	uns	uns	uns	uns
2nd person	ihr	euch	euch	euch	euch
3rd person	sie	sie	ihnen	sich	sich
you (formal, sing. & pl.)	Sie	Sie	Ihnen	sich	sich

DEFINITE ARTICLES AS DEMONSTRATIVE PRONOUNS

The definite articles can be used as demonstrative pronouns, giving more emphasis to the sentences than the personal pronouns **er, sie, es**. Note that these demonstrative pronouns have the same forms as the definite articles. An exception is **denen**.

Wer bekommt *den* Cappuccino? *Der* ist für mich.

	NOMINATIVE	ACCUSATIVE	DATIVE
Masculine	der	den	dem
Feminine	die	die	der
Neuter	das	das	dem
Plural	die	die	denen

INTERROGATIVES

INTERROGATIVE PRONOUNS

	PEOPLE	THINGS
Nominative	**wer?** *who?*	**was?** *what?*
Accusative	**wen?** *whom?*	**was?** *what?*
Dative	**wem?** *to, for whom?*	

OTHER INTERROGATIVES

wann? *when?* **warum?** *why?* **wie?** *how?* **wieviel?** *how much? how many?*	**wie viele?** *how many?* **wo?** *where?* **woher?** *from where?* **wohin?** *to where?*	**welche?** *which?* **was für (ein)?** *what kind of (a)?*

PREPOSITIONS

Accusative	durch, für, gegen, ohne, um
Dative	aus, bei, mit, nach, seit, von, zu
Two-Way: Dative–**wo?** Accusative–**wohin?**	an, auf, hinter, in, neben, über, unter, vor, zwischen

WORD ORDER

POSITION OF VERBS IN A SENTENCE

The conjugated verb is in *first* position in:	yes/no *questions (questions that do not begin with an interrogative)* **Trinkst du Kaffee?** **Spielst du Tennis?** **Möchtest du ins Konzert gehen?** *both formal and informal commands* **Kommen Sie bitte um 2 Uhr!** **Geh doch mit ins Kino!**
The conjugated verb is in *second* position in:	*statements with normal word order* **Wir spielen heute Volleyball.** *statements with inverted word order* **Heute spielen wir Volleyball.** *questions that begin with an interrogative* **Wohin gehst du?** **Woher kommst du?** **Was macht er?** *sentences connected by* **und, oder, aber, denn** **Ich komme nicht, denn ich habe keine Zeit.**
The conjugated verb is in *second* position and the infinitive or past participle is *final* in:	*statements with modals* **Ich möchte heute ins Kino gehen.** *statements in conversational past* **Ich habe das Buch gelesen.** *statements with* **werde** *and* **würde** **Ich werde im Mai nach Berlin fliegen.** **Die Oma würde gern ins Theater gehen.**
The conjugated verb is in *final* position in:	*clauses that begin with interrogatives (* **wo, wann, warum,** *etc.)* **Ich weiß, wo das Hotel ist.** **Ich weiß nicht, wer heute morgen angerufen hat.** *clauses that begin with* **weil, daß,** *or* **ob** **Ich gehe nicht ins Kino, weil ich kein Geld habe.** **Ich glaube, daß er Rockmusik gern hört.** **Ich komme morgen nicht, weil ich zu Hause helfen muß.** **Ich weiß nicht, ob er den Film schon gesehen hat.**

POSITION OF NICHT IN A SENTENCE

To negate the entire sentence, as close to end of sentence as possible:	**Er fragt seinen Vater**		**nicht.**
Before a separable prefix:	**Ich rufe ihn**	**nicht**	**an.**
Before any part of a sentence you want to negate, contrast, or emphasize:	**Er kommt**	**nicht**	**heute.** **(Er kommt morgen.)**
Before part of a sentence that answers the question **wo?**	**Ich wohne**	**nicht**	**in Berlin.**

ADJECTIVES

ENDINGS OF ADJECTIVES AFTER DER- AND DIESER-WORDS

	NOMINATIVE	ACCUSATIVE	DATIVE
Masculine	der **-e** Vorort	den **-en** Vorort	dem **-en** Vorort
Feminine	die **-e** Stadt	die **-e** Stadt	der **-en** Stadt
Neuter	das **-e** Dorf	das **-e** Dorf	dem **-en** Dorf
Plural	die **-en** Vororte	die **-en** Vororte	den **-en** Vororten

NOTE: Names of cities used as adjectives always have the ending **-er: der Frankfurter Zoo, das Münchner Oktoberfest**

ENDINGS OF ADJECTIVES AFTER EIN

	NOMINATIVE	ACCUSATIVE	DATIVE
Masculine	ein **-er** Vorort	einen **-en** Vorort	einem **-en** Vorort
Feminine	eine **-e** Stadt	eine **-e** Stadt	einer **-er** Stadt
Neuter	ein **-es** Dorf	ein **-es** Dorf	einem **-en** Dorf

ENDINGS OF ADJECTIVES AFTER KEIN AND THE POSSESSIVES

	NOMINATIVE	ACCUSATIVE	DATIVE
Masculine	kein **-er** Vorort	keinen **-en** Vorort	keinem **-en** Vorort
Feminine	keine **-e** Stadt	keine **-e** Stadt	keiner **-er** Stadt
Neuter	kein **-es** Dorf	kein **-es** Dorf	keinem **-en** Dorf
Plural	keine **-en** Vororte	keine **-en** Vororte	keinen **-en** Vororten

ENDINGS OF UNPRECEDED ADJECTIVES

	NOMINATIVE	ACCUSATIVE	DATIVE
Masculine	**-er** Salat	**-en** Salat	**-em** Salat
Feminine	**-e** Suppe	**-e** Suppe	**-er** Suppe
Neuter	**-es** Eis	**-es** Eis	**-em** Eis
Plural	**-e** Getränke	**-e** Getränke	**-en** Getränken

MAKING COMPARISONS

	Positive	Comparative
1. *All comparative forms end in* **-er**.	schnell	schneller
2. *Most one-syllable forms have an umlaut.*	alt	älter
3. *Exceptions must be learned as they appear.*	dunkel	dunkler
	gut	besser

Equal Comparisons:	Er spielt **so gut wie** ich (spiele). *He plays as well as I (do).*
Unequal Comparisons:	Sie spielt **besser als** ich (spiele). *She plays better than I (do).*
Comparative adjectives before nouns:	der **bessere** Wagen ein **schöneres** Auto

NOTE: Comparative adjectives before nouns have the same endings as descriptive adjectives (see page 337).

VERBS

PRESENT TENSE VERB FORMS

		REGULAR	-eln VERBS	STEM ENDING WITH t/d	STEM ENDING WITH s/ß
INFINITIVES		spiel -en	bastel -n	find -en	heiß -en
PRONOUNS		stem + ending	stem + ending	stem + ending	stem + ending
I	ich	spiel -e	bastl -e	find -e	heiß -e
you	du	spiel -st	bastel -st	find -est	heiß -t
he *she* *it*	er sie es	spiel -t	bastel -t	find -et	heiß -t
we	wir	spiel -en	bastel -n	find -en	heiß -en
you (plural)	ihr	spiel -t	bastel -t	find -et	heiß -t
they	sie	spiel -en	bastel -n	find -en	heiß -en
you (formal)	Sie	spiel -en	bastel -n	find -en	heiß -en

NOTE: There are important differences between the verbs in the above chart:

1. Verbs ending in **-eln** (**basteln, segeln**) drop the **e** of the ending **-eln** in the **ich**-form: **ich bastle, ich segle** and add only **-n** in the **wir-, sie-,** and **Sie**-forms. These forms are always identical to the infinitive: **basteln, wir basteln, sie basteln, Sie basteln.** Similarly, verbs ending in **-ern,** (**wandern**) drop the **e** of the ending **-ern** in the **ich**-form: **ich wandre** and add only **-n** in the **wir-, sie-,** and **Sie**-forms. These forms are always identical to the infinitive: **wandern.**

2. Verbs with a stem ending in **d** or **t**, such as **finden**, add an **e** before the ending in the **du**-form (**du findest**) and the **er-** and **ihr**-forms (**er findet, ihr findet**).

3. All verbs with stems ending in an **s**-sound (**heißen**) add only **-t** in the **du**-form: **du heißt.**

VERBS WITH A STEM-VOWEL CHANGE

There are a number of verbs in German that change their stem vowel in the **du-** and **er/sie**-forms. A few verbs, such as **nehmen** (*to take*), have a change in the consonant as well. You cannot predict these verbs, so it is best to learn each one individually. They are usually irregular only in the **du-** and **er/sie**-forms.

	e → i			e → ie		a → ä	
	essen	geben	nehmen	lesen	sehen	fahren	einladen
ich	esse	gebe	nehme	lese	sehe	fahre	lade ein
du	ißt	gibst	nimmst	liest	siehst	fährst	lädst ein
er, sie	ißt	gibt	nimmt	liest	sieht	fährt	lädt ein
wir	essen	geben	nehmen	lesen	sehen	fahren	laden ein
ihr	eßt	gebt	nehmt	lest	seht	fahrt	ladet ein
sie	essen	geben	nehmen	lesen	sehen	fahren	laden ein
Sie	essen	geben	nehmen	lesen	sehen	fahren	laden ein

SOME IMPORTANT IRREGULAR VERBS: HABEN, SEIN, WISSEN, AND WERDEN

	haben	sein	wissen	werden
ich	habe	bin	weiß	werde
du	hast	bist	weißt	wirst
er, sie	hat	ist	weiß	wird
wir	haben	sind	wissen	werden
ihr	habt	seid	wißt	werdet
sie	haben	sind	wissen	werden
Sie	haben	sind	wissen	werden

VERBS FOLLWED BY AN OBJECT IN THE DATIVE CASE

antworten, *to answer*	gratulieren, *to congratulate*
danken, *to thank*	helfen, *to help*
gefallen, *to like*	passen, *to fit*
glauben, *to believe*	

Es geht (mir) gut.	Es steht (dir) gut.
Es schmeckt (mir) nicht.	Es macht (mir) Spaß.
Es tut (mir) leid.	Es tut (mir) weh.
Was fehlt (dir)?	

MODAL (AUXILIARY) VERBS

The verbs **dürfen, können, müssen, sollen, wollen, mögen** (and the **möchte**-forms) are usually used with an infinitive at the end of the sentence. If the meaning of that infinitive is clear, it can be left out: **Du mußt sofort nach Hause!** (**Gehen** is understood and omitted.)

	dürfen	können	müssen	sollen	wollen	mögen	möchte
ich	darf	kann	muß	soll	will	mag	möchte
du	darfst	kannst	mußt	sollst	willst	magst	möchtest
er, sie	darf	kann	muß	soll	will	mag	möchte
wir	dürfen	können	müssen	sollen	wollen	mögen	möchten
ihr	dürft	könnt	müßt	sollt	wollt	mögt	möchtet
sie	dürfen	können	müssen	sollen	wollen	mögen	möchten
Sie	dürfen	können	müssen	sollen	wollen	mögen	möchten

VERBS WITH SEPARABLE PREFIXES

Some verbs have separable prefixes: prefixes that separate from the conjugated verbs and are moved to the end of the sentence.

	INFINITIVE: **aussehen**
ich sehe ... aus	Ich sehe heute aber sehr schick aus!
du siehst ... aus	Du siehst heute sehr fesch aus!
er/sie/es sieht ... aus	Sieht sie immer so modern aus?
	Sieht dein Zimmer immer so unordentlich aus?
wir sehen ... aus	Wir sehen heute sehr lustig aus.
ihr seht ... aus	Ihr seht alle so traurig aus.
sie sehen ... aus	Sie sehen sehr schön aus.
Sie sehen ... aus	Sie sehen immer so ernst aus.

Here are the separable-prefix verbs you learned in Level 1 and Level 2.

abheben	aufräumen	fernsehen	vorziehen
abräumen	ausgehen	herausnehmen	weggeben
anprobieren	aussehen	mitkommen	wegtragen
anrufen	einkaufen	radfahren	wegwerfen
anziehen	einladen	vorschlagen	zustimmen
auflegen	einstecken		

COMMAND FORMS

Regular Verbs	**gehen**	**spielen**
Persons you address with **du** (singular) with **ihr** (pl) with **Sie** (sing & pl) "let's" form	**Geh!** **Geht!** **Gehen Sie!** **Gehen wir!**	**Spiel!** **Spielt!** **Spielen Sie!** **Spielen wir!**

Separable-prefix Verbs	**mitkommen**	**anrufen**	**aufräumen**	**anziehen**	**ausgehen**
	Komm mit! **Kommt mit!** **Kommen Sie mit!** **Kommen wir mit!**	**Ruf an!** **Ruft an!** **Rufen Sie an!** **Rufen wir an!**	**Räum auf!** **Räumt auf!** **Räumen Sie auf!** **Räumen wir auf!**	**Zieh an!** **Zieht an!** **Ziehen Sie an!** **Ziehen wir an!**	**Geh aus!** **Geht aus!** **Gehen Sie aus!** **Gehen wir aus!**

Stem-changing Verbs	**essen**	**nehmen**	**geben**	**sehen**	**fahren**
	Iß! **Eßt!** **Essen Sie!** **Essen wir!**	**Nimm!** **Nehmt!** **Nehmen Sie!** **Nehmen wir!**	**Gib!** **Gebt!** **Geben Sie!** **Geben wir!**	**Sieh!** **Seht!** **Sehen Sie!** **Sehen wir!**	**Fahr!** **Fahrt!** **Fahren Sie!** **Fahren wir!**

NOTE: The vowel changes **e → i** and **e → ie** are maintained in the **du**-form of the command. The vowel change **a → ä** does not occur in the command form.

EXPRESSING FUTURE TIME

In German, there are three ways to express future time:

1. present tense verb forms	Ich **kaufe** eine Jeans. Ich **finde** bestimmt etwas.	*I'm going to buy a pair of jeans. I will surely find something.*
2. present tense verb forms with words like *morgen, später*	Er kommt **morgen.** Elke ruft **später** an.	*He's coming tomorrow. Elke will call later.*
3. **werden,** *will,* plus infinitive	Ich **werde** ein Hemd **kaufen.** Er **wird** bald **gehen.**	*I'll buy a shirt. He'll go soon.*

SUBJUNCTIVE FORMS

THE FORMS HÄTTE, WÄRE, KÖNNTE, AND WÜRDE

ich	hätte	wäre	könnte	würde
du	hättest	wärest	könntest	würdest
er, sie, es	hätte	wäre	könnte	würde
wir	hätten	wären	könnten	würden
ihr	hättet	wäret	könntet	würdet
sie, Sie	hätten	wären	könnten	würden

NOTE: In spoken German the forms **wärest** and **wäret** are often shortened to **wärst** and **wärt.**

PAST TENSE VERB FORMS

In this book, you learned the simple past of **haben** and **sein:**

THE SIMPLE PAST OF HABEN AND SEIN

	haben	sein
ich	hatte	war
du	hattest	warst
er, sie	hatte	war
wir	hatten	waren
ihr	hattet	wart
sie	hatten	waren
Sie (formal)	hatten	waren

THE CONVERSATIONAL PAST

German verbs are divided into two groups: weak verbs and strong verbs. Weak verbs usually follow a regular pattern, such as the English verb forms *play — played — has played*. Strong verbs usually have irregularities, like the English verb forms *run — ran — has run* or *go — went — has gone*.

The conversational past tense of weak and strong verbs consists of the present tense of **haben** or **sein** and a form called the past participle, which is usually in last position in the clause or sentence.

Die Schüler	**haben**	ihre Hausaufgaben schon	**gemacht.**
Sabine	**ist**	gestern zu Hause	**geblieben.**

FORMATION OF PAST PARTICIPLES

Weak Verbs	spielen	(er) spielt	gespielt	Er hat gespielt.
with inseparable prefixes	besuchen	(er) besucht	besucht	Er hat ihn besucht.
with separable prefixes	aufräumen	(er) räumt auf	aufgeräumt	Er hat aufgeräumt.
Strong Verbs	kommen	(er) kommt	gekommen	Er ist gekommen
with inseparable prefixes	bekommen	(er) bekommt	bekommen	Er hat es bekommen.
with separable prefixes	mitkommen	(er) kommt mit	mitgekommen	Er ist mitgekommen.

NOTE: For past participles of strong verbs and irregular verbs, see pages 344–346.

WEAK VERBS FORMING THE PAST PARTICIPLE WITH SEIN

bummeln, *to stroll*	ist gebummelt	**surfen,** *to surf*	ist gesurft
reisen, *to travel*	ist gereist	**wandern,** *to hike*	ist gewandert

PRINCIPAL PARTS OF THE VERBS PRESENTED IN LEVELS 1 AND 2

This list includes all verbs included in the **Wortschatz** sections of Level 1 and Level 2. Both strong and weak verbs, including verbs with separable prefixes, stem-vowel changes, and other irregularities are listed. Though most of the verbs in this list form the conversational past with **haben**, a few of the verbs you have learned take **sein** in the present perfect tense.

STRONG VERBS

INFINITIVE	PRESENT (stem vowel change and/or seperable prefix)	PAST PARTICIPLE	MEANING
abheben	hebt ab	abgehoben	*to lift (the receiver)*
anrufen	ruft an	angerufen	*to call up*
anziehen	zieht an	angezogen	*to put on (clothes)*
aussehen	sieht aus	ausgesehen	*to look, appear*
bekommen	bekommt	bekommen	*to get, receive*
beschreiben	beschreibt	beschrieben	*to describe*
bleiben	bleibt	(ist) geblieben	*to stay*
brechen	bricht	gebrochen	*to break*
einladen	lädt ein	eingeladen	*to invite*
essen	ißt	gegessen	*to eat*
fahren	fährt	(ist) gefahren	*to drive, ride*
fernsehen	sieht fern	ferngesehen	*to watch TV*
finden	findet	gefunden	*to find*
geben	gibt	gegeben	*to give*
gefallen	gefällt	gefallen	*to like, be pleasing to*
gehen	geht	(ist) gegangen	*to go*
gießen	gießt	gegossen	*to pour; to water*
haben	hat	gehabt	*to have*
halten	hält	gehalten	*to keep*
heißen	heißt	geheißen	*to be called*
helfen	hilft	geholfen	*to help*
herausnehmen	nimmt heraus	herausgenommen	*to take out*
kommen	kommt	(ist) gekommen	*to come*
lassen	läßt	gelassen	*to let*
laufen	läuft	(ist) gelaufen	*to run*
lesen	liest	gelesen	*to read*
messen	mißt	gemessen	*to measure*
nehmen	nimmt	genommen	*to take*
radfahren	fährt Rad	(ist) radgefahren	*to bicycle*
scheinen	scheint	geschienen	*to shine*
schlafen	schläft	geschlafen	*to sleep*
schlagen	schlägt	geschlagen	*to slam*
schreiben	schreibt	geschrieben	*to write*
schwimmen	schwimmt	(ist) geschwommen	*to swim*
sehen	sieht	gesehen	*to see*
sein	ist	(ist) gewesen	*to be*
sprechen	spricht	gesprochen	*to speak*
tragen	trägt	getragen	*to wear*
trinken	trinkt	getrunken	*to drink*
tun	tut	getan	*to do*
vermeiden	vermeidet	vermieden	*to avoid*
vorschlagen	schlägt vor	vorgeschlagen	*to suggest*

INFINITIVE	PRESENT (stem vowel change and/or seperable prefix)	PAST PARTICIPLE	MEANING
vorziehen	zieht vor	*vorgezogen	*to prefer*
waschen	wäscht	gewaschen	*to wash*
weggeben	gibt weg	weggegeben	*to give away*
wegtragen	trägt weg	weggetragen	*to take away*
wegwerfen	wirft weg	weggeworfen	*to throw away*
wissen	weiß	gewußt	*to know*

*These verbs have a consonant change in the past participle.

WEAK VERBS

INFINITIVE	PRESENT (stem vowel change and/or seperable prefix)	PAST PARTICIPLE	MEANING
abräumen	räumt ab	abgeräumt	*to clear away*
angeln	angelt	geangelt	*to fish*
anprobieren	probiert an	anprobiert	*to try on*
arbeiten	arbeitet	gearbeitet	*to work*
auflegen	legt auf	aufgelegt	*to hang up (receiver)*
aufräumen	räumt auf	aufgeräumt	*to pick up/clean room*
basteln	bastelt	gebastelt	*to do arts and crafts*
bedauern	bedauert	bedauert	*to be sorry about*
bedienen	bedient	bedient	*to serve*
besichtigen	besichtigt	besichtigt	*to sight see*
besuchen	besucht	besucht	*to visit*
bezweifeln	bezweifelt	bezweifelt	*to doubt*
brauchen	braucht	gebraucht	*to need*
bringen	bringt	** gebracht	*to bring*
bügeln	bügelt	gebügelt	*to iron*
decken	deckt	gedeckt	*to set (the table)*
einkaufen	kauft ein	eingekauft	*to shop*
einlegen	legt ein	eingelegt	*to insert*
einstecken	steckt ein	eingesteckt	*to insert (coin)*
ernähren	ernährt	ernährt	*to nourish*
faulenzen	faulenzt	gefaulenzt	*to be lazy*
fotografieren	fotografiert	fotografiert	*to photograph*
s. freuen	freut s.	gefreut	*to be happy about*
s. fühlen	fühlt s.	gefühlt	*to feel*
füttern	füttert	gefüttert	*to feed*
glauben	glaubt	geglaubt	*to believe*
gucken	guckt	geguckt	*to look*
hoffen	hofft	gehofft	*to hope*
holen	holt	geholt	*to get*
hören	hört	gehört	*to hear*
s. interessieren	interessiert s.	interessiert	*to be interested in*
kämmen	kämmt	gekämmt	*to comb*
kaufen	kauft	gekauft	*to buy*
kennen	kennt	** gekannt	*to know*
kosten	kostet	gekostet	*to cost*
leben	lebt	gelebt	*to live*
machen	macht	gemacht	*to do or make*

INFINITIVE	PRESENT (stem vowel change and/or seperable prefix)	PAST PARTICIPLE	MEANING
mähen	mäht	gemäht	*to mow*
meinen	meint	gemeint	*to think, be of the opinion*
passen	paßt	gepaßt	*to fit*
polieren	poliert	poliert	*to polish*
putzen	putzt	geputzt	*to clean*
rauchen	raucht	geraucht	*to smoke*
regnen	regnet	geregnet	*to rain*
sagen	sagt	gesagt	*to say*
sammeln	sammelt	gesammelt	*to collect*
schauen	schaut	geschaut	*to look (at)*
schenken	schenkt	geschenkt	*to give (a gift)*
schmecken	schmeckt	geschmeckt	*to taste*
segeln	segelt	(ist) gesegelt	*to sail*
sortieren	sortiert	sortiert	*to sort*
spielen	spielt	gespielt	*to play*
spülen	spült	gespült	*to wash dishes*
suchen	sucht	gesucht	*to look for*
tanzen	tanzt	getanzt	*to dance*
tauchen	taucht	getaucht	*to dive*
telefonieren	telefoniert	telefoniert	*to call (on the phone)*
verbringen	verbringt	** verbracht	*to spend time*
trocknen	trocknet	getrocknet	*to dry*
wählen	wählt	gewählt	*to dial*
wandern	wandert	(ist) gewandert	*to hike*
s. verletzen	verletzt s.	verletzt	*to injure*
s. verstauchen	verstaucht s.	verstaucht	*to sprain*
wischen	wischt	gewischt	*to dust*
wohnen	wohnt	gewohnt	*to live*
wünschen	wünscht	gewünscht	*to wish*
zahlen	zahlt	gezahlt	*to pay*
zeichnen	zeichnet	gezeichnet	*to draw*
zustimmen	stimmt zu	zugestimmt	*to agree*

**Although weak, these verbs have a vowel and/or consonant change in the past participle.

GERMAN-ENGLISH VOCABULARY

GERMAN-ENGLISH VOCABULARY

This vocabulary includes almost all words in this textbook, both active (for production) and passive (for recognition only). Active words and phrases are practiced in the chapter and are listed in the Wortschatz section at the end of each chapter. You are expected to know and be able to use active vocabulary. An entry in black, heavy type indicates that the word or phrase is active. All other words—some in the opening dialogs, in exercises, in optional and visual material, in the Landeskunde, Zum Lesen and Kann ich's wirklich? sections—are for recognition only. The meaning of these words and phrases can usually be understood from the context or may be looked up in this vocabulary.

With some exceptions, the following are not included: proper nouns, verb conjugations, and forms of determiners.

Nouns are listed with definite article and plural form, when applicable. The numbers in the entries refer to the level and chapter where the word or phrase first appears or where it becomes an active vocabulary word. Vocabulary from the location openers is followed by a Loc and the chapter number directly following the location spread.

The following abbreviations are used in this vocabulary: adj (adjective), pl (plural), prep (preposition), pp (past participle), sep (seperable-prefix verb), poss adj (possessive adjective), sing (singular), dat (dative), acc (accusative), s. (*sich,* or reflexive), and conj (conjunction).

A

ab (prep) *down, off,* II1

ab und zu *now and then,* II4

der Abend, -e *evening,* I; **am Abend** *in the evening,* I

das Abendbuffet, -s *dinner buffet,* II12

das Abendessen, - *dinner, evening meal,* II5

das Abendkleid, -er *evening gown,* II12

abends *evenings,* II1

der Abenteuerfilm, -e *adventure film,* I

die Abenteuerreise, -n *exotic vacation,* II9

aber (conj) *but,* I; **aber sicher!** *but of course!,* II4

die Abfahrt, -en *departure,* II9

das Abgas, -e *exhaust,* II9

abgehakt *crossed off,* II3

abgeschnitten *cut-off,* II8

abgestanden *stale, flat,* II2

abheben (sep) *to pick up,* I; **den Hörer abheben** *to pick up the receiver,* I

abholen (sep) *to come for, pick up,* II11

der Abholschein, -e *check to pick up a prescription,* II6

abladen (sep) *to unload,* II2

das Ablagefach, ̈-er *storage shelf,* II10

ablaufen (sep) *to flow or run off; to elapse, expire,* II11

ablehnen (sep) *to decline, turn down,* II12

abräumen (sep) *to clean up, clear off,* I

der Absatz, ̈-e *shoe heel,* II8

die Absatzforschung, -en *marketing research,* II10

abschneiden (sep) *to cut off,* II5

abschreiben (sep) *to copy,* II5

abschwirren (sep) *to buzz off,* II12

absichtlich *on purpose,* II12

absolut *absolute(ly), unconditional(ly),* II6

der Abstand, ̈-e *distance, gap,* II12

abstellen (sep) *to switch off,* II7

die Abteilung, -en *division, department,* II1

abtrocknen (sep) *to dry off,* II5

abwechselnd *alternating, one after the other,* II3

die Abwechslung, -en *change, variety,* II3

abwechslungsreich *varied, diversified,* II12

abwischen (sep) *to erase, wipe up,* II11

Ach *Oh!,* I; **Ach ja!** *Oh yeah!,* I

Ach schade! *That's too bad.,* II6

achten auf (acc) *to pay attention to,* II12

das Acryl *Acrylic,* II8

der Actionfilm, -e *action movie,* I

das Adjektiv, -e *adjective,* II8

die Adresse, -n *address,* II11

afrikanisch (adj) *African,* II12

die Agentur, -en *agency,* II8

ägyptisch (adj) *Egyptian,* II11

ähnlich *similar,* II7

die Ahnung, -en *idea, notion,* II8; **Keine Ahnung!** *I have no idea!,* I

die Aktie, -n *share, stock,* II8

aktiv *active,* II8

die Aktivität, -en *activity,* II4

aktuell *current, contemporary,* II1

akzeptiert *accepted,* II11

die Alarmanlage, -n *alarm system,* II10

der Alkohol, -e *alcohol,* II4

alkoholfrei *non-alcoholic,* II11

all- *all,* II8

allein *alone,* II2

die Allergie, -n *allergy,* II4

allergisch (gegen) *allergic (to),* II4

der Alltag, -e *weekday, workday routine,* II9

allzu *much too, far too,* II7

als *than,* II7

also (conj) *so, therefore,* II6; (particle) *well, okay;* II1

alt *old,* I

älter *older,* II7

die Alufelge, -n *aluminum rim,* II10

am=an dem *at the*, I; am ...platz *on ... Square*, I; **am Abend** *in the evening*, I; **am ersten (Juli)** *on the first (of July)*, I; **am letzten Tag** *on the last day*, II3; **am liebsten** *most of all*, I; **am Tag** *during the day*, II4; **an der Schule** *at school*, II4; **am besten** *best (of all)*, II5

der Amerikaner, - *American*, II4

amerikanisch (adj) *American*, II11

die **Ampel, -n** *traffic light*, I; **bis zur Ampel** *until you get to the traffic light*, I

an *to; at*, II9

anbieten (sep) *to offer*, II7

anbraten (sep) *to grill, roast*, II12

ander- *other*, I; **ein(-) ander-** *another (a different) one*, II9

andererseits *on the other hand*, II7

der Anfang, ⁼e *beginning*, II8

der **Anfänger, -** *beginner*, II12

angeben (sep) *to indicate, state*, II2

das **Angebot, -e** *offer*, I; **Angebot der Woche** *weekly special*, I

angeboten *offered*, II12

angeln *to fish*, II9

angenommen *accepted, assumed*, II12

angeschlossen *connected to, adjacent to*, II3

der Angestellte, -n *employee*, II12

angezogen *dressed*, II8

angucken (sep) *to look at*, II10

anhaben (sep) *to have on*, II1

anhören (sep) *to listen to*, II6

ankommen (sep) *to arrive*, II12

ankreuzen (sep) *to cross, mark off*, II3

die **Anlage, -n** *grounds, site*, II12; *system, installation*, II2

der Anlaß, (pl) Anlässe *occasion*, II2

der **Anorak, -s** *parka*, II8

anprobieren (sep) *to try on*, I

die Anregung, -en *stimulation, incitement*, II1; **zur Anregung** *as a start*, II1

der Anrufbeantworter, - *answering machine*, II9

anrufen (sep) *to call (on the phone)*, I

anschauen (sep) *to look at*, II7

der **Anschlag, ⁼e** *announcement*, II11

die Anschlagtafel, -n *bulletin board*, II2

anschließend *following, adjacent*, II12

s. ansehen (sep) *to have a look at*, II2

die Ansicht, -en *view, point of view*, II9; **nach Ansicht von** *in the opinion of*, II9

ansonsten *otherwise*, II3

die Ansprache, -n *speech, address*, II3

ansprechen (sep) *to talk to*, II9

der Anspruch, ⁼e *claim; right*, II12

die Anstalt, -en *institute, establishment*, Loc 7

die Anstrengung, -en *exertion, effort, strain*, II6

die Antwort, -en *answer*, II2

antworten (dat) *to answer*, II2

die Anwendung, -en *application, use*, II3

die Anzahl, -en *number, quantity*, II8

die Anzeige, -n *ad*, II10

anzeigen (sep) *to show, indicate or record*, II10

anziehen (sep) *to put on, wear*, I

der **Anzug, ⁼e** *suit*, II8

der **Apfel, ⁼** *apple*, I

der **Apfelkuchen, -** *apple cake*, I

der **Apfelsaft, ⁼e** *apple juice*, I; **ein Glas Apfelsaft** *a glass of apple juice*, I

die **Apotheke, -n** *pharmacy*, II6

der **Apotheker, -** *pharmacist*, II6

der **Apparat, -e** *telephone*, I

das **Appartement, -s** *apartment*, II12

der Appetit: **Guten Appetit!** *Bon appétit!*, II11

die **Aprikose, -n** *apricot*, II4

der **April** *April*, I

die **Arbeit, -en** *work*, II2

arbeiten *to work*, II3

die Arbeitsklamotte, -n *work clothes*, II8

die Architektur *architecture*, II3

arg *very; annoying*, II4

ärgerlich *annoying*, II3

der **Arm, -e** *arm*, II6

das **Armband, ⁼er** *bracelet*, II1

die **Armbanduhr, -en** *wristwatch*, I

der **Ärmel, -** *sleeve*, II1

ärmellos *sleeveless*, II8

die **Armut** *poverty*, II7

der **Artikel, -** *article, commodity*, II2

der **Arzt, ⁼e** *doctor*, II6

der **Atem** *breath, breathing*, II12

der **Athlet, -en** *athlete*, II12

atmen *to breathe*, II12

die Atmosphäre, -n *atmosphere, environment*, II11

attraktiv *attractive*, II1

Au!, Aua! *Ouch!*, II6

auch *also*, I; **Ich auch.** *Me too.*, I; **auch noch** *also*, II9; **auch schon** *also*, II3

auf (prep) *on, onto, to*, II1; **Auf dein/Ihr/euer Wohl!** *To your health!*, II11; **auf dem Land** *in the country*, I; **Auf Wiederhören!** *Goodbye!*, I; **auf einer Fete** *at a party*, II8

der **Aufdruck** *print impression*, II1

die **Aufgabe, -n** *assignment*, II3

aufgeben (sep) *to give up*, II4

aufgelistet *listed*, II4

aufgeschnitten *cut open*, II5

aufgießen (sep) *to brew a drink (tea, coffee)*, II5

aufgrund dessen *because of that*, II9

aufhängen (sep) *to hang out, up*, II4

aufheben (sep) *to lift or raise*, II2

aufhören (sep) *to stop*, II6

der **Aufkleber, -** *sticker*, II10

aufkommen (sep) *to get up; to arise*, II5

die **Auflauf, ⁼e** *soufflé*, II5

auflegen (sep) *to hang up (the telephone)*, I

aufräumen (sep) *to clean up*, I

der **Aufschnitt** *cold cuts*, I

aufschreiben (sep) *to write down*, II12

aufsetzen (sep) *to put or place on*, II5

aufstehen (sep) *to get up*, II6

der **Aufstrich, -e** *spread*, II11

auftauchen (sep) *to turn up, arise*, II10

auftreten (sep) *to appear*, II6

aufwachen (sep) *to wake up*, II12

aufwachsen (sep) *to grow up*, II7

aufwärmen (sep) *to warm up*, II5

aufzählen (sep) *to enumerate*, II11

das Auge, -n *eye*, I

der Augenblick, -e *moment*, II12

die Augenfarbe, -n *eye color*, II1

der **August** *August*, I

aus (prep) *from, out of*, II1; **aus Baumwolle** *made of cotton*, I; **aus dem (16.) Jahrhundert** *from the (16th) century*, II9; **aus den 60er Jahren** *from the sixties*, II8; **aus welchen Gründen** *for what reasons*, II8

die **Ausbildung, -en** *education*, II7

der **Ausdruck, ⁼e** *expression*, II2

ausdrücken (sep) *to express*, II6

der **Ausflug, ⁼e** *excursion*, II11

das Ausflugsschiff, -e *excursion boat*, II11

ausgeben (sep) *to give out; to spend (money)*, II12

ausgehen (sep) *to go out,* II1
ausgeschnitten *low-cut,* II8
ausgewählt *chosen,* II11
ausgezeichnet *excellent, outstanding,* II1
aushöhlen (sep) *to hollow out,* II5
s. auskennen (sep) *to know all about,* II9
die Auskunft, ⁼e *information,* II3
der Ausländer, - *foreigner,* II11
das Ausland *foreign country,* II9
ausländisch *foreign,* II11
die Auslandsreise, -n *foreign travel, trip,* II9
auslegen (sep) *to lay out* (money, etc.), II5
ausmachen (sep) *to make up, constitute,* II12
die Ausnahme, -n *exception,* II8
ausprobieren (sep) *to try out,* II5
ausquatschen (sep) *to have a good chat,* II2
ausrechnen (sep) *to calculate; to figure out,* II8
die Ausrede, -n *excuse,* II6
ausreden (sep) *to finish speaking,* II2
der Ausreißer, - *deserter, runaway,* II11
ausrufen (sep) *to call out,* II2
s. ausruhen (sep) *to relax, rest,* II5
die Ausrüstung, -en *equipment, outfit,* II10
die Aussage, -n *statement,* II7
aussagen (sep) *to state, express,* II9
s. ausschlafen *to sleep one's fill,* II9
der Ausschnitt, -e *excerpt,* II4
aussehen (sep) *to look like, to appear,* I; **der Rock sieht ... aus.** *The skirt looks...,* I; **Wie sieht er aus?** *What does he look like?,* I
die Aussicht, -en *view,* II12
die Ausstattung, -en *equipment, furnishing,* II10
die Ausstellung, -en *exhibition,* II11
die Ausstellungseröffnung, -en *opening of an exhibition,* II11
austauschen (sep) *to exchange,* II2
der Austauschschüler, - *exchange student (male),* II4
die Austauschwoche, -n *exchange week,* II2
die Auster, -n *oyster,* II11
die Auswahl, -en *choice,* II8
auswählen (sep) *to choose from,* II5
s. ausdenken (sep) *to think up,* II5
ausfüllen (sep) *to fill in (a form),* II8

außer (prep) *except for,* II11
außerdem *besides,* II5
außereuropäisch *outside of Europe,* II12
außerhalb (prep) *outside of,* II3
der Auszug, ⁼e *excerpt,* II11
das Auto, -s *car,* I; **mit dem Auto** *by car,* I
die Autobahn, -en *highway,* II10
der Autofahrer, - *driver,* II10
der Automat, -en *vending machine; robot,* II2
die Automatik *automatic transmission,* II10
die Automobilindustrie, -n *automobile industry,* Loc 1
die Autotür, -en *car door,* II7

B

der Bäcker, - *baker,* I
die Bäckerei, -en *bakery,* I
das Backhaus, ⁼er *bakehouse,* II9
baden *to swim,* I; **baden gehen** *to go swimming,* I
der Badestrand, ⁼e *beach,* II3
das Badezimmer, - *bathroom,* II7
die Bahn, -en *train,* II9
der Bahnhof, ⁼e *train station,* I
die Bahnübergang, ⁼e *train crossing,* II7
das Ballett, -e *ballet,* II11
die Banane, -n *banana,* II2
die Bank, -en *bank,* II3
der Bärenhunger *hungry as a bear,* II12
barfuß *barefoot,* II12
die Barockstadt, ⁼e *baroque city,* II3
Basketball *basketball,* I
die Basketballhalle, -n *basketball gym,* II12
der Basketballplatz, ⁼e *basketball court,* II12
basteln *to do crafts,* I
der Bau *construction,* II3
der Bauch, ⁼e *stomach,* II6
die Bauchschmerzen (pl) *stomachache,* II6
das Baudenkmal, ⁼er *monument,* II11
bauen *to build,* II2
der Bauer, -n *farmer,* II10
die Bauernente, -n *farm-raised duck,* II11
das Bauernhaus, ⁼er *farm house,* II9
der Bauernhof, ⁼e *farm,* II3
der Baum, ⁼e *tree,* II7
die Baumwolle, -n *cotton,* I
bayerisch (adj) *Bavarian,* II1
das Bayern *Bavaria,* II4

beachten *to notice, heed, regard,* II7
beantworten *to answer,* II2
der Becher, - *cup,* II2
bedauern *to be sorry about,* II5
bedeuten *to mean,* II1
bedeutend *meaningful,* Loc 1
bedienen: die Kamera bedienen *to operate the camera,* II3
bedienen *to serve,* II3
die Bedienung, -en *wait person,* II1
bedruckt *printed,* II8
beeindruckend *impressive,* II11
beenden *to end,* II10
die Beere, -n *berry,* II4
s. befinden *to find oneself, to be,* II9
befragen *to ask questions,* II9
begabt *gifted,* II12
begeistert *enthusiastic,* II1
beginnen *to begin,* II12
begleiten *to accompany,* II4
begründen *to found; to give a reason for,* II2
beherbergt *given shelter,* II3
bei (prep) *by, near, at,* II9; bei uns *with us at home,* II10; **beim Bäcker** *at the baker's,* I
beide *both,* II2
die Beilage, -n *side dish,* II11
das Bein, -e *leg,* II6
das Beispiel, -e *example,* II1
beitragen zu (sep) *to contribute to,* II7
bekannt *known,* II3
der Bekannte, -n *acquaintance (male),* II7
die Bekleidungsabteilung, -en *clothing department,* II1
das Bekleidungsgeschäft, -e *clothing store,* II12
bekommen *to get, receive,* I
belegen *to cover; to register for,* II5
beliebt *popular,* II9
beliefern *to supply (with),* II7
die Bemerkung, -en *comment, remark,* II10
s. benehmen *to behave,* II11
benutzen *to use,* II6
das Benzin *gasoline, fuel,* II10
der Beobachter, - *observer,* II12
bequem *comfortable,* I
bereit *willing; prepared,* II5
bereits *already,* II12
der Berg, -e *mountain,* II7
die Bergbahn, -en *mountain or alpine railway,* II9
das Bergsteigen *mountain climbing,* II3

die Bergtour, -en *tour or trip in the mountains,* II9
der Bergwanderer, - *mountain hiker,* II9
berichten *to report,* II1
beruflich *professional(ly),* II10
berühmt *famous,* II3
beschäftigt *busy,* II3
die Bescheidenheit, -en *modesty,* II8
beschlossen *decided,* II12
beschreiben *to describe,* II1
die Beschreibung, -en *description,* II1
beschrieben *described,* II1
beschriften *to inscribe,* II8
die Beschwerde, -n *trouble, complaint,* II6
beseitigen *to remove, abolish,* II7
besetzt *busy (on the telephone),* I
besichtigen *to sightsee, visit a place,* II3
die Besichtigung, -en *sightseeing, visit,* II9
der Besitz, -e *ownership,* II1
besonders *especially,* I
besorgen *to provide,* II12
besprechen *to discuss,* II9
besser *better,* I
die Besserung, -en *improvement,* II6; **Gute Besserung!** *Get well soon!,* II6
bestehen *to pass,* II2
bestehen aus *to consist of,* II2
bestellen *to order,* II2
die Bestellkarte, -n *order form,* II8
die Bestellnummer, -n *order number,* II8
die Bestellung, -en *order,* II11
besten: **am besten** *the best,* II5
bestens *very well, best,* II1
bestimmt *certainly, definitely,* I
bestreuen *to sprinkle,* II5
der Besuch, -e *visit,* II2
besuchen *to visit,* I
der Besucher, - *visitor,* II11
betreten *to step on; to enter,* II8
der Betrieb, -e *business, firm,* Loc 10
das Bett, -en *bed,* I
beurteilen *to judge,* II12
die Bevölkerung *population, inhabitants,* II4
bevor (conj) *before,* II2
bevorzugen *to prefer, to favor,* II12
beweisen *to prove,* II12
der Bewerber, - *applicant,* II10
bewundern *to admire,* II9
bezahlen *to pay,* II11
bezahlt *paid for,* II1
bezeugen *to testify to,* Loc 10
beziehungsweise=bzw. *respectively,* II11

das Bezirksamt, ⸚er *local government office,* II11
bezweifeln *to doubt,* II9
biegen *to bend, curve, turn,* II9; **einbiegen** (sep): **Biegen Sie hier ein!** *Turn here!,* II9
der Biergarten, ⸚ *open-air restaurant, beer garden,* II12
das Biertrinken *drinking beer,* II11
bieten *to offer,* II7
das Bild, -er *picture,* II5
bilden *to form, shape, construct,* II1
billig *cheap,* II7
der Bioladen, ⸚ *natural foods store,* II4
die Biologie=Bio *biology,* I
die Biologielehrerin, -nen *biology teacher (female),* I
die Birne, -n *pear,* II5
bis (prep) *until,* II1; bis auf *except for, all but,* II5; **Bis dann!** *Till then! See you later!,* I; bis zu *up to,* II9
der Bischof, ⸚e *bishop,* II3
der Biß, (pl) Bisse *bite, sting,* II12
bißchen: **ein bißchen** *a little,* I
bissel=bißchen *a little,* II4
bitte *please,* I; **Bitte (sehr/schön)!** *You're (very) welcome!,* I; **Bitte! Hier!** *Here you go!,* II10
bitter *bitter,* II1
das Blatt, ⸚er *leaf; page,* II12
blau *blue,* I
die Blaubeere, -n *blueberry,* II4
der Blazer, - *blazer,* II8
bleiben *to stay, remain,* II3
der Bleistift, -e *pencil,* I
der Blick, -e *glance, view,* II3
blöd *dumb,* I
blond *blonde,* I
bloß *only,* I; **Was soll ich bloß machen?** *Well, what am I supposed to do?,* II9
der Blouson, -s *bomber jacket,* II8
die Blume, -n *flower,* I
das Blumenbeet, -e *flower bed,* II7
der Blumenkohl *cauliflower,* II4
der Blumenstrauß, ⸚e *flower bouquet,* I
die Bluse, -n *blouse,* II8
der Boden *floor, ground,* II12
das Bogenschießen *archery,* II1
die Bohne, -n *bean,* II2
das Boot, -e *boat,* II9; **Boot fahren** *to go for a boat ride,* II9
botanisch *botanical,* II3
boxen *to box, punch,* II10
braten *to roast, bake,* II9
der Braten *roast,* II11

die Bratkartoffeln (pl) *fried potatoes,* II11
brauchen *to need,* I
braun *brown,* I
bräunen *to dye brown; to tan,* II8
s. brechen (etwas) *to break (something),* II6; **er/sie bricht** *he/she breaks,* II6
breit *large, wide,* II1
die Bremse, -n *brake,* II10
bremsen *to brake,* II12
das Brettspiel, -e *board game,* I; **ein Brettspiel spielen** *to play a board game,* I
die Brezel, -n *pretzel,* I
der Brieffreund, -e *pen pal,* II6
die Briefmarke, -n *postage stamp,* I
der Briefpartner, - *pen pal,* II7
die Brille, -n *a pair of glasses,* I
bringen *to bring,* II8; zum Ausdruck bringen *to express,* II9; etwas in Ordnung bringen *to get something in order,* II8
der Brokkoli *broccoli,* II4
das Brot, -e *bread,* I
das Brötchen, - *breakfast roll,* II5
der Brotkrümel, - *bread crumb,* II12
der Brotteller, - *bread plate,* II12
der Bruder, ⸚ *brother,* I
die Brücke, -n *bridge,* II9
brüllen *to shout, holler,* II9
der Brunnen, - *fountain,* II9
die Brusttasche, -n *breast pocket,* II8
brutal *brutal, violent,* I
das Buch, ⸚er *book,* I
buchen *to book, reserve,* II9
der Buchstabe, -n *letter (of the alphabet),* II1
die Bucht, -en *bay,* II12
das Buddelschiffmuseum, -museen *museum of bottled boats,* II9
die Bude, -n *hut, room,* II12
bügeln *to iron,* II2
die Bühne, -n *stage,* II12
bulgarisch (adj) *Bulgarian,* II11
der Bummel *stroll,* II1
bummeln *to stroll,* II1
der Bund *bundle, bunch,* II2
das Bundesland, ⸚er *(German or Austrian) federal state,* I
das Bundesligateam, -s *team in the federal league,* II12
die Bundfalte, -n *pleat,* II8
die Bundfaltenhose, -n *pleated pants,* II8
bunt *colorful,* II8
das Bürgerhaus, ⸚er *home of a prosperous citizen,* II9
der Bürgerkrieg, -e *civil war,* II10
bürgerlich *civic, civil,* II11; **gut**

bürgerliche Küche *good home-cooked food*, II11

der **Bürgermeister**, - *mayor*, II3

das **Büro**, -s *office*, II3

der **Bus**, -se *bus*, I

der **Busausflug**, ÷e *bus excursion*, II11

die **Busfahrt**, -en *bus trip*, II9

die **Butter** *butter*, I

die **Buttermilch** *buttermilk*, II2

das **Butterschmalz** *shortening*, I

bzw.=beziehungsweise *respectively*, II12

C

das **Café**, -s *café*, I

der **Camembert Käse**, - *Camembert cheese*, II5

der **Cappuccino**, -s *cappuccino coffee*, II2

die **CD**, -s *compact disc*, I

Ćevapčići (Serbocroat: rolled spicy ground meat), II12

Chanukka *Hanukkah*, I; **Frohes Chanukka-Fest!** *Happy Hanukkah!*, I

der **Charakter** *character, personality, quality*, II8

charakterisieren *to characterize*, II1

checken *to check*, II10

der **Chefkoch**, ÷e *head chef*, II12

die **Chemie** *chemistry*, Loc 7

chemisch *chemical*, II4

chic *smart (looking)*, I

der **Chinese**, -n *Chinese (male)*, II12

chinesisch (adj) *Chinese*, II11

das **Chorkonzert**, -e *choir concert*, II11

die **Clique**, -n *clique*, II4

das **Cola**, -s *cola (also: die Cola)*, I

die **Comics** (pl) *comic books*, I

der **Computer**, - *computer*, II10

cool (adj) *cool*, II8

die **Couch**, -en *couch*, I

der **Court**, -s *court*, II12

der **Couscous=Kuskus** *couscous*, II12

der **Cousin**, -s *cousin (male)*, I

die **Creme**, -s *cream*, II6

die **Cremesoße**, -n *cream sauce*, II12

die **Crêpes** (pl) *crepes*, II12

D

da *there*, II1; **Da hast du (bestimmt) recht!** *You're right about that!*, II10; **da hinten** *there in the back*, I; **da vorn** *there in the front*, I; **Da stimm' ich dir zu!** *I agree with you about that!*, II10

dabei *by it; near it; beside it, with it*, II2

die **Dachrinne**, -n *rain gutter*, II12

dafür *for it*, II10; **Ich bin dafür, daß ...** *I am for doing...*, II11; *I prefer that...*, II11

daheim *at home, in one's own country*, II12

daher *from there; (conj) for that reason*, II7

dahin *to that place*, II9

dahinter *behind it*, II9

damals *then, in those days*, II12

damit *with it; (conj) so that*, II1

der **Damm**, ÷e *dam, dike*, II7

dampfend *steaming*, II12

danach *after that*, I

daneben *next to it*, II1

danebengehen (sep) *to be way off, miss the mark*, II11

Danke! *Thank you!*, I; **Danke (sehr/schön)!** *Thank you (very much)!*, I; **Danke! Dir/Ihnen auch!** *Thank you! Same to you!*, II11; **Danke gleichfalls!** *Thank you and the same to you!*, II11

danken (dat) *to thank*, II1

dann *then*, II1; **Dann nehm' ich eben ...** *In that case I'll take...*, II5; **Dann trink' ich halt ...** *I'll drink instead...*, II5

daran *at it; on it*, II4

darauf *on it; to it*, II3

Darf ich (bitte) ...? *May I (please)...?*, II10

darin *in it*, II8

darüber *over it*, II8

darüberstreuen (sep) *to sprinkle over something*, II12

darunter *under it, underneath*, II8

daß (conj) *that*, I

der **Dativ** *dative case*, II6

die **Datscha**, (pl) Datschen *garden house*, II11

der **Daumen**, - *thumb*, II6

davon *away from it; of it*, II7

davor *in front of it*, II9

dazu *for it; with it*, II2

dazwischen *between it*, II10

der **Decathlet**, -en *decathlete (male)*, II12

die **Decke**, -n *blanket, cover*, II12

der **Deckel**, - *lid*, II5

decken *to cover*, II2; **den Tisch decken** *to set the table*, I

deftig *robust*, II11

dein (poss adj) *your*, I

derselbe *the same*, II3

die **Delikatesse**, -n *delicacy*, II11

denken *to think*, II2

das **Denkmal**, ÷er *monument*, Loc 1

denn (particle), I

denn (conj) *because, for*, I

des *of the*, II1

deshalb (conj) *for this reason*, II2

desinfizieren *to disinfect*, II7

das **Desinteresse** *disinterest*, II8

dessen *of him, it; of whose*, II9

deswegen (conj) *because of that, for this reason*, II1

das **Deutsch** *German (language)*, I; *(school subject)*, I

die **Deutschklasse**, -n *German class*, II2

der **Deutschlehrer**, - *German teacher (male)*, I

die **Deutschlehrerin**, -nen *German teacher (female)*, I

der **Deutschschüler**, - *German student (male)*, II5

deutschsprachig *German-speaking*, II12

der **Dezember** *December*, I

das **Dia**, -s *slide*, II3

die **Diätmargarine** *diet margarine*, II2

der **Dichter**, - *writer, poet*, II3

dick (adj) *fat*, II4; **dick machen** *to be fattening*, II4

der **Dienstag** *Tuesday*, I

dienstags *Tuesdays*, II10

dies- *this*, II5

dieselbe *the same*, II6

diesmal *this time*, II3

das **Diktatschreiben**, - *dictation*, II2

das **Ding**, -e *thing*, II1; **vor allen Dingen** *especially*, II10

dir *to you*, II3

direkt *direct*, II9

die **Dirigentin**, -nen *conductor (of an orchestra) (female)*, II11

die **Disko**, -s *disco*, I; **in eine Disko gehen** *to go to a disco*, I

die **Diskothek**, -en *discotheck*, II9

die **Diskussion**, -en *discussion*, II10

das **Diskuswerfen** *discus throw*, II1

diskutieren *to discuss*, II7

DM=Deutsche Mark *German mark (monetary unit)*, I

doch (particle) *yes, it is!*, I; **Ich meine doch, daß ...** *I really think that...*, II10

der **Doktor**, -en *doctor*, II8

der **Dom**, -e *cathedral*, II3

der **Donnerstag** *Thursday*, I

donnerstags *Thursdays*, II10

doof *dumb*, I

das **Dorf**, ÷er *village*, II7

die Dorfgemeinde, -n *village community*, II3

die Dorfkirche, -n *village church*, II3
dörflich *rural*, II12

der Dorfplatz, ⸚e *village square*, II3

die Dorfplatzeinweihung, -en *village square dedication*, II3
dort *there*, I; **dort drüben** *over there*, I
dorthin *to there*, II9

das Drahtbett, -en *wire-frame bed*, II7
drauf=darauf *on top of it*, II5
draußen *outside*, II5

der Dreck *dirt*, II2
dreckig *dirty*, II7
drehen *to turn*, II7
drin=darin *in it*, II8
dritt- *third*, II1

die Drogerie, -n *drugstore*, II6

der Drogist, -en *druggist (male)*, II6

die Drogistin, -nen *druggist (female)*, II6
drücken *to press, squeeze*, II6

der Druckfehler, - *printing error*, II2

der Druckknopf, ⸚e *snap*, II8
drunter=darunter *underneath it*, II5

der Dschungel, - *jungle*, II9

der Duft, ⸚e *scent, perfume*, II2
dumm *dumb, stupid*, I
dummerweise *stupidly*, II3

das Düngemittel, - *fertilizer*, II4
dunkel *dark*, II1
durch (prep) *through*, II9
durchchecken (sep) *to check through*, II10

die Durchschnittskosten (pl) *average cost*, II10
dürfen *to be allowed to*, II4; **er/sie/es darf** *he/she/it is allowed to*, II4

der Durst *thirst*, II2

E

eben (particle), II5; **Dann nehm' ich eben ...** *In that case I'll take...*, II5; **eben nicht** *actually not*, II9
ebenfalls *likewise*, II5
echt *real(ly)*, II3; *genuine*, II1

die Ecke, -n *corner*, II9
eckig *with corners*, I
egal *alike, equal*, II5; **egal sein: Mode ist mir egal.** *I don't care about fashion.*, II8
eher *sooner; rather*, II3
ehrlich *honestly*, I

das Ei, -er *egg*, I
eigen *(one's) own*, II7

die Eigenschaft, -en *quality, property, attribute*, II1
eigentlich *actual(ly)*, II1; **Eigentlich schon, aber ...** *Well yes, but...*, II4
ein(-) ander- *another (a different) one*, II9
einander *one another*, II7
einbiegen (sep) *to turn*, II9

der Eindruck, ⸚e *impression*, II12
Einfach! *That's easy!*, I
einfarbig *one-colored*, II8
einfüllen (sep) *to fill in*, II5

der Eingang, ⸚e *entrance*, II1

die Eingangstür, -en *entrance door*, II12
eingebildet *arrogant*, II8
eingeweiht *dedicated*, II3
einheimisch *local, native*, II9
einige *some*, II2
s. einigen auf (acc) *to agree on*, II12
einigermaßen *to a certain extent*, II4

der Einkauf, ⸚e *purchase*, II8
einkaufen (sep) *to shop*, I; **einkaufen gehen** *to go shopping*, I, II5

der Einkaufsbummel *shopping through downtown area*, II9

die Einkaufsliste, -n *shopping list*, II5

das Einkaufszentrum *shopping center*, II2

der Einkaufszettel, - *shopping list*, II2

das Einkommen, - *income*, II7
einladen (sep) *to invite*, I; **er/sie lädt ... ein** *he/she invites*, I

die Einladung, -en *invitation*, II1
einlegen (sep): **ein Video einlegen** *to insert a video*, II3
einmal *once*, I; **einmal am Tag** *once a day*, II4
einmalig *unique*, II9
einnehmen (sep) *to take*, II6

der Einreiher, - *coat with one row of buttons*, II8
einrichten (sep) *to arrange*, II7

die Einrichtung, -en *arrangement*, II11
einsam *lonely*, II12
einschalten (sep) *to switch on*, II10

die Einschaltquote, -n *number of viewers*, II10
einschlafen (sep) *to fall asleep*, II12
einschüchtern (sep) *to intimidate*, II7
einsetzen (sep) *to put, fill in*, II7
einsteigen (sep) *to get into, onto a vehicle*, II10

die Einstellung, -en *attitude, outlook*, II8
eintragen (sep) *to record (an entry)*, II2
eintreten (sep) *to enter*, II6
Einverstanden! *Agreed!*, II10

der Einwohner, - *resident*, Loc 1
einzeln *single, individual, solitary*, II2
einzig *only; unique*, II9

das Erlebnis, -se *experience*, II7

das Eis *ice cream*, I

der Eisbecher, - *a dish of ice cream*, I

die Eischeibe, -n *slice of egg*, II5

der Eistee *iced tea*, II5
elastisch *elastic*, II8
elegant *elegant*, II12

die Elektroindustrie, -n *electrical appliances industry*, Loc 1

die Elektrotechnik *electrical engineering*, Loc 4

der Ellbogen, - *elbow*, II6

die Eltern (pl) *parents*, I
empfangen *to greet, receive*, II10
empfehlen *to recommend*, II11

die Empfehlung, -en *recommendation*, II11
empfinden *to feel*, II9

das Ende, -n *end*, II2
endgültig *final(ly), last(ly)*, II12
endlich *at last*, II8

die Endung, -en *ending*, II5

die Energie, -n *energy*, II4
eng *tight*, I
englisch (adj) *English*, II1

das Englisch *English* (school subject), I; (language), I

das Englischlernen *learning English*, II6
englischsprechend *English-speaking*, II12

die Englischvokabel, -n *English vocabulary word*, II6

die Entdeckungsreise, -n *voyage of discovery or exploration*, II12

die Entdeckungstour, -en *discovery tour*, II12

die Ente, -n *duck*, II11
entfernt *far-off, distant*, II3
enthalten *to contain*, II2
entlang *along*, II9
s. entscheiden *to decide*, II9
Entschuldigung! *Excuse me!*, I
s. entspannen *to relax*, II9

die Entspannung, -en *relaxation*, II12
entsprechen (dat) *to correspond to, to agree with*, II2
entstehen *to come into existence*, II12
enttäuscht *disappointed*, II9

entweder: entweder ... oder *either ... or,* II3

entwerfen *to draw up, draft, design,* II5

die Epoche, -n *epoch,* II3

er *he,* I; *it,* I

erarbeiten *to get or gain by working for,* II7

erbaut *built, constructed,* Loc 1

die Erbse, -n *pea,* II2

die Erdbeere, -n *strawberry,* II4

die Erdkunde *geography,* I

die Erdnußbutter *peanut butter,* II5

erfahren *to experience,* II3

der Erfahrene, -n *experienced (person),* II12

erfinden *to invent,* II3

der Erfolg, -e *success,* II12

erfragen *to ascertain by questioning,* II3

erfrischen *to refresh, revive,* II12

erfüllen *to fulfill,* II7

ergänzen *to add to, complete,* II4

ergeben *to produce, yield,* II9

das Ergebnis, -se *result,* II2

erhalten: **gut erhalten** *well maintained,* II9

erhältlich *obtainable,* II9

erhöht *raised,* II6

s. erholen *to recover,* II12

die Erholung, -en *recovery,* II9

der Erholungssuchende, -n *person looking to recuperate,* II12

s. erinnern an (acc) *to remember,* II3

s. erkälten *to catch cold,* II12

die Erkältung, -en *cold (illness),* II6

erkennen *to recognize,* II3

erklären *to explain,* II5

erlaubt *permitted,* II10

erleben *to experience,* II9

das Erlebnis, -se *experience,* II5

ermitteln *to find out,* II10

s. ernähren *to feed, nourish,* II4

die Ernährung *food,* II4

der Ernährungsbewußte, -n *person conscious of his diet,* II12

erraten *solve a riddle, guess correctly,* II1

erscheinen *to appear,* II4

erst *first,* II1

erstellen *to make available,* II9

ersten: am ersten *on the first,* I

erstens *first of all,* II4

ersticken *to suffocate,* II8

ertragen *to bear,* II12

erträumen *to dream of or about, imagine,* II9

erwachsen (pp) *grown up,* II5

erwähnen *to mention,* II3

erwarten *to expect,* II11

erzählen *to tell* (a story), II1

die Erzählung, -en *story,* II12

essen *to eat,* I; **er/sie ißt** *he/she eats,* I

der Eßlöffel=EL *tablespoon,* II5

der Eßtisch, -e *dining table,* I

das Eßzimmer, - *dining room,* II7

etlich- *some, a certain,* II10

etwa *about, more or less,* II4

etwas *something,* I; **Noch etwas?** *Anything else?,* I

euch (pl, acc case) *you,* I; (pl, dat case) *to you,* II3; (reflexive) *yourselves,* II4

euer (poss adj) *your,* II3

der Europäer, - *European,* II12

europäisch (adj) *European,* II12

evangelisch *Protestant,* II9

exklusiv *exclusive,* II12

experimentieren *to experiment,* II8

der Experte, -n *expert,* II12

F

die Fabrik, -en *factory,* II8

das Fach, ̈-er *school subject,* I

fachmännisch (adj) *expert, competent,* II12

das Fachwerkhaus, ̈-er *cross-timbered house,* II3

fahren *to go, ride, drive* (using a vehicle), I; **er/sie fährt** *he/she drives,* I; **Fahren wir mal nach ... !** *Let's go to ... !,* II9

der Fahrgast, ̈-e *passenger,* II11

die Fahrpraxis *driving experience,* II10

das Fahrrad, ̈-er *bicycle,* II4

das Fahrrad-Depot, -s *bicycle racks,* II12

die Fahrradclique, -n *bicycle group,* II1

die Fahrradtour, -en *tour by bicycle,* II9

die Fahrschule, -n *driving school,* II10

die Fahrstunde, -n *driving lesson,* II10

die Fahrt, -en *ride, drive, journey,* II2

die Fahrzeit, -en *travel time,* II11

das Fahrzeug, -e *vehicle,* II7

der Fall, ̈-e *case,* II3

das Fallschirmspringen *sky-diving,* II10

der Faltenrock, ̈-e *pleated skirt,* II8

die Familie, -n *family,* I

das Familienmitglied, -er *family member,* II5

die Familiensendung, -en *family program,* II10

der Fantasyroman, -e *fantasy novel,* I

das Farbbild, -er *color photograph,* II3

die Farbe, -n *color,* I

das Farbfernsehgerät, -e *color TV set,* II10

farblich *colorful,* II8

die Faser, -n *thread, material,* II8

faszinierend *fascinating,* Loc 4

faul *lazy,* II1

faulenzen *to be lazy,* II3

der Februar *February,* I

fechten *to fence,* II1

fehlen: **Was fehlt dir?** *What's wrong with you?,* II6

der Fehler, - *mistake,* II2

die Feier, -n *celebration, party,* II2

der Feiertag, -e *holiday,* I

fein *fine, exquisite,* II12

der Feind, -e *enemy,* II4

die Feinmechanik *precision tool mechanics,* Loc 10

der Fels, -en *boulder,* II9

feminin *feminine,* II5

das Fenster, - *window,* I

die Ferien (pl) *vacation (from school),* II3

das Ferienangebot, -e *special vacation offer,* II9

der Ferienort, -e *resort,* II3

das Ferienparadies, -e *vacation paradise,* II9

der Ferienplan, ̈-e *vacation plan,* II9

das Ferienziel, -e *vacation destination,* II12

die Fernbedienung, -en *remote control,* II10

Fernseh gucken *to watch TV* (colloquial), II10

der Fernseh- und Videowagen *TV and video cart,* II10

die Fernsehanstalt, -en *TV station,* II10

Fernsehen schauen *to watch TV,* I

fernsehen (sep) *to watch TV,* II10

der Fernseher, - *television set,* II10

das Fernsehgerät, -e *television set,* II10

die Fernsehgewohnheit, -en *TV viewing habit,* II10

der Fernsehgucker, - *TV viewer,* II10

das Fernsehprogramm, -e *TV schedule,* II10

der Fernsehrat *TV council,* II10

der Fernsehraum, ̈-e *TV room,* II9

die Fernsehsaison, -s *programming season,* II10

die Fernsehsendung, -en *TV program, show,* II12

der Fernsehzuschauer, - *TV viewer*, II10

fertigen *to finish*, II9

das Fertiggericht, -e *frozen food*, II5

. **fesch** *stylish, smart*, I

fest *firm*, II12

das Festland *mainland*, II9

die Festlichkeit, -en *party, celebration*, II12

der Festtag, -e *holiday, festival*, II8

fett *fat, greasy*, II6

das Fett: **hat zu viel Fett** *has too much fat*, II4

fetzig *really sharp (looking)*, II8

feuerrot *bright red*, II8

das Fieber, - *fever*, II6

der Film, -e *movie*, I; *roll of film*, II3

filmen *to film, videotape*, II3

der Filzstift, -e *felt-tip pen*, II1

die Finanzmetropole, -n *financial center*, II3

finden *to think about*, I; **Das finde ich auch.** *I think so, too.*, I; **Das finde ich nicht.** *I disagree.*, I; *I don't think so.*, II10; **Ich finde es gut/schlecht, daß ...** *I think it's good/bad that...*, I; **Ich finde den Pulli stark!** *The sweater is awesome!*, I; **Wie findest du (Tennis)?** *What do you think of (tennis)?*, I

die Firma, (pl) Firmen *company*, II3

der Fisch, -e *fish*, I

das Fischerdorf, ⸚er *fishing village*, II9

die Fischerhose, -n *pedal pushers*, II8

das Fischgericht, -e *fish entrée*, II11

das Fischstäbchen, - *fish stick*, II5

s. fit halten *to stay fit*, II4

die Fitneß *fitness*, II12

die Fitneßgewohnheit, -en *fitness habit*, II4

der Fitneßraum, ⸚e *training and weight room*, II9

die Fläche, -n *flat area, surface*, Loc 1

flach *flat*, II8

die Flasche, -n *bottle*, II5

die Fledermaus, ⸚e *bat*, II11

das Fleisch *meat*, I

das Fleischgericht, -e *meat dish*, II11

der Fleischsalat, -e *meat salad*, II5

fleißig *hard-working*, II1

die Fliege, -n *bow tie*, II12

fliegen *to fly*, II9

die Fliese, -n *tile*, II12

der Flohmarkt, ⸚e *flea market*, II1

flott *lively, brisk*, II12

der Flug, ⸚e *flight*, II12

der Flughafen, ⸚ *airport*, II3

die Flugstunde, -n *hour of flying time*, II12

das Flugzeug, -e *airplane*, II7

der Flur, -e *hallway*, II7

der Fluß, (pl) **Flüsse** *river*, II7

das Flüßchen, - *streamlet*, II9

folgen (dat) *to follow*, II8

folgend- *following*, II2

fordern *to demand*, II5

die Forelle, -n *trout*, I!4

das Forellenfilet, -s *trout fillet*, II11

der Fortgeschrittene, -n *advanced (person)*, II12

das Foto, -s *photo*, II1

die Fotogeschichte, -n *photo story*, II6

der Fotograf, -en *photographer*, II12

fotografieren *to photograph*, II3

die Frage, -n *question*, II4

der Fragebogen, ⸚ *questionnaire*, II3

fragen *to ask*, II4

französisch (adj) *French*, II11

die Frau, -en *woman; Mrs.*, I

die Frauenrechtlerin, -nen *supporter of equal rights for women (female)*, Loc 7

frei *free*, II9; **Wir haben frei.** *We have off (from school).*, I

freilich *to be sure, quite so*, II11

der Freitag *Friday*, I

freitags *Fridays*, II10

freiwillig *voluntary*, II9

die Freizeit *free time, leisure time*, I

die Freizeitbeschäftigung, -en *free time activity*, II3

das Freizeitzentrum, (pl) -zentren *leisure time meeting area*, II1

fremd *foreign; strange*, II11

der Fremdenverkehrsverein, -e *tourist bureau*, II3

das Fremdwort, ⸚er *foreign word*, II2

die Freude *happiness*, II9

s. freuen auf (acc) *to look forward to*, II4

s. freuen über (acc) *to be happy about*, II4; **Ich freue mich, daß ...** *I am happy that...*, II4

der Freund, -e *friend (male)*, I

die Freundin, -nen *friend (female)*, II1

freundlich *friendly*, II1

friedlich *peaceful*, II7

frisch *fresh*, II2

der Friseur, -e *hair stylist*, II12

froh *happy*, II4

fröhlich *cheerful, happy*, II2

der Froschschenkel, - *frog's leg*, II5

die Frucht, ⸚e *fruit*, II5

das Fruchtfleisch *fruit pulp*, II5

der Fruchtsaft, ⸚e *fruit juice*, II11

früh *early*, II6

der Frühling *spring (season)*, I

das Frühstück, -e *breakfast*, II5

s. fühlen *to feel*, II4; **Ich fühle mich wohl!** *I feel great!*, II6

führen *to lead*, II9

der Führerschein, -e *driver's license*, II10

die Fülle, -n *fullness, abundance*, II4

fünft- *fifth*, II9

fünftgrößt- *fifth biggest*, II3

fünfzeilig *five line*, II7

für (prep) *for*, I

furchtbar *terrible, awful*, I; **furchtbar gern haben** *to like a lot*, I

fürs=für das *for it*, II1

der Fuß, ⸚e *foot*, II6

Fußball *soccer*, I

der Fußboden, ⸚ *floor*, II12

die Fußbremse, -n *foot brake*, II10

die Fußgängerzone, -n *pedestrian zone*, II9

füttern *to feed*, I

G

gähnen *to yawn*, II12

ganz *all, whole*, II1; **Ganz klar!** *Of course!*, I; **ganz wohl** *extremely well*, II4

gar nicht gern haben *not to like at all*, I

die Garage, -n *garage*, II2; **die Garage aufräumen** *to clean the garage*, II2

der Garten, ⸚ *garden, yard*, II7

die Gartenarbeit, -en *yard work*, II2

der Gast, ⸚e *guest*, II3

der Gastgeber, - *host*, II2

das Gasthaus, ⸚er *hotel, bed and breakfast*, II3

der Gasthof, ⸚e *restaurant, inn*, II3

das Gastland, ⸚er *host country*, II9

die Gastronomie *gastronomy*, II3

die Gaststätte, -n *restaurant, coffee house*, II12

der Gastwirt, -e *owner of a restaurant, hotel*, II12

das Gebäude, - *building*, Loc 4

geben *to give*, I; **er/sie gibt** *he/she gives*, I; **Das gibt's doch nicht!** *There's just no way!*, II10

gebeten *asked*, II12

das Gebirge, - *mountains*, II3

geblieben *remained, stayed*, II3

geblümt *flowery*, II8

geboren *born*, II3

das Gebot, -e *commandment*, II4

gebracht *brought*, 8
gebraten *fried*, II11
gebrauchen *to use*, II1
gebrochen *broken*, II6
der Geburtstag, -e *birthday*, I; **Alles Gute zum Geburtstag!** *Best wishes on your birthday!*, I; **Herzlichen Glückwunsch zum Geburtstag!** *Best wishes on your birthday!*, I; **Ich habe am ... Geburtstag.** *My birthday is on...*, I
die Geburtstagsfeier, -n *birthday celebration*, II11
die Geburtstagsfete, -n *birthday party*, II2
die Gedächtniskirche *Memorial Church*, Loc 4
der Gedanke, -n *thought, idea*, II5
das Gedicht, -e *poem*, II7
gefächert *varied*, II11
gefallen *to like;* **Hat es dir gefallen?** *Did you like it?*, II3; **Wie hat es dir gefallen?** *How did you like it?*, II3
das Gefäß, -e *container for liquid*, II3
gefüllt: das gefüllte Ei, -er *deviled egg*, II11
gefüttert *padded*, II8
gegangen *gone*, II3
gegen (prep) *against*, II1
die Gegend, -en *area*, II7
gegenseitig *mutual(ly)*, II1
gegenüber (prep) *across from*, II9
gegessen *eaten*, II3
der Gegner, - *opponent*, II1
gegrillt *grilled*, II11
gehackt *chopped*, II12
der Geheimtip, -s *secret tip*, II12
gehen *to go*, I; **Das geht nicht.** *That won't work*, I; **Es geht.** *It's okay*, I; **Wie geht's (denn)?** *How are you?*, I; **Gehen wir mal auf den Golfplatz!** *Let's go to the golf course!*, II9
geholfen *helped*, II3
der Geigenbau *violin making*, Loc 1
gekauft *bought*, I; **Was hast du gekauft?** *What did you buy?*, I
geknotet *knotted, tied*, II1
gekrönt *crowned*, II3
gekürzt *shortened, abbreviated*, II3
gelaunt: **gut gelaunt** *in a good mood*, II1
gelb *yellow*, I
das Geld *money*, I
die Gelegenheit, -en *opportunity*, II2
gelesen (pp) *read*, I; **Was hast du gelesen?** *What did you read?*, I

gemacht *done*, I; **Was hast du am Wochenende gemacht?** *What did you do on the weekend?*, I
gemahlen (pp) *milled, ground*, II12
das Gemälde, - *painting*, II2
die Gemäldegalerie, -n *gallery*, II3
gemeinsam *in common; joint, together*, II3
die Gemeinschaft, -en *community*, II3
gemietet *rented*, II12
gemischt *mixed*, II11
das Gemüse *vegetables*, I; **im Obst- und Gemüseladen** *at the produce store*, I
die Gemüsefrau *produce vendor (female)*, II2
der Gemüseladen, - *produce store*, I
der Gemüsemann *produce vendor (male)*, II2
gemustert *patterned*, II8
gemütlich *comfortable*, II7
genannt *named*, II3
genau *exact(ly)*, II4
genauso wie *just as ...*, II8
das Genie, -s *genius*, II12
genießen *to enjoy*, II9
genossen *enjoyed*, II3
genug *enough*, I; **Ich habe genug.** *I have enough.*, I
genügend *enough*, II4; **genügend schlafen** *to get enough sleep*, II4
der Genuß, (pl) Genüsse *pleasure*, II6
die Geografie *geography*, II8
gepflegt *well cared-for, well-groomed*, II12
gepunktet *polka-dotted*, II8
gerade *straight*, II2; *precisely, just*, II9; **Das ist gerade passiert.** *It just happened.*, II9
geradeaus *straight ahead*, II9
das Gerät, -e *appliance*, II10
geraten: **in Schwierigkeiten geraten** *to get into trouble*, II4
geräuchert *smoked*, II11
das Gericht, -e *meal, entrée*, II11
gerieben *grated*, II12
gering *small, unimportant*, II7
die Germanistik (sing) *German studies*, II4
gern (machen) *to like (to do)*, I; **gern haben** *to like*, I; **Gern geschehen!** *My pleasure!*, I; **besonders gern** *especially like*, I; **Gern! Hier ist es!** *Here! I insist!*, II10
gerne=gern, II2
der Gesamtpreis, -e *total price*, II8
der Gesamtschüler, - *student at a comprehensive school*, II8

die Gesäßtasche, -n *back pocket*, II8
das Geschäft, -e *store; business*, II5
die Geschäftsleute (pl) *business people*, II11
das Geschenk, -e *gift*, I
die Geschenkidee, -n *gift idea*, I
die Geschichte *history*, I
das Geschirr *dishes*, I; **Geschirr spülen** *to wash the dishes*, I
der Geschmack, -̈e *taste*, II5
geschnitten (pp) *cut*, II12
geschrieben *written*, II2
die Geschwindigkeitsbeschränkung, -en *speed limit*, II7
die Geschwister (pl) *brothers and sisters*, I
geschwommen *swum*, II3
die Gesellenprüfung, -en *apprentice's final exam*, II7
die Gesellschaft, -en *social group; society*, II10
das Gespräch, -e *conversation*, II1
gesprochen *spoken*, I; **Worüber habt ihr gesprochen?** *What did you (pl) talk about?*, I
gestatten *to allow, permit*, II12
gestehen *to admit*, II11
gestern *yesterday*, I; **gestern abend** *yesterday evening*, I
gestiegen *climbed*, II3
gestoßen *shoved*, II12
gestreift *striped*, II8
gesund *healthy*, II4
die Gesundheit *health*, II4
der Gesundheitstip, -s *health tip*, II4
gesüßt *sweetened*, II5
das Getränk, -e *drink*, II11
das Getriebe, - *transmission*, II10
gewesen (pp) *been*, II3
das Gewichttraining *weight training*, II12
das Gewissen, - *conscience*, II4
das Gewitter, - *storm*, I
die Gewohnheit, -en *habit*, II4
gewöhnlich *usually*, II4
das Gewölbe, - *archway, vault*, II3
gewonnen *won*, II8
geworden (pp) *became*, II12; **er ist groß geworden** *he got big, grew up*, II12
gießen *to water*, I; **Blumen gießen** *to water the flowers*, I
giftfrei *non-toxic*, II7
die Gitarre, -n *guitar*, I
das Glas, -̈er *glass*, I; **ein Glas Apfelsaft** *a glass of apple juice*, I
die Glasscheibe, -n *pane of glass*, II9
glauben *to believe*, I; **ich glaube** *I think*, I; **Ich glaube nicht, daß ...** *I don't think that...*, II9

gleich *immediately; equal,* II2
Gleichfalls: **Danke, gleichfalls!**
*Thank you and the same to
you!,* II11
gleichmäßig *even, symmetrical,* II5
glotzen *to stare,* II10; Fernseh
glotzen *to watch TV,* II10
das Glück *luck,* I; **So ein Glück!**
What luck!, I
das Glücksrad, ⸚er *lotto wheel, wheel
of fortune,* II10
das Goethehaus (Goethe's birthplace), II3
Golf *golf,* I
der Golfplatz, ⸚e *golf course,* II9
der Gott, ⸚er *God,* II1; um Gottes
willen *for God's sake,* II11
die Götterdämmerung, -en *twilight of
the gods,* II11
der Grad *degree(s),* I; **zwei Grad**
two degrees, I; **Wieviel Grad
haben wir?** *What's the
temperature?,* I
das Gramm *gram,* I
grau *gray,* I; **in Grau** *in gray,* I
grausam *cruel,* I
die Grenze, -n *border,* II12
der Grieche -n *Greek,* II9
griechisch (adj) *Greek,* II11
groß *big,* I
großartig *wonderful,* II4
die Größe, -n *size,* I
die Großeltern (pl) *grandparents,* I
größer *bigger,* II7
die Großmutter, ⸚ *grandmother,* I
der Großraum, ⸚e *metropolitan
area,* Loc 10
die Großstadt, ⸚e *big city,* II7
der Großvater, ⸚ *grandfather,* I
die Großzügigkeit, -en *generosity,* II8
gruftimäßig *like a Punker,* II8
grün *green,* I; **in Grün** *in
green,* I
der Grund, ⸚e *reason,* II2
der Grundschüler, - *elementary school
student,* II2
die Gruppe, -n *group,* I
gruselig *horrible, frightening,* II9
der Gruselroman, -e *horror novel,* I
der Gruß, ⸚e *greeting,* II7; grüßen *to
greet,* II1; **Grüß dich!** *Hi!,* I;
Grüß Gott *Hello,* II1
die Grütze: Rote Grütze (name of a
dessert), II11
gucken *to look,* II5; **Guck mal!**
Look!, II5; **Fernseh gucken** *to
watch TV* (colloquial), II10
das Gummiband, ⸚er *rubber band,* II8
günstig *favorable,* II9

die Gurke, -n *cucumber,* II2
die Gurkenscheibe, -n *cucumber
slice,* II2
der Gürtel, - *belt,* I
gut *good,* I; **Gut!** *Good! Well!,* I;
gut gelaunt *good-tempered,*
II1; **Gut! Mach' ich!** *Okay, I'll
do that!,* I; gut sein: **Ist dir
nicht gut?** *Are you not feeling
well?,* II6
der Gymnasiast, -en *student in
Gymnasium (male),* II2
die Gymnasiastin, -nen *student in
Gymnasium (female),* II2
die Gymnastik *exercise,
calisthenics,* II4; **Gymnastik
machen** *to exercise,* II4
das Gyros *gyros,* I

H

das Haar, -e *hair,* I
die Haarfarbe *hair color,* II1
die Haarlänge *hair length,* II1
haben *to have,* I; **er/sie hat**
he/she has, I; **Haben Sie das
auch in Rot?** *Do you also have
that in red?,* I
die Hacke, -n *hoe,* II7
das Hackfleisch *ground meat,* I
die Haftung, -en *liability,* II2
das Hähnchen, - *chicken,* I
halb *half,* I; **halb (eins, zwei,
usw.)** *half past (twelve, one,
etc.),* I
halblaut (adj) *whispering,* II11
die Hälfte, -n *half,* II12
die Halle, -n *hall,* II12
das Hallenbad, ⸚er *indoor pool,* II9
Hallo! *Hi! Hello!,* I
der Hals, ⸚e *throat,* II6
die Halskette, -n *necklace,* II1
die Halsschmerzen (pl) *sore
throat,* II6
das Halstuch, ⸚er *kerchief,* II1
das Halsweh *sore throat,* II6
halt (particle), I; **Die Kleinstadt
gefällt mir gut, weil es da halt
ruhiger ist.** *I like a small town
because it's just quieter there.,* II7
halten *to stop, hold,* II4; (für) *to
consider as,* II9; **s. fit halten** *to
keep fit,* II4
die Handbremse, -n *emergency
brake,* II10
die Handcreme *hand cream,* II6
die Hand, ⸚e *hand,* II6
der Handel *business, trade,* Loc 7
handeln von *to be about,* II12
die Handtasche, -n *handbag,* II1

hängen *to hang,* II3
hart *hard, tough,* II6
hartgekocht *hard-boiled,* II5
hätte: Ich hätte gern ... *I would
like...,* II11
der Haufen, - *pile,* II7
häufig *frequent(ly),* II6
das Hauptgericht, -e *main dish,* II11
der Hauptpunkt, -e *main point,* II3
der Hauptschüler, - *(male) student at
the Hauptschule,* II8
die Hauptschülerin, -nen *(female)
student at the Hauptschule,* II8
die Hauptstadt, ⸚e *capital,* I
die Hauptstraße, -n *main street,* II9
die Haupturlaubsreise, -n *main vacation trip,* II9
das Hauptwort, ⸚er *noun,* II11
das Haus, ⸚er *house,* II7; **zu Hause
bleiben** *to stay at home,* II6
die Hausarbeit, -en *housework,* II2
die Hausaufgaben (pl) *homework,* I;
Hausaufgaben machen *to do
homework,* I
hausgemacht *home-made,* II11
der Haushalt, -e *household,* II10
haushalten *to keep house,* II10
die Hausmannskost *simple, hearty
food,* II5
das Haustier, -e *pet,* I
die Haut, ⸚e *skin,* II6
hassen *to hate,* II5
häßlich *ugly,* I
die Heckenschere, -n *pruning
shears,* II7
das Heft, -e *notebook,* I
heftig *vehement, violent,* II10
die Heide *heath,* II7
der Heilbutt *halibut,* II5
das Heim, -e *home; institute,* II10
der Heimatort, -e *native place,* II7
die Heimatstadt, ⸚e *native city,* II7
die Heimfahrt *trip home,* II2
heiß *hot,* I
heißen *to be called,* I; **er heißt**
his name is, I
helfen (dat) *to help,* I; **zu Hause
helfen** *to help at home,* I
hell *bright,* II7
hellbraun *light brown,* II1
das Hemd, -en *shirt,* I
heraus *out,* II3
herausfinden (sep) *to find out,* II5
herauslösen (sep) *to filter out, to
remove,* II5
herausnehmen (sep) *to take
out,* II3
herausschneiden (sep) *to cut
out,* II5

heraussuchen (sep) *to pick out, select,* II8

der Herbst *fall* (season), I; **im Herbst** *in the fall,* I

der Herd, -e *stove,* I

herstellen (sep) *to manufacture, produce,* II5

der Herr *Mr.,* I

herrlich *fantastic,* II9

die Herrschaft, -en *rule, dominion; person,* II3

herumlaufen (sep) *to run around,* II11

das Herz, -en *heart,* II6

herzhaft *hearty,* II11

herzlich *heartfelt,* II12; **Herz-lichen Glückwunsch zum Geburtstag!** *Best wishes on your birthday!,* I

der Herzog, ⸗e *duke,* II1

heulen *to cry,* II9

heute today, I; **heute morgen** *this morning,* I; **heute nachmit-tag** *this afternoon,* I; **heute abend** *tonight, this evening,* I

heutzutage *nowadays,* II8

hier *here,* I; **Hier bei ...** *The ... residence.,* I; **Hier ist ...** *This is ...,* I

die Hilfe, -n *help,* II11

die Hilfsbereitschaft *cooperation,* II8

die Himbeere, -n *raspberry,* II2

die Himbeermarmelade, -n *rasp-berry marmalade,* II5

die Himbeertorte, -n *raspberry cake,* II1

der Himmel, - *sky, heaven,* II6

das Himmelbett, -en *canopy bed,* II7

hin *to,* II1

hinaus *out,* II7

hinausziehen (sep) *to go outside,* II7

hinein *into,* II12

hineinwerfen (sep) *to throw into,* II12

hingehen (sep) *to go to,* II2

hinten *at the back,* II1; **da hinten** *there in the back,* II1

der Hintergrund, ⸗e *background,* II11

hinterlassen *to leave behind,* II9

der Hinweis, -e *hint, direction,* II4

historisch *historical,* II1

die Hitze *heat,* II6

der Hitzschlag, ⸗e *heat stroke,* II6

hob (past) *lifted,* II12

hobbymäßig *for a hobby,* II10

das Hobby, -s *hobby,* II1

hoch *high,* II6

das Hochwasser, ⸗ *flood,* II9

die Hochzeit, -en *wedding,* II12

der Hof, ⸗e *court, courtyard,* II9

hoffen *to hope,* II6

Hoffentlich ... *Hopefully...,* II6; **Hoffentlich geht es dir bald besser!** *I hope you'll get better soon.,* II6

die Hoffnung, -en *hope,* II6

höflich *polite, courteous,* II12

hoh- *high,* II1

höher: noch höher *still higher,* II10

holen *to get, fetch,* I

das Holz, ⸗er *wood,* I; **aus Holz** *out of wood,* I

der Holztisch, -e *wooden table,* II9

hören: **Hör mal zu!** *Listen to this!,* II5; **Hör mal!** *Listen!,* II5; **Musik hören** *to listen to music,* I; **Hör gut zu!** *Listen carefully.,* I

horchen *to listen carefully,* II12

der Hörer, - *listener; receiver,* I; **den Hörer abheben** *to pick up the receiver,* I; **den Hörer auflegen** *to hang up (the telephone),* I

der Horrorfilm, -e *horror movie,* I

die Hose, -n *pants,* I

das Hotel, -s *hotel,* II3

hübsch *pretty,* II1

die Hüfte, -n *hip,* II6

das Huhn, ⸗er *chicken,* II4

der Hummer, - *lobster,* II11

der Hund, -e *dog,* I

hundelieb *fond of dogs,* II12

der Hunger *hunger,* I; **Ich habe Hunger.** *I am hungry,* II6

hungrig *hungry,* II12

hupen *to honk the horn,* II7

der Hürdenlauf, ⸗e *hurdling,* II1

der Husten, - *cough,* II6

der Hut, ⸗e *hat,* II1

I

ich *I,* I; **Ich auch.** *Me too.,* I; **Ich nicht.** *I don't.,* I

die Idee, -n *idea,* II9; **Gute Idee!** *Good idea!,* II12; **Hast du eine Idee?** *Do you have an idea?,* II9

identifizieren *to identify,* II1

s. identifizieren mit *to identify your-self with,* II7

das Idol, -e *idol,* II1

ihm *to, for him,* I

ihn *it, him,* I

ihnen *to them,* II3

Ihnen (formal) *to you,* II3

ihr (poss adj) *her, their,* I; *to, for her,* I; (pl) *you,* I

Ihr (poss adj, formal, pl, sing) *your,* II5

die Illustration, -en *illustration,* II7

die Illustrierte, -n *magazine,* II5

im=in dem; im Frühling *in the spring,* I; **im Januar** *in January,* I; **(einmal) im Monat** *(once) a month,* I; **im Wohn-zimmer** *in the living room,* I

der Imbißstand, ⸗e *fast-food stand,* II2

die Imbißstube, -n *snack bar,* II3

immer *always,* I

das Imperfekt *past tense,* II3

imposant *impressive, majestic,* II9

in (prep) *in, into,* II9; **in Blau** *in blue,* I; **in der (Basketball) Mannschaft** *on the (basket-ball) team,* II4; **in die Apotheke gehen** *to go to the pharmacy,* II6

indem (conj) *in that,* II11

indisch (adj) *(Asian) Indian,* II11

individuell (adj) *individual,* II12

die Industrie, -n *industry,* Loc 1

der Industriestandort, -e *industrial location,* Loc 10

das Infoblatt, ⸗er *information brochure,* II4

die Information, -en *information,* II4

der Innenraum, ⸗e *interior, inside,* II5

die Innenstadt, ⸗e *downtown,* II9

die Innentasche, -n *inside pocket,* II8

innerhalb (prep) *within, on the inside,* II12

die Insel, -n *island,* II12

insgesamt *altogether,* II5

das Instrument, -e *instrument,* I

inzwischen *in the meantime,* II12

intelligent *intelligent,* II1

intensiv *intensive,* II6

interessant *interesting,* II5

das Interesse, -n *interest,* I; **Hast du andere Interessen?** *Do you have any other interests?,* I; **Ich habe kein Interesse an Mode.** *I am not interested in fashion.,* II8

s. **interessieren für** *to be interested in,* II8; **Interessierst du dich für Mode?** *Are you interested in fashion?,* II8

international *international,* II7

interviewen *to interview,* II7

irgendein- *someone, something,* II2

irgendwas *anything, something,* II2

irgendwelch- *some, any,* II2

irgendwie *somehow,* II1

irgendwo *somewhere,* II2

irgendwohin *to somewhere,* II1

das Islandpferd, -e *Iceland pony,* II3
ist: **er/sie/es ist** *he/she/it is,* I;
sie ist aus *she's from,* I; **Ist
was mit dir?** *Is something
wrong?,* II6
der Italiener, - *Italian,* II9
italienisch (adj) *Italian,* II11

J

ja *yes,* I; **Ja klar!** *Of course!,* I;
Das ist ja unglaublich! *That's
really unbelievable!,* II10; **Ja,
kann sein, aber ...** *Yes, maybe,
but...,* II4; **Ja, natürlich!**
Certainly!, II4; *Yes, of
course!,* II10; **Ja, schon, aber ...**
Well yes, but..., II7; **Ja? Was
denn?** *Okay, what is it?,* II5
die Jacke, -n *jacket,* I
das Jahr, -e *year,* I; **Ich bin ... Jahre
alt.** *I am...years old.,* I
der Jahrestil, -e *year's style,* II8
die Jahreszeit, -en *season,* II5
das Jahrhundert, -e *century,* II9; **aus
dem 17. Jahrhundert** *from the
17th century,* II9
jährig *year-old,* II9
jahrzehntelang *for decades,* Loc 4
der Januar *January,* I; **im Januar** *in
January,* I
der Japangarten *Japanese garden,* II9
je *each, every,* II8; **je nach
Gelegenheit** *according to the
occasion,* II8
die Jeans (mostly sing) *jeans,* I
die Jeansjacke, -n *jeans jacket,* II1
die Jeansweste, -n *jeans vest,* II8
jed- *every,* II2; **jede Woche**
every week, II4; **jeden Tag**
every day, I; **jedes Wochenende**
every weekend, II4
jemand *someone, somebody,* II6
jenseits (prep) *on the other side,
beyond,* II12
jetzt *at present, now,* I
der Job, -s *job,* II7
das Jobangebot, -en *job offer,* II12
joggen *to jog,* I
der Jogging-Anzug, ̈e *jogging
suit,* I
der Joghurt, -s (or **das**) *yogurt,* II5
die Jugend *youth,* II3
die Jugendherberge, -n *youth
hostel,* II3
das Jugendlager, - *youth camp,* II9
der Jugendliche, -n *teenager
(male),* II8
die Jugendliche, -n *teenager
(female),* II8

die Jugendpflege, -n *youth
welfare,* II11
der Juli *July,* I
jung *young,* II7
der Junge, -n *boy,* I
jünger *younger,* II7
der Juni *June,* I
der Jux *practical joke,* II12

K

das Kabarett, -e *cabaret,* II11
das Kabelfernsehen *cable TV,* II10
das Kabriolett, -s *convertible,
cabriolet,* II10
der Kaffee *coffee,* I
der Kajak, -s *canoe, kayak,* II7
der Kakao *chocolate milk,* II5
der Kalender, - *calendar,* I
kalifornisch (adj) *Californian,* II11
die Kalorie, -n *calorie,* II1
kalt (adj) *cold,* II4
die Kälte, -n *cold, coldness,* II12
die Kamera, -s *camera,* II3
der Kamin, -e *fireplace, chimney,* II9
s. kämmen *to comb,* II6
die Kammerspiele (pl) *(small)
theater,* II11
kämpfen *to fight,* II12
der Kanal, ̈e *canal,* II1
das Kapitel, - *chapter,* II1
das Käppi, -s *(baseball) cap,* II8
kaputt *ruined, broken,* I, II9
die Kapuze, -n *hood,* II8
kariert *checked,* II8
das Karo, -s (pattern) *check,
diamond,* II12
die Karotte, -n *carrot,* II7
der Karpfen, - *carp,* II4
die Karte, -n *card; ticket,* I
die Karteikarte, -n *index card,* II7
die Kartoffel, -n *potato,* I
der Käse, - *cheese,* I
das Käsebrot, -e *cheese sandwich,* I
der Käsekuchen, - *cheese cake,* II5
die Käserei, -en *cheese dairy,* II9
die Kasse, -n *cash register,* II8
die Kassette, -n *cassette,* I
der Kassettenspieler, - *cassette
deck,* II10
der Kasten, ̈ *box,* II1
der Katalog, -e *catalogue,* II8
die Kategorie, -n *category,* II1
der Katholik, -en *Catholic,* II3
die Katze, -n *cat,* I
kauen *to chew,* II12
kaufen *to buy,* I
das Kaufhaus, ̈er *department store,* II2
der Kaufmann, (pl) Kaufleute *salesman,* II11

der Kaugummi, -s *chewing gum,* II1
kaum *barely, hardly,* II6
der Kavalierstart, -s *jack-rabbit
start,* II7
die Kegelbahn, -en *bowling alley,* II3
kegeln *to bowl,* II3
kein *no, none, not any,* I; **Ich
habe keine Zeit.** *I don't have
time.,* I; **Ich habe keinen
Hunger mehr.** *I'm not hungry
any more.,* I; **Keine Ahnung!** *I
have no idea!,* I
der Keks, -e *cookie,* I
der Keller, - *cellar,* II7
der Kellner, - *waiter,* II11
kennen *to know, be familiar or
acquainted with,* I
kennenlernen (sep) *to get to
know,* II12
das Kilo=Kilogramm, - *kilogram,* I
das Kind, -er *child,* II1
kinderlieb *fond of children,* II1
die Kindheit *childhood,* II3
das Kinn, -e *chin,* II3
das Kino, -s *cinemc,* I; **ins Kino
gehen** *to go to the movies,* I
die Kirche, -n *church,* I
die Kirsche, -n *cherry,* II4
die Klamotten (pl) *(casual term for)
clothes,* I
der Klang, ̈e *sound, ring,* II11; **vom
Klang her** *as far as the sound
goes,* II11
klappen *to go smoothly, work,* II9
klappern *to rattle, clatter,* II12
klar *clear,* II2
Klasse! *Great!; Terrific!,* I
die Klasse, -n *grade level,* I; *class,* II4
der Klassenkamerad, -en *classmate
(male),* II2
die Klassenkameradin, -nen *classmate (female),* II2
das Klassenzimmer, - *classroom,* II2
klassisch *classic(al),* II1
das Klavier, -e *piano,* I; **Ich spiele
Klavier.** *I play the piano.,* I
kleben *to glue, stick,* II8
das Kleid, -er *dress,* I
die Kleidung *clothing,* II1
der Kleidungsartikel, - *article of
clothing,* II8
die Kleidungsreklame, -n *clothing
ad,* II8
der Kleidungsstil, -e *clothing
style,* II8
das Kleidungsstück, -e *piece of clothing,* II12
klein *small,* I
kleingeschnitten *cut small,* II12
die Kleinstadt, ̈e *town,* II7

klettern *to climb*, II9

die Klimaanlage, **-n** *air conditioning*, II10

die Klippe, **-n** *cliff*, II12

der Klops, **-e** *meat ball*, II11

der Kloß, **⸚e** *dumpling*, II11

der Klub, **-s** *club*, II3

das Klubmitglied, **-er** *club member*, II3

die Kluft *gap, crevice*, II12

klug *intelligent*, II8

knabbern *to gnaw, nibble*, II2

knallgelb *glaring yellow*, II8

das Knie, **-** *knee*, II6

knien *to kneel*, II1

der Knoblauch *garlic*, II11

der Knöchel, **-** *ankle*, II6

der Knochen, **-** *bone*, II2

der Knopf, **⸚e** *button*, II8

der Koch, **⸚e** *cook (male)*, II12

das Kochbuch, **⸚er** *cookbook*, II2

kochen *to cook*, II1

die Köchin, **-nen** *cook (female)*, II8

der Kofferraumdeckel, **-** *trunk lid*, II7

der Kohl *cabbage*, II12

der Kollege, **-n** *colleague*, II11

der Kombi, **-s** (Kombiwagen) *station wagon*, II2

kombinieren *to combine*, II8

komisch *funny; strange*, II11

kommen *to come*, I; **er kommt aus** *he's from*, I; **Komm doch mit!** *Why don't you come along?*, I; **Wie komme ich zum (zur) ... ?** *How do I get to...?*, I

die Komödie, **-n** *comedy*, I, II10

das Kompliment, **-e** *compliment*, II1

der Komponist, **-en** *composer*, Loc 1

die Kondition, **-en** *condition*, II4

der König, **-e** *king*, II3

königlich *royal*, II3

können *to be able to*, I; **Kann ich bitte Andrea sprechen?** *Could I please speak with Andrea?*, I; **Was kann ich für dich tun?** *What can I do for you?*, I

konservativ *conservative*, II8

der Konsum *consumption*, II10

die Kontaktlinse, **-n** *contact lens*, II1

konvertiert *converted*, II3

das Konzert, **-e** *concert*, I; **ins Konzert gehen** *to go to a concert*, I

konzertmäßig *as far as concerts go*, II7

der Kopf, **⸚e** *head*, II6

der Kopfhörer, **-** *headphones*, II10

der Kopfhöreranschluß, **-anschlüsse** *headphone outlet*, II10

der Kopfsalat, **-e** *head of lettuce*, II2

die Kopfschmerzen (pl) *headache*, II6

kopieren *to copy*, II1

körperlich *physical(ly)*, II6

die Körpertemperatur, **-en** *body temperature*, II6

der Korridor, **-e** *aisle, passage*, II12

die Kost *food, board*, II4

kosten *to cost*, I; *to taste*, II4

köstlich *delicious, charming*, II2

die Köstlichkeit, **-en** *delicacy*, II11

die Krabbe, **-n** *crab*, II11

der Kraftfahrer, **-** *driver*, II7

das Kraftstudio, **-s** *weight gym*, II12

der Kraftwagen, **-** *motor vehicle*, II7

krank *sick*, II2

das Krankenhaus, **⸚er** *hospital*, II4

das Kraut, **⸚er** *herb*, II5

der Kräutergarten, **⸚** *herb garden*, II7

die Krawatte, **-n** *tie*, II8

der Kreis, **-e** *circle; district*, II7

der Kreislauf *circulation (of the blood)*, II6

die Kreuzung, **-en** *crossing, junction*, II11

kriechen *to crawl*, II12

der Krieg, **-e** *war*, II7

kriegen *to get, receive*, II9

der Kriegsfilm, **-e** *war movie*, I

die Kriegszerstörung *war destruction*, II1

der Krimi, **-s** *detective movie*, I

die Krimiserie, **-n** *detective series*, II10

kritisieren *to criticize*, II7

die Kroketten (pl) *potato croquettes*, II11

der Krümel, **-** *crumb*, II12

die Küche, **-n** *kitchen; cuisine*, I, II7

der Kuchen, **-** *cake*, I

der Küchendienst, **-e** *kitchen duty*, II2

die Kuchenschlacht, **-en** *run for the cake*, II5

der Küchenschrank, **⸚e** *kitchen cabinet*, II12

der Kugelschreiber, **-** *ballpoint pen*, II1

das Kugelstoßen *shot put*, II1

kühl *cool*, I

kühlen *to cool*, II7

der Kühlschrank, **⸚e** *refrigerator*, I

der Kuli, **-s** *ballpoint pen*, I

die Kultur, **-en** *culture*, II9

kulturell *cultural*, II3

die Kulturmetropole, **-n** *cultural metropolis*, II1

die Kultursendung, **-en** *cultural program*, II10

die Kulturstadt, **⸚e** *city of great cultural significance*, II3

der Kummerbund, **-e** *cummerbund*, II12

der Kunde, **-n** *customer (male)*, II1

die Kundin, **-nen** *customer (female)*, II9

die Kunst, **⸚e** *art*, I

die Kunstausstellung, **-en** *art exhibition*, II11

die Kunstfaser, **-n** *synthetic fabric*, II8

die Kunstsammlung, **-en** *art collection*, II8

die Kunstseide, **-n** *synthetic silk, rayon*, II8

der Kunststoff, **-e: aus Kunststoff** *made of plastic*, I

der Kurfürst, **-en** *Elector (of a king)*, II3

der Kurs, **-e** *course*, II9

die Kurve, **-n** *curve*, II7

kurz *short*, I

kürzer *shorter*, II8

die Kuschelecke, **-n** *a place to cuddle*, II7

kuscheln *to cuddle*, II9

die Kusine, **-n** *cousin (female)*, I

die Küste, **-n** *coast*, II12

L

lachen *to laugh*, II2

lachend *laughing*, II2

der Lachs, **-e** *salmon*, II11

der Lackschuh, **-e** *patent leather shoe*, II12

der Laden, **⸚** *store*, I

die Lage, **-n** *setting, place*, II12

das Lagerfeuer, **-** *campfire*, II9

das Lammfleisch *lamb*, II5

die Lampe, **-n** *lamp*, I

das Land, **⸚er** *country*, I; **auf dem Land** *in the country*, I

die Land- und Forstwirtschaft *agriculture and forestry*, II1

der Landesfürst, **-en** *sovereign, prince*, II3

die Landeshauptstadt, **⸚e** *state capital*, II1

die Landeskunde *culture*, II3

die Landeszeitung, **-en** *newspaper (distributed statewide)*, II3

die Landkarte, **-n** *map of the country*, II9

die Landschaft, **-en** *countryside*, II9

die Landstraße, **-n** *highway*, II10

die Landwirtschaft *agriculture*, II9

lang *long*, I

länger *longer*, II8

der Langlauf *cross-country skiing*, II4

langsam *slow(ly)*, II7

längst *long ago, since,* II12
der Langstreckenlauf, -̈e *long dis-*
tance run, II1
s. langweilen *to be bored,* II12
langweilig *boring,* I
der Lärm *noise,* II7
lärmbewußt *conscious of*
noise, II7
die Lärmminderung, -en *lessening of*
noise, II7
Lärmschutzgründe: aus
Lärmschutzgründen *for noise*
protection, II7
lassen *to let, allow;* **er/sie**
läßt *he/she lets,* II10; **Laß**
mich mal ... *Let me...,* II10
lässig *casual,* I
das Laster, - *vice,* II4
lästig *bothersome,* II8
der Lastkraftwagen (Lkw), -
truck, II7
Latein *Latin,* I
der Lauf, -̈e *run,* II1; **der 100-Meter-**
Lauf *the 100 meter dash,* II1
laufen *to run,* II3; **er/sie**
läuft *he/she runs,* II3; **Was**
läuft im Fernsehen? *What's*
on TV?, II10
die Laune, -n *temper, mood,* II12
laut *loud,* II2
lauten *to sound, read,* II2
der Lautstärkeregler, - *volume*
control, II10
leben *to live,* II2
das Leben *life,* II7
die Lebensmittel (pl) *groceries,* I
die Leber *liver,* II2
der Leberkäs *(a Bavarian*
specialty), I
lecker *tasty, delicious,* I
das Leder *leather,* I
die Lederjacke, -n *leather jacket,* II8
leer *empty,* II3
legen *to lay,* II2
der Lehrer, - *teacher (male),* I
die Lehrerin, -nen *teacher*
(female), I
das Lehrjahr, -e *apprenticeship*
year, II7
der Lehrplan, -̈e *teaching*
curriculum, II2
die Lehrstelle, -n *apprenticeship,* II7
leicht *easy, simple,* II1; *light,* II6
die Leichtathletik *track and field,* II1
das Leichtkraftrad, -̈er *motorbike,* II7
leid: Es tut mir leid. *I'm sorry.,* I
leiden: Ich kann dich nicht leiden.
I can't stand you., II10
leider *unfortunately,* I; **Ich kann**
leider nicht. *Sorry, I can't.,* I;

Das ist leider so. *That's the*
way it is unfortunately., II10;
Ich hab' leider nur ... *I only*
have..., II5
der Leierkastenmann *organ*
grinder, II1, Loc 1
das Leinen, - *linen,* II8
leise *soft, lightly,* II12
die Leitung, -en *direction,*
conduit, II3
lesen *to read,* I; **er/sie liest**
he/she reads, I
letzt- *last,* I; **letzte Woche** *last*
week, I; **letztes Wochenende**
last weekend, I
die Leute (pl) *people,* I
das Licht, -er *light, lamp,* II12
der Lichtschalter, - *light switch,* II12
der Lichtschutzfaktor, -en *sun pro-*
tection factor, II6
die Liebe *love,* II1
lieber: **lieber mögen** *to prefer,* I
der Liebesfilm, -e *romance,* I
der Liebesroman, -e *romance novel,* I
liebevoll *loving, caring,* II8
Lieblings- *favorite,* I
liebst: Ich würde am liebsten ...
I would rather..., II11
das Lied, -er *song,* I
der Liederabend, -e *evening of*
songs, II11
liegen *to lie on,* II6; das liegt an
dir *it's your fault,* II12
die Liegewiese, -n *lawn for relaxing*
and sunning, II9
die Liga, (pl) Ligen *league,* II10
die Limo, -s (Limonade, -n) *lemon*
drink, I
die Linie, -n *line,* II8; in erster
Linie *first of all,* II8
die Liste, -n *list,* II1
der Liter, - *liter,* I
der Lkw=Lastkraftwagen, -
truck, II7
das Loch, -̈er *hole,* II12
logisch *logical,* II4
s. lohnen *to be worth it,* II9
das Lokal, -e *small restaurant,* II3
los *detached,* II3
lösen *to solve,* II7
die Lücke, -n *blank,* II9
die Luft *air,* II7
die Luftverschmutzung *air pollu-*
tion, II7
lügen *to tell a lie,* II11
lustig *funny,* I
das Lustspiel, -e *comedy,* II10
der Luxus *luxury,* II8
die Luxusgüter (pl) *luxury items,* II8

M

machen *to do,* I; **Das macht**
(zusammen) ... *That comes*
to..., I; **Gut! Mach' ich!**
Okay, I'll do that!, I; **Machst du**
Sport? *Do you play sports?,* I;
Hausaufgaben machen *to do*
homework, I; **macht dick** *is*
fattening, II4; **Macht nichts!**
That's all right, II5
das Mädchen, - *girl,* I
das Magazin, -e *journal,* II10
der Magenkrampf, -̈e *stomach*
cramp, II6
die Magenschmerzen (pl) *stomach*
pains, II4
mag: *see* **mögen**
mager *lean,* II4
die Magermilch *skim milk,* II4
mähen *to mow,* I
Mahlzeit! *Bon appétit,* II11
das Mahnmal, -e *memorial,* Loc 1
der Mai *May,* I; **im Mai** *in May,* I
mal (particle), I
malen *to paint,* II1
der Maler, - *painter,* II1
malerisch *picturesque,* II1
man *one, you* (in general),
people, I; **Man hat mir gesagt,**
daß ... *Someone told me*
that..., II11
manche *some,* II4
manchmal *sometimes,* I
der Mann, -̈er *man,* I
die Mannschaft, -en *team,* II4
die Margarine *margarine,* II5
mariniert *marinated,* II11
die Mark, - *mark* (German monetary
unit), I
die Markenbutter *brand-name*
butter, II2
der Markt, -̈e *market,* II10
der Marktanteil *market share,* II10
der Marktbrunnen, - *market*
fountain, II9
der Marktplatz, -̈e *market square,*
I, II3
die Marmelade *marmalade,* II5
marschieren *to march,* II3
der März *March,* I
der Maschinenbau *mechanical engi-*
neering, II1
die Mastente, -n *fattened duck,* II11
materiell (adj) *material,* II7
die Mathematik=Mathe *math,* I
die Mauer, -n *wall,* II11
das Mauerwerk *masonry,* II9
die Maus, -̈e *mouse,* II9
die Medaillengewinnerin, -nen *medal*
winner (female), II12

mediterran *Mediterranean*, II11
die Medizin *medicine*, II6
das Meer, -e *ocean*, II9
die Meeresfrüchte (pl) *seafood*, II5
das Mehl *flour*, I
die Mehlspeise, -n *food made of flour*, II5
   mehr *more*, I; **Ich habe keinen Hunger mehr.** *I'm not hungry anymore.*, I
die Mehrfachnennung, -en *repeated reference*, II9
   mehrfarbig *many-colored*, II8
   meiden *to avoid*, II4
   mein (poss adj) *my*, I
   meinen: Meinst du? *Do you think so?*, I
die Meinung, -en *opinion*, II8
   meist *most*, II9
   meistens *most of the time*, II4
der Meister, - *master, champion*, II3
das Meisterstück, -e *masterpiece*, II3
die Melone, -n *melon*, II5
die Menge, -n *quantity, heap*, II8
die Mensa *student cafeteria*, II4
der Mensch, -en *human, person*, II4
die Menschenmasse, -n *mass of people*, II9
   merken *to notice, pay attention to*, II12
die Messe, -n *fair*, II3; *Catholic Mass*, II9
   messen: Fieber messen *to take someone's temperature*, II6; **er/sie mißt** *he/she measures*, II6
das Messer, - *knife*, II12
die Metallkette, -n *metal chain*, II1
der Meter, - *meter*, II9
die Metropole, -n *metropolis*, II11
der Metzger, - *butcher*, II2
die Metzgerei, -en *butcher shop*, I
   mexikanisch (adj) *Mexican*, II11
   mich *me, myself*, I
   miesest *the worst*, II2
das Mietshaus, ⁼er *apartment house*, II7
die Milch *milk*, I
   mild *mild*, II11
die Milliarde, -n *billion*, II12
   mindestens *at least*, II3
das Mineralwasser *mineral water*, I
   mindern *to lessen*, II7
   mir *to, for me*, II3; **Mir gefällt ... besser als ...** *I like ... better than ...*, II7
die Mischfasern (pl) *blended fibers*, II8
   miserabel *miserable*, I
   mißfallen (dat) *to displease, offend*, II12

mit (prep) *with, by*, I; **mit Brot** *with bread*, I; **mit dem Auto** *by car*, I
mitbringen (sep) *to bring along*, II9
miteinander *with one another*, II5
mitgebracht *brought along*, II5
mitgehen (sep) *to go along*, II1
mitgekommen (pp) *come along*, II3
mitgekriegt *understood*, II10
mitgenommen *took along*, II3
das Mitglied, -er *member*, II9
   mitkommen (sep) *to come along*, I
mitmachen (sep) *to take part*, II1
mitnehmen (sep) *to take along*, II2
der Mitschüler, - *schoolmate (male)*, II1
die Mitschülerin, -nen *schoolmate (female)*, II1
der Mittag *noon*, II1
das Mittagessen *lunch*, II3
die Mitte *middle*, II11
   mitteilen (sep) *to communicate; to share*, II4
das Mittelalter *the Middle Ages*, Loc 7
   mittelgroß *middle-sized*, II5
   mittellang *medium-length*, II1
der Mittwoch *Wednesday*, I; **am Mittwoch** *on Wednesday*, I
   mittwochs *Wednesdays*, II10
die Möbel (pl) *furniture*, I
   möchten *would like to*, I; **Ich möchte ... sehen.** *I would like to see...*, I; **Ich möchte noch ein ...** *I'd like another...*, I; **Ich möchte kein ... mehr.** *I don't want another...*, I
die Mode, -n *fashion*, I
die Modefachfrau, -en *fashion consultant (female)*, II8
der Modefachmann, ⁼er *fashion consultant (male)*, II8
das Modell, -e *model*, II8
die Modenschau, -en *fashion show*, II8
die Moderatorin, -nen *moderator (female)*, II11
   modern *modern*, I
   modisch *fashionable*, II8
das Mofa, -s *moped*, II7
   mögen *to like, care for*, I; **Ich mag kein ...** *I don't like...*, II4
   möglich *possible*, II10
die Möglichkeit, -en *possibility*, II9
   möglichst *as ... as possible*, II8
die Möhre, -n *carrot*, II4
der Moment, -e *moment*, I; **Einen Moment, bitte!** *Just a minute, please.*, I; **im Moment gar nichts** *nothing at the moment*, I

der Monat, -e *month*, I; **einmal im Monat** *once a month*, I
   monatlich *monthly*, II10
die Monatsausgabe, -n *monthly expenditure*, II10
   monoton *monotonous*, II8
der Montag *Monday*, I; **am Montag** *on Monday*, I
   montags *Mondays*, II10
das Moped, -s *moped*, I; **mit dem Moped** *by moped*, I
der Mord, -e *murder*, II10
   morgen *tomorrow*, I
der Morgen, - *morning*, I; **Guten Morgen!** *Good morning!*, I; **Morgen!** *Morning!*, I
   morgens *in the mornings*, II2
das Motiv, -e *motif*, II3
der Motor, -en *motor*, II7
das Motorboot, -e *motorboat*, II9
   motorisiert *motorized*, II7
das Motorrad, ⁼er *motorcycle*, II7
   müde *tired*, II6
der Muffel, - *a person not interested in something*, II4
die Mühle, -n *mill*, II11
der Müll *trash*, I; **den Müll sortieren** *to sort the trash*, I
der Müllhaufen, - *pile of trash*, II2
die Münze, -n *coin*, I; **Münzen einstecken** *to insert coins*, I
   murmeln *to murmer; to mutter*, II10
die Muschel, -n *mussel*, II5
das Museum, (pl) Museen *museum*, II3
das Musical, -s *musical*, II11
die Musik *music*, I; **klassische Musik** *classical music*, I
die Musikkapelle, -n *musical band*, II3
der Musikkapellmeister, - *bandleader*, II3
der Musikraum, ⁼e *music room*, II2
das Müsli *grain cereal*, II11
   müssen *to have to*, I; **ich muß** *I have to*, I
das Muster, - *pattern*, II12
die Mutter, ⁼ *mother*, I
der Muttertag *Mother's Day*, I; **Alles Gute zum Muttertag!** *Happy Mother's Day!*, I
die Mütze, -n *cap*, II1

N

Na ja, soso. *Oh, all right.*, II3
Na klar! *Of course!*, II4
nach (prep) *after*, I; **nach der Schule** *after school*, I; **nach**

links *to the left*, I; **nach rechts** *to the right*, I; **nach Hause gehen** *to go home*, I; **nach dem Mittagessen** *after lunch*, II3

der Nachbarort, -e *neighboring town*, II7

nachdem (conj) *after*, II12

nachdenkenswert *worthy of reflection*, II8

nacherzählen (sep) *to retell*, II6

die Nacherzählung, -en *retelling*, II12

nachher *afterwards*, II10

der Nachmittag, -e *afternoon*, I

der Nachname, -n *last name*, II7

die Nachricht, -en *message*, II9

die Nachrichten (pl) *the news*, II10

nachsehen (sep) *to look up, look again*, II10

die Nachspeise, -n *dessert*, II11

nächst- *next*, II2; **die nächste Straße** *the next street*, I

nächstgrößer- *next-largest*, II11

die Nacht, ̈e *night*, II10

der Nachteil, -e *disadvantage*, II7

der Nachtisch, -e *dessert*, II11

nachts *nights, at night*, II9

der Nachtzug, ̈e *overnight train*, II2

nackt *naked*, II12

das Nagelbett, -en *bed of nails*, II7

die Nähe *vicinity*, II3; **in der Nähe von** *near to*, II9

nah *near*, II9

die Nahrungsmittel (pl) *food*, II5

der Name, -n *name*, II4

nämlich *namely*, II2

die Nase, -n *nose*, II6

naß *wet*, I

die Nationalversammlung, -en *National Assembly*, II3

die Natur *nature*, II3

der Naturforscher, - *natural scientist (male)*, Loc 4

Natürlich! *Certainly!*, I

die Natursendung, -en *nature program*, II10

neben (prep) *next to*, II9

nebenan *close by*, II10

der Nebenjob, -s *second job*, II8

die Nebensache, -n *matter of minor importance*, II9

der Nebensatz, ̈e *dependent clause*, II12

negativ *negative*, II4

nehmen *to take*, I; **er/sie nimmt** *he/she takes*, I; **Ich nehme ...** *I'll take...*, I

neidisch *envious*, II8

nein *no*, I

nennen *to name*, II2

nervös *nervous*, II1

das Nesthäkchen, - *baby of the family*, II12

nett *nice*, II1

neu *new*, I

neuerdings *recently*, II12

neuest *newest*, II8

neugierig *curious*, II1

nicht *not*, I; **Nicht besonders.** *Not really.*, I; *Not especially.*, II3; **nicht gern haben** *to dislike*, I; **nicht schlecht** *not bad*, I; **Ich nicht.** *I don't.*, I

der Nichtraucher, - *non-smoker*, II4

nichts *nothing*, I; **Nichts mehr, danke!** *Nothing else, thanks!*, I

nie *never*, I

niemand *no one*, II12

nix=nichts II8

noch *yet, still*, I; **Haben Sie noch einen Wunsch?** *Would you like anything else?*, I; **Ich brauche noch ...** *I also need...*, I; **Möchtest du noch etwas?** *Would you like something else?*, I; **Noch einen Saft?** *Another glass of juice?*, I; **noch höher** *still higher*, II10; **noch nie** *not yet, never*, II3

normal *normal*, II2

normalerweise *normally, usually*, II4

die Normalstärke *normal volume*, II7

die Not, ̈e *need, want*, II5

die Note, -n *grade*, I

notieren *to note, jot down*, II12

nötig *necessary*, II4

die Notiz, -en *note*, II1

der Notizblock, ̈e *note pad*, II9

das Notizbuch, ̈er *notebook*, II1

der November *November*, I

die Nudel, -n *noodle*, II4

das Nudelgericht, -e *noodle dish*, II5

die Nudelsuppe, -n *noodle soup*, I

null *zero*, I

die Nummer, -n *number*, II8

nur *only*, II1; **nicht nur ... sondern auch** *not only ... but also*, II3

der Nußknacker, - *nutcracker*, II11

O

die Oase, -n *oasis*, II12

ob (conj) *whether*, II9

oben *above*, II2

ober- *upper*, II3

die Oberschule, -n *(same as Gymnasium)*, II7

das Obst *fruit*, I

der Obst- und Gemüseladen, ̈ *fresh produce store*, I

obwohl (conj) *although*, II7

oder (conj) *or*, II1

der Ofen, ̈ *oven*, I

offen *open*, II8

öffentliche Verkehrsmittel (pl) *public transportation*, II7

offiziell *official*, II3

die Öffnungszeiten (pl) *opening hours*, II2

oft *often*, I

öfters *quite often*, II6

ohne (prep) *without*, II2

ohne ... zu *without...;* **ohne zu schlafen** *without sleeping*, II4

das Ohrensausen *ringing in the ears*, II6

der Ohrenschmaus *musical treat*, II12

die Ohrenschmerzen (pl) *earache*, II6

der Ohrring, -e *earring*, II1

der Oktober *October*, I

das Olivenöl, -e *olive oil*, II12

olivgrün *olive green*, II8

die Olympiade *Olympiad*, II12

der Olympiasieger, - *olympic champion*, II12

olympisch *olympic*, II12

die Oma, -s *grandmother*, I

der Onkel, - *uncle*, I

der Opa, -s *grandfather*, I

die Oper, -n *opera*, I

die Operette, -n *operetta*, II11

das Opfer, - *victim*, II10

die Orange, -n *orange*, II5

der Orangensaft *orange juice*, II5

die Ordnung *order*, II8

die Organisation, -en *organization*, II9

organisieren *to organize*, II1

das Orgelkonzert, -e *organ concert*, II11

die Orientierungsstufenschülerin, -nen *(student in the beginning years of Gymnasium) (female)*, II8

der Ort, -e *place; location*, II3

die Osterferien (pl) *Easter vacation*, II12

das Ostern *Easter*, I; **Frohe Ostern!** *Happy Easter*, I

österreichisch (adj) *Austrian*, II3

die Ostküste *east coast*, II3

P

paar: **ein paar** *a few*, I

das Päckchen, - *small package*, II5

das Paddelboot, -e *paddle boat*, II9

die Palme, -n *palm tree*, II9
der Palmengarten, ÷ *garden of palm trees*, II9
der Pantoffel, -n *slipper*, II2
das Papier, -e *paper*, II1
die Paradejacke, -n *marching band uniform*, II1
das Parfüm, -e *perfume*, I
parfümiert *perfumed*, II6
der Park, -s *park*, I; **in den Park gehen** *to go to the park*, I
parken *to park*, II9
der Parkplatz, ÷e *parking spot, lot*, II9
der Partner, - *partner (male)*, I
die Partnerin, -nen *partner (female)*, I
partymäßig *for parties*, II7
passen *to fit*, I; **Der Rock paßt prima!** *The skirt fits great!*, I
passend *fitting*, II11
passieren *to occur*, II1; **Das ist gerade passiert.** *It just happened.*, II9
die Patchworkdecke, -n *quilt*, II12
der Patient, -en *patient*, II6
die Pause, -n *break*, I
das Pausenbrot, -e *sandwich (made especially for a school snack)*, II5
das Pausenklingeln *recess bell*, II2
Paßt auf! *Pay attention!*, I
das Pech *bad luck*, I; **So ein Pech!** *Bad luck!*, I; **Was für ein Pech!** *That's too bad!*, II5
die Peking Ente, -n *Peking duck*, II11
die Penne *(casual term for) school*, II7
die Pension, -en *inn, bed and breakfast*, II3
pensioniert *retired*, II4
perfekt *perfect*, II12
die Person, -en *person*, II1
die Personenbeschreibung, -en *personal description*, II7
der Personenkraftwagen, - *(Pkw) car*, II7
persönlich *personal(ly)*, II7
die Persönlichkeit, -en *personality*, II8
die Perspektive, -n *perspective*, II12
die Petersilie *parsley*, II12
das Pfadfinderlager, - *boy scout camp*, II9
die Pfanne, -n *pan*, II9
das Pfannengericht, -e *pan-cooked entrée*, II11
das Pfd.=Pfund *pound*, I
der Pfeffer, *pepper*, II5

der Pfennig, - (smallest unit of German currency; 1/100 of a mark), I
das Pferd, -e *horse*, II9
der Pferdestall, ÷e *stable*, II11
der Pferdewagen, - *horse-drawn carriage*, II9
die Pfingstferien (pl) *Pentecost vacation*, II9
der Pfirsich, -e *peach*, II2
die Pflanze, -n *plant*, II2
die Pflaume, -n *plum*, II2
das Pfund, - **(Pfd.)** *pound*, I
phantasievoll *imaginative*, I
Phantastisch! *Fantastic!*, II3
pharmazeutisch *pharmaceutical*, II10
der Pilz, -e *mushroom*, II4
die Pizza, -s *pizza*, I
der Pkw, -s *car*, II7
der Plan, ÷e *plan*, II1
planen *to plan*, II5
die Planung, -en *planning*, II10
platschen *to make a flapping sound*, II12
der Platz, ÷e *place, site*, II12
plötzlich *sudden(ly)*, II9
der Pokal, -e *trophy*, II1
polieren *to polish*, II2
die Politik (sing) *politics*, I
die Pommes (frites) (pl) *French fries*, II5
das Ponyreiten *pony ride*, II3
der Pool, -s *swimming pool*, II7
der Popstar, -s *pop star*, II1
positiv *positive*, II4
die Post *post office*, I
der Posten, - *place, position*, II2
das Poster, - *poster*, I
die Posthalterei, -en *stable for post horses*, II9
die Pracht *splendor*, II3
praktisch *practical*, II10
die Praline, -n *fancy chocolate*, I
präsentieren *to present*, II12
die Praxis *practice; doctor's office*, II10
der Preis, -e *price*, II1
preisgünstig *cheap*, II9
preiswert *reasonably priced*, I; **Das ist preiswert.** *That's a bargain.*, I
Prima! *Great!* I
das Privathaus, ÷er *private home*, II3
das Privatquartier, -e *private accommodation*, II3
probieren *to try*, II5
das Problem, -e *problem*, II7

die Produktion, -en *production*, II10
produzieren *to produce*, II7
profitrainiert *trained by a professional*, II12
das Programm, -e *schedule of shows*, II10
die Programmanzeige, -n *listing of shows*, II10
das Projekt, -e *project*, II8
das Pronomen, - *pronoun*, II6
der Prospekt, -e *brochure*, II12
Prost! *Cheers!*, II11
das Prozent *percent*, II4
das Publikum *public; audience*, II10
der Pulli, -s *pullover, sweater*, I
der Pullover, - *sweater*, I
der Puls *pulse*, II6
der Punker, - *punker*, II1
putzen *to clean*, I; **Fenster putzen** *to wash the windows*, I

Q

der Quadratkilometer, - *square kilometer*, II1
die Qual, -en *torture*, II11
die Qualität *quality*, II3
der Quark (a soft cheese similar to ricotta or cream cheese), II5
das Quartier, -e *quarter, accommodation*, II3
der Quatsch *nonsense*, II12
die Quelle, -n *source, (underground) spring*, II9

R

der Rabatt, -e *discount*, II9
das Rad, ÷er *bike; wheel*, II1; **mit dem Rad** *by bike*, I
radfahren (sep) *to ride a bike*, II4
die Radfahrgruppe, -n *group of bicycle riders*, II3
das Radio, -s *radio*, II2
die Radiosendung, -en *radio show*, II7
die Radtour, -en *bicycle tour*, II1
die Rangliste, -n *ranking chart*, II10
der Radiergummi, -s *eraser*, I
der Rallyestreifen, - *rally stripe*, II10
der Rasen, - *lawn*, I; **den Rasen mähen** *to mow the lawn*, I
raten *to guess*, II1
die Ratesendung, -en *quiz show*, II10
das Ratespiel, -e *quiz game*, II1
das Rathaus, ÷er *city hall*, I
rauchen *to smoke*, II4
der Raucherfeind, -e *person who dislikes smokers*, II4

der Raum, ⸚e *room*, II4
das Raumschiff, -e *spacecraft*, II10
raus=heraus *out, away*, II11
reagieren auf (acc) *to react to*, II4
der Realschüler, - *student at a Realschule*, II2
rechnen *to tabulate, calculate*, II11
die Rechnung, -en *bill, check*, II1
das Recht, -e *law; right*, II1
recht haben *to be right*, II10
recht- *right, right-hand*, I; **nach rechts** *to the right*, I
reden *to talk, speak*, II4
das Reformhaus, ⸚er *natural food store*, II4
das **Regal**, -e *bookcase*, I
regelmäßig *regularly*, II4
die Regel, -n *rule*, II4
der **Regen** *rain*, I
regnen: Es regnet. *It's raining.*, I
reiben *to rub, grate*, II10
reichlich *plenty*, II12
reicht: Es reicht. *That's enough.*, II11
der Reifen, - *tire*, II10
die Reihe, -n *row; line*, II1
die Reihenfolge, -n *succession, sequence*, II12
die Reihenwörter (pl) *successive words*, II3
der Reim, -e *rhyme*, II2
rein *pure*, II8
die **Reinigung**, -en *cleaners*, II8
reinkommen=hereinkommen (sep) *to come in*, II2
reinschauen=hereinschauen (sep) *to look in*, II1
der **Reis** *rice*, II4
die Reise, -n *trip, voyage*, II3
der Reiseberater, - *travel agent*, II9
der Reisebericht, -e *travel report*, II12
der Reiseleiter, - *tour guide (person)*, II11
reiselustig *wanting to travel*, II12
reisen *to travel, take a trip*, II1
der Reiseort, -e *vacation spot*, II9
das Reiseziel, -e *travel destination*, II9
das Reisgericht, -e *rice dish*, II12
reiten *to ride a horse*, II3
der Reiterhof, ⸚e *horse farm*, II9
die Reithalle, -n *riding court*, II3
die Reithose, -n *riding breeches*, II8
der **Reißverschluß**, (pl) **Reißverschlüsse** *zipper*, II8
die Reklame, -n *advertisement*, II8
die Reklameabteilung, -en *advertising department*, II8

die Reklameseite, -n *page of advertising*, II8
rekonstruieren *to reconstruct*, II12
die **Religion**, -en *religion* (school subject), I
der Renner, - *runner; top product*, II9
das Rennrad, ⸚er *racing bicycle*, II12
renoviert *renovated*, II3
die Reparatur, -en *repair*, II10
reservieren *to reserve*, II11
die Reservierung, -en *reservation*, II11
das **Restaurant**, -s *restaurant*, II3
restauriert *restored*, II11
das Resultat, -e *result*, II4
die Reue *remorse, regret*, II4
das Rezept, -e *recipe*, II12; *prescription*, II6
die Rezeptmenge, -n *amount in a recipe*, II12
s. richten nach *to conform to*, II2
richtig *correct, proper*, II1
riechen nach *to smell like*, II2
das **Rindfleisch** *beef*, II4; **Rind schmeckt mir besser.** *Beef tastes better to me.*, II5
der **Ring**, -e *ring*, II2
der **Ringel**, - *ringlet*, II12
das **Rindersteak** *(beef) steak*, II5
der **Rock**, ⸚e *skirt*, I
rodeln *to sled*, II1
roh *raw*, II11
das Rohr, -e *pipe*, II8
die Rolle, -n *role*, II1
der Rollkragen, - *turtle-neck*, II8
der Rollschuh, -e *roller skate*, II9
Rollschuh laufen (sep) *to roller-skate*, II1
der **Roman**, -e *novel*, I
der **Römer** (name of the city hall in Frankfurt), II3
rot *red*, I; **in Rot** *in red*, I
Rote Grütze (red berry dessert), II11
der **Rotkohl** *red cabbage*, II11
rötlich *reddish*, II1
rüber=herüber *from there to here*, II11
das Ruderboot, -e *row boat*, II3
der **Rücken**, - *back*, II6
die Rückkehr *return*, II9
die Ruhe *calm*, II5
ruhig *calm(ly)*, II7
rund *round*, I
runden *to round*, II11
der Rundfunk *television and radio communications*, Loc 7
der Rundgang, ⸚e *tour, walk*, II9
runter=herunter *from there down here*, II3

das Rüschenhemd, -en *frilled shirt*, II1
russisch (adj) *Russian*, II11
rustikal *rustic*, II11

S

das **Sachbuch**, ⸚er *non-fiction book*, I
die Sache, -n *thing; matter*, II9
sächsisch (adj) *Saxon*, II9
der **Saft**, ⸚e *juice*, I
sagen *to say*, I; **Sag mal ...** *Tell me...*, II4; **Was sagt der Wetterbericht?** *What does the weather report say?*, I
sagenhaft *great*, I
die Sahne, -n *cream*, II4
der **Sakko**, -s *business jacket*, II8
der **Salat**, -e *lettuce; salad*, I
das Salatblatt, ⸚er *lettuce leaf*, II5
die Salatgurke, -n *cucumber*, II5
salopp *casual*, II12
das **Salz** *salt*, I
salzig *salty*, II1
sammeln *to collect*, I
die Sammlung, -en *collection*, II3
der **Samstag** *Saturday*, I
samstags *Saturdays*, II10
sämtlich *entire*, II12
der **Sandstrand**, ⸚e *sand beach*, II9
der **Sänger**, - *singer (male)*, I
die **Sängerin**, -nen *singer (female)*, I
satt *full*, II7
der Satz, ⸚e *sentence*, II2
der Satzanfang, ⸚e *beginning of a sentence*, II10
die Satzlücke, -n *blank*, II2
der Satzteil, -e *part of a sentence*, II11
sauber *clean*, II7
das **Sauerkraut** *sauerkraut*, II5
saugen: Staub saugen *to vacuum*, I
saumäßig *filthy, lousy*, II2
die **Sauna**, -s *sauna*, II9
sauwohl *great*, II8
das **Schach** *chess*, I
Schade! *Too bad!*, I
schaden (dat) *to harm*, II6
schädlich *harmful*, II7
der **Schal**, -s *scarf*, II1
schälen *to peel*, II5
scharf *sharp*, II8; *spicy, hot*, II11
schauen *to look*, I; **Schau mal!** *Look!*, II5
der Schaukelstuhl, ⸚e *rocking chair*, II7
das **Schauspiel**, -e *play*, II11
der **Schauspieler**, - *actor*, I

dreihundertfünfundsechzig

die **Schauspielerin**, -nen *actress*, I

das **Schauspielhaus**, ⸚er *play-house*, II11

die **Scheibe**, -n *slice*, II5

der **Scheibenwischer**, - *windshield wiper*, II10

scheinen *to shine*, I; **Die Sonne scheint.** *The sun is shining.*, I

der **Scheinwerfer**, - *headlight*, II10

schenken *to give (a gift)*, I; **Was schenkst du deiner Mutter?** *What are you giving your mother?*, I

scheußlich *hideous*, I

die **Schichtarbeit** *shift work*, II11

schick *smart (looking)*, I

das **Schiebedach**, ⸚er *sun roof*, II10

das **Schiff**, -e *ship*, II9

schimpfen *to scold*, II11

der **Schinken**, - *ham*, II11

das **Schisch-Kebab** *shish kebab*, II11

schlafen *to sleep*, II4

der **Schlafsack**, ⸚e *sleeping bag*, II9

das **Schlafzimmer**, - *bedroom*, II7

die **Schlaghose**, -n *bell bottoms*, II12

die **Schlange**, -n *line*, II12

schlank *slim*, II1

die **Schlaufe**, -n *belt loop*, II8

schlecht *bad(ly)*, I; **schlecht gelaunt** *in a bad mood*, II1; **Mir ist schlecht.** *I feel sick.*, II6

die **Schleife**, -n *loop, bow*, II2

schließlich *at the end, after all*, II4

schlimm *bad*, II5

Schlittschuh laufen *to ice skate*, I

das **Schlitzohr**, -en *rascal*, II2

das **Schloß**, (pl) **Schlösser** *castle*, II3

schlucken *to swallow*, II6; **Ich kann kaum schlucken.** *I can barely swallow.*, II6

schmackhaft *tasty*, II12

schmalzig *corny, mushy*, I

schmecken *to taste*, II5; **Schmeckt's?** *Does it taste good?*, I; **Wie schmeckt's?** *How does it taste?*, I; **schmeckt mir nicht** *doesn't taste good*, II4; **schmeckt mir am besten** *tastes best to me*, II5

der **Schmerz**, -en *pain*, II6

der **Schmuck** *jewelry*, I

schmutzig *dirty*, II7

die **Schnecke**, -n *snail*, II5

der **Schnee** *snow*, I

schneiden *to cut*, II5

schneien: Es schneit. *It's snowing.*, I

schnell *fast*, II7

der **Schnittkäse** *cheese for slicing*, II2

der **Schnittlauch** (sing) *chives*, II5

das **Schnitzel**, - *cutlet (pork or veal)*, II5

schnorcheln *to snorkle*, II9

der **Schnupfen** *runny nose*, II6

die **Schokolade**, -n *chocolate*, II2

schon *already*, I; **Schon gut!** *It's okay!*, II5; **schon oft** *a lot, often*, II3; **Ich glaube schon, daß ...** *I do believe that...*, II10

schön *pretty, beautiful*, I

die **Schönheit**, -en *beauty*, II8

der **Schönheitswettbewerb**, -e *beauty competition*, II8

schräg *diagonal*, II9

der **Schrank**, ⸚e *cabinet*, I

schreiben *to write*, I

der **Schreibtisch**, -e *desk*, I

der **Schreiner**, - *cabinet-maker*, II7

der **Schriftsteller**, - *author (male)*, Loc 1

der **Schritt**, -e *step*, II9

der **Schubkarren**, - *wheelbarrow*, II7

der **Schuh**, -e *shoe*, II8

die **Schule**, -n *school*, I

der **Schüler**, - *student, pupil (male)*, II

der **Schüleraustausch** *exchange student program*, II3

die **Schülerin**, -nen *student, pupil (female)*, II1

die **Schulfeier**, -n *school celebration*, II11

der **Schulhof**, ⸚e *schoolyard*, II2

das **Schuljahrbuch**, ⸚er *school yearbook*, II7

die **Schulsachen** (pl) *school supplies*, I

die **Schultasche**, -n *schoolbag*, I

die **Schulter**, -n *shoulder*, II6

schützen *to protect*, II6

der **Schutzfaktor**, -en *protection factor*, II6

schwarz *black*, I

das **Schwein**, -e *pig, pork*, II5

der **Schweinebraten**, - *pork roast*, II2

das **Schweinerückensteak**, -s *pork loin steak*, II1

das **Schweinefleisch** *pork*, II5

das **Schweinekotelett**, -s *pork chop*, II5

der **Schweizer**, - *Swiss (male)*, II5

der **Schweizer Käse** *Swiss cheese*, II5

schwer *heavy; difficult*, II4

schwerhaben (sep) *to have a hard time*, II9

die **Schwester**, -n *sister*, I

die **Schwierigkeit**, -en *difficulty, problem*, II4

das **Schwimmbad**, ⸚er *swimming pool*, I

schwimmen *to swim*, I

schwitzen *to sweat*, II2

der **Science-fiction-Film**, -e *science fiction movie*, I

der **See**, -n *lake*, II7

die **See**, -n *ocean, sea*, II9

das **Seebarschfilet**, -s *filet of perch*, II11

das **Segel**, - *sail*, Loc 7

der **Segelkurs**, -e *sailing class*, II9

segeln *to sail*, II9

sehen *to see*, I; **er/sie sieht** *he/she sees*, I

die **Sehenswürdigkeit**, -en *place of interest*, II1

sehr *very*, I; **Sehr gut!** *Very well!*, I; **sehr gesund leben** *to live in a very healthy way*, II4

sei: Sei ... ! *Be...!*, II5

seicht *shallow*, II9

seid: ihr seid *you* (pl) *are*, I

die **Seide**, -n *silk*, I

das **Seidenhemd**, -en *silk shirt*, II8

der **Seidenschal**, -s *silk scarf*, II8

die **Seife**, -n *soap*, II6

sein (poss adj) *his*, I

sein *to be*, I; **er ist** *he is*, I

seit (prep) *for*, II1

die **Seite**, -n *page*, II1

sekundengenau *accurate within a second*, II10

selber *self*, II9

selbst *self*, II1

selbstverständlich *of course*, II12

die **Selbstverteidigung** *self-defense*, II1

selten *seldom*, II4

seltsam *strange*, II1

die **Semmel**, -n *roll*, I

der **Sender**, - *station, transmitter, channel*, II10

der **Sendesaal**, (pl) **Sendesäle** *broad-casting studio*, II11

die **Sendung**, -en *show, program*, II10

der **Senf** *mustard*, I

sensationell *sensational*, I

der **September** *September*, I

die **Serie**, -n *series*, II10

servieren *to serve*, II5

die **Servobremsen** (pl) *power brakes*, II10

die **Servolenkung**, -en *power steering*, II10

Servus! *Hello!; So long!*, II1

der **Sessel**, - *armchair*, I

setzen *to put*, II6

s. **setzen** *to sit down*, II12

das Shampoo, -s *shampoo,* II6
die Shorts (sing or pl) *pair of shorts,* I
sich *herself, himself, itself, yourself, themselves, yourselves,* II4
Sicher! *Certainly!,* I; **Ich bin nicht sicher.** *I'm not sure.,* I; **Aber sicher!** *But of course!,* II4; **Ich bin sicher, daß ...** *I'm certain that...,* II9
sicher *secure,* II7
sichern *to secure,* II9
sie *she; it; they; them,* I
Sie *you* (formal), I
das Silber *silver,* II2; **aus Silber** *made of silver,* II6
sind: sie sind *they are,* I; **Sie** (formal) **sind** *you are,* I; **wir sind** *we are,* I
singen *to sing,* II3
sinnlos *senseless,* II12
sitzen *to be sitting,* II1
der Sitzschoner, - *seat cover,* II10
skeptisch *skeptical,* II5
das Skifahren *skiing,* II4
Ski laufen *to ski,* II1
die Skizze, -n *sketch,* II8
der Smoking, -s *tuxedo,* II12
so *so, well, then,* I; **so lala** *so so,* I; **So sagt man das!** *Here's how to say it!,* I
so ... wie *as ... as,* II7
die Socke, -n *sock,* II8
das Sofa, -s *sofa,* I
sofort *immediately,* II6
sogar *even,* II2
sogenannt *so-called,* II3
der Sohn, ⸚e *son,* II1
die Sojasprossen (pl) *bean sprouts,* II5
das Solarmobil, -e *solar-powered car,* II10
solch- *such,* II9
solid *solid,* II9
sollen *should, to be supposed to,* I
der Sommer, - *summer,* I
die Sonderfahrt, -en *chartered tour,* II9
sondern: nicht nur ... sondern auch *not only ... but also,* II3
der Sonnabend, -e *Saturday,* II11
die Sonne *sun,* II4
s. sonnen *to sunbathe,* II9
die Sonnenallergie, -n *sun allergy,* II3
das Sonnenbad, ⸚er *sunbathing,* II6
die Sonnenbrille, -n *sunglasses,* II12
die Sonnencreme *sun tan lotion,* II6
die Sonnenmilch *sun tan lotion,* II6
der Sonnenschutz *sun protection,* II6

der Sonnenstich, -e *sunstroke,* II6
der Sonnenstrahl, -en *sun ray,* II6
sonnig *sunny,* I
der Sonntag, -e *Sunday,* I
sonntags *Sundays,* II10
sonst: Sonst noch etwas? *Anything else?,* II2
sonstig- *other,* II8
sorgen für *to take care of,* II5
die Sorte, -n *kind, type,* II2
sortieren *to sort,* I
die Soße, -n *sauce,* II5
soviel *as much,* II6
sowas *the like; like that,* II11
sowie *and,* II7
sowohl ... als auch ... *...as well as...,* II7
sozial *social,* II8
spanisch (adj) *Spanish,* II11
spannend *exciting, thrilling,* I
der Spaß *fun,* I; **(Tennis) macht keinen Spaß** *(Tennis) is no fun,* I
spät *late,* II4
der Spaten, - *spade,* II7
später *later,* II10
spazieren *to walk, stroll,* II3
spazierengehen (sep) *to go for a walk,* II3
das Speerwerfen *javelin throw,* II1
die Speise, -n *food,* II5
die Speisekarte, -n *menu,* II5
speisen *to eat, dine,* II11
die Spezialität, -en *specialty,* II3
speziell *especially,* II10
das Spiel, -e *game,* II3
spielen *to play,* I
der Spielfilm, -e *feature film,* II10
die Spielshow, -s *game show,* II10
der Spinat *spinach,* II2
Spitze! *Super!,* I
die Spitzenqualität *top quality,* II2
der Spitzensportler, - *top athlete,* II12
der Spitzer, - *pencil sharpener,* II5
der Sport *sports,* I; *physical education,* I
die Sportanlage, -n *sport facility,* II12
die Sportart, -en *kind of sport,* II1
der Sportartikel, - *sporting equipment,* II2
die Sporteinrichtung, -en *sport facility,* II12
der Sportler, - *athlete,* II12
sportlich *sporty,* II8
die Sportsendung, -en *sports show,* II10
die Sportübertragung, -en *sports telecast,* II10
der Sportwagen, - *sports car,* II10

die Sprache, -n *language,* II4
der Sprachkurs, -e *language course,* II3
die Sprechblase, -n *speech bubble,* II5
sprechen *to speak,* I; **sprechen über** *to talk about, discuss,* I; **er/sie spricht über** *he/she talks about,* I; **Kann ich bitte Andrea sprechen?** *Could I please speak with Andrea?,* I
das Sprichwort, ⸚er *saying,* II11
spritzen *to spray,* II4
der Spritzer, - *splash,* II12
das Spülbecken, - *sink,* I
spülen *to wash,* I
der Staat, -en *country, state,* II3
die Staatssammlung, -en *state collection,* II1
der Stabhochsprung *pole vault,* II1
stabilisieren *to stabilize,* II6
das Stadion, (pl) Stadien *stadium,* II3
die Stadt, ⸚e *city,* I; **in der Stadt** *in the city,* I; **in die Stadt gehen** *to go downtown,* I
die Stadtbesichtigung, -en *city tour,* II3
der Stadtbummel *stroll downtown,* II1
die Stadtkarte, -n *city map,* II9
der Stadtplan, ⸚e *city map,* II9
der Stadtrand, ⸚er *edge of the city,* II7
die Stadtrundfahrt, -en *city sightseeing tour,* II11
der Stadtrundgang, ⸚e *city walking tour,* II9
der Stadtteil, -e *neighborhood in a city,* II3
das Stadttor, -e *city gate,* II9
das Stadtzentrum, (pl) Stadtzentren *downtown,* II7
stammen aus *to come from,* II1
der Stammtisch, -e (table reserved for regular guests), II12
der Stand, ⸚e *stand,* II5
das Stangenbrot, -e *bread stick,* II5
stark *great; strong,* II3
die Stärke *strength,* II12
stattfinden (sep) *to take place,* II9
stattgefunden *taken place,* II3
stattlich *stately; imposing,* II9
der Staub *dust,* I; **Staub saugen** *to vacuum,* I; **Staub wischen** *to dust,* II2
der Steckbrief, -e (here:) *personal profile,* II1
die Steghose, -n *stirrup pants,* II8
stehen: auf etwas stehen *to swear by,* II2; **Das steht dir prima!** *That looks great on you!,* II8; **Wie steht's mit ...?** *So what about...?,* II4

steigen *to climb,* II9

die **Stelle, -n** *position; job,* II7

stellen *to put,* II1; Stell deinem Partner Fragen! *Ask your partner questions.,* II5

das **Stereo-Farbfernsehgerät, -e** *color stereo television set,* II10

die **Stereoanlage, -n** *stereo,* I

das **Stereogerät, -e** *stereo,* II10

der **Sterngucker, -** *stargazer,* II10

der **Steuerberater, -** *tax advisor,* II8

steuern *to steer, operate,* II10

das **Stichwort, ⸚er** *key word,* II3

stickig *stuffy, suffocating,* II7

der **Stiefel, -** *boot,* I

der **Stift, -e** *pencil,* II9

der **Stil, -e** *style,* II8

still *quiet,* II9

stimmen *to be correct,* II2; **Stimmt (schon)!** *Keep the change.,* I; **Stimmt!** *That's right! True!,* I; **Stimmt nicht!** *Not true!; False!,* I; **Stimmt (überhaupt) nicht!** *That's not right (at all)!,* II10; **Stimmt, aber ...** *That's true, but...,* II4

die **Stimmung** *mood,* II3

die **Stirn, -en** *forehead,* II6

das **Stirnband, ⸚er** *head band,* II1

der **Stoff, -e** *material,* II12

der **Stolz** *pride,* II3

stolz auf (acc) *proud of,* II3;

die **Strafe, -n** *punishment,* II2

der **Strahl, -en** *ray,* II6

der **Strand, ⸚e** *beach,* II9

die **Straße, -n** *street,* I; **bis zur ...straße** *until you get to ... Street,* I; **in ...straße** *on ... Street,* I

der **Strauch, ⸚er** *bush,* II7

der **Strauß, ⸚e** *bouquet,* I

das **Streichkonzert, -e** *concert for strings,* II11

der **Streifen, -** *stripe,* II12

streiten *to fight,* II9

der **Streß** *stress,* II7

stricken *to knit,* II7

der **Strumpf, ⸚e** *stocking,* II8

das **Stück, -e** *piece,* I; **ein Stück Kuchen** *a piece of cake,* I

stückeln *to cut into pieces,* II5

der **Student, -en** *(college) student (male),* II4

die **Studentin, -nen** *(college) student (female),* II4

die **Stufe, -n** *step, level,* II1

der **Stuhl, ⸚e** *chair,* I

die **Stunde, -n** *hour,* II3

stundenlang *for hours,* II2

der **Stundenplan, ⸚e** *class schedule,* I

der **Studienkreis, -e** *study circle,* II9

studieren *to study,* II4

suchen *to look for, search for,* I

südlich *southern,* II9

super *super,* I

das **Superangebot, -e** *special offer,* II2

der **Supermarkt, ⸚e** *supermarket,* I

supertoll *really great,* II4

die **Suppe, -n** *soup,* II1

surfen *to surf,* II9

süß *sweet,* II6

süßsauer *sweet and sour,* II1

der **Süßstoff, -e** *sweetener,* II5

sympathisch *nice, pleasant,* II1

das **Symphoniekonzert, -e** *orchestral concert,* II11

das **Symphonieorchester, -** *symphony orchestra,* II11

die **Symphoniker** *(pl) members of a symphony orchestra,* II11

das **Symptom, -e** *symptom,* II6

die **Synagoge, -n** *synagogue,* II11

die **Szene, -n** *scene,* II2

T

die **Tabelle, -n** *table, grid,* II4

die **Tablette, -n** *pill,* II6

die **Tafel, -n** *table, blackboard,* II1

der **Tag, -e** *day,* I; **eines Tages** *one day,* I

die **Tagesfahrt, -en** *day trip,* II9

täglich *daily,* II2

tagsüber *during the day, in the daytime,* II12

der **Tagungsort, -e** *conference site,* II3

das **Tal, ⸚er** *valley,* II9

der **Talkessel, -** *basin of the valley,* Loc 10

die **Talkshow, -s** *talk show,* II10

der **Tandemsprung, ⸚e** *tandem jump,* II10

die **Tante, -n** *aunt,* I

tanzen *to dance,* I; **tanzen gehen** *to go dancing,* I

die **Tanzveranstaltung, -en** *dance,* II3

tappen *to fumble about, to grope,* II12

die **Tasche, -n** *bag; pocket,* II8

die **Taschenlampe, -n** *flashlight,* II9

der **Taschenrechner, -** *pocket calculator,* I

das **Taschenwörterbuch, ⸚er** *pocket dictionary,* II1

die **Tätigkeit, -en** *activity,* II6

der **Tatort, -e** *scene of a crime,* II10

tatsächlich *really, actually,* II11

tauchen *to dive,* II9

die **Tauchschule, -n** *diving school,* II12

tausend *thousand,* II12

der **Taxifahrer, -** *taxi driver,* II11

der **Tee** *tea,* I; **ein Glas Tee** *a glass of tea,* I

der **Teelöffel, -** *teaspoon,* II5

der **Teil, -e** *part,* II1

teilen *to divide, share,* II3

teilnehmen an (sep, dat) *to participate in,* II4

teilweise *partly,* II4

die **Theke, -n** *bar, counter,* II4

das **Telefon, -e** *telephone,* I

telefonieren *to call,* I

die **Telefonnummer, -n** *telephone number,* I

die **Telefonzelle, -n** *telephone booth,* I

die **Temperatur, -en** *temperature,* II6

das **Tennis** *tennis,* I

der **Tennisplatz, ⸚e** *tennis court,* II9

der **Tennisschläger, -** *tennis racket,* II2

der **Tennisspieler, -** *tennis player,* II1

das **Tennisturnier, -e** *tennis tournament,* II1

der **Teppich, -e** *carpet,* I

die **Terrasse, -n** *terrace, porch,* II7

testen *to test,* II2

teuer *expensive,* I

die **Textilindustrie, -n** *textile industry,* Loc 1

das **Theater, -** *theater,* I; **ins Theater gehen** *to go to the theater,* I

die **Theateraufführung, -en** *theatrical performance,* II3

das **Theaterstück, -e** *play,* II11

das **Thema, (pl) Themen** *subject, topic,* II2

theoretisch *theoretical(ly),* II10

tief *deep,* II12

die **Tiefkühlerdbeere, -n** *frozen strawberry,* II5

die **Tiefkühlkost** *frozen food,* II5

tiefschwarz *jet black,* II8

das **Tier, -e** *animal,* II2

der **Tiergarten, ⸚** *zoo,* II11

tierlieb *fond of animals,* II1

die **Tierliebe** *love of animals,* II5

die **Tiersendung, -en** *animal documentary,* II10

der **Tilsiter Käse** *Tilsiter cheese,* II5

der **Tisch, -e** *table,* I

das **Tischtennis** *table tennis,* II3

das **Tischtuch, ⸚er** *tablecloth,* II12

der **Titel, -** *title,* II4

Tja ... *Well...,* I

die **Tochter, ⸚** *daughter,* II1

todlangweilig *extremely boring,* II7

das **Tofu** *tofu,* II5

die **Toilette, -n** *bathroom, toilet,* II7

toll *great, terrific,* I
die Tomate, -n *tomato,* I
die Tomatensoße, -n *tomato sauce,* II12
der Topf, ⸗e *pot,* II9
das Tor, -e *gate,* Loc 4
die Torte, -n *layer cake,* I
die Tour, -en *tour, trip,* II4
der Tourismus *tourism,* Loc 1
der Tourist, -en *tourist,* II9
die Tracht, -en *ethnic costume,* II8
tragen *to wear; carry,* II8; **er/sie trägt** *he/she wears,* II8; **tragen zu** *to wear with,* II8
der Träger, - *strap,* II8
das Trägerhemd, -en *camisole,* II8
trainiert *trained,* II3
das Training *training,* II3
trampen *to hitchhike,* II9
die Traube, -n *grape,* I
der Traubenzucker *glucose,* II5
die Traumanlage, -n *dream spot,* II12
der Traum, ⸗e *dream,* II9
das Traumhaus, ⸗er *dream house,* II7
traurig *sad,* I
der Treff, -s *meeting, rendezvous,* II9
s. treffen *to meet,* II3
treiben: Sport treiben *to play sports,* II4
das Tretboot, -e *pedal boat,* II9
treten *to step on; to pedal,* II6
trinken *to drink,* I
trocken *dry,* I
trocknen *to dry,* II2
der Trödelmarkt, ⸗e *second-hand or flea market,* II8
trollen *to trot, to troddle,* II11
trotz (prep) *in spite of, despite,* II8
trotzdem *nevertheless,* II3
der Trumpf, ⸗e *trump (card),* II9
Tschau! *Bye! So long!,* I
Tschüs! *Bye! So long!,* I
das T-Shirt, -s *T-shirt,* I
das Tuch, ⸗er *towel, rag,* II1
tun *to do,* I; leid tun: **Es tut mir leid.** *I'm sorry.,* I; **Tut mir leid. Ich bin nicht von hier.** *I'm sorry. I'm not from here.,* II9; weh tun: **Tut dir ... weh?** *Does your...hurt?,* II6; **Tut dir was weh?** *Does something hurt?,* II6; **Tut's weh?** *Does it hurt?,* II6
türkisblau *turquoise,* II8
türkisch (adj) *Turkish,* II11
der Turm, ⸗e *tower,* II11
turnen *to do gymnastics,* II2
das Turnier, -e *tournament,* II12

der Turnschuh, -e *sneaker, athletic shoe,* I
das Tüteneis, - *ice cream bar,* II2
der Typ, -en *guy; type,* II8
typisch *typical,* II1

U

die U-Bahn=Untergrundbahn, -en *subway,* I
die U-Bahnstation, -en *subway station,* I
über (prep) *over; about; above,* II1
überall *everywhere; all over,* II8
überhaupt *generally; absolutely,* II2; **überhaupt nicht** *not at all,* I; **überhaupt nicht gern haben** *to strongly dislike,* I; **überhaupt nicht wohl** *not well at all,* II4
s. überlegen *to consider, reflect,* II12
übernachten *to spend the night,* II3
die Übernachtung, -en *overnight stay,* II9
übernehmen *to take over,* II1
überraschen *to surprise,* II12
die Überraschung, -en *surprise,* II11
überstand (past) *overcame,* Loc 4
die Übertragung, -en *telecast, transmission,* II10
überwältigend *overwhelming,* II11
überzeugt *convinced, persuaded,* II8
die Übung, -en *exercise,* II2
die Uhr, -en *watch, clock,* II1
die Uhrzeit, -en *time of the day,* II3
um (prep) *at; around,* II9; **um 8 Uhr** *at 8 o'clock,* I; **um ein Uhr** *at one o'clock,* I; **Wieviel Uhr ist es?** *What time is it?,* I; **Um wieviel Uhr?** *At what time?,* I
um ... zu *in order to...,* II4
die Umfrage, -n *survey, poll,* II2
die Umgebung, -en *surrounding area,* II7
umher *around, on all sides,* II12
umrahmen *to frame,* Loc 10
umrühren (sep) *to stir,* II12
umschreiben (sep) *to rewrite,* II4
die Umwelt *environment,* II7
das Umweltbewußtsein *environmental consciousness,* II4
der Umzug, ⸗e *change of residence, move,* II7
unbedingt *absolutely, by all means,* II1; **Nicht unbedingt!** *Not entirely! Not necessarily!,* II5

unbegrenzt *boundless, limitless,* II12
unbequem *uncomfortable,* I
und (conj) *and,* I
unecht *not genuine,* II12
unentbehrlich *indispensable, absolutely necessary,* II10
unfreundlich *unfriendly,* II1
ungefähr *about, approximately,* I
ungekocht *uncooked, raw,* II12
ungesund *unhealthy,* II4
ungewöhnlich *unusual,* II12
unglaublich *unbelievable,* II10
die Uni, -s=Universität *university,* II3
die Universität, -en *university,* II3
das Universum *universe,* II10
unmöglich *impossible,* II8
unnötig *unnecessary,* II7
unpraktisch *impractical,* II8
uns *us,* I; *ourselves,* II4; *to us,* II3
unser (poss adj) *our,* II5
unsicher *unsure,* II8
unsportlich *unathletic,* II1
unsympathisch *unfriendly, unpleasant,* II1
unten *underneath, below,* II2
s. unterhalten *to chat, converse,* II2
die Unterhaltung, -en *conversation; entertainment,* II3
die Unterhaltungskosten (pl) *cost of upkeep,* II10
die Unterhaltungsmöglichkeit, -en *entertainment option,* II3
die Unterkunft, ⸗e *accommodation,* II3
unternehmen *to undertake, to attempt,* II1
unternommen (pp) *undertaken, attempted,* II12
der Unterricht *class, lesson,* II2
unterscheiden *to distinguish,* II8
unterteilt *subdivided,* II12
unterwegs *on the way, underway,* II3
unwohl *unwell,* II6
der Urlaub, -e *vacation (time off from work),* II3
der Urlauber, - *person on vacation,* II12
das Urlaubsglück *vacation happiness,* II12
der Urlaubsort, -e *vacation site,* II9
das Urlaubsparadies, -e *vacation paradise,* II9
das Urlaubsziel, -e *vacation destination,* II9
das Urteil, -e *verdict, judgment,* II12
usw.=und so weiter *et cetera, and so on,* II1

V

die Vanille *vanilla*, II5

das Vanilleeis *vanilla-flavored ice cream*, II5

die Vanillemilch *vanilla-flavored milk*, II5

die Variante, -n *variant*, II12

variationsreich *full of variations*, II12

der Vater, ∸ *father*, I

der Vatertag *Father's Day*, I; **Alles Gute zum Vatertag!** *Happy Father's Day!*, I

der Vati=Vater *father*, II1

der Vegetarier, - *vegetarian*, II5

vegetarisch (adj) *vegetarian*, II5

die Veranstaltung, -en *performance, show, arrangement*, II11

verändern *to modify, change*, II8

das Verb, -en *verb*, II11

verbessern *to improve, to correct*, II7

der Verbesserungsvorschlag, ∸e *suggestion for improvement*, II7

verbieten *to forbid*, II7

das Verbot, -e *prohibition*, II4

verbracht (pp) *spent*, II3

verbreitet *spread, disseminated*, II2

verbringen *to spend (time)*, I

der Verein, -e *association, club*, II9

vereinigt *unified*, II3

vereint *united*, Loc 4

verfügen über (acc) *to have something at one's disposal*, II12

die Vergangenheit *past*, II3

vergessen *to forget*, II1

vergiftet *poisoned, contaminated*, II7

vergleichen *to compare*, II7

das Verhalten, - *behavior*, II7

das Verhältnis, -se *situation, circumstance; relationship*, II11

verheiratet *married*, II12

verkaufen *to sell*, II7

der Verkäufer, - *salesman*, II1

der Verkehr *traffic*, II7

der Verkehrslärm, - *traffic noise*, II7

das Verkehrsmittel, - *transportation*, II9

verklärt *transfigured, radiant*, II11

der Verlag, -e *publishing house*, Loc 4

verlassen *to leave*, II2; (adj, pp) *deserted, abandoned*, II2

verlegen *embarrassed, self-conscious*, II1

s. verletzen *to injure* (oneself), II6

vermeiden *to avoid*, II4

vermengen *to mix*, II12

vernünftig *reasonable, sensible*, II4; **vernünftig essen** *to eat sensibly*, II4

verrechnen *to miscalculate*, II10

verreisen *to leave on a trip*, II8

verrückt *crazy*, II5

verrühren *to mix, stir*, II5

verschieden *different*, I

der Verschluß, (pl) Verschlüsse *lock, clasp, seal*, II8

versehen *to provide*, II5; (pp) *provided*, II5

das Versehen, - *oversight, error*, II5

die Versicherung, -en *insurance*, II10

versprechen *to promise*, II11

verständigen *to communicate*, II1

verstanden (pp) *understood*, II3

das Verständnis, -se *comprehension; sympathy*, II2

der Verstärker, - *amplifier*, II9

s. verstauchen *to sprain*, II6

verstehen *to understand*, II4

verstellbar *movable, adjustable*, II8

der Versuch, -e *attempt*, II3

versuchen *to try*, II10

der Vertrag, ∸e *contract, agreement*, II12

vertragen: Ich kann das Brot nicht vertragen. *The bread doesn't agree with me.*, II12

vertreiben *to banish, expel*, II7

vertun *to squander, waste*, II2

verursachen *to cause*, II6

verwandelt *transformed*, II3

der Verwandte, -n *relative*, II7

verwenden *to make use of, use*, II4

verwöhnen *to spoil, pamper*, II12

Verzeihung! *Excuse me!*, I; *Pardon me!*, II9

verzichten auf (acc) *to do without*, II4

das Video, -s *video cassette*, I

die Videocassette, -n *video cassette*, II10

die Videokamera, -s *camcorder*, II3

der Videorecorder, - *video cassette recorder*, II3

der Videotext, -e *videotext*, II10

der Videowagen, - *VCR cart*, II10

das Vieh *cattle*, II9

viel *a lot*, I; **viel zu** *much too*, I; **viel Obst essen** *to eat lots of fruit*, II4

viele *many*, I; **Vielen Dank!** *Thank you very much!*, I

vielleicht *maybe, perhaps*, I

vielseitig *versatile*, II11

der Vierbeiner, - *four-legged animal*, II12

vierfach- *quadruple*, II12

das Viertel: **Viertel nach** *a quarter after*, I; **Viertel vor** *a quarter till*, I

viert- *fourth*, II11

die Viskose *viscose*, II8

das Volk, ∸er *people*, II12

das Volksfest, -e *festival*, II8

voll *full*, II5

Volleyball *volleyball*, I

völlig *completely*, II3

das Vollkornbrötchen, - *whole wheat roll*, II5

die Vollkornsemmel, -n *whole wheat roll*, I

die Vollmilch *whole milk*, II4

die Vollpension *all meals included*, II12

vollschlank *not-so-slim*, II1

vollwaschbar *fully-washable*, II8

die Vollwertkost *highly nutritional food*, II4

vom=von dem

von (prep) *from, of*, II9; **von 8 Uhr bis 8 Uhr 45** *from 8:00 until 8:45*, I; von daher *for this reason*, II7; von hier aus *from here*, II9; **von hinten** *from behind*, II8; von vorn *from the beginning*, II8; von zu Hause *from home*, II9

vor (prep) *before, in front of*, II9; vor allem *most importantly*, II8; vor allen Dingen *especially*, II10; **zehn vor ...** *ten till...*, I

das Vorabendprogramm, -e *schedule for the early evening*, II10

vorbei *along, by, past*, II3

vorbeidonnern (sep) *to roar past*, II9

vorbeiführen (sep) *to lead past*, II12

vorbeikommen (sep) *to pass by, drop by*, II9

vorbereiten auf (sep, acc) *to prepare for*, II5

die Vorführung, -en *production, performance*, II3

vorgehen (sep) *to go before; to take action*, II5

vorgeschrieben *prescribed*, II10

vorgestern *day before yesterday*, I

vorhaben (sep) *to intend, plan*, II1

vorher *before, previously*, II12

vorkommen (sep) *to happen*, II4

vorlesen (sep) *to read aloud*, II4

die Vorliebe, -n *preference*, II12

der Vormittag, -e *morning*, II1
der Vorort, -e *suburb*, I
der Vorschlag, ⁼e *suggestion, propo-sition, proposal*, II12; **Das ist ein guter Vorschlag.** *That's a good suggestion.*, II12
vorschlagen (sep) *to suggest*, II9
die Vorsicht *caution*, II6
vorsichtig *cautious*, II5
die Vorspeise, -n *appetizer*, II11
vorspielen (sep) *to act out*, II5
s. vorstellen (sep) *to present, intro-duce; to imagine*, II7
die Vorstellung, -en *presentation; idea*, II11
der Vorteil, -e *advantage*, II7
der Vortrag, ⁼e *lecture, presenta-tion*, II3
vortragen (sep) *to report*, II5
vorüber *past, beyond*, II2
das Vorurteil, -e *prejudice*, II8
die Vorverkaufskasse, -n *advance booking office*, II11
vorwiegend *primarily, prevail-ing*, II12
vorziehen (sep) *to prefer*, II7
vorzüglich *superior, excellent*, II11
der Vulkan, -e *volcano*, II9

W

wachsen *to grow*, II7
die Waffe, -n *weapon*, II3
der Wagen, - *car, truck, wagon*, II10
die Wahl, -en *choice; election*, II9
wählen *to choose; elect*, II5
wahlweise *by choice*, II12
wahnsinnig *insanely, extremely*, II3; **Wahnsinnig gut!** *Extremely well!*, II3
wahr *true*, II3
während (conj, prep) *during*, II3
wahrscheinlich *probably*, I
das Wahrzeichen, - *landmark, symbol*, Loc 4
das Waldspiel, -e *forest game*, II9
der Waldweg, -e *forest path*, II9
die Wand, ⁼e *wall*, II8
die Wanderhose, -n *hiking breeches*, II8
wandern *to hike*, I
der Wanderweg, -e *hiking trail*, II3
wann? *when?*, I
das Wappen, - *coat of arms*, II1
war: ich war *I was*, I
wäre *would be*, II2; **Das wäre toll!** *That would be great!*, II12; **Das wär' nicht schlecht.** *That wouldn't be bad.*, II11

das Warenhaus, ⁼er *department store*, II1
warm *warm*, I
warten auf (acc) *to wait for*, II2
warum? *why?*, I
was? *what?*, I; **Was noch?** *What else?*, I; **Was gibt's** *What is it?*, II5; **Was ist?** *What is it?*, II5
was=etwas *something*, II6; **Ist was mit dir?** *Is something wrong?*, II6
was für? *what kind of?*, I; **Was für ein Pech!** *That's too bad!*, II5
die Wäsche *laundry, clothes*, II2
waschen *to wash*, II6
s. **waschen** *to wash oneself*, II6
das Wasser *water*, I
der Wasserhaushalt *water conserva-tion*, II5
der Wassernapf, ⁼e *water bowl*, II12
der Wecker, - *alarm clock*, II2
weder ... noch *neither ... nor*, II9
weggeben (sep) *to give away*, II8
weggehen (sep) *to go away*, II8
wegwerfen (sep) *to throw out*, II8
weh tun (sep) *to hurt*, II6
weich *soft*, II8
Weihnachten *Christmas*, I; **Fröhliche Weihnachten!** *Merry Christmas!*, I
weil (conj) *because*, I
die Weile *while*, II7
der Wein, -e *wine*, II2
weiß *white*, I
die Weißwurst, ⁼e (southern German sausage specialty), I
weit *far; wide*, I; *big, broad*, II12; Wir sind so weit. *We're ready.*, II11; **weit von hier** *far from here*, I
weiter *further*, II3
weitergeben (sep) *to pass on*, II11
weithin *far and wide*, II3
der Weitsprung *long jump*, II1
welch-? *which?*, I; **Welche Fächer hast du?** *Which sub-jects do you have?*, I
die Welt, -en *world*, II10
der Weltmeister, - *world champion*, II12
der Weltruf *international reputation*, Loc 4
wem? *to whom?, for whom?*, I
wen? *whom?*, I
wenig *few*, II4
wenigstens *at least*, II4
wenn (conj) *whenever*, II8
wer? *who?*, I; **Wer ist das?** *Who

is that?*, I
werben *to advertise*, II10
die Werbesendung, -en *commer-cial*, II10
die Werbung, -en *advertisement*, II8
werden *will*, II10; **er/sie wird** *he/she will*, II10; **Ich werde mir ... kaufen.** *I'll buy myself...*, II10
werfen *to throw*, II12
das Werk, -e *work; factory*, II11
der Wert *worth, value*, II8
wesentlich *substantial(ly)*, II10
der Westen *west*, II7
der Western, - *western (movie)*, I
wetten *to bet*, II5
das Wetter *weather*, I
der Wetterbericht, -e *weather report*, II10
die Wetterjacke, -n *rain jacket*, II8
der Whirlpool, -s *whirlpool*, II9
wichtig *important*, II4
wie? *how?*, I; **wie oft?** *how often?*, I; **Wie spät ist es?** *What time is it?*, I; **Wie steht's mit ...?** *So what about...?*, II4; **Wie wär's mit ...?** *How would ... be?*, II11; **Wie war's?** *How was it?*, II3
wie lange *how long*, II6
wieder *again*, I
wiedergeben (sep) *to repeat*, II9
wiederholen *to repeat*, II2
Wiederhören *Bye!* (on the tele-phone), I; **Auf Wiederhören!** *Goodbye!* (on the telephone), I
Wiedersehen! *Bye!*, I; **Auf Wiedersehen!** *Goodbye!*, I; Wiederschaun! *Goodbye!*, II11
wiegen *to weigh*, I
das Wiener Schnitzel, - *veal cutlet*, II11
die Wiese, -n *meadow*, II3
wieso? *why?; how?*, II11
wieviel? *how much?*, I; **Wieviel Grad haben wir?** *What's the temperature?*, I; **Wieviel Uhr ist es?** *What time is it?*, I
wievielmal *how many times, how often*, II6
die Wildlederjacke, -n *suede jacket*, II12
der Wildwestfilm, -e *wild west film*, II10
willkommen *welcome*, II12
die Windjacke, -n *windbreaker*, II8
windsurfen *to wind surf*, II9
der Winter *winter*, I
wir *we*, I
der Wirbelwind, -e *whirlwind*, II12
wirklich *really*, I

der Wirt, -e *proprietor*, II12
die Wirtschaft *business, economy*, Loc 7
wischen *to wipe*, II2
wissen *to know* (a fact, information, etc.), I; **Das weiß ich nicht.** *That I don't know.*, I; **Ich weiß nicht, ob ...** *I don't know whether...*, II9
witzig *fun, witty*, II8
wo? *where?*, I
woanders *somewhere else*, II2
wobei *whereby*, II4
die Woche, -n *week*, I; **(einmal) in der Woche** *(once) a week*, I
das Wochenende, -n *weekend*, I
die Wochenendfahrt, -en *weekend trip*, II9
wöchentlich *weekly*, II12
wofür? *for what?*, II7; **Wofür interessierst du dich?** *What are you interested in?*, II8
woher? *from where?*, I; **Woher bist du?** *Where are you from?*, I; **Woher kommst du?** *Where are you from?*, I
wohin? *where (to)?*, I; **Wohin fahren wir?** *Where are we going?*, II9
wohl *well*, II1; **Ich fühle mich wohl.** *I feel great.*, II6
wohlhabend *well-to-do*, II12
wohnen *to live*, I
das Wohngebiet, -e *residential area*, II7
die Wohngegend, -en *residential area*, II7
das Wohnhaus, ̈er *residence*, II9
das Wohnmobil, -e *mobile home*, II9
der Wohnort, -e *residence*, II1
der Wohnraum, ̈e *living space*, II12
die Wohnung, -en *apartment*, II7
das Wohnzimmer, - *living room*, II7
wolkig *cloudy*, I
die Wolle *wool*, II8
wollen *to want (to)*, I
das Wollhemd, -en *wool shirt*, II8
woran? *at, on what?*, II9
worauf? *on, to what?*, II10
woraus? *out of, from what?*, II12
das Wort, ̈er *word*, II2
das Wörterbuch, ̈er *dictionary*, I
der Wortschatz, ̈e *vocabulary*, II1
worüber? *about, over what?*, II2; **Worüber habt ihr gesprochen?** *What did you talk about?*, II2
Worum geht's? *What's it about?*, II6
wovon? *of what?*, II12

wozu? *why?; to what purpose?*, II11
wunderbar *wonderful*, II8
das Wunderkind, -er *prodigy*, II12
wunderschön *incredibly beautiful*, II12
wundervoll *wonderful, full of wonder*, II3
der Wunsch, ̈e *wish*, I; **Haben Sie einen Wunsch?** *May I help you?*, I; **Haben Sie noch einen Wunsch?** *Would you like anything else?*, I
s. **wünschen** *to wish*, II5; **Ich wünsche mir ...** *I wish for...*, II7
der Wunschtraum, ̈e *wish-dream*, II7
wurde (past) *became*, II3
würde *would*, II11; **Würdest du gern mal ...?** *Wouldn't you like to...?*, II11
die Wurst, ̈e *sausage*, I
das Wurstbrot, -e *bologna sandwich*, I
würzen *to spice*, II5
würzig *spicy*, II11
die Wüste, -n *desert*, II3

Z

die Zahl, -en *number*, II1
zahlreich *countless*, II12
der Zahn, ̈e *tooth*, II6
die Zahnpasta *toothpaste*, II6
die Zahnschmerzen (pl) *toothache*, II6
zart *tender*, II2
zeckig *hip* (with clothing), II8
der Zehnkämpfer, - *decathlete*, II12
zeichnen *to draw*, I
die Zeichnung, -en *drawing*, II5
zeigen *to show*, II3
die Zeit *time*, I; **zur Zeit** *right now*, II8
die Zeitausdrücke (pl) *time expressions*, II3
die Zeitschrift, -en *magazine*, I
die Zeitung, -en *newspaper*, I
das Zelt, -e *tent*, II9
die Zentrale, -n *center*, II10
die Zentralverriegelung, -en *central locking system*, II10
zerrissen *torn*, II12
zerstört *destroyed*, II3
die Zerstörung, -en *destruction*, II3
der Zettel, - *note*, II2
ziehen *to pull*, II5
das Ziel, -e *goal*, II9
zielen *to aim*, II9

ziemlich *rather*, I
die Zigarette, -n *cigarette*, II4
das Zimmer, - *room*, I; **mein Zimmer aufräumen** *to clean my room*, I
die Zimmerantenne, -n *indoor antenna*, II10
der Zimt *cinnammon*, I
der Zirkus, -se *circus*, II11
die Zitrone, -n *lemon*, I
zögern *to hesitate*, II9
der Zoo, -s *zoo*, I
zu *too; to*, I; **zu Fuß** *on foot*, I; **zu Hause helfen** *to help at home*, I; **zu bitter** *too bitter*, II1; **zu viel** *too much*, II4; **zu viele** *too many*, II4
das Zuhause, - *home*, II4
zuallererst *first of all*, II4
die Zubereitung, -en *preparation*, II5
der Zucker *sugar*, I
zueinander *to one another*, II11
zuerst *first*, I
zufällig *coincidentally, by accident*, II9
zufrieden *satisfied*, II7
die Zufriedenheit, -en *satisfaction*, II8
der Zug, ̈e *train*, II1
zugeben (sep) *to admit*, II12
zugleich *at the same time*, Loc 4
zugreifen (sep) *to grab, take*, II12
zuhören (sep) *to listen to*, II6; **Hör gut zu!** *Listen carefully!*, I
der Zuhörer, - *listener*, II7
die Zukunft *future*, II3
zuletzt *last of all*, I
zum=zu dem: **zum Abendessen** *for dinner*, II5; **Zum Wohl!** *To your health!*, II11
zumachen (sep) *to close*, II5
zunächst *for the time being*, II12
zunehmend *increasingly*, Loc 1
die Zunge, -n *tongue*, II2
zur=zu der: **zur Anregung** *as a start*, II1; **zur Zeit** *right now*, II8
zurechtkommen (sep) *to get on well*, II6
zurück *back*, II1
zurückkommen (sep) *to return, come back*, II1
zusammen *together*, II1
die Zusammenarbeit *cooperation*, II11
zusammenballen (sep) *to conglomerate*, II9
die Zusammenfassung, -en *synopsis*, II11
zusammenkommen (sep) *to come together*, II3
zusammenpassen (sep) *to match*, II8

zusammensetzen (sep) *to put together*, II4

zusammenstellen (sep) *to put together*, II5

die Zusammenstellung, -en *combination*, II1

der Zuschauer, - *viewer*, II10

zuschlagen (sep) *to slam*, II7

zustimmen (sep) *to agree*, II7

die Zutaten (pl) *ingredients*, II5

zutreffen (sep) *to be correct*, II6

zuvor *before*, II10

zwar *indeed*, II7

zweckmäßig *appropriate, suitable*, II12

der Zweifel, - *doubt*, II9

zweimal *twice*, I

das Zweirad, ⸚er *bicycle*, II7

zweisprachig *bilingual*, Loc 7

zweit- *second*, II1

die Zwetschge, -n *plum*, II2

die Zwiebel, -n *onion*, I

der Zwilling, -e *twin*, II1

zwischen (prep) *between*, II9

zwischendrin *in between*, II12

ENGLISH-GERMAN VOCABULARY

ENGLISH-GERMAN VOCABULARY

This vocabulary includes all of the words in the **Wortschatz** sections of the chapters. These words are considered active—you are expected to know them and be able to use them.

Idioms are listed under the English word you would be most likely to look up. German nouns are listed with the definite article and plural ending, when applicable. The number after each German word or phrase refers to the chapter in which it becomes active vocabulary. Entries followed by the Roman numeral I indicate the word became active in Level 1; entries followed by the Roman numeral II indicate the word was introduced in Level 2. To be sure you are using the German words and phrases in the correct context, refer to the chapter and book in which they appear.

The following abbreviations are used in the vocabulary: sep (separable-prefix verb), pl (plural), pp (past participle), sing (singular), acc (accusative), dat (dative), masc (masculine), and poss adj (possessive adjective).

A

a, an *ein(e)*, I
about *ungefähr*, I
across from *gegenüber*, II9
action movie *der Actionfilm, -e*, I
actor *der Schauspieler, -*, I
actress *die Schauspielerin, -nen*, I
advanced: to be advanced (person) *der Fortgeschrittene, -n*, II12
advantage *der Vorteil, -e*, II7
after *nach*, I; **after school** *nach der Schule*, I; **after the break** *nach der Pause*, I; **after lunch** *nach dem Mittagessen*, II3
after that *danach*, I
afternoon *der Nachmittag, -e*, I; **in the afternoon** *am Nachmittag*, I
afterward *nachher*, II10
again *wieder*, I
agree: I agree with you on that! *Da stimm' ich dir zu!*, II10; **Yes, I do agree with you, but...** *Ja, ich stimme dir zwar zu, aber ...*, II7
Agreed! *Einverstanden!*, II10
air *die Luft*, II7; **air conditioning** *die Klimaanlage, -n*, II10
airplane *das Flugzeug, -e*, II7
alarm clock *der Wecker, -*, II2
alcohol: to not drink alcohol *keinen Alkohol trinken*, II4
all *all-*, II8
all right: Oh, (I'm) all right. *Na ja, soso!*, II3
allergic: I am allergic to... *Ich bin allergisch gegen ...*, II4
allowed: to be allowed to *dürfen*, II4
along: Why don't you come along! *Komm doch mit!*, I
already *schon*, I
also *auch*, I; *auch schon*, II3; **I also need...** *Ich brauche noch ...*, I

always *immer*, I
am: I am *ich bin*, I
and *und*, I
ankle *der Knöchel, -*, II6
announcement *der Anschlag, ̈-e*, II11
another *noch ein*, I; **I don't want any more...** *Ich möchte kein(e)(en) ... mehr.*, I; **I'd like another...** *Ich möchte noch ein(e)(en) ...,* I
another (a different) one *ein(-) ander-*, II9
antenna: indoor antenna *die Zimmerantenne, -n*, II10
anything: Anything else? *Sonst noch etwas?*, I, II2
apartment *die Wohnung, -en*, II7
appear *aussehen (sep)*, I
appetizer *die Vorspeise, -n*, II11
apple *der Apfel, ̈-*, I
apple cake *der Apfelkuchen, -*, I
apple juice *der Apfelsaft, ̈-e*, I; **a glass of apple juice** *ein Glas Apfelsaft*, I
approximately *ungefähr*, I
apricot *die Aprikose, -n*, II4
April *der April*, I
archery *das Bogenschießen*, II1
are: you are *du bist*, I; **(formal)** *Sie sind*, I; **(pl)** *ihr seid*, I; **we are** *wir sind*, I
arm *der Arm, -e*, II6
armchair *der Sessel, -*, I
around *um*, II9
art *die Kunst*, I
as ... as *so ... wie*, II7
at: at 8 o'clock *um 8 Uhr*, I; **at one o'clock** *um ein Uhr*, I; **at the baker's** *beim Bäcker*, I; **At what time?** *Um wieviel Uhr?*, I
at *an, in*, II3
athletic *sportlich*, II8

August *der August*, I
aunt *die Tante -n*, I
avoid (the sun) *(die Sonne) vermeiden*, II4
awesome *stark*, I; **The sweater is awesome!** *Ich finde den Pulli stark!*, I
awful *furchtbar*, I

B

back *der Rücken, -*, II6
bad *schlecht*, I; **badly** *schlecht*, I; **Bad luck!** *So ein Pech!*, I; **It's too bad that...** *Es ist schade, daß ...,* II4; **That's not so bad.** *Nicht so schlimm!*, II5; **That's too bad!** *Was für ein Pech!*, II5; *Ach schade!*, II6
baker *der Bäcker, -*, I; **at the baker's** *beim Bäcker*, I
bakery *die Bäckerei, -en*, I
bald: to be bald *eine Glatze haben*, I
ballet *das Ballett, -e*, II11
ballpoint pen *der Kuli, -s*, I
banana *die Banane, -n*, II2
bank *die Bank, -en*, I
bargain: That's a bargain. *Das ist preiswert.*, I
basketball *Basketball*, I
bathroom *das Badezimmer, -*, II7; **toilet** *die Toilette, -n*, II7
bay *die Bucht, -en*, II12
be *sein*, I; **I am** *ich bin*, I; **you are** *du bist*, I; **he/she is** *er/sie ist*, I; **we are** *wir sind*, I; **(pl) you are** *ihr seid*, I; **(formal) you are** *Sie sind*, I; **they are** *sie sind*, I
be able to *können*, I
be called *heißen*, I
beach *der Strand, ̈-e*, II9; **sand beach** *der Sandstrand, ̈-e*, II9

bean (green) *die (grüne) Bohne, -n*, II2

beautiful *schön*, I

because *denn, weil*, I

become *werden*, II10; *he/she becomes er/sie wird*, II10

bed *das Bett, -en*, I; **to make the bed** *das Bett machen*, I

bed and breakfast *die Pension, -en*, II3

bedroom *das Schlafzimmer, -*, II7

beef *das Rindfleisch*, II4

beginner *der Anfänger, -*, II12

behind: from behind *von hinten*, II8

believe *glauben*, I; **You can believe me on that!** *Das kannst du mir glauben!*, II9; **I do believe that...** *Ich glaube schon, daß ...*, II10

belt *der Gürtel, -*, I; **belt loop** *die Schlaufe, -n*, II8

best: Best wishes on your birthday! *Herzlichen Glückwunsch zum Geburtstag!*, I

better *besser*, I, II5

between *zwischen*, II9

bicycle *radfahren (sep)*, II4; *das Fahrrad, ̈-er*, I; **by bike** *mit dem Rad*, I

bicycle racks *das Fahrrad-Depot, -s*, II12

big *groß*, I; *weit*, II12

bigger *größer*, II7

biology *Bio (die Biologie)*, I

biology teacher (female) *die Biologielehrerin, -nen*, I

birthday *der Geburtstag, -e*, I; **Best wishes on your birthday!** *Herzlichen Glückwunsch zum Geburtstag!*, I; **Happy Birthday!** *Alles Gute zum Geburtstag!*, I; **My birthday is on...** *Ich habe am ... Geburtstag.*, I; **When is your birthday?** *Wann hast du Geburtstag?*, I

bitter: too bitter *zu bitter*, II1

black *schwarz*, I; **in black** *in Schwarz*, I

blazer *der Blazer, -*, II8

blond *blond*, I

blouse *die Bluse, -n*, I

blue *blau*, I; **blue (green, brown) eyes** *blaue (grüne, braune) Augen*, I; **in blue** *in Blau*, I

blueberry *die Blaubeere, -n*, II4

board game *das Brettspiel, -e*, I

boat *das Boot, -e*, II9; **to go for a boat ride** *Boot fahren*, II9

bologna sandwich *das Wurstbrot, -e*, I

bomber jacket *der Blouson, -s*, II8

Bon appétit *Mahlzeit!*, II11; *Guten Appetit!*, II11

book *das Buch, ̈-er*, I

bookcase *das Regal -e*, I

boot *der Stiefel, -*, I, II8

bored: to be bored *sich langweilen*, II12

boring *langweilig*, I

bought *gekauft*, I; **I bought bread.** *Ich habe Brot gekauft.*, I

bouquet of flowers *der Blumenstrauß, ̈-e*, I

bow *die Schleife, -n*, II12

bow tie *die Fliege, -n*, II12

boy *der Junge, -n*, I

bracelet *das Armband, ̈-er*, II1

brake: (foot, hand) brake *die (Fuß, Hand)bremse, -n*, II10

bread *das Brot, -e*, I

break *die Pause, -n*, I; **after the break** *nach der Pause*, I; **to break something** *sich etwas brechen*, II6; **he/she/it breaks something** *er/sie/es bricht sich etwas*, II6

breakfast *das Frühstück*, II5; **For breakfast I eat...** *Zum Frühstück ess' ich ...*, II5

bright *hell*, II7

bring: Please bring me... *Bringen Sie mir bitte ...*, II11

broad *weit*, II12

broccoli *der Brokkoli, -*, II4

broken *kaputt*, I, II9

brother *der Bruder, ̈-*, I; **brothers and sisters** *die Geschwister (pl)*, I

brown *braun*, I; **in brown** *in Braun*, I

brush one's teeth *sich die Zähne putzen*, II6

brutal *brutal*, I

bus *der Bus, -se*, I; **by bus** *mit dem Bus*, I

bush *der Strauch, ̈-er*, II7

busy (telephone) *besetzt*, I

but *aber*, I

butcher shop *die Metzgerei, -en*, I; **at the butcher's** *beim Metzger*, I

butter *die Butter*, I

button *der Knopf, ̈-e*, II8

buy *kaufen*, I; **What did you buy?** *Was hast du gekauft?*, I; **Why don't you just buy...** *Kauf dir doch ...!*, I, II8

by *bei*, II9; **by bike** *mit dem Rad*, I; **by bus** *mit dem Bus*, I; **by car** *mit dem Auto*, I; **by moped** *mit dem Moped*, I; **by subway** *mit der U-Bahn*, I

Bye! *Wiedersehen! Tschau! Tschüs!*, I; **(on the telephone)** *Wiederhören!*, I

C

cabinet *der Schrank, ̈-e*, I

café *das Café, -s*, I; **to the café** *ins Café*, I

cake *der Kuchen, -*, I; **a piece of cake** *ein Stück Kuchen*, I

calendar *der Kalender, -*, I

call *anrufen (sep), telefonieren*, I

calm *ruhig*, II7

calories: has too many calories *hat zu viele Kalorien*, II4

camcorder *die Videokamera, -s*, II3

Camembert cheese *der Camembert Käse*, II5

camera *die Kamera, -s*, II3

camisole *das Trägerhemd, -en*, II8

can *können*, I; **Can I please...?** *Kann ich bitte ...?*, II10; **Can I ask (you pl) something?** *Kann ich (euch) etwas fragen?*, II4; **Can you tell me whether...?** *Können Sie mir sagen, ob ...?*, II10

cap *die Mütze, -n*, II1; **(baseball) cap** *das Käppi, -s*, II8

capital *die Hauptstadt, ̈-e*, I

car *das Auto, -s*, I; *der Wagen, -*, II10; **by car** *mit dem Auto*, I; **He's slamming the car door (the trunk)!** *Er schlägt die Autotür (den Kofferraumdeckel) zu!*, II7; **to polish the car** *das Auto polieren*, II2

card *die Karte, -n*, I

care: I don't care about fashion. *Mode ist mir egal.*, II8

care for *mögen*, I

carp *der Karpfen, -*, II5

carpet *der Teppich, -e*, I

carrot *die Möhre, -n*, II4

cassette *die Kassette, -n*, I

casual *lässig*, I; *salopp*, II12

cat *die Katze, -n*, I; **to feed the cat** *die Katze füttern*, I

cathedral *der Dom, -e*, II3

cauliflower *der Blumenkohl*, II4

cellar *der Keller, -*, II7

century *das Jahrhundert, -e*, II9

certain: I am certain that... *Ich bin sicher, daß ...*, II9

Certainly! *Natürlich!*, I; *Sicher!*, I; *Ja, natürlich!*, II4

chair *der Stuhl, ̈-e*, I

change: Keep the change! *Stimmt (schon)!*, I

channel *der Sender, -*; *das Programm, -e*, II10

cheap *billig*, I

check: The check please! *Hallo! Ich möchte/will zahlen!*, I

checked *kariert*, II8

Cheers! *Prost!,* II11
cheese *der Käse, -,* I; **Swiss cheese** *der Schweizer Käse,* II5
cheese sandwich *das Käsebrot, -e,* I
chess *Schach,* I
cherry *die Kirsche, -n,* II4
chicken *das Hähnchen, -,* I; *das Huhn, ̈-er,* II4
child *das Kind, -er,* II1
Chinese *chinesisch* (adj), II11
chives *der Schnittlauch,* II5
chocolate *die Schokolade,* II2; **chocolate milk** *der Kakao,* II5; **fancy chocolate** *die Praline, -n,* I
Christmas *das Weihnachten, -,* I; **Merry Christmas!** *Fröhliche Weihnachten!,* I
church *die Kirche, -n,* I
cinnamon *der Zimt,* I
cinema *das Kino, -s,* I
city *die Stadt, ̈-e,* I; **in the city** *in der Stadt,* I; **city gate** *das Stadttor, -e,* II9; **in a big city** *in einer Großstadt,* II7; **in this city** *in dieser Stadt,* II4
city hall *das Rathaus, ̈-er,* I
class *die Klasse, -n;* **in class** *in der Klasse,* II4
class schedule *der Stundenplan, ̈-e,* I
classical music *klassische Musik,* I
clean *(sich) putzen,* II2; **to clean the windows** *die Fenster putzen,* I; **to clean up my room** *mein Zimmer aufräumen* (sep), I
clean *sauber* (adj), II7
clear: to clear the table *den Tisch abräumen* (sep), I
clever(ly) *witzig,* II8
cliff *die Klippe, -n,* II12
climb *steigen,* II9
clique: in the clique *in der Clique,* II4
clothes (casual term for) *die Klamotten* (pl), I; **to pick up my clothes** *meine Klamotten aufräumen* (sep), I
cloudy *wolkig,* I
coast *die Küste, -n,* II12
coffee *der Kaffee,* I; **a cup of coffee** *eine Tasse Kaffee,* I
coin *die Münze, -n,* I
cold *kalt,* I
cold cuts *der Aufschnitt,* I
collect *sammeln,* I; **to collect comics** *Comics sammeln,* I; **to collect stamps** *Briefmarken sammeln,* I
color *die Farbe, -n,* I
colorful *bunt,* II8
comb *(sich) kämmen,* II6
come *kommen,* I; **That comes to...** *Das macht (zusammen) ...,* I; **to come along** *mitkommen* (sep), I

comedy *die Komödie, -n,* I
comfortable *bequem,* I; *gemütlich,* II7
comics *die Comics,* I; **to collect comics** *Comics sammeln,* I
compact disc *die CD, -s,* I
concert *das Konzert, -e,* I; **to go to a concert** *ins Konzert gehen,* I
conservative *konservativ,* II8
cook *kochen,* I
cookie *der Keks, -e,* I; **a few cookies** *ein paar Kekse,* I
cool *kühl,* I, II8
corner *die Ecke, -n,* II9; **That's right around the corner.** *Das ist hier um die Ecke.,* II9
corners: with corners *eckig,* I
corny *schmalzig,* I
cost *kosten,* I; **How much does... cost?** *Was kostet ...?,* I
cotton *die Baumwolle,* I; **made of cotton** *aus Baumwolle,* I
couch *die Couch, -en,* I
cough: I have a cough and runny nose. *Ich habe Husten und Schnupfen.,* II6
countless *zahlreich,* II12
country *das Land, ̈-er,* I; **in the country** *auf dem Land,* I
court *der Court, -s,* II12
cousin (female) *die Kusine, -n,* I; **cousin (male)** *der Cousin, -s,* I
cozy *gemütlich,* II7
crab *die Krabbe, -n,* II11
cream: hand cream *die Handcreme,* II6
crime drama *der Krimi, -s,* I
cross-timbered house *das Fachwerkhaus, ̈-er,* II3
cruel *grausam,* I
cucumber *die Gurke, -n,* II2
cummerbund *der Kummerbund, -e,* II12
curious *neugierig,* II1
curve: You're taking the curve too fast! *Du fährst zu schnell in die Kurve!,* II7
cut-off *abgeschnitten,* II8
cutlet *das Schnitzel, -,* II5

D

dance *tanzen,* I; **to go dancing** *tanzen gehen,* I
dark *dunkel,* II1
dark blue *dunkelblau,* I; **in dark blue** *in Dunkelblau,* I
dash: 100 meter dash *der 100-Meter-Lauf,* II1
daughter *die Tochter, ̈-,* II1

day *der Tag, -e,* I; **day before yesterday** *vorgestern,* I; **every day** *jeden Tag,* I; **on the last day** *am letzten Tag,* II3
decathlete *der Zehnkämpfer, -,* II12
December *der Dezember,* I
definitely *bestimmt,* I
degree *der Grad, -,* I
delicacy *die Delikatesse, -n,* II11; *die Köstlichkeit, -en,* II11
Delicious! *Lecker!,* I
describe *beschreiben,* II1
desk *der Schreibtisch, -e,* I
dessert *die Nachspeise, -n,* II11
detective movie *der Krimi, -s,* I
dial *wählen,* I; **to dial the number** *die Nummer wählen,* I
diamonds: check, diamond (pattern) *das Karo, -s,* II12
dictionary *das Wörterbuch, ̈-er,* I
different *verschieden,* I
dining room *das Eßzimmer, -,* II7
dining table *der Eßtisch, -e,* I
dinner *das Abendessen,* II5; **For dinner we are having...** *Zum Abendessen haben wir ...,* II5
directly *direkt,* I
dirty *schmutzig,* II7
disadvantage *der Nachteil, -e,* II7
disagree: I disagree. *Das finde ich nicht.,* I
disco *die Disko, -s,* I; **to go to a disco** *in eine Disko gehen,* I
discothek *die Diskothek, -en,* II9
discus throw *das Diskuswerfen,* II1
discussion *die Diskussion, -en,* II10
dish: main dish *das Hauptgericht, -e,* II11
dishes *das Geschirr,* I; **to wash the dishes** *das Geschirr spülen,* I
dislike *nicht gern haben,* I; **strongly dislike** *überhaupt nicht gern haben,* I
diverse *abwechslungsreich,* II12
dive *tauchen,* II9
do *machen,* I; *tun,* I; **do crafts** *basteln,* I; **do homework** *die Hausaufgaben machen,* I
doctor *der Arzt, ̈-e,* II6
documentary: animal documentary *die Tiersendung, -en,* II10
dog *der Hund, -e,* I
done *gemacht* (pp), I
don't you: You like quark, don't you? *Du magst doch Quark, nicht wahr?,* II5; **You like yogurt, don't you?** *Du magst Joghurt, oder?,* II5
doubt: I doubt that... *Ich bezweifle, daß ...,* II9

downtown *die Innenstadt, ̈-e,* I, II9; **to go downtown** *in die Stadt gehen,* I

draw *zeichnen,* I

dress *das Kleid, -er,* I

drink *trinken,* I; **drink** *das Getränk, -e,* II11

drive *fahren,* I; **he/she drives** *er/sie fährt,* I

drugstore *die Drogerie, -n,* II6

dry *trocken,* I

dry clothes *die Wäsche trocknen,* II2

duck: fattened duck *die Mastente, -n,* II11; **Peking duck** *die Peking Ente, -n,* II11

dumb *blöd,* I; *doof, dumm,* I

dumpling *der Kloß, ̈-e,* II10

dust *Staub wischen,* II2

E

each, every *jed-,* II3

earache *die Ohrenschmerzen (pl)* II6

earring *der Ohrring, -e,* II1; **a pair of earrings** *ein Paar Ohrringe,* II1

Easter *das Ostern, -,* I; **Happy Easter!** *Frohe Ostern!,* I

easy *einfach,* I; **That's easy!** *Also, einfach!,* I

eat *essen,* I; **he/she eats** *er/sie ißt,* I; **to eat ice cream** *ein Eis essen,* I; **to eat sensibly** *vernünftig essen,* II4

eat and drink *sich ernähren,* II4

education *die Ausbildung, -en,* II7

egg *das Ei, -er,* I; **deviled egg** *das gefüllte Ei, -er,* II11

Egyptian *ägyptisch (adj),* II11

ehrlich *honestly,* I

elegant *elegant,* II12

entranceway *der Flur, -e,* II7

enough *genug,* I

environment *die Umwelt,* I, II7

eraser *der Radiergummi, -s,* I

especially *besonders,* I; **especially like** *besonders gern,* I; **Not especially.** *Nicht besonders.,* II3

evening *der Abend, -e,* I; **in the evening** *am Abend,* I

every: every day *jeden Tag,* I; **every evening** *jeden Abend,* II3; **every morning** *jeden Morgen,* II3

excellent *ausgezeichnet,* II1

exciting *spannend,* I

excursion *der Ausflug, ̈-e,* II11

Excuse me! *Entschuldigung!, Verzeihung!,* I, II9

exercise *Gymnastik machen,* II4

expensive *teuer,* I

experienced (person) *der, die Erfahrene, -n,* II12

exquisite *fein,* II12

eye *das Auge, -n,* I; **blue (green, brown) eyes** *blaue (grüne, braune) Augen,* I

F

fall *der Herbst,* I; **in the fall** *im Herbst,* I

family *die Familie, -n,* I

fancy chocolate *die Praline, -n,* I

Fantastic! *Phantastisch!,* II3

fantasy novel *der Fantasyroman, -e,* I

far *weit,* I; **far from here** *weit von hier,* I

fashion *die Mode,* I

fashionable *modisch,* II8

fast *schnell,* II7

fat: has too much fat *hat zu viel Fett,* II4; **It is fattening.** *Es macht dick.,* II4

father *der Vater, ̈-,* I

Father's Day *der Vatertag,* I; **Happy Father's Day!** *Alles Gute zum Vatertag!,* I

favorite *Lieblings-,* I; **Which vegetable is your favorite?** *Welches Gemüse magst du am liebsten?,* II5

February *der Februar,* I

feed *füttern,* I; **to feed the cat** *die Katze füttern,* I

feel *sich fühlen,* II4; **How do you feel?** *Wie fühlst du dich?,* II6; **I feel great!** *Ich fühle mich wohl!,* II6; **Are you not feeling well?** *Ist dir nicht gut?,* II6

fence *fechten,* II1

fetch *holen,* I

fever *das Fieber,* II6; **to take one's temperature** *Fieber messen,* II6

few: a few *ein paar,* I; **a few cookies** *ein paar Kekse,* I

fibers: made from natural fibers *aus Naturfasern,* II8

film, videotape *filmen,* II3; **adventure film** *der Abenteuerfilm, -e,* II10

fine *fein,* II12

first *erst-,* I; **first of all** *zuerst,* I; **on the first of July** *am ersten Juli,* I; **the first street** *die erste Straße,* I

fish *angeln,* II9; **fish stick** *das Fischstäbchen, -,* II5

fit *passen,* I; **The skirt fits great!** *Der Rock paßt prima!,* I; **to keep fit** *sich fit halten,* II4

flats *Schuhe mit flachen Absätzen,* II8

flower *die Blume, -n,* I; **to water the flowers** *die Blumen gießen,* I

flowery *geblümt,* II8

food *die Speise, -n,* II4

foods: to only eat light foods *nur leichte Speisen essen,* II6

foot: to walk on foot *zu Fuß gehen,* I, II6

for *für,* I; *denn (conj),* I; **I am for doing...** *Ich bin dafür, daß ...,* II9; **for whom?** *für wen?,* II1

foreign *ausländisch,* II11

fountain *der Brunnen, -,* II9

free time *die Freizeit,* I

French *französisch (adj),* II11

fresh *frisch,* I

fresh produce store *der Obst- und Gemüseladen, ̈-,* I

Friday *der Freitag,* I; **Fridays** *freitags,* II10

fried *gebraten,* II11; **fried potatoes** *die Bratkartoffeln (pl),* II11

friend (male) *der Freund, -e,* I; **(female)** *die Freundin, -nen,* I; **to visit friends** *Freunde besuchen,* I

friendly *freundlich,* II1

fries: french fries *die Pommes frites (pl),* II5

from *aus,* I; *von,* I; **from 8 until 8:45** *von 8 Uhr bis 8 Uhr 45,* I; **from the fifteenth century** *aus dem fünfzehnten Jahrhundert,* II9

from where? *woher?,* I; **I'm from** *ich bin (komme) aus,* I; **Where are you from?** *Woher bist (kommst) du?,* I

front: in front of *vor,* II9; **there in the front** *da vorn,* I

fruit *das Obst,* I, II4; **a piece of fruit** *ein Stück Obst,* I; **to eat lots of fruit** *viel Obst essen,* II4

fun *der Spaß,* I; **(Tennis) is fun.** *(Tennis) macht Spaß.,* I; **(Tennis) is no fun.** *(Tennis) macht keinen Spaß.,* I

funny *lustig,* I, II1

furniture *die Möbel (pl),* I

G

garage *die Garage, -n,* II2

garbage *der Müll,* II2

garden(s) *der Garten, ̈-,* I, II7

garlic *der Knoblauch,* II11

geography *die Erdkunde,* I

German mark (German monetary unit) *DM = die Deutsche Mark,* I

German teacher (male) *der Deutschlehrer, -,* I; **(female)** *die Deutschlehrerin, -nen,* I

get *bekommen,* I; *holen,* I; **Get well soon!** *Gute Besserung!,* II6

gift *das Geschenk, -e,* I

gift idea *die Geschenkidee, -n,* I
girl *das Mädchen, -,* I
give *geben,* I; **he/she gives** *er/sie gibt,* I
give (a gift) *schenken,* I
glad: I'm really glad! *Das freut mich!,* II3
glass *das Glas, ̈er,* I; **a glass of tea** *ein Glas Tee,* I; **a glass of (mineral) water** *ein Glas (Mineral)Wasser,* I
glasses: a pair of glasses *eine Brille, -n,* I
go *gehen,* I; **to go home** *nach Hause gehen,* I; **goes with: The pretty blouse goes (really) well with the blue skirt.** *Die schöne Bluse paßt (toll) zu dem blauen Rock.,* II8
Goethe's birthplace *das Goethehaus,* II3
gold: made of gold *aus Gold,* II2
golf *Golf,* I; **golf course** *der Golfplatz, ̈e,* II9
good *gut,* I; **Good!** *Gut!,* I
Good morning! *Guten Morgen!, Morgen!,* I
Goodbye! *Auf Wiedersehen!,* I; (on the telephone) *Auf Wiederhören!,* I
gown: evening gown *das Abendkleid, -er,* II12
grade *die Note, -n,* I
grade level *die Klasse, -n,* I
grades: a 1, 2, 3, 4, 5, 6 *eine Eins, Zwei, Drei, Vier, Fünf, Sechs,* I
gram *das Gramm, -,* I
grandfather *der Großvater, ̈,* I; *Opa, -s,* I
grandmother *die Großmutter, ̈,* I; *Oma, -s,* I
grandparents *die Großeltern* (pl), I
grape *die Traube, -n,* I, II5
gray *grau,* I; **in gray** *in Grau,* I
great: It's great that... *Es ist prima, daß ...,* II4; **really great** *supertoll,* II4; *Echt super!,* II3; **Great!** *Prima!,* I; *Sagenhaft!,* I; *Klasse!, Toll!,* I
Greek *griechisch* (adj), II11
green *grün,* I; **in green** *in Grün,* I
grilled *gegrillt,* II11
groceries *die Lebensmittel* (pl), I
ground meat *das Hackfleisch,* I
grounds *die Anlage, -n,* II12
group *die Gruppe, -n,* I
guitar *die Gitarre, -n,* I
guy *der Typ, -en,* II8
gyros *das Gyros, -,* I

H

halibut *der Heilbutt,* II5
hair *die Haare* (pl), I
half *halb,* I; **half past (twelve, one,**

etc.) *halb (eins, zwei, usw.),* I
hall *die Halle, -n,* II12
hallway *der Flur, -e,* II7
ham *der Schinken, -,* II11
handbag *die Handtasche, -n,* II1
hand cream *die Handcreme,* II6
hang up (the telephone) *auflegen* (sep), I
Hanukkah *Chanukka,* I; **Happy Hanukkah!** *Frohes Chanukka Fest!,* I
happy: I am happy that... *Ich freue mich, daß ...,* II4; *Ich bin froh, daß ...,* II4
hard-working *fleißig,* II1
hat *der Hut, ̈e,* II1
have *haben,* I; **he/she has English** *er/sie hat Englisch,* I; **I have German.** *Ich habe Deutsch.,* I; **I have no classes on Saturday.** *Am Samstag habe ich frei.,* I; **I'll have...** *Ich bekomme ...,* I
have to *müssen,* I; **I have to** *ich muß,* I
he *er,* I; **he is** *er ist,* I; **he's from** *er ist (kommt) aus,* I
head *der Kopf, ̈e,* II6; **headband** *das Stirnband, ̈er,* II1; **headache** *die Kopfschmerzen* (pl), II6
headlight *der Scheinwerfer, -,* II10
headphones (stereo) *der (Stereo) Kopfhörer, -,* II10
health: To your health! *Auf dein/Ihr/ euer Wohl!, Zum Wohl!,* II11; **to do a lot for your health** *viel für die Gesundheit tun,* II4
hear *hören,* I
heard: I heard that... *Ich habe gehört, daß ...,* II11
hearty *herzhaft, deftig,* II11
heel *der Absatz, ̈e,* II8; **flats** *Schuhe mit flachen Absätzen,* II8; **high heels** *hohe Absätze,* II8
Hello! *Guten Tag!, Tag!, Hallo!, Grüß dich!,* I
help *helfen,* I; **to help at home** *zu Hause helfen,* I
her *ihr* (poss adj), I; **her name is** *sie heißt,* I
Here you go! *Bitte! Hier!,* II10; **Here! I insist!** *Gern! Hier ist es!,* II10
herself *sich,* II4
hideous *scheußlich,* I
high heels *hohe Absätze,* II8
hike *wandern,* I
him *ihn,* I
himself *sich,* II4
hip *die Hüfte, -n,* II6
his *sein* (poss adj), I; **his name is** *er heißt,* I

history *die Geschichte,* I
hobby *das Hobby, -s,* II1
hobby book *das Hobbybuch, ̈er,* I
hole *das Loch, ̈er,* II12
holiday *der Feiertag, -e,* I
home: good home cooked food *gut bürgerliche Küche, -n,* II11; **private home** *das Privathaus, ̈er,* II3; **to stay at home** *zu Hause bleiben,* II6
homework *die Hausaufgabe, -n,* I; **to do homework** *Hausaufgaben machen,* I
honk (the horn) *hupen,* II7
hood *die Kapuze, -n,* II8
hope: I hope that... *Ich hoffe, daß ...,* II6; **I hope you'll get better soon.** *Hoffentlich geht es dir bald besser!,* II6
Hopefully... *Hoffentlich ...,* II6
horror movie *der Horrorfilm, -e,* I
horror novel *der Gruselroman, -e,* I
hot *heiß,* I
hot (spicy) *scharf,* II11
hotel *das Hotel, -s,* I, II7
house *das Haus, ̈er,* II7
how much? *wieviel?,* I; **How much does... cost?** *Was kostet ...?,* I
how often? *wie oft?,* I
how? *wie?,* I; **How are you?** *Wie geht es dir?,* I, II6; **How do I get to...?** *Wie komme ich zum (zur) ...?,* I; **How does it taste?** *Wie schmeckt's?,* I; **How's the weather?** *Wie ist das Wetter?,* I; **How was it?** *Wie war's?,* II3; **How about...?** *Wie wärs mit ...?,* II11
hunger *der Hunger,* I
hungry: I'm hungry. *Ich habe Hunger.,* I, II6; **I'm not hungry any more.** *Ich habe keinen Hunger mehr.,* I
hurdling *der Hürdenlauf,* II1
hurt: Does it hurt? *Tut's weh?,* II6; **Does your... hurt?** *Tut dir ... weh?,* II6; **It hurts!** *Es tut weh!,* II6; **My... hurts.** *... tut mir weh.,* II6; **What hurts?** *Was tut dir weh?,* II6

I

I *ich,* I; **I don't.** *Ich nicht.,* I
ice cream *das Eis,* I; **a dish of ice cream** *ein Eisbecher,* I
ice skate *Schlittschuh laufen,* I
idea: I have no idea! *Keine Ahnung!,* I; **Do you have an idea?** *Hast du eine Idee?,* II9; **Good idea!** *Gute Idee!,* II12
imaginative *phantasievoll,* I
impossible: (That's) impossible! *(Das ist) nicht möglich!,* II10

in *in*, I; **in the afternoon** *am Nachmittag*, I; **in the city** *in der Stadt*, I; **in the country** *auf dem Land*, I; **in the evening** *am Abend*, I; **in the fall** *im Herbst*, I; **in the kitchen** *in der Küche*, I

income *das Einkommen*, II7

Indian: (Asian) Indian *indisch* (adj), II11

injure (oneself) *sich verletzen*, II6

inn *die Pension, -en*, II3

insert *einstecken (sep)*, I; **to insert coins** *Münzen einstecken*, I

instead: I'll drink...instead *Dann trink' ich halt ...*, II5

intelligent *intelligent*, II1

interest *das Interesse, -n*, I; **Do you have any other interests?** *Hast du andere Interessen?*, I; **I'm not interested in fashion.** *Ich hab' kein Interesse an Mode.*, II8; **to be interested in** *s. interessieren für*; **Fashion doesn't interest me.** *Mode interessiert mich nicht.*, II8; **Are you interested in fashion?** *Interessierst du dich für Mode?*, II8; **What are you interested in?** *Wofür interessierst du dich?*, II8

instrument *das Instrument, -e*, I; **Do you play an instrument?** *Spielst du ein Instrument?*, I

interesting *interessant*, I

into *in*, II9

invite *einladen (sep)*, I; **he/she invites** *er/sie lädt ... ein*, I

is: he/she is *er/sie ist*, I

island *die Insel, -n*, II12

it *er, es, sie*, I; *ihn*, I

Italian *italienisch* (adj), II11

J

jacket *die Jacke, -n*, I; **business jacket** *der Sakko, -s*, II8; **leather jacket** *die Lederjacke, -n*, II8; **bomber jacket** *der Blouson, -s*, II8

January *der Januar*, I; **in January** *im Januar*, I

javelin throw *das Speerwerfen*, II1

jeans *die Jeans, -*, I

jewelry *der Schmuck*, I

job *der Job, -s*, II7

jog *joggen*, I, II4

jogging suit *der Jogging-Anzug, ¨e*, I

juice *der Saft, ¨e*, I

July *der Juli*, I

jump: long jump *der Weitsprung*, II1

June *der Juni*, I

just: Just a minute, please. *Einen Moment, bitte!*, I; **Just don't buy...**

Kauf dir ja kein ...!, II8; **That just happened.** *Das ist gerade passiert.*, II9

K

keep: Keep the change! *Stimmt (schon)!*, I

kilogram *das Kilo, -*, I

kitchen *die Küche, -n*, I, II7; **in the kitchen** *in der Küche*, I; **to help in the kitchen** *in der Küche helfen*, II2

knee *das Knie, -*, II6

know (a fact, information, etc.) *wissen*, I; **Do you know whether...?** *Weißt du, ob ...?*, II10; **I don't know whether...** *Ich weiß nicht, ob ...*, I, II9

know (be familiar or acquainted with) *kennen*, I

L

lake *der See, -n*, II7

lamb *das Lammfleisch*, II5

lamp *die Lampe, -n*, I

last *letzt-*, I; **last of all** *zuletzt*, I; **last week** *letzte Woche*, I; **last weekend** *letztes Wochenende*, I

Latin *Latein*, I

laundry *die Wäsche*, II2

lawn *der Rasen, -*, I; **to mow the lawn** *den Rasen mähen*, I; **lawn for relaxing and sunning** *die Liegewiese, -n*, II9

layer cake *die Torte, -n*, I

lazy *faul*, II1; **to be lazy** *faulenzen*, II3; **I want to be lazy!** *Ich will faulenzen!*, II1

leather *das Leder*, I; **made of leather** *aus Leder*, I

left: to the left *nach links*, I

leg *das Bein, -e*, II6

lemon *die Zitrone, -n*, I

lemon drink *die Limo, -s*, I

let, allow *lassen*, II10; **he/she lets, allows** *er/sie läßt*, II10; **Let me...** *Laß mich mal ...*, II10; **Let's go to the golf course!** *Gehen wir mal auf den Golfplatz!*, II9; **Let's go to...!** *Fahren wir mal nach ...!*, II9

lettuce *der Salat, -e*, I

license: driver's license *der Führerschein, -e*, II10

life *das Leben*, II7

light blue *hellblau*, I; **in light blue** *in Hellblau*, I

like *gefallen, mögen, gern haben*, I, II7; **I like it.** *Er/Sie/Es gefällt mir.*, I; **I like them.** *Sie gefallen mir.*, I; **Did you like it?** *Hat es dir gefallen?*, II3; **to like an awful lot** *furchtbar gern*

---

haben, I; **to not like at all** *gar nicht gern haben*, I; **to not like very much** *nicht so gern haben*, I; **I don't like...** *Ich mag kein ...*, II4; **I like to go to the ocean.** *Ich fahre gern ans Meer.*, II9; **I would like...** *Ich hätte gern ...*, II11

like (to do) *gern (machen)*, I; **to not like (to do)** *nicht gern (machen)*, I

linen *das Leinen*, II8

listen (to) *hören*, I; *zuhören*, I; **Listen!** *Hör mal!*, II5; **Listen to this!** *Hör mal zu!*, II5

liter *der Liter, -*, I

little *klein*, I; **a little** *ein bißchen*, I; **a little more** *ein bißchen mehr*, I

live *wohnen*, I; *leben*, II4

living room *das Wohnzimmer, -*, II7; **in the living room** *im Wohnzimmer*, I

lobster *der Hummer, -*, II11

long *lang*, I

look *schauen*, I; **Look!** *Schauen Sie!*, I; *Guck mal!, Schau mal!, Sieh mal!*, II5; **That looks great on you!** *Das steht dir prima!*, II8

look for *suchen*, I; **I'm looking for** *ich suche*, I

look like *aussehen (sep)*, I; **he/she looks like** *er/sie sieht ... aus*, I; **The skirt looks...** *Der Rock sieht ... aus.*, I

lot: a lot *viel*, I; **I saw a lot, too.** *Ich habe auch viel gesehen.*, II12

luck: Bad luck! *So ein Pech!*, I; **What luck!** *So ein Glück!*, I

lunch *das Mittagessen*; **For lunch there is...** *Zum Mittagessen gibt es ...*, II5

M

made: made of cotton *aus Baumwolle*, I; **made of leather** *aus Leder*, I

magazine *die Zeitschrift, -en*, I

make *machen*, I; **to make the bed** *das Bett machen*, I

man *der Mann, ¨er*, I

many *viele*, I

March *der März*, I

margarine *die Margarine*, II5

marinated *mariniert*, II11

mark *die Mark, -*, I

market square *der Marktplatz, ¨e*, I

marmalade *die Marmelade, -n*, II5

math *Mathe (die Mathematik)*, I

may: May I help you? *Haben Sie einen Wunsch?*, I; **May I (please)...?** *Darf ich (bitte) ...?*, II10; **he/she may** *er/sie darf*, II4

May *der Mai*, I
maybe *vielleicht*, I; **Yes, maybe, but...** *Ja, das kann sein, aber ...*, II4
me *mich, mir*, I, II3; **Me too!** *Ich auch!*, I, II12
measure *messen*, II6; **he/she measures** *er/sie mißt*, II6
meat *das Fleisch*, I; **You eat a lot of meat, right?** *Du ißt wohl viel Fleisch, ja?*, II5
mess: What a mess! *So ein Mist!*, I
Mediterranean *mediterran* (adj), II11
Mexican *mexikanisch* (adj), II11
mild *mild*, II11
milk *die Milch*, I, II5
mineral water *das Mineralwasser*, I
minute: Just a minute, please. *Einen Moment, bitte!*, I
miserable *miserabel*, I
modern *modern*, I
moment *der Moment, -e*, I
Monday *der Montag*, I; **Mondays** *montags*, II10
money *das Geld*, I
month *der Monat, -e*, I
monument *das Baudenkmal, ¨er*, II11
mood: in a bad mood *schlecht gelaunt*, II1; **in a good mood** *gut gelaunt*, II1
moped *das Moped, -s*, I; **by moped** *mit dem Moped*, I
more *mehr*, I
morning *der Morgen*, I; **Morning!** *Morgen!*, I
most of all *am liebsten*, I
most of the time *meistens*, II4
mother *die Mutter, ¨*, I
Mother's Day *der Muttertag*, I; **Happy Mother's Day!** *Alles Gute zum Muttertag!*, I
motor *der Motor, -en*, II7
motorcycle *das Motorrad, ¨er*, II7
mountain *der Berg, -e*, II7; **in the mountains** *in den Bergen*, II7
movie *der Film, -e*, I; **to go to the movies** *ins Kino gehen*, I
movie theater *das Kino, -s*, I
mow *mähen*, I; **to mow the lawn** *den Rasen mähen*, I
Mr. *Herr*, I
Mrs. *Frau*, I
much *viel*, I; **much too** *viel zu*, I
museum *das Museum*, (pl) *Museen*, I, II3
mushroom *der Pilz, -e*, II4
music *die Musik*, I; **to listen to music** *Musik hören*, I
musical *das Musical, -s*, II11
mustard *der Senf*, I; **with mustard** *mit Senf*, I

my *mein* (poss adj), I; **my name is** *ich heiße*, I
myself *mich*, II4

N

name *der Name, -n*, I; **her name is** *sie heißt*, I; **What's the boy's name?** *Wie heißt der Junge?*, I
nauseous: I'm nauseous. *Mir ist schlecht.*, II6
nearby *in der Nähe*, I
necklace *die Halskette, -n*, II1
need *brauchen*, I; **I need** *ich brauche*, I
never *nie*, I; **not yet, never** *noch nie*, II3
new *neu*, I
news: the news *die Nachrichten* (pl), II10
newspaper *die Zeitung, -en*, I
next: the next street *die nächste Straße*, I
next to *neben*, II9
night: to spend the night *übernachten*, II3
no *kein*, I; **No more, thanks!** *Nichts mehr, danke!*, I
no way: There's just no way! *Das gibt's doch nicht!*, II10
noise *der Lärm*, II7
non-fiction book *das Sachbuch, ¨er*, I
none *kein*, I
noodle soup *die Nudelsuppe, -n*, I
normally *normalerweise*, II4
North: the North Sea *die Nordsee*, II9
not *nicht*, I; **not at all** *überhaupt nicht*, I; **to not like at all** *gar nicht gern haben*, I; **Not really.** *Nicht besonders.*, I
not any *kein*, I
Not entirely!/Not necessarily! *Nicht unbedingt!*, II5; **actually not** *eben nicht*, II9
notebook *das Notizbuch, ¨er*, I; *das Heft, -e*, I
nothing *nichts*, I, II9; **nothing at the moment** *im Moment gar nichts*, I; **Nothing, thank you!** *Nichts, danke!*, I; **There's nothing you can do.** *Da kann man nichts machen.*, II9
novel *der Roman, -e*, I
November *der November*, I
now *jetzt*, I
number *die (Telefon)nummer*, I; **to dial the number** *die Nummer wählen*, I

O

oasis *die Oase, -n*, II12
ocean *das Meer, -e; die See, -n*, II9
o'clock: at 1 o'clock *um 1 Uhr*, I
October *der Oktober*, I
of *von*, II9; **made of wool** *aus Wolle*, II8
Of course! *Ja klar!*, I; *Ganz klar!*, I; *Na klar!*, II4; **Yes, of course!** *Ja, natürlich!*, II10
offer *das Angebot, -e*, I
often *schon oft*, I, II3
Oh! *Ach!*, I; **Oh yeah!** *Ach ja!*, I
oil *das Öl*, I
Okay! I'll do that! *Gut! Mach' ich!*, I; **It's okay.** *Es geht.*, I; *Schon gut!*, II5
old *alt*, I; **How old are you?** *Wie alt bist du?*, I
older *älter*, II7
olympic champion *der Olympiasieger, -*, II12
on: on ... Square *am ...platz*, I; **on ... Street** *in der ...straße*, I; **to walk on foot** *zu Fuß gehen*, I; **on Monday** *am Montag*, I; **on the first of July** *am ersten Juli*, I; **on a lake** *an einem See*, II7; **on a river** *an einem Fluß*, II7
once *einmal*, I; **once a month** *einmal im Monat*, I; **once a week** *einmal in der Woche*, I; **once a day** *einmal am Tag*, II4
onion *die Zwiebel, -n*, I
only *bloß*, I; *nur*, II5
onto *auf*, II9
opera *die Oper, -n*, I
opera house *die Oper, -n*, II3
operetta *die Operette, -n*, II11
orange juice *der Orangensaft, ¨e*, I
other *andere*, I
Ouch! *Au!, Aua!*, II6
ourselves *uns*, II4
out of *aus*, II9
outstanding *ausgezeichnet*, II5
oven *der Ofen, ¨*, I
over it *darüber*, II8
over there *dort drüben*, I; **over there in the back** *da hinten*, I
own: (one's) own *eigen-* (adj), II7
overcast *trüb*, I
oyster *die Auster, -n*, II11

P

padded *gefüttert*, II8
pain *der Schmerz, -en*, II6
painting *das Gemälde, -*, II2
pair *das Paar, -e*, II1
pan dish *das Pfannengericht, -e*, II11

pants *die Hose, -n,* I
Pardon me! *Verzeihung!,* II9
parents *die Eltern* (pl), I
park *der Park, -s,* I, II9; to go to the park *in den Park gehen,* I
parka *der Anorak, -s,* II8
parking place/lot *der Parkplatz, ⁻e,* II9
pattern *das Muster, -,* II12
pea *die Erbse, -n,* II2
peaceful *friedlich,* 7
peach *der Pfirsich, -e,* II2
pencil *der Bleistift, -e,* I
people *die Leute* (pl), I
perch: filet of perch *das Seebarschfilet, -s,* II11
perfume *das Parfüm, -e* or *-s,* I
perfumed *parfümiert,* II6
pet *das Haustier, -e,* I
pharmacy *die Apotheke, -n,* II6
photograph *fotografieren,* II3; color photograph *das Farbbild, -er,* II3; I took pictures. *Ich habe fotografiert.,* II3
physical education *der Sport,* I
piano *das Klavier, -e,* I; I play the piano. *Ich spiele Klavier.,* I
pick up *aufräumen* (sep), I; to pick up my clothes *meine Klamotten aufräumen,* I; to pick up the telephone *den Hörer abheben* (sep), I
piece *das Stück, -e,* I; a piece of cake *ein Stück Kuchen,* I; a piece of fruit *ein Stück Obst,* I
pizza *die Pizza, -s,* I
place *der Platz, ⁻e,* II12
plastic *der Kunststoff, -e,* I; made of plastic *aus Kunststoff,* I
play *spielen,* I; I play the piano. *Ich spiele Klavier.,* I; to play a board game *ein Brettspiel spielen,* I; *das Schauspiel, -e,* II11; *das Theaterstück, -e,* II11
pleasant *sympathisch,* II1
please *bitte,* I
pleasure: My pleasure! *Gern geschehen!,* I
plum *die Zwetschge, -n,* II2
pocket *die Tasche, -n,* II8; back pocket *die Gesäßtasche, -n,* II8
pocket calculator *der Taschenrechner, -,* I
pole vault *der Stabhochsprung,* II1
political discussion *eine Diskussion über Politik,* II10
politics *die Politik* (sing), I
polka-dotted *gepunktet,* I
pool *der Pool, -s,* II7; indoor pool *das Hallenbad, ⁻er,* II9
porch *die Terrasse, -n,* II7

pork chop *das Schweinekotelett, -s,* II5; pork loin steak *das Schweinerückensteak, -s,* II11
possible *möglich,* II10
post office *die Post,* I
poster *das Poster, -,* I
potato *die Kartoffel, -n,* I; fried potatoes *die Bratkartoffeln* (pl), II11; potato croquettes *die Kroketten* (pl), II11
pound *das Pfund, -,* I
poverty *die Armut,* II7
prefer *lieber (mögen),* I; *vorziehen,* II7; I prefer... *Ich ziehe ... vor,* II7; I prefer noodle soup. *Nudelsuppe mag ich lieber.,* II5; I prefer that... *Ich bin dafür, daß ...,* II11
pretty *hübsch,* I; *schön,* I
pretzel *die Brezel, -n,* I
probably *wahrscheinlich,* I
produce *produzieren,* II7
produce store *der Obst- und Gemüseladen, ⁻,* I; at the produce store *im Obst- und Gemüseladen,* I
program (TV) *die Sendung, -en,* II10; family program *die Familiensendung, -en,* II10; nature program *die Natursendung, -en,* II10
Pullover *der Pulli, -s,* I
put on *anziehen* (sep), I

Q

quark *der Quark,* II5
quarter: a quarter after *Viertel nach,* I; a quarter to *Viertel vor,* I
question *die Frage, -n,* II4
quiz show *die Ratesendung, -en,* II10

R

radio *das Radio, -s,* II2
railroad station *der Bahnhof, ⁻e,* I
rain *der Regen,* I; It's raining. *Es regnet.,* I
rainy *regnerisch,* I
raspberry marmalade *die Himbeermarmelade, -n,* II5
rather *ziemlich,* I
raw *roh,* II11
read *lesen,* I; he/she reads *er/sie liest,* I; What did you read? *Was hast du gelesen?,* I
really *ganz,* I; *wirklich,* I; *echt,* II1; Not really. *Nicht besonders.,* I
receive *bekommen,* I
receiver *der Hörer, -,* I
red *rot,* I; in red *in Rot,* I
red berry dessert *Rote Grütze,* II11
red cabbage *der Rotkohl,* II11

refrigerator *der Kühlschrank, ⁻e,* I
religion *die Religion, -en,* I
remote control *die Fernbedienung, -en,* II10
residence *das Wohnhaus, ⁻er,* II9; the ... residence *Hier bei ... ,* I
restaurant *das Restaurant, -s,* II3; *der Gasthof, ⁻e,* II3; small restaurant *das Lokal, -e,* II3
rice *der Reis,* II4
right: to the right *nach rechts,* I
right: That's all right. *Macht nichts!,* II5; That's not right (at all)! *Das stimmt (überhaupt) nicht!,* II10
right: to be right *recht haben,* II10; You're right about that! *Da hast du recht!,* II10
ring *der Ring, -e,* II2
ringlet *der Ringel, -,* II12
river *der Fluß,* (pl) *Flüsse,* II7; on a river *an einem Fluß,* II7
roast *der Braten,* II11
roll *die Semmel, -n,* I
roll of film *der Film, -e,* II3
romance *der Liebesfilm, -e,* I; romance novel *der Liebesroman, -e,* I
room *das Zimmer, -,* I; to clean up my room *mein Zimmer aufräumen* (sep), I
round *rund,* I
ruined *kaputt,* I, II9
run *laufen,* II3; he/she runs *er/sie läuft,* II3; long distance run *der Langstreckenlauf,* II1
Russian *russisch* (adj), II11

S

sad *traurig,* I
sail *segeln,* II9
salmon *der Lachs, -e,* II11
salt *das Salz,* I
salty: too salty *zu salzig,* II1
sandwich *das Sandwich, -es,* II5; What do you have on your sandwich? *Was hast du denn auf dem Brot?,* II5
Saturday *der Samstag,* I; Saturdays *samstags,* II10
sauerkraut *das Sauerkraut,* II5
sauna *die Sauna, -s,* II9
sausage *die Wurst, ⁻e,* I
say *sagen,* I; Say! *Sag mal!,* I; What does the weather report say? *Was sagt der Wetterbericht?,* I
scarf *der Schal, -s,* II1
schedule of shows *das Programm, -e,* II10

school *die Schule, -n,* I; **after school** *nach der Schule,* I; **How do you get to school?** *Wie kommst du zur Schule?,* I; **at school** *an der Schule,* II4

school subject *das Fach, ⸚er,* I

school supplies *die Schulsachen* (pl), I

schoolbag *die Schultasche, -n,* I

science fiction movie *der Science-fiction-Film, -e,* I

sea *die See, -n; das Meer, -e,* II9

search (for) *suchen,* I

second *zweit-,* I; **the second street** *die zweite Straße,* I

secret tip *der Geheimtip, -s,* II12

secure *sicher,* II7

see *sehen,* I; **he/she sees** *er/sie sieht,* I; **See you later!** *Bis dann!,* I; **to see a movie** *einen Film sehen,* I; **What did you see?** *Was hast du gesehen?,* I

seldom *selten,* II4

sensational *sensationell,* I

September *der September,* I

set *decken,* I; **to set the table** *den Tisch decken,* I

shampoo *das Shampoo, -s,* II6

sharp (clothing) *scharf,* II8; **really sharp** *fetzig,* II8

she *sie,* I; **she is** *sie ist,* I; **she's from** *sie ist (kommt) aus,* I

shine: the sun is shining *die Sonne scheint,* I

ship *das Schiff, -e,* II9

shirt *das Hemd, -en,* I

shish kebab *das Schisch Kebab,* 11

shoe: patent leather shoe *der Lackschuh, -e,* II12

shop *einkaufen (sep),* I; **to go shopping** *einkaufen gehen,* I

short *kurz,* I

shortening *das Butterschmalz,* I

shorts: pair of shorts *die Shorts, -,* I

shot put *das Kugelstoßen,* II1

should *sollen,* I

shoulder *die Schulter, -n,* II6

show *die Sendung, -en,* II10

side dish *die Beilage, -n,* II11

sightsee *etwas besichtigen,* II3

silk *die Seide,* I; **made of silk** *aus Seide,* I; **silk shirt** *das Seidenhemd, -en,* II8; **real silk** *echte Seide,* II8

silver: made of silver *aus Silber,* II2

singer (female) *die Sängerin, -nen,* I; **singer (male)** *der Sänger, -,* I

sink *das Spülbecken, -,* I

sister *die Schwester, -n,* I; **brothers and sisters** *die Geschwister (pl),* I

site *die Anlage, -n,* II12

size *die Größe, -n,* I

skin *die Haut,* II6

skirt *der Rock, ⸚e,* I; **pleated skirt** *der Faltenrock, ⸚e,* II8

sledding *rodeln,* II1

sleep: to get enough sleep *genügend schlafen,* II4; **he/she sleeps** *er/sie schläft,* II4

sleeves: with long sleeves *mit langen Ärmeln,* II8; **with short sleeves** *mit kurzen Ärmeln,* II8

sleeveless *ärmellos,* II8

slender *schlank,* II1

slide *das Dia, -s,* II3

slow(ly) *langsam,* II7

small *klein,* I

smart (looking) *fesch, schick, chic,* I

smoke *rauchen,* II4

smoked *geräuchert,* II11

snack bar, stand *die Imbißstube, -n,* I, II3

snap *der Druckknopf, ⸚e,* II8

sneaker *der Turnschuh, -e,* I

snow *der Schnee,* I; **It's snowing.** *Es schneit.,* I

so *so,* I; **So long!** *Tschau! Tschüs!,* I; **so so** *so lala,* I

soap *die Seife, -n,* II6

soccer *Fußball,* I; **I play soccer.** *Ich spiele Fußball.,* I

sock *die Socke, -n,* I, II8

soda: lemon-flavored soda *die Limo, -s (die Limonade, -n),* I; **cola and lemon soda** *das Spezi, -s,* II11

sofa *das Sofa, -s,* I

soft *weich,* II8

someone: Someone told me that... *Man hat mir gesagt, daß ...,* II11

something *etwas,* I

sometimes *manchmal,* I

son *der Sohn, ⸚e,* II1

song *das Lied, -er,* I

sorry: to be sorry *bedauern,* II5; *leid tun,* II3; **I'm sorry.** *Es tut mir leid.,* I, II3; **Sorry, I can't.** *Ich kann leider nicht.,* I; **Sorry, but unfortunately we're all out of couscous.** *Tut mir leid, aber der Couscous ist leider schon alle.,* II12; **I'm so sorry.** *Das tut mir aber leid!,* II3; **I'm sorry. I'm not from here.** *Tut mir leid. Ich bin nicht von hier.,* II9

sort *sortieren,* I; **to sort the trash** *den Müll sortieren,* I

soup *die Suppe, -n,* II1

Spanish *spanisch (adj),* II11

spend: to spend the night *übernachten,* II3

spicy *würzig,* II11; **spicy, hot** *scharf,* II11

spinach *der Spinat,* II2

sport(s) *der Sport,* I, II1; **sport facility** *die Sportanlage, -n,* II12; **sports telecast** *die Sportübertragung, -en,* II10; **Do you play sports?** *Machst du Sport?,* I

sporty *sportlich,* II8

sprain (something) *sich (etwas) verstauchen,* II6

sprouts (bean) *die Sojasprossen,* II5

spend (time) *verbringen,* I

spring *der Frühling,* I; **in the spring** *im Frühling,* I

square *der Platz, ⸚e,* I; **on ... Square** *am ...platz,* I

stamp *die Briefmarke, -n,* I; **to collect stamps** *Briefmarken sammeln,* I

state: German federal state *das Bundesland, ⸚er,* I

station *der Sender, -,* II10

stay, remain *bleiben,* II3

steak (beef) *das Rindersteak, -s,* II5

stereo *die Stereoanlage -n,* I

stinks: That stinks! *So ein Mist!,* I

stirrup pants *die Steghose, -n,* II8

stocking *der Strumpf, ⸚e,* II8

stomach *der Bauch, ⸚e,* II6; **stomach-ache** *die Bauchschmerzen (pl),* II6

storage shelf *das Ablagefach, ⸚er,* II10

store *der Laden, ⸚,* I

storm *das Gewitter, -,* I

stove *der Herd, -e,* I

straight ahead *geradeaus,* I

strawberry *die Erdbeere, -n,* II4; **strawberry marmalade** *die Erdbeermarmelade,* II5

street *die Straße, -n,* I; **on ... Street** *in der ...straße,* I; **main street** *die Hauptstraße, -n,* II9

stripe *der Streifen, -,* II12

striped *gestreift,* I

stroll *spazieren,* II3

stupid *blöd,* I

style *der Stil, -e,* II8

subject (school) *das Fach, ⸚er,* I; **Which subjects do you have?** *Welche Fächer hast du?,* I

suburb *der Vorort, -e,* I, II7; **a suburb of** *ein Vorort von,* I; **in a suburb** *in einem Vorort,* II7

subway *die U-Bahn,* I; **by subway** *mit der U-Bahn,* I

subway station *die U-Bahnstation, -en,* I

suede jacket *die Wildlederjacke, -n,* II12

sugar *der Zucker,* I, II4

suggest *vorschlagen,* II9; **I suggest that...** *Ich schlage vor, daß ...,* II9;

What do you suggest? *Was schlägst du vor?,* II9
suggestion *der Vorschlag, ⸚e,* II12
suit *der Anzug, ⸚e,* II8
summer *der Sommer,* I; **in the summer** *im Sommer,* I
sun *die Sonne,* I; **the sun is shining** *die Sonne scheint,* I
sun protection factor *der Lichtschutzfaktor, -en,* II6
sun tan lotion *die Sonnenmilch,* II6; *die Sonnencreme,* II6
Sunday *der Sonntag,* I; **Sundays** *sonntags,* II10
sunny *sonnig,* I
sunroof *das Schiebedach, ⸚er,* II10
sunstroke *der Sonnenstich, -e,* II6
Super! *Spitze!, Super!,* I
supermarket *der Supermarkt, ⸚e,* I; **at the supermarket** *im Supermarkt,* I
suppose: I suppose so, but... *Eigentlich schon, aber ...,* II7
supposed to *sollen,* I; **The fish is supposed to be great.** *Der Fisch soll prima sein.,* II11; **Well, what am I supposed to do?** *Was soll ich bloß machen?,* II9; **What's that supposed to be?** *Was soll denn das sein?,* II5
sure: I'm not sure. *Ich bin nicht sicher.,* I; **I'm not sure that/whether...** *Ich bin nicht sicher, daß/ob ...,* II9
surrounding area *die Umgebung, -en,* II7
sweater *der Pulli, -s,* I
swallow: I can hardly swallow. *Ich kann kaum schlucken.,* II6
sweet *süß,* II6
swim *schwimmen,* I; **to go swimming** *baden gehen,* I
swimming: I enjoyed swimming in the Mediterranean Sea. *Ich bin gern im Mittelmeer geschwommen.,* II12
swimming pool *das Schwimmbad, ⸚er,* I; *der Pool, -s,* II12; **to go to the (swimming) pool** *ins Schwimmbad gehen,* I
switch off *abstellen* (sep), II7
synagogue *die Synagoge, -n,* II11

T

table *der Tisch, -e,* I; **to clear the table** *den Tisch abräumen* (sep), I; **to set the table** *den Tisch decken,* I
take *nehmen,* I, II5; **he/she takes** *er/sie nimmt,* I; **I'll take** *ich nehme,* I
talk about *sprechen über,* I; **he/she talks about** *er/sie spricht über,* I

What did you (pl) talk about? *Worüber habt ihr gesprochen?,* I
taste *schmecken,* I, II4; **Does it taste good?** *Schmeckt's?,* I; **How does it taste?** *Wie schmeckt's?,* I, II1; **doesn't taste good** *schmeckt mir nicht,* II4; **Beef tastes better to me.** *Rind schmeckt mir besser.,* II5; **Which soup tastes best to you?** *Welche Suppe schmeckt dir am besten?,* II5
Tasty! *Lecker!,* I
tea *der Tee,* I; **a glass of tea** *ein Glas Tee,* I
teacher (male) *der Lehrer, -,* I; **(female)** *die Lehrerin, -nen,* I
team *die Mannschaft, -en,* II4; **on the (basketball) team** *in der (Basketball)mannschaft,* II4
telecast, transmission *die Übertragung, -en,* II10
telephone *das Telefon, -e, der Apparat, -e,* I; **to pick up the telephone** *den Hörer abheben* (sep), I
telephone booth *die Telefonzelle, -n,* I
telephone number *die Telefonnummer, -n,* I
television (medium of) *das Fernsehen,* I; **TV set** *der Fernseher, -,* II10; **to watch TV** *Fernsehen schauen,* I; *fernsehen* (sep), *Fernseh gucken,* II10; **color stereo television set** *das Stereo Farbfernsehgerät, -e,* II10; **TV and video cart** *der Fernseh- und Videowagen, -,* II10; **TV room** *der Fernsehraum, ⸚e,* II9; **What's on TV?** *Was läuft im Fernsehen?,* II10
Tell me,... *Sag mal, ...,* II4
temperature: What's the temperature? *Wieviel Grad haben wir?,* I; **to take someone's temperature** *die Temperatur messen,* II6; **he/she takes someone's temperature** *er/sie mißt die Temperatur,* II6
tennis *Tennis,* I
tennis court *der Tennisplatz, ⸚e,* II9
tennis racket *der Tennisschläger, -,* II2
terrace *die Terrasse, -n,* II7
terrible *furchtbar,* I
terrific *Klasse, prima, toll,* I;
than *als,* II7
thank *danken,* I; **Thank you (very much)!** *Danke (sehr/schön)!,* I; *Vielen Dank!,* I; **Thank you and the same to you!** *Danke gleichfalls!,* II11; *Danke! Dir/Ihnen auch!,* II11
that *daß* (conj), I; **That's all.** *Das ist alles.,* I; **That's...** *Das ist ...,* I

theater *das Theater, -,* I
them *sie, ihnen,* II3
then *dann,* I
there *dort,* I
they *sie,* I; **they are** *sie sind,* I; **they're from** *sie sind (kommen) aus,* I
think: Do you think so? *Meinst du?,* I; **I think** *ich glaube,* I; **I think (tennis) is...** *Ich finde (Tennis) ...,* I; **I think so too.** *Das finde ich auch.,* I; **What do you think of (tennis)?** *Wie findest du (Tennis)?,* I; **I don't think so.** *Das finde ich nicht.,* II10; **I don't think that...** *Ich glaube nicht, daß ...,* II9; **I really think that...** *Ich meine doch, daß ...,* II10; **I think I'm sick.** *Ich glaube, ich bin krank.,* II6; **I think it's bad that...** *Ich finde es nicht gut, daß ...,* II4; **I think it's great that...** *Ich finde es toll, daß ...,* II4
third *dritte,* I
this *dies-,* II5; **this afternoon** *heute nachmittag,* I; **This is...(on the telephone)** *Hier ist ...,* I; **this morning** *heute morgen,* I
three times *dreimal,* I
thrilling *spannend,* I
throat *der Hals, ⸚e,* II6; **sore throat** *die Halsschmerzen* (pl), II6
through *durch,* II9
Thursday *der Donnerstag,* I; **Thursdays** *donnerstags,* II10
tie *die Krawatte, -n,* II8; **bow tie** *die Fliege, -n,* II12
tight *eng,* I; **It's too tight on you.** *Es ist dir zu eng.,* II8
till: ten till two *zehn vor zwei,* I
Tilsiter cheese *der Tilsiter Käse,* II5
time *die Zeit,* I; **At what time?** *Um wieviel Uhr?,* I; **I don't have time.** *Ich habe keine Zeit.,* I; **What time is it?** *Wie spät ist es?, Wieviel Uhr ist es?,* I
tire: wide tire *der Breitreifen, -,* II10
tired *müde,* II6
to *an, auf, nach,* II9; **Let's drive to the ocean.** *Fahren wir ans Meer!;* **Are you going to the golf course?** *Gehst du auf den Golfplatz?;* **We're going to Austria.** *Wir fahren nach Österreich.,* II9
to, for her *ihr,* I
to, for him *ihm,* I
today *heute,* I
tofu *der Tofu,* II5
toilet *die Toilette, -n,* II7
tomato *die Tomate, -n,* I

tomorrow *morgen*, I
tonight *heute abend*, I
too *zu*, I; Too bad! *Schade!*, I
toothache *die Zahnschmerzen (pl)*, II6
toothpaste *die Zahnpasta*, II6
tour *besichtigen*, I; to tour the city *die Stadt besichtigen*, I; city tour *die Stadrundfahrt, -en* II11
toward *nach*, II9
town *die Kleinstadt, ¨-e*, II7; in a town *in einer Kleinstadt*, II7
traffic *der Verkehr*, II7
train *die Bahn, -en*, II9
train station *der Bahnhof, ¨-e*, I
training and weight room *der Fitneßraum, ¨-e*, II9
transmitter *der Sender, -*, II10
transportation *das Verkehrsmittel, -*, II9; public transportation *öffentliche Verkehrsmittel (pl)*, II7
trash *der Müll*, I; to sort the trash *den Müll sortieren*, I
tree *der Baum, ¨-e*, II7
trout *die Forelle, -n*, II4
truck *der Lastkraftwagen, -, (LKW, -s)* II7
true: Not true! *Stimmt nicht!*, I; That's right! True! *Stimmt!*, I; That's true, but... *Das stimmt, aber ...*, II4
try on *anprobieren (sep)*, I
T-shirt *das T-Shirt, -s*, I
Tuesday *der Dienstag*, I; Tuesdays *dienstags*, II10
Turkish *türkisch (adj)*, II11
turn *einbiegen (sep)*; Turn in here! *Biegen Sie hier ein!*, II9
tuxedo *der Smoking, -s*, II12
twice *zweimal*, I
twin *der Zwilling, -e*, II1
type *der Typ, -en*, II8

U

ugly *häßlich*, I
unbelievable *unglaublich*; That's really unbelievable! *Das ist ja unglaublich!*, II10
uncle *der Onkel, -*, I
under it, underneath *darunter*, II8
uncomfortable *unbequem*, I
unfortunately *leider*, I; Unfortunately I can't. *Leider kann ich nicht.*, I; That's the way it is, unfortunately. *Das ist leider so.*, II9
unfriendly *unsympathisch*, II1
unhealthy *ungesund*, II4; *nicht gut für die Gesundheit*, II4

unpleasant *unsympathisch*, II1
until: from 8 until 8:45 *von 8 Uhr bis 8 Uhr 45*, I; until you get to ... Square *bis zum ...platz*, I; until you get to ... Street *bis zur ...straße*, I; until you get to the traffic light *bis zur Ampel*, I
us *uns*, I, II3
usually *gewöhnlich*, II4

V

vacation (from school) *die Ferien (pl)*, II3; vacation (from work) *der Urlaub, -e*, II9; What did you do on your vacation? *Was hast du in den Ferien gemacht?*, II3
vacuum *Staub saugen*, I
vanilla-flavored milk *die Vanillemilch*, II5
varied *abwechslungsreich*, II12
vegetables *das Gemüse*, I
vegetarian *vegetarisch*; You're vegetarian, right? *Du ißt wohl vegetarisch, was?*, II5
very *sehr*, I, II4; Very well! *Sehr gut!*, I
vest: jeans vest *die Jeansweste, -n*, II8
video: use a video camera/a camera *die Videokamera/die Kamera bedienen*, II3
video cassette *das Video, -s*, I, II3; *die Videocassette, -n*, II10; insert a video cassette *ein Video einlegen (sep)*, II3; take out the video cassette *das Video herausnehmen (sep)*, II3
village *das Dorf, ¨-er*, II7; in a village *in einem Dorf*, II7
violent *brutal*, I
visit *besuchen*, I; to visit friends *Freunde besuchen*, I
visit (a place) *besuchen, besichtigen*, II3; I visited (the cathedral). *Ich habe (den Dom) besichtigt.*, II3
volleyball *Volleyball*, I
volume control *der Lautstärkeregler*, II10

W

walk *spazieren*, II3
want (to) *wollen*, I, II1; What do you want to do? *Was willst du machen?*, II1
war *der Krieg, -e*, II7; war movie *der Kriegsfilm, -e*, I
warm *warm*, I
was: I was (in, at, on)... *ich war (in an, auf) ...*, I, II12; I was at the baker's. *Ich war beim Bäcker.*, I;

he/she was *er/sie war*, I
wash *spülen*, I; to wash the dishes *das Geschirr spülen*, I; to wash (sich) *waschen*, II6; to wash clothes *die Wäsche waschen*, II2; he/she/it washes *er/sie/es wäscht (sich)*, II6
watch *schauen*, I; to watch TV *Fernsehen schauen*, I; *fernsehen (sep)*, II10; (colloquial) *Fernsehen gucken*, II10
water *das Wasser*, I; a glass of (mineral) water *ein Glas (Mineral) Wasser*, I
water: to water the flowers *die Blumen gießen*, I
we *wir*, I
wear *anziehen (sep)*, I; *tragen*, II8; Don't wear anything made of... *Trag ja nichts aus ...!*, II8; Go ahead and wear... *Trag doch mal ...!*, II8
weather *das Wetter*, I; How's the weather? *Wie ist das Wetter?*, I
weather report *der Wetterbericht, -e*, II10; What does the weather report say? *Was sagt der Wetterbericht?*, I
Wednesday *der Mittwoch*, I; Wednesdays *mittwochs*, II10
week *die Woche, -n*, I; every week *jede Woche*, II4
weekend *das Wochenende, -n*, I; on the weekend *am Wochenende*, I; every weekend *jedes Wochenende*, II4
weekly special *das Angebot der Woche*, I
weigh *wiegen*, I
well: Well yes, but... *Eigentlich schon, aber ...*, II4; *Ja, schon, aber ...*, II7; extremely well *ganz wohl*, II4; Get well soon! *Gute Besserung!*, II6; I'm (not) doing well. *Es geht mir (nicht) gut!*, II6; *Mir ist (nicht) gut.*, II6; not well at all *überhaupt nicht wohl*, II4
were: Where were you? *Wo bist du gewesen?*, I, II3; we were *wir waren*, I; they were *sie waren*, I; (pl) you were *ihr wart*, I; (formal) you were *Sie waren*, I
western (movie) *der Western, -*, I
wet *naß*, I
what *was*; What are we going to do now? *Was machen wir jetzt?*, II9; What is it? *Was gibt's?*, II5; *Was ist?*, II5; Okay, what is it? *Ja? Was denn?*, II5; So what about...? *Wie steht's mit ...?*, II4; Yes, what? *Ja, was bitte?*, II5; What can I do for you? *Was kann ich für dich tun?*, I; What else? *Noch etwas?*, I

ENGLISH-GERMAN VOCABULARY

what kind of? *was für?*, I; What kinds of music do you like? *Was für Musik hörst du gern?*, I

when? *wann?*, I

whenever *wenn* (conj), II8

where? *wo?*, I

where (from)? *woher?*, I; Where are you from? *Woher bist (kommst) du?*, I

where (to)? *wohin?*, I; Where are we going? *Wohin fahren wir?*, II9

whether *ob* (conj), II9

which *welch–*, I, II8; Which soup do you prefer? *Welche Suppe magst du lieber?*, II5

whirlpool *der Whirlpool, -s*, II9

white *weiß*, I; in white *in Weiß*, I

who? *wer?*, I; Who is that? *Wer ist das?*, I

whole wheat roll *die Vollkornsemmel, -n*, I

whom *wen*, I; to, for whom *wem*, I

why? *warum?*, I; Why don't you come along! *Komm doch mit!*, I

wide *weit*, I

will *werden*; you will *du wirst*; he/she will *er/sie wird*, II10; I'm going to buy myself a great car. *Ich werde mir einen tollen Wagen kaufen.*, II10

wind surf *windsurfen*, II9

windbreaker *die Wind-, Wetterjacke, -n*, II8

window *das Fenster, -*, I; to clean the windows *die Fenster putzen*, I

windshield wiper *der Scheibenwischer, -*, II10

winter *der Winter*, I; in the winter *im Winter*, I

wish *sich wünschen;* I wish for... *Ich wünsche mir ...*, II7; What would you wish for? *Was wünschst du dir (mal)?*, II7

with *mit*, I; with bread *mit Brot*, I; with corners *eckig*, I

witty *witzig*, II8

woman *die Frau, -en*, I

wonderful *großartig*, II4

wood: made of wood *aus Holz*, I

wool *die Wolle*, II8

wool shirt *das Wollhemd, -en*, II8; made of wool *aus Wolle*, II1

work *arbeiten*, II3; That won't work. *Das geht nicht.*, I

worse than *schlechter als*, II7

would: No, I would rather... *Nein, ich würde lieber ...*, II11; That would be great! *Das wäre toll!*, II12; Wouldn't you like to...? *Würdest du gern mal ...?*, II11; That wouldn't be bad. *Das wär' nicht schlecht.*, II11

would like (to) *möchten*, I; I would like to see... *Ich möchte ... sehen.*, I; What would you like to eat? *Was möchtest du essen?*, I; What would you like? *Was bekommen Sie?*, I; Would you like anything else? *Haben Sie noch einen Wunsch?*, I

wristwatch *die Armbanduhr, -en*, I

write *schreiben*, I

wrong: Is something wrong? *Ist was mit dir?*, II6; What's wrong with you? *Was fehlt dir?*, II6

Y

yard *der Garten, ∸*, II7

year *das Jahr, -e*, I; I am...years old. *Ich bin ... Jahre alt.*, I

yellow *gelb*, I; in yellow *in Gelb*, I

yes *ja*, I; Yes? *Bitte?*, I; Yes, I do! *Doch!*, II4

yesterday *gestern*, I; yesterday evening *gestern abend*, I; the day before yesterday *vorgestern*, I

yogurt *der Joghurt, -*, II5

you *du, Sie, ihr*, I

you're (very) welcome! *Bitte (sehr/schön)!*, I

younger *jünger*, II7

your *dein* (poss adj), I; *Ihr*, II5

yourself *dich, sich*, II4

yourselves *euch*, II4

youth hostel *die Jugendherberge, -n*, II3

Z

zero *null*, I

zipper *der Reißverschluß, -verschlüsse*, II8

zoo *der Zoo, -s*, I; to go to the zoo *in den Zoo gehen*, I

GRAMMAR INDEX

GRAMMAR INDEX

This grammar index includes grammar topics introduced in **Komm mit!** Levels 1 and 2. The Roman numeral I following the page number(s) indicates Level 1; the Roman numeral II indicates Level 2.

NOTE: For a summary of the grammar presented in this book see pages 329–346.

ABBREVIATIONS

acc	*accusative*	dir obj	*direct object*	prep	*preposition*
adj	*adjective*	indef art	*indefinite article*	pres	*present*
art	*article*	indir obj	*indirect object*	pron	*pronoun(s)*
comm	*command*	inf	*infinitive*	ques	*question(s)*
conv past	*conversational past*	interr	*interrogative*	reflex	*reflexive*
dat	*dative*	nom	*nominative*	sep pref	*separable prefix*
def	*definition*	pers	*person*	sing	*singular*
def art	*definite article*	plur	*plural*	subj	*subject*

A

accusative case: def art, p. 123 (I); indef art, p. 123 (I); p. 230 (I); third pers pron, sing, p. 128 (I); third pers pron, plur, p. 180 (I); first and second pers pron, p. 180 (I); following **für**, p. 180 (I); p. 297 (I); following **es gibt**, p. 229 (I); of reflex pron, p. 90 (II); of **jeder**, p. 94 (II); of **kein**, p. 98 (II); of possessives, p. 120 (II); following **durch** and **um**, p. 222 (II)

adjectives: comparative forms of, p. 166 (II); endings following **ein**-words, p. 170 (II); endings of comparatives, p. 176 (II); endings following **der**- and **dieser**-words, p. 189 (II); endings of unpreceded adj, p. 271 (II)

als: in a comparison, p. 166 (II)

am: contraction of **an dem**, p. 65 (II)

am liebsten: use of with **würde**, p. 267 (II)

an: followed by dat (location), p. 65 (II); followed by acc (direction), p. 214 (II)

ans: contraction of **an das**, p. 214 (II)

anziehen: pres tense forms of, p. 131 (I)

article: *see* definite article, indefinite article

auf: followed by dat (location), p. 119 (II); followed by acc (direction), p. 214 (II); use of with **s. freuen**, p. 241 (II)

aufs: contraction of **auf das**, p. 214 (II)

aus: followed by dat, p. 222 (II)

aussehen: pres tense forms of, p. 132 (I)

B

bei: followed by dat, p. 222 (II)

beim: contraction of **bei dem**, p. 222 (II)

s. brechen: pres tense of, p. 145 (II)

C

case: *see* nominative case, accusative case, dative case

class: def of, p. 24 (I)

command forms: **du**-commands, p. 200 (I); p. 297 (I); **Sie**-commands, p. 227 (I); inclusive commands, p. 139 (II)

comparatives: *see* adjectives

conjunctions: **denn** and **weil**, p. 206 (I); **daß**, p. 232 (I); **wenn**, p. 199 (II); **ob**, p. 218 (II)

conversational past: p. 58-59 (II)

contractions: of **in dem**, **im**, p. 65; of **an dem**, **am**, p. 65; of **zu dem**, **zum**, p. 125; of **zu der**, **zur**, p. 125; of **an das**, **ans**, p. 214; of **auf das**, **aufs**, p. 214; of **in das**, **ins**, p. 214; of **bei dem**, **beim**, p. 222; of **von dem**, **vom**, p. 222 (II)

D

da-compounds: p. 241 (II)

daß-clauses: p. 232 (I); verb in final position, p. 89 (II); with reflex verbs, p. 90 (II)

dative case: introduction to, p. 283 (I); following **mit**, p. 283 (I); word order with, p. 284 (I); following **in** and **an** when expressing location, p. 65 (II); with **gefallen**, p. 69 (II); of personal pron, p. 69 (II); plural of def art, p. 69 (II); of **ein**-words, p. 71 (II); following **auf** when expressing location, p. 119 (II); of possessives, p. 120 (II); verbs used with dative forms, **gefallen**, **schmecken**, p. 123 (II); following **zu**, pp. 125, 195 (II); use of to talk about how you feel, p. 137 (II); verbs requiring dat forms, p. 143 (II); reflex verbs requiring dat forms, p. 144 (II); reflex pron, p. 144 (II); use of to express idea of something being too expensive/large/small, p. 149 (II); plur endings of adj, p. 170 (II); endings of

sprechen: present tense forms of, p. 259 (I); **sprechen über**, p. 241 (II)

stem-changing verbs: **nehmen, aussehen**, p. 132 (I); **essen**, p. 155 (I); **fahren**, p. 227 (I); **sehen**, p. 253 (I); **lesen, sprechen**, p. 259 (I); **schlafen**, p. 88 (II); **brechen**, p. 145 (II); **waschen**, p. 145 (II); **messen**, p. 148 (II); **tragen**, p. 194 (II); **lassen**, p. 247 (II); *see also* Grammar Summary, pp. 329–346

subject: def of, p. 123 (I); *see also* nominative case

subjunctive forms: **würde**, p. 267 (II); **hätte**, p. 274 (II)

T

tragen: pres tense of, p. 194 (II)

U

über: following **sprechen**, p. 241 (II)

um: followed by acc, p. 222 (II)

uns: dat personal pron, p. 69 (II); as a reflex pron, p. 90 (II)

unpreceded adjectives: endings of, p. 271 (II)

V

verbs: with sep pref, **anziehen, anprobieren, aussehen**, p. 131 (I); **aufräumen, abräumen, mitkommen**, p. 176 (I); with vowel change in the **du**- and **er/sie**-form, **nehmen, aussehen**, p. 132 (I); **fahren**, p. 227 (I); **sehen**, p. 253 (I); **lesen, sprechen**, p. 259 (I); **schlafen**, p. 88 (II); **brechen**, p. 145 (II); **waschen**, p. 145 (II); **messen**, p. 148 (II); **tragen**, p. 194 (II); **lassen**, p. 247 (II); conv past tense, pp. 58–59 (II); reflex verbs: p. 90 (II); used with dat, **gefallen, schmecken**, p. 123 (II); verbs requiring dat case forms, p. 143 (II); reflex verbs requiring dat case forms, p. 144 (II); **s. wünschen**, p. 169 (II); **passen** and **stehen** with dat, p. 195 (II); verbs requiring prep phrase, **sprechen über, s. freuen auf, s. interessieren für**, p. 241 (II)

verb-final position: in **weil**-clauses, p. 206 (I); p. 165 (II); in clauses following **wissen**, p. 222 (I); in **daß**-clauses, p. 232 (I); p. 89 (II); in **wenn**-clauses, p. 199 (II); in

ob-clauses, p. 218 (II); with **werden** in clauses beginning with **daß, ob, wenn, weil**, p. 253 (II)

verb-second position: p. 54 (I); p. 151 (I); p. 309 (I)

vom: contraction of **von dem**, p. 222 (II)

von: followed by dat, p. 222 (II)

vor: followed by acc (direction) or dat (location), p. 223 (II)

W

waschen: pres tense of, p. 145 (II)

weh tun: as a sep pref verb, p. 143; use of dat with, p. 143 (II)

weil-clause: verb in final position, p. 165 (II)

welcher: forms of, p. 124 (II)

wenn-clauses: verb in final position, p. 199 (II)

werden: use of to express future, forms of, p. 253 (II)

wissen: pres tense forms of, p. 222 (I); p. 299 (I)

wo-compounds: p. 241 (II)

wollen: pres tense forms of, p. 150 (I); p. 302 (I)

word order: ques beginning with a verb, p. 23 (I); ques beginning with a ques word, p. 23 (I); verb in second position, p. 54 (I); p. 151 (I); p. 309 (I); in **denn**- and **weil**-clauses, p. 206 (I); verb-final in clauses following **wissen**, p. 222 (I); p. 299 (I); verb-final in **daß**-clauses, p. 232 (I); with dat case, p. 284 (I); in **weil**-clauses, p. 165 (II); in **wenn**-clauses, p. 199 (II); in **ob**-clauses, p. 218 (II); with **werden** in clauses beginning with **daß, ob, wenn, weil**, p. 253 (II)

s. wünschen: with dat reflex pron, p. 168 (II)

würde: forms of, p. 267 (II)

Z

zu: p. 125 (II); prep followed by dat, p. 195 (II)

zum: contraction of **zu dem**, p. 125 (II)

zur: contraction of **zu der**, p. 125 (II)

zwischen: followed by acc (direction) or dat (location), p. 223 (II)

Map of the Federal Republic of Germany

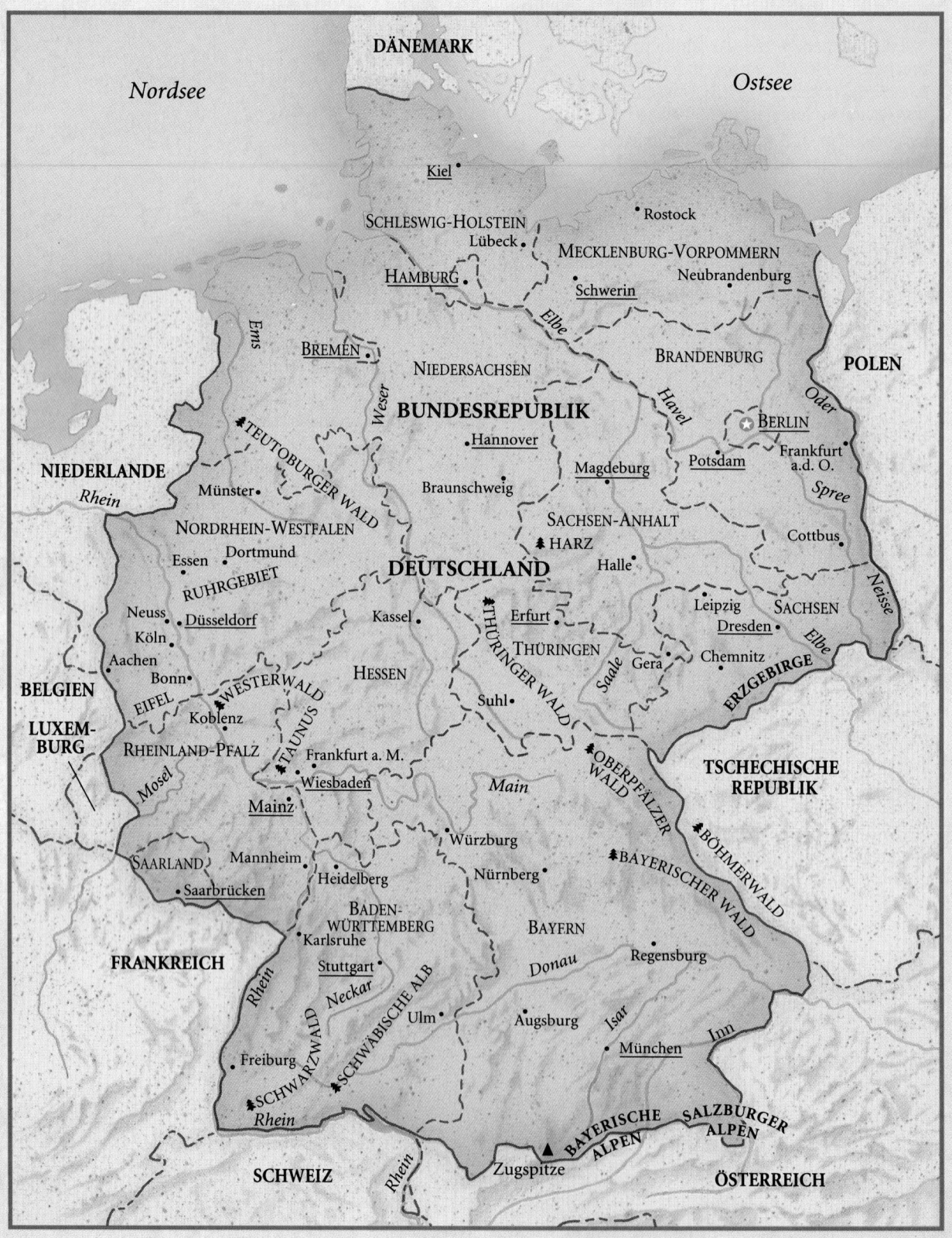

DÄNEMARK

Nordsee

Ostsee

Kiel

Rostock

SCHLESWIG-HOLSTEIN

Lübeck

MECKLENBURG-VORPOMMERN

HAMBURG

Neubrandenburg

Schwerin

Elbe

Ems

BREMEN

BRANDENBURG

POLEN

NIEDERSACHSEN

Weser

Havel

Oder

BUNDESREPUBLIK

BERLIN

Hannover

Frankfurt a.d. O.

NIEDERLANDE

TEUTOBURGER WALD

Magdeburg

Potsdam

Rhein

Münster

Braunschweig

Spree

NORDRHEIN-WESTFALEN

SACHSEN-ANHALT

Cottbus

Dortmund

HARZ

Essen

DEUTSCHLAND

Halle

Neisse

RUHRGEBIET

Leipzig

SACHSEN

Neuss

Düsseldorf

Kassel

Erfurt

Dresden

Köln

THÜRINGER WALD

THÜRINGEN

Elbe

Aachen

Chemnitz

BELGIEN

Bonn

WESTERWALD

HESSEN

Saale

Gera

ERZGEBIRGE

EIFEL

Koblenz

Suhl

LUXEM-

TAUNUS

OBERPFÄLZER WALD

TSCHECHISCHE

BURG

RHEINLAND-PFALZ

Frankfurt a. M.

REPUBLIK

Mosel

Wiesbaden

Main

BÖHMERWALD

Mainz

SAARLAND

Mannheim

Würzburg

BAYERISCHER WALD

Saarbrücken

Heidelberg

Nürnberg

BADEN-

BAYERN

FRANKREICH

WÜRTTEMBERG

Rhein

Karlsruhe

Donau

Regensburg

Stuttgart

Neckar

SCHWÄBISCHE ALB

Augsburg

Isar

Inn

Freiburg

Ulm

München

SCHWARZWALD

Rhein

SALZBURGER

Zugspitze

BAYERISCHE

ALPEN

SCHWEIZ

Rhein

ALPEN

ÖSTERREICH

Map of Liechtenstein, Switzerland, and Austria

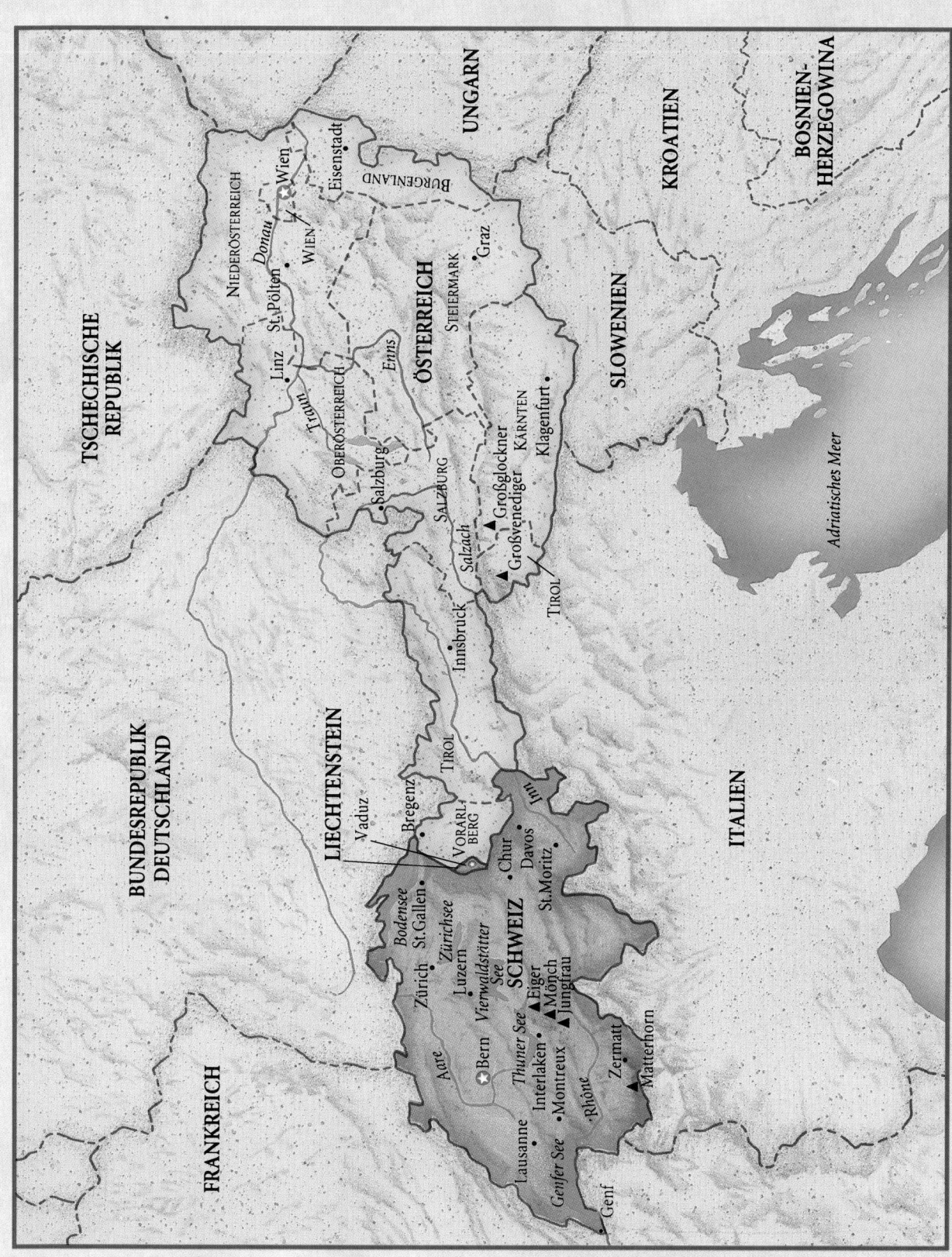

TSCHECHISCHE REPUBLIK

BUNDESREPUBLIK DEUTSCHLAND

FRANKREICH

UNGARN

KROATIEN

BOSNIEN-HERZEGOWINA

NIEDERÖSTERREICH

Wien

Eisenstadt

Donau

St. Pölten

WIEN

BURGENLAND

Linz

Graz

ÖSTERREICH

STEIERMARK

Enns

Traun

OBERÖSTERREICH

Salzburg

SALZBURG

Salzach

SLOWENIEN

KÄRNTEN

Klagenfurt

Großglockner

Großvenediger

TIROL

Innsbruck

Adriatisches Meer

TIROL

LIECHTENSTEIN

Vaduz

Bregenz

VORARLBERG

Chur

Davos

St. Moritz

ITALIEN

Bodensee

St. Gallen

Zürichsee

Zürich

Luzern

Vierwaldstätter See

SCHWEIZ

Eiger

Mönch

Jungfrau

Aare

Bern

Thuner See

Interlaken

Montreux

Rhône

Zermatt

Matterhorn

Lausanne

Genfer See

Genf

ACKNOWLEDGMENTS [continued from page T6]

Rowohlt-Verlag, 1949 Hamburg: "Das Brot" by Wolfgang Borchert from *Das Gesamtwerk*.

RufPress: "Kuren und Bäder" from *Neue Gesundheit*, January 1, 1994, pp. 20–21.

Severin + Kühn: From advertisement "8-sprachige City-Tour/multilingual City-Tour" from *Berlin Programm*, September 1993, p. 59.

Sport-Scheck Reisen GmbH: "Club La Santa auf Lanzarote" from *Sport-Scheck Reisen*, Summer 1993, pp. 172–173.

Süddeutscher Verlag München: "Die Deutschen sind." from *Süddeutsche Zeitung*, no. 44, 1992, p. 36. Copyright © 1992 by Süddeutscher Verlag.

Surya Indisches Restaurant: Advertisement, "Surya Indisches Restaurant" from *Berlin Programm*, September 1993.

Tiefdruck Schwann-Bagel GmbH: "100 Mark für Nichtraucher", from *JUMA: Das Jugendmagazin*, 2/91, p. 4, April 1991. Copyright © 1991 by Tiefdruck Schwann-Bagel GmbH. "Mein Traumhaus ist aus Schokolade" from *JUMA: Das Jugendmagazin*, 1/92, pp. 16–19, January 1992. Copyright © 1991 by Tiefdruck Schwann-Bagel GmbH. From "Tina—das Mädchen aus dem Katalog" from *JUMA: Das Jugendmagazin*, 3/92, pp. i, 10–11, July 1992. Copyright © 1993 by Tiefdruck Schwann-Bagel GmbH. "Zöe" by Zoe L. Smith from *JUMA: Das Jugendmagazin*, 2/93, p. 47, April 1993. Copyright © 1993 by Tiefdruck Schwann-Bagel GmbH. Text from "Hier hab ich meine Ruhe" from *JUMA: Das Jugendmagazin*, 3/93, pp. 6–10, July 1993. Copyright © 1993 by Tiefdruck Schwann-Bagel GmbH. From "Schule im Garten" from *JUMA: Das Jugendmagazin*, 4/93, pp. 32 & 35, October 1993. Copyright © 1993 by Tiefdruck Schwann-Bagel GmbH.

TV Spielfilm Verlag GmbH: Reviews for "Der Junge mit dem großen schwarzen Hund," "Der Prinz von Bel-Air," "Eishockey WM," "Im Reich der wilden Tiere," "Praxis Bülowbogen," and "Raumschiff Enterprise," from *TV Spielfilm/TV Guide*, 9/93, pp. 36–37, 70–71. Copyright © 1993 by TV Spielfilm Verlag GmbH.

Verlag Karl Baedeker GmbH: "Baden-Baden" from *Baedeker Allianz Reiseführer Deutschland, 2*. Copyright © 1992 by Verlag Karl Baedeker GmbH.

Josef Witt GmbH & Co. KG: "Persönliche Bestellkarte" from *Kaufen + Sparen*.

PHOTOGRAPHY CREDITS

ILLUSTRATION AND CARTOGRAPHY CREDITS